FORGING DEMOCRACY

FORGING
DEMOCRACY

*The History
of the Left
in Europe,
1850–2000*

Geoff Eley

OXFORD
UNIVERSITY PRESS
2002

OXFORD
UNIVERSITY PRESS

Oxford   New York
Auckland   Bangkok   Buenos Aires   Cape Town   Chennai
Dar es Salaam   Delhi   Hong Kong   Istanbul   Karachi   Kolkata
Kuala Lumpur   Madrid   Melbourne   Mexico City   Mumbai   Nairobi
São Paulo   Shanghai   Singapore   Taipei   Tokyo   Toronto

and an associated company in Berlin

Published by Oxford University Press, Inc.
198 Madison Avenue, New York, New York 10016

Oxford is a registered trademark of Oxford University Press

Library of Congress Cataloging-in-Publication Data
Eley, Geoff, 1949–
     Forging democracy : The history of the Left in Europe, 1850–2000 / Geoff Eley.
        p. cm.
     Includes bibliographical references and index.
     ISBN 0-19-503784-7; 0-19-504479-7 (pbk.)
        1. Communism—Europe—History. 2. Socialism—Europe—History.
     3. Democracy—Europe—History. 4. Sex role—Europe—History. I. Title.

HX239 .E44 2002
940.2'8—dc21   2001052397

9 8 7 6 5 4 3 2 1

Printed in the United States of America
on acid-free paper

For Anna and Sarah,
who deserve a better world.

Preface

BETWEEN THE LATER 1970s and early 1990s Europe's political landscape was radically rearranged. The 1989 revolutions removed the Eastern European socialist bloc, and the Soviet Union dissolved. Through an equally drastic capitalist restructuring, Western Europe was transformed. Whereas socialist parties recaptured government across Europe during the later 1990s, moreover, these were no longer the same socialist parties as before. Profoundly deradicalized, they were separating rapidly from the political cultures and social histories that had sustained them during a previous century of struggle. Communist parties, consistently the labor movements' most militant wings, had almost entirely disappeared. No one talked any longer of abolishing capitalism, of regulating its dysfunctions and excesses, or even of modifying its most egregiously destructive social effects. For a decade after 1989, the space for imagining alternatives narrowed to virtually nothing.

But from another perspective new forces had been energizing the Left. If labor movements rested on the proud and lasting achievements built from the outcomes of the Second World War but now being dismantled, younger generations rode the excitements of 1968. The synergy of student radicalism, countercultural exuberance, and industrial militancy jolted Europe's political cultures into quite new directions. Partly these new energies flowed through the existing parties, but partly they fashioned their own political space. Feminism was certainly the most important of these emergent movements, forcing wholesale reappraisal of everything politics contained. But radical ecology also arrived, linking grassroots activism, communitarian experiment, and extraparliamentary mobilization in unexpected ways. By 1980, a remarkable transnational peace movement was getting off the ground. A variety of alternative lifestyle movements captured many imaginations. The first signs of a new and lasting political presence bringing these developments together, Green parties, appeared on the scene.

In the writings of historians, sociologists and social theorists, cultural critics, and political commentators of all kinds, as well as in the Left's own variegated discourse, an enormous challenge to accustomed assumptions was generated during the last quarter of the twentieth century. The crisis of socialism during the 1980s not only compelled the rethinking of the boundaries and meanings of the Left, the needs of democracy, and the very nature of politics itself but also forced historians into taking the same questions back to the past. Contemporary feminism's lasting if unfinished achievement, for example, has been to insist on the need to refashion our most basic understandings in the light of gender, the histories of sexuality, and all the specificities of women's societal place. More recently, inspired partly by the much longer salience of such questions in the United States and partly by practical explosions of racialized conflicts in the 1980s and 1990s, a similar examination of race and ethnicity has begun. Many other facets of identity joined a growing profusion of invigorating political debates. In the process, the earlier centrality of class, as both social history and political category, dissolved. While class remained an unavoidable reality of social and political action for the Left in the twenty-first century, the earlier centering of politics around the traditional imagery of the male worker in industry had to be systematically rethought.

Conceived in one era, therefore, this book was completed in another. I began writing in a Europe of labor movements and socialist parties, of strong public sectors and viable welfare states, and of class-centered politics and actually existing socialisms. Though their original inspiration was flawed and the Soviet example was by then damaged almost beyond recall, Communist parties in the West remained carriers of a distinctive militancy. In the public sphere, rhetorics of revolution, class consciousness, and socialist transformation still claimed a place. With Socialists riding the democratic transitions triumphantly to power in Spain, Portugal, and Greece, Polish *Solidarnosc* tearing open the cobwebbed political cultures of Eastern Europe, and French Socialists forming their first postwar government, things seemed on the move. The years 1979–81 were for socialists an encouraging and even an inspiring time.

This gap between optimism and its ending, between the organized strengths of an already formed tradition and the emergent potentials for its succession, is crucial to the purposes of my book. I've written it to capture the drama of a still-continuing contemporary transition. To do so required both a detailed accounting of the past and a bold reconstruction of the present because both the achievements and the foreshortenings of the old remain vital to the shaping of the new. Although the century after the 1860s claims the larger share of the book, accordingly, the lines of the later twentieth-century argument are always inscribed earlier on. In that sense, I would argue, history can both impede the present and set it free. Moreover, beginning in the 1860s, my account moves forward through a series of pan-European revolutionary conjunctures, from the settlements accompanying the two world wars through the dramas of 1968 to the latest restructuring of 1989–92.

Ultimately, despite the endless complexities of detailed historiographical debate, the agonies of epistemology, and the excitements and frustrations of theory, historians can never escape the discipline's abiding conundrum of continuity and change. In some periods and circumstances, the given relationships, socially and politically, seem inert and fixed. Culture signifies the predictable and overpowering reproduction of what "is." It claims the verities of tradition and authorizes familiar futures from the repetitions of a naturalized past ("what has always been the case"). Politics becomes the machinery of maintenance and routine. The image of a different future becomes displaced into fantasy and easily dismissed. The cracks and fissures are hard to find.

But at other times things fall apart. The given ways no longer persuade. The present loosens its grip. Horizons shift. History speeds up. It becomes possible to see the fragments and outlines of a different way. People shake off their uncertainties and hesitations; they throw aside their fears. Very occasionally, usually in the midst of a wider societal crisis, the apparently unbudgeable structures of normal political life become shaken. The expectations of a slow and unfolding habitual future get unlocked. Still more occasionally, collective agency materializes, sometimes explosively and with violent results. When this happens, the formal institutional worlds of politics in a nation or a city and the many mundane worlds of the private, the personal, and the everyday move together. They occupy the same time. The present begins to move. These are times of extraordinary possibility and hope. New horizons shimmer. History's continuum shatters.

When the revolutionary crisis recedes, little stays the same as before. Historians argue endlessly over the balance—between contingency and structure, process and event, agency and determination, between the exact nature of the revolutionary rupture and the reach of the longer running pasts. But both by the thoroughness of their destructive energy and by the power of their imaginative release, revolutionary crises replenish the future. The relationship of the lasting institutional changes to the revolutionaries' willed desires will always be complex. William Morris famously expressed this in *A Dream of John Ball*: "I . . . pondered how [people] fight and lose the battle, and the thing that they fought for comes about in spite of their defeat, and when it comes turns out not to be what they meant, and other [people] have to fight for what they meant under another name."[1] Since the 1930s revolutionary sensibility has become ever more tragic in this way, memorably captured in Walter Benjamin's image of the angel of history, with its back to the future, unable "to stay, awaken the dead, and make whole what has been smashed" and compelled instead to gaze "fixedly" on the seamless catastrophe of the past, piling "wreckage upon wreckage" at its feet. The angel is propelled into an unseeable future by an unstoppable force, "a storm blowing from Paradise." "This storm," Benjamin reflects, "is what we call progress."[2]

Revolutions no longer receive a good press. The calamity of Stalinism and the ignominious demise of the Soviet Union have been allowed to erase almost entirely the Russian Revolution's emancipatory effects. Stalinism's ferocities during the 1930s and 1940s did irremediable damage to Communism's ethical credibility, it should be immediately acknowledged, enabling associative allegations against all other versions of socialist ideas. Justified reminders of capitalism's destructive and genocidal consequences for the world, both inside Europe and without, can never dispose of those histories, as fuller knowledge of Bolshevism's post-1917 record is making ever more clear. Nevertheless, for most of the twentieth century, it's important to note, the Left has more often stepped back from violent revolutionary opportunities than embraced them. Moreover, an honest admission of the dangers released by revolutionary uprisings needs to be balanced by two further recognitions. First, there remains something uniquely inspiring in the spectacle of masses of people in political motion, collectively engaging the future. Second, as this book will argue, the most important gains for democracy have only *ever* be attained through revolution, or at least via those several concentrated periods of change I'll call the great constitution-making conjunctures of modern European history.

I've been privileged in my own lifetime to have experienced two of these revolutionary moments—one successful, the other "failed"—while being formed in my childhood by the extraordinary achievements of a third. The 1989 revolutions in Eastern Europe were the most recent of these experiences, and their lasting democratic significance can be neither subsumed nor discounted by the damage to those societies subsequently wrought by marketization. An earlier revolutionary moment, that of 1968, was formative for my own political adulthood as well as for the larger understanding of the Left this book contains.

Finally, I was also formed in the protective and enabling culture of the post-1945 political settlement. I was a child of the welfare state. I drank its orange juice and received its vaccinations. I lived in its housing. I took for granted its third-pint bottles of school milk delivered daily to my classroom. I throve on its educational opportunities, while hating much of the delivery. I knew about family allowances, the National Health Service, free prescriptions, and the begrudging public respect accorded trade unions. I cried, without quite understanding the reasons, when Nye Bevan died, and I remember my mother's disapproval of his hymnless funeral. I was told a lot about the depression and somewhat less about the war, but I knew why they mattered. I understood how profoundly they had affected my parents' generation. Though I was not born until 1949, I remember the war very clearly; it was all around me. I knew why it was fought.

This book is written from great passion and great regret. It has taken me two long decades. Its writing was shaped and buffeted by a huge amount of contemporary change. It has required a willingness to rethink and surrender some valued assumptions and deeply cherished beliefs. Nonetheless, even allowing for the narratives of knowingness and consistency we like to construct for our intellectual biographies, the main lines of argument remain in many ways consistent with my thinking in the mid-1980s, though I'm sure I understand the implications far better now. It was on one of my returns to England in the spring of 1984, reentering the unique contemplative space of the railway journey (also a thing of the past) and reeling from the brutalized public atmosphere surrounding the miners' strike, that I knew the world had changed.

I can still weep for all the loss this entailed, for the wasted sacrifices and poor decisions, for the unsung everyday heroism as well as the more obvious courageous acts, for the crimes perpetrated in the name of virtue as well as those committed against it, for the gaps between promise and achievement, for the movements, communities, and cultures built painstakingly across generations whose bases are now gone. From my vantage point at the close of the twentieth century, there were many times when this seemed a painful book to be writing. It required a lot of letting go.

However, it is decidedly not an epitaph or an exercise in nostalgia. It is written from the conviction that history *matters,* particularly when some vital stories get mistold. That struggle of memory against forgetting has become something of a commonplace of contemporary writing, but is no less empowering for that. During the 1990s new amnesias brought some essential histories under erasure. The history of the Left has been the struggle for democracy against systems of inequality that limit and distort, attack and repress, and sometimes seek even to liquidate human potential altogether. Moreover, this is a history certainly not completed. If my book concentrates in its first three parts on the building of one kind of movement for the conduct of that struggle, the class-centered politics of the socialist tradition, then it seeks to hold that tradition's omissions and foreshortenings clearly in view. The book's final part then outlines the potentials from which a new politics of the Left can be made. In that sense, it looks to the future.

At various times during the writing of this book I was supported at the University of Michigan by the Richard Hudson Research Professorship in History, Research Partnerships from the Horace H. Rackham School of Graduate Studies and the Office of the Vice-President for Research, a Faculty Fellowship from the Institute for the Humanities, and a Michigan Humanities Award. In the summer of 1992, I held a Guest Fellowship at the Max Planck Institute for History in Göttingen. Very early versions of some chapters were typed by Jeanette Diuble, but the advent of word processing certainly hasn't removed the importance of first-class office support, and at various times I've been hugely dependent on the generosity and skills of Lorna Altstetter, Connie Hamlin, and Dawn Kapalla.

While still at Oxford University Press, Thomas LeBien gave me extraordinary help in the editing stages of this manuscript, and his guiding hand shaped the clarity and effectiveness of the final version. After his departure for Princeton University Press, Susan Ferber saw this book through to completion. Her editorial eye was keen and her guidance always surefooted and astute. I'm grateful to have had the benefit of these two consummate editors and of the anonymous readers' reports they commissioned, and the book reflects their input in numerous ways.

A book of this scale accumulates unmanageable debts. Mine begin with my colleagues at the University of Michigan, who since 1979 have provided an incomparably stimulating intellectual home. In the earliest stage I learned a huge amount from Roman Szporluk, who first educated me properly in the complexities of Eastern European history. Bill Rosenberg left his mark on part II, especially my understanding of the First World War and the Russian Revolution. My debt to Terry McDonald is as long as my presence at Michigan, beginning with a reading group on class and social history we ran in the early 1980s, the first of many settings where I've benefited from his rigorous intellectual generosity. Bill Sewell's presence was invaluable in the later 1980s when approaches to working-class formation were being so extensively rethought, and since the early 1990s so has been that of Sonya Rose. Peggy Somers was equally important across many intellectual fronts. Her head for theory constantly challenged me into clearing my own. For my understanding of contemporary Eastern European politics Mike Kennedy and Kim Scheppele were a wonderful resource. My grasp of contemporary European politics more generally owes an equally large debt to Andy Markovits.

It's impossible to communicate with any brevity the high quality of intellectual life in Ann Arbor, both in the History Department and in the wider interdisiplinary sphere. For almost twenty years the affectionately named Marxist Study Group has been giving me intellectual friendship and ideas, and since 1987 so has the Program on the Comparative Study of Social Transformations (CSST). These collective settings afforded my thinking clarity and confidence. A full accounting of my debts would require pages and pages, but among past and present colleagues I'd like especially to thank the following: Julia Adams, Paul Anderson, Sara Blair, Charlie Bright, Jane Burbank, David W. Cohen, Fred Cooper, Fernando Coronil, Val Daniel, Nick Dirks, Susan Douglas, Jonathan Freedman, Kevin Gaines, Janet Hart, Gabrielle Hecht, Julia Hell, June Howard, Nancy Hunt, Webb Keane, Alaina Lemon, Marjorie Levinson, Rudolf Mrazek, Sherry Ortner, Adela Pinch, Helmut Puff, Roger Rouse, David Scobey, Julius Scott, Rebecca Scott, Julie Skurski, Scott Spector, George Steinmetz, Penny Von Eschen, and Ernie Young.

Kathleen Canning has been my immediate colleague since the late 1980s. I'm not only a much better German historian in consequence but also far more conversant with the challenges of gender history. The clarity of the book's argument regarding class formation and its understanding of the importance of gender rely on the pioneering achievements of her work. She is an unfailing source of excellent friendship, knowledge, and advice. I'm equally privileged by having Kali Israel as my colleague and friend. Without her my relationship to all things British would be immeasurably the poorer. By her constant supply of information and small kindnesses, as well as by the largeness of her intellectual vision and friendship, the quality of this book has been hugely enhanced.

Many of my present and former students have helped with the book, initially via research assistance and the exchange of ideas, but increasingly through the excellence of their published work. I'm enormously indebted to them all. They include Richard Bodek, Shiva Balaghi, Monica Burguera, Becky Conekin, Belinda Davis, Todd Ettelson, Anne Gorsuch, Young-Sun Hong, Rainer Horn, Jennifer Jenkins, Mia Lee, Kristin McGuire, Orlando Martinez, David Mayfield, Amy Nelson, Mary O'Reilly, Kathy Pence, Alice Ritscherle, Chris Schmidt-Nowara, Steve Soper, Julie Stubbs, Dennis Sweeney, and Elizabeth Wood. They have also made Michigan into an extraordinary place.

In the wider world the range of my indebtedness is equally great. In many ways this book originated in conversations in Cambridge in the later 1970s at a time of far greater optimism than now, with a quality of intellectual friendship that permanently grounded my thought. The following will recognize their imprint not only in the book's notes but also in the architecture of its ideas: Jane Caplan, David Crew, Gareth Stedman Jones, Paul McHugh, Stuart Macintyre, Susan Pennybacker, and Eve Rosenhaft. Over the book's long life I've depended for bibliographical and interpretative guidance on the generosity and wisdom of large numbers of colleagues far and wide. More perhaps than they realize, their influence is essential to my intellectual and political bearings. I'd especially like to thank Ida Blom, Friedhelm Boll, Nancy Fraser, Dagmar Herzog, John-Paul Himka, Alf Lüdtke, Jitka Maleckova, Mica Nava, Frank Mort, Moishe Postone, Claudia Ritter, Adelheid von Saldern, Michael Schneider, Bill Schwarz, Lewis Siegelbaum, Carolyn Steedman, Michael Warner, and Eli Zaretsky.

A variety of seminars and conferences gave me the chance to try out parts of the argument, including a conference on "The Crisis of Socialism" in Chapel Hill in 1990; a theme year on "Utopia" at the University of Michigan Humanities Institute (1993); a memorial conference on Edward Thompson at Princeton (1994); a summer school for Eastern European political scientists in Gdansk (1994); a conference on twentieth-century Britain and Germany at Portsmouth (1995); a conference on "Anti-Fascism and Resistance" at the Fondazione Istituto Gramsci in Rome (1995); the Twentieth-Century Seminar in New York (1997); the Sawyer Seminar on "Democratic Detours" at Cornell (1998); and the Congress of Contemporary Spanish Historians in Valencia (2000). To all of these colleagues, and to audiences at the University of California in Davis and Santa Cruz (1993), SUNY-Stony Brook (1994), University of Minnesota (1994), University of Warwick (1995), University of Tel Aviv (1996), University of British Columbia (1999), the German Studies Colloquium in Ann Arbor (1999), and the New School University (2000), I'm exceedingly grateful. Especially valuable in this respect was the workshop on "Women and Socialism in Interwar Europe" organized by Helmut Gruber in Paris in 1994, whose proceedings were published as *Women and Socialism / Socialism and Women: Europe between the Wars,* ed. Helmut Gruber and Pamela Graves (New York: Berghahn Books, 1998).

This book could not have been written without the extraordinarily rich historiography now available for its various parts and dimensions, and I've relied necessarily on the insights and originality of specialists, as the footnotes will confirm. At the most general level of inspiration—intellectually, historiographically, politically—certain influences run throughout the book and indeed shape its basic design. In many ways Eric Hobsbawm has been a career-long mentor, although we've only met a handful of times. His insights shine into the most recondite corners of the Left's history, as well as illuminating its bigger picture, and sometimes one's writing feels like an extended footnote to his work. Similarly, the works of Perry Anderson, Stuart Hall, Sheila Rowbotham, and Hilary Wainwright are the crucial foundations on which my book has tried to build. If they find this a good book to think and argue with, I'll feel satisfied indeed.

Finally, some debts deserve to be especially honored. Books are written not only from libraries, archives, and seminar rooms but also from the wider contexts of personal and everyday life. In the earlier stages Eleanor Anasar provided vital supports. Over many years, through our parenting, working lives, and struggles against the school district she always kept me honest, helping me grasp not only the unity of theory and practice but why the personal has to be made political. The friendship of Karl and Diane Pohrt anchors me in similar ways. Karl's consistent and inventive observance of the ethical life, his civic engagement, and his commitment to the exchange of ideas in the public sphere provide a cast-iron model of political decency. He is the best bridge from the sixties, wonderful testimony to their active meanings in the present. For pleasures and enjoyment, for wisdom and understanding, and for solidarities and fellowship in the sheer arduousness of making a life, I've relied on an essential community of friends. In addition to everyone else mentioned, I can thank Nancy Bogan, Katherine Burnett, Paul Edwards, Eric Firstenberg, Jeff Jordan, Sharon Lieberman, Vic Lieberman, Helga Lüdtke, Armena Marderosian, Brady Mikusko, Bob Moustakas, Debbie Orlowski, Irene Patalan, Hubert Rast, Eli Rosenberg, Laura Sanders, Mike Schippani, and Denise Thal.

My dear friend and comrade Ron Suny has been present in the book from the start. As reader, lunch companion, conference organizer, fellow enthusiast, erudite and good-hearted colleague, latenight interlocutor, and sovereign historian of Bolshevism, his advice and support grounded my writing throughout. During the mid 1980s we worked together on the history of Communism and then watched spellbound as Gorbachev cracked open the Soviet Union's inertia and prised loose the opportunities for change. By the excellence of his own work and in countless conversations, Ron guided me through the complexities of Soviet history and the wider histories of socialism. Loyally and critically, he read the manuscript at every stage. Keith Nield has been there even longer. An article we wrote together in 1979, finished en route to the United States, was part of the preamble to this project. My grasp of the book's larger analytical dimensions, as well as my understanding of modern Britain, owe an enormous amount to his ideas. During the 1990s we shared far more than a common project on the contemporary histories of class, and the final stage of my writing benefited hugely from our long-running conversation.

In more ways than one Germany sits at the center of this book—during the second part as the exemplar of radicalism and then during the third as the vehicle of disaster. Atina Grossmann guided me through those histories, from the exhilirating 1920s into the horrors of the Third Reich and out through the ambivalence of Liberation. Her own writings and an essay we wrote together on the movie *Schindler's List* help me grasp those histories far better than before. My indebtedness to her friendship and wisdom is incalculable. At a crucial stage of the book, Lauren Berlant inspired me to think differently about some of the biggest questions—about the nation and its relationship to the local, about the two-way transmissions between personal everydayness and large-scale social transformation, and about the dialectics of utopia and failure. Though that conversation began with the 1920s and took many routes, its real resting place was sixty-eight, and the entire last part of the book presumes its influence. She unsettles political complacency and discouragement better than anyone I know. Bob Moeller has been the most selfless and reassuring of intellectual critics. His own work on the 1950s vastly helped my understanding, but he also provided a thorough and acute reading of a first draft long enough to test the most reliable friendship. Subsequent versions built gratefully on his detailed critique.

All these friends contributed immeasurably to whatever strengths my book might possess. They offer the best supports for optimism in a world increasingly exhausting its supply. The very best support of all is provided by Gina Morantz-Sanchez. She entered my life as the book approached its most difficult final stage. She challenged me into completing it. She purged my writing of excess and guided me toward clarity. She read every word, of which there were very many. From her great knowledge of U.S. history, the history of feminism, and the history of women, she brought invaluable comparative perspectives. She clarified the book's big ideas and pushed me into strengthening them. The final version breathes her presence. Of course, finishing a book requires other supports, too, and it's impossible to express adequately my gratitude for all the ways she kept me on track, at the cost inevitably of the other parts of life. Of unfailing good judgment, she helped guide this book to its finish.

Contents

List of Abbreviations, xix

Introduction   Democracy in Europe, 3

I MAKING DEMOCRACY SOCIAL

1   Defining the Left: *Socialism, Democracy, and the People*, 17
2   Marxism and the Left: *Laying the Foundations*, 33
3   Industrialization and the Making of the Working Class, 47
4   The Rise of Labor Movements: *History's Forward March*, 62
5   Challenges beyond Socialism: *Other Fronts of Democracy*, 85
6   The Permanence of Capitalism?, 109

II WAR AND REVOLUTION, 1914–1923

7   The Rupture of War: *Crisis and Reconstruction of the Left, 1914–1917*, 123
8   The Russian Revolution, 139
9   Breaking the Mold of Socialism: *Left-Wing Communism, 1917–1923*, 152
10 Germany and Italy: *Two Cases*, 165
11 Remolding Militancy: *The Foundation of Communist Parties*, 176
12 The Politics of Gender: *Women and the Left*, 185
13 Living the Future: *The Left in Culture*, 201
14 Broadening the Boundaries of Democracy, 220

III STABILIZATION AND THE "WAR OF POSITION"

15 Capitalist Stabilities: *Future Deferred*, 235
16 Stalinism and Western Marxism: *Socialism in One Country*, 249
17 Fascism and Popular Front: *The Politics of Retreat, 1930–1938*, 261
18 People's War and People's Peace: *Remaking the Nation, 1939–1947*, 278
19 Closure: *Stalinism, Welfare Capitalism, and Cold War, 1945–1956*, 299
20 1956, 329

IV FUTURE IMPERFECT

21 1968: *It Moves After All*, 341
22 Feminism: *Regendering the Left*, 366
23 Class and the Politics of Labor, 384
24 New Politics, New Times: *Remaking Socialism and Democracy*, 405
25 Gorbachev, the End of Communism, and the 1989 Revolutions, 429
26 New Social Movements: *Politics Out of Doors*, 457
27 The Center and the Margins: *Decline or Renewal?*, 470

Conclusion, 491

Notes, 505

Bibliography, 593

Index, 687

List of Abbreviations

APO	Extra-Parliamentary Opposition
ATP	SAP's Pension Reform
AVNOJ	Anti-Fascist Council of the People's Liberation of Yugoslavia
BCP	Bulgarian Communist Party
BSP	Bulgarian Socialist Party
BTs	*bourses du travail*
Bund	General League of Jewish Workingmen in Russia and Poland
BWSDP	Bulgarian Workers' Social Democratic Party
CEDA	*Confederación Espanola de Derechas Autónomas*
CFLN	*Comité Français de Libération Nationale*
CGIL	*Confederazione Generale Italiana del Lavoro*
CGT	*Confédération Générale du Travail*
CIS	Commonwealth of Independent States
CLN	Committee of National Liberation
CLPD	Campaign for Labour Party Democracy
CND	Campaign for Nuclear Disarmament
CNR	*Conseil National de la Résistance*
CNT	*Confederación Nacional del Trabajo*
Cominform	Communist Information Bureau
CPGB	Communist Party of Great Britain
CPSU	Communist Party of the Soviet Union
CSDSD	Czech Social Democratic Party
CSSD	Czech Social Democratic Party
DA	Danish Employers' Association
DAC	Direct Action Committee
DC	Italian Christian Democrats
DiY	"Do-It-Yourself" politics
DMV	German Metalworkers' Union
DNA	Norwegian Labour Party
EAM	National Liberation Front
ECCI	Executive Committee of the Comunist International
EEC	European Economic Community
EETPU	Electrical, Electronic, Telecommunications, and Plumbing Union
ELAS	National Popular Liberation Army
END	European Nuclear Disarmament

ERP	European Recovery Program
EU	European Union
FAI	*Federación Anarquista Ibérica*
FDP	Free Democratic Party
FGDS	*Fédération de la Gauche Démocratique et Socialiste*
FIOM	Italian Metal Workers' Union
FPO	United Partisans' Organization
FPTSF	Federation of the French Socialist Workers' Party
FVDG	Free Alliance
GDR	German Democratic Republic
GLC	Greater London Council
GLF	Gay Liberation Front
GMB	General and Municipal Workers
HAZ	Housing Action Zone Manor
HSP	Hungarian Socialist Party
IAH	International Workers' Aid in Berlin.
IKD	International Communists of Germany
ILP	Independent Labour Party
ISB	International Socialist Bureau
IWSA	International Woman Suffrage Alliance
JCR	*Jeunesse Communiste Révolutionnaire*
JSDS	Slovenian South Slavic Social Democratic Party
KAPD	Communist Workers' Party of Germany
KKE	Greek Communist Party
KOR	Committee for Workers' Defense, Poland
KPD	German Communist Party
KPJ	Yugoslav Communist Party
KSC	Czechoslovak Communist Party
LCC	Labour Coordinating Committee
LCS	Slovene League of Communists
LCY	Yugoslav Communist Party
LO	Danish Trade Union Federation
LP	British Labour Party
LSDWP	Latvian Social Democratic Workers' Party
LSE	London School of Economics
LSI	Labor and Socialist International
MRP	*Mouvement Républicain Populaire*
MSzMP	Hungarian Communist Party
MSZP	Hungarian General Workers' Party
NAC	National Abortion Campaign
NALGO	National and Local Government Officers Association
NEP	New Economic Policy
NOW	National Organization of Women
NSF	National Salvation Front, Romania
NUM	National Union of Mineworkers

NUPE	National Union of Public Employees
NUSEC	National Union of Societies for Equal Citizenship
NUWSS	National Union of Women's Suffrage Societies
OECD	Organization for Economic Cooperation and Development
OEEC	Organization of European Economic Cooperation
OS	*Organisation Spéciale*
OSE	Spanish State Union
P-2	*Propaganda Due*
PCE	Spanish Communist Party
PCF	French Communist Party
PDL	Slovakian Party of the Democratic Left
PDS	German Party of the Democratic Left
PDS	Italian Party of the Democratic Left
PLA	Albanian Communist Party
POB	Belgian Workers' Party
POUM	*Partido Obrero de Unificación Marxista*
PPR	Polish Workers' Party
PPS	Polish Socialist Party (Russia)
PPSD	Polish Social Democratic Party of Galicia
PS	*Parti Socialiste*
PSDR	Party of Romanian Social Democrats
PSI	Italian Socialist Party
PSIUP	Italian Socialist Party of Proletarian Unity
PSOE	Spanish Socialist Workers' Party
PSP	Portuguese Socialist Party
PSR	Romanian Social Democratic Party
PSU	*Partie Socialiste Unifié*
PSUC	*Partit Socialista Unificat de Catalunya*
PZPR	Polish Communist Party
RAF	Red Army Fraction
RC	*Rifondazione comunista*
RCP	Romanian Communist Party
RSDRP	Russian Social Democratic Workers' Party
RTS	Reclaim the Streets
SAP	Social Democratic Party of Sweden
SDAP	Dutch Social Democratic League
SDF	British Social Democratic Federation
SDF	Danish Social Democratic Association
SDI	Strategic Defense Initiative
SDKPiL	Social Democratic Party of the Kingdom of Poland and Lithuania (Russia)
SDP	Finnish Social Democratic Party
SDPC	Croatian Social Democratic Party
SDPR	Social Democrats of the Polish Republic
SDS	Socialist German Students

SDSS	Slovakian Social Democratic Party
SED	East German Communist Party
SFIO	*Section Française de l'Internationale Ouvrière*
SNR	Slovak National Council
SPA	Albanian Socialist Party
SPD	German Social Democratic Party
SPO	Austrian Social Democratic Party
SPS	Swiss Social Democratic Party
SRs	Russian Socialist Revolutionaries
SSDP	Serbian Social Democratic Party
SSP	Slovakian Social Democratic Party
TAZ	West Berlin's daily *Tageszeitung*
TGWU	Transport and General Workers
UDF	Union of Democratic Forces
UDI	Union of Italian Women
UGT	*Partido Obrero de Unificación Marxista*
UJC-ml	*Union des Jeunesses Communistes, marxistes-léninistes*
USDP	Ukrainian Social Democratic Party (East Galicia)
USDRP	Ukrainian Social Democratic Workers' Party (Russia)
USPD	Independent Social Democratic Party
WAVAW	Women Against Violence Against Women
WIRES	Women's Information, Referral, and Enquiry Service
WSPU	Women's Social and Political Union
WTB	Woytinsky-Tarnow-Baade
YCLs	Young Communist Leagues
ZAG	Central Working Agreement

FORGING DEMOCRACY

Introduction

Democracy in Europe

DEMOCRACY IN EUROPE has been a fragile, contested, unfinished, and relatively recent growth. It dates from the revolutionary crisis following the First World War, and then only fleetingly before being brutally swept away. Only after 1945, as a result of the victory over fascism, were democratic goods really attained. Even then, in socialist Eastern Europe a Stalinist counterrevolution immediately supervened, while in the southern periphery of Spain, Portugal, and Greece right-wing dictatorships prevailed. When democratic polities were finally created in those regions too, democracy became a general European reality.

But what does "democracy" mean? In the realm of law it requires at least the following: free, universal, secret, adult, and equal suffrage; the classic civil freedoms of speech, conscience, assembly, association, and the press; and freedom from arrest without trial. By this standard, democracy was achieved nowhere in the world during the nineteenth century and arrived in only four states before 1914—New Zealand (1893), Australia (1903), Finland (1906), and Norway (1913). If we relax our definition by ignoring women's suffrage, then the male democracies of France and Switzerland may also be added.[1] Though 1918 gave rise to the revolutionary circumstances that expanded juridical freedoms, these still proved short-lived and were only lastingly reinstated after 1945. Only the large-scale socioeconomic mobilizations of world war, it seems, created the societal context for the advancement of democratic politics. Hence the special resonance of 1918 and 1945.[2]

3

Juridical definitions describe democratization but can't explain how it came about. For this we need to go further by examining the dynamics of democracy's actual emergence, period by period and country by country. The obvious political arenas of struggle in parliamentary institutions and around citizenship rights are especially significant, but developments in social relations and culture are equally important. Ambitious packages of social rights implied by the rise of the welfare state expanded definitions of democratic entitlements. These were achieved by various forms of social mobilization and cultural self-assertion that gradually shifted definitions of public and private and made use of an increasingly mass-mediated public sphere.

None of these changes can be addressed convincingly without understanding their gender dimensions. This means assessing both the degree of women's inclusion as well as the impact of those gains on established gender regimes. Examining democratic access to see who exactly was given a voice makes the gendering of citizenship a vital aspect of democracy's story. Feminist critiques have emphasized how heavily post-Enlightenment political understanding relied on binary distinctions between men and women embedded in new notions of citizenship, personhood, and self. They have shown how these assumptions crucially limited "women's access to knowledge, skill, and independent political subjectivity," especially when embedded in languages of collective identity, from class and nationhood to religion and race.[3] For example, the basic category of civil society per se presumed women's exclusion. New distinctions of public and private gendered women primarily as mothers and managers of households, as opposed to social leaders and political actors. By the twentieth century, demanding the inclusion of women would require that concepts like the body politic and social citizenship be radically recast.

Though gender distinctions remained a persistent and pervasive source of conflict in the pursuit of democracy, the struggle against unequal power was at its core. Let there be no mistake: democracy is not "given" or "granted." It requires *conflict*, namely, courageous challenges to authority, risk-taking and reckless exemplary acts, ethical witnessing, violent confrontations, and general crises in which the given sociopolitical order breaks down. In Europe, democracy did not result from natural evolution or economic prosperity. It certainly did not emerge as an inevitable byproduct of individualism or the market. It developed because masses of people organized collectively to demand it.

The spread of democracy had a vital transnational dimension. It was shaped to a great extent beyond the frontiers of the nation itself by a series of horizon-expanding pan-European conjunctures between the eighteenth century and the present. There have been five such moments of transnational constitution-making in modern European history, which laid down limits and possibilities for the decades to come: 1776–1815, 1859–71, 1914–23, 1943–49, and 1989–92. For the purposes of this book, the 1860s form the baseline, establishing the enduring framework for popular politics until a new series of radicalized conflicts began to dissolve it during 1905–14. Likewise, the years 1914–23 produced another generalized redrawing of the map, setting the scene for the polarized politics of revolution and counterrevolution that generated fascism.

In the 1860s, liberal constitutionalism registered an impressive international growth through the reorganization of states and recognition of popular rights, most important in relation to the franchise but also including limited legalization of trade unions on a local and national scale, from Spain to the Habsburg Empire and from Britain to Greece. Moreover, these constitutional frameworks fashioned in the 1860s proved remarkably resilient. Stability sometimes had to be secured through national crises, with major feats of accommodation in response to popular pressure, with a definite quickening of difficulties in the decade before the First World War. But in each case, crucially, the changes occurred through constitutional means. Even if extraparliamentary in form, popular pressure was applied mainly *within* rather than *against* the available liberal constitutional frameworks.

Though democracy's most spectacular gains have always occurred on a transnational scale, national states organized around representative government were also a vital prerequisite. The French Revolution had introduced Europeans to the idea that governments could be "for the people," upsetting the stability of early-nineteenth-century authority structures and inspiring a range of revolutionary movements. But only when a system of liberalized nation-states solidified during the 1860s could movements emerge to organize popular hopes. This was most apparent in Italy and Germany, where unification created territorial states for the first time. The newly established constitutional machinery of German and Italian national politics, linked to liberal precepts of self-government and civic responsibility, created the first viable bases for separately organized popular democratic movements. A strengthening of liberal constitutionalism in Europe's older territorial states had the same effect. Dramatic insurgencies of the people had occurred periodically before the breakthrough of the 1860s—in 1830–34, again in 1848–51, and in many more isolated cases across the continent—occasionally sustaining a longer presence on the national stage, as with Britain's Chartists between 1837 and 1848. But only with the 1860s were the legal and constitutional conditions created for popular democratic parties.

Between the 1870s and 1890s, country by country across the map of Europe, socialist parties were formed to give government by the people coherent, centralized, and lasting political form. Until the First World War and to a great extent since, those parties carried the main burden of democratic advocacy in Europe. For most of the period covered by this book, in fact, the banner of democracy was held up most consistently by the socialist tradition. In the 1860s and 1870s, it was socialist parliamentarians who marked out a distinctively democratic space in the liberal-constitutional polities created by the pan-European upheaval of the time. As national labor movements then established themselves, this advocacy became strengthened, until by 1914 social democratic parties had become fixtures of their political systems—at their strongest in a north-central European "core," where between 25 and 40 percent of the national electorates gave socialists their votes.

SOCIALISM AND THE LEFT

This book was initially conceived in the early 1980s, as a deep crisis in the established forms of the Left's politics was already becoming apparent. For most of the century, the Left was defined by socialist and Communist parties, who, despite their mutual antipathies, also acknowledged a common tradition going back to the late nineteenth century. Even the small Trotskyist and Maoist revolutionary sects, contemptuously dismissive of Communists and social democrats alike, affirmed that longer tradition. Throughout the twentieth century, moreover, other progressive movements also oriented themselves around the dominance of these two main parties, finding it virtually impossible in practice to avoid their embrace. Occasionally, progressive causes were pursued separately—in certain anticolonial movements of the 1950s and 1960s, most feminisms, sexual dissidence, a variety of single-issue campaigns, and every so often a new party, like the Commonwealth Party in Britain during the Second World War. But for public effectiveness and legislative success left-wing causes *needed* socialist and Communist support. They provided the political oxygen, and in that sense, they *hegemonized* the Left.

Between the late 1960s and the 1990s, this ceased to be the case. After the suppression of reform movements in Czechoslovakia and Poland (in 1968 and 1981), governing Communisms had finally exhausted any remaining credibility as agencies of progress, although ironically the Soviet invasion of Czechoslovakia had finally pushed western European Communists into developing an independent political course explicitly critical of the Soviet model. However, by the early 1980s it was clear that this "Eurocommunist" direction had also run out of steam. Communist electoral performance began slipping in Italy, and in France and Spain it entirely collapsed. Determined Eurocommunists drew their conclusions and began shedding their Communist identities altogether.

Concurrently, social democratic parties fell into disarray. The British Labour Party and the German Social Democratic Party (SPD) entered a parliamentary wilderness for 18 and 16 years of opposition, respectively, in 1979 and 1982; the initial euphoria of socialist election victories in France, Greece, and Spain in 1981–82 rapidly palled in the face of austerity programs and rising unemployment; governing socialists in Austria and the

Low Countries vacated any distinctive policies; and the long-dominant Scandinavian socialists lost both their confidence and their lock on office. The context of this crisis was the economic recession beginning in 1973, which abruptly ended the postwar pattern of continuously expanding growth on which social democratic confidence relied. During the long post-war prosperity—a "golden age" of capitalist stability, rising living stan-dards, and broad-based social consensus—social democracy's goals of full employment, rising real wages, and a generous welfare state had been se-cured without damaging capitalist accumulation. But in this new period, the pillars of that earlier arrangement—Keynesian economics, comprehen-sive welfare states and expanding public sectors, corporatism and strong trade unions—crumbled.

In other words, the strength of social democracy was embedded in a larger postwar system of politics, which itself was breaking apart. Here the pan-European antifascist popular consensus of 1943–49, itself forged in the crucible of the defeat of Nazism, had been the key. In contrast to the fragilities of the earlier settlement after 1918, this societal consensus proved extremely robust, enjoying both legitimacy at the level of the state and breadth in popular culture. Drawing on democratic patriotisms elicited by wartime solidarities and fusing hopes for a new beginning with the needs of economic reconstruction, the reform coalitions taking office in 1945 managed to ground their programs in the kind of lasting societywide agree-ment that had eluded their predecessors in 1918. The institutional strength of a liberalized public sphere, with all the necessary legal protections and reasonable latitude for pluralism and dissent, was a vital aspect of this big democratic gain. Above all, the full-scale popular mobilizations needed to win the war delivered the momentum for a generously conceived social contract during the peace. These reformist strengths allowed a remarkable degree of popular identification with the state after 1945, giving it lasting reserves of moral-political capital.

Thus the strength of the postwar consensus in Western Europe required more than the prosperity of the long boom or the negative cement of the Cold War; it also presumed that the image of the good society, so pro-foundly shaped by the antifascism of 1945, was finally becoming a reality. The forms of cohesion in a society—and the conditions allowing their re-newal—depend crucially on the identifications forged in popular memory with that society's political institutions, and here a comparison of the twen-tieth century's two great constitution-making conjunctures, 1914–23 and 1943–49, says a great deal. In each case, the scale of societal mobilization, the radicalism of the institutional changes, and the turbulence of popular hopes all fractured the stability of existing allegiances and ripped the fabric of social conformity wide enough for big democratic changes to break through. But in 1918 building sufficiently strong popular identifications with the new democratic states remained highly contested, as the political polarizations of the interwar years and the rise of fascism so tragically

consensus breaks down
dethrone w/c

revealed. After 1945, in contrast, the Western European consensus proved both broad and deep, producing remarkably resilient popular loyalty to the postwar democratic order.

That postwar consensus lasted for two decades. Beginning in the 1960s, however, powerful new developments challenged its continuation. The post-1973 recession, the capitalist restructuring of the post-Fordist transition, and a drastic reshaping of the class structure emerged as key structural developments. Accompanying them were the political explosions of 1968, the rise of a new feminism, and a proliferating ferment of new social movements, identity-based activism, and alternative political scenes. As a result, socialist and Communist parties of the traditional kind lost their dominance of the Left. For a century before the 1960s, those parties had performed the major work of democratic advocacy in Europe, building support through elections and rooting their influence in finely developed popular organization. They had functioned primarily as popular movements based in communities, binding their constituencies by means of elaborate subcultural solidarities. They now went into unarrested decline. Electorally, they found themselves outflanked by Green parties, left-socialists, and a variety of radical democratic initiatives. Moreover, to a great extent the grassroots energy for Left campaigning now passed increasingly beyond the parliamentary arenas favored by socialism to a new localized, fragmented, and amorphously shifting extraparliamentary milieu.

This book will trace the implications of this vital contemporary transition, partly by historicizing the rise and fall of the classical socialist tradition between the 1860s and 1980s and partly by analyzing the post-1968 realignment. If contemporary transformations have exposed socialism's weaknesses in the present, especially the exclusionary consequences of centering democratic strategy on the progressive agency of the industrial working class, then these insights have much to teach us about socialism's limitations in the earlier periods too. If the centrality of the working class has been deconstructed in contemporary social and economic analysis, what happens if we "dethrone" the working class from its privileged primacy in socialist politics in various periods of the past? Feminist critiques of "class-centered" politics since the 1970s have been especially illuminating here, and the powerfully gendered limitations of the Left's history will be a recurring theme of this account.

The complex relationship between socialism and democracy—or between "socialism" and "the Left"—is a vital theme of this book. For a century after the 1860s, in this regard, two complementary principles held good: socialism was always the core of the Left; and the Left was always larger than socialism. Socialists never carried their goals alone. They always needed allies—whether in fighting elections, forming governments, organizing strikes, building community support, conducting agitation, working in institutions, or professing ideas in a public sphere. As socialists lost their hegemony in the Left after the 1960s and other radicalisms entered the *exclusion*

Left's political space, the terms of such negotiations grew ever more complex. Socialists found themselves forming new types of coalitions, or they overhauled their programs and appeals to accommodate the new constituencies. But even in the earlier periods, this book will repeatedly argue, socialists either broadened their appeals in equivalent ways or else held the "class-political" ground and effectively excluded significant populations from the socialist fold. The contraction of socialist politics around strongly gendered ideals of working-class masculinity, with discriminatory and exclusionary consequences for women, was the most important of these effects.

WHERE IS THE LEFT GOING, NOW? —> 1990s = *crisis end of socialism*

Between the late 1960s and the fall of Communism in 1989–91, the socialist tradition entered a long crisis, from which it has yet to recover. For Communists, this was certainly connected to the Soviet Union's loss of legitimacy and final collapse, but social democracy experienced an equally debilitating loss of compass with the unraveling of Keynesianism during the 1970s and 1980s. In both cases, socialism ceased functioning as a convincing alternative to capitalism. In popular perceptions, certainly in the allowable languages of public debate, socialist ideas lost all resonance. As a credible program for replacing capitalism—for reorganizing the economy on the basis of a centrally planned and bureaucratically coordinated state sector—socialism fell apart. As a forseeable project, it receded from practical view. *political*

Thus by the 1990s, socialist advocacy of traditional kinds became almost entirely silenced. The triumphalist rhetoric of the "end of Communism" gave the reckless dominance of marketizing programs in Eastern Europe almost unstoppable force, while in the West neoliberal dogmas permeated political understandings of feasible governance. Social democratic parties replayed the earlier revisionism of the 1950s, this time almost completely shedding the socialist skin, embracing the new neoliberal frameworks via languages of "modernization." With few exceptions, the Communist parties also dissolved or remade themselves, realigning the identity of the Left with a broad politics of democratic coalition, as against socialism per se. In all of these ways, whatever the electoral success of parties still calling themselves "socialist," socialism as a class-political program for transforming or replacing capitalism seemed to be at an end. *social*

This political crisis had an underlying social history too. Socialist labor movements developed in a particular era between the 1880s and 1930s, with strong continuities lasting till the 1960s. They were shaped by the distinctive infrastructure of urban economies, municipal government, and working-class residential communities produced by industrialization, which delivered the underpinnings of socialist political success during the twentieth century.[4] But this social landscape of industry also started disappearing after the 1960s. For the preceding century, it had been the basic environment in which socialist labor movements convincingly championed the cause of democracy. Not only that, those movements also chalked up huge democratic achievements to their credit.

This historic Left had proved more than simply "good enough." It doggedly and courageously constructed the foundations for democracy in Europe. It consistently pushed the boundaries of citizenship outward and forward, demanding democratic rights where *anciens régimes* refused them, defending democratic gains against subsequent attack and pressing the case for ever-greater inclusiveness. Socialist and Communist parties—parties of the Left—sometimes managed to win elections and form governments, but, more important, they organized civil society into the basis from which existing democratic gains could be defended and new ones could grow. They magnetized other progressive causes and interests in reform. Without them, democracy was a nonstarter. Between the 1860s and the 1960s, they formed the active center of any broader democratic advance. This is the history of socialism that needs to be recovered and given its due.

If in its two-century history the Left stood for democratic constitutionalism, expanding citizenship, egalitarianism, respect for differences, and social inclusiveness, then the centering of this politics around socialist values also entailed some distressing limitations. Precisely because socialists proved such effective advocates of democracy, certain issues became effaced. As well as affirming democracy's indebtedness to the Left, therefore, this book also analyzes the *insufficiencies* of socialist advocacy—all the ways socialism's dominance of the Left marginalized issues not easily assimilable to the class-political precepts so fundamental to the socialist vision. Questions of gender were the most obvious case, but other foreshortenings also recurred: questions of local control and cooperative organization excluded by socialism's state-centered logic; sexualities, family forms, and personal life; agrarian problems; questions of colonialism, nationalism, and the continuing conundrum of "race."

These were the questions that invaded the Left's imagination after 1968. For the crisis of socialism came not just from its collision with the unexpected realities of a transformed real world of capitalism. Equally fundamental challenges came from *outside* socialism's familiar class-political frameworks altogether—within theory, within as-yet-unreflected areas of social practice, and within micropolitical contexts of everyday life. The strongest challenge came from feminism. But others quickly followed: antinuclear campaigning; environmental activism; peace movements; gay-lesbian movements and the wider politics of sexuality; local community politics; squatting and the creation of "alternative scenes"; left nationalist and regionalist movements; and, last but not least, antiracism, both responding to antiimmigrant and related radical-right agitations and creating

extending boundaries of politics

space where racialized minorities themselves started to organize. These new movements allowed contemporary identity politics to emerge.

If the old class-centered paradigm of nationally organized socialisms had lost its hold on the definition of the Left—the primary lesson of the 1990s—then these new movements formed the starting points for a politics capable of taking its place. The making of the socialist tradition into the main agency of democracy's advance was the product of a particular era, 1860–1960, which is now over. But if socialism's importance for the Left can be located in this particular period, in a powerful nexus of social histories and political forms whose possible conditions had dissolved, the next question immediately arises: how should democracy be located in the present? What were the Left's coordinates in the new era opened by the 1960s? How might a new sociopolitical basis for democracy be composed? How can further extensions of democracy take place?

Just as contemporary capitalist changes were recomposing the working class rather than abolishing it, so would the reconfigured forms of socialist politics continue to shape the Left. If socialism no longer offered a systemic alternative to market-based types of economy, socialist critiques of capitalism had not lost their force. Socialists had always demanded that liberals live up to their professions of pluralism, tolerance, and respect for diversity, moreover, while grounding arguments about freedom in their own robustly egalitarian philosophy. Strong and elaborate conceptions of social justice and the collective good also retained their oppositional importance against the individualist shibboleths of the neoliberal ascendancy. In all of these ways, the socialist tradition held vital resources for the remaking of the Left, not least because parties calling themselves socialist remained the most popular and reliable repositories of democratic goods.

But the post-1968 movements had also radically expanded socialism's horizons, charting new territories of democratic practice, whether socialists opted to travel there or not. The *boundaries of politics*—the very category of the political—had been extended by feminists, gay liberationists, environmentalists, autonomists, and others. The possible meanings of democracy had changed. These innovations had proceeded largely beyond the awareness of older Left parties, with very few exceptions. Moreover, the new parties—Greens, left-socialists, and other emergent radicalisms—were small and barely captured much of this energy. Far-reaching political realignment was certainly remaking the national political space—not only by reshaping the relationships between socialist parties and their erstwhile supporters but also in novel processes of coalescence, which gave previously marginalized Greens and other radicals a place. Even more: for a century after the 1860s, with the vital exceptions of 1917–23 and 1943–47, parliamentary politics overwhelmingly dominated democratic political action, but after the 1960s this was no longer so. The relationship between a variegated extraparliamentary sphere of localized and often particularistic *failures + crimes* —→ *Violence*

"movement" politics and the continuing parliamentary arenas was becoming the key front of democratic renewal.

Writing this book has involved a complicated ethics. The history of the Left contains much violence, many wrong turnings, many failures of principle and nerve, a great deal of horrifying excess. Stalinism, in particular, spreads like a noxious and indelible stain across a significant part of this history. Likewise, in the field of extremism created by fascists and revolutionaries, and again by Communists and anti–communists, social democracy frequently chose complicity in democracy's restriction and damage. Conventional histories of the Left are also often periodized around a chronology of revolutionary *failures*—in 1848, 1871, 1917–23, 1936, 1956, 1968, and more. I've tried neither to rationalize the failings and omissions nor to look away from the crimes. I've tried not to romanticize missed opportunities. But while acknowledging the Left's defeats and limitations, this book's perspective is different. It tells a story of democracy's European trajectory, whose uneven success was secured by the Left, sometimes passionately, sometimes painfully, but always as the necessary and most reliable support.

In this achievement, we are all the beneficiaries. If we consider the great dramatic moments of European constitution-making, which moved the frontier of democracy forward, from the 1860s to 1989, the Left's radical democratic agency was always there. The political values the Left fought for in those moments, and in the long and arduous intervals in between, have become the values we all accept. The degeneration of the Bolshevik revolution under Stalin and the Stalinization of Eastern Europe after the Second World War have necessarily compromised socialism's place in this accounting. But elsewhere in Europe socialists have been fundamentally responsible for all that we hold dear about democracy, from the pursuit of the democratic franchise, the securing of civil liberties, and the passing of the first democratic constitutions to the more contentious ideals of social justice, the broadenening definitions of citizenship, and the welfare state. Democracy has always been a shifting frontier, whose idealistic but unrealized projections were as vital as the recorded gains. As we move through the unfamiliar landscape of the twenty-first century, therefore, this is a future we will need to remember. And in constructing our maps, we will need the knowledge contained in the Left's rich past.

MAKING DEMOCRACY SOCIAL

Preparing the Future

IN OCTOBER 1895, twenty-four-year-old Edith Lanchester announced to her family her intention of living with James Sullivan in a "free love" union: they had fallen in love and were opposed on principle to marriage as a social institution because it destroyed women's independence. Both were members of the Battersea branch of the Social Democratic Federation (SDF), the small but vigorous British socialist party formed in 1884, he a self-educated workingman of Irish extraction, she the university-educated daughter of a wealthy middle-class London family. Edith had been an SDF activist since 1892, running unsuccessfully for the London School Board in 1894 and joining the party's Executive in 1895.[1]

The day before the free union was to begin, Edith's father and three brothers arrived at her lodgings accompanied by Dr. George Fielding Blandford, a well-known mental specialist. After a short meeting, during which Blandford discussed the marriage question with Edith, invoking the likely consequences of having children and the dangers of desertion, she calmly reaffirmed her decision. Blandford withdrew and signed a certificate of insanity on behalf of the family, whereupon the brothers dragged Edith from the house, threw her in a carriage, bound her wrists, and delivered her to a South London private asylum. Despite her protests, the medical officer duly admitted her. The goal was to save her from "social suicide" and "utter ruin," Blandford explained, because "her brain had been turned by Socialist meetings and writings."[2]

The SDF and the wider radical public moved immediately into action. Sullivan applied for a writ of habeas corpus and alerted the press; public "Lanchester meetings" were organized, addressed by stalwarts of the movement; and a band of SDF supporters rallied overnight at the asylum. In response to the writ, two commissioners in lunacy found Edith of sound mind, if misguided, and ordered her discharged, though only after a delay. John Burns, an SDF founding member but now Battersea's sitting Liberal MP, wrote to the home secretary and the commissioner of police, expediting Lanchester's release and accompanying her and Sullivan home on 29 October. After this four-day ordeal, Lanchester broke definitively with her family, who remained obdurately convinced of the rightness of their action. She remained an active SDFer, attending the London Congress of the Second International in 1896 and speaking frequently at party meetings around the country.

This "Lanchester case" unleashed an extensive public discussion. The SDF itself defended Lanchester's rights, but while condemning the kidnapping and misuse of the law and nodding to the critique of marriage, it argued for pragmatic observance of "the world as it is" and disavowed individual "anarchistic action or personal revolt."[3] It was concerned most of all to dissociate itself from "free love" doctrines: these alienated potential recruits, inflamed the general public, and intruded personal matters inappropriately into politics. To accuse socialists of wanting a "community of women" was merely a slur, but advocacy of sexual freedom gave socialism's enemies a golden weapon. The rival Independent Labour Party (ILP) broadly agreed. Its leader, Keir Hardie, worried about socialism's bad name: "Enemies of Socialism know that such an escapade as that meditated by Miss Lanchester tends to discredit it among all classes."[4]

There were some contrary views. A few SDFers applauded Lanchester's "noble and altruistic example" as a blow against "this dark age of hypocrisy and ignorance." Robert Blatchford's independent socialist weekly *Clarion* concurred: "Socialists believe that a woman has a perfect right to do what she likes with her own body . . . in defiance of priests, laws, customs and cant."[5] Beyond the immediate SDF leadership, in fact, was a much more variegated radical milieu, where cultural dissidence was nourished. Although the trial and demonizing of Oscar Wilde earlier in 1895 had placed sexual radicals under duress, the Lanchester case gave them a chance to speak back.[6] Herbert Burrows, a founding member of the SDF active in Lanchester's defense meetings, personified this secularist and dissenting strand: "the archetypal 'faddist' . . . he was teetotal, anti-tobacco, a vegetarian and a theosophist as well as being an advocate of women's rights." In 1888 he had helped organize the famous matchgirls' strike and became treasurer of their union, campaigning for women's rights at work through the Women's Trade Union League and the Women's Industrial Council. He was an early supporter of women's suffrage.[7]

After 1900, this milieu burgeoned through the electoral rise of the Labour Party, the broadening of intellectual dissent, a gathering swell of industrial militancy, the seeding of local socialisms, and the spectacular growth of the women's suffrage movement. One speaker prominent in Lanchester's defense meetings was the future Labour MP and party chair, George Lansbury. Another was Mary Gray, with whom Lanchester lodged. From lower middle-class origins, Gray worked in domestic service and in 1876 married Willie Gray, a stonemason who was frequently victimized for his trade unionism. She joined the SDF in 1887, became an active speaker, and served on its Executive during 1896–1903. She created the first Socialist Sunday School in 1892 and in 1895 won election as an SDF candidate to the Battersea Board of Guardians. She was keenly active for women's suffrage, working through the Battersea Women's Socialist Circle.[8]

In comparison to the rest of Europe, Britain acquired a strong socialist party very late, and then somewhat ambiguously, as the Labour Representation Committee of 1900 only slowly solidifed into a Labour Party distinct from the Liberals. But the breadth and vitality of its emergent socialist milieu in the 1880s and 1890s certainly resembled the socialist cultures elsewhere, pulling in secularists and freethinkers, feminists and suffragists, spiritualists and Christian socialists, educators and improvers, and all kinds of progressives, as well as the socialist and trade unionist core. From the turn of the century, Europe's socialist parties blossomed into mass popularity with utopian verve, declaring the confrontation with capitalism the "last great battle of the world," which heralded a "paradise of purity, of concord, of love." Socialism meant "the death of darkness and the birth of light," making possible a "regenerated world."[9]

Socialism's utopian imperative was crucial to its rank-and-file support. At the vital rhetorical and motivational levels, in the multiform micropolitical contexts of everyday life, the sense of a better and attainable future was what allowed the countless ordinary supporters of the socialist parties to commit their sustained support. As the Lanchester case revealed, socialist politics created frameworks in which many other progressive causes could be raised. While those causes were still oppositional, and the existing system mobilized great resources to keep them on the outside, they were already reshaping the terms of debate. Rising to impressive success in elections and organizing an imposing presence in society, by 1914 Europe's socialist parties presented an increasingly resilient democratic challenge.

utopian

Chapter 1

Defining the Left

Socialism, Democracy, and the People

THE VOCABULARY OF "Left" and "Right" came from the radical democratic ambience of the French Revolution.[1] When the French Constituent Assembly divided on the question of the royal veto and the powers reserved for the king during 1789–91, radicals took a position physically on the left-hand side of the chamber as viewed from the president's seat, facing conservatives on the right. As this alignment clarified, the "Left" became identified with a strong democratic stance, embracing abolition of the royal veto, single-chamber legislature, an elected rather than an appointed judiciary, legislative supremacy rather than separation of powers and a strong executive, and—most vital of all—the democratic franchise of one man, one vote. During the climactic radicalization of the Jacobin dictatorship in 1793–94, further items were added, including a people's militia as opposed to a professional standing army, anticlericalism, and a progressive system of taxation. Just as this package outlived the French Revolution to dominate much of the nineteenth-century political scene, so too did the seating arrangements. The terms "Left" and "Right" passed into general European usage.

The French Revolution's great rhetorical trinity—"liberty, equality, fraternity"—also accompanied these origins. Gendered connotations aside, "fraternity" implied an ideal of social solidarity vital to most left-wing movements, while "equality" resided at the Left's philosophical core. In demanding the rule of the people, moreover, the Left sought to bring down the power of something else, an *ancien régime,* a socioeconomic ruling class, or simply a corrupt governing establishment. Sov-

17

ereignty of the people was thought to be denied not just by restrictive and repressive political systems, but also by unequal social structures. In the Left's tradition, some notion of social justice was practically inseparable from the pursuit of democracy.

DEMOCRACY AND SOCIETY: VISIONS OF A JUST WORLD

Calls for democracy were linked during the era of the French Revolution to more elaborate visions of the just society, organized around an ideal of independent small property and local self-government. In traditions of popular democracy, this linkage went back to the English Revolution in the seventeenth century and the ideals of the Levellers; in the eighteenth century it reemerged in the plebian radicalism of the American Revolution and related movements in the Low Countries and Britain. During the 1790s, such movements acquired the general name of Jacobinism. Their pursuit of local democracy was greatly inspired by the insurgency of Parisian trades-men, shopkeepers, and impecunious professionals, reaching its apogee in the militancy of the sans-culottes during 1792–94.[2]

This radical democracy of small property holders dominated the popular insurgencies flaring across Europe at various times in the 1820s, in 1830–31, and during the tumults of 1848. It flourished best amid large concentrations of handicrafts, where commercial growth both stimulated the skilled trades and assailed them with a new business uncertainty or where industrialism degraded them into systems of outwork and "protoindustry." It fed on the teeming environment of Europe's capital cities, which brought artisans together with shopkeepers, small traders, lawyers and other professionals, book dealers, journalists, and grubstreet intellectuals to compose the familiar Jacobin coalition. Democratic movements might extend upward to elements of the recognized political nation or downward into the peasantry. Closer to 1848, they were augmented by students and some proletarianized workers. This pattern first registered in the last quarter of the eighteenth century—in the American colonies; in London, Norwich, and other centers of English Jacobinism; in Belfast and lowland Scotland; in Warsaw; in the Low Countries, Switzerland, northern Italy, and other areas of native radicalism paralleling the French; and of course in Paris.[3]

These were societies experiencing an early capitalist transition, where market forces were already transforming existing relations of production but where older popular ideologies of the just society endured. Inequalities among merchants, masters, and men widened, and large parts of the countryside became proletarianized through the expansion of cottage industry. But this transitional world still supported the idealized political projections of the protesting rural outworker, displaced journeyman, and respectable master artisan, with their belief in a moral economy and the commonwealth of all producers. Desires to protect and restore traditional forms of small-scale production could still be sustained, if not by a paternalist government then via radical visions of federated exchange and cooperation among self-governing units of independent producers. The permanence, future direction, and irreversibility of capitalist industrialization had yet to be clearly perceived.

Yet even as this radical democracy reached its climax in 1848, its bases were being undermined. The same capitalism penetrating the world of the small producer was also forging a very different environment of industry—of factories and mills, capitalists and wage-earners, and new urban populations. Certainly the speed of these developments can be exaggerated. In Britain, the pioneer industrializing economy, capitalist production remained remarkably dependent on both manual skills and small-scale organization, and in many industries this blunted the threat to the artisan's status. Artisans remained proudly distinct from the mass of the unskilled and laboring poor, defending their property in skill, respectability and independence and armored by the sovereignty of the workshop. Between the late 1830s and early 1850s in Britain, Chartism became the first mass political movement of the industrial working class, transcending divisions between "artisanal" and "proletarian" workers to a remarkable extent. But *artisanal* attitudes provided the defining force, both as a distinctive approach to economy and society and in a larger tradition of thinking about the British state. Where industrialization came later, in the rest of Europe, such attitudes also had a long life.

Conditions varied industry by industry. Some divisions of labor and technologies of production were kinder to craftsmen than others. Artisans disappeared rapidly in the more obviously modern industries, like iron and steel from the late nineteenth century and the highly mechanized new sectors of chemicals and electrical engineering from the start of the twentieth, followed by the pathbreaking mass production industries in automobiles, aircraft, appliances, and other forms of assembly between the wars. In less capital-intensive branches like textiles and large areas of light manufacture, artisans fared much better, as these combined outwork and unskilled "sweated" labor with craft production using workshop-based hand technologies. Other industries—like construction, carpentry, printing, leather-working, glass-making, shipbuilding, metalworking, and in a different way mining—continued to need handicraft workers of a very traditional sort.

Yet, whether we focus on newly created categories of industrial labor or reconstituted forms of older skills, the capitalist reorganizing of the economy through industrialization necessarily changed the worker's place in society. Artisans increasingly lost control of their trades to the impersonal forces of the capitalist market. They surrendered the autonomy of the workshop to practical forms of dependence on larger-scale business organization, before eventually becoming integrated directly into superordinate structures of capitalist production, employment, and control. Once that happened, social ideals of small-scale organization, local community, and personal independence became far harder to sustain. That is, under conditions of capitalist industrialization the implications of demanding popular sovereignty became profoundly transformed.

Gradually and unevenly, democracy became linked to two new demands: an economic analysis of capitalism and a political program for the general reorganizing of society. The new ideas didn't follow inevitably from socioeconomic change. But in the most general way, changes in the democratic idea clearly had this material source. They resulted from the serious efforts of political thinkers, and countless ordinary women and men, to understand the disruptions of their accustomed world. It was in that moment of transformation that people began exploring the possibilities of collective ownership and cooperative production. And in that juncture of socioeconomic change and political rethinking the ideas of socialism were born.

Thus democracy was always embedded in social history. Both the radical democracy deriving from the French Revolution and the early socialism emerging from the 1830s entailed packages of practical socioeconomic demands. Such demands were deemed an essential accompaniment of genuine democracy, and this now became measured not by the centrality of small propertied independence but by the advent of a new collectivism. Moreover, socialist ideas had a power and resonance of their own. They became diffused, embodied in institutions, and fixed into social relations; they entered people's consciousness and behavior, becoming powerful motivations in their own right. The replacement of one kind of democracy by another entailed more than merely adjustment to a changing society, through which popular awareness eventually caught up with the new conditions. It was also a contest of ideas, with long and undecided results.[4]

The later nineteenth century became the scene of much confusion, as societies, regions, and economic structures shifted in different ways and at different speeds and as the distinctive socialist ideal of democracy—"the social democracy," as the pioneers called it—struggled to take form. Earlier democratic ideas showed remarkable tenacity in the subsequent socialist movements. Given European unevenness, that "earlier period" in any case meant not just the era between the late eighteenth century and 1848 but extended well into the 1860s in Germany, Italy, and central Europe and later still in the peripheries of the south and east. That older radical heritage was only finally left behind after 1917–18 via processes of dramatic clarification going back to the 1890s. The history of the socialist tradition before 1914 was still in many ways a working-through of older legacies, as socialist politicians tried to decide what they owed to earlier democratic traditions and what these traditions could no longer provide.[5]

DEMOCRACY MADE SOCIAL

If capitalist industrialization transformed the conditions under which democratic ideals had to be pursued, the social meanings of those ideals also changed. As the term "socialism" entered into general currency after 1850, this was the transition it was used to express. "Social" came to signify something more than the common system of institutions and relationships in which people lived and started to imply a desirable contrast to the emergent capitalist form of society. It came to mean "an idea of society as mutual cooperation," as opposed to one based on "individual competition." Indeed, the "*individualist* form of society" associated with the new system of wage labor and private property became rejected as "the enemy of truly *social* forms" in this sense. Thus "[r]eal freedom could not be achieved, basic inequalities could not be ended, [and] social justice . . . could not be established, unless a society based on *private* property was replaced by one based on *social* ownership and control."[6]

In this way, democracy's advocates gradually faced the consequences of progress. In 1848, "social-democracy" had still meant just the far left wing of the radical coalitions.[7] But as capitalist relations penetrated ever-larger regions of socioeconomic life, it became harder and harder to generalize the immediate circumstances of independent small producers into programs for organizing the economy as a whole. This opened the space where socialist thinking could begin to emerge as a new and plausible option.

This space expanded once liberalism crystallized into an ideology celebrating an entirely individualist type of society. As liberal ideas invaded public policy during the mid–nineteenth century, socialism became ever more serviceable for analyzing their harmful effects. The causal connections between private property, individualist philosophies, and an economically founded system of class domination became ever easier to make. On the one hand, that society increasingly conceded certain formal equalities of citizens under the law, including after the 1860s even limited forms of the right to vote. On the other hand, extreme material inequalities were still defended by liberals as essential preconditions for the system.

The economics of democracy became the Left's insistent preoccupation in the second half of the nineteenth century. For radical democrats of an earlier time, private property held within modest limits was a social ideal to be defended against the rapacity of parasites and speculators. But for socialists, private property itself was the source of social ill. While liberals consciously worked for the separation of the economic from the political sphere, socialists came to see that very separation as a debilitating discrepancy. Or, as Jean Jaurès, the French Socialist leader before 1914, put it: "Just as all citizens exercise political power in a democratic manner, in common, so they must exercise economic power in common as well."[8] Accordingly, *social democracy* came to signify not only the most radical form of parliamentary government but also the desire to extend democratic precepts to society at large, including the organization of the economy. This—*the making social of democracy*—was the crucial post-1848 departure.

By the last third of the nineteenth century, socialists were challenging political definitions of democracy with a new question: how can genuine democracy be achieved in a society fundamentally structured by class inequalities of ownership, distribution, and control? On this basis, the main features of socialist economic policy became hotly debated—cooperation, public ownership and the socializing of production, industrial democracy, and planned direction of the economy. But of course, as most socialist governments have found, any attempt to democratize the economy in the name of such policies encounters all manner of vested interests with privileged access to political, bureaucratic, and ideological power. In practice, democratic goals can only ever be pursued against the resistance of dominant social groups.

The decisive political and philosophical question then becomes: how far can attacks on the legitimacy of private interests stay compatible with the democratic principle, without requiring the use of force and the damaging of basic rights, while the new collectivist system is being installed? This question has caused the Left endless difficulties over the years, as I will show. How it tended to be resolved became one of the main dividing lines between reformist and revolutionary movements.

DEMOCRACY'S GENDERED HORIZON

Socialism's belief in democracy's social determinants and constraints—the salience of the social in social democracy—was a fundamental broadening of the democratic idea. But in other ways, the latter remained seriously foreshortened. For most of the early democratic movements, except for the utopian socialists in the earlier nineteenth century, popular sovereignty remained a *male* preserve. Chartism in Britain, as the most impressive of these early movements, made this especially clear, because its famous Six Points for democratizing the constitution drawn up in 1837–38 expressly excluded votes for women.[9] By the end of the nineteenth century, European socialist parties had certainly become the foremost advocates of women's political rights, but female enfranchisement had still made virtually no progress by 1914. Women had the vote only in certain parts of the North American West and four of the world's parliamentary states: New Zealand in 1893, Australia in 1903, Finland in 1906, and Norway in 1913.[10]

In labor movements, women's second-class citizenship was linked to explicitly discriminatory thinking consigning them to the family, household management, and ancilliary economic roles, whether paid or not. In agrarian and preindustrial societies, these patriarchal forms of the household economy were secured via systems of property holding and inheritance. In handicrafts, they found their urban counterpart in systems of apprenticeship, legal regulation, and guild exclusion, defining skill and the practice of a trade as a form of property privileged to men. Industrialization then added its own aggressively gendered images of the imagined family economy, in which the wages of skilled working men would support orderly and respectable households where wives had no need of a job. Few working-class households actually matched this ideal. Working-class wives mustered unbounded resourcefulness for economic survival, supplementing their husbands' wages by foraging, marginal cultivation, casual services like laundry, cleaning, and childminding, petty trading, cottage industry and home work, and waged work of many kinds. But through the norms of the male "breadwinner" and the "family wage," the ideal exercised powerful effect. Whatever their *actual* economic behavior, working-class wives were placed ideologically inside the home and beyond the waged economy.

Thus, socialism's official supportiveness for women's rights usually concealed a practical indifference to giving them priority in the movement's work. Where neither working men nor working women possessed the vote, left-wing movements refused to back women's suffrage until the men's franchise was won. But where *man*hood suffrage already prevailed, women's rights became subordinated to economic issues. Either way, women were expected to wait. Here, socialism's grasp of democracy's social context worked to women's specific disadvantage, because the primacy of economics reduced everything else to a secondary concern. The more consistent the socialism, one might even say, the more easily feminist demands were postponed to the socialist future, because a sternly materialist standpoint insisted that none of these questions could be tackled while capitalism perdured.

Such an attitude precluded a more radical approach to the "woman question," as it came to be known. But this wasn't simply a failure of political perception or a consequence of the socialist tradition's more materialist theory. It was also the result of deeper ideological structures, deriving from older systems of masculine superiority. These were located partly in the family, partly in the strength of society's dominant values, and partly in gendered divisions of labor in the economy. But precisely because such patterns were so deeply embedded in the conditions of working-class life, they proved extraordinarily resistant to anything but the most forthright of political critiques. And this the socialist tradition was manifestly unwilling to provide. Behind the labor movements' neglect of women's issues were historically transmitted patterns of gendered culture, which left-wing politicians consistently failed to challenge and invariably endorsed.

This was one of democracy's most egregious limitations. While it led to broader codification of women's demands in socialist party programs, industrialization not so much subverted older patterns of female subordination as reproduced them in new ways. Just as the earlier democratic politics bequeathed lasting legacies to the socialist parties, which were only consciously sorted through in the decades surrounding the First World War, so the earlier assumptions about women's place constrained the Left's ability to imagine a gender politics that was genuinely egalitarian. Until the specific concerns of women were consciously addressed—until socialism also became feminist—the pursuit of democracy would stay severely incomplete.

Socialist downgrading of women's issues was all the worse for the prominence before 1914 of impressive women's mobilizations—in the various national suffrage movements, in educational politics and social reform, in relation to women's industrial work, and in largely intellectual or bohemian movements for sexual emancipation. It was precisely in many such areas that masculine privilege was directly called into question. Strong notions of women's reproductive rights and liberated sexuality were already emerging, reaching fuller expression in the 1920s. As those movements made clear, deficiencies of left-wing thinking in gender terms could only be remedied by bringing politics directly into the personal sphere.

But a full exposure of such questions has only really dated from the 1960s with the emergence of present-day feminism, which challenged the older Left across a broad front of previously neglected issues. The late-nineteenth-century transition from radical to socialist democracy established a pattern lasting for the next hundred years: namely, principled support for women's rights on the basis of a broadened social program but within an overall economism that in practice consistently downgraded the priority of the women's struggle. Post-1968 feminism proved vital in bringing these questions onto the Left's agenda. Both for the character of the contemporary Left in the last third of the twentieth century and for revisiting the earlier periods, recent feminist critiques became indispensable. Indeed, by battling its demands to the center of public debate, via painful conflicts that were certainly not complete, contemporary feminism compelled a rethinking of the viable terms of the socialist project and in the process profoundly redefined the Left.

THE PARTY AND THE PEOPLE

The modern mass party, which became the prevailing model of political mobilization in general between the 1890s and the 1960s, was invented by socialists in the last third of the nineteenth century. By our own time, it had fallen into disrepute and was described increasingly as the enemy of democracy rather than its bulwark. Late-twentieth-century radical democrats condemned bureaucratic centralism and secretive decision-making as distortions of democratic process, whether in their Communist or social democratic guise. Parties were no longer seen as the vectors of the people's will but as instruments of manipulation, anonymous machines removed from the grass roots, protected against popular accountability. In light of such disillusionment, therefore, it's important to grasp the democratic purposes the socialist model of the party was originally meant to serve, and this is best accomplished by examining the earlier organizational forms that preceded the turn to socialist parliamentarianism after the 1860s.

One of these was the local workers' association. From their beginnings between the 1840s and 1860s, working-class clubs subsequently became adapted into the cellular basis for the new national labor movements, whether in the form of the socialist party local in northern and central Europe or as the syndical "chamber of labor" in the south. During the first half of the nineteenth century, though, the Left was also identified with the spectacle of revolution—with the imagery of barricades, popular uprisings, and the toppling of monarchies from power. Before the importance of the party for socialism could be established, therefore, an older model of political transformation had to be laid to rest, namely, the conspiratorial tradition most associated with the indefatigible revolutionism of Auguste Blanqui.[11]

Inspired by the drama of the French Revolution's most radical phase in 1792–93, Blanquism conceived the revolution as an exemplary act triggering a general uprising of the people, directed by a secret revolutionary brotherhood whose dictatorship would secure the results. This thinking originated with Gracchus Babeuf and his quixotic "Conspiracy of the Equals," which sought to salvage the French Revolution's radical momentum in 1796. Babeuf's legacy was then transmitted through the career of his surviving comrade, Filipo Buonarroti, and thence to Blanqui.[12] The "art of insurrection" flourished during the most overbearing phase of the post-1815 Restoration in Europe, whose climate of censorship and repression forced democrats into conspiratorial methods. Personifying in one dimension an ideal of selfless revolutionary heroism and passionate egalitarianism, Blanqui was also an ascetic and egocentric optimist, treating the masses as always available for revolution, if the right moment could only be seized. This seemed vindicated by the great revolutionary explosions of 1830 and 1848, which owed so little to organized preparation. But the fiasco of Blanqui's failed Parisian uprising of 1839 was a far more fitting verdict on his conspiratorial ideal.

The point about Blanquism was its profoundly *undemocratic* character. The conspiratorial ideal postulated a small secretive élite acting on behalf of a popular mass, whose consent was to be organized retroactively by systematic reeducation but who in the meantime couldn't be trusted. Logically enough, Blanquists opposed universal suffrage until after the revolution. They were bored if not repelled by the popular democratic politics actually developing between the 1830s and 1870s, as the repression originally justifying conspiratorial methods slowly and partially eased. In contrast, Karl Marx and the social democratic tradition inaugurated in the 1860s decisively repudiated conspiratorial vanguards and their fantasies of insurrection. The possible need for the revolution's armed defense against counterrevolutionary violence by the ruling class was left open. But between 1871 and 1917 the dominant model of revolutionary politics for socialist parties now hinged on the democratic promise of an irresistible parliamentary majority. The Paris Commune of 1871, which displayed both the heroism and the tragic limitations of the earlier insurrectionary tradition, became the key watershed. Its failure showed the need for democratic methods beyond the conspiratorial horizon.

Henceforth, the pure insurrectionary mode became the property of anarchists, for whom in this respect Michael Bakunin became the leading voice.[13] After the decisive debates of the First International in 1868–72, which secured the victory of parliamentarist perspectives within the Left, Blanquism lost coherence. Conspiratorial methods lacked purpose in an age of popular suffrage, elections, and parliamentary debates. Insurrectionism survived among the Spanish anarchists, with a wider European revival during the syndicalist pursuit of the revolutionary general strike after 1900. But for anarcho-syndicalists, the insurrectionary fantasy became divorced from the ealier conspiratorial precepts. A genuine uprising of the people had no need of any directive leadership in that sense. "Strong men need no leaders," Spanish anarchists like to say.

Conspiratorial methods resurfaced from time to time. Spanish anarchism remained the main source. The libertarian anarcho-syndicalist federation formed in 1919, the *Confederación Nacional del Trabajo* (CNT), was the opposite of a centrally managed trade-union bureaucracy or party machine. But it was matched by the clandestine *Federación Anarquista Ibérica* (FAI) formed in 1927, the quintessence of elitist and conspiratorial revolutioneering. This contradiction between high-flown libertarian rhetoric, which inspired ordinary supporters to acts of life-endangering militancy, and the authoritarianism of the underground plotting that sent them to their deaths, was Michael Bakunin's main legacy. Such activity spilled easily into terrorism. Its temptations remained strongest at times of repression or defeat, when chances for public agitation were most reduced: in tsarist Russia in the later 1870s and early 1880s and again in the early 1900s and in Spain, France, and Italy in the 1890s.[14]

The more troubling of these earlier legacies remained *vanguardism*—the idea that minorities of disciplined revolutionaries, equipped with sophisticated theories and superior virtue, could anticipate the direction of popular hopes, act decisively in their name, and in the process radicalize the masses. Given democracy's imperfections and the complex reciprocities of leaders and led, this remained a recurring problem of political organization in general, because even in the most perfect of procedural democracies a certain latitude necessarily fell to the leadership's discretion, beyond the sovereign people's practical reach. As a rule, however, except when driven underground, the socialist and Communist parties of the twentieth century organized their supporters on the largest scale via systems of procedural democracy, competed in elections, worked through parliaments and local government, and participated in the public sphere.

In that vital sense, socialist constitutionalism was founded on the ruins of the older Blanquist understanding of how revolutions were made. The socialist model of the mass party, campaigning openly for public support and parliamentary representation on a national scale, and organizing its own affairs by the internal democracy of meetings, resolutions, agreed procedures, and elected committees, was *the* vital departure. It was the crucial democratic breakthrough of the nineteenth century's last four decades.

SOCIALISM: UTOPIAN AND DEMOCRATIC

The other major precursors of the labor movements establishing themselves after the 1860s were the utopian socialists, traditionally patronized and dismissed by the later tradition, from moderate parliamentarians and trade unionists to social democrats and Communists alike. Marxists in particular, taking their cue from Friedrich Engels's tract *Socialism: Utopian and Scientific,* repeatedly translated and reprinted after its initial appearance in 1878–80, saw these early exponents of socialism as naïve philosophers inadequately capturing the social logic of the new capitalist age, at best anticipating bits and pieces of the "scientific socialism" developed after the 1840s by Karl Marx.[15] Lacking the moorings of a "mature" working-class presence in society, it was implied, thinkers like Claude Henri de Saint-Simon, François-Charles Fourier, and Robert Owen could only ever have produced visionary blueprints of an ideal society, which the realities of the class struggle and the collective agency of the future labor movements would inevitably supersede.

Their writings—Saint-Simon's *Letters from an Inhabitant of Geneva* (1802), Fourier's *Theory of the Four Movements* (1808), and Owen's *New View of Society* (1812–16)—gave much license for this verdict. In deliberate contradistinction to organized Christianity, they centered a new "science of man" on human nature, advancing social cooperation against the egotism, individualism, and competition that currently reigned. Saint-Simon gave rational and progressive centrality in the new society to all those performing productive functions, from industrialists to scientists and engineers, professional men, and laborers. In the absence of aristocrats, kings, and priests, these "industrialists" would replace privilege, competition, and laziness with functional hierarchy, mutualism, and productivity. Relying on a more elaborate and fanciful psychology, as well as a frequently bizarre cosmology, Fourier projected minutely specified self-contained communities, whose intricate complementarities of tasks and functions would guarantee the happiness of all. Owen designed his New Lanark cotton mills to show the origins of cooperation in healthy social arrangements, including generous working hours and conditions, social insurance, educational provision, rational recreation, and good housing.[16]

The utopians' chosen medium of small-scale experimental communities, Fourier's "phalansteries" and Owen's "Villages of Cooperation," had no connection to labor movements, because their ideas were conceived well before working-class political activity developed, and indeed before the term "socialist" itself was coined in the late 1820s and early 1830s. Utopian socialism contained no critique of capitalist economics, focusing rather around religious and philosophical issues—"equality *versus* hierarchy, human uniformity *versus* differentiation of human types, the speed of social transformation, self-interest or 'devotion' (altruism) as the mainspring of human and socialist progress, the relationship between socialism and religion."[17] It prioritized popular education, seeking to reveal "the mystery of social harmony and human happiness" through the ideal social arrangements of its communities. Religiosity was "inherent in the structure of early socialist thought." Its main enemy was less the undemocratic state or the structure of the capitalist economy than the moral authority of established Christianity. "Its yardstick of judgment was its knowledge of the true nature of man, which excluded original sin and the laws and coercion based upon it."[18]

Having failed to interest the governing élite in his theories of human perfectibility, Owen spent 1824–28 in the United States, where he sponsored the model community of New Harmony in Indiana amid a broader rash of North American communitarian experiments.[19] In the wake of these Owenite and similar initiatives by followers of Fourier and Saint-Simon, utopian ideas circulated remarkably widely, forming a vital reservoir for the labor movements already emerging in western Europe in the early 1830s.[20] The explosive history of the Owenite Grand National Consolidated Trade Union, which flared briefly across Britain's agitated political landscape in 1834, was especially notable. By the spread of Étienne Cabet's "Icarian" movement in the 1840s, named after his utopian novel *Voyage of Icarus* (1839), this culture of socialism, or "communism" as Cabet's followers preferred, had become widely diffused in France too, particularly among those artisanal trades that were being industrialized via the use of cheap and unapprenticed labor, such as tailoring and shoemaking.[21] Through the ferment linking the British reform agitation of 1829–32 with Chartism, and the 1831 and 1834 uprisings of the Lyons *canuts* (silk-weavers) with the 1848 Revolution, "socialist" language now came to define a specifically working-class interest.[22]

In contrast to either radical democracy or the future social democratic tradition, utopian socialism implied retreat from state-oriented thinking about democracy. Yet by the 1830s Owenites had become integral to British radical agitations, as had Saint-Simonians like Philippe Buchez and Pierre Leroux in France. After his early indebtedness to Babeuf, moreover,

Cabet learned much from Owenite trade unionism during his British exile in 1834–39, and after he returned to Paris his newspaper *Le Populaire* helped broaden French republicanism in socialist directions. Both Cabet and Pierre-Joseph Proudhon influenced early French socialism far more than historians have allowed, enunciating demands for government action and national political organization that belied the more naïve utopianism often ascribed to them. Rather than embracing the full-scale communitarian ideal of secession from the existing competitive and selfishly individualist society, in fact, working-class politicians owed Owen, Fourier, and Saint-Simon a much looser general debt: ideals of "association," "mutualism," and "cooperation"; the rationalist and humanist critique of bourgeois society; and the practical conviction that human affairs could be differently and better ordered.[23]

For democracy's longer term, utopian socialists left countervailing legacies. On the one hand, they clearly did retreat into apolitical and often outlandish forms of experimental community building, which left little usable experience for labor movements trying to organize on a national scale. This flight from politics, and indeed from society itself, into small communal enclaves, symbolized by the transatlantic journey to the New World, left a silence on the subject of how the transition to a new type of society was politically to be carried out.[24] Utopian socialists were similarly indifferent to political economy and the structural origins of class-structured inequality. Post-1860s social democrats explicitly repudiated both these aspects of the earlier heritage.

On the other hand, the creative commitment to forms of small-scale community-based cooperation, extending more ambiguously toward participatory democracy, left a far more positive legacy. In the politics of Louis Blanc and other socialist radicals during the 1848 Revolution, the ideals of "association" supported concrete demands for producer cooperatives and "social workshops" to be financed by the French state, while for workers in central and eastern Europe during the 1860s cooperative ideals of collective self-help provided the commonest early encounter with socialism.[25] Ideas of the "emancipation of labor" bespoke simple but passionate desires for a juster world, often framed by mythologies of a lost golden age, which in a crisis like 1848 could easily sustain belief in revolutionary transformation. Likewise, the impulse for self-government, localized earlier in the physical spaces of New Harmony and the other utopian settlements, resurged in the Paris Commune of 1871 as a more programmatic revolutionary demand.

Most interestingly of all, the utopians practised an extremely radical politics of gender. Thus Fourier espoused the full equality of women with men, sexual freedoms, and the dismantlement of marriage, while Owenites attributed capitalism's moral degradation ("the contagion of selfishness and the love of domination") to "the uniform injustice . . . practised by man towards woman" in the family, which thereby functioned as "a center of absolute domination."[26] Indeed, for Owenites the "competitive system" grew not just from the values inculcated by factories, churches, and schools but also from the familial organization of personal life: "*Homo oeconomicus,* the atomized, competitive individual at the center of bourgeois culture, was the product of a patriarchal system of psycho-sexual relations."[27] Any new way of life thus required a complete rethinking of intimate relations, so that the privatized family and its oppressive marriage laws could be replaced by communal arrangements and true equality. If mutuality became established both communally and between the sexes, one Owenite feminist argued, "then would woman be placed in a position in which she would not sell her liberties and her finest feelings."[28]

This early feminism was enunciated at a time of generalized resistance to capitalist industry, when socialists could imagine saving society by remaking human character in the mold of cooperation. But if it was feasible during the 1830s to project a space of reformation *beyond* the capitalist framework, by the second half of the nineteenth century, as Barbara Taylor says, "there was far less 'outside' to go to," and working-class organizations now accepted the given basis of the wage relation.[29] In the meantime, commitment to gender equality was lost. Visions of sexual freedom and alternatives to the patriarchal family were pushed to the dissident edges of the labor movements. Women were no longer addressed by means of an independent feminist platform but were treated as either mothers or potential workers. The earlier belief in sexual equality ("women's petty interests of the moment," as the German Social Democrat Clara Zetkin put it) became swallowed into the class struggle. Or, as Eleanor Marx exhorted in 1892: "we will organize not as 'women' but as *proletarians* . . . for us there is nothing but the working-class movement."[30]

Thus utopian socialism proved a moment of exceptional radicalism on the gender front, which remained unrecuperated until the late twentieth century. While Owen's and Fourier's foregrounding of moral reformation was easily dismissed by later nineteenth-century socialists, along with their indifference to a nationally organized politics of the class struggle, their critiques of the family and women's subordination also fell casualty to these same dismissals. Henceforth, questions of sexuality, marriage, childraising, and personal life were largely consigned to a private sphere away from the central territory of politics. They ceased to be primary questions of socialist strategy.

TOWARD THE 1860s

During the nineteenth century, the Left forged its independence above all through its conflicts with liberalism. Liberals bitterly resisted democratic citizenship. In liberal theory, access to political rights required possession of property, education, and a less definable quality of moral standing—

what William Ewart Gladstone called "self-command, self-control, respect for order, patience under suffering, confidence in the law, and regard for superiors."[31] From Edmund Burke and Alexis de Tocqueville to the ideologues and practitioners of liberalism during its ascendancy of the 1860s and 1870s, including the most generous of radicals like John Stuart Mill, liberals consistently disparaged the civic capacities of the masses, reaching a crescendo of fear during the 1848 revolutions and the first pan-European surge of popular enfranchisement in 1867–71. In liberal discourse, "the democracy" was synonymous with rule of the mob.

Varying by country, labor movements accordingly separated themselves from liberals during the middle third of the nineteenth century. Just as socialists turned their backs on the locally organized cooperative utopia, they also substituted popular sovereignty for the free and sovereign liberal individual. From the 1860s, a socialist constitutionalism took shape that had little in common with the local projects of communal self-administration that first inspired socialist thinking earlier in the century. Socialists had previously functioned as junior elements in broadly liberal coalitions, occasionally gaining greater prominence through the radicalizing opportunities of a revolutionary crisis, as in 1848–49. They had also lobbied for intermediate forms of producer cooperation backed by a reforming government, including national workshops or a people's credit bank, bordering on the more ambitious schemes of Proudhon, Cabet, and other utopians. And finally, the Blanquist temptation of revolutionary conspiracy had also remained.

In all respects the 1860s proved a decisive break. Thereafter socialists in most of Europe put their hopes in a centrally directed party of parliamentary democracy coupled with a nationally organized trade union movement. The case for this kind of movement was successfully made in a series of bitterly conducted debates dominating the European Left from the early 1860s to the mid-1870s, for which the main forum was the International Working Men's Association, or the First International, a new coordinating body created in 1864 and eventually closed down in 1876.[32] Moreover, the rise of this social democratic model was decisively furthered by the growing prevalence in Europe of parliamentary constitutions linked to the principle of the national state, which received a spectacular push forward in the 1860s from German and Italian unification and the broader constitution-making upheavals of that decade. The enabling opportunities of the resulting liberal constitutionalism crucially affected the progress of the social democratic model.

The centralized politics of socialist constitutionalism now coalesced over a 50-year period within the framework of parties that began to be founded, country by country, in the 1870s. But local cultures of socialism and democracy needed much remolding before social democracy could fully prevail. At the grassroots the interest in socialism kept a much stronger emphasis on the local sovereignty of popular democratic action, bespeaking that earlier radical heritage, which social democracy only partially managed to express. Mid-nineteenth-century popular movements had registered exceptionally impressive levels of politicization, carrying the Left's momentum far beyond its usual boundaries. In villages and small towns, as well as the larger urban agglomerations, militants fought the authorities over schooling, recreation, religion, and other aspects of local everyday life. British Chartism was the most impressive of these movements, followed closely by the popular radicalisms of 1848–51 in France, where political clubs and workers' corporations attained high peaks of activism in Paris and other towns and the Democratic-Socialists ("democ-socs") permeated the villages. More localized counterparts could be found in many other countries too between the 1840s and 1860s.[33]

How successfully such energies could be captured and remolded for the purposes of democratic empowerment in Europe's new capitalist societies, both as memories of popular struggle and as active potentials for a still to be imagined future, was the challenge facing the emergent socialist movements of the last quarter of the nineteenth century.

Chapter 2

Marxism and the Left

Laying the Foundations

WHEN KARL MARX died in 1883, socialist organization barely existed in Europe—a united Socialist Workers' Party in Germany, Danish and Dutch Social Democratic associations, fledgeling parties in the Czech and Hungarian parts of the Habsburg Empire, a French Socialist Federation, tenuous networks in Portugal and Spain. Even these were fragile growths, subject to persecution. Yet within a decade, socialist parties existed in all but the remoter reaches of the east. By the time Friedrich Engels, Marx's lifelong collaborator, died in 1895, all Europe's main regions—German-speaking central Europe, the Low Countries, Scandinavia, the Catholic south, tsarist Poland and Habsburg Croatia, even the new states of the Balkans—had acquired, country by country, an organized socialist presence. The remainder rapidly followed—all the Slav peoples of the Habsburg Empire; Jews, Ukrainians, Finns, and Latvians under tsarism; and finally a Social Democratic Workers' Party for Russia itself. By the early 1900s, the map of Europe was entirely occupied by socialist parties, providing the main voice of democracy, anchored in popular loyalties and backed by increasingly impressive electoral support.

This sense of forward movement was a far cry from the crushing isolation of the 1850s, when Marx began his critique of capitalism. After three years of plotting, barricades, fiery journalism, and unremitting revolutionary excitement during 1848–50, Marx found himself stranded in decidedly unrevolutionary London, surrounded by the disappointments of exile and defeat, suffering the hardships of penury, ill health, and family loss. Connected

to the earlier hopes of a general European revolution mainly via the wan-
derings and fantasies of refugees, Marx then sank his energies into books,
laboring in the British Museum, intensively thinking and writing, giving his
faith to the subterranean workings of history, where the "old mole" of
revolution was still surely "grubbing away."[1] It was a decade before popular politics began moving discernedly again. Only in the 1860s did the
apparently solid stabilities of the post-1849 reaction come unstuck.

Bridging this huge gap—between the revolutionary defeats of 1848–49
and the permanent rise of socialist parties by the 1890s—is the task of this
and the following chapters. Democracy in Europe exploded violently across
the continent in the 1790s, flaring from its French revolutionary source,
only to be extinguished with the restorations of 1815. It flashed brilliantly
again in 1848, before order was inexorably restored. Of course, the European narratives of democratic advance recorded many local achievements
between the 1800s and 1860s, with dramatic exceptions to the main story
of stability in transnational crises like 1830–31 or in national movements
like Chartism and its predecessors in Britain in the 1830s and 1840s. The
reemergence of democratic politics in the 1860s also presupposed longer
and less visible accumulations of local experience, patiently built by unsung
pioneers and invariably borne by small-scale community-based action.[2]

But it was only with the pan-European constitution-making of the 1860s
that durable legal and political frameworks were created—national states
with parliamentary institutions and the rule of law—through which democratic aspirations could achieve organized and continuous form. When
democratic parties emerged from the 1870s, they were usually socialist.
And the most important source for their guiding political perspectives was
the thought and legacy of Karl Marx.

WHO WERE MARX AND ENGELS?

Karl Marx (1818–83) and his collaborator Friedrich Engels (1820–95) were
scions of the very class they hoped to destroy: the self-confident and prosperous bourgeoisie, whose spokesmen were slowly emerging in Prussia's
western provinces into a belief in their progressive role in history. Marx
seemed poised to repeat his father's career as a successful lawyer in Trier,
enrolling at Bonn and Berlin Universities; Engels was apprenticed in the
Barmen family firm of Ermen and Engels in 1836, moving to a merchant's
office in Bremen. Their early lives neatly revealed the main axis of the
developing social order—*Bildung und Besitz*, education and property, the
twin pillars of German bourgeois respectability.[3]

Both lives were blown off course by intellectual radicalism. Marx joined
the Berlin circle of Young Hegelians in 1837, Engels the Young Germany
movement in 1841. But while the textile industry and Bremen's commercial
traditions faced the young Engels toward the dynamism of British indus-

trialization, the Rhineland's recent Francophone history pointed Marx to the progressive heritage of the Enlightenment and the French Revolution. Both comparisons gave the German intelligentsia a sense of urgent inferiority during the *Vormärz,* or "Pre-March," in the years preceding the 1848 revolutions. Well before those events would sweep across Europe, Marx and Engels had ample chance for reflection—Marx by returning in July 1841 to the progressive western corner of Germany, where he deepened his philosophical critique of the Prussian state; Engels by a two-year stay in Manchester, observing industrialization's social effects at first hand. Meeting in Brussels in August 1844, they began their intimate collaboration.

While writing together, they worked politically among migrant German artisans in Brussels, Paris, and London, joining the German Revolution in 1848–49. After the triumph of European counterrevolution in 1849, Marx withdrew to London for the rest of his life, while Engels ran the family business in Manchester. The 1850s were bleak for Marx, with financial difficulties, family tragedies, and little to show for his efforts. This changed in 1857, when a first Europe-wide crisis rocked the record-breaking capitalist boom then underway. It spurred Marx to resume his "economics," pursing this feverishly until the end of the 1860s. He also returned to politics, connecting with the nascent labor movements in Germany and elsewhere, especially via the First International, which he helped found in 1864. This decade climaxed in 1867–71, with the publication of the first volume of *Capital,* Marx's intended life work, and the brief success of the Paris Commune, the workers' revolution in action. But the Commune's aftershock and Michael Bakunin's machinations wrecked the First International. Though Marx extended his international range in his final years, he published little and participated in events rarely, his ailments exacting a heavier toll. In 1870, Engels moved to London and took a much stronger role in the relationship.

What influence did Marx and Engels have in their own time? To answer this question requires suspending the endless debates about Marxism as a whole. It means forgetting about 1917, the Russian Revolution, and what we know about Communism. It means forgetting about Marx's philosophical writings of the 1840s, which had little relevance to the 1860s and were entirely unknown to contemporaries. The question of what Marx "really meant"—for example, whether or not the early philosophical arguments about "alienation" still informed the theory of economics in *Capital*—clearly matters for other purposes. But here, it can be safely set aside. Instead, we should ask: What political goals did Marx and Engels argue for in the 1860s and 1870s, which the first generation of social democratic politicians also took for themselves? How was their general theory of society understood?

The Marx we know was not the Marx of contemporaries. Our images are shaped not only by the Marxist tradition's later course but also by those of Marx's writings that were unavailable before his death. Posterity—and the labors of ideologists hostile and sympathetic—have placed Marx and Engels outside of history, blocking our access to their contemporary standing. To grasp that influence, we need to concentrate on the perceptions of socialist politicians and labor activists in the last third of the nineteenth century. What was distinctive about Marx's ideas by the end of his career? How were they used in politics?

It was only with the events of the 1860s that Marx's political influence arrived. Few of his writings were available in his own lifetime. These included a few early philosophical tracts; the journalistic commentaries on the European revolutions (1847–53) plus the *Communist Manifesto* (1847–8); two works of economic theory (1857 to late 1860s); and political writings from the First International (1864–72). These appeared in various languages (German, French, English), passing quickly out of print. Marx's theoretical reputation rested on the great economic writings—the *Critique of Political Economy* (1859), and the first volume of *Capital* (1867). Politically, he was known vaguely for his exploits in 1848; he had some notoriety as a leader of the First International who backed the Paris Commune; and he had a growing reputation as an economic theorist and historian. But in most of Europe, knowledge of his ideas stayed within the small networks of British and German socialists who adopted his intellectual authority.[4]

Marx first encountered workers in the educational meetings of German migrant artisans in Paris during early 1844. By early 1846, he had formed the Communist Correspondence Committee with fellow revolutionaries in Brussels, seeking links with workers through the London-based and semi-clandestine League of the Just. Typically for revolutionary societies of the time, this combined a secret inner core with a public front of cultural action, namely, the German Workers' Educational Union. When the Brussels Communists merged with the Londoners in the Communist League in summer 1847, accordingly, they likewise formed a German Workers' Association in Brussels. By this strategy, democratic radicals sought a broader working-class base, aiming to move it in a socialist direction.

This organizational norm of local working-class association was common to the available models of popular radicalism in the 1840s: the conspiratorial and insurrectionary tradition of Babeuf, Buonarroti, and Blanqui; Chartism in Britain; and the practical trades socialism associated with Proudhon and the apolitical schemes of utopian socialists. These were not totally separate traditions. The communitarian experiments of the utopians blurred with the co-operative ideals preferred by most politically active workers, a convergence strongest in the Owenite socialism of the early 1830s and the utopian communism of Cabet's Icarians in the 1840s. Ideas of producer co operation also ran through Chartism, as did some openness to insurrection. If Blanqui and his coconspirators had a social program, it was on the ideas of Proudhon and the utopians that they naturally drew.

The 1840s saw a key transition, from the purer Blanquist model of revolutionary action to more broadly based popular agitation. While Marx painstakingly broke with the conspiratorial habits of existing revolutionary groups, he remained trapped in Blanquism's practical logic during the 1848 Revolution itself: moving ahead of popular consciousness, he still aimed to steer the masses toward insurrectionary showdown. But he stressed the "bourgeois-democratic" limits of the 1848 Revolution; opposed premature confrontations; and in the revolution's final crisis urged the Cologne workers against any last-ditch uprising. Above all, Marx was explicitly committed to public agitation and the democratic voice of the masses themselves rather than the Blanquist fantasy of a secret revolutionary élite exercising dictatorship for a people not mature enough to govern for themselves.

Yet the practical conjuncture of 1848—with a highly self-conscious revolutionary intelligentsia summoning an industrial proletariat yet to be formed in a Europe of extremely uneven development—made vanguardism hard to avoid. Marx and his friends claimed to know the future by virtue of understanding history's inescapable progress. This put them in a superior relation to the masses, divining the true direction of their interests.[5] In this way revolutionary democrats in 1848 raced ahead of the social movements needed to carry their programs through. Such movements could only succeed, according to Marx, if capitalist industrialization occurred first.

In 1848, Marx radically misread the signs. As Engels ruefully acknowledged, what he and Marx mistook for capitalism's death throes were actually its birth pangs. This sent Marx back to his desk. He already regarded the economics of exploitation as the motor of change, with the oppressed proletariat providing the new revolutionary impulse: no longer small groups of revolutionary conspirators supplied the agency, but social classes defined by conditions of economic life. But after 1848, he reapplied himself to the underlying theoretical inquiry that eventually produced *Capital*. He broke politically with the Communist League, which in defeat hankered for the old Blanquist temptation. As he argued in the key meeting of its Central Committee, revolutions were no mere feat of the will but came from gradually maturing conditions. Workers faced a politics of the long haul: "If you want to change conditions and make yourselves capable of government, you will have to undergo fifteen, twenty or fifty years of civil war." This was also a general principle: "While this general prosperity lasts, enabling the productive forces of bourgeois society to develop to the full extent possible within the bourgeois system, there can be no question of a real revolution. Such a revolution is only possible when two factors come into conflict: the modern productive forces and the bourgeois forms of production." And: "A new revolution is only possible as a result of a new crisis; but it will come, just as surely as the crisis itself."[6]

The year 1850 was the watershed in Marx's career. He felt the rush of revolutionary optimism only once more, during the first great cyclical crisis of the European capitalist economy in 1857, when he set down the basic framework of his economic theory in the seven notebooks of the famous *Grundrisse,* which remained unpublished for a century. This produced a much tougher emphasis on the social forces and objective structures that, while constraining people's abilities to change their environment, ultimately made this possible. From this central insight then came the political perspectives separating Marx and Engels so sharply from the rival traditions of the nineteenth-century Left.

MARX'S AND ENGELS'S LEGACY

For Marx and Engels, economics were fundamental. This began as a general axiom of understanding: "The mode of production of material life conditions the general process of social, political, and mental life. It is not the consciousness of people that determines their being, but, on the contrary, their social being that determines their consciousness." Or: "According to the materialist conception of history, the ultimately determining element in history is the production and reproduction of real life."[7] This philosophical materialism dated from the 1840s. It now became a general theory of economics—of the capitalist mode of production and its general "laws of motion"—to be fully explicated in *Capital*. Explicitly linked to a political project, bringing 1848–49 into perspective and explaining the circumstances of a future capitalist collapse, this general theory was Marx's most important legacy for the pre-1914 social democratic tradition. It became what contemporaries mainly understood by "Marxism"—the role of the "economic factor" in history, the determining effects of material forces on human achievement, and the linking of political opportunities to movements of the economy. In a nutshell: revolutionary politics had to wait for the social forces and economic crises needed to sustain them.

The 1860s galvanized such hopes. In a fresh drama of constitution-making, Italy and Germany were unified. And after the long gap of the 1850s, labor movements resurged, including the craft unions of the Trades Union Congress in Britain and workers' associations in the various states of Germany. Labor organizing spread geographically through the European strike wave of 1868–74, dramatized by the great event of the 1871 Paris Commune. What excited Marx was not just the return of class conflict but its connections to politics, which gave the impetus for the First International in 1864. Just as vital as labor's revival, moreover, was the changing constitutional context in which it happened. For Marx and Engels, new nation-states in Germany and Italy became the key progressive gain, promoting capitalism in those two societies and creating circumstances favorable for workers' advance. Added to the Second Reform Act in Britain (1867), replacement of the Second Empire by the Third Republic in France (1871), constitutional compromise between Austria and Hungary in the

Habsburg Empire (1867), liberal revolution in Spain (1868–69), constitutional reforms in Greece (1864) and Serbia (1869), and even reforms in Russia (1861–64), this was a fundamental redrawing of the political map. In the 1860s, liberal constitutionalism gained the ascendancy in Europe, giving labor movements their first shot at legal activity on a national scale.

This inspired a new type of working-class politics, the independent mass party of labor: independent, because it organized separately from liberal coalitions; mass, because it required broadly based public agitation; labor, because it stressed the need for class-based organization; and a party, by proposing permanent, centrally organized, programmatically coordinated, and nationally directed activity. Marx consistently advocated this model, which the First International was created to promote. Workers needed a *political class movement,* which valued trade unionism and other reforms but hitched them to the ulterior goal of state power, taking maximum advantage of the new parliamentary and legal frameworks. Marx didn't expect this to happen overnight, and during the First International there was only one case of a nationally organized socialist party, the German Social Democratic Party (SPD) and its predecessors.

The case for national trade union and party organizations "as organizing centers of the working class in the broad interest of its complete emancipation" could only be won by defeating older Left traditions.[8] Opposition to Marx in the First International had various sources: the liberal-reformist proclivities of many union leaders, especially the British; French Proudhonists, hostile to both trade unionism and political action via the state; the unpolitical revolutionism of Bakunin and the anarchists, who opposed the centralist structure of the International and its stress on party organizing; and what remained of Blanquism.

Marx had mixed success in dealing with these enemies. With British trade unionists, whose International involvement ran through the London-based crafts, he failed: his modest goal of a break with the Liberal Party showed few returns, and after 1872 the International's English section disappeared. With the followers of Proudhon and Bakunin, he decisively won: the former were defeated via the policies on public ownership adopted during 1866–68, and the latter were outmaneuvered at the Hague Congress in 1872, when Marx countered Bakunin's challenge by transferring the General Council from London to New York. Though in practice this meant closing the International down and abandoning those parts of Europe under Bakunin's sway, principally Italy, Switzerland, and Spain, it gave Marx's allies control of the International's symbolic legacy. Henceforth, anarchism was a permanently marginalized political creed, with regional impact on Europe's southern rim, but never again challenging political socialism's general dominance in Europe's working-class movements.

Marx was most successful against the Blanquists. Outside Britain, Blanquism was the main revolutionary tradition before 1848. Until the Paris Commune, its imagery of barricades, popular insurrection, disciplined conspiratorial leadership, heroic sacrifice, and necessary dictatorship still defined what revolutions were supposed to be. Marx and Engels repudiated conspiratorial politics in the 1840s, and 1848 confirmed this hostility to vanguardism. Instead, they urged the broadest popular democracy, in both public agitation and internal organization. Linked to the idea of the working class as the agency of progress, whose majority followed from capitalism's unfolding, this transformed the image of revolution. Henceforth, it meant not a voluntarist uprising hatched by a self-appointed conspiracy but the coming to power of a class, the vast majority of society, whose revolutionary potential was organized openly and democratically by the socialist party for dispossession of an ever-narrowing circle of exploitative capitalist interests. In this respect, the victory of Marx's perspective was complete.

In Marx's view, each of these factors—the practical import of his social theory; the 1860s and the new opportunities for legal politics; the fight against opponents; and the necessity of publicly conducted mass campaigning—pointed to the same conclusion: that the emancipation of the working class was a *political* question. This was true in three senses: it had to be organized politically, coordinated by a class-based socialist party; the party had to concentrate the workers' collective strengths in a centrally directed movement capable of challenging the political authority of the ruling class; and because the existing state was an expression of class rule, it couldn't simply be taken over but had to be destroyed. This necessitated a transitional state authority, namely, the "dictatorship of the proletariat."[9]

In Marx's own thinking, the "transitional proletarian state" was unequivocally democratic. By democracy, he meant something different from liberal parliamentary institutions. For Marx, it was a system of participatory decision-making, which demolished the walls of professionalism and bureaucracy separating the people from government or from the special categories of politicians and officials who mystified power and severed it from the people's control. Marx never set this down systematically. But he saw the Paris Commune as an example of participatory democracy in action. He urged the return of all offices (armed forces, civil service, judiciary) to the citizenry by direct election. The separation of legislative, judicial, and executive powers would be abolished; a "political class" would cease to exist; and "leadership functions" would be diffused as widely as possible. This was a "vision of democracy without professionals," quite distinct from the social democratic heritage before 1914, which saw democratic rule in mainly parliamentary terms.[10]

Finally, to return to Marx's and Engels's basic materialism: if one side of this was cautionary—avoiding premature revolutionary adventures before the social forces and economic contradictions had matured, with the need for patient political building—the other side was more optimistic. If one side was the power of objective processes over human political agency and "the subordination of politics to historical development," the other was the ultimate inevitability of the victory of socialism. Marx believed in the historical necessity of workers' emancipation, because the processes of capitalist accumulation themselves created "a class constantly increasing in numbers, and trained, united, and organized by the very mechanism of the capitalist process of production."[11] Politics that neglected these underlying processes could not hope to succeed; politics that built from them were assured of victory. This powerful mixture of optimism and certainty—in the inevitable victory of history's massed battalions—was decisive for pre-1914 social democracy.

There were gaps in Marx's thought. He never systematically addressed the problem of the state, nor the transition to socialism and the character of postrevolutionary society. Nor have I addressed every aspect of his thought, most notably internationalism. But there, Marx and Engels had less to say that was original. International solidarity predated the First International and mattered less than the idea of national party organization, which was new. Marx's and Engels's belief in revolutionary war came from the Jacobin tradition. And on nationalism they often repeated the prejudices of the age. Finally, some aspects of Marx's thinking, like his apparent openness in the 1870s to Populist strategies based on the peasantry in Russia, were not widely known at the time.[12]

Marx's and Engels's ideas should be judged for their contemporary significance as opposed to their future or abstract meanings. Marx's activity in the First International has often been seen as a sideshow or a distraction from his finishing *Capital*. In fact, it delivered the vital political perspectives for the socialist parties about to be founded, particularly when contrasted with the older radicalisms of the 1830s and 1840s. Organizationally the First International had limited impact. In 1869–70, it became riven with conflicts and by 1872 it was a dead letter. But certain policies had been publicly stated—for example, the practical program of labor legislation and trade union reforms in Marx's "Instructions" for the delegates to the Geneva Congress in 1866; or the resolution on public ownership at the Brussels Congress in 1868; or the resolution on the "Political Action of the Working Class," which called for "the constitution of the working class into a political party," adopted by the London Conference in 1871. These became fixed referents for the later socialist parties. In other words, through their influence in the First International Marx and Engels supplied the guiding perspectives for the first generation of social democratic politicians and the movements they tried to create.

THE DIFFUSION OF MARXISM

The period between publication of Engels's *Anti-Dühring* in 1877–78 and his death in 1895 saw "the transition, so to speak, from Marx to Marxism."[13] This was orchestrated by Engels himself. As Marx's literary executor with Eleanor Marx, he made the popularization of Marx's thinking the mission of his final years. He edited *Capital*'s remaining volumes for publication, with volume 2 appearing in 1885 and volume 3 in 1894, volume 4 becoming the three-volume *Theories of Surplus Value* (1905–10) edited by Karl Kautsky.[14] Engels revived older works, published new ones, and codified Marx's thought into a comprehensive view of the world.[15]

Engels also managed an extraordinary network of international socialist contacts, rapidly expanding with the new socialist parties and the founding of the Second International in 1889. He advised these national movements, especially the German, French, Austrian, Italian, and Russian ones, and helped launch the new International. He represented Marx not only via the printed word but in constant communications and personal visits, with countless practical interventions. He tutored the first generation of continental Marxist intellectuals. His influence "provided the formative moment of all the leading interpreters of the Second International" and a good number of the Third as well.[16]

Making Marx's heritage secure thus established a "Marxist" political tradition. Older veterans eschewed this label as a "sectarian trade-mark," an aversion Marx and Engels had shared, preferring "critical materialist socialism," or "scientific" as against "utopian socialism."[17] Kautsky, however, had no such compunctions. Using his closeness to the SPD leaders August Bebel and Wilhelm Liebknecht and to Marx's and Engels's leading protegé in the 1880s, Eduard Bernstein, he maneuvered skilfully through the party debates of the 1880s and made Marxism into the social democratic movement's official creed. His vehicle was the monthly theoretical review *Neue Zeit*, which he founded in 1883. He assured his standing as theoretical heir by publishing *The Economic Doctrines of Karl Marx* in 1887, which swiftly became the standard introduction.[18]

If Engels was the final arbiter of Marx's authority, Kautsky was its faithful mouthpiece. Kautsky's orthodoxy systematically expunged non-Marxist traces. Other leading thinkers of the first generation—Eduard Bernstein, Victor Adler, Georgy Plekhanov, Antonio Labriola—were less dogmatic but shared the same commitment. They wished "to systematize historical materialism as a comprehensive theory of man and nature, capable of replacing rival bourgeois disciplines and providing the workers' movement with a broad and coherent vision of the world that could be easily grasped by its militants." This meant validating Marxism as a philosophy of history and dealing with themes Marx and Engels had not developed, like literature and art, or religion and Christianity.[19]

This work had practical urgency. Within two decades of the SPD's foundation in 1875, every European country acquired a movement aligning itself with Marx's ideas. New generations of militants needed training in the movement's basic principles, not only as a cadre of socialist journalists, lecturers, and officials but also to impart socialist consciousness to the rank and file and the great mass of the yet unconverted. The culture of Europe's labor movements began to organize.

We can track this organization by the availability of Marx's own writings in Europe. The original German edition of *Capital* appeared in 1867, the French translation in 1875, and a Russian one in 1872. The *Communist Manifesto* was revived in over nine editions in six languages from 1871 to 1873, during which time Marx's statements on the Paris Commune also became widely known. European diffusion continued apace, with editions of *Capital* in Italian, English, and Polish and abridgements in Spanish, Danish, and Dutch. By 1917, translations had followed in Bulgarian, Estonian, Czech, Finnish, and Yiddish. By 1918, the *Manifesto* had appeared in 30 languages, including Japanese and Chinese. Aside from Germany, Austria, Italy, and France, the liveliest interest was in east-central Europe and the tsarist empire, with 11 editions of the *Manifesto* in Polish, 9 in Hungarian, 8 in Czech, 7 in Yiddish and Bulgarian, 6 in Finnish, 5 in Ukrainian, 4 in Georgian, 2 in Armenian, and a remarkable 70 in Russian. The countries of weakest diffusion were those of the Iberian peninsula, where anarchism dominated, and the Balkans and parts of eastern Europe where there was no labor movement yet and little popular literacy.[20]

Most evidence—memoirs, print runs for particular titles, catalogues and lending records of socialist and union libraries, questionnaires on workers' reading habits—shows that Marx was read mainly by movement intellectuals. Even in a broad definition of these, embracing not only recognized theoreticians, journalists, and parliamentarians but also activists who ran the workers' libraries, taught party education classes, organized discussion circles, and lectured at public meetings, we are still dealing with minorities. In addition, the SPD, for example, contained a plurality of outlooks. Even the Party School, founded in 1906 under Marxist control, gave a mixed picture. Having won the fight for an orthodox curriculum, with tight theoretical training and screening of enrollees, the Marxist instructors were chagrined by many students' revisionist ideas. Moreover, the 240 students graduated by the Party School during 1906–14 were offset by the 1,287 passing through the Trade Union School, with its highly practical curriculum. The actual diffusion of Marxism among the cadres was limited, and as we move outward to the unschooled outlook of ordinary members, this becomes plain. Only 4.3 percent of borrowings from workers' libraries were in the social sciences, with another 4.4. percent covering philosophy, religion, law, and miscellaneous subjects. The vast bulk, 63.1 percent, were in fiction, with another 9.8 percent in children's books and another 5.0 percent in anthologies.[21] Works by Marx and Engels (and for that matter Kautsky) were mainly absent from the chosen reading.

The diffusion shouldn't be too narrowly understood. Even if Marx's own writings were hard to get hold of, there were many commentaries about them—some three hundred titles in Italy alone from 1885 to 1895, or over two books a month on Marxism and socialism for a decade.[22] Not surprisingly, then, early socialist intellectuals acquired garbled versions of Marx. They knew a few basic ideas: the primacy of economics in history; the natural laws of social development; the scientific basis of socialism; the class struggle as the motor of change; the proletariat as the agency of progress; the independent political organization of the working class; the emancipation of labor as the emancipation of society. To this degree, Kautsky's popularization had already succeeded: awareness of "Marxism" preceded awareness of Marx himself and supplied rudiments of popular socialist consciousness.

The socialist press was key. In Germany, the SPD's daily and periodical press was the most popular working-class reading matter. By 1913, there were 94 party newspapers, all but four appearing six times a week, with a combined circulation of one and a half million, or a sixfold increase over 1890. This press achieved blanket coverage of party members. In Berlin in 1906, less than 3 percent of the 48,352 SPD members were not reading *Vorwärts* (the party daily) or another party paper, and elsewhere subscribers often outnumbered party members. Moreover, party newspapers were consumed collectively, passed hand to hand, and available in cafés, clubs, and bars. Most decisive were the rhythms of daily communication in working-class communities. Joining in the life of the movement, with its politicized sociability, cultural opportunities, and face-to-face interaction, made people into Social Democrats.[23]

It's unclear how consciously Marxist this everyday culture of the socialist movement was. On some interpretations, the SPD's official Marxism was disconnected from its practical life, whether in unions, daily propaganda, cultural and recreational clubs, or general consciousness of members.[24] But this can go too far. Most people most of the time don't hold an explicit philosophy, let alone sophisticated doctrinal bases for their beliefs. That doesn't preclude deeply felt political values, which in the early labor movements meant ideas of social justice, separateness from the dominant culture, an ethic of working-class community and collective solidarity, a class-combative anger against the powerful, and so forth. Marxism wasn't the only creed sustaining those beliefs. But its contribution was clear, especially in derivative values and popular discourse. A cadre of more consciously Marxist militants was also created before 1914, and during wider popular agitations this cadre clearly came into its own. *agreed*

Pre-1914 labor movement values were broadly congruent with the political legacy of Marx and Engels. This was true of the basic materialist outlook; the new opportunities for national politics created by the 1860s constitutional reforms; the antipathy to anarchism; the sense of the need for strong union and party organization to wrest gains from government and employers; and the general conviction that history was carrying the working class to its rightful inheritance in society. This congruence was especially strong in Germany, where the SPD lacked rivals in the working-class movement, whereas in Italy and France socialists competed with syndicalists in the movement's overall culture. There were some discordances. The SPD had no unequivocal belief in the ultimate revolutionary confrontation Marx thought inevitable. Socialist parties' growing parliamentary strengths also posed dilemmas of revolution versus reform Marx was spared. But Second International parties broadly accepted the politics Marx pioneered so consistently in his final two decades. If Marxism is defined like this rather than by detailed knowledge of *Capital*, popular socialist consciousness appears in a far more Marxist light.

In two respects the legacy changed in the passage from Marx to Marxism. One was the bifurcation of labor movements into political and industrial arms. As each pursued their own reformist ends, the unified struggle for workers' emancipation conceived by Marx fell apart. Marx's other commitment to participatory forms of direct democracy was also lost, making the main versions of democracy almost completely parliamentary in form. Second, Engels's and Kautsky's renditions of Marx's thought brought evolutionism and naturalism into historical materialism. Engels had already set the tone in his speech at Marx's funeral, drawing parallels with Charles Darwin: "Just as Darwin discovered the law of development of organic nature, so Marx discovered the law of development of human history."[25] Engels elaborated this claim in his works of the 1880s, which Kautsky then consummated in his further works of popularization.

In most accounts of Second International Marxism, this "scientific" language was its hallmark. A natural-scientific outlook formed by reading Darwin and the works of Ludwig Büchner and Ernst Haeckel permeated Kautsky's pre-Marxist thinking. This encounter with evolution proved intellectually liberating for Kausky's socialist generation. In *Neue Zeit*, the dual affiliation to Marx and Darwin was virtually on the masthead. The class struggle—"the struggle of man as a social animal in the social community"—mirrored the biological struggle for existence. What was true of Kautsky characterized the SPD at large. Bebel declared confidently: "Socialism is science, applied with full understanding to all fields of human activity." After Bebel's own *Women and Socialism*, popularizations of Darwin and evolutionary theory were the favorite nonfiction reading in workers' libraries.[26] The same applied to Italian socialism, where the architect of a remarkably vulgar Darwinian Marxism was Enrico Ferri, a leading party official and long-time editor of the party newspaper *Avanti!*[27] When the young socialist agitator Benito Mussolini began editing a party newspaper in Forli in 1910, he called Marx and Darwin the two greatest thinkers of the nineteenth century.[28]

The hallmark of popular socialist consciousness, however, was robust eclecticism. In shaping a socialist political tradition, certain general principles—the labor movement's basic values—mattered more than the exclusive and esoteric grasp of any one theory. Non-Marxist influences, including Lassalleanism in Germany, Mazzinianism in Italy, Proudhonism in *eclectic movement*

France, the nameless amalgam of Carlyle and Ruskin, secularism and free thought, and residual Chartism in Britain, all influenced the socialist tradition. By 1900, a string of others were added, varying across the continent—the theories of Henry George, the ethical teaching of Leo Tolstoy, Edward Bellamy's socialist fiction, an assortment of futurist utopias, and the "Darwinist" ensemble of evolutionist theories. Socialist propagandists could also use the languages of popular religion, "presenting socialism as both science and faith, as at once religion or faith in human kindness and as the heir to the humanitarian condition."[29] In autobiographies, working people describe coming to Marxism via these eclectic and circuitous routes, with a thirst for unifying and ecompassing philosophies of the world. Engels and later Marxists might decry the woolly-headed popularizers, but works like *Anti-Dühring* did as much to strengthen as negate the impact of simplified materialist accounts.[30]

A large centrally organized socialist party like the SPD strengthened the resources available to the worker wanting to learn. But this proceeded largely beneath the level of official party ideology, whether avowedly Marxist as in Germany or an obstinately non-Marxist ethical socialism as in the British Labour Party after 1900. At the movement's grassroots was an eclectic and autodidactic type of working-class socialism, where Marxism was only the most powerful in a larger "constellation of socialist ideologies."[31] A special set of circumstances made this eclecticism possible—after opportunities for popular literacy had grown, but before these individual efforts at self-learning became preempted by comprehensive systems of state schooling and more doctrinaire approaches to party educational work.[32]

Underpinning the organized efforts of socialist movements, moreover, were the momentous social changes produced by capitalist industrialization, which assembled massive concentrations of working-class people in the new urban environments. Collective action became essential to the hopes and material well-being of these new populations, and it was here that the relevance of Marxist ideas decisively converged. Before considering the emergent socialist parties in more detail, therefore, it is to industrialization and the making of the working class that we must turn.

Chapter 3

Industrialization and the Making of the Working Class

DURING THE "DUAL revolution" between the 1780s and 1840s—industrialization in Britain, political upheaval in France—class became the modern name for social divisions. No less than "industry" or "democracy," "class" became a modern keyword. "Socialism," "working class," and "proletariat" all appeared in Britain and France by the early 1830s, in Germany a decade later. Terminology then became truly polarized into "worker" and "bourgeois" during the third quarter of the nineteenth century in the wake of the failed 1848 revolutions, as capitalism began its first worldwide boom.[1] The progress of machinery, steam power, factories, and railways became increasingly the markers of progress in Europe, and as the first industrializing society Britain pointed toward an exciting and necessary but forbidding future. Moreover, the novel concentrations of industry presaged a dangerous new presence in society, one troublesomely resistant to social and political control.

Industry brought the "social problem." New forms of regulation were needed for public health, housing, schooling, poor relief, recreation, and criminality. Worse, industrialization contained a political threat. Industry brought the rise of a working class, with no stake in the emerging order or its laws. For polite society, collective action by the laboring masses became a constant anxiety, and to cope with such fears distinctions were drawn between "respectable" workers and the rest. To such thinking, the skilled working man became demoralized by an unhealthy urban environment, corrupted by the criminally indigent and seduced into radicalism by socialists

workers = social + pol threats

47

and other agitators. But for their own part, the agitators drew the opposite conclusions. The socialist advocates of the class-conscious proletariat found in workers' communities an essential unity of purpose, borne forward by the logic of capitalist growth. This chapter, by sketching the working class as it emerged into social history, provides a framework for measuring those claims. In what ways were socialist hopes justified?

A NEW WORLD OF INDUSTRY

Unevenness was decisive for European industrialization before 1914. Capitalism rarely transformed the old landscape comprehensively, turning trees into smokestacks and fields into factories. The pace of development varied too widely, both between and within societies, generating complex combinations of advanced, backward, and hybrid production in contiguous regions, often mutually dependent on each other's forms of specialization. Dynamism actually required backwardness in this dialectic of dependency, producing turbulent new labor markets, mass migrations from the countryside, and a novel urban topography, but with far richer interconnections between industry and agriculture, "modern" and "traditional" production, and large and small-scale enterprise than the more aggressive predictions had assumed.

This unevenness of industrialization across countries and regions, and the resulting variations in working-class populations, created huge strategic problems for the Left. Socialist parties presented themselves as parties of the working class, which modern industry was supposedly making into society's overwhelming majority. Yet everywhere in Europe those parties faced mixed populations, with millions still employed in agriculture and other "traditional" occupations. Industrial workers failed to become the overwhelming mass of society, although masses of proletarians certainly concentrated in particular places and often entire regions. Even in Britain, where proletarianization *had* gone far, the First World War proved the peak: thereafter, manual workers gradually contracted in numbers, from three-quarters to less than a third of the employed population by 1990. This became the general trend of industrial economies. Even as industrial labor reached its furthest extent, long-term restructuring was already tipping employment toward white-collar and other jobs in services.

These trends challenged the Left's given assumptions. If the logic of class formation disobeyed Marx's predictions, what did this mean for working-class politics? If the typical image of the proletariat—manual workers in factories, foundries and mines, on the docks, in the shipyards, and on the railways—was increasingly unlike the actually employed population during the twentieth century, where does that leave the working class in the "founding" periods earlier on? How else might the working class be defined?

By the simplest Marxist definition, the working class were those with no ownership or control over means or conditions of production. Workers were a class of direct producers who—in contrast to peasant farmers or skilled artisans—no longer owned independent means of subsistence or even their own tools. All they had was their ability to work, which they sold to an employer, a capitalist, for a wage. To create such workers, active proletarianization was needed. Small producers in town and country had to be robbed of their independence—whether in free peasant cultivation, servile labor on great estates, household mixtures of subsistence farming and domestic industry, rural handicrafts, or small urban workshops. Labor power had to be released from its traditional legal, social, and cultural restraints, converted into a commodity, and freed into the capitalist market. The direct producers had to be separated from the means of production and forced into dependent labor. Access to means of subsistence had to be available only via the wage, in a labor process controlled by the capitalist. The laborer had to be made doubly "free," from old feudal obligations and from all propertied bases of independent livelihood.

Marx called this "primitive accumulation." It created the preconditions for capitalist industrialization in Britain during 1500–1800. Peasants were forced off the land and converted into landless laborers, either working for capitalist farmers or migrating for jobs in the towns. Small-scale handicrafts simultaneously fell to centralized manufacture, either controlled financially by merchants or physically concentrated under a single roof in factories. This severance of country people from subsistence also created new markets for commodities, stimulating commercialized agriculture and growth of industry.

The countryside's transformation impelled capitalist industrialization. If manufacture gave capitalists control over means of production via the new property relations, mechanization brought control of the labor process by completing the worker's subordination to its technical needs. Replacing a division of labor based on handicrafts by one based on machines was the really revolutionary step in capital's progress, making production less dependent on the worker's manual skills and enormously boosting productivity.[2] Concentration in factories could then accelerate, reorganizing workplaces and harnessing the reserves of labor power released by rural dispossession. All the long-term logic of capitalist industrialization now unfolded, from the relentless polarizing of the class structure between a minority of capitalists and an ever-expanding category of workers to the continued proletarianizing of intermediate groupings like surviving small farmers, artisans, and small businessmen and the growing homogenization of the working class. In the political sphere, this created the basis for labor movements, in the growth of class consciousness around workers' collective interests.

Treated as a universal description, rather than a conceptual framework based on the British case, however, there are two big problems with this

① process of indus)

Problems w/ Marxist

Interesting b/c Hand Machines makes Great Britain ought to be so superior on technology ↑

model. First, it oversimplified the process. Machines and factories mattered less than was supposed. Industrial revolution involved cumulative changes and not a big bang. Hand technologies rather than mechanization, and the dispersal of small-scale, labor-intensive production in the countryside rather than mass production in towns, were the norm. Early capitalism exploited cheap labor supplies in the countryside, where simple technologies could be used and where rural families' contribution to their own subsistence kept wages low. There might be little incentive to make the leap into factories. And these weren't "preindustrial" holdovers doomed to disappear in the march of progress. By 1914, British industry still used manual labor more than machines, relying on the worker's physical effort. Coal-mining output roughly doubled in 1875–1914 but only by doubling the workforce, with minor advances in methods. British industry avoided mechanization by exploiting an abundance of labor and refining the use of manual tools. Its labor process relied "on the strength, skill, quickness and sureness of touch of the individual worker rather than upon the simultaneous and repetitive operations of the machine."[3]

Several conclusions follow. For one, because there were many paths to industrialization, class relations between capitalist and worker could be shaped in varying ways. Next, industrial capitalism can't be identified simply with factories and machines. Not only did older patterns of hand labor and smaller units persist but also capitalism continuously invented new small-scale forms, including "sweating" or homework, and specialized skilled manufacture. Finally, if industry didn't simply call for mechanization, the urban pooling of labor, or an expanding market, then the changing relations in workplaces become all the more key. It was not just the ownership and nonownership of means of production that mattered but all the ways in which work itself was done.

② w/c formation

This raises the second problem with a classical Marxist approach. Linear models of industrialization oversimplify working-class formation. They imply too close a fit between the progress of capitalism and the growth of class consciousness. As the growing proletariat became ever more concentrated in new urban-industrial centers, as machinery eliminated distinctions between types of labor, and as the wages system equalized workers' conditions of life, Marx thought, the working class would acquire unified consciousness. In this model, workers were forced by exploitation into solidarity, at first defensively through local and industry-based clubs for mutual self-help, then more confidently in nationally organized unions, and finally politically in a revolutionary party. Throughout, the dialectic of class and class consciousness was linked to changes in the economic base: the laws governing the capitalist mode of production had social effects, which determined the rise of the working-class movement. Marxists expressed this by a famous couplet, distinguishing between the class "in itself" and the class "for itself." In this way, they believed, the forms of working-class collective organization (and eventually the victory of socialism) were inscribed in the very processes of capitalist production themselves. As capital expanded, it also created the conditions for the working class to organize.[5]

As a guide to working-class behavior in actual societies, this powerful analysis was always misleading. The working class was identified too easily with the wage relationship in a pure form: the authentic worker, the true proletarian, was the factory worker. As this argument ran, the unevenness of industrialization and its diverse settings were certainly important, but ultimately mass production in factories (and mines, construction sites, transportation systems, docks) still mattered more. From this, strong labor movements were easily identified with "truly modern industry." In this view, small-scale forms of production, notably craft-based industry in small workshops, even if longer-lasting than once supposed, were transitional and doomed to die. As industry became bigger, more machine-based and more concentrated class formation became more "advanced" and the labor movement more "mature." The whole of the working class would never be subsumed into the "pure" proletarian relationship of the deskilled and propertyless worker against the capitalist. There would always be forms of ancillary production. Nevertheless, industrial workers would form the vanguard, and other workers would follow.

History proved this view flawed. Workers were recruited by many different means, among which primitive accumulation and expulsion of peasants from the land was only one. Workers were pushed into wage-dependency by many other routes—via commercialized farming, cottage industry, urban handicrafts, the urban infrastructure's dense service economies, casualized trades and "sweating," as well as factories, mines, and industrial production in the stereotypical sense. Across Europe, different labor regimes were mixed together. Eastern Prussia used both a dependent small-holding peasantry and large masses of migrant labor on its commercialized estates. The Po Valley's estates used both wage labor and share-cropping. Cottage industry and peasant farming were by definition inter-mixed. Further, some settings proletarianized more than others. Large-farm systems, cottage industry, and substantial factory production necessarily entailed the creation of proletariats, but "specialized farming, peasant farming, and urban craft production" might not.[6]

Such processes varied richly by region. In Saxony, as in many other regions, the proletariat was recruited mainly in the countryside from people already earning wages rather than from people passing freshly out of another class. Before the 1820s, most British industry developed like that, including the pioneering textile industry. In other cases, social dislocation was sudden and sharp, and the later and faster the industrialization, the more drastic this was. The massive late-nineteenth-century coalfield expansions in the Ruhr, Silesia, South Wales, and parts of France recruited mostly from in-migrating rural populations, as did new industries in Italy and Russia. Clearly, these differing paths toward proletarianization had huge implications for the specific working-class societies that would result.

GENDER, SKILL, AND SOCIALISM

In fact, the "unity" of the working class was an idealized projection, an abstraction from the disorderly and unevenly developing histories of industrialization in the nineteenth century, whose visible concentrations of laboring poor certainly impressed contemporaries but required sustained action before settling into a pattern. Beginning in the 1830s, new cohorts of interpreters armed with new languages of "class" began organizing this social world. "Class" became a way of rationalizing the divisive facts of industrialization—capitalism's manifold accumulation regimes, labor markets, divisions of labor, technologies of skill, workplace relations, wage systems, and all the ways of dividing workers and aggregating them together. It also described the new social landscape, both the emerging patterns of residence and urban segregation, and the inequalities structuring the life-chances of different groups. When organized practices also formed around these new understandings, including government action, religious and charitable work, political clubs, and eventually socialist parties and trade unions, the class languages gained further weight. Thus, class offered a powerful armory of definitions, shaping disparate experiences into a unified social identity.

As labor movements started to form in France, Belgium, Germany, and Britain, they drew workers of a particular type: skilled workmen in small to medium workshops, strongly identified with their trade. Such male workers were artisans, with a proprietorial sense of skill and the rules of the trade, autonomy on the job, and distinction from the mass of the unskilled poor. But this status was threatened on many fronts—loss of control over local markets; introduction of machinery and labor-saving methods; entrepreneurial separation of masters from men; cheap mass production outside the boundaries of trade regulation; and centralization in factories. Such changes might set masters against men or rally them both against merchants and factory entrepreneurs. Once economies were affected by the vicissitudes of the business cycle, all trades felt the uncertainty in wages and employment. Specialized producers, whether northern English hand-loom weavers or Lyon silk weavers, could be dramatically hit by technical and organizational change. Lower-status trades like shoemakers and tailors came universally under pressure, soon joined by other crafts vulnerable to rapid market expansion. The male "artisan" was being turned into the "worker," who might retain the scarcity of skill but controlled little more than the capacity to work. Customary independence within complex hierarchies of skill was replaced by growing subordination in a capitalist division of labor.

Craftsmen defending their independence against the slide into the proletariat galvanized radical agitations in the 1830s and 1840s, helped ignite the 1848 revolutions, and shaped early socialism. Such agitations were drawn naturally to producer cooperation for alternatives to capitalism, employing ideas of "mutualism" or the "cooperative commonwealth." Until 1914, French labor movements recurred to an ideal of "federalist trades socialism," which imagined organizing collective ownership through a democratic federation of self-governing skilled trades and local communes. This "socialism of skilled workers" was inscribed in a larger "idiom of association," carried forward in two spurts of radicalization. In 1830–34, the term "association" became extended from the original meaning of workers' corporations (mutual aid societies adapted from the corporative traditions of the *ancien régime*) to the idea of producers' cooperatives, and thence to the socialist project of a crosstrade federation of all workers.[7] Then in 1848–51, it joined the revolutionary politics of a popular movement. This idiom of association also reflected patterns of popular sociability, through which male workers fashioned a public sphere, grounded not just in the trade and mutual aid leagues but in the cultural world of choral societies and social clubs and the everyday life of workshops, lodging houses, taverns, and cafés.[8]

In the first industrializing society, Britain, skilled male artisans also proposed the idea of a general working-class interest. The shipwright John Gast for the London skilled trades, Gravener Henson for outworkers in the northern manufacturing districts, and John Doherty for the cotton-spinners (a new type of semiartisanal skilled worker) represented early trade unionism at its climax in 1829–34.[9] Artisan radicalism was embedded in broad popular movements demanding socioeconomic redress but especially democratic reform between the 1810s and the Reform Act of 1832, sometimes on a revolutionary scale. After embittering setbacks in 1832–34, when antidemocratic parliamentary reform was followed by the social policing of the 1834 Poor Law, radicals regrouped under the banner of Chartism, with its extraordinary unity across working-class differences—handicrafts and new manufactures; skilled, semiskilled, and unskilled; organized and unorganized; men and women; natives and migrants; different regions, industries, and religious denominations.

Nonetheless, Britain's radical culture of the 1820s depended heavily on male artisans in the "old specialist, unrevolutionized handworking trades," invariably the better-off "mechanics," as contemporaries called them.[10] Capitalist expansion pushed the London trades, especially tailors, shoemakers, cabinet-makers, and carpenters, into crosstrade solidarity for demanding renewal of traditional regulations and democratic reform, using litigation, strikes, and parliamentary lobbying on tariffs, wages, machinery, and hours. A similar logic pushed the Birmingham trade societies "to redefine their relationships, not only with the employers, but also with other trades who shared the experience of change in the workplace."[11] But the broader mass of proletarianized wage-workers fitted uneasily into this artisanal culture. The "aristocratic" craft workers treated farm laborers, factory and detail workers, Irish migrants, the unskilled, paupers, casual laborers, and vagrants with disregard if not contempt, leading to serious conflicts. Such tensions were better handled in Chartism, but ideals of producer democracy only slowly subsided before more inclusive doctrines of socialism.

Apart from the followers of Robert Owen, Charles Fourier, and other utopian socialists, the democracy of early radical movements was also a male preserve. Chartism's Six Points for democratizing the British constitution in 1837–38 expressly excluded votes for women.[12] Such discrimination repeatedly emphasized women's place in the home and the proper ordering of sexual difference. Women were certainly active in Chartism and other radical agitations, but when they spoke, they did so only within the walls of the embattled popular community itself. It was men who addressed the outside world "in the first person for the community as a whole." Public discourse proper—including socioeconomic discontents, campaigns for civil freedoms, struggles over the law, and demands for the vote—was closed to women.[13]

For radical working men—the modest master craftsmen, displaced domestic workers, artisans and mechanics, and skilled factory operatives providing the backbone of Chartism and contemporary movements—the household's integrity was basic to political identity. Whatever the reciprocities between women and men in the household division of labor, as a system of domestic authority the family was centered on masculine privilege. Thus in raging against capitalist industry, which undermined their skills and pulled their wives and children into factories, radical artisans were also defending their own sexual and economic regime within the family. "Their status as fathers and heads of families was indelibly associated with their independence through 'honorable' labor and property in skill, which identification with a trade gave them." Women had no access to that independence. They were excluded from most trades, practising a craft only by virtue of their male kin. Woman's "skill" was in her household, her "property in the virtue of her person." But "separated from the home, her family and domestic occupations, or outside the bonds of matrimony, a woman was assured of neither."[14] A woman's political identity was subsumed in the man's. Rare proponents of female suffrage also limited their advocacy to "spinsters and widows," because wives and husbands were simply deemed to be one.[15]

This thinking adapted easily to industrialization. Demands for "protective" legislation became clamorous by the 1830s. Protecting women and children against the degrading effects of work in the new mills meant defending an idealized notion of family, hearth, and home, where benevolent patriarchy and healthy parental authority ordered the household economy by "natural differences and capacities" of women and men. When wives and children were forced into factories by the unemployment and depressed earning power of the husband-father, this natural order was upset.[16] To this dissolution of moral roles—the "unsexing of the man," in Engels's phrase—were added the effects of women's cheap labor, whose attractions for capitalists spelled loss of jobs, status, and skill for the men.[17] This fusion of anxieties—resistance to the capitalist reorganization of industry; the desire to quarantine the family's moral regime—powerfully motivated those skilled workers with a strong enough bargaining position. After 1850, with Britain's new prosperity and greater political stability, such groups came into their own.

Women's work was crucial to this system of distinction. Women were certainly a strong presence overall—around a third of employment in Britain, Germany, France, and Italy by 1914, a fifth in Sweden—but appeared only in certain industries, mainly textiles and clothing. In basing their working-class ideals not only around workplace solidarities and crosstrade cooperation but also around sharply gendered notions of respectability placing women in the home, nineteenth-century democratic movements affirmed models of dignified masculinity, which consigned women to dependency. Such positive models of working-class domesticity were also a direct rejoinder to bourgeois attacks on the moral disorder and degradation of the poor. Working-class radicals celebrated their own ideals of responsible manliness and womanly virtue in reply. But this politics of respectabilty militated against gender equality and women's public participation, precluding other models of civic mobilization asserting women's rights. By choosing certain strategies of community defense over others, working-class radicals shaped an enduring ideology of domesticity, limiting effective citizenship to men.

The result was a recharged domestic ideology of masculine privilege, embodied by those skilled men whose earning power supported their wives and children. Irregular and seasonal labor markets invariably meant that male earnings needed to be supplemented by whatever income the rest of the family could secure, usually in casual, sweated, or home-based employment or in the local informal economy. But if the skilled craftsman keeping his wife in domesticated unemployment was in a privileged minority in that sense, early trade unionism was virtually predicated on the system of female exclusion, and the new ideal of the "family wage" was a main mechanism separating the small élite of unionized craftsmen from the rest. Not only did it strengthen that élite's material advantages but it also normatively marginalized women's employment as something exceptional and undesirable, confining it to the low-paid, unskilled, and often hidden areas of waged work.[18]

In this respect too, therefore, the working class was a complex social formation. Though based on common social structures produced by capitalist industry and urbanization, as a social identity it was structured around differences not easily stabilized into a unity for political purposes. To the divisions already mentioned—gross sectors of industry, agriculture, and services; various branches of industry; regional disparities; diverse demographics of proletarianization; the major faultline of skill—should be added gendered differences between working-class women and men. Across industrializing Europe, the ideal of a household managed by the nonworking wife was available to only a minority. Women's earning power may have been vital to working families, but its status was practically and explicitly devalued. Thus in building the collective ideal of the working class—in shaping the disorderly facts of industrialization into a basis for politics—socialists embraced only some parts of working-class life while derogating others. In the centering of class identity, some working-class experiences became valorized, others ignored or effaced.[19]

As independent labor movements began forming in the 1860s, including trade unions and socialist parties, they inherited these gendered traditions. The earliest initiatives, in the European strike wave and political upheavals of 1868–74, were borne by representatives of the skilled crafts. Subsequent heavy-industrial expansion—in coal, iron and steel, shipbuilding, transport, chemicals, heavy machine-building—directly generated few jobs for women. So labor movements institutionalized precisely the systems of distinction that were least conducive to a genuinely inclusive and gender-blind working-class political presence. While invoking the interests, authority, and collective agency of the working class as a whole, those movements were actually far more narrow and exclusionary.

THE POLITICS OF WORKING-CLASS FORMATION

How a working class was recruited also shaped the possible forms of working-class politics. Where industry grew slowly, from protoindustrial communities with long histories of industrial or semiindustrial employment, the labor movement's prospects differed from those where industry was freshly introduced. This contrast is dramatically illustrated by the west German cities of Hamborn and Remscheid. From 1861 to 1910, Remscheid, a metals center since the seventeenth century, grew steadily from 16,000 inhabitants to 72,000, recruiting its workers from the immediate countryside and preserving the small scale of its craft-based industry. In contrast, Hamborn exploded from a village of 6,000 in 1895 into a huge company town of 103,000 by 1910. Its workforce was recruited from far and wide, brutally inducted into a new proletarian life.[20]

The two environments could hardly have been more different: Remscheid, with its slowly accumulating continuity of working-class culture, securely rooted in the self-improving ethos of skilled artisans; Hamborn, with its uprooted mass proletariat, dragooned into the mines and iron and steel works, crammed into the company-owned rental barracks, lacking either the dignity of work or the reserves of a self-confident labor movement culture. Across many criteria, including housing conditions, occupational health, infant mortality, educational provision, violent criminality, drunkenness, levels of poverty, and regimes at work, Hamborn workers were by far worse off.[21] Hamborn's extremely unrespectable and turbulent workers were the very epitome of the brutalized and exploited factory proletariat.

Yet Remscheid workers had the more developed class consciousness, measured by strong union and party organizations. The Remscheid parliamentary seat was SPD from 1895, and reforms were also wrested from the liberal city council. In Hamborn, the SPD was weak, and union relations with the bulk of Hamborn workers were fraught with mutual suspicion, even contempt. This contrast surfaced vividly in the German Revolution of 1918–19. Remscheid's labor movement took local power behind a left-socialist but orderly program of political demands. Hamborn workers showed more violent rank-and-file militancy, rallying behind economistic demands over wages, work, and control of industry but outside the framework of any left-socialist party and ultimately lacking in political direction.[22]

Neither one nor the other, the skilled craft-conscious trade unionist nor the unskilled and unorganized laborer, formed the "authentic" working class in pre-1914 Europe.[23] One set of conditions was superficially more conducive to socialist organizing. Yet the other conditions generated workplace militancy that seemed more radical—violent, spontaneous, less respectful of authority and established procedures, ready for confrontation. How far different conditions directly determined different forms of action, in the sense of ruling out the alternatives and how far they left socialists with space for maneuver was unclear.

What *was* clear was that socialists had a problem—how to devise a politics for both. Then to this starker contrast came a still wider diversity of working-class experience. "Typical" workers included not only skilled metalworkers in Remscheid and heavy-industrial proletarians in Hamborn but also a multiplicity of manual occupations: dockers, seamen, transport-workers, construction workers, skilled machinists and semiskilled machine-minders, textile operatives, laborers in the chemicals, woodworking, food and drink, and clothing industries, skilled workers in specialized manufacture, and all manner of traditional craftsmen, including printers, book-binders, tailors, leather-workers, shoemakers, carpenters, masons, house-painters, potters, and the like. Still others tended to be marginalized from the emerging imagery of the industrial working class, including domestic servants, agricultural laborers, shop-assistants, clerks, uniformed workers on the state railways and mails, and, last but not least, women home-workers in textiles, clothing, tobacco, and other trades. Just as fundamentally, whole areas of work—like housework, family maintenance, and domestic labor or the "assistance" provided by women and children to male breadwinning heads of household—rarely counted as "work" at all.

Moreover, workers of whatever kind led lives beyond the workplace, however overshadowed by the daily grind of recuperating to face the next working day. They lived in neighborhoods, residential concentrations, and forms of community, cheek by jowl with other types of workers and alongside other social groups as well. They lived in complicated households, sometimes resembling the stereotypical nuclear family but more often not. They came from diverse regions and birthplaces, spoke different languages or dialects, and bore profoundly different cultural identities from religious upbringing and national origins.[24] They were young people and mature adults, and of course women and men. How all this might be fashioned into a single working-class identity was the operative question for socialists.

The rise of the urban working-class neighborhood was crucial to this project. Initially, lower-class loyalties were held within superordinate structures of deference and paternalism, often ordered by religion, and increasingly dominated by liberals. Across Europe, government policies and party actions regulated popular culture by interacting with the social histories of urbanization in ever more ramified ways. From the 1890s, states intervened with gathering intensity in the everyday lives of working people, assisted by new knowledges and professions and targeting social stability and the national health via powerful ideas of family. In the process, powerfully gendered images of the ideal working father and the responsible mother permeated the politics of class. Then socialist parties, too, began organizing working people into collective political agency beyond the neighborhood and workplace, with an impact on government, locally and municipally, in regions, and eventually the nation. All these processes helped shape class identities institutionally.

But no less vital were the complex ways neighborhoods spoke and fought back.[25] If the workplace was one frontier of resistance, where collective agency could be imagined, the family—or more properly, the neighborhood solidarities working-class women fashioned for its survival—was the other:

> Working men faced industrial capitalism . . . in long, cold walks to the job, exhausting labor, occupational injuries and diseases, and grim periods of unemployment. The wives met the forces of the industrial system at other points: sometimes at their own paid jobs, always at the local market street, with the landlord, with the charities, and with such state institutions as hospitals, schools, and sanitary authorities.[26]

The challenge for the Left was to organize on *both* fronts of social dispossession. The practical policies of socialist parties inevitably registered the separation, but usually by adopting the normative gender assumptions rather than bringing them into critical and truly democratic focus. This remained one of the Left's most perduring misrecognitions: "labor movements" implied a socialism beginning from the workplace, centered on strikes, and borne by militant working men; yet those movements were actually more broadly founded, also requiring women's efforts in households, neighborhoods, and streets. Even where this duality was acknowledged, the primacy of the male-gendered class-political languages was seldom escaped.[27]

By 1900, the new urban societies were starting to solidify and coalesce.[28] In Britain, some 80 percent of working-class marriages were now made from common backgrounds, while residential segregation encouraged the extended family networks of working-class community life. Dense sociability of pub and street and the spread of collective associations—friendly societies, working men's clubs, cooperative societies—thickened the infrastructure of common identity, while new organized hobbies, mass sports, betting on horses and dogs, the continuity of home and street, and new commercial entertainments all separated working-class people from the rest. This was "the working class of cup finals, fish-and-chip shops, *palais-de-danse,* and Labour with a capital L," recognizable "by the physical environment in which they lived, a style of life and leisure, by a certain class consciousness increasingly expressed in a secular tendency to join unions and to identify with a class party of Labour."[29] This urban sociopolitical coalescence implied a certain kind of manageable and interconnected community, "places where work, home, leisure, industrial relations, local government, and home-town consciousness were inextricably mixed together."[30]

Organizing political consciousness was easier in smaller single-industry towns like Remscheid or Solingen in Germany with an older trade union culture, or their British equivalents like Sheffield, or "Red Limoges," Roubaix, Lille, and Montluçon, where French socialists were capturing municipal government in the 1890s, or the northern Italian socialist municipalities enabled by local government laws of 1903.[31] Working-class institutions also afforded citywide frameworks of action, like the friendly societies councils and trades councils in Britain; "Chambers of Labor" in Spain, Italy, and France; or the labor secretariats of the German SPD. These allowed some influence over the urban environment, where workers still lacked full democracy in the vote. The earliest cases of municipal socialism, such as the Labour Group's brief rule in East London's West Ham in 1898–1900, made housing, public health, and social improvement into vital sites of action. But the first goal was mastering the casualized labor market, by creating a municipal works department, promoting investment, using public contracts, and requiring union rates.[32] Such political action was key to class formation, as unions and work-based organizing still tended to privilege the older craft societies.

Once urbanization passed a certain threshold, the city's everyday life—notably in transport and rented housing—became a practical infrastructure binding working people together, particularly as reforming city administrations built mass transit systems and public housing of their own. Resulting concentrations of working-class people loyal to the city became a vital resource for socialist city governments after 1918, the bedrock of socialist electoral success. Red Vienna was the most imposing example of a general pattern, where municipal housing, public transport, direct labor, and the city payrolls grounded the Left's twentieth-century urban hegemonies. In 1914–45, expanding central government provision of social goods, such as unemployment relief, health, education, housing, and social security, were also disbursed locally, giving the working poor key incentives for organizing. It began really to matter who was sitting in the council chamber or wearing the mayor's chain of office.[33]

However, the local weight of a city's working class needed the franchise to be felt. It was only after 1918, via revolutionary insurgencies, new constitutions, and a wave of popular enfranchisement that socialist parties came to local power. This was startling in its rapidity in northern Italy during 1918–21, before Fascism violently brought an end to it. But in Weimar Germany, many urban locations of Scandinavia, Britain, and France, and especially Red Vienna, socialist city governments pursued impressive programs of general working-class reform. These rendered sectionalism more manageable, especially once the post-1918 union expansion finally loosened the dominance of skilled workers and craft traditions, easing new partnerships with industrial and public-sector unions. Craft exclusiveness was also complicit in ideologies of domesticity keeping women from public voice, and so *its* decline potentially weakened the masculinity of socialist political cultures too. Municipal socialism, with its expanding welfare apparatus, gave women new opportunities everywhere, but in Scandinavia and Britain these brought wider political participation. Following enfranchisement in 1918, women moved the Labour Party toward a stronger social agenda during the 1920s (via nursery education, maternal and child welfare, public health), shifting it further from the old trade-union ground. By the mid-1920s, Labour's women's sections had 200,000 members, with 155,000 in 1933, or 40 percent of the whole.[34]

CONCLUSION

Thus, working-class formation was no simple result of industrialization. Capitalism certainly brought a distinctive social structure via common processes of dispossession, exploitation, and subordination, until working people kept few means of livelihood past selling their labor power for a wage. Capital's regimes of accumulation, the practical circumstances of industrial production, and patterns of urbanization also shaped working-class life in powerful ways. The spatial architecture of the working-class presence in society—the social geography of industrialization, the growth of cities, the concentration of working people in segregated quarters, the visible massing of workers in all these ways—likewise structured common trends of collective belonging. Working-class cultures displayed strong unifying regularities across neighborhoods, occupations, industries, regions, religious and linguistic barriers, and Europe's national frontiers. In light of these convergent processes, "the working class" became a resonant and meaningful term of social and political address. By 1900, it described a palpable reality of European politics, social administration, and everyday life.

Yet workers were not the only popular class in European society. They coexisted with peasants and lower middle classes, usually in equivalent numbers with continuing societal strength. Moreover, distinctions within the working class remained strong, not just outside work but in the multiple differences of the workplace itself, in wages, security of employment, seniority, job control, and of course skill, quite apart from sectional divisions from industry to industry and firm to firm. Despite the wage relation's universalizing logic, industrialization itself continuously invented new distinctions, notably around new technologies. The most troublesome divisiveness, in variable but persistent forms, centered on gender and work. Relatively small numbers of workers commanded higher wages and better conditions via their skill, as against the low wages, irregular work, and stricter subordination of the mass of the working poor. And not only did working women fall consistently on the disempowering side of this skill line, but the prevailing structures of working-class respectability also silenced and marginalized women via cultures of family, home, and public masculinity.

How these complex and countervailing logics of unity and difference worked with and against each other in particular times and places depended crucially on politics—on the fashioning of working-class organizations and on the rivalry of religious, philanthropic, party, and governmental interventions seeking to shape and secure working-class allegiance. In this respect, social administration, public health, policing, the law, and the ramified institutional machinery of local and national government, as well as constitutional frameworks and the character of public spheres, all determined the course of working-class formation. As the working class made its collective appearance in European history, these were not external forces acting on a working class already made from economics and sociology but an intimate part of the making of the working class *tout court*.

Chapter 4

The Rise of Labor Movements

History's Forward March

THE 1860S WERE a key watershed for the Left. Older traditions became eclipsed, while others like anarchism moved to the margins of the international movement. A new ideal emerged of nationally organized parties of labor focused on the parliamentary arena. This socialist constitutionalism arose from the dramatic liberalizations of 1867–71, which allowed many labor movements their first legal agitation on a larger-than-local scale. It was also actively promoted by the First International, whose influence far exceeded the modest memberships of its affiliates. Its perspectives were those of Marx and Engels, who assumed during these years their lasting role of senior consultants to the European socialist movements.

The 1860s sowed the seeds of organization. Some party foundations coalesced from earlier initiatives, as in Germany, where the SPD's two tributaries dated from 1863.[1] Others anticipated things to come, as in Britain and the tsarist empire, where stronger foundations came only around 1900. Others still led a marginal or semiclandestine existence before 1914, as in Iberia, the Balkans, and most of eastern Europe. But these were all social democratic parties, distinct from other strands of the Left, like anarchist or syndicalist movements, radical democratic parties, peasant parties, or the populist Socialist Revolutionary Party in Russia (see table 4.1). They were parties aligning themselves with the Second International formed in 1889, consciously identifying with the legacy of Karl Marx.[2]

These movements were a novel departure for Europe's Left. They were the first nation-

TABLE 4.1 The First Socialist Parties 1871–1905

1871	Portuguese Socialist Party (PSP)
1875	German Social Democratic Party (SPD)
1876	Danish Social Democratic Association (SDF)
1878	Czech Social Democratic Party (CSDSD)
1879	Spanish Socialist Workers' Party (PSOE)
1880	Hungarian General Workers' Party (MSZP)
	Federation of the French Socialist Workers' Party (FPTSF)
1881	Dutch Social Democratic League (SDAP)
1882	Polish Proletariat Party
1883	British Social Democratic Federation (SDF)
	Russian Group for the Emancipation of Labor
1885	Belgian Workers' Party (POB)
1887	Norwegian Labor Party (DNA)
	Armenian Hanchak Party
1888	Swiss Social Democratic Party (SPS)
1889	Austrian Social Democratic Party (SPÖ)
	Swedish Social Democratic Workers' Party (SAP)
1891	Bulgarian Workers' Social Democratic Party (BWSDP)
1892	Serbian Social Democratic Party (SSDP)
	Italian Socialist Party (PSI)
1893	Polish Socialist Party (Russia) (PPS)
	Social Democratic Party of the Kingdom of Poland (Russia) (SDKPiL)
	Romanian Social Democratic Party (PSR)
1894	Croatian Social Democratic Party (SDPC)
1896	Slovenian South Slavic Social Democratic Party (JSDS)
1897	Polish Social Democratic Party of Galicia (PPSD)
	General League of Jewish Workingmen in Russia and Poland (Bund)
1898	Russian Social Democratic Workers' Party (RSDRP)
1899	Ukrainian Social Democratic Party (East Galicia) (USDP)
1900	British Labour Party (LP)
1903	Finnish Social Democratic Party (SDP)
1904	Latvian Social Democratic Workers' Party (LSDWP)
1905	Ukrainian Social Democratic Workers' Party (Russia) (USDRP)
	Slovakian Social Democratic Party (SSP)

ally organized socialist parties with any continuous existence. There were smaller groups before, but only in local and ephemeral ways, and during 1849–60 state repression and poor national communications stifled anything more. Despite labor associations based on the skilled trades, political efforts struggled until the 1870s and belonged to earlier Left traditions. This didn't change overnight. The new parties competed with rival tendencies in some countries and endured splits and fragmentation in others. Nevertheless, they registered a qualitative shift in socialist activity, beginning a new epoch of the Left's history.

THE GEOGRAPHY OF SOCIALISM

The new parties varied enormously in significance. The strongest were in Scandinavia and German-speaking central Europe (including the Czech lands of the Habsburg Empire), the weakest in the Mediterranean. Where industry made little progress, so did socialism, as in southeastern Europe. But industrialization was no infallible guide. The success of Bulgarian socialists in the 1913 elections or the Ukrainian Social Democrats among the East Galician peasantry, and the socialist advance in Finland, Norway, and Sweden all show socialist parties winning rural support. Legality, a functioning parliamentary constitution, and a democratic franchise were just as enabling as industrialization. Conversely, Russian autocracy held back democratic expression of popular militancy, and a discriminatory franchise artificially depressed the Belgian socialists' electoral showing. Thus, early liberal democratic political frameworks could compensate for the absence of capitalist industry, just as the absence of liberalization could hamper a labor movement's progression toward a "German" or "Scandinavian" model of social democratic success in the more industrial economies. In this sense, the constitutional factor could anticipate or impede the consequences of industrial class formation.

There are two further complications in this geography of socialist support. First, in the western Mediterranean the picture was muddied by anarchism and, after 1900, by the related antiparliamentary, anticentralist, direct-action politics usually called syndicalism. This applied most to Spain, where Bakunin's supporters preempted those of Marx in the late 1860s and where economic backwardness and liberalism's fragility impeded the Spanish socialists. But it also applied to Italy, where the PSI failed to supplant a vigorous anarchist tradition. Anarchists imparted localist and insurrectionary violence to the militancy of the northern Italian working class in the great popular explosions between the 1890s and the victory of Fascism. The most anomalous case was France. By 1914, French republicanism had bequeathed the Left a century of parliamentary democratic experience, in a strongly if unevenly industrializing economy. Yet socialist votes remained surprisingly low, given French workers' record as the vanguard of European radicalism in 1830, 1848, and 1871.

In all three countries, the medium of labor action was less the local branch of the centrally organized socialist party than the "Chamber of Labor"—the workers' *centro* in Spain, the Italian *camere del lavoro,* the French *bourse du travail.* These were active centers of socialist culture, mixing the functions of labor exchange, trade-union syndicate, educational resource, recreation facility, meeting place, citizens' advice bureau, agitational nucleus, and fount of socialist morality. They came from older traditions of self-help, mutual aid, and cooperation. But they were also new, improvised collectively by proletarianized urban or rural wage-earners, forming a counterpoint to the social democracies emerging from the 1860s and 1870s. In Spain, workers' chambers were the cellular basis for an anarcho-syndicalism that marginalized socialists in industrial Catalonia and rural Andalusia, confining them to the mining regions of the north. In Italy, in contrast, they fed the growth of socialism, especially among the agricultural laborers of the Po Valley. In France, they fell in between.

The second complication before 1914 was Britain. Here was a paradox, for the nation with the most advanced capitalism and the most proletarian society had one of the weakest socialist votes. Contrary to the rest of Europe, working-class activism continued through the Liberal Party, keeping specifically socialist politics marginal until shortly before 1914. Yet, starting with the socialist revival of the 1880s, vibrant socialist subcultures coexisted locally with Liberal electoral representation, particularly in the north.[3] It was the Labour Representation Committee after 1900, first as a parliamentary lobby for unions within the Liberal framework but then as an emergent party in its own right, that eroded the Liberal Party's hold on workers' support. The shift to Labour was slow and uneven, and the First World War finally effected the change. But beginning with 1906 and the two 1910 elections, Labour was claiming its own space.[4]

Nowhere else did labor stay so comfortably in an older liberal framework. With this one exception, there were three distinct geographies of socialism before 1914: the social democratic "core" of Scandinavia and central Europe, where the new model of socialist parliamentarianism and associated trade unionism dominated labor movements; the western Mediterranean, where anarcho-syndicalism weakened the socialist parties and rendered working-class politics more volatile; and the eastern European rim of Russia, the Balkans, and much of Austria-Hungary, where economic and political backwardness delayed socialist parties or forced them underground.

Socialist parties came in two phases: the first occupied the gap between the First and Second Internationals, ending with the Italian party in 1892; the other beginning with the Balkan and Polish foundations of the early–1890s and ending in 1905 with the revolution in Russia. This sequence followed Europe's developmental gradient, sloping downward from west to east and north to south. Apart from the British Labour Party, later foundations came where conditions had retarded popular politics, either through absent or uneven industrialization, low levels of literacy and public culture, or a repressive political system. Examples included not only the Russian and Habsburg east but also the southern periphery of Spain, Portugal, and much of Italy. In the east, socialists succeeded best where either local industrialization or less repressive local regimes made the environment less inhospitable. For socialist activity to take off, either capitalist development or liberal political traditions were needed, however limited (see table 4.2).

TABLE 4.2 The Progress of Social Democracy before 1914

Country/Party	Founded	Peak Electoral Performance (%)	Peak Membership
Finland (SDP)	1903	43.1 (1913)	85,027 (1906)
Sweden (SAP)	1889	36.5 (Sept. 1914)	133,388 (1907)
Germany (SPD)	1875	34.8 (1912)	1,085,905 (1914)
Czech lands (CSDSD)	1878	32.2 (1911)	243,000 (1913)
Denmark (SDF)	1876	29.6 (1913)	57,115 (1914)
Norway (DNA)	1887	26.3 (1912)	53,866 (1914)
Austria (SPO)	1889	25.4 (1911)	89,628 (1913)
Italy (PSI)	1892	22.8 (1913)	47,098 (1901)
Belgium (POB)	1885	22.5 (1900)	
Bulgaria (BWSDP)	1891	20.2 (1913)	6,168 (1912)
Switzerland (SPS)	1888	20.0 (1913)	29,730 (1913)
Netherlands (SDAP)	1881	18.6 (1913)	25,708 (1913)
France (SFIO)	1880	16.8 (1914)	93,218 (1914)
Britain (LP)	1900	7.0 (Jan. 1910)	

SOCIALISM, PARLIAMENTARY GOVERNMENT, AND THE FRANCHISE

From the constitutional upheavals of 1867–71 to 1914, north-central Europe was surprisingly stable. Europe certainly saw strains—the endemic violence of the Italian state's response to popular protests, suffrage crises in Belgium, British labor unrest in 1911–13, the Tragic Week in Spain in September 1909, and all the turmoil surrounding the 1905 Russian Revolution—but the constitutional frameworks of the 1860s proved remarkably resilient. During these decades, stability required major feats of constitutional accommodation, as in the British Third Reform Act (1884), the Belgian Constitution (1893), universal manhood suffrage in Austria (1907) and Italy (1912), and the Scandinavian liberalizations in Norway (1898), Denmark (1901), Finland (1905), and Sweden (1907). But these settlements were negotiated precisely *through* the available constitutional means. Democratic aspirations were channeled *into* the liberal constitutional framework. Stability was secured through the available parliamentary forms.

The 1860s established the lasting parliamentary-constitutional norms for European political life, which both the Left and their opponents accepted. After 1905, inspired by the St. Petersburg Soviet and European mass strike agitations, socialist radicals began criticizing these parliamentary perspectives. But their critiques came to fruition only in 1917–23. Earlier, most socialists observed the parliamentary norms; and where they didn't exist, extraparliamentary agitation was meant to create them. Likewise, outside Russia, the Balkans, and Iberia, where parliamentary constitutions remained weak, Europe's dominant classes proved reluctant to jettison these for reactionary governing systems less vulnerable to popular pressure. Even where the labor movement's freedoms became restricted, as in Germany under the Anti-Socialist Law of 1878–90, parliamentary frameworks remained intact. If German socialists suffered police harassment and unions were illegal, the SPD was still permitted to fight elections.

For the new socialist parties, one principle was axiomatic: labor's politics needed the available parliamentary forms. These could be used partly as a platform for rousing the masses, partly for winning short-term reforms. Moreover, the further struggles for a democratic franchise directly affected the Left's relations to liberalism, because so long as *anciens régimes* resisted reform, liberals commonly joined oppositional fronts with socialists and other radicals. But once votes for workers were won, splits occurred. Democratizing the constitution, however modestly, cleared the way for other conflicts. Having secured a more democratic franchise, socialists seized their political independence.

Britain was one extreme, where labor's junior status in a popular liberal coalition outlasted anywhere else. The Gladstonian Liberal Party, shaped into a national movement in the 1860s, was the classic party of limited reform, leading the respectable working class through two Reform Acts in 1867 and 1884 and mobilizing against a perceived corrupt aristocratic establishment. Yet the very limits of reform—and the practical disfranchisement of half the male and all the female working class—impeded a separate party of labor. This, and the weight of tradition, powerfully justified the Liberal alliance, until wartime conditions and a further Reform Act in 1918 enabled the Labour Party's complete independence.

Germany was an opposite extreme, with the rupture of labor and liberalism coming exceptionally early in the 1860s. The reasons were complex, involving deep divergences over the forms of German unity. Inclusion of universal manhood suffrage in the North German and Imperial Constitutions of 1867–71 freed the infant socialist party from its earlier dependence on the liberals. It took another two decades for German Social Democrats to become a mass party, but the political conditions of independence were laid.

Against these extremes, Scandinavia and the Low Countries were in between. In the 1890s, Norway's Labor Party was a loose federation of local workingmen's associations. Moved by the national question of Norwegian separation from Sweden, it backed the farmer-based Liberal *Venstre* party, virtually winning universal manhood suffrage in 1898 for its pains. Danish Social Democrats likewise joined the Liberal *Venstre* party in a democratic alliance against the government's resistance to parliamentary accountability. From the 1890s, Swedish Socialists and Liberals also collaborated against Conservatives for suffrage reform. In each case, winning parliamentary government with manhood suffrage upset these longstanding liberal-socialist alliances—in Norway after separating from Sweden (1905), in Denmark after constitutional reform (1901), in Sweden after the suffrage reform of 1907.[5] Once the constitutional question was resolved, socialists' increased parliamentary strength encouraged independence, and realignment could occur. Similarly, Belgian socialists usually aligned with liberal coalitions for anticlerical educational policies and suffrage reform, oscillating between mass working-class protests (suffrage actions of 1886, 1893, 1899, 1902, and 1913) and parliamentary cooperation with radical liberals. But after the 1902 mass strike met defeat, they formed a more stable liberal alliance, as did the Dutch socialists after their failed suffrage action of 1903.[6]

The constitutional question had a further twist. The franchise was one thing. The larger framework of parliamentary accountability, which might bring socialists into government, was another. Here too was wide variation. Parties' relationship to the state, and the state's response to their rise, shaped their radical propensities. Where parliamentary traditions were old and popular ideology identified democracy with their strength, as in Britain, or where the state backed civil liberties and industrial arbitration, as in Sweden and Denmark, labor movements favored gradualism or reformism. Where socialists lacked parliamentary representation and the state behaved repressively—as in Iberia, Italy before 1912, the Hungarian half of the Habsburg Empire, or imperial Russia—labor militancy became intransigent. The Anti-Socialist Law, police harassment, barring socialists from public employment, demonizing them as "antinational"—these German conditions solidified the SPD's loyalty to revolutionary Marxism. Seeing the state as a tool of the ruling class, not to be reformed but destroyed, grew from the movement's daily maltreatment, not least because its rising electoral strength was negated by the government's freedom from parliamentary control.[7] This governing system eased the SPD's adoption of a Marxist program at its Congresses in Gotha (1875) and Erfurt (1891), while silencing efforts to change it. This didn't preclude welcoming reforms far short of capitalism's overthrow. Socialists accommodated to German capitalism's given institutions, in trade unionism, local government, and parliamentary committee work. As the movement proliferated bureaucratically after 1890, greater organizational conservatism followed. Yet, while this was happening, state repression helped keep the party officially revolutionary.

In a counterexample, Denmark showed how early compromise between state, capital, and labor could give the movement's politics a reformist mold. In 1899, a national carpenters' dispute pulled in the Danish Trade Union Federation (LO) and Danish Employers' Association (DA), each nationally organized the previous year, resulting in a sixteen-week general lockout. In the September Agreement ending the dispute, the employers won respect for managerial prerogatives but also conceded rules for strikes and lockouts, including arbitration courts staffed by the two sides' nominees and a presiding judge. Thus employers had conceded Danish unions' essential legitimacy, including rights to organize, negotiate, and strike and the key principle of collective bargaining. With no European parallel as a national corporative arrangement before 1914, the September Agreement defined the framework of labor relations in Denmark for the twentieth century.[8]

France presents yet another pattern. The republican tradition commanded powerful popular solidarity in France, despite the Third Republic's origins in a counterrevolutionary massacre of 20,000 supporters of the Paris Commune. When the Republic was in danger, the French labor movement backed coalitions of republican defense. Despite the repression of the 1870s, workers also saw the anticlerical republic as the natural ally against authoritarian and catholic employers, while republican politicians were concerned "to present the republic as something other than the guard-dog of the employers."[9] Beginning with the legalizing of unions in 1884, incremental labor reforms were the result, bringing industrial arbitration (1892), employer liability for industrial accidents (1898), and a ministry of labor under Alexandre Millerand (1900). Governments hardly advocated working-class interests in the socialist sense. But the republican tradition's leftward tilt encouraged an ambivalence in the French labor movement's attitudes to the state that was missing from the direct antagonism in Germany.

In social democracy's founding era, it was a dialectic of integration and exclusion that favored the largest parties: sufficient measures of parliamentary government for the party to take off but sufficient measures of repression to sharpen its radical edge. Socialist parties didn't rely purely on parliamentary institutions to flourish. The rapid rise of the Russian, Jewish, Ukrainian, and Latvian parties in the Russian Empire showed socialism's adaptability to illegal conditions. Parties could also retool for forming governments once parliamentary democracy was won; witness the impressive staying power of Scandinavian social democracy in government between the 1930s and 1970s. But in social democracy's pre-1914 oppositional culture, it was the intermediate situation—enough democracy, but not too much—that gave the movement its élan. Beyond this, the ability to identify positively with the existing state, as something susceptible to influence, change, and eventually control, was a key divider for European parties. Where that ability to identify was strong, the more reformist parties emerged; where the ability was weak or impaired, the greater the potential for a more revolutionary stance.

TRADE UNIONISM

Almost all socialist parties had close relationships with nationally organized trade-union federations. Indeed, they were instrumental in launching such national organizations, which, with Britain's exception, postdated the foundation of the socialist party itself (see table 4.3).

TABLE 4.3 Social Democracy and Trade Unionism

Country		National Union Federation
Britain (LP)	(1900)	1868 Trades Union Congress
Spain (PSOE)	1879	1888 General Union of Spanish Labor
Germany (SPD)	1875	1891 General Commission Free Trade Unions
Hungary (MSZP)	1880	1891 Trade-Union Council
Austria (SPÖ)	1889	1893 Trade Union Commission
Czech lands (CSDSD)	1878	1897 Trade Union Commission
Belgium (POB)	1885	1898 General Federation of Belgian Labor
Denmark (SDF)	1876	1898 Trade Union Confederation
Sweden (SAP)	1889	1898 Trade Union Confederation
Norway(DNA)	1887	1899 Trade Union Confederation
Bulgaria (BWSDP)	1891	1904 General Workers' Trade Union
Netherlands (SDAP)	1881	1906 Federation of Trade Unions
Italy (PSI)	1892	1906 General Confederation of Italian Labor

The growth and forms of trade unionism varied greatly across Europe. When other national movements remained embryonic, British unions had 674,000 members by 1887, as against 139,000 in France and 95,000 in Germany. British unions were also recognized, both under law and by employers. The liberalizing economic legislation and constitutional reforms of the 1860s legalized workers' combinations elsewhere too, but antilabor policies commonly returned, and unions were rarely protected under law outside Britain, the Low Countries, and Scandinavia. If by 1914 laws had improved, state power was routinely used against workers in strikes, and unions seldom escaped surveillance. Levels of unionization still varied, sliding in 1913 from peaks of 25 percent in Britain and 20 percent in Denmark through 15–16 percent in Belgium and Germany and down to only 10–11 percent in Norway, France, and Italy.[10]

In gross terms, trade unionism was a matter of economics, spreading with the rates and forms of industrialization. There were three types of experience before 1914, starting with Britain and Belgium as the pioneer industrializers of the earlier 1800s. Industrialization then followed in Germany and Scandinavia in the second half of the century, accelerating after the 1890s on a massive scale. Finally, industrialization elsewhere was weaker, although from the 1890s France, Italy, and Russia developed impressively advanced industrial sectors, as did Bohemia, Vienna, and Budapest in the Habsburg Empire and Barcelona in Spain. In all cases, small and exclusive craft unions based around skill gave way to the mass unionism made possible by industry.

Everywhere, it was less the factory hands who forged early labor movements than skilled men in small workshops. The earliest unions came from friendly societies, journeymen's clubs, and educational associations filling the space left by the guilds. In Germany before 1890, craft societies were at the labor movement's core—printers, carpenters, masons, glovemakers, smiths, molders, and others, including local specialties like ships' carpenters in Hamburg or cutlery grinders in Solingen. Such male artisans possessed specialized knowledge of production and an ability to regulate labor markets by custom and apprenticeship. They eluded the "sweating" found in more employer-dominated labor markets, which killed crafts like tailoring and shoemaking. They boasted collective organization, which rural artisans or factory workers lacked.

Printers were the typical pioneers, forming the first unions in Switzer- ⟵ land (1858), Bohemia (1862), Austria (1864), Hungary (1865), Germany and the Netherlands (1866), Spain (1868), Italy (1872), Norway (1882), and Bulgaria (1883).[11] When trade unionism began among the Polish artisans of Lvov in the late 1860s, printers were naturally there first, emulating Progressive Societies in Vienna, Prague, Budapest, Brno, and Trieste and organizing a successful strike in January 1870, that sparked a general Galician strike wave. By 1890, they were still there, providing the core for the Galician Workers' Party, precursor of the Galician Social Democratic Party launched in 1897.[12]

In the transition from this craft unionism, Britain was unique. There, unions grew inside an existing craft framework of exceptional strength. This came from British industrialization's slow accumulation before the 1860s—small-scale, unmechanized, reliant on plentiful skilled labor. It allowed skilled craftsmen's organizations to stabilize via the so-called new model unions during 1848–75. Nowhere else did craft unions expand by "colonizing the basic industries of the country" rather than being confined to skilled minorities of particular trades. In Britain, craft unions became the model even for skilled workers created by industrialization itself, like the cotton spinners, who then excluded the less skilled. This dominance also made possible another distinctive British phenomenon after 1889, the polymorphous general unions, which moved into all those industries the craft unions' traditionalism led them to ignore.[13]

These general unions differed from two other models on the continent: industrial unions, which recruited everyone in a single industry, regardless of skill or even the collar-line; and general laborers' unions, which collected all the unskilled who were left, either because of craft exclusiveness or because their jobs defied traditional classification; when enough of these unskilled had been recruited, they were reassigned to the appropriate industrial union, ideally merging with the relevant crafts.[14] Industrial unionism spread unevenly. In Germany, it was strongest among metalworkers and woodworkers (beginning 1891 and 1893), followed by construction workers (forming one union in 1912 from bricklayers and laborers), transport workers, textile workers, and miners.[15] But in Britain, the ubiquity of craft unions made industrial unionism a nonstarter. That situation invited a broader general unionism, reaching from unspecialized general laborers to the neglected skilled and semiskilled across many industries—"a changing conglomerate of miscellaneous local and regional groups of workers in particular industries, occupations and plants."[16]

General unions appeared in Britain with the New Unionism in 1889–92, which shifted the movement decisively toward the unskilled and established the lasting future pattern. Of the ten largest unions in 1885, only one kept its place in 1963 (engineers), whereas seven at the later date originated during 1880–1914: Transport and General, General and Municipal, Miners, and Electricians (all 1888–89), Shop and Distributive (1891), Railways (1889), and Local Government (1900s).[17] This produced the striking dualism of British union growth: craft unions doggedly defending dearly won privileges in labor market and workplace and emergent mass unionism gathering up the slack. The latter flourished in the new branches of modern industry, of which automobiles and armaments became the emblematic twentieth-century examples.

In less industrial countries, the smaller opportunities didn't prevent embittered conflicts over opposing models—as in the Budapest-centered Hungarian union movement or the small but vigorous Bulgarian one, passionately split after 1903 between centralist advocates of revolutionary industrial unionism and reformist defenders of "nonpolitical" craft-based federalism. In northern Italy, Spain, and France, unions followed local and federalist paths—municipal coalitions of labor around a craft core, based on multifaceted chambers of labor and capable of citywide actions going well beyond the regularly unionized skilled workers. There, centrally organized unions affected only the public sector, railways, and mines. Only in the heavily proletarianized Spanish and Italian countrysides did general unions grow. The huge Italian *Federterra* (agricultural workers' union, founded 1901) was uniquely successful in organizing an agricultural proletariat, although membership fluctuated wildly: in 1913 there were 469,000 organized farm workers, as against 503,000 oganized in industry.[18]

National federation, in the French CGT (1895) and Italian CGL (1906), made little impact on this proud localism. Apart from the remarkable Federterra and the Metal Workers' Union (FIOM) formed in 1901, Italian Socialists failed to dislodge the locally rooted craft societies. The local arena of the workers' chamber blurred the boundary of unions and politics, so that *bourse du travail* and *camere del lavoro* substituted for the local socialist section. In Italy, the two were complementary, as local Socialists worked in the *camere*'s enlarged cultural milieu. Against this, the French CGT rejected all "political" affiliations: indifferent to the advantages of centralism, CGT unionism mobilized around individual militants, who operated through the *bourse*. In syndicalism, this strategy competed directly with parliamentary socialism, which in France had a very specific regional and socioeconomic niche.[19] Centralism and localism in Spain polarized into adversarial federations, the Socialist UGT and the anarcho-syndicalist

CNT. This differed profoundly from the national model proposed by Marx and broadly realized in the north, which combined parliamentary socialism with centralized unions.

If Britain had a mixture of nationally organized craft and general unions, while France, Spain, and Italy produced decentralized and heterogeneous, locally based coalitions, Germany showed the clearest developmental progression, with craft traditions succumbing to mass industrial unionism. The German labor movement also grew from local or citywide artisans' associations. But German craft unions never broadened their base like the British: deprived of legal protection by the Anti-Socialist Law in 1878, they were overtaken by the speed and greater modernity of German industrialization. Before the Law banned coordinated union and party activity, there were 27 national craft unions, from the tobacco-workers (with 8,100 members), printers (5,696), and joiners (5,500) down to the saddlers (260), basket weavers (100), and sculptors (35). After a year, there were only four left: the printers, lithographers, glovemakers, and hatters. State repression cut the movement back to its local roots.[20]

After the Anti-Socialist Law, the movement exploded outward, as Germany's rapid industrialization outstripped craft societies' abilities to integrate new types of workers. During 1892–1914, national unions dropped from 57 to 46, but members rocketed from 215,000 to 2.5 million. This growth reflected two key shifts. Craft influence was slashed: by 1914 over half the 1892 unions had gone, as organization spread into mining, construction, engineering, transport, processing, and general manufacture. Second, centralism triumphed over localism. In 1895, 45 percent of Berlin trade unionists were still in local unions, grouped in the Free Alliance (FVDG) based in engineering and construction. But in 1907–8, Berlin metalworkers were finally integrated into the national union, and FVDG membership was banned.[21] By 1914, the big seven—six industrial unions (metals, wood, construction, transport, textiles, mining) plus general factory workers—each had a six-figure membership, making 70 percent of the total.

The stark lines of this typology can be softened. Until the mass unionism after 1895, the German movement resembled the pre-1889 "old unionism" in Britain, although craft unions never had the British breadth. Moreover, German craft unions hardly disappeared altogether. Carpenters, painters, stone-layers, and asphalt-layers all resisted absorption into the construction union.[22] Conversely, de facto industrial unions could also emerge inside the British general unions, as with dockers in the Transport and General Workers Union (TGWU). After the First World War, moreover, European unionism converged generally toward centrally federated movements operating corporatively in relation to economy and state.

Two final points arise. On the one hand, political contexts decisively shaped trade unionism's national characteristics. If the German movement differed from the British in the 1860s, this came less from industrial sociology than the repression German unions had to face. This political adversity encouraged German militants into socialism, while in Britain union toleration and parliamentary reform sealed ties with liberalism. Thereafter, Bismarckian repression blocked a more "British" course. Loss of union rights under the Anti-Socialist Law raised socialist loyalties to practical primacy, simply because the SPD in parliament was the only legal representation left. When national unions reemerged after 1890, their socialist affiliations then promoted the centralized industrial-unionist model. In this manner, national political contexts shaped how unions were organized and behaved.[23]

On the other hand, economics also remained key. The compressed and accelerated aspects of German industrialization, plus German capitalism's highly organized character, made the most compelling case for centralized industrywide unions. German industrialization generated new types of workers faster than locally grounded craft societies could ever absorb them. Moreover, concentration of capital elicited concentration of labor, for it was only by the most determined centralizing of resources that workers could hope to fight the big employers. In SPD thinking, this was linked to larger visions of capitalist development, where concentration, rationalization, and technical progress all furthered the advent of the centrally planned economy. This necessitated equivalent union organization—equal to the struggle against capital and to taking control of the economy after revolution. Such arguments weren't relevant in backward economies where industry was small scale and geographically dispersed. There, the national economy had yet to acquire its salience for collective bargaining, and localist forms survived.

LABOR MOVEMENTS EXPAND

The rhythm of union advance was linked both to the boom and bust of the business cycle and to politics. A dialectic of political liberalization and booming economy had shaped the first pan-European strike wave of 1868–73, when militancy extended far into the underdeveloped periphery, from Spain to Galicia. Liberalization then interacted with the end of the depression in 1895–96 to help the transition to mass unionism. Politics also drove the continental labor explosion of 1904–7, when Austrian unions tripled, German, Norwegian, and Swedish more than doubled, and Hungarian almost doubled in membership, not to speak of localized militancy in France, Italy, and Spain and the revolutionary turbulence in Russia, where unions appeared legally for the first time. Suffrage questions and Russia's revolutionary inspiration were the impetus, although economic upswing certainly helped.

One effect of depression was decisive. Outside Britain, 1873–96 changed free trade to protection, sucking government into the economy. In heavy industry and emerging sectors of chemicals and electrical engineering, this also drove concentration, with imposing levels of vertical and horizontal integration in and across sectors, ruthless market regulation via cartels, and new corporate lobbies influencing government. This was most marked in Germany. But it described dynamic sectors everywhere, establishing a new pattern for industrializing economies in Italy, Russia, and Scandinavia. Capitalism was far more organized—larger in scale, more interconnected via the national economy, more politicized, and more integrated corporatively with the state. This reshaped the environment where unions had to operate, with big consequences for their likely success.

The breakthrough to mass unionism was impressive. By 1913, British unions had added roughly 3.4 million, German unions just under 3.8 million, and French around 900,000 workers to their membership of the late 1880s.[24] Unions finally invaded the factory floor, as against the building site, coal mine, and small workshop, where they already had a presence. In Britain, where 1911–13 added 1.5 million workers (66 percent of unions' earlier strength), this embraced distributive workers, local government employees, civil servants, and teachers, as well as workers in transport and manufacture.[25]

These new recruits had industry-specific skills without craft training in chemicals, food manufacture, and new branches of engineering like bicycle and car production where the engineering union was weak. In older engineering branches, union demands took familiar craft forms, focusing on apprenticeship, demarcation, and machine manning, plus broader issues of piecework, overtime, and the eight-hour day. But craft unionism's weakness in newer sectors freed organizers to focus on the semiskilled and skilled machinists whom mechanization was starting to invent.[26] Moreover, if in Britain this expansion occurred beyond existing craft unions, which balked at organizing the less skilled, on the continent metals unionism became adapted for exactly that purpose. But in both cases a new vanguard was emerging: the semiskilled production worker trained on the job.

Localized bargaining became ever harder to operate. Campaigns like the eight-hour day *demanded* national coordination. Employers also aggressively forced the pace. The power of big capital in Germany deployed an imposing antiunion repertoire, from company housing and welfare schemes to the operation of blacklists and "yellow" unions, to which this new political coordination was now added. This in turn put huge pressure on unions to centralize. Government also took a new interest in labor disputes. In Britain, industrial conciliation developed through the Labour Department of the Board of Trade, aided modestly by the 1896 Conciliation Act. The strongest cases were Denmark, via the September Agreement (1899); and Sweden, via agreements for engineering (1905) and textiles (1909). Similar trends appeared in France (arbitration legislation 1892, Ministry of Labor 1900); and Italy (Supreme Council of Labor 1902, arbitration code 1905). Repression was never far away. In 1901–4, when the Liberal Italian government was negotiating with reformist Socialists, 40 strikers were killed by police. But in Germany, linked to the social insurance legislation pioneered there in the 1880s plus the uneven spread of collective bargaining, a national system of industrial relations promised to reshape the framework for unions.[27] Ultimately, it was the First World War that brought this about.

Trade unionism's mass basis made it a key factor in national life. In Britain, the scale of strikes changed: "while the outbreak of 1889 had consisted largely of a wave of local and generally not very large strikes propagated by chain reaction, the 1911 outburst was dominated by national confrontations, or battles deliberately engaged by national armies."[28] On the continent, the fulcrum was the great labor militancy of 1904–7. This partly reflected the changing national economy and its integrated corporate structures. But it was politically driven, too, dramatized by the suffrage agitations and the 1905 Russian Revolution. Here, questions of work and democracy—wages and citizenship—were inextricably linked. With the growth of a national public sphere and the rise of mass socialist parties, trade unionism crystallized larger hopes and fears. Labor conflicts symbolized larger principles. As trade union struggles grew in scale, so did this national political dimension.

Centralism had its costs. Members felt disempowered as permanent officials and delegate structures replaced decisions by general meeting. Tensions between national organizing and local initiative were worst over strikes. Centralizing resources was essential for fighting the employers, but the constitutionalizing of strike decisions sacrificed members' democracy to the authority of national executives. Input from rank and file was minimized, whether through ballot or general meeting. If workers in a particular locality, branch of production, or occupation wanted to strike, it wasn't easy to win official backing, as leaders prioritized "building the organization," providing benefits and conserving resources for the "real" trial of strength, which by the psychology of responsible trade unionism could be infinitely deferred. Conversely, top-heavy centralism became a big spur to unofficial militancy.

In Germany, the Ruhr miners were a good illustration. The great coal strikes of 1889, 1905, and 1912 built a reputation for militancy. These were coalfield-wide strikes of high participation, 80 percent in the first two, 60 percent in the third. Intervening years saw intense localized militancy—for example, at least 17 strikes in the Bochum area from 1889 to 1914. Such militancy contrasted with the Ruhr's other big sector—iron, steel, and heavy engineering—with few industrial actions and low unionization.[29] But the first two coalfield strikes and most smaller ones began spontaneously against the union leaders, in unofficial actions where the younger haulers rather than more senior face-workers took the lead. Otto Hué, the miners' leader from the 1890s, was unbudgingly hostile to such militancy, invoking the disastrous strikes of 1889–93, when the union had tried vainly to capitalize on the impetus of 1889. Hué's caution was predicated on weakness. The miners were divided by religion and ethnicity, with Catholic (1894) and Polish (1902) rivals to the SPD union.[30] Given the power of employers, policing their workers via company paternalism, this put socialist trade unionists at huge disadvantage. Hué advocated a cautious style of labor leadership in response, stressing discipline, continuity of organization, political "neutrality," and conserving resources for the future, rejecting a more confrontational approach.

The strategy made rational sense. It bespoke a reformist rather than a revolutionary vision but implied no lack of "class consciousness" by Hué and other leaders. The success of the 1889 and 1905 strikes required the crossconfessional and crossnational solidarity of SPD, Catholic, and Polish unionists, whereas the 1912 strike was called by a coalition of socialist and Polish unionists and the small liberal union against the Catholic union's opposition and collapsed in a week. Yet the strategy's rationality couldn't hide its modest success. At its 1905 peak, the SPD union organized only 29.4 percent of the Ruhr miners, dwindling to 15.8 percent by 1913. It failed to integrate the localized rank-and-file militancy that gave the union its bitterly secured advances. Nor would the problem disappear if the union achieved its reformist breakthrough, through either prounion laws or collective bargaining agreements with employers. As the First World War revealed, this could as easily lead to co-optation, driving a further wedge between union bureaucrats and alienated rank and file. This conundrum—reconciling the case for centralism with the demands of internal democracy and grassroots militancy—would be the source of enormous internal conflict.

It also raised vital issues of socialist principle, which were to explode violently during 1914–23. One source of tension was the predicament of trade unionism's skilled artisan pioneers, who were the mainstay of early socialist organizing in its tough formative decades after the 1860s. By 1900, labor movements were being reshaped by the larger industrial unions, where a different type of worker set the tone, and many craft socialists were unhappy with the results. Such conflicts not only reflected differences in the image of socialism but also reemphasized socialism's dependence on local working-class cultures.

In Germany, the knife-grinders of the Solingen cutlery industry provide an excellent illustration.[31] In contrast to the forgers who prepared their metal, the grinders had preserved their craft against mechanization while reaping the benefits of improved energy, first from steam and then electricity. By 1900 the divergence between production stages was glaring: in the 1850s, two highly skilled forge-workers were needed for every three grinders, yet by 1908 a single forger kept over six grinders supplied with steel. While grinders' ranks swelled fivefold, those of the forgers stayed virtually the same. While forgers saw a few master-entrepreneurs getting rich at their expense and steam hammers replacing their skills, grinders guarded their independence. Instead of centralizing grinding under their own control, cutlery manufacturers subcontracted to "independent" craftsmen clustered around the factories. Grinders thereby blocked machines and enforced craft exclusiveness. In the post-1895 boom, when Solingen surpassed Sheffield in world cutlery trade, this worked very well. But the 1908–9 recession called it into question. Whereas earlier the grinders had been assailed only by "rogue" entrepreneurs like Gottlieb Hammesfahr, whose efforts to bring grinding "indoors" provoked successful strikes in 1899 and 1905, now they were vulnerable to attack.

While defending themselves against "dequalification," grinders became outflanked by a new enemy in labor's own camp, the Metalworkers' Union (DMV), which after 1900 finally began organizing wage-earners in the Solingen area.[32] These new recruits worked in smaller tool shops on the edge of the cutlery trades proper—fitters, turners, smiths, plumbers, moulders, and especially general forge and foundry workers, who now unionized for the first time. Such workers resented the aristocratic grinders. Parallel union drives developed: grinders merged with other local craft societies into the Solingen Industrial Workers' Association, while the DMV advanced.[33] In 1905, rivalry became open war. When the grinders struck against the Hammesfahr firm's latest trick, the DMV gave and then withdrew support, calling a general strike of forge workers that starved the grinders of blades.[34] This was a cynical ploy to break the knife-grinders' craft organization, apparently in collusion with the firm.[35]

This was more than a clash of sectionalisms. It bespoke diametrically opposing attitudes to industrial progress and contrary visions of socialism. For the DMV, grinders' resistance to machines was an arrogant craft mentality, and their guildlike privileges damaged the rest of the class. Technical progress was the harbinger of the socialist future: "World history cannot be turned back for the sake of the knife-grinders."[36] But for the artisans who built the Solingen labor movement, socialism meant "the concrete utopia of a cooperatively organized 'people's industry,' " based on the "association of free producers" in local frameworks of the artisan economy.[37] Solingen's veteran socialists were indifferent to Kautsky's centrally planned and managed economy. For DMV spokesmen, in contrast, the end-goal was quite abstract: socialism was projected beyond the maturation of productive forces, to whose technical possibilities the workers could only adjust. In the meantime, unions should organize all of the working class, not just its aristocratic sections, to promote "the social improvement and trade union representation of all workers in capitalism."[38]

These rival visions of socialism opened a bitter split in the Solingen SPD, beginning after the Anti-Socialist Law and lasting to 1914.[39] This happened in other bastions of Germany's early labor movement too, including neighboring Remscheid, Lennep, Ronsdorf, and Elberfeld-Barmen and areas of Saxony, Thuringia, and Württemberg. Where groups like the Solingen cutlery grinders clung to older ideals of a locally rooted cooperative commonwealth based on craft autonomy, the new DMV strategists celebrated technical progress, mass material improvement, and an industrial unionism proper to the structures of a continuously rationalizing capitalism. This major gap—replicated many times in European industry, wherever craft traditions faced the organizing drives of mass unionism—provoked wide-ranging discussion among labor activists. Such debates concerned workers' ability to exercise control over production once the favorable environment of the craft workshop had gone; the possibilities of immediate reform under developing capitalism; and the nature of the socialist project itself.

SOCIALISM, NATIONAL POLITICS, AND EVERYDAY LIFE

By the mid-1890s, European labor movements had reached a first watershed. One cycle of party foundations was complete, covering northern and western Europe; and the second phase was under way, beginning with the parties of Poland and the Balkans in the early 1890s, continuing across the Russian Empire, and completed by 1905. The parliamentary states established by the constitutional settlements of the 1860s had stabilized, with extensions of the franchise in the Low Countries and Scandinavia. Economic boom after 1895–96 brought the first period of sustained unionization. The socialist parties of the first cycle made steady electoral gains, establishing a parliamentary presence, permeating the public sphere, and deepening their roots. Together, these processes generated the north-central European "social democratic core."

By 1914, seven parties commanded at least a quarter of their national electorates—those in Finland, Sweden, Germany, the Czech lands, Denmark, Norway, and Austria. The Finnish SDP's remarkable rise after 1903, benefiting from the constitution seized by general strike during the 1905 Russian Revolution, made it the voice of national independence, immediately winning 37 percent in the first elections of 1907. Its membership shot from 16,610 to 82,328 between 1904 and 1907, in a population of barely 3 million.[40] After incremental broadening of the constitution between 1898 and 1906, Norwegian socialists also began surpassing their liberal rivals as a national force. Sweden's SAP recorded 133,388 members at its prewar peak in 1907, in a population of 5.5 million. Its local cells were the 427 "labor communes," coordinating union activity along the lines of British trades councils and seeding the party's community presence. They founded People's Halls as the movement's meeting places, around which agitation, educational work, and sociability all coalesced. A youth movement and women's clubs were launched in 1892.[41]

The best-known example of a socialist subculture before 1914 was in Germany, where the SPD's growth followed the fitful progress of civil freedoms.[42] The party adopted a new constitution in 1905, creating its first uniform organization and a central bureaucracy with permanent officials. By 1910, all but 16 of the 397 parliamentary districts had committees. Party membership grew from 384,000 to over a million during 1906–14. In 1898 the SPD became the largest party in popular votes (27.2 percent) and in 1912 the largest in parliamentary seats (110 out of 397). The movement rapidly diversified, with national organizations for Worker Athletes, Popular Health, Worker Singers, Worker Gymnasts, Worker Cyclists, Worker Swimmers, Worker Samaritans, Workers' Temperance Union, Nature Lovers, Workers' Theater Union, and Proletarian Freethinkers. Its cultural presence was organized via its press, educational activities, libraries, lecture series, and public meetings, quite aside from the output of pamphlets, flyers, posters, and more substantial reading matter. It built a finely ramified presence in the lives of its militants and general supporters. The local labor secretariats numbered 120 by 1914, when they dispatched a total of 692,000 items of information and legal advice.[43]

Faced with this imposing machinery of identification and the apparently inexorable progress of socialist parties as popular movements, it was easy to believe in the "forward march of labor." The liberal constitutionalism arising normatively from the 1860s powerfully supported this belief, because once they had the vote, the industrial masses soon realized the advantages of a national party, as Marx had foreseen. The growing integration of the national economy within the legal frameworks of the 1860s further enhanced this trend. If far from homogeneous, working people acquired compelling reasons for seeing themselves as a class, because their patent powerlessness in society made the ballot box hugely valuable, especially as their other collective resource, workplace combination in unions, remained elusive until the upheavals of 1910–20. The suffrage struggles of 1890–1914 were the engine of political class formation. Moreover, once workers possessed the franchise, they used it, as the extraordinary surge of socialist electoralism in 1907–14 showed. The "politically defined nation" became "the effective framework of their class consciousness."[44]

Structural arguments for the inevitability of class conflict further strengthened this confidence in working-class agency, whose dynamics Marx located in the labor process of capitalist industry. Strong class identities also formed in particular industries, occupations, and residential communities. Miners became a powerful archetype of this process. Living in isolated and self-contained settlements, united by the muscular solidarities of the coal face, and hardened by the dignity of their exceptionally difficult labor, coal miners evoked heroic associations of the class struggle. A rugged culture of collectivism developed around the work-team's underground autonomy, which even displaced the functions of managers and foremen on the job. Managerial recourse to harshly administered wage-systems or paternalist social provision via company housing and company colonies then only welded the miners more firmly together. Mining communities' capacities for collective self-help, whether through families' mutual aid in hard times, lodging arrangements, and drinking clubs, or through cultural institutes, were well known. The facts of mining life simply made for cohesion.[45]

More generally, workers' everyday lives revealed many small solidarities. In the workplace, horseplay and enjoyable time-wasting, ritualized practical jokes and hazing, plus the endemic pilfering and petty sabotage, were as vital to the growth of shopfloor cultures as unions. Such mundane self-assertions carved a niche of work-time for "being-by-oneself and with one's workmates" at the bosses' expense. They also produced resilience and self-respect in circumstances where authority deprived workers of immediate control. Small acts of self-affirmation may not have expressed a consciously "political" outlook, but at a more basic level this everyday culture laid the foundations of militancy. If workers seemed indifferent to organized politics, this didn't mean they had no idea of the good life, simply that such thoughts were often locked in a "private" economy of desires. How to release them was the question facing the Left's cultural politics.[46]

Only a minority of workers were ever members of socialist parties and their unions, and still fewer knew the finer points of socialist theory. But the experience of everyday life, where abstract power relations were practically encountered, spawned attitudes of independence with obvious political potential. Under circumstances of general social and political crisis, like the European insurgencies of 1904–7, the revolutionary years 1917–21, or particular national and local mobilizations, such cultures of resistance might gain fuller political meaning. Then the worlds of politics and the everyday could move together.

There was nothing natural or predetermined about such a juncture—about the synchrony of socialist politics and broader working-class cultures of everyday life—although the parallelism of labor movements and industrialization certainly encouraged this belief. As the stronger socialist parties acquired permanent bureaucracies and full-time officials and parliamentary delegations developed autonomy, politics in the conventional sense became removed from the participation of ordinary workers, complicating the connections with everyday life. Socialist leaders and union officials easily fortified themselves against the elemental democracies of the shopfloor and the street, especially when important gains—a legislative reform, a parliamentary victory, a favorable contract—dictated patience and the disciplined restraint of militancy. Miners, the earliest and strongest instance of industrial unionism, showed this tension between the "formal" and "informal" regions of collective action particularly well.

The class consciousness of the Ruhr miners epitomized a powerful contradiction. In the great strike of 1905, and again in the socialization drive of early 1919, a rolling wave of militancy washed across the moderation of the miners' union and SPD. These movements grew from informal solidarity structures, where demands for public ownership and workers' control expressed the miners' immediate needs: "Socialization was no mere utopia or abstract construction, it was also the sum of [the miners'] experiences; not just projection, but also a taking up of elements and structures grounded in the everyday; a continuation of the everyday."[47] In responding to these direct actions, labor leaders parroted the social fears of the Ruhr bourgeoisie, charging miners not only with lack of discipline and immature consciousness but also with straightforward lack of "culture." In this view, the workers' problems would pass once the labor movement had organized, educated, and reformed them. Yet, while union and party leaders saw only roughness, turbulence, and disorder, the miners already possessed a culture of great resourcefulness.

The contexts of everyday life revealed the deficiencies of the labor movement's socialist culture. The Göttingen SPD, for example, was a small party in a semiindustrial provincial town, with 190 members among the thirty-thousand inhabitants in 1908. Its subculture was thin—forty members of a gymnastics club, a consumers' cooperative, and not much else. Given its political marginality, the local party focused heavily on educational work, within a wholly conventional framework of cultural values. "The party activists wanted to live worthy, upstanding, moral, moderate, and disciplined lives: on the one hand, to show the workers who were not yet organized a good example; on the other hand, to show bourgeois society that one was up to all tasks, that one deserved good standing and respect." The party sought to appropriate existing "high culture," whether in classical literature, theater, art, and music or more widely in matters of taste and morality. While the SPD was politically excluded, these attitudes remained tied to oppositional goals. But when it joined the system after 1918, the conservatism came to the fore—values of hierarchy and authority, militarized language, fetishism of discipline, patriotism, and patriarchal attitudes toward family, child-raising, and the place of women.[48]

There was little challenge to hegemonic values. In the Göttingen party's early days, members were inducted into the movement culture via common readings of newspaper articles, assignment of political reports, and use of a question box at meetings. But even this atrophied, with barely a single collective reading a year during 1904–7, as against eight in 1900 and 1901. There was little wider agitation: public meetings were held indoors; May Day festivities were party affairs rather than public rallies; meetings occurred around lectures, with little spontaneous exchange; strikes were carefully depoliticized. Socialist politics lacked connection to the members' everyday lives, let alone to workers at large. Daily life was measured against certain established precepts for the rational ordering of social behavior, which left entire areas of working-class conservatism unchallenged, especially attitudes to women and children, sexuality, and private life. Other aspects of workers' culture—the "roughness" beyond the Göttingen party's small domain—were attacked. This was a far-reaching failure to ground the party's socialist ideals in any prefigurative approach to everyday life.

CONCLUSION

Thus the socialist parties' impressive growth before 1914 contained some clear limits. They not only reached a ceiling of electoral support—somewhere between a quarter and a third of the electorate at best—but were structurally outside the governing order, kept there as much by their own irreconcilable opposition to the system as by its desire to exclude. In those few cases where universal suffrage and full parliamentary government arrived without the First World War, these limits were loosened. But elsewhere, the parties kept their outsider status, trusting in the longer-term logics of capitalist development and crisis to bring them to power. When reformists emerged, like the French Possibilists in the 1880s or SPD moderates in Germany's more liberal southwestern states after the 1890s, they were disavowed. Nonparticipation in "bourgeois governments" remained the Second International norm. In 1913, the Dutch SDAP refused a place in government on this basis.

This policy of abstention implied enormous confidence in the future, a steadfast belief in the inevitable working-class majority and the ever-expanding power of socialism's working-class support. These parties built slowly from their early artisanal core and diverse radical traditions, growing in the lawful spaces provided by the constitutional settlements of the 1860s. As labor movements grounded their electoral presence in the subcultures of particular cities, urban districts, and occupational communities, socialism's appeal grew. From the 1890s, favorable economic conditions, accretions of social legislation and national labor law, and the incremental strengthening of parliamentary systems allowed the parties to expand. Whether via the new mass unionism, freshly created party machines, and cultural activities or the early achievements of municipal socialism, they became powerful fixtures of their political systems.

Yet they never came close to universal working-class support. Many working-class allegiances remained conditional, pragmatic, volatile, and extremely uneven across industries, occupations, regions, and cultural differences. Loyalties were contested—by liberalism in Britain, organized Catholicism in Germany, Belgium, France, and southern Europe, and many other rivals. Socialism's ability to harmonize heterogeneous interests was always insufficient. Running through these other divisions were the contradictions of gender, because socialist parties fudged the issues of equality between women and men. In fact, those parties mobilized only certain kinds of workers. The biggest distinction of all was between those workers who had joined the cause and all those remaining outside, including the superstitious and religiously devout, the sexually transgressive, the frivolous young, the ethnically different and other marginalized minorities, and the rough working class of criminal subcultures, casualized labor markets, and the migrant urban poor. Centering their appeal so fervently on industrial workers' class-political agency left socialist parties poorly equipped for handling these "other" identities, which made many workers resistant to socialism's appeal.

Once democracy expanded again after the First World War, the most successful socialist parties stepped outside this more exclusive class-political tradition to broaden their appeal. They began speaking for broader progressive blocs in their societies, attracting the hopes of larger masses of workers as well as other social groups, cutting through the somewhat exclusionary definitions of working-classness that prevailed before 1914. This broadening was most apparent in the Scandinavian social democratic parties, in the British Labour Party's electoral rise, and in the Austrian SPÖ's dominance of Red Vienna. But earlier, as the Second International parties emerged into the greater popularity of the early 1900s, they still represented mainly a particular sector of society. They were parties of the organized and respectable male working class. Until 1914, they were still only partially accepted within the polities of Europe and excluded from the governing orders, with no prospects of breaking out of their political isolation. This was an isolation they had defiantly embraced.

Chapter 5

Challenges beyond Socialism

Other Fronts of Democracy

,2 causes

SOCIAL DEMOCRACY BECAME the Left's main force in most of Europe between the 1870s and the First World War. The collectivist élan of the new socialist parties grew from a shared working-class experience, which critiques of capitalism as a system of inequality compellingly described. But equally vital was the hostility of European governments to the masses, whom they consistently excluded from citizenship. Where the franchise was partly won, popular democracy was still largely denied; where the franchise was lacking, it came only through bitter confrontations. To that degree, the pre-1914 political climate *required* the Left's revolutionary stance, because its opponents' intransigence offered no choice.

The strongest movements presented a common pattern: single parties organizationally united but ideologically diverse, without serious rivals, and rallying mixed interests around broadly social democratic values. But this model was unequivocally established only in the north-central European social democratic core. Elsewhere, Left politics proved more contentious, parties more fractious. In Britain, locally vigorous socialist initiatives in the 1880s and 1890s still made little headway against the popular liberalism shaped in the 1860s. In Italy and Spain, socialists contended with acute regional disparities, state violence, and strong urban anarchist movements. In France, socialists were notoriously split, identifying with rival strands of the French revolutionary traditions, appealing to earlier non-Marxist legacies, and taking contrasting lessons from the Paris Commune. Only in 1905 was sectarianism overcome, when the

Marxist followers of Jules Guesde joined forces with the ethical socialism of Jean Jaurès, forming the Section Francaise de l'Internationale Ouvrière (SFIO) as a parliamentary socialist party comparable to those in the north.

Moreover, these early socialist parties weren't the only source of democratic advocacy before 1914, and the Left's possibilities beyond social democracy also need to be explored. For one thing, the parties' internal disagreements provided seedbeds for alternative visions, and during 1905–13 the older frameworks of orthodoxy and loyalty started to break down. Second, socialism's contemporary rivals also marked out a space for alternatives—various anarchisms, syndicalisms, populisms, and forms of agrarian radicalism. Third, feminists added vital areas of democratic priority, which socialists had recognized only in the most partial of ways. Finally, all these tensions increased during 1905–14, when the political frameworks created during the constitution-making efforts of the 1860s teetered, threatened to collapse, and then fell.

THE SECOND INTERNATIONAL AND ITS DIVISIONS

On 14 July 1889, rival international congresses met in Paris during the French Revolution's centenary celebrations. One, called by Paul Brousse and convening French Possibilists, British trade unionists, and other moderates, remained focused on the eight-hour day and improving working conditions. The competing congress, instigated by the SPD, presented the Marxist face of Europe's emergent socialist parties. Its concluding resolutions addressed four areas: the eight-hour day and working conditions; peace, war, and the virtues of national militias over standing armies; universal suffrage; and May Day as a proposed demonstration of international working-class solidarity. The week's proceedings saw impassioned polemics both within and between the rival events. Both were also disrupted by anarchists.

Attended by 391 delegates from 20 countries, the Marxist congress inaugurated the Second International.[1] Its subsequent congresses included Brussels (1891), Zurich (1893), London (1896), Paris (1900), Amsterdam (1904), Stuttgart (1907), Copenhagen (1910), and Basel (1912). After 1900, the permanent Secretariat was created in Brussels, with an International Socialist Bureau (ISB) to coordinate Congress resolutions. By the Zurich meeting, an Australian delegation was present, and at Amsterdam Sen Katayama attended for the Japanese Socialist Party, formed in 1901. Otherwise, the International was overwhelmingly Eurocentric.

Early debates followed old First International tracks, marking double distance from anarchism and "bourgeois democracy." The 1893 Congress's general resolution balanced revolutionary principles with practical improvements, allowing maximalist goals and short-term amelioration to inhabit a common political language. Anarchism's violent posturing was rejected, but so was direct collaboration with nonsocialist reformers. A broad *agenda* agenda of democracy and social reform was laid out for parliamentary action, stressing universal suffrage, emancipation of women, the eight-hour day, and opposition to war. But this could only be achieved by the independent parties of labor advocated by Marx during the First International, freed from bourgeois tutelage.

Until the 1890s, socialists kept apocalyptic hopes alive, basing their image of the inevitable revolution on earlier nineteenth-century experience, when social crises spawned rapid breakdowns of authority and popular insurrections. Blanqui had epitomized this revolutionary psychology. Revolutionary expectations were further fueled by police repression and violent confrontations, exemplified in the drama of the German Anti-Socialist Law. For August Bebel, one of the Second International's main personalities, the *Kladderadatsch,* or great collapse of the system, was always round the next corner.[2] In place of collapse, however, increasingly came inclusion. By 1900, socialist parties were themselves entering the "bourgeois" political constellation, winning seats in national elections, participating in parliamentary culture, and campaigning for reform. For parties of revolutionaries, accordingly, questions of purity or compromise, maximalism or constructive participation, revolution or reform, increasingly shadowed the agenda.

The first big scandal was the "Millerand Affair" in France. At the height of the Dreyfus crisis in 1899, a government of Republican Defense formed under René Waldeck-Rousseau, joined by Alexandre Millerand, a leading Independent Socialist, as minister of commerce.[3] This polarized French socialists, with ex-Possibilists and other reformists rallying to the Republic, and the French Workers' Party, the Central Revolutionary Committee, and other radicals declaring a plague on both bourgeois houses. Millerand secured significant reforms: reducing the work week, strengthening the industrial inspectorate, creating labor councils, and using public contracts to improve working conditions. But the symbolics of joining a government containing General Gaston Gallifet, the butcher of the 1871 Paris Commune, were intolerable for Edouard Vaillant, the ex-Communard. Moreover, government behaved as repressively as ever. After three strikers were shot in Chalon-sur-Saône, Jules Guesde commented that "the war on the working class has never been so implacable as under the Waldeck-Rousseau-Millerand government."[4]

In adopting the Dreyfus cause, Jaurès, in keeping with his Radical past, committed himself to an ethical defense of French liberties, seemingly removed from socialist advocacy per se. On the other hand, this helped shape the broadest republican unity, opening government to socialists for the first time. In consequence, democracy could not only be strengthened but gradual progress to socialism might also occur. Such perspectives were not exactly foreign to socialism's history. In Britain, progressivism in municipal politics graduated toward the formal Lib-Lab collaboration of the 1906 elections and subsequent Liberal government, where the Labour Party became a junior partner.[5] In this light, the Millerand Affair was the first chance to go a stage further by actually joining government itself.

Nor was this inconsistent with socialist parliamentarianism. Since the 1860s, social democrats had seen parliaments as vital to their effectiveness, both for winning working-class gains via legislation and for building popular support in elections. However, Jaurès's critics took a sterner view. For Vaillant, the state was no neutral framework available for working-class "penetration" but was defined by the repressive machinery of army, police, and judiciary. Class inequalities worked in the same way, allowing the bourgeoisie to "govern by the vote as it rules by religion and . . . the gun."[6] Instead, workers advanced by their own militancy, forcing concessions from governments or waging the class struggle in industry. The Republic's main value was to have freed politics for the "real" struggle of labor and capital. In this view, socialists should use parliament and elections and should certainly defend the Republic and its freedoms, but without illusions. The larger goals of revolution should always prevail.

Guesde's view was sterner still: the Republic was a sham; no genuine reforms could be expected; bourgeois republicans were no better than royalists or the Right. This issue dominated the International's fourth Congress in Paris in September 1900, when the SPD asserted its authority. Liebknecht's first reaction was peremptory: "a socialist who enters a bourgeois ministry either deserts to the enemy, or he surrenders to the enemy."[7] But this gave way to Kautsky's revolutionary pragmatics, which upheld democratic rights as a good in themselves and approved tactical alliances. Seeing nonsocialists as "one reactionary mass" was profoundly mistaken, particularly as socialists grew stronger, "already powerful enough to influence the course of events, but not strong enough to be the dominant power."[8] The key was socialist clarity and independence: "As long as we preserve our proletarian character, corruption from . . . other parties is not to be feared . . . [I]f we give up [our] proletarian character, we lose the firmest ground under our feet and become a ball of the most contradictory interests. . . . Compromises in action are not dangerous, but those in program are."[9]

The clearest case for coalition was a national emergency, when a society's "fundamental democratic institutions" were endangered.[10] During the Millerand Affair, an Italian political crisis met exactly this standard. The right-wing government of General Luigi Pelloux, formed after the May 1898 massacre of demonstrators in Milan, unleashed draconian repression against the Left, imposed by royal decree. In response, Liberals formed a common front with the extreme Left. This emerged from elections with big gains, eventually forming a new government in February 1901, endorsed by the PSI. The French scenario repeated itself. Filippo Turati pushed social reforms, including the Labor Office, social insurance, protective laws against female and child labor, and public works. Likewise, defending the Constitution didn't inhibit Liberals from using troops against strikers, which soon exposed the limits of this progressive front. However, by contrast with Millerand, Turati refused ministerial office, and the PSI eventually abandoned the government.[11]

These experiments with reformism provoked recriminations. They immobilized the PSI for much of the prewar period. In France, the opposing camps coalesced into the French Socialist Party and the Socialist Party of France, the former rallying to Jaurès's defense of the Republic, the latter combining supporters of Guesde and Vaillant.[12] The International itself had passed a compromise resolution in 1900, leaving coalitions to the discretion of national parties. Millerand was condemned, but supporting the government from the outside made sense. Bourgeois coalitions might be justified, but only temporarily and from a position of clear independence and distinct "proletarian" identity.[13]

Thus the scandal over "ministerialism" revealed two models of socialist politics, whose tensions were to recur. One was the proud upholding of socialism's revolutionary goal—the destruction of capitalism and the building of a different society—which required determined opposition, complete noncooperation with "bourgeois" parties, and nonparticipation in existing institutions. Karl Kautsky, the "pope" of socialism, was the model's most noted articulator. Final victory would come from the inevitable workings of history, as the workers' movement became ever more organized and popular, capitalism collapsed amid irresolvable contradictions, and socialists inherited the state, whether through overwhelming force of numbers or last-ditch confrontation with the dying old order.

The second model imagined a similar outcome, in scarcely less utopian terms. This stressed the ecumenical pursuit of principle and an ethical and democratic humanism, treating socialist values as the bridge to larger coalitions, based on democracy and social justice. If the economic theory of socialism made victory inevitable, socialists would be best placed to take power where working-class citizenship was strongest, and this meant working on the broadest front for democratizing the constitution. Outside Germany, the pioneering generation of socialist politicians shared this perspective, including Jaurès in France, Vandervelde in Belgium, Victor Adler in Austria, Hjalmar Branting in Sweden, and Turati in Italy.

It had its supporters in Germany too. By 1900 the SPD was incomparably the strongest socialist party, and its Erfurt Program was the model for social democratic parties elsewhere.[14] Kautsky's commentary on the program, *The Class Struggle*, intended as a "catechism of Social Democracy," was translated into sixteen languages by 1914, and other Marxists deferred to his views. While building an increasingly elaborate organization and implanting itself in the national polity (becoming by 1898 the largest German party in popular votes), the SPD remained explicitly revolutionary. Its goal was nothing less than "the overthrow of capitalist society."[15]

As the SPD advanced in parliamentary strength, though, preserving its revolutionary purity became a problem. While standing proudly apart from bourgeois society, after 1890 the party was continually drawn into the "system"—cooperating with nonsocialist progressives in elections and political maneuvers, joining parliamentary committees, supporting or opposing legislation. Into this gap between revolutionary theory and immediate practice then came a series of articles by the SPD's senior intellectual, Eduard Bernstein, in its premier journal, Kautsky's *Neue Zeit,* collected as *The Preconditions of Socialism and the Tasks of Social Democracy.* Here, Bernstein argued that capitalism had surmounted its proneness to crisis. Marx's doctrine of pauperization—ever-widening polarization between rich and poor, inscribed in the labor theory of value—was falsified by improving standards of living. Working-class movements could hope to win reforms under capitalism, therefore, gradually transforming the state toward democracy. Against the castastrophic theory of revolutionary transition, Bernstein proposed a continuous model of improvement, or "evolutionary socialism."[16]

Bernstein's arguments provoked a storm of outrage from orthodox Marxists, including the young Rosa Luxemburg. Urged on by August Bebel, Kautsky joined the attack against his old friend, and at the 1899 Hanover Congress Bernstein was officially repudiated. As in the Millerand Affair, the real fight was over strategy. Bernstein's critique of Marxist economics mattered less than his political conclusions. If "[the] peasants do not sink; middle class does not disappear; crises do not grow ever larger; [and] misery and serfdom do not increase," he said, then socialists needed to recruit nonproletarian supporters and cooperate with liberals and other nonsocialist progressives.[17] Indeed, the SPD's future lay with the coalition building advocated by Turati in Italy, Jaurès in France, and Fabians in Britain. But Bernstein underestimated the power of the SPD's revolutionary ethos, not to mention the Imperial state's antidemocratic hostility to reform.

Defeating revisionism inspired a powerful rallying of orthodoxy in the SPD, which hugely constrained coalition building in the future. Kautsky treated this as a zero-sum game: the primacy of the class struggle precluded cooperating with bourgeois parties, and vice versa. This was also transported into the International. At Amsterdam in 1904, Jaurès valiantly upheld the case for broad democratic cooperation, arraigning the "powerlessness" of the SPD instead, whose embattled isolation he called a pseudorevolutionary posture imposed by the Imperial constitution's lack of democracy. In this view, Kautsky's purist formulas were a smokescreen for enforced inaction. But Bebel was obdurate. Monarchy and republic were both "class states"—"both are a form of state to maintain the class rule of the bourgeoisie, both are designed to protect the capitalist order of society." Following Jaurès would only confuse and split the working-class movement.[18]

A compromise, which would have repeated the Paris formula of 1900 allowing national variations, was narrowly defeated by a single vote. The SPD's resolution, banning reformist alliances as distractions from the class struggle, then passed 25 to 5, with 12 abstentions. Opponents and abstainers came from countries with stronger parliamentary constitutions; supporters from those where democracy was weak. This already presaged the later constellation of 1914–17, for the vocal opponents of revisionism included several members of the revolutionary opposition during the war— Christian Rakovsky of Bulgaria, Rosa Luxemburg, and Vladimir Ili'ich Lenin.[19] While the Amsterdam decision gave the impetus for the unification of the SFIO in France, therefore, its long-term future effects were divisive.

Questions of imperialism and nationalism produced similar divisions. Significantly, colonialism first entered the International's agenda at Paris in 1900 during the Boer War, British imperialism's assault on a white settler republic; and neither the exploitation of colonial peoples nor eastern European nationality questions troubled the International until 1907.[20] Likewise, new critiques of imperialism, like Rudolf Hilferding's *Finance Capital* (1910) and Rosa Luxemburg's *Accumulation of Capital* (1913), said little about the colonial world per se, as against capitalist dynamics in the metropolis. After some vacillation, "capitalist colonial policies [which] must, by their nature, give rise to servitude, forced labor and the extermination of the native peoples," were condemned by the Stuttgart Congress in 1907.[21] This debate had a familiar look—Bernstein and his fellow SPD reformist Eduard David, the Dutch SDAP's Henri van Kol and British Labour's Ramsay MacDonald dragging their feet and Kautsky, SPD leftist Georg Ledebour, the Guesdist Alexandre-Marie Desrousseaux, the Pole Julian Marchlewski and the British SDF's Harry Quelch strongly in favor.[22]

Socialists found various grounds for accepting imperialism. It created jobs, especially in shipyards, docking, armaments, and industries dependent on colonial trade. And while positive colonialist enthusiasm among socialists was rarer, assumptions of racial superiority and acceptance of the "civilizing mission" were not.[23] More seriously, escalating great-power rivalries fed the growth of patriotism, especially via national emergencies and fears of foreign invasion. Tsarism was a synonym for reactionary backwardness in the European Left's collective imagination, and even Kautsky talked of defending German civilization against possible Russian attack. French socialists saw analogous contrasts between French revolutionary traditions and German authoritarianism, and when the SPD blocked SFIO antimilitarist initiatives in the International after 1905, relations became frayed. In fact, the issue of preventing war became the vital test of the International's cohesion. If war was to be stopped, armies, munitions, and railways had to be immobilized in all combatant countries, and from 1904 calls for a general strike against war never left the agenda.

Inside the socialist parties, inspired by the Russian Revolution of January 1905, the mass strike debate was the engine of radicalization. For the

SPD left, it was vital leverage against its Executive's growing caution, a means of keeping the movement revolutionary. But the party's qualified endorsement of the mass strike tactic in September 1905 was reversed a year later by union pressure. The SPD leaders were increasingly unwilling to risk their organization in political confrontations with the state, and this bureaucratic conservatism was strengthened by the unions' growing weight in the movement. What is more, the SPD arrogantly guarded itself against external purview. While happily using the International's authority to seal revisionism's defeat, it shielded its own practice from scrutiny, consistently diluting Congress resolutions. When the French began pressing antiwar demands, under Vaillant's slogan "Rather Insurrection Than War!" the Germans stonewalled. Formally, the 1907 Stuttgart resolution fused antiwar and revolutionary principles, committing socialist parties "to utilize the economic and political crisis created by the war to rouse the masses and thereby to hasten the downfall of capitalist class rule."[24] But SFIO calls for concerted action were always blocked by the SPD. From pragmatic and patriotic motives, national defense became the SPD's tacit policy.[25]

If socialists proved vulnerable to superordinate national loyalties in the decade before 1914, habituating to the hegemonic rhythms of the national interest, they were equally negligent of national minorities. This was not invariably true—Scottish and Welsh radicalisms had a decisive role in shaping the British labor movement, for instance. The social democracies of the subject nationalities of the Russian Empire also coexisted with the central Russian party before 1914. On the other hand, the SPD had a poor record of either integrating the German Poles or honoring their separate organizations.[26] But the key test was the multinational Habsburg Empire, with its chaos of nationalities, where the dominant Germans and Hungarians were only the largest minorities of many.

The Austrian Social Democrats envisaged a single party for the state as a whole. They wanted to preserve the Empire's territory while transforming it into a "democratic federation of nationalities," in the words of the 1899 program. Once the imperial state democratized, cultural self-determination for the nationalities would be uncoupled from territorial independence. And, as the larger economic region was the progressive basis for development, the Empire's existing boundaries should survive. This arrangement could model multinational cooperation for the rest of the International. Victor Adler called the project a "little International" in itself.[27]

The problem was that the SPÖ's precedence mirrored the dominance of the Germans in the Empire. The party of one nationality, the Germans, doubled as the umbrella for the state as a whole. Moreover, faith that class identities would inevitably triumph over national differences in the industrialized future, leaving only a variety of cultural-linguistic residues behind, proved naive. The Czech Social Democrats (CSDSD) proved fully as well organized as the Austrians, and on a rising tide of tensions the two parties pulled apart. By 1911, the "little International" of the multinational Habsburg state was dead.

Thus when the outbreak of war in August 1914 threw the Second International into disarray, it was not just antimilitarism that was ruined but also socialists' classical approach to the national question. Marxist theoreticians, from Kautsky to Luxemburg, Trotsky to Lenin, believed that rising class consciousness would allow the national identities of workers to die away. There was plentiful evidence to the contrary in the 20 years before 1914, in the popular mobilizations around crises like the Dreyfus Affair, in socialists' countless invocations of national traditions, and in the resentments of multinational movements like the Austrian and Czech. Socialist leaderships had tacitly accepted this reality, from Bebel and Jaurès to the practising reformists increasingly running the union and party machines. Some right-wing socialists aggressively declared their patriotism. But in official declarations there was largely silence. No congress of the Second International placed the "national question" as such on its agenda. The First World War changed all this, almost overnight.

POPULISTS, ANARCHISTS, AND SYNDICALISTS

If nationalism posed problems for the Left, the countryside posed more. Social democrats expected their working-class voters to become "the great majority of the population," whose vast numbers promised unimpeachable democratic legitimacy.[28] Yet even in Germany, agriculture accounted for 28.4 percent of employment in 1907, with 5 million small farmers. Society was far more complex than the binary picture of two forces polarizing around the class struggle allowed. It comprised other popular classes— peasants, self-employed, lower-rank civil servants and professions, white-collar workers. To win elections, socialists needed these other groups, with peasant farmers heading the list. Thus, it was no accident that by 1895 the agrarian question was exercising socialist parties in Germany, France, Belgium, Italy, Denmark, and Russia.[29]

Sometimes, socialists could protect orthodoxy by treating country dwellers as a rural working class. But small and middling peasants with little wage labor were hard to attract with that approach. A peasant-based strategy advocating regulation of mortgages, insurance, and credit, plus strengthening of communal rights, gained momentum in the SPD, only to be rejected in 1895. Kautsky asserted the orthodoxy: support for the peasantry merely salvaged an archaic form of agriculture, doomed to vanish with capitalist expansion; the party's real priority was farm laborers on big estates. Though Bavarian policies went unchanged, Kautsky's intervention silenced the national debate.[30]

Like related controversies, this German agrarian debate hardened the orthodoxy internationally. This applied par excellence in tsarist Russia, where the illegal RSDRP originated in extreme disillusionment with the peasantry as a revolutionary class. The earlier revolutionary tradition in Russia, Populism, pursued a strategy of peasant organizing combined with insurrection, including exemplary terror against the tsar and top officials (culminating in the assassination of Alexander II in 1881). Its theorists saw peasant communal institutions as both the best medium of mobilization, the local basis for democracy, and the key to collectivized agriculture. Against these perspectives, the earliest Russian Marxists stressed the necessity for capitalist development. The Group for the Emancipation of Labor, formed in 1883, defined themselves via polemics against the Populists, denying the relevance of the peasant commune and staking their future on Russian capitalism.

This dismissal of the peasantry reflected Marxism's rigidification after Marx. Plekhanov approached Russia "as a 'not yet' Germany or England" in the early stage of a predictable path, which would bring Russia to socialism only after "a prolonged period of capitalism under liberal bourgeois rule."[31] For orthodox Marxists, this future developmental convergence was key, not Russia's existing differences from the West. Though societies might begin from diverse origins, capitalism would iron such messiness out. Meanwhile, it was pointless vesting hopes in classes fated to disappear like the peasantry.

As the twentieth century confirmed, this confidence in a uniform capitalist model was misplaced—the European peasantry itself took a century to disappear; class polarization didn't occur; and industrial workers became a diminishing rather than an expanding part of society. Yet whatever the truth of the predictions, abandoning the peasantry to one's opponents was still a mistake. In 1917–23, the countryside became a counterrevolutionary reservoir in Italy and Germany and a powerful source of inertia against Bolshevism in the USSR. Marx himself learned much from the Populists during his last decade, immersing himself in Russian sources to understand Russia's specificities. In 1871–83, he based his thinking not on Plekhanov but on the perspectives of the People's Will: the uneven development of European capitalism, the coercive Russian state's leading economic role, the Russian peasantry's primacy as a revolutionary force, and the democratic potential of peasant communal organization. It was a huge error to ignore all this in building a socialist movement.

It was again Kautsky who fixed discussion around doctrinaire positions. Tragically, he was followed most faithfully in agrarian societies where peasant strategies were most needed—imperial Russia, the Balkans, eastern Europe, the Mediterranean.[32] Yet behind the Kautskyan orthodoxies was plentiful evidence of rural success. In the SPD itself, the south German parties doggedly resisted the national Executive's discipline, pursuing peasant-friendly strategies down to 1914, and in southern France, the SFIO built notable strength among the farmers of the Mediterranean basin. Scandinavian socialism's success was also rooted in types of farmer-labor alliance.[33]

A striking "non-Kautskyan" case of peasant-based socialism developed in one of Europe's most impoverished agrarian regions, eastern Galicia in the Habsburg Empire, where Ruthenian peasants suffered under the regional rule of Polish landowners. When young intellectuals around Ivan Franko formed the Ruthenian Radical Party in Lvov in 1890, their program took the standard form, following its commitment to "scientific socialism" with a detailed catalogue of reforms. But the latter were wholly focused on the peasantry, "aimed at preventing the rapid proletarianization of the rural population."[34] This movement flourished into one of the strongest peasant radicalisms of pre-1914 Europe. Like Czech Social Democracy, it fused its social program to the national question, in a political space beyond Second International socialism. It laid the basis for the West Ukrainian People's Republic in October 1918 and the strength of the West Ukrainian Communist Party in interwar Poland.

The strongest counterphilosophy to socialism on the Left after the 1860s, anarchism, encapsulated democracy's dilemmas with special poignancy. On the one hand, anarchists passionately decried Marxist idealizing of centralized organization, whether in the economy or the state. They rejected social democracy's focus on parliament and elections. Still more, they denounced the state and political authority per se, affirming the sovereignty of individuals. Instead, they defended democratic values that socialists like Kautsky tended to forget—local control, direct participation, small-scale community, and federative cooperation. On the other hand, their revolutionary conspiracies dispensed with all democratic process. In the existential moment of the terrorist act, anarchist secrecy and violence produced the purest authoritarianism.

Anarchism had an amorphous existence before 1914, as little more than a synonym for any violent revolutionism, localized militancy or direct action beyond the Second International's parliamentarist and trade union frames. It was identified with larger-than-life individuals, like Pierre-Joseph Proudhon, Michael Bakunin, Errico Malatesta, and Peter Kropotkin, making their own rules rather than serving political movements of the socialist kind. Their international impact, notably Bakunin's conspiratorial antics in the First International and the accompanying Italian agitations of the 1870s, was heightened by the counterrevolutionary panic of European governments surrounding the Paris Commune. Until the 1890s, anarchists rivaled socialists in Europe as a whole, and so the failure of the Bakuninist Anti-Authoritarian International to establish a comparable political tradition deserves some discussion.

Some anarchist beliefs were homologous with the socialist cultures coalescing after the 1870s—an ethics of cooperative sociality, ideals of human improvement, militant secularism, basic collectivism—and for a while the two remained porous, especially locally. They divided over questions of the state, organizational strategy, and the nature of revolutionary change. Anarchists rejected state authority, all forms of centralized government in fact, in favor of locally based self-administration, linked to common ownership and cooperative economy. They opposed parties and unions as bureaucratic prefigurements of coercive power, valuing the dialectic of conspiratorial organization and popular spontaneity instead. They rejected electoral politics in favor of direct action. Finally, they upheld the classical revolutionary imagery of barricades and violent insurrection. All these commitments ran counter to Second International socialism.

Once Marx controlled the First International's Hague Congress in 1872, the Bakuninists launched their own Anti-Authoritarian International, based in Italy, Spain, Belgium, and the Swiss Jura Federation. It met four more times before dying in London in 1881.[35] Lacking the labor-based contexts of popular militancy associated with the European strike wave of 1868–73, the constitutional upheavals of the 1860s, and the Paris Commune, anarchists turned their isolation into a cult of individual protest. Conspiratorial cells and "propaganda of the deed" substituted for the genuine democracy of popular organization. After an earlier terrorist flurry in 1878, with bombings in Italy and failed attacks on the German, Spanish, and Italian monarchs, the assassination of Alexander II in 1881 began the long romance with exemplary terror, the fantasy that dynamiting public property or killing public figures could inspire popular revolt. Absent the socialists' public proceduralism, individual hotheads knew no constraint. Anarchism became forever identified with the political desperation of passionate but frequently deranged young men.

Rather than exposing the emptiness of authority and making it accountable, terrorism confirmed its coercive power and attracted its wrath. One cycle of provocation and repression occurred in France, climaxing in 1883 in the show trial of 65 anarchists, including Kropotkin.[36] A more lethal phase occurred in the 1890s, as anarchism's isolation increased. Eleven bombings occurred in France during 1892–94, including one in the Chamber of Deputies and the assassination of the president, Sadi Carnot. Concurrent campaigns were waged in Italy and Spain. A rash of major assassinations followed, including those of Antonio Canovas, the Spanish prime minister, in 1897, Empress Elizabeth of Austria in 1898, and King Umberto of Italy in 1900. Repression was draconian, subjecting working people to intrusive policing and loss of political freedoms. Rather than inspiring citizens to revolt, this anarchist strategy deprived them of voice.[37]

Anarchist disregard of open and accountable frameworks (like a party or public society) was self-disabling. Bakunin's revolutionary maximalism—his belief that popular uprisings could bring the "total destruction of the world of the legal state and of all bourgeois so-called civilization"—remained a Blanquist fantasy.[38] His conspiratorial ethic was profoundly authoritarian and élitist. The anarchist avengers of the 1880s and 1890s had no relationship to the southern European social movements of the 1860s and early 1870s. By the 1890s, anarchists had no base comparable to that of the socialist parties now emerging into mass activity. They had only a wrecking presence in the Second International and after the London Congress in 1896 were definitively excluded. Eventually, they managed an international gathering of their own in Amsterdam in 1907, but with no results.

Despite anarchist affinities, syndicalism in the 1900s was a new departure, most identified with an upsurge of working-class militancy in France. The *bourses du travail* (BTs), local chambers of labor originally sponsored to promote "responsible" trade unionism and handle unemployment, were a key source, boosted by the CGT, the first national union movement launched in 1895. In 1902, the CGT and BTs merged, enacting the Charter of Amiens in 1906, in polemical counterpoint to the coalescence of French socialism in the SFIO. While the Charter declared neutrality from "the parties and sects," CGT militants were passionately hostile to socialist parliamentarianism.[39]

Instead of parliamentary process, syndicalists celebrated the direct action of sabotage and strikes; rather than central bureaucracies, they demanded rank-and-file initiative; against elections, they upheld the revolutionary value of the general strike. In France, this activist élan certainly contrasted with the factionalized weakness of electoral socialism and its weak unions. But the spread of European labor militancy also brought syndicalist influences into the socialist mainstream. The new economic upswing after 1896, socialist electoral growth, and the forming of mass unions all inspired big debates over strategy. Then the radicalizing effects of the 1905 Russian Revolution kicked in, adding a revolutionary charge. Radicals saw class consciousness rising through an unfolding chain of mass strikes, ending in capitalism's overthrow. Momentum would come from the shopfloor, from industrial rather than craft or sectional unions, and through direct action, including sabotage and wildcat strikes. This ran counter to social democracy's main features—electoralism and parliamentary politics, the primacy of party over unions, centralized organization, and socializing the economy via the state.[40]

By 1914, syndicalism was hard to distinguish from the general unrest.[41] Britain saw a huge density of labor protest, with union members surging from 2.5 to 4.1 million in 1910–13. Giant disputes rocked the economy, including national coal and rail strikes, transport strikes in London and Dublin, a general strike in Liverpool, a construction lockout in London, and continuous battles in South Wales and elsewhere. The Industrial Syndicalist Education League formed by Tom Mann in 1910 was certainly influential. The grassroots of militancy inspired powerful advocacy of working-class power, most famously in *The Miners' Next Step,* a withering attack on the official union's reformism, counterposing industrial democracy to the "delusion and snare" of parliament.[42] Coherent syndicalist statements like this focused impassioned debates and circulated widely in the labor movement.

Nevertheless, the main energy passed ultimately into national trade unionism of the conventional kind. The pre-1914 labor unrest brought new categories of the semiskilled into unions, as in the growth of the British Workers' Union (5,000 to 160,000, 1910–14), but the syndicalist panacea of the revolutionary general strike never arrived. The strongest industrial action by a European union federation, the Swedish general strike of August 1909, was a disaster, setting the movement back a decade. Ironically, the most successful mass strikes were political demonstrations by socialist parties—the Habsburg suffrage strikes of 28 November 1905 and the Finnish National Strike of November 1905, both of which achieved their goals. Neither, though, kept syndicalism alive.[43]

Ultimately, organized syndicalism receded beside the broader radicalization of 1905–14 it helped dynamize. Syndicalist rhetoric resonated with the revolutionary temper of a new Marxist Left, inspired by 1905, who disputed the Second International's Kautskyan orthodoxies in an extraparliamentary resurgence. Ironically, syndicalist ideas strengthened socialist political agitations for universal suffrage. But mass strike debates also rejuvenated revolutionary hopes for left-wing socialists, for whom Rosa Luxemburg's *Mass Strike, Party and Trade Unions* (1906) became the manifesto.[44] In this looser sense, syndicalist agitations appealed to desires for workplace autonomy and control, which took revolutionary strategy away from Kautsky's stress on the state. Syndicalists hoped that unions could become "the basic organizations for production and distribution" after the revolution, basing socialism "not on the oppressive centralized state but on the functional self-governing producers' groups."[45] The strike became an all-purpose panacea, the much-needed solvent for party caution and union bureaucracy, which were dragging the proletariat's spontaneous class consciousness down. In this sense, syndicalism did reconnect to anarchist ideals of the 1870s. But it also anticipated the Council Communisms of 1917–23.[46]

Some continuity between syndicalism and earlier anarchists ran through the sympathies of intellectuals. The appeal of Georges Sorel's eclectic fusion of materialism and activism to many syndicalists was well known, and his critique of bourgeois civilization in the name of the revolutionary myth of the general strike evoked the irrationalist and vitalist philosophical currents of the 1900s.[47] Such radicalisms helped open the first cracks in the self-confident cultures of science and rationalism so crucial to the labor movements' origins. Closer to 1914, there were links with the artistic and aesthetic avant-garde, especially in Italy, where the PSI's stability dissolved after 1911 in explosive radicalizations. Earlier, in the 1880s and 1890s, Parisian anarchism existed most densely in the bohemian milieu of cabarets, cafés, and newspapers in Montmartre, and its affinities with postimpressionist artists and symbolist writers were also paralleled in the interactions of art and anarchism in Pablo Picasso's turn-of-the-century Barcelona.[48]

This was an experimentalism beyond the organized uplift of official socialist culture. In Britain, Edward Carpenter and his friends pursued change outside the main arenas of party and trade-union action, seeking "to release the creativity and artistry in everyone" by healing "the breach between the heart, the body and the mind":

> They saw socialism as an inner transformation which meant change in the here and now. They sought this new life in the everyday, in their stress on the warmth of fellowship and comradeship, in their clothes and furnishings, in a network of associations from cycling clubs to Socialist Sunday Schools, which could sustain them through isolation, hardship and despair.[49]

These links between personal life and socialism—extending into areas of gender equality and sexual freedom—were barely acknowledged in the official life of the socialist parties. They never ruffled the surface of the Second International's agenda or entered the urgencies of socialist public debate. In this prefigurative sense, late-nineteenth-century anarchist traditions remained influential. For Carpenter, or for another hugely popular maverick like Oscar Wilde, anarchism offered inspiration where Marxism in its dominant scientistic and materialist versions did not.[50]

FEMINISTS, SOCIALISTS, AND THE EMANCIPATION OF WOMEN

Nothing underscores the Left's lost opportunities like socialism's difficulties with feminism. Theoretically, socialists were radical advocates of sexual equality. The program of the Parti ouvrier francais (POF) of 1882 called for women's full political and economic emancipation, while the SPD's Erfurt Program demanded full citizenship for women in the vote plus "abolition of all laws which place women at a disadvantage to men in public and civil law."[51] The SPD introduced the first parliamentary motion for women's suffrage in Germany in 1895, and when women acquired rights of political association in 1908, its women's movement rapidly grew. August Bebel's *Woman under Socialism* (1878) was German socialism's founding text, with 50 editions by 1909 and 15 translations, rivalling Kautsky's commentary on the Erfurt Program as the movement's best-read book. It expounded the maximum program of women's rights, from suffrage and access to professions through divorce and married women's property to modernist ideals of dress reform and emancipated sexuality. Women were doubly oppressed—by "economic and social dependence upon man" and by capitalist exploitation. Legal and political emancipation alone couldn't be enough. Women would only truly be freed by socialism, via the economic independence of working beyond the home. The "woman question" would be really solved if "the existing state and social order were radically transformed."[52]

Thus socialists combined political rights with wider socioeconomic demands, including socialized childcare for working mothers, equal pay, equal education, egalitarian households, abortion reform, and contraception. But the "social question" always came first. Once women were at "work," meaning regular employment in industry, all else would follow. Even more: once capitalism was overthrown, childcare and housework could be socialized and women freed from the family's domestic prison, becoming productive workers like men. In making women's emancipation fundamentally an economic question like this, socialists invoked another founding text, Engels's *Origins of the Family, Property and the State* (1884), which explained women's oppression by the family's relation to the prevailing mode of production.

Socialist practice was more equivocal. The SPD's founding Congress in 1875 initially advocated only manhood suffrage, and Bebel's amendment for "citizens of both sexes" was rejected for one mentioning simply "all citizens." Many male socialists viewed women as a "backward" force for conservatism, superstitiously in thrall to priests and lacking in class consciousness: "Women don't want to know about politics and organization ... they appreciate a May Day festival, with singing and speeches and dancing ... but they don't appreciate political and trade union meetings."[53] The exclusivist misogyny of skilled artisans, familiar from early labor movements, transmuted into generalized cultures of aggressive masculinity, unwelcoming to women. When Klara Haase joined the SPD committee in her Berlin parliamentary district, she was marginalized by an offensive barrage of bravado: "the men tried to show their courage by using the vilest expressions and the foulest words in order to annoy me."[54] In Hamburg, the party men forbade their wives and daughters to attend the women's meetings: "they should only look after the household, darn stockings, and suchlike."[55] This might take explicitly antifeminist form. For Edmund Fischer, a parliamentarian on the SPD's revisionist wing, women's "natural occupation" was "the care and upbringing of young children, the embellishment and stabilization of family life." The party should return women to the family.[56]

The feminism of pre-1914 labor movements had distinct limits. Women workers were no priority for unions. After legalization in 1890, only 1.8 percent of German unionists were women, rising only to 8.8 percent by 1913. The Copenhagen cigar makers' constitution (1872) said baldly: "Any cigar maker who teaches a woman, apart from his wife, how to roll a cigar cannot be a member."[57] Women became routinely excluded, union by union, from entering skilled trades. If boundaries were sometimes breached, prejudices still prevailed. French printers passed a resolution in 1910 admitting women if they earned union rates, but when Emma Couriau applied to join the Lyon section it not only refused but expelled her husband Louis for letting her work.[58]

The gap between socialist rhetoric ("There can be no antagonism between the men and women of the proletarian class") and union practice was most painful in the one industry where women were always strong, textiles.[59] Well over half the 275,000 British cotton unionists in 1910 were women, but female activists never qualified for leadership in the Labour Party or the Trades Union Congress (TUC). Women textile workers of the Nord were a bastion of Guesdes's POF, but from 1897 socialists sacrificed their interests to male-dominated unionism and electoralism. In Belgium, the Flemish women textile workers of Ghent built a remarkable socialist movement after 1885, only to be marginalized after 1902 by the Brussels-based Francophone leadership of the POB/BWP (Belgian Workers' Party).[60] The SPD's textile union founded in 1891 had 11 percent female membership in 1897, rising to 36 percent in 1907–13, while the smaller Christian union had 30 percent. But women's militancy met running complaints from male union leaders: wildcat strikes constantly disrupted top-down decision-making, and women's strike participation outstripped their willingness to join the union. The union's male bureaucracy denied women official positions, resisted equal pay, and ignored women's extra burdens of family obligations, discriminatory workplace rules, and sexual harassment.[61]

Indeed, union men translated these conditions of women's labor into accusations of "backwardness": "female workers often figured in union rhetoric as passive, apolitical workers who because of the double burden of wage work and housework/child rearing were at best a costly burden upon the labor movement and . . . betrayed the union's struggle by acting as wage cutters and strikebreakers."[62] Such antifeminism denied legitimacy to women's work. This was clearest in the "sweated trades" and casualized labor markets so vital to industrialization. Aside from clothing, laundry, and food workers, these included "a great host of artificial-flower makers, box makers, brush makers, book folders, paper-bag makers, wood choppers, envelope makers, cigar and cigarette makers and wrappers, ostrich-feather curlers, lace makers, straw-plait makers, and many more."[63] Lumped together as "[a]ll labor employed in manufacture which has escaped the regulation of the Factory Acts and the trade unions," sweating became pathologized into a female problem requiring legislation rather than union action. A liberal-socialist campaign emerged in Britain via the National Anti-Sweating League for a Minimum Wage, culminating in the Trades Boards Act of 1909, which created a regulative framework for chain-making, box-making, lace-making, and tailoring.

The London strikers of 1910–14 ("jam and pickle workers, rag pickers, bottle washers, laundry women, envelope, biscuit, cocoa and tin box–makers, and distillery and confectionary workers") included many previously unorganized women.[64] But reformers' belief that sweatshops and home-work would progressively die out implied prejudicial assumptions about where the "real" working class should be found. Protective laws for women's work, regulating working hours, night work, maternity leave, and heavy labor implicitly removed women from the core working class, defin-ing them as dependents rather than citizens in their own right. Though socialist women often joined other feminists in opposing sex-based protec-tive laws, socialist parties mainly took the paternalist approach. Protecting women workers involved genuine reforms, especially when integrated with goals like the eight-hour day and equal pay. But socialists often implied something else—that women shouldn't be working in the first place. They belonged at home.[65]

The SPD women's movement contained mainly housewives (married nonwaged women over 25) rather than factory workers.[66] Recruitment ac-celerated after 1904–5, using issues like food prices, family welfare, and cost of living.[67] Indeed, far from destroying the family as antisocialists al-leged, the SPD made the "social democratic family" its ideal, anchoring working-class respectability. "Family wage" ideals, allowing male bread-winners to support households free of wives' employment, were no less prevalent than elsewhere. From 1905, *Die Gleichheit* expanded its "non-political" content aimed at housewives, mothers, and children, turning a profit for the first time and massively boosting circulation. The ideal so-cialist woman became the architect of a socialist home, raising socialist children and providing succor and comradeship for a socialist husband, with "an untroubled understanding of his aspirations, his struggles, and his work." "When the proletarian then says 'my wife,' he adds to this in his mind: 'the comrade of my ideals, the companion of my exertions, the educator of my children for the future struggle.' "[68]

This translated into public policy. In the 1890s, in line with Second International precepts, the SPD prioritized women's industrial work but shifted after 1905 to family welfare. It formed Child Protection Commit-tees, agitating for maternity homes, school meals, creches, and playgrounds and organizing activities for children and youth; SPD women worked in elections to local health insurance councils. Some were employed by local social services. This certainly had radical potential. Socialist women forced new issues into politics, demanding democracy in everyday life. "Mother-hood in its wide sense" signified "pure food, a municipal milk supply, healthy schools, the raising of the school age, sound moral training, without any squeamish holding back knowledge of the facts of life that boys and girls should know, the abolition of sweated labor."[69] Margaret McMillan, a British socialist and suffrage campaigner, used Bradford's school board as her platform, campaigning for school-based healthcare and later organ-izing camps for poor children and founding an open-air school in Deptford, London. By lobbying, speaking, and journalism, she pushed tirelessly on political boundaries, theorizing childhood into a metaphor for remaking the world.[70] Yet socialist parties marginalized these issues as inferior "women's questions." Women's emancipation became subsumed into programs of family-based welfare.

Socialist fudging on the "woman question" was worst on the central issue of democracy itself, the suffrage. Where working-class men had the vote, socialist parties failed to prioritize votes for women. Where struggles for manhood suffrage continued, they relegated female suffrage to the future. In choosing electoral politics by 1900, French and Belgian socialists marginalized strong women's labor movements in the Nord and Ghent, because voteless female workers didn't matter. If strong enough, socialists sharply opposed "bourgeois" women's rights campaigns. Complex calculations were in play. Antifeminism made manhood suffrage easier to achieve by itself, socialists assumed. But bourgeois suffragists had their own partial strategy, demanding the limited property franchise enjoyed by men as a realistic goal, moved by class fears of democracy. Where mass socialist parties monopolized arguments for democracy, the gap with "womens-rightsers" widened, stigmatizing "feminism" as a self-interested middle-class demand. Given the masculinist culture of labor movements and their family-centered ideology, the space for democratic feminism in socialist parties was small.[71]

The Czech lands and Britain offered counterexamples. British feminism descended from the suffrage movements of the 1860s and earlier campaigns for divorce reform and married women's property. Absent a mass socialist party, these became organized by the National Union of Women's Suffrage Societies (NUWSS) and the Women's Social and Political Union (WSPU), through which other influences intersected, including the Women's Cooperative Guild, the Women's Trade Union League, the ILP, and the Women's Labour League. Public attention was commandeered after 1905 by the WSPU's direct-action militancy under Emmeline and Christabel Pankhurst, with disruptions of political meetings, civil disobedience, violence against property, and spectacular individual acts, most famously when Emily Wilding Davison threw herself under the king's horse at the 1913 Derby. Militancy escalated after "Black Friday" (18 November 1910), when police violently humiliated WSPU demonstrators outside Parliament. From 1909, prison hunger strikes were met with force-feeding and the "Cat-and-Mouse" Act of 1913, which allowed release and rearrest of imprisoned militants.

The militancy of the WSPU certainly radicalized the context, not least via the stylistic inventiveness of its great collective actions, notably "Women's Sunday" in June 1908, a march of 30,000 ending in a rally of 250,000 in Hyde Park, and "From Prison to Citizenship" in June 1910, a procession of 15,000 two miles long. Yet NUWSS also had its equivalents, like the three-thousand-strong Mud March of 1907 or the 13 June 1908 Procession, followed later by the lantern-light Pageant of Women's Trades and Professions in 1909 and the Hyde Park rally of 23 July 1910. Most spectacular of all was the Women's Coronation Procession in 1911, uniting both wings of the movement to rival the official Coronation a week later: "40,000 women from at least 28 women's suffrage organizations marched five abreast in a gala procession with floats, banners, music and historical costumes . . . seven miles long."[72] So if WSPU militancy delivered the initial shock to political norms, the ensuing activism worked on wider political fronts. "Votes for Women" produced generalized momentum before 1914, reshaping the meanings of citizenship, as NUWSS converged democratically with the emergent Labour Party.

Behind the drama of militancy was a wider ferment among working-class women in the localized socialist subcultures of the north, particularly around ILP organizers like Isabella Ford, Selina Cooper, Ada Nield Chew, Hannah Mitchell, Teresa Billington-Greig, Ethel Snowden, and Mary Gaw-thorpe. If WSPU leadership became isolated in London around the Pank-hursts' autocracy, "militancy" as such became diffused through the wider suffrage movement elsewhere. Organizational weight was in NUWSS and its broader coalitions, especially via the Women's Cooperative Guild and the East London Federation of Sylvia Pankhurst. This was reemphasized by the Women's Freedom League, launched in protest against the Pank-hursts' decision to break with the ILP. The intransigence of the WSPU was vital in clarifying the Liberal government's hostility to women's suffrage, but Christabel Pankhurst's sectarian and messianic dominance also blocked alternative progressive coalitions. Instead, the rise of "democratic suffrag-ism" enabled NUWSS to break with Liberalism and realign with Labour. Labour's unequivocal rejection of any franchise reform excluding women in 1912 opened the way.[73]

In the febrile political mood of Britain in 1910–14, defined by syndi-calism, labor unrest, and crisis in Ireland, women's suffrage became the opposite of a single-issue campaign. In its forms of association, languages of citizenship, and everyday ethics, it radically changed how democracy might be imagined. As the working class coalesced into a political identity via labor organizing and municipal socialism, gender regimes were also remade, resonating with images of the "new woman." This came partly via the new social agenda ("better schools, healthier housing, public baths and wash-houses, and improved maternity services"), where "social redistri-bution and democracy were linked," and partly via older influences, from Chartist legacies of parliamentary reform, secularism, religious equality, and democratic internationalism, to "root and branch land reform," tem-perance, Irish Home Rule, and free education. Here, "radical Christianity, temperance groups, the Freewoman Circle, and socialist speakers fostered criticism of conservatism of all kinds."[74] Selina Cooper, a Lancashire "mill-girl" in Nelson, came to the NUWSS from exactly this working-class mi-lieu—not just SDF and ILP but also the Women's Cooperative Guild, the St. John Ambulance Committee, the Literary and Debating Society, the

Mutual Improvement Class, Women's Temperance Association, the Cooperative Education Committee, the National Home Reading Union, the Co-operative Holiday Association, and the Clarion Cycling Club, as well as chapel and the weavers' union and eventually the Labour Party.[75]

The suffrage movement complicated the boundaries of public and personal life by questioning family, domesticity, and sexual culture, revisiting motherhood, and imagining the forms of women's independence in work and the public sphere. Suffragists attacked "the double standard of morality, prostitution, and the sexual objectification and abuse of women."[76] This was most associated with Christabel Pankhurst's book *The Great Scourge and How to End It* (1913), which denounced the hypocrisies of men's sexuality with its reduction of women to "the Sex," urging cessation of sexual relations under the slogan "Votes for women and chastity for men." Pankhurst's opponents accused her of "feeding and flattering a sexual ideology which juxtaposed the perfection of women against the bestiality of men."[77] But such critiques of masculinity took many forms. Most shared some belief in the moral-political empowerment of gaining the vote, including the chance to reform men's sexual exploitation of women. This moral crusading dimension went back to the campaign against the 1864 Contagious Diseases Act and its attack on prostitution and male-dominated medicine. It ranged from refusals of sexuality per se to radical advocacy of women's sexual freedom. Far more than other parts of the Left, suffragists brought politics and personal life into creative tension, enacting a running moral-political challenge.[78]

This British suffragism—by far Europe's strongest movement of women—flourished in the absence of a socialist party on the central-north European scale. The national coordinates of the constitutional settlements of the 1860s were again the key. Britain's exceptionally resilient popular liberalism created frameworks of radical advocacy, especially in northern England, where women could act. Municipal franchise gave them access to public life in areas of welfare and schooling. From the Langham Place circle of Barbara Bodichon and others and John Stuart Mill's defeated amendment to the 1867 Reform Act, British feminism was never without a parliamentary voice in the Liberal Party's radical wing.[79] The remaking of British radicalism from the ground up after the 1880s, in the localized mushrooming of socialist societies, enabled the intermingling of feminist and labor activism in ways disallowed by the success of centralized parliamentary socialist parties in central and northern Europe.[80] If the WSPU repudiated existing progressive coalitions, Emmeline and Richard Pankhurst had also been leading ILPers after 1894, formed by Manchester's radical political culture.[81] Though Emmeline and Christabel split from the ILP, grassroots interconnectedness proved stronger, and the WSPU lost the popular initiative, reflected in the secession of Sylvia Pankhurst's East London Federation. The NUWSS-Labour alliance was the stronger departure by 1914.

In the Czech lands in 1912, a similar convergence of socialist and non-socialist feminists succeeded, this time on the common ground of the national question. In protest against the Habsburg government's continued denial of Czech self-determination, the nationalist writer Bozena Viková-Kunetická was elected to a vacant seat in the Bohemian Diet, supported by Progressive, National-Socialist, and Young Czech Parties.[82] The CSDSD had run their own candidate, Karla Máchová, editor of the socialist journal *Ženský list,* but they generally cooperated in the pluralist framework of the Czech Women's Club, formed as a radical alternative to the Central Association of Czech Women. The CSDSD's efforts paralleled those of the Committee for Women's Suffrage under Frantiska Plamínková, although the latter equivocated over the long-term principle of universal equal suffrage. Like the CSDSD itself, socialist women overwhelmingly backed separating from the Austrian Socialists, and this allowed convergence with the democratic nationalism of the Progressives and National-Socialists. Thus in the Czech case, socialists and "bourgeois" feminists converged in the democratic framework of national self-determination, not unlike progressive nationalisms in Iceland, Finland, and Norway.

✓ Elsewhere, the strongest women's movements developed in Scandinavia, where liberal constitutionalism was well established before 1914.[83] In Russia, the Balkans, and much of eastern Europe, where constitutional legality was barely established, women's rights were raised mainly by circles of pioneers. In Catholic Europe, women's suffrage lacked large-scale mobilization. In German-speaking central Europe, where class politics polarized around the democratic presence of socialist parties, feminism's independent space was slight. In Austria, it paralleled the SPÖ, whose women's movement counted 28,058 members in 312 sections six years after its founding in 1907–13, organizing Vienna's first Women's Suffrage Day with 20,000 marchers in March 1911. Independent feminists campaigned for women's economic and legal equality, abolitionism, settlement work, "life reform," and public voice, with 40,000 aggregated members in 80 affiliates of the umbrella League of Austrian Women's Associations. But neither the activist General Austrian Women's Association, with its three hundred members, nor the Committee for Women's Suffrage were more than adjuncts to socialist-dominated action.[84] In Germany, the League for Protection of Motherhood and Sex Reform advocated "New Morality" (legal contraception and abortion, equality for unmarried mothers, sexual freedom). They were dwarfed by the Federation of German Women's Assocations, which after 1908 welcomed diverse conservative organizations, with an aggregate membership of 250,000.

By 1914, campaigning for women's rights bifurcated between socialist partics, which gave precedence to class-political and male trade union goals and "bourgeois" women's movements, which rallied around individual emancipation or equality with middle-class men (as in the property-based limited franchise). Britain was exceptional in its intermixing of feminist and socialist organizing, because the inchoateness of the Labour Party during 1900–1914 allowed suffragism to develop broader democratic aspirations and independent social goals. Elsewhere, mass socialist parties like the SPD preempted the space for democratic suffragism but then filled it with socially conservative policies subsuming women's identities in the family. Official policy was conveyed by the twin goals of Zetkin's resolution to the Women's Conference of the Second International's Stuttgart Congress in 1907—universal suffrage for men and women, no alliances with bourgeois women's-rightsers.[85]

Nonsocialist feminists also pursued international organization, from Marie Goegg's short-lived Swiss-based International Association of Women in the late 1860s, which opened links to the First International before post-Commune repression closed it down, to the International Woman Suffrage Alliance (IWSA) launched in Berlin by affiliates from the United States, Canada, Australia, Britain, Germany, the Netherlands, Norway, and Sweden in 1904.[86] However, most women's groups joined the nationalist solidarities of the First World War, from socialists to suffragists; and their belief in women's "cultural mission" put them inside the prevailing nationalist and ethnocentric ideologies, whether or not they supported the war. No less than socialists, feminists failed to question assumptions of national character, imperialist entitlement, and racial superiority, seeing women in the colonized world as the potential beneficiaries of European women's advance.[87] Those pacifists who identified with the Women's International League for Peace and Freedom in 1915 also used Eurocentric images of "womanliness" to make their case. Nonetheless, it was labor movement activists in the prewar suffrage movement who provided British opposition to the First World War.[88] Alice Wheeldon, a Derby secondhand clothes trader, WSPU activist, and ILPer, was jailed for conspiracy after sheltering conscientious objectors. With her schoolteacher daughter, Hettie, she sustained a "defiant culture" of war resistance, growing from the pre-1914 unrest: "the women in this rebel network cut their hair short, read feminist, socialist and pacifist papers, and discussed Shaw's plays."[89]

CONCLUSION

Like anarchists, syndicalists, and agrarian radicals, pre-1914 feminists marked out democratic possibilities beyond the boundaries of parliamentary socialism. Such challenges came not just from organized suffrage or women's rights campaigns or the women's activism enabled by Second International parties themselves but also from the exemplary lives of remarkable pioneers. Thus Rosika Schwimmer was the leading activist in the Hungarian Union for Women's Rights, which campaigned vainly among Liberals and Social Democrats during the prewar suffrage crisis. She became IWSA secretary in London in 1914, before leaving for the United

States on the outbreak of war. From a freethinking bourgeois Jewish family in Budapest, she founded the Hungarian Association of Working Women and headed the Women Office-Workers' Association in the 1900s, translating Charlotte Perkins Gilman's *Women and Economics* into Hungarian. She developed a wide-ranging feminism, "from suffrage to pacifism, from childcare and marriage reform to equal pay and employment for women," campaigning for birth control, dress reform, antimilitarism, and abolition of child labor.[90] Her charismatic energy migrated naturally from the constricting Hungarian context to the transnational theater of progressive action. The First World War temporarily marginalized her ideals, as the machineries of militarized state power rolled across earlier political conflicts and submerged dissidence in the resulting xenophobia. But lives like Schwimmer's created inspiring precedents, which after 1917–18 came back into their own.

These exemplary lives charted territories that socialists didn't map, especially in sexuality, reproductive freedoms, family, and personal life. In many ways, an agenda was being assembled for the future, which only the massive societal mobilizations and revolutionary crises of the First World War brought to fruition. Women's suffrage actually arrived via that later pan-European democratization—in Denmark and Iceland completing prewar changes, elsewhere through the invention of new states like Czechoslovakia, Poland, Ireland, and Russia and the remaking of constitutions in Britain, Germany, and Sweden. The turmoil of 1917–23 allowed other prewar radicalisms to revive. Union growth was resumed on even larger scale. Prewar syndicalism was replicated, with militancy radically outgrowing established union frameworks. Rank-and-file movements targeted the workplace rather than national agreements or legislation, demanding factory councils and workers' control. These movements failed but decisively shifted the balance of industrial power in emergent corporatisms that labor movements hoped to control. The prewar movements for women's emancipation also had their postwar analogues, linked to new freedoms beyond the family, public visibilities, and long-term changes of employment and education, which winning the vote helped to frame. In this sense, the nonsocialist radicalisms before 1914 remained a series of incitements and rebukes, which during the following decades the Left only partly and unevenly addressed, if at all.

Chapter 6

The Permanence of Capitalism?

BETWEEN THE 1860s and the First World War, socialist parties became the torchbearers of democracy in Europe. Country by country, they provided the strongest and most consistent democratic advocacy. They did so by defeating two of the Left's earlier traditions—radical democracy focused exclusively on the franchise and frequently allied with liberalism and the utopian socialisms and other communitarian experiments of the earlier nineteenth century. In both respects, the 1860s were a decisive break. Socialist parliamentarianism substituted popular sovereignty for the free and sovereign individual of the liberals but simultaneously turned its back on the locally organized cooperative utopia. This was a momentous change.

Thereafter, socialists pursued maximum parliamentary democracy on a basis usually resembling the Six Points of the 1838 People's Charter in Britain. In most of Europe, the dominant Left vehicle became a national social democratic party in tandem with nationally federated trade unions. This new political model was centralist, stressing national rather than local forms of action; parliamentarist, privileging the parliamentary arena as the source of sovereignty; and constitutionalist in the given meaning of the term, adopting representative over direct methods of governing. This preference for centralized forms over the looser federated ones prevalent between the 1820s and 1860s brought a new theme into the Left's discourse, namely, the key role of the party.

After the divisive debates of the 1860s and 1870s, the idea of the party seemed unavoidable. Throughout these conflicts, the arguments for different types of state organization and different types of movement were homologous, contrasting once again with what came before. Before the 1860s, the locally based associational activity of radical democrats and early socialists had coalesced mainly around certain common ideals, focused by newspapers, pamphlets, itinerant lecturers, and a few national parliamentarians and similar charismatic figures. The impetus came from once-off campaigns that left little permanent structure behind them. Likewise, the imagined democratic state presupposed similar principles of decentralized association, usually expressed through an ideal of loosely federated, self-governing units of cooperatively organized small producers.

An analogous continuity of movement and state characterized the new social democracy, with the form of the future socialist constitution being abstracted from socialists' organizational experience under capitalism. Thus, both the socialist parties and their unions strongly preferred representative forms of national organization over direct democracy based on rank and file at the local level and on the shopfloor; and this was repeated in the preference for a parliamentary constitution. Likewise, centralized bureaucracy allowed both party and unions to concentrate the movement's strengths and equalize resources among its stronger and weaker sections; and by the same logic, central institutions of economic planning would give the future state maximum resources for building socialism.

In other words, pre-1914 socialist parties showed little interest in decentralization, whether this meant the cooperative and communitarian self-governing schemes of earlier socialist pioneers or the soviets and workers' councils about to appear in 1917–21. Indeed, leading theorists like Karl Kautsky specifically rejected workers' control, arguing that the complexities of the advanced industrial economy and the modern enterprise precluded bringing democratic procedures directly into the economy itself. Instead, the only effective watchdog over the managerial bureaucracies of the economy, no less than over the civil bureaucracy of the state, was a strong parliament. In this manner, the model of democratic responsibility fashioned by labor movements for their own affairs—permanent officialdom accountable to the constitutional authority of an elected assembly of trade-union or party delegates—became transposed to government in the form of a socialist parliamentary state.

...AND LIMITS

Of course, social democracy seldom established an exclusive ascendancy over the Left and still shared space with other movements. At the continent's two extremities, for example, British socialists remained overshadowed by radicals in the Liberal Party until shortly before 1914, while lack of constitutional freedoms in Russia forced the Left there into illegal revolutionary action.[1] Further, the rivalry with anarchists gave socialists in southern Europe a more "maximalist" or confrontational style, making them more receptive to direct action than their solidly parliamentarian counterparts to the north. And after 1900, syndicalism also challenged the parliamentary model, migrating from its southern European baselands to Britain, parts of the Low Countries, Germany, and Scandinavia.

But even inside the social democratic tradition older influences remained active. Democratic nationalism offered one such continuity with the earlier nineteenth century. The networks of migrant artisans and political exiles linking Paris, London, Brussels, and the Rhineland had been fertile ground for the young Marx and Engels in the 1840s and 1850s, joining Polish, Italian, and Hungarian patriotisms to the causes of Chartists and French republicans. Here, nationalist forms of radical democracy resonated through the international popularity of Lajos Kossuth and Giuseppe Mazzini, lasting in southern and eastern Europe well into the 1880s and beyond. The ideas of Jean Jacques Rousseau, with their celebration of participatory democracy and local self-government, also permeated these midcentury national intelligentsias, subtly displacing the ideal of the citizen-democrat onto the collective image of the oppressed patriot-people struggling for national freedom.[2]

Social democracy's dominance of the Left was clearest in central and northern Europe, forming a German-speaking and Scandinavian social democratic "core"; it was weaker in the south and east, with French-speaking Europe in between. A key variable was liberal constitutionalism. Social democracy made least progress where that national institutional framework was least developed—parliamentary government, civil liberties and the rule of law, trade union recognition, a legally guaranteed national public sphere. Where constitutionalism hadn't yet been established, as under the full-scale repression of tsarist Russia, or remained weak, as with the narrowly oligarchic polities of Italy and Spain, socialist parties had less chance to flourish. Agrarian backwardness, with its glaring rural inequalities, a land-hungry peasantry, and flagrantly exploited agricultural workers, also required a different left-wing politics than in the industrial northwest. These nonindustrial settings described a further space of democratic politics beyond socialism's new frame, namely, the populist agrarian radicalisms of Russia and eastern Europe, reminiscent in some respects of the anarchisms and cooperative radicalisms earlier in the west.

But alternative visions weren't confined entirely to Europe's geographical margins or its economically backward periphery. For one thing, democratic traditions in the more developed societies needed reshaping over a longer period before the social democratic model became fully established. Socialist activity was invariably pioneered among artisanal workers as a "federalist trades socialism," which stressed local cooperation based on workers' control rather than a national economy run by a collectivist state, and such ideals didn't entirely die away.[3] In France, they rivaled social democracy throughout the later nineteenth century. They inspired the ear-liest socialists in Germany and the Habsburg Empire in the 1860s and 1870s, while further to the east notions of consumer and producer coop-eration invariably gave people their first encounters with socialism.[4] They persisted most impressively among anarcho-syndicalists in Spain as far as the Civil War. And they also persisted in the Low Countries and Switzer-land up to 1914.[5]

These ideas remained an alternative source of inspiration to the cen-tralist social democratic model. They resurfaced in a new form under the impact of the war economy after 1914, reaching dramatic definition in the movements of soviets and workers' councils flourishing across Europe dur-ing the revolutionary years of 1917–21. By emphasizing the local sover-eignty of democratic action, therefore, these later movements reconnected with the localist traditions of mutualism described earlier, which social de-mocracy only imperfectly supplanted. In this respect, the dominance of the new socialist parties over the Left remained incomplete.

Finally, over the longer term two further limitations had big effects. The first concerned colonialism. Europe's socialists noticed the question of de-mocracy in the colonial world only very exceptionally before 1914: not only were non-Western voices and peoples of color entirely absent from the counsels of the Second International, but its parties also failed to condemn colonial policy and even positively endorsed it.[6] Socialists commonly af-firmed the progressive value of the "civilizing mission" for the underde-veloped world, while accepting the material benefits of jobs, cheaper goods, and guaranteed markets colonialism brought at home. Critical insight into imperialist culture and its legitimizing of exploitation was rare indeed, from racialized forms of understanding and ideologies of racial inequality to gen-ocidal practices and acceptance of colonial violence. Here, the early-twentieth-century stirrings of colonial revolt leveled a powerful rebuke against Europe's Left. When Lenin began insisting in 1916–17 that national self-determination also applied to the colonial world, therefore, he fore-grounded the critique of colonialism for the first time. The presence of non-Western delegates at the Communist International's founding Congress in 1919 was something quite new, as was its backing for nationalist move-ments campaigning for anticolonial independence.[7]

Second, feminism also raised democratic demands beyond the socialist framework altogether. While socialist parties certainly formed their own women's organizations, gender politics remained their greatest weakness. They failed to develop a consistent approach to the emancipation of women, constantly sidelining it for the male-defined priorities of the class struggle. This inability came from deeply ingrained working-class attitudes, from family values to the cultures of workplace discrimination, bordering frequently on misogyny. Socialist politicians and trade unionists often ex-pressed these views. Relegating women's issues to low priority and refusing cooperation with "bourgeois" women's rights groups was a strategic choice by most socialist leaderships. When in some countries large and ebullient women's movements developed before 1914, accordingly, they did so entirely independently of the socialist parties, defining a separate space of women's democratic politics usually focused on the suffrage. From self-interest alone, failing to take these movements seriously was extremely shortsighted, because, once enfranchised, women had no reason to turn to socialists, given this poor pre-1914 record. Much more seriously, socialist parties' claims to be the vanguard of democracy, rallying all progressive causes to their banner, foundered on this gender neglect.

THE CULTURE OF SOCIALISM: EXPECTING THE FUTURE

Socialism's claims to the mantle of democracy were founded on its organized popular support—on its relationship to the massed ranks of male industrial wage-earners, on its assumptions about the necessary direction of social change, and on its belief in the inevitability of the future working-class majority. In other words, socialism's strengths came not only from the rising curve of electoral success but also from connecting this parliamentary strength to a wider coalescence in society. Socialist labor movements forged a special relationship to the results of capitalist industrialization. They rationalized these into a compelling narrative of capitalist crisis and the resulting socialist future, organized around the new collective identity of the working class. Socialism's appeal before 1914 rested on its ability to weave the myriad working-class experiences of societies undergoing rapid transformation into a single story. It promised to shape the disorderly aggregations of dispersed and heterogeneous circumstances defining working-class lives into a unified political agency. Around this powerful working-class core, which socialists expected to expand inexorably into the overwhelming majority of society, other social interests and progressive causes could then be gathered.

The resulting movement cultures had several key aspects. One was the all-embracing mass party. Between the First International's founding debates and the self-confident growth accompanying the launching of the Second International after 1889, socialists invented the modern political party.[8] By this I mean the new model of a permanent campaigning organization geared to fighting elections, which established a continuous presence in its supporters' lives, bound them together through elaborate machineries of identification, and built lasting cultures of solidarity from the social architecture of everyday life. By the turn of the century, this was establishing a new norm of political action, which other political parties ignored at their peril. Before 1914, Catholic and Christian-social parties were the most successful emulators, but after the First World War, the model became universal.[9]

Second, among the Second International's leading activists, socialist culture was nothing if not internationalist. Karl Kautsky himself was born in Prague, joined the Austrian party, and settled in Germany after sojourns in Zurich and London; the Russian exile Anna Kuliscioff became Filippo Turati's lifelong companion at the head of the Italian party; Rosa Luxemburg, Leo Jogiches, and other leaders of the Polish Social Democrats found their way to the SPD from Russian Poland via Switzerland before retraversing the borders back and forth after 1905; the Romanian-born future Bolshevik Christian Rakovsky became a roving emissary for the Balkan revolution, the crucial connection between the Serbian and Bulgarian parties and the SPD; Anton Pannekoek was as much at home in the German as in his native Dutch party. These and many other complex biographies required "a genuine international community . . . a body of men and women conscious of being engaged on the same historical task, across national and political differences."[10] Such a transnational network, cemented by its confidence in the common socialist future, reemphasized socialists' apartness from their respective national scenes, pointing them away from potential intranational coalitions.

Third, socialism's rising electoral and organizational strength, combined with the expanding ranks of the working class and the impression of an unstoppable forward march, kept the movement's utopianism alive. For many pragmatists the revolutionary end-goal became increasingly abstract, yet even the more prosaic reformists held onto the image of a shining socialist future. Socialists sought to organize working-class solidarities into a movement capable of making the world over. In the stronger parties of central Europe and Scandinavia, an imposing array of organizations fashioned a distinctive social democratic way of life—"reading and library associations, proletarian theater and concert clubs, organizations specializing in the preparation and equipping of festivals and celebrations, choirs," plus the Freethinkers, Workers' Abstinence Leagues, the Worker Cremators, the Friends of Nature, workers' sports clubs, and recreational clubs for every aspect of life.[11] Certain values were iterated over and over again, like self-improvement and sobriety, commitment to education, respect for one's body, egalitarian relations between men and women, the progressive heritage of humanistic culture, the dignity of labor, and a well-ordered family life. Through this restless cultural striving and the ambition to remake society entirely anew, the working class became conceived as the inevitable guardian of the future, both the inheritor of existing civilization and the triumphal bearer of a new and progressive collectivist ethic.

This socialist culture was defined by its extraordinary optimism and by the unabashed certainty of its political desire, surrounding the movement's organizational muscle with a halo of utopian fervor. This shone from the working-class autodidact's chosen reading, from the rhetoric of socialist stump orators, from the imagery of the movement's banners and emblems, and from the iconography of socialist parades and festivals, which offered solemn but exuberant displays of loyalty to the movement, to the image of the class, and to the certainty of the socialist future.[12] "Oh, when will [the socialist world] come?" asked a British socialist election flyer in 1895. "God is ready, nature is ready," it replied; "When will you, the producers of wealth . . . stretch out your hands . . . and will this thing? Then—then—that very minute, it shall come."[13] The best-loved writings were not the austere summaries of Marxist economics but wide-ranging disquisitions like August Bebel's *Woman and Socialism,* or the writings of utopians like William Morris and Edward Bellamy, or the massively translated works or Edward Carpenter, which originated beyond organized social democracy altogether.[14]

In this world, to take the British example, the labor churches and socialist Sunday schools were just as important as local branches of the Independent Labour Party or the Social Democratic Federation.[15] In larger parties like the German party, Proletarian Freethinkers, temperance enthusiasts, and partisans of Esperanto took their place with the mass formations of Worker Singers and Worker Gymnasts.[16] Socialists expected the world to be comprehensively remade, from the reign of universal peace to the adoption of a universal language. Progress was indivisible, because the emancipation of the workers would be the emancipation of all humanity, bringing the freedom of women, sexual liberation and the new life, the conquest of science over nature, a new world of plenty, and a just distribution of its riches, "from each according to their abilities, to each according to their needs."[17]

TOWARD A CRISIS?

These heady aspirations were not put to the test before 1914; for even the strongest socialist parties commanded little more than a third of their national electorates and by themselves had no prospects of forming a government. In any case, most states retained constitutional mechanisms for keeping the Left at bay. In most countries, the other parties continued to close ranks against the socialists, amply backed by the state's coercive powers, and the Left reciprocated in kind, proudly defending its isolation. This permanent standoff showed few signs of relaxing. On the other hand, a barricades revolution on the style of 1848 was obsolete, it was generally agreed, and power could only come via the ballot box, whatever confrontations might be needed along the way to deal with ruling-class violence or efforts at suppressing the suffrage. Thus the socialists' dilemma was acute: on the one hand, despite their impressive growth, they were fixed in opposition, permanently on the outside; on the other hand, access to government could only come from coalition, for an avowedly limited program, by modifying or postponing the revolutionary goal.

The dilemma sharpened after 1905, when the political settlements of the 1860s finally came apart. In response to the revolution in Russia and to the strike waves and suffrage agitations elsewhere, the political temperature went dramatically up, radicalizing the extremes of Left and Right and sending reformers in search of possible realignments. The years 1905–13 became an important moment of fission. Often this strengthened the socialist Left's independence. At the continent's two extremes, renewed social polarization in Russia during 1912–13 confirmed the irrelevance of the parliamentary arena, while in Britain the fracturing of Liberal unity over Irish Home Rule, women's suffrage, and syndicalism created clearer space for the Labour Party's parliamentary separation. In some cases—Scandinavia, the Habsburg lands, the Netherlands—labor movements emerged with added oppositional weight, rallying broad coalitions for the extension of democracy. In Italy and Germany, on the other hand, socialists began pulling themselves apart: the parliamentary PSI became overwhelmed by a new maximalist militancy in the country; while at the SPD's 1913 Jena Congress for the first time it proved impossible to hold the conflicting viewpoints over revolution versus reform together.

Above all, the radicalizations of 1905–13 destabilized the existing constitutionalist frameworks. As the socialist labor movements built greater popular momentum during the 1890s, they kept steadfastly to the given parliamentarist rules—defending the progressive gains of the 1860s, campaigning for suffrage reform and other measures of democracy, fighting for civil freedoms, and strengthening trade unions under the law. But during the pre-1914 decade, a new radical temper complicated the continuance of this tradition. Larger-scale suffrage agitations, direct action, burgeoning industrial militancy, extraparliamentary radicalisms, new forms of mass action—all these transgressed the limits socialists had previously observed. Not only the constitutional settlements of the 1860s, therefore, but also socialist parliamentarianism started to break down.

Strong drives for democracy now arose independently of parliamentary socialist parties altogether—most notably in the campaigns for women's suffrage. In Europe's multinational empires, moreover, nationalists also disputed socialist leadership in the struggle for democracy. In that setting, some socialist movements, like the Finnish or Czech, or the Jewish Bund in the Russian Empire, made the advocacy of national self-determination their own, but more often nationalists closed ranks against the socialists, denouncing them as "enemies of the Fatherland." Moreover, once socialist parties began debating political strategy in national terms, this divisiveness opened inside their own ranks, ranging "social patriots" and reformists against internationalists and revolutionaries.[18] Of course, socialists had always faced this dilemma in the older national states of Europe, where ownership of the nation was already exercised by dominant classes, sometimes brutally. Socialists countered with their own ideas of the nation, drawing on democratic patriotisms of 1789 and 1848, but in the Europe of nation-states they could only do this from the outside, banging to be let in. In those nations still seeking their own states, socialists often found it easier to claim a place, joining the democracy of citizens' rights to the nationalist panacea of self-determination.[19]

Equally dramatic, matching the suffrage movements of women and the nationalist undermining of multinational empires, a new industrial rebelliousness swept across Europe. Often identified by their most self-conscious syndicalist elements, new movements of industrial militancy stressing direct action and the futility of parliamentary politics aggressively outstepped the available social democratic frameworks of election campaigns and responsible trade unionism. Rather than seeking to strengthen socialist influence in parliaments to reform the system from within, these radicals opposed the state per se, disputing its openness for capture. In Germany, early SPD parliamentarians had seen the Reichstag instrumentally as the best available platform, "speaking through the window" to the masses outside, and the new militants now revived this idea, dismissing the parliamentary talking-shop and celebrating the revolutionary potential of the mass strike. After 1905, and especially during 1910–13, Europe's socialist parties faced a revival of extraparliamentary revolutionary politics in this way.

Thus, on the eve of 1914, the European Left presented a split picture. In many ways, socialist predictions were bearing fruit. The parties and unions were stronger than ever before; socialist electoral strength was rising; unions slowly acquired legitimacy; socialist culture became ever more elaborately organized; municipal socialism offered concrete utopias of local reform. As unions built themselves into the institutional machinery of capitalist industry, socialist parliamentarians also asserted themselves, joining legislative committees and trading their votes, amassing expertise, consulting with government spokesmen, and constructively participating in the status quo. To this extent, socialists were no longer on the outside. Large parts of the party leaderships, from national executives down to local functionaries, saw themselves as practical reformers by 1914, patiently awaiting their rightful inheritance and tacitly shedding the revolutionary skin. The logic here, coming to a head in various crises between 1900 and 1914, country by country, was certainly toward integration.[20]

Yet this picture of gowing acceptance was hard to reconcile with the pre-1914 explosions of radicalism. Europe's parliamentary polities were sliding into chaos—with, for example, 10 separate governing coalitions in France between 1909 and 1914 and five Italian governments in only four years. Amid such instability, labor unrest became all the more threatening. Its scale was certainly immense. After the initial transition to mass unionism around the turn of the century, the continental strike wave of 1904–7 began a broadening of industrial militancy, which in 1910–13 was then aggressively continued. If we add the working-class mobilizations accompanying the Russian Revolution and the end of the First World War, the years 1910–20 become the great age of European unionization, not to be matched until after 1945. But this unruly expansion also outgrew the movement's patiently cultivated framework of behavior. The pre-1914 cultures of socialism had coalesced around desires for respectability that forthrightly rejected the aspects of the working class now bursting to the fore, especially the rough and disorderly cultures of the poor, which the incorrigibly self-improving social democrats always passionately disavowed. The turbulent pre-1914 militancy left these cultures of respectability looking surprisingly exposed.

By 1914 socialists may have been stronger than ever before in their parliamentary and trade union arenas, but those arenas had themselves grown increasingly insufficient. Whether among women, Irish and eastern European nationalists, or industrial militants, huge mobilizations were passing the Left's existing politics by. Socialist parties had passionately pioneered the cause of full-scale parliamentary democracy after the 1860s, pushing patiently against liberalism's confining limits. Without that advocacy, democracy was a slender growth indeed. Yet, those parties neither exhausted the full range of nineteenth-century socialist practice and belief, as I have shown, nor encompassed the broader reservoir of popular democratic experience. During 1910–13, this was becoming more painfully clear. How Europe's socialist parties would rise to this challenge the dramatic events of 1914–23 would soon reveal.

WAR AND REVOLUTION, 1914–1923

IN MARCH 1921, a violent social crisis exploded in the Mansfeld-Halle region of central Germany, when employers and government moved to assert control over an exceptionally militant working class, who had been armed since the defeat of the right-wing Kapp Putsch against the Republic a year before. Seeing this as the opening of a revolutionary situation, the Communist Party (KPD) called a general strike, though without the national resources to carry this off. As the action began, Max Hölz arrived by train from Berlin and proceeded to organize mineworkers into fighting units, making an army two thousand strong. While the strike movement rolled unevenly along, this guerrilla band dominated the Mansfeld mining district for the next week, robbing banks, sacking government buildings, ransacking stores, and dynamiting railway lines, while fighting with security forces. The general strike failed to take off with sufficient force beyond Mansfeld, and by the end of March the authorities had suppressed the insurgency, with some 35,000 arrests, including that of Hölz himself.[1]

Hölz was a remarkable figure, a mixture of Robin Hood, working-class hero, and revolutionary brigand. Born in 1889 amid the impoverished cottage industry of the Vogtland region of Saxony, he was politicized by the

First World War and the 1918 German Revolution. During the latter he organized the unemployed in his home town of Falkenstein, quickly acquiring a reputation for revolutionary intransigence and joining the KPD in 1919. In March 1920, he shot to prominence during the Kapp Putsch by organizing workers into a red army, whose regional exploits translated the defense of the Republic into a revolutionary uprising—fighting the army and liberating the prisons, attacking and burning public offices, robbing and looting in order to feed the poor. As order was reimposed, Hölz fled across the Czech border and after a spell of internment returned secretly to Germany via Vienna, attending political education classes in Berlin while organizing his own "expropriations." He was imprisoned for his role in the 1921 March Action but was amnestied in 1928 and went to the Soviet Union, where he died in 1934.[2]

This story says a great deal about the character of the revolutionary circumstances dominating much of Europe in the wake of the First World War. Hölz was a revolutionary freebooter and insurrectionary entrepreneur, with little educated relationship to the Communists or any other Left organization. Indeed, he was expelled by the KPD for his role in 1920 and while underground moved closer to the ultraleft Communist Workers' Party (KAPD), which for a year after its foundation in April 1920 rivaled the KPD in popular support. Yet the real gap was neither between moderate socialists and Communists nor between KPD and KAPD but between the Left's national party apparatuses in general and the turbulence of the grass roots, where the main energy for revolutionary militancy was being produced. During 1919–21, the passions and hopes of rank-and-file insurgents constantly outstripped the capacity of existing Left organizations to represent them.

Hölz was not a wholly exceptional figure. During 1920 Karl Plättner (born 1893) also organized robberies of banks, post offices, and mines in Thuringia, Saxony, and Brandenburg in the name of the revolution, rivaling Hölz in 1921 as the March Action's leading insurgent commander. He proposed converting the KAPD into an armed underground and when rebuffed organized his own outfit. By mid-1921 he was in prison, where he died in 1933. Herbert Kobitsch-Meyer (born 1900) was radicalized by the Russian Revolution while interned as a sailor in Siberia, made his way back to Germany, and joined the Communists. He made contact with the Plättner organization during the March Action and after a spell in Essen organized his own gang in Hamburg in 1924. By 1925 he was also in prison, where he died five years later. Young men radicalized by the war, whose training was the revolution itself, figures like these made insurgency into a way of life, substitutiong summary acts of social justice, "expropriations," bombings, and armed struggle for public democratic process. They rejected "parties" as such. "So away with professional leaders, with all organizations that can only work with leaders at the helm," another of these mavericks declaimed. "Away with centralism, the organizational principle of the ruling class. Away with all central bodies."[3]

This German pattern dramatized the problem facing the Left in the new postwar conjuncture. Traumatized by the First World War and inspired by the Russian Revolution, Europe's working classes produced the only instance under capitalism of a pan-European revolutionary crisis in which popular uprisings for socialism seemed to have a chance. As such, the years 1917–21 massively stand out in modern European history. The ambition to challenge capitalism's permanence by seizing power behind a revolutionary socialist program was at its strongest in Italy and Germany but certainly moved the most radical sections of the national labor movements in other parts of Europe too. By the early 1920s, these challenges had clearly failed. Yet in the meantime, country by country, their presence and effects had decisively shaped the future political force field.

During these years, insurrection wasn't the sole option for socialists. Pragmatists in the pre-1914 social democratic parties had clearsightedly collaborated in their countries' war efforts and hoped for big reformist concessions in return. Indeed, this moderate socialist option chalked up major democratic gains in 1918–19, from the franchise to extensive social reforms and trade union recognition. At the same time, these gains necessarily placed moderates at odds with the revolutionaries, who from 1919–20 were being powerfully courted by newly established Communist parties, enjoying all the prestige of their links with the successful Bolsheviks in Russia. The ensuing confrontations—between moderate socialists, who insisted on sticking to the parliamentary rules of electoral majorities and coalition building, and revolutionaries who wanted to ignore them—proved disastrous for the Left.

This embittering split between socialists and Communists displaced some vital democratic priorities from the future agendas. A genuine politics of women's equality was one such casualty. Developing a constructive approach toward popular entertainment cultures was another. The split certainly undermined the Left's abilities to shape the new forms of capitalist stability that materialized during the mid-1920s. Equally serious, it preempted any effective strategizing in response to the world economic crisis after 1929. Most disastrously of all, it prevented a united response to the rise of fascism.

The most complex questions facing the Left's politics during this period lay somewhere inside the polarity of insurrectionaries versus parliamentarians. On the one hand, moderate socialists proved so cautious in their conciliating of the old orders that the lasting import of their democratic achievements became undone; on the other hand, the insurrectionaries created so much anxiety in governing circles that the resulting repression preempted any longer-term concessions through reform. But if moderate socialism undermined itself and revolutionary socialism was unrealistic, what intermediate supports for democracy might the Left have pursued? And following from this: if socialist revolution was *not* on the agenda, then what kind of Left politics would emerge when the postwar crisis was over?

Chapter 7

The Rupture of War

Crisis and

Reconstruction of the

Left, 1914–1917

THE FIRST WORLD WAR dramatically changed socialism's place in the polity. From being the enemy within, social democrats throughout Europe joined the patriotic consensus, upholding national security against foreign aggression and keeping the domestic truce while the war was on. As states pushed their subject populations to unparalleled sacrifices, the resulting transformations of public culture were extraordinary. This extended wartime emergency stoked nationalist loyalties to unprecedented intensity, easing the integration of labor movements into the patriotic consensus and making the "national interest" into moderate socialism's new hegemonic frame. Remarkably, given the pre-1914 histories of intransigent exclusion, socialists also entered governments for the first time.

During the same period the major revolutionary upheaval centered on Russia profoundly changed Europe's political geography. Initially, the Left's enthusiasm for events in Russia was entirely ecumenical, inspiring moderate socialists no less than anarchists, syndicalists, and other radicals. But sympathy for overthrowing tsarism, the epitome of reactionary backwardness, was one thing; supporting the Bolsheviks was quite another. Welcoming Russia into the democratic camp in February 1917 became by October something far more sinister: for the first time, a revolutionary socialist party had come violently to power. Renouncing the Left's traditional parliamentarism, Bolshevism claimed the new class-based legitimacy of the soviets instead. The ominous-sounding "dictatorship of the proletariat" entered public circulation.

Few countries went untouched by popular insurgencies in 1917–18, and shorter-lived revolutionary experiences in Germany, Austria, Hungary, and Italy followed Russia's example. In the east and on Europe's western periphery in Ireland, moreover, the twin motifs of "the national" and "the revolutionary" powerfully coincided as "national revolutions" transformed the wreckage of the Habsburg, Romanov, Ottoman, and Hohenzollern multinational empires. The war in the west was "primarily a struggle between states and armies for the redistribution of power," whereas in the east "the war released from state control crucial national, class, and social antagonisms," opening a veritable Pandora's box of subversion.[1] The revolutionary turmoil following 1917 was decisive for the future, not least by provoking counterrevolutionary opportunities for fascism. More immediately, it split the European socialist movement: after benefiting from long-term social democratic coalescence before 1914, working-class movements were henceforth irreparably divided between socialists and Communists.

With the possible exception of the 1860s, the war brought the single most concentrated pan-European societal transformation since the French Revolution. Quite apart from the appalling death toll, the Eastern Front's more mobile warfare shifted huge populations around the map. And the war's impact reached into every sphere of social life. It recast the relationship between government and economy, bringing unforeseen centralization to production, distribution, and consumption, promoting the expansion of some sectors over others (arms and war-related production over consumer goods), and spawning new triangular relations between state, capital, and labor. This required as much political and ideological as economic mobilization. The patriotic upswing of the war rested on a new form of the social contract: in making their demands on popular loyalties, governments encouraged expectations of postwar reform, and in popular perceptions wartime sacrifices would certainly be rewarded by an expansion of citizenship. This meant a huge change of consciousness. In the popular imagination, it was understood: at war's end things would have to change.

THE CRISIS OF THE SECOND INTERNATIONAL

The war ambushed Europe's socialists. Ironically, it came at the peak of a European peace campaign, as both the Tenth International Socialist Congress and the Twenty-first Universal Peace Congress were scheduled to meet in August–September 1914 in Vienna, precisely the storm center of the diplomatic crisis that launched the war. Balkan tensions were certainly long familiar, and hopes of containing Franz Ferdinand's assassination at Sarajevo on 28 June also persisted, even after the Austrian ultimatum to Serbia on 23 July. Yet by the time the International Socialist Bureau (ISB) convened on 29–30 July, war between Austria and Serbia was set.

The Bureau kept a brave face, moving the forthcoming Congress from Vienna to Paris and appealing for international arbitration. As Hugo Haase, cochairman of the SPD, said, antiwar protests by the Second International might be ineffective, but at least "we can have the satisfaction of having done our duty."[2] But within a day Russian general mobilization had destroyed prospects of confining the war to the Balkans. By 1 August the parameters had completely changed. The International was powerless to stop the war. Even the socialists' more prosaic fallback option, coordinating country-by-country parliamentary opposition to war credits, proved a forlorn hope.[3]

Recognizing the International's powerlessness, socialists rapidly moved into actively supporting the war. On 4 August, German and French Socialists voted their government's war credits, the former after an agonized debate. Socialists in Belgium, Britain, Austria, and Hungary adopted "national defensism," as did the socialist parties in neutral Switzerland, Holland, Sweden, and Denmark. Dissident minorities barely dented the shield of patriotic resignation. In the belligerent countries, only the Serb and Russian Lefts diverged from the pattern—the two Social Democrats in the Serbian legislature condemned both the Austrian ultimatum and their own government's nationalism, while in the Russian Duma Bolsheviks and Mensheviks joined Alexander Kerensky's Labor Party in opposing the war. Among the neutrals, both the Italian Socialists and the "Narrow" faction of the Bulgarian Social Democrats condemned the war in 1914, keeping this stance even after their governments entered the conflict in 1915. But despite these exceptions, for all practical purposes the old internationalism was buried.

In the climax of the July Crisis, the Left's eyes had turned to Berlin, for the SPD was the International's senior party, the defender of its stated traditions. Initially, the party executive had called mass rallies for peace, reaching their climax on 28–30 July, just as Austria-Hungary declared war on Serbia. This was a big show of strength—with 30,000 demonstrators in Berlin, 35,000 in Dresden, 50,000 in Leipzig, 20,000 in Düsseldorf and Hanover, 10,000 in Bremen, Cologne, and Mannheim, and so forth. But the meetings were indoors, with no unfolding campaign of open-air rallies and street demonstrations. There was certainly no thought of a general strike. The SPD avoided directly contesting the public mood of ebullient chauvinism, and this made it easier to demobilize the membership when "peace" turned to "national defense." *Vorwärts* already sounded that note on 30 July, and on 2–3 August the Free Trade Unions and SPD Reichstag group made it official. On 4 August 1914, the party voted unanimously in the Reichstag for the German government's war credits.[4]

Motivations varied. Resignation played a big part, reflecting exaggerated fears of the Prusso-German state's repressive powers. The leadership refused to risk the organization's accomplishments in all-or-nothing show-downs and dismissed the efficacy of revolutionary actions. Besides, French labor would not reciprocate a German general strike, they thought, a skep-ticism confirmed by the assassination of Jaurès, internationalism's most pas-sionate French defender. With mounting evidence of popular war enthu-siasm, SPD leaders doubted even their own militants' response to an antiwar call. The government's casting of the conflict as a war against tsar-ist aggression was the *coup de grace*. Given the historic connotations of tsarist reaction and Slavic backwardness for the German Left, this gave the SPD positive arguments for joining the patriotic bloc. Of course, this kind of "progressive" justification worked for the French too, allowing them to vilify the Germans. As Haase told a French comrade over lunch in Brussels: "If France alone were involved our attitude would be simple. But there are the Russians. What the Prussian boot means to you the Russian knout means to us."[5]

Beneath the duress lurked ulterior agendas. Most SPD leaders evinced a hardheaded but class-conscious pragmatism, infused with nationalism. They expected a reformist breakthrough once labor had shown its loyalty. As one leading SPD reformist, Eduard David, told the government, "the hundreds of thousands of convinced Social Democrats who are giving their all for the war effort expected some acknowledgement of their own wishes in return."[6] This meant the long-demanded introduction of universal suf-frage in Prussia, plus a package of social reform. For the unions, it meant legally sanctioned collective bargaining and full involvement in running the economy. In short, the wartime emergency promised the lasting basis of the labor movement's acceptance into the nation.

"Purely" nationalist motives were inseparable from this reformist cal-culation. Deserting the fatherland in its hour of danger was a stigma the SPD refused to bear, not least when the aggressor seemed the standard-bearer of European reaction. The summons to national unity was the chance to come in from the cold. For Ludwig Frank, one of the movement's reformist stars, who volunteered in 1914 and died on the Western Front in the first German offensive, this took particularly dramatic form. As he wrote from the front: "Instead of a general strike we are waging a war for the Prussian suffrage." Or, in another of his phrases: "We are defending the fatherland in order to conquer it!"[7]

The case for renouncing revolutionary internationalism in favor of German-bound democratic reform was not new, but wartime allowed such thinking to bloom. Reformists spoke more confidently of converting social democracy into "national democracy," of achieving a "parliamentary dem-ocratic form of government headed by the monarchy."[8] The most forthright advocates had opened contacts with the government in 1914: Eduard Da-vid, Albert Südekum, and Max Cohen-Reuss. With backing from the SPD Executive and Karl Legien, chairman of the Free Trade Unions, they quickly set the tone in parliament and the SPD's public statements. Party discipline was tightened, and left-wing strongholds, like the board of *Vorwärts*, were eventually purged. The logic became clearer as the war wore on. This SPD right adjusted with remarkable ease to Germany's violation of Belgian neutrality and the invasion of France, tacitly abandoning the formula of an antitsarist defensive war. By August 1915, they were opposing the party's initial line of peace without annexations. The SPD adopted a war aims statement, drafted by David, which was indistinguishable from more moderate expansionist programs in the nonsocialist camp.

THE LEFT REGROUPS

Socialists elsewhere matched the Germans in patriotism.[9] In Britain and France, the consensus absorbed them more deeply: Jules Guesde and Marcel Sembat joined the French government on 28 August 1914; six months later three members of the British Labour Party accepted office. Socialists on all sides produced high-sounding justifications. Austrians and Hungarians were defending European culture against eastern despotism; Germans were doing the same, while freeing oppressed peoples from tsarist tyranny; the British and French were defending democracy against the Prussian jackboot. The Jacobin heritage of revolutionary war was adapted for nationalist purposes in France, as was the democratic anathema of tsarism in Germany. In contrast, the Italian Socialists' antiwar stance becomes all the more impressive, despite the PSI's practical passivity after Italian intervention in May 1915. In Russia, a politically reactionary tsarism made it easier for the Left to hold out against the war, whereas Italian Socialists faced similar pressures to their German, French, or British counterparts.

Embracing patriotism came more easily in Britain and France, where longer traditions of parliamentary or republican government allowed the war to be packaged as a defense of democracy against militarism. But for the SPD in Germany, "national defensism" became a route to the same parliamentary ideals. Heavily trade-unionized in its wartime politics, the SPD advanced confidently toward a reformist future, contemptuously dismissing its left-wing critics, while keeping a nervous eye on popular discontent. Across Europe, the Left were simply disarmed by patriotism's apparent universality in 1914. "The workers were swept by an irresistible wave of nationalism," Albert Merrheim later claimed, "and would not have left it to the police to shoot us. They would have shot us themselves." But there was also a sense of historic opportunity, which called on the Left to act. In the words of Leon Jouhaux, the CGT secretary-general: "We must give up the policy of fist-shaking in order to adopt one of being present in the affairs of the nation. . . . We want to be everywhere where the workers' interests are being discussed."[10]

By the autumn of 1914, right-wing socialists were digging themselves into the new nationalist positions. At their Vienna meeting in April 1915 the socialist parties of the Central Powers might speak the rhetoric of national independence and anti-Russian defense, but the German army's march through Belgium had placed the SPD at an acute moral disadvantage, accused by their former comrades in France, Belgium, and Britain of endorsing their government's military aggression. In London on 14 February 1915, all three of the latter parties, plus Socialist Revolutionaries from Russia (neither Bolsheviks nor Mensheviks were invited), waxed eloquent in these denunciations: the war against Germany was a war for democracy, and Germany defeated was democracy saved.

Socialists in the neutral countries attempted mediation. Several initiatives were rapidly hatched—from the United States, Sweden, the Netherlands, Italy, and Switzerland—but to no avail. The efforts at reforging socialist unity caught hold only later with two external events: Woodrow Wilson's peace initiative, begun in December 1916, and the Russian Revolution of February 1917. Feverish activity ensued, as the SPD, western socialists, and the neutral socialist leaders each maneuvered for influence with socialist groupings in Russia. The Dutch, led by Pieter Troelstra, finally bypassed the recalcitrant Belgians and on 15 April 1917 called an international conference in Stockholm under their own name, forming a Dutch-Scandinavian organizing committee on 10 May. All ISB affiliates were invited to attend, including minority factions produced by the war. But whether the Allied socialists would sit down with the Germans remained the crucial question.[11]

Over the same period in Switzerland, an avowedly oppositional, largely unofficial movement sought to recapture national parties from the "social patriots" and reformists. By the spring of 1915, there were indeed signs of a left-wing revival. In Germany, a third of the SPD's parliamentary group now opposed the war credits. Radicals formed the Group International, while moderates ventured into public criticism of the leadership.[12] On May Day in France the Metalworkers' newspaper opposed the war. Meanwhile, international conferences of women and then youth met in Bern, while the Swiss left-socialist journalist Robert Grimm fanned the flames, helped by the Italian party and Russian and Polish exiles. International conferences in the villages of Zimmerwald (September 1915) and Kienthal (April 1916) near Bern were the result.

Zimmerwald was a vital forum of the emergent left, giving rise to the International Socialist Commission (ISC). Psychologically, after the debacle of 1914, its significance was immense, although under wartime conditions it was less clear what could be done. Lenin's answer, at one Zimmerwald extreme, was to demand a new International. But this was a distinctly minority viewpoint, confined to the notoriously fractious Bolsheviks and a few others. The rest, notably the French and Germans, balked at breaking the civil truce. Most delegates couldn't write off their old allegiances. Only a campaign for peace, rather than new revolutionary slogans, they argued, would overcome the workers' demoralization. The main consensus was an amorphous commitment to peace in a revived Second International.[13]

By Kienthal, things had radicalized. The main resolution now attacked the reformist leaderships of the belligerent parties and the passivity of ISB. Originally, it also proposed sanctions: first, the ISB executive should be rebuilt from the nonbelligerent parties; then affiliated parties should expel socialists still holding government office, refuse the war credits, and break the civil truce. This marked a clear leftward shift. Only the French delegates applied a brake, opposing the submitted resolution at every point, while Pavel Aksel'rod, the Menshevik, acted the incorrigible conciliator. Real intransigence came from Lenin's Bolsheviks, who denounced all cooperation with ISB. They couldn't carry the majority, which still shied from a break. But the core of the Zimmerwald Left had grown from 8 to 12, with fluctuating support on particular issues.[14]

What was the Zimmerwald constellation? Most obvious was the prominence of the Russian and east European periphery, which provided the strongest cluster of national parties officially joining Zimmerwald. These included the Bolshevik and Menshevik factions of the Russian Social Democrats, the Latvian party, the Bund, the Social Revolutionaries, the SDKPiL, and the Serb, Romanian, and Bulgarian (Narrow) Social Democrats. The roster was completed by the PPS-Left, the Polish strand of SPD opposition (Rosa Luxemburg, Leo Jogiches, Karl Radek), and the Parisian *Golos/Nashe Slovo* group influential in French antiwar circles. The groundwork was laid by Christian Rakovsky, the Romanian delegate and future Bolshevik, who solidified contacts in Milan, Paris, and Switzerland before uniting the Romanian, Bulgarian, Greek, and Serbian parties into the Revolutionary Balkan Social Democratic Federation, the first internationalist regroupment of the war. Finally, the southern periphery was also key. The Portuguese Socialists affiliated, sending Edmondo Peluso to Kienthal. But the Italian Socialists were the decisive organizational support and the largest western European party to join.

The Swiss Social Democrats were the other major affiliate: though the leadership disavowed Grimm in October 1915, party Congress vindicated him overwhelmingly next month, accepted the Zimmerwald Manifesto, and joined ISC.[15] Otherwise, ISC attracted small oppositional groups in the west: the Tribune Group in Holland; the Social Democratic Youth League in Sweden; the International Socialists of Germany, formed by Julius Borchardt after Zimmerwald, plus the more circumspect Group International; the Committee of International Action formed by French Zimmerwaldians in November 1915; and the British Socialist Party (BSP) and ILP in Britain.

Broader Zimmerwald sympathies were crystallizing in Germany and France. In 1915, the SPD's antiwar opposition reached from the radical Group International to moderates around Haase, Kautsky, and Bernstein, with local pockets in Berlin, Bremen, Stuttgart, and Dresden. Then the SPD majority pushed things to a split: Liebknecht was expelled from the parliamentary group by 60 to 25 votes, whereupon a second radical, Otto Rühle of Dresden, resigned in solidarity. Joined by 18 deputies expelled for voting against the emergency budget, they formed the Social Democratic Working Group inside the existing party. Throughout 1916, left-wing resolutions also advanced in the French SFIO.

How far was there a coherent antiwar position between the extremes of right-wing social democracy and Lenin's revolutionary demand for a split? Did antiwar grievances imply politics that were revolutionary rather than simply "pacifist"? Did opposing the war entail anticapitalist intent? Certainly, linking peace abstractly to the victory of socialism no longer satisfied the Bolsheviks, who wanted a clean break with the Second International. But they rallied only 8 of the 38 Zimmerwald delegates and 12 of the 39 at Kienthal, and the broader left still shied from a break.[16] Yet the main thrust at Zimmerwald was peace, to get the Left moving again; by Kienthal, Lenin's drive for clarity was enlisting the avowed revolutionaries. During 1916, this galvanized the bigger delegations—the Italians, Poles, non-Bolshevik Russians, somewhat the French, and the Spartacists (as Group International became known), the Bremen Left, and International Socialists in Germany. Next, the broader Franco-German parliamentary lefts needed moving too.

These alignments prefigured the revolutionary years 1917–21. The broader antiwar Left often reverted to social democracy during the 1920s Communist-Socialist split. This applied to the Swiss Zimmerwaldians, some of the French, most leading Italians, and most German oppositionists. On the other hand, younger Zimmerwaldians born in the 1880s helped launch the same countries' Communist parties and figured prominently in the Comintern. Polish Zimmerwaldians formed the nucleus of the interwar Polish Communist Party, and continuity from Group International to the German Communist Party was especially strong. Above all, Bolshevik leadership remade itself via Zimmerwald. The future Central Committee of the 1917 Bolshevik Party and leading personalities of the Soviet state descended from the internationalists of 1914–17. Originally heterogeneous, their outlooks were sharpened into focus by Lenin's relentless revolutionary line.

Finally, what was missing from Zimmerwald? First, no big western or central European party was officially present, including the prewar north-central European social democratic core: British Labour, SFIO, the Belgian and Dutch parties, the Scandinavian parties (partly excepting the Norwegian), and German, Austrian, Czech, and Hungarian Social Democrats; only their sectarian rivals and vocal minorities joined the ISC. Second, the tsarist empire's non-Russian nationalities were unrepresented. Latvian and Polish Zimmerwaldians explicitly *rejected* national self-determination, and the Jewish Bund sent no delegates for exactly that reason. None of the national revolutions of 1917–21 in ex-tsarist lands—Finland, Ukraine,

Georgia—ruffled Zimmerwald's surface; nor did those of ex-Habsburg east-central Europe in 1918–19.[17] Third, aside from three American affiliates and the International Socialist League of South Africa, the extra-European world was entirely missing. This contrasted markedly with the global interest aroused by the Russian Revolution and the Third International.

THE RADICALIZATION OF LABOR

Beyond Zimmerwald was a slowly emerging grassroots resentment against the war's privations.[18] Of course, popular politics were severely constricted by wartime conditions. Not only were civil liberties curtailed by emergency regulations but the public climates of civil truce directly attacked dissent. Constraints were as much ideological as police-repressive. An enormous commitment—either moral courage or bravado—was needed to come out publicly against the war. Indeed, many local labor movement institutions responded to the war by positively mobilizing social solidarity. This was especially marked in France, where socialists organized massive social provision for soldiers' families and others in need during 1914–15, offering communal meals and other supports.[19] Even when discontent emerged, the civil truce perpetuated a particular language, taking the idealized patriotic consensus for its common ground.

As the war dragged on, the Left found this a weakness and a strength. Appeals to patriotic community created potential openings for left-wing agitation as well as initially silencing it. In the Right's calculation, war was certainly intended to banish opposition. As Wilhelm II famously declared on 4 August 1914: "I know no more parties; I know only Germans."[20] But this could easily backfire. Patriotic consensus bent not only to the insistent pressure of trade union pragmatists for a reformist payoff but also to popular ideals of social justice. Placing themselves inside the consensus freed working-class advocates to demand a more equitable distribution of the war's burdens, often via militant direct action, secure in the moral justifications that government appeals to common sacrifice delivered. War enthusiasm gave the Left vital leverage once hardships started to pinch, because grievances could employ the very language that official patriotism approved. Class inequities aggravated by the scarceties of the war economy were an obvious ground for populist complaint.

Within a year, working-class hardships tugged on the rhetoric of patriotic sacrifice—as shown by, for example, the food protests in Berlin in the spring of 1915 or the Clydeside rent strikes of May–November 1915. Civil truce couldn't stifle class combativity in the economic sphere. As war continued, the egalitarianism in socialist editorials was matched by broadening working-class resentments of food shortages and the black market, declining real wages and worsening conditions at work, the militarization of the economy and escalating carnage at the front.[21] The gap between government exhortations to common sacrifice and most people's experiences of inequality fueled discontent.

In Germany, the watershed was the summer of 1916. Food shortages brought demonstrations in Düsseldorf, Frankfurt, Kiel, and Hamburg, with extensive rioting elsewhere, especially violent in Leipzig, Worms, Offenbach, Hamborn, and Hamburg. This coincided with the Battle of the Somme and the worst casualties of the war. Antiwar demonstrations by SPD leftists occurred in Dresden, Stuttgart, Braunschweig, and Bremen. At the center were partially spontaneous actions supporting Karl Liebknecht, sentenced to penal servitude in June 1916 for opposing the war. Some 60 percent of workers in 65 Berlin factories (55,000 workers) responded to the strike call of shop stewards in the metalworkers' union, with similar actions in Braunschweig and Bremen.

Behind this activity lay the restructuring of the working class in the war economy. Enormous numbers of men were in the army, which more than doubled in Germany from 5 to 11 million during the war. This not only depressed the industrial workforce but also required massive recruitment of women and youth into previously male industries. By 1918, women workers had risen from 22 to 34 percent of the total. In two years, female labor in German metalworking rose from 7 to 23 percent of the total and in electricals from 24 to 55 percent. In France, a quarter of the war industry workforce was female by 1918, and in the Paris metal industries it was a third. In German mining, iron, steel, metalworking, and chemicals there were six times more women in 1918 than 1913. A similar increase occurred in France, and in Britain the number of women in metals and chemicals grew from 212,000 to 947,000 by November 1918.[22]

Economic mobilization involved comprehensive retooling of the economy. Industries disconnected from the war necessarily suffered. Labor shifted into branches producing directly for the war, whose workforce increased by 44 percent in Germany 1914–18, with "peace" and "mixed" industries declining by 40 and 21 percent, respectively.[23] In tracking labor radicalism, historians have focused on the big conglomerations of war production, such as the German metal and engineering centers of Berlin, the Ruhr, and Stuttgart; the chemicals plants of Leverkusen, Ludwigshafen, and Merseburg; comparable munitions complexes of Vienna, Budapest, Pilsen, and Turin; and the equivalent centers of Britain and France. But in smaller centers of industrial conversion the impact was hardly less intense.

Recruitment for war also involved huge migrations. In Italy, Turin's population grew by one-fourth during 1911–18, doubling its wage-earners from 79,000 to 185,000 (or a third of total population).[24] Other economies couldn't meet their labor needs from the countryside: Britain's alternative source was women, Germany's, conscripted foreigners.[25] It was the interaction of these newcomers with the labor movement's existing traditions that proved explosive. In the most radical centers, an unruly influx of female, young, and unskilled or semiskilled new recruits proved ready "to follow the lead of the highly paid, exempted skilled workers who capitalized upon both their indispensability and their self-conceived role as the vanguard of the working class."[26] Such "war" workers might be relatively protected against conscription and less badly hit by eroding standards of living. But "dilution" by hastily trained new labor threatened the work hierarchies, wage differentials, and craft traditions of the skilled men, the backbone of prewar unions and socialist parties.

In this sense, the war transformed the labor movement's relationship to the overall working class, which was being drastically recomposed. By 1917, 64 percent of German trade unionists were at the front, and SPD membership had plummeted from over a million to only 243,000. Not surprisingly, socialism's most stalwart supporters—nonconscripted skilled men in metalworking—started resenting the civil truce and its effects. Yet they found themselves surrounded by workmates—female, young, untrained—who were the opposite of the stereotypically class conscious. This changing sociology of labor was key for the snowballing grassroots militancy of 1917–18. Neither previously unorganized "new" labor nor politically experienced "old" labor could be contained. Where one lacked the formative loyalties of the movement's pre-1914 traditions, the other felt those traditions damaged by the war economy's needs.

By opening unprecedented access to decision-making in state and industry, the centrally regulated war economy brought genuine gains for union and socialist party leaders. Right-wing socialists expected to parlay their patriotism into reforms by astutely managing organized labor's newfound influence. But shopfloor workers mainly experienced these institutional gains as hardships. Beyond the war's human misery of killing, maiming, and separation and the horrible effects of a long war on living standards, official labor's influence was bought at the expense of the worker's shop-floor needs. If regulating the war economy was perceived as a form of "socialism" by right-wing socialists and union bureaucrats, for the ordinary worker it meant speedups, suspension of factory regulations, lower safety standards, the freezing of basic union rights, and general loss of control.

Thus the socialists' integration into government was matched by rank-and-file alienation. In Britain, for example, national control of the labor supply was achieved via the Treasury Agreement of government and unions in March 1915, greatly toughened by conscription via the Military Service Acts of January–July 1916. For overriding established labor rights and practices in this way, labor leaders certainly secured something in return: a system of military exemption for skilled workers; a framework of industrial conciliation, including the Ministry of Labour, Industrial Unrest Commissions, and the Whitley Committee on Industrial Councils; and postwar promises of social reform. When the Lloyd George Coalition was formed in December 1916, Labour's entry to the Cabinet and the creation of the Ministry of Labour were essential to this political realignment.[27]

This dovetailed with the official labor movement's own reformist hopes, articulated in Britain via the War Emergency Workers' National Committee.[28] Elsewhere in Europe, the state's regulatory actions were more authoritarian, involving rapid militarization of the labor force and tighter controls. This was notably so in Italy, where Central and Regional Committees of Industrial Mobilization administered a draconian system of military discipline in all firms linked to the war effort, subordinating workers to given terms of employment on pain of dismissal, military prison, or dispatch to the front. In the war's last 10 months, 19,018 workers were sentenced to hard labor and another 9,522 to ordinary prison for abandoning their jobs or other infractions, representing some 10 percent of all "military" or "exempted" workers in designated "auxiliary" industries.[29]

So the gains enjoyed by labor's leaderships could be hard for ordinary workers to see. Unions were represented on the Italian Committees of Industrial Mobilization, became heavily involved in arbitration, and acquired the de facto legitimation the British unions gained from managing conscription. But while the Metalworkers' Union (FIOM) and its secretary, Bruno Buozzi, might feel well pleased, they were resented among metalworkers, including the FIOM's own members, who grew from 11,000 to 47,000 during the war. Italian rank-and-file militants turned increasingly against the Mobilization system, organizing via their own Internal Commissions. Here, the promise of labor's integration started generating its opposite—a combative movement of class hostility, stressing the incompatibility of labor's interests with capital. The British version of the Internal Commissions was the shop stewards' movement, spreading from Clydeside in 1915–16 to Sheffield and other centers of munitions. In the words of the Clyde Workers' Committee: "We will support the officials just so long as they rightly represent the workers, but we will act independently immediately if they misrepresent them."[30]

After two years of war, this created big tensions in all national labor movements. The German Patriotic Auxiliary Service Law (December 1916) encapsulated the contradiction. On one side, it was a striking success for the trade union and SPD right. Though aimed originally at full-scale militarizing of labor to channel workers into industries needing them most, the measure was partially stolen by Karl Legien and his fellow socialists as it passed through the Reichstag. It created arbitration boards with union representation, extending potentially to general questions of wages and working conditions. For Legien, this was a decisive gain of union recognition, wrested from government over employers' bitter opposition. It stopped the drainage of union membership. For the SPD right, it was a key fruit of the new collaborative course. Yet the Law deepened unions' complicity in policing their own members. If in practice the job-changing of skilled metalworkers was little reduced, the Law scarcely allayed their grievances. In the depths of the war's worst winter, the leadership's latest patriotic act only widened the gap between the movement's official policies and its rank-and-file desires.[31]

THE BROADENING OF DISCONTENT

By late 1916, a conjunction of factors brought radicalization on a European scale. The cruel hardships of the war, the return of rank-and-file industrial militancy, the regroupment of the revolutionary left at Zimmerwald, and the growth of antiwar politics in the socialist mainstream all brought the patriotic consensuses of 1914 under strain. The dominant grouping still comprised the reformist majorities of most prewar socialist parties, whose leaderships opted for national defense in August 1914. These included not only the parties of the main combatants, with the ambiguous exception of imperial Russia, but also the northern neutrals in Netherlands, Denmark, and Sweden. Exceptions were the parties in Italy, Switzerland, the Balkans, and the territories of the Russian empire, but even there opposing the war didn't prevent strong reformist currents from emerging.

As war dragged on, it grew harder to keep the broadest patriotic consensus together. Opposition grew in the French and German movements during 1916, with an evenly balanced executive at the SFIO's December Congress and the forming of the SPD opposition in March. By early 1917, this had gone further. While none of the German opposition wanted to break with the larger movement and their own past, the SPD leadership left them no choice. The party executive moved against the Left's strongholds and seized control of its newspapers. When the opposition tried to defend themselves against further reprisals, the executive moved for expulsion. A separate party became the only choice, and on 6–8 April 1917 the Independent Social Democratic Party (USPD) was launched.

For the USPD's leaders, the split had more moral than clearly thought-out political grounds. They were moved by distaste for the SPD's collaboration in a war of aggression that was increasingly oppressive for the mass of workers, which compromised the movement's proudest traditions. But it was unclear where the USPD differed from the parent party. By invoking the movement's revolutionary traditions, its leaders implied a mixture of extraparliamentary agitation and parliamentary obstruction and not the full-scale revolutionary politics advocated by Lenin. They were reaffirming the old rather than proclaiming the new; they were the SPD's troubled conscience, calling from a previous era. Like the broad-left oppositions elsewhere—in France, or the national rank-and-file convention called by the British antiwar Left in Leeds in June 1917, or the Italian "maximalism" around Giacinto Serrati—the USPD lacked either a coherent vision or a solid popular organization.

On the extreme left, Zimmerwald's explicitly revolutionary affiliates had more coherent goals but with scarcely more popular backing. To be sure, the small numbers of German Spartacists or the Italian Intransigent Revolutionary Faction could be deceptive, because under wartime conditions the determined vanguardism of a few agitators went a long way.[32] But none of these groups damaged the hold of social democratic traditions on politically conscious workers. The Bremen Left's neosyndicalist orientation toward the shopfloor was more of a break, forming the basis for the shadowy International Socialists of Germany. In Italy, syndicalist traditions converged with the future council communist movement in Turin around the journal *Ordine nuovo,* launched on May Day 1919. But the resonance of such groups was limited. Broadly based popular opposition to the labor movement's reformist leaderships was preempted by the wartime restriction of politics, which strengthened tendencies to sectarian fragmentation.

However, movements of the rank and file were beyond any of these groupings. One barometer was the number of strikes. In Britain, this never dipped as low as on the Continent with the start of the war: in 1915–16, total strikes dropped from 672 to 532 (and from 401,000 strikers to 235,000) but at a level still higher than both the peacetime years 1902–10 and the continental strike rate of the war; and in 1917–18 disputes recovered the immediate prewar levels, from 730 to 1,165 strikes and 575,000 to 923,000 strikers, respectively. Elsewhere in Europe, the decline and resumption of militancy were more dramatic. From the low points of 1914–15, French strikes increased from 314 and 41,000 strikers in 1916 to 696 and 294,000 in 1917, at a level comparable to pre-1914 but with more strikers involved in fewer disputes. The pattern was clearest in Germany, where the abrupt suspension of industrial conflict in August 1914 was followed by a gradual resumption in 1915–16 and a major escalation in the next two years.[33]

The German case showed disputes changing markedly in character: they became more concentrated and more political, mirroring the wartime concentration of the munitions industry, the interlocking of state and industry in the war economy, the growth of popular antiwar feelings, and the crucial absence in wartime of opportunities for political expression. The typical prewar pattern was the localized strike in small and medium-sized firms, dictated by union weakness in the more concentrated sectors of heavy industry, machine-building, chemicals, and electrical engineering. But these were now precisely the expanded sectors of war production manifesting the returning militancy. Wartime conditions also dissolved the boundary between economic and political actions so carefully preserved by the prewar labor movement: in one munitions strike at the Knorr-Bremse works in Berlin-Lichterfelde in April 1917, a mass meeting of 1,050 strikers (some 60 percent of the workforce) listed eminently political demands, including the freeing of Liebknecht and other political prisoners, the removing of restrictions on association and other freedoms, an adequate system of rationing, the lifting of the state of siege, and an end to the war without reparations and annexations.[34]

April–September 1917 saw a rupture in Europe's popular political climate. Without exception, patriotic consensus dissolved. In Britain and France, labor unrest was matched by mutinies in the army.[35] Equally serious, the relentless accumulating of food protests and women's direct actions in Germany made social disorder a daily occurrence, fatally corroding popular belief in the effectiveness of the German state. Since 1914–15, women had protested publicly against shortages, inequalities of distribution, and official corruption, eliciting remarkable responsiveness from government "in a cycle of protest and appeasement that officials could not escape."[36] And by the summer of 1917, popular patience was exhausted, as the imperial state's centralized machinery failed to surmount the effects of shortages, inefficiency, and the Allied blockade. Women's food actions now fused with industrial militancy—itself borne increasingly by women—to challenge public authority.

These everyday struggles over food and distribution of the war's material burdens, with their practical logic of negotiation and empowerment, gave decisive impetus to popular opposition. While the German government trumpeted patriotic solidarity via egalitarian rhetorics of sacrifice, participation, and community, actual inequalities stoked an angry new politics centered around the female citizen-consumer. When the "food dictatorship" failed to handle the hardships of the disastrous "turnip winter" of 1916–17, government credibility was profoundly shaken. The failure of Georg Michaelis, first as provisioning commissar in February 1917 and then as chancellor from July to November, signaled "the end of trust in the competence, good faith, and legitimacy" of the state. In Berlin, the gulf between government and people widened: "In so far as civil society remained intact, it was outside any relationship or obligation to the state, except an inimical one. The state no longer had any right to call upon [Berlin's] residents for anything."[37]

A similar crisis of the state exploded in Italy, where Socialists were jolted from antiwar passivity on 21–28 August by a popular uprising in Turin, provoked by a breakdown of bread supplies. The city's working class confronted the state's armed power, throwing up barricades before being beaten into defeat. Generated from below, this rising immediately galvanized local and national PSI radicals, while the attendant repression dramatized divisions between reformists and radicals in the movement.[38] As in Berlin, food protests led by women drove radicalization along, converging with industrial militancy that was likewise borne by women. Female workers were recruited in Italy in ever-growing numbers from late 1916; they composed a majority of strikers the following year and 21.9 percent of Italy's workforce by 1918. Direct actions were massed and violent: "shops were looted, tramlines torn up and the trams burnt . . . barricades constructed, telephone and telegraph wires cut, and town halls attacked."

Proximate causes were "lack of bread . . . low wages . . . cost of living . . . departure of soldiers . . . [and] punishment of workers." But actions were "always against the war and for peace."[39]

Mass actions also hit Austria, rolling through a series of strikes—in Donawitz at the end of March 1917, on the railways in late April, in Vienna's industrial quarters in May, and in St. Pölten, Fohnsdorf, Knittelfeld, and Graz during June–July. The same synergy recurred: food actions and strikes; collapse of belief in government; angry disavowals of Socialist and union officials. In Germany, massive protests exploded in the spring: a metalworkers' strike on 16–23 April, mainly in Berlin (some three hundred thousand workers in some three hundred plants) and Leipzig (30,000 workers) but with further outbreaks in Braunschweig, Dresden, Halle, Hanover, Magdeburg, and elsewhere. Reduced bread rations precipitated broader political demands, sharpened into an antigovernment challenge by the nascent shop stewards' movement and the freshly founded USPD. Actions continued into the summer. In the Münster military district covering the Ruhr, authorities reported 22 separate disputes between 22 June and 5 July, from a three-day strike of miners at Westhausen near Dortmund to a large-scale walkout of 3,500 at Düsseldorf *Rheinmetall*.[40]

While owing much to left-wing activists, this popular anger crystallized its own organization. The Clyde Workers' Committee of 1915 and national shop stewards' movement presaged this in Britain, followed by Berlin and Leipzig metalworkers' actions in April 1917. But huge central European munitions strikes in January 1918 gave the real push. A million workers in Vienna and Lower Austria, Upper Austria, Styria, and Budapest struck for general economic and political demands against the war (14–22 January), followed by week-long nationwide actions in Germany (28 January), with half a million workers in Berlin and perhaps 4 million overall. This was not only the largest mass protest of the war; it was the largest strike movement in Austrian and German working-class history. When the strike receded, it left in place a permanent organization, the Berlin Committee of the Revolutionary Shop Stewards.[41]

These mass actions of 1917 came to a head *before* the Bolshevik revolution of October. Whatever role the Bolsheviks played for the rest of Europe in 1918–19, before October 1917 the German, Italian, and Austrian movements were setting their own pace. Yet the February events in Russia had an enormous impact on the climate elsewhere, releasing previously pent-up desires for a democratic peace. They rendered the original Austro-German socialist justification for the war—a necessary defense against tsarist reaction—nugatory. Accordingly, it is to the impact of the Russian Revolution that I must now turn.

Chapter 8

The Russian Revolution

ON 27 FEBRUARY 1917, as agitation escalated in the Petrograd streets, public order collapsed. Women from the textile mills and bread lines supplied the drive, urging each other forward until three hundred thousand workers joined a citywide general strike. Troops mutinied. Workers and soldiers commanded the streets. Tsar Nicholas II provided no lead but suspended the Duma and State Council. By nightfall, the Duma had taken procedure, if nothing else, into its hands, forming the Temporary Committee for a new government. Earlier, workers and soldiers had invaded the Duma's home in the Tauride Palace, where they revived the Petrograd Workers' Soviet, whose 50 days in October–December 1905 symbolized the popular legacy of the 1905 revolution. So when the Temporary Committee finally appointed the Provisional Government of 10 liberal ministers, on 1 March 1917, it was sharing not just the Tauride Palace but the exercise of sovereignty. The Provisional Government was formed in consultation with the Soviet's Executive, and together they created the joint Military Commission to keep public order. The tsar, abdicating on 2 March, was gone. But no undivided authority took his place.[1]

This was the famous "dual power." While the Provisional Government sought future legitimacy from a parliamentary constitution, the Soviet claimed the rougher and more immediate legitimacy of the streets. Demanding democratizion of the army while raising an unmistakable note of class war, the Soviet proclaimed its military authority. Real power—"the power to call people into the streets, defend the city, make things work or

139

fall apart"—lay with the Soviet, not the government.[2] And this institutional separation was matched by social polarization: between the privileged society of the propertied classes and the egalitarian hopes of the people.

DUAL POWER: THE DYNAMICS OF RADICALIZATION

Initially, this division ran conveniently between Right and Left, pitting the moderate liberalism of the Provisional Government against the socialisms of the Soviet. The Government would organize elections and a constituent assembly, establish the rule of law, and generally implement the "bourgeois revolution"; the Soviet would handle practical administration and secure the strongest benefits for the working class in the parliamentary system now to be created. The two would march separately in the same direction.

Popular hopes, however, outpaced the limited goals the Soviet's early leadership set for the revolution. The peasantry needed immediate land reform; workers wanted a say in the economy. Workers also expected soviets to be institutionalized in the constitution, in a way hard to square with a parliamentary system. More important, the "national defensism" advocated by the Soviet Executive was out of step with the people's mood. On the factory floor, in the streets, and among the soldiers, attitudes were cut and dried: end the war and bring the armies home.

Social polarization rapidly exploded the political framework of bourgeois revolution. Instead of responding to pressure from below, the Soviet's leaders entrenched behind avowedly moderate goals. After the Miliukov crisis in April 1917, leading socialists joined the coalition to broaden its base, only to suffer the inevitable burden of its failures.[3] In theory, the Left's new portfolios—ministries of labor, agriculture, food supply, posts and telegraphs, justice, and war—gave ample scope for revolutionary initiative. But the new incumbents were hamstrung by limited readings of the revolution's potential, while even modest reforms remained blocked. Just as popular opinion turned against the Provisional Government, therefore, moderate socialists became inveigled into defending its policies, disastrously compromising their popular credentials. Herein lay the true key to the April crisis, the unresolved "problem of dual authority, social polarization, and the revolution's future goals and direction."[4]

April–October 1917 was a story of escalating contradictions. Popular expectations outgrew the government's intentions on every front; and as Russian society mobilized, the government's capacity dwindled. By simply seizing the lands, peasants indicted its dissembling over land reform. When the government failed to bring peace, it lost the loyalty of the troops. The June military offensive was a disaster. Morale collapsed. Popular demonstrations followed on 18 June, with massive disorders on 3–5 July, the July

Days. The Kornilov rising of 25–28 August, a counterrevolutionary coup by the recently appointed commander-in-chief, was defeated by working-class resistance, with a resurgence of popular revolutionary hopes and further damage to government. Most of all, amid general economic collapse, the honeymoon of workers and employers expired. Organized workers increasingly assumed practical control through factory committees and the Soviet's coordination. On all three fronts—land, army, and industry—pressure for resolving dual power in favor of the Soviet reached a crescendo.

Following the April crisis, the group consistently urging that resolution was the Bolsheviks. Immediately after February, the Bolsheviks had joined other socialists in loose coalition around the Soviet. But with Lenin's return from exile on 3 April, this abruptly changed. Next day, he read his "April Theses" to a mixed socialist audience and urged for the first time pushing the revolution into a socialist stage: "The peculiarity of the current moment in Russia consists in the transition from the first stage of the revolution, which gave power to the bourgeoisie as a result of the insufficient consciousness and organization of the proletariat, to its second stage, which should give the power into the hands of the proletariat and poorest strata of the peasantry." The present regime would never end the war, implement reform, and restore economic life. A new state was needed: "Not a parliamentary republic—a return to that from the Soviet of Workers' Deputies would be a step backward—but a republic of Soviets of Workers', Poor Peasants', and Peasants' Deputies throughout the country, growing from below upwards." The economy would be reorganized by nationalizing land, converting large estates into model farms, creating a single national bank, and taking production and distribution into soviet control. This would ignite revolutions in the advanced capitalist countries of western Europe. Bolsheviks should campaign for this among the workers until a Soviet majority was secured. An insurrection to seize power could then be launched.[5]

Lenin's audience listened in disbelief. On 8 April, the party's Petrograd committee rejected his Theses by 13 votes to 2, with one abstention. It was only after intensive persuasion that majorities swung around: first in the Bolshevik Petrograd City Conference (14–22 April) and then in the All-Russian Party Conference immediately following. Debates centered on dual power. For Lenin, this could only be transitional, inherently conflict ridden. Victory of one authority over another was unavoidable: "There cannot be two powers in the state."[6] The Bolsheviks should effect transfer of sovereignty to the Soviet, which could then supervise the revolution's second stage. But for Lenin's opponents, this was adventurist. The bourgeois revolution had not run its course. Russia was not ripe for immediate transition to socialism. The Soviet could exercise "the most watchful control" over the Provisional Government but certainly not overthrow it. The debate was settled decisively in Lenin's favor. Henceforth, the slogan "All Power to the Soviets" sharply divided Bolsheviks from the other Left.

By June–July, popular frustration was turning into class anger. The July Days provided frenetic impetus: the first real crackdown against popular militancy also loosened upper-class inhibitions, exciting popular fears of a counterrevolution—an anxiety soon vindicated by Kornilov's abortive coup. The economy deteriorated to nearly systemic collapse. Workers experienced this as inflation-driven pressure on real wages, factory shutdowns, shortages, and government ineffectuality—which they increasingly attributed to "bourgeois" interests. Over the summer, economic crises became linked in the popular imagination to capitalist "sabotage." Employers' impatience with revolutionary militancy gave grist to this mill. A notorious statement to the Trade and Industrial Society on 3 August by the leading Moscow financier and industrialist Pavel Riabushinskii brought class enmity to a head: "It will take the bony hand of hunger and national destitution to grasp at the throat of these false friends of the people, these members of various committees and soviets, before they will come to their senses."[7]

For socialists advocating national unity, social polarization had disastrous effects. But as the only group untainted by the Provisional Government's drift, the Bolsheviks rode it into power. When the First All-Russian Congress of Soviets convened in early June, Bolsheviks were still weaker than Mensheviks and Social Revolutionaries (105 delegates, as against 248 and 245, in a total of 822). But June–July worked compellingly in their favor. Kornilov's defeat was the final increment of radicalization. The Petrograd and Moscow Soviets voted the Bolshevik program, their executives passing quickly under Bolshevik control. The party's membership confirmed this ascent: in February, it numbered only 2,000 in Petrograd and 600 in Moscow, but by October the figures were 60,000 and 70,000, in a national total of 350,000.[8] With the government paralyzed, the other socialists compromised, the masses keyed for action, and the Soviet apparatus firmly under Bolshevik control, the seizure of power, on the night of 24–25 October 1917, proved relatively simple.

MENSHEVISM IN 1917: REVOLUTION BY THE BOOK

Russian events exercised decisive influence on the Left elsewhere, stamping its image of what a socialist revolution should be, positively or negatively. One view saw the pathology of backwardness. Tsarism suffered beneath the contradictions of modernization and collapsed from the added strains of war. In the resulting chaos, power fell to the group ruthless enough to impose its will. In anti-Communist versions, centralism became the logical expression of Bolshevik ideology, with Lenin as villain-in-chief. It descended from the Jacobin dictatorship via the insurrectionary vanguardism of nineteenth-century conspiratorial traditions. That lineage, severed by

Western social democracy, had a second life under Russian conditions. The key to Bolshevik success, accordingly, was the model of the tightly disciplined party of professional revolutionaries Lenin presented in *What Is to Be Done* (1902), allowing manipulation of the masses via superior organization.[9] Russian backwardness plus Bolshevik centralism fundamentally distinguished the situation from the West.[10]

In certain respects, Russian circumstances followed the West. Despite the unaltered repressiveness of tsarist rule, in 1914 "social patriotism" was certainly not missing from the Russian scene. Plekhanov called for national defense: unless German militarism was stopped, European freedoms would be extinguished, retarding socialism's chances by decades. This entailed all the compromises of right-wing socialists in Britain, France, and Germany, made all the nastier by imperial Russia's reactionary character. It placed Plekhanov and his cothinkers against the very movement they had worked to create. Plekhanov embraced this contradiction with shocking enthusiasm: "If I were not old and sick I would join the army. To bayonet our German comrades would give me great pleasure."[11]

The real test of the civil truce in imperial Russia would be the openings toward trade union recognition and parliamentary reform promised by the war. Early on, there was reason to hope.[12] Two-thirds of the Duma joined a group from the State Council in the Progressive Bloc, which in late August 1914 gave the tsar a program of national unity. This requested minimal liberalizing of the cabinet: clemency for political and religious offenders; relaxing of police measures; Jewish emancipation; concessions to Poles, Ukrainians, and Finns; equality of rights for peasants; geographical extension and legal strengthening of the zemstvos. This would ground imperial government in what existed of Russian civil society, in a rudimentary step towards social consensus. The Petrograd War Industries Committee also had limited representation for labor: 10 workers out of 150 members, indirectly elected from factories of over 500 workers. This created the usual dilemmas of participation for the Left, compounded by the continued illegality of trade unions, the vehicles of corporatism in the West. The Bolsheviks boycotted. The Mensheviks, in contrast, were divided: the proboycott Secretariat in Exile was opposed by sections in Petrograd.

Unattainable under tsarism, democracy to strengthen working-class rights was the Menshevik goal for the revolution. The February Revolution conformed exactly to Menshevik theory: tsarism collapsing from its own immobility, via rising popular pressure and upper-class exasperation. "Society"—public institutions, bureaucratic and capitalist modernizers, the forces of the Progressive Bloc—had invited the tsar to broaden the autocracy's base; he refused; so prewar polarization of state and society resumed. Political revolution became essential to free the way for modernizing. For Mensheviks, this would liberate the potential for capitalism, with all the liberal reforms—constitutional, legal, social, economic—connoting capitalism's rise in the West. The Left would be the democratic watchdog in this bourgeois revolution. It could *not,* in the minds of most Mensheviks, push forward to socialism.

This Menshevik reading was perfectly consistent with the Second International's main traditions and indeed mirrored reactions to the February Revolution in the social democratic parties of northern Europe. Second International Marxism reflected powerfully deterministic readings of capitalist accumulation and crisis, after all: capitalism would experience escalating structural crises via its own laws of development, reaching a final moment of revolutionary collapse. This encouraged social democrats into both fatalism and certainty. Their parties sought maximum democracy in the existing system, for both short-term reforms and the best positioning when capitalism fell. Like the evolutionist determinism, this parliamentary model implied a peaceful transition to socialism, not barricade revolutions like 1789 or 1848. The pre-1914 tradition stressed building the movement by national organization. Where capitalist societies acquired parliamentary and local government institutions, parties should use them for legal propaganda and practical work.

This was the politics Mensheviks pursued. If the 1917 revolution was a bourgeois revolution, then a broadly based legal labor movement was needed, with political and trade union arms, and the social and cultural resources to carry labor's cause through the ensuing capitalist transformations. Because of Russia's backwardness, and the bourgeoisie's pusillanimity, the working class would be thrust to the fore. But it could not force things prematurely toward socialism. This Menshevik view required what Kautsky called "masterly limitation"—an activist politics, even leadership of revolutionary coalitions, but observing the limits history imposed: "To how great an extent socialism can be introduced must depend upon the degree of ripeness which the country has reached. . . . [A] backward country can never become a pioneer in the development of socialist form."[13] The Left should facilitate conditions for socialist possibilities to ripen— uprooting backwardness and traditionalism, while preparing the ground for capitalism. When Russian capitalism had matured, perhaps several generations later, the working class could seize its inheritance.

Principled and realistic as an assessment of Russia's existing developmental resources, this strategy remained doctrinaire, abysmally fitted for the popular mobilization of 1917. The one, Menshevik sense of responsibility before History, militated directly against the other, Menshevik responsiveness to popular radicalism. Mensheviks found themselves constantly trying to hold popular hopes back, within the bourgeois revolution's normative limits. This applied par excellence to the Soviet. In theory, dual power allowed socialists both to pursue immediate working-class interests and to toughen the bourgeoisie's resolution, but without overstepping the revolution's structural limits. But in practice, the working-class movement could never confine itself to a watchdog role. It was drawn ineluctably into ever greater responsibility for the government per se, not least because liberal failures were so dire.

This trapped Mensheviks into a debilitating logic of incorporation. National defensism was a disastrous policy, because the masses were demanding peace. The economy ensnared Mensheviks in the same way. In the factories, city administrations, and economy at large, working-class leaderships in the soviets, unions, and factory committees were drawn ever further into managing the chaos. In 1917, strengthening the working class under capitalism meant taking responsibility for capitalism's problems, and this carried working-class hopes past the limits Mensheviks set for the revolution. The way out was a countervailing logic of popular democratic leadership, where the Left took full responsibility by ditching the liberals and forming an exclusively socialist government. But this was the leap most Mensheviks would never make. It was the soviets and factory councils—an emergent infrastructure of working-class self-administration—that were assuming the tasks of social organization and economic management in 1917. Willy-nilly, the Mensheviks acknowledged this by accepting responsibility for government between April and October. But they never drew the further conclusions. They continued substituting for the social force—the liberal bourgeoisie—they believed the rightful bearer of the revolution.[14]

BOLSHEVISM: MAKING THE REVOLUTION

For Bolshevism in 1917, social polarization was the key. This was a dual process: the autocracy's *political* isolation was increasingly overburdened by a deepening *social* gap inside the antitsarist camp between "privileged" and "unprivileged," the "propertied" and the "people." Even as political society coalesced into an antitsarist opposition, the working class pulled away from the privileged sectors into generalized confrontation with respectable society. Moreover, the new militancy's "workerist" mentalities threatened to maroon moderate socialists on the wrong pole of this developing confrontation. This made 1912–14 very different from the buildup to the 1905 revolution, when a broad front of the intelligentsia embracing liberals, Marxists, and Populists alike had spoken for the people. By 1914, working-class militancy disordered the simplicity of that earlier antitsarist confrontation.[15]

Initially, workers seemed open to cooperation, in an exchange of reform for productivity, ratified by a 10 March accord introducing the eight-hour day, factory committees, and the Central Conciliation Board, drawn equally from Petrograd employers and the Soviet. Strikes slowed, while workers focused on the political arena and other forms of protest. Ritual "cartings-out" from the workplace, petitions, demonstrations, and attacks on unpopular officials were aimed more at rectifying abuses and affirming community values than at stopping production or questioning managerial prerogatives.[16] It was the failure to end the war that prevented this *modus vivendi,* and by extension the politics of coalition, from stabilizing. Bitterly frustrated antiwar feelings undermined the prospects, not least through the mass presence of a vocal and discontented soldiery, numbering a quarter of a million in Petrograd alone.

In April–October 1917, a graduated radicalization occurred in the scale, forms, and content of working-class unrest. The July Days marked the transition from the politics of revolutionary unity to a more class-divided discourse, in which the government's priorities lurched toward law and order, while employers and workers resumed their mutual suspicions. In the Trade-Industrialist conference of 3 August, its president Riabushinskii denounced the socialists in the government as "a pack of charlatans" hindering the politics of bourgeois stabilization; and by October, after the Kornilov fiasco, amidst ever-worsening economic disintegration, and with the Petrograd and Moscow Soviets now under militant control, workers responded in kind. In September–October they struck in vast numbers with far more violence, arresting and abusing managers and owners, blocking the movement of materials and goods, forming Red Guards, and seizing factories. Street actions over food shortages escalated.[17] The politics of social polarization had resumed.

Bolshevism rose to power by organizing this popular radicalization. Bolshevik success is often reduced to superior organization—in the model of the disciplined, monolithic, highly centralist party of professional revolutionaries ascribed to Lenin's *What Is to Be Done?* of 1902. Yet from the moment of Lenin's return to Petrograd, Bolshevik strategy evolved through disagreements, whether around Lenin's April Theses, in the confusion of the July Days, or in Lev Kamenev's and Grigory Zinoviev's opposition to the seizure of power.[18] This atmosphere of debate belies the stereotypical image of the vanguard party. In any case, the conditions of political life in these months, the activist volatility of the masses, and the flooding of the Petrograd party by tens of thousands of workers and soldiers unaware of the esoteric debates of 1902–14 about organization, rendered the fantasy of a ruthlessly disciplined cadre party absurd. The Bolsheviks' success derived from their consistent nonparticipation in the government, which gave them access to the revolutionary counterlegitimacy of the Soviet. Unlike their rivals, for whom popular turbulence threatened the revolution's orderly progress, they wanted to drive the popular movement forward.

Lenin's belief that workers would displace the bourgeoisie as the revolution's leading force came from the idea of "combined and uneven development." A crushingly backward society, Russia entered a Europe already dominated by advanced capitalist economies. This gave Russia access to foreign capital, new technologies, and the latest managerial expertise, capitalist industry's most modern characteristics. But they were grafted onto the worst aspects of backwardness, from a reactionary political structure to a hopelessly underdeveloped civil society and a vast peasant majority. Because Russian capitalism developed from state intervention and foreign capital, rather than "organically" from indigenous enterprise, Russia's bourgeoisie remained weak. In contrast, because of its physical and economic concentration, the Russian proletariat was exceptionally strong. This enhanced working-class cohesion, boosted class consciousness, and gave workers central political importance.

So far, little separated this from Menshevism. Two factors allowed Lenin—and Trotsky, the argument's earlier pioneer—to claim that workers themselves could seize power. First, the dynamics of working-class mobilization left the revolutionary party no choice; workers would always demand socialist measures, and any party seeking to hold them back would be swept aside. Second, the global process of uneven and combined development delivered the material conditions for this course. As Trotsky said: "it is possible for the workers to come to power in an economically backward country sooner than in an advanced country."[19] The surrounding backwardness of Russian society and the bourgeoisie's political weakness, plus Moscow's and Petrograd's disproportionate primacy as political, administrative, and cultural capitals where workers were also concentrated, gave the working class a political capacity beyond its numbers. Thus, "the numbers, the concentration, the culture, and the political importance of the industrial proletariat" determined its leading role. This was the theory of "permanent revolution."[20]

Yet, however "advanced" in itself, the working class was still a minority in an overwhelmingly peasant country. For Lenin, revolution in the countryside complemented workers' mobilization in the towns. This meant not only commitment to land reform but also to its immediate implementation, which neither the Mensheviks nor Socialist Revolutionaries (SRs) could accept. This was the worst failure of the non-Bolshevik Left. Under a decree of 21 April 1917, land committees were preparing agrarian reform, but government intransigently deferred action. Bolsheviks demanded transfering the land immediately to the peasants, without compensation, and without waiting for the Constituent Assembly. Lenin's commitment to the poor peasant, formulated after 1905, was prominently displayed in the April Theses. It was voiced consistently during 1917. In late August, he took the "model decree" of the SRs (compiled from 242 demands from the All-Russian Peasants' Congress in May) and stitched it to the Bolsheviks' anticapitalist program. He endorsed peasant land seizures, and the Bolshevik government's first two acts on 26 October—the decree on peace, the decree on land—were a ringing validation of the previous nine months' frustrated peasant aspirations.[21]

This propeasant orientation shouldn't be overstated. Bolshevism had no members beyond the towns. It had no practical, visible presence in the countryside. Lenin's own thinking on agrarian policy went through many turns, before and during 1917. However positive Bolshevik attitudes to the peasantry were during the revolution, the later 1920s were a different story. Yet in 1917 itself, their record was singular. They alone took the peasants seriously.[22] Even more, Lenin grasped the dynamics of radicalism in the countryside. In this, the Bolsheviks sharply departed from the socialist tradition. Second International socialists rarely troubled themselves with the peasantry. Even when social democrats were supported by the peasantry, as in Menshevik Georgia in 1905–21, they misrecognized this sociology.[23] Given this blind spot, Lenin's opening of Bolshevik politics to the agrarian question was crucial for the party's popular legitimacy in 1917.

Bolsheviks also grasped the importance of soviets. Despite his critique of workers' spontaneity in *What Is to Be Done?* Lenin saw immediately the Soviet's significance in October 1905: on their own initiative, workers had fashioned a new revolutionary democracy. The soviet became the primary arena for revolutionaries to intervene, and Lenin's slogan of "All Power to the Soviets" identified Bolshevik strategy. Whatever Lenin's personal sincerity, it was in the soviets—and the factory councils, where Bolsheviks won their earliest elections in 1917—that Bolshevism secured its democratic credentials. Crucially, the Petrograd Soviet's newly created Military Revolutionary Committee also organized the seizure of power in October, rather than the Bolsheviks acting in their own name. Soviet democracy provided the legitimacy that carried the Bolsheviks into power.

Less appealing was Lenin's belief in splitting—his drive for polemical clarification, brutally distancing his rivals. Accentuating differences typified his *modus operandi,* both in the original Bolshevik-Menshevik split of 1903 and the intense politicking of 1907–14.[24] It also described Zimmerwald, where he aimed to split the Second International and create an alternative revolutionary center. It was a well-honed strategy by 1917, stressing noncooperation with Mensheviks and SRs from the start, freeing Bolshevism's revolutionary mandate in October from the government fiascos of the previous six months. This was also Lenin's willingness to exercise power given the chance, his absolute determination to seize the revolutionary moment. In contrast, Mensheviks made almost a virtue out of hesitancy. They held their imagination back, tethered to the limits of the bourgeois revolution. But when Tsereteli famously insisted at the All-Russian Soviet Congress in June 1917 that no party was willing to say: "Give the power into our hands, go away, we will take your place," Lenin defiantly contradicted him from the hall.[25] This was a powerful unity of conviction and action, the certainty that revolution could be made to happen. It made the Bolshevik Party's accelerating popular momentum in July–October a magnet for all the revolution's frustrated activism.

In Bolshevik internationalism, pragmatism met conviction. Lenin's internationalist imperative came from his analysis of capitalism in its monopoly and imperialist phase—his belief that capitalism exhausted its progressive potential by needing to expand on a world scale, with resulting exploitation of the underdeveloped world and sharpening of contradictions in the metropolis. National liberation movements in underdeveloped countries would upset the process of imperialist accumulation, he argued, undermine prosperity in the capitalist economies, and trigger renewed popular militancy. Capitalist concentration had meanwhile brought the productive forces to their fullest potential, leaving the economy's commanding heights ripe for socialization. Finally, the war and the great powers' intensified competition had accentuated all these conditions, with explosive consequences for any power that was defeated. As Lenin said, "the war has given an impetus to history which is now moving with the speed of a locomotive."[26] As "the weakest link in the imperialist chain," tsarist Russia was especially vulnerable to the destabilizing effects, particularly as imperial society buckled under the war's strain.

This internationalist perspective functioned in a particular way. It countered Menshevik belief that Russian backwardness precluded the building of socialism. Such objections had long pedigrees among socialists, and when Lenin's April Theses proposed moving directly to socialist revolution many Bolsheviks also balked. Socialism could not be built from scarcity, only from material abundance, once capitalism had released the forces of progress: "Whence will arise the sun of the socialist revolution? I think that with all existing conditions, with our standard of living, the initiation of the socialist revolution does not belong to us. We have not the strength, nor the objective conditions, for it."[27]

Neither Lenin nor Trotsky disputed this as such. Indeed, Trotsky added a further dimension: "the real obstacle to the implementation of a socialist program . . . would not be economic so much—that is, the backwardness of the technical and productive structures of the country—as political: the isolation of the working class and the inevitable rupture with its peasant and petty-bourgeois allies."[28] But here, internationalism supplied a solution, via sympathetic revolution in the West. Problems would disappear in the larger context of a federated socialist Europe: the more advanced economies delivered the missing developmental resources, compensating the proletariat's Russian isolation with the international solidarity of broader-based workers' states to the west. This was vitally enabling for the Bolsheviks: if seizing power was to be justified before the court of history, revolution in the West had to occur. Lenin and Trotsky entered the October Revolution with this explicit realization. Otherwise, Menshevik taunts of adventurism were much harder to dispel.

These, then, were the main ingredients of Bolshevik success: a sharper grasp of specifically Russian conditions, embracing precocity as well as backwardness; advocacy for the peasantry; the Soviet's institutional centrality; activist demarcation against the other Left parties; and a global analysis of the overall European situation, bringing confidence in the prospects of sympathetic revolution in the West. Other factors were important too, including the personalities of Lenin and Trotsky. But it was above all the combination of relentless activism and remarkable clarity of perspective, under conditions of soaring popular radicalism and extreme social polarization, that brought the Bolsheviks to power.

FROM DUAL POWER TO DICTATORSHIP OF THE PROLETARIAT

After the October Revolution, political concentration was rapid and extreme. Once the Bolsheviks seized power, their relations with other left groupings became crucial. The Mensheviks and SRs seceded from the Second All-Russian Soviet Congress on 25 October. They formed the All-Russian Committee for the Salvation of the Country and the Revolution, preparing a rising to join the expected attack on the capital by General Petr Krasnov and his Cossacks. Krasnov was easily beaten on 29–30 October, but this gave the Bolsheviks grounds to sever talks and tighten discipline in their own ranks. The Left SRs now broke decisively with their party, refused to join the walkout of 25 October, endorsed the Bolshevik seizure of power, and on 15 November joined the Bolsheviks in coalition.

Conflicts hinged on the issue of legitimacy and the revolution's fundamental definition, "bourgeois-democratic" or "proletarian-socialist," now centering on the soviets. The Bolshevik rising was deliberately timed for the opening of the Second All-Russian Congress of Soviets, and once the original soviet leaders had gone, nothing could stop popular militancy flowing through this framework. As the Bolsheviks desired, political choices were being polarized. On one side was the formal legitimacy conferred by the imminent Constituent Assembly and the parliamentary system advocated by the Provisional Government; on the other was the new revolutionary legitimacy of the soviets. In ostentatiously leaving the Soviet Congress, the Mensheviks and Right SRs left no doubt where their allegiance lay. This destroyed all chances for giving the new regime a nonpartisan socialist basis. The Bolshevik rising commanded powerful support, especially with militants in the army and factories. But, equally, there were strong unity sentiments for a coalition of all socialists, providing it was antibourgeois. This was the potential the Mensheviks and Right SRs fatally squandered. As the Menshevik Nikolai Sukhanov later conceded, "we completely untied the Bolsheviks' hands, making them masters of the entire situation and yielding to them the whole arena of the revolution."[29]

Thus the Constituent Assembly was already delegitimized even before the elections of 12 November 1917. In those elections, returns were good for the SRs—410 seats out of 707, as against the Bolsheviks' 175. But the Bolsheviks' other rivals were erased. Bolsheviks carried the towns, with 36 percent of the vote in provincial capitals, as against 23 percent for Kadets, the sole surviving bourgeois party, and 14 percent for SRs. The political alignment, with urban allegiances concentrated around Bolsheviks and Kadets, now directly registered the social polarization. While SRs held some ground, it was paltry compared with the summer, and the Mensheviks were completely wiped out.[30]

As the Left's dominant party in the cities, the Bolsheviks throve on the still evolving urban radicalization. The gap between Bolshevik leadership in the soviets and their weaker standing in the Constituent Assembly left them undismayed. When the Assembly convened on 5 January 1918, they corrected the imbalance by dissolving it. This was consistent with the slogan "All Power to the Soviets" and the logic of urban popular loyalties. To legitimize the closing of the Constituent Assembly, the Bolsheviks called not only a third All-Russian Congress of Soviets (after those in June and October 1917) but also an All-Russian Congress of Peasants' Deputies, for mid-January 1918. The founding document was its "Declaration of Rights of the Toiling and Exploited Peoples," drafted on 3 January, adopted by the All-Russian Soviet Congress on 15 January, and inscribed in the new Constitution in July. The worker-peasant axis was central here, but the self-presentation of the Bolsheviks themselves—the revolutionary élan of Bolshevik political culture—was unambiguously proletarian. Adapting this self-understanding to the needs of a worker-peasant alliance became a crucial issue in the further course of the revolution.

Other problems were looming. How to institutionalize the direct democracy of the Soviets and factory committees was one. Pluralism—how to deal with organized opposition—was another. The question of nationalities, flagged in the Declaration of the Rights of the Toiling and Exploited Peoples, was still another. Each goes to the heart of the relationship of socialism and democracy. The salient theme was the turn from parliamentary to soviet democracy, a decisive break, whose only forerunner in the social democratic tradition of the first two Internationals was the Paris Commune. To the previous ideal of the democratically elected parliamentary majority, Bolshevism counterposed the ominous-sounding formula of the dictatorship of the proletariat. Something important had clearly changed. The All-Russian Soviet Congress greeted the suppression of the Constituent Assembly by singing the *Marseillaise* (the anthem of the French Revolution) as well as the *Internationale* (the anthem of the workers' international), so that the transition from the epoch of the bourgeois to that of the proletarian revolution would be marked.[31]

Chapter 9

Breaking the Mold

of Socialism

Left-Wing Communism,

1917–1923

RUSSIAN EXTREMES CREATED chances for the Left that weren't available elsewhere in Europe. Some wartime circumstances were generic—notably, the labor movement's incorporation via patriotism, bringing gains for leaders but hardships for the rank and file. But in other ways, Russian circumstances were least like the others, because the thinness of civil society left Russia exceptionally vulnerable to generalized breakdown, which the West's more developed institutional resources forestalled. This left a vacuum during 1917, which the highly mobilized working class of Moscow and Petrograd acted to fill. Seizing such chances required a revolutionary imagination, which Lenin, Trotsky, and the Bolsheviks supplied.

Bolshevism broke the mold of the socialist tradition, jolting European Marxists from their fatalism. Socialism was no longer the necessary exit from inevitable capitalist crisis; instead, revolutions could now be made. Not simply the objective result of history's laws, they required a creative political act. For the radicals of European socialist parties, for working-class militants of 1917–18, and for many younger intellectuals fresh to the Left, the Russian Revolution enlarged a sense of political possibility. It created a new horizon. It incited a general sense of movement and opportunity, of pushing on the frontiers of political imagination. For Antonio Gramsci, Lenin was "the master of life, the stirrer of consciences, the awakener of sleeping souls." The Bolsheviks had made "man the dominant factor in history, not raw economic facts—men in societies, men in relation to one another, reaching agreements with one another, developing through these contacts a collective, social will." Russian backwardness was no problem: "The revolutionaries themselves will create the conditions needed for the total achievement of their goal." Revolution was the crucible of opportunity.[1]

Briefly—varying across Europe, but concentrated in 1917–20—the political imagination was unleashed. And before the revolutionary tide ebbed, much had changed. Working-class revolution did not succeed elsewhere, and some national movements experienced crushing defeat. Most movements became bitterly split between surviving socialist parties and new Communist ones. There were also limits to the new politics. Postrevolutionary constitutions were still conceived in parliamentary terms. The new revolutionaries neglected building the coalitions so crucial to the practical survival of revolutionary regimes, given the social, religious and ethnic heterogeneity of all European countries. Even where most ambitious, as in the *Ordine nuovo* group around Gramsci, their cultural politics rarely transcended traditional class-political frameworks, which downgraded the interests of women and other vital questions.[2]

Yet, when the imagination was recalled from the frontier to more prosaic tasks by the uneven stabilization of 1921–23, the landscape was fundamentally transformed. In much of Mediterranean and eastern Europe—in Hungary, Italy, Bulgaria, Spain—stabilization took authoritarian forms, leaving strong radical movements of town and country defeated and underground. But in the prewar central and north European "social democratic core," comprising Austria, Germany, Czechoslovakia, Switzerland, and Scandinavia, together with France, the Low Countries and Britain, the Left was far stronger than before. While in some cases improvement followed the collapse of old imperial regimes amidst revolutionary turbulence and in all others there were large-scale popular pressures, this was no specifically socialist advance. Instead it brought a strengthening of parliamentary democracy, an expansion of workers' rights under the law, further union recognition, the growth of civil liberties, and the beginnings of a welfare state. The enhancement of the public sphere—in parliamentarian, publicistic, and cultural terms—was also a big gain, especially in countries where public freedoms were cramped and harassed before.

To judge the revolutionary years 1917–23 we have to bring this whole picture into view, assessing the limits as well as the strengths of the new politics, precisely what had and had not been achieved. This means assessing the reformist as well as the revolutionary chances—the slow, uneven, and reversible gains of the Left, not just the dramatic bursts of willed revolutionary action.

THE GEOGRAPHY OF REVOLUTION

Outwardly, Bolshevik predictions of general European revolution bore fruit. Signs of a potential revolutionary crisis came with the great strikes of January 1918. Protesting the German handling of peace negotiations with the Bolsheviks at Brest-Litovsk and spreading outward from Vienna and Budapest, these snowballed into massive working-class actions against the war, embracing Berlin and much of Germany, the Czech lands, and Krakow before subsiding.[3] Lack of coordination ultimately blunted the challenge, but the Bolshevik wager on Western antiwar sentiments clearly had some basis. Another dramatic turn of the war—a worsening of popular hardships or military defeat—might bring a less manageable crisis.[4]

It came eight months later in October 1918, with the collapse of the Bulgarian front, the breakup of Austria-Hungary, and imperial Germany's demise. The first act was a sequence of "national revolutions," erecting new republican sovereignties on the ruins of the Habsburg monarchy: first Czechoslovakia (proclaimed on 28 October 1918), followed by Yugoslavia (29 October), "German-Austria" (30 October), Hungary (31 October), Poland (28 October–14 November), and West Ukraine (Eastern Galicia), where the People's Republic was proclaimed on 31 October.[5] These new states, except West Ukraine, which was annexed by Poland in July 1919, secured their constitutional legitimacy, not least via international recognition at the peace conference in Versailles. The chain of republican revolutions was concluded, moreover, with the toppling of the Hohenzollern monarchy and the proclamation of a German Republic on 9 November 1918.

Overall, these events were hardly less imposing than the February revolution in Russia. They carried revolution to the Rhine and the Alps and upturned the sociopolitical order across a massive central European swathe. Like Russian events, the German Revolution reverberated elsewhere. Without evidence of working-class readiness, the Dutch Social Democratic leader Pieter Troelstra quixotically proclaimed the revolution in the Netherlands in two speeches on 11–12 November, with some damage to the SDAP's morale and credibility. German events helped precipitate a crisis in Sweden (10 November–6 December), where only Hjalmar Branting's and the SAP's skill kept the demand for a democratic constitution from spilling into more radical socialist desires. In Switzerland, a long-brewing confrontation between government and the left-moving labor movement was sparked in a general strike on 12–14 November.[6] South of the Alps, Italian Socialists watched German events closely.

Six months of radicalization ensued. The German Revolution reached crisis point with a renewed SPD-USPD split in December 1918, the ill-fated Spartacist Rising in early January, and the murders of Rosa Luxemburg and Karl Liebknecht. Though a bloody defeat, the Left read this as a sharpening of the contradictions, from which revolutionary apocalypse would result. The Third International's launching in a hastily convened congress in Moscow on 4–6 March 1919 dramatized this belief. The period opened by the central European national revolutions seemed one of continuously rising opportunity, in which ever greater initiative devolved to the working class, just as dual power had worked for the Bolsheviks.

This dynamic came through in Hungary. Social Democratic unions were the solid core of Count Michael Karolyi's coalition government of 31 October 1918. With deteriorating economic conditions—demobilization and reconversion of industry, materials shortages, chronic unemployment, and an escalating crisis of production—they became increasingly drawn into managing industry, sowing thoughts of workers' control. Over Christmas, as workers formed councils and red guards, the demand for democratizing industry coalesced. The systematic nationalization program of the new Communist-Socialist government taking office on 21 March 1919 grew logically from these developments. Karolyi had resigned in protest at Hungary's losses at Versailles, but the dialectic of dyarchy—a situation of dual power resembling that in Russia—had given the new regime birth. Its leader, Bela Kun, saw himself as Lenin to Karolyi's Kerensky.[7]

The Hungarian Soviet Republic lasted only four months, from March to August 1919. But coming immediately after the Comintern's foundation and coinciding with Soviet Republics in Bavaria (7 April to 1 May) and Slovakia (16 June to 1 August), it preserved the revolutionary momentum. The main axis was now central European, with a strong leftward shift in Czechoslovakia and violent radicalization in Germany. Spurred by anti-Left repression, German workers were switching from SPD to USPD, whose membership grew from 300,000 to 750,000 between March and November 1919. Revolutionary ferment also spread further afield, through the *Trienio Bolchevista* of 1918–20 in Spain and the *biennio rosso* of 1919–20 in Italy.

The most concentrated European revolutionary agitation was framed by the First and Third Comintern congresses of March 1919 and June 1921. The Second Comintern Congress (July 1920) was the apex, reflecting the Red Army's advance on Warsaw in the Soviet-Polish War.[8] But by August, the tide was running the other way. After the Polish counteroffensive of 16 August, the Red Army was in full flight till the armistice of 12 October, followed by the Peace of Riga in March 1921. This was matched by dramatic turns elsewhere. In October 1920, the factory council movement in Milan and Turin brought Italy to the point of general revolution before subsiding into demoralization. In Germany, the Communist Party's March Action proved a fiasco. Finally, the same month, in a dangerously disintegrating situation, the Bolsheviks relaxed the tempo in Russia itself with the New Economic Policy (NEP) and began normalizing their relations with the capitalist world through a trade agreement with Britain. This brought the most advanced Bolshevik radicalism—and decisive revolutionary politics west of the Vistula—to a close.

THE RANGE OF REVOLUTIONARY
EXPERIENCE

After Russia, there were no socialist revolutions in 1917–23, except the short-lived Hungarian Soviet. However, there were many revolutionary situations: popular insurrections that toppled existing regimes; radicalizations tending toward "dyarchy," where extreme Left confronted new constitutional governments, inspired by Bolshevik example; popular militancy pushing nonsocialist regimes into preemptive reform, which was commonest of all in 1917–23; isolated acts of revolutionary insurgency; and of course counterrevolution.

Extraordinary drama was concentrated into these years. The chain of central European revolutions creating the so-called successor states between 28 October and 14 November 1918 did so via demonstrations, strikes, riots, mutinies, and the forming of workers' and soldiers' councils. The new democratic constitutions in Poland, Czechoslovakia, Yugoslavia, Austria, Hungary, and Germany were founded in popular insurgencies, which also affected Bulgaria. Expansions of democracy occurred in Britain and France, the Low Countries, and Scandinavia. Only in Hungary did the Bolshevik example briefly inspire a revolutionary state. But in 1919–20, massive radicalizations occurred in Germany, Czechoslovakia, and Italy, with street-fighting, repeated challenges to authority, and regional uprisings, bringing those countries to the point of civil war. The defeat of these insurgencies brought their opposite: repression and police terror. After the Hungarian White Terror of 1919–20, during 1922–23 a resurgent Right destroyed the Left's gains in Italy, Spain, and Bulgaria.

Reform responding to radical pressure was a common syndrome of these years. As revolutions elsewhere maximized governments' anxieties about their own societies, even revolutionary minorities had disproportionate effect. This was true during 1919 in Belgium and France. The Dutch case was especially clear, as the revolutionary challenge was entirely rhetorical. Troelstra proclaimed the Dutch revolution on 11–12 November 1918 in response to events in Germany, thereby galvanizing his horrified party and trade union comrades into a major reform statement, which demanded nationalization of suitable industries, repeal of the 1903 strike ban for public employment, the eight-hour day, old-age pensions, and abolition of the upper chamber. While the SDAP had managed only 22 percent in the first democratic elections in July 1918, a strong reform package resulted, including votes for women. Most of all, a new corporative deal was framed for organized labor, including the Ministry of Social Affairs and the consultative High Council of Labor in October 1919, which convened the four main employers' associations, three trade union federations, government agencies, and private expertise.[9]

Fear of Bolshevik contagion was vital in western Europe, but other factors also favored reform. Social harmony and patriotic consensus were the watchwords: the impetus was not sectional class interest but "the new democratic consciousness and the new social consciousness which have come to birth in the long agony of the present struggle" (the war).[10] The nonpartisan appeal of this belief in social regeneration can't be underestimated. In Britain, the proposals of the Ministry of Reconstruction set up in July 1917, plus the Ministry of Pensions (1917), the reports of the Board of Education (1917–18), plans for the Ministry of Health (formed 1919), and a more democratic franchise offered a grand vision of the social contract. The corporative arrangements of the Ministry of Labour formed the political cornerstone. As King George V said in his address to Parliament in February 1919: "We must stop at no sacrifice of interest or prejudice to stamp out unmerited poverty, to diminish unemployment, to provide decent homes, to improve the nation's health, and to raise the standard of well-being throughout the country."[11]

These reformist opportunities were inconceivable without the staggering growth of trade unions in 1918–20.

> The trade-union density in Britain, Germany, Denmark and Norway at the end of World War I was between twice and three times the percentage of 1913, in Sweden and the Netherlands more than three times, in Belgium almost five times as high. . . . [I]n some cases—notably Britain and Germany—the strength of trade unions as a percentage of the labor force was higher than it has ever been since, in others—France, Denmark, perhaps Norway—it was not reached again before the middle or late 1930s.[12]

These phenomenal figures came from the short-lived boom as industry reconverted for peacetime. With pent-up demand for goods, a lag in productive capacity, availability of investment capital, relaxed government controls, and inflationary fiscal policies, a remarkable upswing occurred in spring 1919–summer 1920 (lasting somewhat longer in central Europe), ending in an equally sharp contraction. After a flash flood of unemployment in winter 1918–19, therefore, returning troops were rapidly absorbed into an expanding labor market. Neither the reform-proneness of governments, the scale of militancy, nor the massive union expansion were possible without this boom. When it abruptly passed, unemployment rose alarmingly high, and workers were cast unceremoniously onto the defensive.

Postwar circumstances briefly gave union leaders enormous leverage—an opening for which wartime corporatism had prepared them. Under conditions of nearly revolutionary turbulence, as workers practised flexing their industrial muscle, "responsible" union leaders became the best hope for holding disorder at bay.[13] With British labor unrest approaching its peak in early 1919, Winston Churchill elaborated: "The curse of trade unionism was that there was not enough of it, and it was not highly enough developed to make its branch secretaries fall into line with the head office."[14] That was precisely the point. Union leaders faced their own loss of control. The revolutionary climate after 1917–18 raised the entire temper of working-class hopes, such that workplace militancy could already be passing the leaders by.[15]

In eastern Europe, the revolutionary upheavals of 1917–23 had powerful nationalist dimensions too, because the post-1918 political settlement involved not only social changes and political reform but also territorial revision and new relations among states. The Treaty of Versailles (June 1919) was followed by the east European supplements, most of which were preceded by wars. Not accidentally, most involved the great power absent from Versailles, Soviet Russia. Most also had the dimensions of civil war.

In November 1918, when the war in the West was lost, the German army still occupied a line from Finland to the Caucasus. This German impact on eastern Europe severely complicated the building of stable governing orders after the Bolsheviks seized power, with big implications for the non-Russian nationalities of the old Russian Empire. In western Europe, the weakening of some states (Germany) and aggrandizement of others (Britain and France) via the First World War was momentous for the Left as nationalism favored the Right, but territorial revisions were qualitatively different in the east, where they accompanied the collapse of existing states. These revisions involved less the adjustment of older boundaries than the creation of entirely new countries, whose political systems had to be invented from scratch. This was clearest in German-occupied Russia in 1917–18, where the German military sledgehammer smashed whatever was left of the old social fabric in much of the Baltic, Belorussia, and Ukraine. As the rapacious German administration receded at the war's end, it left a calamitously anarchic situation, compounded by the death of tsarism.[16]

By intruding itself between the peoples of the Empire and their self-determination in the very moment of revolutionary change—after the old order had gone but while the new was struggling to be born—the German army suspended democracy before it had barely begun. Bolsheviks, autonomists, left-nationalists, separatists, and counterrevolutionaries found themselves in confused relationships to local populations, but in most cases nationalism's practical logic worked against Moscow's need for consolidation. Bolsheviks might endorse national self-determination theoretically, but movements for independence invariably aligned themselves with Bolshevism's foes, first with the Germans (until late 1918) and then with the British and French (1919–21), who also backed the Whites in the Russian Civil War. In this way regional events—in Finland, the Baltic, Ukraine, Caucasus, even Belorussia—devolved into separate revolutionary processes with an integrity of their own. In strategic vision, popular experience, and practical delimitation, these were *national revolutions,* in ways that confused conventional political or social labels.[17]

Competing claims of nationality and class shaped these revolutionary dynamics in the former tsarist territories during 1917–23.[18] This was no simple dichotomy in which one identity precluded the other. Appealing to national solidarity could suppress or deemphasize class hostilities, harnessing working-class politics to larger patriotic coalitions led by conservatives or liberals, where socialist departures were practically ruled out. But the Left might also claim leadership of national coalitions for itself, by offering distinctive programs inside the developing nationalist framework. At least, it could advance specifically working-class or other popular interests in more modest and defensive ways. Assumptions about the national bases of political identity could enable socialist strategy rather than undermining it.

The creation of the new eastern European nation-states in 1918 shaped politics into this framework of national revolution, and socialists found few prospects outside the heterogeneous founding coalitions of the new republics, with temporary exceptions in Bulgaria and Hungary. The small Romanian Social Democratic Party was entirely marginal to this process, as was the breakaway Communist Party of 1921, which had no impact before being banned in 1924. In Poland, the Communist Workers' Party formed from various Zimmerwaldians in December 1918 had stronger native roots but lost all influence on the new state's founding coalition because of its antiparliamentary revolutionism and dogmatic internationalism. Its self-marginalizing was sealed in the summer of 1920 by its identification with the invading Red Army. In the new Yugoslav polity, where party formation was badly fragmented along national lines, the unified Communist Party of 1919 showed more potential: but if the 1920 Constituent Assembly elections brought much success, in 1921 it too was banned.[19]

In these countries, the dominant nationalist framework militated against the Social Democratic and Communist Left. But one case of socialists winning space inside the new nationalist framework was Czechoslovakia, where Social Democrats formed a new government with Czech Socialists and Agrarians after the local elections of June 1919, and the left began enlarging its strength in the party. This Social Democratic left stayed avowedly within the parent party rather than splitting it, giving critical support to the government and party right for the April 1920 elections. When the split eventually arrived, this strategy of consolidation allowed a sizeable majority of the CSDSD to follow the left into the Communist Party, which retained strong continuities with the national labor movement's earlier traditions, unlike other Communist parties of 1918–21. Czech Communist strength grew from "organic" radicalization inside the framework of national revolution, whose legitimacy the left leaders had carefully accepted and whose constitutional conditions allowed a strong CSDSD left to flourish. Moreover, the Czech Community Party—like the Yugoslav—was the only party in its nationally fragmented state that was proving genuinely national in structure, basing itself deliberately on all national territories rather than on single constituent nationalities.[20]

COUNCIL COMMUNISM AND THE REVOLT OF THE RANK AND FILE

The distinctiveness of revolutionary activity in 1917–23 lay in the workers' councils, though militancy varied greatly in exact forms. These ranged from unofficial strike committees developing larger political aims, like the shop stewards' movements of Clydeside, Sheffield, or Berlin, to sophisticated revolutionary innovation, like the factory councils in Turin.[21] In between came a rich assortment: the *Räte* in Germany and Austria, claiming functions of class representation in a locality; councils based in factories, firms, or other economic units; and local action committees for specific ends, like the Councils of Action opposing British military intervention against Soviet Russia in summer 1920 or the revival of councils in Germany to oppose the Kapp Putsch in March 1920.[22]

A new medium of working-class activity, councils differed from both socialist parties, which acted through parliamentary and state institutions, and unions, which worked on the capitalist economy's given assumptions via the wage relation. Their supporters departed from the mainstream of European labor movements between 1864–75 and the First World War, sharing some affinities with prewar syndicalists, particularly in their enmity toward union officialdom and party machines. But the militantly distinctive council communist vision materialized only during the radicalizations of 1918–21. Few council activists originally saw them as a permanent alternative to parliamentary institutions, rather than transitional bodies during the initial breakthrough to democracy, possibly with lasting watchdog functions in the future republican constitution.

Stronger versions of the council idea were hostile to orthodox trade unionism and socialist electoralism, recoiling from the accepted model of separately organized, centralized, nationally focused political and economic movements. Instead, councils were based within production: inside the unit of production itself, in the factory, the plant, or the shop. Councils raised issues of industrial democracy, workers' self-management, and workers' control. They transcended the fractured pursuit of "political" and "economic" goals typical of the pre-1914 labor movements, joining industrial direct action to the political project of a workers' government. Measured against the socialist mainstream since the Paris Commune, this interest in workers' democracy, as against the parliamentary representation of the people, was new.[23]

One model of council activity was community based but linked to factories via shop stewards or similar workplace networks. Another was production based but connected to broader social arenas. In national emergencies like the Kapp Putsch, the socialization campaign in the Ruhr and central Germany in spring 1919, or the northern Italian factory occupations, the two converged. In Germany, for example, it was only after the demise of the original Räte, in the radicalization after the Spartacist Rising and the January 1919 elections to the National Assembly, that a more radical council movement developed. Earlier, constitutional respect and loyalty to the parliamentarist SPD kept Räte from expanding their competence. Once radicalized, councils articulated extraparliamentary, direct-democratic, self-consciously class-based alternatives to the labor movement's existing strategies and institutions. The strongest version was the Russian system of dual power around the Petrograd Soviet.

For the most part, local councils coexisted in parallel with legal government and local state representatives. The key was how far workers' councils overturned existing legality. In moderate versions, councils confined themselves to general supervisory roles, leaving local administration practically intact. But supervision could also be highly intrusive, with purging and replacement of local government personnel and strict accountability for implementing new left-wing policies. In 1918–21, Germany provides the richest evidence of this variation, especially in the distinctive "council communist" movement.[24]

German council communism crystallized around demands for "socialization"—a strong combination of public ownership and workers' control.[25] On 18 November 1918, government appointed a commission of inquiry on the subject, but the real impetus was the militancy of the miners in the western Ruhr, escalating on 15 December into strikes over wages and hours. After a partial settlement on 28 December, actions resumed in January, incited by the Spartacist Rising in Berlin. The Essen Workers' and Soldiers' Council formed a nine-person commission for socializing the coal industry, occupied the mineowners' headquarters, and confirmed these steps in a regional conference. The SPD government dissembled, while launching a military pacification of the Ruhr. Miners responded with a general strike (18–23 February), which was bloodily suppressed. By now the socialization campaign had spread to Halle, Anhalt, Thuringia, and Saxony (23 February–10 March); Berlin (3–8 March); and Upper Silesia (5–15 March). Actions repeated the cycle of impressive mobilization, brutal suppression, and embittering defeat. The workers' exasperated militancy produced one further round of conflict: another general strike in the Ruhr (1–30 April), involving 73 percent of all Ruhr miners at its peak; a Braunschweig sympathy strike (9–16 April); a Württemberg general strike (31 March–7 April); and the events of the Munich Soviet Republic (7–30 April).

An immense gulf separated militants from official leaders. The local SPD met actions with contempt, denouncing miners as criminals and ruffians, whose violence undermined the union's policy. Such attacks were hugely resented, sowing the very violence they alleged. But if the movement was driven by anti-SPD bitterness, it was steered by neither USPD nor KPD. Militancy was spontaneous, though not unorganized. It proceeded beyond the framework of any parties and against the official union from a pithead democracy of delegates and mass meetings. In its local base in production, its informal agitational methods and mine-to-mine coordination, its preference for decentralized nationalization via mine-based workers' control, and its suspicion of national bureaucracies, the movement echoed the themes of syndicalism—and indeed, a local syndicalist, Heinrich Heiling, a leader of the small syndicalist miners' union formed in 1908, was prominent in the Hamborn agitation.[26] In the volatile circumstances of early 1919, the boundaries separating an older syndicalist tradition, a newer brand of industrial unionism, the infant KPD, and unaffiliated grassroots militancy were blurred. The key was the alienation of militants from the SPD and its unions.[27]

This was the conjuncture that produced "council communism." Council communism—and the rank-and-file militancy it sought to theorize—dismissed the political complexities of revolution. There were huge areas council communists ignored. Questions of women, the family, and the sexual division of labor were one. Coalition building was another, for the council movement refused to worry about peasants, petty bourgeoisie, and other nonproletarian social groups. Council militants were untroubled by the administrative consequences of organizing revolutionary government around the point of production. If the councils had a factory rather than a territorial basis, training workers for running production rather than society in general, then how would the noneconomic functions of government be addressed? How would the councils deal with social welfare and education? How successfully could they represent the interests of nonworkers?

Council communism's "productivism"—the conviction that true revolution began from the workplace—was so axiomatic that such questions were never posed. This was exacerbated by the movement's towering voluntarism. If 1917 was a "Revolution against Capital," in Gramsci's phrase—against the Second International's economic determinism—council communists carried this to its sublime extreme.[28] Their approach presupposed western Europe's ripeness for revolutionary transformation. If so, politics became necessarily confrontationist. A strategy was needed in which "absolute opposition to all non-revolutionary forces and the greatest possible purity of revolutionary principles . . . would empower the working class to construct the dictatorship of the proletariat."[29] Consciousness came exuberantly to the fore. Minds were to be revolutionized: "In the German Revolution the subjective elements play a decisive role. The problem of the German Revolution is the problem of the development of the self-consciousness of the German proletariat."[30]

Relations between the councils and trade unions were chronic, reflecting opposed ideals of organization. It was hard even for unions with a strong left, like the metalworkers in Germany (DMV) and Italy (FIOM), to assimilate factory or plant-based systems of council representation. Councils undermined union ability to negotiate national agreements and more generally to provide leadership in national affairs. Collective contracts were trade unionism's centerpiece before 1914, and devolving decisions back onto locals would delight employers, who wanted nothing better than to deal exclusively with their own workforce. Union resources would no longer be mobilized to benefit weaker, less organized parts of the membership. Unions' ability to influence national policy would be undercut, whether from reformist or revolutionary perspectives. Moreover, demands for local control came at the worst possible time: just as unions acquired corporative leverage through the war economy, a disorderly shopfloor militancy threatened from the rear. Unions devoted great efforts in 1919–20 to neutralizing the councils' challenge, not just from bureaucratic self-interest or resistance to democratization but from legitimate disquiet that workers' collective interests were being undone.

In Italy, trade union leaders moved to contain the councils' demands. The FIOM national agreement of February 1919 included the Internal Commissions as grievance committees, but conflicts over prerogatives only radicalized the council ideal. As workshop commissars were elected in November–December 1919 and council supporters won control of the Turin PSI, the unions proposed their own ideas for institutionalizing them. These included the workers' "Centurians" adopted by the Chemical Workers' Union in October 1919 (one delegate for every hundred workers, with no nonunion voters); the Rome Gas Workers' system, which allowed votes to nonunion members (November 1919); and the "Baldesi Project" (named after the CGL's Gino Baldesi), which crafted an agreement between unions and the Turin council movement in May 1920. The Baldesi Project typified union tactics: conceding limited factory functions to councils and giving nonunion workers the vote but reserving key policies for the unions, making councils ancillary to union structures, and preserving union primacy in national affairs.[31] Though the Italian ferment lasted another six months and the Turin council movement briefly imposed itself via the factory occupations of September 1920, jockeying between unions and councils was abruptly ended by Fascism.

In Germany, counterrevolution was hardly less violent in 1919–21 but unfolded within the parliamentary framework rather than overturning it. The pact of unions and big employers in the throes of the 1918 revolution, the Central Working Agreement, already envisaged workers' committees as part of trade unions' own local machinery, and as SPD and unions labored in 1919 to produce legislation, this was the bureaucratic model they favored. The Works Councils Law of 4 February 1920 carefully protected union primacy. All radical aspects of industrial democracy and workers' control were gone—sovereignty of the mass meeting; direct democracy and power of recall; access to the books; control of hiring, firing, and the labor process; rights of negotiating with management; and independence from union bureaucracy. Employer sovereignty was intact. All key issues were reserved for the union's collective bargaining machinery. Councils were reduced to the latter's adjunct, with merely consultative status.[32]

In a moderate trade union perspective of reform under capitalism, these measures were a solid gain. Centralized, national organization was defended unbudgingly, just as in Italy. As the guidelines agreed by a conference of union chairmen put it: "The basis of industrial democracy is the collective agreement with legal force."[33] But the reform can't be divorced from surrounding events. It was meant to defuse the council movement's more radical demands, and this badly compromised the progressive value. The point was brought tragically home at the climax of the German law. A mass demonstration called by the USPD to the Reichstag steps was massacred by troops, leaving 42 dead and 105 wounded. Ultimately, an unprecedented rank-and-file movement's hopes for workplace democracy, public ownership, and workers' control, based on autonomous councils, had shrunk to a limited union gain. Implementing it required the bloody policing of the original movement.

The workers' council movement was destined for failure once a national revolutionary breakthrough didn't occur. In Italy, that moment passed with the factory occupations in September 1920. In Germany, the USPD and other left groupings still pursued permanent government by councils, whether linked to a parliamentary constitution or not, until the Weimar Constitution and accompanying legislation, like the Works Councils Law, laid these ideas to rest. But the real hub was the socialization issue. The strongest drive for socialization came only in early 1919, mainly locally, in the Ruhr and parts of central Germany, recalling the national movement to the united socialist action of November 1918. The suppression of that movement, and of the local soviets that flickered across the spring of 1919, changed the character of the later conciliar actions. Henceforth, the councils were forced back to the local level, either as vehicles of revolutionary agitation no longer linked to serious prospects of local administrative power or as the committees of action in a political emergency, like the Kapp Putsch of March 1920. As a movement, with national political hopes, council communism was gone.

Chapter 10

GERMANY, 1918–1923: THE SOCIAL DEMOCRATIC REPUBLIC

THE MOST STRIKING thing about the German revolution was the unrelenting intransigence of the SPD's moderation. Rather than harnessing working-class militancy, the leaders did their best to suppress it. The SPD upheld the constitutional reforms of late September 1918 in the hour of Germany's military defeat, as the old regime tried to legitimize itself for negotiating with the Western Allies. For the SPD Right, this constitutional transition completed the policies of August 1914. It vindicated their patriotism. The measures making Germany a constitutional monarchy, reached after the SPD joined the coalition government on 3 October, already satisfied the party's cochairmen, Friedrich Ebert and Philipp Scheidemann. The party's impending parliamentary dominance seemed sufficient guarantee of further reforms.

The situation was transformed between 27 October and 5 November 1918, when naval mutinies in Kiel escalated via election of sailors' councils, a garrison revolt, and a general strike into a local seizure of power by workers' and soldiers' councils.[1] During the previous month the removal of censorship and release of political detainees had stoked popular expectations, while recognition of the lost war brought troops to the point of mutiny.[2] Popular insurgency spread across Germany, until a Bavarian revolutionary government was formed in Munich on 7–8 November, followed the next day by the kaiser's abdication in Berlin. Although government now passed to Ebert and the SPD, they made no concessions to these profound changes. They called the constituent assembly, while managing an orderly transition. They focused on bringing the troops home without disorders, maintaining the food supply, and at all costs avoiding Allied military intervention.[3] This replicated the political logic of the civil truce: patriotic discipline and public order; exaggerated fears of mass action; angry contempt for the "irresponsible" left; practical compromise with the old order.

The SPD leaders displayed no glimmers of doubt. They evinced the inevitabilism of their pre-1914 outlook, now transposed to the necessary triumph of a parliamentary constitution. They made a virtue of hardheaded realism, of taking the tough decisions left-wing dreamers refused to face. The latter shirked responsibility, they complained, beguiling the masses with unattainable utopias and flirting with chaos. "The path from 4 August 1914 to 5 October 1918 was difficult," Eduard David recorded in his diary, "But what would have been achieved by a revolutionary tactic?" Only "the most frightful dangers and suffering," he answered, ending "in the triumph of reaction."[4] The SPD leaders savored the complacencies of power. The October changes made them arbiters of a rapidly disintegrating political situation, where the old order had lost popular legitimacy. Their left-wing rivals lacked the same certainty, resources, and support. The Independent Social Democrats (USPD) acquired a stronger profile in the freer atmosphere of October but were no convincing alternative. The Spartacists and far left were too fragmented. And while Karl Liebknecht personally commanded enormous popularity, he was too purist a revolutionary to join the new government.

The Council of People's Commissars formed on 9–10 November gave the left parity, with three SPD nominees (Ebert, Scheidemann, Otto Landsberg), and three USPD (Hugo Haase, Wilhelm Dittmann, Emil Barth, the last also representing the Berlin Shop Stewards), cochaired by Ebert and Haase. On 10 November, the Berlin Shop Stewards called workers' and soldiers' delegates to the Circus Busch to confirm the new government, and it too elected a parity-based Executive.[5] But while the Circus Busch issued a socialist declaration—for "the speedy and thorough socialization of the capitalist means of production"—it was the SPD's pragmatism that called the shots.[6]

On 12 November 1918, the government issued its manifesto. With the aim "of realizing the socialist progam," it listed its immediate commitments: the eight-hour day; full employment and unemployment legislation; expanded social insurance; housing reform; universal, equal, secret, and direct suffrage, with proportional representation and no distinction of sex; the calling of a constituent assembly; and an end to all wartime restrictions on civil freedoms and the free movement of labor. This was a solid catalogue of reforms. But after the initial declaration, it made no mention of socialism as such and specifically omitted salient demands like socialization. It also made no mention of the Räte. Dittmann called it "the Revolution's

Magna Carta."[7] But between the lines the SPD leaders were thinking less of socialist construction than of the orderly transition to a parliamentary republic.

This was made clear by three vital decisions. Most notorious was Ebert's "alliance" with the military against "Bolshevism," broached on the telephone by Quartermaster-General Wilhelm Groener to Ebert after the Circus Busch assembly. By committing the field army to Ebert, the High Command protected the officer corps against democratization via soldiers' councils. For his part, Ebert dismissed the democracy of soldiers' councils, focusing only on demobilizing the army within the time limits of the Armistice. He ignored not only traditional socialist demands for a people's militia but also the SPD's own prior resolutions. He preferred the framework of the old order rather than something new. In a crisis, this would easily license repression. When Ebert approved the formation of voluntary units (the *Freikorps*) in late December against the Left, this is precisely what happened.[8]

If SPD leaders showed little desire to reform the army, deferring gratuitously to its prestige, the same applied to the civil service. In early November, city administrations commonly coexisted with the Räte, giving the latter watchdog functions while keeping charge of day-to-day affairs, and this was repeated at the national level. The new government appealed to all levels and departments of the civil service to stay at their posts, including the judiciary. There was no thought of purging or democratizing the bureaucracy.[9]

Third and most decisive of all, on 15 November 1918 the Free Trade Unions came to agreement with the big employers, in the crucial sociopolitical compromise of the revolution. Under this Central Working Agreement (ZAG), the employers recognized the unions as collective bargainers, accepted the principle of collective agreements, conceded the right of all workers to join a union, and abandoned company unions. They agreed to the eight-hour day. Works committees would be formed in any establishment of at least 50 workers. Unions and employers agreed to cooperate for demobilization. In return, the unions tacitly dropped socialization. Overall, the big employers showed remarkable flexibility, considering their earlier dogmatism. For union leaders, the Agreement was a triumphant vindication of their collaborationist line since August 1914.[10]

In the abstract, added to the constitutional transition and the SPD's program of social reforms, these union advances seemed impressive. But the actual circumstances—widespread working-class insurgency and democratic hopes racing far ahead of the SPD's more moderate constitutionalism—tarnished the luster of this success. Initially, the current of working-class sympathies flowed strongly in the SPD's favor. But as the SPD and USPD broke apart, the unity of popular opinion fractured. In a series of dramatic incidents between 6 and 28 December 1918, the SPD government members moved unilaterally against the revolution's radical wing—first suppressing a Spartacist demonstration, with 16 fatalities, then trying to disarm the People's Naval Division, whose occupation of the royal palace symbolized the popular aspects of the 1918 revolution. These actions aligned the SPD with the reassembling forces of order. On 28 December, the USPD left the government.

Superficially, the SPD had won an imposing victory. It had consistently outmaneuvered the USPD to control the council movement's central organs in Berlin. The unions had gained a powerful corporative place via the ZAG. The revolution's parliamentary parameters were secured by making the constituent assembly the fixed focus of discussion. Advocates of a more "Bolshevik" approach were marginalized in the labor movement's forums, from the Circus Busch assembly of 10 November to the National Congress of Workers' and Soldiers' Councils on 16–21 December. The climax from the SPD's point of view came with the far left's defeat in the Spartacist Rising of 5–15 January and the elections to the National Assembly four days later. On the one hand, the popular insurrection called against the Ebert government by the Revolutionary Shop Stewards and the newly founded Communist Party (KPD) was decisively crushed, Karl Liebknecht and Rosa Luxemburg were murdered, and "Order Rule[d] in Berlin." On the other hand, the SPD polled 37.9 percent of the vote in the elections, against only 7.6 percent for the USPD, and with the Democrats and the Catholic Center achieved a clear republican majority. The elections seemed a resounding popular endorsement of the SPD's approach.[11]

By other criteria, however, this achievement looked less secure. By refusing a confrontation with militarism, by not reshaping the bureaucracy and judiciary, by shying away from land reform, and by dissembling on socialization, the SPD deprived the republican political order of solid social foundations beyond the ZAG and the various welfare measures. This was all the more shortsighted because the disordering of social-political arrangements had created such unsurpassed readiness for radicalism. Wartime traumas, immediately followed by the upheavals of revolution, had upturned the expectations of what might realistically be stabilized or restored, making citizens unusually receptive to change.[12] Yet, disabled by a sense of constitutionalist responsibility and patriotic mission and full of traditional prejudices about the undisciplined instincts of the non–Social Democratic masses, the SPD's political imagination failed to escape from a remarkably moderate legalism.

What is more, holding the revolution to a narrowly constitutionalist path meant restraining and then repressing the popular movement. The workers' councils were the main basis for a "third way" between the SPD's constitutionalism and the insurrectionary politics inspired by the Bolshevik revolution, and Ebert and his colleagues were lamentably unimaginative in failing to harness this popular upsurge. Here was the energy and institutional leverage for the further-reaching democratization whose neglect was so fateful for the Weimar Republic's survival. But not only did the SPD fail to grasp this positive opportunity; the party's own preferred strategy required the councils' active liquidation. In the name of one kind of democracy—parliamentary constitutionalism—another kind had to go.[13]

From this contradiction came a popular radicalization that left much of the SPD's achievement nugatory. As repression of the left continued and government shilly-shallied on socialization, the SPD's hold on working-class loyalties slipped. Mass actions surrounding the defeat of the Kapp Putsch in March 1920 dramatized the widening gap between the SPD and many working-class hopes, and in the June 1920 elections the USPD now attained 18.6 percent of the vote against the SPD's 21.6, with another 1.7 percent for the KPD. In the labor movement's old industrial strongholds the trend was all the more marked. Thus January 1919 saw less the end of the revolution than its radical beginning—and one proceeding both outside and against the framework of SPD policies.[14]

By its own lights, the SPD had done a lot. The constitutional, corporative, and welfare state advances could even sustain an optimistic projection, in which structural reforms transmuted into socialist transformation. The Social Democrats saw themselves progressing in that direction. But their constitutionalist course was imposed at a double cost: the bases of authoritarianism in the state and economy had been saved, indeed renewed, in their time of greatest vulnerability; and the best expressions of popular democracy had been rebuffed, even brutally repressed. The real tragedy of 1918–19 was not the failure to force through a socialist revolution. The abstract merits of such a course may be endlessly debated, but it could only have succeeded through a long and bloody civil war, and for many socialists this was too high a price to pay. The real tragedy was the SPD's excessively legalistic, stolidly unimaginative, and wholly conservative notion of what a democratically ordered polity might be. In 1918, the SPD had an unprecedented chance to expand the frontiers of democracy, both by dismantling the bases of authoritarianism in the discredited ancien régime and by harnessing the new popular energies the councils movement released. The chances of a further-reaching reformism were squandered. It was by its own democratic lights that the SPD failed the test.

ITALY: COUNTERREVOLUTION TRIUMPHANT

In Italy, revolutionary turbulence was still more impressive than in Germany. It grew from the consequences of the war economy, from popular hopes for the postwar future, from the favorable circumstances of massive union expansion, and from the dialectic between popular militancy and established labor leaderships stretched to the limits of their representative capacities. Italy also replicated many of the Russian conditions: the timing and speed of industrialization since the 1890s; high levels of capitalist concentration; industry's geographical concentration in the northern triangle of Turin-Milan-Genoa; the state's forward role in the economy; and the extremes of development and backwardness inside the country. Both Germany and Italy passed through revolutionary crises after the First World War, but whereas in Germany the left's defeat led to the consolidation of a parliamentary republican regime, in Italy it brought the Fascists to power. How do we explain this difference?[15]

The Italian Socialists were more intransigent, more united, and more left-wing. The PSI stood out among west European socialist parties for refusing to support the war. Even after Italy entered the war in May 1915 the PSI voted against the war credits. As the war's end approached, the movement rejected government proposals for economic reconstruction. Likewise, the PSI vetoed the demand for a constituent assembly as another form of collaborationism. Instead, party eyes were on Russia. In September 1918, the party reaffirmed its maximum program of socialist revolution. Then, on 7–11 December, fortified by the central European revolutions of the previous month, the PSI Directorate called for the immediate "institution of the Socialist Republic and the dictatorship of the proletariat."[16] This was the party's declared goal over the next two years. It fought the November 1919 elections on that basis and had no interest in using its parliamentary strength as a springboard into government. In contrast to the SPD, therefore, the PSI never backed a reformist program of parliamentary stabilization. It was only in the summer of 1922 that Filippo Turati's reformists declared for a politics of coalition—18 months after the PSI had split, after Fascism had already broken the movement.

During the "red two years" of 1919–20, the Italian Left had a remarkable upsurge of support. The PSI's membership soared, as did the unions', whether in the CGL, the syndicalist USI, or the freshly founded Catholic Unions. This popular upsurge occurred in a general atmosphere of social confrontation—massive strike waves in industry and agriculture, direct action in the factories, local food and price actions, land occupations, and constant displays of collective strength in rallies, marches, and processions. It produced powerful concentrations of local and regional strength.

The PSI dominated the north. Nationally, it did better in cities than rural areas. But the northern countryside was just as red: the agriculture of the lower Po Valley complemented the industrial triangle of Turin-Milan-Genoa. In Bologna province, nearly three-quarters of the rural electorate voted for the PSI in 1919. The key was the imposing presence of the Federterra, the agricultural laborers' union, which by 1920 had some nine hundred thousand members. The Federterra rested on an interlocking system of its own local leagues, the *camera del lavoro*, the cooperatives, Socialist local government, and public works contracts, subsidies, and credits, in which PSI branches might play little formal role outside the Socialist town councils themselves. By late 1920 this rural hegemony had brought the lower Po Valley and its economy under Socialist control, putting the dominant classes under a deeply humiliating state of siege.

This rural Socialism luxuriated in its new public power, savoring the taste of class revenge. In Ferrara, the PSI provincial administration took over the castle, painted *Viva il socialismo* in luminous paint, draped it with red flags, made it the headquarters of the camera del lavoro, and, to the horror of their fellow resident, the prefect, threw it open to all manner of working-class meeting and celebration.[17] In this climate of manifest class confrontation, in which union boycotts and attacks on blacklegs were mixed with cost-of-living riots, attacks on the police, and general taunting and intimidation of the bourgeoisie, many rural agitators were deliberately escalating tensions for purposes of revolution. This was a combative, exuberant socialism, in which even the PSI Directorate's revolutionary Maximalism lagged behind the direct-action militancy of the rank and file. The PSI's electoral success depended directly on identifying with social struggles that the SPD in Germany had bitterly opposed. In the 1920 local elections the Socialists were most successful where agricultural militancy was most intense: in Rovigo they won all 63 communes; in Mantova, 59 out of 68; in Bologna, 54 out of 61; in Reggio Emilia, 38 out of 45; and so forth.

Faced with this uncompromising revolutionism, the Italian bourgeoisie could be forgiven for expecting insurrection. But in practice the Maximalist leadership lived permanently in the gap between word and deed: "The declared objectives were always uncompromisingly extreme, and verbal violence, with its proclamation of subversive intentions, its insults, and threats against adversaries and the established institutions, reached a very high pitch."[18] Nor was there any shortage of local activism. But whenever a general insurrectionary opportunity arose, the Maximalists hung resolutely back from the brink. This was true of the massive cost-of-living disturbances in June–July 1919, true also of the Piedmont general strike of 13–24 April 1920, and true again in late 1920, when factory occupations conjoined with another climactic struggle of the Federterra and the 5 November local elections. In a joint meeting on 9–11 September, the question of converting the factory occupations into a national revolutionary challenge was referred by the PSI leadership to the CGL National Council, which rejected the idea by only 591,245 to 409,569 votes.[19]

Maximalism's bizarre mixture of verbal intransigence and strategic procrastination remains perplexing. The narrow élitism and antipopular violence of the prewar Italian state, successively overlaid by the wartime polarization and the popular utopianism of the peace, also played their part, as did the shibboleth of unity, which militated against alienating a sizable, more cautious part of the movement. But Maximalism also came from the Second International's automatic Marxism, the Kautskyian faith in History and objective process. Only the extreme left groupings of the party, the emergent communist factions around Gramsci and Amadeo Bordiga who embraced Bolshevik voluntarism, escaped this inherited culture. The Maximalists themselves justified their inaction by the international conjuncture, waiting for radicalizations elsewhere.[20] But the ingrained assumptions behind this rationalization, the entire idiom of classical social democracy, were more important: "We, as Marxists, interpret history; we do not make it."[21] The revolution was always just around the next corner.

Maximalist failings were an object lesson in how not to conduct a revolution. They fed expectations without resolving them. They fanned a mood of revolutionary excitement but refused to shape it into a revolutionary challenge. They fashioned socialism into a barrier against the bourgeois world and from behind this ideological stockade released a fusillade of rhetorical provocation. But when the masses took them at their word and acted, they counseled discipline and patience. Understandably, this bred resentment. By late 1920, the movement was directionless and demoralized, racked by recriminations, and generally falling apart. The Fascists beckoned as an agency of counterrevolutionary pacification. Localized paramilitary activity had been brewing since early 1920 and now spread violently in organized form. Class struggle abruptly left the land of posturing, rhetoric, and symbols for the world of guns, beatings, and militarized terror. Schooled in the protocols of a much-maligned liberal polity, Socialists had no answer to this systematic political violence. Without the advantages of legality, shocked by a brutal assault on the premises of the labor movement's popular-democratic ethos, the PSI's local hegemonies crumbled. It became "a revolution of blood against a revolution of words."[22]

One lesson of Maximalist failings, then, was organizational: the need for revolutionary leadership, a Bolshevik party. This was Bordiga's position, and during 1920 Gramsci joined him. The issue was renewal versus secession: winning the party to a "communist" perspective, which could require expelling the reformists or launching a new party to the left. It proved insoluble. When the PSI Congress finally met in Livorno on 15–21 January 1921, the party split three ways: 98,028 votes for the Unitarian Communist motion, 58,783 for the Communists, and 14,695 for the Socialist Concentration. The Communists immediately left, forming the Communist Party of Italy.[23]

DILEMMAS OF REVOLUTION: PARLIAMENTS, FACTORIES, AND STREETS

Italian Socialism encapsulated the Left's dilemmas in the postwar revolutionary conjuncture. The obstacles to socialist revolution, in Italy no less than Germany, were formidable. But among them was a failure of revolutionary leadership, which "faded away at the moment of truth."[24] One of the worst consequences of this was the isolation of the urban revolutionary movement—from the middling strata, from the expanding small-holding peasantry, from the burgeoning ex-servicemen's movement, and from any effort at cooperating with progressive groupings of the bourgeoisie.[25] By September 1920, this isolation was a fact. But during 1919 things were more fluid, and the PSI's failure to speak for the multiform yearnings and discontents of that time had its roots in Maximalism.[26]

Localism, both in its specifically Italian form and in the general bias of council-based activity, also stalled the PSI Directorate's capacity for action. A rolling revolutionary chain reaction might have been imagined, similar to the November revolution in Germany. But bringing such a movement to climax required decisive intervention by the Directorate, and here the well-ensconced autonomies of the movement's local cultures were a hindrance rather than a help.[27] This was exacerbated by geography and the physical separation of the labor movement's strongholds from the political and administrative capital in Rome. By contrast with Berlin (and Petrograd or Budapest), Rome was no magnet for radicalism. The PSI's centering in Milan, Turin, and Emilia made it much harder to bring insurrection to the portals of state power. In effect, storming the latter would have required the PSI's own "march on Rome," an infinitely more complicated matter than if the movement was centered in the capital city.

If an Italian October was unlikely, how should we conceptualize the radical Left's realistic agenda? There were two other models of socialist action in 1917–23. One came from Germany and Austria, where a social democratic party's commanding position in government opened a path for democratizing state and society and for decisively tipping the balance of socioeconomic power in the workers' favor, even inside the limits of the capitalist system. The other was common to much of western and northern Europe, where the radical climate created by the Russian and central European revolutions and the peculiarities of the postwar conjuncture allowed labor movements to exert unique pressure on nonsocialist governments. Reforming social democrats and union leaders enjoyed passing political leverage, often from a new base in coalition governments, as in Sweden and the Low Countries.

In theory, both models promised lasting increments of legitimacy and corporative power for working-class movements, with solid institutional foundations for further gains. In practice, the ebbing of the revolutionary threat between the autumn of 1920 and the spring of 1921 combined with the end of the postwar boom to undermine labor's temporary bargaining power and restore conservatives' confidence. What should have been the transition to a new social democratic era became the prelude to a restabilizing of capitalism. Nonetheless, these partially realized chances are a useful framework for considering the Italian case.

There were two obvious occasions for radical parliamentary intervention by the PSI. The first was the PSI's victory in the November 1919 elections. These elections were "a 'historic opportunity' for the renewal of

Italian public life through the implementation of reforms that could have eliminated, or at least substantially reduced, the distance still separating the masses from the life of the state." Aside from wartime restructuring of the economy, the popular mobilizations in town and country, and constitutional reform, the legislature also experienced an infusion of new blood (304 of 501 deputies were new), and procedural innovations strengthened party government. This was a major turning point in the Italian polity, when the traditional power bloc, whose constancy survived the earlier reforms of 1882 and 1912, was finally dislodged.[28] The PSI potentially claimed enormous parliamentary leverage as a result, either from within government or from a nonministerial position of parliamentary support. The second occasion came at the height of the political crisis of the factory occupations in September 1920. By that time, Maximalist intransigence had narrowed the room for parliamentary maneuver, but key liberals saw bringing the PSI and CGL into government as the best chance for stability, and a last opportunity again opened up.

In both cases, the Left's best hope was in joining—and helping to shape—a broader democratic bloc. Such a bloc was a possible basis for further-reaching socioeconomic reforms. Once the high tide of popular militancy had passed and the Fascists were on the march, it could also enable democratic defense. Italy and Germany produced complementary histories in this respect. The SPD claimed impressive strength in the parliamentary arena but lacked strategic vision, building its republican coalition around the most moderate possible consensus; the PSI abandoned coalition building to pursue extraparliamentary mobilization but produced, ironically, the best blueprints of reform. If the SPD was stuck in the most cautious version of a coalition, sacrificing democratic energies to the narrowest constitutionalism, in a counterrevolutionary perspective of law and order, Italian reformists had the opposite problem, a coherent and ambitious program but without any access to power. This was the tragedy of the two revolutionary movements. A successful non-Bolshevik Left needed the best of both worlds: radical yet democratic extraparliamentary energies mobilized and channeled through the parliamentary process.

Of course, neither the SPD nor the PSI completely controlled their situations but contended with ebullient and unmanageable popular movements, whose militancy and hopes set the agenda as much as followed it. But in 1918–19 the masses were primed for a lead, and both parties enjoyed remarkable loyalty from their working-class supporters until the dialectic of disillusionment and radicalization set in. If reformist socialists had developed the courage of their convictions and instead of demonizing Bolshevism or dismissing the agency of ordinary people had built bridges from their parliamentary strength to the grassroots democracy of the councils and the activism of the streets, the gap between national leaderships and the socialist rank and file might not have widened. Conversely, if the German insurgents of 1919–21 (whether council communists, syndicalists,

KPDers, or USPD left) and the Italian Maximalists had committed to the parliamentary arena, the broad socialist electorates of 1919 might not have dispersed. Either way, lasting popular enthusiasm for democracy was not created. As the success of Benito Mussolini's Fascists and the limited resilience of the Weimar Republic after 1929–30 both confirmed, the costs were huge.

Could argue that Flex was like Faine a revolutionary

Ex: Civil rights movement through Martin Luther King

Chapter 11

Remolding Militancy

The Foundation of

Communist Parties

I LEFT THE INTERNATIONAL initiatives of European socialism in early 1917, stymied in Stockholm. The northern neutrals vainly confronted the anti-Germanism of the British, French, and Belgian socialists, hoping to revive the pre-1914 Second International. The Zimmerwald movement looked for a renewal of revolutionary politics but without breaking irrevocably with the past. Both were focused on Russia, where the Left's revolutionary prestige had increasingly become the standard.

Thus on the eve of the Bolshevik revolution the Left's politics were very amorphous. The basic split between antiwar opposition and "ministerial socialists" backing the war was clear enough, as was the latter's pragmatic vision of postwar reforms. But the terrain between the militant reformism of a Philipp Scheidemann or Albert Thomas and the single-minded revolutionism of a Lenin remained indistinct. Even Lenin couldn't bring his own party entirely behind the demand for a Third International, and non-Bolshevik support was small. The choice Lenin offered the Zimmerwaldists—"to remain a temporary shelter for revolutionary socialists and war-weary opportunists, or become the basis of a Third International"—was one most Italian, Swiss, French, and German Zimmerwald supporters wouldn't make.[1] But this reluctance to burn bridges was not just fuzzy-headedness and cold feet. It reflected fundamental differences over democracy, national particularities, and vanguardism, which had no easy resolution and dogged the Third International's history in years to come. Where most Zimmerwaldists awaited the revival of mass revolutionary agitation from below, Lenin insisted on superior organization and a strong lead.

THE DIVISIONS OF INTERNATIONAL SOCIALISM

Once the Bolsheviks took power and the armistice gave right-wing socialists freer rein, both extreme wings moved to institutionalize the wartime split. As Stockholm discussions faded away, Allied socialists appointed a three-person committee of their own and called a conference in Bern for February 1919 to reestablish the Second International. In parallel, the Bolsheviks launched the Third International, with a founding congress in Moscow for March 1919.[2] Yet, much socialist opinion was aligned with neither—essentially the old Zimmerwald majority, greatly expanded now that legal politics were back. Some parties either boycotted the Bern meeting, like the Italians and Swiss, or else went and later withdrew. Between the First and Second Congresses of the Communist (Third) International in March 1919 and July 1920, such official secessions made the Second International mainly a northern European affair, based on majority socialist parties in Britain, Germany, Sweden, Denmark, the Netherlands, and Belgium. The first to leave was the Italian party in March 1919, followed by those in Norway, Greece, Hungary, Switzerland, and Spain. In early 1920, the German USPD, the French SFIO, the British ILP, and the Austrian SPÖ all followed suit.[3]

While some of these parties gravitated toward Moscow, Second International losses weren't immediate gains for the Third. Those came later, after the Second Comintern Congress in July 1920 issued its Twenty-One Conditions for joining, which then provided criteria for defining a Communist party (CP).[4] With this instrument, Grigorii Zinoviev and other Bolshevik emissaries toured sympathetic Socialist parties in winter 1920–21, cajoling the pro-Bolshevik Left into finally breaking with their opponents, either by expelling the latter where they were strong enough or by themselves forming a new party. This occurred first at the Halle Congress of the USPD in October 1920, which voted 237 against 156 to accept the Twenty-One Conditions: the right kept 340,000 members and most of the apparatus, but the left claimed 428,000 members, taking 370,000 of them into the united KPD in December.[5] The SFIO came next, voting at its December Congress in Tours to join the Third International and create the French Communist Party (PCF).[6] In Livorno in January 1921, roughly half the PSI's membership left to form the Italian Communist Party, and in May the same occurred in Czechoslovakia.[7] These new parties joined the smaller CPs established around Europe after 1918 (see table 11.1).

This new round of splitting gave large groupings no international home, so yet a third international body took shape, emerging from two confer-

TABLE 11.1 The Foundation of Communist Parties

Country	Name of Party	Year	Membership
Austria	Communist Party of German Austria (KPÖ)	1918	3,000
Belgium	Communist Party of Belgium (PCB)	1921	517
Bulgaria	Bulgarian Communist Party (BKP)	1919	
Czechoslovakia	Czechoslovakian Communist Party (KSC)	1921	170,000
Denmark	Danish Communist Party (DKP)	1920	25,000
Finland	Socialist Workers Party(SSTP)	1920	2,500
France	French Communist Party (PCF)	1920	109,000
Germany	Communist Party of Germany (KPD)	1918	106,656
Great Britain	Communist Party of Great Britain (CPGB)	1920	3,000
Greece	Socialist Workers Party of Greece (SEKE)	1918	
Hungary	Hungarian Communist Party (KMP)	1918	
Iceland	Icelandic Communist Party (KFI)	1930	
Ireland	Communist Party of Ireland (CPI)	1921	
Italy	Communist Party of Italy (PCI)	1921	70,000
Luxemburg	Communist Party of Luxemburg (CPL)	1921	500
Netherlands	Communist Party of Holland (CPH)	1918	1,799
Norway	Norwegian Communist Party (NKP)	1923	16,000
Poland	Polish Communist Workers Party (KRPP)	1918	
Portugal	Portuguese Communist Party (PCP)	1921	
Romania	Romanian Communist Party (PCR)	1921	2,000
Spain	Spanish Communist Party (PCE)	1919	1,000
Sweden	Communist Party of Sweden (SKP)	1921	14,000
Switzerland	Communist Party of Switzerland (KPS)	1921	
Yugoslavia	Communist Party of Yugoslavia (KPJ)	1919	

ences in Bern and Vienna in December 1920 and February 1921 as the International Working Union of Socialist Parties. This Vienna Union, or "Two-and-a-Half International," rallied the left-socialist rumps who rejected the Twenty-One Conditions, including the USPD, the Czech Social Democrats, the SFIO, and the full array of Balkan Social Democratic groups. They were joined by the Swiss Social Democrats, who first affiliated and then left the Third International in summer 1919; anti-Bolshevik Russians among the Mensheviks and Left SRs; and the British ILP. The moral lead came from the Austrian Socialists, who during 1919–20 stayed consistently independent between the camps.[8]

The Vienna Union was exactly what Lenin condemned in the latter-day Zimmerwald movement, officially disbanded by the Third International in March 1919—a temporary refuge for antireformists who couldn't stomach a split. But for Friedrich Adler, its secretary and moving spirit, it was a bridge to socialist unity. He brokered a unity conference in Berlin in April 1922, to which each International—the Second, Third, and Two-and-a-Half—sent 10 delegates, with the remaining executives as observers. It was perhaps remarkable that this conference—the first since the old ISB's final meeting in Brussels in July 1914 where all tendencies of the international movement were present—met at all, at least creating a "Committee of Nine" for future cooperation. But by the Committee's first meeting the following month the framework was already lost. The Third International withdrew, amid violent recriminations now only too familiar in Left political exchange.[9] By fall 1922, the Two-and-a-Half International was in unity talks with the Second International. In May 1923, they merged as the Labor and Socialist International (LSI) in Hamburg.

This universalized the split in the socialist movement opened by the war, a split disfiguring the Left's politics until the flux of 1956–68 and beyond. Two camps faced each other across a minefield of polemical difference. Yet a nonaligned center had sought to escape these polarized outcomes imposed by the Second and Third internationals, and in much of Europe still carried the Left's hopes. Its leading voices—Friedrich Adler, Giancinto Serrati, Jean Longuet, and in a different way Karl Kautsky—were infuriatingly wishy-washy when it came to acting on their revolutionary principles. By Bolshevik standards, parties like the USPD and SPÖ were certainly no advertisement for revolutionary decisiveness. But in the light of later history—not just the Russian Revolution's degeneration and the murderous stain of Stalinism but the Left's return in the 1970s and 1980s to classical democratic perspectives—their scruples deserve to be taken seriously. However ineffectual its bearers on a scale of revolutionary success, the line from Zimmerwald to the Vienna Union charted principles of national diversity and classical democracy, which the Third International sacrificed to its cost.

LAUNCHING THE COMMUNIST INTERNATIONAL

Once Bolshevism was in power, Lenin had his way, and a new International was formed. Scope was initially limited by wartime communications. In early February 1918, a Moscow meeting of leftists from Scandinavia and eastern Europe wanted to call a conference, but the Soviet regime's renewed military problems supervened. Nevertheless, a Federation of Foreign Groups of the Russian Communist Party was formed in May, and plans resumed with the end of war and the central European revolutions. In a radio appeal to Europe on Christmas Eve 1918, the Bolsheviks rallied supporters openly to the "Third International," "which, for all intents and purposes, has already been launched."[10] On 21 January 1919, a small group drafted an invitation to "the first congress of our new revolutionary International" in Moscow, broadcast three days later in the names of the Russian, Latvian, and Finnish Communist Parties, the Revolutionary Balkan Federation, and the Foreign Bureaus of the Communist Workers' Parties of Poland, Hungary, and Austria.[11] Originally called for 15 February, the meeting actually convened in the first week of March.

The call mentioned 39 groups in 31 separate countries, all European apart from the United States, Australia, and Japan; others from the colonial world were added later. The Congress drew 52 delegates from 35 organizations in 22 countries. After national reports and credentialing, proceedings revolved around analysis of the world capitalist order, recorded in four detailed statements: "The Platform of the Communist International"; Lenin's "Theses and Report on Bourgeois Democracy and the Dictatorship of the Proletariat"; the "Attitude toward the Socialist Currents and the Bern Conference"; and the "Manifesto of the Communist International to the Workers of the World." Communism was contrasted with the moribund system of "bourgeois democracy," which not only the "social patriots" but also "the amorphous, unstable Socialist center" were now defending. To parliaments and classical liberal freedoms were counterposed the soviets or workers' councils as "the conditions and forms of the new and higher workers' democracy." The dictatorship of the proletariat was the instrument of the workers' class emancipation, just as "insurrections, civil wars, and the forcible suppression of kings, feudal lords, slaveowners, and their attempts at restoration" were the unavoidable medium of the bourgeoisie's rise before. Forming an international vanguard was the utmost priority.[12]

There was no dissent. On the third day of the Congress, 4 March 1919, the motion to found the Communist International, submitted by Austrian, Hungarian, Swedish, and Balkan delegations, was passed unanimously with one abstention. While the Congress was a small and vaguely representative gathering, in the Left's longer history it was a momentous occasion, whose significance needs careful explication.

The Bolsheviks' own phenomenal success, the central European upheaval of fall 1918, and radicalization in Italy and elsewhere, fueled the sense of an impending world-historical break. Even in the face of immediate disaster—like the German repression and the murders of Luxemburg and Liebknecht preceding the Congress—the new Communists saw contradictions moving inexorably in their own favor. The drama of the occasion, and the sense of revolutionary anticipation, of being on the cusp of a new era, was palpable. Arriving in the midst of the second day, the Austrian delegate Karl Steinhardt captured the mood: dirty and disheveled, striding straight up to the podium to declare his credentials, ripping them from his tattered greatcoat by knife, and immediately receiving the floor. After a stirring and grossly inflated account of Austrian Communist strength, he ended on a heroic note:

> For seventeen days we have been underway from Vienna to Moscow. We travelled the whole way like hoboes; on coal cars, locomotives, couplings, in cattle cars, on foot through the lines of Ukrainian and Polish robber bands, our lives constantly in danger, always driven by the single burning desire: we want to get to Moscow, we must get to Moscow, and nothing will stop us from getting there![13]

European revolutionary advance was thought to be imminent. The new International would soon be headquartered in the West, in Berlin or Paris, depending on where the breakthrough occurred.

Yet, revolutionary enthusiasm aside, what exactly the Congress represented was unclear. Despite the search for appropriate affiliates and the Credentials Commission's meticulous standards so familiar from pre-1914 international socialist culture, the Moscow meeting was an arbitrary miscellany of self-appointed radicals. Simply disseminating the invitation was a problem, given the Allied blockade of Soviet Russia, the Civil War, and the Soviet government's diplomatic isolation, which lasted into late 1919. The call appeared in Austria and Hungary as early as 29–30 January 1919 but wasn't properly published in Germany until a month later. Some two dozen emissaries tried to carry the invitation through the blockade, but only a few reached their destinations. Most participants resided in the Soviet Republic itself.[14]

This problem of representation—of the Communist International's actual, rather than rhetorical, relationship to an international movement—becomes clearer from the overall picture of the Congress. Delegates fell into five categories. With the exception of the Germans and Hungarians, those representing Communist parties already in existence came exclusively from the Russian empire's former territories, including Finland, Estonia, Latvia, Lithuania, Belorussia, Poland, Ukraine, and Armenia. Second, nationalist intellectuals spoke for areas of the Middle and Far East, where Communist organization barely existed, including Turkestan, Azerbaijan, the Volga Germans, and the United Group of the Eastern Peoples of Russia, together with Turkey, Persia, China, and Korea. A special case was Georgia, where the socialist intelligentsia had exceptional popular support but took a Menshevik rather than a Bolshevik path.

Next came small left-wing sects with little working-class support, perhaps calling themselves Communist parties, but not particularly "Communist" in character: groups from Austria, Switzerland, Netherlands, Sweden, and the United States, plus the Balkan Revolutionary Social Democratic Federation. Fourth, a few delegates came from mainstream social democratic parties, including those in Norway, Switzerland, Bulgaria, and France. Last, several delegates already in Moscow—from the Czech, Bulgarian, Yugoslav, British, and French Communist Groups—represented only the Russian party's Federation of Foreign Groups rather than any distinct connections at home.

There was thus a big gap between the International's revolutionary élan—its sense of purposeful forward momentum—and the European labor movement's continuing allegiances. The spread of radicalism was patent enough, but how to capture it for Communist parties, and indeed what defined "Communism" in the first place, remained unclear. The new International's opening toward the colonial world was a far stronger distinction. A quarter of the delegates, 12 out of 52, came from Asia, and in this sense the Russian Revolution brought anticolonialism freshly into the heart of the Left. The Bolsheviks' early international policy included an audacious bid to revolutionize the non-Western world, turning its sights deliberately "toward the Orient, Asia, Africa, the colonies, where this movement [for national self-determination] is not a thing of the past but of the present and the future."[15] Here, the Congress launched a vital longer-term tradition, to which the Baku Congress of the Peoples of the East in September 1920 became the bridge.

The Congress also marked the arrival of a younger activist generation. One category of delegates, from Russia itself and eastern Europe, had become social democrats in their teens and twenties, either in the founding upsurge of eastern socialist parties in the 1890s or during the radicalizing experience of 1905. But most of the rest were formed by the First World War, including the western Europeans, Transcaucasians, and broader Asian contingent. Here the contrast with the prewar Second International Congresses—and with the Bern Congress of February 1919—was sharp: "Instead of all the well-known 'esteemed' fathers of international Social Democracy; instead of the theoreticians, hoary with age; instead of the leaders of the workers' movement of the previous half-century; here, with a few exceptions, were gathered new people, whose names were still little known."[16]

But neither these youthful energies nor the general revolutionary optimism could conceal the fledgeling International's dependence on events in Russia. Bolshevik leaders assumed that the Moscow headquarters were temporary. Zinoviev anticipated "transferring the Third International's place of residence and executive committee as quickly as possible to another capital, for example, Paris." He was echoed by Trotsky: "to Berlin, Paris, London."[17] But despite this genuine internationalism, Bolsheviks retained the decisive voice, particularly when pan-European revolutionism subsided after 1921. Once defending the Soviet Union became an overriding priority for Communists elsewhere, the Comintern dwindled unavoidably into a resource for Soviet foreign policy.

WHAT KIND OF COMMUNISM?

Given the uncertainties of the Third International's relation to the Left country by country, the big unanswered question concerned the kind of Communist parties to promote. Lenin's "Theses . . . on Bourgeois Democracy and the Dictatorship of the Proletariat" defined strict criteria for affiliation with the Comintern, incorporated into the "Platform" of 6 March. Here, Communist politics meant soviet as against parliamentary state forms. Yet this prescription worked only while insurrections were on the agenda. Once they receded, the Left again faced participating in the existing order—parliaments, elections, and the general institutional world of "bourgeois democracy." Lenin would find himself, willy-nilly, conceding the importance of parliamentary, trade union, and other "legal" fields of action, however tactical, subordinate, or cynical these concessions claimed to be.

Furthermore, the Third International's impact beyond the Soviet Union's own borders and contiguous areas of the colonial world required making serious inroads into Europe's established socialist movements. Its success depended on breaking into these existing formations and their popular support, just as Zimmerwald had needed the broader antiwar sentiments of the much maligned center. Lenin might hammer on the need for a new start and a clean break. But new parties couldn't be fashioned from nothing. They needed to reshape existing traditions and contexts of militancy. Where such parties were launched into a vacuum, without splitting an existing movement, they seldom escaped sectarian marginality.

This gave the Comintern a dilemma. Once the affiliated groups expanded in 1919–20, particularly with the hemorrhage of support from the Bern International and the possible regroupment of the socialist center, the ambivalence of the Comintern's potential supporters over soviet versus parliamentary democracy couldn't be ignored. By 1920 and the buildup to the Second Congress, the affiliated parties embraced the gamut of left-wing politics, from parliamentary socialism of the prewar kind, through council communism, to syndicalism and an extreme ultraleftism that refused all truck with parliaments. Resolving this question became the Third International's key dilemma as it entered its second year.

The Twenty-One Conditions of July 1920 were only a partial solution. These were certainly effective in drawing the lines more sharply against reformists, digging a deep ditch between Communist parties and the older social democratic ones still shaping the Left in Scandinavia, the Low Countries, and Britain. But they brutally excluded a much wider range of socialist opinion and support, that expressed through the short-lived Two-and-a-Half or Vienna International, which included not only Mensheviks and other defeated factions, or smaller Left parties like the British ILP, but also the prestigious Austrian Socialists and larger left-socialist groupings from Germany, Czechoslovakia, and France unhappy with the discipline and loyalty the Third International now required. Over the longer term, the new CPs could only prosper by winning the confidence of these groupings and their support. For most of the 1920s and 1930s, however, Communists only accentuated their differences, driving left-wing socialists back into the arms of the social democratic right.

Equally serious, the most impressive revolutionary insurgencies during 1919–21 reflected violent, volatile, and localized forms of working-class radicalism, which the new parties had little ability to organize or control. This was clearest in Germany, Italy, and Czechoslovakia, where the strongest CPs faced mobilized workers angrily resistant to any leadership seeking to implement national strategy or develop a coordinated political line. Indeed, as much activism existed *beyond* the organized frameworks of Communist and left-socialist allegiances as within them: in late 1920, for instance, as the 78,000 KPD members awaited the influx of former USPDers, the council-communist KAPD and its associated General Workers' Union may have counted another one hundred thousand supporters, not to speak of the kaleidoscopically shifting patterns of unaffiliated neosyndicalist militancy.[18] These working-class mobilizations simultaneously sustained and frustrated Communist revolutionaries, producing the most reckless challenges to authority but without lasting supralocal effect. This was the infant Communist parties' thorniest dilemma: how successfully they shaped such militancy would decisively influence the *kind* of Communist parties they would become.

FOR WOMEN IN the revolutionary years, the ambiguities of change were acute. The war's end brought the first breakthrough of female enfranchisement. Before 1914, women voted in only Finland (1906) and Norway (1913), but by 1918 they shared in Europe's democratization. First in Russia, then in the central European revolutions of Czechoslovakia, Austria, Hungary, Poland, and Germany, and finally in Ireland (1922), the new states included women as voting citizens, as did the liberal polities of the north—Denmark and Iceland (1915), Sweden (1918), Britain (1918), Luxemburg (1919), and the Netherlands (1920). If women's suffrage wasn't universal—in Belgium, France, and Italy reforms were blocked—the trend was clear.[1]

In contrast, women's economic dependency was scarcely improved. Wartime entry into protected male occupations was crudely reversed. Women stayed in waged jobs, because working-class households still needed their incomes, but the priority of demobilized male "breadwinners" was quickly restored. Right and Left shared a desire to restabilize gender relations upset by the war. In short, while winning constitutional gains, women became the objects of social policies implying that little really had changed.

The Politics of Gender

Women and the Left

CITIZENS, MOTHERS, AND CONSUMERS

In a nutshell: women were enrolled into citizenship and men's and women's political rights finally grew the same, only for social policies to reassert their difference. The leading edge of this gender politics was *maternalism*—ideas and policies foregrounding motherhood as crucial for the nation's public health, global competitiveness, and moral order. Two intersecting anxieties were involved. One was the war's demographic catastrophe. Europe lost 50–60 million to military and civilian casualties, starvation and disease, and war-induced birth deficits, and 20–25 million were permanently disabled, leaving a stark gender imbalance among younger women and men. Second, the war disordered "normal" family life. It snatched husbands and fathers from patriarchal roles and required new female responsibilities—not just the obvious burdens but ambiguous freedoms and opportunities too. Added to demobilization and men's reentry into the labor market, which spurred talking about women's place, these effects harnessed attention to the health of the family.

Population policy became an obsession of interwar public life. The surplus of women and shortage of men, the declining birth rate, the war's visible human wreckage, and fears of social degeneration all combined with women's new political rights and the enhanced welfare state to bring women to the political fore. Pronatalist policies for raising the birth rate and the quality of society's human resources and maternalist policies for strengthening women's family roles converged. The resulting policy regimes—and the debates and battles surrounding them—varied country by country in complex ways but described a space of political intervention common to interwar Europe. Questions of reproduction (birth control, abortion, sterilization), child welfare, medical advice, household efficiency, and social services composed the shared battleground of politics. They incited diverse projects of social policing and improvement, with openings not only for the efficiency-maximizing ambitions of bureaucracies and experts but also for the altruism of reformers, from professionals and social activists to labor movements and women's organizations, as well as ordinary women themselves. Consequently, it mattered enormously what particular balance of political forces pertained.[2]

The Right sought to confine women at home, invoking "traditional" family values or nationalist demands for "purifying" the population pool, for which Nazism's racialized policies in 1933–45 became a terrible extreme. But this wasn't the prerogative of the Right alone. Whether in the USSR, the French Third Republic's population policies, Fabian social policies in Britain, or sex reform in Weimar Germany, the Left were active too. Biological politics—removing issues from contention by "naturalizing" them, referring them to medical and scientific expertise rather than democratic debate—were common ground of discussion for welfare issues, child-raising, public health, sexuality, and sex differences between the wars.[3] Other public discussions also revolved round this central theme, from the memorializing of the First World War to the linking of patriotism with masculine ideals of virility and domesticized images of female patience and virtue.[4] The "feminizing" of social policy, education, and family life into women's distinctive domain reflected this syndrome too.[5]

Left and Right occupied a single frame. Family reform implied women's advancement, whether via positive recognition as wives and mothers or recruitment into voluntary agencies and "caring" professions for the same familial needs. In the meantime, analyses of fascism and post-1968 feminist critiques have explored the disempowering consequences of such biologically based familialism confining women to the home. Seeing women's emancipation in a "separate sphere" of familial, domestic or feminine virtues has become more problematic in light of these critiques, because separation undermined civic and legal equality as often as securing it. But in 1918, these issues were blurred. Even the strongest radicals, like the Bolshevik Aleksandra Kollontai, retained some notion of a "natural division of labor" affecting women's innate roles as mothers.[6]

Initially, validating motherhood and domesticity could be empowering. Social feminism—protection for motherhood, family-oriented social policies, education for girls, protective labor legislation, a politics of women's special nature—had focused feminists' vision of women's emancipation before 1914 as much as legal equality and the vote.[7] "Advanced" thinking among emancipated women and men enlisted eugenicist ideas for regulating human procreation, blurring the lines between feminist control over reproduction and "national efficiency" arguments for survival of the race. Unless reforms made motherhood more attractive, it was commonly argued, only "inferior" mothers would have children.

There was one last complication. If tensions endured between civil equality and constructions of sexual difference, they also defined the new consumerism—between social policies confining women to the family and consumer promises tempting them out. Housewives became household managers, joining the public sphere as purchasing agents for husbands and children. Even more destabilizing, a new culture of cheap entertainment— in dream palaces and dance halls, and the lure of lipstick, smoking, and fashion—captured attention. Younger women found an expressive independence, a stylistic escape from domestic and public oppressiveness of male control, in a commercially driven culture of possibility, "playing on fantasy and desire."[8] Advertising and the cinema transported this reality from the socially restricted culture of the metropolis to the general topography of women's imaginations.[9]

How the Left reacted to the commercial culture of mass entertainment became a key question of politics. For feminists and socialists alike, young women embodied this challenge. On the one hand they were egregiously neglected by the Left; on the other consumerism offered an escape from domesticity. Feminist campaigners dimissed the new fashions as distraction, while male socialists slipped easily into misogynist contempt. The pleasure-seeking young had no place in the socialist imaginary—those "silly girls in their synthetic Hollywood dreams, their pathetic silk stockings and lipsticks, their foolish strivings."[10] Yet consumerism, like the politics of the family and welfare, described a key site of politics. These were the new realities the war and the contemporary transformations of capitalism engendered. They elicited a new right-wing political repertoire, to which the Left had a remarkably slow response.

COMMUNISM AND WOMEN

What did women gain in the revolutionary years? Lenin insisted proudly on Bolshevik success: "Not a single state . . . has done even half of what the Soviet Government did for women in the very first months."[11] Allowing for nongendered exclusions of property owners from the franchise in the 1918 and 1923 constitutions, women had full citizenship in the Soviet state, sharing equally in the new political community of labor. Equality was grounded in economic independence, as the right—and obligation—to work. Impediments to equality were removed—the gendered apparatus of nineteenth-century liberal reforms no less than the patriarchalism of tsarist law. Residential, property, and inheritance laws gave women equal rights in land, households, and communes. Radical labor laws provided extra protections and equal pay. New family law addressed the household dominance of fathers, introduced civil marriage and divorce on demand, abolished illegitimacy, and legalized abortion. Women's treatment in Muslim Central Asia was also addressed. This was Western feminism's maximum program, to which no government in the West ever came close to agreeing.[12]

Treatment of motherhood as a social responsibility was the dark side. If childbearing was a collective good (as against individual and family fulfilment), political egalitarianism and sexual radicalism could be twinned with equally strong programs of maternal and child welfare. For Kollontai at the Commissariat for Social Welfare, collectivized living freed women from the family to discharge their duties as workers and mothers. Indeed, she argued, attaching intimate relations, child-raising, and social reproduction to the nuclear family was historically outmoded: "The family ceases to be necessary."[13] But few Bolsheviks were comfortable with Kollontai's advocacy of sexual freedom and antifamilial critique, and by 1923 her ideas were being attacked as irresponsible. Sexual danger replaced sexual freedom in Bolshevik rhetoric. The family form allowed sobriety and discipline to be restored. N. Semashko, People's Commissar for Health, hammered this lesson home in 1925: "Drown your sexual energy in public work. . . . If you want to solve the sexual problem, be a public worker, a comrade, not a stallion or a brood-mare."[14]

This conservative turn decided the fate of Zhenotdel, the CPSU Women's Department, created from the First All-Russian Congress of Working Women in November 1918. Charged with raising women's political consciousness, it was disregarded by most party men. It came to be channeled in the usual ways—to socialization of housework and childcare, provision of social services, food distribution, caring for homeless children, or nursing the wounded in the Civil War. Kollontai colluded, distinguishing the public sphere of men from women's everyday life. Zhenotdel, initially used for other purposes, was seen as a troublesome diversion and in 1930 was closed.[15]

If the Russian Revolution's legacy for women was inconclusive, Stalinism consigned the issue to silence. In 1917–30, there were 301 Party decrees and resolutions on "women"; in the next thirty years only three.[16] This pattern was repeated in the Communist International. The second Comintern Congress launched an International Women's Secretariat with sections in Moscow and Berlin, unified under Klara Zetkin in November 1922, but Soviet insistence on a single model of women's agitation created tensions from the start. In April 1926, the Comintern Executive replaced the Secretariat with a new women's department directly under itself.[17] In the individual CPs, the record varied. In the early years, women's membership was weakest in Catholic countries where women's suffrage had failed: 6 percent in Belgium, 1.5 percent in Italy, 2 percent in France. It was stronger where Communists carried larger numbers from the existing labor movements with them in the splits of 1920–21, notably in Germany (12 percent) and Czechoslovakia (20 percent).[18]

Particularly in the smaller or illegal Communist parties, a women's strategy barely arose, as priorities were elsewhere. In Italy, socialists had seen the "woman question" in strictly "workerist" terms, ruling anything else, from women's suffrage to social policies, dogmatically out of order. But the salience of women's wartime protests changed the terrain, and after the 1921 split the new CP immediately made the *questione femminile* a leading cause, seeing women's political rights as essential to the missing democratic revolution. Communists still focused on women as workers, treating them otherwise "as a potentially conservative force." But Antonio Gramsci forced discussion onto the ground of culture, where noneconomic issues of family, schooling, and religion could be raised. From 1921, he persuaded Camilla Ravera to address these questions in *l'Ordine nuovo*—"problems of contraception, abortion, the burden of housework, . . . the commercial nature of marriage . . . the most radical aspects of the Soviet experience . . . [and] the implications of socialism for the transformation of the traditional family."[19] But this was terminated by Fascism, which after 1922 smashed the labor movement, dismantled democracy, and reinstated the most reactionary of gender regimes against women.[20]

A small CP like the British, with less than five thousand members in the early 1920s, couldn't mobilize women *as* women. The party's industrial strongholds (mining in Scotland, South Wales, and the north, engineering in south Yorkshire and greater Manchester) were precisely the labor movement bastions of skilled masculinity most exclusionary against women. Female militants themselves opposed separate women's sections, preferring an ideal of emancipated and egalitarian comradeship instead. Female recruits—young women from socialist families, individual worker militants, teachers, and educated women radicalized via the war—entered the mainstream of party work. This worked for women with some economic independence, but ordinary female "supporters" were connected vicariously through their husbands. Relieving husbands of domestic duties itself counted as "party work." Women's Sections held afternoon meetings in houses, keeping party wives loyal to their husbands' political activity, providing a chance for political discussion, and counteracting housewifely isolation. Yet this replicated the wider society's sexual division of labor, with women servicing their men—as "a sort of housewife to the party," as one Communist husband disarmingly put it.[21]

Some of this came from the British party's smallness. Recruiting outside the recognized working-class core was beyond its resources. It also resisted taking noneconomic oppression seriously. Conflict over birth control climaxed in the summer of 1922, for example, leading the advocates of women's reproductive rights, Stella Browne, Cedar Paul, and Maurice Eden Paul, either to leave or take minor roles. Feminists radicalized by the pre-1914 suffrage campaigning were one of the CPGB's founding groups, and it squandered the chance to build on this start. The failure reflected both socialism's gender blindness and the tightened discipline imposed by Comintern in 1922–24.[22]

The somewhat larger French party, 60,000 strong in 1924, showed a similar trajectory. In the early years it became a gathering point for diverse radicalisms frustrated with available political options, including feminists and sex reformers, offering a home for experimental ideas before "discipline" imposed a more orthodox frame. In contrast to the Socialists and Radicals, the PCF consistently advocated women's suffrage, proposing bills in 1924, 1927, and 1928, and vigorously pressed women's interests at work. Most impressively of all, it championed the cause of birth control and abortion reform, setting itself against the vociferous pronatalist consensus of French public life and collaborating with Madeleine Pelletier and other radical feminists.[23] On the other hand, Comintern directives steadily reduced the PCF's openness, until after 1928 the party hardened its sectarianism, asserting ownership over working women's struggles, cutting its ties to feminists, and sharpening an aggressively masculine style. As membership halved by 1930, women's issues inevitably receded.[24]

The German Communist Party (KPD) seemed utterly typical. It declared the primacy of the class struggle in industry for mobilizing women and ascribed emancipation to productive employment, backed by socialization of childcare, housework, and other domestic services. In the mid-1920s, it demanded exclusive focus on the factory, assigning women an essential psychology whose "petty-bourgeois backwardness" required undeviating emphasis on the class struggle. True proletarian consciousness, Ruth Fischer claimed, was impossible in the four walls of the household, and working-class housewives needed the "hard reality" of wage work to escape their backward mentality.[25] Yet the KPD was an unruly party, fluctuating wildly in membership: from a notional peak of 450,000 after fusing with the USPD in October 1920, it veered crazily up and down, before plummeting from 294,230 to 121,394 between September 1923 and April 1924. This alone made the party hard to control. Further, while the KPD became accused of unimaginative Stalinist orthodoxy, it became despite itself a home for more complex agitations.

A large party like the KPD had contacts with women that were denied to a small cadre party like the British. Aside from wage workers themselves, it had three bridges to working-class women: consumer cooperatives; educational work; and protests against shortages and prices. The last affords the best example. Beginning as spontaneous protests by housewives and youth in late 1919 and summer 1920, repeated in winter 1921–22, and peaking in the second half of 1922 with a major coda in summer 1923, such actions negotiated fair prices with shopkeepers and local authorities but also escalated into riots, with looting of food, shoes, and clothing, and battles against police. The KPD tried to shape this activity for its own ends by forming "control committees" based on works councils to monitor local prices, blurring the link to women's direct actions. Such committees had diverse origins, including citywide parliaments of works councils, local union initiatives, mass meetings at big firms, or informal assemblies of workers and housewives. But the KPD typically imposed its own structure. It hitched women's militancy to the works councils, subsuming it in the "class struggle" of the (male) worker in production. The 840 delegates to the national congress of works councils in November 1922 included only 16 housewives and 16 working women. Women's grassroots militancy was coopted into a bureaucratized revolutionary posture. A separately initiated women's movement was demoted to auxiliary support for the old factory-based ways.[26]

The KPD practice was based in the dogma of the emancipatory necessity of wage labor. Yet, however well-grounded in Marxist economics, this approach scarcely appealed to hard-pressed working-class mothers: in one course for female cadres, the class bridled at the idea that housework was "unproductive." Women's discussion evenings in Berlin-Neukölln in 1922 replaced the factory struggle's exclusive primacy with a battery of women's demands: cooperative households to ease the domestic burden (as against the KPD's program of factory canteens, municipal provision, and nationalization of services); the "real eight-hour day" (in the home as well as the factory); wages for housework; free choice of profession for women (rejecting assumptions about women's work); and genuine sexual freedom (beyond abortion reform and civil marriage).[27]

The KPD leaders tried to make this local militancy conform with its official line. And the KPD's size and militancy continued to attract radicals angry with the SPD's compromising: this applied to radical women no less than radical men. Among German parties, the KPD did have the strongest program of women's liberation, including not only freeing women from the home, via the right to work, socializing domestic labor, and complete civil and professional equality, but also reproductive rights to birth control and abortion. In short, the KPD's assumptions about women's "backwardness" hardly encouraged women's equality in the movement, but it was still a place where women's political militancy could be articulated. Later in the 1920s, this took surprisingly developed forms.[28]

SOCIAL DEMOCRACY AND THE GENDERING OF CITIZENSHIP

One effect of the war was a new prominence of the state in domestic life: if husbands, fathers, and male "breadwinners" were absent, then women's resulting new "presence" needed attention. The earliest example was help for soldiers' wives, and as war continued expenditure escalated. By July 1918 in Britain, 1.5 million wives and 1.5 million dependent relatives were receiving army separation allowances (plus several million children), requiring 120 million pounds per year, or two-thirds of annual central government spending before 1914. Government became involved in four additional areas: general income support and poor relief for the hardships of the war; controlling shortages and prices (especially food and rents); social services for working women; and moral anxiety about the absence of men, stressing disruption of marriages and the crisis of fertility, the spread of prostitution, sexually transmitted diseases, youth criminality and control of children, and women's sexual independence.

Just when the family was not "there," it became vital to insist on its presence. Women's de facto independence—the "unhusbanding of women," in a phrase of the time—fed fears of moral endangerment. It not only made women heads of households and breadwinners, it also conjured huge anxieties around female autonomy, lack of restraint, and the "abnormal excitement" following removal of the husband's or father's moral authority. The further connection, from unhusbanding and immorality to militancy and troublemaking, was easy.

Domestic surveillance of women and families by police and social workers was universal among the First World War's combatant governments. Welfare payments gave the leverage. In Britain, soldiers' allowances were tied to the domestic competence and sexual chastity of wives, first through the volunteer casework of the Soldiers' and Sailors' Families Association and then directly via government in the Statutory Committee of military, political, and philanthropic representatives (1915) and the new Ministry of Pensions (1916).[29] In France and Germany, factory nurses or social workers ("company housewives") coordinated working women's needs for childcare, housing, nutrition, and health, while encouraging sobriety and orderly living. The German state created the Women's Department attached to the new War Office in November 1916, under the social worker and future liberal parliamentarian Marie-Elisabeth Lüders. It wanted to ensure "healthy social relations" for "after the war," which meant "in the first instance protection of the family."[30]

Despite women's unprecedented autonomy, these measures carefully constructed their entitlements as a dependency on men. Payments of allowance directly to women undoubtedly reinforced their wartime independence: "It seems too good to be true, a pound a week and my husband away," in one British wife's words.[31] But supporting women and children remained a strictly male responsibility for which the state temporarily stood in. This model of social citizenship made "motherhood" the ideological complement to "soldiering." If recognition of women's wartime contribution was mediated through their husbands, the effects of their independence as workers and household managers might be contained. This over-determining impact of the war decisively changed the meanings of welfare for women, both as recipients and practitioners, tightening the institutional and discursive links to the state.[32]

Here, social democrats were entirely complicit. They found recognition of public responsibility very attractive. Soldiers' allowances fixed the principle of the state's obligation to its (male) citizenry in a language of social citizenship, attaching social rights to social roles like soldiering or working. Charities, the private apparatus of middle-class moral reform, were finally replaced by state-provided welfare, which socialists would eventually control. The Labour Party in Britain saw the Ministry of Pensions, headed by the trade-union parliamentarian George Barnes, as a building-block for the welfare state. The SPD in Germany was less successful in establishing public control. As in Britain, the labor movement's local government strength de facto dominated social services delivery after 1918, but the religiously organized private charities survived in the confusing tangle of laws composing the Weimar Republic's welfare sector. Nowhere were women's rights given autonomous recognition. When women's benefits were extended—in Britain for unemployed workers' dependents (1921) and widows' pensions (1925, 1929)—it was in virtue again of dependent status. Women remained secondary beneficiaries of their husbands' rights.

Reformist socialists congratulated themselves. Social needs were removed from the moralizing of middle-class charitable visitors to become the nation's public responsibility. Family welfare became a class demand, legitimately voiced by the labor movements. Social rights became attached to citizenship. These lines ran directly to post-1945 welfare states. But the erasure of working-class women as democratic agents with rights separate from husbands reflected deeply conservative assumptions about women's proper place. This emerged instantly in the revolutionary turbulence of 1917–23, when German and Austrian Social Democrats anxiously defended their own moral reliability, as women arrived for the first time as voters. They had no interest in free love, in introducing a "whore economy," or in removing children from mothers to the charge of the state, they insisted. These were "fairy stories" spread by demagogues and priests.[33]

The SPD was the protector of the working-class family. It upheld civil equality and equal pay, but its priority for women was the family: supporting families-in-need via benefits, home visiting, and advice centers; maternal and child protection; contraception and abortion, ideally through citywide "family care agencies"; adequate housing and a "family" wage; ethical partnership in marriage and democratic child-raising. This was the "social worker's–eye view" of working-class daily life. It reflected both the SPD's local government dominance in newly democratized urban Germany and a new professional cadre of socialist doctors, teachers, and social workers in public life. Social Democrats took a didactic and patronizing view of the working-class poor, separating respectable working families from the rough and disorderly residuum, whom the state needed to manage. Working-class family life became either the solid fundament of socialist culture or the pathology requiring cure. The social democratic family was an ideal in which the roughness of the poor could be recast. The skilled, regularly employed, unionized working class displayed the orderly family living that SPD ideology desired.

These family images had little emancipatory promise. As mothers and social workers, women appeared as agents of family moralization, not the autonomous political subjects whom dismantling the family could free. Whether through the budding welfare-statism of SPD cities or housing reform and campaigns for rationalizing housework, socialist social policy made dependent places for women, bounded by the home. In the domestic sphere, socialist creativity mostly concerned the young—free school experiments, "child republics," and youth movements—leaving sex-gender distinctions in the family alone. At the SPD's Heidelberg Congress in 1925, one Leipzig woman delegate accused SPD men of failing "to introduce socialism into their own families."[34] But such critiques were rare.

Validating motherhood in a separate-spheres ideology was institutionalized in the SPD after the opening of female membership in 1908.[35] Before 1914, the SPD still stressed the oppressiveness of private property organized through the family and the liberating necessity of women's productive labor. But with the wartime split, Marie Juchacz and others now celebrated women's reproductive contribution to the nation: as mothers of future generations, they became a priority of national policy. In taking its place inside the maternalist consensus, the SPD typified the socialist parties of the old north-central European social democratic core—Germany and Austria, the Czech lands, the Low Countries, Scandinavia.[36]

In the British Labour Party, women's activism was less wholly shaped by the politics of social work. Women activists were still shunted into education, health, and social services. Union bloc voting rigged annual Conferences against feminist resolutions, and comparable worth strategies failed to budge the traditional line of "equal pay for equal work," which directly benefited women less. Yet in 1929 Labour's first woman cabinet minister, Margaret Bondfield, took the Ministry of Labour rather than a welfare brief, and other leading women MPs, like Susan Lawrence and Ellen Wilkinson, made a point of speaking for the whole movement, without distinction of gender. During the 1920s Labour women enlivened municipal socialism by strong grassroots movements around working-class welfare, including birth control and family allowances, insisting that "sex" issues were really "class" issues. What most separated Labour women from feminists in single-sex organizations, notwithstanding overlaps of membership, was the feeling that the latter were middle-class individualists insensitive to the working class.[37]

FEMINISM BETWEEN THE WARS

What about feminism per se? Enfranchisement problematized feminism's future direction. Suffrage agitations had always raised other issues, concerning women's social, sexual, and civil identities. But wartime patriotism—with the exception of the Women's International League for Peace and Freedom, formed in 1915—largely narrowed the debate. Following through on equality of citizenship by attacking sex discrimination and campaigning for equal pay was one response to winning the vote, but it was eclipsed in most countries by a "new feminist" maternalism. By 1917–18 prominent British feminists like Eleanor Rathbone and Maude Royden were advocating a "national endowment for motherhood," and Rathbone's tireless propaganda through the Family Endowment Committee captured postwar feminist agendas. Her tract, *The Disinherited Family* (1924), sought to shift feminism primarily onto maternalist ground.

Rathbone was president of the National Union of Societies for Equal Citizenship (NUSEC), British feminism's umbrella organization, during 1919–28.[38] The NUSEC initially backed an orthodox "equality" feminism, embracing equal suffrage, equal pay, equal opportunities for employment, equal moral standards for divorce, equal parental rights, and pensions for widows with dependent children. But by 1925, Rathbone added birth control and family allowances in a very different overall perspective, invoking patriotic motherhood-as-citizenship arguments to insist that "real equality" transcended equal opportunities with men. It stressed what was valuable and different in women themselves:

> True equality meant freeing these women from economic dependence on their husbands by granting equal honor and financial support to their work in "women's sphere." This could not be done through "old

feminist" campaigns for equal pay and open access to men's jobs; labor market reforms would not answer the needs of the unwaged. Only State intervention could do so; welfare programs could circumvent the labor market to provide independent support for mothers.[39]

Equality feminism vigorously resisted—via the London Society for Women's Service under Ray and Pippa Strachey, the Women's Freedom League, the Six Point Group, and the weekly journal *Time and Tide*. When new feminists pushed another maternalist demand, protective legislation for women workers, equality feminists regrouped in the Open Door Council in May 1926. The NUSEC annual council passed a motion supporting protective legislation by 81 to 80 votes in March 1927. An attempt to reassert equal pay as the main priority over birth control and family allowances was defeated, and 11 of the 23 members of the newly elected executive resigned. This divisive debate—plus the completion of women's enfranchisement in 1928—ended British feminism's unity between the wars.

The conflict reflected larger visions.[40] For equality feminists, equal pay struck at the heart of the underlying gender assumptions whose persistence family allowances helped entrench; by foregrounding the latter, new feminists were perpetuating inequality's root cause. New feminists, on the other hand, saw themselves mounting a more imaginative challenge to existing gender relations, which were based on the male breadwinner norm and the ideology of the family wage. Family allowances payable directly to the mother would break the chain of female subordination, recognize the national interest in maternity, and constitute motherhood as citizenship. But in practice, Rathbone's proposals were easily stolen by the state, as in the laws for widows' pensions in 1925 and 1929, which efficiently assimilated her thinking to the prevailing masculinist rationale. In this sense, maternalist feminism was a trap. Severed from political alliances and lacking economic and institutional power, Rathbone and other new feminists couldn't win by rhetoric alone: "in the end their maternalist, 'separate but equal' ideology was pressed into service in the creation of policies encoding dependence, not the value of difference."[41]

By the 1930s, feminists in Europe more generally were at an impasse. In north-central Europe, the vote was won. In the USSR, legal emancipation seemed very advanced, although the outlawing of abortion, restriction of divorce, and criminalizing of homosexuality would shortly tell a very different story. In western Europe, equality legislation begrudgingly ensued. In Britain, this included the Sex Disqualification (Removal) Act in 1919, technically opening public appointments and professions; the Matrimonial Causes Act of 1923, equalizing divorce; and the Guardianship of Infants Act in 1925, improving mothers' rights. But such reforms mainly sought to head feminists off. Discrimination typically regrouped to impede women's progress via marriage bars in teaching, civil service, and public employment. Economic dependency negated women's ability to enjoy legal equalities of choice.

If women joined social democratic parties, they were typecast as "caring" auxiliaries in fields like welfare or health, finding feminist goals blocked by male decision-making structures.[42] Communist parties were more promising but also stifled gender politics by unrelenting "proletarianism." The daily practice of left-wing movements was riddled with masculine prejudices that rarely were honestly faced. Even worse, counterrevolutionary repression—in Hungary, Italy, and Europe's eastern and southern peripheries—reversed postwar gains or hardened existing gender oppressions. New right-wing mobilizations, disastrously threatening for women, started in Germany, Austria, and elsewhere in the West.

Feminist maternalism—working sexual difference into a program—sought to make women's special nature into an instrument of empowerment rather than oppression. Given male resistance to admitting women on equal terms, this took men at their word, coopting the idea of irreducible differences based in biology and asserting motherhood's centrality as a public value. It, rather than the fruitless quest for equal pay, would be the basis of women's independence, the argument ran, because once the state "endowed" women's role in the family through a system of direct payments, the case for the male breadwinner norm, the need for men to support a family on their own wage, fell away.

But social conservatives already commanded the language of maternalism. Policy-makers—in government, business, parties, unions, churches, press—made motherhood key to postwar normalizing. Maternalism was the medium of gender restoration, returning women to the home; and by equating motherhood with citizenship, British new feminists like Rathbone moved women's demands exactly where conservatives preferred. As maternalism seemed the only game in town, feminists joined in, bending things toward their own agenda. Antifamily radicalism promised only marginalization. But left-wing maternalism remained a fateful choice: by embracing maternity's virtues, new feminists learned a language that already assigned women a lesser, poverty-ridden, and dependent place.

Rathbone's was not the only British feminist voice, and her opponents stayed active in many areas of public, professional, and intellectual life, as new political agendas became composed.[43] By the 1930s, moreover, the contrast between "equal rights" and "new" feminist positions was often blurred, not least in the Labour Party, where they were caught "in a rich and complex web of interlocking dialogues about the nature of the party and its relationship to the British state."[44] But in most of Europe, Communist and left-socialist support for women's civil and economic equality, social democratic welfarism, and the variety of reformist and right-wing maternalisms left European feminists little independent space—as, for example, the contrast between Madeleine Pelletier's Communist period in

1920–25 and her individualized efforts of the 1930s only too tragically showed.[45] On the other hand, social changes were proceeding that over the longer term *required* feminist response: "the birthrate did decline, families did become smaller, women were more visible in public, the 'woman and sex questions' were discussed differently, and the role of doctors did increase."[46] In the 1920s, these and other questions affecting women were still awaiting the Left's programmatic attention.

EMANCIPATION AND ITS DISCONTENTS

Official socialist and Communist views of sexuality itself were extremely conservative. While youthful working-class sexuality inevitably found its own way, party cultures stressed self-control. The Austrian Socialists were typical. Sexuality should be "shaped and constrained" to produce an "*ordentliche* (orderly, decent and respectable) family," laying the ghost of sexual decadence and promiscuity and bringing the party credit. There was no space for the sexual independence of women. Such thoughts bowed to the family's affective needs. Measured by the latter, youth sexuality was an unhealthy disturbance, comparable to smoking and drink, for which the "cold showering" of physical exercise—in the Workers' Association for Sports and Body Culture—was the answer.[47]

Nevertheless, sexology, or the scientific construction of sexual knowledge around naturalized ideas of health and well-being, began to authorize a new openness about sexual pleasure. A new genre of marriage manuals encouraged women to see themselves as sexual agents, including Marie Stopes's *Married Love* (1918), selling four hundred thousand copies by 1923; Theodor van de Velde's *Her Volkomen Huwelijk* (1926), translated by Stella Browne as *Ideal Marriage: Its Physiology and Technique* (1928), with editions in all other European languages; and Helena Wright's book *The Sex Factor in Marriage* (1930). Fiercely rejecting "the conventional estimate of women's sexual apathy" as a mechanism of male control, Stella Browne expounded a politics of reproductive rights focused on birth control, abortion, and women's sexual self-determination.[48] Population politics, maternalism, and the growth of women's citizenship were also bringing sexual relations into political vision.

In Weimar Germany, a remarkable sex reform movement flourished. Growing from local working-class birth control leagues, it blossomed into a panoply of educational, counseling, and clinical services, guided by a militant ideology of working-class entitlement. By 1928, the movement converged with medical networks and labor movement welfare organs. The League for Birth Control and Sexual Hygiene formed a national umbrella with the Society for Sexual Reform, broadly aligned with the SPD but rivaled in 1929 by the apolitical League for the Protection of Mothers and Social Family Hygiene. Despite the divisive launch of a rival Communist organization in April 1931, cooperation continued among Communist, SPD, liberal, and nonaligned left-wing doctors, social workers and other activists, reaching its zenith in the 1931 campaign for abortion reform and the undergrowth of sex clinics in Berlin, Hamburg, and elsewhere.[49] The movement's leadership was still mainly male centered, indebted to maternalist and eugenicist assumptions. But it did make ordinary people's sexual enjoyment and women's right to reproductive freedom into serious political matters and came closest to allowing a woman-centered sexual politics to break through.

Sex reform reflected the politicizing of domesticity during 1914–18. Child-raising, motherhood, and housewifery entered politics under broadly maternalist auspices, and once "the working-class home was opened up, not only to closer state regulation, but also as a legitimate sphere of political struggle," sexual relations came to the fore.[50] But sex reform had contrary potentials. If claiming privacy and everyday life for politics could encourage emancipation, new opportunities for women, and new political alliances, it was also an invitation to control. Evoking Frederick Taylor and Henry Ford under the banner of "social rationalization," new managerial ideologies engendered a powerful conception of the mobility-oriented nuclear family: "comprising a skilled worker risen to plant engineer, a hygiene-conscious housewife, a boy in whose education a maximum of money and effort was invested, and a decently educated daughter who worked in the office until marriage, with a well-groomed, discreetly fashionable appearance."[51] Ideas like this also captured the Left's imagination in the 1920s, permeating the common sense of the labor movement.[52]

Grandiose speculations were voiced. Reflecting on Fordism, Gramsci saw modernity requiring a transformation of sexual culture, for "the new type of man demanded by the rationalization of production . . . cannot be developed until the sexual instinct has been suitably regulated."

> It seems clear that the new industrialism wants monogamy: it wants the man as worker not to squander his nervous energies in the disorderly and stimulating pursuit of occasional sexual satisfaction. The employee who goes to work after a night of "excess" is no good for his work. The exaltation of passion cannot be reconciled with the timed movements of productive motions connected with the most perfect automatism.[53]

But the Left shared too easily in this discourse not of its own making. Women were unlikely to benefit from ideas clinically subordinating their sexuality, where the "wife waiting at home" became just another "permanent machine part."[54] If sex reform promised women's emancipation, rationalization returned it to a new regime of regulation.

Rationalization also invaded the sphere of consumption, shaping new languages of advertising, fashion, and design. But if "efficiency" provided one model of consuming, in kitchens, furnishings, and the products of modern cheap design, "dreaming" was another, borne by new entertainment media of radio, gramophone, and film, in the expressive codes of fashion and style. The emerging culture of consumption had collective expressions, partly in the physical arenas of picture palaces and dance halls, partly in the sociability of tightly knit working-class neighborhoods. Another context was supplied by the newly flourishing "keep fit" movements of the 1930s, sometimes regimented by the state, as in Fascist Italy and Nazi Germany, but often affording a new space of female companionship, self-affirmation, and "autonomous pleasure in [the] body."[55] The British Women's League of Health and Beauty, with its 170,000 members—"where standardized precision movement was performed by women voluntarily seeking fun and fitness"—reflected the same cult of rationalization. Its members were "women of the Machine Age, for whom the machine meant employment, consumer goods, modernity, individuality, pleasure."[56]

The Left rarely grasped the importance of the "new woman." Feminists were dismayed. "Can [young women] really follow a difficult scientific demonstration or a complex piece of music, can they really feel the intensities of admiration or love when a good part of their thoughts is concerned with the question 'Is it time to powder my nose again'?"[57] Young women's pleasure-seeking was frivolous and tawdry, male socialists complained. On his travels through northern England, George Orwell saw only "the same sheeplike crowd—gaping girls and shapeless middle-aged women dozing over their knitting."[58] Worse, female consumers betrayed their class. They were a fifth column of bourgeois materialist values and "cheap luxuries which mitigate the surface of life." "Of course, the postwar development of cheap luxuries has been a very fortunate thing for our rulers. It is quite likely that fish and chips, artificial silk stockings, tinned salmon, cut-price chocolate (five two-ounce bars for sixpence), the movies, the radio, strong tea and the football pools have between them averted revolution."[59]

Interwar socialists had no political language for new generations of young working women, for the shopgirls, hairdressers, typists, assembly-line workers, and cleaners—for the "destructive" pleasures of "the young prettily-dressed girls" pouring from the shops and businesses at the end of the working day.[60] Large movements like the SPD saw the problem. The behavior of working-class daughters was a serious hemorrhaging from working-class culture. But moralizing talk of traditional working-class values was hardly an appealing answer. The SPD's solution was simply to strengthen the subculture's socializing institutions—to find working-class daughters reliable working-class husbands before the corruption began.

Chapter 13

Living the Future

The Left in Culture

THE YEARS 1914–23 were a time of revolutionary change in the arts. The high-cultural landscape was buffeted by storms of innovation. New artistic movements—Fauvism, Cubism, Futurism, Expressionism, Dadaism, Neo-Plasticism and De Stijl, Vorticism, Verism, Purism, Constructivism, Productivism—appeared in bewildering profusion. Centered on painting, they spilled across the arts and national cultures. Yet the convergence with politics was no foregone conclusion. The avant-garde had flouted the concert-going and gallery-visiting public before 1914, but this antibourgeois outlook shared little with the labor movement's socialist culture, whose view of the arts remained resolutely conventional. The pre-1914 avant-garde also eschewed political engagement. They assailed the art world's decorums and attacked the social order but did so in the name of authenticity, *Geist*, and art itself (or alternatively, "life"). It took the war and the Russian Revolution to fuse this creative energy with politics.

Socialists mobilized Enlightenment ideals against inequality and injustice, but to broaden access to high culture rather than challenge it—democratizing the old culture rather than creating a new. Conversely, the avant-garde's cultural radicalism was apolitical: the Parisian extravagance of the Russian Ballet might scandalize bourgeois sensibilities but expressed creative license rather than political emancipation.[1] Beyond both was the emerging "mass" culture of leisure, moreover, which neither socialists nor avant-garde had faced. If political radicals and cultural radicals ignored each other, this new challenge outflanked them both.

BRINGING ART TO LIFE

Pre-1914 avant-gardes were nothing if not international—a "spray of intellectuals which in this period distributed itself across the cities of the globe, as emigrants, leisured visitors, settlers and political refugees or through universities and laboratories." The École de Paris seemed to have fewer French painters than "Spaniards (Picasso, Gris), Italians (Modigliani), Russians (Chagall, Lipchitz, Soutine), Romanians (Brancusi), Bulgarians (Pascin) and Dutchmen (Van Dongen)."[2] London, Berlin, Paris, Vienna, St. Petersburg—all functioned as magnets. But if there was a regional nucleus for international modernism in revolutionary Europe, it was the Berlin-Vienna circuit of the German-oriented central European intelligentsia.

There is a paradox when we turn to 1918. In a time of national revolution, when the Habsburg Empire's multinational framework collapsed and Czechs, Hungarians and others celebrated ethnocultural achievement, a vibrant cosmopolitanism flowered. This came partly from a bourgeois Jewish literary and academic intelligentsia, who identified with an enlightened model of dominant German culture and valued supranational supports in the anti-Semitic atmosphere after 1917–18. The international excellence of the German universities in science, philosophy, and social science also played a part. So did repression. It was no accident that Hungarians rather than, say, Czechs distinguished this cosmopolitan scene, because the Hungarian Soviet's destruction sent an entire generation of liberal, radical, and Marxist intellectuals into Austro-German exile. This is what changed with the war: artistic radicalism was joined by an international political filiation, inspired by the Bolshevik revolution but regrouping around the West's main revolutionary hope, the German Communist Party (KPD).

During the Weimar Republic (1919–33), Berlin was modernism's engine room. Radicals from smaller countries—the Low Countries and Scandinavia—came naturally into its orbit. Two major countries secluded from international modernist discourse—Britain by the complacencies of its conservative imperial culture, Italy by Fascism—found it vicariously, as in Christopher Isherwood's writings with their memorable portrait of Berlin in its last pre-Nazi phase.[3] This was a notable shift in Europe's cultural center of gravity. It brought the temporary eclipse of Paris, till a fresh chain of events—Surrealism's impact, Nazism's coming to power in Germany, the French and Spanish Popular Fronts (1934–37)—supervened. If Paris was the "capital of the nineteenth century," Berlin promised to be the capital of the twentieth, until Nazism brutally broke the spell.[4]

The early twentieth century was crucial for the modern history of the arts. The dramatic political, economic, and technological changes fired a new sensibility, which saw itself as their specific expression. And in attacking the rules of artistic production and form, new avant-gardes were certainly assailing social convention—using "art" to speak about "life." In Filippo Tommaso Marinetti's Futurist Manifesto of 1909, hymning the speed and dynamism of modern industrial life, the language of revolution and the language of the avant-garde seemed to coincide:

> We will sing of great crowds excited by work, by pleasure, and by *riot*
> . . . the multicolored, polyphonic tides of revolution. . . . So let them come, the gay incendiaries with charred fingers! Here we are! Here we are! Come on! Set fire to the library shelves! Turn aside the canals to flood the museums. . . . Take up your pickaxes, your axes and hammers, and wreck, wreck the venerable cities, pitilessly![5]

Denouncing the past and celebrating aggression, movement, and revolt, Marinetti hailed machines as liberating weapons of disorder, embracing war as the world's sole redemption. Before 1914, this appeal to violence and the crowd, the misogynist celebration of physical power, and the turn to the irrational made its insurrectionary language the opposite of progressive; by 1922, the Fascist potentials were distressingly real. But still, the target—the complacencies and rigidities of bourgeois civilization—was also the target of socialism. By 1916–17, the shocks of war and revolution were sending many of the avant-garde to the Left. To take the most self-consciously and militantly subversive of the new artistic movements, for example, if Dadaism was an assault on meaning, this was also the meaning legislated by the given principles of the established social order; and the assault was also the assault on the bankruptcy of a specifically bourgeois sensibility.[6]

DESTROYING THE OLD, BUILDING THE NEW: CULTURAL REVOLUTION IN RUSSIA?

Culturally, the Russian Revolution produced glorious confusion. The Petrograd and Moscow masses cleared a path for cultural no less than political experimentation. The masses themselves, as much as the Bolshevik Party, repudiated the given culture—expropriating bourgeois, gentry, and aristocratic property, occupying apartments, manor houses, palaces and museums, redefining public and private space, and physically destroying the old regime's symbols, from buildings and paintings to fancy furniture and books. The youthful avant-garde luxuriated in joyful destruction. For the poet Alexander Blok, the revolution was "to remake everything. To organize things so that everything should be new, so that our false, filthy, boring, hideous life should become a just, pure, merry, and beautiful life."[7]

The revolution's destructiveness, which for its enemies meant only the irrational violence of the "mob," cleared an imaginative space for fresh thinking. The symbolic radicalism of the avant-garde's assault on bourgeois civilization, given the latter's descent into the morass of the First World War, shaped the Left's emerging cultural agenda. If by 1918 the Italian Futurists had dispersed into Fascism, a Russian Futurist like Mayakovsky grasped the opportunities of the Russian Revolution with alacrity. "The streets are our brushes, the squares are our palettes," he wrote, and he threw himself with gusto into preserving the new revolutionary state.[8]

Bolshevism's alliance with the avant-garde in the revolution's crucial first phase (from Civil War to New Economic Policy, 1918–21) was eased by the appointment of Anatoly Lunacharsky to the Commissariat of Enlightenment in November 1917. A prewar associate of Aleksander Bogdanov, the independent Bolshevik philosopher who had clashed with Lenin over culture, Lunacharsky worked with Trotsky in Paris during the war and rejoined the Bolsheviks in 1917. At his new ministry, he practised a shrewd and generous utopianism, moved by an emancipatory ideal for the working class—"to acquire, in the course of many years, genuine culture, to achieve true consciousness of its own human worth, to enjoy the salutary fruits of contemplation and sensibility."[9] But this was tempered by the pressures of a collapsing economy and the rival advocacy of utilitarian technical education. Popular education was in disastrous straits. By 1925, less than half the school population had finished even three years of schooling and total enrollments were less than 50 percent of 1913 levels.

Still, Lunacharsky's ideal of cultural emancipation created a framework of excitement, and his Commissariat gave ample scope for avant-gardists and cultural visionaries. It housed a museum department; sections for theater, music, art, literature, cinema, and photography; the Telegraph Agency; the arts schools; the Higher State Art-Technical Studio; and the Institute of Artistic Culture. It was responsible for schools, universities, scientific-technical education, and child welfare too. Lunacharsky was ecumenical. While harnessing Fururism's energy, he rejected its iconoclastic absolutism. He also wished to preserve, maintaining classical traditions and protecting museums against vandalism. While enlisting the youthful avant-garde, he also worked with nonsocialists among the old intelligentsia. He saw the vitality of the new and needed innovators like Mayakovsky but refused to privilege them in the revolution's agenda.[10]

Lunacharsky saw that art needed its freedom—tolerating diversity and excess was the key virtue. This was clearest his in relations with *Proletkult,* the proletarian culture movement inspired in 1917 by Bogdanov and the *Vpered* group.[11] Urging a culture of workers themselves, free of experts, analogous to workers' councils in production and economics, Proletkult clashed with Bolshevism's primacy of the party. For Lenin and other Bolsheviks, it seemed merely a refuge for intellectuals chafing against party discipline, a magnet for potential opposition. Leaders like Nadezhda

Krupskaya and Lenin himself sought Proletkult's subordination, while Proletkultists defended themselves as the voice of an authentic proletarian culture.

Lunacharsky was caught in the middle. His use of Futurists antagonized party leaders, who wanted "more proletarian simplicity [in] our art."[12] But Proletkultists also inflamed Bolshevik preferences for centralism and political control: Proletkult factory cells threatened Party jurisdiction. Proletkult's scale, with four hundred thousand in its studios and workshops, made this dissonance a serious matter. When the Proletarian University, launched in Moscow on Proletkult initiative in early 1919, became forcibly merged into Sverdlov Communist University, with its narrower model of political education, the writing was on the wall. Pressures for moving Proletkult directly under the Commissariat grew immense, and at the end of 1920 it was subordinated via the new Chief Committee for Political Education.

Proletkult's history showed the central postrevolutionary tension—between revolutionary creativity and revolutionary consolidation. For most Bolsheviks, the revolution's survival dictated single-minded concentration, from which the avant-garde was a frivolous and costly diversion. For Trotsky and Lenin, immersed in administrative and military details, while struggling to preserve a longer-term vision, artistic autonomy seemed a luxury when the regime was fighting for its life in the Civil War. People might not live by bread alone, but for now the overwhelming demand was indeed for "bread and coal." Lenin looked at Proletkult's fertile heterodoxy and saw only an "abundance of escapees from the bourgeois intelligentsia" who treated educational work "as the most convenient field for their own personal fantasies."[13]

In such circumstances, asserting control over cultural policy came as no surprise. In fact, Proletkult's subordination to the Commissariat bespoke the larger administrative stabilization of the New Economic Policy (NEP), ratified at the Bolsheviks' Tenth Congress in March 1921. This declared limited toleration of market relations and private property, especially in the countryside. It was conceived as a breathing-space, sheltering the exhausted Soviet regime after the Civil War and adjusting to revolution's failure in the West. As Lenin said, the time-scale of socialist construction was different from the pace of revolution: "Learn to work at a different tempo, reckoning your work by decades not by months, and gearing yourself to the mass of mankind [sic] who have suffered torments and who cannot keep up a revolutionary-heroic tempo in everyday work." This call to the prosaic, to "a mood of patience, caution and compromise," was echoed by Kamenev: "We have come out of the period of landslides, of sudden earthquakes, of catastrophes, we have entered on a period of slow economic processes which we must know how to watch." In politics and economics, dramatized in early 1921 by military suppression of the Kronstadt commune, the disciplining of left-wing opponents, and the welcoming of nonsocialist specialists for their much-needed skills, the change was abrupt. But in culture, the painful contraction of radical futures took longer to work itself out.[14]

In 1917, the revolution had released the imagination—a sense of no holds barred, of being on the edge of possibility, of "blast[ing] open the continuum of history," in Walter Benjamin's words.[15] It brought an ecstasy of transgression, in which the people occupied the palaces and art suffused the texture of life, dissolving dichotomies between high culture and low. In the vast popular festivals, like May Day 1918 in Petrograd and the Bolshevik revolution's first anniversary in Moscow or the four great Petrograd festivals of 1920, the masses staged symbolic dramas of history, while the artists seized the potential of the streets—of carnival and circus, puppetry and cartoons, and other popular media. Carrying art to the masses took many forms in 1918–20: the ubiquitous posters; street theater; factory arts groups, with genres of industrial writing and performance; and the "agittrains" that used art and film to politicize the peasants. The forms were carnivalesque rather than monumental, the aesthetic one of movement rather than order.

But this synergy of artists and people required the Civil War's hiatus of public authority, when "culture" was left to its own devices, sheltered by Lunacharsky's generosity. It was the full flower of revolutionary culture; far more so than the official projects for recasting public values, like the formal calendar of revolutionary festivals, new flags, and anthems, or Lenin's plan for covering Moscow with monuments to past revolutionary heroes. Vitality dissipated once Proletkult was disciplined and NEP was inaugurated in the winter of 1920–21. Excitement still occurred. Mayakovsky was irrepressibly active. Constructivism, the revolution's most coherent artistic movement, forever epitomized by Vladimir Tatlin's famously unbuilt Monument to the Third International, climaxed after the shift. Agitational culture survived. Soviet film was just getting started.[16] But the mood had nonetheless changed.

In all these respects, the Bolshevik Revolution staged a paradigmatic debate over the shaping of socialist culture and its translation into policy. The most attractive position—a generous-spirited socialist humanism, too abstracted from practical urgencies of state-building to carry the day—was Lunacharsky's. Another stance, shared by Proletkultists and avant-garde, was a confrontational "left modernism," demanding breaks with the past and the invention of new forms. Both were defeated by the dominant mentality after the Civil War. This new mood contained an extreme utilitarianism, approaching education exclusively via the Soviet economy's desperate needs for technical skills. It was reinforced by Marxist reductionism, which viewed culture as a secondary phenomenon shaped by material forces, something to be measured by the prevailing socioeconomic conditions. A new culture could not be immediately created, in this view. It could only arrive through the future economic transformation.

Consequently, the Bolshevik revolution's cultural legacy was ambiguous. On one side was the joy of creative release, by which extraordinary achievements, in the formal arts and popular culture, could occur. On the other side, though, was NEP's normalized official culture, a straitening of revolutionary imagination, which brought greater toleration for prerevolutionary and classical traditions but less readiness for cultural risks. Beneath this new "moderation" was an uneasy awareness of popular conservatism, of the smallness of the socialist working class and its exhaustion in the Civil War, and of the recalcitrance of everyday behavior. As Trotsky reflected: "Politics are flexible, but life is immovable and stubborn. . . . It is much more difficult for life than for the state to free itself from ritual."[17] How the Left would deal with this question, in the Soviet Union and elsewhere, was vital for the post-Bolshevik era.

THE LEFT AND INTELLECTUALS

In the 1919 Hungarian Soviet, the efforts of the Commissariat of Education under Georg Lukács mirrored Lunacharsky's in Russia. These included a broadly conceived school reform, literacy campaigns, adult education programs, and the Workers' University in Budapest; support of the arts via the Artists' and Writers' Registries; opening the Academy of Art to modernism, with a new teaching studio stressing public decoration, poster design, and other mass forms; and a fraught but tolerant relationship with the avant-garde, like the self-aggrandizing poet Lajos Kassak and his Futurists. Lukács balanced democratizing the classical European heritage with radical innovation.

The pioneer film theorist Bela Balázs transformed the repertoire of the newly nationalized theaters, combining progressive national drama with classical and modern European plays and distributing subsidized tickets via trade unions. He created traveling theater troupes and an imaginatively run Film Directorate. He produced 31 films (adaptations of world literature for working-class audiences); ran a documentary and newsreel unit; published a lively journal, *Vörös Film* (Red Film); and planned a film actors' school. Balázs prioritized children, with traveling puppet shows and "afternoons of fables" and a children's film unit. Assumptions were challenged in extreme ways. Lukács wanted to ban nonrecognized newspapers, destroy all property records, prohibit alcohol, and promote liberated sexuality and opposition to parental authority among children. He pursued an "earthly paradise which we thought of as communism" in an avowedly "sectarian, ascetic sense": "There was absolutely no thought in our minds of a land flowing with milk and honey. What we wanted was to revolutionize the crucial problems of life."[18]

The Hungarian Soviet matched young intellectuals like Lukács and Balázs with younger trade unionists, all radicalized by the war.[19] Before 1914, the Habsburg Empire's ramshackle disorder had stoked desires for political regeneration, increasingly in exclusionary nationalist ways. In Hungary, an interlocking public culture had shaped this opposition—the review *Huszadik Század* (Twentieth Century, launched 1 January 1900) and the associated Social Science Society a year later; the Free School of Social Sciences for workers' education classes (1906); the Galileo Circle for students at Budapest University (1908); several Freemason lodges; and the élitist Sunday Circle around Lukács and Balázs after 1915, with its esoteric seminar and lecture program. These prewar networks already included socialists, influenced by Ervin Szabó. The Sunday Circle produced the cultural cadres of the future revolutionary government, including Lukács and Balázs, Béla Fogarasi (the Soviet's director of higher education), Frigyes Antal (deputy head of the Art Directorate), and a team of art historians, philosophers, and writers working for Lukács, including Lajos Fülep, Tibor Gergely, Arnold Hauser, Anna Lesznai, Karl Mannheim, Ervin Sinkó, Wilhelm Szilasi, Charles de Tólnay, and Janos Wilde.[20]

This cohort's passage from romantic anticapitalism and ethical critique to revolutionary politics was a pan-European phenomenon. Universities had grown hugely during 1870–1913, tripling student numbers in most countries, while secondary schooling expanded two to five times.[21] Publics for "high culture" also grew. Theater and concert-going flourished: in Germany, for example, the number of theaters increased from two hundred to six hundred during 1870–96. The fine art market boomed; big-city and monumental architecture, and the fashion for public statuary, boosted demand for architects and sculptors; reproductions of great masters and mass editions of literary classics serviced the cultivated public. Industrialized structures of public communication expanded careers in the literary, visual, and technical arts, with massive growth of the daily and periodical press, expansion of photography and illustration, the rise of advertising and the poster, and the arrival of cinema, to be followed after 1918 by public broadcasting. New opportunities for employment, accreditation, and subsidy changed the artist's relationship to the market, private patronage, and the state.[22]

This was the sociology for a dissenting intelligentsia—larger numbers of the academically educated and artistically active, in a different working environment. Before 1914, the rhetoric of the "artist or intellectual in society" quickened, vesting *Geist* ("intellect" or "the spiritual") with special responsibilities for national well-being during massive social change and lost bearings. A clash between ethicocultural values and industrial-capitalist civilization pitted the realm of the spirit against sociopolitical life. German expressions ranged from the apolitical aestheticism of the Stefan George circle to the political messianism of the journal *Die Aktion,* launched in 1911. But by 1914, the future emergence of a self-conscious radical intelligentsia claiming a voice in politics could be glimpsed. The intelligentsia had also acquired a big technical and professional component, the "new middle class" of managers, engineers, civil servants, lawyers, doctors, teachers, social workers, clergy, journalists, and public administrators. The Hungarian Soviet's leaders included not only socialist activists, trade unionists, and newly radicalized creative intellectuals but also engineers and other white-collar professionals of this ilk.[23]

The war brought cultural unease to a political head. The shock of the trenches was the radicalizing event. Nearly all the writers, artists, musicians, and filmmakers of Weimar Germany's left-intellectual culture were born in the early 1890s and after (architects tended to be a decade older), making them 20 and younger when war began, acutely vulnerable to its shattering effects.[24] Artists like Max Beckmann, Otto Dix, and George Grosz were profoundly marked by the front, as were dramatist-poets like Erwin Piscator, Ernst Toller, and Carl Zuckmayer. Politics was preceded by humanist revulsion and existential trauma—mental hospital and breakdowns were common. Radicalism was borne by the expressive qualities of a new art, galvanized by Berlin Dada in 1917–18. Protests were angry and symbolic—both Grosz and his friend John Heartfield (Helmut Herzfelde) legally anglicized their names against the reigning anglophobia. An older generation, like the leading *Jugendstil* (art nouveau) painter Heinrich Vogeler, could also be radicalized: "The war has made a Communist of me. After my war experiences I could no longer countenance belonging to a class that had driven millions of people to their death."[25]

Amid the horrors of war, popular protests and military collapse then posed a moral and political choice. Bela Balázs pondered the prospects of revolution: "I would not participate . . . (I would participate only in a revolution of the soul). . . . But if, by accident, the battle reached me on the barricade, I would no longer run away. The question is this: where does the barricade begin?"[26] By 1918, abstract musings had gone. Zuckmayer, Piscator, Toller, Vogeler, the young Bertolt Brecht, students like Max Horkheimer and Herbert Marcuse (future members of the Frankfurt School), and many others joined the German Revolution. Intellectuals organized themselves in the "Revolutionary Central Committee of Dada"; the short-lived Political Council of Intellectual Workers in Berlin and Munich; the November Group for the interests of radical artists; and the longer-lasting Working Council for Art, lobbying official policy in architecture and design. Piscator, Grosz, Heartfield, and his brother Wieland Herzfelde were founder members of the KPD. The ill-fated Bavarian Soviet in April 1919 depended heavily on intellectuals, including Toller, the anarcho-communist writer Erich Mühsam, and the intellectual anarchist Gustav Landauer. This Budapest and Munich pattern was repeated in Prague, where a Socialist Council of Intellectual Workers rallied to the revolutionary banner on 6 July 1919; and Turin, where Gramsci and the *Ordine nuovo* group urged an encompassing cultural program on the factory councils in 1919–20.

How far did this mirror the experience of revolutionary Russia? There was the same explosion of creativity, inseparable from war and revolution. For many, the creative act could never be the same again. Heinrich Vogeler recorded this rupture perfectly. From prewar success in art nouveau ("lapdog of the big bourgeoisie"), he turned to full-time activism under Weimar, first as a council communist and then in the KPD till his expulsion in 1929. He turned his Barkenhoff estate near Bremen into a socialist commune, then into a home for children of victimized workers. He formed the Association of German Revolutionary Artists in 1928, before emigrating to the USSR, dying in 1942. The war was the pivotal experience. He volunteered in 1914 but by January 1918 was committed to mental hospital for sending Wilhelm II a peace letter. He turned to socialist theory and surfaced in the Workers' and Soldiers' Council in Osterholz near Bremen. He became a painter of political murals. Those in the Barkenhoff home became a *cause célèbre* when the state ordered them removed in 1927. After protests, they were covered up instead, only to be destroyed by the Hitler Youth in 1939.[27]

Such changes were never totally abrupt. Vogeler was in the Garden City Society before 1914, drafting blueprints for workers' settlements and visiting Britain to study Glasgow slums and the model town of Port Sunlight. Bruno Taut was another example. Designer of the Falkenberg garden city (1912–14) and the "Glass House" at the Cologne *Werkbund* exhibition in 1914, he advocated housing reform and a visionary architectural philosophy, fusing "the social and rational skills of the architect with the fantasy and subjectivism of the painter."[28] His postwar activities, chairing the Council of Intellectual Workers and the Working Council for Art till March 1919, continued these commitments. Yet neither the utopian fancies of the "Alpine Architecture" folio, begun in 1917, and the *Glass Chain* (1919–20) nor his interest in Proletkult were conceivable without war and revolution. Likewise, the next period produced a further turn. If revolutionary turbulence brought construction projects to a halt, the stability of the mid-1920s put socialist architects back to work. The distance from the Taut of the *Gläserne Kette,* spinning his crystal castles in the air, to the Taut of *Die neue Wohnung* (The New Dwelling, 1924), settling down to the famous public housing projects in Berlin, was a paradigmatic contrast.[29]

SOCIALIST CULTURE AND MASS CULTURE

Younger artists, writers, and academics joined revolutionary movements from a mélange of utopian, anarcho-communist, radical bohemian, or plain nihilistic motives, often with an élitist thrust. The German Political Council of Intellectual Workers, for example, naively expected workers' councils to welcome their leadership.[30] Such intellectuals celebrated the destruction of the old without seeing clearly the new. George Grosz was emblematic, with his savage caricatures of militarists, judges, civil servants, and bourgeois philistines, his burning humanist morality, and his radical links to Dada, Malik-Verlag, and the KPD.[31] But if Grosz joined the Communists with fellow artists like Vogeler and the brothers Heartfield/Herzfelde, it remained unclear what this meant.

One theorist offering answers was Antonio Gramsci. Gramsci's cultural and educational initiatives in Turin—the Clubs of Moral Life (1917), the School of Culture and Propaganda (1919), and the Institutes of Proletarian Culture (1920)—paralleled Bogdanov's vision of Proletkult, to which the 1920 Institutes were affiliated. The project of *l'Ordine nuovo* (1919–20) was guided by an ideal of working-class self-realization in the new agency of the factory councils. From 1916, Gramsci had pressed for a Socialist cultural association to match the party and Cooperative Alliance, as "the third organ of the movement."[32] He was inspired by a broader generational challenge to the provincialism of Italian high culture, drawing on the activism associated with Georges Sorel, Henri Bergson's voluntarism, and Benedetto Croce's general philosophy. Here, culture was not just the arts and scholarship but "exercise of thought, acquisition of general ideas, habit of connecting causes and effects." For Gramsci, "everybody is already cultured because everybody thinks." The goal should be promotion of critical thinking, or "thinking well, whatever one thinks, and therefore acting well, whatever one does." This couldn't be left to the schools or spontaneous workers' experience. It had to be actively promoted: "Let us organize culture in the same way that we seek to organize any practical activity."[33]

Unless political revolution was accompanied by cultural change, Gramsci argued, it would never breach capitalism's less visible defences, the entrenched bourgeois values and social relations of civil society. Socialists had a double task. Ordinary people should be empowered in their own deliberative capacities, so that intellectual functions could be freed from the monopoly of a specialized élite; and the working class should be raised to moral-political leadership in society. The practical agency was the factory councils of 1919–20. For Gramsci, the councils' revolutionary character was precisely this cultural potential. They were media of working-class self-education, "schools of propaganda." This should happen on the broadest cultural front. They should raise workers to a sense of their full capacity to govern production and thence society.

While the victory of Fascism liquidated the legal preconditions for Gramsci's ambitious cultural-political program in Italy, by the 1920s there were already strong traditions of socialist culture-building in Europe.[34] These were commonly found in self-contained and internally cohesive communities, where priorities were superficially the opposite of a grandiose cultural program. In such local strongholds, the goals were usually the mundane ones of defending and improving working-class living standards.

Progress was measured very prosaically by the delivery of services in housing, unemployment assistance, job creation, educational access, public health, public transportation, and other aspects of welfare and public good.

But in another dimension, these local solidarities raised countercultural challenges to authority—against courts, schools, regional government, church, and the national state, all of them enmeshed with the power of local capitalists. In "little Moscows," small towns and villages across Europe where socialists had established local dominance, culture was a battleground. These local communities had the familiar texture of working-class collective life: "the banners, the bands, the evening socials and sport, the youth groups, the Friends of the Soviet Union, and so on."[35] But this quotidian culture also disclosed an explicitly political identity. Here, the working-class life-world—organized around basic values of community and cooperation, fellowship and mutuality, independence and resistance to authority—was shaped in unusually politicized ways. Face-to-face democracy was key: "industrial activities, cooperative societies and other organizations were all constituted on the sovereignty of the membership," and democracy was kept to a public arena of open and collective decision-making, "at public meetings or in open air."[36] But two questions arise. Whereas this politicized culture could be both subversive and empowering, how far did it really challenge the dominant culture in Gramsci's sense? And: what were its blind spots?

We can get closer to some answers by considering two of the strongest cases of a prefigurative socialist strategy in cultural terms. To take the first of these, "Red Vienna" was Europe's most imposing showcase of municipal socialism between the wars.[37] Its centerpiece was public housing, with 64,000 apartments in large housing blocks, servicing one-seventh of the city at 5 percent of a worker's wage. Financed by a luxury tax, this was a directly redistributive strategy. Moreover, the program's scale and ramifications gave it a special edge. This was the first socialist party "to preside over a city with over a million inhabitants, and 'Red Vienna' was the first practical example of a long-term Socialist strategy of reforming the entire infrastructure of a metropolis."[38]

The housing blocks were a project of "anticipatory socialism," designed to express collectivist goals and an integrated communal life. The plans allowed for greenery, usable courtyards, and cultural space: meeting places and club rooms, common baths and laundries, cooperative stores and restaurants, nurseries, playgrounds, and the general run of civic provision, from schools and libraries to parks, swimming areas, gymnasia, health facilities, and clinics. The infrastructure of civic life was relocated inside a physically demarcated socialist public sphere, further solidified by the 21 districts of SPÖ organization, with their electoral subdivisions and house-cum-street associations and citywide subcultural apparatus of clubs. Housing policy was complemented by an innovative public health program and a progressive educational reform, based on the common school, cooperative pedagogy, abolition of corporal punishment, and extensive adult education. The new housing blocks—"worker palaces" or "red fortresses"—formed a symbolic counterlandscape to the ruling architecture of monuments, palaces, and museums.

There were limits to this prefigurative vision. If the housing blocks provided for collective life and political culture, they failed to promote a participatory ethic, treating tenants as passive beneficiaries of a paternalist administration.[39] Socialist city planners celebrated standardization and the economies of scale, discarding other models. In 1918–20, though, a massive squatters' movement had arisen on Vienna's outskirts involving 55,000 residents. These were organized into cooperative housing associations, which practised self-management and projected garden cities based on owner occupancy and collective facilities. But by 1921 the socialist city had asserted control; participatory culture dissolved; and the alternative model of the one-family home was wholly exchanged for the new superblocks.[40]

Red Vienna remained an imposing fortress of working-class solidarity. Austrian Social Democracy was "the most massive and comprehensive . . . of the mass proletarian parties" formed before 1914, avoiding splits and the rivalry of a sizeable Communist Party: the Vienna working class was solidly in its fold, joining or voting for the party or belonging to its manifold clubs and associations, from Worker Choirs and Worker Sports to Worker Stamp Collectors and Worker Rabbit Breeders.[41] Beyond its national electoral strength (42.3 percent, 1927) and municipal power, the party organized its own militia after 1923, the *Schutzbund*, which was larger than the official army.

Yet political passivity brought the movement's ruin between the crisis of 15 July 1927 and the civil war of February 1934, and the ease of the its suppression questions the efficacy of the SPÖ's socialist culture in Gramsci's sense. In the 1926 Linz Program, Otto Bauer and other leaders evinced revolutionary intentions and expected to come to power. At the opening of the Vienna stadium in July 1931, 240,000 watched a mass pageant of the movement's history, which climaxed with worker-actors toppling "a huge gilt idol-head representing capital from its metal scaffolding."[42] Yet these cultural energies and symbolic creativity were never translated into revolutionary action—that is, into the confrontational readiness needed to convert the party's democratic legitimacy into actual power.

In these lights, Vienna's socialist subculture starts to seem like a displacement, both a retreat into the municipal arena after the loss of national government power in 1920 and compensation for the new period of waiting. Something similar occurred in Germany, where the SPD's "cultural socialism" forms my second example. Also excluded from national government in June 1920 yet firmly ensconced in Prussia and other states, bunkered into the Republic's labor-corporative and welfare-statist arrangements, the SPD and its unions were practically integrated into the parliamentary system. Propagating socialist values fell to the cultural organizations, the "third pillar" of the movement, which also nurtured the movement's revolutionary élan. Socialism regrouped as a prefigurative project: "the picture of a new order has to be strongly anchored in the minds before it is possible to erect the building. And every political influence is pointless if the acquisition of education, knowledge and culture does not take place at the same time."[43]

This recalled Gramsci's language. Socialist cultural activism was certainly impressive, prospering under Weimar's new freedoms. Worker Sports grew from 169,000 members to 770,000 between 1912 and 1928, Worker Singers from 192,000 to 440,000, and Worker Cyclists from 148,000 to 220,000. Worker Athletes (boxers, wrestlers, weightlifters) grew from 10,000 members to 56,000, and "Nature Lovers" (ramblers, rock-climbers, skiers, canoeists) from 10,000 to 79,000. There were leagues for chess, sailing, angling, hunting, bowling, and gliding. They all nourished alternative values, including cooperative ideals of discipline and mutuality, and a noncompetitive ethos of participation and collective endeavor as against the star system and the individualist cult of winning. It became harder to resist pressures for competitive reward (trophies, medals, certificates of merit), to be sure, and the modern sporting spectacle was also gaining ground. But cultivating fellowship—common socializing, taking trips together, sing-songs, and collective recitation of workers' poems—kept these trends reasonably at bay.

There was a huge upswing after 1918 in "life reform"—natural living, exercise and fresh air, sensible nutrition, abstinence from alcohol and tobacco, rational dress, therapy, preventive medicine, and sex counseling. These interests were served by Proletarian Nudists' Clubs and especially in the sex reform movement, with its birth control leagues, progressive doctors, women's groups, and Socialist and Communist welfare organizations. "Lay sex reform groups, with their illustrated journals filled with advice of sexual technique, contraception, eugenic hygiene, health, and the protection of mothers; their centers for the distribution of contraceptives; and their many therapeutic question-and-answer lectures, were an integral and crucial part of the working-class subculture of the Weimar Republic."[44] The People's Health League, based in Dresden, practised holistic medicine, homeopathic remedies, and nudism. The changed climate for such activities was illustrated by the Proletarian Freethinkers, who advocated secularized rites of passage, abolition of religious instruction in the schools, cremation, and leaving the church. From 6,000 members in 1914, this movement attained mass status with 590,000 members in 1929.[45]

Cultural socialism promoted its collectivist ethic via team sports, massed gymnastic displays, and experiments with group forms like synchronized swimming. The massed choirs gracing most party festivals symbolized the relationship of cultural emancipation, collective effort, and mass form: 50,000 amateur musicians attended the first Workers' Song Festival in Hanover in 1928.[46] These activities seemed to meet Gramsci's ideal. The SPD now mobilized progressive intellectuals outside its own ranks, permitting a stronger challenge to the dominant culture's legitimacy than the pre-1914 subcultural ghettoization had ever allowed. It also kept its own educational machine, enhanced by the subsidized adult educational systems of big SPD-run cities like Berlin, Hamburg, and Leipzig.

In its end goals cultural socialism expected workers' daily lives to be transformed. But in trying to prefigure this utopia in the capitalist present, it organized an artificially separate cultural sphere—"a sort of holiday culture, a culture for the rare moment."[47] It bracketed precisely the arenas—workplace, party-political structures, family—where the new values needed to be most tenaciously pursued. Above all, the forthright masculinity of socialist movement culture was almost never brought self-consciously into focus.[48] In this sense, the tripartite division of labor that the cultural movement accepted in order to call itself the "third pillar" was profoundly reformist. It stopped short of the fully integrated conception of "anticipatory socialism" that a genuinely "Gramscian" centering of cultural struggle would imply. As Gramsci knew, culture was too important to leave to "culture" alone.[49]

MASS ENTERTAINMENT, POLITICS, AND PLEASURE

This hallowing of culture, which removed it from the everyday, was fateful. Popular culture was already being transformed by cheap technologies of mass entertainment and leisure. This preceded 1914—with photography, film, phonograph, and radio, plus bicycle, motor car, telephone, and typewriter. But the possibilities came fully to fruition between the wars. In 1919 there were 2,386 cinemas in Germany, slightly less than 1914; but by 1929 there were over 5,300, making Germany the largest European film market. The cinema's physical setting was also changing, with itinerant film shows and smaller houses giving way to the picture palace, including Britain's first four-thousand-seaters in Glasgow (1925) and Croydon (1928). In much smaller Sweden, cinemas more than doubled, from 703 to 1,719, in the first postwar decade.[50]

Radio grew spectacularly. Regular broadcasting began in the early 1920s, instantly generating new listening publics. Britain and Germany led in subscribers (4.5 and 4.0 million, 1931), but Sweden was proportionately just as high (1.5 million, 1940). This extended far into the working class, composing a quarter of the German listening public by 1930. In the major British city of Liverpool, 9 out of 10 families had a radio by 1936. Print media also expanded. Newspapers were transformed by technology, advertising, expanding urban populations, and a new demotic tone. British sales of national dailies climbed from 3.1 million to 10.6 million between the wars. Other commercial forms, owing less to technology, transformed popular culture in similar directions, notably dancing and spectator sports.[51]

How did this commercialized culture of leisure, seeing itself as entertainment rather than art, diversion rather than uplift, affect the labor movement's organized culture? One response was to "tame" the new media by nationalizing the film industry and regulating radio, or by using "softer" forms of public control. The SPD proposed state participation in Germany's second largest film company, Emelka, in 1928, and secured access to radio via legislation in 1926. In both cases, it treated new media as novel means for old ends, either educationally via radio lectures and arts programs (like the "Workers' Hour" series provided by the Hamburg Workers' Board of Trustees on social aspects of the Weimar Constitution), or agitationally via specially produced films and mobile propaganda units (like the Braunschweig SPD's "People's Red Cinema"). More ambitiously, the SPÖ had its own film company, operating 13 cinemas directly and supplying another 25 before the movement's destruction in 1934. But independent programing couldn't compete with the glitter and excitement of commercial cinema and either appealed to smaller audiences of the converted or compromised with commercial operation.[52]

Many socialists rejected the new media altogether, neither seeing the technical potentials nor validating the pleasures. Traditionally, socialists disparaged plebeian culture, stressing sobriety and self-improvement over the disorderly realities of many worker's lives. Socialists drew sharp moral lines between their own self-educated respectability and the apolitical roughness of the working-class poor—or between "the W.E.A. study-in-spare-time-class" and "the pub-dance-and-girl-class of young men," as one English working man put it.[53] Commercial entertainments, like music halls, circuses, fairs, and rough sports, seemed a source of frivolity and backwardness in working-class culture. Instead, socialists held "the ideal that working people should collectively organize their own free time in morally uplifting ways."[54] Thus film seemed just a new source of escapism and corruption in a still-uneducated working class. In 1919, a Frankfurt USPD newspaper lamented the moral decline: "The path to the gambling dens of the big city begins in the dance halls and the cinemas. . . . Surrounded by superficial din and deadened in their souls, the misled section of the proletarian youth dances its way into depravity."[55]

Yet commercial cinema's mass audience was heavily working-class. This reflected significant social changes, including lasting gains in real wages, increased leisure time, and the remarkable cheapness of cinema tickets.[56] "Going to the pictures" became a central fixture of working-class life, popular culture's real location as against the idealized imagery of socialist culture. The gap between socialist ideas of cultural progress and actual workers' behavior disconcertingly widened, because with greater leisure workers turned only partially to the socialist cultural organizations yet flocked in masses to capitalist-organized commercial entertainment. Too often, left-wing critics blamed the workers. Movies were a capitalist trick, a medium of ideological manipulation "cleverly used to dope the workers," a form of "pseudo-culture," "whereby [workers'] attention is diverted from the class war and . . . their slave status is maintained." For too many socialists, everyday working-class culture was a problem, something to moralize and improve.[57]

But the emergent apparatus of the "culture industry," from the razzmatazz of the cinema and the dance hall to the rise of spectator sports, the star system, and the machineries of advertising and fashion, proved remarkably successful in servicing popular desires in the 1920s. It invaded precisely the human space of everyday life that socialists were neglecting to fill. Moreover, once the labor movement's infrastructure had been smashed by fascism in Italy and Germany, this private recreational domain proved the fascist state's most successful sites of intervention. Fascism was not just the instrument of antidemocratic repression and a system of terror (although it was certainly both) but also harnessed psychic needs and utopian longings the Left neglected at their peril. By the same argument, the emerging popular culture was not simply an empty and depoliticized commercial corruption of traditional working-class culture but possessed democratic validity of its own. The fantasies produced in Hollywood were a bridge to ordinary desire, the daydreams of poverty and depression. They described an imaginary space ready for occupation, whether the Left wanted to move there or not.[58]

CONCLUSION: SOCIALIST VERSUS MASS CULTURE

Measured by a "Gramscian" model of cultural politics, the socialist achievements of the 1920s only partially fit the bill. Radicalized intellectuals vitally assisted the revolutionary upswing. Socialist politics became linked to anticipatory change in culture. Many on the Left agreed that cultural struggle had to be organized. But this invariably occurred in paternalist ways, as something provided *for* the masses, either by the movement's cultural and educational auxiliaries or via growing control of central and local government, in an improving but ultimately controlling manner. The masses' cultural empowerment, via experimentation and self-directed creativity rather than reception of ready-made cultural goods, rarely occurred outside the revolutionary situations of 1917–21, when party discipline fell away. The SPD's "cultural socialism," with its collectivist ethic and mass participation, was a partial exception. But even here, the watchwords were discipline, coordination, and rational control, rather than imagination and worker-initiated creativity. There was little sign of Gramsci's extended conception of culture as the general faculty of thinking—of the idea that "culture is ordinary" and involves the making and remaking of a society's "common meanings." There was little attempt to locate the possibilities of a democratic and alternative culture in the workplace and the domestic arenas of the everyday.[59]

The creativity of working-class solidarity, and the complex texture of working-class community life, remained impressive. Socialists successfully fashioned these strengths into a collective agency for achieving social and political goals—conducting strikes and campaigns, building local hegemonies, winning national elections, or fighting fascism and other forms of reaction. Whether the main forms of collective organization were adaptable for the challenges of continuing social change (like the new cultures of entertainment and mass consumption), however, was less clear. How far did these movements create fully fledged alternative cultures, strong enough to replace society's existing value system? How capable were they of providing a new morality, of generating counterhegemonic potentials in Gramsci's sense? *Pace* the remarkable achievements of local socialisms, it was here—in the fall of the PSI's regional bastions to Fascism, in the limits of the SPD's cultural socialism, and in Red Vienna's ultimate defeat—that the failures of the Left's cultural politics were most tragic.

Beyond the dramatic violence of these defeats, in Italy (1920–22), Germany (1930–33), and Austria (1927–34), were fundamental omissions, going to the heart of socialism's prefigurative project. Socialists consistently failed to challenge the most basic of working-class cultural attitudes in the family, concerning organization of households, domestic divisions of labor, sexuality, child-raising, and the proper roles of women and men. Instead, they validated conservative models of respectability, counterposing them against the roughness of the disorderly poor, as the best defense against hardship and misfortune. Increasingly, they also affirmed the virtues of the solid and respectable working-class family against commercialized cultures of entertainment, decrying the latter's corrupting effects. But this cleaving to conventional and reassuring ground left powerful territories of dominant ideology intact—including the patriarchal ordering of the entire domestic sphere, prevailing distinctions of public and private, and established gender beliefs.

Socialist family values and the wholesomeness of worker sports were an increasingly compromised resource against the attractions of the new mass culture. This isn't to diminish the democratic values of self-improvement, emancipation through education, and equality of access to established cultural goods. The cultural movement gave invaluable opportunities for fulfilment and enjoyment in an atmosphere of equality and fellowship, as many memoirs movingly attest. But by attacking mass culture, socialists were isolating themselves from the bulk of the young working class, women and men, for whom "independence meant precisely what [the] militants abhorred, namely consumerist eroticism and leisure, new styles in dress, smoking, drinking, dancing and sport." From providing "an ideal towards which others could strive, now for the first time since the 1890s" socialists "were becoming ideologically marginal within the working class."[60] Tensions were growing between socialist culture and popular culture in the 1920s, despite cultural socialists' creativity with a more open collectivist ethic. While the SPD's cultural experts orchestrated the massed choirs and choreographed the gymnasts and dancers, the popular imagination was already migrating elsewhere, to the dance halls and dream palaces of the entertainment industry.

Chapter 14

Broadening the Boundaries of Democracy

A EUROPE OF CONSTITUTIONS: THE LEFT ENTERS THE NATION

THE YEARS 1914–23 stand out in modern European history as an exceptional moment of general revolutionary upheaval, certainly comparable to the French Revolution and Napoleonic Wars. This momentousness began with the sheer scale of the military violence of the "Great War" and the societal efforts needed to wage it. The combatant societies were traumatized both by the mass killing at the front and by the privations at home, requiring large changes at the war's end if society's cohesion was to be salvaged. But if victory in Britain and France brought significant reforms during 1918–19, defeat for Russia, Austria-Hungary, and Germany spelled social and political disintegration. First the Russian Revolution toppled the tsarist empire, unleashing an extraordinary chain of radicalization between February and October 1917, bringing socialists to power. Then the German and Austro-Hungarian states collapsed amid massive popular insurgencies. By the fall of 1918, the multinational empires previously dominating central and eastern Europe were gone.

This outcome completed the nineteenth-century processes of state formation, dramatically furthered by the 1860s, which formed Europe into a system of nation-states. If the 1860s had brought Italy and Germany onto the map, this new bout of constitution-making added the so-called successor states of east-central Europe, the Baltic states, and the Irish Republic, while rationalizing borders in the Balkans. But this political settlement didn't simply revise territorial relations among states; it also involved revolutionary transformation. Political instability was so acute in east-central Europe because territorial changes occurred amid the collapse of existing political authority. It proceeded not through the readjustment of existing borders but by the making of completely new states, whose internal social and political arrangements had to be built up from the ground.

While the socialist Left was strong in some of these new states, especially Czechoslovakia and Austria, in the rest it was quickly marginalized and in Hungary brutally suppressed. But the revolutionary turbulence of 1918 was a broader pan-European phenomenon, resulting from the generic consequences of the war—both from the interventionist war economy and associated changes in state-society relations and from popular resistance to the oppressiveness of the sacrifices. From 1918 to the early 1920s, large-scale working-class insurgencies blazed across Europe's social and political landscape—from the main storm centers of German-speaking Europe and Italy to the more dispersed and sporadic turbulence of the rest of Europe and from Spain to the various borderlands of the former Russian Empire.

Behind these revolutionary outbreaks was a common dialectic of the Left's tense and incomplete political integration. On the one hand, state-economy and state-society relations, country by country, became profoundly reshaped via the demands of war, bringing organized interests into new corporatist collusion with the state and hugely expanding the latter's demands on its citizenry. Union officials and moderate socialists reaped big benefits from brokering popular acquiescence in this process, bringing them for the first time into government orbit. On the other hand, by 1917–18 war weariness had severely damaged popular belief in the governments, propelling rising numbers into protests of increasingly radical temper. In this sense, the new patriotic unities forged in the summer of 1914—the overpowering appeals to national loyalty and common sacrifice—proved a double-edged sword. If those appeals had initially defused the Left's radicalism by drawing socialist parties and their unions into an unprecedented national consensus, they could also backfire, giving the Left new moral-political leverage once the inequities of the war's hardships grew too hard to bear.

Thus the war changed the Left's place in the nation. Compared to pre-1914, when even the strongest socialist parties were kept in opposition, 1918 brought them to the brink of governing. In Germany, Austria, and Czechoslovakia they briefly captured government itself, charged with stabilizing new democratic polities amid widespread working-class insurgency.[1] Socialists were clearly the beneficiaries of universal suffrage, expanding their electorates and forming coalitions with other parties willing to accept democracy. The resulting changes went far beyond the modest parliamentary constitutions that had prevailed in Europe since the 1860s. While parliamentary sovereignty and civil freedoms remained basic to democratic citizenship, other gains were now added, from an emergent package of social rights to changing definitions of the public sphere. Extraparliamentary social movements decisively sustained this process, ranging from the massive trade union growth and associated industrial militancy to women's movements of various kinds and a wide array of single-issue campaigns, many of them locally based.

Altogether, this brought a massive increment of reform. In a big part of Europe, the Left emerged with unprecedented positions of strength, not just in the earlier social democratic "core" of north-central Europe where socialist parties cleared 20 percent of the vote in prewar elections but also in states where socialist votes had lagged behind, like France, the Low Countries, and Britain. Yet, as I have shown, this strengthening of the Left came not from any breakthrough to socialism, certainly not in Bolshevik terms. It depended on the enlargement of parliamentary democracy—via universal manhood, and sometimes women's, suffrage—linked to stronger citizens' rights, an opening outward of the public sphere, a pushing forward of social services, and clear protections for unions under the law.

Socialists had often disparaged such gains in the past, implying that "real" emancipation could only come from abolishing capitalism or, worse, that "bourgeois" democracy was merely the fig leaf for capitalist oppression and a mask for ruling-class power, functioning as "the best possible political shell for capitalism," in Lenin's phrase.[2] Yet where revolutionaries scorned these formal rights, democracy suffered grievously as a result. Strong legal protections were indispensable for the democratic potentials organized by the stronger social democracies of the 1920s, whether in Germany and Austria, Scandinavia, or many local strongholds elsewhere. The achievements of Red Vienna and its counterparts were not imaginable without protection of the law. This was apparent no less from the demise of the German and Austrian republics in 1933–34, which spelled the destruction of those labor movements, than from the republics' birth, which first brought them to plausible national leadership. Indeed, the failures of central European socialists to break through to socialism during the revolutions of 1918–19 mattered far less than the new democratic capacities and legal resources that the improved constitutional frameworks now supplied.

In the political outcomes of 1918, there was a vital difference between military winners and losers. If the war brought a general toughening of the state across the combatant countries, by 1917–18 it had catastrophically weakened those states that were defeated—namely, the Russian, Austro-Hungarian, and German multinational empires. To them may be added Italy, technically on the winning side but experiencing this victory largely as defeat. In these cases, the war's final stages destabilized authority to the point of general dissolution when the war was lost, producing stronger popular mobilizations and greater measures of reform. Where existing states remained intact, on the other hand, enhanced by the prestige of a military victory, as in Britain and France, the settlements proved more modest on both crucial counts, namely, a less complete extension of the franchise and a compromised social deal.

On one vital front of democracy, the gendered dimensions of citizenship, the settlements fell profoundly short. Measuring women's citizenship mainly by their capacities as mothers counteracted their admission to citizenship in the vote, undermining political equality and fixing them in the domestic sphere. By the 1930s, the postwar gains had in any case been erased in most of central and eastern Europe, while women's greater visibility in the labor market and the public sphere attracted a vicious antifeminist backlash. In Catholic Europe, women hadn't even received the vote. There, socialist support for women's emancipation was at best ambivalent or lukewarm.

THE MEANING OF OCTOBER: BOLSHEVISM AND NATIONAL REVOLUTION

As socialists in the West struggled to assert themselves within parliamentary frameworks, sometimes bolstered and sometimes undermined by extraparliamentary movements, the Russian revolutionaries faced the more momentous tasks of advancing socialist goals in the East. Indeed, as the Bolsheviks emerged successfully from their Civil War during 1919–20, the complexities of postrevolutioonary state-building were already presenting their sympathizers elsewhere with an acute political dilemma. Western socialists were being urged not just to endorse the Bolsheviks' policies and behavior inside Russia but to take these as the best political model for their own societies' needs.

Bolshevik success in making their revolution—in seizing state power, winning the Civil War, and consolidating a socialist regime—has understandably dominated perceptions of these revolutionary years in Europe. The chances of revolutionary change elsewhere have usually been judged against this Bolshevik model, which implied armed insurrection, leadership by a disciplined revolutionary party, extreme social polarization, collapse of the liberal center, and a pitched confrontation between the Left and the recalcitrant forces of the old order, ending in "the dictatorship of the proletariat" or some equivalent of the short-lived Hungarian Soviet of 1919. The strongest insurgencies elsewhere, like the Italian occupation of the factories in fall 1920 or the German and Austrian revolutions in 1918–19, are then judged by their failure to generate scenarios of that kind.

However, the Bolshevik model of social polarization and successful insurrection was not the only or even the dominant pattern of revolutionary change. The dramatic instances of violent militancy in Italy and central

Europe, which partially mirrored the Petrograd mass actions of 1917, shouldn't obscure their national specificities. In fact, the far commoner pattern was one in which the fear of "Bolshevism" inspired major reformist departures, either by forcing the hand of a nervous government or by encouraging farsighted nonsocialist politicians into large-scale preemptive gestures. The interaction of working-class militancy, massive union growth, and extreme government anxieties provided the strongest impetus for radical change in the immediate postwar years. And of course in some cases, most notably Germany and Austria, the scene was initially set by a genuine revolutionary uprising.

The strongest reformisms—those capable of further extension during the 1920s—were precisely the ones with some guiding social democratic vision or intelligence, where the parties concerned could build on a strong prewar parliamentary tradition, effectively brokering the relations of government and people. The German, Austrian, and Scandinavian socialist movements did this, reemphasizing once again the importance of the north-central European social democratic core. The more fragile reformisms, on the other hand, occurred in societies without this mediating social democratic intelligence, where the main push for radical changes during 1918–20 came from the more transient pressure of the postwar union expansion, as in France and Britain.

In other words, in parliamentary Europe—the existing constitutional states of the west and north, plus the new national republics of central Europe and the east—socialist politics expressed not the extreme social polarization and insurrectionary confrontation coming from Russia but the Left's impact on much broader sociopolitical coalitions. Here, revolutions involved the prosaic but decisive institutional gains denounced by the Bolsheviks as meaningless reformism—namely, the full array of democratic gains in the franchise, union rights and labor laws, welfare measures, more generous civil rights, and the strengthening of the public sphere. In that case, the most inspirational element of 1917 for the rest of Europe was less the Bolshevik call for confrontation with "bourgeois democracy" than the affirmation of the rights of peoples to national self-determination—whether by creating entirely new democratic republics or by bringing the people of existing states into their rightful inheritance. In *this* sense, we can find four types of revolutionary context.

Most immediately, the western and southern peripheries of the former Russian Empire, from the Baltic states and Finland through Ukraine to Transcaucasia, produced separate revolutionary processes in 1917–20, distinct from the main Petrograd-Moscow axis of the Bolshevik revolution and each with their own dynamism and integrity. Second, there came between 28 October and 9 November 1918 a separate central European sequence of revolution, collectively no less significant than events in Russia. This erected new republican sovereignties on the ruins of the Habsburg and Hohenzollern monarchies in a chain linking Czechoslovakia, Yugoslavia,

"German-Austria," Hungary, Poland, West Ukraine, and Germany, with the socialist Left as major actors. During the founding period, the main pattern in these "successor states" was one of new parliamentary polities with a strong Left presence.

Third, the Bolshevik revolution accelerated the early stirrings of anti-colonial nationalist revolt—in the Middle East and Central Asia, China, India, and over the longer term Latin America, Southeast Asia, and South Africa. Here, Russia's economic backwardness and the overwhelmingly agrarian context of the Bolshevik revolution supplied the resonance, combined with Lenin's prioritizing of the principle of national self-determination during 1917–18. For the longer future, this surpassed Bolshevism's impact in Europe itself. For the first time, between the February and October revolutions, delegations of various extra-European peoples began appearing at the international gatherings of the Left in their own right. This was a momentous change.

Finally, the main pattern in the established national states of northern and western Europe was one of revolutionary pressure from within the existing institutional frameworks, in a setting of densely organized civil societies and emergent democracy. Here, the radical Left certainly generated much revolutionary heat and light, though on a far more sporadic and localized basis than in central Europe and the south. But the main changes came from the bending of governments to radical pressure, acceding reluctantly to the logic of democratic growth. The resulting sociopolitical packages amounted to a renegotiated social contract, producing not just extensions of the franchise, union recognition, and social laws but the toughening of civil society and the enhancement of the public sphere. In Scandinavia, the Low Countries, Britain, Switzerland, and France, this created a legitimate and structural place for the Left. Compared to the pre-1914 situations, this was also a momentous change.

SOCIAL DEMOCRACY AND COMMUNISM: A HOUSE DIVIDED

Bolshevism overturned socialist assumptions about how revolution would occur. Second International theorists had expected it to come naturally, after ever-sharpening polarization of society and the amassing of unstoppable working-class majorities in elections. Even as more apocalyptic visions tacitly receded, most pre-1914 socialists still nourished this belief: capitalist accumulation would eventually make the economy ripe for socialist control, and once socialists dominated parliament it would fall logically into their grasp.

Democracy was essential here, both in allowing the socialist movement to grow and in delivering the mechanisms for bringing economies under control. In Germany, therefore, which contained Europe's most dynamic capitalism and most prestigious socialist party, everything seemed to depend on replacing the imperial governing structures with a full-scale parliamentary republic. Once that democratic revolution was won, the governing socialists could turn to socializing the economy, bringing its private power under public control and redistributing its abundance. In that sense, the German changes of fall 1918, and their equivalents in Austria and elsewhere, brought the long-awaited scenario to fruition. Yet there were three problems.

For one thing, pre-1914 social democrats "systematically shied away from considering the issues involved in the actual exercise of power at the national level."[3] They entered government in 1918–19 ill-equipped for decisive action and with no program for moving to socialism. Worse, they did so in Austria and Germany amid the chaos of national military defeat, where practical emergencies of food supply, epidemic disease, lawlessness, and demobilizing the troops overshadowed thoughts of socialist construction, which in any case were increasingly consigned to rhetoric. Governing socialists, from the right-wing steadfastness of Friedrich Ebert and Philipp Scheidemann in Germany to Otto Bauer's troubled leftism in Austria, concentrated on managing an orderly transition to elections, so that new constitutions could be written, the revolution's gains be approved by a grateful electorate, and the social democrats be duly elected, after which the real business of reform could begin.

Unfortunately, neither the SPD nor the SPÖ secured a lasting popular mandate, and by 1920 they were back in opposition. While the fundamental democratic gains remained and vital enabling laws were passed, social democrats had failed to seize their time. The more radical spirits continued to advocate structural progress toward socialism, particularly those intellectuals schooled in Marxism and visionary cultural theorists. Their movements still pushed on the frontier of reform, especially in the economy and welfare state. But now change was pressed from within existing frameworks, and socialists spent their time increasingly defending the 1918 gains. Henceforth, socialist politics shriveled back into the parliamentary sphere, limiting any action to the new machineries of social administration and public education, forms of trade union corporatism, and ritual displays of movement support. Revolutionary expectations were shed.

This was a definitive "constitutionalizing" of social democracy. Its effects were not entire and immediate, because most socialist parties retained wider cultures of militancy during the interwar years, with major upswings of extraparliamentary activism from time to time, especially during the Popular Front campaigning against the rise of fascism in the mid-1930s. But the shift to moderation had a strong and definite logic, capturing the official strategies of the parties concerned—Labour in Britain, the SPD and SPÖ, the socialist parties of Switzerland, the Low Countries, and France. Only in Scandinavia did socialist parties keep a more open relationship to projects of structural transformation.

Second, however, this embracing of a strictly constitutional approach to further reform, which tied changes to the unambiguous verdicts of elections, had to be forced through against the racing revolutionary desires of a burgeoning extraparliamentary movement. It was this doubled quality that defined the new social democracy—not only its readiness to become a "responsible" party of government, cooperating with other parties and observing constitutional channels, but also its willingness to police any wider-reaching militancy, if necessary by suppressing revolutionary opponents by force. This trapped social democrats into alliances with the dominant classes, stymied their radical will, and constantly pitted them against the very popular movements they had always claimed to represent. The most egregious case was the SPD, which repeatedly preferred the priorities of "order" over the endorsement of popular democratic energies, from its maneuvering in November 1918 itself through the suppression of the Spartacist Rising and the socialization campaigns in early 1919 to the repression of the renewed popular militancy that defeated the Kapp Putsch in 1920.

Third—and this was the really disastrous consequence of social democracy's defense of law and order—the extraparliamentary militancy of the revolutionary years was captured by a new rival on the Left, the freshly established Communist parties aligned with the Bolsheviks in Russia. So it was not just that social democrats condemned rank-and-file militancy and used troops to put it down, in other words; it was also that Communists were now waiting to give such militancy voice.

In fact, many socialists expressed acute misgivings at the rightward drift as it first occurred. Discouraged by the mood of anti-Bolshevism, some larger parties seceded from the Second International in late 1919, including the German USPD and the Austrian, Swiss, French, and Norwegian parties, joining the Italian Socialists who had left it in March. These departures reassembled the broader Zimmerwald grouping from 1916–17, suggesting that Lenin's goal of reuniting revolutionaries around the nucleus of the Third International was in sight. To further this, Lenin published *"Left-Wing Communism"—An Infantile Disorder* in spring 1920, which, by criticizing the ultra-Left's extreme revolutionism sought to make the Communist parties into more attractive rallying points for disaffected socialists.[4]

Then, as the pan-European turbulence approached its height, the Twenty-One Conditions were adopted as the entrance ticket to the Third International, as a litmus test of revolutionary seriousness. By setting such stringent rules for joining, including extreme centralism of organization, the expulsion of pacifists and other heterodox radicals, and a willingness to submit to the discipline of the Third International's Executive, these Conditions played a vital part in defining the kind of movements the putative Communist parties could become. Between October 1920 and January 1921, substantial CPs were created by splitting existing socialist parties in Germany, France, and Italy (USPD, SFIO, and PSI); the Norwegian Labor Party joined the new International; there were mass CPs in Bulgaria and Czechoslovakia; and a significant affiliate existed in Finland, though partially underground. In Britain and Ireland, the Low Countries, Denmark and Sweden, Switzerland, Iberia, and the rest of eastern Europe, on the other hand, CPs could only be established on a marginal basis.

The fateful significance of this new division cannot be overemphasized. If the ground was laid for distinctively revolutionary parties, these were held to a new standard of international conformity that contrasted starkly with the frustrating but capacious pluralism of the past. Of course, the breakdown of tolerance and an increasingly embittering divisiveness already dated from the war, driven as much by right-wing social democrats as by the future Bolsheviks, and the counterrevolutionary violence of 1918– 20 then whipped this further along. Moreover, the rampant adventurism of the new radicalisms exploding across industrial Europe made some decisive initiative to shape that militancy almost inevitable. Certainly by late 1920, as the Soviet regime became marooned in isolation and revolutionary activism contracted in the West, some means of stabilizing the far Left was urgently needed.

This didn't yet mean crude uniformity of line. In 1921–23, some Communists continued cooperating with other parts of the Left, especially in the large German and Czechoslovak parties, helped by the policy of United Front approved by the Third International's Fourth Congress in December 1922.[5] By the Fifth Comintern Congress in July 1924, though, the collapse of Communist support in Europe tightened the pressure for conformity. A new policy of "Bolshevization" was adopted, which dragooned the CPs toward stricter bureaucratic centralism. This flattened out the earlier diversity of radicalisms, welding them into a single approved model of Communist organization. Only then did the new parties retreat from broader Left arenas into their own belligerent world, even if many local cultures of broader cooperation persisted.[6] Respect for Bolshevik achievements and defense of the Russian Revolution now transmuted into dependency on Moscow and belief in Soviet infallibility. Depressing cycles of "internal rectification" began, disgracing and expelling successive leaderships, so that by the later 1920s many founding Communists had gone. This process of coordination, in a hard-faced drive for uniformity, was finalized at the next Congress of the Third International in 1928.

Thus the extraordinary hopes of the years 1917–23 ended in disappointment. The Left's exuberant breakout from prewar isolation had culminated in a rigidly policed standoff between mutually hostile camps: an avowedly reformist social democracy, certainly committed to strengthening democratic goods but aggressively rejecting any greater radicalism and jealously guarding its new influence; and a dourly revolutionary Communism, digging itself down into redoubts of proletarian militancy, bitterly denouncing social democrats for betraying the revolution, and uncritically upholding Soviet superiority. At the core of this divisiveness was the defining experience of the revolutionary years themselves. On the one hand, social democrats had refused to harness the momentum of a tremendous democratic upsurge and on the contrary had endorsed its suppression; on the other hand, angry and fragmented working-class militancies, whose best impulses were thereby demonized and traduced, took their succor in Communism.

Under the circumstances, the new Communist parties discharged a difficult task remarkably well—namely, shaping the disorderly and localized radicalisms of the postwar years into lasting form by creating a focused continuity out of their revolutionary restlessness. But this also narrowed and simplified the possible trajectories, imposing an approved pattern whose rigidity was only sharpened by social democracy's unbending anti-Communism. The popular democratic optimism of the revolutionary years became broken and demoralized in these pincers: revolution was first defeated in the West; and its mantle was then captured by an ever-rigidifying Bolshevism. If 1917–23 was an exceptional time, a unique moment of pan-European insurrectionary revolution never to be repeated, then one of its consequences—the split in socialism—had permanent twentieth-century effects.

III

STABILIZATION AND THE "WAR OF POSITION"

ON 15 JULY 1943, Jacob Gens, Jewish dictator of the Vilna ghetto, met with the leaders of the United Partisans' Organization (FPO), the ghetto's underground resistance movement. While banking on ruthless compliance with Nazi demands to secure whatever Jewish survival was possible, Gens had been keeping lines open to the FPO from cynical self-interest of his own. The FPO dated from January 1942, when the ghetto's Communists and main Zionist groupings made common cause in preparing armed resistance. Finding agreement had not been easy: on the ghetto's formation in September 1941 existing political leadership collapsed, and prewar enmities could only be painstakingly handled. The initiatives came from younger men and women, especially Abba Kovner (born 1918), who was in many ways the FPO's leading inspiration, even though a respected and somewhat older Communist, Itzhak Witenberg (born 1909), was made commander, partly because of his Communist contacts outside the ghetto.

Unbeknownst to the FPO, Gens had a hidden motive for calling the meeting. Some weeks before, the Nazis had broken the Communist underground cell in the city and secured knowledge of its contacts with Witenberg inside the ghetto, though without suspecting his role in the FPO or even the existence of a Jewish fighting organization. On 8 July they demanded that Gens surrender Witenberg, who meanwhile had gone into hiding. Unable to fend the Nazis off any longer, Gens tricked the FPO Command into coming to his residence and had Witenberg arrested.

Events now moved very fast. Alerted independently to what was happening, an FPO detachment ambushed the Lithuanian police escorting Witenberg, who escaped into hiding. The remaining FPO leaders reconvened with Witenberg and agreed to defend him, if necessary by force. At 3 A.M. Gens addressed his ghetto police and the so-called *shtarke* ("strong ones," the underworld thugs he used for coercing the ghetto), accusing Witenberg and the Communists of bringing the general population into danger. Unless Witenberg was handed over, he claimed, the Nazis would liquidate everyone. The shtarke proceeded to attack the FPO refuge, backed by larger crowds whipped up by the police. The FPO's situation became impossible. They could only protect Witenberg and launch an uprising by firing first on their fellow Jews. Gens had successfully isolated Witenberg against the mass of the ghetto (by that stage some 20,000 inhabitants), who felt themselves imperiled by his links to Communists outside. The Nazis now issued their own ultimatum: surrender Witenberg alive, or they would enter the ghetto.

Gens sent a delegation of ghetto notables to negotiate directly with the FPO. After tortured discussions, the latter decided that Witenberg must surrender, a decision also reached earlier by the Communist group. Amid further anguish, after exploring all possible options, Witenberg agreed. After meeting personally with Gens, he was escorted to the ghetto gate, where the Nazis were waiting. It was the evening of 16 July. Overnight he committed suicide with cyanide supplied by Gens.[1]

Living under Nazi occupation during 1939–45 imposed intolerable decisions on Europe's citizens, in ways becoming ever more brutalized and atrocious the further to the east one looks, reaching their unimaginable worst for the Jews. Political decisions were simultaneously elevated and compromised—reduced on the one hand to the most basic issues of everyday survival and infused with the most complex and momentous ethical meanings on the other. In the Vilna ghetto, any of the courses available to the *Judenrat*—meeting Nazi demands in order to modify them, selecting certain categories of people for deportation over others, distributing welfare to the poor rather than radically collectivizing resources, and so on—involved heavy moral expenditure.[2] The most useful of the ghetto leadership's protective measures, like the assigning of work papers, involved harming some to benefit others. No one was untouched by these dilemmas. Constraints on ethical behavior were unimaginably hard. As Kovner, Witenberg, and their comrades knew, the very act of resistance invariably penalized one's immediate fellows rather than helping them. Success was minimal, reprisals ferocious.

Witenberg's dilemma was replicated endlessly across Europe. For example, Hanna Lévy-Hass, a teacher in Montenegro, was active in the Yugoslav Communist underground when war broke out. When the Germans moved into the area formerly occupied by their Italian allies in the fall of 1943, she found herself in the village of Cetinje among 30 other Jews. She was preparing to join the Communist resistance in the mountains, when a deputation of three young Jews arrived. "Can your conscience," they asked, "bear the thought that in order to go and join the partisans, you will be sacrificing thirty other people? If you go, we shall all be shot." She stayed, was imprisoned with the rest, and in the summer of 1944 was deported to Bergen-Belsen, where she barely survived.[3]

The rise of fascism in Europe not only put the democratic gains of the post-1918 period into jeopardy but threatened civilized human values per se. Defeating Nazism required not only the international anti-Hitler alliance but also a new breadth of coalition building for the defense and furtherance of democracy inside European societies, for which the growth of antifascist resistance during 1943–45 became the sign. Much as the Vilna ghetto fighters found common cause in the FPO, all across Europe Communists, socialists, radicals of many hues, liberals, and Christians proved willing to bury their enmities in the higher cause. A new democratic momentum developed as a result—a less sectarian and more generous Communism, inspired by ideas of "national roads to socialism" rather than the all-valid Bolshevik model; a reradicalized socialism; a liberalism more reconciled to democracy's specific claims; and a Christian Democracy urgently repudiating the compromised and collaborationist conservatisms of the past.

These new formations were animated by a palpable shift in popular attitudes. As they emerged from the horrors of the war, Europe's citizens expected better worlds to be built. There was enormous tiredness, relief, and a desire for the normal, the return of the predictable and reassuring everyday. But there was also great elation, an optimism, a belief in reachable futures. There was "a spirit in Europe," as the title of one idealistic tract put it.[4] This was connected to the privations endured during the 1930s. These were partly political—Witenberg had been active in the trade union movement, chairing the Leather Workers' Union, with long experience in the Polish Communist underground; his fellow Communist in the FPO Command, Sonia Madeysker (born 1914), had spent eight years in Polish prisons.[5] But for the mass of Europeans a sense of righteous entitlement also fed on the Depression's social miseries. Europe's post-1945 political cultures fused both these powerful memories: sacrifices in common struggle and inequalities that were patently unjust.

Chapter 15

Capitalist Stabilities

Future Deferred

BY CONTRAST WITH 1871–1914, when European peace was broken mainly by colonial violence overseas, 1918–39 was a time of revolutionary and counterrevolutionary strife, civil war, unprecedented economic depression, and renewed social polarization. State terror and acute international tension culminated in the Second World War and the genocidal destruction of peoples. But one huge fact stands out: 1917–21 was the last pan-European uprising of the peoples, a chain reaction of barricade revolutions on the classic nineteenth-century model, in which old regimes toppled and new orders promised to take their place. Particular insurgencies happened later on—the Spanish and French Popular Fronts in 1936, Balkan resistance struggles in the Second World War, the Hungarian uprising of 1956, the May events in Paris in 1968, the Portuguese Revolution of 1974, the eastern European revolutions of 1989. But that intoxicating sense of the masses in motion, of generalized societal crisis during which previously solid structures suddenly tottered and history was available for the turning, had passed. The sense in 1917 that everything was possible, what George Lukács called "the actuality of the revolution," had gone.[1]

By the mid-1920s, the revolutionary vision changed. Before 1914, socialists rarely explained how power would be seized, let alone the practicalities of building socialism. Kautsky and his contemporaries banked on capitalist development's iron logic. Social polarization and inevitable capitalist crisis would bestow power on the waiting socialists, already legitimized (it was assumed) by huge majorities in elections. Rejecting such "automatic Marxism" at Russia's crucial juncture in 1917, in contrast, Lenin and Trotsky imagined further breakdowns of public authority in the West, allowing revolutionaries to force events along rather than waiting for them to happen. Preconditions were charted: radicalization of the masses via immiseration, divisions of the dominant classes, mutinies of the army. Popular uprisings under revolutionary parties would allow the citadel of the state to be stormed. This activist view of revolution was also vital to Bolshevism's own survival: once those conditions arrived in the West, the Russian Revolution could be supported in spite of Russia's poorly developed industrial economy.

This strategizing of revolution had an afterlife through the Comintern, in the ultraleftism of some CPs, in rank-and-file utopianism, and among the smaller revolutionary sects. The 1929 depression, fertile ground for political extremes, also revived such thinking. Revolutionary agency was exercised on gargantuan scale in the Soviet industrialization drive after 1929, as Bolsheviks transformed their society from above. But this was the action of state on society rather than a bid for state power mounted from within the social domain. Elsewhere, imagining revolutionary transitions took far less activist forms, and by the mid-1930s voluntarism was definitely in recession.

RETHINKING THE MEANINGS OF REVOLUTION

For large parts of the Left, the goal wasn't "revolution" at all but reforming the given system, meaning both the capitalist economy and the democratized parliamentary constitutions forged from the First World War. Such reformism remained radical, because making society more equitable and humane entailed conflicts and confrontations. Five categories of reforms usually came into play: democratization per se, via universal suffrage and maximum parliamentary government, though often with restrictions against women; labor law and trade union rights, turning after 1929 increasingly on employment and workers' protection; social insurance, including unemployment benefits, low income support, sickness benefits, pensions, and healthcare; housing reform, usually via city-based public sectors; and educational reform to expand equality of access. Strategically, these reforms relied on the abundance generated by the fully matured capitalist economy. Socially, they coalesced increasingly into the idea of a welfare state.

Such reforms could be prefigurative. In Austria, the Socialization Commission of April 1919 was conceived as the enabling framework for step-by-step restructuring of the national economy, taking socialized industries into common trusteeship by labor, capital, consumers, and the state, joined by factory councils in democratization from below. But this goal became stymied in parliament, and the collapse of coalition in June 1920 ended the SPÖ's governing spell. Throughout, its radicalism was caught in the democratic socialist dilemma: in 1918–19 it had decisively rejected force, an option acutely posed by the existence of the short-lived Hungarian Soviet, when winning a civil war was still imaginable; but having rejected insurrection and left the Hungarians to their fate, the SPÖ was now aligned against the Communists. And securing conservative acquiescence in the Republic's early reforms proved poor compensation for this divisiveness on the Left.

After 1920, this decision—for democracy over dictatorship, in contemporary rhetoric—returned the SPÖ to opposition. It took refuge in the optimistic scenario of ever-growing electoral support, where the only acceptable road to power was the coming of the socialist parliamentary majority. The party's Vienna reforms became pedagogical in purpose, preparing the masses for the future rather than directly contesting power. But however creative the redistributive fiscal policies behind Red Vienna, they depended ultimately on a prosperous capitalism, and this was the reformist conundrum.[2] The labor movement wielded impressive social power, as a subcultural complex organizing the community solidarity and everyday lives of the working class in all the ways Red Vienna professed. Yet the bridge from this subaltern collectivism to genuine political leadership over society—hegemony in Gramsci's sense—had yet to be found. Translating the labor movement's subcultural influence into power in the state, through a non-insurrectionary revolutionary strategy, was the problem.[3]

The German case gave some pointers. Under Weimar, the SPD's expectations stayed tethered to the habits of Marxist political economy, where economics provided the preconditions of political success—cyclical fluctuations, the tendency of the rate of profit to fall, crises of capitalist accumulation. In the 1920s, Rudolf Hilferding defined a new stage of capitalist development—"organized capitalism"—in which rising concentration of ownership and control in the economy's dynamic sectors, and the state's growing responsibility for national economic management, gave democratically elected governments increasing leverage. International trade and capital flows through world financial markets also enhanced government's role in the national economy, as did industrial rationalization and the corporatism securing organized labor's cooperation. Indeed, as capitalism became ever more self-organized and ever greater coordination was required of government, public control of the economy for the common good became easier. International trade, prices, technology, planned investment, the labor market, workplace organization, producing socially needed skills through education—all were increasingly regulated politically. As government became sucked into managing the economy, therefore, the chances of bringing it under democratic control also grew.[4]

Between the SPD Congresses of Breslau (1925) and Hamburg (1928), Fritz Naphtali and a group of economists organized these claims programmatically into *Economic Democracy: Its Character, Means and Ends.*[5] This envisaged four priorities of intervention—nationalization of the commanding heights; central cooperative institutions; industrial democracy; and a national wages policy. The goals were broken down impressively into specifics, making an ambitious catalogue of eminently practical measures. It was a strategy for changing capitalism from within, gradually extending the frontier of control, until prerogatives of private property passed under public command, in a government of the overwhelming noncapitalist majority of the people.

Ideas like economic democracy widely influenced interwar left-socialist circles as a revolutionary alternative to the CPs' Leninism. If the human and democratic costs of abandoning parliament for the dictatorship of the proletariat seemed too great, then socialists also worried that observing parliamentary rules would neutralize their challenge. Either reformism might ease capitalism's continuation by coopting the working class or, by imposing redistributive and regulative burdens, it might provoke capitalists into withdrawing their cooperation. Accordingly, a strategy was needed to transcend capitalism's given structures, by winning diverse and majoritarian popular support, extending democratic control, and allaying capitalists' immediate fears, in a process of organic socialist transition.

Here, the interwar non-Communist Left had two projections. One held that "reformism can have revolutionary consequences; that, if conceived within a correct political perspective, reforms which apparently strengthen the capitalist order may simultaneously establish the conditions for its transformation." The other was classically "Kautskyan" in the pre-1914 sense: "socialistic" logic in the capitalist organization of production—through state intervention and planning, public investment and regulation, selective nationalizations, growing monopoly organization—would ultimately necessitate formal socializing of the economy, to rationalize the already accumulating change. In the meantime, "since the time is not ripe for socialism, the object of socialists should be to actively promote the maturation of capitalism in a direction favorable to socialist goals."[6] Socialism's future would be nurtured in the womb of capitalism's present.

This reliance on capitalism's future foundered on the 1929 crash. In the fiscal crunch, the SPD caved in to cuts in public spending and wages, seeing profitability as the only way of reviving production, consumption, and employment in the future. Alternative proposals from the unions, like the Woytinsky-Tarnow-Baade (WTB) program for reflating the economy via public works in 1931–32, were rejected by Hilferding, Naphtali, and other SPD theoreticians as remedial measures for capitalism, restoring its stability rather than hastening its demise. Actually, the WTB program included detailed "Guidelines for Restructuring the Economy" (July 1932), implying incremental steps to socialist planning similar to Naphtali's economic democracy.[7] But SPD leaders balked at the intransigence needed for that program. They ceded economic initiative to business and its government allies.

The labor movement won the worst of all worlds. Lacking electoral majorities or reliable allies after 1930, the SPD was excluded from power, while backing an unsympathetic conservative government from fear of worse. Its defensive strength let business blame it for the crisis of profitability, while the socialist rank and file suffered creeping demoralization.

THE CONSTITUTIONALIZING OF SOCIAL DEMOCRACY

Structural reform's inability to burst the fetters of social democracy's entrenched inevitabilist assumptions is most striking. For guardians of economistic orthodoxy like Hilferding, both a respected theoretician and twice minister of finance, proto-Keynesian proposals were irrelevant tinkerings with capitalism's fundamental processes, without purchase on its ultimate collapse. Likewise, elder statesmen like Kautsky reaffirmed their faith in labor's inevitable democratic inheritance. Yet, faced with the practical emergencies of economic crisis, social distress, and right-wing political extremism, socialist leaderships brooked no alternatives to the parliamentary arena, which in practice left them striving for defensive coalitions from positions of institutional weakness, excluded from government power. Meanwhile, other parts of the movement, through the unions and party militia, sustained rhetorics of militancy that frightened their opponents without ever being put to the test. As democracy became dismantled—with the dissolving of the SPD government in Prussia in July 1932 or Nazism's seizure of power itself in January–March 1933—the workers' troops never received the call.[8]

The other big case of interwar structural reform was the Plan of Labor adopted by the Belgian Socialists in December 1933, known as the *Plan de Man* after its architect, the heterodox socialist thinker Hendrik de Man. Like economic democracy, this broke with the reified binarism of "revolution" and "reform," which counterposed the necessity of securing the workers' immediate interests against the future goal of capitalism's end. Instead, it proposed a seamless transition, in which skilfully crafted reforms cumulatively shifted the balance in socialism's favor. In 1933–35, the Plan de Man dramatically captured the public imagination, with wide international effects.[9]

The campaign of the Belgian Workers' Party (POB) for the Plan was exceptionally creative, using print media, radio, theater, cabaret, song, speaking choruses, film, study courses and retreats, mass meetings, and teams of bicycle agitators for the countryside. Aside from planning per se, the strategy connected the needs of economic recovery to a specifically socialist future. De Man offered a dynamic model of the mixed economy, in which centralized control of the commanding heights and generalized regulation combined with support for small-scale enterprise to initiate socialist transition. Joined to immediate nationalization of big monopolies, a comprehensive national plan for all areas of fiscal, commercial, and social policy would begin transferring the economy under democratic control, embracing investment, trade, labor markets, training, industrial relations, and social insurance. Protection for private ownership and supports for small business, appealing deliberately to the middle class, would lay the specter of an overpowerful state bureaucracy. Amid the demoralization of the depression and increasingly frightening political setbacks, from the Nazi seizure of power in Germany to the defeat of the workers' rising of February 1934 in Austria, the Plan of Labor was a much-needed Left counteroffensive. It rallied the Left's unity, while inviting "non-proletarian strata" to give support. It was this seizing of the political initiative that proved so inspiring.

The Plan's radical hopes, however, came to nothing. In early 1935, as the conservative government of Georges Theunis began another round of social cuts, de Man and the POB leaders faced the strategic dilemmas both SPD and SPÖ evaded—whether to stake the movement's future on a pitched confrontation with government or to go for defensive and minimalist compromise. An emergency conference of POB and unions narrowly rejected a general strike by block votes of 581,412 against 481,112. Then the Theunis government resigned. The Socialists joined the Christian Democrats in coalition on 26 March 1935, with de Man as a POB minister. Another emergency congress endorsed this on 30–31 March by 519,672 votes against 41,902. De Man himself had become dismayed by the gathering social crisis. Faced with the choice of open rebellion and accompanying bloodshed or forming a moderate coalition, he took the latter.[10]

This Belgian experience—the meteoric rise and fall of "radical planism" as a distinctively socialist answer to the Great Depression, attuned to planning and managerialism, mobilizing working-class hopes, and appealing to nonworkers—was highly instructive. The most innovative structural strategy aimed at circumventing the need for a Bolshevik-style uprising, the Plan de Man ended by just confirming the unavoidability of a showdown. If socialists were serious about transforming capitalism, it showed, the need for insurrection—pitched battles, via general strike or massed demonstrations, aimed at bringing the Left to power—couldn't be avoided. Radicalizing the political agenda meant popular mobilization, in extraparliamentary and thus dangerously transgressive ways, which pushed on the normative limits of politics, frightening the dominant classes and their popular support and raising the Bolshevik specter just the same. Where the radical Right were already mobilizing their own extraparliamentary power, against both liberal states and the Left's popular democracy, the logic of a showdown was even more dramatically posed. Radical planism could only postpone questions of confrontation, direct action, and insurrection, not supersede them.

When tested, social democrats—and, except rarely, Communists too—could never take the insurrectionary plunge. Whether in August 1914, in the turbulence after 1917–18, in the central European crisis of democracy in the early 1930s, or in the French Popular Front of 1936, various motives kept socialists from abandoning legality and challenging state power—respect for the law, fear of bloodshed, anxieties about failing, ingrained weddedness to electoralism and the parliamentary arena, a patriotic ideology of the national interest. The choice was very clear. Lacking absolute electoral majorities, should the Left go for confrontationist politics, entailing violence; or should it go for coalition, diluting its demands and settling for modest reform? In face of this choice, Belgian radical planism promised a third way. It combined maximalism and legality, holding out for the whole demand ("The Plan; All of the Plan; Nothing but the Plan") while rallying diverse popular support and directly attracting the middle strata rather than negotiating with their parties. But then, as usual, socialist leaders stepped back from the brink. The POB's vote against general strike in March 1935 mirrored the Italian movement's analogous decision of September 1920. Having rejected the risks of the showdown, socialists reoccupied their political isolation, watching power from the sidelines, or joined coalitions for avowedly limited goals. Meanwhile, fascism advanced.

The lasting effect of the post-1918 settlement and the constructive achievement of those farsighted conservative politicians who faced up to the working-class insurgencies of 1917–23 was thus the definitive "constitutionalizing" of social democratic parties and their unions, those wings of the labor movements deciding not to join the Third International in 1920–21. Britain was typical: "Labour never looked afterwards like a social force capable of taking over leadership of society or of reconstructing the state."[11] Henceforth, the Labour Party always disavowed extraparliamentary and direct-action militancy and craved the legitimacy of official recognition, desiring nothing more than to perform its moderation, as a responsible party of constitutional government. Decorousness and propriety became the rule. Having rejected the Bolsheviks' vanguardist model of proletarian democracy as authoritarian and counterproductive, a recipe for destructive violence and self-isolating dictatorship, social democrats adhered rigidly to parliamentary rules, trapped in a psychology of proceduralism and forever shying from the fight. This hardwiring of social democratic imaginations into the integrated circuits of parliamentary legality was the key to the post-1918 period.

CORPORATISM AND PARLIAMENTARY GOVERNMENT

The political stabilizations of the early 1920s faced the Left with varying national alignments, which supported authoritarian, fascist, and some parliamentary outcomes. The clearest regional pattern was in the economically backward eastern and southern European periphery, which contained agrarian economies of a particular kind—economies that were mixtures of inefficiently organized big estates and poorly endowed family farms and were labor intensive, undercapitalized, low in technology, and demographically overloaded—with a distinctive social structure to match.

Such societies had specialized industrial sectors that were usually concentrated around the capital cities, a few mining centers, rural manufacturing, and the major ports. But these industrial enclaves were dwarfed by agricultural populations and authoritarian polities. Urban middle classes were chronically factionalized between state-dependent and entrepreneurial sectors as well as by ethnicity and religion. Building multiclass political alliances was hopelessly complex. Consensus building in these societies proved fragile. Most reverted to authoritarianism, either in counterrevolutionary response to postwar democratic uprisings or by incremental attacks on democratic life such as banning parties, restricting the franchise, and attacking civil liberties. By the time of a coup d'état—Poland and Lithuania in 1926, Yugoslavia in 1929, Bulgaria, Estonia, and Latvia in 1934, Greece in 1936—democracy was already hollowed out.[12]

The Left's prevailing pattern in southern and eastern Europe had three elements. First, Communist parties, as rallying points for committed revolutionaries among worker militants, dissident intellectuals, and Moscow-trained professional cadres, were either banned or persecuted. Second, radicalism in these overwhelmingly agrarian societies involved peasants. After suppressing urban revolutionary organizations and targeting known individuals, authoritarian regimes isolated and controlled the countryside via policing, paternalist social discipline, legal discrimination, and restricted franchise. And finally, if social democrats repudiated Communists and avoided the countryside, authoritarian regimes sometimes allowed them back.[13]

This authoritarianism differed from fascism. After immediate counter-revolutionary brutalities, eastern European dictatorships observed limited constitutional forms, allowing elections and some legalities for organized labor. By contrast, labor movements in Italy and north-central Europe were incomparably stronger. They were larger, better organized, and deeply integrated into the social life and public culture of their countries. Uprooting the Left from this historic embeddedness in complex civil societies required a comprehensive assault on the status quo. Thus fascism was vastly more radical as it faced an immensely stronger working-class adversary. It "sought to disenfranchise, in the fullest sense, the working classes, and to destroy political and labor market gains that had been generations in the making." This required a different kind of regime, one that systematically attacked the given bases of political life. Accordingly, fascism knew no restraints.[14]

New system of politics which stabalized Western European capitalism after '45

But despite the fascist extremes, a new system of politics was fashioned in 1914–23 in western Europe that not only resolved the political breakdowns occurring at the end of the First World War but delivered the lasting bases of stabilization for western European capitalism after 1945.[15] "Corporatism," institutionalized cooperation between employers and unions mediated by the state, crystallized from the postwar crises. It required containing labor's challenge in the factories as well as blocking larger-scale plans for socialization. The path was then freed for rationalization—mechanization and enlargement of capacity; Taylorization, scientific management, and deskilling of work; control of the labor process, the production line, and the shedding of redundant labor. But this also allowed limited collective bargaining, regulated ideally on national, industrywide bases. This doubled quality was crucial to the stabilization—not only repression of the working-class insurgency and its revolutionary desires but also calculated concessions to some categories of workers, explicitly furthering employers' control. Even fascism devised these forms of corporatist recognition.

More than this, stabilization sustained a general political settlement, redesigning relations among government, economy, and parliamentary arenas. Faced with both the insurgencies of 1917–23 and dysfunctions of the international economy and fresh from wartime interventionism, western European governments claimed an expanding responsibility for managing the national economy. But parliaments couldn't handle the central problems of the crisis—the crucial "disputes through which the basic distributions of power were contested or exposed: conflicts over nationalization, taxes, and inflation; relations between capital and labor; reparation quarrels; tariff negotiations." They were being displaced by a new system of "constant brokerage" between the state and major organized interests. "Classical parliamentarism was shifting toward patterns of interest group representation."[16]

Labor movements became drawn into the managerial structures of national economies in this way. But the interaction of parliamentary politics and corporatism was complex. This was no zero-sum game, where the new brokerage of interests required the decline of parliaments and the rise of one was the loss of the other. Instead, social democracy became simultaneously "constitutionalized." Just as unions were entering new partnerships with employers and government in systems of corporatist negotiation over wages and workplace authority, social democratic parties were also committing themselves to visions of parliamentary reform. Existing parliamentary arenas were less the obstacle to corporatist solutions than a complementary source of legitimation. If corporatist arrangements helped discipline rank-and-file militancy by breaking the shopfloor accountability of union leaders and using them to police their own members, then parliamentary democracy could focus popular political hopes. Corporatism developed from a crisis of political representation, in which working-class mobilization took avowedly revolutionary forms. But if it was to work, working-class expectations still needed a credible political arena.

Stabilization in the 1920s needed *both* the new corporatism *and* the strengthening of parliaments. In Britain, Labour became the voice of reform in a two-party system only amid wider democratic ferment in 1910–26, when a gradualist or constitutionalist perspective wasn't yet assured. Joining the patriotic consensus of 1914–18 certainly privileged moderate union leaders and Labour parliamentarians, while the 1918 Representation of the People Act (votes for men over 21 and women over 30) lent this dominance popular electoral momentum. But Labour also faced the British version of the European working-class insurgency of 1917–21. What became a taken-for-granted constitutionalism had to be bitterly secured against more radical socialist perspectives. The Labour Party's new constitution in 1918 linked socialism's achievement to public ownership (clause 4) but by an exclusively parliamentary road that repudiated the direct-action militancy of many of its strongest working-class supporters.

Ramsay MacDonald and the Labour leadership discovered a common interest with Conservatives in securing Labour's status as the second party, because the more radical forms of "the democracy" could only be defeated by ensuring that the masses "were properly and moderately represented within the councils of state." As the Conservative leader Stanley Baldwin said, the first goal was "the disappearance of the Liberal Party. . . . The next step must be the elimination of the Communists by Labour. Then we shall have two parties, the Party of the Right and the Party of the Left."[17] The dual purposes of the democratic reform of 1918—the stabilizing of capitalism, the cohesion of society—were vital. New arrangements for running the capitalist economy, via representation of corporately organized interests, was one dimension. But corporatism per se contributed little to other political needs—the competition of ideas in the public sphere, the building of broader social coalitions, and the winning of popular consent for the defense or critique of existing political arrangements.[18]

PATTERNS OF STABILIZATION

From 1917 to the early 1920s, the Left's challenge placed democracy onto the European agenda in the most radical socialist and participatory ways. The 1920s also framed a longer epoch, through which two vital constitution-making conjunctures (1859–71, 1917–23) ordered and reordered state-society relations democratically. The framing events of this epoch in Britain were the 1867 Reform Act and the Representation of the People Act of 1928, which created "for the first time a fully-fledged, formal, mass democracy," inside a broader transition to collectivist ideas of state and society.[19] Here the "constitutionalizing" of Labour's vision remained decisive, as it ruled out the extraparliamentary direct action that might have expanded citizenship and the constitution. Holding the parliamentary line—and complementary corporatist arrangements—meant disavowing other types of agency, from councils of action, rent strikes, and protests of the unemployed to "Poplarism" and imaginative local socialisms. Above all, it meant repudiating "unconstitutional" political confrontations, like the ill-fated General Strike of May 1926.[20]

The strength or weakness of parliaments was the key variable shaping successful corporatisms, and British distinctiveness emerges when compared to weaker parliamentary systems. In Italy, for example, the confrontational politics of the PSI—which in 1917–22 rejected being "constitutionalized"—exhausted the liberal state's intermediary capacities and drove the dominant classes to Fascism. Corporatist innovation occurred in both countries, but while the Left's defeat in Italy led to Mussolini's March on Rome, its defeat in Britain through the 1926 General Strike led to the 1929 election of a Labour government. Thus in Britain parliamentary and corporatist fields weren't incompatible but on the contrary were complementary. Parliamentarism legitimized corporatism for the masses. The stability promised by corporatism presupposed a constitutional framework that guaranteed the juridical rights of citizenship and enabled the populace to feel itself free. Like the Italian, Weimar Germany's corporatism lacked the firm machinery of parliamentary legitimation, in contrast, and the eclipse of parliamentarism after 1930 was a symptom of German corporatism's instability, not its strength.[21]

Europe's patterns of political stabilization ranged from authoritarian dictatorships in the east and south to relatively stable liberal democracies in western Europe. Full-scale recourse to fascism came in Italy, Germany, and Spain, where working-class mobilizations outgrew liberal democracy's capacities for containment. Finally, the Scandinavian pattern of state-incorporated social democracy, based on cross-class coalitions, in the doubled context of economic corporatism and functioning parliamentarism that I have emphasized earlier, was the strongest case of reform.

Some countries are admittedly hard to place in this typology. A dominant clericalism, organized around confessional parties and unions, marked the Belgian and Dutch polities. Czechoslovakia, eastern Europe's surviving parliamentary democracy, showed signs of the Scandinavian pattern in the mid-1930s, brutally interrupted by the country's dismemberment in 1938–39. Austria fell somewhere between authoritarian dictatorship and fascism, given the radicalized right-wing assault on the labor movement's highly mobilized socialist culture.

Finally, this typology maps interestingly onto the main pre-1914 pattern, that of the north-central European social democratic core, which contained the strongest labor movements. Here, the division runs down the middle. In Germany, the SPD failed to institutionalize the Scandinavian success story of social democratic corporatism, as the consensus-sustaining capacities of the Weimar parliamentary system collapsed in 1930–33. In Czechoslovakia, a putative Scandinavian trajectory was terminated by Franco-British acquiescence in Nazi Germany's imperialist aggression. In Austria, the German experience of suspended parliamentary government was replicated in 1927–34, while any pragmatic arrangement between the post-1934 authoritarian regime and the socialists was precluded by the former's international dependence on Fascist Italy and the Third Reich. The key difference, dividing the Scandinavian experience from these cases, was the labor movements' ability to sustain a larger crossclass coalition.

Neither the ineffectuality of the SPD's coalition building nor the Scandinavian success story were inevitable. In France, the chances of fascist-driven polarization in the 1930s were stronger, and the parliamentary system more fragile, than is often assumed. But in the stable democracies of the western European cluster, the settlement endured. These countries were governed continuously between the wars by the center-right. In Britain, apart from two Labour interludes in 1924 and 1929–31, Conservatives were permanently in office, either alone or in coalition. In France, the center-right also dominated, with short-lived breaks for center-left and Popular Front governments in 1924–25 and 1936–38. In Switzerland, a similar center-right formula reigned in 1918–43. In each case, this system was directed against the socialist Left. The corollary was related subordination of national trade unionism, secured via the climacteric of a defeated general strike—in Switzerland (November 1918), France (May 1920), and Britain (May 1926). Socialist weakness also resulted from an absence of major cleavages, like "language, region, religion," which had previously divided the middle-class parties, thereby delivering the socialists potential allies, and enabling "lib-lab" coalition. The very primacy of class politics after 1918 placed labor movements in permanent electoral isolation, forever the losers in "a clear-cut choice between a working-class party and an anti-socialist party or coalition."[22]

In the fascist cases, neither condition obtained. Before the fascist victory, German, Italian, and Spanish labor movements were not marginalized but embedded in national, regional, and local government; and the middle-class sector was not unified but split. While implying left positions of strength, these contexts actually produced catastrophic defeat. Left institutional strengths weren't converted into control of the state. Middle-class fragmentation was overcome not via democratic coalition building to the left but through fascist concentration in a triumph of the radical Right.

Fascism succeeded where it became feasible for dominant classes to take such extreme solutions seriously. Turning to fascism became most likely where the Left made inroads into state administration and private capitalist prerogatives, even when excluded from national government. In Italy and Germany, combinations of entrenched reformism and defensive militancy blocked the resolution of economic crisis and the restoration of order. The post-1930 crisis of Weimar resulted from the persistence of social democratic corporatism in trade union law, the Ministry of Labor, compulsory arbitration procedures, unemployment insurance, and other welfare legislation, which angered the Right into leaving the constitutional framework of pluralism behind. The more labor defended its post-1918 gains, the more determined the Right's recourse to extrademocratic means became. When we add the Left's strengths in regional and local government (the PSI in 1919–20, the SPD up to 1932–33), the impressive militancy of its rank and file, and the vitality of a Marxist vision among the party intelligentsia, the attractions of radical authoritarianism for the dominant classes become all the clearer. It seemed the only means of clearing the way. Fascism's rise as a credible mass movement then delivered the popular basis for "extrasystemic solutions."[23]

Finally, the Scandinavian pattern of state-incorporated social democracy gave socialists unique national leadership via long-lasting governments in Denmark (from 1929), Sweden (from 1932), and Norway (from 1935). Successfully centralized industrial relations, institutionalized around national federations of employers and unions very early before 1914, anchored the Scandinavian social settlements of the 1930s. Business acknowledged the legitimacy of social democratic government, with its commitment to high wages, social welfare, and full employment, while socialists conceded the sanctity of private property, guaranteed private control of capital markets, and restrained union militancy in the interests of social peace. Nationalization and public ownership were dropped in favor of redistributive strategies using taxation and public spending, easing both corporatist resolution of industrial conflicts and working-class social gains. A state-backed compact of employers and unions was the centerpiece—the Kanslergade Agreement in Denmark (1933), a similar bargain in Norway (1935), and the Saltsjöbaden Agreement in Sweden (1938).

This corporatist centerpiece also needed political foundations in a parliamentary coalition. A constructive politics of the countryside was decisive here. The relative absence of agricultural wage-earners encouraged more flexible socialist policies and rural coalition building, while farm-based parties proved receptive to socialist alliance. In contrast to Italy, where the PSI mobilized laborers but alienated smallholding farmers, and Germany, where the countryside was dominated by anti socialist movements eventually feeding into Nazism, Scandinavia supported a distinctive farm-labor coalition.

In both dimensions—corporatist détente with nationally organized employers, political trade-off with the countryside—Scandinavian social democrats marked their distance from the reformisms imagined by socialists in Germany, Austria, and Belgium. Public ownership, in the sense of nationalization, production planning, and the command economy, receded before more flexible proto-Keynesian and redistributive ideas of public control. Rather than entering a direct confrontation with private interests in the economy, whether over ownership in industry, small business, or the land,

Scandinavian socialists preferred a different approach, joining corporatist pragmatics to fiscal steering, redistributive taxation, and an active social policy. This strategy—"a détente with, rather than a takeover of, the private economy"—had distinct benefits, shifting economic conflicts into the political arena, where socialists "could maximize the use of their principal asset—state power—and thus their control over the labor movement and economy."[24]

Chapter 16

Stalinism and Western Marxism

Socialism in One Country

DURING 1917–21, the left became permanently split between those who joined the Third International and those who did not. For Communists, Soviet events played an ever more decisive part, proceeding from the power struggle surrounding Lenin's illness and death in 1923–24. The factional maneuvering—which first isolated Trotsky and then broke the authority of Kamenev and Zinoviev, while relentlessly concentrating power around Stalin—profoundly influenced how Communism elsewhere would be shaped. In particular, Stalin produced the new thesis of "Socialism in One Country," which claimed, for the first time, that socialism could be built without revolution in the West. This line was taken up by others, hardening into a system within the year. As Stalin pronounced in *Problems of Leninism* in January 1926: "We mean . . . the possibility of the proletariat assuming power and using that power to build a complete socialist society in our country, with the sympathy and the support of the proletariats of other countries, but without the preliminary victory of the proletarian revolution in other countries."[1]

This insistence on the primacy of building socialism in Russia imparted a new tone to international socialist discussion. From being seen as the first spark of a general European conflagration, the Russian Revolution became its main flame. Soviet socialism under Stalin came to be increasingly celebrated as the foundation for socialism elsewhere, rather than the reverse. This demoted the importance of other Communist parties and redefined their roles. Henceforth, they were to defend the Soviet Union and harness their strengths to its needs. In this new perspective, Soviet survival had become decisive for the prospects of revolution in the West; it was "the foundation, the mainstay, the refuge for the revolutionary movement of the whole world."[2]

FROM BOLSHEVIZATION TO THIRD PERIOD, 1923–1928

The Third International's dependency on the USSR was meant to be temporary, but its thinking inevitably prioritized the Soviet state's foreign policy needs. This soon produced tensions for both Soviet policy-makers and the Left elsewhere—between sponsoring revolution on a world scale and coexisting in a capitalist global economy or between supporting Communist parties against foreign governments and normalizing Soviet relations with the same states. It was no accident that the Anglo-Soviet Trade Agreement of March 1921, the first real breach in the new state's isolation, accompanied the introduction of the New Economic Policy (NEP), which modified the radicalism of domestic socialist advance.[3] By Comintern's Fourth Congress in 1922, the main principle of international solidarity for Communists had shifted from independent revolutionism to supporting the Soviet Union. The European stabilization of 1923–24 only strengthened this trend.[4]

If the Bolsheviks' immense prestige made it hard for foreign Communists to argue against them in the 1920s, this was exacerbated by the polarized 1930s, with most CPs illegal and the Soviet Union seemingly alone against fascism. The smaller, the more embattled, the more persecuted the CP, moreover, the more vital a psychological resource Bolshevik success became. From exile or the darkness of a fascist jail, identifying with the Soviet Union became the indispensable lifeline. Genuine internationalism was certainly involved: many Communists had frequent misgivings, but honoring Soviet primacy expressed an internationalist discipline the Second International had failed to deliver.

International Communism in the 1920s was volatile and confused, as revolutionaries adjusted to the nonrevolutionary circumstances after 1923. From the Third Comintern Congress in 1921, which acknowledged a period of nonrevolutionary stabilization, to the Sixth Congress in 1928, battles for control in individual CPs brought violent oscillations, as "right" and "left" fought over Soviet favor. Such swings meant frequent changes of leadership, with the German party offering an extreme case. In 1920, the KPD retained a "right" leadership under the surviving Spartacist Paul Levi; and after the 1921 March Action and a brief ascendancy of the "left" brought Levi's expulsion, a renewed "right" leadership under Ernst Meyer and Heinrich Brandler resumed control. In 1922, the United Front strategy was seriously pursued, followed in 1923 by a delicate balance of "right" leadership under Brandler and "left" minority. By 1924, in reaction to the botched Hamburg insurrection and the old leadership's insufficient Bolshevism, a new "left" faction under Ruth Fischer and Arkadi Maslow was installed but was soon followed by another purge and a fresh controlling group around Ernst Thälmann and Ernst Meyer.[5]

But these twists and turns reflected structural facts, including massive turnovers of membership, rather than just Moscow control via dictatorial or capricious meddling in a foreign party's affairs. From almost 300,000 members on the eve of the Hamburg uprising, the KPD plummeted to 120,000 in spring 1924, where membership stayed until the renewed growth after 1930. With rapidly changing rank-and-file support, sudden and frequent reversals of political fortunes, and a general dashing of revolutionary hopes, KPD behavior could hardly be anything *but* erratic.

This made sense of the Bolshevization drive—the instructions issued by the Fifth Comintern Congress in 1924 for reshaping CPs in the Bolshevik image. It was meant precisely to fortify the infant Communist parties against changes of line and leadership. "Bolshevization" meant strict centralism of organization; disciplined respect for Comintern directives; and "Leninist" theory. Again, this wasn't simply imposed by Moscow. The CPs were ripe for such regularizing. The Russian Revolution's overpowering prestige for the mainly small and struggling fellow parties and the felt need for international solidarity if the Revolution was to be defended were very persuasive. But discipline was urgently needed for organizational effectiveness in the foreign CPs, where such disparate mixtures of ex–social democrats, syndicalists, anarchists, left sectarians, feminists, trade union militants, and the previously unorganized all gathered.

On the one hand, the Bolsheviks took an increasingly Moscow-centric view of the International, reducing its autonomy, solidifying Soviet control of the Executive (ECCI), and imposing conformity with Soviet needs. Where Soviet foreign policy dictates diverged from the needs of revolutionary strategy in the West, as in the secret pacts with the German government in the 1920s for military aid or the German trade deals during the first Five Year Plan after 1928–29, Soviet leaders disregarded Western revolution. Instead, the setting of a uniform line through the Comintern rigidified after 1928, regardless of national circumstances. The Soviet-dominated ECCI suppressed debate and imposed its own clients on individual CPs. On the other hand, the CPs had a desperate need of their own for stability, and the discipline demanded by Comintern became seductively functional for institutional consolidation in that sense.

When the Third International had its Sixth Congress after a four-year hiatus in 1928, these issues came to a head. The so-called Left Turn now stressed the opening of a new, "Third Period" in capitalism's history since 1917. If the First Period marked revolutionary crisis (till 1923) and the Second relative stabilization (1924–28), the Third supposedly resumed the crisis, intensifying Western economic difficulties, with renewed openings for revolution. This required ironclad discipline from national CPs and strict separation from reformists. It demanded that Communist parties become the sole anticapitalist rallying points, destroy reformist illusions in the working class, and oppose all cooperation with social democrats, who became the main enemy. This last instruction, denouncing social democrats through the infamous formula of "Social Fascism," repudiated coalition building in the working class. Rather than repairing the 1917–23 splits, Communists now deepened them. Reformists were vilified as fascism's trailblazers. Communism degenerated toward sectarian isolation.

This sectarianism had its precedents, but the 1928 Turn's uniform application began a lasting pattern for the future. It became the instrument of orthodoxy, disciplining the CPs' often turbulent independence. The Sixth Congress suppressed debate—as in the final reckoning with Brandler and neutralizing of Meyer in the KPD or the humbling of Jules Humbert-Droz, the Comintern's independently minded Latin European expert. It also installed long-term loyalist leaderships inside national parties.[6] The crudity of the process contrasted with the febrile, if frequently embittered, openness of inner-party debates earlier on, but most CPs produced no dearth of supporters for the 1928 line. The ultraleft proclivities of the KPD—a party never happier than when assailing the SPD's criminal reformism—made it the most zealous advocate of the Soviet proposals. Newer militants in the Young Communist Leagues (YCLs), molded by the new culture of antagonism to social democracy, supplied much of the indigenous sectarian momentum. Given this support in the membership, and most CPs' weakness (some were already illegal), the Soviet leadership's immense authority precluded opposition.

British Communists, for example, had definite misgivings. But if Tom Bell attacked the Comintern's use of "bad second-rank specialists in the business of detecting deviations" and Tommy Jackson lamented "the process of 'Inprecorization' " as the death of critical thought, in the end "discipline" got the better of "conviction," and the CPGB swung round.[7] Italy's PCI put up the hardest fight. At the Sixth Congress, Angelo Tasca and Palmiro Togliatti stuck by their principles and resisted the now familiar browbeating from ECCI's Soviet contingent, even leaving the hall in protest at Togliatti's treatment.[8] But while Tasca left the PCI, decrying Stalin's role and the Comintern's "degeneration," Togliatti made his peace: "If we don't give in, Moscow won't hesitate to fix up a left leadership with some kid out of the Lenin School"; or, in Stalin's version: "Either complete capitulation or we could leave."[9]

Thus the Left Turn remade Communist leaderships and rigidified inner-party life. The quality of Comintern debate declined. The gap between Congresses lengthened: there were annual meetings during 1919–24 and then four years before the Sixth and seven before the Seventh (and last) Congress. Comintern functionaries changed from facilitators of national revolutionary initiative, roving consultants to the world revolution, into loyal Soviet servants. There was always an unreality earlier, as ill-informed emissaries parachuted fleetingly into unfamiliar national situations. But that system also produced formidable individuals, like the Swiss Communist Jules Humbert-Droz, whose Comintern responsibilities embraced southern Europe, with a decisive role in the PCF in 1924–28; or the German Willi Münzenberg, who orchestrated a remarkable range of humanitarian, political, economic, and cultural activities through the International Workers' Aid (IAH) in Berlin.[10]

In Moscow's relations with foreign Communist parties, therefore, the Third International's Sixth Congress was the watershed. Soviet leaders brought the international movement uniformly behind the Third Period's new strategy, enforcing new standards of uncritical obedience to their decisions. In the nonrevolutionary circumstances after 1923, the CPs might have developed broader coalitions, given encouragement by a friendly Comintern leadership. The 1928 Left Turn countermanded such national integration, severing earlier links to the non-Communist Left.

SHAPING A COMMUNIST TRADITION

Communist parties were stamped by two early experiences—anger at the Left's older social democratic traditions and ambivalence toward the popular insurgencies of 1917–21. The workers' councils have often been claimed as a possible "third way" between a hopelessly compromised social democracy beholden to the forces of order and an alien Bolshevism plying a misguided extraneous model. But in the 1920s the councils inspired less by their alternative revolutionary example than by their ineffectuality and failure. Like the 1871 Paris Commune, they were a glimpse of how socialism might be organized. But otherwise, the turbulence of 1919–21 revealed the fragmentation of the "revolutionary movement" into violently adventurist localisms, sometimes avowedly syndicalist but driven by blanket antipathies against remote political machines. The Left's problem was how to unify this militancy for political ends and how to organize the frustrated revolutionary hopes for a period of prosaic recuperation. This was the problematic of Bolshevization. It was also at the center of Gramsci's and other leading Communists' thinking in 1923–28.

Given Bolshevism's bedrock assumptions, articulated by Lenin between the Zimmerwald movement and the October Revolution, the CPs needed to demarcate themselves as sharply as possible from their Second International predecessors. For Lenin, this was how the amorphous left-socialisms of 1918–19 could be converted into durable party alternatives, and so something like the Twenty-One Conditions became unavoidable. As the European revolutionism contracted during 1921–23, Comintern Congresses tracked foreign Communist faithfulness to Bolshevik methods, particularly after the "German October" of 1923, whose failure was attributed to inadequate "Bolshevization." The injunction to foreign CPs to make this deficit good was the key outcome of the Fifth Congress in June–July 1924.

Yet this was not the only option in the mid-1920s. In theory, the Comintern's 1922 framework of United Front made reintegration with left social democracy an equally logical course. But Bolshevization sharpened distinctions between Communist and non-Communist affiliations. It required definitive transformation of the new CPs from parties rooted in their national labor movements into wholly new formations. This was the process that was brought to a climax in 1928. The CPs not only emerged with new leaders, often trained in Moscow, especially if the party was underground; they also began recruiting new sections of workers with no previous labor movement backgrounds. Communists now stressed their apartness from the rest of society, including the rest of the working class.

The Czechoslovak CP (KSC) was an extreme case. Formed in 1920 under Bohumir Smeral, an ex–Social Democrat schooled in the Austro-Marxist tradition, it seemed well adapted to the stabilized 1920s. Instead, the Comintern severed these existing working-class roots. In 1928, the KSC massively purged itself, reducing membership from 150,000 to only 25,000 by 1930. Most party members and Red trade unionists returned to Social Democracy. The party Bolshevized itself at the cost of losing "its roots in the mainstream of the Czechoslovak working class" and migrating "from the 'center' of the working class to the 'periphery.' "[11] Its collective self-differentiation created a rare form of disciplined corporate élan, and in the conditions of the Third Period this took a specifically Stalinist form, with bureaucratic decision-making, reduction of inner-party democracy, uncritical conformity to the party line, and obedience to Moscow. Many excesses wouldn't easily be forgotten. Given Klement Gottwald's maiden speech to the Czechoslovak Parliament in 1929, his later protestations of democratic affinities after 1935 hardly inspired instant belief: "We are the party of the Czech proletariat and our headquarters are in Moscow. We go to Moscow to learn from the Russian Bolsheviks how to twist your throats. And as you know, the Russian Bolsheviks are masters at that."[12]

In Togliatti's PCI a similar process came to inspire self-confidence in the party's indigenous tradition. In 1926, Togliatti adjusted cannily to Stalin's incipient ascendancy, while Gramsci stayed heterodox on workers' councils, party education, and appeals to nonproletarian strata. Yet Gramsci had still supported Bolshevization, which empowered the internal fight against Amadeo Bordiga and helped demarcate a Communist as against a social democratic identity. If that identity became colored by Stalinism after 1928, the process of self-demarcation had already conferred important strengths. The Lyon Theses—steered through the PCI's Third Congress in January 1926, just before Gramsci was arrested and Togliatti called to Comintern work in Moscow—were a foretaste of the Popular Front's discussions after 1934–35. Neither Gramsci, removed from the Left Turn's vicissitudes by imprisonment, nor the shrewdly circumspect Togliatti ever abandoned this thread. For the PCI, the 1928 Turn disastrously interrupted a national strategy moving toward what we might term "left Popular Frontism." By contrast with the KPD, which was always happiest denouncing Social Democrats, the PCI's instincts stressed the broadest cooperation against the Fascists.

So the Third Period's meanings for the Communist political tradition were complex. The Communist parties were new political formations, unfixed in character, and it's easy to forget their often chaotic fluidity in the 1920s, when the Communist political tradition was still being shaped. That degree of internal volatility hardly favored stable policies, and the post-1928 regularities consequently came as a relief. Communism as a distinctive and unitary tradition—lasting a quarter-century up to 1956—was certainly shaped decisively by the Third Period. Unfortunately, this simultaneously expressed the Stalinist ascendancy inside the Soviet Union, which now fully coopted the Comintern into its orbit.

NATIONAL COMMUNISMS?

Third International Communism was something qualitatively new in European labor movements.[13] It demanded a special loyalty, expanding into all parts of an activist's life, especially where parties remained small cadre organizations. Joining the CP required full-time daily commitment, marking Communists off from other workers. Passionate identification with the Soviet Union and the discipline of international solidarity were vital to Communism's positive appeal. A key part of this political culture was Stalinism, whose main manifestations were the demonizing of Trotsky; silencing of inner-party and wider public dissent; purges and show trials; and uncritical ex post facto endorsement of Soviet events like the Nazi-Soviet Pact, via the dependency instated so crudely by Comintern's Sixth Congress in 1928. This sad abjection—belying so many Communists' courageous independence on home ground and deforming their internationalism's underlying generosity—required socializing the members into the history and practices of the movement.

In 1938, the famous "Short Course" on the *History of the Communist Party (Bolshevik) of the Soviet Union* was published, and its massive worldwide dissemination had no parallel in the international labor movement until Mao Zedong's little *Red Book* in the 1960s and 1970s. This manual invented *diamat* (dialectical materialism) and the "axiomatic simplification" of Marxism. It privileged Bolshevism as the exemplary experience. It kept a deafening silence over the history of the International, let alone other parties. It was "the sacramentalization of party history."[14] There was a world of difference between the drafting of the Short Course in the later 1930s and the revolutionary years after 1917, when Gramsci reflected so creatively on Communist political education. The new stale conformities reduced Marxism's intellectual vitality and the breadth of Communism's popular appeal. Yet there were also times when Comintern's iron discipline became relaxed and individual CPs might protect certain areas of autonomy.

In "Little Moscows"—local Communist strongholds—a CP could integrate creatively into the rhythms of local community life. In Mardy in South Wales, Lumphinnans in Fife, and the Vale of Leven in western Scotland, Communists subsisted on local solidarities, which they strengthened and transformed. These were compact, homogeneous working-class communities, dominated by single staple industries like coal and textiles experiencing a crisis of contraction after 1918, with no alternative sources of employment, and with an unbalanced and incomplete class structure (no resident capitalist or rentier class), allowing the working class to dominate the local political scene. If struggles were defensive ones over unemployment, basic union rights, and evictions, they presupposed a broadly based oppositional culture enabling the whole community to be mobilized rather than manual workers alone. Communists rooted themselves in all the organized structures of everyday life. CP members weren't particularly numerous. But the party's legitimacy and leadership—its local hegemony—grew from organizing defense of the community's way of life. Yet this was not solely a story of localized political culture. Militants drew essential inspiration from the larger international movement they tried to represent.[15]

The specifically *Communist* part of Little Moscows' oppositional culture included the USSR's popularity as an idealized workers' state, diffused through the Friends of the Soviet Union. Comintern's official culture also reshaped British Marxism, with an older socialist autodidacticism disappearing into the official Marxism-Leninism, stressing the need for practical involvement in the labor movement and working-class community life. Yet by 1930, party theory had rigidified into orthodox rehearsals of given positions, with Moscow's authority substituting for "indigenous understanding and debate." "Theorists" increasingly were university-trained intellectuals conversant with Soviet Marxism rather than self-taught "proletarian philosophers" from a Marxist theoretical culture within the working class. This was another aspect of the specifically "Communist" affiliations of the CP.[16]

Paradoxically, Third Period sectarianism produced much creativity in cultural politics, because withdrawing from cooperation with other parties threw the CPs back on their own resources. An array of innovations resulted in theater, film, the rest of the arts, activities for youth and children, sports, the organization of leisure, and the general cultural sphere, which recaptured some of the verve of 1917–23.[17] This was especially true of sexual politics and women's rights, given socialism's poor existing record of challenging established notions of sex, gender, motherhood, and women's place. In Germany during the Third Period, Communists came closer to breaking this particular barrier.[18]

With its aggressively "proletarian" identity contrasting starkly with its actual members, who gathered on street corners rather than factory floors (80 percent being unemployed after 1930), the KPD found itself willy-nilly the voice of broader-based "nonclass" mobilizations around women, youth, tenants, welfare claimants, and others during its period of growth in 1930–32.[19] Sex reform agitations over abortion and contraception were part of this, with surprising cooperation among Communist, Social Democratic, liberal, and nonaligned left-wing doctors, social workers, and other activists. The KPD—or individual Communists and their professional organizations and the coalitions and forums the party sponsored—energized the 1931 campaign for abortion reform and the remarkable sex counseling clinics that flourished before 1933.[20]

Even as the Comintern's Left Turn committed the KPD to a disastrously sectarian national strategy, in other words, its behavior at the base became more flexible. While its public ideology relentlessly reiterated its credentials as the archetypically proletarian party, it was joined by people who were the very opposite of the classically proletarian. The KPD's tragedy during the early 1930s was not just that it lost the working-class party's traditional workshop and factory base via unemployment, the victimizing of militants, and the SPD's control of labor's old institutional world, because this forced it into creative alternatives. The real tragedy was that the party stumbled on solutions that its own self-understanding disallowed. Such a politics— focused on women and youth as well as employed and unemployed working men, on the "private" as well as the "public" sphere, and on broad democratic values as against the misplaced triumphalism of the impending proletarian revolution—offered a chance to transcend the labor movement's narrower class-based vision. Indeed, this politics expanded the boundaries of the political itself, bringing the intimate domains of sexuality and domesticity into politics and questioning the traditional boundaries of private and public life.

There were many reasons why this possibility—an oblique Popular Frontism, from below and *avant la lettre*—never took off. But one was certainly the subordination of the KPD's official thinking to the Comintern's 1928 line. This can't be said too strongly. Recent histories of individual CPs have placed them carefully in the social and political history of their own societies rather than seeing them as the ciphers of interests and policies originating elsewhere, in the apparatus of Comintern and the power centers of Moscow.[21] But the Third International remained the authority that Communist parties all acknowledged. The new histories have shown the potentials for creative "national-popular" politics an imaginative Communist party could release. But such possibilities were only ever fitfully realized. The Stalinist culture of the Third International was crucial to how they were stifled.[22]

WESTERN MARXISM

While Western CPs rigidified in the wake of Stalinism, creative forms of Marxist thought survived. Before 1914, Marxism was almost entirely co-terminous with the socialist political tradition. Marxist thought was absent from universities, academies, and other contexts of formal intellectual life. Declaring oneself a Marxist meant taking a place within the socialist movements themselves, making a living from journalism, lecturing, and socialist educational work. While Second International theoreticians (Labriola, Mehring, Kautsky, Plekhanov, Lenin, Hilferding, Luxemburg, Bauer) came from middle-class or gentry backgrounds, few others brought an academic education. Pre-1914 socialist culture was mainly fashioned by self-educated labor activists, typified by the SPD's twin founders, Wilhelm Liebknecht and August Bebel. There were exceptions—the PSI recruited more successfully from university graduates and academics before 1914—but the main relationship of Marxism and mainstream intellectual life before the First World War was mutual isolation.

This changed after 1918. The radicalizing of intellectuals through war and revolution brought a younger generation of writers, artists, and the academically educated into the Left, often without organized party affiliation. After 1918, for the first time one could be a Marxist and hope for an academic or professional career. Conversely, one could teach in a university, work for a newspaper or publisher, manage a theater or gallery, or build a career in the educational, welfare, health and housing bureaucracies and take Marxist ideas seriously without losing one's post. This was true of Germany, Austria, Scandinavia, Czechoslovakia, France, the Low Countries, and Britain. Intellectual radicalisms never achieved more than grudging toleration from the dominant culture and reckoned with harassment, bordering on outright suppression. Nonetheless, socialist ideas developed a presence beyond the organized tradition itself, with certain shifts in Marxist theory as a result. If Marxist thinkers focused originally on politics and economics, expounding the laws of development of capitalism and the theory of the class struggle in the direct service of their parties, after 1918 they turned to philosophy and aesthetics.[23]

Exponents of this "Western Marxism" worked in relative isolation, both from the practical activism of labor movements and from each other, without the translation, circulation, and exchange of Marxist ideas common before 1914. Three major figures of the 1920s exemplified this trend: Karl Korsch, Georg Lukács, and Antonio Gramsci. Each thought within a specific idiom, defining Marxism's originality against dominant pre-Marxist philosophical traditions—Hegel and his legacies in particular, or in Gramsci's case the massive influence in early twentieth-century Italy of Benedetto Croce. Their early works—Korsch's *Marxism and Philosophy* (1923), Lukács' *History and Class Consciousness* (also 1923), Gramsci's writings in

L'Ordine nuovo during 1919–20—belonged quintessentially to the postwar revolutionary moment. They stressed the subjective elements in Marx and the room for creative revolutionary agency (Gramsci's "revolution against *Capital*") against the Second International's orthodox determinism, already reviving via the economistic rigidities of Marxism-Leninism and Stalinized Third International thought. With the removal of their authors—Korsch was expelled from the KPD in 1926, Lukács recanted his dissent from the 1928 Turn and withdrew into literary work, and Gramsci was imprisoned—these early texts of Western Marxism became forgotten.[24]

A further site of Western Marxist innovation, the Institute for Social Research in Frankfurt, founded in 1923 and transplanted to New York in 1934, severed the links to politics even more completely. Some collaborators had Communist links, including Karl Wittfogel, Henryk Grossmann, and Walter Benjamin; others supported the SPD, like Franz Neumann and Otto Kirchheimer. Most, like Herbert Marcuse, were radicalized in 1917–18. The Institute's presiding patriarchs, Max Horkheimer and Theodor Adorno, made a virtue of independence. The Frankfurt School's theoretical concerns—the contradictory meanings of the Enlightenment, emancipation, and the critical theory of society, the rise of mass culture, the dialectic of reason and domination, and the impact of psychoanalysis—took them exclusively to philosophical aspects of Marxism, in an esoteric mode disconnected from the labor movement, with no interest in influencing working-class militants. This was a conscious stance. The Frankfurt School's leading voices (Marcuse, Horkheimer, Adorno) despaired of working-class political agency, a pessimism doubly induced by the logics of quiescence they detected in the workers' relationship to mass culture and by the labor movement's disastrous defeats under fascism. Exile played a big part too, for in the United States the Institute was divorced entirely from a labor movement with socialist or Marxist traditions.[25]

Marxist thought between the wars—and over the longer term to 1968—displayed a striking paradox. Rigid and formulaic in the officially sanctioned discourse of the CPs, it developed impressive creativity in specific areas like philosophy and aesthetics, sometimes in a tolerated space inside the parties, sometimes in the universities or the public sphere of letters and the arts, where Marxism for the first time achieved limited acceptance, at least in societies with stable democratic polities and legally secured freedoms of expression. Thus Western Marxism's distinctive features contrasted with the period before 1914. Classical Marxists—the Second International theorists, coming after Marx and Engels themselves—were usually full-time revolutionaries, who united theory and practice, cut their teeth on Marxist economics, and devoted their writing to current political problems, supported by their parties rather than by positions in universities and other academic institutions. Western Marxists after 1918 were invariably isolated from direct political involvement—either because they avoided party membership, pursued purely theoretical studies, or lived in a Fascist prison. They wrote mainly about philosophy, culture, and aesthetics rather than economics and politics. They were mostly professional academics.

This was a Marxism of defeat. It came from pessimism, political disconnectedness, and sometimes despair. But this disempowerment had a double source. On one side, the revolutionary movement had contracted in the West, certainly by 1923, leaving Marxists with profoundly different circumstances from the unbounded opportunities beckoning so excitingly in 1917–21. Then, in the world economic crisis after 1929, the working-class movements suffered disastrous setbacks, when their proudest, largest, and most self-confident exemplars—in Germany and Austria—went down, crushingly, to defeat.

Yet on the other side, the surviving space of revolutionary optimism, the Soviet Union and its organizationally impressive Third International, was cramped and unsympathetic for intellectuals, bluntly and aggressively intolerant of critical theoretical work. Worse, it was increasingly undemocratic. The Stalinization of the CPs after 1928 was a political defeat for committed, creative, and generous-minded socialist intellectuals almost as depressing as the crisis of European democracy, especially during the purges in the Soviet Union after 1934. Through Stalinism, Marxism lost much of its public creativity as a theoretical tradition. Independent thinkers were forced to the margins of the Communist movement or out of it altogether. Western Marxists suffered beneath this complex burden, a triangulated sense of defeat. They retreated before the failed revolution in the West, the victory of fascism, and Soviet Stalinization.

Chapter 17

Fascism and Popular Front

The Politics of Retreat, 1930–1938

BY 1930 THE LEFT'S prospects were bleak. Despite apocalyptic wagers on the world crash, out-and-out revolutionaries remained minorities in their national movements, even, as in the KPD, where they enjoyed mass support. Socialist parties were further from power than ever, while even the scaled-down hopes authorized by the post-1918 settlements wore thin. Democratic franchise, civil freedoms, welfare legislation, and an expanded public sphere characterized those settlements, rather than socialist measures per se, and even these gains were moot. On Europe's periphery—the Baltic, Balkans, and Iberia—democracy lost to authoritarianism. In first Hungary (1919–20) and then Italy (1920–22), virulent counterrevolutions were unleashed. Only in Scandinavia was democracy secured. In France, government scandals energized the extraparliamentary Right during 1933, and in Britain the debacle of the 1929–31 Labour government split the party and slashed its parliamentary strength, paralyzing it indefinitely.

This made democracy's fate in central Europe all the more vital. And it was here that democratic breakdown was far advanced—on 15 July 1927 Austria entered incipient civil war after a confrontation of government and Socialists, while in March 1930 parliamentary government was suspended for rule by Presidential Decree in Germany.[1] These conflicts interacted with the Wall Street crash of October 1929 in crises of enormous proportions. By 1933, industrial unemployment ran from 36.2 percent in Germany and 33.4 percent in Norway to 28.8 percent in Denmark, 26.9 percent in the Netherlands, 19.9 percent in

261

Britain, and 14.1 percent in France.[2] As Nazi electoral support rocketed from a tiny 2.6 percent in 1928 to 37.4 percent in 1932, things were clearly coming to a head. Once the Nazis entered government, not only labor's hard-won corporative gains of 1918 but also the larger democratic foundations would fall.

The Nazi seizure of power (30 January 1933) was a democratic catastrophe whose effects reverberated across Europe. By spring, the SPD and KPD, Europe's most prestigious Social Democratic and Communist parties, had gone; terror was unleashed against the regime's opponents; and German democracy was dead.[3] The impact elsewhere was immense. While the term "fascism" already existed, its overpowering valency was new—as the future that had to be stopped. It named the main threat, internationally in the Third Reich's foreign aggressions, nationally in one's own society—a danger to the rights of labor and socialism, to the Soviet Union, to democracy, to peace, to cultural freedom, to decent and civilized values, to individual liberties, to progress. As Communist militants, rank-and-file socialists, and Left intellectuals contemplated possible futures, the rise of fascism reshaped their rhetoric. "Stopping the fascists" dominated discussion.

In the later 1920s, Italian Fascism graduated into a full-blown postdemocratic regime. Spain, Portugal, Poland, Lithuania, Albania, and Yugoslavia all buried parliamentary democracy in the same decade, while Hungarian authoritarianism radicalized under Gyula Gömbös in 1932. In 1933, social democracy's central European heartland also fell—Austria via the clerico-authoritarianism of Engelbert Dollfuss and Germany via the Nazi assumption of power, leaving only Czechoslovakia among 1918's democratic republics. In 1934, the Right's inexorable advance continued in Bulgaria, Latvia, and Estonia, with Greece falling in 1936. Facing these disasters, three dramas stamped Left perceptions: the Austrian Schutzbund's desperate attempt to resist further police repression by an armed rising in Linz on 12 February 1934; the nationwide Socialist and Communist general strike against the growing violence of the French Right, also on 12 February 1934; and the Spanish Socialist uprising of October 1934, including the 14-day insurrection of Asturian miners.[4]

Two of these initiatives—the Austrian and Spanish—were bloody failures. The Linz Schutzbund failed to galvanize SPÖ leaders, and the belated Vienna uprising experienced terrible defeat. Yet the very decision to resist—in contrast to SPD passivity—had huge resonance and inspired the Asturian fighters, emblazoning their actions with the slogan "Better Vienna Than Berlin."[5] The Spanish rising, also suppressed, proved vital for later radicalization. Only the French events spelled success. After a crescendo of right-wing violence against the Republic, stopping short of a coup but paralyzing the moderate Left and returning the Right to government, demonstrations and streetfighting pervaded the week, until CGT and Socialists called a general strike on 12 February and Communists and their unions followed suit. Separate marches converged unpredictably on the

Place de la Nation, where a highly emotional unification ensued. Spontaneous solidarity maximized the pressure for burying the sectarian hatchet. The preceding week's Right offensive—the precipice of fascist violence, fear of a Nazi repetition—brought the Left together. In European terms, this was the countervailing moment, when the Left finally recorded a success. This was the first sign of what became the Popular Front.[6]

FORGING THE POPULAR FRONT

Until the last minute, unity was overshadowed by fierce Socialist-Communist animosities. The PCF sternly applied the Comintern's 1928 line, denouncing the SFIO not only as a tool of the bourgeoisie but as "an instrument of the capitalist attack against the working class." "Social Fascism" obliterated distinctions between fascism and other "bourgeois" politics, indicting socialists precisely for defending liberal institutions and fostering reformist illusions, diverting workers from the revolutionary path. Unfortunately, such slogans conveyed the PCF's experience of the system. In 1928, the party's million first-ballot votes brought only 14 parliamentary seats, while the same support for the right-wing *Union Républicaine Démocratique* brought 142! Preventive arrest was used routinely against Communists, and the PCF's 1929 Congress was surrounded by police. Socialists ceded nothing to Communists in enmity. *Le Populaire* declared: "We shall never ask anything from the Bolsheviks, we'll kick their teeth in."[7]

Moves toward unity in France took a double track. First, party leaderships buried the hatchet. On 27 July 1934, a unity pact was signed, followed by a joint memorial for the assassination of Jean Jaurès—nicely symbolizing the mixture of history, solidarity, and patriotic countermemory identifying the Popular Front. These events were carefully watched elsewhere, and a month later PSI and PCI also signed a pact. Reviving the United Front was a badly needed boost to left-wing morale. Between December 1933 and August 1934, initiatives occurred in Catalonia, Asturias, the Saarland, Austria, and Belgium, plus many localized actions. In Spain, independent socialists set the pace. Local Communists were pulled along too, but the Comintern still dragged its feet.

This was the second track. Comintern endorsement was needed for national pacts of Socialists and Communists to stick. The domestic preoccupations of Soviet leaders in 1930–35 made enough room for allies of a United Front to maneuver, but the vital impetus was the fascist threat. The Nazi seizure of power, and right-wing violence in France and elsewhere, impelled the first United Front initiatives in 1933–34, reopening debate in ECCI for the first time since 1928. Georgii Dimitrov moved the Comintern toward antifascism, backed by Dmitri Manuilski and Comintern's man in the PCF, Evzhen Fried ("Clément").[8] On 28 May 1934, *Pravda* endorsed an SFIO-PCF pact. The German, Hungarian, and Bulgarian CPs still balked, but the French, Italian, Czechoslovak, and Polish parties were now on board. From June 1934, "United Front from Above" became the official Third International line.

In the Labor and Socialist International (LSI), the Comintern's social democratic rival, resistance to unity was more entrenched, so while the Third International was emerging from its bunker, the Second continued digging itself in. Alignments in the LSI Executive repeated the battle lines of 1917–23, when an anti-Communist northern bloc had squelched left-socialist efforts led by the SPÖ to keep lines open.[9] After an LSI Emergency Conference rebuffed Comintern overtures in August 1933, the Austrian, French, Italian, Spanish, and Swiss socialist parties joined the Menshevik and Polish sections in a left-wing "Group of Seven," and the divisions paralyzed social democracy internationally. Despite informal contacts from Comintern in autumn 1934, LSI still refused talks.[10]

Comintern sought alliances elsewhere, shifting from the United to the broader Popular Front in May and June 1935.[11] French Communist language shifted dramatically from the class struggle to "people" and "nation" instead. Extraparliamentary mobilization of the masses gave way to institutional vocabularies of parliament and constitution. In Spain, the PCE also moved officially from sectarianism to support for United Fronts, appealing to "socialists, anarchists, republicans, nationalists; everyone in one bloc facing the fascist bloc of the various monarcho-fascist parties of the bourgeoisie."[12] On 20 May 1935 the PCE's pact with the Republican parties was signed.

Any doubts about Stalin's support were removed by the Franco-Soviet defensive treaty of 2 May 1935, with an accompanying Moscow Declaration on the two countries' needs for strong armies. Acknowledging the legitimate security needs of an imperialist power was a hard pill for a party like the PCF to swallow. But Thorez could now wear the Jacobin mantle of 1792, and embracing national defense helped the Communists' credibility as coalition partners. Defense of the Soviet Union was de facto substituting for the world revolution. But the debacle of the Third Period's sectarianism after 1928 lent this more modest strategy greater appeal.

All this set the scene for the Third International's Seventh Congress in Moscow, on 25 July 1935. The ritualized triumphalism of the occasion couldn't disguise realities of loss and retreat. Dimitrov delivered the main address, presenting ECCI's freshly minted definition of fascism—as "the open, terrorist dictatorship of the most reactionary, most chauvinist, and most imperialist elements of finance capital."[13] This badly misrecognized Nazism, which was never an instrument of big business or the straightforward vehicle of capitalist interests in that way. But by contrasting the pro-fascist parts of the dominant classes with the democratic ones, it created a basis for antifascist alliance with the latter. By contrasting fascist regimes with bourgeois states respecting democracy, an opposition rejected at the Sixth Congress in 1928, Dimitrov embraced "bourgeois democratic" freedoms per se as something worth defending in their own right, as a source of lasting political good.

In a time of retreat, the Left should not only emphasize working-class unity for defending democratic rights, Dimitrov argued, but embrace other social groups interested in democracy too, including parts of the dominant classes. It should work with nonsocialists—liberals, radicals, and republicans; peace movements; humanitarian organizations; where possible the churches; even conservative groups willing to defend democracy. It should support bourgeois governments upholding democratic rights, especially in the interests of international antifascist coalitions, both for containing Nazi Germany and Fascist Italy and for removing the Soviet Union's isolation. In short, the politics of the revolutionary Left underwent a major post-1917 reorientation.

This was the People's Front. It was a defensive regroupment—for raising obstacles to fascism's spread and encouraging resistance where it had won. It was meant to overcome CP isolation by finding the Left's common ground. But building the broadest cooperation required democratic rather than socialist principles, because working-class parties by themselves weren't strong enough to win. Furthermore, if the Left managed to establish its democratic credentials, coalitions might pass beyond existing democracy to the groundwork of socialist transition. The Popular Front strategy had this other, ulterior dimension: it "was more than a temporary defensive tactic, or even a strategy for eventually turning defeat into offensive. It was also a carefully considered strategy of advancing to socialism."[14]

This Popular Front strategy contained some vital recognitions. It was the first revision of the revolutionary optimism driving Communism since the foundation years of 1919–21 and the first questioning of the Bolshevik model from the inside. Communists began withdrawing from their vanguard claims: they were not the workers' sole legitimate voice, and their working-class support was not guaranteed but shared with others. Nor could a country's working class achieve victory by itself. It needed social allies, whether peasants, white-collar and professional groups, or intelligentsia, or even the small business class. The more complex the society, the more essential alliances became. Only exceptionally could CPs entertain seizing power alone. Above all, their sectarian isolation needed to be overcome.

In contrast to the short-term and instrumental strategies of the 1920s, this was a new departure. Alliances had to be principled, because alliances to deceive one's partners (supporting them as the rope supports a hanging man, in Lenin's notorious image) were self-defeating. To achieve them, Communists should even be willing to relinquish their "leading" role and take a junior place. As the Popular Front strategy evolved, it envisaged concentric circles of cooperation: United Fronts of workers for elections, general strikes, and other mass actions to heal the splits of 1914–21; antifascist "People's Fronts" embracing nonsocialists to resist foreign aggression from Hitler, Mussolini, and Japan; and an international front of governments against fascism and war.

Democracy became the unifying theme of this approach. Internationalism was still upheld, but democratic patriotism replaced the purism reigning since Lenin's extreme Zimmerwaldism of 1915–16. This meant speaking the language of national democracy, in the syntax of what Gramsci called the "national-popular," drawing on a country's distinctive traditions—the radical Leveller and Chartist versions of parliamentary democracy in Britain, Jacobinism in France, democratic traditions of Risorgimento in Italy. As Thorez said: "We will not abandon to our enemies the *tricoleur,* the flag of the great French Revolution, or the *Marseillaise,* the song of the soldiers of the Convention." The CPs now claimed the mantle of a nation's best democratic traditions.[15]

Popular Frontism recast socialism as the highest form of older progressive traditons rather than their implacable opponent, and this affirming of universal humanist values also implied a different politics for culture and the arts. In marking the distance from "bourgeois" culture, the Third Period's sectarian isolation had forced Communists into greater inventiveness, embracing agitprop, a formalistic left modernism, and the avant-garde. In contrast, Popular Fronts now resutured the Left's cultural imagination to the progressive bourgeois heritage, rallying it to the antifascist banner. Antifascist appeals were directed especially toward intellectuals in literature, theater, and the arts, as well as popular arts like film.[16]

The Popular Front was a huge departure, produced by the scale of the fascist threat. For Otto Bauer, for example, fascism was an ultraright attempt to burst the fetters of 1918–19, because the costs of democracy, typified by the welfare state and union rights, exceeded what the needs of capitalist restabilization and political order could bear. While capitalism had tottered in 1918, the Left had failed to realize its revolutionary advantage, and "a temporary equilibrium" of class capacities ensued. Initially, Bauer had seen this transitional equilibrium optimistically, stressing the potential for socialism's future gains. But by the end of the 1930s, he saw the scope for fascist counterrevolution instead. It was not a revolutionary crisis that provoked the rise of fascism, in Bauer's view, but the Right's desire to sweep away the democratic gains in the republican system. Nazism fed not on Communism per se but on hatred of the Weimar Republic's freedoms: "The turn to fascism is provoked less by capitalist fear of revolution than by a determination to depress wages, to destroy the social reforms achieved by the working class, and to smash the positions of political power held by its representatives; not to suppress a revolutionary situation but to wipe out the gains of reformist socialism."[17]

If, contrary to the Third Period's maximalism, Europe wasn't on the verge of revolution during the Great Depression but direly vulnerable to fascism's counterrevolutionary assault, then the Left's priorities shifted accordingly. The Comintern's new leadership edged toward this view in

1932–34. And while ultraleft proclivities survived in parts of the Comintern (some Communists believed nothing had changed; that the Popular Front was simply a short-term expedient), the more "democratic" view implied reevaluating revolution in the capitalist West. This went furthest in the PCI—via Gramsci's influence and the strategizing of Togliatti, Gramsci's legatee. For Gramsci and others, something had fundamentally changed. Their thinking was

> based on the assumption that the lost opportunity of 1917–20 would not recur, and that Communist Parties must envisage not a short front offensive but a lengthy war of position—a policy of the long haul. In effect, they must win the leadership of a broad alliance of social forces, and maintain this leadership during a prolonged period of transition, in which the actual transfer of power was only one episode.[18]

This was now the revolutionary Left's main division. On one side was the classic insurrectionist approach: a mass uprising of the oppressed; violent destruction of the state; confrontation with the dominant classes to uproot the bases of their power; retribution and reprisals against the old order; extreme vigilance for the security of the revolution. This originated in the French Revolution's Jacobin phase, continuing through the nineteenth-century insurrectionary tradition of Buonarotti and Blanqui. Under the Second International, it survived where parties faced illegality and police repression, as in Russia, resurfacing in the Bolshevik seizure of power.[19] On the other side was gradualism. This stressed not the revolutionary climacteric but a different set of modalities: building popular support slowly over a long term, drawing progressive aspirations from all parts of society, commanding ever greater public influence via existing institutions, building the working-class movement's moral authority into the democratic foundations of the transition. This approach redirected attention from armed struggle and pitched confrontations to changing the system from within by incremental advance.

The democratic quality of the restructuring was crucial. The Left was to build the new society in the frame of the old, both prefiguratively by exemplary institutions and behaviors in the working-class movement and legislatively by reforms. This more gradualist perspective was built on some key recognitions: the lower-than-expected electoral ceiling of support for socialism (rarely more than 40 percent of the vote at best, usually much lower); the necessity of coalitions with nonsocialist forces; the inevitability of periods of moderation, defensive consolidation, and slow advance. Above all, confrontational violence, intolerance, and coercion isolated the Left from the rest of society. Breadth of consensus was essential to socialist success.

By its gradualism, this second perspective confused the differences opened by the splits of 1917–21—between Communism and social democracy. The "Gramscian" understanding of Popular Front converged in many ways with the left-socialist strands of the Second International. There was also much congruence with reformist socialism since 1917, both in the foregrounding of democracy and in the gradualist stress on existing institutions. A third convergence occurred with a new radical liberalism, most developed in Italy in the ideas of Piero Gobetti and Carlo Rosselli, who opened liberal thinking to the permanence of conflict and an ethics of civic activism.[20] It was unclear where the boundaries were now drawn.

THE POPULAR FRONT GOVERNMENT IN FRANCE

The French Popular Front took off when the Radicals joined the mass meeting of PCF and SFIO on Bastille Day in 1935. Moved by distaste for Pierre Laval's right-wing government of June 1935, with its deflationary social agenda and profascist foreign policy, and by fear of the right-wing Leagues, the Radicals realigned with the Left. The tripartite coalition was sealed in the Popular Front Program of 11 January 1936. The Left mobilized for another huge demonstration of over half a million when the SFIO leader Léon Blum was almost lynched by the *Action Francaise* on 13 February 1936 and the momentum built impressively toward the elections of May 1936, which brought the Popular Front a decisive majority, with the balance shifting markedly from the Radicals to the SFIO and PCF.[21] The new government took office in June 1936 under Blum, with the PCF supporting from outside the cabinet. The masses gave spectacular acclaim on 24 May, when six hundred thousand marched to commemorate the dead of the Paris Commune.[22]

The twin coordinates of this Left resurgence, antifascism and economic distress, were immediately visible. On 11 May 1936, a week after the election, in the hiatus before the new government, the previously nonmilitant workers of the Bréguet aircraft works in Le Havre occupied their factory, secured immediate victory via the arbitration of the local mayor, and then flocked into the CGT, thereby triggering a massive strike wave. By June, two million workers had downed tools, complementing the Popular Front with a general strike.[23]

The strikes were remarkable in form. Three-quarters of them were factory occupations, challenging employers' prerogatives and evoking the European direct-action insurgencies of 1917–21. Not planned by unions or politically organized militants, the strikes were a spontaneous response to the labor movement's entry into government, which reversed the European trend of fascist success and left-wing defeat. The mood of popular empowerment was palpable. This was an explosion of popular desire, composing scenes of extraordinary visual power. In the Paris suburbs, "building after building—small factories and large factories, even comparatively small workshops—were flying red, or red and *tricoleur* flags—with pickets in front of the closed gates."[24] The joy was licensed by political expectation.

On 7 June 1936, the employers met with the CGT in the Hôtel Matignon, and made remarkable concessions.[25] The Matignon Agreement honored union rights and recognized the CGT, with collective agreements industry by industry, wage increases of 7–15 percent favoring the lowest paid, and elected works committees in factories of over 10 people. Blum attached a political rider, promising collective bargaining, the 40-hour week, and two weeks paid vacation. This was an extraordinary victory for labor, reminiscent of European trade unionism's dramatic gains of 1918–19. In one fell swoop, it gave the CGT leadership national corporative influence, instituted shopfloor representation, and committed a Left government to social reform. It was a moment of rare decisiveness by a newly elected socialist government. For once, the Left seemed ready to act.

There were three dimensions to the departure. First, it was trade unionism's historic breakthrough in France. The 40-hour week was one longstanding central demand. The CGT also gained a legitimate national voice. In one year, CGT membership scaled unprecedented heights, from around 778,000 when the strikes began to almost 4 million in March 1937. Second, the government showed an impressive political will—not only banning the right-wing Leagues (where the SPD had tolerated them, for instance) but also acting immediately on its program. It passed 133 new laws in only 73 days, including partial nationalization of the Bank of France, nationalization of arms industries, public works, creation of the Wheat Marketing Board, and raising the school leaving age to 14. Third, the Left invaded the public sphere. The exuberant theatricality of the factory occupations pervaded the atmosphere. The rally of 14 July 1936 mobilized a million people for the most spectacular pageant of the streets; new paid holidays brought workers into the countryside and onto the beaches, disrupting established topographies of social privilege. In year one, six hundred thousand people benefited from the people's annual holiday ticket that was introduced by the Socialist minister responsible for sports and leisure, Léo Lagrange.[26]

From this peak, however, came rapid descent. The Popular Front's program was a wager on consumption: it sought to reflate the economy via increased purchasing power and the social legislation's stimulus to productivity. Capital went on strike. Between April and September 1936, the Bank of France gold reserves dropped from 63 to 54 billion francs, with another 1.5 billion fleeing the country during 4–16 September. Blum reneged on a central commitment by devaluing the currency. Production also failed to respond. By October, Blum demanded a change of pace, and his New Year message sacrificed further reforms to social "reconciliation."[27] The fiscal policies of March 1937 reverted to extreme conservatism, cutting public spending and abandoning the promises on pensions, unemployment benefits, indexing of wages, and public works. Blum became isolated in his own governing coalition. The PCF criticized from the left, the Radicals broke to the right. On 22 June 1937, Radical defections in the Senate denied Blum the powers for the new fiscal emergency, and he resigned. There were no protests in the streets.

What explained this plummeting from the proud heights of June 1936? The PCF was the Popular Front's true beneficiary, as it passed from margins to mainstream, raising its membership from 40,000 (1934) to some 330,000 (1937). It straddled both worlds of the movement, with one foot in the legislature and one in the streets. It held Blum to the common program, while shaping popular militancy into disciplined support. While the PCF deployed its militants in the factories and recruited strikers, it sought to leash militancy as much as driving it on. In the bright glow of the government's inception, this strategy could work. Restraint, respect for procedures, high productivity for the national economy, discipline, unity—all were needed for the government's success. But workers would buy the rhetoric if gains ensued. Given Blum's retrenchment after September 1936, these abruptly ceased.[28]

After Blum's resignation, things fell apart. Dramatic strikes occurred in December 1937, with a huge battle at the Goodrich tire factory and a public services strike in the Seine region. In March–April 1938, 150,000 Paris metalworkers came out. In November 1938 wildcat strikes against increasing the 40-hour week climaxed in an abortive general strike on 30 November. The problem had already been dramatized at Clichy on 16 March 1937: the Communist council and Socialist deputy called a counterrally against a fascist meeting the government had refused to ban; the police fired on the Left, with five deaths and several hundred wounded; and the gap between the government and its working-class supporters was exposed.

The post-Matignon political logic was depressingly familiar.[29] It recalled the SPD's situation in Germany after November 1918: early strength created by an extraparliamentary movement, temporary collapse of the dominant classes, and initial decisiveness in the legislative arena; compromises and deals with the forces of order; the alienation of a disappointed but still mobilized rank and file; and finally the loss of government power amid demoralization, repression, bitter recriminations, and a deep political split. In retrospect, this logic was inscribed in SFIO attitudes from the start. Amid the strike wave, the new minister of the interior, Roger Salengro (driven to suicide by right-wing vilification later that year), a key architect of Matignon and the reforms, declared; "For my part I've made my choice between order and anarchy. I will maintain order in the face of all opposition."[30] The wonder was that Blum ever began. After the panic of May–June 1936, the dominant classes also recovered their nerve, subjecting the government to ever-tightening constraint, in an unstoppable logic of disablement, for which the Radicals became the unfailing barometer.[31]

DECISION IN SPAIN

How might this have been avoided? The Blum government had two sources of momentum: its party-political breadth and its popular support. Both gave the Left unparalleled inclusiveness, stretching its legitimacy past the previous boundaries of socialist strength. But if one key to the Popular Front's initial momentum was its temporary ownership of patriotism, another was its equally fleeting political resolve. Far from dissipating post-elections, the Popular Front's impetus grew—through immediate introduction of popular reforms, domination of public space (the massive demonstrations and their iconography), social breadth of the rhetoric, appeals to history, and the bid for leadership of the nation-in-general. This situation needed leaders of vision who commanded the necessary political will—capitalizing on the opening of June 1936, feeding the sense of historic opportunity, driving the advantage home against the dominant classes, and finding the broadest unity in the PCF's sense.

The Spanish Civil War—beginning with the nationalist uprising of 17–18 July 1936 against the Spanish Popular Front government formed from the elections of 15 February—was the test. The electoral victory of Popular Fronts in two large and contiguous countries was a golden chance for cross-national solidarity. Indeed, the polarized rhetoric of the 1936 elections marked the new Spanish government as a bulwark against fascism's further advance. The military rebellion produced an outpouring of emotional solidarity from what survived of democratic Europe. Aid for Spain seemed an obvious priority for the Blum government to pursue.

However, rather than honoring the Republic's military contracts with Spain, Blum caved in to pressure from the French Foreign Office, the British government, the Radicals in his own administration, and the right-wing press and suspended military aid, substituting an international Non-Intervention Agreement to block Italian and German aid for the nationalist rebels instead. This was a catastrophe for the Spanish Republic. But it also undermined the Popular Front in France. It disregarded left-wing morale's international dimension in 1933–36. It squandered the potential for anti-fascist rallying via combined internationalist and patriotic identification. Polarization in France would have ensued—but on the Left's own terms rather than via constant retreat and with rhetorical advantage constantly given away.[32]

Spain's Popular Front was ambiguous from the start. It embraced the broadest spectrum of the Left—Socialists and their unions (the UGT), Communists, smaller ultraleft sects, and left Republicans. But its core was more specific, the Republican-Socialist coalition of 1931–33. In the 1933 elections, the PSOE had broken with left Republican prime minister Manuel Azana, opening the way for a right-wing victory.[33] The ensuing backlash was appalling, reversing progress toward land reform and labor laws and wreaking endless harassment on the labor movement. While the reactive PSOE uprising of October 1934 symbolized resistance to fascism, it provoked vicious repression. In response, a potent dialectic of electoral coalescence and popular mobilization was released. Azana rallied Socialists and left Republicans for democratic restoration, capturing popular imagination by his oratory in massive rallies during May–October 1935. But popular hopes raced past these parliamentary horizons, embracing more radical desires for change.[34]

The government elected in February 1936 needed to rally republican defense without driving the middle classes to the Right. However, the PSOE was bitterly split.[35] The rightist Indalecio Prieto backed coalition with Azana. But the PSOE majority, based in Madrid, the Socialist Youth, and militant parts of the UGT had veered to the left. Under Francisco Largo Caballero—veteran PSOE leader for three decades, architect of the UGT's accommodation to Primo de Rivera's dictatorship in the 1920s, minister of labor 1931–33, and now freshly declared revolutionary—the Socialists abstained from constructive government politics just when they were needed most. In November 1933, Largo exchanged bourgeois democracy for the dictatorship of the proletariat. He was behind the fiasco of October 1934 and the intransigence of 1935. He refused talks with Azana, thereby disabling Prieto's republican defense. By 1936, he left the PSOE Executive to form an alternative leadership. He eventually endorsed the Popular Front but from outside the resulting government, fueling the verbal polarization and incipient violence of the coming months. He demanded a wholly Socialist government but tolerated the drift to civil war, denying the Popular Front its own majority party's full support.

Largo was a disaster for the Republic, strutting on the stage of history while its real chances were missed. A Johnny-come-lately of revolution, he hijacked the militancy of 1933–36, denouncing reformist illusions and firing utopian hopes but with no idea of how power could be seized, given the Left's divisions and the Right's fearsome strength. Largo was a consummate corporatist politician—now the labor bureaucrat, negotiating a *modus vivendi* from regimes in power and securing his members the best available deal (the Primo de Rivera years); now the reforming Socialist minister (1931–33); now the neosyndicalist voice of militancy (1933–34). But Spain's societal crisis required greater political vision than this. When Largo struck the pose of revolutionary tribune after 1933, he sidestepped this responsibility, urging the masses into confrontations he had no strategy for winning. As things fell apart in May 1936 and Prieto secured Azana's elevation to the presidency, leaving the premiership for himself, Largo still withheld PSOE support. Yet, when forming a government two months after the military revolt, his reformist course was indistinguishable from the one he refused in May. After forming his government on 4 September 1936, he abandoned Madrid to the Nationalist advance on 6 November, leaving its defense to General José Miaja, with no prior warning and no plans for arming the people.[36]

Madrid was saved by its citizens. Largo had left a vacuum, into which the Communists stepped, fortified by the International Brigades and the all-important Soviet aid arriving from November 1936.[37] Aided by Largo's self-styled "bolshevism," the PCE already had its foot in the Socialist door, with the Communist CGTU joining the UGT and the two youth movements merging under Santiago Carillo, who was already attending PCE meetings. Communists drew huge prestige from the defense of Madrid, boosting membership from a few thousand to a quarter of a million by May 1937. With direct lines to government under Largo, they relentlessly pressed the Comintern's guidelines for Popular Fronts, urging the need at all costs to avoid alienating either the British and French governments or bourgeois democrats inside Spain by fear of revolution. Winning the war took utmost priority over social reforms. The PCE stood for centralizing authority, conventional military discipline, and respect for small property.

These goals were advanced against the popular hopes unleashed by the Republic's defense. A vast militant sector was unintegrated into the Popular Front, the anarcho-syndicalism of the CNT, based in Aragon, Valencia, Andalusia, and industrial Catalonia (where it dwarfed the Socialists).[38] In the summer of 1936, even the CNT was outflanked by revolutionary spontaneity. After defeating the military rebels in five of the seven biggest cities and half the countryside, militants pushed on to form revolutionary committees, seizing local government, and collectivizing industry and agriculture. In Barcelona, anarcho-syndicalism's urban capital, CNT leaders were paralyzed: neither willing to run the Catalonian government nor ready to proclaim the revolution, they simply called for solidarity with the Republic, and watched while their supporters seized the city regardless. The social landscape exploded—flags, banners, insignia, posters, badges, workers with rifles, everyone in blue dungarees, the exuberant stylistics of the people capturing public space. As a Communist railwayman, Narciso Julián, who arrived in Barcelona the night before the popular insurrection and was swept up in its fervor, said, "It was incredible, the proof in practice of what one knows in theory: the power and strength of the masses when they take to the streets. Suddenly you feel their creative power; you can't imagine how rapidly the masses are capable of organizing themselves. The forms they invent go far beyond anything you've dreamt of, read in books."[39]

Julián's next sentence was: "What was needed now was to seize this initiative, give it shape"; and this was the rub. Barcelona's anarchism was inspiring, everything a revolution should be. But anarcho-syndicalists refused state power once the people controlled the economy via self-managed collectives, and this apoliticism removed CNT leaders from the republican coalition. The movement's utterly incorrigible localism was worsened by the autonomy of workplace collectives, rogue militias, the shadowy influence of charismatic bosses, and the violent intransigence of the FAI, the

CNT's interior vanguard.[40] This spelled irresponsible disorder to the Catalan government, where the newly formed PSUC and the *Esquerra* were dominant.[41] By the spring of 1937, half the Communists' members were now peasant owners, shopkeepers, artisans, and white-collar workers worried by collectivization in town and country. As the Republic's military fortunes sank, the "passive dual power" of the anarchists—keeping their parallel power structures but abstaining from government—became intolerable. The government moved to evict them from the Telephone Exchange, and after a week of street fighting (3–8 May 1937) took control of Barcelona. Largo was replaced as prime minister by the moderate Socialist Juan Negrín.

The Republic's defeat—Bilbao fell to the Nationalists in June 1937, Gijón in October, Aragon in March–April 1938, Barcelona in January 1939, and finally Madrid on 27 March 1939, with the Republic's surrender on 1 April—owed much to this internal strife. Largo had squandered the chance to stabilize the government in early 1936, immobilizing the one party capable of grounding the Popular Front. Then, by abruptly switching to republican consolidation on forming a government, he left his supporters' militancy dangerously high and dry. The PSOE was also haughtily hostile to the CNT, and these two Lefts dominated separate regions. To political divisions was therefore added geographical fragmentation, plus the rivalries of countless local committees, jealously guarding their autonomy. Communists, easily the most effective republicans, embraced these divisions. Licensed by the indispensible Soviet aid and by their own vanguardism (undiminished by Dimitrov's strictures at Comintern's Seventh Congress), the PCE behaved with increasing arrogance—maneuvering to monopolize key positions, especially in the reprofessionalized army; showing sectarian disregard for allies and contempt for opponents; ignoring democratic procedures; and finally resorting to terror against rivals in 1937 (notably the Partido Obrero de Unificación Marxista (POUM), stigmatized as "Trotskyist" and so for Stalinists tantamount to fascism), in a disgraceful copy of the Soviet purges.

This Stalinism reflected a larger weakness. Restraining revolutionary experiments to win the war was not the problem, because everyone (including CNT leaders) paid lip service to that. But making this into a dichotomy was a mistake. Prosecuting the war with a central command while securing the revolutionary gains were not mutually exclusive. As one PCE organizer said, it was not a matter of sacrificing the revolution altogether but of deciding "what sort of revolution should be made" and how it could help the war.[42] Losing sight of this was the PCE's big failure. After the showdown with anarchists in Barcelona's May Days, it moved completely to a bureaucratic style. In the summer of 1937, agrarian collectives in Aragon were rationalized. In Catalonia, workers' control was replaced by nationalization and central planning. The PCE aligned itself wholly with the PSOE right, with conciliating the middle classes, and with conventional warfare. This was a far cry from the heroic days of the defense of Madrid, when the PCE mobilized the people.

The PCE had another priority—to keep pressure on Britain and France to intervene, or at least to avoid scaring them from Soviet cooperation. British and French non–intervention, when Nazi Germany and Fascist Italy were pumping support to the Nationalists, was an unmitigated calamity for the Republic, matched by the LSI's passivity. But the Republican government also excluded anything that would lead to "the enemies of Spain considering her a communist republic," as Stalin put it.[43] This precluded guerrilla warfare to capitalize on the Republic's popular enthusiasm, building on the improvised mobilizations of the summer of 1936, while activating indigenous traditions ("guerrilla" was a Spanish term from the anti-Napoleonic struggle). Ignoring irregular warfare was one of the Popular Front's worst omissions. As one young peasant Communist, an officer in the Republican army, later said with regret, "If we hadn't been convinced that the democratic countries would come to our aid, different forms of struggle would have developed. . . . This wasn't a traditional war—it was a civil war, a political war. A war between democracy and fascism, certainly, but a popular war. Yet all the creative possibilities and instincts of a people in revolution were not allowed to develop."[44]

FAILURE AND DEFEAT

Not only did the Republic lose the Civil War, leading to brutal reprisals and three decades of authoritarian rule, but the Comintern's strategy also failed. The Comintern hoped to combine both the United Front of working-class parties and the broader Popular Front. This was formally realized in the Largo Caballero government of September 1936, extended in November toward the CNT. But many divisions undermined the effort. The biggest of these pitted the Comintern's advocacy of self-limiting republican defense, from which specifically socialist demands were dropped, against the desires of the people militant, for whom revolution was all.

As an international strategy, the Popular Front also failed. British and French support for nonintervention made it a nonstarter. Their refusal to support Spanish democracy ensured the Republic's destruction. As the Republic died, the western democracies were simultaneously appeasing Hitler in central Europe, first at the *Anschluss* with Austria in March 1938 and then in the dismemberment of Czechoslovakia in September. As the Nationalists took Madrid, Hitler's armies marched into Prague. When Hitler immediately turned his aggression on Poland and Britain and France still gave the USSR no response, collective security for containing Nazi Germany was in shreds. Stalin drew his conclusions, signing the Non-Aggression Pact with Hitler in August 1939. With the destruction of the Spanish and Czechoslovak republics, two more of Europe's remaining democracies had gone. So far from rallying to their defense, the western democracies preferred to dig their graves. At the CPSU's Eighteenth Congress (March 1939), the Popular Front strategy was tacitly dropped.[45]

The scale of Spanish atrocities was appalling. Republicans were not innocent (six thousand priests were estimated killed), especially in the embittered countryside of anarchist Andalusia, where rough justice was dispatched to the rulers.[46] But as the Nationalists retook the south, the worst antirepublican killings were unleashed. In a fury of retribution, immediate eruptions of brutalized class hatred were succeeded by systematic terror—not just against the Left's activists but also their presumed supporters among workers and rural laborers. The odious Gonzalo de Aguilera, a Nationalist officer, despised the Spanish masses as "slaves" and "lined up the laborers on his estate, selected six of them and shot them in front of the others—'*Pour encourager les autres,* you understand.' " When the Nationalists took Badajoz, the *Chicago Tribune* correspondent reported a massacre in the bullring of 1,800 leftists. Another American journalist saw a mass execution of six hundred captured militiamen on the main street of Santa Olalla. Colonel Juan de Yagüe, the butcher of Badajoz, made no bones: "Of course we shot them. What do you expect? Was I supposed to take 4,000 reds with me as my column advanced. . . . Was I supposed to turn them loose in my rear and let them make Badajoz red again?"[47] For the European Left, the Spanish Civil War was a lesson in what to expect if the fascists won again.[48]

But the lessons of the Spanish Civil War weren't all bleakness and defeat. The Civil War signified Guernica, not just as the scene of atrocity (on 26 April 1937, when the German Condor Legion bombed the town into destruction) but as Picasso's painting, the most famous instance of artistic creativity in the Republican cause. For progressives, the Republic symbolized the defense of humane and forward-looking values, the place where the vision of a better, more egalitarian world could be upheld. Here is the sculptor Jason Gurney: "The Spanish Civil War seemed to provide the chance for a single individual to take a positive and effective stand on an issue which appeared to be absolutely clear. Either you were opposed to the growth of Fascism and went out to fight against it, or you acquiesced in its crimes and were guilty of permitting its growth."[49]

The International Brigades—40,000 volunteers from over 50 nations, including 15,400 French, 5,400 Polish, 5,100 Italians, 5,000 Germans and Austrians, over 3,000 each from the United States, Britain, Belgium, and Czechoslovakia—carried this solidarity. They included political exiles from the already fascist or authoritarian parts of Europe; Communists, socialists, and independent idealists; students; artists and creative intellectuals; politically conscious workers, like most of the 169 volunteers from Wales—all united by a sense of political momentousness, of needing to take a stand.[50] For those who stayed at home, Spain was also a noble cause, a chance to halt Europe's drift toward fascism, the place where "Our thoughts have bodies; the menacing shapes of our fever / Are precise and alive," as W. H. Auden's great poem put it.[51] In Britain, where a Popular Front was opposed by the iron control of the Labour Party right, an international solidarity campaign was coordinated by the National Joint Committee for Spanish Relief that involved many autonomous local and union groups. This less tangible effect of the Popular Front in Spain, the symbolics of popular antifascist identification, remained for the future.

Chapter 18

People's War and People's Peace

Remaking the Nation, 1939–1947

WHEN DIMITRI MANUILSKI delivered his Comintern report at the CPSU's Eighteenth Congress on 10 March 1939, the hopes of 1935 were in shreds. Illegality was now the norm of Communist existence: the German, Austrian, Italian, Spanish, Portuguese, Czechoslovak, Yugoslav, Greek, Bulgarian, Romanian, and Hungarian parties were all underground. With the onset of the Second World War, the PCF too was banned, soon followed in 1940 by CPs in countries invaded by Germany and in Switzerland. The Swedish and British CPs became the only ones remaining above ground. So by 1939 the split in the European Left seemed as bitter as ever. The CPs were not only illegal but back in their former isolation, returned to the margins.

The Soviet Congress met in the shadow of the Munich Conference where Britain and France surrendered Czechoslovakia to Hitler's aggression, ceding the so-called Sudetenland directly to Germany while Poland and Hungary also grabbed territory, leaving behind a demoralized and defenseless rump. Manuilski's address was delivered amid the ruins of European collective security: Hitler had just occupied what remained of Czechoslovakia and then seized Memel, provoking fears of war against Poland. While acquiescing in this further aggression, Britain issued bilateral guarantees to Poland, Romania, Greece, and Turkey.

The Left's fate was now tied to war and peace. Crucially, the Soviet Union abandoned calls for anti-Nazi alliance.[1] Instead, it accused "English reaction" of wanting to embroil it in a destructive war of survival against Nazism. Maxim Litvinov, the advocate of collective security, was replaced as foreign minister by Viacheslav Mikhailovich Molotov. The British and French approached the USSR but wilfully dragged their feet in negotiations. Hitler trumped them by a nonaggression treaty with Stalin signed on 23 August 1939. This provided for Poland's partition, while assigning Estonia and Latvia to a Soviet and Lithuania to a German sphere of influence. Freed from a two-front war, Hitler invaded Poland on 1 September 1939. Against type, Britain acted on its Polish guarantee. On 3 September the European war began.

THE NAZI-SOVIET PACT: COMMUNISM EMBATTLED

In most accounts, the Nazi-Soviet Pact was the Popular Front's great betrayal, exposing Soviet hypocrisy while negating antifascism. But for Communists, it was less apocalyptic. The Popular Front was already dead, strangled by northern socialist parties and the British government, buried by the sacrifice of Czechoslovakia. It was hard to see the new Pact as a violation of international morality after the Munich Agreement. In Communist estimation, the great betrayal had already occurred when the British and French governments—and the Labour Party and SFIO—ignored the Spanish Republic, destroyed Czechoslovak democracy, and refused Soviet offers of anti-Hitler cooperation. The Labor and Socialist International (LSI) had long abdicated responsibility, as socialist internationalists well knew, and in June 1939 the LSI's secretary, Friedrich Adler, declared it dead. Its more radical sections, the Austrian, Menshevik, Italian, and Spanish, were illegal with little weight; the dominant sections in Britain, France, the Low Countries, and Scandinavia were wholly focused on their own affairs. As a collective body the LSI was gone.

The Soviet deal with Hitler seemed a sensible effort at buying time, at holding the Nazi aggressor at arm's length while ditching the hollow diplomacy with the West. If some "dedicated comrades were left without a compass," most were secure in their antifascist credentials and could rationalize a pragmatics for the Pact.[2] Western governments' own behavior was grist for such rationalizations and the new antiimperialist line. Even before war began, the French government banned the PCF daily newspaper *L'Humanité* and arrested Communists. On 26 September, the party itself was banned, lasting until August 1944. By March 1940, 2,778 Communist city councillors were dismissed, 629 Communist-led trade unions were dissolved, and 3,400 militants were imprisoned. In March–April 1940, 44 PCF parliamentarians were tried for treason: all but three, who recanted, received long prison sentences. On 10 April 1940, Communist propaganda became punishable by death.

The Nazi-Soviet Pact was certainly a bitter pill to swallow. The French-based Italian Anti-Fascist Alliance fell apart; its president, Romano Cocchi, was expelled from the PCI for condemning the Pact, and the PSI repudiated unity. But most CPs assumed their antifascist struggles would continue. It wasn't the Pact as such that shook them but how it was carried out. Communists distinguished between defending the Pact (Soviet security needs) and their own politics (continuing an antifascist line). It was a month before Stalin cracked the whip. Thus, in Britain the lone Communist MP William Gallacher was the sole parliamentary voice protesting Prime Minister Neville Chamberlain's trip to Munich in September 1938, and once war came the CP affirmed this moral stance. As Harry Pollitt said in *How To Win the War* on 14 September: "To stand aside from this conflict, to contribute only revolutionary-sounding phrases while the fascist beasts ride roughshod over Europe, would be a betrayal of everything our forbears have fought to achieve."[3] Defeating Chamberlain's government ("British imperialism") would allow a progressive coalition to fight the war better.

But the same day, Moscow described the war in a radio broadcast as "an imperialist and predatory war for a new redivision of the world, a robber war kindled from all sides by the two imperialist groups of powers" and suppressed the differences between Hitler's Germany and other capitalist regimes. The party was instructed to oppose the war and drop its attacks on fascism. On 2–3 October 1939, the CPGB Central Committee reconvened and by 21 votes against 3 condemned the "imperialist war."[4]

After a brief hiatus, therefore, Moscow imposed conformity: the Non-Aggression Pact required antiwar agitation; attacks on Nazi Germany should cease. This evasion of the main danger was not one-sided, because both the French state and the SFIO preferred attacking the PCF to building anti-Hitler coalitions.[5] Even so, the Communist line was confusing and morally suspect. Calling the war an imperialist war was an abrupt *volte-face,* an irresponsible conflation of the western allies with the Rome-Berlin Axis. For Communists in Germany itself, Italy, Spain, and eastern Europe, any future still presupposed Nazism's defeat, and when Mussolini invaded Greece (October 1940) after Hitler's subjugation of the Low Countries and France (May–June), the equivalence of "imperialist aggressors" became even more strained. As fascism overran continental Europe during 1939–41 and bedraggled CP leaderships reassembled in Moscow, accordingly, Communists were in disarray. Togliatti, barely escaping a French prison, just ahead of Hitler's invading armies, reached safety at the movement's lowest point. Biding one's time was the best he could offer: "Let us not lose our heads, but concentrate on gaining as much time as possible."[6]

Togliatti's counsel came not only amid fascist terror but at the end of the Great Soviet Purges.[7] These stood out by their use of show trials and by the sheer scale of the victims. People were not just expelled from the party but incarcerated and killed: 680,000 were executed in 1937–38, three million detained.[8] The terror targeted the veteran party leadership itself, alleging a vast anti-Soviet conspiracy in a series of staged trials: first Kamenev, Zinoviev, and others, as the "Trotskyite-Zinoviev United Center" in the summer of 1936; then Piatakov, Radek, and leading Comintern officials, as the "Anti-Soviet Trotskyite Center" in January 1937; and then Bukharin, Rykov, and 19 others, as the "Anti-Soviet Bloc of Rightists and Trotskyites" in March 1938. This effected a massive turnover of leadership: of 1,966 delegates to the Seventeenth Party Congress in February 1934, only 59 were back at the Eighteenth Congress in 1939; and of 139 Central Committee members, only 24 remained, with 98 convicted of treason and shot. This was replicated in the regions: Leningrad was particularly badly hit; after the May 1937 Congress of the Georgian party, 425 of the 644 delegates disappeared. No institution was safe; in the Red Army some 35,000 officers were eliminated.

This savagery caught foreign Communists in its net. Most exile groups suffered, notably Germans, Hungarians, and Yugoslavs, as well as anyone connected internationally, like veterans of the Spanish Civil War or Comintern officials. Only Togliatti and Dimitrov secured their comrades some protection. The Polish party was brutally treated, officially dissolved once its leaders and exiled militants were killed. These atrocities indelibly stained Soviet Communist history. Perhaps the worst came after the killings were over but when the detained population still grew. Under the Nazi-Soviet Pact, in February 1940, some five hundred German exiles (mostly Communists) were taken to the border and given to the Nazis, who transported them to concentration camps.

The democratic impoverishment of the Comintern's internal regime, the Great Purges, foreign Communists' uncritical adulation of Stalin, and instrumentalizing of national CPs by Soviet foreign policy—all these features of Communist history disfigured the Left's political experience between the Third Period and the CPSU's Twentieth Congress in 1956. If individual CPs had been moving away from sectarianism under the Popular Front, rejecting proletarian isolationism for coalitions of diverse social support, the Comintern remained decisively beholden to Stalinism. When directives from Moscow changed, foreign Communists fell into line. Required by the Nazi-Soviet Pact to abandon the antifascist war, Maurice Cornforth, the CPGB's Eastern Counties organizer, performed the consequent somersault: "I must say that I have got that sort of faith in the Soviet Union, to be willing to do that, because I believe that if one loses any of that faith in the Soviet Union one is done for as a Communist and a Socialist . . . the fact of the matter is that a socialist state, I believe, in that position can do no wrong, and is doing no wrong, and this is what we have to stick to." Or as the Yorkshire Communist Bill Moore recalled, looking back across 50 years: "the defense of the Soviet Union was decisive, absolutely decisive, which it still is, to my mind, despite all the criticisms we may have of the Soviet Union."[9]

Here was the rub. Communists were strongly rooted in working-class communities, well aware of national and local particularities, and not slavishly dependent on the Moscow line. Yet CPs prided themselves on the "steel-hardened" discipline of following Soviet dictates if required. While Communists advocated democratic alliance in a broadened spectrum of the Left in the Popular Front era, they acted from a Communist culture of loyalty to the line—a political culture further entrenched via the Purges, when Comintern was dragooned into Soviet dependency. "The duty of a Communist is not to disagree but accept," intoned Rajani Palme Dutt, the *éminence grise* of British Stalinism.[10] This political tradition of Stalinism came from Bolshevization and demarcation against social democrats in the 1920s and lasted for three decades. But while this international dimension of Stalinism sometimes delivered political strengths, as in the anti-Nazi Resistance movements, at other times it repeatedly got in the way.

It was paradoxically the wartime adversity that broke through this dilemma, briefly interrupting the rigidity of Comintern directives and allowing Communist initiative to flourish. Even before Hitler invaded the USSR on 22 June 1941, and despite Comintern instructions to oppose the war, CPs under Nazi or Italian military occupation were organizing resistance in the old antifascist way. This was true in Greece after the Italian invasion of 27 October 1940; Yugoslavia after the fall of the pro-Nazi government on 27 March 1941 and the ensuing German invasion; and Bulgaria after the quartering of German troops in March 1941. In all three cases, the radicalizing of wartime pressures overrode Soviet instructions.

In France, where the large CP was now underground, antifascism re-emerged under German occupation and the creation of the Vichy regime in June 1940. Communists easily opposed Vichy as a reactionary throwback: "Pétain at Versailles, Jesuits in the schools, Communists in prison; it is the dictatorship of army and priest."[11] Despite some misguided episodes, they moved rapidly into opposition in the north too. An *Appeal* was issued by Maurice Thorez and Jacques Duclos, followed by a *Letter to Communist Militants* and a Central Committee *Manifesto* in November 1940. Each attacked both Vichy and German occupation in the name of French independence and a people's government. Communists formed clandestine committees and stockpiled arms, establishing the *Organisation Spéciale* (OS) to coordinate activity. The party issued a *Letter to a Socialist Worker* (October 1940) and *Letter to a Radical Working Man* (December), building unity from below. In May 1941, it launched the National Front of Struggle for France's Independence. Finally, in May–June 1941, PCF militants were crucial in shaping a strike of one hundred thousand miners.[12]

It was another "external" event, the Nazi invasion of the USSR, that changed the rules, finally imposing the international alliance the Popular Front had envisaged. British aid was immediately pledged by Winston Churchill, prime minister since May 1940 in a National Coalition now including Labour. On 3 July 1941, Stalin described the war as an antifascist democratic crusade, "a united front of the peoples standing for freedom and against enslavement."[13] For a while Hitler's armies carried all before them, sweeping through Ukraine, placing Leningrad under siege, and only halting before Moscow on 8 December 1941. The following summer, German military success continued, concentrated in the south. But with the massive defeat at Stalingrad between August 1942 and February 1943, the war turned.

Meanwhile, the conflict had broadened after the Japanese attack at Pearl Harbor on 7 December 1941 and Hitler's declaration of war on the United States. Events in the West moved slowly. After the battle of El Alemain (October 1942), the tide turned in North Africa, leading to the invasion of Sicily and Mussolini's fall in July 1943. In June 1944, Rome was occupied and Normandy invaded, beginning the methodical advance of British and U.S. armies through northern France into Germany. In the East, the Red Army advanced steadily during 1943, reaching the borders of Eastern Europe by August. By autumn 1944, the Baltic and half of Poland had been regained, Romania and Bulgaria had realigned with the Allies, and the Germans were leaving Greece. In the winter, while the British and US armies halted before a German counteroffensive in Belgium, the Red Army resumed its advance, taking Warsaw in January and pressing on to Berlin. Between February and May, the central European capitals of Budapest, Vienna, Prague, and Berlin were liberated, and Italy was free. The war came to an end on 7 May 1945, when the German army unconditionally surrendered, a week after Hitler's suicide.

AGAINST HITLER FASCISM: NATIONAL COMMUNISMS, NATIONAL FRONTS

Italian and central European leftists had known since 1939 that their best hope was a European antifascist war, and after the confusing interlude of the Nazi-Soviet Pact in 1939–41, the Grand Alliance of Britain, the USSR, and the United States delivered this condition. How the three Allies saw the postwar world now decisively affected the Left's fate—from Stalin's desire for a regional system of eastern European security to Churchill's federalist schemes of anti-Communist containment, and the United States' belief in the free movement of the world economy. The most famous example was Churchill's Moscow agreement with Stalin over Eastern Europe in October 1944:

> Let us settle about our affairs in the Balkans. Your armies are in Romania and Bulgaria. We have interests, missions, and agents there. Don't let us get at cross-purposes in small ways. So far as Britain and Russia are concerned, how would it do for you to have 90 percent predominance in Romania, for us to have 90 percent of the say in Greece, and go 50–50 about Yugoslavia?[14]

The practical ground for the Left was laid by the three great summit meetings of Teheran in November–December 1943, Yalta in February 1945, and Potsdam in July 1945.[15]

On 10 June 1943, in the interests of the Grand Alliance, the Comintern was dissolved. Once the USSR entered the war, it had been turned over to radio propaganda, broadcasting on liberty, democracy, and national independence in 18 languages 24 hours a day. In October 1941 it moved to Ufa near the Urals under Togliatti's direction, while Manuilski and Dimitrov worked with central government. Comintern publications shed their revolutionary language, barely mentioning the Comintern's name. The dissolution occurred in a small meeting in Kuibyshev, without Togliatti's presence. For Stalin, the International had become an encumbrance, a relic of an earlier time that needlessly annoyed his American and British allies. Disbanding it would be an act of good faith, placating non-Communists and easing postwar continuance of the Grand Alliance.

The domestic correlate of the Grand Alliance was the "national front," the broadest possible cooperation of forces in each society opposing Nazism and therefore a resumption of the Popular Front. These national coalitions varied across occupied Europe, but Communists usually made the running, sometimes joined by new intellectual groupings, and easily outpacing their Socialist rivals, who faced the Nazi disaster in utter disarray.

In France, the PCF wasted no time. In July 1941, it revived its drive for the broadest national coalition. In the words of one official appeal: "there is no difference at all among Communists, Socialists, Radicals, Catholics, and followers of Charles De Gaulle . . . there are only French people fighting Hitler."[16] After rocky negotiations with De Gaulle and his London Committee for Free France, the PCF was eventually accepted. In May 1943, the unified Resistance council, *Conseil National de la Résistance* (CNR), gathered all anti-German parties, the various trade unions, and De Gaulle's French National Committee. The military resistance was unified in February 1944 into the *Forces Françaises de l'Intérieur,* based around the PCF's own *Francs-Tireurs et Partisans.* In January 1943, the PCF joined De Gaulle's London Committee. In June 1943, a provisional government was formed, the *Comité Français de Libération Nationale* (CFLN), recognized by Stalin but not the western Allies. The SFIO also joined De Gaulle's Committee but was deeply compromised by the capitulation of June 1940 and the creation of Vichy, as well as by the persecution of the PCF in 1939–40. The PCF also mobilized intellectuals in the *Comité National des Ecrivains,* formed in 1943.[17]

Mussolini fell in Italy on 25 July 1943. The Fascist Grand Council handed power to King Vittorio Emanuele, with Marshal Pietro Badoglio as premier. Italy became divided between the Nazi-occupied north, the Allied military front, and Badoglio's expanding zone in the south. The Left formed the Committee of National Liberation (CLN) on 9 September 1943, uniting Communists, Socialists, and the small Action Party with Catholics, liberals, and Ivanoe Bonomi's small Democracy of Labor. In August, the Italian Socialist Party of Proletarian Unity (PSIUP) had formed from French and Swiss exiles, reemerging PSI veterans, and the ultraleft Movement of Proletarian Unity around Lelio Basso and younger militants in Milan. The PCI resurfaced as an inchoate blend of new liberal recruits like Giorgio Amendola and older Leninists like Luigi Longo, Pietro Secchia, and Mauro Scoccimarro, inspired by the insurrectionary potential of northern resistance. Uncertainties were resolved on 27 March 1944, when Togliatti arrived in Naples and committed the PCI to Badoglio. First the PCI and then the PSIUP joined the government, relaunched under the CLN president and pre-Fascist prime minister Bonomi in June 1944. Togliatti's goal was to contain the ardor of the PSIUP, Action Party, and the PCI's own partisan units, while extending cooperation to liberals and emergent Christian Democrats.[18]

Czechoslovakia was the eastern European country closest to this Franco-Italian pattern.[19] The KSC's Moscow leadership already floated a national front in May 1941 before the Nazis invaded the USSR, and Edward Benes, head of the exiled government in London, shared this approach, seeking to neutralize Soviet domination by absorbing the KSC under his own lead. For their own part, Communists hoped Benes could broker east-west relations in the region. Stalin recognized him as postwar premier in December 1943 in return for key Communist demands, including the banning of political forces compromised by the Munich betrayal and the forming of National Committees for the liberation. Benes's formula of "national revolution" required expulsion of the German minority and refusal of Slovakian autonomy, but while the Communists agreed to the former they strongly backed the launching of the Slovak National Council (SNR) in December 1943, which sponsored the Slovak National Uprising in the fall of 1944. The SNR was also part of the Kosice Program, negotiated in Moscow in March 1945, which divided government posts among the KSC, Social Democrats, and National Socialists.[20]

Czechoslovak Communism had strong indigenous roots and reaped the benefits of Soviet opposition to the 1938 Munich Agreement; Communists and non-Communists shared common ground; and the KSC led by its genuine strengths. In Poland, none of this applied. Dissolved in 1938, the Polish CP reemerged as the Polish Workers' Party (PPR) in occupied Warsaw in January 1942. Its program called for a broad national front, in common with Communist strategy elsewhere, but by April Stalin's relations with the London-based Polish government in exile had collapsed, and the PPR reverted to extreme opposition. Thus in Poland Communists remained isolated. Few non-Communists backed the National Council of the Homeland, launched in December 1943, and even Moscow loyalists found its radicalism a liability in talks with London. Communists veered between official national front rhetorics imposed by Moscow's security needs and militant opposition to the London-backed underground. On the one hand, the Polish Committee of National Liberation, formed in July 1944, called for broad political cooperation and dropped its socialist demands. On the other hand, in October 1944 Stalin reverted finally to a harder line, giving Vladislav Gomulka and other PPR leaders their way, devolving national front rhetoric into a Communist drive for power.[21]

Yugoslav Communists faced a brutal partisan struggle with no political allies, a rival resistance on the extreme Right, and an exiled royal government they refused to support. Here, Moscow's advocacy of national fronts had no purchase.[22] The Communist Party of Yugoslavia (KPJ) began armed resistance on 4 July 1941 from a liberated zone in western Serbia known as the Uzice Republic, which they held until December. Talks between Tito and Dragoljub-Draza Mihailovic, leader of the ultraright Serb royalist resistance, the Cetniks, collapsed in November 1941, leaving Communists alone against the Germans. By March 1942, five "Proletarian Shock Brigades" with pan-Yugoslav composition complemented the bulk of locally based partisan units. The Anti-Fascist Council of the People's Liberation of Yugoslavia (AVNOJ) was launched in November with sole KPJ membership, becoming a year later the government of liberated Yugoslavia. On 7 March 1945, it became the official Provisional Government, to which Tito reluctantly admitted the exiled royalists. Stalin had been furious at AVNOJ's formation ("a stab in the back for the Soviet Union"),[23] but the polarized Yugoslav situation compelled Tito to go it alone. Here national front was a nonstarter.

Greek circumstances were similar. The Communists (KKE) launched the National Liberation Front (EAM) in September 1941, followed in December by the National Popular Liberation Army (ELAS), starting operations in spring 1942. But in contrast to Yugoslavia, the British backed the right-wing resistance linked to the royal government in exile. In March 1944, the KKE formed the Political Committee of National Liberation as the political voice of "Mountain Greece" but after much agonizing joined the British-backed government of national unity on its entry to Athens in October; EAM-ELAS forfeited a chance to fill the vacuum left by the Germans and were outmaneuvered. Amid rising bitterness, Left ministers resigned from the government, and on 3 December 1944 EAM called a mass rally as the prelude to a general strike. Police fired on the crowd, accelerating the impending civil war. The British army backed the political élite, treating liberated Athens as a conquered city; EAM-ELAS accepted a ceasefire in January 1945, but with no improvement. But Stalin was satisfied, as Greece stayed in the British sphere agreed on with Churchill. In neither Yugoslavia nor Greece did the Soviet Union aid the successful partisans or their revolutionary hopes. But the British left Yugoslavia to Tito; in Greece, they backed the Right.[24]

Elsewhere, national fronts were less central, either because the Left was weak (Romania, Hungary) or because Communists were dwarfed by social democrats in a more centrist coalition (the Low Countries, Scandinavia).[25]

Albania followed Yugoslavia under the KPJ's lead. Bulgaria was an intermediate case. The Fatherland Front, formed in July 1942 by Communists, left Agrarians, Social Democrats, and *Zveno* (supraparty reformers), flourished only with the Red Army's arrival, after which Bulgarian Communist Party (BCP) growth was impressive, rising from 15,000 to 250,000 members between October 1944 and January 1945.[26] Britain, as the last unoccupied anti-Nazi combatant, was in a category by itself: the CPGB's role was not insignificant, especially at the grassroots of the war effort among trade unionists and intellectuals, but it played no part in the wartime government, which owed nothing to the specifically Communist idea of antifascist war.

EUROPE'S HORIZONS: BUILDING A BETTER WORLD

Communist parties briefly entered the accepted political nation in most of Europe. As stalwarts of the European Resistance, they prospered in postwar elections, becoming the Left's majority force in Italy, France, Czechoslovakia, Yugoslavia, Albania, Bulgaria, and Greece. Here the Third International's legacy was ambiguous. All the qualities of post-1928 Stalinism equipped CPs for clandestine resistance against repressive regimes, from "steel-hardened" discipline to centralist decision-making and selfless loyalty to the "line." Yet after 1943 they were swamped by new recruits untrained in vanguard beliefs about how Communists behaved. Stalinist leadership styles, unchallenged by the war and even validated by the Resistance, now faced new mass support shaped by egalitarian solidarities of the partisan struggle, whose hopes of postwar change ignored the embittered prewar divisions. Wartime also limited the practical control party leaderships could wield, whether from exile in Moscow or the "interior." Peculiar wartime conditions made the space where a different kind of Communism, based on the Resistance and each society's progressive traditions, emerged.[27]

The Resistance movements subsumed older rivalries, making European unity into a redemptive good. A Geneva conference in July 1944 outlined a federal Europe with written constitution, armed forces, and directly elected supranational government.[28] Popular hopes had a generalized utopian quality. Not only democracy in the constitutional sense—free elections, civil rights, rule of law—but the root-and-branch rebuilding of society was involved. This required decisive reckoning with the past—with the prewar élites who had sacrificed democracy to appease dictators. Europe should be purged of the old divisiveness and class privilege, and the Resistance ideals delivered the momentum. This moral crusade of reconstruction expected the prosecution of war criminals and collaborators, from fascists themselves to the élites who cooperated with their rule.[29] It projected postwar political forms true to the anti-Nazi solidarities, possibly as a single "Resistance party." Economic planning would avoid the capitalist dysfunctions so crucial to the prewar societal collapse. Egalitarian social policies would sustain the wartime spirit of common sacrifice.[30]

Rhetorically, the Grand Alliance endorsed these hopes. The 1943 conference of Allied Foreign Ministers in Moscow linked democracy to antifascist committees of liberation. But by the Yalta meeting held in February 1945, the Declaration on Liberated Territories mentioned only free elections. This contrasted with the political documents still emerging from Resistance movements themselves, whose desires for radical transformation were undiminished. The French Resistance Charter of 1944 called for nationalization, comprehensive social security, workers' control, trade union guarantees, a rational reorganizing of the economy, and the ideal of "a more just social order." How this desire for change would unfold, in the practical circumstances of liberation, was the big question of the postwar world.

The Left's situation in 1945 was close to what the 1935 Popular Front strategy had imagined. The international coalition against fascism had worked. Mussolini was deposed, Hitler defeated; of the other rightist dictators only Franco in Spain and Antonio de Oliviera Salazar in Portugal remained. The "workers' state," the Soviet Union, had emerged triumphantly from a war that had immensely boosted its prestige. Broad coalitions for democracy and reform, so-called national fronts, were formed in most countries. United fronts between Socialists and Communists were also common, especially locally all over Europe. Radical changes seemed afoot.

The chance was fleeting. It lasted from 1942–43, as fascism retreated in the south and east, until 1947–48, when the Cold War fully began. Wartime dynamics—Nazi occupation, fascist rule, and Resistance—laid the first basis for politics. Nazism's unparalleled violence trumped all abstract debates over differences between fascism and liberal democracy, and the misguided Communist ultraleftism of 1928–35, which denied this distinction, died away. The vast scale of destruction—the Nazi genocide of Jews and other peoples, the murderous foundations of Nazism's new order—rallied all those committed to even minimal standards of democracy and human rights. This human devastation was vital in solidifying beliefs in reconstruction, in rebuilding Europe democratically. Nonpartisanship and crossparty unity were the order of the day.

The years 1943–47 were a rare moment of European history—the moment of antifascist unity—whose opportunities compared with 1917–18. Reading Cold War divisions back into this time distorts its dynamics, which on the contrary produced a radical openness. The war brought a powerful shift to the Left, bringing socialists and Communists center stage in entirely new ways. The only mass transference of loyalties from one set of Left parties to another since 1917–23 now occurred, in a second "great wave of communization within popular and labor movements, especially in Eastern and Central Europe."[31] The CPs in Yugoslavia, Albania, Greece, and

Czechoslovakia became leading national forces; the Italian Communist Party (PCI) became an imposing mass movement; the PCF became the dominant working-class party in France; and the smaller CPs in Scandinavia, the Low Countries, and Britain reached their highest popularity.[32] By leading Resistance movements, at huge sacrifice, Communists finally joined the legitimate political nation. They earned popular recognition, with begrudging acceptance from antifascist conservatives and liberals as well as non-Communist parts of the Left. They rose to political leadership in the liberation struggles of 1944–45 by organizational effectiveness, ideological clarity, and popular support.

While the political psychology of the Red Army's victories was vital, Communism's prestige came above all from the Resistance. The brutality of Nazi rule required exceptionally hardened commitment, with qualities of discipline that Communists prized. The resulting political cultures were also heavily patriotic: the Resistance produced unique identification of the Left with the nation. Class fused with popular struggles, breaking socialists and Communists from working-class isolation into broader coalitions, even claiming leadership in the nation. Winning the intellectuals mattered enormously, beginning with the Popular Front campaigns of the 1930s, when fascism began threatening Western culture's best humanistic achievements. The Left's ability to mobilize languages of "civilization versus barbarism" in its own favor was also key to the time.

Given its pre-1941 isolation, Communism's arrival into the political mainstream was remarkable. The first postwar elections brought powerful evidence of broadly based reforming desires, borne by rhetorics of national reconciliation and new beginnings.[33] This pattern characterized Scandinavia, the Low Countries, Italy, and France. From the fall of 1945 to the summer of 1946, varying configurations of Socialists, Communists, and Christian Democrats commanded three-quarters of the popular vote—74.9 percent in the French elections to the Constituent Assembly of October 1945, 74.6 percent in Italy (June 1946), 86.8 percent in Belgium (February 1946), and 72 percent in the Netherlands (May 1946) (see table 18.1).

TABLE 18.1 Anti-Fascist Governing Coalitions: First Postwar Elections, Percentages of Popular Vote

	Belgium 1946	France 1946	Italy 1946	Netherlands 1946
Socialists, Social Democrats	32	21	21	28
Communist parties	13	26	19	11
Christian Democrats and Catholic People's parties	43	26	35	31
Liberals	9			13
Total	97	73	75	83

TABLE 18.2 The Communist Vote in the First Postwar Elections

Country	Election Year	Percentage of Popular Vote
Austria	1945	5.4
Belgium	1946	12.7
Czechoslovakia	1946	37.9
Denmark	1945	12.5
Finland	1945	23.5
France	1946	26.0
Germany, Federal Republic	1949	5.7
Hungary	1945	16.9
Iceland	1946	19.5
Italy	1946	19.0
Luxemburg	1945	13.5
Netherlands	1946	10.6
Norway	1945	11.9
Sweden	1944	10.3
Switzerland	1947	5.1

Communist parties made universal gains—at their strongest in France, Finland, Iceland, and Italy, while those in Luxemburg, Belgium, Denmark, Norway, and the Netherlands made double figures for the first time (see table 18.2). They were matched by a new Christian Democratic conservatism: the French *Mouvement Républicain Populaire* (MRP), identified with De Gaulle; the Italian Christian Democrats; the Belgian Catholic Party; and the Dutch Catholic People's Party. In the democratic upswing of the Liberation, progressive strands of political Catholicism came to the fore, stressing voluntary service and social solidarism in their approach to the welfare state but also standing tentatively on the new ground of republicanism, democracy, and egalitarianism.[34] Socialist parties also reasserted their presence, including the SFIO, the PSIUP, the Belgian Socialist Party, and the Dutch Labor Party.

When people imagined a different future, what did they see? New constitutions in France (1946), Italy (1947), and West Germany (1949) restored parliamentary democracy, civil rights, and the rule of law, enfanchising women in Italy and France for the first time. They were also republican. In France and West Germany this reaffirmed earlier decisions from 1871 and 1918–19, but Italy required a bitterly fought referendum in June 1946, when republic defeated monarchy by 54.2 to 45.8 percent. These constitutions included decentralization and regional autonomy, progressive taxation, antitrust laws, workers' codetermination, and public ownership. The economic provisions were mainly enabling and in Italy included land reform, which was buried by Christian Democrats after 1947.

Beyond the remaking of democracy, there were three unifying themes: comprehensive social security; abolition of unemployment by rational management and planned modernizing of the economy; and moral renewal, by purging collaborators and the "old gang" from the civil service, judiciary, and economy. This was the program of the French Resistance Council (CNR), which the government of 1945–46 now deployed. It also restored the 40-hour week and union rights, introduced elected works committees for social and cultural activities funded by employers, nationalized banks and basic industries, and created the *Commisariat Général du Plan* under Jean Monnet, with its ten Modernization Commissions. This suggested an emerging corporatism of state, employers, and unions, shadowing the tripartite coalition of PCF, SFIO, and MRP in government. It was paralleled in Belgium, where a National Conference of Labor convened every six months under the prime minister, bringing together employers and unions for corporatively framed welfare reform, including wage restraint matched by food programs and child allowances, public housing, and poverty-related benefits.[35]

The destructive hiatus in governing orders created by Nazi rule, the discrediting of prewar élites, the confused end-of-the-war transitions, and the heady hopes of the Liberation created openings for radical transformation, bringing Europe as close to a revolutionary situation as it had been since 1917–23. Revolutionary uprisings comparable to 1917 or the German and Italian insurgencies of 1918–21 didn't occur, but guerrilla warfare often brought the Left to the threshold of power. This occurred in Yugoslavia, whose liberated territories were revolutionized from the ground up. In contrast, a comparable partisan struggle in Greece ended in an urban insurrection in Athens in December 1944, which failed. In Italy, partisan struggle in the north climaxed in a chain of well-executed uprisings in Genoa, Turin, and Milan on 24–26 April 1945, suggesting the momentum for a seizure of power. How far was this a missed revolutionary opportunity?[36]

ITALIAN COMMUNISM AND THE BOUNDARIES OF CHANGE

In 1944–45, Italian Communists avoided the polarizing maximalism of 1917–20 and upheld the antifascist priority—national unity, winning the war, restoring democracy. For Togliatti, the Bolshevik model was inappropriate, because "the dictatorship of the proletariat" would only fuel anti-Communist anxieties and isolate the party. The priority was a Constituent Assembly to restore democracy. In the spring of 1944, he committed the PCI to the Badoglio government as Communists, Socialists, and Christian Democrats regrouped for a governing coalition. Already, direct democracy was discarded in favor of parliamentary institutions. The idea of an Italian soviet republic was consigned "to history's utopias."[37]

Disavowing revolution involved dismantling local Resistance committees and disarming the partisans. After protesting de Gaulle's dissolution of the Resistance militias in October 1944, the French Communists had accepted this step, rejecting the militias and liberation committees as a potential system of dual power. At its Tenth Congress in June 1945, the PCF backed "a government of broad national and democratic unity," as "the recovery of France cannot be the task of a single party" but "of the whole nation."[38] However, rhetorics of collective sacrifice would stretch only so far in keeping supporters happy. A "neosovietism" at the grassroots, reflecting insurrectionary nostalgia by older cadres and impatient militancy from youth, could easily revive. Tensions between demonstrating the ability to govern, as responsible "statesmen" and true leaders of the nation, and maintaining popular credibility, by sustaining their movement's élan, were the bugbear of Togliatti and Thorez in 1944–47.

The legislative program was meant to service this dialectic. In Italy, the best case of popular mobilization from inside the government was land reform. The PCI agricultural minister, Fausto Gullo, coordinated this with the unified union federation, *Confederazione Generale Italiana del Lavoro* (CGIL), formed in June 1944. At the height of the agitation in 1946, with uncultivated lands being occupied, cooperatives litigating under Gullo's enabling laws, and the CGIL fighting for the rights of wage laborers to contracts, the southern countryside was in uproar. In 1944–49, at least 1,187 cooperatives with a quarter of a million members took over 165,000 hectares of land. Using magistracy and the Mafia, landowners fought back with utmost brutality, as well as with legal obstruction. Cooperatives lacked adequate resources and credit support. Poor peasant employers of casual labor were also threatened by the CGIL's drive for contracts. Nonetheless, the campaign implanted the Left in the southern countryside for the first time, created a political culture of collective action among the peasantry, and gave the PCI a new constituency for the future. It was an extraordinary achievement.

From the larger revolutionary perspective, though, the Italian land agitation was paradigmatic for the PCI's failure, promising a fundamental realignment of Italian society but ending in a readjustment of the old divisions. Togliatti staked everything on the PCI's ability to ensnare the Christian Democrats into progressive democratization, hoping to ratchet structural changes into place, pull left-wing Catholics along, and eventually split the new party. The PCI would rally an ever larger bloc of social forces under its leadership, he hoped. Everything depended on maintaining the Resistance coalition to keep society from repolarizing on the lines of 1917–22. Compromises were needed to hold the Christian Democrats by the national alliance, while ultra-revolutionary hotheads were contained.

The corollary to the national front was the broad social alliance, freeing the Left from its working-class ghetto. In Italy, the peasantry and middle strata were potential allies, including "the intellectuals" in Gramsci's sense, "from the schoolteachers and the priests to the various categories of professional people and to the men of great culture such as poets, artists, scientists, and writers."[39] The PCI's postwar strength in the "red belt" of Emilia, Umbria, and Tuscany, with their variegated rural economies, reflected this broader appeal. For Togliatti, winning such constituencies over was another dimension of conciliating the DC, which contained "a mass of workers, peasants, intellectuals, and young people, who basically share our aspirations because like us they want a democratic and progressive Italy."[40]

Togliatti sought to defuse the power of religion in Italian politics—by neutralizing Catholicism's hostility to the PCI and loosening the Church's resistance to progress. The automatic identity of conservatism and religion needed to be broken—no easy task, given the Left's anti-clerical traditions and the Church's concentrated institutional power. Arguments centered on the Concordat between the Church and Mussolini in 1929, which the papacy wanted in the new Constitution. In March 1947, Togliatti broke ranks in the lay coalition, swinging the PCI behind the Concordat to avoid further polarization. He meant to show the PCI's respect for pluralism; clear the ground for other priorities; and sustain long-term dialogue between Communists and Christians. Bracketing religion as a site of contention was essential in this profoundly Catholic country, he argued. However, a rogue Communist, Giovanni Grilli, tabled a constitutional amendment declaring the family not indissoluble, thereby implying the future possibility of divorce. Despite this breach of discipline, the party joined the rest of the lay Left in voting the amendment through (194 votes to 191).

The PCI settled into the centerground of postwar Italian culture. "To counter the ferocious campaign conducted by Fascism and capitalism against the shaggy Communists with knives in their teeth," one young Communist remembered, "Togliatti wanted to demonstrate conclusively that we were, in fact, a civilized, educated, advanced party."[41] The PCI rallied intellectuals to the Communist cause, launching the journal *Rinascita* in June 1944 and winning impressive support in the universities, press, cinema, and arts. It participated imaginatively in the national public sphere, shaping cultural debate. The systematizing of Gramsci's legacy held a key place in this process, especially the canonizing of his *Prison Notebooks*, the first commentaries from which started appearing in 1946, with a full edition in 1948–51. This claim to moral leadership in the refounding of Italian democracy culturally grounded the PCI's postwar success.

Each of these aims—holding the PCI to its parliamentary course, while deflating insurrectionary desires; balancing the DC coalition with extra-parliamentary pressures for reform; building the broad social alliance in a framework of Communist political culture—required the molding of a new mass party. The PCI's spectacular growth—from barely 5,000 to over 1,750,000 members between mid-1943 and late 1945—made it entirely different from the small and battered cadre party of 10 years before. Italian Communists had always been independent-minded, but two generations were now added, the antifascist Resisters from the war and the influx of 1945.[42] The goal was a Gramscian party, the *Partito nuovo*, able to organize a progressive bloc of Italian society into a counterhegemonic potential. Ancillary organizations were essential for this purpose from the CGIL and the cooperatives and peasants' leagues to the National Association of Ex-Partisans (ANPI) and Union of Italian Women (UDI). Aside from the party sections themselves, the local "Houses of the People" and the annual *feste dell'Unità* were key. "For Every Bell-Tower a Communist Party Branch" was the 1945 slogan.[43]

The ambition to become a genuine national force was crucial to Togliatti's strategy for the PCI.[44] Unlike the case of France, the combined Communist-Socialist vote in 1946 fell short of a majority (39.6 percent), and this precluded greater radicalism. A Communist bid for power could only polarize antifascist forces, negating democratic reconstruction before it even began. The split between north and south was also a problem. In the rural south old political structures perdured, and the Resistance was a purely northern affair. Insurrection could only pit the two regions against each other. The unfinished business of the "southern question" was vital to Togliatti's and Gramsci's reading of Italian history, going back to *l'Ordine nuovo* in 1918–20. The parliamentary strategy was meant to forestall the national paralysis that opened the way for Fascism in 1919–20, while designing a national framework for further Left advance. Here the Allied military presence added a huge constraint. As well as dividing the country, any insurrection would have been suppressed by Allied troops: "A whole generation of militants would have been decimated and the working-class movement put back by many years."[45]

The PCI missed some chances for reform in 1944–47, whether in purging Fascists from the judiciary and civil service, sustaining the land reform, strengthening urban labor, or attacking the power of the Church. But the situation was incredibly finely balanced. Before the April 1948 elections, as Communists were being redemonized as the "enemy within," George F. Kennan urged U.S. Secretary of State George C. Marshall to ban the PCI: "Communists would presumably reply with civil war. . . . This would admittedly result in much violence and probably a military division of Italy; but we are getting very close to the deadline and I think it might be preferable to a bloodless election victory, unopposed by ourselves."[46] This posed the Left's dilemma. It made the practical parameters very stark. The goal could not be a seizure of power, the dictatorship of the proletariat, and socialist construction but only more modest radical gains: confronting the legacy of the Fascist past, constituting the strongest basis for Italian democracy, and creating conditions where the Left's mass party could thrive.[47]

RADICAL DEMOCRACY AND THIRD WAYS

In judging the opportunities for radical change in 1945, historians have used an extremely constricting framework of "revolution" versus "reform." The idea of a missed revolutionary opportunity has focused on a popular uprising, for which the armed militancy of the Italian partisans seemed the best chance. Conversely, reform has been viewed in the most limited way— as parliamentary democracy plus economic planning. But while insurrection was unrealistic in Western European conditions, where the Left was at best a contested majority in a pluralist system protected by British and U.S. military power, the reform model applies the narrowest version of the postwar transition, falling far short of the radical reconstruction the Left was actually pressing. The issue really concerns the intermediate ground, the space between these polar options—the opportunity for radical democratic change, or a "third way."

The Left set the agenda for the coalitions taking office with the Liberation. For all its cautions, the PCI drove Italian democratization forward. If the PCF lost its bid to head the French government, its reform package was also adopted under the tripartite coalition. Social reform, modernization of industry, and strengthening of democracy characterized this program, with mainly foreign policy, especially decolonization, dropping out.[48] When the British Labour Party took office in July 1945, it implemented its program forthwith, including demobilization and full employment; comprehensive social security; family allowances; the National Health Service; expanded secondary education; and extensive nationalization, bringing one-fifth of the economy into public ownership, including the Bank of England, cable and wireless, electricity, gas, civil aviation, road and rail transportation, coal, iron and steel. Again, the deficit was overseas: weak decolonization and relentlessly anti-Communist foreign policy.[49]

So the weakness was less in the Left's legislative agenda than in the form and manner of reconstruction. In Britain, nationalization was adopted at Labour's December 1944 Conference against the leadership by a floor resolution from the left-wing backbencher Ian Mikardo. But the resulting "mixed economy" had little radical about it. In selecting only infrastructural industries for public ownership, "the Government was . . . conducting a socialization of loss, not profit," and the one exception, iron and steel, proved highly contentious.[50] Any self-management or workers' control, or alternatives to capitalism in a systemic sense, were avoided. Levels of compensation were absurdly high. The preferred model of the public corporation substituted one managerial bureaucracy for another, with little change for the workers. As implemented, nationalization gave no leverage for managing the national economy, and no agency was responsible for central or long-range planning.

Thus public ownership lacked strong socialist content: it gave neither impetus for economic planning nor an arena for democratic self-management or social accountability. The Labour Government's main model of reform was paternalistic and bureaucratic. A blend of Fabian administrative progressivism (giving people what was good for them) and authoritarian trade unionism, it had little room for participatory democracy. There were other examples. Housing was British voters' single biggest concern in 1945. Chronic shortages provoked the 1946 squatting campaign, when spontaneous occupations of empty military camps ignited a national movement under the Communist Party's lead. At its peak, some 45,000 people were occupying the camps, with thousands more squatting in empty housing around the country, and direct actions were targeting luxury flats. The CPGB saw this as a chance to revive popular pressure for democracy in peacetime planning, building on its wartime success in mediating between shopfloor militancy and productivity needs in industry.[51] The level of debate about "active citizenship" among Labour-linked intellectuals and policy groups may have been quite rich, but the Labour government per se neglected to build such ideas into its legislation, whether for nationalization, schooling, the National Health Service, or elsewhere.[52]

Participation was the democratic fault-line of the postwar settlements in Western Europe, separating the normalized parliamentary regimes established by 1950 from the new Europe the Resistance movements had imagined. "Politics as usual" resumed after the Liberation, as old leaders returned from exile in Moscow or London, reemerged from prisons and camps, and revived old political habits, including working with those civil servants, judges, managers, and professionals who had collaborated with the wartime regimes. This was a sad contraction of the democratic imagination. Politics were squeezed back into parliamentarist frames; other forms were forgotten.

The PCI was an exception, both in the remarkable energy of the land campaign and in the excitement of building the party, which substituted for power in the nation, for the popular revolution militants were denied. Elsewhere, the mood turned to private desire, as 1945's jubilation gave way to the hard slog of reconstruction, and people reassembled the fragments of interrupted lives—"education, careers, marriage, children, homes."[53] As wartime conditions of austerity, shortages, emergency, and regulation persisted into the peace, the public power seemed ever less susceptible to the popular control that the wartime ethos of common sacrifice had imagined. Withdrawal from politics and "the pursuit of private solutions to public problems" were one result.[54]

This shift reemphasized how fleeting the antifascist opportunity had been. Most of the key changes came in the full flush of Liberation. By the end of 1947, the time had gone. As the French Socialist André Philip predicted: "Everything can be done in the first year following the Liberation. ... What is not done in the first year will never be done, because by then all the old habits will have been resumed."[55] But this presumed new forms of popular participation equivalent to the resistance activity in Nazi-occupied Europe or the production drive on the British home front. This was the practical core of the Communist rhetoric of "new" or "progressive democracy" in 1945. Public ownership without public participation, planning without democracy, and a welfare state without popular accountability would make reform an unfinished thing, bureaucratic and paternalistic superstructures lacking democratic roots.

Disbanding the Resistance organs had been a key defeat. These were the molecular forms of a different course, analogous to the workers' councils that mushroomed across Europe in 1917–21. Both movements aspired to remake society in just and egalitarian ways, organizing food supplies, social administration, and public order in the end-of-the-war emergency, while enlisting ordinary people's energies and skills. But they challenged the authority of existing intitutions as local government and parliaments were restored. As in 1917–21, neither the dominant classes nor the moderate Left—nor the Damocletian presence of Allied military power—could accept a system of dual power, and so the Resistance committees were demobilized preemptively, with the acquiescence of Communist and other Left leaderships, before any protorevolutionary challenge could arise. The chance for creative intermediate solutions was lost—for harnessing the energy, idealism, and commitment of the people-in-motion, by building new participatory forms into the emerging constitutional settlement, bridging the gap between national arenas and the local everyday.

The fate of German *Antifas* was sadly paradigmatic. As the Allies advanced into Germany, local "Anti-Fascist Committees" formed in the empty space left by the collapsing public authority, usually organized by reemerging Communists and Social Democrats. Disarming local Nazis, providing improvised shelter for refugees and homeless, and organizing supplies of food, fuel, and clothing, such Antifas offered themselves as the potential building blocks for the coming democratic Germany. Tenuous democratic manifestations in a society comprehensively disorganized in its older associational culture by 12 years of fascism, they were the available indigenous basis for redemocratizing German society from the ground up. Yet they were peremptorily brushed aside by the Allies, who preferred the respectable scions of some notional pre-Nazi bourgeois society in the western zones and the returning Communist cadres in the east.[56]

Despite the missed chances, the collapse of antifascist consensus, and the narrowing of vision, postwar Europe was still a happier and more democratic place than before. Even in the east, the reconfiguring of social chances, the provision of welfare-state securities, and the very removal of the Nazi occupation profoundly changed conditions of life, despite the brutal conformities Stalinism was about to impose. Less tangibly, the Left had come in from the cold, welding its traditional advocacy of working-class rights to the patriotics of popular citizenship in an unparalleled national emergency, acquiring new legitimacy, and claiming its place in the nation. The exigencies of the antifascist Resistance compelled liberals, conservatives, and the dominant classes to acknowledge the patriotism of those previously stigmatized as traitors. Whatever the rollback effected by the Cold War, which banished Communists rudely back to the margins, this common occupancy of the national ground, secured by the antifascist legacy, was a lasting transformation. The discursive unity of democracy, socialism, and the nation was a recurring refrain. In February 1944, the Resistance movement *Défense de la France* summarized its aspirations in a letter to de Gaulle as "the idea of the Republic, the idea of Socialism, and the Idea of the Nation."[57]

The antifascist war had lasting cultural effects. People's hopes for a better world—and their knowledge of survival's fragilities—filled the political space of the nation, rhetorically and emotionally, displacing other conflicts and powerfully relativizing social distinctions, economic inequalities, and the divisiveness of political life. The longer-term cultural aspect of the postwar settlement cemented its strength—the fields of popular political identification wartime experiences brought into being, the ways these became linked to a postwar system of politics, the legitimation they gave postwar states, and the supports they delivered for one kind of politics as against another. The cohesion in postwar society depended crucially on the loyalties forged in popular memory to national political institutions. Here, the enduring cultural narratives of the postwar settlement became key.

The catastrophic nature of the Second World War was vital. The scale of the fighting, the massive demands of states on their societies, the unparalleled mobilizations involved in conscript armies and on the home fronts, the extraordinary numbers of casualties, and the pervasiveness of violence and death—all these gave postwar electorates a new grasp of just how far governments were able to go. This worked powerfully with the grain of another popular memory store, focused on the shame of the 1930s—the misery of mass unemployment, the ineffectiveness of earlier governments, and the discrediting of old élites, based on their failure before the rise of fascism and their subsequent collaboration with the Nazi occupiers. This potent brew energized popular expectations after 1945 behind a vision of reconstruction containing strong ideals of democratic citizenship, egalitarianism, and social justice. Tragically, the rapid reprocessing of those desires under the impact of the Cold War quickly reduced the more radical possibilities. But powerful traces of the popular script still survived, embedded in a broad consensus of the collective good—certain default assumptions about what the state could be expected to provide, and popular confidence in the efficacy of governance, especially via the welfare state.

Chapter 19

Closure

Stalinism, Welfare

Capitalism, and Cold

War, 1945–1956

DESPITE TENSIONS AMONG Britain, the United States, and the USSR, compounded when France joined occupied Germany's Allied Control Council, there was no open conflict in the summer of 1945.[1] There was no formal division of Europe and no assumption that the east would pass under Soviet rule. The Potsdam Summit of 17 July–2 August 1945 opened no fissures in the antifascist alliance. Straight lines linked the Atlantic Charter of August 1941 through the Yalta Declaration on Liberated Territories of February 1945 to the postwar coalition governments. The mood seemed further confirmed by the 50-nation conference that launched the United Nations Charter on 26 June 1945.

Trouble began outside Europe in the colonial world. After September 1945, Britain restored French colonialism in Indo-China, despite the declaration of Vietnamese independence by Ho Chi Minh, the Communist leader of the anti-Japanese resistance. Similar conflicts followed in the future Indonesia, the Philippines, and Malaysia, while in China civil war resumed between Communists and Chiang Kai-Shek's Nationalist government. The biggest test in Europe came in Greece, where the right-wing government was terrorizing the Left: the local Communist party boycotted corrupt elections, and civil war began in October 1946.

By early 1946 the collaborative atmosphere was evaporating. On 5 March, Churchill delivered a speech in Fulton, Missouri, denouncing Soviet power: "From Stettin on the Baltic to Trieste in the Adriatic, an iron curtain has descended across the Continent. Behind that line lie all the capitals of the ancient states of Central and Eastern Europe."[2] During the next year this story acquired specificity. In January 1947, manifestly rigged Polish elections gave Communists 80.1 percent of the vote and the opposition Peasants Party only 10.3. After Britain ceased financing anti-Communist governments in Turkey and Greece, President Truman asked Congress for funds on 12 March 1947 for that purpose, declaring a global struggle of totalitarianism and freedom. Rhetorics of postwar reconstruction were transmuting into Communist "containment." For Dean Acheson, the U.S. undersecretary of state, this was "Armageddon":

> "Soviet pressure on the Straits, on Iran, and on northern Greece had brought the Balkans to a point where a highly possible Soviet breakthrough might open three continents to Soviet penetration. Like apples in a barrel infected by one rotten one, the corruption of Greece would infect Iran and all to the East. It would also carry infection to Africa through Asia Minor and Egypt, and to Europe through Italy and France. . . . The Soviet Union was playing one of the greatest gambles in history at minimal cost. We and we alone were in a position to break up the play."[3]

In June 1947, Truman's containment doctrine was joined by the Marshall Plan, an ambitious proposal providing economic aid for Europe. By September 1947 sixteen countries were enrolled in the Organization of European Economic Cooperation (OEEC) in Paris, and during 1948–52 the resulting European Recovery Program (ERP) disbursed 13 billion dollars in cash and essential supplies.[4] Even before Marshall Aid, however, dollars were pumped into France and Italy for political "stabilization" against the Left, while a 1945 loan to Britain already carried political conditions. Moreover, by releasing pressure on domestic consumption, Marshall Aid preempted radicalizations to the Left. This anti-Communist calculation made the Truman Doctrine and Marshall Aid two sides of the same coin. In Truman's words, the latter "helped save Europe from economic disaster and lifted it from the shadow of enslavement by Russian Communism."[5]

European polarization proceeded apace. The French, Italian, and Belgian CPs were expelled from government in May 1947. In September 1947, Stalin launched the Cominform (Communist Information Bureau) at a conference in Poland of ruling CPs plus those of Italy and France. Designed to solidify the Eastern Bloc, it signaled the end of Stalin's tolerance for Western Communist "national roads," substituting the uniform "Two Camps" line of Andrei Alexandrovich Zhdanov, his ascendant lieutenant. Conformities were toughened in Eastern Europe, most dramatically through the Czechoslovak Revolution of 19–25 February 1948. When the western Allies presaged the West German state via currency reform in June 1948, the USSR retaliated by blockading Berlin, a move defeated by the famous airlift. In 1949, the division of Germany into East and West became fixed, symbolizing the larger division of Europe and indeed the world.

The weaving of world events into a single story of global confrontation marked these years. In Asia the anticolonial revolts had mixed results. The proclamation of the Chinese People's Republic on 21 September 1949 gave them a massive boost, but if antiimperialist movements succeeded in Indonesia and Burma, elsewhere they were either bloodily suppressed or entered generations-long wars of liberation. The Korean War (1950–53), a major turning point, impelled the full-scale remilitarizing of Europe. Back in Europe, the Greek Communists, abandoned by Stalin, lost their Civil War during 1948, while the United States poured resources into the bitterly fought April elections in Italy, bringing Christian Democrats to victory over the Communist-Socialist Left. In Eastern Europe, Stalin imposed brutal uniformity, symbolized in the expulsion of Tito's Yugoslavia from Cominform in June 1948 for refusing that discipline. The binding of the two camps ensued.

Postwar politics were under massive constraint. After antifascism had eased the Left's western acceptance, the Cold War removed it again, returning left-wing socialists and Communists to the margins. Western foreign policies shaped a mood of conformist repression, demonizing Communism as the USSR's political tool and the source of unfreedom, identifying radicalism with national disloyalty and the enemy within. In the East, this tightening of hostility was worse, as the People's Democracies descended into conspiracy paranoias and brutal pathologies of control and terror. But on both sides the Cold War became a new system of disciplinary power, limiting what could be said and thought. The Cold War decisively shaped possible agendas from the late 1940s to the late 1960s, with profound consequences down to the present.[6]

MAKING DEMOCRACY SAFE FOR CAPITALISM

In 1943–47, between the battle of Stalingrad and the expulsion of Communists from the French and Italian governments, the momentum of the antifascist war worked strongly for the Left and the promise of socialist-driven democracy. After 1947, the Cold War militated as powerfully against the democratic agendas of the Resistance coalitions, foreclosing possibilities rather than opening them up, dampening rather than energizing the desire for change. This containment—the reconstituting of prewar political boundaries, the fettering of democratic imagination—marked the closure of the postwar settlement and the hopes it inspired.

Theaters of conflict persisted in Greece and Italy, while Spain and Portugal remained mired in fascist repression. But in the north and west—Scandinavia, the Low Countries, Britain, even France—anti-Communism became subsumed in the economics of reconstruction. Marshall Aid was both the gift that put Europe "back on its feet" and the cynical instrument of U.S. power, a potent unity of moralizing and self-interest. Capitalism—as economic recovery and eventual prosperity—would lay democracy's foundations, overcoming wartime destruction and the radical threat of the Left; democracy would be made safe for capitalism, blocking more radical hopes. This unity of capitalism and democracy, interest and altruism, was the Marshall Plan's defining aim.[7]

A multilateral trading order would secure Europe's social peace while guaranteeing U.S. economic growth. This vision included a revived West German economy, whose political effects Western European cooperation would then contain. Britain was originally to broker this process, but when the Labour Government retreated from Europeanism, France assumed that role. Aside from the capital inflows for economic recovery, therefore, Marshall Aid shaped the political framework of the postwar settlement in Western Europe, pioneering transnational integration from the Schuman Plan to the Treaties of Rome, complemented by NATO.[8] Domestically, it promoted corporatist cooperation among business, agriculture, unions, professions, and the state. Socially, it was meant to "underwrite industrial modernization projects, promote Keynesian strategies of aggregate economic management, overhaul antiquated systems of public administration, and encourage progressive tax policies, low-cost housing programs, and other measures of economic and social reform."[9] This seamless package wasn't introduced into a vacuum, however. Western Europe was governed not just by the modernizing architects of a multilateral trading order and its social supports but also by social democratic, liberal and Christian reformers, flanked by Communists and other radicals. Measured against these radical hopes for reconstruction, the significance of the Marshall Plan's reformist ambition greatly recedes.

Faced with Western Europe's fast-moving openness in 1945–46, U.S. policy applied the brakes to reform rather than driving it along. Indeed, Marshall Aid was the political leverage for a new postwar pattern, conjoining intimately with anti-Communism to inaugurate the Cold War and thereby negating its own reformist wish. Anti-Communism encouraged alignments with European society's most reactionary sectors, squeezing the room for reformist experiments to virtually nothing. In Greece, for example, it was precisely the moderate social democratic option that was immediately scotched. After the Civil War, Greek peasants and workers bore the costs not only of brutal right-wing repression but also of economic policies perpetuating their poverty. Western aid coalesced with the reactionary effects of anti-Communism to impose a long-term frame of dependency onto Greek society. There, U.S. policy was primarily anti-Communist, undermining whatever reformist agenda Marshall Aid professed.[10]

The crucible of postwar societal conflict, Italy was an excellent laboratory for the Marshall vision: Italian labor should trade its militancy for higher wages and increased productivity, backed by a package of social reforms and higher social spending. But this required utterly reshaping an Italian labor movement backed by Communists, Socialists, and radical Catholics, freshly unified by antifascism. The anti-Communist imperative took over. The U.S. aid was crudely applied to splitting the CGIL, whose freshly minted unity in June 1944 eloquently expressed the wartime solidarities. Right-wing forces in Italy itself were anxious to neutralize the PCI, but excluding the Communists from the antifascist coalition was unimaginable without massive U.S. support, and Marshall Aid provided that leverage. Between the PCI's expulsion from government in May 1947 and the splitting of the CGIL after the general strike of July 1948, the United States completely realized its goal.[11]

What exactly was won? The U.S. policy entailed reviving conservative authority, including the Church's societal power, and breaking the labor movement's unity. It meant a repressive system of labor relations: from 1948 to 1955, productivity rose 100 percent in Italy, while wages rose only 6 percent. PCI voters, between a fifth and a third of the national electorate, were permanently excluded from the polity. This was no unfortunate side effect of Marshall aid or an unforeseen hijacking by "traditional" Italian interests. It was the express purpose of the Plan: "With the ascendancy of anti-Communism over reform, Italian industry was able to pursue untroubled an economic policy based on low internal consumption, low wages, and authoritarian industrial relations."[12] As the war ended, Italian society displayed the most impressive democratic mobilization in Western Europe. By the 1950s, however, "the Italian labor movement was among the weakest in Europe."[13]

The Cold War's effects were also clear in Britain, where Labour's post-1945 mandate was huge, untrammeled by coalitions. A key figure was the foreign secretary, Ernest Bevin, fresh from the wartime Ministry of Labour, with a militant but right-wing trade union history. Incorrigibly authoritarian and antiintellectual to a fault, Bevin was the archetypal labor bureaucrat, crudely hostile to rank-and-file activists and socialist thinkers alike, belligerently intolerant of democracy, whether on the shopfloor, in the general meeting, or in the committee room, let alone on the streets. Beside Prime Minister Clement Atlee, Bevin was the government's dominant personality and brooked no criticism, bullying parliamentary critics into acquiescence and overriding his cabinet colleagues. He subscribed wholly to the "official" Foreign Office view of British policy—preserving Britain's role as a great power, within some adjusted version of the imperial world role and an independent nuclear capability—in full continuity with the Churchillian policies that came before. This included the "special relationship" with the United States, axiomatic anti-Communism, and extreme anti-Soviet animus.[14]

Labour's defense of Britain's military obligations had dire fiscal effects. After 1947, the Atlee government abandoned social projects, opting instead "to end controls of the economy and to augment private capital by limiting increases in working-class living standards and restraining social spending."[15] Marshall Aid vitally helped, allowing high military spending without squeezing living standards more tightly. Again, the nexus of postwar economics, international Cold War, and anti-Communism decided how the boundaries of politics could be drawn. Across Europe and indeed the world, the rhetoric of the Soviet menace disguised local histories of exploitation and destroyed experiments in self-determination and democracy. Revolutionary conflicts in places like Greece, Southeast Asia, and Iran were never simply the by-products of great power rivalries or of opposing "free-world" and Communist principles but movements in their own right. It was this world of plural histories that the Cold War now suppressed.[16]

By wielding economic aid so ruthlessly to block radical options, U.S. policy-makers ensured that non-Communist reformers—the Socialists and social democrats, liberal intellectuals and radical Christians they wanted to bribe and cajole from Communist cooperation—were left with no effective choice.

> By transforming European economic conditions, the [Marshall Plan] not only reversed collectivist trends but also the political conditions that granted respectability to Communists. . . . But that Plan was not a non-political aid package; it was a cornerstone of the containment doctrine and had a major political aim: to isolate the Soviet Union and European Communist Parties. This goal succeeded, forcing the blame for rejecting aid onto the Soviets and thereby securing a great propaganda victory.[17]

PROSPECTS OF DEMOCRACY IN EASTERN EUROPE

International constraints for the Left were especially clear in Eastern Europe. Nazism in the east had been immeasurably more brutal, obliterating sovereignties in favor of a racialized New Order. The scale of destruction was truly staggering, imposing a common experience of military repression, ruthless exploitation, forced labor, mass deportations, and genocide. Europe's Jews, concentrated by deportation and the "Final Solution" in Eastern Europe, were decimated, as were Sinti and Roma. Six million Poles died, or one-fifth of prewar population. The migrations at war's end were huge: 12.3 million Germans moved west from East Prussia, Poland, Czechoslovakia, and the dispersed outposts of Nazi rule; 4.5 million Poles and 1.9 million Czechs took their place; 2.3 million Russians moved west into the Soviet Union's newly annexed territories; and millions of displaced persons were stranded amid the ruins of the Third Reich.[18]

These two experiences—Nazism's destructive ferocity and the astonishing mobility of massed populations, as armies, prisoners, deportees, forced laborers, and refugees roamed across Eastern Europe's brutalized landscape—were crucial to postwar circumstances. Civil society's prewar fabric was shredded. The predictabilities on which the multinational coexistence of Eastern Europe's peoples depended were smashed. The churches, landowning society, and the professions were discredited by Nazi collaboration. Even without the Red Army, whose presence overshadowed Eastern European reconstruction, this vacuum powerfully pulled in the energy and ambition of the Communists, who had few scruples in rising to the challenge.

In 1945 there was still room for indigenous Eastern European Lefts to maneuver. They did so within broadly common circumstances.[19] The region's economies were underdeveloped, with a catastrophically war-damaged infrastructure. Industrializing would be painful no matter what, and the Soviet model of revolution from above, which prioritized heavy industry and capital goods, meant big consumer sacrifices. This decisively separated the East from Britain, France, and northern Europe, while revealing Marshall Aid's Western premises, which linked industrial modernizing to consumption. The lack of a Soviet equivalent gave Eastern European economies huge handicaps, particularly as Stalin took a crudely self-interested view, ransacking former enemy economies in Hungary, Romania, Bulgaria, and the Soviet zone of Germany and binding the region into dependency. Another priority for such overwhelmingly peasant countries was land reform to replace neofeudal estates with cooperatives and family farms, but after an early interlude the Soviet model of collectivization bluntly took over.

Throughout Eastern Europe, recent political experience was overwhelmingly one of dictatorship. Self-governing institutions were either suspended between the wars or terminated by Nazism. Repression, imprisonment, exile, and resistance had also decimated generations of Leftists, as had the Soviet purges, which depleted foreign CPs no less than the Communionist Party of the Soviet Union (CPSU), especially those of Hungary, Poland, and Yugoslavia. Here, Resistance and Liberation brought extensive new recruits, however, plus broader popular constituencies, particularly once people began seeing the future and protecting themselves opportunistically for the new postwar situation. Politically, reconstruction required capitalizing on this antifascist momentum—isolating reactionaries and fascist collaborators, building grassroots participation, and strengthening social linkages across the working class, peasantry, and intelligentsia.

In pursuing such aims, Eastern European Lefts were well positioned. The region's emergent pattern—coalitions of national unity creating "people's democracies"—was guaranteed by the Red Army, whose presence precluded Western scenarios of conservative restoration at Left expense. On the other hand, Soviet security interests were narrow and indifferent to socialism per se. The Soviet model of command economy and single-party rule meant "socialism" only in an impoverished technical sense, purged of democracy. Since 1925, the USSR had cumulatively lost its socialist name. By 1935–38 at the latest, democracy was also gone from the CPSU, the Soviet state, the economy, organized social life, and everyday transactions, replaced by bureaucracy and police coercion. As Spain revealed, Soviet policy had ceased backing revolution elsewhere, hijacking Europe's Lefts for its own great-power goals. On the other hand, Soviet structural changes did promote socialist economics, if only negatively by destroying capitalism. Public languages also remained socialist, however crude the Marxism, allowing some space for future socialist revival. Moreover, socialist values in the USSR might still be renewed via political struggles for democracy.

Initially, Soviet dominance in Eastern Europe varied. The slogan of "national roads to socialism" already characterized Communist policy in Western Europe in 1945, and from the summer of 1946 until late 1947 applied in the East too.[20] The actuality of "national roads" varied. Elections ranged from thoroughly corrupt in Poland to genuinely free in Czechoslovakia.[21] Aside from attacking Nazi collaborators, Communists moved earliest against their strongest rivals, typically the peasant-based parties, either by coopting them into governments or treating them as enemy magnets.[22] After 1945–46, genuine pluralism became rare. Typically, Communists took key ministries like transportation and the interior, controlling mobility and public space while dominating economic planning. Precise rhythms varied, but CPs throughout Eastern Europe secured their rule during 1947–48 with a single-mindedness belying the rhetorics of people's democracy and national roads. The Hungarian Communist leader Mátyás Rákosi's "salami tactics," cutting the ground out from under the opposition piece by piece, was the reality behind the pluralist claims.[23]

Communist-Socialist relations were central. Peasant parties proved indecisive, and "third way" proponents like the Hungarian populists Gyula Illyes and István Bibó managed nothing comparable to the strategies of Communist and Socialist planners. Once Cold War raised the stakes in the spring of 1947, Communists outmaneuvered their rivals, but social democrats backed the radicalizations too. Ensuring regime survival moved many non-Communists, who remembered the disasters of 1918–20 and 1933–34. Breaking through to socialism was a compelling goal, especially under rising international pressure and anxieties about right-wing plots and economic destabilization. Joining with Communists for a practical socialist agenda, when history seemed about to close the door, became a credible choice. The Hungarian left Social Democrat György Marosán was one who took it. Well aware of Stalinism, he weighed the danger from the Right and cast his lot with Rákosi's government in 1948 as minister of light industry. He then lived the consequences, disappearing in the purges in August 1950 and resurfacing in 1956 to reform the regime that had earlier destroyed his career.[24]

In sum, the chances for Eastern European democracy were fragile and brief. Even allowing for the handicaps of backwardness, the wreckage of fascism, and the impact of Cold War, Stalinism—as Soviet influence and local practice—proved insurmountable. The region's economic underendowment was compounded by Soviet exploitation and the East's exclusion from Marshall Aid. Stricter Soviet control after spring 1947 ended the "national roads." Tightening conformities—via rigidly centralist states, excluding non-Communists from office, restaffing state positions, converting to single-party government, withholding civil liberties and constitutional guarantees, and obedience to the USSR—deprived People's Democracies of their popular support. Centralized control through ministries of the interior (with police machines shaped by Soviet security "advisers") not only destroyed potentials for democratic political culture of the masses but also liquidated the Communist parties themselves as creative organs. The appalling purges of 1948–52 decimated the region's CPs just as they emerged from the isolation of the Resistance.

STALINIZING THE PEOPLE'S DEMOCRACIES

Until 1947, futures remained relatively open. Sometimes, strategic security needs and weak CPs led to Soviet control directly, concentrating power quickly around the CP, as in Poland, Romania, and Bulgaria. Elsewhere, Communists took key ministries (interior, police and security, justice, propaganda and information, transportation), while proving more cautious on the economy than their socialist rivals. But before the spring of 1947, national roads—parliamentary democracy, national autonomy, and gradual transition—still held sway. As the Hungarian Communist Bela Szasz later reflected, "the general opinion in Hungary, and not only in Communist circles, was that the way of Hungary could not be the way of Russia. You see, it was a different country with different traditions and different people."[25]

What changed? The Cold War simply pulled the rug from under democratic initiatives. A relentless sequence of events in 1947—the Truman Doctrine, the expulsion of the PCF and the PCI, the Marshall Plan, the founding of Cominform—irrevocably changed the scene. After the national roads strategy failed in the West, Stalin prioritized Communist conformity for the East. Even then, Czechoslovak Communists defended their approach. Gottwald sought Marshall Aid by hoping to join the ERP, but Stalin's veto stopped him in July. The absence of positive signals from the United States, contextualized by Britain's abandonment of Czechoslovakia in 1938 and disregard for the exiled government during the war, then further demoralized the non-Communist members of the coalition.[26] The launching of Cominform—the Information Bureau of Communist and

Workers Parties—at Szkalarska Probea in Poland in September 1947 was the *coup de grace.*

Cominform's contrast with Comintern starkly defined the international movement. The meeting was small, with two delegates each from Poland, Romania, Bulgaria, Hungary, Czechoslovakia, Yugoslavia, Italy, and France. The Soviet spokesmen, Andrei Zhdanov and Georgii Malenkov, presided. Key notables—Tito, Togliatti, Thorez, Dimitrov, Gottwald, Rákosi, all general secretaries of their parties—were missing. The East Germans and Albanians were also absent. The meeting was no proud display of revolutionary strength. The Greek CP was not invited, nor was the Spanish, an emblematic late Comintern party, nor the Finnish, which was particularly strong. There was no nod to colonial liberation. The referents were Eurocentric in the extreme. The purpose was loyalty to Soviet foreign policy.[27]

The world was redivided into two camps. Ranks were closed: People's Democracies became Communist regimes; nongoverning CPs led resistance to Americanization in the West. Instant casualties were "national roads," with the PCI and PCF berated for compromising with parliamentary democracy and conciliating Catholics. The immediate effect was confrontation with non-Communists and the launching of a second phase of Soviet power, that of Stalinization proper from mid-1947 to late 1948. In the accompanying radicalization, vanguardism revived. Third Period Comintern veterans returned, their instincts hardwired to Bolshevism. Dramatized by the February 1948 revolution in Czechoslovakia and replicated elsewhere, anti-Communist newspapers were shut down and the rest purged.[28] Civil society—universities, professional associations, publishers, sports clubs, the church—was attacked, as were the civil service and army. Surviving parties became mere shells, while Social Democrats forcibly merged with the CPs. Collectivization of agriculture began and nationalization was completed, climaxing in multiyear plans, that coordinated the Eastern European economies with the USSR.[29]

The Tito split began Stalinization's final phase, from the summer of 1948 to Stalin's death in 1953. Stalin was furious at the revolutionary independence of the Yugoslav party (KPJ). After 1945, that party championed dictatorship of the proletariat against parliamentary roads, affirming international revolution and backing the Greek Communists, while Stalin kept his wartime agreement with Churchill for noninterference. At Cominform's launch, Stalin used the KPJ to berate the other CPs into line, but now Tito detected a similar move against himself. Tensions crackled at a consultation of Soviet, Yugoslav, and Bulgarian parties in Moscow in February 1948, when Stalin accused Tito of creating an alternative Communist center. Stalin recalled Soviet advisers in March, denouncing Yugoslav deviations. When the KPJ defended itself, Stalin expelled Tito's party from Cominform, exploiting this for a monolithic display of loyalism. The international movement was wheeled into action, orchestrated into a chorus of anti-Tito abuse.[30]

The impoverished tones of anti-Tito polemics were dreadful. The initial attacks were straightforward, focusing on KPJ deviations from Soviet policy. They soon turned worse: Tito and his comrades were nationalists, Trotskyists, "dubious Marxists," "murderers and spies," a criminal clique, counterrevolutionaries, fascists.[31] Condemning Tito became the litmus test of Communist loyalty. James Klugman for example, a sophisticated CPGB intellectual who had fought with KPJ Partisans during the war, now had to denounce his comrades. His book-length diatribe, *From Trotsky to Tito* (1951), was a disgraceful betrayal and a traducement of ethics, an index of Cold War polarization and the extreme choices Communists now faced. It was an excruciating test of Klugman's "faith in Communism, of his intellectual integrity, of his moral courage. He chose, what certainly could not have been the easy way, to prove himself a steadfast Communist by denouncing the object of his past ardor."[32]

Eastern European stakes were deadly.[33] Vladislav Gomulka was the first to be disgraced, removed as Polish party chief in September 1948 and then imprisoned. Enver Hoxha's pro-Tito rival Koçi Xoxe was expelled from the Albanian party in November 1948, tried in May, and executed in June. Trajco Kostov, leader of the Bulgarian Communists' wartime underground, was dismissed from all offices in March 1949, arrested in June, and tried and executed in December. László Rajk, head of the Hungarian wartime underground, deputy leader, and interior minister, was arrested in June 1949, tried in September, and executed in October. These were show trials, with "the usual implausibility, mendacity, paranoia and degradation of such affairs." The accused recited formulaic scripts of conspiracies, treason, and service to U.S. imperialism and Tito. Hungary's purges were ferocious: 2,000 Communists executed, 150,000 imprisoned, 350,000 expelled from the party. "Rákosi killed more Communists in five years than Horthy had in twenty-five, and the entire society was cowed into a condition of bewilderment and terror."[34]

As this Stalinist juggernaut gathered momentum, KSC leaders came under immense pressure to follow suit. They tightened party discipline after the Tito split but resisted general hysteria. On the eve of the Rajk trial, Rákosi demanded Gottwald's support, and Soviet security experts arrived in September 1949 to hunt the "Czechoslovak Rajk," ratcheting up the paranoia. New sweeps began, aimed at the pre-1948 coalition parties and the church, leading to trials in 1950. "Slovak bourgeois nationalists" were attacked next, taking investigations into the CP's heart. One case centered on Foreign Minister Vladimir Clementis, but this was trumped in October 1950 by the arrest of Otto Sling, the Brno regional party secretary, whose connections rationalized a huge operation. The self-cannibalizing of the party reached the general-secretary himself, Rudolf Slansky, who was arrested in November 1951. The "Czechoslovak Rajk" was found. The trial arraigned 14 codefendants, the KSC's cream, in November 1952; 11 were hanged, three imprisoned for life.[35]

What did this extraordinary bloodletting mean, in which Communists turned state terror against themselves? The Tito split is the best clue. Tito was actively pursuing Balkan and Eastern European confederation. This was an old Comintern idea of the 1920s, with obvious virtues of economic integration, given the region's backwardness. Dimitrov had floated a general confederation of the People's Democracies and Greece, where civil war was approaching its climax: "When the question [of a federation] matures, and it must inevitably mature, then our peoples, the nations of people's democracy, Romania, Bulgaria, Yugoslavia, Albania, Czechoslovakia, Poland, Hungary and Greece—mind you, and Greece!—will settle it. It is they who will decide what it shall be . . . and when and how it will be formed."[36] Stalin nipped this in the bud. Imposing Stalinism per se—rigid top-down centralism, systematic surveillance, bureaucratic conformity, disciplined obedience to the line, and unquestioning belief in Soviet infallibility—was the purpose of the purges.

The key was the attack on "National Communists" or "local undergrounders," like Rajk in Hungary, Gomulka in Poland, or Kostov in Bulgaria, whose Resistance backgrounds separated them from Moscow exiles. For Stalin, "cosmopolitanism" or western links made a broader cohort of "outsiders" automatically suspect—ex–Social Democrats and unaffiliated leftists, International Brigaders from Spain, Jewish intellectuals, exiles from London as against Moscow. The exact victims varied across countries. Earlier drives in Poland, Albania, and Bulgaria were accomplished with less bloodletting, targeting leading figures and immediate allies. Hungary brought the larger scale. Then, the Czechoslovak scenario spiralled wildly out of control, because techniques were perfected, the KSC was especially strong, and the country's frontline status magnified the paranoia.

This sad and sordid story had many terrible parts. Contempt for legality, democracy, political ethics, and socialism's best traditions mocked Communism's progressive claims. The purges were a shocking indictment of Soviet policies and the Communists who went along. The descent from the Liberation of 1945 into the brutalized passivity of the early 1950s wrought a violence to the socialist idea from which it never recovered. Communism's best achievements—service in Spain, anti-Nazi solidarity with peoples of the West, the free-ranging internationalism of the Popular Front era, generous identification with the progressive goods of European culture, and of course the democratic pluralism of the Czechoslovak national road—became prima facie evidence of crimes. Jewish suffering in concentration camps was converted into anti-Semitic denunciation. On first encountering his "Teachers" (Soviet interrogators), Eugen Loebl faced "a long tirade against the Jews that would have done honor to any Gestapo man." Anti-Semitism, recoded as anti-Zionism, permeated the Slansky trial, where 11 of the 14 accused were Jews.[37] This was the degrading paradox of the entire process: the best Communist virtues were redefined as betrayal. "The worst, perhaps, was the knowledge that one was the victim of one's own Party, for which one had lived and given everything."[38]

The Slansky trial was the last, loathsome act in the Stalinizing of Eastern Europe, a brutal and hardfaced normalizing of 1945, when Liberation from Nazism promised not only social transformation but new measures of democracy and well-being. Power was now centralized in the party-state's inner leadership, with no constitutional checks or legal opposition, a supine press and an administered public sphere, and a local political life frozen into paranoid conformity, whether inside the party or out. Communist parties had their long-heralded dominance in the working class but only as a sterile administrative consummation in which compulsory mergers with the socialists were an early step: Romania in February 1948, Hungary and Czechoslovakia in June, Bulgaria in August, Poland in December.

The Eastern European CPs were Stalinism's real casualties. In aggregate, an estimated 2.5 million people, or a quarter of total membership, were expelled between 1948 and 1952, with perhaps a quarter of a million imprisoned. These parties were destroyed as creative movements and in the process totally remade. This had a sociological dimension: in Czechoslovakia "between 1948 and 1953 an estimated 200,000 to 400,000 workers were promoted from the shopfloor into state administration: in the economy, but more particularly in the army and the police." Conversely, "in 1951 alone the authorities fired some 77,000 intellectuals who were 'recycled' into the industrial sector."[39] Thus in one way, the working class had its social revolution. But Stalinization descended onto Eastern Europe as a political counterrevolution. If the Marshall Plan made democracy safe for capitalism, then Soviet policy in Eastern Europe made socialism safe for Stalin.

PATTERNS OF WESTERN EUROPEAN REFORM

In East and West, the Cold War closed down the radical openings of 1945. But if the sharpening of international tensions in 1947 began a conservative resurgence in Western Europe, the conservatism emerging from the 1940s was still different from the one before the war. In contrast to the settlements of 1918–19, whose democracy proved unstable and was reversed, the democratic gains of 1945 endured. Besides new constitutions and the enfranchisement of women, these new settlements included nationalization and public ownership, organized around mixed economies and central planning, linked to strong welfare states and an active labor policy. European integration also moved forward, initiated through Marshall Aid, reinforced by the division of Europe and NATO, and continuing via the Council of Europe and Franco-German economic cooperation.[40]

Collectivism, as a complex amalgam of patriotism, public responsibilities, and public goods, defined this mood. Above all, labor movements became integrated into the state's active life through union recognition, free collective bargaining, and expanded civil liberties, which now joined the entailments of citizenship in Western Europe for the first time. Not only had the labor movements moved to the polity's center, but labor itself was a social good. The postwar settlement transitioned from liberal democratic ideals of 1789, which saw political rights as sufficient guarantees of freedom, toward social democracy and rights in the socioeconomic sphere.

Social citizenship was a decisive breakthrough. A political abstraction from wartime collectivism, this also drew on Christian ideals of social duty and the humanistic liberalism of many social policy professionals appalled by the depression.[41] In Britain, the practical egalitarianism of "everyone pulling together" was integral to the public rhetorics of the war itself, while in continental Europe such ideas formed in the planning circles of Resistance and exile. If the people were to exercise their democracy effectively, it was argued, minimum standards of living were needed. Otherwise, social inequalities undermined citizenship in the vote. Political rights needed complementing with social rights too—rights to jobs, unemployment and sickness insurance, old age pensions, universal health care, decent housing, equal educational chances, a minimum wage. These longstanding demands of European labor movements now became general entitlements via postwar reconstruction and remained so until the mid-1970s.

Women were central to the welfare state—as objects of policy, as subjects of the new socially inflected citizenship talk, as addressees of political campaigns. Women finally had the vote in France, Italy, and Belgium, regaining rights interrupted by fascism elsewhere, for only in Scandinavia and Britain did female suffrage exist continuously after 1918. Women's wartime mobilization also raised expectations of equality, although once again the resulting citizenship claims centered around maternity. The pressure of returning soldiers for jobs, unions' defense of the gender bar, deep prejudices about women's place, desires to rebuild society on the "healthy" basis of a reassembled familialism—all these factors remasculinized the world of work and the public sphere, ascribing women to family. In fact, female employment still rose, and women didn't simply return to the home. But the public languages imagined they did. Women participated in the postwar romance of democracy but on terms already familiar from the post-1918 maternalist gender regimes.[42]

This was an obvious front of normalization. Catholic Europe used familial rhetorics of the most reactionary kind. For the Italian Christian Democrats (DC), family was the battle site for reviving the nation after Fascism and defending it against Communism, a "fortress" of true values. For the

West German Christian Democratic Union (CDU), "restoring" the family was also key, reaffirming privacy, male prerogatives, female domesticity, and the sanctity of motherhood as the primary markers of denazification, the ideal bulwark against Communism, and the core of the "Christian occidental" tradition. Family policy became a vital weapon of the Cold War, with "totalitarian" control of the family in the Communist East an ever-present figure of fear. The SPD also affirmed this nexus of "a healthy economy, a self-supporting welfare state, large families, good mothers, and national vitality."[43] The same applied in Britain, where the reforms of 1946 made family a male-headed economic unit and placed women firmly inside the home. Women's big gain, family allowances paid directly to mothers, reflected similar maternalist assumptions.

Yet women activists saw maternalism as a way of contesting the trade unionist nostrum of the "family wage" by addressing women's specific needs. This suggested the ambivalence of postwar reforms—the meanings of women's gains and the underlying hegemony of the family form, where women's futures were subsumed. Women may have felt validated by recognition of mothering, in a vision of the "equality of worth [that] acknowledges difference," as one SPD spokeswoman called it. But "that vision was completely consistent with a legal order that fully legitimated a normative vision of the home as women's most important [domain]."[44] Much rested on what exactly women's maternal citizenship allowed.

Here, the language of entitlements associated with social citizenship made a climate conducive to other claims. If later feminisms weren't directly created by the postwar settlement, it did provide contradictions where they could work. The 1960s feminisms logically extended earlier arguments to women, for if effective citizenship required legislative action for social rights, other forms of affirmative action could follow—against gender as well as class inequalities via equal pay, antidiscrimination laws, reproductive rights, and so forth. In complicated ways, therefore, welfare state measures and citizenship reforms of the antifascist period accumulated languages of rights and capacities that later radicalisms could also deploy.

Reforms were multivalent. Postwar welfare states involved population policy and industrial modernization, international competitiveness and national efficiency, as much as social improvement and democratic progress in altruistic ways. Technocratic policies of economic recovery also defined the postwar settlement—social policies for strengthening the family and securing social reproduction, for maintaining gender regimes and sexual divisions of labor, and for promoting new models of mass consumption. Educational reforms met the needs of the changing economy for skilled and unskilled labor. The ability to harmonize such functionalist arguments with the hopes of large social movements and to combine the goal of capitalist prosperity with the reformist project of a Left political base was vital to the stability of the new political arrangements during the Cold War.[45]

POSTWAR SOCIAL DEMOCRACY

Here was the terrain of the Left's main non-Communist tendency after 1945—a social democracy increasingly shedding the Marxist tradition, increasingly nervous about the class struggle, and increasingly skeptical about transforming capitalism by revolution. The strongest parties were in Scandinavia, where Swedish, Norwegian, and Danish socialists won repeated elections with programs of structural reform based on liberal democracy, mixed economies, trade union corporatism, and strong welfare states. In a second set of cases, strong socialist parties with consistently high support (20–45 percent of the vote) joined coalitions on an institutionalized multiparty basis: the Benelux countries, the remaining Scandinavian ones (Finland and Iceland), Switzerland, and Austria, where a bilateral "great coalition" ruled.

Elsewhere, socialists suffered continuous opposition. In Britain and West Germany, strong parties were blocked by popular conservatisms. Labour lost successive elections on very high popular votes—48.8 percent in 1951, 46.4 percent in 1955, 43.8 percent in 1959—while the SPD hovered at disappointingly low levels: 29.2 percent in 1949, 28.8 percent in 1953, 31.8 percent in 1957. Irish Labour was permanently marginalized by the nationalist political frame, scoring at best 12 percent (1957) in the five elections of 1948–61. In France and Italy, socialists faced strong CPs and vacillated between left-wing posturing and mere pragmatics on a dwindling electoral base: the former SFIO sank from 23.4 to only 12.6 percent during 1945–62; while the PSI declined from 20.7 to 14.2 percent during 1946–58, with another 4.5 percent in 1958 for the right-wing Partito Socialista Democratico Italiano (PSDI). The French Socialists even joined 21 of the 27 governments during 1944–58, but in centrist coalitions of minimal reform. Finally, socialists were underground in Spain, Portugal, and Greece until the mid-1970s after the end of dictatorships.

The strongest social democracies were general vehicles of progressivism, but in much of Western Europe conditions militated against this happening. Mass Communism blocked the chances in Italy, France, Finland, and Iceland, as did religious or ethnolinguistic divisions among workers in West Germany, the Low Countries, Italy, and Switzerland. The SPD's strong doctrinal traditions and Marxist attachments also hampered its reformist reorientation. But where these factors were absent and pragmatic social democracy dominated national labor movements, socialist parties became the dominant voice of 1945, rallying broad coalitions to the labor movement's progressive flag. This applied to Britain, Scandinavia, and Austria. These were the only parties consistently breaking the 40 percent electoral barrier from 1945 to 1960 (see table 19.1).

International factors secured social democratic success. Marshall Aid underpinned Labourism in Britain, while Scandinavian Communism's elec-

TABLE 19.1 Highest Social Democratic Vote, 1945–1960

Country	Election Year	Percentage of Popular Vote
Austria	1959	44.8
Belgium	1954	38.6
Denmark	1954	41.3
Finland	1951	26.5
France	1946	21.1
Great Britain	1951	48.8
Germany, Federal Republic	1957	31.8
Iceland	1956	18.3
Ireland	1954	12.0
Italy	1946	20.7
Luxemburg	1951	41.4
Netherlands	1956	32.7
Norway	1957	48.3
Sweden	1960	47.8
Switzerland	1947	26.2

toral growth was abruptly canceled by the Cold War.[46] This dualism—Marshall economics, anti-Communist politics—cemented the postwar settlement. As Europe divided—inside societies, no less than geopolitically—defense of "the West" supplied social democracy's identifying vocabulary. Both European integration and interests overseas became harnessed to the Western political community of the Cold War. Bevin tied the Labour Party to imperial defense, and in the festering sequence of late-colonial wars in Africa and Asia, French Socialists took a leading role. Guy Mollet, who led the SFIO in the name of "that fundamental reality, the class struggle" in 1946, headed a government in 1956–57 that was notable for its draconian response to Algerian anticolonialism, not to speak of the disastrous Suez adventure.[47] The deepest cleavage of the 1950s was between those socialists who were ready to identify themselves with NATO and those parts of the Left who were not.

Where the social agenda behind the Marshall Plan—a modernizing package of high productivity, high wages, redistributive taxation, and mass consumption—met a militant labor movement led by Communists, it clashed with the Truman Doctrine's anti-Communism and so gave way, as in Italy and Greece. Where, by contrast, the CP was small and the labor movement securely social democratic, as in Britain, the Low Countries, and Scandinavia, Marshall Aid went with the grain of indigenous reformisms and made them robust. Here the north and west European group of parties, who had formed the right-wing Second International bloc against Zimmerwald in 1915–17, dug themselves into anti-Bolshevism after 1917, and immobilized the LSI's antifascist potential in the 1930s, came into their own.[48]

Keynesianism, designed to tame capitalism's cycles of boom and slump, grounded this social democratic agenda.[49] Accepting the permanence of capitalism but seeing the necessity of state intervention for correcting market dysfunctions, Keynesianism advocated macroeconomic steering mechanisms of aggregate demand management via fiscal policy and large-scale public spending, with a view to evening the process of economic growth via high wages, stable prices, and full employment. It allowed popular patriotism to be rewarded with a strengthening of democracy and social justice, without denying capitalism as the source of future prosperity. Capital's interests would be guaranteed by national economic management, social peace, and rising productivity. The people would be served by full employment, rising incomes, expanding social services, and the government's commitment to social equality.

CORPORATISM

The guarantors of this implied social contract were national union barons. Epitomized by Ernest Bevin, they brokered industrial discipline and their members' productivity. Sections of workers—organized, skilled or semi-skilled, male—won unprecedented security, with not only full employment and rising real wages but a new shopfloor self-respect. New workplace deals brought union recognition, legally fixed seniority and demarcation rules, job protections, fringe benefits, and the constraining of management's power in production, all secured by national agreements of unions and employers backed by the state. Conversely, management invested in higher productivity, via new plants, new machines, and new techniques of production, without worrying about union attacks on its rights of control. Production lines spread, with automobiles as the classic industrial model. This new factory regime—high wages, no strikes, high productivity—would feed a new consumer-oriented boom, where profits could escape older challenges to the nature of the system.

At the apex was the state. Postwar industrial relations required a corporatist triangulation: labor won tangible economic benefits and political influence; capital won the space for a new accumulation strategy based on Fordism, meaning workplace deals combining high wages, productivity, and a modernized labor process, linked to consumer-driven growth; and the state won a new role overseeing this large-scale societal compromise. This corporatism was held together partly by national systems of consultation between government, employers, and unions and partly by Keynesianism's ending of mass unemployment. It produced a system of "reform or managed capitalism." This held a central place for organized labor, while bypassing socialism as such.[50]

The entire package presumed a future of economic growth. An unparalleled capitalist boom incited social democrats to amazing optimism, now guided not by belief in capitalism's inevitable collapse but by the humanized certainty of its prosperous future. "Traditionally socialist thought has been dominated by the economic problems posed by capitalism, poverty, mass unemployment, squalor, instability, and even the possibility of the collapse of the whole system," Anthony Crosland argued, but now "[c]apitalism had been reformed out of all recognition."[51] By 1960, socialists were over-hauling their social analysis. Steadily rising living standards, accelerating after 1960 into a full-blown consumer economy, were matched by the upward mobility of educational qualifications, not least via expanding public employment. In short, the Keynesian formula deradicalized the social democratic imagination.

Socialist strategists took prosperity's permanence as an appealing substitute for abolishing capitalism, for which in any case they had no plan. The rhetoric of revolution, as a challenge to state power, was long gone. But any extraparliamentary politics, via local government, workplace democracy, or direct action, however vestigial, now too disappeared. Languages of class, claiming irreconcilable conflicts in the economy, atrophied. The new strategists shifted priorities—away from the primary agency of the working class and toward slow ameliorations of the class structure and broader social coalitions. Instead of the class struggle, revisionists opted wholly for elections. Socialist parties became "people's parties" with varied support.

The SPD's 1959 Program, adopted at its Godesberg Congress, pioneered this "modernizing" approach.[52] All talk of ending capitalism ended, as did Marxism and indeed the word "socialism" itself. Remaining was the desire to govern after winning an election. The mixed economy, with its architecture of welfare state, full employment, and strong public sector, reconciled social democrats to private ownership and control. By the 1960s, this stance wholly dominated the SPD, British Labour, socialist parties in the Low Countries and France, and Scandinavian social democracy. Further, while socialists had shaped the postwar settlement, it was conservatives who reaped the benefits, and parties like Labour and SPD were back in opposition, supporting consensus from the outside. But neither the 13 years of Conservative rule in Britain (1951–64), nor the 17 of the West German "CDU state" (1949–66) could have worked without union cooperation. Traditional socialist analysis was losing its force.

The strongest Keynesian-welfare-state synthesis, taking explicitly social democratic form, with the labor movement in the driving seat, was Sweden.[53] The SAP rested historically on exceptionally effective representation of the working class, reflecting a particularly cohesive class formation. By 1917, the SAP was Sweden's largest party, governing continuously between 1932 and 1976; by 1991, it had governed Sweden for 80 percent of democratic time, averaging 44.8 percent of the vote during 1921–85. This solidity involved an integral relationship with the unions (LO), corporatively established via the 1938 Basic Agreement with Employers. The party mostly avoided acrimony with the small CP, and from the 1960s developed a parliamentary alliance. By allying with the Agrarian Party during 1936–57, it also preempted a farming interest hostile to the Left.

Foundations were laid in the 1930s. The SAP governments adopted Keynesian-like policies, starting in 1933 with public works programs at standard union rates, plus agricultural price supports. Social reforms included work creation and the Manpower Commission, unemployment insurance, "People's Pensions," preventive health and social services, family allowances, and rent subsidies. The SAP respected the advanced corporatism of the 1938 Basic Agreement, eased by highly centralized organization of unions and employers. With one interlude during 1944–48, it abandoned nationalization and planning projects in favor of forecasting and demand management, freeing the welfare state from the specter of state ownership in the economy.

The idea of the "People's Home," coined in 1928 by Per Albin Hansson, party chair from 1928 and prime minister from 1932, conveyed an ethic of consensus and mutuality, based on the absence of hierarchy and privilege:

> In the good home equality, consideration, cooperation, and helpfulness prevail. Applied to the great people's and citizens' home this would mean the breaking down of all the social and economic barriers that now divide citizens into privileged and misfavored, into rulers and dependents, into rich and poor, the glutted and the destitute, the plunderers and the plundered.[54]

This freed an ideal of social justice from the more divisive productivist rhetoric of the primacy of the working class. It evoked most Swedes' rural links, for the demographic balance tipped to the towns only in 1930–35. It reflected belief in coalition building, if socialists were to win society's moral leadership. For the welfare state, it proposed universalism, making social rights part of citizenship rather than means-tested relief. By presenting solidaristic social policies in languages of family, home, and community, it seized the high ground of the nation.

Uniquely for the Left, Scandinavian social democracy governed in the 1930s, building the welfare state's legitimacy in expansive national-popular terms. Alva and Gunnar Myrdal's *Nation and Family* (1934) established the unity of population policy, social welfare, and national interest from an avowedly democratic perspective, making social security "part of Swedish national identity."[55] Welfare policy was guided by the principle of universalism, extended by national health insurance in 1956 and education reform in 1962. In the 1950s the LO also advocated solidaristic wage bargaining, coordinated with the employers. In return for wage increases, the low-paid were encouraged toward dynamic industries through retraining and relocation; and by accepting wage restraint to benefit the lower-paid, high-wage workers endorsed productivity-based policies for their own more successful sectors. Thus, a redistributive mechanism for low-wage workers was combined with a dynamic industrial policy for Sweden's international competitiveness. A national wages policy joined to an active labor market policy integrated different groups of workers and boosted industrial modernization.

Then, in 1959 the SAP's Pension Reform (ATP) refocused the welfare-state ethos, replacing the "proletarianizing" egalitarianism of flat-rate contributions linked to minimum standards with a "middle-class" leveling-up based on earnings-related schemes and income maintenance. This was a divisive struggle, which remade the social basis of the SAP's governing hegemony. The ATP shrewdly gave the growing white-collar interest a material stake in the welfare state, shifting socialist strategy away from the old labor-farmer alliance. In sacrificing equality of benefits, it hoped to preempt better-organized skilled and white-collar workers grabbing supplementary retirement income via collective bargaining, binding them instead to the welfare state. The resulting wage-earner coalition promised to secure the SAP's electoral future.

The three pillars of postwar social democracy—Keynesianism, corporatism, welfare state—were an integral unity in Sweden, where high-quality leadership shaped a coherent vision of societal reform. The key enabling conditions were also present: a united labor movement untroubled by a mass CP; cultural homogeneity, denying the wedge of ethnocultural differences to antisocialism in the working class; and doctrinal flexibility. The corporatist promise—wage restraint for economic reconstruction, in return for social reforms and full employment—was actually delivered upon by the SAP. Swedish workers could identify with the reforming state, with more than rising real wages as a stake, an identification skilfully extended toward white-collar and professional middle classes. Other social democracies rarely emulated the national leadership, government competence, humane political values, and strategic understanding of the SAP's unbroken ascendancy from 1932 to 1976.[56]

By 1960, socialists had mostly abandoned ideas of abolishing capitalism. Radical factions remained but mainly among intellectuals or the remnants of local socialist cultures or sections of the youth. Social democrats put their faith in economic growth, industrial prosperity, and rising standards of living, imagining societies where "ideological questions" and the "class struggle" had died away. Maintaining full employment, reducing inequality by progressive taxation and social reform, improving life chances via education and social services, making society more humane—these goals no longer implied abolishing capitalism. Social democrats could still claim credit for the postwar settlements. But by 1955—outside Scandinavia—they were watching from opposition. This was a far cry from 10 years before. At the birth of the British wartime coalition, in a speech before two thousand union leaders on 25 May 1940, Ernest Bevin, then newly appointed minister of labour, asserted the unity of socialism and patriotism in the promise of a Labour-dominated political future:

> I have to ask you virtually to place yourselves at the disposal of the state. We are Socialists and this is the test of our Socialism. It is the test whether we have meant the resolutions which we have so often passed. . . . If our Movement and our class rise with all their energy now and save the people of this country from disaster, the country will always turn with confidence to the people who saved them.[57]

By 1945 this promise had been fulfilled. The war years endowed an ethic of collectivism that resonated for another three decades. But the larger vision, of exercising moral-political leadership in the nation, in the manner Gramsci or the architects of Red Vienna or the militants of little Moscows had imagined, or the Swedish Social Democrats still pursued, was lost.

WOMEN IN THEIR PLACE (AND MEN IN THEIRS)

Women's experience between Popular Front and Cold War told a familiar tale. Popular Fronts in Spain and France seemed to bring women into a public sphere, whether through the franchise and the Republican cause in the Civil War, or the French strike wave of June 1936. The Second World War then mobilized rhetorics of patriotic service across Europe, in women's work for the British war economy, and the sacrifices of Resistance in Nazi-occupied Europe. Wartime massively disrupted family life, confused boundaries of public and private, and brought women into normally male-defined roles, upsetting given gender norms. Yet after 1945, older continuities were reinstated; instead of women gaining full participation in democratic citizenship, motherhood and domesticity again usurped the results.

In Spain, the Popular Front immediately improved women's legal status and access to divorce, civil marriage, and even voluntary abortion in Catalonia. Republican mobilization recruited women into industry and public services, agricultural collectives, and initially the militias. But women were still addressed mainly as mothers and wives. They were soon running field kitchens, washing and sewing, staffing hospitals, and organizing refugees, as well as filling jobs vacated by fighting men. If committed to emancipation, the *Agrupación de Mujeres Antifascistas,* launched in 1933, was wholly conventional on this front.[58] The anarchist *Mujeres Libres* formed in summer 1936 wished to liberate women from their "triple enslavement to ignorance, as women, and as producers," but it also ran afoul of the entrenched sexism of the CNT.[59] Of course, the issue was brutally tabled by Nationalist victory in the Civil War, which returned women to an unrelenting subordination.

France was the same. "Universal suffrage," the pride of French republicanism, still denied votes to women, and juridical citizenship served them no better: the reformed Civil Code of February 1938 removed some disabilities but kept the husband *chef de la famille*. Blum's appointment of three women subministers in 1936 was a cynical sop.[60] Only the Resistance forced the issue: if Radicals kept female suffrage out of the CNR Charter in March 1944, the Algiers assembly in April put it in, and in 1945 the vote was won. Yet public policy left women's place unchanged. The SFIO and PCF mouthed the old nostrums—productive labor as a condition of emancipation—while their unions perpetuated female exclusion, family wage, and unequal pay. In the 1936 strikes, women had been beholden to male militancy in shopfloor committees and the public languages of unions and parties, as CGT leaders applauded women strikers for "defending [our] bread, the home, the survival of our children."[61] In working-class women's memories, "the crisis, the recession, unemployment, newspapers, trade unions and politics were all domains or concepts reserved for men."[62] With the Popular Front, the PCF had moved loudly into the French pronatalist consensus.[63] Antifascist radicalism stopped at the family hearth.

Italy, the other big Catholic country of the south with a strong CP, varied the pattern. In September 1944, the Resistance launched the Italian Women's Organization (UDI) as a classic expression of Togliatti's alliance strategy, appealing to non-Communist women through its journal *Noi Donne* and counting 3,500 local circles and a million members by 1954.[64] But UDI broke women from "home and church" into public roles without challenging gendered relations in families or the secondary status of "women's sphere." Its 1947 slogan was "For a happy family, for peace, and for work."[65] Communists addressed the "social function" of housework and maternity by demanding maximum social security and the classic socialist solutions of universal technology and collectivized services. But the party's gender politics were at best unsure, and women militants saw UDI as implicitly second rank, "a form of exile from the real business of the party."[66] Moreover, the alliance strategy downplayed sensitive issues like contraception, abortion, and divorce, pushing UDI further toward motherhood, childraising, and family.

The PCI claimed high female membership, 25.9 percent by 1959. But this went unreflected at the top, where only 5–6 percent of leaders were women from 1945 to the 1960s. Difficulties were clearest in Turin, with its powerful workerist traditions. The CGIL unions lobbied to keep UDI safely away, confining it to "women's issues," and when UDI began its 1950s campaigns for equality at work, PCI unions were too weakened by the Cold War to help. One UDI local circle described its aim as "women's emancipation, which must be the human and political motif which animates all our activity." But it was uncoupled from main party life. The circle met biweekly in the house of an activist's mother:

> On 8 March (Women's Day), the local girls' choir and ballet gave a performance and the trousseaus of the members who were to be married that year were put on display. Other activities included petitions for public housing and for peace, the selling of the journal *Noi Donne,* assistance to older and sick women during the winter months, solidarity with women workers sacked at the local shoe factory, the organization of a children's camp by the sea, bus trips to local museums.[67]

Thus women's admission as voting citizens failed to unlock existing gender regimes. If 1918 enfranchised women in northern and central Europe, 1945 did so in Catholic Italy, Belgium, and France, while restoring votes that fascism had taken away. Only Portugal, Spain, Greece, and Switzerland kept exclusively male polities. But again the dialectic of equality and difference supervened: even as women exercised political rights, postwar social laws tried to keep them at home. "During marriage most women will not be gainfully occupied," Beveridge flatly declared, and the welfare states constitutively privileged the male "breadwinner" in his delivery of the "family wage."[68] In reproductive rights, the normalizing logic was the same. The returning German sex reformers after 1945 found their radical legacy reduced to pronatalism, marital harmony, and family health, removed from earlier ideals of affirmative sex counseling, abortion reform, and homosexual rights. By the time the West German version of Planned Parenthood was launched in July 1952—the aptly named *Pro Familia,* with the unnoticed scandal of Hans Harmsen as its president—Weimar utopias of emancipated sexuality were truly no more. The goal was now "[t]he healthy family in ethical, sexological, and psychological perspective."[69]

The Left's inability to escape this maternalist frame marked the limits of antifascism. Communists reached out to "nonproletarian" groups but addressed women stereotypically, while social democrats cleaved even closer to conservatively gendered terrain. Socialism always promised far-reaching liberation of women. "After the revolution" women would attain true equality via an independent working-class identity, supported by collectivist social policies for childcare and domestic living. Inspired by that ethos, the party youth movements nurtured ungendered cultures of socialism beyond the privatized familialism where female dependency began, modeling the egalitarian comradeship of women and men.

Yet misogyny, separation of spheres, and simple indifference by heavily masculine movements remained the norm. Labor movements dismissed feminism per se as middle-class careerism, using "feminist" as a derogatory term. For democratic purposes, labor politicians and feminists might cooperate, but class-political animus against "bourgeois feminists" more often prevailed. While before 1918, Keir Hardie and the ILP supported women's suffrage in Britain and Sylvia Pankhurst's East London Federation co-founded the CPGB, in Germany the SPD refused all such collaboration. After 1918, the distinction shifted: Labour's rise as a class party raised a new boundary against interwar feminisms, while in Weimar democracy common ground formed between SPD and activist women in education, social policy, sex reform, and health.

The Second World War reduced the barriers. In 1938, Florence Keyworth, a respectable working-class teenager in Sheffield fleeing her parents' conservatism, was rebuffed by the Young Communist League's exclusively male culture of union militancy. Four years later, toughened via the League of Nations Union and the Left Book Club and empowered by women's greater public roles, she joined the CP with two women friends, becoming a journalist on the *Daily Worker* in 1945.[70] In occupied Europe, where women joined the Resistance, stakes were far higher. In Italy, 70,000 were in Defense Groups and 35,000 fought with partisans.[71] Twenty-six and pregnant, Ave Albertini worked as a courier in Modena before joining her husband's unit in the field, acting as their seamstress and giving birth during a battle in August 1944. Others trained for combat, including several all-female units, but rarely escaped familiar roles. Teresa Testa found herself acting as "political commissar, cook, laundress, and courier" for her unit near Turin. Communist women lived "schizophrenically," Luciana Viviani recalled, because political identity was always overdetermined by being "a good wife, a good mother."[72]

Through experiences like these, women certainly acquired a stronger sense of their own political agency, but by 1950 normative expectations were strongly reinstated. In wartime Britain, women's politics were already subsumed in social services, providing day nurseries and municipal restaurants for working mothers and defending these against post-1945 closure. For Keyworth, the hierarchy hadn't changed: "many Communist women (I was one) decided we were not interested in 'women's work' which we despised." The labor movement's masculinity remained a default characteristic. In Yorkshire, the CPGB subsisted in the occupational cultures of the engineering and mining unions, from which women were excluded; at a week-long party school in Rotherham in 1944, Keyworth was alone among 17 men.[73] Unemployment marginalized women as workers, but full employment added its own twist: women's politics disappeared into the family, whether through breadwinner rhetorics and the family wage, restrictive union practices for married women, or the welfare state.

The strength of Communist and socialist parties in the antifascist era was their general progressivism. The Left emerged from Liberation exercising moral leadership in the nation and rallying a rich repertoire of causes around the central goals of reform—or hegemonizing them, in Gramsci's term. Here, the maternalist normalizing of politics was a major symptom of failure. Antifascism, so creative in transcending the class-political ghetto, allowed safe repetitions of working-class attitudes when it came to women. Wartime patriotism, whose rhetorics privileged older gender lines—men soldiering, women keeping the home fires burning—was limiting after all. As in 1914–18, women were wrenched out of domesticity, brought into employment and other public roles, and mobilized for the collective good. This was guided by promises of citizenship, equality in the nation at the war's end. Yet by 1950, women were back in the old secondary place.

Is that all there is to say? Differences between East and West do reveal certain patterns of longer-term change. In socialist Eastern Europe women became socialized comprehensively into employment during the postwar decades, reaching 45–50 percent of the workforce by 1988, with Bulgaria and the USSR at the top. In Western Europe, rates were lower: 43.3 percent in Britain, 42.7 percent in France, 38.5 percent in West Germany. Likewise, 83.2 percent of working age women were employed in the GDR, 70.1 in Hungary, and 65.0 in Poland but only 67.7 percent in Britain, 59.2 in France, and 55.4 in West Germany. By 1980, socialist countries led Europe in numbers of women students, at parity or more. In the GDR (German Democratic Republic), 82 percent of women workers had completed vocational qualifications, while 30 percent of lawyers and 52 percent of doctors were women, compared with only 4 and 16 percent in Britain and 14 and 23 percent in West Germany. No less than in the West, women concentrated in the the caring professions, health, education, the service sector, and historically female industries. In the GDR, 69 percent of textiles and clothing workers were women, as were 100 percent of trainee secretaries and 95 percent of trainee salespersons and hairdressers but only 9 percent of apprentices in machine building and 8 percent in construction. Women's presence also thinned out within professional status hierarchies: women became 77 percent of the GDR workforce in education but only 32 percent of principals and only 7 percent of university lecturers.[74]

There were more women legislators in Eastern than Western Europe outside Scandinavia, with the same gap between lower levels and the top. By the 1980s, 25 percent of the GDR's local mayors were women, plus 40 percent of county, district, and borough councils and 35 percent of party members, but only 13 percent of the Central Committee and none of the Politburo. Above all, household divisions of labor went unchanged. By 1989, 80.2 percent of GDR children were in a creche (ages 0–3 years) and 95.1 percent in a kindergarten (ages 3–6), as against 3.0 and 67.5 percent for the West German Federal Republic (FRG). But the party accepted the permanence of women's double burden: women's policies should allow them to "reconcile the demands of their job still more successfully with their duties towards child and family," in order "to better harmonize employment, social commitment, and maternal duties, which generally benefits family life."[75]

Following the war, women didn't always leave paid employment, where the underlying upward trend remained. In 1901, women were 29 percent of the British workforce, remaining stable until 1939–45, when numbers steadily grew, reaching 39 percent by 1982. Figures for France and West Germany were similar, and Italian women's share of jobs rose from 23 to 34 percent and Swedish from 24 to 46 percent between 1950 and 1982. Numbers of all women working also increased—from 41 to 56 percent in Britain, from 32 to 40 percent in Italy, and from 35 to 76 percent in Sweden. The married part of the female workforce in Britain had been 13–16 percent before 1939, but by 1951 it was 40 percent, and in 1960 married women were already a majority. Women were still concentrated in certain industries; unequal pay and job discrimination persisted. But this feminization of the workforce had huge consequences for women's political place.

Welfare state maternalism disabled women politically by fixing them in domesticity but might also validate participation. In Italy, both the Maternity Law of 1950 and the Equal Pay Convention of 1956 owed much to PCI support and established legal openings for women after the 1960s.[76] In Sweden, this was even clearer. Exceptionally, Sweden produced no movement against married women's work in the 1930s. Swedish women's groups coalesced around "a host of issues, such as paid vacations for housewives, decriminalizing contraceptives, increased political representation of women, support for single mothers . . . and mothers' right to work," fashioning exceptional unity across party and class lines, exemplified in the "Call to Swedish Women" issued by 25 women's groups in 1936.[77] Crucially, the LO raised no opposition to women's demands, partly because the highly segregated Swedish labor market made women's competition less of a threat. Moreover, Hansson's notion of the "People's Home" captured the high ground of national interest for the Left in the 1930s, giving women positive connections from everyday life to politics, via "housing policies, maternal health and welfare, and fertility."[78] Key Parliamentary Commissions on Married Women's Work and Population Policy (1935–38), which laid down progressive policies in both areas, were decisively influenced by the new cohort of Social Democratic feminist women.

Finally, peace movements provided a context of women's activism going back to the 1900s, when the International Women's Suffrage Alliance advocated international conciliation. In Britain at that time, the NUWSS, the East London Federation, and even the WSPU combined with the Women's Cooperative Guild and the ILP in supporting peace. After 1918 this tradition was reactivated through the Women's International League of Peace and Freedom, founded in 1919, itself descending from the International Committee of Women for Permanent Peace, launched at the Hague Women's Congress of April 1915. In Britain these contexts included the No Conscription Fellowship of 1914–19, the No More War Movement launched in 1920, and the Peace Pledge Union formed in 1934, merging with No More War in 1936, as well as the League of Nations Union and War Resisters International.

The key forum in the Popular Front campaigns of the 1930s was the Women's World Committee Against War and Fascism, which gave women access to a public sphere, especially locally. In Manchester, for example, the Women's Sub-Committee of the Northern Council Against Fascism worked through the annual International Women's Day campaign, a Women's Conference on Unity in June 1937, the various Aid Spain groups, Maternity Mortality committees, and a variety of local campaigns linked with the Women's Cooperative Guild, the Labour Party, the ILP, and the CPGB. After 1945, the Cold War reduced the scope, and the World Peace Council formed in 1950 was too identified with the USSR. The Council's Stockholm and Warsaw Appeals in 1950 for banning the atomic bomb drew 500 million signatures, but 90 percent of these came from the East. Once peace campaigning revived on a broader basis after 1956, pioneered in Britain through the Direct Action Committee and the Campaign for Nuclear Disarmament, however, women's prominence was no surprise.[79]

BETWEEN THE PERSONAL AND THE POLITICAL

The 1950s were an intermediate time for women, suspended between the newness of juridical citizenship and the normalizing of domesticity, in a gender regime of public and private that entailed the opposite of emancipated personhood. Here the maternalist framing of the welfare state was key, especially in the strongest pronatalist forms, with their valuing of the working-class child. Even progressives distinguished between housewife-mothers—the "real" mothers that working-class women should have the right to become—and women who worked, who deprived their children of mothering. The popular association of "feminism" with single or childless professional women opting for careers over family was much strengthened as a result.

This was not inevitable. The needs of growing labor markets for female workers, plus wartime innovations like nurseries for working mothers, suggested an alternative scenario. But the ideal of the fulltime housewife-mother triumphed—supplied with social services, free milk, and orange juice, trained into technical competence, sharing roles with the husband-breadwinner bringing home the wage. The elaboration of technical and common-sense knowledges for the needs of children and mothering by John Bowlby and others, via theories of maternal deprivation, and attachment and loss, helped secure this consensus.[80] Women's increasing participation in the economy, via employment, higher education, and consumer spending, which was redefining women's relation to the public world, became thereby obscured. Even the most politically conscious left-wing women could barely escape.

This silencing of radicalism, amid profamily conformities, was also an effect of the Cold War. Mobilizing patriotism against Communism after 1947, in distorted continuity with anti-Nazi solidarities, went easily with rhetorics of family and home, suturing an idealized domesticity to the threatened integrity of the nation and its way of life, only recently saved from fascism. If women were positioned as mothers in this discursive economy, men were constructed not only as fathers but as bearers of public responsibility, in rigid systems of gender difference. Sexual dissidence— specifically, male homosexuality—became marked as a danger to the community's self-security. It became the window of society's moral vulnerability, and nonconforming behaviors were anxiously policed. Prosecutions for homosexuality increased fivefold in Britain during 1939–54. Legacies of fascism went unnoticed: in West Germany and France, Nazi and Vichy legislation against homosexuals lasted unchanged. While the political community of "the West" was being elaborated in the 1950s, "the scourge of homosexuality" marked an inner edge of anxiety, functioning in public discourse as a boundary of normal behavior.[81]

Despite enclaves of intellectual toleration, the Left was no less blunt in disavowals, incomprehension, and outright hostility, and by staying inside these limits—of heteronormative thinking about family, sexuality, and the public-private split—socialists and Communists cohabited the bottom line of postwar conformity.[82] Sexualities were the uncharted territory of Left politics in the mid–twentieth century, the unreflected ground of a conservatism more visible after 1968. When the pro-Labour *Daily Mirror* urged British women to "Vote for Him," meaning their soldier husbands, in the 1945 election, it not only sold the promise of female citizenship unacceptably short but bespoke an entire universe of gendered social and political assumptions. After the interlude of independence in the Second World War, of self-confident entry into the public goods of the nation, postwar normalizing had to be experienced by women as a contraction:

> Come 1945: a letter in the post one Friday morning: "This nursery shuts today (for good) at 6 pm. Please remove all your belongings with your child this evening." And I was a single parent; no more nurseries. The Government needed jobs for the returning heroes; women had to make their homes and beautify them with feminine charm (up the birthrate). Came Macmillan and we'd never had it so good. Came Bowlby who told us that it was all our fault if anything went wrong with our children's lives if we left them for any time at all. Came demand feeding, babies inseparable from mothers on slings around our backs and fronts; came television, washing machines, and durable goods to make us feel wanted in the home. Came Do It Yourself. Came Guilt—never think of yourself as a person, never have sex outside marriage, never never never leave your child, be content with

Uncle Government's lovely domestic hardware; never breathe a word of the orgiastic nights on the gun site (or the warmth of the all-women's residential Nissen huts and officers' buildings, not a man for miles).

Just remember, everything is always your fault. You don't have rights. The children have rights. The children are always right. You are always wrong. Just get on and do the washing and bake a cake. Don't speak. Be silent. You are no-one (except a machine to spend money).[83]

Chapter 20

1956

"NEVER THE DICTATOR, never one to lay down the law, always eager and willing to listen, to understand another's point of view. . . . No words, no monuments, no tributes can ever do justice to the revolution in people's minds and actions, in changing world history, in freeing millions from darkness, oppression, poverty, and misery that have been brought about by the work of Comrade Stalin. . . . Eternal glory to the memory of Joseph Stalin."[1]

Harry Pollitt's grotesque peroration typified the eulogies that flooded the Communist world when Stalin died on 5 March 1953. These were not cynically intended. Stalinism's political psychology in the West subsisted on three decades of isolation and defeat, counterposed to the stirring narrative of the USSR's heroic success—victory in the civil war, socialism in one country, industrialization and the five-year plan, defeat of fascism—a polarity confused during 1941–47, but now freshly dramatized by the Cold War. Moscow loyalism reflected western Communism's siege mentality in 1947–53, constantly charged by Soviet demands. But the abjection of so many independent minds, entire movements in fact, before the cult of Stalin's personality still eludes understanding.

Stalin's succession seemed straightforward. Nikita Khrushchev defeated first Lavrenty Beria, who was arrested in June 1953 and shot in December, and then Georgii Malenkov, replaced as Premier in February 1955. The Cold War continued with lowered intensity. The Warsaw Pact was formed in response to West Germany's rearmament and admission to NATO in May 1955, while the United

States deposed the reforming government of Jacoba Arbenz in Guatemala in June 1954. But halts were brought to the wars in Korea and Indochina, and the Philippine and Malayan insurgencies also neared their end. Conciliatory moves were made in Europe, where Soviet leaders normalized relations with Tito and agreed to Austrian neutrality in May 1955, placing a German rapprochement on the agenda. They accepted a summit with the United States, Britain, and France in Geneva in July 1955, the first since Potsdam. They opened relations with West Germany, inviting Chancellor Konrad Adenauer to Moscow in September 1955. But inside the socialist countries dramatic changes were afoot.[2]

DE-STALINIZATION AND THE TWENTIETH CONGRESS

Popular unrest threatened to destabilize the postfascist international order. The East German Uprising of 17 June 1953 grew from protests of East Berlin construction workers against higher production norms, raising political demands for free elections. Military repression was swift, but both the SPD and the Allies in West Berlin observed restraint, closing the border against possible solidarity.[3] A general Eastern European strike wave developed after Stalin's death, with over a hundred factories affected in Czechoslovakia, including the Skoda arms complex in Pilsen, where troops were sent. Strikes spread through Hungary, Bulgaria, and Romania, reaching the USSR itself in July, in the camps of the Vorkuta mining complex in Siberia, following earlier risings in 1948 and 1950. Eastern European industrial unrest prompted economic liberalization and loosening of repression. In Hungary, Rákosi was partially disavowed and replaced as prime minister by the reform Communist Imre Nagy. The prisons were massively cleared out.

Then, at the Twentieth Congress of the CPSU in February 1956, Krushchev denounced Stalin. The Congress began with the familiar fanfares and speeches, but anticipation was in the air. Vittorio Vidali, a delegate from Trieste and transnational citizen of Communism, with spells in Italy, Germany, the United States, France, the USSR, Spain, and Mexico since 1917, exchanged news of disappeared comrades in the corridors: "Every day the tone is more shrill, the accusations more specific."[4] Appalling stories, banished to the Communist unconscious, returned:

> At dinner Germanetto informed me that a certain Bocchino from Trieste wanted to meet me. He has served 17 years in jail; now he has been rehabilitated . . . and Russified. There are other "rehabilitated" Italians with him; nearly all of them have spent half of their lives in concentration camps. They came here to work as specialists, techni-

cians. One fine day they were arrested, accused of sabotage and sent to prison. Probably to avoid torture or death, they confessed to crimes they had not committed, and so they ended up in Siberia. It happened to many people. When I asked about Edmondo Peluso, or Signora Monservigi (whose son died at Stalingrad), or Parodi's wife, about Gorelli, Ghezzi, etc., I received no answer. Robotti, too, was in jail for more than a year, but he signed nothing and so they had to release him; but he went through hell; he is made of steel. The same thing happened to Gottardi, but he "confessed" to what he had not done. They asked Robotti to "confess" that Togliatti was a spy![5]

Detailed revelations were delivered by Khrushchev at midnight on 25 February in closed session, with foreign Communists excluded. Detailing the cult of personality and Stalin's megalomania, the "secret speech" focused on the gross arbitrariness of Stalin's power, Soviet ill-preparedness for war, and the dictatorial "violations of socialist legality" in the terror of the 1930s. Though Stalin's *behavior* in the 1920s was attacked, his *policies*—socialism in one country, Bolshevization of the Comintern, central planning, industrialization, collectivization of agriculture, and of course democratic centralism and the one-party state—were not.[6]

Communism was cast into disarray. Senior nongoverning Communists were informed, and knowledge quickly circulated. Leading Communists killed in 1948–52, like Rajk in Hungary and Kostov in Bulgaria, were rehabilitated. Stalinist leaderships kept the lid closed, but events in Poland and Hungary moved too fast. Gomulka's successor as Polish general secretary since 1948, Boleslaw Bierut, died just after the Twentieth Congress, and Edward Ochab now took the Khrushchev route, releasing political prisoners and encouraging open debate. Intellectuals urged freedom of expression; industrial militants moved toward workers' councils; and events exploded into a workers' uprising in Poznan on 28 June 1956. A crisis meeting of Polish and Soviet leaders brought Gomulka back to power on 19–20 October. He initiated economic reform, cultural liberalization, and compromise with the Catholic Church. In return, Khrushchev removed the hardline Polish minister of defense, Marshall Konstantin Rokossovski, who had been ready to march on Warsaw. Crucially, Gomulka observed the lines of the postwar Eastern European settlement: the single-party state, the centrally planned economy, and Soviet military rule.[7]

Hungarian events were more extreme with different results. While Rákosi had surrendered the Premiership to Nagy in July 1953, he continued blocking reforms and forced Nagy's dismissal in March 1955. But civil society was starting to stir, with writers, students, Catholics, and eventually workers forming associations, galvanized by attacks on Stalin and stories of returning prisoners. The Petöfi Circle, a student discussion club, called for honoring the purge victims. Rajk's widow Julia denounced Rákosi at a Petöfi meeting on antifascist Resistance and prewar illegal work in June

1956:"Murderers should not be criticized–they should be punished. I shall never rest until those who have ruined the country, corrupted the Party, destroyed thousands and driven millions into despair receive just punishment. Comrades, help me in this struggle!" The Circle's last meeting before suspension occurred on 27 June, the day before the Poznan Uprising. A huge overflow crowd heard calls for press freedom, Nagy's reinstatement, and changes in the system.[8]

On 18 July, the USSR replaced Rákosi with another Stalinist, Ernö Gerö, balanced by two returned victims, János Kádár and György Marosán. An alternative leadership crystallized on 6 October during Gerö's absence in Moscow, when Rajk and three others were reinterred in the Kerepesi National Cemetery on a hugely emotional occasion. New voices were demanding reform—the Writers' Union, the Central Council of Trade Unions, the reactivated Petöfi Circle, and a new student association. On 22–23 October, as demonstrations spiraled out of hand, inspired partly by Gomulka's appointment in Poland, Gerö handed over to Nagy and Kádár as premier and general secretary. Budapest lurched into turmoil, as fascists and freebooters joined democrats and reformers on the streets. On 30 October, Nagy restored the multiparty system, backed by a four-party coalition of Communists, Smallholders, Social Democrats, and National Peasants, with Christian Democrats forming in the wings. On 1 November, he withdrew Hungary from the Warsaw Pact. On 4 November, the Red Army occupied Budapest and all the major cities.[9]

Here, a second international crisis supervened: Israel had invaded Egypt on 29 October in collusion with Britain and France. Gamal Abdel Nasser, Egypt's nationalist leader since 1954, had nationalized the Suez Canal on 26 July 1956, challenging Western authority in a formerly colonial territory. The Israeli invasion was the pretext for an Anglo-French ultimatum calling on both sides to withdraw, so that British and French troops could "protect" the Canal. Against U.S. warnings, Britain and France began bombing Egypt on 30 October, invading a week later. On 6 November, the freshly reelected U.S. president, Dwight D. Eisenhower, imposed a ceasefire on the British and French.

Perversely, these dramatic disruptions confirmed the lasting stability of the 1945 settlement, with each side tacitly conceding the other's freedom of action—the USSR's in Eastern Europe, the West's in the colonial and postcolonial world. But this very coincidence of police actions finally shattered the Cold War's disciplines, leaving a new oppositional space beyond the Communist and social democratic battlelines. If Soviet behavior disastrously compromised Communism's remaining credibility, the equivocations of right-wing Socialist and Labour leaderships over the Suez invasion renewed a nonCommunist antiimperialist critique. As the British Left demonstrated for a Suez ceasefire on 4 November, the Red Army was entering Budapest, and this painful symmetry inspired a "new" Left to emerge.

Khrushchev's revelations tore Communist loyalties open. The secret speech elicited agonized self-criticisms, personally and collectively, with great divisiveness and calls for reform. Then, at the height of this soul-searching, the Hungarian invasion suggested that nothing had changed after all. As Communists stared at the freshly exposed Soviet reality, first in the wake of the Twentieth Congress and then "through the smoke of Budapest," facing not only the record of repression, but the public lies and massive self-deceptions that Moscow loyalties had entailed, conformities cracked.[10] The resulting debates surpassed anything since the mid-1920s, when Bolshevization sacrificed internal democracy to revolutionary élan.

This was Communism's big trauma: in two years, the PCI lost four hundred thousand members and the CPGB dropped from 33,095 members to 24,900. In some smaller CPs, like the Austrian, West German, and Portuguese, Moscow loyalists merely bunkered down.[11] Some nongoverning parties developed greater autonomy, usually after losing members, often via splits. This applied to Scandinavia, Spain, Greece, Switzerland, Britain, Ireland, and the Low Countries. Finally, in the larger Icelandic, Italian, and French CPs, 1956 worked with the grain of existing history. If the Icelandic People's Alliance avoided the vagaries of international Communism altogether, the PCI used 1956 to enhance its autonomy, while the PCF flaunted its Moscow orthodoxy. If Thorez minimized destalinization out of ingrained pro-Soviet loyalism, Togliatti pursued an explicitly independent course.[12]

But whatever the independence from Moscow, internal centralism remained. The CPGB's Commission on Inner-Party Democracy recommended against reform: once the dissidents had left, they became "renegades" and the party circled its wagons.[13] The PCF dissent broke on the rock of Stalinist discipline. Even in the PCI, the least Stalinist of CPs, whose support for pluralism and civil liberties was boosted by 1956, Togliatti adhered to the party's centralism. At the PCI's Eighth Congress in December 1956, dissenters were easily defeated. Some prominent individuals left, but the party's structure perdured.

Talking to *Nuovi argomenti* in June 1956, Togliatti stepped out of the self-referential Communist public sphere, however, and rebuked Khrushchev for confining criticism to Stalin's person rather than the system itself. He advanced the notion of polycentrism: "there are countries in which the road to socialism is being pursued without the Communist Party being in the lead. . . . The whole system is becoming polycentric, and even in the Communist movement we cannot speak of a single guide, but of progress which is achieved by following roads which are often diverse."[14] These were oblique references not only to China and Yugoslavia but also to Italy itself and the People's Democracies, invoking the "national roads" philosophy of 1943–47. Togliatti reiterated these views many times after 1956, culminating in his Yalta Testament of September 1964, just before he died. A new diversity characterized the international conferences of CPs in Moscow in November 1957 and December 1960, which denied the USSR the blanket loyalism it had earlier presumed. In April 1956, Cominform was dissolved, and the PCI blocked Soviet initiatives for any new international organization.[15] Instead, regional conferences of Western European CPs met in Brussels in 1965 and Vienna in 1966. The PCI reopened relations with the Yugoslav League of Communists and began meeting regularly with the PCF.

Thus the crisis of Communism in 1956 provided crucial pointers for the future. On the one hand, the revival of grassroots democracy was extraordinarily moving and courageous. The main Hungarian resistance to the Red Army had come from workers' councils, which reappeared in Europe for the first time since 1917–23. Resistance committees in 1943–45 had been a partial revival, as were the French factory occupations in summer 1936 and the anarcho-syndicalist collectives in Spain. But Hungarian events revived the conciliar form, mainly after the Nagy government's fall. Industrial towns, the main coalfields, and the Budapest district of "Red Csepel" resisted the Red Army during 4–11 November, forming the Central Workers' Council (CWC) of Greater Budapest, with three permanent officials and seven commissions. It negotiated with the Kadar government; handled relations with the Soviet military; coordinated a citywide strike; and prepared a National Council in a conference of 21 November. But in December, the authorities regained the initiative. They began picking the councils off, outlawing the CWC. But the councils remained an impressive display of grassroots democracy, based in the working class, mobilizing the best of rank-and-file Communism. They established a precedent for future episodes of working-class democracy.[16]

On the other hand, the Nagy government provided vital precedents for Communist reform. The Hungarian revolution was much disputed, with anti-Communists upholding its democratic authenticity and pro-Soviet apologists attacking its counterrevolutionary dangers, as former fascists, Horthy supporters, and Western agents came out of the ground. Hungary's leaving the Warsaw Pact also threatened to drive a Western wedge into the Soviet sphere. But the Nagy government stood for Communist reform, based on Nagy's own ministerial record from 1945–49 and his manifesto on the eve of the Twentieth Congress, On Communism. Nagy invoked Lenin's NEP as a better model of socialist construction than Stalinist five-year plans, with slower industrialization, priority for consumer goods, and an end to collectivization. Nagy's socialist-humanist credo and language of the national road was close not only to the reform Communism of the 1968 Prague Spring but also to the Eurocommunism of the mid-1970s and the unrealized antifascism of 1945. These perspectives characterized the clandestinely published *Hungaricus* pamphlets in December 1956–February 1957, calling for "new roads, different from Stalinist terror-communism or the social democratic trends fawning upon capitalism," in effect a "premature Eurocommunism."[17]

WEST OF SUEZ

The Suez Crisis was a watershed of international relations, marking both US primacy over Britain and France and a disastrous defeat for the old imperialist powers, whose inability to block colonial liberation was now exposed. Resistance to decolonization continued, but mainly where European settlers hijacked colonial rule—in Algeria, the Belgian Congo, Portuguese Africa, and British southern Africa. Otherwise, Suez drew a thick line between two moments of decolonization: before 1956, when colonial independence came mainly through bloody wars of liberation, and after Suez, when negotiated independence took over.[18] In Cyprus, the Communist sympathies of the nationalist movement under Archbishop Makarios made this shift to negotiation especially dramatic. British Colonial Office spokesmen had declared that Cyprus would never be independent, exiling Makarios to the Seychelles in early 1956; in March 1957 he was released, leading to independence in three years.[19]

Unfortunately, decolonization owed little to the Left as such. Paternalist favoring of colonial development notwithstanding, Labour disregarded the rights of colonial peoples to self-determination. The French Left also emerged with little honor: it was a Socialist prime minister, Guy Mollet, who presided over Suez; and neither the PCF nor the SFIO managed a principled anticolonial politics over Algeria. In Western Europe no less than the East, 1956 demanded a reckoning with existing Left politics—"with the depressing experiences of both 'actual existing socialism' and 'actual existing social democracy.' "[20]

The main story of the early 1950s was one of closure—of stepping down from the big expectations accompanying the end of war, of giving up the sense of agency in a changeable present, of forgetting what the victory over fascism could bring, of shedding the optimist's skin, the sense of history still being made. The postwar settlement brought large and lasting change, and capitalism's slow but dependable recovery in the West was about to deliver a different kind of plenty, a prosperous future of consumer largesse. But as Europe emerged from austerity after the war, it was the the Cold War's conservatism that delivered the main truth.[21]

The dual crisis of 1956 broke through "the climate of fear and suspicion which prevailed" during the 1950s, when "the 'Cold War' dominated the political horizon, positioning everyone and polarizing every topic by its remorseless binary logic." For Stuart Hall, a student at Oxford in the early 1950s, freshly arrived from Jamaica, the converging tragedies of Hungary and Suez dramatized the lack of appeal of both the Left's primary traditions, Communism and mainstream social democracy. These two events "unmasked the underlying violence and aggression latent in the two systems which dominated political life at that time—Western imperialism and Stalinism." The year 1956 "symbolized the break-up of the political Ice Age." It pointed the way forward to a new or "third" political space, where a "New Left" could form.[22]

IV

FUTURE IMPERFECT

IN FEBRUARY 1983, the British Labour
Party lost a disastrous by-election in Bermondsey, a South London docklands district
held continuously by the party since 1918. In
a microcosm of the difficulties befalling urban
Labour parties in the late twentieth century,
deindustrialization and demographic change
had removed the labor movement's social underpinnings, leaving behind an entrenched
party oligarchy in the Southwark Borough
Council linked to a union machine. In an increasingly familiar patterm, younger activists
moved into the local party, selecting its new
secretary, Peter Tatchell, in 1982 to succeed
the retiring MP Bob Mellish. The contrast was
stark: Mellish, the right-wing associate of former Prime Minister James Callaghan, in bed
with the union power brokers of the Borough
Council and the sworn enemy of change;
Tatchell, a 30-year-old former sociology student in public employment, an Australian
with no local roots, and equivocally on the
left. Tatchell was also gay.

Under pressure from Mellish and the party
right, Michael Foot, the new elected Labour
leader, publicly disavowed Tatchell as Bermondsey's parliamentary candidate, citing an
article Tatchell had written in *London Labour
Briefing* and accusing him of membership in
Militant, a Trotskyist caucus inside the party.
The local Labour Party refused to back down,
and Tatchell fought the bye-election amid vi-

ciously homophobic attacks from the press, from a "Real Bermondsey Labour" candidate, and from his Liberal-SDP Alliance opponent, who won
the seat.[1] But Tatchell had no links to Militant. A grassroots socialist, he
typified a generation of post-1968 activists who graduated from the student
movement into forms of community-based politics and during the course
of the 1970s saved local Labour Party branches from decay. In the offending article in *London Labour Briefing,* he had called merely for broad extraparliamentary mobilization by and for the unemployed in a "Siege of
Parliament" to restore "the radical and defiant spirit" of Labour's early
days. He was a pacifist. He supported gay and lesbian rights. He was in
tune with Ken Livingstone's recently elected left-wing administration at the
Greater London Council (GLC).[2]

The Bermondsey by-election revealed the collision of Left cultures. It
was a dramatic case of the so-called "loony Left" syndrome. Throughout
the 1980s, Conservatives and the press pilloried Labour politicians in local
government for supporting antiracism, feminism, and lesbian-gay rights.
Labour's national leadership reacted cravenly by disavowing the policies.
Faced with the new political agendas, it recurred to the safest political
ground, presenting a "respectable, moderate, trade-unionist, male-
dominated working-class" account of itself, through which the post-1968
ideas were denied.[3] The Right's demonizing of these New Left causes scared
the Old Left leaders so effectively that the issues were simply excised from
the agenda. In a later by-election in Greenwich in February 1987 and likewise in the runup to a general election, the Labour candidate Deidre Wood,
a former GLC member, faced the same vilification with no official Labour
support and lost again to the SDP. As the Labour leader aide Patricia Hewitt commented: "The 'loony Labour left' is taking its toll; the gays and
lesbians issue is costing us dear among the pensioners."[4]

These conflicts recurred across Western Europe. On one side were left-
wing generations shaped by the legacies of the Second World War and the
postwar settlement, complacent from the climactic prosperity of the 1960s
and increasingly intolerant of dissent, settling into their anticipated future
as natural parties of government. On the other side were the generations
of 1968 and beyond, whose sense of the future was very different. Participatory politics and direct democracy; feminism, gender difference, and the
politics of sexuality; issues of peace and ecology; racism and the politics of
immigration; community control and small-scale democracy; music, counterculture, and the politics of pleasure; consciousness raising and the politics of the personal—these were the issues that inspired younger generations
of the Left during the 1970s and 1980s. For the generations of 1945, such
preoccupations were simply not intelligible. The resulting clash fundamentally shifted the Left's overall ground.

For the first time in a century, the parliamentary party of socialism
linked to trade unions lost its hegemony over the democratic project of the
Left. Aside from the litany of particular issues just mentioned, the last third

of the twentieth century saw a resurgence of interest in locally focused direct action to the point where extraparliamentary agitations frequently supplanted the parliamentary sphere as the main center of left-wing energy. Concurrently, the infrastructures of capitalist industry, urban class formation, and autonomous city governent previously sustaining the class-oriented parties of socialism also began to break up. In a surrounding economic context after 1973 of recession, massive unemployment, and ravaged welfare states, that old socialist and Communist Left experienced profound disorientation.

In the midst of these changes, the Soviet Union entered a dramatic period of upheaval and reform, which ended with its dissolution in 1991. Along the way, and after a succession of earlier crises, the governing Communisms of Eastern Europe collapsed, bringing the region into the pan-European system of democratic states via the Revolutions of 1989. In conjunction with the longer-run changes mentioned earlier, these events signaled the end of a long era. The politics of democracy were clearly opening out.

Chapter 21

1968

It Moves After All

There'll be marching on

the streets, Little victories

and big defeats.

—Joan Baez,

"Song for Bobby"

ON 2 JANUARY, Fidel Castro, Cuba's charismatic leader, declared 1968 the Year of the Heroic Guerilla in memory of Ernesto Che Guevara, killed in Bolivia the previous October.[1] An international Cultural Congress in Havana, with four hundred intellectuals from the Americas and Europe, then focused international enthusiasm for the Cuban Revolution.[2] Meanwhile East Asia captured attention, from China's Cultural Revolution (1965–69) to student tumults against the USS *Enterprise* in Japan and the seizure of the intelligence vessel USS *Pueblo* in North Korea. On 30 January, the National Liberation Front, or Vietcong, launched the Tet Offensive against major cities in South Vietnam, pitching U.S. policy there into crisis. By the time U.S. and South Vietnamese troops reoccupied Hue, their credibility was in shreds.

European radicalism in 1968 was nothing if not internationalist, inspired by non-Western revolutionary movements or anger at the counterrevolutionary United States. Students passed easily across borders, from one theater of radicalism to another. The Bertrand Russell Peace Foundation's International War Crimes Tribunal promoted this process, centering its efforts on the Vietnam War.[3] The world had shrunk, practically through travel and communications and culturally through taste and style. Television was key. Events in Saigon—or Paris, Prague, and Chicago—could be shared simultaneously in student bars and common rooms in London, Stockholm, Rome, Amsterdam, or West Berlin:

for the first time, the world, or at least the world in which student ideologists

341

lived, was genuinely global. The same books appeared . . . in the student bookshops in Buenos Aires, Rome and Hamburg. . . . The same tourists of revolution crossed oceans and continents from Paris to Havana to Sao Paulo to Bolivia. The first generation of humanity to take rapid and cheap global air travel and telecommunications for granted, the students of the late 1960s, had no difficulty in recognizing what happened at the Sorbonne, in Berkeley, in Prague, as part of the same event in the same global village.[4]

LEAVING NORMAL

On 5 January, Antonin Novotny, Czechoslovakia's Stalinist President, was replaced as the KSC first secretary by a reluctant reformer, Alexander Dubcek.[5] By March 1968, the KSC had liberalized the press, abolished cultural censorship, and recognized academic freedom. It rehabilitated Purge victims. Its Action Program of 10 April focused political hopes in what became known as the Prague Spring. Concurrently, student protests precipitated crises in Poland and Yugoslavia, climaxing in March and June. Students clashed with police, spreading demands for civil freedoms across Poland. Warsaw Polytechnic University was occupied as students demanded a "Czechoslovak" process of reform.[6]

Students were on the move in Western Europe too. In Spain's universities they demanded educational reform, physically battled the state, and pressed for democracy with militant workers and illegal opposition groups. Faculty and administrators were suspended or resigned, police occupied buildings, and universities were closed.[7] Italian students occupied universities in Trento, Milan, and Turin, then Rome and Naples, until 26 universities were struck and higher education was immobilized. When students in Rome tried to occupy the faculty of architecture on 1 March, police brutality was answered in kind: "It was the first time we hadn't retreated in front of the police. . . . It gave us a sense of strength, of doing what we hadn't been able to do before. We were profoundly convinced that we were right to be doing it. We ripped up the wooden park benches and used the planks as clubs."[8]

This violent confrontation, the "Battle of Valle Giulia," became the 1968 norm. In West Germany, violence had already erupted during protests against the Shah of Iran's visit to West Berlin in June 1967, anger spilling over into other universities. In Britain, a sit-in at the London School of Economics (LSE) during March 1967 sparked the same pattern, with further flare-ups at universities in Leicester, Essex, Bristol, Aston, Hull, Bradford, Leeds, and Hornsey College of Art. Two London Vietnam demonstrations in October 1967 and March 1968 captured the rising propensity for violence: one was an orderly march of 10,000, but the other drew 30,000 who battled police at the US Embassy in Grosvenor Square.[9]

Paris had the same combustible ingredients as in Italy and West Germany—hugely expanding student numbers, hopelessly inadequate facilities, alienating environments, uncomprehending administrations—but it took time to draw the spark. Protest began at the new university of Nanterre, built on an air force depot in northwest Paris, in "a brutalist construction of glass and steel cubes, set down where industrial wasteland meets the ready-built slum housing of the Spanish and Algerian immigrant workers."[10] In November 1967, Nanterre was paralyzed by a student strike, and campus surveillance by plainclothes police ratcheted up the tensions. Daniel Cohn-Bendit emerged as the audacious and charismatic agitator of Nanterre's discontents.[11]

On March 22, six Nanterre activists were arrested after Vietnam rallies, and students occupied the chancellor's offices in response. The 22 March Movement was born, forging a common front beyond the Left's sectarian divisions—"without formal leaders, without common theoretical positions ... divided by their different political beliefs but united by a common will to act, and a pact that all decisions would be taken by general assemblies."[12] Hostilities spiraled: classes were suspended while police cordoned off the campus; sociology students boycotted exams; the university closed three days later. Authorities disciplined the leaders, summoning Cohn-Bendit and seven others to a hearing in the Sorbonne on 6 May. Parisian Maoists ("with helmets, clubs, catapults and ball-bearings") arrived after an ultra-Right threat to "exterminate the leftist vermin," and Nanterre closed indefinitely.[13] A manifesto of the 22 March Movement was endorsed by 1,500 students: "outright rejection of the capitalist-technocratic university, of the division of labor, and of so-called neutral knowledge—supplemented by a call for solidarity with the working class."[14]

By May, the signs had multiplied. Other French campuses were affected, and students sometimes connected with workers—at the Saviem works in Caen, the Dassault factory in Bordeaux, and Sud Aviation in Nantes. Unrest reached the schools, with a teachers' strike and High School Student Action Committees forming on 26 February. Student anger at the Vietnam War was shaped by an International Congress hosted by the Socialist German Students (SDS) in West Berlin in February. An attempted assassination of SDS leader Rudi Dutschke on 11 April produced immediate international solidarity, with Cohn-Bendit coordinating French protests for the 22 March Movement, joined by the Maoist *Union des Jeunesses Communistes, marxistes-léninistes* (UJC-ml) and the Trotskyist *Jeunesse Communiste Révolutionnaire* (JCR). French radicalization joined a general European tumult, with student risings in Spain, Italy, and Poland, widespread demonstrations in West Germany and Britain, and further militancy in Belgium, Sweden, and elsewhere, all in a framework linking Vietnam to student issues and revolutionary critiques of capitalism.

Student movements discarded conventional politics in favor of direct action and the streets. Student radicals ignored parliaments and elected representatives, behaving in passionate and unruly ways and looking for agency and meaning beyond the confines of the "system." Their actions were embedded in broader generational rebellion, as world events magnified images of change. Tensions heightened following the 1967 Arab-Israeli War, the Nigerian Civil War (1967–70), confrontations of state and students in Algeria, and the war in Southeast Asia. United States events shattered the Cold War's domestic stabilities: Democrats divided over Vietnam as President Lyndon B. Johnson withdrew from reelection; black radicalization accelerated after the urban riots of summer 1967, with the growing militancy of the Black Panthers, black nationalism, and the civil rights movement's conversion into the Poor People's Campaign. The transcontinental rioting after Martin Luther King's assassination on 4 April blazed across Europe's television screens.

PARIS, FRANCE: THE MAY EVENTS

When student revolution exploded in Paris on 3 May 1968, it was no bolt from the blue. Through television, Europe had grown used to mass demonstrations, red flags over occupied universities, and young people battling police. Burning cities and streetfighting were also familiar. Moreover, France was no bastion of tranquility. The Fifth Republic had barely surmounted the political ravages of the Algerian War, between the violent divisiveness of its foundation in 1958 and an abortive military coup in 1961. De Gaulle's presidency sat uneasily on the emerging prosperity of the mid-1960s. Yet the sheer scale of the May events came as a huge surprise, an abrupt counterblast to the West's complacencies.[15]

Things began on a Friday, as the eight Nanterre students arraigned on disciplinary charges strategized for their Monday hearing with comrades in the Sorbonne. A crowd gathered in the University's courtyard. The rector called in the police, who arrested those present. As the police vans were leaving, other students attacked them. The police ran riot, clearing the cobblestoned streets of the Latin Quarter and swinging their batons. There were 596 arrests and countless injuries. One leaflet vividly conveyed the drama:

> The CRS were leading the fight. They even charged into the halls of apartment houses, invaded several hotels and came out with young people whom they beat up while the public booed. . . . The police reaction reached its climax when the order was given to "clear everything." Blackjacks held high, the CRS attacked, hitting with all their might in all directions. Old women were caught in the general turmoil. A passing motorist shouted his indignation. CRS swooped down on his car and tried to pull him out of it, hitting him while he was still seated.[16]

The students' reactive anger had taken police unawares. Television and newspaper images of police brutality stunned the wider public. Outrage at police behavior propelled student militancy beyond expectations. The leaders bundled into police vans were "amazed as bottles, ashtrays, and mustard pots taken from cafés rained against [the] van[s]." The women from the courtyard meeting, who had been allowed to leave, led the attack. Hélène Goldet, from a wealthy Parisian family and the Trotskyist JCR, was one:

> It was great! Who started it, I don't know, nobody knows to this day. People just didn't like seeing that huge column of black police vans carting off those who'd been arrested. They ripped up the iron gratings from around the trees on the pavement to block the vans, threw everything they could lay their hands on at them, burnt newspapers to prevent the motorcycle police getting through. It was a great battle, a festival! I felt happy.[17]

Over the weekend, courts gave suspended sentences but sent four students to prison. The Sorbonne stayed shut under police guard. The freed leaders called a strike for Monday—release the students, withdraw the police, reopen the Sorbonne—and Friday's battle was repeated on a ferocious scale. Twenty thousand police faced a crowd of demonstrators that meandered through the city, diverted by roadblocks, building in numbers, and dangerously frustrated. By late afternoon, swollen to 30,000, the crowd turned back to the Sorbonne. Police charged with brutal abandon, smashing and kicking behind a barrage of tear gas, and the students replied in kind, sheltering behind cars and an improvised arsenal of cobbles. After holding the police off, they reassembled and marched to the University, where battle resumed. The violence was simultaneously exhilarating and shocking, spreading sympathy for the students. An opinion poll showed four-fifths of Parisians behind them.

Tuesday–Wednesday saw large peaceful marches of 30,000–50,000 people, followed on Thursday by intensive debate. Ultraleft sects competed with the Communists for attention and control, but both were eclipsed by the Movement of 22 March, the nonsectarian coalition forged in Nanterre, stressing sovereignty of the rank and file.[18] Activism was grounded in local Action Committees, ranging from study groups and faculty caucuses to neighborhood committees, with existing national associations providing an official voice. From 3 May, this comprised a triumvirate of the French National Union of Students under Jacques Sauvageot, the lecturers' union under Alain Geismar, and Cohn-Bendit.

As the violence of 6 May subsided, thoughts of settlement grew. But the silence of de Gaulle and his prime minister, Georges Pompidou, incited further mobilization, which was called for the evening of Friday, 10 May.

Last-minute negotiations over live radio between Geismar and the Sorbonne's vice-chancellor foundered on the demand that prisoners be released. The government also refused to speak with Cohn-Bendit. The stakes had become increasingly high. As Geismar pointedly said on live radio: "We have put forward our positions publicly, in front of the people who are listening. If the government is not prepared to assume its responsibility in the matter, then it is the people who will have to."[19]

The battle occurred that night. To prepare for police attack, some 20,000 demonstrators occupying the Latin Quarter broke the streets into cobblestones. Henri Weber, a JCR militant, described the symbolic power:

> It was a real stroke of genius. People were beginning to make the piles into barricades. Militarily speaking, it was probably silly. But politically, it was exactly the thing to do. The image of barricades in French history is associated with all the heroic moments of popular uprisings: in 1830, 1848, the Paris Commune. The barricade is a symbol, the defense of the poor, of the workers against the armies of the kings and reactionaries.[20]

The barricades were an unmistakable statement. Fifty to sixty were erected, some 10 feet high, and violence was sure to follow. At 2 A.M., the police attacked, with a savagery carried by radio into the living rooms of France: "the exploding plop of tear gas grenades, the vicious, brutal shouts of the riot police as they stormed barricades, the thud of exploding car petrol tanks, the groans of wounded students being carted off to ambulances."[21] Police assailed anyone in sight, including the occupants of apartments, which they invaded indiscriminately. No one escaped the frenzy: professors, tourists, nurses, medical personnel, or pregnant women. Misogyny and xenophobia ran rampant. By dawn, barricades were cleared, and 180 vehicles smouldered. There were a thousand recorded injuries and 468 arrests. On the radio, Cohn-Bendit called for a general strike.

Until now, the PCF response had been a sneer, denouncing the ultraleft as provocateurs, harping on Cohn-Bendit's Germanness, and calling students "pseudorevolutionary" foes of the working class. But as events unfolded, rank-and-file Communists inevitably joined the actions. Aware that no broader antigovernment challenge could happen without them, the CGT reluctantly combined with the other unions in a one-day protest strike on 13 May, when eight hundred thousand workers marched in a massive validation of the students' actions.[22] Georges Séguy, the CGT head, was forced to include Cohn-Bendit in the front rank, publicly uniting old and new Left. This was also the tenth anniversary of de Gaulle's rule, so the march naturally acquired anti-Gaullist momentum. It ended in triumph: Pompidou withdrew the police and reopened the Sorbonne. The students proclaimed a liberated zone.

Once Pompidou reopened the Sorbonne and the CGT took its troops home, the crisis seemed to have passed. But even as students reveled in their freedom, the aftershocks began, in a societal mobilization unparalleled in capitalist Europe since 1936. Momentum passed from students to workers. The spark came from Nantes: the student union and the the CGT brought demands to the prefect on 13 May, and after a pitched battle of "cobblestones against tear gas," he gave in; the next day, two thousand workers at Sud Aviation locked managers in their offices and occupied the plant.[23] Actions also occurred at Renault in Cléon, Flins, Le Mans, and Boulogne-Billancourt.[24] By the weekend, a strike wave was in progress, centered on the Paris red belt, Normandy, and Lyon. Automobiles, aeronautics, engineering, coal, chemicals, and shipbuilding were all affected, plus the public sector with municipal transit, railways, gas and electricity, the mails, sanitation, and channel ferries all on strike. Technical professionals, like air traffic controllers and radio and television personnel, were also out. By 18 May, 2 million were on strike, including 120 factory occupations. With the new week, strikers numbered from 4 to 6 million. The next day, 8 to 10 million were out.

Two movements were coming together. Students made universities into sites of euphoric experimentation, dismantling hierarchies, democratizing administrative process, redesigning curricula. The famous slogans, posters, and graffiti now appeared—"All power to the Imagination," "Their Nightmares Are Our Dreams," "Be Realistic—Demand the Impossible," "Take Your Desires for Realities," "Revolution Is the Ecstasy of History."[25] The Odéon theater housed a round-the-clock circus of endless debate: "Since the National Assembly has become a bourgeois theater, all bourgeois theaters should be transformed into national assemblies." In the *École des Beaux Arts,* students formed the *Atelier Populaire,* a daily source of collectively produced posters, a factory of the revolutionary gesture.[26] But workers were also claiming their agency. Inspired by the students' example, their audacity took not only employers and government but also the unions by surprise. In Nantes, the Sud Aviation action galvanized a generalized strike movement, culminating in city hall's seizure by the central strike committee of workers, peasants, and students on 27 May, displacing the prefect and mayor.

The CGT leadership remained dourly committed to keeping the two movements apart. Communists had painstakingly built up their organization in the industries agitated by the May events and bristled against imported fantasies of revolutionary change. French unions were among Europe's weakest—membership fell by two-thirds during 1947–55, and by 1968 union density was barely 20 percent. For Communists this spelled strategic caution, and once actions spread to workers they became desperate to assert control. During May, they doggedly reiterated their line— "defense of the republic" by a popular government of the Left, plus higher wages. Superficially it was a strategy with excellent historical credentials, especially from the Popular Front.

But the PCF's parliamentary strategy had three vital flaws. First, their parliamentary allies—Francois Mitterrand and the loosely formed *Fédération de la Gauche Démocratique et Socialiste* (FGDS), subsuming the moribund SFIO, and Pierre Mendès-France for the tiny *Partie Socialiste Unifié* (PSU)—were broken reeds. Second, the PCF's Left unity excluded the students. It red-baited them shamelessly.[27] Communists instead offered themselves as the party of order, set against extremists. Third, both factors undermined the PCF's credibility against de Gaulle. It could never compete with him on the terrain of "order." Consequently, while his government was paralyzed and the main hope was to press forward with change, the PCF failed to capture the momentum. At the height of the strikes, Séguy still denounced the radicals, arguing that "such empty formulas as self-management, structural reforms, plans for social and university reforms, and other inventions" only stymied the wage demands.[28] When students tried to join a CGT rally on 24 May, Communist marshals kept the processions strictly apart. "The General Will against The Will of the General"—one of the students' best slogans—was light-years away from the PCF's goals.

On 18 May, de Gaulle pronounced: "Reform, yes; shit-in-the-bed, no!"[29] Violence in Paris continued, with clashes at the Gare de Lyon, arson at the stock exchange, and attacks on three police stations; it was barricades and cobblestones again. The state was losing control of some cities like Nantes and Lyon, while Marseilles was under general strike. Then Pompidou's talks with employers and unions on 25–26 May produced terms: a 35 percent increase in the minimum wage, a 10 percent all-round increase, and progress toward the 40-hour week. For Séguy, this was a decisive breakthrough. But, dramatically, 10,000 Renault workers at Billancourt, the emblematic CGT bastion, rejected the accords; workers repeated this action elsewhere; and the stalemate returned. Workers wanted quality-of-life changes: more self-respect, greater shares in decision-making, more control over everyday life—everything implied by self-management.

The gap between the popular movement and the Left's existing national leaderships now really mattered. The former had no national structure. Ideal for some purposes, anticentralism was disabling in a general crisis of the state. The National Students Union called a rally to the Charléty stadium for 27 May, with 30,000 students and workers attending; but the 22 March Movement were opposed, the PCF went their own way, and the occasion slipped to the PSU and Mendès-France, who had no strategies to offer. On 28 May Cohn-Bendit, recently banned from France, returned clandestinely but failed to recreate his earlier energizing role. The same day, Mitterrand declared his willingness to replace de Gaulle, with Mendès-

France as prime minister. On 29 May, the PCF and CGT led their own huge anti-Gaullist march.

This tortoiselike step toward trying to form a government was rudely interrupted by de Gaulle. Having secured the loyalty of the French Army on the Rhine, he broadcast to the nation on 30 May, in a threatening four-minute statement: "No, I shall not stand down!" Parliament was dissolved for elections; the French people were summoned to "civic action" against "totalitarian Communism"; participatory democracy was dismissed; the army would be used against disorder. Half a million Gaullists poured into the streets, releasing a month's pent-up political rage. Their slogans were a brutal reminder of the divided society: "France back to work!" "Clean out the Sorbonne!" "We are the majority!" and "Cohn-Bendit to Dachau!" During de Gaulle's broadcast, an Eastern European emigré, turned to his colleague in the Sorbonne, and said: "It's all over now."[30] Government and respectable society had recovered their nerve.

RETURNING TO NORMAL

Although strikers began returning to work, a million were still out by 10 June, especially in the engineering and automobile industries. On 7 June, a military assault of 3,000 police with armored cars and helicopters evicted the 11,000 Renault workers at rural Flins west of Paris, with three days of resulting violence. This was repeated at Peugeot in Sochaux on 8 June, but after returning to work, the workers reoccupied the plant and fought the police for 36 hours, and two workers were shot. In the associated protests in Paris, 72 barricades reappeared, resulting in 400 injuries and 1,500 arrests.[31] Briefly, student militants could convince themselves that the movement continued.

But workers were now divided. Hostilities flared between pickets and those returning to work. The CGT and PCF amplified their denunciations: student militants were "agents of the worst enemies of the working class" and "specialist[s] in provocation."[32] While student militants had multiplied, the broader mobilization was dissipating, as were popular sympathies. The authorities isolated student radicals, reclaimed the universities, and purged the Odéon. On 16 June, they retook the Sorbonne.

In the elections of 23–30 June, the ruling coalition easily won. The Fifth Republic's electoral system helped (Gaullists took 60 percent of seats on 40 percent of the vote), but the Left's demoralization was no match for anti-Communist rhetorics of order. The PCF lost 39 seats; the Socialists lost 61; the PSU's 3 seats were gone. The government returned with 358 seats out of 485. Young people under 21, the active bearers of the May events, were excluded from the vote.

POLITICS IN A TIME OF DESIRE

Two Lefts faced each other across the frontier of de Gaulle's 30 May address—one anxiously awaiting normal politics to resume, the other disbelieving they ever could. The first was shaped by war and Liberation, through the political mythologies and social histories of the Resistance, the Cold War, and reconstruction. The second was nascent, arising from the 1960s themselves—the national crisis of the Algerian War, the social fallout of Gaullist modernization, the promises of prosperity, and the perceived drawbacks of the new consumer capitalism. These two positions displayed mutual incomprehension. The PCF typified the old Left (after the Italian, it was the largest Western CP), and its conservatism warrants some discussion.

Communists weren't passive. Once strikes began, the CGT supplied organizational muscle, and after Pompidou's wages package was rejected the PCF magnified its call for a government change. But the PCF reacted formulaically, without imagination, lagging behind at every stage. This had structural origins. French unions lacked density and political clout. Operating from weakness, the CGT tuned its militancy to the frequency of the PCF's political line, the party staking everything on parliamentary maneuvers. And while the PCF jockeyed for position, disavowing the revolutionary fervor, it wasn't surprising that Mitterrand sought to coopt popular energy for himself. This mutually reinforcing opportunism paralyzed the prospect of a united front. It was also reflex behavior: the old Left either held their ground as tribunes of the oppressed, deploying their strength as an oppositional bloc, or struck a parliamentary pose, unconnected to activism.

The dialectic of Cold War repression and social modernization marginalized the PCF, entrenching its reliance on defensive resources of class solidarity. While society was shifting behind de Gaulle's post-1958 rule through a stepped-up version of 1945 *dirigisme,* the PCF held the old ground. In 1962–68, the rural population sank from 41 to 29 percent, industry became more concentrated and capitalized, comparative growth in GDP improved, and France joined the world economy. State-sponsored economic plans promoted specific sectors—chemicals, telecommunications, construction, electronics, aeronautics, pharmaceuticals, data processing. Yet Communists lived in the older world of coal mines, mechanical engineering, municipal employment, and factories. As urbanization, mass schooling, and technology transformed the social landscape, modernization reshaped the economy, and consumerism flooded the culture, the PCF sheltered its ingrained routine.

This was the old Left's decisive failure, because May 1968 cleared a space for something new. The militancy's antiauthoritarianism was the main force, exploding through the widening cracks of Gaullist political culture. This was the Left's second politics—the antiauthoritarian socialism of Cohn-Bendit and the 22 March Movement. It could be found in the Odéon and Atelier Populaire, the collective culture of sit-ins and demonstrations, the anarchist wall newspapers, the endless debates, the practical tasks of supply and distribution, and the collectivizing of private space. It was in the general meetings and action committees. These were the sites where ordinary people's agency appeared. Ebullient desires for self-actualization were uncorked: "The unthinkable had happened! The strikes were like a flame, like everything we'd been saying at Nanterre. Fuck hierarchy, authority, this society with its cold, rational, elitist logic! Fuck all the petty bosses and the mandarins at the top! Fuck this immutable society that refuses to consider the misery, poverty, inequality, and injustice it creates."[33]

By June, Paris had 450 action committees. They grew from general assemblies wherever workers were striking, not only in factories but also in offices, transit depots, research centers, and broadcasting stations. The general strike of Paris lycées on 10 May led to three hundred reports questioning exams and grades, curricula, teaching methods, and schools' role in society. Teachers, ex-students, parents, and 3,700 students seized the Lycée Janson de Sailly, electing a central committee and four working commissions.[34] Action committees attacked hierarchies and democratized decision-making. Government by general meeting rebuked the hollowed-out parliamentary system and presidential regime of the Fifth Republic. In Nantes, the committee took over the running of the city. At the Berliet truck plant, workers switched the firm's name to read *Liberté*.

Animating the antiauthoritarian revolt was an ideal of self-management, officially adopted as *Autogestion* by the new *Parti Socialiste* (PS) in 1973–75. It envisaged democratizing the economy—via calls for plant-based workers' control, self-managing cooperatives, and constitutionalizing of businesses, and by means of participatory decision-making, opening the books, decentralized management, and general workplace enrichment. It was antistatist, the opposite of bureaucratic nationalization, and hostile to CGT unionism. It repudiated the post-1945 Left. It questioned parliamentary socialism, denying that liberal proceduralism (voting in elections, parliamentary representation, rule of law) ensured democracy under capitalism.[35]

Autogestion bypassed the hegemonic principles of representative democracy. It expressed workers' resentment at the unfairness of modernization, for while the French middle classes relished the booming consumerism, workers' incomes languished. Anomie was paralleled for students in the oppressive gap between promises of careers and the present tense of boredom, marginality, and disempowerment. French youth felt the excitements of cultural change in a public culture that "spoke endlessly of things that were totally foreign to us: national independence, . . . [the] independent nuclear strike force, the role of the constitution."[36] In these class and generational gaps, violent discontents arose, directed against consumer capitalism, the work ethic, regimentation, and authority. "Alienation" was the buzzword. It issued a powerful accusation: "that modern society is a confidence trick offering high standards of material comfort in exchange for slavery to the industrial machine; that modern learning has acceptance of this situation as its main goal."[37] As Cohn-Bendit recalled: "The students wanted to know: why are we learning this? To do what? To have what function in society?"[38]

The 22 March Movement pioneered this critique, with its absence of bureaucracy, idealizing of local autonomy, and permanent democracy of the general meeting. Once the Sorbonne was occupied, experiments could flourish. Students rebelled against perceived logics of modernization—against "the politico-economic power's entire depersonalized, 'rationalized,' bureaucratic plan of action."[39] Such logics seemed continuous across industry, education, and personal life: from deskilling and automation, to "machine-like preparation for a circumscribed role in a big organization" and everyday fragmentation and isolation.[40] Thus, if the positive program of 1968 seemed a highly rhetorical and abstract desire for "wholeness," "liberation," and the reclaiming of an integrated self, it was in the multiple settings of everyday life—workplace, school, lecture hall and exam room, shopping center, car, television, family, bedroom, the generalized imaginative space of commodification and mass-mediated culture—that this became compellingly concrete. Politics were coming down to the ground.

Connecting everyday life to politics required disobedience and lots of noise. It implied a breaking of rules—overturning public life's given protocols, the boundaries of what could and couldn't be said. This flew in the face of entrenched wisdom. Conversely, therefore: "To bring politics into everyday life is to get rid of the politicians."[41] Thus, debating democracy redefined the very category of the political itself. Hitherto, making a revolution had implied seizing power in the state, linked to reorganizing the economy. In the Marxist tradition, Cohn-Bendit reflected, two decades later, you had "to change all the structures to change life." But in 1968, "[w]e discovered . . . that the revolutionary process is a summary of changes in daily life. This was new. It was interesting for other students. We didn't propose a change in the next life, after you die for the revolution, but today where you live. . . . We wanted to be in charge of our lives. That's still the main issue today."[42]

This building of the new politics from the starting points of everyday life—making the political personal—generated the immediacy and excitements of the time. It also made explicit an emerging agenda the old Left could barely perceive. The consumer prosperity of the 1960s combined with the rise of the new student populations and the stylistic rebellions of youth to perforate the postwar settlement's stabilities. From the fascination with direct democracy and participatory forms through "permissiveness" to the enabling of sexuality and the counterculture's hedonistic excess, from the practical experiments with autogestion to the obsessive critiques of alienation—in all these respects "1968" challenged the hegemony of "1945." The resulting conflicts took many years to work themselves out, but over the longer term their effects were huge. They redefined the ground of politics. They complicated notions of the Left. They changed established assumptions about where radical democratic agency could be found.

CONSUMER CAPITALISM, GENERATIONS, AND THE POLITICS OF CULTURE

In its distinctiveness, the French student revolt was linked to a crisis of the French state, whose democratic arrangements were among the West's least functional. But the effects of the new consumer capitalism were general throughout Western Europe. Rising living standards included not only housing and nutrition and the pervasive security of full employment and the welfare state but also greater disposable incomes from rising real wages. Novel access to consumer goods meant electric irons, vacuum cleaners, washing machines, refrigerators, and of course television sets and cars. Such change came suddenly, concentrated in the early 1960s. In Britain, consumer spending increased by 45 percent from 1952 to 1964, and consumer durables' share in household budgets more than doubled. Between 1958 and 1965 in Italy, refrigerator ownership rose from 13 to 55 percent of households, washing machines from 3 to 23 percent, televisions from 12 to 49 percent. The same pattern characterized West Germany, where refrigerators became nearly universal by 1968.[43]

This new consumerism became linked in public minds to acquisitive individualism and a privatized lifestyle. Cultures of sociability shriveled into the private space of the home, where commercial values corroded the family's cohesion and authority. Both conservatives and the Left found this troubling. For Italian Christian Democrats, materialism produced "the decomposition of the traditional structures of Italian society," while for Communists, it spelled lower attendance at party meetings, the seductions of commercial entertainment, and the atrophe of working-class collective pastimes.[44]

Such debates had longer provenance, linked to fears of "Americanization" and popular cultures stigmatized as "vulgar" and "mindless"—conveyed now by pop music, jukeboxes, Coca-Cola, blue jeans, comic books, milk bars, and slang. Television's arrival undermined not only the political sociability of the Left but also older commercial entertainments—English soccer crowds declined by a third (1949–66) and British film-going by three-quarters (1946–62). Public attention obsessed over the decadence of U.S. rock-and-roll, from Elvis Presley and Bill Haley's *Rock around the*

Clock to British television's *Juke Box Jury, Oh Boy,* and the *6:05 Special.* Technologies drove this along—amplification and electric guitars, long-playing records and "45s," and transistor radios.[45]

Contempt for and identification with the consumer economy's modest pleasures broke along ageist lines. New youth markets brought self-conscious solidarities, further magnified by the Beatles, the Rolling Stones, and the explosion of indigenous rock, which fed on grassroots creativity. For David Fernbach, about to be radicalized at the LSE and a future gay activist, the rock band he formed meant "a whole new way of being," expressing "a basic aspiration to live our own life in a way that accorded with things that gave us pleasure." Such desires crossed national barriers but also those of gender and class. For Laura Derossi, a middle-class 16-year-old in Milan in 1962, buying cosmetics and dresses and viewing adult movies were the "first acts of rebellion": they made "a special type of friendship, a generational union, in place of the traditional family-based friendships, like my mother's. We changed everything, inherited nothing."[46]

This defiance was bitterly upsetting for adults. Fernbach's parents had modest means: "They were keen for me to study hard and get a good professional job. Throughout my teens, there was this conflict between what they wanted for me and doing my own thing here and now."[47] Rock music, clothes, long hair, sex, and drugs flouted parental values, the more painfully where parents were themselves left-wing, wielding "the blackmail of past hardships" against present critiques: "Older generations, those that went through Fascism, war, Resistance, hard times in the factories, poverty, and the Depression, often think they have a monopoly on history, and blackmail the younger generations with it."[48] For Gaetano Bordoni, a Communist barber in San Lorenzo (Rome), his daughter's political complaining and casual treatment of hard-won comforts dishonored his own generation's earlier anti-Fascist sacrifice. "By leaving her steak uneaten on her plate," Bordoni's daughter diminished the meaning of her father's life, where material improvements blurred into the winning of democracy: "By claiming that 'this isn't freedom' and calling for more radical forms of struggle, the younger generation questions both the achievements of the anti-Fascist struggle and the current politics of the working-class Left."[49]

Radical youth faced a dominant politics—right and left—entrenched around such wartime and postwar experiences. Its rebelliousness had antipatriarchal qualities—against the power of fathers in families but also against long-established political authority, embodied in the governing gerontocracy of Adenauer (born 1876), de Gaulle (1890), Franco (1892), and Macmillan (1894). In return, antifascist generations—who had experienced the Second World War as adults and now led the Communist and social democratic parties—despised the student Left:

> These people are not Socialists. They are not even respectable Marxists. They are a new brand of anarchists, very different from the en-

dearing characters whom many of us knew. . . . They are wreckers who . . . are concerned only to disrupt society. Their weapons are lies, misrepresentations, defamation, character assassination, intimidation and, more recently, physical violence.[50]

This "generation gap" was embraced on both sides: "The best poster on the walls of my faculty, I remember it really distinctly, out of all the posters there: 'I want to be an orphan.' "[51]

Students multiplied in the 1960s—trebling in France, Greece, and Scandinavia, doubling in Italy, the Low Countries, West Germany, Britain, and Iberia.[52] Spectacular unrest affected Italy, West Germany, and France, countries where university entrance required only completing academic high school rather than selection. The baby boom contributed—with birthrates 30 percent higher for 1946–50 than 1935–39 in Britain and France and West German and Italian increases following later. School leaving age was also raised, and youth straddled childhood dependence and adult "responsibility," creating a new category of young people with time, knowledge, money, and growing self-consciousness, targeted as a market and concentrated in distinctive institutions but juridically excluded from citizenship.

Student radicalism reached beyond the university to a broader rebelliousness of youth. If Paris saw the synergy of students and workers, London had the counterculture. Entrepreneurial freebooting and creative experimentation exploded across publishing, music, design, theater, and performance in London, with new careers in media, arts, and entertainment. In 1966–68, the British "Underground" was a kaleidoscope of institutions, including the Notting Hill Free School, the Anti-University, Indica Gallery, the Arts Lab, Apple, the Electric Cinema, the Macrobiotic Restaurant, a series of clubs, and a mosaic of "happenings" and festivals. One climax, marked by the drug prosecutions of John Hopkins, a leading counterculture impresario, and the Rolling Stones, was the Fourteen Hour Technicolor Dream at the Alexandra Palace and the release of the Beatles' *Sergeant Pepper's Lonely Hearts Club Band*. This scene, imbricated with the arts and theater avant-garde, suffused with the drugs aesthetic, and luxuriating in stylistic rebellion, drew provincial talents like a magnet.[53]

In Britain's New Left, ideas had coalesced around the Campaign for Nuclear Disarmament (CND) formed in 1958, linking an annual march from the Atomic Weapons Research Establishment in Aldermaston with wider agitation and a campaign in the Labour Party for unilateral nuclear disarmament. By April 1962, the four-day Aldermaston March drew 15,000 participants, with 150,000 at the final rally in Hyde Park. Key departures also occurred on CND's left, with the Direct Action Committee (DAC) pioneering civil disobedience, increasingly against the Labour Party, which refused to outstep parliamentary channels. In October 1960, the DAC merged into the Committee of 100, organizing mass sit-downs at the Ministry of Defense (February 1961), Parliament Square (April), and Trafalgar Square (September). The state's response hardened, with mass arrests of 826 in April, and 1,314 in September.[54]

The DAC anticipated key aspects of 1968—not only these forms of direct action but also appeals to workers, international solidarity with Ghana against French nuclear tests in the Sahara, and impatience at the old Left of Labour and the CP. It meant the "extension of politics away from the party machines and into the community."[55] Here, it connected with the Communist dissidence of 1956 and the post-Suez revival of broader left-wing activity, themselves cohering around the New Left Review and its Clubs.[56] This New Left developed critiques of Communism and social democracy, projected an internationalism beyond the Cold War camps, and analyzed contemporary changes in capitalism. It advocated participatory democracy inside an ethics of "commitment." Most of all, it argued that the boundaries of politics were changing:

> We raised issues of personal life, the way people live, culture, which weren't considered the topics of politics on the left. We wanted to talk about the contradictions of this new kind of capitalist society in which people didn't have a language to express their private troubles, didn't realize that these troubles reflected political and social questions which could be generalized.[57]

In 1958–62, this inchoate movement started coming together. It owed much to an earlier dissenting Communism, with its antiimperialism, internationalist networks, and ethical nonconformity. But it owed more to postwar social and cultural changes. The CND and the associated New Left swam in the cultural dissidence of the time—inspired by public intellectuals in literature, theater, and arts but also by bohemianism and the Beats. As a 12-year-old in Slough, David Widgery watched the Aldermaston March:

> the march passed through the streets with great clamor and glamor. People with battered top hats playing the cornet out of tune and girl art students with colored stockings—the whole parade of infamy came through the town. It was terribly enticing. At school, we were told to beware of them, not to fraternize. There was a lot of quiet pandemonium about CND and these beatniks. It wasn't just that they were campaigning for nuclear disarmament, they were political in a different kind of way, into linking up with local and direct action groups. They were passionate, evangelical, calling upon you to do things now, to sit down, to stand up and be counted.[58]

The world of jazz and R & B, poetry in pubs, little magazines, and art schools grounded the prehistories of 1968 as much as CND. Michael Horovitz's poetry magazine New Departures (launched 1959), with its five hundred jazz and poetry readings, complemented New Left Review and its

Clubs. CND's "carnival of subversion" regrouped in the 1965 International Festival of Poetry, where an unprecedented audience of 7,500 witnessed the counterculture's explosion into the light of day.[59] The Festival was the "transition between the two parts of the 60s," and "a pre-indication of what was to come."[60] By July 1967, the Congress of the Dialectics of Liberation sharpened this cultural radicalism to a political edge. It marked a "shift away from the CND nuclear pacifist orientation to an attitude which identified strongly . . . with revolutionary movements in the Third World."[61]

THE PRAGUE SPRING: "SOCIALISM WITH A HUMAN FACE"

In Eastern Europe, a New Left was also forming in Czechoslovakia. Communism there was a paradox. Europe's largest CP between the wars and the strongest in Eastern Europe after 1945, the KSC enjoyed genuine popularity in 1945–48. Yet it developed the region's nastiest Stalinism in the purges after 1948–49 and postponed de-Stalinization until 1962–63. By that time, Eastern Europe's socialist economies were languishing, and in Czechoslovakia the crisis was severe. Following experiments with market socialism in Hungary and Poland, socialist states began modestly shifting priorities from heavy industry to consumption and services, and by 1964–65 the KSC was considering proposals for market reform. This occurred amid intellectual ferment and brewing nationality problems.[62]

A complex dynamic produced the Prague Spring. It began in the Central Committee between October 1967 and January 1968, culminating in Novotny's replacement by Dubcek as party first secretary. The implications remained unclear, for if attacks on Novotny were borne by demands for democratization, the new KSC leadership was indistinctly committed to reform. Convinced radicals in the Presidium were few—Frantisek Kriegel, Josef Smrkovsky, Josef Spacek, and the secretaries Cestmír Císar and Václav Slavík—but conservatives only coalesced after May, and the key axis was provided by Dubcek and Prime Minister Oldrich Cerník, assisted by the candidate member Bohumil Simon and the secretary Zdenek Mlynár, who consistently pressed reform.[63] Still more important, the Presidium's will to change depended on pressure from below.

In the ranks party members mobilized quickly during January–April 1968, with the freeing of the press and intensive inner-party debates, especially via the district conferences convening in March. The Action Program of 10 April revived the party, and the calling of the Fourteenth Congress for September focused a process of radicalization. But once the public sphere was reopened, the energy for democratizing outgrew party channels, and broader popular hopes revitalized civil society. This occurred via thousands of public meetings, mass rallies, and new associations like the organization of victims of Stalinism (called K-231) and the Club of Non-Party Engagés. Non-Communist parties were refounded, including the illegally revived Social Democratic Party. The pivotal event was the "2,000 Words Manifesto," drafted by the writer Ludvík Vaculík and distributed in three hundred thousand copies on 27 June, focusing the popular identification with reform. This radicalized the public temper, polarized conservatives and reformers, and pushed things beyond the KSC Presidium's control.

An increasingly nervous Soviet Union watched these events spiral out of conservatives' grasp. Repeatedly demanding promises of normalization, Leonid Brezhnev moved toward military intervention, collaborating secretly with the KSC Presidium's antireformers.[64] But the Prague Spring had renewed the suppressed vitality of Czechoslovakia's Communist tradition, activating varied hopes and reactions. Even as reformers and conservatives worked at stabilizing the party's legitimacy, accordingly, the public sphere grew ever more unruly, as student assemblies, public meetings, and the press institutionalized a censorship-free ferment of opinion.[65] Early May was a turning point. Flushed with the excitement of May Day, which galvanized huge spontaneous support, KSC leaders went to Moscow seeking Soviet endorsement. Yet Brezhnev denounced popular demonstrations as counterrevolutionary, demanded imprisonment of non-Communist critics, and told Dubcek's group to start behaving as "real leaders of this party."[66] Despite the reformers' naively lingering optimism, therefore, by 29 July the Soviet position had become brutally clear: "we could occupy your entire country in the course of twenty-four hours."[67]

By then, popular hopes were beyond recall. The Presidium went to the final summit at Cierná nad Tisou on 29 July backed by an appeal in *Literární listy* by Pavel Kohout called "Socialism, Alliance, Sovereignty, Freedom" and ending: "We are with you, be with us!" which drew a million signatures. On arrival, they received a local petition of 20,000 names from virtually every adult in the district. The radicals now invoked a broader-than-Communist mandate. Smrkovsky approached Cierná with two objectives: "to defend the post-January policy as expressed in the Party's Action Program and to prevent any break with the Soviet Union." He had secretly approved the public pressure of Kohout's appeal to constrain pro-Soviet loyalists in the Presidium from breaking ranks.[68] But by this time, the Soviet leaders had already decided on their course, actively conspiring with Presidium conservatives to remove Dubcek and restore control.[69] For Brezhnev and the CPSU, the Prague Spring's revival of National Communism had broken the bounds of tolerable Communist practice.

The Prague Spring, like the Hungarian Reform Communism in 1956, problematized the CP's political monopoly, reaching the edge of the Stalinist systems established in 1947–49. The bases of those systems—single-party rule, administrative justice, censorship, Marxist-Leninist orthodoxy, and the autonomy of security services—were nonnegotiable in Soviet minds. Ending single-party rule was unacceptable. Freedoms of speech, association, and assembly, abolishing censorship and freeing the press, instituting cultural freedoms, and protecting universities and the arts all clashed with Soviet rules. Dubcek's pluralism was still indistinct, and the KSC's existing proposals permitting non-Communist political activity begged many questions. But the Action Program of 10 April had clearly crossed the rubicon of democratic reform, violating the strict code of Soviet rule descending from 1956.

Here was the site of irreconcilable KSC–Soviet differences. The principle of pluralism itself defined the Action Program from the start. In the latter's words, the CP had to "earn" its leadership by deeds. It had no right to "monopolistic concentration of power." It was not "the instrument of the proletarian dictatorship." It had to act by persuasion, on the basis of democracy. Stalinism was a bureaucratic degeneration impeding future progress. The KSC had the chance of building something better—"to blaze a trail under unknown conditions, to experiment, and to give a new shape to socialist development" based on "creative Marxist thinking" and a knowledge of Czechoslovak conditions, with the advantages of "a relatively mature material base, unusual standards of education and culture among the people, and incontestable democratic traditions."[70]

In this respect, there was no gap between KSC reformers and the country in August 1968. Soviet hostility had brought opinion massively behind the government. Reform's "real enemies" were in "the repressive and ideological sections of the party apparatus, security and judiciary officials, older Communists, higher officers of the army, and the People's Militia," while other opponents simply feared for their futures—"the whole of the central economic bureaucracy, managers without education, workers in heavy industry, and certain parts of the party apparatus." But there were equally big constituencies for change, including the technical intelligentsia, cultural intellectuals, students, journalists, "workers in certain non-preferred branches of industry, and in transport and communications, farmers, women and working youth." Reformers drew many managers, trade unionists, party officials, and soldiers into this gathering coalition.[71]

The USSR's implacable conservatism ended the Prague Spring. Brezhnev lost patience with Dubcek's delaying tactics, and the Warsaw Pact armies arrived in Prague on 20 August to reestablish normal rule. However, the conspiracy arranged with conservatives in the KSC's Presidium was botched. Two of its members voted with the Presidium majority (7 to 4) to condemn the invasion. The conspirators left the government building in disarray, while the reformers awaited their fate.[72] The Prague City Committee called the Fourteenth KSC Congress to the Vysocany industrial district, where delegates rallied secretly against the invasion. Dubcek, Cernik, Smrkovsky, Kriegel, Spacek, and Simon were abducted to Moscow, joined by President Ludvík Svoboda on his own decision. The conspiracy's debacle left Brezhnev no choice but to talk with the kidnaped KSC leaders. After traumatic negotiations, a protocol was agreed. Dubcek and the others returned to Prague. They had fended off the conservatives, dropping only some radicals and resisting blanket disavowals of reform. But in signing the protocol, they surrendered the Action Program. Only Kriegel had refused.

The reformers were soon trapped into demeaning and irreversible retreat. The Vysocany Congress was annulled. Censorship was reintroduced. Reform of the security apparatus was shelved. The public sphere was closed down. Gustav Husák, based in the Slovak CP, took charge.[73] Continuing protests against the invasion between October 1968 and March 1969 only hardened the normalizing line. By April 1969, the reformers were entirely dispossessed, the party purged of 21.7 percent of its membership, and Soviet order restored.[74] Among reformers who persisted, few kept any integrity. Dubcek was broken. Smrkovsky and other stalwarts of the Action Program were gone. Cernik had horribly compromised himself: "I have shat away my position and my honor."[75]

COMMUNISM AND THE LEFT

We saw the dour Czechs slowly coming to life, gaining expression, smiling at one another in trams, appearing on TV without ties. Together with the foreign friends, scattered in flats over our housing estate, we saw this face pushed into the mud by olive-green Soviet tanks, these being driven by catatonic pink-faced eighteen-year-olds from rural Russia. . . . As Robin and I watched the nervous Soviet tank crews and anguished crowds in the debris-covered Wenceslas Square, he asked me whether it was not time to break with Communism.[76]

The Soviet invasion of Czechoslovakia ended socialism's Eastern European prospects. For Soviet leaders, it was plain; liberalization was ipso facto counterrevolution. There were three fixed points in the Soviet system that preempted any genuine Left in Eastern European CPs after 1968. These were also huge liabilities for Western Lefts, whose socialist advocacy was disastrously handicapped by "actually existing socialism."

The first was the iron fist of Soviet military rule, based on Europe's geopolitical division in 1945–49, solidified by NATO and the Warsaw Pact. Socialist economics—collective property, bureaucratic management, and central planning—was the Soviet system's second fixed point. Economic reform always halted at state ownership and the command economy, whether targeting regional and sectoral decentralization, profit mechanisms, new accounting methods, enterprise autonomy, or self-management. The third fixed point was Communist political monopoly and single-party rule. Policing the public sphere, penalties for dissent, administrative solutions for political differences, and confinement of thinking within narrow orthodoxies—all these marked Communist political life. When reform outstepped these precepts, the boundaries of the possible were reached.

National roads, market extension, and political reform went against the Soviet grain. In the Soviet imperium's first quarter-century, reform always involved complex synergies between social pressures and inner-party renewal. Communist traditions themselves fed into the Hungarian revolution and the Prague Spring. And this was the possibility terminated by 20 August 1968. Henceforth, dulled conformity, social apathy, bureaucratic privilege, Moscow loyalism, and at best a kind of technocratic ambition became generalized across Eastern Europe's governing cultures. After 1968, no democratic impulse could begin from Eastern Europe's Communist parties. Left politics had to originate in opposition to the CPs rather than through them.

The Czechoslovak invasion was a watershed for Western CPs too. By contrast with 1956, Soviet actions were almost universally condemned. Soviet contempt for the world movement was shocking, and world Communist unanimity had dissolved.[77] By the CPSU's Twenty-Fifth Congress (February 1976) and the long-postponed Conference of European CPs (East Berlin, June), diversity was institutionalized. Western European CPs demanded "independence," "sovereignty," and "equality and respect for the autonomy of all parties," supporting individual and collective freedoms under socialism. A shared position coalesced around the Italian, British, Swedish, and even the French speakers, whom Soviet leaders denounced. In East Berlin, an unparalleled debate ensued, the resulting document stressing "equality and sovereign independence of each party, non-interference in internal affairs, [and] respect for free choice of different roads." It validated debate, international non-alignment, and "dialogue and collaboration with democratic forces." Leninist talk—where parties were "vanguard forces," with "identical objectives" and "a common ideology"—was gone.[78]

Equality

This was the slow working-through of de-Stalinization. Until 1956, one could support the USSR or one's own CP, even despite Stalin's crimes. Resisting fascism and the Nazi new order had been compelling reasons for doing so, as were the Cold War's battlelines. Communist parties were the most consistent opponents of imperialism. They organized the most militant workers, particularly in countries of mass Communism (Italy, France), or where Communists led resistance to dictatorship (Spain, Portugal, Greece), but also in the northern heartlands of social democracy (Britain, the Netherlands, Scandinavia), where Communists rallied the more radical Left. Isolating oneself from working-class radicalism was the cost of rejecting the CP. This was the argument of Jean-Paul Sartre and many intellectual "fellow travelers" between the rise of fascism and 1956.[79] But it was true more generally of trade unionists, social activists, peace campaigners, radical Christians, and reformers of all kinds, who disliked Stalinism but couldn't stomach the pragmatism, machine politics, and moral compromising of social democrats. For revolutionaries, this reflected longer-term perspectives:

> these societies were economically ossified and politically repressive. And yet, the Left . . . have continued to side with them. Why? Because they saw these societies as the main line of trenches in the war of position against the bourgeois bloc, the only secure front after the defeats of the twenties in Europe. As a result, the West, which had not made its revolution, came to console itself with the revolutions that had occurred elsewhere, while these revolutions bore, in their own lack of freedom and impasse, the consequences of the failure of revolution in the West.[80]

After 1956, this changed. Krushchev's revelations wrecked the USSR's progressive credibility, compounded by the Hungarian invasion. His other initiative of "peaceful coexistence" of East and West, which disavowed traditional revolutionary ambitions under capitalism, also allowed the Chinese Revolution to emerge as a militant counterpole for the international Left. Sino-Soviet conflict divided the world movement further, with new Maoist groups inside national lefts. By 1960, Communism's granite orthodoxies were severely cracked. The aftershocks of 1956 moved some parties into realignment. Others gradually rethought.

The 1960s also saw remarkable revivals of Marxism, which shattered the Stalinist ideological mold, breaking Marxist ideas from the self-referential isolation of the Cold War. Sometimes this began inside Communist frameworks—the *Praxis* group of philosophers in Yugoslavia; the influence of Lukács in Hungary, Leszek Kolakowski and others in Poland, and Karel Kosík in Czechoslovakia; Marxist sociologies in Hungary and Poland; or Louis Althusser's circle in France. In countries without a large CP, Marxism spread from the universities, as in West Germany with the Frankfurt School and Ernst Bloch. In France and Italy, Communism's role in the Resistance and organized Left culture made Marxism an accepted part of intellectual life through writers like Sartre, the journals *Les Tempes modernes* (1945–) or *Arguments* (1956–62), and the influence of structuralism. In Britain, Marxism found space between the CPGB and the labor movement's cultural institutions, broadening in the 1960s with university expansion and the opening of the arts and television. Ex-members of the CP Historians' Group, the founding of cultural studies around Richard Hoggart, Raymond Williams, and Stuart Hall, and broader New Left activity were all key. Finally, Trotskyism also energized Marxist intellectual work, as did smaller intellectual groupings like *Socialisme ou Barbarie* around Cornelius Castoriadis and Claude Lefort in France. These influences were a bridge from the crisis of Stalinism in 1956 to the explosions of 1968.[81]

By 1968, the lines between these variegated Marxisms and the slowly de-Sovietizing CPs were blurred. But two decisive manifestations of official Communist conservatism—the PCF's failures in the May events and the Soviet invasion—called the future of Western European Communism into doubt. Either the CPs would separate from Stalinism by condemning the Soviet invasion, or they would condemn themselves to political insignificance. In 1968, opposing the USSR meant embracing new ideas of democracy and the other meanings of the May events. Post-Stalinist trajectories of the Scandinavian, Dutch, British, Greek, Spanish, and Italian CPs after 1956, and the Prague Spring's inspiration, suggested that Western European CPs—though not the governing Communisms of socialist states—were still capable of renewal. But would Communism go the way of the PCF, in its traditionalist refusal of new times? Or would it learn from 1968?

GATEWAY TO THE FUTURE?

By their own lights, the movements of 1968 everywhere failed. In Western Europe, university reforms were enacted and the worst *in loco parentis* paternalism (gate hours, sexual regulations, social rules) abolished. But overcrowding wasn't reduced; curricula weren't transformed; and universities weren't democratized, let alone becoming "red bases," as some revolutionaries dreamed.[82] In France, the toppling of de Gaulle never happened. The May events precipitated a national political crisis, but the June elections left Gaullism apparently unscathed. The equally vigorous West German and Italian student revolts also failed. The great Vietnam actions of 1968 failed to move their governments from uncritical pro–United States support. In Spain, Francoism survived. In Eastern Europe, the Polish and Yugoslav student movements were beaten back, leading to general repression. In Czechoslovakia, reform Communism expired.

But the new radicalisms were as much disorderly symptoms as consciously directed movements. Militancy seldom cohered in other than temporary or local ways—an individual university, a particular event, a campaign like the Vietnam solidarity actions. These were more the unanticipated effects of sociocultural changes during the postwar boom—rising standards of living, new consumer capitalism, highly visible stylistic subcultures of youth, and expanding universities. Such processes were transforming the landscapes where politics occurred. They defined new spaces, where new ideas and practices were needed. Eastern agendas were clearer, for the Prague Spring involved dynamics of de-Stalinization deriving from 1953–56. But the Western European consumer economies had only just appeared. The movements of 1968 provided flashes of a future still being shaped—class structures being recomposed, labor movements losing their distinctive cultures and community ground, service industries dominating the labor market, new technologies and labor processes linked to new discourses of self-management and alienation. But it was only through the explosions of 1968 that social theorists, activists, and citizens began to grasp what that future contained.

Necessarily, student movements had a short life. Partly by the brevity of the student career, partly by the worsening labor markets after 1973–74, conditions for free-ranging radicalism disappeared, barely outlasting 1967–74. The two most visible legacies—the growth of Trotskyist and Maoist ultraleft sects and the turn to terrorism in West Germany and Italy—were the least prefigurative. If "party building" was an extreme reaction to the amorphousness of movement culture, "armed struggle" dramatized feelings of disempowerment resulting from the immobility of established political structures. The widening gap between public authority and the antiauthoritarianism of the young in the early 1970s ironically encouraged the tacit and ambivalent sympathies on which terrorism—an ineluctably authoritarian course—perforce relied.[83]

A third legacy of the student movements was the opposite of this extreme disaffection from parliamentary politics—namely, permeation, or what Rudi Dutschke called "the long march through the existing institutions."[84] This meant some version of a Gramscian "war of position"— mining the stabilities of the system by sapping the earthworks and outer defenses of civil society, working through education, social work, healthcare, law, civil service, professions, trade unions, and so on, until the state's resistance gradually fell away. The infusion of activists into the mainstream parties of the Left during the 1970s was a similar manifestation.

Two other legacies of 1968 were more important for the Left's future by far. One was the revival of extraparliamentary politics—as direct action, community organizing, ideals of participation, smaller-scale nonbureaucratic forms, the stress on grassroots, the bringing of politics down to everyday life. The other was feminism and the rise of new women's movements, which during the 1970s were also the most creative instance of extraparliamentary opposition.

Of course, behind all the excitements of 1968, parliamentary socialism still perdured. Social democracy revived for the first time since the defeats of the early Cold War. In 1964, British Labour returned to government after 13 years. The SPD entered national government for the first time in West Germany, first with the CDU in a Grand Coalition in 1966 and then heading its own government in 1969. Social Democrats and Communists formed a Popular Front government in Finland in 1966. From 1970, the SPÖ began governing without the Christian Democrats in Austria. The PSI joined a center-left coalition in Italy in 1963. In Sweden, Denmark, and Norway, Social Democrats continued their postwar dominance. Thus, it seemed immaterial whether socialist parties were in or out of government when the explosions of 1968 occurred.

Not the least of the shocking revelations of 1968 was the angry contempt separating Old from New Left. With the merest of individual exceptions, an older generation of socialists and Communists proved incapable of responding to student radicalism sympathetically, let alone with enthusiasm. Any broader generational groupings, such as the British May Day Manifesto Committee during 1966–68, were themselves marginal to the main Left party and were in any case quickly supplanted by the year's events.[85] But if old and new Left found each other mutually incomprehensible, the new radicalism had certainly assembled a new political agenda, which over the next two decades socialist and Communist parties inescapably addressed. How far would these older formations—the social democracies and Communisms of Cold War and postwar boom—manage to assimilate the new movements, coopting their radicalism and defusing any transformative challenge? Or would these movements find their own political expressions, somewhere between extraparliamentary social movements and a new parliamentary front, putting the ideas of 1968 into practice through new types of democratic coalition?

Chapter 22

Feminism

Regendering the Left

IN EARLY 1969, women organized a session on women's liberation during a "revolutionary festival" at Essex University. The occasion was tense. Men, as well as women, were present and responded by dismissing the issues. "At various times it seemed as if the meeting would go over the edge and end in acrimony and ridicule":

> For a moment the women's resentment focused on a man who'd made a speech about political priorities. He said very self-importantly that in a revolutionary movement you couldn't waste time on trivia, and the fact was that women simply weren't capable of writing leaflets. In the smaller meeting we held later a girl [*sic*] hissed venomously through her teeth, "I always change his fucking leaflets when I type them anyway."[1]

Such stories fill women's accounts of 1968. If young women were clearly present in demonstrations and sit-ins, marching in CND and opposing the Algerian War, they were decidedly not on the podium. In 1968, girlfriends and wives were present with their men. They made the coffee and prepared the food, wrote the minutes and kept the books. They handled the practical tasks, while decision-making, strategizing and taking the limelight stayed with the men. Flagrantly contradicting the antihierarchical and participatory ideals of the 1968 movements, this taken-for-granted status soon led to anger: "We really have to battle to have a turn to speak," one French woman militant complained, but "when we've finished, we might as well not have bothered, they haven't even been listening."[2]

Sometimes there were public clashes, most notoriously at the Frankfurt Congress of the West German student movement SDS on 13 September 1968. Fed up with the male-sidedness of the West German movement's taboo-busting sex radicalism, a West Berlin Women's Liberation Action Council began advocating radical childcare arrangements (*Kinderläden*, or storefront daycare centers) to begin democratizing relations between women and men. At the SDS Congress, Helke Sander now demanded attention to "the specific problems women face," so that "problems previously hidden in the private sphere" could become "the focus for women's political solidarity and struggle." She then challenged SDS leaders to acknowledge their own alienation. The links between the strain of continuous public militancy and private unhappiness had to be addressed: "Why do you talk about the class struggle here and about the problem of having orgasms at home? Isn't the latter worthy of discussion by SDS?"[3]

The all-male podium responded with ribald belittlement, whereupon Sigrid Röger, the leadership's token woman, pelted one of them with tomatoes. By November, when the SDS Congress reconvened in Hanover, eight autonomous women's groups had formed. They turned the movement's antiauthoritarian axioms against the sexism of its own political culture. "Liberate the socialist stars from their bourgeois pricks," urged the Frankfurt "Broads' Committee" (*Weiberrat*) in its so-called lop-them-off leaflet. The accompanying cartoon showed a woman proudly reclining with an axe. Mounted as hunting trophies on the wall were two rows of idiosyncratic penises, each bearing an SDS leader's name.[4]

CREATING MOVEMENTS: FEMINISM OF THE SECOND WAVE

These stories say two things. First, Women's Liberation Movements, sometimes called the Second Wave after earlier movements petering out in the 1920s, were dramatically linked to 1968. The West German movement crystallized inside SDS. Various small Parisian groups converged in the French *Mouvement de Libération des Femmes* during 1967–70, including *Feminism-Marxisme-Action; Nous sommes en marche;* Antoinette Fouque's and Monique Wittig's group, which became *Politique et Psychanalyse,* or *Psych et Po; Les oreilles vertes;* and the Thursday Group.[5] In Italy, the *Movimento de Liberazione della Donna* launched in Rome in June 1970 was linked to the Radical Party and open to men, while other groups— *Collettivo della Compagne* in Turin; *Il Cerchio Spezzato* in Trento; *Rivolta Femminile* in Milan; *Lotta Femminista*—formed directly in the crucible of 1968–69.[6] Second, the moment of feminist truth was an infuriating experience with Left misogyny, the shock of the sexist encounter.[7]

This brought a dialectic of inspiration and anger. The British revolutionary newspaper *Black Dwarf,* launched by socialist academics, poets, and activists amid the volatile intermixing of counterculture and New Left in June 1968, exemplified the tensions. Sheila Rowbotham ran a theme issue on women's oppression in January 1969 containing articles on single motherhood, contraception, women in unions, Marxism and psychology, and sexual humiliation, with a centerfold manifesto called "Women: The Struggle for Freedom." Yet the newspaper's designer ("a young hippy," radicalized via the Vietnam Solidarity Campaign) initially "overprinted [the manifesto] on a naked woman with the most enormous pair of breasts imaginable." The general response of the editorial collective to the theme was patronizing. One "left man" said "he supposed it had helped me express my personal problems." But it had "nothing to do with socialism."[8]

Nevertheless, change was afoot. Rosalind Delmar went to her first women's meeting at the London School of Economics in summer 1968: "A male trade unionist came in and started telling us what to do. We told him to go away, no one was going to listen to him. There had always been a tendency on the student left to defer to industrial workers because they were felt to be more strategically important than anyone else—certainly more than women. I was very impressed with what we had done."[9] Like Delmar, many came to Women's Liberation through the student movement and its internationalist campaigns, further pushed by the seeming irrelevance to women of many established labor movement concerns. In the setting of embittered divisiveness produced by the student movement's distinctive politics, as Old Left politicians arrogantly disparaged direct action, participatory democracy, and the ethics of commitment, younger women who were tired of being disregarded easily looked elsewhere.

Thus 18-year-old Aileen Christianson entered politics in 1962 by marching with CND to Glasgow. After five years of university education in Aberdeen, she moved to a research position at Edinburgh University and during 1969–70 became radicalized through the Defence of Literature and the Arts Society, antiapartheid direct action, and the campaign against secret files. She was inspired by reading Germaine Greer's *Female Eunuch* in December 1970. She helped run a local election campaign "on a platform of grass roots democracy" and laid the foundations for a Residents' Association. Then in 1974, she briefly attended the Edinburgh Women's Liberation Conference.[10]

Born in 1937 from a working-class background, with a grammar school and university education, Audrey Battersby was a social worker living on her own in Islington with three children. She went with a friend to Juliet Mitchell's course at the Anti-University and helped form the Tufnell Park women's group.[11] "My socialism . . . was totally male-dominated. I always took a back seat, I rarely said anything. I went, and did, and demonstrated and whatever, but I was still the little woman." Her older loyalties were now remade: "I'd always been a socialist, anti-nuclear marcher, antiapartheid, that sort of thing, but this was different because it was our own struggle."[12]

The first National Women's Liberation Conference met in Ruskin College, Oxford, on 27 February 1970, drawing five hundred women (plus 60 children, 40 men) from around the country. They came from the handful of London groups, Coventry, Birmingham, Nottingham, Sheffield, Leeds, Bristol, and elsewhere; from International Socialism and Trotskyist and Maoist sects; and from the National Joint Action Committee for Women's Equal Rights. It was a convergence of many individuals, mainly in their twenties, primed by immediate political experiences, personal biographies, and countercultural incitements for breaking away. Accounts agree on the newness, the empowering sense of an unexpected and clarifying collectivity.

Some participants brought a wealth of cosmopolitan backgrounds in Europe and North America, while others "felt a bit like young girls from the provinces." Another strikingly different feature was the presence of children: "there were all these children, and there was going to be a creche, run by men." For Sally Alexander, one of the organizers, the event was a "mind blowing" experience, which brought dispersed "bits of myself . . . more together." There was a general feeling of breaking through: "And I never went back to—or was ever remotely interested in—those sorts of bits and pieces of male left politics that I had picked up on and had seen a bit of."[13]

The practical outcomes were a National Women's Coordinating Committee and the Women's Liberation Movement's Four Demands: equal pay; equal education and opportunity; 24-hour nurseries; and free contraception and abortion on demand. The first national women's march was planned for International Women's Day next year, and the Conferences now met annually until 1978, when factionalism supervened.[14] But the movement's real presence lay in the local groups and campaigns. The London Women's Liberation Workshop was a loose federation of small groups in the 1970s, for example, with 80 affiliates at its peak. It was antihierarchical and decentralized, deliberately contrasting with "the traditional Left from which many of us had come." It registered the passionate desire to rethink what politics involved: "We wanted to redefine the meaning of politics to include an analysis of our daily lives."[15]

The founders came through the student movement and similar experiences but were alienated by the gendered culture of militancy. They were often isolated by motherhood, highly educated but undervalued. They had professions in education, health, media, and the arts. They were mainly born in the 1940s. Of 10 founders of the Belsize Lane group still active in 1979, seven were aged 26–33 in 1969; seven were already mothers or pregnant; eight were in the arts (theater, film, photography, writing, pottery); all had a profession (two social workers, two health workers, two writers, an acupuncturist-photographer, a potter, a film editor, an academic).[16] There were no links to earlier twentieth-century feminism. There was a sense of "all these people who were really new to politics [being] suddenly released to express themselves."[17]

The Ruskin Conference came in a wider cluster of events.[18] The earliest had the strongest old Left links—the equal pay strike at Ford Dagenham on 7–28 June 1968, where women sewing machinists demanded wage parity with welders, metal finishers, and body repair workers.[19] This strike provided the impetus for the National Joint Action Committee for Women's Equal Rights, whose campaign culminated in the Trafalgar Square Equal Pay rally of May 1969. Second, Anne Koedt's mass-circulated pamphlet, *The Myth of the Vaginal Orgasm* (1969), brought women's sexuality into politics, distinguishing it from reproduction, separating pleasure from the penis, and converting individual "problems" into political ones. Thirdly, the Tufnell Park group leafleted the Ideal Home Exhibition in the spring of 1969 to reach women "in their roles as housewives, consumers, and mothers." The action raised issues of housework, childcare, family, and the sexual division of labor via critiques of consumerism and advertising. It questioned the Left's assumed "real" priorities—the "frozen notions of the proletariat and/or point-of-production politics."[20]

Especially notable was the disruption of the televised Miss World pageant in November 1970. Women demonstrated outside the Albert Hall and infiltrated the audience, storming the stage at a prearranged signal, throwing smoke bombs and bags of flour. Four women stood trial for the action, using the dock as a platform. In 1969, protestors had worn sashes saying "Mis-Fit Refuses to Conform," "Mis-Conception Demands Free Abortion for All Women," "Mis-Fortune Demands Equal Pay," "Mis-Treated Demands Shared Housework," "Mis-Nomer Demands a Name of Her Own," and seven similar slogans. This 1970 action mixed creativity, anger, direct action, and mass media in turning the spectacle of women to spectacular use. It expressed 1968's typical hostility against consumer capitalism— "Graded, degraded, humiliated. . . . Legs selling stockings, corsets selling waists, cunts selling deodorants, Mary Quant selling sex. . . . Our sexuality has been taken away from us, turned into money for someone else." Absolving the contestants, they attacked "our conditioning as women, and our acceptance of bourgeois norms of correct behavior."[21]

The national demonstration of March 1971 brought all this together: the Four Demands; links to working-class women and the labor movement via the campaign for equal pay; critiques of women's confinement in the family; public voicing of sexuality and politicizing of the body; attacks on consumerism, commercial exploitation, and public representations; an inventive political style. Childcare campaigners parodied the nursery rhyme with a 12-foot-high Old Woman's Shoe; another float showed childbirth "bedecked with strings of cardboard cut-out babies and sanitary towels"; banners displayed cosmetics, bras, and corsetry, "appropriating the adman's appropriation of the movement"; women danced to Eddie Cantor's "Keep Young and Beautiful" on a wind-up gramophone on wheels.[22]

WOMEN'S LIBERATION AND THE NEW POLITICS

Compare w/ the earlier British Feminist movement

For British feminism, defense of the 1967 Abortion Act was the most salient national campaign. Women's slow, uneven progress in unions was another. After the Ford equal pay strike came the protracted night cleaners' campaign from the autumn of 1970. A women's rights conference of the National Council for Civil Liberties at the TUC in February 1974, with 550 union and Women's Liberation delegates, was the first explicit coalition. The campaign for the 10-point Working Women's Charter grew from grassroots alliances of feminists and local union branches, often coordinated via trades councils. In 1975, the TUC incorporated these demands into its own Charter for equal pay and opportunities, maternity leave, nondiscriminatory tax laws, and social security, later adding a proabortion statement and universal childcare in 1978. The TUC's official march for abortion rights in October 1979 mobilized one hundred thousand people.

But the Women's Liberation Movement's real center of gravity was the small consciousness raising (CR) group (with 30–50 varying participants in its weekly meetings), often attached to a women's center, around which circulated many other actions—community childcare initiatives and drop-in centers, claimants unions, squatting and housing campaigns, family allowance campaigns, women's health groups, wages for housework, Working Women's Charter groups, links to individual unions, National Abortion Campaign groups, women's therapy centers, groups on nonsexist education, women's literacy classes, newsletters and local newspapers, and of course study groups, all of them with leafleting, public meetings, research, and direct actions. Feminists agitated other contexts, from local meetings of national campaigns (including the Labour Party) and Women and Socialism events to new initiatives like Women's Aid for battered women, Gingerbread for single parents, Under Fives community nursery groups, and so on. There was a big multiplier effect: "Every action taken leads outwards, has wider repercussions. For instance, those members of consciousness-raising groups live in families, belong to unions or political parties, talk to the neighbors, take children to school, post letters, ring up friends. Ideas get around."[23]

What was distinctive about this new feminism? The small Consciousness Raising group was the quintessential Women's Liberation form: an ideal of unstructured, decentralized, nonbureaucratic association. For the British pioneers, who were often young mothers isolated from the public worlds they desired, this reflected everyday needs; neither workplace and profession nor parties and public institutions gave usable supports. The CR group made the personal political, building collective identity around matters that politics conventionally ignored—children, daycare, schooling, careers, health, housing, loneliness, and of course husbands, boyfriends, and partners. It encouraged expression of feelings and thought, the finding of voice. It was where the most difficult issues were aired. It was the ur-democratic form, where every member could speak and be heard.

This small-scale, participatory basis of Women's Liberation expressed a vital 1968 legacy—the revival of direct democracy and direct action, the critique of alienation, the interest in self-actualization. This was a new voluntarism, a politics of subjectivity, making personal change the key to emancipation. It also meant extraparliamentary politics, beyond the frameworks of electoral and party action, usually on a local footing. The "personal" meant less an individualistic private domain than the contexts of everydayness—the quotidian and the local. This politics was profoundly contrary to old Left thinking about "the party." Plurality and flexibility were the rule: " 'movement' implied dynamism, adaptation, lack of rigidity, while 'organization' implied hierarchy, immobility, fixed structures."[24]

Women's Liberation also practised a subversive and exuberant political style. It meant taking the culture's trappings and symbols, its most cherished beliefs, and disordering them, playing with them, turning their meanings around, in acts of public transgression. It was a calculated acting-out, a purposeful disobedience, a misbehaving in public. It was a questioning of national institutions, designed to startle the complacencies of the largest public—like the laying of a wreath "to the unknown wife of the unknown soldier" at the Tomb of the Unknown Soldier in Paris in August 1970.[25] Street theater and agitprop were essential, from the Electronic-Nipple Show at the 1970 Miss World protest and the general parodying of conventions to the flourishing of feminist theater, as troupes like Monstrous Regiment and Gay Sweatshop brought new themes to the stage.[26] In the Italian unions, feminists stepped outside the time-honored ritual culture: "They carried multicoloured banners (instead of the obligatory red), shouted feminist slogans, and publicly celebrated sisterhood where the traditional terms were fraternity."[27]

Women's Liberation was separatist. In Britain, the Skegness Conference of September 1971 showed that men's participation wouldn't work, a lesson repeated in small groups ("We met with the husbands at first, but they took over, so we had to stop").[28] Broader coalition building often mattered less than giving women a separate political space. In France, abortion reform was carried by *Choisir,* formed in April 1971, the French branch of International Planned Parenthood, and the *Mouvement pour la libération de l'avortement et contraception,* an umbrella federation formed in April 1973, while Women's Liberation itself preferred women-only small groups, producing parallel campaigns also found in Britain and elsewhere. This principle of autonomy brought a stronger separatist logic toward radical or revolutionary feminism and thence often to political lesbianism. Radical feminism became a generalized stance against male power, not capitalism or bourgeois society. By the mid-1970s, this had a new edge. Radical feminists attacked heterosexuality as such, dismissing straight women for sleeping with the enemy.

In excluding men from its new center in Covent Garden in November 1973, the London Women's Liberation Workshop forced socialist feminists onto the defensive.[29] Its newsletter serialized "The Clit Statement," an extreme polemic against heterosexual women by New York radical lesbians in summer 1974. Sheila Jeffreys's pamphlet *The Need for a Revolutionary Feminism* in 1977 advocated overthrowing the ruling power of men. Leeds Revolutionary Feminists made political lesbianism the rule in 1979: "men should be avoided not because of sexual preference but as a political duty . . . all men were regarded as potential rapists and heterosexual women were branded as collaborators."[30] Separatists' rising intolerance conflated feminist authenticity with sexual orientation. It narrowed Women's Liberation's organized framework just as it was taking off, sending socialist feminists and nonaffiliated women to other settings.

Still, expanding the Four Demands to include financial and legal independence and calling for "[a]n end to all discrimination against lesbians and a woman's right to define her own sexuality" was a vital change. "Sexual liberation" was big in the counterculture, which wanted sex "out in the open, an all-pervasive element of daily life: No boundaries, no taboos, no deviants, no hostages to guilt and repression; more sex, better sex, different sex was on the agenda." But Women's Liberation made this an egalitarian ideal, "committed to extending knowledge about the body and being frank about female physiology," while bringing women's sexuality and erotic desires into public voice.[31] It claimed the "private" sphere for change, seeing family and sexuality as key sites of power. Orgasm, contraception, abortion, body knowledge, control of sexuality, all joined the agenda. This body politics differed from that of the 1920s and 1930s: rather than rationalizing sexuality, it stressed experimenting with female agency in an ethic of choice and personal change, while questioning accepted definitions. In the early 1970s, these ideals converged with gay liberation. Despite much embitterment, the gain was huge: not only was lesbianism affirmed but the complicated factors shaping masculinity and femininity were brought into the political arena, as was the question of pleasure.[32]

With the radicalizing of separatism into political lesbianism came a stress on violence against women. The first British battered women's refuge was created in Chiswick in 1972: when the National Women's Aid Federation was launched in 1975, there were 111 similar groups, and by 1986 there were 179. Women Against Rape was formed, with Britain's first rape crisis center in North London in 1976; by 1985, there were 45 centers nationwide. Both areas displayed the feminist dualism of public lobbying and grassroots élan—bringing guilty secrets into the open, agitating opinion, pressing government for support; yet organizing women for self-help in locally grounded collective action.

"Take Back the Night" actions pushed this further, attacking the climate of fear restricting women in public—red-light districts, porn shops, X-rated cinemas, men-only bars, violent and demeaning imagery in advertisements. Women marched rowdily through the streets of London and other cities on 12 November 1977, demanding freedom "to walk down any street, night or day, without fear." This progression, from exposing physical violence to attacking violent representations in culture, was spurred in Britain by public sensationalism and police sexism surrounding the serial rape-murders of the "Yorkshire Ripper" in 1977–80. On 27 November 1980, 10 days after the thirteenth killing, Women Against Violence Against Women (WAVAW) was founded in Leeds: "women demonstrated outside cinemas, glued up the locks of sex shop doors, smashed windows of strip clubs, daubed angry messages on walls ('MEN off the streets'), and marched to 'Reclaim the Night."[33]

For WAVAW, male violence was a single system of control: "Sexual harassment at work . . . rape and sexual assault . . . sexual abuse in the family . . . obscene phone calls, pornography, rape in marriage (unrecognized in law), gynecological practice which violates women's bodies . . . we discussed them all."[34] This campaigning captured big public space for feminist ideas and by 1980 also linked to the new peace movement. "Take Back the Night" grew from the International Tribunal of Crimes against Women in Brussels in 1976, which made sexual violence a call to action: one hundred thousand women joined the Italian marches in fall 1976, and the first West German marches occurred shortly thereafter.[35] The first German "Women's House" for battered women opened in West Berlin in November 1976; by 1979, 14 cities had shelters; by 1982, there were 99. These and other initiatives had the British mixture of local militancy, public agitation, and city funds. But in West Germany, foregrounding violence also made it easier to form coalitions. The Declaration on "Violence Against Women" issued by the Democratic Women's Initiative in Düsseldorf in October 1979 explicitly linked this to "structural violence" elsewhere, in work, the arms race, and the environment. The Women's Congress against Nukes and Militarism in September 1979 made the same connections.[36]

Women's Liberation also changed perceptions of work. Not only by campaigning on low and unequal pay but also by demanding that homework, casual service work, and housework be valued, feminists redefined the very category. Wages for housework drew the most publicity. *Lotta Femminista*'s Manifesto of Housewives in the Neighborhood (1971) in Italy demanded state payments to men and women, linked to neighborhood services, housing reform, and reorganizing the working day.[37] While unrealistic when the welfare state was under attack and as likely to entrench as subvert existing sexual divisions of labor, this manifesto proposed expanding control over daily life in precisely those "community" matters that the Left's traditional focus on the factory neglected, like housing, transport, town planning, childcare, worktime and leisure time, and public services. This new approach connected with contemporary transformations of class. Not only women's growing presence in the workforce but also a new awareness of the sexual division of labor and a changing grasp of what counted as work upset traditional left-wing assumptions about what working-class politics should contain.

Women's Liberation created a new feminist public sphere. First came newsletters linking local groups, like *Shrew* for London Women's Liberation Workshop (originally *Bird,* then *Harpie's Bizarre,* from the spring of 1969), followed by national magazines—*Spare Rib* in Britain (launched July 1972 by Rosie Boycott and Marsha Rowe); *Le Torchon brûle* (1970–73) and its successors in France; *Effe* (1973) and *Quotidiano Donna* (1978) in Italy; *Courage* (1976) and *Emma* (1977) in West Germany. Women's centers followed. In London, these ranged from the main gathering point at Covent Garden from 1973 to more improvised local centers. In Islington, the York Way Women's Center (1972–73) was followed by Essex Road (1974–76) and a third in 1978; each time a women's health center, childcare arrangements, local campaigns, legal advice, research and writing projects, and a simple meeting place were the main goals. Activity in the Netherlands crystallized around cafés and bookshops, Consciousness Raising groups, and women's education classes: in 1977, 37 Dutch towns had centers; by 1982, there were 160.[38]

British Women's Liberation created the National Information Service in Leeds for the huge volume of queries and contacts outside London, with a bimonthly newsletter from 1975, which developed into WIRES (Women's Information, Referral, and Enquiry Service). GLIFE was the equivalent in France from 1975, plus a 24-hour emergency hotline, *SOS Femmes Alternatives.* Feminist publishers began with Virago, Women's Press, Onlywomen Press, and Sheba in Britain; *Edizione della Donna, I libretti verdi,* and *La Tartaruga* in Italy; the Munich *Frauenoffensive* in West Germany; and *De Bonte Was* and *Sara* in the Netherlands. Feminist networks, like the British Women's Film, Television and Video Network, formed in the media. By 1980, women's studies had gained a foothold in universities. Early grassroots activity became an elaborate feminist scene of alternative bookshops, publishers, magazines, Women's Summer Universities, women's studies research centers, ongoing campaigns, and safe houses, plus broader subcultures of self-help, medical self-care, and women's heath networks. This activity recalled the social democratic subcultures after the 1880s, though without the centralized resources of national parties and unions.

FROM WOMEN'S LIBERATION TO FEMINISM

Women's Liberation movements coalesced nationally via abortion campaigns.[39] In France, this was dramatized in April 1971 by the "Whores

Manifesto" signed by 343 women in *Le Nouvel Observateur* declaring their experience of illegal abortions, a tactic repeated in West Germany in July, with 374 names and photographs appearing in *Stern* (plus another 2,345 women over the next six weeks, with 86,100 declarations of support). The French action achieved the freeing of four working-class women in Bobigny accused of procuring an abortion for a teenage daughter.[40] In West Germany, the campaign built from the first National Women's Conference in Frankfurt in March 1972; 1971 surveys showed 71 percent of women supporting legalization, rising to 83 percent in 1973. In Italy, the Collective of 6 December emerged from a 1975 rally to coordinate the campaign, and eight hundred thousand signatures were collected for a national referendum.[41] When laws were passed (France 1975, West Germany 1977, Italy 1978), they did not provide for free abortion on demand and usually regulated access with time limits, counseling requirements, and sociomedical conditions. But the campaigns had decisively shifted public climates. In both Britain and Netherlands, abortion had been legalized in 1967. The National Abortion Campaign (NAC) and the broader Coordinating Committee in Defense of the 1967 Abortion Act then worked to neutralize the backlash in Britain, as did We Women Demand and its successors in the Netherlands.

Abortion campaigning displayed the full repertoire of Women's Liberation politics: "big splash" events like demonstrations; subverting the law by self-help and lay provision; and lobbying inside the system. Women's reproductive rights meant control of sexuality and languages of autonomy—*Our Bodies, Ourselves,* in the title of the universally translated handbook, or "My Belly Belongs to Me," in the West German slogan.[42] Abortion rallied a gender-based collectivity of women from all backgrounds, ages, and classes. Campaigns consistently linked abortion to economics, social rights, equality in households, sexuality, and family, all in critiques of male domination. Thereby, feminists escaped the abstract sloganeering against "capitalism," "bourgeois society," and "women's oppression" to more concrete ground, where links to other issues were preserved. Feminists "transformed abortions from being a civil rights issue into a struggle over how power was being exercised in society," involving "not just the state or the Church as institutions, but the 'micro' relations of power in everyday life."[43] Demands for controlling one's body grounded more general claims to political identity. "Abortion" redefined the boundaries of politics per se rather than remaining an issue by itself. Reproductive freedom issued a challenge to society's dominant values by questioning existing religious, medical, and political authority. It brought the "body politic" itself into question.[44]

Internationalism was essential, in a shared mobilization across not only Western Europe but also the Atlantic. United States Second Wave feminism predated European events. From the early books like Betty Friedan's *Feminine Mystique* in 1963 and the creation of a national women's lobby in

NOW (National Organization of Women) from 1966 to the radicalizing collisions with the sexism of Student for a Democratic Society, Women's Liberation happened first in the United States.[45] But transnational circuits remained active. Young American women were in the earliest Women's Liberation groups in London. West German SDSers were also in London in 1968–70. Helke Sander's speech of September 1968 circulated widely, while translations, like Shulamith Firestone's *Dialectic of Sex,* Kate Millett's *Sexual Politics,* and Germaine Greer's *Female Eunuch,* as well as Anne Koedt's pamphlet, were common. British Reclaim the Night marches were directly inspired by West German predecessors. After the transition to democracy in 1975–77, Spanish Women's Liberation deployed precedents from Britain, West Germany, and France. The publication of *New Portuguese Letters* by the so-called three Marias in 1973, and the authors' subsequent trial, became an international *cause célèbre.*[46]

There were important crossnational differences, however. The strongest Women's Liberation movements were in Britain, France, Italy, the Netherlands, and West Germany.[47] Each grew from "1968," while angrily rejecting its sexist and gendered limits. They had a common pattern—small localized groups, with a participatory ethos of direct action, evolving toward separatism, with sexual politics ever more primary, and achieving through national abortion campaigns wider mobilization among women and broader alliances in the Left. As national movements, Women's Liberation crested with these 1970s campaigns. But as conflicts opened along the fundamental divide between radical or revolutionary versus socialist feminisms, the momentum was dissipated.

Interestingly, Scandinavia lacked distinct Women's Liberation movements in the 1970s. In April 1970, 12 Danish women (so-called Redstockings) organized a public protest against fashion and makeup called "Keep Denmark Clean," which was followed by other small groups. In Norway, the first battered women's helpline appeared in Oslo in 1977, producing the first refuge in 1978, with 53 shelters and three thousand activists by 1991.[48] But the broader framework of separately organized feminism didn't coalesce for various reasons: legal equality within marriage had already been achieved in Scandinavia by 1929; civil equality was matched by unusually high female employment; relatively "depatriarchalized" welfare states offered positive citizenship for women; and the right to an abortion was already won.[49]

In Austria, Belgium, and Switzerland, conservative gender regimes inhibited strong women's movements. Smaller-scale feminisms focused either on winning the vote, as in the Zurich Manifesto of the Swiss Women's Liberation Movement in June 1968, or achieving civic equality, as in the Austrian family law reforms of 1975–78 or the later Swiss counterparts of 1988. Women's movements emerged via the democratic transitions in Portugal, Spain, and Greece in 1974–75 but were more attuned to parliamentary politics than Women's Liberation per se. In Eastern Europe, there were no comparable feminist movements, whether in the Prague Spring or the Polish and Yugoslav student movements.

By 1979–80, Women's Liberation was running out of steam. Movements had divided over sexuality and separatism, over political alliances, over organization. The conflicts of radical versus socialist feminists were a main case, but in 1972–74 British socialist feminism too became divided, as women from Marxist sects sought to capture the agenda, alienating others by their tactics and trying to corral the women's movement into a single mass campaign focused exclusively on abortion, coordinated via a central committee.[50] Gaps opened between theorists in universities and activists in the trenches, and by 1978–79 unity was gone. Black British women also held a separate conference in 1979, attacking Women's Liberation for ignoring race. In October 1983, the Reproductive Rights Campaign seceded from the NAC to place black and Third World women at the center.

In Italy, fragmentation took a dramatic turn. The Communist leadership simply dissolved the UDI at its Eleventh Congress in May 1982, converting it from "a formal, centralized, hierarchical association to a loose network of local women's groups." UDI had become a gathering point for "every type of autonomous women's initiative ranging from gymnastic classes, handicraft cooperatives, and holistic medical groups, to women's legal aid collectives." But this was a huge strain for its leadership—beholden to political strategy decided elsewhere by the PCI, used by the wider women's movement as a default resource, yet with dues-paying members whose outlook fell far short of the new self-actualizing Consciousness Raising ideals. "The old model of militancy no longer holds up," the UDI leaders now insisted and withdrew from an impossible situation.[51] In one form or another, disunity overcame Women's Liberation politics throughout Europe.

THE WOMEN'S MOVEMENT AND THE LEFT

Second Wave feminism failed to institutionalize itself nationally, and in the case of the UDI a major existing movement specifically sacrificed itself to build élan from the base.[52] The "tyranny of structurelessness" was a particular problem. The desire to overturn the Left's calcified proceduralism, where podiums ruled meetings and executives set agendas, was basic to Women's Liberation, counterposing the egalitarian democracy of face-to-face groups, where all had a voice and decisions crystallized by consensus. But the resulting free-for-all allowed hidden leaderships to form, and "the anti-institutional, directly participatory perspective created real barriers to continuity, communication, and critical analysis."[53] Women's liberation thrived on its spontaneity. But the same quality vitiated its staying power as a cohesive political force. Creativity flashed brilliantly and then dispersed.

One response was to enter the Left's mainstream. Feminists found niches in the Left's existing frameworks. One place was local government, via funding and facilities for childcare, legal aid, women's health, and adult education. Legislation and labor movement traditions provided links—via public services in Scandinavian social democracies or the PCI Red Belt of the Po Valley and industrial cities like Turin and Milan. The Italian 150 Hours movement—work-study release first won by metalworkers in 1972— became a key area, as were publicly funded free women's clinics from 1975.[54] Similar converging of Women's Liberation with Left local government occurred via Labour in Britain, as in the campaign of the Women's Action Committee, formed in 1981, for party recognition of women's issues, or the projects of the Women's Committee of the Greater London Council and other Labour-controlled cities.

Left parties dealt with new feminisms unevenly, to say the least. "What do you want to do that for? To discuss Lenin's views on lingerie?" was the Labour Party secretary's reaction to the forming of a women's section in Newcastle East.[55] The two largest CPs, the French and Italian, suggested the poles. Both had the classic record on the "Woman Question"—economistic stress on women as workers, plus broader campaigning on maternity, social issues, and consumption, within movement cultures of sexism. Feminism per se was seen as a bourgeois diversion. Both parties sought to break these habits in the Eurocommunist turn by integrating the new women's movements. Yet if Italian Communists responded in good faith, the French instrumentalized the women's movement in 1976–78 only to shed feminist garb when the Union of the Left was gone. At the PCI Women's Conference in February 1976, Geraldo Chiaromonte used "liberation" affirmatively, pledging the PCI to a feminist course. In Paris South, one of the PCF's strongest Eurocommunist sections, a feminist influx sustained a Women's Commission with regular monthly attendance of 50, but once the party resumed a strong workerist line in 1978, Women's Liberation motifs became squelched, militants left, and by 1979 the Women's Commission was dead.[56]

Socialist feminism had very low success in transforming existing Left parties. These addressed women's issues in old-style institutional ways. In France, Mitterrand's 1981 Socialist government created the Ministry of the Rights of Women under Yvette Roudy, and some laws were eventually passed, like Penal Code revisions on sexual harassment in 1992. But the French Socialist governments attended more to equality-style lobbies, like *Choisir* or *La Ligue des droits des femmes*—to the "representation of interests" rather than a Women's Liberation politics of "collective identity."[57] In Spain, the PSOE government created the Institute of Women in 1983, with regional institutes in Andalucía, Valencia, the Basque country, and Catalonia and smaller ones elsewhere. This gave the women's movement access to resources, influence in the Ministry of Social Affairs, and elaborate public responsibilities—for coordinating equality policies and public campaigns, running programs for employment and training, health and social services, culture and education, generating research, and funding projects.[58] The Socialist government's longevity gave feminist policy-making an important continuity from 1983 to 1996.

Women's Liberation did assure greater visibility in the public sphere. By the early 1990s, women's parliamentary presence was still languishing below 10 percent in Greece, France, Britain, Portugal, and Belgium; in Italy, it actually declined from 16 percent to 12.9 percent during the 1980s and to a mere 8.1 percent in 1992. On the other hand, Spanish women's share of ministerial posts and parliamentary seats rose from 5 to 13 percent. Quotas became one way of improving women's presence: French Socialists finally gave women one-third of party lists and government posts in 1997, and the PSOE adopted a target of 25 percent in 1988. For the first time, the Italian Communists also moved in 1986–87 to a system of women's quotas in party positions.

In Norway, such progress was dramatic. An early campaign of 1967–71 reduced the prevalence of all-male municipal councils, boosting women's representation in nine large cities to parity. The Socialist Left Party used quotas from 1974, copied reluctantly by Labor in 1984. Women held 36 percent of parliamentary seats by 1989 and 42 percent of government posts in 1995. By the 1990s, women's parliamentary presence was high elsewhere in Scandinavia—33 percent in Denmark, 38.1 in Sweden, and 38.5 in Finland—followed by the Netherlands, Austria, and West Germany.[59] By 1992, women in the main parliamentary delegations of the Left varied from roughly parity in Norway and Sweden through 18–35 percent in Denmark, the Netherlands, West Germany, Austria, Italy, and Spain and down to less than 10 percent in Greece, Belgium, France, and Britain.[60]

Thus several continuing patterns of feminism emerged. Autonomous activity remained vital—intellectually and culturally, socially, and in myriad local forms—though rarely as a centered women's movement with national organization. Spectacular actions and national mobilizations also still occurred—usually to defend existing gains, such as the efforts in 1979 and 1982 to defend abortion in France. The most impressive was in Iceland, where feminists called a general strike for equal pay and other antidiscriminatory demands in 1975, bringing 90 percent of all Icelandic women out; this was repeated on the tenth anniversay through the Women's Alliance, which in 1987 went on to win six parliamentary seats.[61] Where socialists governed, as in France, Spain, and Scandinavia, and in many cities across Europe, women's interests were pursued more conventionally via funding, legislation, and institutional supports, inflected with Women's Liberation radicalism.

Above all, the new feminism devolved onto civil society—onto multiple sites, sometimes inside the distinctively feminist public sphere, sometimes in the universities, media, and arts, sometimes in professionalized spheres of healthcare and social services, sometimes in the world of unions and work, and sometimes in varieties of social activism. This was a variegated ground from which politicals could begin, intermediate between formal politics and the everyday. It was not often connected to traditional Left mobilizations, through socialist or Communist parties organizing via elections to form a government. More often, a sympathetic government—nationally, in cities, in small communities—gave resources and an umbrella for decentralized action, as in many Italian examples. This politics built from the ground, seeding possibilities for a still undefined future.

CONCLUSION

Mary Kay Mullan, born in 1950, was an 18-year-old student at Queen's University Belfast when she joined People's Democracy in the Northern Irish Civil Rights Movement. After a year's frenetic agitation ("marches, meetings, pickets, leafleting, sit-ins, traffic disruption, and all types of nonviolent public direct action"), she marched with People's Democracy from Belfast to Derry in January 1969, when the brutality at Burntollet Bridge radicalized the civil rights struggle into a 30-year civil war.[62]

After traveling abroad in 1972–75, she returned to Derry to teach, focusing her feminism in a Consciousness Raising group and a course on "Women in Irish Society." She helped found a Woman's Aid Refuge—"squatting, negotiating, publicizing, fundraising, learning about Social Security, housing laws, and laws affecting women's status . . . organizing petitions, lobbying MPs and Ministers." She helped organize campaigns against rape, domestic violence and sexual abuse, while coming out as a lesbian. In November 1978, inspired by Centerprise in Hackney, East London, she opened Bookworm Community Bookshop in Derry city center, which flourished into a workers' cooperative. By 1988, activity had diversified still further: a women's health collective; the Rape and Incest Line; the Family Planning Association branch; the Women in Trade Unions group; Women's Aid; creche campaigns and playgroups; study groups; assertiveness classes; the monthly Derry Women's Newssheet; and a set of connections to Sinn Fein and Prisoners' Relatives Action Committees, from an independent feminist standpoint.[63]

This example eloquently makes the point: by the 1980s feminism had not "transformed society," but the utopianism of Women's Liberation—"its wild wish"—had redefined "the scope and conceptualization of what is politics."[64] As politics moved right, this changing of categories happened increasingly in the private zones—in personal relationships, in small groups, in alternative spaces, and in fashioning new cultures, away from the main throughfares of party and state, although still shaped and enabled by larger structural changes in employment, social policies, education, public health, family organization, and popular culture much as before. Women's Liberation's distinctive arguments remained urgently relevant to how those changes could be handled—"for rethinking work, time, the social forms of technology, the utilization and distribution of resources and power, the role of the state, the bringing up and educating of children."[65] Feminist insistence on politics' relationship to ordinary living, on the importance of sexuality, on the interconnections of body and mind, on pleasures rather than disciplines, consumption rather than production, has transformed the starting points for thinking about political change, expanding the Left's assumptions about what the category of politics contains. "The personal is political" gave individual autonomy new meanings. It brought principles of equality and democracy into human relationships in new ways.

In reaffirming and simultaneously recasting feminism's historic goals of women's equality and emancipation, the new women's movement had also effected a remarkable public breakthrough. In spearheading the growth of democracy in the earlier twentieth-century reform settlements of 1917–21 and 1945–47, socialist and Communist parties had certainly brought women's demands into the political foreground. But political and civil equality was always compromised, and often badly undermined, by the persisting systems of gendered economic discrimination and welfare state innovation, whose dominant maternalist presuppositions continued to assign women a dependent and subordinate place. Whenever the socialist Left came close to power, it seemed, established gender norms invariably prevailed, from the imposing municipal socialisms of the 1920s through the Popular fronts to the reforming social democracies after 1945. During that era, once the suffrage was won, feminisms observed the same dominant strictures: motherhood was the appropriate foundation for citizenship claims; the family was the primary referent for women's political identity.

It was this powerful framework that Women's Liberation broke apart. Through the anger and tumults of the pioneering years, initiated by the courageous and determined acts of small groups but broadening into mass campaigning around issues of reproductive rights, safety, and health, public political agendas became unsettled, fractured, and then unevenly but lastingly recomposed. At the center of this feminist political process, for the first time, was an unequivocal critique of the *family*. By shifting the burden of women's emancipation onto the family's importance in the shaping of personhood, Women's Liberation opened a space where questions of sexuality, child-raising, gendered divisions of labor, ideologies of the family wage, the tracking of girls into feminine futures at school and work, and the generalized masculinity of the public sphere could all be addressed in new ways. Feminists compelled the Left to reconsider its assumptions regarding the coordinates of democracy and the good life. Henceforth, public policy was to be judged not just by its contribution to the provision of basic social goods, vital those these remained, but also by its role in perpetuating or changing gender relations.

How exactly Left politics would be affected, given the crisis of social democracy, the failure of Eurocommunism, the changing composition of class, and the dissolution of the postwar settlement, remained to be seen. The force of these developments, which placed the Left so powerfully on the defensive in the 1980s, diminished the divisiveness of the conflicts within feminism. While the heyday of Women's Liberation was over, feminists found ways of cooperating both with each other and in overarching frameworks of the Left. The ascendancy of the Right—Thatcherism in Britain, Kohl and Christian Democracy in [West] Germany, the DC and Craxi's Socialist Party in Italy, and the variegated hegemony of neoliberal policies throughout Europe—overrode differences for the purposes of common action. The rise of the new Cold War, the threat of nuclear destruction, and the growing consciousness of the world environmental catastrophe all gave impetus to feminist convergences within the Left. The transnational Peace Movement and the rise of Green politics supplied the practical terrain on which new alliances could begin.

Chapter 23

Class and the

Politics of Labor

FROM THE 1860s until the last third of the twentieth century, the centrality of the working class was an axiom of socialist thinking. It rested on a duality of actual movements and visionary social understandings—of the rise of labor movements and the belief in the working class as the bearer of history, the indispensible collective agency of progressive change. Going back to Marx and Engels, the origins of trade unions, and the forming of socialist parties, this dialectic of movement and representation shaped the prospects of democracy in Europe. Class-centered politics was a constant of the Left's self-definition. The collective agency of the working class was the defining referent of left-wing sociopolitical understanding. It was central to the sociology of socialist and Communist parties. It was key to trade unionism's role as the vector of progressive social change. It was decisive for the Left's popular electorate. It was basic to both the iconography and the manifest social landscape of the democratic imagination in the century after the 1860s. The working class's ever-expanding numbers and deepening exploitation were the long-term surety of socialist political success.

Before 1914, this meant an evolutionary determinism, the Second International's automatic Marxism, where capitalist development would make workers the overwhelming mass of society and therefore (under parliamentary democracy) the source of an unstoppable socialist majority. The revolutionary conjuncture of 1917 dramatically upset this inevitabilism, but by 1930 it was back, in its variant social democratic and Stalinist forms. After 1945, Communist parties kept ideas of the polarization of society and proletarian immiseration alive, but with declining relevance to Western capitalism's unfolding prosperity. In contrast, social democrats accepted the realism of reforms inside a stabilized capitalism. But either way, the working class was still the fixed point.

DECLINE OF THE WORKING CLASS?

From the 1960s, the hard-and-fast assumptions about the centrality of the working class were thrown into question. In most of Europe the manufacturing workforce still expanded during the 1950s, but thereafter the industrial proletariat shrank. In 11 Western European economies, industrial employees in the early 1950s ranged from a high of almost 50 percent in Britain and Belgium to a low of 25.1 percent in Spain. West Germany and Sweden were at the higher and Italy at the lower ends of this hierarchy, with the rest, Austria, Denmark, France, the Netherlands and Norway, falling in between. After 1973–74, declines were steep. In Britain, industrial employment had dropped from 49.2 to 30.2 percent by 1985–87; in Belgium from 48.3 to 28.7 percent; in Norway from 36.5 to 26.5 percent; and in Sweden from 40.6 to 30.2 percent.[1] Manufacturing revealed an equally stark pattern. In 1970–93, British manufacturing plummeted from 32.4 percent of jobs to only 18.9 percent; Belgian from 32.1 to 17.7 percent; Norwegian from 26.7 to 14.3 percent; and Swedish from 28.3 to only 16.8 percent. Even stronger economies like Germany and Austria succumbed, while still-industrializing Italy dropped from 31.1 to 19.8 percent. Only in the developing economies of Portugal and Greece were levels modestly maintained.[2]

Other transformations occurred. Agrarian jobs massively declined, confining peasants by 1980 to Europe's far peripheries. At the same time services expanded, with their white-collar legions in retail and offices; burgeoning supervisory, managerial, and administrative positions; proliferating technoprofessional functions in research, education, and communications; and massively expanding public bureaucracies. In Sweden, services and industry both grew modestly in the 1950s, but in 1960–80 services soared to 61 percent of total employment, industry sinking to 34. In Denmark, the pattern was repeated: both sectors growing modestly in the 1950s but widening disproportionately thereafter. The Austrian case was especially clear: services were stable in the 1950s at 30 percent, with industry rising from 37 to 46 percent; but proportions reversed by 1980, with services predominating at 54 percent and industry dropping to 37 percent. The pattern was universal, with variations. The more advanced the capitalism, the greater the structural shift.

This contemporary transformation had profound implications.[3] First, capitalist economies deindustrialized, as "old" industries like coal, iron, and steel, railways, shipbuilding, docking, machine tools, and textiles decayed and "newer" ones like automobiles fled. Second, despite "high-tech" growth in computers, pharmaceuticals, electronics, and aerospace, new jobs came overwhelmingly in three tertiary areas: food and catering, health, and business and information services. Third, this new work—part-time, unprotected, insecure, geographically concentrated, low-waged, and non-unionized—was beyond the established reach of the labor movement and its cultures and institutions. Fourth, these labor markets were typically "feminized": the bulk of new employment for women was part-time.[4] Last, "community, social, and personal services" grew especially fast, embracing public employment associated with the welfare state. This area expanded everywhere after 1960. In the Low Countries and Scandinavia, it became 31–38 percent of all jobs by 1992.[5]

The British example was dramatic.[6] Elected in 1979, Margaret Thatcher's Conservative government recklessly deindustrialized. After four years, British industry's share of employment was down to 34 percent. In 1978–83, 179,000 jobs were lost in automobiles, 173,000 in textiles, 110,000 in iron and steel, 51,000 in coal-mining, 42,000 in shipbuilding, and 23,000 in machine tools. Even in growth industries, hemorrhaging occurred: 25,000 jobs were lost in instrument engineering, 21,000 in aerospace, and 11,000 in electronics. Over 28 percent of industrial jobs disappeared in the north, Wales, the West Midlands, and Northern Ireland; 23–27 percent in Scotland and the rest of the north; and 18–21 percent in the East Midlands, London, and the southwest. From 300,000 workers in 1974, British iron and steel fell to 183,000 by 1983. In automobiles, half a million workers became only 290,000. Coal-mining vanished: after nationalization in 1947, it dwindled through rationalization, redundancies, and closures from 690,000 miners in 1950 to 287,000 20 years later, and by 1989 there were only 60,000 left.

Britain also showed the shift to services. If industrial employment sank from 49 to 34 percent during 1963–83, services rose from 48 to 64 percent. If 2.2 million industrial jobs were lost from 1971 to 1983, 1.7 million tertiary jobs were created, mostly in hotels and catering, business services, health, and education. The British labor market underwent egregiously unregulated restructuring, with huge social costs. Tertiary jobs were also hit after 1979. Public sector employment in the welfare state stagnated. From 1971 to 1981, with attacks on public spending, such jobs dropped from 27.3 to 23.7 percent of total employment, before recovering slightly to 25.5 percent in 1992. Most tertiary jobs went to women rather than men on a part-time basis. Regional disparities increased, concentrating opportunities in London and sharpening enmities between the metropolitan south and the northern industrial wastelands. No work was created where it was most missing.

Thus the shift from skilled industrial work to white-collar labor in services entailed other changes—preferences for women over men, part-time working, rising joblessness, extreme gaps between regions, new computer-based high-technology industries, and the collapse of the industrial economy's old manufacturing core. Deindustrialization remapped the capitalist economy. Industry's flight from city centers had dated from 1939–45 but now became general. In Britain from 1951 to 1976, 40–60 percent of manufacturing jobs, branch by branch, left the inner city. By the 1980s, major urban economies like Clydeside, Tyneside, Teesside, Liverpool, Manchester, Leeds-Bradford, and London in the East End and south of the river were gutted of industry. Conversely, countrysides reaped the benefit. In 1960–81, rural manufacturing jobs increased by 24 percent. But in London, metropolitan areas, other cities, and larger towns, the decline was harsh.

Several historic patterns of industry were coming to an end. In decline were capital cities, with their traditional mass markets, luxury consumption, and specialized manufactures, plus wider infrastructures of construction, transportation, and communication. So too were port cities, with their docklands, shipyards, shipping, and ancilliary industries mushrooming around export and import trade. Older nineteenth-century urban concentrations also started to disappear, from coalfields, railway yards, and steel mills to heavy engineering, specialized light manufacture, and textiles. Finally, "Fordist" mass production had stamped the years 1930–60 with its monstrous plants and huge populations dominating a city or region, sometimes as a company town and invariably backed by the state. Fordism had used new technologies based on electricity and oil rather than coal and steam, armies of semiskilled and unskilled labor, and a labor process organized around assembly lines. Now it too was in decline.[7]

TRADE UNIONS AND THE CRISIS OF CORPORATISM

To grasp the political implications, we need to look at the changing place of unions. During the capitalist restructuring of the post-1973 recession, corporatist variations vitally influenced the Left's future. Where unions were weak, as in Italy and France, corporatism was heavily statist, interweaving business and government and excluding organized labor. In West Germany, Austria, and Scandinavia, in contrast, with higher union density and organizational strength, labor movements helped shape the resulting system. After 1973, postwar settlements survived best where this strong labor-corporatist backbone existed. Britain was in between, with especially strong unions producing political crises, in which a violent anti-Keynesian backlash could occur.[8]

After Labour's defeat in the 1951 elections, Conservative governments followed a pragmatics of corporatist conciliation. The emblematic figure was R. A. Butler, whose name was joined to that of the Labour leader Hugh Gaitskell in the term "Butskellism," a sobriquet for consensus.[9] Likewise, through successive appointments to the ministries of Health, Labour, and the Colonies during 1952–61, Iain Macleod also preserved key continuities from before 1951. He headed off strikes with conciliation procedures, treating union leaders as responsible participants in the national enterprise of growth. The big unions were also ruthlessly ruled by a rightist oligarchy: they happily policed their own memberships, rigidly performing their anti-Communism while stifling dissent in an economistic culture of conformity and wage-driven improvement.

Things changed when shopfloor militancy outgrew this control. Strike rates more than doubled during 1963–70, as initiative passed from union head offices and full-time officials to shopfloor representation. Between 1961 and 1978, shop steward numbers in Britain soared from 90,000 to a quarter of a million, while public sector unions massively expanded: NUPE (National Union of Public Employees) grew from 200,000 to 700,000, and NALGO (the National and Local Government Officers Association) from 274,000 to 782,000; in health services, unionized workers went from 370,000 to 1.3 million and union density from 38 to 74 percent, in one decade. This challenged existing arrangements, which rested on moderate but class-conscious Labour-loyalist union leaders in classic industries. Shop stewards inserted a new volatility into relations between union officers and members, relocalizing militancy and the effective unit of negotiation. Public sector unionism simultaneously increased the onus on the state as employer. In response, the Labour governments of 1964–70 and 1974–79 tried to strengthen national corporatism, wagering politically on the TUC's centralized authority.[10]

This corporatism's aspiring form was a voluntary incomes policy with the TUC, whose failure brought the Prices and Incomes Act of 1966 as a statutory alternative. By 1967, this was also collapsing. Unofficial strikes persisted, and a wages revolt led by public sector workers finally buried the policy. In 1969, unions also defeated a proposal for state regulation of strikes, which bitterly divided the Labour Party. After a Conservative interlude during 1970–74, whose debacle further raised the stakes, new Labour governments of Harold Wilson (1974–76) and James Callaghan (1976–79) repeated the search for union cooperation, this time via the "Social Contract," whose architect was the Transport and General Workers (TGWU) leader, Jack Jones.[11]

The Social Contract proposed wage restraint in four stages, beginning with a flat-rate increase favoring the lower-paid, and reverting by stage 3 to percentages. Unions held this arrangement, but then in July 1978 stage 4 pegged increases unrealistically low at 5 percent. The Ford Motor Company blew a hole through the policy by settling a two-month strike at 16.5 percent in November 1978, followed by a national truckers' strike with a settlement of 17–20 percent. Public service unions reacted with a one-day strike and publicly disastrous stoppages by health workers, dustmen, civil servants, and grave-diggers. This "winter of discontent" killed the Callaghan government, and Labour lost the upcoming election of May 1979, bringing Conservatives back for the next 18 years.

The failure was in the political payoff. An incomes policy unmatched by political gains became merely punitive wage restraint. Two decades earlier, Jones' predecessor at the TGWU, Frank Cousins, succeeding the crudely right-wing Arthur Deakin in 1956, had stated this sharply enough, tying cooperation to socialist advance: "when we have achieved a measure of planning and a Socialist Government, and if I have to say to my members, 'we must now exercise restraint,' I will say it and when I say it, I will mean it."[12] By these lights, the Social Contract qualified. It envisaged abolishing Heath's Industrial Relations Act of 1971, increasing union rights, and moving to industrial democracy. It required a radicalized Keynesianism by way of price controls, public investment, nationalization, control of capital, and a strengthened welfare state, with food and transport subsidies, expanded public housing, better social services, and redistributive social justice, prioritizing pensioners and the lower-paid. Jack Jones backed this program, giving the "Alternative Economic Strategy" some much-needed social idealism and ethical drive.[13]

But the Labour goverment saw only crisis management. Jones was never admitted to the government's counsels, and after the EEC Referendum in June 1975 and International Monetary Fund (IMF) crisis of December 1976, the party's Left was marginalized.[14] Some laws were passed—on Trade Union and Labour Relations, Sex Discrimination, Health and Safety at Work, and Employment Protection, plus measures for youth employment. But this was the honeymoon, before government capitulated to recession and dumped the left. By 1978, nothing remained of the vision. Callaghan had surrendered all moral authority needed to forestall the politically debilitating strikes of 1978–79, which produced maximum disruption of everyday life.

Absent political rewards, unions reverted to default economism. "We will not have wage restraint, whoever . . . wraps it up for us," Cousins had said.[15] This outlook was integral to the postwar settlement, legitimated by social democratic celebration of the West: "free collective bargaining" was the axiom of British labor's commitment to democracy. "Statutory enforcement of wage and salary levels" was "unacceptable to free men, freely bargaining in a free society." When a government "takes that basic principle from democracy . . . democracy no longer exists." Industrial bargaining was "outside the realms of the law": "you cannot have a social democracy and at the same time control by legislation the activity of a free trade union Movement;" that was the drift "into the totalitarian type of control." These attitudes were deeply ingrained post-1945: the "oft worn phrase that the Government must govern" was "so repetitious that one is beginning to think that we are in Portugal or Spain or Eastern Europe" rather than the Free World.[16]

To move trade unionists from their obduracy, some sociopolitical gain was needed, resuming the progressive advance of 1945. Earlier languages of productivity and economic reconstruction had been matched by precisely such a vision, for the strengthening of democracy, the welfare state, rising standards of living, and a universalist ethic of public goods. Then trade unionists, from right to left, had less problem with restraint, and larger progressivist rationales could surely be found again. Otherwise, unions would recur defiantly to their bloody-minded but principled ground. As the Miners' president in the 1974 coal strike, the solidly right-wing Joe Gormley, asked: "Who are they as a government to say what should be the wages of men who work at the coal face five days a week? Who are they to lay down the law in this democratic society we have?"[17]

THATCHERISM, "BUSINESS UNIONISM," AND THE DUAL LABOR MARKET

If one response to the shop steward was corporatist reliance on the TUC, a second was the opposite of a national system of industrywide bargaining—namely, plant or company-based deals. One way of neutralizing shop stewards was to recentralize union power in central office, but another was to suck them into management and surround them with rules. One survey found workplaces with written procedures rising from 50 to 80 percent during the 1970s. Removing health and safety rules, tea breaks, and firing from shopfloor negotiation became management's goal. In normalizing shop stewards, therefore, new legislation in 1974 also put constraints on their power. Productivity and job evaluation schemes did the same. Company-level bargaining sapped both the industrywide strength of unions like the Engineers and TGWU *and* the steward's shop-based role. In the resulting arrangements, designated unions would concede management prerogatives (including antistrike pledges) in return for high wages and company benefits, like pension plans, equity-ownership schemes, and private insurance. This model of bargaining liberated big companies from the national system of industrial relations.

But it required fierce confrontations and a determined political will. Shop stewards and big unions had too much at stake.[18] Abandoning corporatist precepts meant repudiating the postwar consensus, and under Margaret Thatcher's post-1979 right-wing government this was done. Empowered by business and middle-class opinion, Thatcher waged war on unions per se. The employment Acts of 1980, 1982, and 1984 attacked picketing and other rights, regulated union elections and decision-making, and defined "free collective bargaining" by narrowly legal rules. The centerpiece was the extraordinary miners' strike of 1984–85, when the most militant big union, whose 1972 and 1974 strikes had shamed the Heath government, was targeted for destruction. Thatcher staged a confrontation, stockpiling coal and preparing massed policing against pickets. The dispute became a battle over British governance. The miners' own view of the strike as a test of democracy and the labor movement's survival failed to enlist Labour or the TUC. The strike's defeat in March 1985 banished unions from government counsels. Later labor struggles—the attack on print unions in 1985–86 or the final erasure of coal in 1992–93—were merely a coda.

In Britain, joblessness rose steadily in the 1970s but soared under Thatcher to 13.2 percent by 1984. It became long-term, heavier among the young, and regionally uneven. Union membership initially survived: British union density was constant from 1953 to 1968, passing 50 percent in 1974 and peaking at 55.4 percent in 1979 with 13.5 million members. But thereafter decline was steep, down to 37.7 percent of the workforce, or 9.9 million members, by 1990 and only 30 percent by 1997.[19] Individual unions were hugely affected: coal-mining had virtually disappeared by 1993; in the five years after Thatcher's election the TGWU lost 29 percent of its membership; and other big unions declined by a quarter to a fifth. Unions elsewhere in Europe also suffered from the post-1973 recession. But if the decline was equally bad in France, Netherlands, Austria, Spain, Portugal, and Italy, elsewhere union density even improved. Where government favored them and public values backed full employment, unions survived, whether socialists or conservatives governed. Swedish union density rose from 67.7 percent in 1970 to 82.5 percent by 1990. Even in deindustrialized Belgium, where unemployment was 14 percent in 1984, union density rose from 45.5 to 55.9 percent during the 1970s, holding at 51.2 percent in 1990.[20]

Thus the politics of an antiunion drive explained the TUC's new weakness in Britain, as did less virulent antiunion politics in the comparable French, Iberian, and Dutch union declines. As labor was bludgeoned onto the defensive, reeling from unemployment, legal attacks, and the miners' strike, the mainstays of the TUC's progressivist axis after 1967–68, the Engineering and Transport Workers, both moved right. The third largest industrial union, the Electricians and Plumbers (EETPU), aggressively embraced the changes, identifying with company profitability and driving the best deal, regardless of any general ethic of solidarity. It negotiated private health insurance, betraying labor's axiomatic support for the National Health Service. When the print unions were broken in 1985–86, it recruited from the new workforce, violating taboos against scabbing and poaching. The EETPU pioneered business unionism: " 'We're in a free market for trade unionism,' said one of their officers. The fittest survive; the weak can go to the wall."[21]

This Thatcherized ethos showed how easily militant economism worked against the Left, once the postwar settlement's corporatist scaffolding was gone. Soon, half of all collective bargaining agreements had a single-employer basis, by company or plant. Workers under collective contracts also fell from 68 to 51 percent from 1984 to 1990. Big industrial unions abandoned industrywide collectivism for company-by-company deals, necessarily favoring workers in the economy's most profitable branches. In contrast to this new model, national agreements covered the less skilled and lower-paid, lacking the industrial muscle and favorable labor markets needed for action on their own. The case for national agreements had always entailed collectivist visions of the general interest in that way, for which the Social Contract was a final try.

For capital, keeping negotiations inside the company, ideally plant-by-plant, minimized trouble. Unions were stopped from mobilizing their full national strength, while employers kept their own central control. Plant agreements stressed local performance, not national rates for the job. Wages increasingly required bonuses and profit-sharing deals, with basic pay shrinking in the overall wage packet. In the 1980s, such schemes grew from 15 percent of all collective agreements to half. Companies slimmed their direct workforce to a protected and higher-paid "core," while "outsourcing" the rest, for whom job security, wages, and conditions became worse. For the core, company identification could be solidified through company pensions and health schemes, leisure facilities, employee equity-ownership, consultative mechanisms, and so on.[22]

PROGRESSIVISM AND THE PUBLIC SECTOR

The British example bespoke a general trend: in this period Western European capitalism increasingly acquired dual labor markets. Best-paid workers were divided from the rest by company-negotiated contracts dispensing with the old corporatist ground rules. The latter entailed industrywide collective bargaining, the national strength of big unions, social security and a national health system, and the universalist welfare state. Those older industrial relations certainly hadn't disappeared, and by 1990 half the collective bargaining in Britain still occurred nationally or regionally in that way. In the public sector, it was still the rule, and given the shift from industry to services and the rise of the latter's unions, this was vital. After TGWU and Engineers, the three largest unions were now the General and Municipal Workers (GMB) with 1.1 million members, NALGO, with 796,000, and NUPE, with 704,000. All were based in the public sector, organized women, and grew dramatically after 1960.[23]

As big industrial unions retreated to sectionalism, public sector unions took up their progressive role. As Thatcherism celebrated individualism and the market, EETPU's business unionism was applauded as the harbinger of modernization, enlisting other skilled unions like the Engineers.[24] But the lower-paid reacted differently, angered by the Callaghan government's betrayals, Thatcher's assault on the welfare state, and their own enduring sense of public value. The labor movement's local organs (trades councils, local Labour parties) already reflected the rise of public sector unions, and now these moved left. The general secretary of the GMB, David Basnett, known as "the reassuring face of trade-union barony," had been a byword for unimaginative centrism, a Labour loyalist who never rocked the boat. But an active membership wrought changes, culminating in the election of Basnett's successor, John Edmunds, in 1985.[25]

These unions led defense of the public sector—against attacks on local government, cuts in welfare and social security, hospital closures, and privatization of services; NUPE became a key force in the Labour Party. By 1987, its general secretary, Rodney Bickerstaffe, was chairing the TUC Economic Committee, and his deputy, Tom Sawyer, Labour's Home Policy Committee. NUPE prioritized the minimum wage, for which industrial militants traditionally had little time, and stressed equal pay, antidiscrimination, childcare provision, and other issues for women at work (its members were 65 percent women), as well as women's public representation.[26] It was committed to political education, stressing activism, participation, and democratic accountability.

Against EETPU business unionism, this public sector activism upheld an ethos of labor solidarity—organizing the workforce, bargaining collectively for wages, benefits, and conditions, securing rules and rights at work, and lobbying for influence. But it linked this to the broader public good the Social Contract had failed to express. As the Left's strength in industrial unions sank, progressivism migrated to the public sector. Indeed, unions like NUPE *had* to argue on broader political fronts. They provided services to the general public rather than producing goods for a market. This changed a strike's impact on ordinary people (as the "public," taxpayers, consumers, clients of services, citizens) in ways unions couldn't afford to neglect, as public sector unions learned in 1978–79 to their cost. Public employees had no access to the private schemes and company-provided benefits that EETPU chose to pursue. They confronted a different labor market. They needed the welfare state for themselves—for both social security and jobs.

Given the changing occupational structure, the rise of public sector unions encouraged thoughts of reviving old-style social democracy. If industrial unions had either lost their clout or retreated to sectionalism, rising service sector unions might fill the breach. If the older industrial economy of Fordism and mass production was passing away, then the post-Fordist economy of services and information technologies had its own proletariat, upholding the labor movement's collective organization in a time-honored way. If the sociology of working-classness had changed, it was hoped by many, the traditional coordinates of working-class politics survived. Whatever the changing shape of economy and class structure, the socialist politics associated with the postwar settlement could be reaffirmed—trade union corporatism, the Keynesian package of demand management, public investment, and full employment, the reduction of social inequality through the welfare state, progressive taxation, planning. By the 1990s, it was time for the force of these arguments to be judged.

NO GOING BACK

Analytically, class kept its centrality. It was necessary for making sense of society under capitalism—from the organizing of social life and the mapping of human differences to the charting of inequalities in the social distribution of value produced in the economy. The core of socialist definitions of the working class, wage-labor—meaning the sale of labor power for a wage, as the source of livelihood under relations of dependency and subordination, without alternative means of support—had become ever more universal. Certainly, the visible markers and wider cultural meanings of working-classness had changed. Where and how people lived, ate, drank, and played, as well as the nature of the workplace, the kind of work they did, and how they did it, were all transformed in the twentieth century, whether measured from the First World War, the post-1945 settlement, or the accelerating transformations of recent decades. But the central organizing fact of working for a wage (even when wages were salaries), and the straightforward material necessity of doing so, was more true for more people than ever before, even if mediated and obscured in subtle and complex ways.

Class as an analytic category, and as an organizing condition of social life, may have remained, but its structure and manifest forms had profoundly changed. With new employment patterns, the geography and gender of working-classness changed, as did the architectures of everyday life in housing, family, sexuality, friendship, schooling, recreation and leisure, and taste and style. So too did the cultures of identification. It made a difference if the representative trade unionists were coal-miners, dockers, steelworkers, machine-builders, and other men applying muscle and intelligence to arduous physical tasks or men and women sitting behind computers, canteen or laundry workers in public institutions, or nurses' aids in big city hospitals. The valencies of class as a basis for politics were different.

Class took its meanings from the historical circumstances where its boundaries and capacities, its terms of inclusion and exclusion, its constraints and promises, were shaped. So in 2000, the class-based social democracy of 1945–68 couldn't simply be revived. An organized working-class presence in politics involved more than the multiplication of wage-earning positions in a social structure or the systematic production of social inequalities or the cultural existence of working-class collective identities per se. Post-1945 histories of the working class were shaped by common experiences of government action, social reform, material betterment, and collective memory, summarized in this book as the postwar settlement. War, Liberation, and reconstruction after 1945, in the moment of antifascist opportunity and its later normalizations, in an enduring structure of constraints and possibilities, defined class in its political reach.

There was thus a political dimension to class formation under the postwar settlement, which helped establish what the limits and potentials of working-classness could be. The postwar boom was essential to this political history too, entering European popular experience around 1960 via greater disposable incomes, access to consumer durables, new forms of commercialized leisure, and the commodification of style and display. Fordism, as a distinctive regime of accumulation, combining mass production and mass consumption in workplace packages of productivity bargaining and high wages, provided the infrastructure of the social consensus this prosperity sustained. But post-1945 national political arrangements made a crucial difference. It *mattered* whether the postwar regime of accumulation was administered by a social democratic state committed to regulating capitalism and expanding democracy, at its strongest in Scandinavia, or whether it was managed on the backs of workers after labor movement defeat, as in southern Europe, either via dictatorship or coalitions excluding the Left.

Rather than flowing logically from the economics of growth and postwar prosperity's sociologies of improvement, labor's importance was constructed by politics. It was constructed partly by anti-Communism and the Cold War, in a system that countered 1945's more radical hopes—that is, by the limits on democratic advance. But it was also constructed by reform's humanizing achievements—by the Keynesian regulation of capitalism, the political culture of the welfare state, the practice of social citizenship, and the habitus of an expanding democratic ideal. Between postwar reforms and the later 1960s came a political hiatus, defined by the Cold War, and by the hard work and self-denials of reconstruction. But by the time these conformities were loosening and the political imagination bestirred, the corporatist frame had coalesced, and habits had hardened into norms of consultation between government and unions. British cycles of negotiation around incomes policy, from the Wilson government to the Social Contract, presumed this prehistory, when labor's influence cohered from postwar reforms.

When its prolabor institutional framing was removed, the postwar settlement fell apart. Governments brokered the long boom's benefits into material improvements and sociopolitical recognition—rising real wages and higher standards of living on the one hand and promises of reform on the other, which by 1960 included educational opportunities and access to leisure, plus extensions of social justice, the welfare state, and democracy at work. Such reforms had to come, or corporatist compromise would founder. When rising inflation and declining productivity damaged popular optimism in the economy, the political stakes were raised, especially if wage restraint was imposed. Without one or the other, economic betterment or reform, postwar settlements couldn't survive. And into the gap came the self-interested militancy of the Western European strike wave of 1968–74, sometimes energizing socialist radicalism but turbulently bursting the frameworks of national union representation in new repertoires of shop-floor mobilization.

During 1965–75, the postwar settlement's scaffolding fell away. The breakdown of Bretton Woods and the international monetary order, US difficulties resulting from the Vietnam War and the crisis of the Nixon presidency, the oil embargo and world recession—all hit Keynesianism's international framework. The Fordist regime of accumulation based in mass production entered a long-term crisis, leading to capitalist restructuring. The hegemonic form of macroeconomic governance in the nation-state, Keynesianism, was abandoned. Planning, public investment, and deficit financing were opposed by monetarism, privatization, and neoliberal ideologies of the market. Redistributive systems of direct taxation linked to social justice entered disrepute. Public expenditure and high taxation became objects of public hostility. Social democracy was stigmatized for its politics of "tax and spend." The welfare state was cut back and even dismantled, with a retreat from universalism ("social security from the cradle to the grave"), reversion to individualism and charity, and the return of services to the market, from healthcare to pensions.

Further, after their 1970s peaks in membership and density, unions lost legitimacy, with restrictions under law, tensions with socialist parties, and heavy membership attrition via recession. Unions lost their special relationship to government as corporatism dissolved. The high-wage, full-employment economy of Fordism and Keynesianism, secured by industry-wide collective bargaining and national agreements, with vigorous cultures of shopfloor militancy, ended. National systems of industrial relations attaching to corporatism and unified labor movements dissolved. They were replaced by new dualisms: high-wage workers in dynamic industries, with flexibility and valuable skills, opting for company-based agreements; and lower-paid unskilled workers in smaller-scale industry and public employment, for whom traditional collective bargaining and national agreements remained the necessary norm.

Developments across Europe weren't uniform. In Scandinavia, union density remained high, even increasing. In France, Portugal, and Spain, it sank catastrophically low. In Scandinavia and Austria, national union federations kept influence. In Germany, Austria, the Netherlands, and Scandinavia, electoral consensus for social services perdured. French abandonment of Keynesianism occurred under the Socialist government elected in 1981. Tax revolts were early, virulent, and successful in Britain and Denmark. But the key Western European variable was the political strength of 1950s corporatism. Where postwar Keynesianism was built on the labor movement via union federations and their policy units, the consequences of recession, deindustrialization, and post-Fordist restructuring were less damaging to the Left's political survival. But if corporatism excluded labor or presumed its defeat in the early Cold War, Left parties lost control over the crisis, adopting neoliberal economic policies even in power. Britain was in between, combining strong wage and work-related corporatism organized around unions' industrial strength and a civil service Keynesianism. But the Wilson government failed to integrate the TUC into the Keynesian economy's national institutions, producing a fracture between Labour and unions and the debacle of the Social Contract.[27]

THE UNMAKING OF THE WORKING CLASS

By the 1970s, the Left had a central problem. As parties traditionally based on the industrial working class, socialists and Communists were appealing to ever smaller populations. Furthermore, the remaining workers no longer saw themselves collectively in the same way. As an operative identity—as the socialist tradition's organizing myth, capable of inspiring collective action, of uniting disparate categories of working people inside the same solidarity, with enduring efficacy in politics—the "working class" was losing its motive power.

In this double sense—in social structure and social understandings, as the social aggregation of wage-earning positions in industrial economies and as an organized political identity—the working class declined. This was a complex story. Perceptions of decline reflected the demise of one *kind* of working-class aggregate—the skilled or semiskilled male proletarians of the "old" industries and the electrochemical complex of the "second industrial revolution." By stricter definitions of wage-labor, after all, working-class positions still increased. The declining peasantry, shopkeepers, tradesmen, and other self-employed more than replenished the wage-dependent labor force, likewise women's entry into employment. Assumptions about working-class identity lagged behind actual changes in work and the continuing creation of new types of worker, as growth of the service sector and public employment made clear. Yet the "decline of the working class" was not just an illusion.

The working class was never only a homogeneous category of wage-earners. Whatever the stage of capitalism, the working class was always in process of being formed. It had to be made into an operative unity—one with recognized public meanings and an active political presence. It was always a complex of communities and occupations, divided by gender, age, seniority, skill, training, type of work, religion, language, ethnicity and national origin, residence, region, and other distinctions. It became a collectivity for political purposes only via creative and continuous efforts.

Moving from class as social facts to class as sociopolitical understandings—from an aggregate of wage-earners in structurally dispersed class locations to a collective agency in politics—was never "given."[28] It involved unpredictable political histories. The political fixing of class could certainly acquire stability, in solid institutional frameworks like the Keynesian, welfare-state, and corporatist ones of the postwar settlement. But keeping multiform divisions in forward-moving tension, within broadly framed common solidarities, remained inevitably incomplete. Many categories of workers in purely wage-earning terms fell outside the realized unity of "the working class" at particular times. Many have resisted appeals to "working-class consciousness." The ambivalence of multiple and conflicting interests can always be found operating eloquently inside individual lives.

Some generalizations about the differences complicating or impeding the "unity" of the working class in the present were evident.[29] One split concerned blue- and white-collar workers. White-collar personnel in offices held different social standing and had different everyday experiences from workers in mines or factories. Unionizing or appealing across these distinctions engendered tensions. Differences inside the manual working class itself also widened after the 1970s. Dual labor markets set higher-paid skilled workers, with privileged bargaining positions and company benefits, against the reserve of casualized and unskilled, subject to low-waged irregular work and lack of insurance. This emerging "two-thirds, one-third society" stigmatized the impoverished minority into an "underclass," like the "residuum" of pre-1914 or the "undeserving poor." Still worse, in an alternative analysis the tendential "third-third-third society," spreading insecurity upward into the "newly insecure," left only an upper third free from risk.[30] Intermediate categories of semiskilled workers, the mass recruits of earlier industrial unions, declined. Social fragmentation now complicated the traditional rationales for solidarity, both among unions and in labor's political cause.

These differences mapped onto a third set, those between men and women. Women dominated new areas of tertiary employment. They also joined the less skilled, part-time, and lower-paid workers in industry. Women's growing union presence, recruitment to local government and parliaments, and electoral weight compelled a momentous regendering of the Left. Yet Left leaderships stayed overwhelmingly male. Labor movements were still riddled with sexism. The Left's prioritizing of women's workplace interests was painfully uneven, whether in relation to job segregation, discriminatory hiring, sexual harassment, childcare arrangements, or unequal pay.[31]

Age was also a key divider. Apprenticeship declined, even if age-related white-collar and other hierarchies remained. Employed workers became severed from the elderly and youthful never-employed; dependence of the former on ever-larger social spending (pensions, healthcare, social services) and the latter's subcultural aggressions produced tensions, which earlier solidarities of family, neighborhood, and community, themselves disrupted by change, couldn't contain. Deindustrialization—manufacturing flight from inner cities, the collapse of old industries and ancilliary labor markets, the death of single-industry communities—also meant huge inequalities among regions, which also handicapped political coalescence. Examples included long-term economic decline (closing entire coalfields or shipyards), technological change (containerization in the docks), rural depopulation (the Italian south), and internal colonialism (postunification eastern Germany after 1990).[32]

Finally, race and national identity sharply disrupted working-class solidarities.[33] Labor needs of booming Western economies sucked immigrants from the Mediterranean to West Germany, the Low Countries, and Scandinavia, or from ex-colonies in South Asia, North Africa, and the Caribbean to Britain and France. By 1990, European Union (EU) countries had 13 million migrant nonnationals, with consistently rising tensions. Antiforeigner violence erupted in Germany after unification, and Left parties largely evaded the challenge of this popular divisiveness. But workers also supported neofascist initiatives, like the French National Front. Working-class racism festered in Austria, Germany, Belgium, and Britain. Similar conflicts marked post-Communist Eastern Europe from the late 1980s, in Yugoslavia to the point of state disintegration, societal collapse, and civil war. Divisiveness sometimes merged with regional disparities, as in politicized attacks against southern migrants in the Italian north. Cultural divisiveness—whether grasped in nationalist, ethnic, racial, or religious terms—resisted superordinate languages of class solidarity.[34]

THE LOOSENING OF CLASS AFFILIATION

Mobilizing for general class solidarity, whether for demonstrations, elections, or an uprising, always encountered divisions among workers. The unity of the working class was always a projection, the goal of socialist politics, rather than a given quantity determined by economics or social inequality. As a collective agency, the working class was always in motion, affected by economic fluctuations, the contingencies of everyday life, and government action, locally and nationally. It was always in process of being "made."

From the late nineteenth century, though, there was a logic to this making. It united workers' loyalties around the political cause of labor, within a broadly conceived socialist consciousness maturing between the wars, whatever the party infighting produced by 1914–23. The postwar settlements then solidified this coalescence after 1945, even as the social effects of the new postwar prosperity undermined its existing communal supports, slowly disordering working-class solidarities via new processes of fragmentation. The late twentieth century thus brought an epochal change: from the socialist parties' foundation to the high tide of antifascism, the main trend was class coalescence; from the 1960s, the emergent story was dis-integration. Contemporary changes gave divisions among workers new po-litical valency. The backbone of class affiliation became broken.

By 1960, sociologists and cultural critics were already marking the pass-ing of the "traditional working class" in debates about "affluence" and the effects of postwar boom. Yet this had been a very specific working-class formation, coalescing via late-nineteenth-century industrialization, acquir-ing stronger shape in following decades, and stabilizing through the post-1945 settlements. In this sense, the socialist tradition's self-confident and successful organizing of class-centered aspirations was the finite effect of a distinctive period, lasting some eight decades.

This "historic" working class developed only partly from industry per se and far more from its spatial location in special communities—small single-industry settlements around mines or factories, big metropoles like ports or capital cities, and especially medium towns or bounded inner-city districts, like West Ham or Woolwich in London, Wedding in Berlin, Sesto San Giovanni in Milan, or Sans in Barcelona.[35] Municipal socialism on this community scale was vital for the movement before 1914. Socialist cadres, unionized workers, the clerical and direct workforce of the city, and con-stituencies benefiting from services gave the Left formidable political ma-chines. The post-1918 democratic franchise placed them in charge. During 1920–60, labor conquered the city. It dominated local government in cap-ital cities and industrial regions long before winning national office. Class formation was a politically driven process of social coalescence, "nurtured in the womb of municipal government." A collective identity "was forged for the working class, and by reaction for the lower middle class" in these new urban settings: "Urban society moved a long way in the interwar years from being a cellular society to being a class society."[36]

In organizing urban neighborhoods and inner-city wards, socialist par-ties became "the agent[s] of class formation."[37] Formed during 1880–1930, this tradition outlasted the conditions of its rise. The Left's dominance sur-vived through the 1950s and 1960s, as in the Labour Party's rule in large parts of Scotland, South Wales, and the north or the PCF's in the Paris "red belt." But these urban hegemonies became continuously eroded. Local working-class political cultures became ever harder to find. Between the wars, suburbanization undermined communities where municipal social-isms had formed, sometimes promoted by slum clearance and new town development.[38] Such processes accelerated from the 1970s—via manufac-turing decline, industrial flight, deindustrialization of regions, labor force recomposition, and dismantlement of welfare states. In Britain, the struc-ture of local government finance and delivery of services, which first sus-tained experiments like "Poplarism" and socialism's vision of the city, be-came destroyed, most egregiously in the abolition of the Greater London Council in March 1986.[39] Work and residence became ever more split. Enjoyment became displaced from music halls, cinemas, theaters, and clubs into the privacy of "entertainment centers" in the home. City centers became abandoned to commercial development, gentrification, and the miscellaneous poor.

After 1945, class became slowly a less reliable predictor of voting.[40] In countries like Austria, Scandinavia, and Britain, class had strongly determined voting before, while in West Germany, France, and Italy it was complicated by religion, and in the Low Countries and Spain it predicted weakly. But now its decline became a general trend. In Sweden, "the predictive value of class fell from 53 percent of the variance in 1956 to 34 percent by 1985, with young and female voters being least influenced by class position."[41] As workers declined in numbers, socialist parties also found it harder to keep their support.[42] From 1945 to 1983, British Labour's share of working-class votes sank from 62 to 42 percent. In 1983–87, only 39 percent of union members supported Labour, a quarter less than in 1979, with 6 in 10 trade unionists voting elsewhere; Labour won only a fifth of the white-collar electorate, and less than half the semiskilled and unskilled voters—figures that were barely bettered in 1992, when Labour's popular vote improved. During the 1980s Thatcherism had successfully reduced Labour's electorate to a demoralized working-class minority.[43]

Thus class voting became weaker: "the Labour vote remains largely working-class; but the working class has ceased to be largely Labour."[44] New workers were ambivalent about the labor movement's traditions, while former loyalists defected. In 1979, anti-Labour swing among skilled workers was 10–11 percent. Old Left formulas lost effectiveness. High taxes, welfare bureaucracies, inefficient nationalized industries, and other degenerative aspects of the postwar settlement eroded workers' loyalties. Old appeals were exhausted. Emergent labor market dualisms cut through individual industries, pitting worker against worker: "part-time against full-time, core versus periphery, Fordist production against post-Fordist, temporary against permanent employment, in-house versus contracted-out workforce, and so on."[45]

Through these changes trade unionism lost its credentials as a progressive force. Unions had always been intimately connected with socialism. Beyond party–union relations was the larger sense of trade unionism as the weapon of the weak, mobilizing workers' collectively organized strength as their only defense against exploitation, social inequalities, and the power of capital. Trade unionism was a class capacity, through which masses acting in unison could have effects. Industrial strength was essential for immediate improvement in wages and working conditions. But trade unionism was also a larger vision, a collectivist ideal of the general good, a desire for improving society, a general ethic of social solidarity. Until 1914, working-class militants hankered after the revolutionary chimera of the general strike. In the more radical, usually syndicalist, versions, this would start the socialist transition. More generally, it forced recalcitrant dominant classes into political change, as in pre-1914 general strikes for suffrage. Industrial action also conveyed more modest political hopes: workers with trade union strength helped workers who were weak, because higher standards of wages and working conditions leveled the rest up. Unions carried the torch for progressive reform.

After 1918, and especially since 1945, trade unionism's centrality for workers' political consciousness subtly changed. Until socialist parties could change the law, workers' social security required their collective organizations in the economy. Between the wars, the Left only rarely formed governments outside Scandinavia. But the democratic franchise made unions a legitimate bloc of interests, so that even in the depression their legal rights survived (where fascism didn't destroy them altogether). After British labor's massive setback in the General Strike (1926), the Labour government's collapse (1929–31), and the disasters of mass unemployment, unions were spared reactionary legal assault. On the contrary, they reemerged during the patriotic mobilization of the Second World War's with renewed strength. They attracted general progressive hopes, not just from existing union members but from the not-yet-unionized and the larger mass of working-class poor.

Under welfare states, however, trade unionism stopped carrying these hopes of the poor. New supports in social services and national health systems freed unions for wage bargaining and defending interests at work. With ideas of social citizenship and social wage, workers' well-being derived from a wider public charge, supplying genuine measures of security. Collective bargaining slid more easily into sectionalism, less attentive to a general working-class interest or to effects on other unions and categories of workers. Poverty was handled by the welfare state. If it came from low wages, then militancy of the higher-paid would pull these up. But poverty now became demonized into the pathologies of decaying regions and inner cities, from single mothers and ethnic minorities to violent and drug-abusing youth, in hidden economies of casualization and permanent underemployment. In this racialized and criminalizing discourse, movements shaped historically by appealing to white male workers in regular employment had less and less to say. The more visionary trade unionists still voiced an ethics of solidarity, as in Jack Jones's idea of the Social Contract or Swedish unions' more persistent efforts in the 1970s and 1980s. Equal pay and antidiscrimination legislation (and union support for women's rights) became new forms of commitment to a general cause. But mainly trade unionism narrowed into sectionalism.

FAREWELL TO THE WORKING CLASS?

By 1980, socialism's class-centered politics was in crisis. In the new democracies of Spain and Greece, socialist parties had ascendancy. In France, Socialists won the presidency and a parliamentary majority for the first time. In Austria, Socialists remained dominant. In Norway and Sweden, they returned to office after brief opposition. Yet in West Germany, a tired and lackluster SPD vacated government after 13 years in 1982. British Labour left office in 1979 for 18 years in opposition. But even *in* office, socialists found it ever more difficult to avoid policies pioneered by their conservative opponents. Social democracy's pillars—full employment and Keynesian economics, welfare states and expanding public sectors, corporatism and strong unions—were crumbling and under attack. In Communist Europe, things were also bleak. The main source of an optimistic critique of social democracy, the PCI's Eurocommunism, was in retreat. The greatest mass movement to emerge in a socialist country, Polish Solidarity, was suppressed by the military. Eastern European Communism was out of creativity. The USSR was a byword for stagnation. The Marxist intellectual tradition was in trouble.

Leading commentators took apocalyptic tones. "Socialism Is Dead," sociologist Alaine Touraine declared. "Farewell to the Working Class," echoed radical social theorist André Gorz.[46] Reeling from the disappointments of the 1970s, British socialist intellectuals made searching reviews of class-political thinking, from the given model of the party to the automatic assumption of the leading role of the working class.[47] Reflecting on deindustrialization, the right-wing radicalism of Thatcher's attack, and the recomposition of the working class, they concluded that "the world has changed, not just incrementally but qualitatively." The new social order was "characterized by diversity, differentiation and fragmentation, rather than homogeneity, standardization and the economies and organizations of scale which characterized modern mass society."[48] Post-Fordist transition was changing the place in politics of the working class. The Fordist regime of mass production implied one type of politics, and the post-Fordist regime of "flexible specialization," spreading in the 1980s, implied another:

> The huge mass-production plant built around the conveyor belt, the
> city or region dominated by a single industry, as Detroit or Turin were
> by automobiles; the local working class united, welded together by res-
> idential segregation and workplace, into a multi-headed unity—these
> seemed to have been characteristics of the classic industrial era. . . .
> The classic "post-Fordist" industrial regions—for instance the Veneto,
> Emilia-Romagna, and Tuscany in North and Central Italy—lacked the
> great industrial cities, the dominant firms, the huge plants. They were
> mosaics or networks of enterprises ranging from the cottage workshop
> to the modest (but high-tech) manufactory, spread across town and
> country.[49]

By 1990, the Left was divided between advocates of change and defenders of the faith. The former carried the day. Contemporary transformations were not the "death of class" or the "end of the working class" per se. They were the passing of one type of class society, the one that was marked by working-class formation between the 1880s and 1940s and the resulting political alignments, with its apogee in the postwar settlement. As long-term changes in the economy combined with the attack on Keynesianism, the unity of the working class ceased to be available in that old and well-tried form as the natural ground of left-wing politics.

While classic male proletarians in mining, transportation, and manufacture declined, with their unions, residential concentration, and family living, another working class made up of mainly female white-collar and menial workers in services and all types of public employment unevenly materialized in its place. The operative unity of this new working-class aggregation—its active agency as an organized political presence—remained very much in formation. The making of the first working class via the rise of labor movements had displayed a necessary political dimension, which shaped the socialist tradition into a class-centered politics of democracy and emancipatory social reform, as an egalitarian drive for the civilizing of capitalism. To rebuild the socialist tradition, some new vision of collective political agency was needed, one keyed to conditions of capitalist production and accumulation at the start of the twenty-first century. Class needed to be reshaped, reassembled, put back together again in political ways. To use a Gramscian adage: the old was dying, but the new had yet be born.

Chapter 24

New Poltics, New Times

Remaking Socialism and Democracy

DURING 1970–90, the bases for socialist movements of the classical kind dissolved in Europe. This meant not only the old class solidarities but also the industrial capitalism behind them—factory and small workshop concentrations of machine production; heavy manual labor in mines and metal mills; labor-intensive docklands, railways, and urban transit systems; huge and ramified complexes of mass production organized in big cities, coalfields, chains of factory towns, and single-industry settlements. Having dominated European society from the 1880s to the 1960s, this landscape now slowly disappeared. Government infrastructures of socialist reform were also dismantled, from the sovereignties of the parliamentary state and national economy to the urban community resources of local government. Collective self-organization, ideals of improvement, club life, an ethics of collectivist progress and public good—these supporting cultures of socialism dwindled. Labor movements' resilient masculinities became subject to change too, from the patriarchy of working-class households to the gendered practices of unions and parties and their inveterate sexism. The socialist tradition's default assumptions, its axiomatic class-political orientation, no longer held good.

On the other hand, socialism's democratic ideals remained as vital as ever, as did the constitutional, organizational, and cultural frameworks of democracy, for which social democratic and Communist parties had been so indispensable—in times of democracy's greatest danger no less than in the great constitution-making breakthroughs after the world wars. As the conditions sustaining the classical tradition disappeared, therefore, the questions inevitably arose: what kinds of socialism could still be imagined, and what new forms of politics would secure democracy's future?

END OF THE POSTWAR BOOM

A world economic downturn followed the oil crisis of 1973–74, ending the postwar boom and its promises of continuously rising prosperity. The OPEC raising of oil prices surrounding the Arab-Israeli War derailed capitalist Europe's already teetering economies, which suffered the first absolute decline in output since 1929–32. In the years that followed, individual countries entered periods of extreme domestic crisis. British social polarization under the Heath government climaxed in the miners' strike of February 1974, while in Italy societal crisis spiraled outward from student uprisings and labor unrest. For Western Europe more generally, high inflation, rising unemployment, and low growth became the new norm.

The boom's end magnified the effects of far-reaching changes in the economy—the reorganizing of labor markets, manufacturing decline and deindustrialization, class recomposition, and general capitalist restructuring. With economic stagnation, welfare states went into crisis. They were constantly attacked for being too costly, too inefficient, too bureaucratic, too corrosive of individual morale, and too subject to abuse. Their machinery of public provision and the language of public goods were corrupting, their critics complained. Services should be privatized. As the postwar boom's Keynesian orthodoxies also fell into disarray—deficit financing, demand management, strong public sectors, full employment—the common sense of politics began to change. The reliable verities of the Fordist era started to crumble, from the economics of mass production and the associated corporatist arrangements to the prized securities of rising real wages and full employment. The new priorities of a "post-Fordist transition" supervened.[1]

Profound ruptures occurred with the past. Post-1945 political systems had brought the Left fundamental gains, endowing organized labor's new influence with powerful democratic meanings. The postwar settlements had celebrated democratic sovereignties of the people, formally so in the new constitutions of West Germany, Austria, the Low Countries, and Scandinavia. If the synthesis of Keynesian economics, welfare states, and corporatism was less relevant in southern Europe, the French and Italian constitutions also delivered vital democratic goods. After 1945, the Left dominated local government too, via strongholds in particular industries, cities, and small communities, often covering entire regions. Left advance became institutionalized first where poor relief, housing, schooling, wider services, and public jobs could be expanded using local taxes and disbursing central government funds. These were the urban-political contexts of class formation, the bedrock of socialism after 1945.

But contemporary transformations made any simple continuation of this socialist tradition impossible. For the century 1860–1960, twin axioms prevailed: if socialism always provided the Left's core, the Left was still always larger than socialism. Socialists could never win politically by themselves. Their goals could only be realized through coalitions—whether for the purposes of elections, for forming a government, for planning and organizing a strike, for rallying community solidarities, for waging effective local campaigns, for capturing existing institutions, or for arguing ideas in the public sphere. In handling this wider process of politics, three factors became crucial: one organizational, affecting the type of movement socialists invented; one cultural, involving broader popular identifications with the gains of 1945; and one structural, concerning the national and transnational contexts of Left activity.

To take the first of these, the pre-1914 era had established the lasting model of the parliamentary socialist party and allied union federation, geared to elections and harnessing mass memberships via the socialist clubs and the big auxiliaries for women and youth. Communist parties followed the same pattern. This socialist associationism aspired to the entirety of its supporters' lives, ideally backed by local government and the future socialist state. It grounded the parliamentary party in the lives of its members. Socialism's promise also had wider-than-proletarian appeal, attracting white-collar workers, professionals, intellectuals, nonemployed family members, discriminated national and other minorities, and so on. Yet postwar changes slowly destroyed the infrastructures for such broad-gauged socialist cultures, and by the 1990s the classical party, as a movement simultaneously rooted in working-class communities and magnetizing broader aspirations, was gone.[2]

Second, "1945" signified democracy, social justice, and national independence, forming a template for the collective political imagination. The legacies of antifascism and reconstruction delivered a persuasive narrative— hardships and struggle, plus reform and improvement—which stabilized the postwar settlement's popularity. A popular culture of improvement and appreciation cemented the welfare states and associated practices of government, deepening a broadly social democratic consensus. But by the 1960s, this was less effective. For new generations, stories of sacrifice and improvement spelled political complacency. Their own sense of a future felt blocked by conformity. "1968" was thus a crisis of postwar political culture in a double sense: it brought the impatience of dissident generations to an explosive head, and it opened public space for a right-wing backlash—against not only the cultural radicalism of the sixties themselves but also the lineaments of consensus around the legacies of the war. A battle of ideas ensued, through which socialist parties lost their grip on political common sense. This badly damaged the Left's broader progressive project.

Finally, both the socialist party and the postwar consensus presumed the nation-state's operative sovereignty, because the channels of political action and the Left's legislative program required this setting. International factors always set limits, but now a new international conjuncture exerted its power. After 1973, globalization compromised national governments' autonomy—through the collapse of Bretton Woods, through deindustrialization and capital's transnational mobility in multinational corporations, and through the profitability available in newly industrializing countries. European integration demonstrated this transnational logic through the expansion of the EEC, adding Britain, Denmark, and Ireland (1973), Greece (1981), Spain and Portugal (1986), and Austria, Sweden, and Finland (1995) to the original six, with post-Soviet Eastern Europe pressing close behind. The Single Europe Acts of 1986–1992 and the Treaty of Maastricht, through which the EEC became the European Union in 1994, removed the option of national Keynesianism. Sovereignty shifted decisively to the EU's unwieldy and undemocratic institutional frame.[3]

Thus, national models of socialist politics, identified with distinctive class-political movements, popular memories of war and reconstruction, and the sovereignty of territorial states, passed into disarray. The basic conditions for this tradition were gone. As Soviet Communism entered its terminal crisis in the 1980s, the Communist parties reinvented themselves as broader Left parties or dwindled away. Established socialist parties continued, usually as the strongest formations in Western European national Lefts, but no longer relied on the same infrastructure of dense organization, mass membership, community mobilization, and class-political allegiance as before. What would replace them as the main organized formations of the European Left? In this respect, the consequences of the explosions of 1968 were still unclear.

EUROCOMMUNISM, 1968–1980: WAR OF POSITION

For the international Communist movement, the Soviet invasion of Czechoslovakia in 1968 was a decisive parting of the ways. With it, reform Communism died in Eastern Europe. After the Prague Spring, Warsaw Pact governments never again deviated from the central axioms of Moscow loyalism; namely, cohesion of the Soviet bloc, bureaucratic structures of the command economy, and the Communist political monopoly. In Western Europe, on the other hand, the Soviet invasion moved Communists to unprecedented anti-Soviet critique.

Internationally, the mid-1970s were a threatening but exciting time. In 1974–75, southern Europe's three dictatorships collapsed. Radical officers of the Armed Forces Movement initiated the Portuguese revolution in April

1974, and seized power from Marcelo Caetano; the Greek dictatorship resigned after provoking a Turkish invasion of Cyprus in July 1974; and Franco's death in November 1975 began the democratic transition in Spain.[4] In each case Communists had been the sole sustained opposition, expecting grateful citizenries to reward them with their votes. All three Communist parties adopted strategies of constitutionalism and broad alliance, backed by extraparliamentary demonstrations but opposing all insurrectionary or "Bolshevik" temptations. This applied to the solidly Moscow-loyalist PCP under the veteran Stalinist Alvaro Cunhal no less than the PCE under Santiago Carrillo, who took a pronounced anti-Soviet stance. Each of these situations seemed finely poised. Not only were Communists seeking to establish democratic credentials and position themselves to govern, but the dangers of right-wing coups also seemed acute.

Meanwhile, democracy in Italy was dangerously close to breaking down. After three bombs exploded in December 1969, one in Milan killing 16 people and two in Rome injuring 18, anarchists were rounded up, but neo-Fascists linked to the Secret Service had perpetrated these atrocities. Their "strategy of tension," using an anti-Left backlash to rationalize restrictions on civil liberties, emergency laws, and even a coup d'état, required intricate connections across government, military, Secret Service, business, Vatican, and Mafia, for which a secret anti-Communist masonic lodge, *Propaganda Due* (P-2), founded by the ex-Fascist Licio Gelli, was apparently the key.[5] In 1974, bombs killed 8 at an anti-Fascist rally in Brescia in May and 12 on the Florence-Bologna train in August, while neo-Fascist street violence in northern cities escalated. In the 1972 elections, the neo-Fascist Movimento Sociale Italiano (MSI) had won 8.7 percent, its highest-ever vote. Concurrently, the Red Brigades also passed from violent propaganda (attacks on property, beating up managers and foremen, kidnapings) to dramatic armed hits, beginning with the seizure of the Genoa judge Mario Sossi, who was released after 35 days in April 1974. During 1974–76, police raids and shootouts kept left-wing terrorism in public view.[6]

Amid these tensions and the delicately balanced transitions in Greece, Portugal, and Spain, Communists foregrounded threats from the Right. These were dramatized by the military coup of September 1973 against Salvador Allende's Popular Unity government in Chile, whose parliamentary socialism had inspired so many left-wing hopes. The PCI leader Enrico Berlinguer drew the political moral. Invoking Togliatti's legacy, he urged the broadest democratic consensus to defend and extend the Republic. Chile warned against the "pressing danger of the nation being split in two," because antidemocratic forces always turn to violence when popular movements record fundamental gains. Thus the PCI should seek to revive Italian democracy's founding coalition, by rallying not only the Socialists but also the third component of the "popular movement," the Catholic. Opening

Christian Democracy to the Left would secure the Republic against the Right, prevent society's division into polarized blocs, and allow new progressive advance.[7]

This was Berlinguer's "historic compromise"—rallying Italy's three great popular traditions, Communism, socialism, and Catholicism, for renewed democratic change. Electoral demographics were on his side. In 1972, the PCI managed 27.2 percent of the vote, and adding the Socialists made only 36.8 percent, way short of a majority. In 1968, the combined Left reached 45.8 percent, because anti-Communist Social Democrats briefly joined the PSI. But rallying the Left on that basis presaged the very societal polarization that Berlinguer feared—the secular bloc of Communists, Socialists, and Social Democrats on one side, the DC forced into bed with neo-Fascists on the other. Even if such a bloc could be forged, which was improbable, and it passed 50 percent, then governing against the DC, which occupied commanding heights of state, economy, and society, still wouldn't work. Given existing signs—the MSI's growth, right-wing terrorism, the Right's "strategy of tension"—a socialist bloc might expect sabotage on a Chilean scale. For Berlinguer, "the central political problem in Italy" was avoiding that end.[8]

Instead, he wanted to bring Christian Democrats along. On this analysis, the DC was at an impasse, humiliated by progressive victory in the divorce referendum of May 1974, reeling from corruption scandals, and accused of using the "strategy of tension" for a Gaullist-type coup.[9] Italian politics were at a standstill. Neither Left nor Right could establish hegemony. Nor could the Right govern via force, because society's oppositional capacities were too strong. This "precarious balance of forces between the two main parties," with the Communists "not sufficiently strong to rule without the center, and Christian Democrats no longer able to rule in the old way," required a new initiative.[10] Otto Bauer had argued this in the 1920s, when the SPÖ's simultaneous dominance of Vienna and exclusion from national power created a similar equilibrium. That was a source of great danger but also gave the Left an unprecedented chance. In Austria, it had ended in destruction of the labor movement and the triumph of clerico-fascism in 1934. But for Berlinguer, this merely reemphasized the necessity of getting the strategy right.

The prize was the fundamental realignment of Italian society which Gramsci and Togliatti had both imagined. And Berlinguer's strategy seemed to work. Regional and local elections in June 1975 raised the PCI's vote to 33.4 percent (7.6 more than 1970), and the DC's dropped slightly to 35.3. The existing PCI-PSI strongholds of Emilia-Romagna, Tuscany, and Umbria were now joined by Lombardy, Piedmont, and Liguria, plus all the major cities except Palermo and Bari. A year later, national elections confirmed the trend. Despite overt pressure from the U.S. secretary of state, Henry Kissinger, recalling anti-Communist intervention in 1948, the Communists raised their vote to 34.4 percent. The rest of the Left brought this to 46.7 percent.

This was the setting for Eurocommunism. The tag was invented by liberals as a tocsin, denouncing a seemingly reformed Communism as merely a smokescreen for Europe's creeping sovietization.[11] But Berlinguer seized the label, extolling the Left's common commitment to a distinctive Western road to socialism. Santiago Carrillo, seeking to lead Spain's democratic transition, then deployed the term more ambitiously, as "the 'Eurocommunist' road to power." His book, *"Eurocommunism" and the State*, helped focus a summit of Italian, Spanish, and French CPs in Madrid in March 1977, where the silent referent had remained the Prague Spring. Berlinguer and the others marked their difference from Moscow, continuing to criticize the Soviet invasion of Czechoslovakia, upholding the rights of individual countries to their own "national roads," and defending human rights in the USSR.[12]

Eurocommunism was inseparable from the legacies of fascism, because the Left's defeats in Italy and Spain between the wars inspired this new antimaximalist strategy of broad democratic alliance. Now that Franco was dead, Spanish Communists hoped to repeat the PCI's experience of 1944–47, when antifascism brought lasting popular success. Eurocommunism's architects, Berlinguer and Carrillo, evoked antifascism's heroics, while guiding their parties toward a different political future—away from permanent opposition, away from "dictatorship of the proletariat," and away from the handicaps of Moscow loyalism. Their strategy was constantly shadowed by dangers of counterrevolution, whether via the Italian Right's "strategy of tension" or fears of Francoist coups. Antifascism was reactivated as "a symbol of national unity."[13]

The PCI broke the deadlock, supporting the DC government from opposition and negotiating common programs. Pietro Ingrao, leader of the PCI left, became the first Communist president of the Chamber of Deputies. Berlinguer cast this as accepting national responsibility amid economic crisis and democratic danger. The time when "the old political élite" could do as they wished had "gone for ever," he argued; they now had to "ask us" and not simply "impose sacrifices on the working class." By stepping up to the mark, the PCI would establish its right to govern. There would be "a profound change in the economic and social structures, in the functioning of the state and the whole public sector, in relations of power, in the way of life and habits of the country."[14] This vision was Eurocommunism's zenith. It united the party. It concentrated progressive energies around the PCI for the 1976 elections. It inspired enormous hopes in the Left elsewhere.

The strategy ran into the sand. Rather than bringing structural reform, the Historic Compromise merely blunted the PCI's challenge. Events certainly played their part. As the Government of National Solidarity began, the Red Brigades kidnapped Aldo Moro, the DC's main bridge to Berlinguer's hopes, and in March 1978 threw the Republic into crisis. The PCI took the hardest line: giving in could only encourage terrorism; democracy was at stake. This was correct: Moro was killed, but armed revolutionism was bankrupted, and after further violence and intensified policing, terrorism petered out.[15] Yet politics had been hijacked. The PCI became "the party of law and order, the bulwark of democratic legality, the shield of the constitution"—all sound Togliattian precepts but hitched to a corrupt state still honeycombed with DC vested interests, a well-oiled machinery of paybacks and private enrichment.[16] By restricting public rights and expanding police powers, the antiterrorist stance painfully compromised the PCI's guardianship of civil liberties. By realigning so strongly with the DC, Communists damaged their links to the broader Left. As Luciano Lama, head of the trade union movement (CGIL), said: "the battle [against terrorism] completely absorbed us, and so we did not see all the rest with the necessary clarity."[17]

In the Historic Compromise, the PCI rehearsed an old socialist dilemma, familiar from Weimar and Red Vienna. By accepting the system's premises—NATO, the DC, Catholicism, and capitalism—the PCI took a deck already stacked. In 1977–78, they espoused a version of Jack Jones's Social Contract in Britain: wage restraint plus productivity for jobs and investment, linked to political empowerment and social reform. Flat-rate increases, tied to the *scala mobile* (indexing of wages to inflation, agreed in 1975), favored the lower-paid, at the cost of alienating higher-paid skilled workers if promised political goods didn't arrive.[18] Berlinguer's ethical defense of austerity, as a redistributive opportunity to attack "the waste, injustice, privilege and the excesses of private consumption," required this political payoff. By their sacrifices, workers would not only save the economy but would enable its reconstruction on more equitable bases, linked to social reforms and stronger democracy.[19]

But by 1979, there was little to show for this compromising. Inflation was down to 12.4 percent, and unions made big concessions on wage indexing, redundancies, and productivity. But unemployment was rising and workers' disaffection was rife. As Berlinguer told Lama, "without an army we won't be able to fight any battles at all."[20] The PCI was also no closer to entering government, however intricate the consultations. The DC inveigled the PCI into responsibility and stifled its initiatives with consummate skill, while silencing its traditional opposition.

Berlinguer was done. The PCI declared its opposition, accusing Giulio Andreotti, the DC premier, of reneging on reform. Rather than reopening talks, Andreotti called elections for June 1979. The Historic Compromise was rebuffed: Communists lost 1.5 million votes, dropping to 30.4 percent, while the DC steadied at 38.3 percent. The PCI had lost momentum, especially among militant workers, the poor in the south, and the young. Berlinguer drew the conclusions: after initially reaffirming the Historic

Compromise, he replaced it with the "Democratic Alternative," a return to courting the PSI.

Eurocommunism passed its moment. From the high-water mark of 1976, it was already receding. The Spanish Communists had a crushing disappointment. After maneuvering through the post-Francoist minefield with exemplary forebearance, the PCE received 9.3 percent in the first elections in 1977, rising to only 10.7 percent in 1979. Carrillo's Eurocommunism was unequivocal—a parliamentary democracy and multiparty system, independent unions, complete civil and cultural freedoms, and total independence from the USSR. During the long march of opposition, he prioritized the broadest coalitions, from the Pact of Liberty in 1969 and Catalan Assembly movement of 1971 to the various coalitions leading to the final talks in 1975–77. The PCE's democratic credentials couldn't be faulted. It upheld the integrity of parliament, while mobilizing popular pressure. By accepting a back seat—after carrying the burden of anti-Franco resistance—it protected emergent democracy against right-wing retaliation. Berlinguer's fears for democracy were writ all the larger in Spain, and the abortive counterrevolution of February 1981 vindicated Carrillo's cautions against provoking a Francoist coup.[21]

But Carrillo's ultracaution compromised the radicalism that had sustained the party's militants in 38 years of opposition. To get the PCE legalized, he recognized the monarchy, shelved the constituent assembly, accepted the continuity of judiciary and civil service, and committed to a future social contract. This became the *Pacta de la Moncloa* in October 1977, an all-party austerity program, which balanced wage restraint against promises of welfare reform and a tax on wealth. While this consensus matched Carrillo's vision and compensated for the PCE's electoral defeat, it disoriented supporters. Carrillo's moderation jettisoned "the party's historic identity as the fulcrum of resistance to Franco's dictatorship," suspending militancy without the prize of government.[22] The PCE was losing members—from 201,757 to 171,132 a year later. A reinvented PSOE, irrelevant under the dictatorship but now massively funded by the Socialist International, supplanted the Communists. As the PSOE's star rose, so the PCE's fell; by December 1983, its membership was only 84,562. The PCE travails were also internal, for Carrillo kept the strictest centralism within, wielding the Stalinist axe repeatedly against critics. This left a salutary moral: under conditions of democracy, Eurocommunist strategy into a Stalinist party wouldn't go.[23]

This was confirmed in France. The French Left, headed by Francois Mitterrand for the new PS, Georges Marchais for the PCF, and Robert Fabre for the Left-Radicals, agreed to the Common Program in July 1972, where the Communists seemed ascendant. Their policies were mostly adopted, while the PS remained politically amorphous, a medium for Mitterrand's presidential future. When Michel Rocard's PSU merged with the PS, autogestion marked greater difference from the PCF but compounded the vagueness.[24] The 1973 elections also confirmed the old balance, with 21.4 percent of first ballots going to Communists and 17.7 to their Socialist rivals. Marchais moved the PCF behind the Union of the Left, deferring to Mitterrand as presidential candidate in May 1974 and bringing him within one percentage point of success. The PCF took its own Eurocommunist turn, abandoning dictatorship of the proletariat at its Twenty-Second Congress in February 1976, criticizing lack of Soviet freedoms, and affirming a French road to socialism. It abandoned opposition to French nuclear arms. Yet these changes came from above, with little debate. With the new pluralist rhetoric and growing membership, from 410,000 to 600,00 during 1974–77, the Stalinist style became dysfunctional. As the generations of 1968 entered the PCF—salaried and technical workers, women, and those aged 16–25—its political culture had to change.

Marchais withdrew from the Common Program in September 1977 as abruptly as he'd entered. Right-wing Socialists were certainly angling for a break, but Communists were scared of losing their primacy. Polls put them behind the PS, which merely bolstered the internal opponents of Eurocommunism. The pact collapsed: Left-Radicals launched an anti-Communist attack, happily endorsed by the PS right, and Marchais severed the alliance. For the 1978 elections, the PCF reverted to sectarianism, securing its traditional constituency, while vilifying the ex-allies. It took 20.6 percent on first ballot, but for the first time since 1945 Socialists won more, 22.6 percent. For second ballots, 96 percent of Communist voters obeyed discipline and voted for the PS; only 66 percent of Socialists switched to PCF. After the earlier certainties of Left success, the debacle was laid at the PCF's door. There was a major inner-party revolt, suppressed in time-honored Stalinist style. By the next elections in 1981, a quarter of PCF votes and a third of its members had gone. The Eurocommunist interlude was over, and French Communism never recovered.[25]

The West's strongest CPs reached the edge of power and failed.[26] Eurocommunism offered a vision of democratic normalization, through which Communists broke with the USSR, upheld national democratic traditions, and showed their fitness to govern. Officially revolutionary, these parties attempted to rethink their role under capitalism by imagining structural reforms leading to socialism, and their failures spelled not just immediate disappointments but long-term decline. As dictatorships collapsed and the PCI went from strength to strength, southern European Lefts seemed on the verge of a breakthrough and Eurocommunism emerged as a final effort at strategizing socialist transition in the capitalist West. However rhetorical or deferred the references to "revolution" might have become, as opposed to visions of "fundamental" or "structural" reform, Eurocommunism's failure finally marginalized the last organized advocacy of revolutionary socialism in Western Europe. Henceforth, there were no major parties where this language could any longer be realistically used, whether by activists or theoreticians.

On the other hand, Eurocommunism produced some lasting results. Without the PCI's stand on the Constitution or the PCE's loyalty to negotiated transition, right-wing dangers would have been far worse. In Spain, this stance bridged to the democratic Constitution, passed by referendum in December 1978, but also to a more general liberalization, including police reform and abolition of capital punishment, outlawing of sex discrimination, access to contraception, and decriminalizing of morality. These changes profoundly enhanced the quality of life, as did freeing the public sphere. In Italy, the PCI also secured reforms during 1977–78: strengthening the regions; urban planning; fair rents; public housing; mental health; community-based national health; legalized abortion; and expanded services, including sports facilities and kindergartens. Negation of these measures by the endemic graft of Italian public administration can neither entirely nullify their meaning nor be blamed on Communists. If not a "profound change in economic and social structures" (Berlinguer's test for the Historic Compromise), they at least mapped some desirable terrain.[27]

Eurocommunism brought southern Europe into the fold of social democracy. While Scandinavia, the Low Countries, and German-speaking Europe comprised a north-central European "social democratic core" from 1900 to the 1960s, Mediterranean Europe had a different labor movement, one shaped by anarcho-syndicalism and then in the Cold War by strong CPs marginalized by regimes of the Right. Only after 1960 did southern European Lefts win leverage on government via organized labor followed by electoral growth. Socialist parties challenged Communist primacy, in France through the dialectic of the Common Program, in Italy in Eurocommunism's aftermath, and in Iberia via massive financing from northern European socialism, which manufactured the Portuguese Socialist Party (SP) of Mário Soares and the Spanish PSOE afresh. But Communists themselves adopted perspectives indistinguishable from the more ambitious forms of social democracy associated with the Swedish SAP, Austro-Marxism, and left-socialists between the wars. In Berlinguer's statements, still more in Carrillo's, the specifically Communist faded away.

The Italian reforms of 1968–72 owed as much to unions as to the Left in parliament.[28] The Workers' Charter of May 1970 secured workplace protections familiar from northern Europe, like rights of assembly, trade union access, safety regulations, and rights of appeal against dismissal. But the unions also campaigned over health, housing, transport, town planning, redistributive taxation, and a progressive investment strategy. A corporatist triangulation on northern European lines materialized willy-nilly, but initially only giants like Fiat and Pirelli saw unions as a counterweight to militancy on the shopfloor. *Confindustria*, the national industrial federation, remained hostile till the presidency of Giovanni Agnelli in 1974. The PCI also overcame its misgivings, and the Historic Compromise allowed a full-fledged Italian corporatism to emerge, steered by Luciano Lama through the CGIL Congress in 1978. If this Italian social contract collapsed with the PCI's break from government in 1979, the new cooperation of unions, government, and employers remained paradigmatic.

Eurocommunism rejected the Leninist model of the cadre party. If stringent discipline had been indispensible for the PCE in the Franco years, with legalization and elections this abruptly changed. Moreover, a massive shift to commerce and services forced the PCE to rethink its primary focus on workers in industry.[29] These changes challenged its old *modus operandi*. Eurocommunism also broke the French Communists from their self-consciously proletarian ghetto, boosting membership from 250,000 to 650,000. But then sectarian enmity against the Socialists returned the party to its core after 1978, which meant a precipitously declining electorate and the much lower membership levels of the 1960s. The PCF lost 3 million voters between 1978 and 1988, sinking to only 9 percent of the electorate in the 18–25 age group. Even the lastingly Eurocommunist PCI found its support contracting around a reliable core: by 1985, less than 10 percent of its members were under 30, while over 30 percent were older than 60.[30]

Under Eurocommunism broader appeals were made to socially diverse support, from new professionals and white-collar strata to the university-educated and women, particularly on the generational axis of 1968. This implied a different kind of party from before—*away* from the Leninist party of militants, with its demands of time and energy, and exclusive Communist loyalties; and *toward* the broadly campaigning electoral party, with its looser structure of alliances and less exacting identification, based in varied social constituencies. Eurocommunist calls to democratize the party meant not only dismantling centralism but also opening the party to diverse currents and issues. Such calls posed a distinct challenge for parties of the Left, given their powerful class-political reflexes. *This* agenda remained on the table.

Finally, Eurocommunism opened greater space on the Left for radical democracy, suggesting a "third way" between Western European social democracy and the official Communisms of the East.[31] This had happened before—in the New Lefts of 1956–68. But now some established parties moved in this direction. After breaking with the USSR, they embraced pluralism, multiparty competition, free elections, and parliamentary government, with associated democratic rights. Eurocommunists prioritized issues that couldn't be subsumed within class-struggle perspectives based on the industrial working class. Such issues included everything from the big identity axes of gender, ethnicity, religion, and race to problems of youth, sexuality, ecology, international relations, and a cultural politics embracing both uplift and entertainment.

These departures converged with the legacies of 1968, for which Eurocommunism became a main conduit to the party system. Eurocommunism in narrower terms failed—as a project of the Italian and Spanish CPs in the later 1970s, which briefly captured the French. But it permanently shaped the PCI. It inspired smaller CPs in the Low Countries and Scandinavia. When the European Left began rebuilding itself in 1985–95, faced with profound deradicalization of the social democratic parties and the bankruptcy of Soviet-style Communism, those CPs with a lasting Eurocommunist presence were able to become vitally involved.

WEST GERMANY: FROM APO TO THE GREENS

West Germany, in contrast to Italy, France, and Spain, lacked a strong CP. The KPD had shriveled into an imprint of East German Stalinism. West German Communists, banned in 1956, neither were rivals for the SPD nor offered ideas from the margins as did some other small CPs like the British and Scandinavian. The SPD had the field to itself. Permanently stuck in opposition until 1966, facing the recharged authoritarianism of Konrad Adenauer's "CDU state" and its "economic miracle," the SPD formed the vanguard of Western European revisionism. The Godesberg Program of 1959 shed the Marxist heritage, declaring its loyalty to Western consensus and the politics of growth. The SPD staked its claims to govern by rejecting radicalisms further to the Left.[32]

In West Germany, 1968 saw exceptionally bitter polarization between the student movement and the mainstream Left. The SPD had systematically marginalized earlier dissent, opposing the campaigns against rearmament, nuclear arms, and the new Emergency Laws. It treated its own student affiliates with crass shortsightedness, expelling first SDS in 1960 and then its successor, the Social Democratic Higher Education League, once it turned left in 1969–72. The violence of student activism in 1967–68 was fueled by this highhandedness, and successive SPD mayors stoked the anti-SDS hysteria in West Berlin, endorsing police illegalities and denouncing students with contempt. Both the streetfighting militancy of the demonstrations and the wantonly provocative sex radicalism of Dieter Kunzelmann's Kommune I (formed January 1967) fed the backlash in return. The very form of the student movement's direct action politics, the Extra-Parliamentary Opposition (APO) formalized in December 1966, violated the SPD's parliamentarist identification with the "Free Democratic Basic Order" of the 1949 Constitution.[33]

Conflict was fired by emotionally charged languages of antifascism, as students accused older generations, SPD and CDU alike, of evading Nazism's continuing legacies. West German antiauthoritarianism subsisted on this historical critique. The Adenauer government's attacks on civil liberties, the rise of the neo-Nazi New Democratic Party, and students' physical encounters with state power, dramatized in the police murder of Benno Ohnesorg during protests against the Shah of Iran in June 1967, were all grist for the mill. The SPD's entry to a Grand Coalition with the CDU under the ex-Nazi Kurt Georg Kiesinger in December 1966 seemed to confirm attacks on the its compromised character. Antifascism became the APO's default demeanor, the accusing anger of children against the guilty silence of parents. After hearing about concentration camps at school when he was 15 in 1963, Detlev Claussen

> came home very upset and talked about it. Without explanation, my father responded by talking about the Communists after 1945. He simply refused to deal with the Nazi past. The East is now, the past is past, he was saying in effect. I never heard him voice any concern about the past. I took that very badly, something broke between us, and later it led to a split between the rest of the family and my brother and me.[34]

The student movement's "culture of insubordination," which "challenged almost every shibboleth of Western society," certainly pushed West Germans into facing their authoritarian habits, opening the boundaries of what could be thought and said.[35] But the high point of direct actions themselves, in May 1968, ended in collapse. The assassination attempt on Rudi Dutschke in April provoked an explosion of violence nationwide, and then in May the failure of a national rally against the Emergency Laws to spark a general strike dashed hopes of worker-student alliance. The SDS intensified actions on campuses, in extremes of physical militancy. Discipline and "party building" became the watchwords. A profusion of Maoist groups joined Trotskyists and Spartacus, the student affiliate of the re-legalized Communists, beside localized and eclectically Marxist radicalisms, feminisms, and the partially anarchist counterculture and "alternative scene." The fragmentation was disastrous, severing radicals from the broader mass of sympathetic but semipolitical students and other young people.

This coincided with the SPD's breakthrough to government under Willy Brandt in 1969, in a "social-liberal" coalition with the small Free Democratic Party (FDP).[36] The SPD returned to office as the main governing party for the first time since 1930, followed by its highest-ever support in 1972, finally surpassing the CDU. Resulting reforms, especially the normalized relations with the USSR, Eastern Europe, and the GDR, boosted its membership from 732,000 to 991,000, and that of the Young Socialists from 150,000 to 350,000 during 1968–74.[37] *Bürgerinitiativen,* or Citizens' Initiatives, also flourished. But the oil crisis and Brandt's succession by a dourly conservative Helmut Schmidt supervened. The government's imagination narrowed. From 1972–74, antiterrorist measures and loyalty tests for civil servants, including teachers and academics, tightened the public sphere against emergent cultures of participation. The SPD squandered its chance to harness 1968's energies. Rather than "daring more democracy," in Brandt's evocative phrase, it battened down the hatches, reopening the cleavage to the left.

Here West Germany diverged from Britain, Italy, and France, where generational radicalism flowed back through existing Left parties. In West Germany, two factors stopped this from happening and renewed the antagonism between extraparliamentary Left and the SPD, which was now compromised rather than boosted by its governing status.[38] One was the campaign against terrorism, whose damage to civil liberties recharged the antiauthoritarian movement. The other was antinuclear campaigning.

Massive environmental protests based around resistance to large-scale nuclear energy projects combined with the danger to civil liberties in reviving extraparliamentary actions.[39] The SPD lost democratic credibility. Citizens' Initiatives originated in the SPD's own voter drives but were now demonized as extremist. While protests celebrated grassroots democracy via unparalleled civic activism, government replied with authoritarianism, a chasm vividly recalling the battles of 1968. Yet the rhythm was quite different now. Earlier confrontations isolated SDS, drawing the broader progressive electorate to the SPD and driving the APO into violence and fragmentation, including the militarist Red Army Fraction (RAF). Now the state's criminalizing of extraparliamentary action as "anticonstitutional" in the name of antiterrorism had the opposite effect, as protesters coalesced nationally in the name of participatory democracy. Antinuclear protests became generalized into an ecological program. And from 1979, the peace issue further strengthened this process.

"The peace movement of the 1980s was by far the largest social movement West Germany had ever seen, [reaching] into an incredibly wide array of social groups."[40] Resisting NATO's "dual-track" decision to deploy Cruise and Pershing II missiles in Western Europe, it sustained remarkable breadth, from dissident Social and Free Democrats, left-wing Christians, and Communist-influenced campaigning groups to the burgeoning post-1968 social movements.[41] In opinion polls, sympathizers increased from 46 to 61 percent during 1981–83, including not just the young and better-educated but also 65 percent of workers, and 59 percent of the over-60s. Its Coordinating Committee grew to include SPD and FDP dissenters; the CP and pro-Soviet groups; pacifists; the National Association of High School Students; some Christian groups; the Union of Environmentalist Citizens' Initiatives; radical feminists of the Association of Women for Peace; independent socialists from *Sozialistisches Büro;* grassroots groups like the libertarian-socialist Federation of Non-Violent Action Groups, the Conference of Independent Peace Groups, and the Coordinating Office of Civil Disobedience; and Third World solidarity groups linked through the National Congress of Development Aid Groups with its 1,100 affiliates.[42]

The Peace Movement mirrored the practices of feminism and the student radicals' participatory ideals of 10 years before. Some six thousand local initiatives drew 20–50 members for weekly or fortnightly meetings in an avowedly antihierarchical form. With ecology and the women's movement, this reflected remarkable density of crosscutting grassroots activity. It shaded into the "alternative movement," which lived 1968's countercultural values in a politicizing of everyday life. Rejecting norms of discipline, productivity, competition, and commercialized social relations in favor of experiment and spontaneity, the alternative scenes of big cities like West Berlin, Frankfurt, Hamburg, Munich, and Cologne sustained squats and communes, self-help and advice agencies, clinics and education centers, design and arts studios, galleries and cinemas, bookshops and printers, restaurants and cafés, an array of alternative businesses, and an alternative press, crowned by West Berlin's daily *Tageszeitung* (*TAZ*). West Germany had an estimated 11,500 alternative projects, with 80,000 active members and 350,000 sympathizers, ranging from West Berlin's "Factory for Culture, Sport and Handicrafts" to food co-ops in small towns. By February 1982, 15,000 volunteers ran 1,500 self-help groups in West Berlin alone, affecting 100,000 people.[43]

This public defined itself against parties per se. The trajectory from APO to antinuclear protests shaped by government's antiterrorist turn involved profound alienation from normal politics. In a 1978 survey, half of the the 5.4 million West Germans aged 17–23 were dissatisfied with state and society. [44] In January 1978, West Berlin's *Tunix* festival (a corruption of the German for "do nothing") drew 20,000 revellers, enjoined by its slogan "Departure from Model Germany" to "sail away to Tunix Beach," an alternative utopia "beneath the cobblestones of this country."[45] Government and Spontis faced each other in mutual incomprehension. One minister told an audience of incredulous students: "We all are the state." One replied: "We are excluded from all real participation. Our alternative ways of living only receive two responses: discrimination and police."[46]

In the "German Autumn" of 1977, tensions climaxed. In the wake of two dramatic assassinations, the RAF kidnapped the Daimler-Benz chairman and employers' federation chief the ex-SS officer Hanns Martin Schleyer. Ultraleft terrorism and neo-McCarthyite attacks on the Left were locked by now in a spiral of anger and fear, further stoking the direct action militancy of environmental protests. Activists were criminalized; government was assailed as fascist in response. In October, a Lufthansa jet was hijacked to Mogadishu in Somalia to demand the freeing of RAF leaders imprisoned since 1972. A West German commando freed the hostages, as the RAF leaders Andreas Baader, Gudrun Ensslin, and Jan-Carl Raspe were found dead in Stammheim maximum security prison in Stuttgart. Schleyer's corpse appeared in Alsace the next day. This brutal tit-for-tat laid a climate of menace onto West German public life. The "Free Democratic Basic Order" became invoked relentlessly against any and all left-wing dissent. Democracy's health was tied rhetorically to stronger police powers.[47]

The RAF managed further spates of violence, disbanding only in 1998. But the physical confrontations practised by militants now became better contained in their effects and instead national political coalescence occupied the agenda, as ecological activists moved toward fighting elections. Here the SPD's obduracy—its adherence under Schmidt to the politics of growth, its rigidities over nuclear energy, its support for law and order, and its uncritical NATO loyalism—opened the space for new initiatives.

In 1978–79, ecology slates contested regional elections in Hamburg, Lower Saxony, Hesse, Bavaria, Rhineland-Palatinate, West Berlin, and Schleswig-Holstein. A list ran for European Elections in June 1979 as "Miscellaneous Political Union—The Greens." Delegates met in Offenbach in October to discuss Federal Elections, uniting around an ecological and social program of grassroots democracy and nonviolence. In the Bremen and Baden-Württemberg regional elections, ecology lists scraped past the 5 percent barrier regulating parliamentary representation. During 1980, a Karlsruhe Congress launched "The Greens" (avowedly not a "party"), leaving questions of program and structure for later congresses in Saarbrücken and Dortmund to decide. By then, right-wing ecologists had seceded, and Left activists from West Berlin, Hamburg, Frankfurt, Bremen, and western Germany set the tone. The consensus on ecology and peace was expanded toward gay rights, the 35-hour working week, immigration, and abortion.[48]

The Greens were a remarkable departure. West Germany's party system had been exceptionally stable, dominated by three parties since 1953. A new party with parliamentary staying power implied a major realignment, however small its support. Despite setbacks in the 1980 Federal Elections, when they won only 1.5 percent, in the next three years Greens took off. They entered legislatures with 7.9 percent in West Berlin and 7.7 percent in Hamburg, followed by Lower Saxony and Hesse. By the next Federal Elections in 1983, they had joined the Bundestag, also passing the 5 percent barrier in 6 of 11 state parliaments, in many localities with a 10–15 percent vote. Red-Green coalitions became imaginable in Hamburg and Hesse. "In less than two years, this motley crew of environmentalists, sixty-eighters, radical leftists, and disillusioned social democrats forged a political coalition which was poised to change the landscape of German politics and the Left."[49]

In the professional, educational, and generational backgrounds of Green supporters, 1968 was a clear presence. Feminism was a vital bridge: women became a majority of the Green parliamentary delegation in 1987 and in one year provided an all-women leadership. Green politics resumed the APO ideals, with their antiauthoritarianism, critiques of domination and alienation, and participatory forms, as well as direct action and subversive political style. Countercultural beliefs in alternative ways of living bore this continuity, as did feminist consciousness raising. The Greens were not a party of the centralized sort but a movement. The APO had been the first of the "new social movements" in that sense.

The Greens formed in the new spaces between old and new Lefts. The takeoff coincided with the peace movement's height. The "Eco-Pax" alliance of ecologists and peace activists was a natural conjunction. A 1980 forum in Krefeld declared nonnegotiable opposition to the missiles, drawing eight hundred thousand signatures within six months and 2 million after another year. The first national demonstration against the missiles in Bonn drew three hundred thousand people in October 1981, surpassed by the half-million protesting President Reagan's state visit a year later. At the climax in October 1983, a million joined the "people's rallies" in four separate cities, with 2–4 million attending weeklong events. After the Bundestag approved deployment, the movement fell away, although 400,000 still formed human chains around military bases in the fall of 1984 and the Easter Marches drew 450,000 earlier that year. This extraordinary mobilization fueled Green election success, hoisting them into the Bundestag.[50]

The Old Left viewed Green politics askance; SPD voices were arrogantly disparaging. When the FDP bolted and brought the SPD government down in 1982, Schmidt flatly vetoed dialogue with the Greens. In Hamburg and Hesse, the SPD premiers Klaus von Dohnanyi and Holger Börner had to talk, but after earlier denunciations this smacked of opportunism. In Hesse a Red-Green coalition actually governed in 1985–87. But Börner acted purely from parliamentary weakness, briefly beholden to his own left wing, while SPD machine bosses were temporarily silenced. Richard Löwenthal, the veteran cochair of the SPD's Commission on Basic Values, named the party's choice—either affirming class-political identification with industrial workers or choosing the new social movements. It couldn't do both. Reactions to Green politics were usually more base. On the SPD's right, Börner had contempt for protesters against the Frankfurt airport expansion, denouncing them as "chaotics," "vandals," and "alternatives." As he sneered: "I regret that my high government office forbids me to pop these [demonstrators] one in the face myself. It used to be that you took care of things like this on the construction site with a two-by-four."[51]

SPAIN: SOCIALISM WITHOUT WORKERS

"Spain" had special meaning for the European Left, symbolizing the fight against fascism and the tragedy of revolutionary hopes lost. Throughout Francisco Franco's long reign, 1939–75, democracy was imagined heroically, as resistance exploding after the dictator's death. The Workers' Commissions gave this credence after 1964 via recurring mass protests and the crescendo of militancy in 1974–76. Yet democratic transition proved prosaic. It was handled remarkably smoothly, controlled by Franco's named successors, King Juan Carlos and the technocratic minister Adolfo Suarez, behind closed doors. The old order was dismantled from within, not by a revolutionary confrontation. Democracy took a parliamentary form via carefully managed consensus. Voting, negotiated compromise, and legal ratification—elections, the Pact of Monocloa, and the new Constitution—marked the normalizing of a new system. This contradiction, between heroic image and prosaic reality, popular mobilization and negotiated deals, went to the heart of the new Spanish Socialist Party (PSOE) emerging from the process.[52]

For the Left, democracy's return was a double disappointment. First, the Spanish Communists (PCE) failed. The core of the Workers' Commissions, the mainstay of illegal opposition, and pioneers of Eurocommunism, the PCE and its leader Santiago Carrillo expected to become victors of transition. But by backing Suarez and Juan Carlos in a "strategy of responsibility" rather than building from the grassroots, the Communists squandered their political capital. In refusing to endanger transition by unpredictable popular actions and avoiding at all costs polarizations favoring the Right, the PCE aided the conditions of its own defeat. Meanwhile, Carrillo belied Eurocommunist principles with a Stalinist innerparty regime. The PCE's electoral support crashed from already modest levels in 1977 and 1979, while Carrillo's dysfunctional highhandedness left the party's organization in shreds.[53]

Second, disappointment was replicated in the trajectory of the PSOE, the transition's real beneficiary. From sectarian irrelevance during illegality, the Socialists emerged from their 1976 Congress and relegalization as the Left's main electoral force, with a landslide of 48.4 percent in 1982. The 1976 program promised socialist transformation beyond "simple reform of the system." Yet by 1980, this was gone. The party became ruthlessly centralized around Felipe Gonzalez. On taking office in 1982, the Socialist government dumped its remaining radicalism, including commitments to halve unemployment and leave NATO. From posing as Europe's most radical socialist party, the PSOE behaved as its most technocratic, in a spectacular version of socialist betrayal.[54]

The PSOE's metamorphosis occurred against the background of Spanish modernization. In Franco's later years, Spain underwent extraordinary transformation. Agricultural employment fell from 50 to only 14 percent during 1950–80, most dramatically after 1960. Masses were on the move. Two million workers left for elsewhere in Europe. Three million migrated from agricultural south to industrial north. In 1960, 19.1 percent of population lived in cities of over one hundred thousand while only five years later the figure was 32.7. Between 1960 and 1965, the GNP grew annually by 9.2 percent. In an amazingly short time, Spain acquired a social structure comparable to those of Italy and France. The Spain of the Spanish Civil War was gone.

Greater Barcelona, the engine of Spanish industrialization since 1900, saw a huge concentration of change. In two decades the city grew from 1.0 to 1.75 million, while the metropolis saw growth "equivalent to the creation each year of a city of 100,000 inhabitants."[55] Older industries like textiles and engineering expanded, while new ones like chemicals and food processing arrived. The old textile town of Sabadell grew from 60,000 to 160,000. The new industrial settlement of Cornella, an indistinct blotch southwest of the city, grew from 11,000 in 1950 to an agglomeration of 76,000 two decades later. Aside from its generic forms—massive reorganizing of labor markets, restructuring of class relations, and transformation of the lived environment—industrialization had two key effects. It disorganized a "traditional" working-class culture of residential and occupational communities into a featureless urban sprawl. It flooded Catalan society with rural nonnative immigrants, mainly from the Andalusian south. By 1970, 40 percent of Catalan population came from outside.

By the 1970s, the working class was entirely recomposed. In size, concentration, employment, ethnicity, residence, organization, and collective identity, this was not the same class that had fought the Civil War. Repression also extirpated union and political traditions. In all Spain, 22,000 were executed during 1939–50, with 3,385 in Catalonia and masses of unrecorded killings. In Sabadell (population 74,000), 59,000 files were opened on enemies of the regime. Trade unionism became impossible: 17 successive national executive committees of the Anarchist CNT were arrested, as were 7 of the Socialist UGT. This decimating of pre-1939 militants severed workers from their own traditions. The Labor Ministry legally controlled industrial relations, banning strikes and requiring workers' compulsory registration in 28 "vertical" branches of the State Union (OSE). Continuity in working-class culture, so necessary for collective political agency, was decisively broken. Strikes still occurred. But the Barcelona tram boycott and general strike of March 1951 was the last display of the old culture of militancy. Anarchist and Socialist trade unionism and associated political cultures were wiped out by savage repression, criminalizing of organizations, and Francoist regulation.[56]

Thus when a labor movement reemerged, it took a different form. In 1958, the Ministry of Labor ceded responsibility to employers via industry or plant-level collective bargaining, linked to shop steward–like representation under the aegis of the OSE. When the wage freeze was lifted, this system moved into place but led immediately to strikes. A key initiative followed in September 1964: a citywide committee of engineering shop stewards in Madrid, keyed to the metal industry's new bargaining structure, and organized within OSE's legal framework.[57]

These Workers' Commissions were specifically allowed by the new laws. They officially used the OSE's resources and legitimacy, arising "organically out of the bargaining process."[58] The Commissions recalled European industry's shopfloor representation in 1914–18 and British shop stewards in the 1960s. They were sustained by new activists, transgressing the old Civil War alignments. They were sometimes industry based, as in Madrid metals, sometimes city- or districtwide, as in Barcelona, and sometimes company or plant specific. They were "in practice the first democratic broadly based union organization to be set up in Spain since the Civil War."[59] Anarcho-syndicalism had no presence. Nor were these Commissions embraced by Socialists or the UGT. Instead, they provided openings for the PCE's strategy of infiltration—of working in the space Franco's system allowed—and attracted new Catholic activists. When this new labor movement materialized in official union elections, it immediately provoked the Commissions' suppression as subversive organizations. But militancy was released. Protest continuously rose, from 8.7 million strike-hours in 1970 to 28.4 million in 1974–75 and a final climax of 106.5 million working hours lost in 1976.

With this revolt, the earlier smashing of the Spanish Left's organized capacities acquired all the more importance. After brutally liquidating earlier leaderships, the dictatorship deprived new ones of the chance to cohere. Repression stunted the new labor movement's growth into a national force. The prosperity of the 1960s and its new consumer cultures also played their part. A passive consensus, based around individualized consumption, was actively contrived by the regime's liberalizers. Industrial militancy was compatible with a hardnosed and self-interested outlook, with no necessary oppositional logic. The head of the Catalan OSE greeted the new prosperity accordingly. He wanted "a new type of worker who knows which side his bread is buttered on, who can tell what's fair and what isn't. The greatest achievement of our organization is in having produced a change of mentality, a new syndical culture, an ability to negotiate."[60]

Yet at the end, workers in Catalonia, Madrid, and other industrial centers were clearly militant and angry. Collective action, responding to brutality or coercion, burgeoned when the dictatorship's wraps were off. As in Germany and Italy, fascism had disorganized a highly sophisticated working-class movement, first by viciously smashing its organizations, killing and driving out its leaderships, and breaking its capacity for resistance and then by regulating the public sphere that was always essential for the Left's popular strength. But given the Workers' Commisions' new potential and the militancy's impressive scale, why did the new working-class radicalism fail to graduate into greater national effectiveness when the dictatorship died?

The Spanish Socialists were negligible under the dictatorship, except for Asturias and parts of the north. The PSOE and the UGT were especially weak in areas of Francoist industrialization, Catalonia, and greater Madrid. Exiled leaderships in North Africa, Mexico, and France were chronically divided. Factionalism paralyzed the party inside Spain. Yet this mutual isolation of factions also allowed a revisionist tendency to emerge without interference. Renovation occurred most of all around Gonzalez in Seville, who captured control after 1972, culminating in his 1974 election as party secretary.[61]

Under Gonzalez, the PSOE internalized its factionalist heritage. It lacked any culture of internal democracy. Gonzalez consistently overrode accountability, silencing internal critics and immunizing the party against pressure from below. For a party riding such an unprecedented electoral wave, the PSOE had remarkably thin membership: only 1.5 percent of its voters joined the party, as against 49 percent in Sweden or 30 percent in Austria. While membership then doubled from 107,000 to 210,000 during 1981–88, reaching 309,000 in 1991, the gap between leaders and base perdured. The Gonzalez government was uniformly technocratic. It contained no women, no workers, none of the beleaguered party left. Manual workers were the largest category of members but the most underrepresented relative to population. The party ceased recruiting youth. It was top-heavy: half the membership held public office owed to the party, including 70 percent of Congress delegates by 1988; office-holding became its own justification, with rampant corruption.[62] Policies were militantly technocratic: neocapitalist modernization and industrial restructuring in the interests of European integration; dismantling the public sector; massive unemployment. It was unclear what remained "socialist" at all.

Although corruptibility was in depressingly big supply, this "betrayal"—of the PSOE's traditions, of working-class militancy, and of the 1976 program—needs explanation beyond the moral failings of leaders. The specific dynamics of transition supplied one answer: the PSOE's meteoric rise followed the unexpected collapse of Communists and the conservative Democratic Center, and these events allowed the Gonzalez faction's managerial ruthlessness free rein. Lacking any popular challenge from countervailing political forces, Gonzalez loosened his party's working-class moorings. But the background of postwar industrialization under Francoism's repressive frame was also key. The disabling effects of long dictatorship—the disorganizing and corporatizing of working-class culture and the segmented and localized bases of the new labor movement, plus the absence of civil freedoms and a public sphere—left a vacant field of national representation, which the PSOE under Gonzalez astutely filled.

The PSOE reappeared inside Spain amid extraordinary democratic upheaval. But it entered the political process via backroom negotiations, not by integrating with popular protests. It tried neither to ground itself in rank-and-file militancy and the Workers' Commissions, where Communists already held sway, nor to build links to broader agitations around "social" concerns like housing, prices, transportation, and schooling, which especially mobilized women. Instead, once in government the PSOE demobilized the working class, severing the party's thin symbolic and emotional links to the labor movement's traditions per se. It deployed neoliberal economics comparable to those of the right-wing Thatcher government in Britain, implemented under the economics minister Miguel Boyer, in a shameless dumping of the 1982 program's Keynesianism, replicating the French Socialist government's volte-face of the time.

Privatization, support for multinational capital, closing down industries, and tight money and wage restraint, plus Spanish entry to the EC, delivered a catastrophe of deindustrialization for the working class.[63] Spain's historic industries—steel, shipbuilding, electrical engineering, textiles—were massively gutted. Unemployment, already 17 percent in 1982, hit 22 percent in 1986 and was 50 percent for those aged 16–19 and 40 percent for those aged 20–24. Unions' patience expired. After rising labor protests and a one-day general strike in December 1988, Gonzales conceded a social program, with long-demanded pension reform, expanded healthcare, and educational opportunity. This gesturing to earlier social democratic commitments of 1976–82 gained him reelection in 1989 and 1993. But the neoliberalism remained confirmed. In the reign of Gonzalez, the politics of socialism was disengaged from trade unionism. UGT lost half its members in four years. Spanish union density became the lowest in Europe outside France.[64]

This was the Spanish lesson in European terms. Under recession, a post-Fordist transition brought long-term convergence of public policy in Europe overall. Sharply differing politics centered around a common story of severe welfare cuts, privatization, market hegemony, and declining organized labor, to the point of unions' marginalization from national political process. These new policy-making logics trumped political differences of socialists and conservatives in government. Sometimes, the Left rather than the Right set the pace. After 1982, Mitterrand's France and Gonzalez' Spain rivaled Thatcher's Britain in neoliberal economics. Where social democratic corporatism was strongest—Scandinavia, Austria, West Germany—damage to the working class could be contained, whether in jobs, incomes, benefits, political representation, union organization, the socially organized capacities of working-class communities, or the social value accorded to labor and its culture and traditions. There, even under retreat, organized labor kept better resources and self-confidence in the political arena. But where this labor-corporatist hardwiring was missing, as a matrix of interrelations among unions, socialist party, and state, labor's political fortunes experienced terrible loss.

Spain was the most extreme case. The PSOE had one of the European Left's biggest electoral landslides since 1945 (48.4 percent in 1982), won three later elections, and governed for 14 years. Yet its behavior bore scant resemblance to socialism's theory and practice, even in the sadly reduced forms established in social democratic parties by the 1970s and certainly by the standard of the PSOE's own 1976–82 program. The pressures acting on Left governments now were huge. The Gonzalez regime was not the only socialist party failing to deliver the goods, calling on the labor movement for sacrifices and upholding instead the superior priorities of "the economy," "modernization," or "the national interest." But in Spain, 36 years of dictatorship deprived the PSOE of the rootedness in working-class communities and organization that otherwise afforded some bearings.

The PSOE under Gonzalez pioneered an extreme version of socialism's severence from its working-class roots. There was a massive gap between the towering popular mobilization of the democratic transition in 1975–76 and the gutting of popular democracy that actually established the

PSOE's ascendancy. This left the paradox of a phenomenally successful electoral socialism with no living relations to organized popular support. The PSOE's brilliantly successful maneuvering for high political advantage in 1976–79 fashioned a narrow conception of "the political" from the hard-won democracy of the anti-Franco struggle, which it then confined in a technocratically circumscribed parliamentary arena. There it stayed, removed from the everyday interests of Spanish working people.

As such, the PSOE repeated a familiar history. But in Spain, liberal democracy was tragically disjoined from the radical possibilities preceding it. Likewise, the destruction of Spain's recently assembled manufacturing base concentrated century-long development into just several decades, and here the PSOE discharged with alacrity Spanish capitalism's modernizing agenda. But its management of this conjuncture—between the democratic transition's popular dynamic and the technocratic dictates of capitalist restructuring—demoralized the working-class movement. Spanish socialism enacted a familiar scenario of the passage from authoritarian to democratic political systems, contrasting the euphoria of massive popular democratic mobilization with the hard-nosed pragmatism of negotiated transition, disciplining emancipatory hopes with exigencies of economic change. Spain confirmed the difficulty of institutionalizing a diverse and richly localized popular mobilization in nationally effective forms, when dictatorship had disorganized the available democratic traditions.

Chapter 25

Gorbachev, the End of Communism, and the 1989 Revolutions

STALINISM WAS AN utter disaster for the Left. As a general name for the rigidities of Communist parties after the late 1920s, it massively handicapped their credibility. Secrecy, manipulation, ruthlessness, taking orders from elsewhere—these charges against Communists became generalized to Leftists of every stripe. All were lumped together, tainted as forever suspect, as "enemies within," Moscow stooges, or "reds under the bed." Such anti-Communist scare-mongering drew credence from Stalinist political culture, which celebrated "steel-hardened" discipline behind the "party line." At the height of Stalinism, 1948–53, Communists unleashed horrendous polemics against opponents, while sheltering their own inner-party practices, which were the opposite of democratic. Western Communists' ability to emerge from this dark night of the Cold War, reclaiming democratic legacies from the mid-1940s and beyond, required a long and difficult struggle, for which Eurocommunism proved the decisive push.

In Eastern Europe, Soviet-style centralism had deadly force. In 1943–47, the region's CPs had much independence, emerging renewed from the rubble of Liberation and unencumbered by the legacies of Bolshevization. But with the Cold War, Moscow asserted control, terminating the national roads to socialism and imposing repression brutally across the region. The purges destroyed the CPs' potential creativity by a machinery of arrests, interrogations, surveillance, trials, imprisonment, and judicial killing, hanging a pall of conformity across the political horizon. As the crises of 1956 and 1968 confirmed, Soviet security interests had hardened into an imperium. Within the system's rigid limits—command economy and one-party rule—Soviet leaders refused to budge.

The Soviet system was more than Stalin's personal rule. Soviet Communism was a program of forced industrialization, based on state ownership and the centrally administered plan. It required centralized control of investment, materials, production targets, and the distribution of goods, prioritizing heavy industries, capital goods, transportation, and energy. It was an accelerated drive from above, unleashed on a society locked in backwardness. It entailed huge inefficiencies, worsening the human hardships of such vast social transformations. But as a crude developmental drive, it was astonishingly successful, attracting widespread admiration between the 1930s and 1950s. It allowed the USSR not only to survive the Nazi onslaught but to win the war. It became a prestigious precedent for Eastern Europe's impoverished and devastated societies after 1945. Soviet industrialization became a natural model for the East, where only the GDR, the Czech lands, greater Budapest, and parts of Poland had any appreciable industry. It also inspired anticolonial movements as they confronted their own societies' economic underdevelopment.

But the Soviet system had glaring structural flaws as it entered the postwar era, which deteriorated over the years. Soviet agriculture was a failure. Soviet economic bureaucracy was an unfailing source of inefficiencies. The bias toward capital goods continuously militated against satisfying consumers, who in any case had no market to register their demand. In basic necessities, the system did reasonably well, certainly as it emerged from war and reconstruction. It delivered jobs, heavily subsidized food, clothing, housing, and transportation and created access to healthcare and schools. But it failed desperately to organize services, so that even relative successes—the social minimum and the welfare state—became undermined. People became ingenious in circumventing shortages via the indispensable black economy.[1] With the growth of trade, the loosening of travel, advanced telecommunications, and the internationalizing of taste and style, the Iron Curtain became ever more permeable. By the 1980s, socialist citizens painfully compared the drabness of their personal lives with their counterparts in the West.

But Stalinism was not only a "program for transforming backward economies into advanced ones."[2] It was also a polity. It was not only the development strategy of "socialism in one country" announced in 1926 but also the Bolshevik factional struggle after Lenin that concentrated power around Stalin, silenced his opponents, and ended democracy. The Civil War had squeezed the life from Soviet democracy, and Lenin sanctioned much that eased Stalinism's arrival. But it was Stalin who in his unobtrusively power-engrossing way relentlessly squelched democracy's latent promise. War Communism, the regime's isolation, and the social dynamics of NEP all pushed in that direction. The ban on factions, restricting inner-party debate, already dated from the 1921 Kronstadt Uprising. But Stalin created the personal dictatorship, endowed it with the cult of personality, and instituted political terror. This broke profoundly with pre-1914 socialisms, which were democratic if nothing else. Stalin's ambition to regulate the entirety of the Soviet citizenry's thoughts and lives was wholly foreign to the Second International.

Stalinism's political system presumed the sole power of the Communist Party, encompassing a command economy, monopoly of public life, and control of culture. Party and state were completely integrated. The party controlled appointments to the state and economy. It regulated access to higher education, cultural life, the arts, and the public sphere. It secured popular conformity by elaborate systems of censorship, surveillance, policing, official ideology, and at times physical coercion and terror. Under Stalin, the system became a personal autocracy. This was the system that became generalized to the People's Democracies in the late 1940s. Through it, socialism's actuality became not only an oppression for the immediate region but also an enormous albatross for socialists in the West.[3]

SOLIDARNOSC: DEMOCRACY AND WORKING-CLASS INSURGENCY IN POLAND

Despite the huge crisis of 1968, Eastern Europe's neo-Stalinist regimes seemed secure. Czechoslovak normalization followed the Hungarian pattern, with resistance giving way to weary resignation. Economic indicators seemed good. The region's growth rates for 1966–70 were positive and improved in 1971–75. International legitimacy was assured. The West German government's "Eastern Policy" was unaffected by the Soviet invasion of Czechoslovakia, and the 1972 Treaties normalized relations between East and West, licensing Soviet action in its own sphere. The Helsinki Accords of the Conference on Security and Cooperation in Europe, signed by the United States, the USSR, 30 European countries, and Canada in 1975, recognized sovereignty, noninterference, and the inviolability of borders, while promising East-West cooperation. Detente eased the Cold War but institutionalized its geopolitical effects, in a " 'long decade of the Brezhnev doctrine," from 1968 to the opening of the Soviet crisis in 1986.[4]

Appearances deceived. Socialist stability fissured dramatically through Poland. Massive strikes followed food price increases, announced without warning first in 1970 by Gomulka's government and again in 1976 amid economic crisis by Edward Gierek's. Both times, the state backed down in the face of working-class militancy—strikes, marches, formal protests, and direct actions, with sacking of buildings, battles with police, and workplace occupations. In 1970–71, events began in the Baltic shipyards and spread through Katowice, Poznan, Wroclaw, Krakow, Warsaw, and Lodz. Tanks entered the Baltic ports, and Warsaw was under general strike. The new general secretary, Gierek, dealt directly with the occupying Szczecin shipyard workers, eventually announcing a two-year price freeze at 1966 levels, enabled by a Soviet loan. In 1976, this cycle was repeated more rapidly: increases were announced; workers took to the streets; and the government backed down.[5]

Polish opposition was distinctively working class. In 1970–76, it began outside the Party, owing little to intellectuals or students.[6] But it was the opposite of a narrow wage-related movement and made political demands from the start. Just as the French general strike of 1968 presupposed the student rising and the crisis of Gaullism, Polish actions necessarily challenged the party-state.[7] Despite the workers' extreme combativity, Gierek refrained from general repression but conciliated instead, holding 13 "consultations" with mass meetings in the shipyards and 10 in Lodz during 1971–75. Gierek launched industrial modernization with Western credits, to be financed via the intended growth in exports, while favoring private farmers for agricultural productivity. This had some success, but consumer demand remained unsatisfied, and by 1975 Poland's foreign indebtedness was extreme. Food prices were being subsidized to the tune of 12 percent of GNP.

Gierek bought time by appeasing protests. Communist rule relied on its social contract of the social minimum and the welfare state, linked to high wages, cheap food, and social recognition. Working-class membership in the Party increased, becoming at 46 percent the highest of the Soviet bloc, but this coopting of workers was counterbalanced by bureaucratic entrenchment. Workers were "consulted," visibly enhancing the party's legitimacy. But decision-making remained centralist as ever. Gierek also used selective repression. In response, opposition now broadened. In 1976, intellectuals formed the Committee for Workers' Defense (KOR) to raise support for imprisoned workers, helping shape collective identity through a Charter of Workers' Rights. Parts of the Church also defended victimized workers. The hierarchy's main advocate of human rights, Cardinal Wojtyla of Krakow, became Pope John Paul II, and his June 1979 visit to Poland inspired both public dissent and social organizing.

A third insurgency began in August 1980, again after price increases but this time in a nonviolent national movement. The government bought off the first strikes, but workers occupied the Lenin Shipyard in Gdansk, with a victimized electrician, Lech Walesa, at their head. Szczecin followed suit, and actions spread through the centers of 1970–76, plus Silesia and Poznan. Workers made an inventory of political demands, with independent unions at the top. The government agreed to the Inter-Factory Strike Committee's 21-point Charter on 31 August, while adding its own principles of collective property, the Party's leading role, and international alliance. Gierek was replaced by Stanislaw Kania on 6 September. The Accord was secured, region by region, by strikes and confrontations with the authorities, who dragged their feet. The Independent Self-Governing Trade Union, or Solidarity, was founded on 17 September, consolidated through a national strike on 3 October and officially registered on 10 November. By the end of September, it had 3 million members, doubling in a month, rising to 8 million after two. A year later, it claimed nearly 9.5 members in a total workforce of 12.5 million.[8]

The Party and Solidarity were in constant confrontation. As a result, any strategic vision was lost to the absolutism of intransigents on either side—Party hardliners urging normalization, Solidarity militants opposing any collaboration. Then the naming of General Wojciech Jaruzelski, the military commander-in-chief, as prime minister in February 1981 suggested growing Soviet nervousness at the Party's failing political center. And in Moscow on 4 March, Soviet and Polish leaderships agreed "to reverse the course of events" and "eliminate the peril looming over the socialist achievements of the Polish nation."[9]

Solidarity was torn between coexisting under Communism, which required abstaining from political ambitions, and the dynamism of its own growth, which constantly pulled politics in. It tried identifying "politics" with the corrupted party-state, to be brought under "social" control and public accountability. But this approach was unrealistic, given the membership's huge moral investment in the movement's potential: "In the eyes of the people, the new trade unions should do everything: they should fulfil the role of trade unions, participate in the administration of the country, be a political party, and act as a militia, that is, detain drunkards and thieves."[10] Walesa and his Catholic advisers imagined bypassing the Party with a corporatist division of labor or a social compact with a reformed Communist government. That was Jaruzelski's preference too, offering a corporatist deal in November 1981 as an alternative to martial law. But if this might have worked earlier, events had now gone beyond ready conciliation.

At its first Congress in September-October 1981, Solidarity dropped its trade union stance and called for "a self-governing republic," attacking the CP's "leading role." The planned economy was rejected in favor of autonomous "self-managing" enterprises, with syndicalist intimations of a democratized economy beyond the Party's sphere of command. When the Program declared that "[p]ublic life in Poland requires profound and comprehensive reforms which result in a permanent introduction of the principles of self-government, democracy, and pluralism," it was entering the territory of the Prague Spring and leaving the land of "actually existing socialism" behind.[11] The outcome was inevitable. On 12 December, Jaruzelski declared martial law, rounded up Solidarity leaders, and formed a Military Council of National Salvation.

Given the Soviet system's three pillars—the Soviet military power and right of intervention, the socialist command economy, and the CP's sole rule—martial law was a foregone conclusion. Solidarity's leaders had been acutely conscious of the need to keep the Red Army at bay, and so it was amazing how far Polish workers went. Their sophistication was impressive. The Gdansk Workers' Charter integrated social egalitarianism and radical democracy: a wage package angled for the low-paid; an end to privileges for Party appointees; equitable price controls and rationing; and expansion of welfare but also freedoms of press, speech, and publication. This reflected the wider cultural dissidence of the late 1970s, inspired by KOR's activities, a growing *samizdat* press, and the unofficial circulation of ideas. It also presumed prior histories of militancy, equivocally tolerated by the Party. No less than political movements in the West, Eastern European oppositions grew from longer-term sedimentations of political culture. They had national genealogies and international determinations.

With an eye to the future—the end of Communism in 1989—Solidarity's history had a fourfold significance: it brought the final demise of the Communist Party; it fatally delegitimized the language of socialism; it saw the rise of a uniquely powerful, nationally organized working-class democracy; and it embodied the utopia of a separately organized "civil society" that could remain somehow uncontaminated by the state.

The Polish winter confirmed the lesson of the Prague Spring: reform would never come from governing Communist parties while Soviet rule survived. For Soviet leaders, any relaxing of Communist political monopoly was unacceptable. Yet the Polish Party encompassed a sizeable bloc of society, and Solidarity overlapped with it locally, notably in the largest industrial plants targeted for Party recruitment in the 1970s, the "citadels of socialism," with the best-paid workers and largest factory branches. Local Communists were active in the 1980 strikes, and by December half Solidarity's regional activists were Party members. During early 1981, the so-called Horizontal Structures movement cohered around the Gdansk provincial secretary, Tadeusz Fiszbach, seeking to use coalition with Solidarity to democratize the Party. Its April conference represented half a million Party members, calling for a new Party leadership and program.[12]

Here was a space for Poland's Prague Spring, a golden chance to unite Solidarity's energies with party reformers from below. But this was precisely the democratization placed under Soviet ban. After the ineffectual Party Congress in June 1981, the state began attacking Solidarity, while Jaruzelski and the army tightened their hold on government. Kania's liberal center had missed its chance. The desire for reform at the Party's base and its interlacing with Solidarity undermined the Party leadership's ability to reimpose control; yet any gestures to reform automatically pushed Moscow's buttons; the Kania group's paralysis was the result. When the promise of reform proved empty, Solidarity's supporters left the Party in droves.

Conversely, Solidarity ignored this inner-party struggle. Social democrats like Jacek Kuron of KOR and their Catholic allies preferred sidelining the Party by solidifying corporatist relations between Solidarity and the government, in a strategy Adam Michnik called the "New Evolutionism."[13]

The Horizontal movement took them by surprise.[14] The Church also had no desire to see the Party renewed. Most Solidarity intellectuals favored marketization plus plant self-management based on reformers in the state apparatus. Finally, working-class activists wished to keep the Party at arm's length, and most radicals boycotted it on principle. By summer 1981, the temper of the militants had radicalized, pushing Solidarity's October Congress in anarcho-syndicalist directions. In all of these ways, Solidarity had no base for alliances to the Party.

Martial law, declared on 12 December 1981, was a total displacement of the Party. It destroyed not only the vision of peaceful democratic transition but also the agency of the Polish CP. The latter was paralyzed by the Czechoslovak precedent: it could neither ally with reform nor escape from its popularity. Thus when repression arrived, it came through the army and security forces rather than a purged and re-Stalinized Party. No Kádár or Husak was waiting in the wings. The Party's collapse as an active agent—its complete replacement by the army—had no precedent in socialist states.[15]

The outcome of the Polish crisis had a second crucial dimension. From the Gdansk Charter of August 1980 to the Program of 16 October 1981, Solidarity had seemed a radical social democratic movement, comparable to the central European insurgencies of 1918–19 or the French Popular Front of 1936. Borne by extraparliamentary militancy and direct action, these were movements for parliamentary democracy and social reform. Solidarity likewise contained diverse radicalisms, including neosyndicalist belief in purely working-class democracy organized around production, which inspired the movement's militant core in autumn 1981. In its union of class-political self-assertiveness, egalitarian social outlook, belief in public goods and the welfare state, and radical-democratic commitment to a "self-governing republic," Solidarity belonged squarely within socialist traditions.

Many Solidarity militants gave practical expression to socialist values. Yet the language, legacies, and iconography of socialism were missing from Solidarity's self-representations, because Communist rule had delegitimized socialism as an available political language. The Soviet invasion of Czechoslovakia identified "socialism" with an oppressive opposite of the democratic and egalitarian ideals Solidarity espoused. Stalinism—as a system of command economics, inefficiency and waste, as a social machinery of privilege in the inequitable distribution of goods, as a Communist political monopoly, and as a public culture of simplistic exhortation—was a degenerate version of socialist public address. Socialism was contaminated by its existing usage. It was owned by official Communist culture, and ipso facto no good. Into its space, other political languages—Catholic, nationalist, democratic, liberal-economic—were able to rush. In Eastern Europe, it was peculiarly hard to argue in socialist terms. The Polish events made it impossible, even in the form of Western European social democracy.

Yet sociologically, Solidarity was a classic working-class movement. The alliance with KOR was vital, but labor militants bristled against strategies brought from outside. This relationship, where KOR acted as advisers (or performed specialist functions, as in the press), without becoming leaders per se, lasted through 1980–81. The movement's élan and political idiom were self-consciously proletarian, charismatically figured in Lech Walesa, whose ordinary origins—an electrician in the shipyards since 1967, the father of eight children—were emblematic. Solidarity encompassed the full complexity of the working class, mobilizing across industries, regions, generations, both genders, and all grades of wage-earners. It was continally managing these differences, including those between the shopfloor and the technicians and white-collar grades who were disproportionately active in its regional executives. But it was centered on the big industrial plants in each region, huge monoliths of Fordism—the Lenin and Paris Commune shipyards of Gdansk-Gdynia; the Warski yard and Police chemical plant in Szczecin; the Marschlewski works in Lodz; ZISPO in Poznan; Huta Lenina in Krakow; Huta Katowice and the July Manifesto mine in Upper Silesia; the Pafaweg railway car plant in Lower Silesia; Zeran, Ursus, and Huta Warszawa in Warsaw.

Solidarity was sui generis in the history of the Left. As a movement uniting union and political goals, it recalled the earlier syndicalist ideal of "one big union" from 1900–1921. But that had always competed with social democratic and Communist models of organizing national labor movements, while Solidarity was the only game in town. The extreme risks of Soviet invasion provided huge incentives for negotiating differences inside Solidarity, much as the earlier danger had concentrated the Prague Spring's unity in April–August 1968. This shaped the movement's neosyndicalist "one-big-union" quality into a framework of political coalition. It fused the workerist logic, which implied an alienated refusal of the "politics" of the CP monopoly, with a social democratic one, which required a political approach to the state. If Solidarity the social movement kept its neosyndicalist virtue, Solidarity the political coalition developed a strategy for corporatist power sharing, in which government would concede control of social policy, while devolving the economy into a system of self-managing enterprises, with a radically shrunken role for the Party as a result. This slippage between neosyndicalist and social democratic conceptions in a single national movement was unique in the history of the European Left.[16]

Finally, Solidarity also became an agency for society's moral renewal, where the virtues of citizenship could be nurtured in a non-Party public sphere.[17] This aspect of the movement, a project of moral-political reconstruction, had powerful Gramscian overtones. During its 18 months, Solidarity came close to organizing Polish society into a counterhegemonic potential. It was certainly Europe's most impressive working-class insurgency since 1917–23. There were comparable mobilizations—Hungary in 1956 or France in 1936. But only Solidarity sustained itself over a period of time with self-generated institutional forms. Its origins in a purportedly socialist state were bitter irony for the Left. It was only appropriate that the PCI, the Gramscian party par excellence, should draw the moral. In a series of debates and resolutions, the PCI drew a line beneath the epoch of the Bolshevik Revolution:

> we must accept that this phase of socialist development (which began with the October Revolution) has exhausted its driving force, just as the phase which saw the birth and development of socialist parties and trade union movements mustered around the Second International also ran out of steam. The world has moved on, it has changed, thanks, also, to this turn that history took. The point is to overcome the present by looking ahead.[18]

GORBACHEV

Once the Cold War began, the USSR affected the Western European Left as a series of disruptions—as a politics profoundly at odds with parliamentary socialism, as the scene of dictatorship and police rule, and as the source of a disastrous crisis of socialism's moral credibility. In 1956 and after, Western socialists were constantly apologizing for Soviet behavior. With the invasions of Hungary and Czechoslovakia, embarassment turned to anger. The USSR might give resources to the Cuban and other Third World revolutions, but its treatment of dissidents and disrespect for civil rights, both at home and in Eastern Europe, were a disgrace. It trampled on democracy and destroyed the three strongest reform movements developing in socialist countries—the Hungarian Revolution (1956), the Prague Spring (1968), and Solidarity (1980–81). Each time, Communism's vital signs became weaker. Despite Eurocommunism, the Soviet Union under Brezhnev all but destroyed the space where Communist parties in the West might flourish. The Soviet example was the greatest weapon the Right could ever have wanted against the Left in Western Europe.

In 1985–86, all of this changed. After 18 years of deadening conservatism, Brezhnev died in November 1982.[19] He was replaced by Iurii Andropov, long-time KGB head, with a reputation for efficiency and rectitude. Andropov began replacing the ridiculous gerontocracy then ruling the USSR—the Politburo's average age was over 70, and only three of its members were born after 1917. After Andropov's unexpected death in 1984, the still shorter reign of Konstantin Chernenko failed to halt renewal. When he too died in March 1985, the Politburo's youngest and most dynamic member, Mikhail Gorbachev, previously nominated by Andropov, was immediately appointed his successor.[20]

No one was prepared for what ensued. From being set in stone, the Soviet system turned into a roller coaster. Gorbachev began a program to move Soviet Communism into a modernized future, which actually led to its implosion. He was the first genuine reformer since Khrushchev. He was stylistically the opposite of his predecessors, back through Stalin himself. University educated (already a difference), he marshaled a distinctive generational culture—wartime childhood, youth in the ideological *Sturm und Drang* of the early Cold War, adulthood during reconstruction and the lessening of international tensions by the 1960s. Sophisticated and intellectually urbane, Gorbachev recuperated non-Stalinist reform traditions identified with NEP, Bukharin, and much of the Khrushchev era. As Gorbachev's program took shape, it recalled the Prague Spring.[21]

Gorbachev's first priority was new blood, and by March 1986 half the Politburo, Secretariat, and Central Committee owed their places to his new broom.[22] In policy, he began cautiously enough, continuing Andropov's drives for productivity and against corruption. At the Twenty-seventh Congress in March 1986, mainly the rhetoric of deepening "socialist democracy" was new. It was during this Congress speech that Gorbachev launched his defining slogans—*perestroika* (restructuring or radical reform), and *glasnost* (openness). After years of empty and mendacious posturing, it was hard to take the rhetoric seriously. But when Gorbachev said, "Communists want the truth, always and under all circumstances," remarkably enough, he meant it.[23]

Something was desperately needed to jolt the economy from stagnation. The command economy's chronic malfunctioning fused with bleak conditions of life—from food shortages and other scarcities to deteriorating services and worsening health and mortality—to create the needed sense of emergency. But the main issue was political—cutting through the accumulated layers of lethargy and corruption where the economic bureaucracy was now buried. The nuclear disaster at the Chernobyl power station in Ukraine in April 1986 dramatized the problems—poor construction standards, inferior materials, bad design, lax maintenance, inadequate safety rules, dismal training, irresponsible management, layers on layers of bureaucratic cover-up. Chernobyl exposed all the problems of inefficiency and misinformation that glasnost was meant to address.

To make economic reform work, the public sphere had to be freed. Liberal editors were appointed to journals, censorship was dismantled, the arts freed, history reexcavated. Public life became unrecognizable. Gorbachev met with writers, social scientists, and intellectuals. He welcomed dissidents back from prison or abroad. Dramatically, he telephoned the regime's eminent critic, the physicist Andrei Sakharov, recalling him from exile in Gorky in December 1986. "The old does not give up without a fight," he declared, and appealed over the Party to the people, "who wish for change, who dream of change."[24] Gorbachev made audacious moves to end the Cold War, which had been freshly escalating via NATO's deployment of cruise missiles and Ronald Reagan's foreign policy. To ease the pressure on domestic budgets, the USSR needed a break from the arms race. Gorbachev consistently pressed a new detente, refusing to join the confrontation announced by Reagan's Strategic Defense Initiative (SDI).[25] At the Geneva summit in 1985, he crafted a joint statement that nuclear war was unwinnable; at Reykjavik in 1986, he proposed cutting strategic arms by 50 percent, initially to Reagan's spontaneous agreement; at Washington in 1987, agreement was reached for eliminating some land-based missiles.[26]

Under Khrushchev and Brezhnev, Soviet support for antiimperialist movements in the Third World had continued. Gorbachev withdrew from this adversarial stance, proposing instead a "comprehensive system of international security." For the first time, the Twenty-seventh CPSU Congress in 1986 made no commitment to national liberation movements, shifting foreign aid from arms to welfare. Rather than "two camps," Gorbachev stressed common human values, mutual respect, and sovereignty of independent states. Via the Geneva Agreement, Soviet troops left Afghanistan by February 1989. Most remarkably of all, Gorbachev disengaged from Eastern Europe. Renouncing the Brezhnev Doctrine as early as March 1985, he unilaterally withdrew half a million Warsaw Pact troops on 7 December 1988. By 1987, Western Europeans were persuaded of his genuine commitment to peace and democracy; he received the Nobel Peace Prize in 1990.[27]

By 1988–89, the reconfiguring of Eastern European politics had already begun, with Hungary and Poland in the lead. And once democracy was broached for Eastern Europe, it became posed for the Soviet republics too. A third logic of Gorbachev's international strategy—after ending the Cold War and freeing Eastern Europe—was the breaking-up of the USSR. This had been the great anxiety of 1968—once Czechoslovakia had its national road, Soviet leaders had feared, not only the other socialist countries, but the Soviet nationalities would demand theirs too. By 1988–89, this anxiety proved prophetic.

In the summer of 1987, protests greeted the anniversary of the 1939 Nazi-Soviet Pact, which had brought Soviet seizure of Lithuania, Latvia, and Estonia in August 1940, and by the fall of 1988 "Popular Fronts" were demanding national independence in all three states. Each Supreme Soviet declared its sovereignty; the Popular Fronts embraced secession; and in the summer of 1989 the Baltic CPs seceded from the CPSU. On the fiftieth anniversary of the Pact, 2 million people formed a human chain across all three republics. Similar movements emerged in Belorussia, Moldavia, and Ukraine. In the Caucasus they turned violent. War erupted between Armenia and Azerbaijan in February 1988 over the mountain region of Nagorno-Karabakh, three-quarters Armenian but administered by Azerbaijan since 1923. In February 1989, big independence rallies occurred in Georgia on the anniversary of the republic's Soviet annexation in 1921, with further protests in April, when a nationalist rally in Tbilisi was attacked by Soviet troops, with 16 deaths.[28] Georgians clashed with Osetin and Abkhaz national minorities. In June 1989, intercommunal violence exploded in the Ferghana valley of eastern Uzbekistan between majority Uzbeks and Meskhetian Turks, deported from Georgia in 1944.

Changes of this magnitude on the periphery required decisions at the center, but Gorbachev's intentions evolved fitfully. By recruiting new leaders, releasing the flow of ideas, and shedding the siege mentality of the Cold War, he hoped to move the CPSU into a Soviet Prague Spring, inspiring popular belief along the way. But cajoling the party-state into action, after decades of deals and dissimulation, was hard. To crack the Party's inertia, society had to be set into motion. If Communists would not go to the mountain, the mountain would be brought to the Communists. But Gorbachev still needed the Party. The dialectic of party and society was supposed to recharge the former, concentrating society's hopes in a revitalized agency of change. But society was discovering its own multivariate interests and capacities. With so much incitement—freeing debate, removing taboos, uncovering the past, and speaking the unspoken—a new pluralism was unavoidable. While Gorbachev sought to channel its energies, civil society was seeking its own forms.

Gorbachev kept the courage of his convictions: "We must not retreat. We have nowhere to retreat to." On television, he called a Party conference for "further democratizing the life of the Party and society as a whole."[29] It eventually convened on 28 June 1988, exposing the Party's divisiveness to public view, while endorsing Gorbachev's proposal for the elected Congress of People's Deputies. The subsequent election of the Congress in March 1989 then became the hinge of the Gorbachev years, comparable to the French Estates-General of 1789. It was a moment of authentic, if procedurally cumbersome and juridically inadequate, popular democracy. It began the forming of parties, pulling together the "informal movements" crystallizing during 1986–87 and providing the impetus in 1990–91 for the real thing.

The Congress involved a free electoral process and open debates. By a mixed system—one-third of the 2,250 deputies were appointed, two-thirds elected—the Soviet citizenry chose among candidates nominated by the CP and other organizations. The campaign polarized society over reform, and while 87 percent of those elected were CPSU members, debates were freed from party discipline. The Congress opened before live cameras for 12 days of free-ranging debate. The vital effect was the process of public disagreement itself. Gorbachev had "moved *perestroika* from liberalization toward democratization of the system." By 1989, the impetus for change passed beyond his reach: "power flowed away from the party and its leader, into the streets, the national republics, and the meeting rooms of independent political and social organizations."[30]

Gorbachev's ideal of controlled reform ("I want a stage-by-stage, step-by-step process that will not stimulate disintegration and chaos") vanished in a new polarization. The Union was breaking up. Lithuania (11 March 1990), Estonia (30 March), and Latvia (4 May) each declared independence. Violence flared in Azerbaijan against Armenians in January 1990. Gorbachev sent troops and only worsened nationalist alienation from the center. By the time institutions began democratizing—between the Party Conference of June 1988 and elections to the Congress of People's Deputies—the non-Russian republics were already in motion. As the peripheries entered crisis, the center failed to hold. Gorbachev's charismatic opponent, Boris Yeltsin, became chair of the freshly elected Russian Congress of People's Deputies in May 1990 and proclaimed Russian sovereignty. "If the center does not overthrow us in the next 100 days," he declared, "Russia will be independent in everything."[31] It was no longer clear what the "center" still meant.

The Communist Party was opposed by an ever-broadening coalition, from national republics to radical reformers. On 15 March 1990, the Congress of People's Deputies elected Gorbachev to the newly created presidency, accountable to the Congress and assisted by a cabinet—a far cry from the old governing system centered on the Politburo. On Gorbachev's urging, the Central Committee had renounced article 6 of the Soviet Constitution, which guaranteed the CPSU's leading role. However unavoidable, it was a procedural death knoll. As the national republics peeled away and Yeltsin's Russia contested central jurisdiction, Gorbachev was marooned on a federal island of abstracted all-Union institutions. Without the CP's unifying instrument, his powers could only shrink.

Gorbachev missed two big chances. One was the long gap between January 1987, when he announced the Party Conference, and June 1988, when it met. His speech for the Revolution's seventieth anniversary in 1987 revealed the problem. Its "jumbling of critique and praise," attacking Stalin's abuses but upholding his policies, recalled Khrushchev's formulas of 1956 and conveyed vacillation. Trying to mediate between old-party conservatives and new reformers impeded any strategic vision. "One style of leadership, self-confidently based in a dying political culture, was being pitted against an incoherent, improvised movement toward greater democracy and an uncertain future."[32]

The second chance came in summer 1990, as economic reform came to a head. Against the government's main proposal for a five-year transition to a regulated market ("shock without therapy," according to one critic), another policy group offered a "500-day" transition, based on radical privatization via sale of assets to citizens. Gorbachev and other policy-makers no less than the broader public remained concerned about high unemployment and other hardshops, and big-bang marketization was anything but predictable. But the ideals of democracy and market were so sutured together now that intermediate solutions were becoming exceptionally squeezed. Gorbachev held back and adopted a heavily modified market reform, while in September 1990 Yeltsin introduced the 500-day plan in Russia. Whatever the rational arguments, the political costs were vast. Gorbachev seemed to be appeasing his conservatives again; Yeltsin seemed to hold the grail of reform.

Gorbachev had gone as far as he could without shedding the Party. He had disavowed Marxism's absolute truth. He had repudiated the invasion of Czechoslovakia and endorsed Eastern European change. He strategically shifted authority from party to state. But he could act no further without abandoning the Party per se. Democrats had become anti-Communist. They were casting their lot with nationalists in the Baltic and Russia. In local and republican soviet elections during 1990, the CPSU consistently lost, because even if winning candidates held party cards, they were now in transit to new "Democratic" affiliations. Yeltsin was the coming man. During 1990, he dug himself into a strengthened Russian Republic. In a triumphal presidential election in June 1991, he took 57 percent of the vote. While Yeltsin was making republican statehood the medium of democratization, Gorbachev was trapped into acting as federal policeman, most painfully in the Baltic crisis of January 1991, when troops fired on Lithuanian and Latvian demonstrators. Yeltsin had stolen the initiative: "The so-called revolution from above has ended. The Kremlin is no longer the initiator of the country's renewal or an active champion of the new. The processes of renewal, blocked at the level of the center, have moved to the republics."[33]

In 1991, Gorbachev followed twin goals. He renegotiated the Constitution's federalism around the republics, with the Union as a reduced executive. Second, he edged toward breaking with the Communist tradition. The Central Committee accepted a broadly social democratic program in July 1991, and Gorbachev affirmed the mixed economy and market socialism, with Scandinavian social democracy as the implied model. Given these two conditions—the Union Treaty and a refounding of the CPSU— he could be cautiously optimistic.

But both Yeltsin and Leonid Kravchuk, head of Ukraine, were already ditching the treaty. Then, on 18 August 1991, an eight-man State Committee for the Emergency arrested Gorbachev on vacation in the Crimea and tried to seize power. This coup lasted three days. Its leaders were senior CPSU bureaucrats in key state positions. They suspended all freedoms; declared an economic emergency to be addressed by central action through cutting prices, raising wages, and equitable food distribution; central planning, law and order, and Soviet international prestige would all be restored. The coup was abysmally executed, unsupported by the army and KGB élite units. Gorbachev refused to endorse it. More dramatically, Yeltsin mounted a tank outside the Russian Parliament, denounced the coup, and called for defense of democracy. Massive crowds responded. Next day, the coup collapsed and Gorbachev flew back. He condemned the coup and applauded Yeltsin's resistance. He resigned the CPSU general secretaryship and called on the Central Committee to dissolve. The CPSU was suspended and its assets seized.

The victor was not Gorbachev or his project of perestroika—a democratized USSR and a revived CP, reinvented as a social democratic party committed to market socialism—but Yeltsin and the Russian Republic. Gorbachev doggedly pursued the chimera of a viable Union Treaty, but the basis had evaporated. During the coup, the Baltic Republics were joined by the rest in full independence—Ukraine (24 August), Belorussia (25 August), Moldova (27 August), Azerbaijan (30 August), Uzbekistan (31 August), Kirgizia (1 September), Tajikistan (9 September), Armenia (23 September), Turkmenia (27 October), and Kazakhstan (16 December). Moscow now had two rival executives—Gorbachev, whose raison d'être was gone; and Yeltsin, "swelled with new powers, sucking the sense out of an all-union government."[34] On 8 December, Yeltsin joined Ukraine and Belorussia for a Commonwealth of Independent States (CIS). Eleven republics (excepting Georgia and the Baltic) signed a declaration at Alma Ata to this effect. On 25 December 1991, Gorbachev resigned the presidency of the USSR, which had ceased to exist.

POST-COMMUNISM: THE REVOLUTIONS OF 1989

The events of the fall of 1989 were extraordinary.[35] They were comparable to the east-central European revolutions of 1918: like them, they created national sovereignties from a decayed imperial system; as in 1918, they were overshadowed by events in Germany, which had profound implications for the new democracies to the East. The revolutions displayed a common pattern—replacement of single-party Communist governments and command economies by multiparty democracies and market capitalisms based on private property and the rule of law. The revolutionary transitions, through which Communists surrendered their monopoly, were generic. They were linked in a single chain, each sparking and inspiring the next. This connectedness came partly from common belonging to the Warsaw Pact and partly from regional circuits of opposition from the 1980s. But it also resulted from the communications revolution apparent in 1968. These revolutions were televised.[36]

Gorbachev had indicated since 1985 that the Brezhnev Doctrine was defunct. At the United Nations, he renounced "the threat of force," describing "freedom of choice" as a "universal principle" for "both the capitalist and socialist systems."[37] Roundtable negotiations with the Polish and Hungarian oppositions began respectively on 6 February and 13 June 1989, as Communists sought to preserve a special role within the putative pluralist arrangements. Events outstripped this goal. In Poland, agreement was reached for elections to the freely elected Senate and the Sejm, with 65 percent of the seats reserved for the Communists, but on 4–18 June Solidarity carried 65 percent of the vote, with 92 of 100 Senate seats and 160 of 161 contested seats in the Sejm. It rejected a coalition of national unity and formed its own government on 20 August, with Jaruzelski remaining as president. So ended Communist rule in Poland.[38] It happened as the Congress of People's Deputies was opening up the political process in the USSR, the new US president, George Bush, was declaring the Cold War to be over, and Soviet troops were already leaving Hungary.

Since February 1989, the Hungarian CP had agreed to a multiparty democracy, and by June reformers had outflanked the general secretary, Karoly Grósz, to capture the Party.[39] The struggle for reform acquired mass dimensions around the country's commemorative calendar, as the opposition established Hungary's 1848 revolution as a rival national holiday to the Bolshevik revolution. The government agreed to Imre Nagy's ceremonial reinterment on 16 June, the date of his 1957 execution, and a quarter of a million attended the ceremony.

By then, however, international attention was turning to East Germany. From 2 May, Hungary had begun defortifying its Austrian border, and East Germans found an escape path to the West. In July, GDR citizens crammed the West German embassies in Budapest, Warsaw, and Prague as refugees. Hungary freed the Austrian border (10 September), and by the end of October 50,000 East Germans had fled. On 30 September, the GDR allowed refugees to leave Prague and Warsaw for West Germany in sealed trains, but this only stoked popular discontent. As one train passed through Dresden, 10,000 demonstrators fought police while attempting to board it, and numbers continued to escalate. The Hungarian exodus became a flood. It was visible, uninhibited, and angry and came at the worst possible time. As the GDR approached its fortieth anniversary, the socialist citizenry was doing everything possible to leave. In 1989, 343,854 voted with their feet.[40]

By October 1989, Eastern Europe was on the edge of revolution. Gorbachev's new internationalism had not only buried the Brezhnev Doctrine but was now leaving the ground of Yalta too. It was unclear until now just how far he would go. In East Berlin for the GDR's fortieth birthday, he told the Socialist Unity Party (SED) Politburo: "life punishes those who come too late."[41] Erich Honecker, general secretary since 1971, refused concessions. The Party was demoralized. Protests on 7–8 October throughout the country were attacked brutally by police. The key test was a weekly rally in Leipzig the next day. Starting from small peace meetings in the Nikolai Church since 1982, these Monday actions had grown tenfold from 4 September to 2 October, when 15,000 demonstrated. Amid fears of a "Chinese" repetition, 70,000 now gathered. Local negotiations between Kurt Masur (director of the Leipzig Gewandhaus Orchestra), two theologians, and three Party secretaries prevented police violence, paralleling a pact in Dresden the previous day. The rally passed without incident.

No reformers emerged in the SED to contest Honecker's rigidity. When he was replaced by Egon Krenz on 18 October, opposition had massively grown, now crystallizing into new organizations, from a Social Democratic Party to a variety of Left, feminist, and democratic networks. Protests acquired enormous dimensions, affecting most cities and smaller towns by late October and spreading to universities, factories, and the GDR's entire institutional landscape. In Leipzig, the weekly actions became a massed crescendo of democratic hope: from 110,000 on 16 October to 225,000 a week later and half a million by 6 November. On 4 November in East Berlin, a million rallied for democracy, free speech, human rights, a change of government, and socialist renewal. While Krenz desperately reshuffled his government, opened the public sphere, and searched for a workable travel law, the party's local machinery collapsed. On 9 November, under confused circumstances, the Berlin Wall came down.[42]

These events were revolutionary: popular protests escalating to an antigovernment challenge; the state's repressive machinery crumbling; the regime and its supporters paralyzed; a new government committed to free elections and democratic transition. A process of restructuring in the USSR, geared to an unspecified "democratization," had widened the space for negotiated transitions in Poland and Hungary. Soviet perestroika had excited popular mobilizations in the Baltic and Caucasus. An organized civil society was emerging in Hungary, a process already advanced under Solidarity in Poland. But the GDR was the first socialist country whose government was directly toppled by a mass uprising. November 1989 brought the political process from the committee rooms into the streets. In November–December 1989, a revolutionary chain reaction carried democracy into Eastern Europe.

On 10 November, a Politburo coup replaced Todor Zhivkov, Party leader in Bulgaria since 1954. Bulgarian Communist Party reformers announced a program of pluralism and democracy. Dissidents were rehabilitated, political freedoms instated, and opposition legalized. The party's leading role was renounced. The Bulgarization campaigns against ethnic Turks were ended. Free elections were promised and Roundtable talks opened with the newly formed Union of Democratic Forces (UDF).[43]

In Czechoslovakia, police violence against students began the crisis on 17 November. The Czech Civic Forum and Slovak Public Against Violence were founded by intellectuals, and by 20 November huge crowds of 200,000 to 350,000 were in the streets of Prague daily. The dissident Václav Havel and a newly reemerged Alexander Dubcek addressed the crowds on 23 November. A two-hour general strike showed the movement's popular breadth. The KSC now folded: its leading role was removed from the Constitution; the People's Militia disbanded. A new Government of National Understanding was dominated by the Civic Forum. President Husak resigned and was replaced by Havel; Dubcek chaired the National Assembly; free elections and the transition to a market economy were announced.[44]

Romania closed the cycle of Eastern European revolutions, when Nicolae Ceauşescu was deposed on 22 December by the National Salvation Front (NSF), headed by Ion Iliescu and other Communists and backed by the army. This was a carefully staged coup, secured by popular uprising. The spark was a massacre on 17–18 December in Timişoara, where people were defending the dissident Hungarian Reformed minister László Tökés against deportation. Protests against the Hungarian minority's maltreatment broadened into an attack on the regime, with a local general strike. Protests spread to Arad and Cluj. At a televised mass rally in Bucharest, Ceauşescu was visibly unnerved by heckling. Fighting began on 22 December, insurgents invaded the Central Committee building, and the Ceauşescus were captured that night. They were tried and executed on Christmas Day. In a confused situation, the NSF claimed victory over Ceauşescu's hated *Securitate*. Iliescu became president, with Petre Roman as prime minister, pending elections in April 1990.[45]

Finally, convergent moves to democracy reached a climax in Slovenia, the strongest economy among Yugoslavia's constituent republics. The Slovene League of Communists (LCS) had encouraged independent parties and "the opening up of political space" since the fall of 1988, while actively pursuing economic reform, internal democracy, and closeness with the West.[46] The legislature declared Slovenia a "sovereign and independent state," removing the Party's leading role from the Constitution. In December, it declared democratic elections for April 1990. The LCS challenged the extreme ethnonationalist course of the Serbian Communists under Slobodan Milosevic, and at the all-Yugoslav Party Congress on 20 January 1990 it proposed a multiparty system, secret ballots, and a federated Communist League of independent parties. Milosevic denounced this, and the Slovene Communists walked out. Back in Ljubljana, they relaunched themselves as a social democratic Party of Democratic Renewal. The Yugoslav League of Communists ceased to exist.[47]

LEFT STANDING

What did the 1989 revolutions achieve? These were democratic revolutions in a strict sense. Primary demands recurred: free elections, parliamentary government, civil freedoms, multiparty competition. Conditions of pluralism were secured, not just by party competition in free elections but via rule of law and a guaranteed public sphere. Party and state were to be separated, as were state and civil society. So too were the state and economy: the biggest future agenda was marketization. Finally, it all happened without bloodshed—without the collective violence of repressive authorities and insurgent crowds. The exception, in Romania, where armed clashes, streetfighting, and the execution of deposed leaders described the revolutionary process, also saw the least structural change.[48]

Thus the 1989 revolutions involved genuine structural transformation. New constitutions were written; institutional landscapes were rebuilt; and the rule of law was established, with independence of the judiciary, control of police, enforceability of contracts, security of property, and protection of civil liberties. Public spheres were created. Norms of public life were remade. Institutional changes of this magnitude created conditions for profound cultural reformation, with implications across every sphere—high culture and the arts, entertainment and recreation, popular culture, associational life, family forms, sexualities, schooling, intellectual exchange, and the general texture of public language. In Eastern Europe, it became possible to speak, write, act, and think differently.

In modern Europe, three earlier conjunctures brought big increments of democracy: the 1860s; 1917–23; and 1944–49. Other times saw huge popular mobilizations but without comparable results: in 1848 and 1968, democratic hopes met defeat. Another transnational constitution-making moment was 1989. If 1945 brought a strengthening of liberal democracy in Western Europe, making universal suffrage normative for the first time, 1989 brought equivalent gains in the East. Free elections were held, as promised—in the GDR (March 1990), Hungary (March–April), Slovenia (April), Romania (May), Czechoslovakia (June), Bulgaria (June), and Poland (October 1991).[49] Juridically, democratic gains were consolidated, and in the meantime democratic procedures—electoral outcomes, alternation of parties in government, and civil rights—were respected. Democratic capacities involve far more than this, of course, but as a public culture parliamentary democracy was the defining good of 1989.

If one dimension of 1989 was change at the top, the other was a shift from below. Pluralism presupposed the self-organizing of "society" in contradistinction to the party-state. Polish Solidarity in 1980–81 had been the organized expression of such autonomy, to the point of becoming "counterhegemonic" in Gramsci's sense. Polish workers' collective militancy had allowed wider social forces to convene through a new ethic of refusal. Earlier reformers had worked in the party institutions themselves, especially the universities and research institutes, policy commissions and journals, seeking links with the leadership. This was the model of 1956 and 1968. But those violent defeats, and the crude normalizing of 1968–73 in Poland, Yugoslavia, and Hungary no less than Czechoslovakia, exhausted Communism's credit. Thereafter, opposition became withdrawal to a defiant noncooperation, or "antipolitics," in György Konrad's term.[50] Dissenters "ceased addressing the party-state and turned directly to society."[51] Their home ground became "civil society," organized beyond official frameworks altogether. This was Adam Michnik's "new evolutionism," projecting the system's collapse from its cumulative loss of societal control. Michnik called it "living in dignity," Havel "living in truth."[52]

As a program, this relied on the Helsinki Final Act of 1975. In Czechoslovakia, it dated from "Charter 77," a key post-1968 European political initiative: signed openly by 243 intellectuals, it preferred the language of human rights to a "political" critique of the regime.[53] Concurrently, the KOR formed in Poland in 1976, gradually seeding a kind of countersociety. In Hungary, intellectuals signed petitions for Charter 77 and launched the Hungarian Flying University, accompanied by a flourishing samizdat of journals and publication. By the 1980s, this Eastern European activity spanned all the issues of Western new social movements, including ecology, peace, and even, in Slovenia, feminism and gay rights. These oppositions mirrored the cultural politics of 1968. This came partly through student movements themselves—Michnik and others were active in 1968—partly through the arts, and partly via counterculture. Both Czechoslovak and Slovene oppositions were galvanized by official attacks on youth subcultures—in the former by the prosecution of the Plastic People of the Universe and other rock musicians in 1976, in the latter by attacks on punks in 1980–81.[54]

The common organizational medium in the revolutions (except Romania) was the "Forum"—a broad informal front, hastily improvised, comprising mainly intellectuals, with unclear popular support and not representative in any procedurally democratic sense. When talks began, these self-constituted committees sat at the table, not organized parties with memberships and programs. These Roundtables were very ambiguous affairs. They were partly confrontations of irreconcilable opposites: corrupt and undemocratic party-states facing revived civil societies where democracy could be regrounded, the sites of a "parallel polis."[55] Here—as a challenge of ethics to power—there seemed to be no compromising. Yet such Roundtables were remarkably successful vehicles of immediate transition. The oppositions proved to be hardheaded negotiators, and some Communists emerged as respected interlocutors, credible partners in the democratic future. Many wanted the opposition not to develop into parties. The point was to speak openly and ethically on behalf of civil society by calling rulers to moral account: the general "movement" quality of the opposition seemed its best asset, which would be lost if "forums" became partisan parties.

Measured by this—rebuilding the "civicness" of society via an ethic of responsibility, by perpetuating movements like Civic Forum or Solidarity—the revolutions failed. The East German civic movement was ruthlessly outflanked by West German Chancellor Kohl's offer of a united Germany, making the CDU overwhelmingly the largest party in the first GDR elections in March 1990. The elections became a referendum on German unity, particularly when Kohl dangled the bait of monetary union and large-scale funding. The civic ideal of a reformed GDR making its own future was crushingly defeated. Advocates of GDR's democratic renewal swam against an irresistible tide. The political infrastructure had completely dissolved, and Western politicians muscled into the vacuum. Mass migration of youth and talent to the West continued. Waste, obsolete technologies, and horrendous pollution revealed East German industry hopelessly unable to compete. Revelations of pervasive surveillance by the *Stasi* produced demoralization and fury. By the time Germany was unified on 3 October 1990, there was nothing left to renew.[56]

Elsewhere, Forum frameworks fractured into parties. The Hungarian elections brought a dual alignment: one multiparty camp was rural, populist, nationalist, and committed to marketization, while protecting Hungarian interests and smaller business, in the language of a "third way"; the other camp was urban, Westernized, and committed to neoliberal economics, based in the metropolitan dissenting intelligentsia of 1980s Budapest.[57] In Czechoslovakia, Bulgaria, and Slovenia, democratic fronts lasted the first elections, winning easily except in Bulgaria, where UDF remained the largest opposition. But by the next round of elections, unity had gone. In the Czech Republic and Slovenia, liberal parties emerged far ahead of the field, as did Vladimir Meciar's Movement for a Democratic Slovakia. But in Poland the largest party, Tadeusz Mazowiecki's new Democratic Union, had only 12.3 percent in a disastrously fragmented party field.[58]

The very first post-Communist elections were exciting referenda on democracy, clearly breaking with the past. But Forum politics' larger hope of regrounding politics in an ethical revival, vanquishing the "lies" of totalitarianism with civil society's "truth," failed. The 1989 revolutions expressed the opposition between "official" and "extraparliamentary" politics that was so characteristic of the European Left after 1968. The "Forums" also recalled the tension of "party" and "social movement" that was increasingly central to the Western Left after the 1970s. The intense moment of the revolution as an immediate event was an extraordinary laboratory of popular democratic initiative—especially in the massed insurgencies of Czechoslovakia and the GDR but also in the popular ferment of the negotiated transitions as well, and in every small and everyday statement of rebellion and dignity across the region. Both existentially, in the defining dramas of individual lives, and mythologically, in the collective memory of peoples, the 1989 revolutions profoundly affected the future of democratic values. Post-Communist polities were founded in courageous acts of collective motion, in languages of inclusion, reason, nonviolence, pluralism, and democracy. These were all values the Left could claim.

MAKING THE MARKET

Post-Communist governments shared a neoliberal belief in marketizing. After three decades of misfired economic reform, many Communists now agreed.[59] This was a painful dilemma for the Left. Control of the economy via central planning and public ownership, regulation of the labor market, and distribution of the product was axiomatic for socialists. Political economy was the starting point of socialist thought. Separating politics from economics and conceding that good economics and the democratic interest might clash, was hard. But going further, to seeing economic inequalities—"the market" in the neoliberal sense—as functional for democracy, was always beyond the line. Private property, the market, capitalism—these were what socialists wanted to overturn. Socialist readiness to embrace the market, not in some Keynesian version of the mixed economy but in a more absolute sense, was a profound change. It became the common ground of Eastern European reform.

The special case of a "big bang" was the former GDR, where German unification totally dismantled the old state-run economy. This was done through the *Treuhandanstalt,* created to manage the privatizing of East German enterprises. Smaller companies were sold off in a year, the rest by 1995. Huge investment went to rebuilding the infrastructure. But while massive transfers also came from unemployment relief and other social payments, the main effect in East German industry was destruction. The east became Germany's backward hinterland, with the typical features of a colonized region. Civil servants, administrators, and professions came from the west; skills, qualifications, and youth deserted the east. Carpetbaggers descended, and assets were stripped. The former GDR's welfare state was dismantled, with disastrous results for women. By 1992, 1.2 million east Germans were unemployed, with another 2 million on short hours. In October 1998, joblessness remained 1.2 million, or 16.3 percent of the workforce, double that of the west.[60]

Otherwise, the two cases of "Shock Therapy" were Poland and Czechoslovakia. The Polish finance minister, Leszek Balcerowicz, imposed the market, freeing prices to promote immediate privatization. This succeeded in securing credits from the West. But the result for jobs and living standards was a disaster. Moreover, if banking, commerce, and small business privatized successfully and consumption conspicuously thrived, industry per se barely changed. By 1993, organized labor had also applied the brakes: a pact brought government, employers, and unions to the table, and under a new left-wing government, Tripartite Commissions began slowing transition down. In Czechoslovakia, Finance Minister Václav Klaus was unequivocal: "We want to construct an ideological turnpike, not travel the winding roads from one system to another."[61] The economy was brutally restructured. Laws were passed backing foreign capital, privatizing industry and land, gutting the tax system, rationalizing welfare, and balancing the budget. As in Poland, a voucher plan was adopted giving citizens investment shares, conveying the ideological unity of capitalism and democracy. The Czech transition to capitalism was a boom. But again, social results were dire, and the momentum didn't last. By 1998, a Social Democratic government was elected in response.

In the euphoria of escaping from Stalinism, this neoliberal triumphalism overwhelmed the ideals of democracy. Blasting a path for capitalism was fully as disordering as the earlier establishment of Soviet-type economies after 1947–48. This wasn't the "removal" of the state from economic life but systematic use of the state for radically transformative ends. It was a massive project of "social engineering," replacing "regimes of strong economic and social protection" with regimes exposed to the West's superior economies, with "an extreme form of open door for products and capital, including hot, short-term money flows."[62] The EU governments had no interest in democracy per se, moreover, but used all their fiscal leverage for gaining access to Eastern European markets on favorable terms. The IMF and the EU dictated the form of transition: dismantling the welfare state, selling off the public sector, deregulating the economy.[63] New kinds of states were being founded—ones where fewer socioeconomic protections were possible than capitalist states of the West already possessed. This was less the transition to democracy than the region's brutal subjection to the global capitalist system.

It was most complete in the ex-GDR. In Poland and Czechoslovakia, Balcerowicz and Klaus envisaged the same result. By 1996, IMF leverage had equally crude effects in Bulgaria. Western pressure undermined projections of a revised social contract based on distributive justice, social citizenship, and the welfare state. Alternatives to radical marketization were present, recalling the models of mixed economy explored by Gorbachev and some Communist reformers. Such ideas were still functioning in parts of Western Europe too, despite the dominant neoliberalism of the 1980s; Scandinavia, West Germany, the Netherlands, Austria, even France come to mind. They were presaged in Solidarity's Program of October 1981, reiterated in its negotiating "Positions" for the Roundtable. They also appeared in Czechoslovakia in 1989–90, echoed by returning Left governments in Poland (September 1993) and Hungary (May 1994) and more complexly in Bulgaria and Romania. These were strategies of nationally protected capitalism, with modified welfare states and practical corporatisms based on post-Communist trade unions.

Communist reformers in Hungary and Poland envisaged exactly such a future once democracy was introduced, aspiring to become the Left in the emerging capitalist polities of the region. Imre Poszgay thought like this, as did the Polish party secretary, Mieczyslaw Rakowski. The CPs accordingly reinvented themselves in this image after 1989. Once their "leading role" in the constitutions was removed and pluralism introduced, they took new names as social democratic parties, mirroring the transformations undertaken by the PCI and other Communist parties in the west. (See table 25.1).

TABLE 25.1 Post-Communist Parties, 1989–1998

CP	Refounding	New Party	Peak Vote
Hungary (MSzMP)	Sept. 1989	Hungarian Socialist Party (HSP)	33.0 (5/1994)
Poland (PZPR)	Feb. 1990	Social Democrats of the Polish Republic (SDPR)	20.0 (9/1993)
GDR (SED)	Feb. 1990	Party of the Democratic Left (PDS)	20.0 (10/1994)
Yugoslavia (LCY)	Feb. 1990	[Dissolved]	
Bulgaria (BCP)	April 1990	Bulgarian Socialist Party (BSP)	47.0 (6/1990)
Slovakia (KSC)	1990	Party of the Democratic Left (PDL)	14.4 (6/1992)
Albania (PLA)	June 1991	Albanian Socalist Party (SPA)	26.0 (3/1992)
Romania (RCP, NSF)	July 1993	Party of Romanian Social Democrats (PSDR)	22.0 (11/1996)
[Czech][KSC]	[———]	[Continuing Communist Party]	[14.3] [6/1992]
Czech	Dec. 1989	Social Democratic Party (CSSD)	32.3 (6/1998)
Slovakia	Dec. 1989	Social Democratic Party (SDSS)	6.0 (6/1992)

What did these new parties stand for? They were supported partly by ex–civil servants, pensioners, and everyone for whom Communism's end spelled loss of livelihood or the collapse of a social world. One-eighth of the Bulgarian population—or one-sixth of adults and a quarter of households—had been Communist. Many others suffered by marketization, with plant closings, deindustrialization, and job loss on a mass scale. Moreover, before 1989 ruling CPs had retained substantial popular acceptance, recording approval ratings of 25–30 percent in opinion polls in Poland, Hungary, and the GDR. The strong electoral showing of ex-Communist Lefts soon after 1989 was in this sense a recovery to those prerevolutionary levels of support.[64] Ex-Communist unions also kept strength in the 1990s. In Poland, they far surpassed Solidarity, with 4.5 million members as against 2.3 million in 1995, a pattern extending across Eastern Europe.

The new parties' democratic credentials were ambiguous. Suspicions of opportunism and bad faith, of Stalinist deep structures, were understandable. Parties with such records, filled with time-servers and ex-functionaries, plus legions of informers and ex–secret police, had huge public convincing to do. Some CPs made few concessions to the post-Communist era. The KSC's Slovak successor took a clear social democratic turn, but the CP of Bohemia and Moravia, organized electorally as the Left Bloc, did not. Successive transmutations of the Romanian CP changed its policies more than its political culture. Yet all the ex-CPs followed the democratic rules. With the exception of the Czech, they all redescribed themselves as social democratic, identifying with the Socialist International's Stockholm declaration of July 1989. Some transformations could be dramatic. The East German SED repudiated its past at the emergency Congress in December 1989, reemerging under Gregor Gysi as the Party of Democratic Socialism (PDS). Under Peter Weiss, the Slovak Party of the Democratic Left (PDL) took an especially strong social democratic course.

This "social-democratizing" of the CPs preempted the space for freshly created social democratic parties—apart from the Czech Republic, where the Social Democrats surpassed the CP in 1996 elections, before coming to power in 1998. Elsewhere, ex-Communist parties were back in government, with Poland (1993) and Hungary (1994) joining Bulgaria and Romania.[65]

How far such parties converged with post-Communist Lefts in the West, in a belated "Euro-post-Communism," remained to be seen. The Polish and Hungarian parties had more in common with western Europe's centrist social democratic parties than with the former CP in Italy or the Scandinavian Left-Socialist parties. Moreover, eastern ecoradicals and other new social movements often found a home with the most anti-Communist of the democratic forces in the east, especially in Hungary, Bulgaria, and Czechoslovakia.[66] The mainly eastern-based PDS in Germany was a kind of hybrid, aspiring to become a bridge between the salvageable legacies of the Communist era and an emergent progressivism in the West, adopting much of the program typical of Green parties and Scandinavian Left-Socialists, while still being rejected by the Greens and the SPD in Germany itself.[67] Otherwise, the Eastern ex-Communist parties cleaved to a modified form of social democracy that was all but abandoned in the West, defending versions of national Keynesianism and resisting the wholesale erosion of welfare states.

This was potentially their best hope. By the mid-1990s many citizens of the new democracies were expressing greater skepticism about the material benefits of marketization and its redemptive effects. The more utopian fervor of the immediate transition had certainly gone. Broad constituencies of the disadvantaged, the palpably damaged, the discarded, and the left-behind were waiting for a well-organized protest party to represent them, and the vestigial socialism of the new post-Communist parties still fitted them for this purpose. Directly hit by the dismantling of the old welfare systems and extruded from the new labor markets in disproportionately huge numbers, while facing new conflicts around reproductive rights, women formed an especially broad reservoir of disaffection. The post-1989 climate was notoriously inhospitable to feminism per se. The hollowness of the old CP rhetorics combined with the intrusiveness of pre-1989 family policies to delegitimize any advocacy of specifically women's politics, while "feminist" claims were contemptuously disparaged as Western self-indulgence irrelevant to the region. Yet a series of issues directly affecting women—restrictive abortion laws, high unemployment and the feminization of poverty, maternal and child welfare, domestic violence, and discrimination in the professions—were potentially available to an emergent social democratic agenda.[68]

In this sense, the scope for a social-democratized post-Communist Left in eastern Europe rested less on the conscious survival or adaptation of the old Communist traditions than on the continuing efficacy of the social practices and expectations shaped by the long histories of Communist political culture. These sometimes connected, however obliquely, with the deliberately promulgated official values before 1989, as in many aspects of collectivism and the public good or the social centrality of the workplace or the methods of political mobilization, but often they came from less consciously managed histories, accumulating behind the backs of the old party-state machine. That was true of the mundane—of everyday social exchanges in the informal economy, at work, or in family life—and of the grandiose, in the definitions of cultural value and the imagery of "the nation."[69] In a narrower self-interested sense, the evident continuities of identification and personnel gave the reinvented CPs a ready-made place in the post-1989 polities. But their broadening electoral support during the 1990s suggested that they had more to build on than the greying resentments of pensioners, displaced functionaries, and ideological diehards.

Fifty years of "actually existing socialism" had left lasting imprints on the region's societies. Given eastern Europe's earlier histories of dictatorship and authoritarianism, including virulent indigenous fascisms, for example, post-1945 social change had thoroughly disorganized the institutional, cultural, and socioeconomic bases for straightforward revival of the traditional radical Right. Despite many fears, the post-1989 ethnoreligious nationalist parties never graduated into serious antidemocratic threats, with the special exception of Serbia and Croatia in former Yugoslavia. If "real socialism" laid down anything lasting in the political cultures of eastern Europe, it was a complex of powerful popular expectations about the state's responsibilities for society. A guaranteed basic income, free and equal access to education, cheap and accessible services, protections for jobs, the strength of the welfare state—these issues described the political space where post-Communist Lefts might grow.[70]

ENDINGS AND BEGINNINGS

Was Communist reform foredoomed to fail? In 1968, Brezhnevites denounced any opening to democracy as counterrevolution—an unstoppable slide to socialism's dismantlement, the thin end of a wedge, the breach in the dyke. Gorbachev's experience in 1985–91, the fate of Polish and Hungarian Communist reformers, and the marginalizing of the GDR's civic opposition suggest they may have been right. Was Stalinism—as the command economy and single-party rule—the only way of keeping Eastern Europe socialist? Were the claims of CP conservatives borne out, that pluralism and democracy meant inevitable restoration of capitalism, by destabilizing the Soviet-type systems? Were Stalinists and anti-Communists both correct, equating democracy with capitalism and the CP's political monopoly with the state-socialist economy? Were they right all along, vindicated by Communism's collapse and the headlong drive to the market?

In some crude realist sense, the answer was yes. The state-socialist regimes of the USSR and post-1945 Eastern Europe had gone. The era of the Bolshevik revolution turned out to be a finite period. But "real socialism" recorded real achievements to its credit, given the economic and political devastations wrought during the Second World War and the preceding histories of backwardness and dictatorship, because after fascism's brutalizing of civil society the alternative to Communist dominance in Eastern Europe had not been liberal democracy but violent and divisive authoritarian rule. After the appalling oppressions of Stalinism proper in 1948–53, Eastern Europe also had its periods of stability and improvement, just as the USSR moved forward under Khrushchev. It was the modified Stalinism of the Brezhnev era, the "years of stagnation," that destroyed the options. The Italian Communists declared the Bolshevik era closed with the 1981 imposition of martial law in Poland. But by then, Communist government's surviving legitimacy had eroded to a meager and reduced trace of the social contract, held together by popular cynicism and pragmatic commitment to making it through rather than any positive consensus of loyalty and belief. The credible turning point was 1968. In the Prague Spring, a dynamic package of pluralism, democratization, and mixed economy retained some chance, given the prevailing international situation and such ideas' strength in Western Europe, as the postwar prosperity experienced its final ebullient phase.

But by 1985, the climate was exceptionally unpromising for any mixed solution or "third way." Gorbachev was trying to convert the Soviet economy into a mixed model and the CPSU into a social democratic party precisely when such ideas were weakest in the West—capitalism was in difficulties, social democracy in retreat and disarray. Under the impact of Reaganomics and Thatcherism, the postwar settlement was dismantled. Keynesianism became anathema, viewed as the source of contemporary disorder, self-evidently out of time. Neoliberal economics provided the new hegemony, the primacy of the market the new totalizing frame, an all-purpose social good. There was no room for strong public sector economics or even welfare states. Socialism itself was a bad word, not least because of earlier Soviet behavior.

Holding a broad reforming coalition together, a progressive bloc of party and society, was too late in the day. It might have happened in 1968, when the Prague Spring inspired such hopes. In the 1960s, post-Stalinist improvements were coming to fruition, the long boom was at its global peak, and social democratic ideals of mixed economy were ascendant. But in the 1980s, Gorbachev couldn't carry a broad enough section of the CPSU along. Fashioning larger alliances in the newly liberated public sphere also proved elusive, because radicals bolted for political independence, incited by Yeltsin's destructive grandstanding and self-serving democratic advocacy. Moreover, the United States was on the rebound after the defensiveness and international weakness of the 1970s, buoyantly and aggressively posing neoliberalism as the counteroption, in fact *the* option, if the West's support was to be won. The stakes for the reform course were set brutally high. Whether in Kohl's offer of German unification to the population of the GDR, in the treatments of "shock therapy" offered to newly elected governments of eastern Europe, or in the polarized alternatives in the USSR in 1990–91, large majorities in post-Communist societies found this bargain good enough.

New Social

Movements

Politics Out of Doors

IN EUROPE, THE insurrectionary type of revolutionary politics was bound in time. Before 1914, with the Paris Commune as a guide, the revolutionary crisis was still imagined as a popular uprising, a pitched battle for the state amid the sudden collapse of the system. When things fell apart, barricades would still be needed. The revolutionary turbulence of 1917–23 seemed to vindicate this belief, making the storming of the Winter Palace into the Bolshevik revolution's emblematic event. But thereafter, insurgencies became rare. There was one case of popular insurrection under late capitalism, namely France in 1968, where liberal democracy was brought to a halt. And the revolutions of 1989 produced systemic change on a transnational scale. But otherwise, the insurrectionary fantasy—of a massed uprising, paralyzing government and violently seizing power—largely disappeared.

This hasn't prevented minorities from chasing insurrectionary dreams. After the disappointments of 1968, some student radicals recreated the Leninist model in the form of small and hyperdisciplined revolutionary sects, rejecting participatory ideals for this panacea of the party. For a decade, ultraleft sectarianism consumed many activists, especially in larger polities like France, West Germany, and Britain, where established Left parties dogmatically refused the new radicalisms legitimacy. In 1968–74, for example, many West German activists joined the SPD, doubling membership of its Young Socialists to three hundred thousand and capturing the latter's 1969 Congress with an anticapitalist program of grassroots mobilization. Yet by 1974, the parent party had reimposed its control, and the goal of moving the SPD leftward was blocked. Otherwise, the West German APO fragmented into an absurdly proliferating mosaic of mainly Maoist groups, which seldom managed aggregate memberships of more than a few thousand.[1] This ultraleft milieu persisted until the broader coalescence of the Greens in 1978–79.

Sectarian militancy was thus little more than a noisy sideshow, sometimes attracting broader support through industrial struggles or community campaigns. In Britain and France, it was Trotskyism that provided the main sectarian energy.[2] The largest British sect, International Socialism, built a strong National Rank-and-File Movement with 15 union newspapers by 1974, leading a Right to Work campaign and launching the Anti-Nazi League against the racist National Front in 1976. Other Trotskyists preferred "entrism," the strategy of building influence in the Labour Party behind the cover of a journal: the Militant Tendency successfully controlled the Labour Young Socialists and certain previously decayed city branches, notably in Liverpool, where Labour regained the city council after 11 years in 1983.[3] As a result, Militant became subject in the 1980s to sustained party and wider public attack, vilified by Labour's leader Neil Kinnock as "a maggot in the body of the Labour Party" and ultimately expelled.[4]

In both countries, 1968ers gradually found their way back to the main Left parties. During 1974–78, this was eased by the PCF's Eurocommunist turn, while Mitterrand's revived Socialist Party (PS) ignited great optimism too. Mitterrand coopted the non-Leninist Unified Socialist Party, which stood for one of the prime ideas of 1968, autogestion, or self-management, and made its spokesman Michel Rocard into a leading PS personality.[5] In Britain, younger radicals also joined the Labour Party during the 1970s and struggled to shift a deeply resistant party leftward, first following the industrial militancy of 1970–74 and then after the 1979 election defeat. The CPGB likewise recruited 1968ers, who then cultivated the party's Eurocommunist line.[6]

The generation gap proved more extreme in Italy, where the post-1968 profusion of Leninist party building created a hybrid milieu of an ultraleft and an alternative scene rivaling that in West Germany. The largest Italian revolutionary group, *Lotta Continua,* formed in 1968–69, claimed 30,000 members by 1971 and fought the 1976 elections in coalition with other radical groups before disbanding in response to the dismal results (only 1.5 percent of the vote). The extreme Left regrouped into Proletarian Democracy, but it too failed to win more than 2.0 percent in national elections between 1979 and 1987. Despite the Italian extreme Left's greater popularity—Lotta Continua and Proletarian Democracy were far stronger than any of the new post-1968 parties in West Germany, France, or Britain—there seemed no viable space left of the PCI. Symbolically, the *Il Manifesto* group of Rossana Rossanda, Lucio Magri, and Luciana Castellina, who had broken with the PCI in 1969 over New Left issues of democracy, rejoined it in 1984.[7]

Finally, deformed versions of traditional revolutionary politics marred the 1970s in the form of clandestine armed struggle—or "terrorism," as it became known. The Italian Red Brigades and the West German Red Army Fraction saw their violence—bombings, kidnapings, assassinations, hijackings—as exemplary acts aimed at heightening social polarization as a basis for general working-class revolt. As such, the strategy proved entirely disastrous, only strengthening the state's repressive powers and sharpening the antirevolutionary backlash. After the double climax of the Aldo Moro kidnaping in the spring of 1978 and the analogous Schleyer killing in the "German Autumn" of 1977, both national movements petered out.[8] Elsewhere in Europe, terrorism mattered much less, with the special exceptions of the I.R.A in Northern Ireland and Basque nationalism in Spain. For instance, the British Angry Brigade set off several bombs in 1970–71 before being caught, but this was an isolated action of anarchist and Situationist inspiration.[9]

AUTONOMISTS AND THE ALTERNATIVE SCENE

Terrorism presupposed extremes of alienation, where people lost respect for the system. This went furthest in big cities with masses of younger people marginal to mainstream society—with higher educational qualifications yet displaced from career paths, partially employed, stylistically rebellious, and living and working in distinctive collective arrangements and quarters, often with bohemian or multicultural links, like the Hafenstrasse in Hamburg's St. Pauli or Kreuzberg in West Berlin, with its 40,000-strong alternative scene, 40,000 Turks, and 50,000 "normals" in 1989. Cooperative living and alternative scenes went with squatting—illegal occupations of empty buildings. These "liberated zones" flouted respectable society via style, music, drugs, sex, and indifference to rules of property.[10]

These subcultures presupposed the countercultural militancies of 1968. They preferred subverting politics to its constructive renewal. The Metropolitan Indians' Manifesto of 1 March 1977 in Italy demanded squats of all empty buildings to create alternatives to the family, free drugs, destruction of zoos, destruction of patriotic monuments, destruction of youth prisons, and the "historical and moral reevaluation of the dinosaur Archeopterix, unfairly constructed as an ogre."[11] This stance, for all its irony, encouraged nihilistic displays of public disrespect—a profaning of democratic values. It produced violence, not just against police but against unions and other Left organizations. Pitched battles in PCI-governed Bologna and the barracking of Luciano Lama in occupied Rome University exposed a savage gulf between Communists and the youth revolt.[12]

Similar battles involved the SPD in West Berlin and Hamburg. Progressive cities elsewhere fared no better. In the 1980s, the Dutch *kraakers*, whose squats dated from 1968, resisted long siege warfare in Amsterdam before succumbing to landlord and police assaults. In Copenhagen, a self-governing commune on Christiania Island secured official toleration, while in the city the Occupation Brigade were active from 1981, seizing buildings and disappearing just ahead of the police, most spectacularly in the guerilla seizure of Ryesgade neighborhood in September 1986. In Ryesgade, support services were organized for "normal" inhabitants, barricades were defended, the free radio network mobilized wider support, and food, blankets and other supplies were delivered by supporters from the outside. Nine days later, as the army prepared to attack, the media arrived for a press conference to find the Brigade had flown. The political thrust of these actions was clear: the targeted buildings were owned by multinationals involved in arms trade and South African investments.[13]

Activity was highly organized, but on the anticentralist and participatory lines of 1968. The Kreuzberg squatters were represented by the Squatters' Council, linked to the Autonomist Plenary, modeled on those in Hamburg. Inspiration was transnational, flowing north from Italy in 1977 and through Zurich, where demands for an autonomist youth center exploded in 1980–82, to Amsterdam, West German cities, Copenhagen, and Britain. Antinuclear actions, wider ecological protests, and the Peace Movement paralleled these squatters' movements. The political forms—direct-action militancy, no permanent officials, democracy by general assembly—came from 1968.[14]

PARTIES AND MOVEMENTS: A DIFFERENT POLITICAL SPACE

How should we put this together—squatters, alternatives, autonomists, Metropolitan Indians, Marxists, and wider movements surrounding the West German Greens, including ecologists, antinuclear protesters, peace campaigners, and the feminists common to them all? They came from the polity's grassroots. They involved a politics of refusal, showing at best ambivalence to the parliamentary system. They faced mainstream Lefts that seemed exhausted, despite an ability to continue winning elections—a Eurocommunism (Italy, France, Spain) that failed to break through; a sclerotic social democracy (West Germany, the Low Countries, Britain) stuck in its accommodations to capitalism, dogmatically dismissing the new left; and a technocratic socialism (France, Spain) shedding all relation to unions or movement cultures of the working class.

Established parties were melting away, and even where socialist parties kept support, they became a different kind of party—drastically losing active members and no longer able to rely on traditional "solidarity communities" among a shrinking working class. Instead, they were busily remaking themselves into exclusively electoral machines.[15] And beyond them emerged "new social movements"—feminisms, ecology, peace, Third World solidarities, gay-lesbian rights, and antiracism, as well as squatting and the broader alternative scenes. While most socialist parties ignored this extraparliamentary arena, these new movements composed an expanding political space. Transnationally, peace movements had the largest scale, loosely coordinated through European Nuclear Disarmament (END) launched in London on 28 April 1980, which also pioneered cooperation "from below" across Europe's two blocs. At the climax on 22–23 October 1983, a million West Germans rallied against the missiles; between 500,000 and a million in Rome; 250,000 in London; 400,000 in Brussels; 100,000 in Madrid; followed by 550,000 in The Hague and 40,000 in Bern. The West German Greens translated this into electoral success.[16]

Elsewhere, moves into national politics varied. Three British feminists, Sheila Rowbotham, Lynne Segal, and Hilary Wainwright, published *Beyond the Fragments* in 1978, based on talks to a Socialist Unity Symposium and Socialist Centers in Newcastle and Islington. They presented "the women's movement as an example of new ways of organizing, independent of the Labour Party and suspicious of self-defined vanguards."[17] They sparked a chain of meetings, including a conference in Leeds. Then, like other 1968ers, *Beyond the Fragments*' authors found their way to the Labour Party. When in 1981 Labour captured the Greater London Council (GLC) on a radical program, Wainwright joined an Economic Policy Group and the Popular Planning Unit, where Rowbotham also worked.[18] With Labour out of office nationally, local government became a key site. If Labour lost four hundred thousand paper members in 1975–81, it was acquiring a new activist cohort, a missing generation—supporters from the early 1960s, who left, joined community action or the sects, and returned in the late 1970s.[19]

Such activists appealed outside the old class-political framework. For the GLC leader Ken Livingstone, Labour had to go beyond "the organized working class" to "articulate the needs of the minorities and the dispossessed" and "single-issue groups" as well, because people no longer saw themselves in the "broad class concepts" of "thirty years ago." *London Labour Briefing*, started by Livingstone's circle in 1980, recalled Women's Liberation in the 1970s, which had joined feminism to local activisms around housing and rents, public transport, welfare rights, recreational facilities, childcare, adult and further education, cultural and arts activity, and the plethora of single-issue campaigns from Northern Ireland and antiapartheid to Vietnam and other Third World solidarities. The GLC's agenda in 1981–86 paralleled that of the German Greens but with the resources and problems of a huge metropolitan region. Its policies—cheap fares for public transit, creative development strategies for mass unemployment—captured popular sympathies, while setting a collision course with Thatcher's Conservative government. It welcomed inflammatory causes, including Irish Republicanism and gay-lesbian rights. It promoted a new Left coalition based on "skilled and unskilled workers, unemployed young and old, women, black people, as well as the sexually oppressed minorities."[20]

This urban left subcontracted with the grassroots, directing funding to "small, relatively informal, community groups who were able to develop projects too politically controversial for councils themselves to engage in."[21] This was a decisive breakthrough. It was helped by Labour's crushing local election defeats in 1967–68 and subsequent corruption scandals, which dislodged many self-perpetuating oligarchies linked to union machines whose enmity against activists was entrenched by the Cold War.[22] When Labour began recapturing local government in 1971, its political profile was already different. In 1983, 20 of Manchester's 22 Left councillors were aged 30–45, having joined the party in the mid-1970s. On expulsion from Labour for refusing to accept spending cuts in 1980, they built alliances beyond traditional frameworks with feminists, gays, antiracists, housing campaigns, community centers, and public sector unions, returning to win the council in 1984.[23] The culture shift was extreme: "Councillors in jump suits and jeans; clenched fist salutes in the council chamber; the singing (and flying) of the Red Flag; employees wearing CND badges; office walls decorated with political posters and cartoons; disdain for many established practices and procedures."[24] "At the first meeting of the Labour group," the GLC's head administrator remembered, "there was a baby and cans of coke. Senior officers found it a great upheaval."[25]

THE BRITISH LABOUR PARTY: LEFT IN THE LURCH

But if the urban left and the GLC captured a sense of opportunity, the national Labour Party reflected chances missed. Labour's Left acquired a tribune of the people in Tony Benn.[26] His *New Politics: A Socialist Reconnaissance* (1970) declared politics more than "the marking of a ballot paper with a single cross every five years." He contrasted Labour's governing debacle with rising extraparliamentary activism—"community associations, amenity groups, shop stewards' movements, consumer societies, educational campaigns, organizations to help the old, the homeless, the sick, the poor or under-developed societies, militant communal organizations, student power, noise abatement societies." Benn set out to bridge the gap between Parliament and the extraparliamentary arena, intensifying his efforts after 1970.[27]

Benn was "hoping to start a great new debate within our movement."[28] He rode the militancy of 1970–74, determined to prevent new betrayals in which Labour governments ignored the party's wishes. His supporters spearheaded pressure for Labour's constitutional reform via the Campaign for Labour Party Democracy (CLPD) and the Labour Coordinating Committee (LCC). Where CLPD operated inside the party, LCC addressed Left groups more widely, from the National Council for Civil Liberties, Amnesty, Child Poverty Action, and Shelter to the Socialist Education Association, Counter Information Services, and Friends of the Earth. After the 1979 election defeat, mandatory reselection of MPs was achieved, establishing the principle of accountability. Then the Special Party Conference at Wembley in January 1981 passed new rules for electing the leader by membership, unions, and parliamentary party rather than by the last-named alone. Michael Foot, the parliamentary party's longstanding radical voice, had already succeeded James Callaghan as leader in November 1980. The left's position seemed stronger than ever before.[29]

Yet by 1982 it was in retreat and by 1987 utterly beaten. In protest against Wembley, the "Gang of Four"—Shirley Williams, William Rodgers, David Owen, and Roy Jenkins—launched a new Social Democratic Party (SDP) on 25 January 1981, taking 29 Labour MPs with them.[30] Left and right traded bitter accusations of splitting the party.[31] The right vilified Benn for contesting the deputy leadership, and after his defeat in October 1981 by less than a single percent, the Foot-Healey leadership counterattacked ruthlessly, removing Benn and his allies from their committees. The 1983 elections, stamped by the patriotism of the Falklands-Malvinas War, proved a nightmare, as Labour crashed to its worst defeat since 1935.[32]

This fiasco hastened the realignment. Under a new leader, Neil Kinnock, the party was drastically restructured. The National Executive's control of policy was dismantled, supplanted by the Campaigns and Communications Directorate, which replaced democracy with market research. Kinnock answered another election defeat in 1987 with a policy review, and when the 1989 Conference approved the results, the left's policies had all gone— nationalization and a strong public sector, union corporatism, unilateral nuclear disarmament, opposition to the EEC, and the guiding thread of democratizing the party. Kinnock bequeathed a party more united, more centrist, less distinctively socialist, and wholly demobilized.

This story showed nothing better than the tenacity of right-wing and centrist social democrats in resisting change. For Benn, democracy required more than simply changing Labour's Constitution: "If democracy is based on a moral claim to equality, the issues opened up are as wide as life itself," he argued, and included women's equality, nuclear energy, gay liberation, racial discrimination, immigration, youth culture, pensioners' rights, and more.[33] But even under left-wing influence, Labour's 1983 Manifesto had barely integrated these issues with the Alternative Economic Strategy. The latter invoked a Keynesianism already under fatal attack, in a national-economic framework superseded by global interdependence and the EEC. It said little about the changing nature of work and was innocent of feminist ideas on unequal pay, part-time working, or domestic labor. The Manifesto adopted new social issues without new social movements. Instead, it cobbled together the old Left goals least appealing to a broader electorate— like nationalization, union power, anti-Europe, and unilateral disarmament—with a ragtag mixture of new causes conjuring respectable England's worst nightmares, from Irish Republicanism and lesbian-gay rights to abolition of the House of Lords and antihunting. Issues of potentially broad appeal, like feminism, peace, or the environment, were squandered.

There were no thoughts about uniting the parliamentary party with extraparliamentary actions in a single movement. And this was precisely the strength of Livingstone's GLC and other Labour councils—their ability to lower the boundaries between party control and broader activism. The GLC's real popularity, after the defeat of the Fares Fair campaign in 1982, was perhaps unclear.[34] Its relations with community activists, particularly on the racial front, were often vexed. Local socialisms—in parts of London but especially in Liverpool, where Militant ruled—sometimes followed dogmatically class-centered approaches keeping other issues like gender, sexuality, and race away. But the possibilities were there, and the Labour left's national strategy passed them by.

LEFT FOR THE FUTURE?

Thus the space for new politics in the national polity remained unfilled. On the one hand, like most of its fellow socialist parties, the Labour Party remained stuck in a parliamentarist groove. On the other hand, the new activism, with its direct-action, participatory, and community-based practices, achieved uneven entry into the Left's political mainstream and sometimes stayed completely outside. This tension defined much of the potential for the left's renewal in the 1980s, and the urban Left's fusion of "class" with "identity" issues, at its most earnest and exuberant during Livingstone's reign at the GLC, brought this home especially well. Two other examples from Britain made the fronts dramatically clear: the confluence of feminism with the mass peace movement and the great miners' strike.

The Women's Peace Camp was founded at Greenham Common US airbase on 5 September 1981 by the Women for Life on Earth Peace March, who walked from Cardiff protesting the siting of cruise missiles. In February 1982, the Camp became women-only. It was maintained continuously until 1994, when the missiles were decommissioned.[35] The biggest Greenham actions were held annually on the anniversary of NATO's original decision to house the missiles there, including 35,000 protesters for "Embrace the Base" in December 1982 and 50,000 in 1983, together with repeated blockades and many symbolic protests. Invasions, courtroom actions, small-scale sabotage, and protests of all kinds occurred, including monitoring and harassment of cruise missile convoys. Above all, the Camp's permanence entailed constant inventiveness. This incorporated the legacies of 1968, declaring a new, distinctively feminist presence:

> Whether linking together 30,000 women to "embrace the base" or entering time after time, through the lethal-looking fence of the base, to

plant snowdrops, have a picnic, dance on the silos, occupy a sentry box or a traffic control tower, or paint peace signs on a US spy plane; whether tearing down mile after mile of fencing and padlocking the gates, dressing up as witches or taking two hours to walk 200 yards, women at Greenham have been able for years to mock at and disrupt the efficiency, security and routine of a key military installation of the most powerful country in the world.[36]

Separatist banning of men caused tensions with the general peace movement, and the ecological and spiritualist dimensions of Greenham philosophy made many in the Campaign for Nuclear Disarmament nervous, worrying about public reactions to the Peace Camp's misbehavior. The spectacle of an unruly and unfeminine women's collective, excluding men and often rejecting husbands, living roughly, celebrating lesbianism, and generally ignoring the rules, was an affront to "normal" society. But this transgression—the decision of so many women, grandmothers and school students, lesbians and straights, middle and working-class, professional and unemployed, to step unconscionably outside society—was precisely the point. Greenham women were unassimilable.

The second emblematic event, the miners' strike, called in March 1984 against the government's brutal reduction of the coal industry, was the longest and most violent industrial dispute in Britain since 1926. At its height, 10,000 pickets faced 4,000 police in full riot gear with truncheons and horses. A massive paramilitary operation deploying eight thousand police cordoned off the Nottinghamshire coalfield against pickets; roadblocks prevented Kent miners leaving for the north; and violence surrounded working mines. Hostility between militant areas hit by closures (Yorkshire, Scotland, Kent, South Wales) and richer coalfields opposing the strike (Notts) contrasted starkly with the unity of 1972–74. Aggressive policing intensified the violence, placing Yorkshire mining villages under the equivalent of martial law: 9,750 were arrested during the strike, of whom 7,874 were charged. The National Union of Mineworkers (NUM) failed to overcome the state's assaults, disapproval from Labour leaders and the TUC, and its own internal divisions. The strike lasted a full year, but 71,000 of 187,000 miners had returned to work, and it ended without a settlement.[37]

For the charismatic NUM president, Arthur Scargill, the miners expressed the unchanged centrality of the traditional working class for socialism, the classic labor movement in motion. Miners were class consciousness incarnate: heroic champions of the class struggle, defiant embodiments of working-class masculinity, overwhelming their opponents via their collective strength. The strike evoked equally classic images of working-class community in the mining villages' homogeneous solidarities. It was a protest against deindustrialization itself, defending a whole way of life against vandalism. It made an extraordinarily powerful class-political statement.

As such, it condensed the hopes of socialist traditionalists. Thatcherism had to be reversed: "We want to pave the way for an economic recovery, a general election, and the return of a Labour government."[38] Conversely, Thatcher intended to break the NUM. The new head of the Coal Board, Ian MacGregor, had a brief to close mines and weaken the union. For Mick McGahey, NUM's Communist vice-president, the political stakes were also clear: "In order to dismember the welfare state they had to break the trade union movement, and they needed to break the miners first." Rhetorically, unions were being demonized. Early in the strike, Thatcher declared: "In the Falklands, we had to fight the enemy without. Here the enemy is within, and it is more difficult to fight, and more dangerous to liberty."[39] Put like this, radicals on the Left had little choice but to support the strike.

But the strike lacked broader working-class enthusiasm. It came during union retreat, as the main unions shifted right, unemployment rose, and strikes became restricted under law. British Steel was savaged after a 1980 strike, under MacGregor's previous assignment. In 1984, the "Triple Alliance" of coal, steel, and rail failed to cohere, as did the broader workers' coalitions needed for mass picketing. Worst of all, the NUM itself was split: 20 percent of miners continued working, leading to the Union of Democratic Mineworkers, formed in Nottinghamshire by a 72 percent ballot, with 30,000 members. During the strike, neither TUC nor Labour gave official support. More generally, the labor movement's breadth was eroding. In 1979–83, Labour's electoral strength among trade unionists shrank from 51 to 39 percent, while unions lost popularity with the public.[40]

However, the strike inspired big solidarity along urban Britain's Left networks. Left councils gave moral support. Supporters were twinned to coalfields or individual mines, as in the Durham-Docklands Miners' Support Group, or the Cambridge Support Group, which sent six hundred pounds weekly to the Notts villages of Blidworth and Rainworth. A key bridge from the coalfields to the cities was Women Against Pit Closures, originating in Sheffield and Barnsley. From organizing kitchens to joining the picket lines, the women's movement developed a parallel organization connected to women's groups beyond the coalfields, including Greenham Women. The Sheffield group gathered food for local mines, produced a leaflet, and publicized itself via the Trades Council; it consisted of "local authority workers, unemployed, nurses, engineers, housewives, pensioners, students, bus drivers, and also the mining women from the villages."[41] In South Wales, such activity amounted to "an alternative welfare state" and helped sustain a wider political initiative, the Wales Congress in Support of Mining Communities.[42]

So the strike did produce a politics. "Mines Not Missiles" provided a common link to antinuclear campaigns. Ann Suddick, a clerical worker in the Durham Women's Support Group, made connections between Blyth Power Station and the pit closures, thence to Greenham Common, and finally to the global context of nuclear fuels; she organized a conference in

1986 called "Make the Links—Break the Chain," also involving anti-apartheid and peace groups.[43] The strike's cultural politics involved theater, agitprop, and regional film and video workshops.[44] The Cambridge Support Group's weekly meetings drew 15–50 people, "intellectuals and white-collar strata in general, together with people active in issue-politics, particularly feminism and the nuclear question." It worked through concerts, socials, house meetings, jumble sales, art sales, college collections, and concerted Saturday street collections. The Milton Keynes Support Group was based in the Unemployed Workers' Center, linked to the Sikh Society, the Afro-Caribbean Club, the Peace Group, and Ecology Party, and a membership of 150–200.[45] Multiculturalist support in the cities was especially striking among Afro-Caribbean, Cypriot, Asian, and Turkish groups. There were Lesbians and Gays Support the Miners groups in London, Southampton, Cardiff, Manchester, York, Edinburgh, and Glasgow. In December 1984, a national conference of 1,500 Support Groups was held in Camden Town Hall.

TWO LEFTS: PARLIAMENT AND PEOPLE

The British miners' strike dramatized the European Left's dilemmas more powerfully than any other event. It evoked precisely those traditions of class-political militancy now under erasure. Languages of socialism had always presupposed the collective agency of industrial workers, backed by broader community solidarities, in the ways the miners now asserted. A more powerful example of traditional class consciousness could hardly be imagined, but now the latter's relationship to socialist politics was becoming increasingly decoupled and disavowed.

Socialist parties had always mediated their accountability to the working class, whether viewed as the labor movement, an aggregation of interests, or a social abstraction. As a project of democracy, the Left's agenda was also larger than any class-based vision of socialism. Once socialist parties started accepting government responsibility, and certainly when they became governing parties, presenting themselves in parliaments and elections as voices of the nation, their relationship to the working class became displaced. Given the power of the changes since 1968–73—capitalist restructuring, with deindustrialization and massive class recomposition—socialist politics and traditional images of the industrial proletariat became ever more disjointed. The main axis of progressive politics changed, diminishing the centrality of labor movements and demanding that the Left's basic appeals be rethought. During the 1980s, socialist and Communist parties began disengaging more explicitly from class politics. The British miners' strike was only the most dramatic commentary on this process.

German Social Democrats pointed the way. A younger cohort around General Secretary Peter Glotz and Saarland Premier Oskar Lafontaine produced the Berlin Program in December 1989 after a five-year policy review. Internationally, this proposed a "common security" approach, plus a "federalized" EC and "social Europe." Qualitative growth was addressed by energy-saving, environmental protection, "clean" industries, humanizing the workplace, and a shorter working week. Arguments about gender equality, flexible employment, and role sharing marked feminism's arrival, although unions still balked. Glotz even suggested the slogan "Patriarchy Must Die."[46]

But rhetorically listing these new issues wasn't enough to recast the politics. It was one thing for Glotz to extend the agenda via discussion documents, reaching out to new social movements, translating Italian Communist texts, and even talking to feminists; it was another thing to change the SPD's operative language. Its 1987 election campaign remained boring and gray, treating the Greens as troublemakers rather than allies. New issues might be noticed as slogans and sound bites—common security, international economic justice, gender equality at work, rational technology, qualitative growth, quality of life, new forms of democracy based in the liveliness of civil society. The SPD might eventually convert these slogans into a winning strategy. But the quality of political action was also at stake—the empowerment of participation, the promise of 1968. That was what really lay behind the civic upsurge of the 1980s.[47]

This was the difference: between an additive approach to new identities and interests, grafting them onto established policies and constituencies, in a revamped "people's party" updating Godesberg for the 1990s and, on the other hand, imaginatively binding the latter into a new philosophy of the future, harnessing new social movements to the remaining socialist cultures and working-class solidarities of the old Left, in a new radical vision. The new social movements had a different kind of drive. They were not based in high-intensity membership parties like the socialist subcultures and solidarity communities of old. Parties in that traditional sense were in decline. Instead, the new activisms implied loose federations of the like-minded, through which autonomous citizens and local groups pooled their electoral hopes.

What did this splitting into party and movements mean? Left-wing parties' ability to generate activist identification, binding their members together with wider progressive networks, had gone. They became parliamentary operations. In the extraparliamentary world, on the other hand, vigorous social movements developed locally, unconnected to a national party, for in truth socialist parties were scared of extraparliamentary energy. Broad social movements formed without the backing of socialist parliamentarians—peace movements, abortion campaigns, West German anti-nuclear protests, Sicilian anti-Mafia campaigns, squatting in Copenhagen, Amsterdam, and West Germany, support actions for British miners, and so on. A national politician like Benn was exceptional in endorsing that activity. Communists were more open to it, although only the PCI matched socialist parties in weight, given the PCF's Stalinist decline. The countless neighborhood and city-based agitations of these years overlapped with the local socialist parties but rarely agitated their national parliamentary surface.

The model of the nationally organized socialist party and its affiliated union federation, so effective from the later nineteenth century to the 1960s, was at an end. For the first time since the rise of labor movements, the main impulse for democratic enlargement came from elsewhere—not only outside the socialist parties but often against them too. But if new social movements were potential sources of renewal, how in practice would this occur?

Chapter 27

The Center and the Margins

Decline or Renewal?

NEW SOCIAL MOVEMENTS grew from the wider sociocultural changes of the post-Fordist transition. From 1960 to 1985 professional, technical, and administrative categories at least doubled in Western Europe's workforce, attaining 13–18 percent in most countries and sometimes even more; and these new specialists in education, communications, health, and social services became disprotionately visible in the new movements. British CND drew heavily from the "welfare and creative professions," for example, as did the exceptionally broad peace movement in the Netherlands, where 3.8 million signed the People's Petition against the missiles in 1985, or a quarter of the entire population.[1]

"Post-industrial" economics rested on accumulation and management of information, so that social conflicts revolved increasingly around control and processing of knowledge, access to education, and accountability of bureaucratic power.[2] Post-Fordist economies retained plenty of conflict around social inequality, part-time employment, low pay, safety and health regulations, and job-related benefits, to be sure. But other issues also demanded public attention, concerning self-esteem and self-expression, aesthetic and intellectual satisfaction, identity and belonging, and quality of life. Such "post-materialist" values especially moved the generations coming of age in the 1960s and after. They inspired protests against risks and insecurities of social life, like the threat of nuclear war and the catastrophe of the environment. They encouraged desires for conservation, clean energy, gender equality, plural sexualities, multiculturalism, international understanding,

470

and free artistic and stylistic expression. Critiques of alienation were key, affirming values of control and empowerment, autonomy and individualism, self-actualization and choice.[3]

"Post-materialist values" reflected rising postwar standards of living, including the greater security provided by welfare states. Memories of hardships imprinted the older generations who had experienced postwar shortages and the hardships of war and the Depression, but those born later developed different images of cultural well-being. Not just a political interest in nuclear disarmament and ecology but also changing attitudes to work and leisure, childraising and marriage, sexuality and sexual orientation all correlated with the demographic transition. Generational conflicts appeared in this light too, as parents' hard-won achievements faced the ungrateful rebellions of children. Moreover, by 1980 the political elders were passing from the stage.

Born in 1913, a Liverpool docker's son with two railwayman brothers, for example, Jack Jones had been raised among trade unionists. He was a runner in the 1926 General Strike, educated in Labour colleges, and a Labour Party ward secretary at 16, suffused in cultures of socialism and solidarity. He fought in Spain, worked in the Coventry car industry during 1939–45, and rose through the movement to become TGWU general secretary and mainstay of Britain's trade union Broad Left. By the 1970s, he embodied the best mainstream version of the British Left's labor-centered progressivism, carrying its remaining hopes through his advocacy of the Social Contract. When he retired in 1977, however, an entire culture was coming to an end—and not just its continuities of class identification, the memories of poverty and struggle as well.[4]

These were the increasingly bifurcated circumstances facing European Lefts at the end of the twentieth century. Two distinct constellations of left-wing politics coexisted and were often angrily counterposed. On one side were the established cultures of labor movements, whose values and institutions were shaped by needs of diminishing relevance in the new post-Fordist capitalist societies coalescing since the 1960s. And on the other were the still emergent political cultures of these different formations just described, for which industrial collectivism could no longer be the central organizing principle but only a lesser component in much wider coalitions of interests and desires. Meshing these two constellations together in a common political project was not easy, particularly when the existing parties were so proudly wedded to the old practices and programs. To older generations, the new Left politics were often incomprehensible, and vice versa. But the Left's political efficacies, and with them the future resilience of democracy, depended crucially on bringing them together.

THE NEW POLITICS OF IDENTITY

By the 1980s, urban radicalism had settled around a grassroots repertoire of varied social causes, including "inadequate housing and urban services, rampant building speculation, the lack of community health clinics and day care centers, outdated hospitals, and inhuman prison conditions."[5] Second Wave feminism was active in a similar forest of local campaigns, while the politicized subcultures of alternative scenes further thickened this extra-parliamentary sphere. In aggregate, such contexts of localized activism might seem not so different from the labor movement's earlier twentieth-century coalitions of community-based progressive reform. Now, however, these local agitations lacked the coordinating center of a nationally organized party. Indeed, just as often they found themselves fighting against the local power bases of the old socialist parties, whose policies and practices had meanwhile congealed into the institutionalized vested interests that blocked progressive change. Moreover, the sites and methods of action were now different: consumer prosperity, communicative technologies, and mass-mediated public spheres afforded new resources, potentially democratizing access to the polity.

Not assimilable to class politics in any narrow sense, wider social issues had always been vital to socialist campaigning. But the focus on "identity" was now different. During the 1970s, silenced or marginalized populations began demanding recognition, either by asserting their full rights of citizenship or by claiming public personhood in authentic selves. Women's Liberation was followed by gay liberation and then by racial and ethnic groups, all seeking "to translate 'the personal is political' into everyday practice."[6] Such initiatives began outside the Left's established arenas. But after the initial explosions of self-recognition, local groups and individuals started finding their way to socialist parties, arriving via the urban politics of the 1980s.

Their outlook easily celebrated the sovereignty of particular selves, so that being a woman or gay or black became the principle of political organization, with exclusive claims over recognition. Radical feminisms affirmed a specifically women's culture, building separatist embankments around a space where truthful lives could be lived. Political lesbianism radicalized this separatism, complicating not only cooperation with left-wing men but even with heterosexual feminists. As critiques of sexual violence concentrated radical feminist energies in the late 1970s, setting the terms under which women were exhorted to join radical feminist campaigns, that divisiveness grew. In Britain, the National Women's Liberation Conferences ceased meeting after 1978. The first black women's conference met in London in 1979, beginning a fresh set of particularizing demands. After proposing the unity of all women, feminists experienced an angry proliferating of identities.

The hardest conflicts were around race. In the 1980s, greater space for black feminists in Britain was made via the GLC and London boroughs, but only painfully. Black women's interests were addressed by splitting the abortion movement, with a new Reproductive Rights Campaign in October 1983. Blackness itself experienced the dialectic of unity and fragmentation. In 1970s Britain, antiracist politics invented a black identity for all ex-colonial peoples of color—Caribbean, West and East African, Indian, Pakistani, Bangladeshi. This facilitated speaking back to racism, with institutional recognition in local Labour Parties and Labour local government. But it fixed differences around a central identity claim, the common circumstance of not being white. Blackness authorized one identity, usually also masculine, over others. But by the mid-1980s, Asian women asserted their distinct claims, and localized constructions of ethnicity became stronger, mobilizing not only differences of gender but also geography, religion, generation, and class. Blackness became pluralized.[7]

This was a different pluralism from the polite lobbying of pressure groups, which had brought the liberalizing reforms of the 1960s on homosexuality, abortion, censorship, and capital punishment. Now, pressure came at the grassroots, from new political actors—women, blacks, ethnic minorities, gays, and lesbians—thickening civil society with new collective organization. Given these new claims, it was pointless to invoke the great master categories of the past—"those great stable collectivities of class, race, gender, and nation" that had previously centered identities for politics. Identity had become something "more fragmented and incomplete, composed of multiple 'selves'... something with a history, 'produced,' in process." Politics now had "to address people through [their] multiple identities."[8]

Some of these claims inspired great fear and loathing among inhabitants of dominant cultures, particularly those identities affirmed by the new sexual politics. Cold War sexualities had been dangerous ground, the Left's uncharted territory, and same-sex relations provided the frontier that was most assiduously policed. Homosexuality was partially decriminalized in Britain in 1967, joining the Netherlands, Sweden, and Denmark, followed by West Germany (1969), Austria (1970), Finland (1971), and Norway (1973). But liberalization barely affected the underlying homophobia, against which civil rights groups like the British Campaign for Homosexual Equality, formed in 1969, had only cautious response. When 1968 broke open the continuum of conformity and repression, moreover, the new gay activists quickly polarized sensibilities. Older advocates of homosexual rights were appalled by "the vulgarity of frenetic faggots frolicking through the streets demonstrating defiance, bad taste, disregard for the susceptibilities of others, and adherence to the bogus and the base."[9]

Emboldened by the cultural transgressions of 1968 and inspired by New York's Stonewall rebellion of the summer of 1969, 19 students formed London's Gay Liberation Front (GLF) at the LSE on 13 October 1970, bursting into visibility with guerilla actions against everyday homophobia, or "zapping." Their example inspired the French *Front Homosexual Action Révolutionaire* of 1971 and the *Italian Frente Unitario Omosessuale Rivoluzionario Italiano* of 1971–72. West German Homosexual Action Groups also formed, while Dutch and Scandinavian activists joined existing homophile federations. All this was inseparable from 1968. The London GLF Manifesto declared a long list of oppressions headed by "family," followed by school, church, media, words, employment, law, physical violence, psychiatry, and self-oppression. It demanded "abolition of the family, so that the sexist, male supremacist system can no longer be nurtured there." It rejected the existing "gender-role system" and "compulsive monogomy," advocating consciousness raising groups and gay communes instead. It attacked "plastic gays who are obsessed with image and appearance." The GLF strategy was "changing society, rather than adapting to it. We understood the need for a cultural revolution."[10] Or as one French counterpart put it: "Our asshole is revolutionary."[11]

The GLF spread to Birmingham, Manchester, Leeds, Edinburgh, Bristol, and Cardiff but by 1974 was "torn apart by tensions between women and men, drag queens and machos, socialists and counterculturalists."[12] Women had seceded in February 1972, after the familiar frustrations of "being patronized and having to fight for any space."[13] But the GLF had already launched the future, in an increasingly dense subculture of organizations—the London Lesbian and Gay Switchboard; *Gay News;* the Gay Men's Press; Gay's the Word Bookshop; the First Out cafe collective; Gay Sweatshop and Bloolips in the theater; Icebreakers, a politicized counseling and befriending service, partly an offshoot of the Counter-Psychiatry Group; the Gay Marxist Group; the Gay Left collective; and so on. This legacy reemerged in Labour's urban Left in the 1980s. Yet, despite Benn's and Livingstone's support, the Labour Campaign for Lesbian and Gay Rights in 1982 met virulent homophobia surrounding Peter Tatchell's defeat in the Bermondsey by-election in 1983. While bridges were built via gay and lesbian support for the miners' strike, leading to equal rights resolutions at the Labour Party Conferences in 1985 and 1986, these were bridges to a Labour left in full-scale disarray.[14]

After media demonizing of the "loony left," Labour leaders were running scared: "What doesn't exist in the Labour Party is any of the social movement agenda of the '70s and '80s—that doesn't seem to have really influenced the party at a top level."[15] A conference aimed at overcoming this gap in November 1987 drew five hundred delegates but ended in factionalism. Then, in the campaign for equalizing the age of consent, which was anomalously high for homosexuals (21 as against 16), two initiatives arose: the Stonewall Group for parliamentary lobbying; and OutRage, focused on direct actions. Each involved activists from GLF days—Angela Mason, Stonewall's executive director; and Simon Watney, Peter Tatchell, and others at OutRage.[16]

In the post-1968 decade, gay and lesbian rights had entered the European Left's agenda. Antidiscrimination laws, including antidefamation provisions, were passed in Norway (1981), Denmark and Sweden (1987), and the Netherlands (1992), extending earlier equality legislation. Domestic partnership laws were passed in Denmark (1989), Norway (1993), Sweden (1994), and the Netherlands (1998). Proposals for gay and lesbian adoptions emerged in the Netherlands in 1998, where large majorities in surveys pronounced gays and lesbians good parents. Britain, West Germany, and Austria saw partial liberalizations, while discriminatory laws remained. In southern Europe, gay-lesbian rights entered Left programs, with French and Spanish Socialist governments decriminalizing homosexuality and passing equality laws. Gay candidates were elected to PCI city governments in Milan and Bologna; and the PCI had a gay organization from 1980, with 13,000 members by 1989. Throughout Eastern Europe, semiclandestine gay-lesbian groups formed during the 1980s, and after 1989–91 decriminalization was achieved in Russia, Ukraine, Estonia, Latvia, Lithuania, and all eastern European countries except Romania.[17]

In the 1980s, gay activism was heavily shaped by the crisis of HIV-AIDS. In Britain, the London Lesbian and Gay Switchboard pioneered public awareness, and 1970s activists helped initiate the Terrence Higgins Trust and the National AIDS Helpline, as well as Body Positive, Positive Theater, and other self-help forms. Like Stonewall and OutRage, AIDS activism centered around early GLF militants such as Simon Watney and Cloud Downey. The AIDS epidemic dramatized the dialectic of demonization and solidarity, at the same time empowering homophobic attacks and broadening the field of gay-friendly action. The epidemic sharpened visibility of the gay presence, while complicating the Left's ability to evade it.[18]

While profoundly implicated in work, unions, and the specifics of working-class life, lesbian-gay politics formed an "identity" movement distinct from class-centered old Left politics of the economy. This movement was indelibly marked by 1968. Internationalism was one strand, radiating from Gay Liberation Fronts in the United States and Britain to Western Europe and institutionalized in the Belgian-based International Lesbian and Gay Association, founded in 1979, with three hundred affiliates in 50 countries by 1995. The GLF methods also descended from 1968—small-scale, participatory, direct-action, movement rather than party based. So did the political stylistics—theatrical and spectacular, challenging the personal and the everyday. The GLF redefined the category of the political itself, via critiques of the family and sexism, politics of the body, and politicizing of sexuality. Like Women's Liberation, this movement sutured the personal and political, making sexuality the language of radicalism rather than its unmentionable other side. This was true not only of the young. The veteran anarcho-socialist and sexual philosopher Daniel Guérin brought his politics and gayness together only in the crucible of the May 1968 events.[19]

Lesbian-gay politics kept the radical edge of the misbehavior of 1968 alive, if even here critiques of the family became less common than expanding its definition to same-sex partnerships as well.[20] Like feminisms, gay and lesbian movements were the new social movements most unsettling to the mainstream Left, challenging the deepest assumptions of citizenship in the national culture by questioning the naturalness of the family form. Queer politics, with its attacks on heteronormative values as a dimension of social relations in general, picked up these threads of GLF radicalism in the 1990s.[21]

DO IT YOURSELF POLITICS (DIY)

West German extraparliamentary action, rooted in student revolts and Green activism, peaked during 1979–83 in the Peace Movement, antinuclear protests, and squatters' struggles. Britain's rhythm was similar: a climax of direct action in the miners' strike, the Peace Movement, and the urban riots of the early 1980s, linked to an earlier countercultural politics in the Rock Against Racism carnivals of 1977–78, punk rock, and the Free Festivals starting in 1971–74.[22] British direct action also resurged in the 1990s between the resistance to the Poll Tax and the Criminal Justice Act of 1994.[23] It embraced antiroad protests, animal rights blockades, and the cultural politics of the acid house/rave scene, northern warehouse dances, and free parties.

After the Labour left's defeat in the mid-1980s, this "Do-It-Yourself" politics (DiY) proceeded entirely independently, as successive Labour leaderships obviously preferred. Mass dance culture, with impromptu squatting of disused warehouses, sophisticated mobile sound systems, and elaborate communications, beginning around London in 1986–87, was the opposite of a politics legible to the mainstream Left. But the "Second Summer of Love" declared by ravers in 1988 began a cycle of cultural radicalism comparable to the Italian youth revolt of the late 1970s or the West German, Dutch, and Danish autonomisms of the 1980s. State repression, culminating in the 1994 Criminal Justice Act, also generated its own resistance, forging links with other direct actions.[24]

Clubs like Manchester's Haçienda and commercial underground raves were joined by the improvised spaces of provincial civil society. The depressed mid-Lancashire town of Blackburn had some 10,000 dancers in clubs and warehouse parties at their height, in a utopian fervor of collective pleasure and repeated battles with police. Extraordinary convoys raced the motorways to beat police to the nightly venue. On 22 July 1990, police violence climaxed at Gildersome near Leeds, when sound systems were smashed, records impounded, and 836 ravers arrested. Repression tamed the warehouse scene just as Allan Deaves, an ex-punk fresh from New York's arts and club scene, started an art and dance collective called ART

LAB in Preston in November 1994. The LAB became "a breeding ground of renegade art, and a launch pad for autonomous action."[25] The hedonistic compulsions of dance culture harbored acute avant-garde commitments, anger at the social wreckage of deindustrialized Lancashire, and alienation from mainstream politics.

Alienation became politicized by police overkill, itself fashioned in the repressive laboratory of the miners' strike. Another DiY site was the campaigning against highway construction in the antiroads movement, which attracted New Age travelers, broad if tense coalitions with local residents, and radical ecologists from Earth First![26] These protests invented new techniques, from ditch-digging, squatting the land, and chaining bodies to machinery to passive resistance and collective rituals and symbolics; they also produced the mystique of the "eco-warrior," a creed of nonviolent direct action, and the Dongas Tribe. One of the more exotic manifestations of the protest culture, the Dongas were "an amazing mixture of the wildly New Age . . . and the eminently and stubbornly practical," a type of "political paganism" consciously playing off history and myth, with invented rituals and language.[27] The M11 protests in East London brought ecomilitancy into the city in an urban encampment, with blockading and booby-trapping of the site in "a non-stop performance." From this came Reclaim the Streets (RTS), which mounted spectacular disruptions of London thoroughfares in Camden High Street in May 1995 and Upper Street Islington in August 1995, with banners, dancing, food, agitprop, and an inventive theater of activism.[28] Later protests added tree-sitting, tunnel-dwelling, hill forts, digging up and planting road surfaces, and so-called free states.

How does this relate to the Left? One debt was to Greenham Women and the 102 other peace camps established at U.S. airbases in Britain after 9 November 1983. Ecoradicalism recalled West German antinuclear actions as well as squatting in West Berlin, Hamburg, Copenhagen, and Amsterdam. It expressed the countercultural agitprop strand of 1968, the politics of spectacle, arriving via Women's Liberation and the Gay Liberation Front. Ecowarriors, the urban confrontationism of RTS and warehouse parties, and mass actions like the Trafalgar Square Poll Tax riot of March 1990 carried the other strand, the streetfighting maximalism. Finally, DiY politics carried the legacy of Situationism, the most self-conscious of the efforts during the 1950s and 1960s to establish links between anticapitalist politics and the public disruptions of an aesthetic avant-garde.[29]

Situationist influences took various routes. One of the most striking was *Aufheben*, a magazine collective formed from a Marx reading group in the Anti-Poll Tax campaign, whose annual issues covered themes from the 1992 Los Angeles uprising and the European Monetary Union to the Twyford Down struggle. Its main influences included Situationism and Italian autonomism.[30] Brighton-based Justice? formed in 1994 with its free weekly *schNEWS,* was similar. Reclaim the Streets (RTS) bore the Situationist imprint with flamboyance. At the 1995 Islington street party, a ton of sand was poured onto Upper Street, as three thousand people danced to the sound systems in the car-free space.[31] At the third street party on 13 July 1996, 10,000 people occupied the Shepherd's Bush Flyover on a Saturday afternoon, turning the hard shoulder into a café and stalls, the center into a picnic site and stage, and the fast lane into a sandpit, as they danced and mingled. These were conceived as "temporary autonomous zones," or TAZs.[32]

These new militancies flourished as the parliamentary Left reverted to its most cautious mode and unions barely emerged from a long decade's repression. In this context, they offered new outlets for working-class grievances increasingly disenfranchised by the available Left party. While RTS street parties linked transport and environmental issues with the union struggles of London Underground workers and Liverpool dockers, the anti-road fight at Pollock Free State in 1994–95 brought ecoradicals and working-class communities together, in a city with strong Left traditions, which was also the home of the Anti-Poll Tax Federation. The 20,000-strong RTS March for Social Justice on 12 April 1997, three weeks before the Labour Party's landslide election victory, linked radical ecology to union rights and defense of the National Health Service. The rally ended in an illegal party in Trafalgar Square, complete with mobile sound system, as police battled for control. The banner proclaimed: "Never Mind the Ballots, Reclaim the Streets."

This slogan—invoking a punk emblem of 20 years before, the Sex Pistols album entitled *Never Mind the Bollocks, Here's the Sex Pistols*—provided links to earlier countercultural histories. Crass, "a radical anarcho-pacifist, anarcha-feminist, vegetarian collective" ("nine male and female musicians, artists, filmmakers and activists living in a commune in Essex"), arrived with their album, *The Feeding of the Five Thousand*, in 1978. Defiantly noncommercial, they worked provincial alternative circuits with groups like the Poison Girls, drawing audiences of "self-confessed misfits" in "village halls, old theaters, tents, free festivals" and combining music with performance art in "the fostering of puzzlement." They raised money for "marginal political campaigns (mental health and animal rights)" and advocated peace, enraging the Right with attacks on the Falklands/Malvinas War via singles like *Sheep Farming in the Falklands* and *How Does It Feel (To Be the Mother of a Thousand Dead)?* which became the best-selling punk title of 1983. Their first live gig was the Huntley Street squatters' festival in London in 1977, their last a miners' benefit during the great strike in 1984. They were a troublemaking disturbance from the margins—against "the Church, unemployment, patriarchy, family values, the state, war, nuclear weapons, Third World exploitation, the environment, the meat trade." As the drummer Penny Rimbaud said, the band set about producing contradiction, a "confusion that put people in the middle and said, make your own fucking minds up."[33]

Beyond the Left's mainstream, rallying to the miners' last stand, Crass were a transmission from 1968. Themes recurred, from feminism and peace to ecology and Third World solidarity, in a Situationist aesthetic of subversion. Links were crosscutting. Penny Rimbaud was a hippy organizer of Stonehenge Free Festivals energized by the impact of Sex Pistols; Greenham Women learned many techniques of encampment from the New Age travelers; the Peace Convoy wove in and out of peace camps and protests. Police violence unified these links via the eviction of Rainbow Fields Village from the former air force base at Molesworth in February 1985 and the smashing of the Peace Convoy at Beanfield in June of the same year. Such police actions came hot from the pitched battles of the miners' strike.

DiY made its own public sphere, with decentralized alternative media binding local circuits together. The internet and other technologies joined the print media of newsletters and magazines. Thomas Harding and Paul O'Connor founded Undercurrents in 1993—an alternative news service, training five hundred activists in video technology by 1997, plus a pool of 50 contributors to Undercurrents itself. In London, Exploding Cinema held screenings for homemade video in squats and disused buildings, and similar movements developed around Conscious Cinema in Brighton and Headcleaner Collective in Coventry. By 1996, Undercurrents's local networks were being partly mediated through the Community Organizing Foundation. Other initiatives accompanied the fight against the Criminal Justice Act in 1994, including Forgive Us Our Trespasses in Leeds, which kept a national register of actions, with 52 events in May 1994 alone; The Book, a directory of the same campaign published by Justice?; and United Systems, a collective of sound systems. These intersecting networks thickened an already ramified alternative public sphere, in which feminism, lesbians and gays, HIV-AIDS education, ecology, peace, animal rights, music and dance, and the arts all had their place.[34]

DiY, like West German alternative scenes and Amsterdam and Copenhagen squats, generated its own economies, enclaves of oppositional living challenging the dominance of neoliberalism in the new post-Keynesian era. Justice? seized the derelict Brighton courthouse as an ironic focus for the campaign against the Criminal Justice Act, converting it to "a thriving community center with café, meditation space, crèche, and free entertainment for a free people": "Overtly political activities—like workshops held on the continental squatting movement, prisoner support, and contradictions in the anti-roads movement, and meetings to discuss the group's activities and direction—competed for space with the poetry readings, Tai Chi, massage, cinema, drumming workshops, and arts displays etc."[35]

Exodus Collective in Luton went a stage further. Luton had been a bastion of postwar prosperity, where the "affluent workers" of the car industry reaped high wages, private comforts, and consumer plenty.[36] But by 1980, this dream had collapsed, amid recession and joblessness. Arising in the Fordist economy's social ruins, Exodus began with a DiY loud-speaker stack for an open-air party outside Dunstable in June 1992, grow-ing by New Year's Eve to a stack 30 feet long and 12 feet high, partying with many thousands. Exodus grounded this dance culture in political am-bition by organizing a social movement, "Bringing back community / To a town that's lost it totally," as one of its poems said.[37]

Exodus supported a homeless squat in an abandoned hotel. Evicted two months later, it occupied a derelict nursing home, renaming it HAZ (Hous-ing Action Zone) Manor.[38] Forty residents were given space, with com-munal areas (kitchen, gym, community room, patio, allotments), craft workshops, and a repair shop for loudspeakers. Next, the Collective re-opened a disused farm, building a sizeable herd of animals.[39] This inven-tiveness rebuked the disorder of industrial decline, youth unemployment, and homelessness. Systematic police harassment, culminating in a trumped-up drugs charge against Paul Taylor, the Collective's leading black member (he was acquitted), failed to suppress the energy.[40] The Collective sustained itself by a cooperative ethic and the pooling of modest resources: "So being part of that, all of a sudden your idea of betterment, your idea of progress changes. You can see a new future, without going in and apparently bet-tering yourself by stealing a credit card or whatever. So that's what we've done. We've set an example of a different form of betterment, a different form of self-help. We all get better together."[41]

Exodus mobilized a remarkable range of mainly young people—"em-ployed and unemployed; politically aware, or just wanting a good time; black and white; male and female; urban and rural youth; old hippies, punks, and Hell's Angels; New-Age and traditional travellers; road-protesters and squatters."[42] At the height of their tensions with police in summer 1995, Exodus resolved a violent confrontation on Marsh Farm Estate, extending over several days, by emptying the estate for a party. Where job prospects of working-class youth were gutted, with casual crime and drinking the main compensations, the ability to organize local discon-tents around a collective project, in an architecture of everyday pleasures, was essential.

World-making, however inventive the local energies, needs political space. After Taylor's acquittal and the discrediting of the police, Bedford-shire County Council voted unanimously for a public inquiry headed by Michael Mansfield, a leading civil rights lawyer. Public sympathies shifted to Exodus. Land was offered for licensed summer festivals. In 1997, the rabidly hostile Conservative MPs for Luton were replaced by Labour. The Collective began creating Ark Community Center in a warehouse equipped with recording studios, cost-price food and Marley's bar, workshops, a craft area, local radio, and a press, supported by modest subscription. This was classic community-based organizing, if removed from recognizable La-bour politics or union action. Glenn Jenkins, himself a former train driver and shop steward, 35 years old in 1997, issued the political challenge:

It's about time the politicians . . . stopped talking bollocks about green shoots in the economy and told the people the truth about work. We're not drop-outs, we're force-outs, people who are not wanted any more. There's no future for a lot of people in the present set-up, no chance of decent work. So people need something else, a new existence. The system needs to assist us to diversify. Politicians should support this diversification, because it'll have positive effects on their world. We're on a mission. We're at the cutting edge of a way, an answer.[43]

SOCIALISM FOR NEO-LIBERAL TIMES

Exodus Collective's inventiveness, like the economies seeded by West Germany's alternative scene, suggested how collectivism might be reclaimed. National Keynesianism, bureaucratic nationalization, and centralized planning were discredited by neoliberalism's unstoppable post-1973 advance. Instead, Exodus evoked other traditions of socialist economics based in cooperation, focused less on the economy's commanding heights than local initiative.[44] Decentralized models of community-based planning generated jobs, revitalized community, and crystallized new links between work and everyday life. Democratic planning offered modest chances for the Left, once back in government. National governments' restricted maneuverability in the globalized economy of the 1990s didn't exclude creative strategies of public investment. By sponsoring local initiatives, resources could be returned to regional and urban economies devastated by industrial decline. Such resources included not only capital but organizational support, information and its technologies, and moral-political energy. Thereby, an ideal of public goods could be restored.

Modified Keynesianism was feasible. Decentralized public enterprise, tax concessions and public funds for local initiatives, use of public resources like land and planning permissions for smaller-scale projects, community-based planning—these didn't mean reversing privatization or relegitimizing nationalization per se. The GLC's Popular Planning Unit in the early 1980s was "a resource, research and education center which ensured that the material and political resources of the GLC were shared with grass-roots, trade union, and community organizations across London."[45] Of course, the GLC's short history was contentious. The central state raised all possible obstacles (fiscal, organizational, political) before finally abolishing local democracy itself. But the GLC accomplished many things—an integrated industrial strategy for low-waged and casualized sectors; six Technology Networks to aid innovation; the People's Plan for the Docklands against the commercial program of Thatcher's London Docklands Development Corporation; neighborhood campaigns like the Coin Street

Action Group; broad public health coalitions via the London Health Emergency founded in 1982–83; and so on.[46]

This defied a brutally adversarial national climate, where government drove the opposite course, promoting property deals severed from community. The GLC welcomed new social movements, promoted collaboration among unions, employers, and consumers of services, and waged imaginative campaigns—Fares Fair in 1982, Peace Year in 1983, Anti-Racist Year in 1984, and the hugely successful Jobs for a Change Festivals in 1984 and 1985, which drew crowds of one hundred thousand and five hundred thousand, respectively. Elsewhere in Europe, Mondragón cooperatives in Spain's Basque country had 19,500 workers in over one hundred enterprises; and in PCI-run Emilia-Romagna, Modena textile producers organized their design, marketing, and financial needs cooperatively through a centrally provided organization. Socialist governments of France and Spain seeded activity via research and development, women's initiatives, and community support, much as Scandinavian governments had done. But in this post-Keynesian era, socialist governments lacked the wherewithal to make such piecemeal experiences into a national economic plan.[47]

The end of the 1990s presented a confusing picture. Socialists were governing almost everywhere. The SPD swept the German elections in October 1998, after British Labour's triumph in May 1997, and only the PSOE's 1995 defeat in Spain broke the general pattern. In the post-Communist east, Social Democratic victory in the Czech Republic in June 1998 offset Socialist defeat in Hungary. European government had a socialist uniformity unparalleled since the antifascist coalitions of 1945. Yet this was a chastened and cautious socialism. The distinctive ideals of 1945 had been beaten down. Socialists returned to office with no economic design. They accepted the neoliberal changes, including not only capitalism's permanence but also the aggressively remarketized ideologies of economic freedom pioneered by Thatcherism in the 1980s, for which socialists had no new response. There were no visions of a different socialist future.[48]

The Left was back in office but in disabling overall retreat. As transnational jubilation in October 1998 at the London arrest of the Chilean ex-dictator, General Augusto Pinochet, showed, older radicalisms could still be memorialized.[49] But the larger projects animating the Left in the 1970s were defunct—the Alternative Economic Strategy in Britain, variants of the Swedish model, Eurocommunism. Absent prosperity and growth, even the modest aims of Crosland and Godesberg were gone. For the SPD's official intellectual, Peter Glotz, they had become simply "centralist megalomania." The "obsessive conviction that the State can effectively manage the whole economy" was an outdated dogma alienating voters. Instead "the Left must stand up for consumer rights, free investment decisions, the free disposal of assets, and a decentralized decision making process." But how this would further the goal of "exerting control over the market economy" was unclear.[50]

This emergent stance was a neorevisionism guided by electoral pragmatics and leavened by an ethics of social justice and rhetorics of "modernization." Socialist strategists had jettisoned planning, nationalization, redistributive taxation, and public spending. The ubiquitous language of "newness" implied precisely repudiating such "old" or "traditionalist" ideas—leaving the established socialist tradition behind, embracing capitalism's ascendant forms, accepting that "the market" ruled. Socialists had lost their confidence in the state. Without this Archimedean point, their capacity for imagining anticapitalist alternatives dissolved. "Neorevisionism" was the cumulative outcome of this loss.

SOCIALISM UNDER ANY OTHER NAME: REMAKING THE LEFT?

Without traditional labor movements and their class-political identities, collectivist ideals were hard to sustain. Socialism began as the ambition to abolish capitalism, to build an egalitarian democracy from the wealth that capitalism endowed. Such hopes lasted for many years. While the insurrectionary drama of 1917–23 was never reenacted, the belief in socialism as a reachable destination, as a stage of history clearly distinguishable from the capitalist present, still inspired socialist thinkers. But after defeats and disappointments, socialists settled for more modest aims of civilizing capitalism, stressing democracy, social citizenship, and rights at work. By the 1990s, socialism was an even more diffuse ideal, an abstract political ethics based on social justice. Even the strong social democracies of Scandinavia revised their language. Norwegian Labor's ideals moved from "a socialist society" in 1969, through "the generic values [of] freedom, democracy, and equality" in 1981, to individualism by 1989. Scandinavian parties slid inexorably toward the generic predicament: "mass unemployment, pressures to contain inflation, the end of centralized bargaining, a flexible labor market, the collapse of the manufacturing sector, the loss of national control over the economy."[51]

The main sociopolitical changes in capitalist Europe since the 1960s—the post-Fordist transition—steadily undermined the socialist Left. These far outweighed Communism's collapse in their demoralizing effects. The USSR had long ceased being an inspiration, apart from shrinking minorities of Moscow loyalists. True, Gorbachev reactivated hopes, but their collapse in 1991 wasn't remotely comparable to earlier shocks in 1956 and 1968. Western socialists were already in retreat. The headlong rush to marketization confirmed their beleaguered isolation. They doubted the scope for specifically socialist policies.

Yet the end of the Cold War cleared some vital space. The "End of Communism" meant the end of anti-Communism in a potentially liberating way. From the late 1940s, anti-Communism had placed Western politics under extraordinary constraint—shaping the possible terms of public life, structuring political agendas, ruling alliances in and out of order, policing the forms of dissent, generally defining the boundaries of what could and couldn't be thought. If Communists practised self-censorship in defending the USSR, social democrats also internalized anti-Communism as an insidious constraint, and Gorbachev's reforms now loosened the hold of these habits on Western political imaginations. Western European electorates also appreciated that Cold War militarism was being dismantled mainly at Gorbachev's instigation. When the Soviet imperium ended, anti-Communist mechanisms no longer worked as before. In principle, a "third space" opened between the old polarized alternatives of Stalinism and right-wing social democracy—not as a ready-made "third way" but as a new set of parameters where Left initiatives might form.

This was where new social movements had disproportionate effect. Between the West German Greens and Belgian Ecolo in 1980 and the eastern European Green parties of 1988–90, each country acquired new parties calling themselves Green (see table 27.1).[52] Their success was striking, given the problems of gaining a foothold in congested political systems. For the

TABLE 27.1 European Green Parties, 1980–1998: Performance in National and European Elections

	Founded	National	European 1984	European 1989
Britain (Green Party)	1973	1.3 (1992)	2.7	14.9
West Germany (the Greens)	1980	6.7 (1998)	8.2	8.4
Belgium (Ecolo)	1980	13.9 (1991)	9.8	16.5
Ireland (Green Alliance)	1981	1.5 (1989)		
Sweden (Environment Party)	1981	5.0 (1994)		
Belgium (Agalev)	1982	7.9 (1991)	7.1	12.2
Denmark (the Greens)	1983	0.8 (1990)		
Netherlands (the Greens)	1983	4.1 (1989)	5.6	7.0
Switzerland (Green Party)	1983	6.3 (1987)		
France (the Greens)	1984	6.8 (1992)		10.6
Luxemburg (Green Alternative)	1984	4.1 (1989)	6.0	6.1
Spain (the Greens)	1985	0.7 (1989)		0.9
Austria (Green Alliance)	1986	4.8 (1990)		
Finland (Green Union)	1987	6.8 (1991)		
Italy (Green List)	1987	3.0 (1992)		3.8
Estonia (Green Movement)	1988			
Poland (Party of Greens)	1988			
Lithuania (Green Party)	1989			
Hungary (Green Party)	1989			
Slovenia (Greens)	1989	8.8 (1990)		
Slovakia (Party of Greens)	1990	3.5 (1990)		
Latvia (Green Party)	1990			
Bulgaria (Green Party, Ecoglasnost)	1990	7.2 (1990)		
Croatia (Green Action)	1990			

1984 Euro-elections, seven Green parties signed common declarations in Brussels, and votes ranged from below 1 percent in Britain and Ireland to 8.2 percent in West Germany. By the next Euro-elections in 1989, Green votes had grown: in three EU countries, they reached double figures; in three others, 6–8 percent; in Italy, a Green List debuted; and only in Denmark, Greece, and Ireland was performance poor. These parties had established themselves on the scene. The best showing in national elections came in the familiar north-central European "social democratic core." The combined Belgian parties also scored high returns: 5.1 percent for Ecolo (Flemish-speaking) and 4.9 percent for Agalev (Walloon) in 1991. Otherwise, scores ranged between 4 and 9 percent. By 1990, eastern european Greens did well in Slovenia and Bulgaria too.

By the 1990s, these parties were credible coalition partners, with extensive governing experience in the cities. Their importance exceeded the modesty of their electorate. They visibly marked the wider disjunction between parliamentary and extraparliamentary arenas, and beyond the Greens was the wider universe of new social movements and amorphous alternative scenes. Moreover, these new parties were not membership parties in the traditional socialist sense, showing on the contrary very low ratios of members to electoral support. This was a key paradox: while political activism had been growing since 1968, measured by the signing of petitions and the joining of campaigns, party memberships were dropping, especially among the young.[53] The *meaning* of party was in decline, and this implied no lessening of activism but rather an activism directed elsewhere. Energy for the Left was generated beyond the party walls, with ever weaker reverberations as it entered socialist parliamentary groups. This explained the gap between the Peace Movement's big popularity in the early 1980s and the lackluster conservatism of socialist leaderships on the same issue or the vitality of the British new urban Left as against the centrist obduracy of Labour's national leaders. Greens were themselves uneasily partnered with these extraparliamentary constituencies, linked not via machineries of party discipline but by a more fluid process of identification.[54]

Green parties were not the only new Left form. In Iceland, the functional equivalent was *Kvennalistinn,* or the Women's Alliance, formed in March 1983, with 5.5 percent in that year's elections, doubling to 10.1 percent in 1987. In the Netherlands, the right-wing and marginal Greens were distinct from the Green Progressive Accord, which united several small Left parties for the 1984 Euro-elections and won 5.6 percent of the vote. This Accord embraced Radicals, who pioneered Green issues in the late 1970s, Pacifist-Socialists, and the Eurocommunist CPN, adding the Evangelical People's Party for the 1989 Euro-elections and improving the vote to 7.0 percent; it relaunched itself as the Dutch Green Left. In Denmark, the Socialist People's Party, the Eurocommunist successor to the tiny Stalinist CP, channeled ecological and peace activism in the 1970s, seeking reciprocity with grassroots movements and committing 40 percent of its committees to women.

Its popular vote reached 14.6 percent in 1987. By the 1990s, it governed with Social Democrats or held the balance of power in two-thirds of city councils.[55]

In these cases, Green parties were preempted by Left alternatives adopting green platforms. Conversely, successful Greens generalized their radical stance. The Paris Declaration of April 1984, *Think Globally — Act Locally!* called for "a different, non-aligned and decentralized Europe." After eco-radicalism per se, it opposed nuclear missiles in West and East; attacked unemployment and welfare cuts; demanded equal rights for women; and affirmed civil liberties as the precondition for an emancipatory society.[56]

Greens belonged in a broader hybrid category of radical parties after the 1960s, around which 5–10 percent of the electorate to the left of the main socialist parties gathered. These included older left-socialist parties in Scandinavia dating from the crisis of Stalinism in 1956–68; explicitly Red-Green initiatives like the Dutch Green Left and Finland's Left-Wing Alliance; the Spanish Communists' broad electoral front, *Izquierda Unida;* the Icelandic Women's Alliance; and the Scottish National Party and *Plaid Cymru* (Welsh Nationalist Party) in Britain.[57] Within this broader category, "real" Green parties—freestanding formations occupying radical space—emerged largely in Belgium, Sweden, Finland, and German-speaking Europe.

This spelled a long-term dealignment of European politics.[58] In the 1950s, Britain's two main parties took 93.9 percent of the overall popular votes in elections, but by the 1980s only 71.6. Belgium moved from a two-party system in the 1950s to extreme fragmentation by 1995, magnified after 1980 by the subdividing of parties on Walloon-Flemish lines. These were extremes. But from the 1950s to 1980s, big declines happened in Denmark, Iceland, and Luxembourg as well. In (West) Germany, a two-party system peaked in the 1970s but by 1998 was back to the lower levels of dominance of the 1950s.[59] Moreover, allegiances were loosening in other ways. Even the most independent Communist parties had suffered under the stigma of Stalin, and only the USSR's removal in 1991 finally qualified them as coalition partners. Thus by 1998 Swedish Social Democrats could no longer marginalize the ex-Communist Left Party (VP), especially when its strength was added to the Greens. In 1998, German Greens formed a government with the SPD; and even the ex-Communist PDS was no longer entirely beyond the pale, supporting an SPD minority government in Saxony-Anhalt and joining a coalition in Mecklenburg-Vorpommern.

This new fluidity was striking in the two countries where anti-Communism had cemented the governing blocs after 1947, Italy and France. Here, permanent exclusion of large CPs stabilized otherwise refractory systems. In France, party fragmentation had been partly overcome by de Gaulle's rallying of the Right after 1958, and in the 1960s the two largest parties commanded 56.4 percent of the voting electorate. The Socialists' rise then augured a two-party system, arranged around the PS and the Gaullist Right. Yet by 1990, the electorate was in volatile confusion. The Right was disunited, exacerbated by the xenophobic National Front, which during 1986–97 increased its vote from 9.8 to 14.9 percent. The PCF crashed from 20–23 percent during 1962–78 to only 9–11 percent after 1986. But the Socialists veered wildly from the heights of the 1980s, when they averaged 35.8 percent, down to a disastrous 20.3 percent in 1993 and an improved 25.6 in 1997.

Having fulfilled its anti-PCF mission, the Socialist electorate assembled by Mitterrand during the late 1970s and early 1980s flew apart. On the eve of the 1993 elections, Michel Rocard called wishfully for a "big bang" solution, a new unity of the Left, for "all those who believed in solidarity and transformation, from ecologists to socially minded centrists to re-formed Communists."[60] But by the 1994 Euro-elections, the explosion had rather produced fragments, a disorder of initiatives.[61] In the 1995 presidential elections, Lionel Jospin's surprisingly strong showing presaged a PS revival, confirmed by its return to government in 1997. But 11 million voters supported six antimainstream candidates in the first round for the 1995 presidency, or 37.3 percent of the overall vote. In the second ballot, 6.0 percent of the votes were spoiled. The Socialists' 1997 victory was hardly grounded in stable social support.

In 1992–94, the Italian republic fell apart. The Clean Hands campaign, an extraordinary anticorruption drive radiating from Milan, toppled an entire establishment, from Bettino Craxi and his Socialist Party brokers to Andreotti and the Christian Democrats.[62] Popular anger undid the DC's long-entrenched electoral primacy. In 1992, its vote slid from 34.3 to 29.7 percent, while the PSI faltered from 14.3 percent to 13.6. As scandals spiraled, these two parties decomposed. By the next elections in 1994, the DC's main successor, the *Partito Popolare Italiano*, scraped 11.1 percent, and the PSI had completely gone. The regionalist Northern League, a blustering brew of neoliberal xenophobia, burst into prominence. But 1994's main victor was an entirely new party, *Forza Italia* (Go Italy!), fashioned by the Milan media tycoon Silvio Berlusconi, who rode on populist attacks against the "Italy that is so politicized, statist, corrupt, and hyper-regulated," winning 21 percent, and forming a government with the Northern League and the neo-Fascist Allianza Nationale.[63] Berlusconi played anti-Communism to the full, counterposing "freedom and slavery" and predicting "show trials and prison" if the Left won. His government lasted seven months before it too collapsed in recriminations and corruption.[64]

The key was held by the former PCI, which in 1989–91 finally remade itself as the Party of the Democratic Left (PDS) under its secretary, Achille Occhetto.[65] At one level, this brought Berlinguer's Historic Compromise of the late 1970s to belated fruition. But the party was also the repository of proud militancy and long self-sacrifice, the bearer of revolutionary tradition—a Communist party in that sense—and its leaders, from Togliatti to

Occhetto, constantly balanced strategy against this élan. Breaking out of that framework, as Europe's largest surviving CP, against the backcloth of Gorbachev's reforms, was no simple matter. By now, internal Stalinism, as against bureaucratic inertia, had gone, and since Berlinguer's time the party had always affirmed democratic freedoms, nonviolence, and the parliamentary road. But the contemporary changes were potentially highly divisive. They entailed further "downsizing" the party's radicalism; accepting the decline of the traditional working class; acknowledging its own shifting sociology in the graying of membership, the declining recruitment of youth, and the growing salience of white-collar workers and professionals; joining the Socialist International; and generally coming to terms with its own past.[66]

This was the PCI dilemma: it was joining the social democratic camp just as social democracies elsewhere fell into disarray. On the other hand, it was already receptive to new social movements, which parties like the SPD opposed. When the Historic Compromise had failed in 1979–80, Berlinguer had welcomed new social movements like feminism and the peace movement. Occhetto revived this invitation, making ecology and the women's movement central to contemporary anti-capitalist critique. He brought the PCI out of its Communist past rather than idealizing the latter in Berlinguer's style. Yet Occhetto's PDS declared itself the rallying point for the Left just as its ascendancy tottered. Craxi's PSI disputed that primacy for itself; the Greens refused the embrace; and a large minority, *Rifondazione comunista* (RC), reaffirmed the Communist tradition when the PDS was launched in January 1991, gathering 150,000 pledges of support. Beyond hardline neo-Stalinists, RC rallied *Il Manifesto,* many left-wing Communists, and the surviving New Left groups like Proletarian Democracy. In the 1992 elections, the PDS scored only 16.1 percent, and even with RC's 5.6 percent, this was still 4.9 lower than 1987, the PCI's worst showing since 1963. The wider electorate showed the same fragmentation as France. Together, the "protest" parties—RC, Northern League, neo-Fascists, Greens, Radicals, and the *Rete* or Network, left-wing Sicilian Catholics disgusted with the DC's Mafia connection—took 25.3 percent of the vote.[67]

After a year's clarification, under the technocratic premiership of the ex-DC banker Lamberto Dini, elections were held again in April 1996. The PDS forged a center-left alliance of 12 parties in the *Ulivo* (Olive Tree), plus a pact with RC, under another technocrat, the economist Romano Prodi. Berlusconi's Forza joined with neo-Fascists in the *Polo* (Pole of Liberty), while the Northern League ran alone. Ulivo carried the election with 43.7 percent, defeating Polo with 42.1 percent.

This was a momentous watershed. The Italian Left formed its first ever government, and (ex-)Communists entered office for the first time since 1947. Change was also structural. The two blocs stabilized around the two main parties. The two-party system projected by PCI-PDS reformers in electoral reforms was now close, while party alternation between government and opposition would prevent repetition of the DC's post-1947 single-party dominance, which had permanently marginalized the Communist electorate before. By 1996, the joint PDS-RC vote had regained the PCI levels of 1968–83. This resembled a Scandinavian situation rather than the Italian reformers' idealized British model: a strong social democratic party (PDS) flanked by left-socialists (RC) and the equivalent of Greens, facing a non-unified bloc of the Right. If the PS could ever stabilize its support, this situation beckoned in France too.

Christian Democracy's demise via the anticorruption drive finally realized Togliatti's and Berlinguer's old goal—reconstructing the governing consensus glimpsed in 1943–47 by breaking open the unity of political Catholicism and detaching its democratic parts. Nationally, less than a quarter of practising Catholics voted for the DC's successors in 1996. The Vatican also declared its neutrality, conceding the passing of an era. As against the vast weight of the pre-1992 DC statocracy, 1996 brought only fragments of center-left Catholics on the Left and another small successor party on the Right. The Togliattian strategy had come to pass.

Ulivo's victory typified the European Left in the post-Fordist transition, especially the decoupling of party preferences from class identification. Ulivo took more of its support from the working class than did the Right, but the gap was relatively small and the absolute significance hugely less than in 1976. While Ulivo's final 150,000-strong rally in the Piazza del Populo on 18 April 1996 evoked the mass movements of the past and the RC's campaign used the time-tried methods of mass meeting and printed word, the old mass party, "that great political invention of the late-nineteenth century," was dead.[68] The PDS pioneered a new kind of electoral front, one more loosely linked to its supporters. Ulivo recalled the complex relations described earlier between parliamentary leaders and extraparliamentary social movements. It was a prototype for one possible form the Left might begin to take.

CONCLUSION

In October 1998, Massimo D'Alema, who succeeded Occhetto as PDS secretary, formed a government, placing a Communist at the head of a Western European country for the first time.[69] This was Europe's third major change of government in 1998, in which Swedish and German Social Democrats opened alliances to their left, joining the Franco-British election wins of 1997. This modified Europe's uniform neoliberal hegemonies and generalized market-speak. In the big four—Germany, France, Italy, and Britain—the Left formed governments in 1997–98, while Scandinavian social democracy restabilized its hold on office. With the PCI's passage into PDS and the recycling of Eastern Europe's ex-ruling parties as social democratic, the Left's main voice, country by country, became remarkably continuous. It spoke a deradicalized centrist version of social democracy. This was entirely uninterested in revolution, accepting of capitalism, even enthusiastic about the market, and distanced from the older imagery of the male and muscular working class. Its socialism seemed increasingly residual, based in programs of social justice and the defense of what remained of the welfare state.[70]

Yet socialism's substance still meant more than this. Socialist governments were stronger advocates of democracy, more likely to uphold civil rights, and more generous guardians of citizenship. They were better on race and immigration, though only just. While the democracy deficit varied country by country (in Britain the challenge of reform was greatest), constitutional questions affected Europe as a whole, and here socialists' presence in government could certainly make a difference. European integration was foremost on the agenda. If parliamentary constitutionalism was primary to the 1860s, democracy to 1918, and corporatism and the welfare state to 1945, then the constitutional priority of 2000 was Europe. Socialist parties had a crucial agenda to discharge—from strengthening the European Parliament to regulating European capital and labor markets and making the Social Charter a reality. Socialism's importance was now less in the preceding heritage, from the Second International to the post-1945 settlements, than in the new politics—for Europe and globalization rather than the national state—that socialist governments needed to define.[71]

The real potentials for radicalism were to be found less in the socialist parties themselves than in two new kinds of political space. The first linked dominant socialist parties with the smaller left-socialist and Green parties to their side. The second was the wider connectedness between parliamentary arenas and extraparliamentary social movements. Whether in the diffuse generational and countercultural effects of 1968; in the aesthetic radicalisms of Situationists and their progeny; in the continuing challenge of feminisms; in the queering of politics by feminists, lesbians, and gays; in the rave cultures and alternative scenes; in the antiroads protests; in the burgeoning territories of DiY; in the questions posed by immigration and Europe's growing multicultural diversity; in the politics of the environmental catastrophe; or in popular opposition to militarism, state violence, and war—in all of these areas a new political space could potentially cohere. They all fell beyond socialism's traditional core, and between the 1960s and 1990s neither social democrats nor Communists had responded to them with much generosity or imagination. In fact, more often they were ranged in opposition. But socialist values—collectivism, social justice, egalitarianism, mutualism, democracy—remained best for helping them thrive.

Conclusion

ENDINGS

IN JULY 2000, the former Italian Communist Party (PCI) newspaper, *L'Unita*, closed its doors. First printed in 1924, *L'Unita* had reached its peak of prestige in the 1970s with a quarter of a million daily sales, soaring past a million on Sundays. As the PCI turned itself into the Party of the Democratic Left (PDS) in the 1990s, however, and the newspaper opened its pages to the new pluralism, it lost its identity. Circulation slumped to 50,000. Threatened with bankruptcy, *L'Unita* went into receivership. Meanwhile, the PCI-PDS prepared to vacate its historic Rome headquarters for less costly premises, while the party's old northern citadel, the showcase city administration of Bologna, passed out of its control for the first time since 1945.[1]

Clearly an era had ended. The generation whose lifetimes framed the histories presented in this book was passing. Its members were born into a time shaped by the mature socialist parties formed between the 1860s and the First World War. Those movements provided an architecture of solidarity and hope. The children of socialist parents in the 1920s entered a world shocked into insurgency by the Great War and then emblazoned with the excitement of the Russian Revolution. Yet a short decade later, after a brief democratic prelude, dictatorships were spreading across southern and eastern Europe. Then the Great Depression and the rise of fascism burdened the future with unimagined dangers. Not just democracy and social progress but the most elementary values of human decency were placed under deadly threat. For anyone reach-

Gramsci said: "Turn your face violently towards things as they exist now." Not as you'd like them to be, not as you think they were ten years ago, not as they're written about in the sacred texts, but as they really are: the contradictory, stony ground of the present conjuncture.

—Stuart Hall,

"Then and Now"

491

ing adulthood during the 1930s, political choices became stark. In large parts of Europe—a zone of darkness growing darker by the year—the resources for defending democracy and upholding humane values were growing desperately sparse. By 1940, as Nazism rolled its brutalities across a subjugated continent, there were few safe places left.

Under these circumstances, socialist and Communist parties offered a political relationship to the future. Nazism could only be defeated militarily, to be sure. But the wartime groundwork of democratic renewal was being relaid by socialists, Communists, radical liberals, and Christian democrats, as they came together in a broadening category of the Left. Their efforts profoundly shaped the character of victory. In the resulting postwar settlements, despite all the disappointments and the new disasters of Stalinism in the East, a better world was imagined and made. Socialists born in 1917 entered this postwar world still in their twenties, schooled by the immediacy of hardships and dangers, thankful for survival, and looking to a future of citizenship and security. That future was to be assembled via the welfare state. Reconstruction would honor the contributions of working people to the nation's survival and well-being, not just rhetorically but by a new ethics of public goods. Governments of antifascist unity would organize the transition to this new world. Trade unions would be welcomed as valued and legitimate partners. Last but certainly not least, for the first time democracy could become genuinely universal, because women finally received the vote.

Despite the narrowing of those hopes during the Cold War and the normalizing of postwar society along more conservative lines, the embedding of democracy in western Europe proved a lasting achievement. Crucially assisted by an unprecedented capitalist prosperity, the postwar settlements gradually delivered an improved material life and reliable social security, all within the assured political framework of democratic values, toughened by a popular culture of justified entitlement. But this era also created the conditions of its own transcendence. The 1960s brought generations of young people with different needs and desires, constructing their own understandings of personhood, citizenship, and the future. These generations increasingly disengaged from everything signified by 1945. Their new personal and material circumstances coincided with capitalist restructuring and long-range social changes during the last third of the twentieth century, and this new conjuncture destroyed the environment the socialist tradition had needed in order to grow.

The Eastern European version of this story was extremely bleak. Liberation in 1943–47 had produced a politics not dissimilar from that in the West, especially given the region's specificities of backwardness, its prewar records of dictatorship, and the huge wreckage wrought by Nazism. It was the devastating counterrevolution of Stalinization during 1948–53 that drove democracy from the agenda. Even so, the aspirations of 1945 remained lodged in collective memory, rekindled in the various reform movements following Stalin's death. By the 1960s, moreover, this "actually existing socialism" was bringing Eastern European societies to a similar pass of possible renewal. Given the loosening of police control, the foundations of a democratic revival were being laid—through reasonable economic improvements, the crude egalitarianism bringing working-class sons and daughters to social advancement, and the guaranteed social minimum of the welfare state, leavened by the limited restoration of cultural freedoms, the reopening of debate, and the recovery of earlier ideas. These possibilities varied widely across the Soviet bloc. The Czechoslovak Prague Spring was a final inspired but tragic attempt to bring them to fruition.

By the end of the 1990s, the generational histories I've been describing could be tracked through the obituary columns of the departing century, as an entire collective biography seemingly was laid to rest. Thus in June 1999, Jiři Pelikan, head of Czechoslovak State Television during the Prague Spring and a leading Communist reformer, died in Rome. Pelikan had first joined the Communists as a 16-year-old in 1939 as the Nazis occupied the Czech lands. After five months in a Gestapo prison, he spent the war in the Resistance, emerging after the Liberation as a young Communist functionary, primed for making the new social order. Fighting the Nazis had also entailed the tragedy of loss, for his brother was imprisoned for the duration of the war, his parents taken as hostages, and his mother killed. He spent the 1950s heading the Soviet-aligned International Union of Students before being appointed head of Czechoslovak television in 1963. In 1968, he put the medium to work for the reform movement. After the Soviet invasion, he chose exile in Italy, where he published *Listy,* a journal for exiles, which later developed links with Charter 77. Stripped of citizenship in 1970, he became a naturalized Italian, sitting as a Socialist in the European Parliament during 1977–89 focusing on social and environmental issues. After 1989, he shuttled between Prague and Rome. Despite campaigns of anti-Communist defamation—being smeared with allegations of Gestapo collaboration during the war—he was eventually honored for services to the Czech Republic.[2]

Another Czech reform Communist, Ladislav Lis, died in March 2000. Born the son of a stonemason and apprenticed as a locksmith, he joined the Communist anti-Nazi Resistance as a 17-year-old in 1943. He was quickly promoted through the party after the 1948 revolution, rising to head the Union of Youth. Expelled for dissidence in 1961, he worked on construction sites until he was recalled in 1968 to the KSC's Prague city leadership. Expelled again after the Soviet invasion, he worked from 1969 as a lumberjack, turning his small farm into a haven for dissidents. When Charter 77 was launched, he signed its declaration and in 1978 helped form the Committee for the Defense of the Unjustly Persecuted. He spent most of the 1980s under detention and arrest. During the 1989 revolution, he was active in Civic Forum, serving in Parliament until 1992 as an opponent of Vaclav Klaus's extreme promarket course. After 1994, he joined the

Social Democrats, tirelessly advocating human rights, taking up the cause of Czech Roma, and organizing relief for Kosovo refugees. The Social Democratic government elected in 1998 appointed him to its Human Rights Council.[3]

In December 1999, the longest-serving president of the Italian Chamber of Deputies, from 1979 to 1992, the veteran Communist Nilde Iotti, also died. Born in 1920, the daughter of a railwayman and a washerwoman in Reggio Emilia, Italy's red heartland, Iotti won a scholarship to university in Milan and graduated in 1943, quickly joining the Resistance. Emerging from the Liberation as a young, working-class, academically educated woman Communist, she was elected to the Constituent Assembly in 1946 and helped draft the postwar Constitution. Lover and companion to the much-older Palmiro Togliatti, she met resentment within the heavily masculine culture of the PCI; while elected to its Central Committee in 1956, she was confined to leading the Union of Italian Women. After Togliatti's death in 1964, she built a political identity in her own right. Committed to Enrico Berlinguer's Eurocommunist course, she condemned the invasion of Czechoslovakia in 1968, Soviet intervention in Afghanistan in 1979, and the military coup of 1981 in Poland. A lifelong atheist, she campaigned for divorce and abortion, while respecting the views of Catholic women. In 1979, she was elected to the presidency of the Chamber of Deputies, where she served two further terms. By the end of her career—ironically enough, given the socialist tradition's deep-seated masculinity—she embodied the virtues of socialist parliamentarianism. "Before the state funeral, an all-woman guard of honor stood by the coffin in the hall of the chamber of deputies where she had spent her life."[4]

From a very different part of the Left, Goliardo Fiaschi, one of Italy's leading anarchists, died of cancer in August 2000. A quarry-worker's son in the Tuscan city of Massa di Carrara, the "cradle of Italian anarchism," Fiaschi falsified his birth certificate in 1943 to join the wartime partisans at age 13. At the war's end, he entered liberated Modena in April 1945 as the mascot and standard-bearer of the Costrignano Brigade. During the 1950s, he was active among Spanish anarchist refugees and joined the guerilla struggle in Franco's Spain in August 1957, where he was immediately arrested. Amnestied in 1966, he was sentenced to further imprisonment in Italy and released only after an international campaign in 1974. He returned to Carrara as organizer of a cultural center and bookshop, which occupied the key building in the city's main square, seized originally by anarchist partisans in 1945.[5]

These careers reflect the extraordinary risks that democracy's twentieth-century attainments required. This was true even in countries like Britain, which escaped the oppressiveness of Nazi occupation or indigenous dictatorships. Bill Alexander was born in 1910 in southern England, the son of a rural carpenter and freethinking mother. After qualifying from university as an industrial chemist, he joined the Communist Party (CPGB) in response to the hunger marches of the depression. He was active in the Print Workers' Union and fought the British Union of Fascists in the famous Battle of Cable Street in 1935. He volunteered for the International Brigades in the Spanish Civil War, serving as political commissar to the anti-tank battery and then as commander of the British battalion before being wounded in June 1938. He was commissioned as an officer during the Second World War, serving with great distinction in North Afica, Italy, and Germany. He returned to hold various party offices in the Communist Party, rising to assistant general secretary during 1959–67. While teaching chemistry in southeast London, he devoted the last part of his life to the International Brigade Association, whose legacies he tirelessly memorialized through written and spoken word.[6]

These lives were indelibly marked by the Second World War. They were infused with meaning by the struggle against fascism and by a powerful sense of responsibility for the postwar future. They were also nurtured in the early-twentieth-century cultures of socialism. Another lifelong Communist dying in February 2000 was Dora Cox. Born in 1904 to a father of mixed British-Russian parentage and a Lithuanian Jewish mother and educated in a socialist Sunday school, she came to adulthood amid the febrile political excitements of 1917–23. She kept the socialist 10 commandments in her scrapbook. She remembered "her father bursting into their home with news of the 1917 revolution and twirling her mother around the living room." She helped found the Young Communist League, visited the Soviet Union for the Revolution's tenth anniversary, and stayed three years at a trade union college. Back in Britain, she worked for the CPGB, first in Lancashire among cotton workers and then in the South Wales coalfield, where she coorganized the Welsh section of the 1934 national Hunger March. After coordinating solidarity work for Republican Spain, she returned to London with her husband, the leading Communist Idris Cox, who was appointed editor of the *Daily Worker*. The couple continued working for the CP after the war, eventually retiring to South Wales. In her eighties, she joined a miners' wives support group during the 1984–85 coal strike.[7]

Another "behind-the-scenes socialist and unsung heroine of the labor movement," this time in the British Labour Party, was Joan Bourne, who died in June 2000. Born in 1909, she was active in the Labour Students' Federation, graduating in math from Reading University in 1930 and teaching for two years before moving to full-time Labour Party work in London. By 1939, she was appointed London women's organizer and began focusing on welfare state questions, especially child benefit and maternity care. In 1949, she had an affair with the married Scottish Labour Party organizer John Taylor, bearing an illegitimate daughter. In the ensuing cover-up, Bourne was shunted into a backroom research position, where she labored throughout the 1950s and 1960s on everything from arts policy to prison reform and crime prevention. She leaned to the party's left, rejecting the leadership's anti-Communism and strongly supporting the Campaign for Nuclear Disarmament (CND). Impressively, her personal lifestyle was consistent with her politics. In the face of much disapproval, she raised her daughter alone, accompanying her political work with eloquent campaigning for single mothers, including an important work of advocacy, *Pregnant and Alone,* in 1971.[8]

Democratic values and accomplishments could be pursued away from the thoroughfares of the Left's party politics, particularly by women, whose political roles remained heavily circumscribed by male attitudes. Barbara Kahan, who died in August 2000, became a preeminent influence on British child welfare policies after the war, pioneering enlightened practises as head of Oxfordshire's Children's Department from 1950 to 1970 and becoming a senior civil servant during the 1970s. She chaired the National Children's Bureau in 1985–94 and as a primary expert on residential care co-authored a report on abuse in 1991, *The Pindown Experience and the Protection of Children,* which laid a basis for reform. Kahan was a classic product of a dissenting left-wing milieu, born 1920 the daughter of a railwayman in southern England, in "a Methodist and Labour Party supporting home that revered books." Her railwayman grandfather "read to her everything from fairy tales to *The Pigrim's Progress* and the Bible," while her mother schooled her in good works. The 1926 General Strike was one benchmark experience, as was the sponsoring of a refugee Jewish girl in the 1930s. The Second World War was again decisive. Kahan was trained at Cambridge University and the London School of Economics, then in the prime of its left-wing influence. There, she worked both through the Labour Party and in Richard Acland's Commonwealth Party, which briefly focused many of the wartime's radical hopes.[9]

Democracy's enlargement often proceeded beyond the organized efforts of the socialist and Communist traditions. This was especially true for women, whose practical disfranchisement until after 1945 combined with the prevailing maternalisms of public discourse and the discriminatory cultures of labor movements to force women's agency into other tracks. For example, Alix Meynell, who died in September 1999, built an illustrious career in the British civil service, specializing mainly at the Board of Trade and attaining one of the highest ranks by her retirement in 1955. She began this career after graduating from Oxford in 1922 as one of the first women entering the administrative class. Over the next 30 years, partly by the force of her professional example and partly by determined campaigning, she helped lower the gender barriers: equal eligibility was established for all civil service ranks in 1946, when the ban on married women was also lifted; parity of salary scales was achieved in 1961. Meynell's career was shaped again by the challenges of the Second World War. She was a guiding intelligence behind the planning of wartime economic controls, including the management of trade flows and the regulation of materials and design for domestic products. She ran the new Reconstruction Department in January

1943. She pioneered the utility furniture scheme and other initiatives designed for wartime shortages, often brilliantly improvised, applying the modernist principles that inspired progressive intellectuals between the wars—"plain, functional and modernist," reflecting "the ideals of rationalist living."

Alix Meynell's life strikingly conveys those other strands of Left history, which descended from the modernist ideals of the pre-1914 women's suffragist movements and visionary projections of "the new life," while embracing ideas of personal freedom, sexual experimentation, and women's independence during the 1920s. She came from the virtually fatherless Kilroy family in Nottingham, the second of four sisters, with a mother of strong Unitarian and suffragist background who was herself trained as a nurse. She entered adulthood after the First World War, as British women were acquiring their citizenship, and emerged from an Oxford education committed to career, independence, intellectual seriousness, and the ideal of a truthful self. "Her two bibles were Maynard Keynes's *The Economic Consequences of the Peace* and Virginia Woolf's *A Room of One's Own.*" She cherished a lifelong and open relationship with the poet and typographer Francis Meynell, founder of the Nonesuch Press, whom she met in 1929 and eventually married in 1946. Briefly a Communist, he was "a notorious political firebrand, a courageous supporter of the suffragettes, a conscientious objector during the First World War and founder, with Bertrand Russell, of the No Conscription Fellowship, an active supporter of the General Strike in 1926." In this relationship, her "own politics moved further to the left." By the 1930s, she exchanged pacifism for the urgency of antifascism. In retirement, she "joined the protest against Suez in 1956 and campaigned energetically for CND." In 1981, she became a founding member of the Social Democratic Party, running unsuccessfully in 1986 for local government.[10]

The progressive commitments shaping Meynell's biography in the 1920s owed less to the organized presence of socialist and Communist parties, although they certainly delivered vital supports. Margarete Schütte-Lihotsky, whose life encompassed the century's full duration, from 1897 to January 2000, was Austria's first woman architect, having trained at the Imperial Arts and Crafts School during 1915–19, at a time when "noone could possibly imagine anyone allowing a woman to build a house—not even me." She became involved immediately with the Vienna housing movement, collaborating with the pioneer modernist Alfred Loos in the design of affordable single dwellings, as against the integrated housing blocks preferred by the municipal socialists of Red Vienna. She was recruited by the progressive German architect Ernst May to the Frankfurt housing department in 1926, where she invented the so-called Frankfurt Kitchen, designed to simplify household tasks from a working woman's point of view, using principles of function and efficiency. Her designs considered all aspects of domestic everydayness, including kindergartens, children's furniture, laundries, and self-assembled fittings. In 1930, she visited the Soviet Union with May and her husband, the architect Wilhelm Schütte, and stayed for seven years "developing standardized designs for kindergartens, nurseries and children's furniture for the newly developed heavy industry cities."

A Communist from the early 1920s, Schütte-Lihotsky returned from the Soviet Union to Vienna after working briefly in Istanbul and connected with the anti-Nazi Resistance. She was almost immediately arrested and spent the rest of the war in a Bavarian prison. After 1945, she again returned to Vienna but found little acceptance in the new Cold War environment. Only in the 1980s did she receive public recognition, receiving the Vienna City Prize for Architecture, followed by a belated exhibition honoring her career in 1993. In 1998, she "oversaw a project for a housing estate in north-east Vienna designed for women by women—the largest project of its kind in Europe."[11]

BEGINNINGS

In these lives, the Second World War stands out as the defining experience. It either marked the passage to young adulthood, invariably dramatized by joining the anti-Nazi Resistance or serving in the antifascist war, or saw the peak of careers already begun. It was a time of palpable significance, when left-wing lives had readily accessible *meaning*, connected to the unfolding of a great and unifying cause. It was a time when everything meshed together. The Left had come in from the cold, welcomed from the margins to the centerground of national consensus. By 1945, it was a broader and more inclusive category. It appealed more honestly across gender divisions too, insisting on votes for women and honoring their citizenship, even if the latter still settled around familiar gendered distinctions.

The resulting postwar settlements realized many of the hopes the struggle against Nazism had encouraged. Above all, democratic citizenship was lastingly institutionalized in western Europe, for both women and men. There were limits too: participatory forms of democracy, also nourished via the wartime dynamics of Resistance and everyone pulling together, were quickly preempted or abandoned. The Cold War's arrival during 1947 then imposed an abrupt halt, recasting political agendas and opening a sharp new division between Right and Left. This dour normalizing of postwar possibilities sent Communists, left socialists, and other dissidents back to the margins in the west, while viciously policing them in the east. But however fleeting the antifascist unity was in its strongest forms, the Second World War's meanings still formed a baseline of political culture—a template of popular expectations—for the next two decades.[12]

In stark contrast, the previous moment of general European change, the First World War and accompanying revolutionary crises, had been one of *fission*. That first wave of democracy had broken earlier, and the democratic gains, from the franchise to union recognition and the eight-hour day, failed to last. Instead, societal polarization and political extremism became the rule, leading to the rise of fascism and the Second World War. Of course, it also led to the fateful split in socialism. The catastrophic contribution of the mutual enmity between social democrats and Communists to the early triumphs of fascism can hardly be overstated. Despite the cooperation of the war years, moreover, it was only after 1989–91 that this divisiveness was fully overcome.

A comparable moment of fission occurred in 1968. By that time, the exemplary lives described earlier were at their midpoint or older. From their perspective, in Western Europe many of the old goals seemed to have been won: permanently established parliamentary democracies; secure civil rights; regulated labor markets via strong systems of union recognition, full employment policies, and public planning; social security through the welfare state; equitable tax systems; public values emphasizing social justice and collective goods. By the 1960s, most Western European Communists had also accepted these gains as the best they were likely to see. "After 1956, my activism was transformed into something different and more detached," one of them reflected. "From that time, it was clear to me that the dream was over."[13]

But in 1968, new dreams arrived. In Eastern Europe, they took particular form. In Czechoslovakia, as well as in Yugoslavia and Poland, demands for cultural freedom and the opening of debate allowed the suppressed possibilities of the immediate postwar years to reappear. But the crushing of the Prague Spring by the Soviet invasion of August 1968 finally killed the prospects of Communist reform. The next time opposition exploded—in the Polish rebellions of 1970, 1976, and 1980–81—pro-reform factions inside the ruling CP no longer played a part. The Prague Spring's aspirations certainly remained: pluralism and free elections, mixed economy, cultural freedoms, democratization across the board. But anti-Communism now became the default agreement of Eastern European reformers, and in this sense the break was definitive. On the other hand, this loss of Communist legitimacy in the East spurred its renewal in the West, because breaking with Moscow over the invasion of Czechoslovakia laid the basis for Eurocommunist independence.

Between the start of the Cold War and the late 1960s, Communists were the strongest guardians of radicalism in Western Europe, though increasingly as more militant oppositional versions of social democracy rather than genuinely revolutionary critics of capitalism. But the new radicalisms of 1968, arising first among students and then more generally among the young, were no respecters of seniority. They aimed their fire as much against the old Left as against Conservatives and the Right. Bitter generational gaps were opened in the Left as a result.

The energies released in 1968 revived participatory democracy and direct action, while pushing democracy's challenge into new territories of personal life. From the resulting disorder came a variety of new activisms whose style seemed exotic and unimportant to the old Left of socialists and Communists—including feminisms, gay and lesbian politics, the wider politics of sexuality, health and associated lifestyle movements, radical ecology, squatting and other aspects of the alternative scene, peace movements, antiracism and multiculturalism, free festivals and traveling, and more. Such movements ripped open existing political agendas. They redefined the boundaries between public and private, the personal and the political, opening up the meanings of political action and recasting the very category of the political itself. As a result, the main grounds of politics radically shifted.[14] Moreover, the focus of the new movements was extraparliamentary. They agitated beyond the confines of the socialist committee room and the labor movement's historic institutional subculture.

Belatedly, Communists began responding to these developments in the 1980s, from the large Italian party through the medium-sized Scandinavian CPs to the smaller ones in Britain, the Netherlands, and elsewhere. Their socialist rivals lagged behind: the SPD remained stolidly hostile toward the new Left and its ideas, while the Labour Party tore itself apart in the 1980s, successfully containing that challenge. In most countries, wide gaps opened between the Left's main electoral force and the extraparliamentary social movements, whom parliamentary socialists either denounced or showed little interest in recruiting. By the 1990s, Green parties, reconstituted left-socialist parties, and various electoral groupings began speaking for the new movements instead, occupying small but important niches to the left of the main socialist party and occasionally joining it in coalition. But much of the new energy remained untapped in electoral terms.

Crucially, these generational splits occurred in a surrounding context of profound structural changes. On the one hand, both the Left's major strands since 1917–23, social democratic and Communist, were politically exhausted. The Communist tradition was already in deep crisis after 1968, its Eastern European legitimacy in shreds, and Mikhail Gorbachev's bold initiatives of the later 1980s failed ultimately to realize Communist reform inside the USSR itself. Meanwhile, social democracy had entered a crisis of its own. It both lost momentum by the 1960s, having realized its main reforms, and rejected 1968 as a source for renewal. Most decisively of all, the end of the postwar boom in 1973 removed the main prop of social democratic success, because postwar corporatisms couldn't function without the continuously rising prosperity. Ironically, just as Western Communist parties sought to shed the Soviet handicap by remaking themselves in the social democratic image, most notably via Eurocommunism, social democracy of the established kind became politically a dead end.

On the other hand, the post-1973 recession brought drastic changes in the capitalist economies and their social structures, with huge implications for the effectiveness of government in national states. The final part of this book has explored the consequences of these shifts in great detail. Changes in the world economy undermined the Keynesian thinking behind social democratic policy since the 1940s. Sometimes dramatically, as in the British Labour government's volte-face of 1975 or the French Socialist one in 1981–82, or by steady erosion, social democrats found themselves abandoning old beliefs in public spending. By the 1980s, and neoliberalism's full-scale assault on the Keynesian-welfare state system, social democratic parties were hopelessly adrift. Concurrently, the historic heavy industrial and manufacturing sectors of the European economies, and large parts of newer industries, were gutted. If globalization deprived social democrats of their ability to manage national capitalism in the interests of their working-class supporters, deindustrialization was drastically reducing the size of the old working class itself. During the last third of the twentieth century, capitalist restructuring transformed the accustomed meanings of class.

Finally, socialism's distinctive organizational world also dissolved. The modern mass party, with its continuous and ramified presence in its supporters' lives, sustained by sociability and everyday identification as well as by election campaigns, invented by socialists in the late nineteenth century, had gone. Even the most impressive of those movements, like the postwar counterculture of the Italian Communists, no longer existed in the old way. Between the 1880s and the 1930s, those cultures of socialism, linked to residential working-class communities, trade unionism, and pliable local government resources, formed the solid foundation of socialist party success, with a long afterlife lasting well into the 1960s. Once they were gone, socialists needed to design other strategies for building and holding their support. In light of the structural changes mentioned earlier—capitalist restructuring and globalization, deindustrialization, and the re-composing of the working class—this death of the party spelled the end of the socialist tradition dominating the Left between the 1860s and 1960s.

REMEMBERING THE FUTURE

There is much this book hasn't discussed. In particular, the inchoate political arrangements briefly glimpsed at the end of the 1990s, which returned socialist parties to government, need definition. Detailed treatment would focus on the tentative alliances linking those parties with Greens and other smaller radical groupings, exploring the relations of both with their supporters, which differ profoundly from the ties previously binding socialist parties to the working class. These emerging modalities of political action are still only dimly understood. The depoliticizing of national politics—relentlessly contracting around media-managed election campaigns, which replace strategy with market research, election rallies with focus groups, and citizens with consumers—is matched by the liveliness of grassroots activism, which eschews the centralized approach of the Left in earlier times, seeking shifting coalitions and informal localized forms instead. The interrelationship of these trends, in times of declining electoral turnout and steadily encroaching apathy, remains very unclear. Interactions between voting and longer-lasting political identifications, and between voting and class, are critical to puzzling this out. Given the effects of capitalist restructuring on labor markets and income distribution, the decline of historic industries, and the transformations of the working class, the contemporary logics of class formation badly need to be understood.

Likewise, the transnational dimension of the European Left's history is becoming ever more important. This book has tried to approach its subject in genuinely European terms. Rather than concentrating on a few major countries and allowing European history to become French and German history by default, I've tried to draw out the more general trends and distinguish the common patterns—for example, the long-run importance of the north-central European social democratic core—while making many particular contrasts and comparisons. At the same time, outside the histories of the various Internationals, I have not addressed the forms of cross-national cooperation either among sections of the Left or affecting them. With the growing strength of European integration, from the 1957 Treaty of Rome to the 1992 legislation and the Treaty of Maastricht, this domain requires ever greater attention. Action through the European Union has become a key enabling condition for effective national governance. One future challenge for the Left will involve translating its politics of democratic enlargement onto this European stage—whether via democratizing the EU's central institutions and making its executive accountable to the European Parliament or by implementing a radical social agenda. If national Keynesianism has been increasingly precluded by the impact of globalized capitalism, a European context for regulative intervention is available for the capture.[15]

Globalization requires creative political attention—that is, practical strategizing beyond the glib rhetoric of universalizing values and standardized practices and beyond the fatalistic recognition of the disempowering consequences of global capital flows for national economic sovereignty and government action, all of which vacate the critical analysis of capitalism per se.[16] Moreover, we need to ask: what are globalism's distinctive social relations; what forms of culture and belief are being generated; and what forms of politics might be predicated around them. Or, more radically: what is globalization's utopia? If socialism's classical utopia died slowly with the degeneration of the Russian Revolution, what are the visions, even in the prosaic guise of social goals, that replace this vanished ideal? During the 1990s, neoliberalism proposed only the diffuse and empty languages of "modernity" for this vacant space, which also became the surviving so-cialist parties' derivative response.[17] But vacuous and underspecified notions of a "New Center" or "Third Way," pragmatically sited on the already assembled new terrain, are no substitute for visionary analysis of feasible democratic change.[18]

However, a programmatic or detailed discussion of the tasks facing the European Left at the start of the twenty-first century lies beyond the scope of this book. In the end, this is a history and not a prospectus. It reviews an evolving and then established political tradition, assesses its strengths and failings, and explores its apparent demise. More important, it seeks to place that tradition—*socialism* in its varying forms between the 1860s and the present—in the wider setting of struggles for democracy, because *that* context brings both the splendid achievements and the distressing limita-tions of the socialist tradition better into view. Furthermore, by identifying "the Left" not with socialism but with a more capacious and exacting framework of democracy, in all its appropriate social, economic, cultural, and personal dimensions, the disabling implications of the crises of social-ism during the last third of the twentieth century might be brought under control. If socialism has been essential to democracy's best achievements, I've insisted, then democracy's possibilities always exceeded socialism's range. This becomes especially clear in the period since 1968.

Thus my book is avowedly *not* an epitaph. If its final part narrates a series of endings, as Communisms of East and West lost their projects, social democracies shriveled in ambitions, and the Soviet Union left the map, then it also explores the spaces where new politics can arise. Socialism in certain reified and discredited versions may now be "dead" or appro-priately consigned to an archive, but rich resources nonetheless reside in the socialist tradition. Unless questions of social justice are to be banished definitively from the political agenda, and unless capitalism finally immu-nizes itself against ethical and egalitarian critique—two conditions now perilously close—socialist arguments will remain vital to radical democratic hopes.

Throughout their history, socialists' democratic advocacy fell woefully short on a series of vital fronts, gender and race primary among them. Nonetheless, *socialist* values still provided the best available place to start. Likewise, however cramped and parched the peculiarly centrist versions of socialism currently prevailing in Europe may be, they still hold a place for a democratic politics potentially more generous. For anyone adhering to radical visions of a more just social order—for socialists—it's hard to imag-ine a contemporary political climate less hospitable.[19] Making the case for socialist policies, in the relentlessly triumphalist neoliberal climate that be-came generalized during the 1980s, has become extraordinarily difficult. In these terms, socialists and other radical democrats face a dispiriting politics of the very, very long haul. Yet, as feasible forms of democratic enlargement begin to be imagined again, both the existing socialist parties and the deeper reservoir of their histories will continue to play an indispensible part.

The individual lives recounted earlier in this conclusion are meant to stand in for a much larger historic generation. That generation helped bring to fruition a century of democratic struggle described in this book. They had the joy and the challenge of putting into place, albeit imperfectly, institutions and policies their forbears could only imagine, many giving their lives along the way. With the passing of these activists, of lives lived passionately and tenaciously in a generous and enduring cause, we run the risk of seeing their legacy permanently smeared. In our profoundly conservative context of capitalist restructuring and its globalized market order, words like "socialism," "democracy," and "freedom" are being wrenched from their appropriate histories and translated out of all recognition. However, in imagining the fruits of a fully democratized Europe, despite all the continuing imperfections and exclusions of the present, we are living part of the future the twentieth-century Left had pursued. In meeting the challenge of further democratic change, the rest of that future will need to be remembered.

Notes

PREFACE

1. William Morris, *A Dream of John Ball* (1887), quoted by Thompson, *William Morris,* p. 722.
2. Walter Benjamin, "Theses on the Philosophy of History," in Benjamin, *Illuminations,* pp. 259–60.

INTRODUCTION

1. New Zealand and Australia count as "full democracies" only if we disregard exclusions by race in relation to Maori and Aboriginal populations and nonwhite immigration.
2. For the dynamics of democracy's international diffusion, see Therborn, "Rule"; Markoff, "Really Existing" and *Waves;* Borón, "Latin America."
3. Alexander, "Women, Class," p. 282.
4. Social histories of industrialization weren't enough by themselves to sustain successful socialist movements; parliamentary socialist parties also needed the juridical order created by the European constitutional settlement of the 1860s, while the First World War brought labor movements broader popular acceptance, access to government, and incorporation within the emergent structures of the national economy. This book takes great pains to emphasize the complex interactions between social and political histories in this sense; both are essential.

PART I INTRODUCTION

1. After being forced from teaching because of her socialism, she retrained as a secretary and in 1896–98 was employed as such by Eleanor Marx. The son of an Irish London policeman, James ("Shamus") Sullivan was a factory hand who taught himself bookkeeping and shorthand, working subsequently as a railway clerk and typist. Their union was lifelong, he dying in 1945, she in 1966. Their second child, Elsa Lanchester Sullivan (born 1902), became a renowned actress. Details from Hunt, *Equivocal Feminists,* pp. 94–106, 270, 272–3; Kapp, *Crowded Years,* p. 621; Lanchester, *Elsa Lanchester.*
2. Hunt, *Equivocal Feminists,* p. 96.
3. This was the editorial commentary in the SDF weekly, *Justice,* 2 November 1895. Quoted ibid., p. 99.
4. Ibid., p. 102.
5. Ibid., pp. 102, 103.
6. Weeks, "Havelock Ellis," p. 153.
7. Hunt, *Equivocal Feminists,* p. 266; Liddington, *Life,* pp. 48–9; Pierson, *Marxism,* pp. 71, 169–71, 226; Kapp, *Crowded Years,* pp. 267–9, 319, 355, 481, 525, 636.

8. Hunt, *Equivocal Feminists,* p. 267.

9. The phrases are quoted from various British socialist statements of the 1880s in Pierson, *Marxism,* pp. 226–7.

CHAPTER 1

1. Caute, *Left,* pp. 26–44.

2. See Soboul, *Sans-Culottes;* Williams, *Artisans.*

3. Such coalitions interacted with the faction fighting of respectable politicians, occasionally breaking through to short-lived revolutionary triumphs. In the turmoil of revolution, they produced bewildering mosaics of rapidly shifting alignments. Classic examples may be found in contemporary accounts of 1848 by Karl Marx and Friedrich Engels. See Marx, *Revolutions.*

4. My aim in this section is to suggest the general interrelationship between political programs (Jacobinism, radical democracy, early socialism) and social interests and implies no causal dependency of the former on the latter. On the contrary, the programs concerned themselves shaped the operative presence of those interests, from the *menu peuple* and sans-culottes to the emergent working class. Nor am I presenting a full account of nineteenth-century social movements, whose rhythms and forms of mobilization were far more complex than I have space to discuss. See Tilly, "Social Movements," "Britain Creates," and "Contentious Repertoires"; Tarrow, *Power.*

5. My account of the transition to industrial capitalism and its consequences for democratic thinking builds on the accumulated social history of the past half century, whose findings have hugely accelerated since the 1970s. Any full accounting would be impossible, but the following are a place to start: Hobsbawm, *Labouring Men;* Thompson, *Making;* Conze, "From 'Pöbel' "; Samuel, "Workshop"; Taylor, *Eve;* Sewell, *Work;* Katznelson and Zolberg (ed.), *Working-Class Formation.*

6. See the entries on "Socialist" and "Society" in Williams, *Keywords,* pp. 238–47.

7. Bottomore, "Social Democracy," p. 441.

8. Caute, *Left,* p. 31.

9. The Six Points were as follows: universal male suffrage over twenty-one; secret ballots; no property qualifications for MPs; payment of MPs; equal electoral districts; annual parliaments. See Cole and Filson (eds.), *British,* p. 352. The Six Points originated with the London Working Men's Association and other London radical organizations in early 1837 and were codified into the People's Charter in May 1838. During these intensive discussions, women's suffrage was dropped. See Ward, *Chartism,* p. 78; Thompson, *Chartists,* p. 124; Clark, *Struggle,* pp. 220–32; and more generally, Schwarzkopf, *Women.*

10. Female enfranchisement in the capitalist world came in two main waves with the world wars—first in Austria (1918), Germany (1919), Denmark (1915), Sweden (1918), Netherlands (1919), Canada (1920), the United States (1920), and Britain (1928); then in France (1945), Italy (1946), Belgium (1948), and Japan (1952). Women could not vote in Switzerland till 1971. See Therborn, "Rule," based on 17 states, excluding Greece, Iceland, Ireland, Luxemburg, Portugal, and Spain.

11. Blanqui's ideas sought to rationalize the great Parisian uprisings of the

1790s into a program, celebrating the relationship between the Jacobin dictatorship and mass insurrection, with revolutionary conspiracy as the key. See Spitzer, *Revolutionary Theories;* Bernstein, *Auguste Blanqui.*

12. See Rose, *Gracchus Babeuf;* Eisenstein, *First Professional;* Lehning, *From Buonarroti.*

13. See Lehning, *From Buonarroti;* Kelly, *Mikhail Bakunin;* Ravindranathan, *Bakunin;* Joll, *Anarchists,* pp. 84–114; Woodcock, *Anarchism,* pp. 134–70.

14. See Joll, *Anarchists,* pp. 117–48; Sonn, *Anarchism,* pp. 69–98.

15. *Socialism: Utopian and Scientific* comprised three chapters from Engels's work *Herr Eugen Dühring's Revolution in Science,* originally published in German in 1878. Known as the *Anti-Dühring,* the larger work was the first systematic exposition of "Marxism" as a single body of thought. For socialist thought before Marx and Engels, see Hobsbawm, "Pre-Marxian Socialism," a model of dense reference and distilled understanding.

16. See Lichtheim, *Origins;* Spencer, *Charles Fourier;* Beecher, *Charles Fourier;* Riasonovsky, *Teaching;* Manuel, *New World;* Claeys, *Citizens and Saints;* Harrison, *Robert Owen;* Carlisle, *Proffered Crown;* Evans, *Social Romanticism.*

17. Jones, "Utopian Socialism," p. 139.

18. Ibid., p. 142. See also Crowder, *Classical Anarchism;* Morland, *Demanding.*

19. Royle, *Robert Owen;* Harrison, *Robert Owen;* Taylor, *Visions;* Kolmerton, *Women.*

20. See Garnett, *Cooperation;* Harrison, *Robert Owen;* Claeys, *Citizens and Saints;* Hardy and Davidson (eds.), *Utopian Thought;* Beecher, *Victor Considérant.*

21. See Johnson, *Utopian Communism.*

22. See Sewell, *Work,* pp. 194–276; Bezucha, *Lyon Uprising;* Berenson, *Populist Religion;* Beecher, *Victor Considérant;* Moss, *Origins.*

23. See Vincent, *Pierre-Joseph Proudhon;* Ehrenberg, *Proudhon;* Johnson, *Utopian Communism.*

24. Garnett, *Cooperation;* Royle, *Robert Owen;* Harrison, *Robert Owen;* Hardy and Davidson (eds.), *Utopian Thought;* Taylor, *Visions.*

25. Loubère, *Louis Blanc;* Himka, *Socialism.*

26. The Owenite socialist William Thompson (1783–1833), quoted by Taylor, "Socialist Feminism," p. 160.

27. Ibid.

28. Ibid., p. 158. More generally: Taylor, *Eve;* Kolmerton, *Women.* For French feminism in the wake of Saint-Simon and Fourier: Moses, *French Feminism* and "Saint-Simonian;" Weil, "Feminocentric Utopia;" Scott, *Only Paradoxes,* pp. 57–89, and "Men."

29. Taylor, "Socialist Feminism," p. 161.

30. Ibid., pp. 160, 162.

31. Arblaster, *Rise,* p. 273.

32. See above all Collins and Abramsky, *Karl Marx,* esp. pp. 101–57, 287–303.

33. The Democratic-Socialists were the broad grouping of the republican Left coalescing during the first year after the 1848 Revolution in France. See Berenson, *Populist Religion.* For Chartism, see Yeo, "Some Practices," and Epstein, "Some Organizational"; also Yeo, "Culture."

CHAPTER 2

1. Marx borrowed the metaphor of the "old mole" from Shakespeare's *Hamlet*, working it into his pamphlet *The Eighteenth Brumaire of Louis Bonaparte*, originally written for a short-lived New York journal in May 1852. See Marx, *Surveys*, pp. 143–249.

2. Beneath the legal repression of the 1850s, popular cultures of solidarity clearly survived, notably in the clubs and associational life of the skilled trades. For Germany, see Offermann's now classic *Arbeiterbewegung* and his summary in Offermann, "Lassallean Labor Movement," plus Gotthardt's intensive treatment of local dynamics in northwest Germany, *Industrialisierung*. For France, see Berenson, *Populist Religion;* McPhee, *Politics;* Aminzade, *Ballots;* Merriman, *Red City*, pp. 103–33; Faure, "Public Meeting," and Dalotel and Freiermuth, "Socialism," in Rifkin and Thomas (eds.), *Voices*, pp. 181–234 and 235–328; Johnson, *Paradise*.

3. Marx never entirely renounced the trappings of bourgeois respectability in his private life, even during his family's impoverishment in the 1850s. Similarly, Engels lived the schizoid existence of revolutionary and businessman while managing the family interests in Manchester, before buying out of the partnership in 1869.

4. Engels's main published works in Marx's lifetime were *The Condition of the Working Class in England* (1845), and the *Anti-Dühring* (1878), from which *Socialism: Utopian and Scientific* (1880) was also excerpted. He also produced a large amount of journalism and collaborated closely with Marx on most of his key writings, coauthoring two of these published in Marx's lifetime, *The Holy Family* and the *Communist Manifesto* (1845 and 1848). Of Marx's early writings, only two, *The Eighteenth Brumaire of Louis Bonaparte* (1869) and the *Manifesto*, were republished in his lifetime. The latter was not widely diffused until the 1872 German reprint, the first edition actually to bear Marx and Engels's names.

5. When knowledge of a future outcome is claimed, a manipulative approach to popular politics easily follows, in which the masses are moved to the appropriate destination, whether or not they understand. During 1905–17 Leon Trotsky formulated this belief that revolution would pass through distinct but continuous stages, bourgeois-democratic and proletarian, one growing from the other in a preordained pattern, as the concept of "permanent revolution," but it was anticipated fairly exactly by Marx and Engels in 1848–50. See their *Address of the Central Committee of the Communist League* from March 1850, in Marx, *Revolutions*, especially the final paragraphs, pp. 329–30. For a good commentary, see Löwy, *Politics*.

6. The first of the Marx quotations is from the *Minutes of the Central Committee Meeting of the Communist League*, 15 September 1850, in Marx, *Revolutions*, p. 341; the second from Karl Marx, *The Class Struggles in France: 1848 to 1850*, in Marx, *Surveys*, p. 131. Engels's comments on the misperceptions of the 1848 crisis are in his famous introduction to the 1895 German edition of *The Class Struggles in France* (Moscow, 1968), p. 12, which remains an excellent guide to the change in Marx's and Engels's politics in 1850. See also Williams, "Eighteenth Brumaire."

7. Karl Marx, preface to *A Contribution to the Critique of Political Econ-*

omy, in Marx, *Early Writings,* p. 425; Engels to Joseph Bloch, 21–22 September 1890, in Marx and Engels, *Selected Correspondence,* p. 417.

8. Karl Marx, "Instructions for Delegates to the Geneva Congress of the First International" (Sept. 1966), in Marx, *First International,* p. 92.

9. Lichtheim, *Marxism,* p. 128. While Marx saw the need for decisive and even repressive measures to ensure the revolution's immediate survival, he uses the term "dictatorship of the proletariat" (often mistakenly attributed to Blanqui) as a general synonym for the democratic rule of the working class, as the overwhelming majority of the population, over the rest of society. See especially Hunt, *Political Ideas,* and Johnstone's two essays, "Marx, Engels," and "Marx, Blanqui."

10. See especially Hunt's conclusion in *Political Ideas,* 2:363–7.

11. Marx, *Capital,* p. 929. The phrase "subordination of politics and historical development" is taken from Hobsbawm, "Marx, Engels, and Politics," p. 256.

12. See Shanin (ed.), *Late Marx.*

13. Jones, "Engels," p. 19.

14. By 1888 Engels's deteriorating eyesight often limited his work to two hours a day. Only he and the family could read Marx's almost indecipherable handwriting, and it was vital to train younger people before he died. Kautsky agreed to make a fair copy of the manuscript for volume 4 (over 750 pages) in 1889 but made only slow progress, much to Engels's irritation. See Henderson, *Life,* 2:658–60, 728–30.

15. See Hobsbawm, "Fortunes."

16. Jones, "Engels," p. 19.

17. Engels often quoted Marx's ironic quip that he was not himself a "Marxist." See Engels to Bernstein, 2–3 November, 1882, in Hirsch (ed.), *Bernstein,* p. 154.

18. This paragraph follows the argument in Haupt, "Marx."

19. Anderson, *Considerations,* p. 6. In keeping with the effort at sealing Marx's heritage, plans were also floated for a collected edition of the works. Franz Mehring coordinated the first edition of the Marx-Engels correspondence in 1913 and published the first biography in 1918.

20. Details from Hobsbawm, "Fortunes," pp. 328, 342, 331, and from a number of specialized bibliographies, including Andréas, *Le Manifeste.* See also Hanisch, "Neuere Studien."

21. Langewiesche and Schönhoven, "Arbeiterbibliotheken." This article is based on a comprehensive synthesis of the surviving records of workers' library borrowings before 1914, which counted over a million borrowings in total. The findings are also summarized in Lidtke, *Alternative Culture,* pp. 178–89.

22. Andreucci, "Diffusion," p. 215. For Labriola's testimony on the difficulty of procuring Marx's works, see Piccone, *Italian Marxism,* pp. 54–66.

23. This is the conclusion of the most comprehensive analysis of workers' autobiographies and related evidence for Germany. See Lorreck, *Wie man,* esp. pp. 27–30, 103–58, 247–54.

24. Lidtke, *Alternative Culture,* p. 194.

25. Henderson, *Life,* 2:569.

26. See Langewiesche and Schönhoven, "Arbeiterbibliotheken," and Hans-Josef Steinberg, "Workers' Libraries." Kautsky and Bebel are cited from Steenson,

Kautsky, p. 65; and Bebel, *Women,* p. 371. The best introduction to the question of Kautsky's Darwinism is Geary, "Kautsky," pp. 130–35.

27. Andreucci, "Diffusion," p. 217.

28. Mack Smith, *Mussolini,* p. 15.

29. Rizzi, "Socialist Propaganda," p. 474. For the eclecticism of the late-nineteenth-century socialist milieu, see the following articles on Britain: Yeo, "New Life"; Barrow, "Socialism" and "Determinism"; Kean, "Vivisection," pp. 26–9.

30. See here the remarkable influence of the German worker philosopher Joseph Dietzgen (1828–88), whose monist and dialectical philosophy of materialism was perhaps the commonest introduction to Marxist philosophy for most working-class autodidacts in Britain between 1906 (when his works first became available in English translation) and the mid-1920s (when Soviet-sponsored "dialectical materialism" began displacing it from Marxist education). Dietzgen's influence was a classic instance of eclecticism—that is, of Marxism's "impurities" as the ideas entered the new socialist parties. See Macintyre, *Proletarian Science,* pp. 129–32, and "Dietzgen"; Rée, *Proletarian Philosophers,* pp. 23–45.

31. Andreucci, "Diffusion," p. 219; and for more detail, Andreucci, *Il marxismo.*

32. For the ethical emphases of Swedish socialism, see Hurd, *Public Spheres,* pp. 115–24, 141–8, 191–237; and for the Austrian movement, Mattl, "Austria," p. 2.

CHAPTER 3

1. See Williams, *Culture,* pp. 13–9, and *Keywords,* pp. 60–9; Briggs, "Language of 'Class,' " and "Language of 'Mass' "; Jones, "Rethinking Chartism"; Sewell, *Work;* Conze, "From 'Pöbel.' "

2. This distinction between control over the means of production and control over the labor process, where the former entailed the "formal" subordination of labor to capital but the latter made it "real," is discussed by Hall, "The 'Political,' " esp. pp. 28–36.

3. Samuel, "Workshop," pp. 8, 45. For the authoritative account of steam power and its progress, see von Tunzelman, *Steam Power.*

4. See especially Sabel and Zeitlin, "Historical Alternatives"; Berg, *Age.*

5. The exposition in this paragraph is essentially a paraphrase of the famous passages in the *Communist Manifesto.* See Marx, *Revolutions,* pp. 75–77.

6. Tilly, "Demographic Origins," pp. 25–6. For the relationship of these complexities to the gender dynamics of working-class households, see Gullickson, *Spinners;* Accampo, *Industrialization;* Quataert, "Shaping"; Levine, *Family Formation.*

7. See especially Moss, *Origins;* Sewell, *Work;* Johnson, *Utopian Communism;* Vincent, *Proudhon.*

8. For this argument, see especially Agulhon, *Republic.*

9. Thompson, *Making,* p. 194.

10. Prothero, *Artisans,* p. 5.

11. Behagg, "Custom," p. 480.

12. See chapter 1, note 9.

13. Alexander, "Women," p. 136.

14. Ibid., pp. 137, 139.

15. See Thompson, *Chartists,* p. 125, citing pamphlets by the Manchester Chartist Reginald John Richardson and the London Chartist John Watkins.

16. Family strategies of male artisans in resisting industrial capitalism varied with local circumstances. Thus handloom weavers in western France preserved their craft independence precisely by sending their daughters into the new "sweated trades" of garments and shoes, exploiting their daughters' proletarianized earning power in the higher interest of their trade. See Liu, "What Price," and *Weaver's Knot;* also Bull, "Lombard."

17. Engels, *The Condition of the Working Class in 1844,* in Marx and Engels, *On Britain,* p. 179.

18. In general, see the essays in Frader and Rose (eds.), *Gender,* and Rose, " 'Gender,' " together with three national case studies: Canning, *Languages;* Coffin, *Politics;* and Rose, *Limited Livelihoods.* For an example of the varying complexities of long-term changes in gendered divisions of labor, see Sommestad, "Gendering Work."

19. For an interesting comparison of three industrial regions with radical political culture, see Cooke, "Radical Regions."

20. Lucas calls class formation in the two cities "two different kinds of proletarianization"—"the freeing of labor power through the destruction of handicrafts on the one side [Remscheid], the soaking up of human masses from agrarian provinces and regions through the fully developed capitalist centers on the other [Hamborn]." See Lucas, *Zwei Formen,* p. 41.

21. For example, Hamborn working-class society was dominated by the hard-drinking culture of aggressive masculinity, as opposed to the family-centered culture of sobriety and self-improvement, a feature linked to the big sexual imbalance in Hamborn's demographic profile. This in turn was connected to the absence of a labor market for women in Hamborn, again by contrast with Remscheid, where women's wage-work contributed to working-class family budgets.

22. For a cognate comparison of Hamborn with Düsseldorf, see Nolan, "Workers."

23. Since the 1960s social historians have mainly preferred the "artisanal," model stressing the leading role of male craft workers in the shaping of labor movements. For a compact example of the resulting debates, see Andreucci, "Italy," pp. 195–208, and Davis, "Socialism," pp. 197–210; plus three differing studies of Milan: Bell, *Sesto;* Hunecke, *Arbeiterschaft;* and Tilly, *Politics.*

24. For the importance of religious differences, see Zarnowska, "Religion"; Ritter and Tenfelde, *Arbeiter,* pp. 747–80; Brose, *Christian Labor;* Schneider, "Religion" and *Christlichen Gewerkschaften;* Wintle, *Pillars;* McLeod (ed.), *European Religion, Piety,* and *Religion.*

25. For a fine study of the prehistory of this process, focusing on the casual laborers, ragpickers, beggars, prostitutes, and other categories of the urban poor pushed to the dangerous periphery of the city during the early stages of industrialization, see Merriman, *Margins.*

26. Ross, *Love,* p. 8. See also Jones, *Outcast London.*

27. Few historians have managed to bring both spheres of class articulation together. But see Ross, *Love;* von Saldern, *Häuserleben;* Lindenberger, *Straßenpolitik;* Davis, *Home Fires;* and Lüdtke, *Eigen-Sinn.*

28. For the general argument about urbanization, spatial settlement, and new neighborhood networks between the 1890s and 1920, see Cronin, "Labor Insurgency," pp. 35–41; Savage and Miles, *Remaking,* pp. 57–72. For two illuminating case studies, one (West Ham) commenting on the other (Preston), see Marriott, *Culture,* pp. 1–26; Savage, *Dynamics.*

29. Hobsbawm, "Making," p. 184. For a strong counterargument to Hobsbawm's, stressing the internally divided cultures of the urban working class, with particular stress on gender and ethnicity, see Davies and Fielding (eds.), *Workers' Worlds;* Davies, *Leisure;* and Fielding, *Class.*

30. Hobsbawm, "Labour in the Great City," p. 144.

31. See Lucas, *Zwei Formen;* Boch, *Handwerker-Sozialisten;* Smith, *Conflict and Compromise;* Magnusson, *Contest;* Merriman, *Red City;* Scott, "Social History"; Davis, "Socialism," pp. 196–7, 222–3.

32. Fink, "Forward March."

33. Municipal socialism depended heavily on both the national political climate and election law in the particular city. For the contrasting opportunities available to the highly organized socialists of Red Vienna after 1918 and to the Progressive coalition in pre-1914 London County Council, see Gruber, *Red Vienna,* and Pennybacker, *Vision.*

34. Savage and Miles, *Remaking,* p. 85; Graves, "Experiment."

CHAPTER 4

1. Rival federations of Workers' Associations were formed in 1863, one associated with the maverick journalist Ferdinand Lassalle, the other originally aligned with left liberals. During 1864–65, the latter broke with its liberal sponsors over universal suffrage and moved toward explicitly socialist positions, eventually merging with its rival in the Socialist Workers' Party of Germany at the unification Congress of Gotha in 1875. The party renamed itself the SPD in 1891.

2. Table 4.1 conceals many complexities. German socialism preceded the SPD's foundation by a decade, going back to 1863. The Austrian SDP of the Hainfeld Congress in 1889 technically refounded the movement launched in 1874. Parties also changed their names, especially in the early years, with the French movement presenting an especially confused picture. Finally, the table includes both the first Marxist circles in the tsarist empire (the Russian Group for the Emancipation of Labor, the Polish "Proletariat," the Armenian "Hanchak") and the full-blown social democratic parties launched 10–15 years later.

3. See Thompson, "Homage"; Yeo, "New Life"; Howell, *British Workers;* Crick, *History;* Hill, "Requiem"; Levy, "Education"; Laybourn (ed.), *Centennial.*

4. The Labour Representation Committee was formed in 1900 after discussions among trade unions and the "socialist societies," including both the Social Democratic Federation (SDF) formed in 1883 and the Independent Labour Party (ILP) formed in 1893. The SDF soon seceded from sectarian motives, leaving the ILP as the standard-bearer of socialism. For details, see Pelling, *Origins,* and for the wider question of socialist unity, Laybourn, "Failure."

5. For a taut analysis of the Swedish complexities, see Hurd, *Public Spheres,* pp. 21–30, 93–148.

6. See Kossmann, *Low Countries,* pp. 501–16, and Polasky, *Democratic So-*

cialism, pp. 23–52. For the segmented complexities of the Belgian polity, in which socialists competed with Catholics and nationalists for working-class allegiances in sharply varying urban and regional contexts, see above all Strikwerda, *House Divided*.

7. Under imperial Germany's Constitution, the kaiser (simultaneously king of Prussia, the largest federal state) appointed the chancellor, who then governed with a cabinet of Prussian ministers and imperial secretaries. This national government was not accountable to the majority parties in the Reichstag, which was elected by universal manhood suffrage. Thus the SPD could become the largest party in the Reichstag with no chance of forming a government. The Prussian franchise was also narrowly restricted.

8. See Galenson, *Danish System*, pp. 291–3.

9. Magraw, *France,* p. 286.

10. Rates varied hugely across industries and regions. Generally, they climbed during the decade before 1914. Swedish unionization reached record-breaking levels of 35 percent until the disastrous defeat of the 1909 General Strike, plummeting thereafter to 12 percent. After one year of legalization, Russian unions reached a density of 8.6 percent in 1907. Data are compiled from the following: Bain and Price, *Profiles;* Bonnell, *Roots*, p. 211; Hohorst, Kocka, and Ritter, *Sozialgeschichtliches Arbeitsbuch,* p. 136; Esping-Anderson, *Politics*, p. 64; Cronin, "Strikes," p. 73; Boll, "International," p. 84; Cook and Paxton, *European,* pp. 320–2.

11. National print unions were also important in Britain (dating from the early nineteenth century), and France (founded 1833, relegalized 1867) but were less pioneering, given the broader trade union foundations. The German printers' union had a precursor in 1848.

12. See Himka, *Socialism,* pp. 29–31, 188, 170.

13. Hobsbawm, " 'New Unionism,' " pp. 28, 24. For the British pattern of "closed" unionism between the 1850s and 1889, see Turner's classic study of the cotton spinners, *Trade Union*. Though noncraft unions appeared briefly in the 1870s, British unionism hardened around the sectionalism of skilled workers, who protected their bargaining power by restricting access to the trade. Where such unions were established, organizing of the unskilled was held back.

14. This was the Norwegian pattern, where mass unionization (1905–20) ran mainly through the Union of General Workers, quadrupling its membership in 1905–10 to become half the LO's strength. It was also the pattern in Denmark and Sweden. See Hobsbawm, " 'New Unionism,' " p. 23; and Knut Heidon's entry on Norway in Mielke (ed.), *Internationales*, p. 844.

15. See Schönhoven, *Expansion*, p. 341.

16. Hobsbawm, " 'New Unionism,' " p. 20.

17. Ibid., p. 16.

18. Exceptionally, the *Federterra* also organized women. See Zappi, *If Eight*. Organizationally, the Italian labor movement presented a confused picture: not all the farm workers' leagues were in the Federterra; the socialist union federation (CGL) competed with the syndicalists (USI), and both faced Catholic and independent rivals. The best guides are Seton-Watson, *Italy*, pp. 297–306, and Davis, "Socialism," pp. 210–9.

19. Parliamentary socialism flourished in the textile industry of the Nord, where political socialism substituted practically for weakened trade unions, and

the coalfields of Pas-de-Calais/Nord, Carmaux, and the Loire, where miners pursued collective bargaining via state regulation (achieved precociously for mining in the 1891 Arras Convention), an interest also shared by railwaymen. By contrast, antisocialist syndicalism appealed to skilled craftsmen in smaller-scale industry. See the city-based and regional studies by Scott, *Glassworkers;* Reid, *Miners;* Hanagan, *Logic;* Hilden, *Working Women;* Merriman, *Red City;* Amdur, *Syndicalist Legacy,* pp. 15–55. For general analyses, see Magraw, "Socialism"; Baker, "Socialism"; Stuart, *Marxism,* pp. 20–54, 180–222.

20. In Hamburg, there were craft associations in 1882 for engravers, brushmakers, basket weavers, cartwrights, masons, ship carpenters, blacksmiths, shoemakers, ropemakers and twisters, decoraters, gold-platers, dockers, and cigar and cigarette makers. Details from Ritter and Tenfelde, "Durchbruch," p. 120; Schönhoven, "Localism," p. 220.

21. Müller, "Syndicalism," pp. 239–49.

22. Schönhoven, "Localism," p. 228.

23. In Denmark and Sweden, a more conciliatory framework had the same effect, as government and employers gave unions greater legitimacy and thereby encouraged them toward centralism. Later, the First World War drove centralism forward in Europe as a whole by furthering union leaderships' political integration.

24. Totals include white-collar workers and in Germany nonsocialist unions. British expansion proceeded from the largest base (674,000 to 4,107,000, 1887–1913), while German unions went from 146,361 to 3,928,900. French unions grew more modestly from 140,000 to 1,027,000.

25. Hyman, "Mass Organization," p. 260. By 1913, roughly the same proportion of overall union membership—39 percent—was accounted for in both Britain and Germany by transport workers, metalworkers, and factory workers.

26. See Hyman, "Mass Organization," p. 260, and in more detail, Hyman, *Workers' Union.* For the eroding distinction between "craftsman" and "laborer," see Hobsbawm, "Artisans and Labour Aristocrats."

27. For a challenging argument to this effect, made in the context of Britain, see Melling, "Welfare Capitalism."

28. Hobsbawm, " 'New Unionism,' " p. 20.

29. The Bochumer Verein, a major conglomerate of foundries, rolling mills, and metalworking plants, experienced no strikes in 1889–1914. The few recorded stoppages affected smaller firms among single occupational categories of metalworkers. For comparison of miners and metalworkers, see Crew, *Town,* pp. 159–94. See also Hickey, *Workers,* pp. 169–225.

30. See here Kulczycki, *Foreign Worker* and *Miners' Union.*

31. This is based on Boch, *Handwerker-Sozialisten.* For the labor process in the cutlery industry, see Pollard, *History,* pp. 50, 125; and for the specificities of Sheffield, White, "We Never Knew."

32. In its first year (1891), DMV recorded 164 members in Solingen. Figures rose notably from 109 to 2,469 during 1899–1905. See Boch, *Handwerker-Sozialisten,* pp. 152–7.

33. In 1900–1912, DMV grew nationally from 100,762 to 561,547, expanding from the metal trades' historic centers (Berlin, the Hansa cities, Saxony, Brunswick, Solingen, Remscheid) into mainly medium and small-scale plants, as against large-scale heavy industry and engineering plants in the Ruhr and Silesia.

The union also incorporated gold and silver workers (1900), moulders (1901), shipbuilders (1905), engravers (1907), and smiths (1912). The first craft group to join the Solingen DMV were the grinders and finishers of the pocket-knife branch in 1906, raising membership from 2,469 to 4,025.

34. A limited grinders' action against Hammesfahr was turned by the DMV into a damaging stoppage affecting grinders in general. The grinders counted on sufficient orders from elsewhere to keep working, with only the Hammesfahr grinders as a charge on strike funds. When the DMV called the forge workers out, grinders in general were idled. See Boch, *Handwerker-Sozialisten,* pp. 158–66.

35. The DMV eventually ended the forge workers' strike, after being condemned by all other local unions and the SPD. Ensuing court actions exposed the DMV action as a cynical maneuver against the grinders.

36. Boch, "Lokale Fachverein," p. 175; Boch, *Handwerker-Sozialisten,* p. 161.

37. Boch, *Handwerker-Sozialisten,* p. 292.

38. Ibid., p. 277.

39. Ibid., pp. 257–87. Rival Social Democratic candidates fought the 1893 and 1898 elections. In 1893, Georg Schumacher, leader of the craft-based labor movement and victor in 1890, easily defeated Hermann Schaaf, candidate of the SPD younger generation after 1890. In 1898, Schumacher opposed an official SPD candidate, Philipp Scheidemann, and this time the National Liberal stole the seat. Thereafter, the old craft socialists receded, although divisions flared again in 1913–14, with the SPD expelling leading individuals.

40. See Kirby, "Workers' Cause."

41. Gidlund, "From Popular," pp. 100–105.

42. After the Anti-Socialist Law's abolition (1890), government efforts to renew exceptional laws by restricting trade unions and the law of association were defeated (1895–99). Cross-state organizing was fully legalized (1899), and political association for women and youth was freed (1908).

43. Fricke, *Handbuch,* 1:1022–42, 996.

44. Hobsbawm, *Age of Empire,* p. 129.

45. See Brüggemeier, *Leben,* pp. 52–74, 142–61; Brüggemeier and Niethammer, "Lodgers." For an example of miners' cultural self-help through the founding of institutes and libraries, see Francis, "Origins."

46. See Lüdtke, "Organisational Order," pp. 305, 311, 322.

47. Brüggemeier, *Leben,* p. 251.

48. See von Saldern, *Auf dem,* pp. 235, 130–201, 222.

CHAPTER 5

1. The following countries were represented: France, Germany, Austria, Czech lands, Switzerland, Belgium, the Netherlands, Britain, Denmark, Norway, Sweden, Italy, Spain, Hungary, Poland, Bulgaria, Serbia, Romania, Russia, and the United States.

2. "Every night I go to sleep with the thought that the last hour of bourgeois society strikes soon." August Bebel to Friedrich Engels, 7 December 1885, cited by Lidtke, *Outlawed Party,* p. 233.

3. Elected to the Chamber in 1885, Millerand adopted socialist affiliations,

legally defending socialist militants and advocating social reform. His "Saint-Mandé Program" of 1896 became a minimum basis for mediating French socialism's discordant forces.

4. Gildea, *Barricades,* p. 400.

5. Municipal activism joined isolated parliamentary victories in the 1890s to create a new socialist presence in northern England, industrial Scotland and Wales, and parts of London, driven by the Independent Labour Party (ILP, formed 1893) and older Social Democratic Federation (SDF, 1883). Antiunion offensives pushed unions into seeking a stronger political voice, coalescing with socialists in the Labour Representation Committee (LRC, 1900). By 1903, the LRC secretary, Ramsay MacDonald (1866–1937), concluded a pact with the Liberals for the next elections, resulting in the return of 29 Labour MP in 1906. Later accessions, especially the group of miners' MPs, who left the Liberals in 1909, brought Labour's strength to 45, reduced to 42 after the two 1910 elections.

6. Magraw, "Socialism," p. 76.

7. Wilhelm Liebknecht to the POF, 10 August 1899, in *Dokumente und Materialen,* 4; 31.

8. Karl Kautsky to Victor Adler, 5 May 1894, in Adler (ed.) *Adler,* p. 152.

9. Steenson, *Kautsky,* p. 114.

10. Ibid., p. 116. Ominously (in light of the SPD's decision to support the the German government's war credits in 1914), Kautsky's second example of justified coalition was fighting a "people's war" against Russian invasion.

11. See Miller, *From Elite,* pp. 25–9; and Seton-Watson, *Italy,* pp. 237–46.

12. French socialism's factional histories are best approached through a series of fine biographies: Derfler, *Millerand;* Howarth, *Valliant;* Goldberg, *Life;* Stafford, *From Anarchism;* Vincent, *Between Marxism;* Derfler, *Lafargue.* For the Guesdists, see Stuart, *Marxism at Work;* for the Blanquists, Hutton, *Cult;* and for general overviews, Magraw, "Socialism," and Kergoat, "France."

13. Joll, *Second International,* p. 95.

14. Adopted in 1891, the Erfurt Program became a template for the Norwegian (1891), Swiss (1893), Belgium (1894), Dutch (1894), Swedish (1897), and eastern European party progams, while the contemporaneous Czech (1888), Austrian (1889), and Hungarian programs (1890) followed the same lines.

15. This was Liebknecht's peroration to the SPD's 1898 Congress. See Dominick, *Liebknecht,* p. 399.

16. Tudor and Tudor (eds.), *Marxism,* p. 168. An ex–bank clerk who joined the socialists in 1871, Bernstein (1850–1932) edited the SPD's organ, *Der Sozialdemokrat* (1878–90), from London (1880–1901), where he joined the Marx-Engels circle, becoming Engels's literary executor. He fell under the Fabians' influence in the 1890s. During the Revisionism Controversy, he returned to Germany, taking a Reichstag seat (1902–6, 1912–18, 1920–28). During the First World War, he advocated a peace settlement, opposing war credits and joining the Independent Social Democrats (USPD) in 1917. After 1918, he rejoined the SPD.

17. Quoted by Gay, *Dilemma,* p. 250.

18. Quoted by Joll, *Second International,* pp. 102–3.

19. See *Internationaler Sozialisten-Kongress zu Amsterdam, 14. bis 20. August 1904* (Berlin, 1904), pp. 31–49, in *Kongress-Protokolle.*

20. For general surveys, see Tichelman, "Socialist 'Internationalism' "; Haupt

and Rebérioux (ed.), *La deuxième Internationale*. At particular times, colonial questions preoccupied national movements, as in Britain during the Boer War (1899–1902) or in Belgium over the legal status of the Congo between the mid-1890s and 1908. See Price, *Imperial War;* Gupta, *Imperialism;* Polasky, *Democratic Socialism*, pp. 53–82.

21. Braunthal, *History*, 1:318–9.

22. See especially Karrsholm, "South African War."

23. This mixture of humanitarianism, paternalism, and materialist realism was especially clear in the Belgian socialist mobilization against atrocities in the Congo, where Vandervelde defended the rights of indigenous peoples while affirming the necessity of "commerce and civilization." See Polasky, *Democratic Socialism*, p. 80. For the SPD, see Fletcher, *Revisionism;* Schröder, *Sozialismus;* and *Sozialistische Imperialimusdeutung*. For Britain: Winter, "Webbs."

24. Braunthal, *History*, 1:363.

25. See especially Howarth, "French Workers," and Schröder, *Noske*. For detailed treatment of the view from Britain: Newton, *British Labour*.

26. See Kulczycki, *Foreign Worker* and *Miners' Union;* more generally: Wehler, *Sozialdemokratie*.

27. Joll, *Second International*, p. 118. In general: Mommsen, *Sozialdemokratie*, pp. 362–422; Löw, *Zerfall;* Mommsen, "Otto Bauer", Najdus, "Relation"; Redzič, "Die österreichische Sozialdemokratie"; Tomac, "Die sozialdemokratische Partei"; Šolle, "Die tschechische Sozialdemokratie"; Kořalka, "Czech Workers' Movement"; Rupnik, "Czech Socialists"; Skilling, *Masaryk*, pp. 14, 53–62, 109–10.

28. Kautsky, *Class Struggle*, p. 210.

29. See Friedrich Engels, "The Peasant Question in France and Germany," cited by Hussain and Tribe, *Marxism*, p. 1.

30. Salvadori, *Kautsky*, p. 51.

31. Shanin (ed.), *Late Marx*, p. 275.

32. The Spanish PSOE was especially rigid, barely deviating from the orthodox script. In Bulgaria and Austrian Poland, vigorous socialist movements effectively ceded the countryside to agrarian parties, the Bulgarian Peasant Union of Alexandru Stamboliiski (founded 1899) and the Polish Peasant Party (founded 1895). In Italy, the remarkable success of the PSI among agricultural workers in the north via the Federterra was matched by its general indifference to peasantries in the center and south.

33. In Denmark, this alliance developed from the structural weight of agricultural production in the industrial economy. In Sweden, Norway, and Finland, it came from the interpenetration of industry and agriculture via timber, paper and woodworking, fisheries and forestry, mining, textiles and other rural manufactures. Town and country antagonisms bedeviling socialist parties elsewhere were preempted, and socialists emerged after 1918 with credible claims to speak for the people in general. See especially Simonson, "Sweden," pp. 98–100. For an excellent study of rural socialism in France, see Judt, *Socialism*.

34. Himka, *Socialism*, p. 167.

35. This Bakuninist International encompassed Belgium and France, Switzerland, southern Europe, Russia, and Latin America, with some links to Germany and Britain. Its successes were in Spain and Italy: galvanized by Bakunin's emissaries after the 1868 Revolution, the Spanish Federation was founded in 1870

with 150 associations and 40,000 members; the Italian Federation followed in 1872 with 32,450 members in 155 sections. The Spanish movement imploded after the Alcoy paper workers' uprising near Valencia in 1873, while Italian insurrections in Bologna and Apulia in 1874 brought down the full fury of state repression. Practically, the Anarchist International then "swung on the axis of Belgium and the Jura, the two regions where political conditions allowed sustained and open activity." But in 1876–77 the Belgians defected to social democracy, and by 1879 the Jura Federation was a conventicle of exiles. See Woodcock, *Anarchism*, p. 239. For Spanish anarchism, see Esenwein, *Anarchist Ideology*; Kaplan, *Anarchists*. For Italy: Levy, "Italian Anarchism"; Pernicone, *Italian Anarchism*; Ravindranathan, *Bakunin*.

36. Kropotkin (1842–1921) came from the highest Russian nobility and resigned a military commission before turning to politics and leaving for Switzerland in 1871. After a spell in prison back in Russia, he joined the inner circles of western European anarchists, founding the journal *Le Révolté* in 1878 from his base in Switzerland. From 1885, he lived peacefully in London, elaborating his ideas in a series of books, *The Conquest of Bread, Mutual Aid, Memoirs of a Revolutionist*, and *Fields, Factories and Workshops*. With the revolution, he returned to Russia in summer 1917, emerging as a critic of Bolshevism. See Miller, *Kropotkin*; Cahm, *Kropotkin*.

37. For this phase, see Sonn, *Cultural Politics*; Oliver, *International Anarchist Movement*; Romera Maura, "Terrorism." See also Carlson, *Anarchism*.

38. See Bakunin's description of his program to Sergei Nechayev, 2 January 1870, cited by Joll, "Anarchism—A Living Tradition," p. 215.

39. Thorpe, *"Workers Themselves,"* p. 24; Joll, *Anarchists*, p. 199; Schöttler, *Entstehung*. The first BT was founded in 1887; by 1895 there were 51, rising to 157 by 1907. The key personalities included two journalists with anarchist backgrounds—Fernand Pelloutier, secretary of the Federation of BTs, and Emile Pouget, CGT assistant secretary and editor of its journal *Voix Du Peuple!* CGT membership grew from 420,000 to over a million between 1895 and 1914, based strongly in construction, leather, and woodworking. Under General Secretary Victor Griffuelhes in 1901–8, it promoted confrontation, with strike rates climaxing in 1906. Under Léon Jouhaux, who became general secretary in 1909, syndicalist aggression receded, intimidated by state repression and higher levels of employer organization. See Vandervort, *Griffuelhes*; Milner, *Dilemmas*.

40. The best guide to the mass strike debate is via two classic accounts: Schorske, *German Social Democracy*, pp. 28–58; and Nettl, *Luxemburg*, pp. 295–312, 365–9, 397–428, 513–6. See also Geary, *Kautsky*, pp. 60–72.

41. See esp. White, "1910–1914."

42. Holton, *British Syndicalism*, p. 87. *The Miners' Next Step* was drafted by Noah Ablett, Will Hay, Noah Rees, and others and published by the Unofficial Reform Committee of the South Wales Miners Federation in early 1912 (reprinted London, 1972). It focused debates between state-socialist supporters of public ownership and revolutionary advocates of industrial democracy. For the transcript of a formal debate between the two sides at Trealaw, South Wales, 13 November 1912, see Morgan, "Socialism," pp. 22–36.

43. Syndicalists did manage an International Congress in London in September–October 1913, with representation from 12 countries—Britain, Sweden, Denmark, Germany, Holland, Belgium, France, Spain, Italy, Cuba, Brazil, and Argen-

tina. Acrimonious divisions opened over the issue of banning political action. The dogmatism of the French and Italian delegates contrasted with the political mobility of the British, who combined industrial militancy with elected office in unions, trades councils, and local government. See Thorpe, *"Workers Themselves,"* pp. 73–4. The strongest affiliate was the USI, founded in 1912 after long tensions with the PSI-affiliated CGL. It claimed a membership of 101,729, one-third CGL strength, based among farm workers, construction workers, and metalworkers. It was linked to the local chambers of labor, whose aggregate membership by 1910 far surpassed the CGL's—504,841 against 165,192.

44. Another center of radicalism was the Dutch journal *De Tribune* (1907) around Anton Pannekoek, Hermann Gorter, and Henriette Roland-Holst, who were expelled by the SDAP and formed a new Social Democratic Party in 1909. These Tribunists had close ties with Luxemburg and the SPD left. Swedish Young Socialists broke from the SAP in 1908, forming a separate Swedish Young Socialist Party. In both cases, these pre-1914 left socialists formed the initial core for later Communist parties, linked through the revolutionary internationalist Zimmerwald movement. See especially Gerber, *Pannekoek.*

45. Hobsbawm, "The 1970s," p. 274.

46. For the specialized literature on syndicalism, see Schöttler, "Syndikalismus"; van der Linden, "Second Thoughts." Syndicalism survived longer via synergy with Barcelona anarchism in Spain. See Smith, "Anarchism."

47. Georges Sorel (1847–1922) was a retired engineer, when he began writing about Marxism in the 1890s, moving from orthodox materialism through a Bernsteinian reformism to revolutionary syndicalism. His best-known work was *Reflections on Violence* (1906). After 1909, he gravitated toward the authoritarian Right. See Vernon, *Commitment;* Jennings, *Sorel.*

48. See for instance Sonn, *Cultural Politics,* especially pp. 49–94; Leighten, *Re-Ordering;* Kaplan, *Red City.*

49. Rowbotham, "In Search," p. 132. For the more polite version of this personal and intellectual experimentalism, see Walkowitz, "Science"; and for anarchist problems with feminism see Hutton, "Camile Pissarro."

50. See Rowbotham and Weeks, *Socialism;* Yeo, "New Life." An ex-cleric, Edward Carpenter left Cambridge in 1874 to pioneer the University Extension Movement in northern England, settling in the rural cottage "Millthorpe" near Sheffield from 1882 to 1916. Retaining his Cambridge intellectual ties, he formed close friendships with local socialists, communitarians, and working-class radicals, cofounded the Sheffield Socialist Society in 1886, and lectured widely, making Millthorpe into a retreat for dissidents. His many books included *Towards Democracy* (1883), *Civilization: Its Cause and Cure* (1889), *Love's Coming of Age: A Series of Papers on the Relations of the Sexes* (1896), *Prisons, Police and Punishment* (1905), and *Towards Industrial Freedom* (1917), plus extensive journalism, poetry and literary work, and an autobiography, *My Days and Dreams* (1916). His works enjoyed huge circulation, including German, French, Italian, Dutch, Swedish, Russian, and Japanese editions. His critique of capitalist civilization drew on romantic-idealist traditions, Christianity and Eastern religions, anarchism and ethical philosophy, anthropology, Marxism, syndicalism, and socialist ideas. He advocated everyday self-transformation ("simplification of life") and communal experiments, linking spiritual change to changes in economy and social relations. He was a homosexual and feminist, supporting sex reform and

women's emancipation. His companion from 1891 to 1927 was a Sheffield work-ingman, George Merrill. Emblematically influential before 1914, Carpenter became marginalized by the mainstream twentieth-century socialist tradition.

51. Frevert, *Women,* p. 141.

52. Bebel, *Women,* pp. 4–5.

53. *Sächsisches Volksblatt,* describing the defeat of a miners' strike in Zwickau in early 1900. See Evans, "Politics," p. 269.

54. Ibid., p. 275. Haase noted the offending language and threatened to report its authors to the Party Executive.

55. Evans, *Sozialdemokratie,* p. 88, citing a complaint in a Hamburg women's meeting in December 1886.

56. Fischer made his arguments in *Sozialistische Monatshefte* (1905), cited by Frevert, *Women,* p. 141. For detailed treatments of French and British socialism, see Hunt, *Equivocal Feminists;* Sowerwine, *Sisters.*

57. Smith, *Changing Lives,* p. 304.

58. See Sowerwine, *Sisters,* pp. 135–6. Syndicalists had no better record of integrating women into their leadership or taking women workers seriously. At the Syndicalist International (September 1913), there was only a single woman delegate. See Thorpe, *"Workers Themselves,"* p. 71.

59. The quoted declaration was carried on the masthead of the French socialist women's newspaper, *La Femme socialiste* (launched March 1901), edited by Elisabeth Renaud (1846–1932) and Louise Saumoneau (1875–1950). See Sowerwine, *Sisters,* pp. 82–97.

60. See Hilden's two books, *Working Women* and *Women.*

61. For compelling detail of argument and evidence, see Canning, *Languages,* pp. 314–21; also Lambertz, "Sexual Harassment."

62. Canning, *Languages,* p. 317.

63. Rowbotham, "Strategies," p. 152. The definition of sweating that follows was Beatrice Potter's, given in parliamentary evidence in 1881. See above all Blackburn, "Connection," and "Ideology."

64. Rowbotham, *Century,* p. 24.

65. For a study of gendered labor markets in Scotland, where the organized labor movement became centered around the "real" working class of men in mining, shipbuilding, and other heavy industries while women workers in textiles, lower-paid factory jobs, and sweated trades became hidden, see Gordon, *Women.*

66. Evans, "Politics," pp. 263–6. In the Hamburg socialist women's society (1886), 16 were factory workers, 33 domestic servants, and 74 unwaged; by 1913, only 13.7 percent of the Hamburg SPD's 11,684 women members had paying jobs, and "the majority . . . were the non-working wives of the organized comrades." See Ullrich, *Hamburger Arbeiterbewegung,* p. 77. Records for Cologne (1914) and Leipzig (1909) show 70–75 percent of women members aged 25–50. Evans, "Politics," pp. 281–2.

67. In the final years before women acquired rights of political association (1908), SPD women's educational societies multiplied from 3,000 to 10,500 (1905–7). Women's party membership then rose from 29,458 (1908) to 107,693 (1911) and 174,754 (1914).

68. The quotations are from Clara Zetkin in *Die Gleichheit,* 19 January 1898, pp. 9–10, cited by Evans, "Politics," pp. 271–2.

69. Mabel Harding, "Social Motherhood," *Daily Herald,* 19 April 1912, quoted by Rowbotham, *Century,* p. 18.

70. See Steedman, *Childhood.* As well as fiction for and about children, McMillan published voluminous journalism and campaigning writings, including the influential *Child Labour and the Half-Time System* (1895), also delivered as a lecture, and *Education through the Imagination* (1904). Anomalously, women could be elected to school boards in Britain, a franchise that was removed by the 1902 Education Act.

71. For Anna Kuliscioff's advocacy of universal suffrage in the Italian Socialist Party, see Ascari, "Feminism."

72. Tickner, *Spectacle,* p. 122.

73. Debates concerning adult versus limited suffrage were complex and ranged feminists and socialists on either side during 1890–1914. Fears that adult suffrage would enfranchise only working-class men won credence from the record of socialist parties elsewhere, leading some women suffragists to support equal franchise on the existing limited basis as an empowering first step. Some socialists took a straight class line (only universal equal adult suffrage would do), while others accepted the limited case. Others still opposed female enfranchisement *tout court,* including SDF leaders Henry Hyndman, Ernest Belfort Bax, and Harry Quelch. The events of 1907–14, with the rise of democratic suffragists in NUWSS and the commitment to adult suffrage in the Labour Party, allowed these complexities to be resolved.

74. Rowbotham, *Century,* pp. 17, 19, 8.

75. In the 1890s, Cooper was reading Tom Paine's *Rights of Man* (reprinted 1893) and Bebel's *Woman under Socialism.* See Liddington, *Life,* pp. 17–88. Also Rowbotham, "Travellers," and "Our Party."

76. Kent, *Sex,* p. 7.

77. Teresa Billington-Greig, quoted by Tickner, *Spectacle,* p. 224.

78. See especially the works of Holton, "Suffragist"; *Feminism;* and *Suffrage Days;* also Clark, "Gender, Class." For one collision between the freethinking readiness to challenge sexual conventions, which inspired many individuals in the suffragist and socialist movements, and the strait-laced morality of the official labor movement, see Collette, "Socialism."

79. See Hirsch, *Bodichon.*

80. Analogous cases might be the labor movements of Ghent and the Nord before the Belgian and French socialist parties opted for parliamentary strategies in the 1890s. For the emergent connections across suffragist and socialist radicalisms on the eve of war, see Fletcher, "Prosecutions" and "Star Chamber"; Mayhall, "Reclaiming"; and Holton, *Suffrage Days.*

81. Richard Pankhurst (1835–98) was a classic product of northern radicalism and an advocate of women's rights from the 1860s, serving on the executive of the Manchester Suffrage Society and crafting the various parliamentary initiatives for women's suffrage and married women's property. He married Emmeline Goulden (1879), and after moving to London (1885) they formed the Women's Franchise League (1889). Returning to Manchester (1893), the Pankhursts became leading activists in the newly founded ILP.

82. Under the 1867 Constitution, limited property franchises to the Bohemian Diet and cities (except Prague and Liberec) had survived for women, and in the suffrage conflicts of 1906–13 the Habsburg government abolished these. In 1908–

12, the Czech Committee for Women's Suffrage promoted female candidates as a protest. The governor blocked Viková-Kunetická's election, and the Diet was abolished (1913). See David-Fox, "Czech Feminists"; Nolte, "Every Czech"; Maleckova, "Emancipation"; Skilling, *Masaryk*, pp. 114–28.

83. See Blom, "Struggle"; Jallinoja, "Women's Liberation"; Quist, "Policy"; Christiansen, "Socialist Feminists," pp. 479–82; Frangeur, "Social Democrats," pp. 429–30; Pugh, "Rise."

84. See Anderson, *Utopian Feminism*.

85. The Socialist Women's International was inaugurated at Stuttgart, where the Women's Conference was dominated by Zetkin and the Germans. Delegates attended from Britain, Germany, Austria, Czech lands, Hungary, Belgium, the Netherlands, France, Switzerland, Italy, Norway, Sweden, Finland, Russia, and the United States.

86. The IWSA was a radical offshoot of the International Council of Women (1888), a general umbrella organization that avoided political contention. It was joined by suffrage organizations from Hungary, Italy, and Russia (1906); Bulgaria, Denmark, Finland, Switzerland, and South Africa (1908); Belgium, France, Austria, the Czech lands, and Serbia (1909); Iceland, Polish Galicia, Portugal, and Romania (1911). See Rupp, *Worlds*, pp. 21–60.

87. See especially Burton, "Feminist Quest," and *Burdens*.

88. They included Margaret Bondfield, Selina Cooper, Kathleen Courteney, Margaret Llewelyn Davies, Charlotte Despard, Isabella Ford, Catherine Marshall, Sylvia Pankhurst, and Ethel Snowden. Davies led the Women's Cooperative Guild (1889–1922). Bondfield was an activist in the Shop Assistants Union in London, passing through SDF to ILP, the Women's Trade Union League, and the Women's Labour League. She was president of the Adult Suffrage Society (1906–9). As secretary of the Manchester NUWSS (1908–10), Courteney prioritized recruitment of working women. As NUWSS national secretary (1910), she joined with Marshall (appointed NUWSS parliamentary secretary 1911) in building the Labour Party alliance. Marshall joined ILP (1914). Despard came from wealth, and in middle age she turned to mission work among the London poor, moving through SDF to ILP. She became active in WSPU (1906) but left when the Pankhursts broke with the ILP, helping to form the Women's Freedom League in protest (1907).

89. Rowbotham, *Century*, p. 67, and Rowbotham, *Friends*. Though she was amnestied, Wheeldon's health was destroyed by prison. She died in the influenza epidemic (1919). See also Weller, *"Don't,"* pp. 74–81.

90. Wenger, "Radical Politics," p. 68. After participating in pacifist campaigns in the United States, Schwimmer was persecuted during the Red Scare of the 1920s and denied citizenship, though she remained in the United States until her death.

CHAPTER 6

1. How far the Labour Party was supplanting the Liberals in Britain before 1914 remains subject to historiographical debate. For the revitalizing of the Liberals, see Clarke, *Lancashire* and *Liberals;* for the rival view of Labour's rising organizational strength linked to the unions, see McKibbin, *Evolution;* and for the thesis of the two parties' convergent reform politics or "progressivism," see

Tanner, *Political Change*. For useful commentaries, see Laybourn, "Rise"; Lancaster, "Rise."

2. For the resonance of nationality struggles in the later nineteenth century: Collins and Abramsky, *Karl Marx*, pp. 11–13, 17–26, 66–7, 112–14, 285–6; Cummins, *Marx, Engels*; Finn, *After Chartism*; Sarti, *Mazzini*; Griffith, *Mazzini*.

3. The term "federalist trades socialism" was developed for France. See Moss, *Origins*; also Sewell, *Work and Revolution*; and especially the groundbreaking essays in Hobsbawm, *Laboring Men*.

4. See the excellent analysis in Himka, *Socialism*.

5. Siegenthaler, "Producers' Cooperatives," p. 21: the bases for producer co-operation in Switzerland were "a comparatively small scale of enterprise in all sectors of industry; considerable influence of Latin socialist programs in the labor movement; and the long-term, pre-industrial, agrarian-cooperative and political-cooperative tradition of the country." See also Furlough, *Consumer Cooperation*; Scholliers, "Social-Democratic World"; and Furlough and Strikwerda (eds.), *Consumers*.

6. The non-European presence in the Second International was confined to the United States, "white" colonies like Australia and South Africa, and Japan.

7. The basis for Lenin's thinking about anticolonial movements was laid down by *Imperialism, the Highest Stage of Capitalism* (1916), and other writings during the First World War. See Mayer, *Wilson vs. Lenin*, pp. 293–312. The influence of Marxism among nationalist movements in China and southeast Asia, India, central Asia and the Middle East, Latin America, and parts of Africa dates from the Third International and the impact of the Bolshevik Revolution. Pre-1914 socialists had little impact in this respect.

8. Britain was a major exception to this chronology, because the Gladstonian Liberal Party forged in the 1860s anticipated a comparable process much earlier, based in similar reciprocities between Parliament and people. For the classic account, see Vincent, *Formation*; and subsequently, Biagini and Reid (eds.), *Currents*; Biagini, *Liberty*; Lawrence, *Speaking*; Barrow and Bullock, *Democratic Ideas*; Smith, "Labour Traditions."

9. See especially Strikwerda, *House Divided*.

10. Eric Hobsbawm, preface, to Haupt, *Aspects*, p. xi. For an excellent case study, see Haupt, "Model Party."

11. Mattl, "Austria," p. 320.

12. For an excellent discussion of socialist festivals, see Lidtke, *Alternative Culture*, pp. 75–101; for socialist iconography, Gorman, *Banner Bright*; and in general, Hobsbawm, "Mass-Producing Traditions."

13. Liddington, *Life*, pp. 62–3.

14. See especially Thompson, *William Morris*; Rowbotham and Weeks, *Socialism*; Nield, "Edward Carpenter."

15. See especially Yeo, "A New Life"; and Waters, *British Socialists*, esp. pp. 1–16, 65–96; Thompson, "Homage."

16. For Esperanto, the attempt to invent a new world language to express the internationalism of the workers' movement, see Forster, *Esperanto Movement*; Boulton, *Zamenhof*.

17. This sentence is adapted from Hobsbawm, *Age of Empire*, pp. 338–9.

18. In Poland, rival parties occupied these positions, with the patriotic Polish Socialist Party (PPS) facing the dogmatically internationalist Social Democrats of

the Kingdom of Poland and Lithuania (SDKPiL), both of them dating from 1893. See Rojahn, "Poland," pp. 510–9; Blobaum, *Rewolucja,* pp. 35–39; Blobaum, *Dzierzynski;* Cottam, *Limanowski;* Naimark, *History;* Nettl, *Luxemburg,* 1:69–104. On the eve of the First World War, the national question also divided the Czech Social Democrats, pitting the separatist majority against a smaller internationalist element that remained with the parent Austrian party.

19. The socialist Left was consistently marginalized by some nationalist movements, of which the Irish was the clearest example. The influence of some remarkable individuals notwithstanding, notably the trade unionist James Larkin or the socialist theoretician-activist James Connolly, Irish republicanism was profoundly antisocialist. See Howell, *Lost Left.*

20. The French Millerand affair was the first crisis of this kind in 1899, but during 1910–13 the ban on "ministerialism" became subject to severe strain. The willingness of SPD parliamentary caucuses in Baden and Württemberg to cooperate with their state governments produced widespread dissension in the German party. Tensions were most extreme in Italy, where younger radicals outflanked the established parliamentarianism of the PSI. In 1912, Leonida Bissolati was expelled for proposing to join a Radical coalition government; and the youthful Benito Mussolini, then carving a reputation as a Socialist *enragé,* described universal suffrage as "the oxygen pump administered to a dying patient, parliamentary liberalism." See Stone, *Europe Transformed,* p. 103.

PART II INTRODUCTION

1. The best account of the March Action is still Angress, *Stillborn Revolution,* pp. 105–96; also Winkler, *Revolution,* pp. 503–20.

2. For Hölz, see Angress, *Stillborn Revolution,* pp. 146–51, 159–60, 165, 167; Fowkes, *Communism,* pp. 46, 67; Bock, *Syndikalismus,* pp. 308–12, and *Geschichte,* p. 303; Hölz, *White Cross.*

3. The quotation is taken from the anonymous autobiography, "Erlebnisse und Schlußfolgerungen eines Revolutionärs," in *Proletarische Zeitgeist,* 10 (1931), cited by Bock, *Geschichte,* p. 97. For Plättner and Kobitsch-Meyer, see Bock, *Syndikalismus,* pp. 328–31, 430, 437–8, and *Geschichte,* p. 303.

CHAPTER 7

1. Hajdu, "Socialist Revolution," p. 102.

2. Official record of the ISB session, Brussels, 29–30 July 1914, printed as an appendix in Haupt, *Socialism,* p. 255.

3. The classic account of the Second International's response to 1914 is Haupt, *Socialism.* See also Kirby, *War,* pp. 27–48

4. For reactions inside the SPD, see now Kruse, *Krieg,* pp. 17–151, superseding Miller, *Burgfrieden.* For popular war enthusiasm: Verhey, *Spirit;* Chickering, *Imperial Germany,* pp. 13–7.

5. Hugo Haase, in conversation with Charles Rappoport, cited by Haupt, *Socialism,* p. 208.

6. Kuczynski, *Ausbruch,* p. 207.

7. Miller, *Burgfrieden,* p. 72; Boll, *Frieden,* p. 124.

8. See Fischer, *Germany's Aims,* pp. 330–3; Boll, *Frieden,* pp. 119–29.

9. For Britain, see McKibbin, *Evolution,* pp. 88–111; Fox, *History,* pp. 280–300; Harrison, "War Emergency"; Harris, *Beveridge,* pp. 198–231; Winter, *Socialism,* pp. 121–233. For France: Downs, *Manufacturing,* pp. 21–30; Godfrey, *Capitalism.* For Belgium: Polasky, *Democratic Socialism,* pp. 113–39. See also Horne, *Labour.*

10. Bernard and Dubief, *Decline,* p. 5; Joll, *Europe,* p. 200.

11. Details from Kirby, *War,* pp. 69–94.

12. The SPD voting on war credits had two stages—first in the party's caucus, then on the Reichstag's public floor. On 3 August 1914, the fraction voted 78–14 for war credits in its own meeting and unanimously in the Reichstag next day. In the second war credits vote on 29 November, the fraction divided 82–17, and on 2 December only Karl Liebknecht broke parliamentary ranks. By the third vote, the fraction divided 68–31 (17 March 1915), but now Otto Rühle joined Liebknecht publicly, with 30 deputies absenting themselves (20 March 1915). On 14 December 1915, the fraction split 58–38, while 18 deputies joined Liebknecht and Rühle in the Reichstag (18 December), with 24 abstaining.

13. See Riddell (ed.), *Communist International;* Nation, *War,* pp. 29–168.

14. Zimmerwald was attended by 38 delegates, Kienthal by 39. At Kienthal, the Left included four from Zimmerwald itself (Lenin, Gregory Zinoviev, Karl Radek, Fritz Platten); an additional Bolshevik (Inessa Armand-Petrov), and two from the SDKPiL opposition (Miecyslav Bronski, Wladislaw Stein-Dabrowski); they were joined by five newcomers (the Swiss Ernst Nobs and Agnes Robmann, the Serb Trisa Kaclerovic, the French nonaffiliated journalist Henri Guilbeaux, and Paul Fröhlich from the German Bremen Left). Seven others signed the statement condemning French support for war credits: Paul Graber (Switzerland), Giacinto Menotti Serrati (Italy), M. A. (Marc) Natanson-Bobrov, M. A. Savalyev, and Vlasov (Russian Socialist Revolutionaries), Edmondo Peluso (Portugal), and Willi Münzenberg (as secretary of the Socialist Youth International).

15. The Swiss party had broken the civil truce in the summer of 1915. See Blänsdorf, *Zweite Internationale,* p. 23.

16. "Circular Letter of the ISC," February 1916, in Gankin and Fisher (eds.), *Bolsheviks,* p. 388.

17. A Ukrainian Social Democratic grouping around the journal *Borotba* in Lausanne joined the ISC, with antiwar politics close to the Zimmerwald Left but severed by advocacy of national-cultural autonomy. See Gankin and Fisher (eds.), *Bolsheviks,* p. 370.

18. For a fascinating local study of Islington in north London, which explores the disorientation and regroupment of the wartime Left in the microcosm of the much weaker British socialist movements, focusing on socialists, anarchists, feminists, Christian socialists, and other pacifists, see Weller, *"Don't."*

19. See Robert, "Mobilizing," pp. 80–1.

20. The kaiser's declaration was delivered in his speech from the throne before the Reichstag meeting that approved the war credits. See Cecil, *Wilhelm II,* p. 209.

21. This is the conclusion of both Boll, *Frieden,* pp. 100–117, and Becker, *Great War,* pp. 64–102. See also Bush, *Behind;* Melling, *Rent Strikes.*

22. Figures culled from the following sources: Kocka, *Facing;* Frevert,

Women, pp. 155–7; MacMillan, *Housewife*, p. 131.; Marwick, *Women*, p. 73, 166. For detailed studies: Daniel, *Arbeiterfrauan*; Thom, *Nice Girls*; Woollacott, *On Her*; Downs, *Manufacturing*, pp. 47–78.

23. See Kocka, *Klassengesellschaft*, p. 161, note 104.

24. The 1911 figure was 427,000; 1918, 518,000. Milan's population rose from 599,000 to 719,000 in 1911–21; Rome from 542,000 to 692,000. The wartime expansion of the working class was proportionately greater in Italy than elsewhere. For its gender dimensions, see Foot, "Socialist-Catholic."

25. By 1917, 668,621 registered and perhaps 250,000 unregistered foreigners were working in German industry and agriculture. The largest contingent (395,122) came from Russian Poland. From October 1916 to February 1917, 61,000 Belgians were forcibly drafted into German industry, followed by 100,000 "voluntary" recruits during 1917–18. By August 1916, the German economy was using 1.6 million prisoners of war, plus 80,000 domestic prisoners (normally in agriculture). See Herbert, *History*, pp. 87–119.

26. Feldman, "Socio-Economic Structures," p. 161. See also Dobson's important study of Leipzig, which concretely demonstrates the dialectic of continuities and wartime disruption, using a coherent time frame of 1910–20: Dobson, *Authority*, esp. pp. 2–3, 293–6.

27. See Fox, *History*, pp. 288–300. For a case study, Schneer, "War."

28. This committee was formed on 5 August 1914 to protect labor's interests in the war, adapted from a "peace protest committee." It was composed from the Labour Party, TUC, and rival General Federation of Trade Unions, plus individual trade union leaders and Labour intellectuals. It was a vital forum for postwar reconstruction and the Labour Party. See Harrison, "War Emergency"; Winter, *Socialism*, pp. 184–233.

29. Of 905,000 in classified auxiliary industries in 1918, 311,000 (36 percent) were "military" (seconded from the army) or "exempted" from military service by their skill; 304,000 were men without military obligations; 196,000 were women; 60,000 youths; and 14,000 POWs or colonial workers. See Clark, *Gramsci*, pp. 24–5.

30. Quoted by Hinton, *First*, p. 119. The Clyde Workers' Committee was formed in October 1915, succeeding the Clyde Labour Withholding Committee of the previous February. Though formed through the dilution struggles to preserve the exclusive privileges of craft workers, the new Committee was led by socialists committed to anticapitalist struggle. See esp. Burgess, "Political Economy"; and Reid, "Dilution."

31. The classic account of the Patriotic Auxiliary Service Law is Feldman, *Army, Industry*, pp. 197–249; see also Domansky, "Rationalization," pp. 348–55. For the French context, see Downs, *Manufacturing*, pp. 119–46; Hatry, "Shop Stewards"; Horne, *"L'Impot"*; Fridenson, "Impact."

32. Spartacus grew from the Group International, strengthened via two national conferences on 33 January and 19 March 1916 and taking the name Spartacus from the pseudonym on its first newsletter. The Intransigent Revolutionary Faction came from a clandestine meeting of the extreme PSI left in Florence (July 1917) under Amadeo Bordiga from Naples; its name was borrowed from an in transigent revolutionary faction of the PSI in 1910.

33. See for example, Boll, *Massenbewegungen*; Weitz, *Creating*, pp. 64–78;

Nolan, *Social Democracy,* pp. 251–68; Tobin, "War." For France, see Lagrange, "Strikes"; and for Italy, Bezza, "Social Characteristics."

34. Kuczynski, *Geschichte,* p. 276.

35. See Becker, *Great War,* p. 217; and Dallas and Gill, *Unknown Army.*

36. Davis, *Home Fires,* p. 6.

37. Ibid., pp. 218, 225. The failure of the state-sponsored public meal halls in Germany during 1915–17 contrasted with the success of communal meals in France, sponsored disproportionately by local initiatives of SFIO sections and Socialist town halls. See Davis, *Home Fires,* pp. 137–58; Robert, "Mobilizing," pp. 80–8.

38. After Italy's entry to the war in May 1915, the PSI slogan became "Neither Support nor Sabotage." Repression following the Turin insurrection and the surrounding unrest of the summer pushed Socialists into overt opposition.

39. Procacci, "Popular Protest," p. 43. Women provided 34.4 percent of Italian strikers in 1915; 43.9 percent in 1916; and 64.2 in 1917. See Tomassini, "Industrial Mobilization," p. 74, and for the industrial mobilization of women, pp. 69–73. For the broader political context of the Socialists' gender politics, see Foot, "Socialist-Catholic." For women's similar role in precipitating the Russian Revolution in February 1917: McDermid and Hillyar, *Midwives.*

40. Details from: Cronin, *Industrial Conflict,* pp. 206, 208; Bernard and Dubief, *Decline,* pp. 54, 48–52; Cronin, "Strikes," pp. 67–68; Williams, *Proletarian Order,* p. 58; Hautmann and Kropf, *Österreichische Arbeiterbewegung,* p. 122; Kirby, *War,* pp. 135–37; Kuczynski, *Geschichte,* p. 278.

41. See Bailey, "Berlin Strike."

CHAPTER 8

1. For general accounts of the February Revolution, see Hasegawa, *February Revolution;* Rabinowitch, *Bolsheviks;* Mandel, *Fall;* and Galili, *Menshevik Leaders,* pp. 3–156. For women workers: McDermid and Hillyar, *Midwives;* Smith, *Red Petrograd,* pp. 23–7, 192–5; and Wood, *Baba,* pp. 35–7.

2. Suny, "Toward," p. 36.

3. Pavel Miliukov, leading Kadet politician and foreign minister in the First Provisional Government, issued a Note to the Western allies on 18 April 1917, declaring Russia's intention of continuing the war. It triggered huge demonstrations against the Government from the Left, eventually resulting in the resignations of Miliukov and Alexander Guchkov, minister of war.

4. Rosenberg, *Liberals,* p. 108.

5. Lenin, "The Tasks of the Proletariat in the Present Revolution (April Theses)," in Lenin, *Collected Works,* 24:21–6.

6. Carr, *Bolshevik Revolution,* 1:93.

7. Koenker, *Moscow Workers,* p. 132.

8. The most useful source for these estimates is Rigby, *Communist Party.*

9. With few exceptions, this view prevailed until the 1970s, when social and political histories of the revolutionary movement gradually produced a change. For the Bolshevik Party and Lenin's thought, see Service, *Bolshevik Party;* Harding, *Lenin's Political Thought;* and *Leninism.*

10. This anti-Bolshevik critique echoes the Menshevik attacks of the time,

which accused Lenin of reverting to the conspiratorial adventurism of a Bakunin or Blanqui.

11. Baron, *Plekhanov*, p. 324.

12. Liberal hopes focused on the zemstvo, the limited institutions of local self-government created in 1864. See Emmons and Vucinich (eds.), *The Zemstvo*, esp. essays by Gleason and Rosenberg. A War Industries Committee was also created at the start of the war, headed by Alexsander Guchkov, a leading figure of the Octobrist Party and later minister of war in the First Provisional Government, of which he was a main architect. By the end of 1915, there were War Industries Committees in 28 provinces and 74 cities. The Central War Industries Committee had 19 separate departments, each concerned with a different area of war production and supply. See Siegelbaum, *Politics*.

13. Kautsky, *Georgia,* p. 68.

14. For the Mensheviks, see above all Galili, *Menshevik Leaders.*

15. Haimson, "Problem," is the original source of this interpretation.

16. Rosenberg and Koenker, "Limits," pp. 296–7.

17. Ibid., p. 324; and in more detail, Koenker and Rosenberg, *Strikes.*

18. Kamenev's and Zinoviev's opposition to Lenin illustrated the pluralism of viewpoints in the Bolshevik leadership in 1917. They led dissent against the April Theses and in October opposed the majority's decision for insurrection. Against all Bolshevism's apparent precepts, they mobilized support in the party, and Kamenev even used a nonparty newspaper for a platform. Despite Lenin's demand for expulsion, the Central Committee issued only reprimands. After 25 October, they demanded an all-socialist coalition, again contradicting a Central Committee decision; when faced with an ultimatum, Kamenev, Zinoviev, and three others resigned. As before, this had little practical effect: they finally buried the hatchet after the formation of the Bolshevik-Left SR coalition and resumed leading positions. These conflicts are best followed through Rabinowitch, *Bolsheviks,* pp. 202–8, 219–33, 305–10.

19. Trotsky, *Permanent Revolution,* p. 63.

20. Ibid., p. 65.

21. Bolshevik treatment of the peasant question in 1917 is still surprisingly neglected in the literature. But see Figes, *Peasant Russia;* Kingston Mann, *Lenin.* The Land Decree, together with the Law on the Socialization of Land of 19 February 1918, nationalized the land.

22. The baldness of this assertion is for effect. Some SRs were closely attuned to peasant needs too and advocated immediate land reform rather than waiting. This was one basis for Left SR coalition with the Bolsheviks in October-November 1917. But there was no coherent viewpoint of the SRs *as a party.* Only Bolshevik decisiveness focused the intentions of the more radical SRs.

23. N. Zhordaniya, the leading Georgian Menshevik, consistently evaded the implications of his party's dependence on the countryside between 1905 and the Bolshevik invasion of May 1921, basing his regime programmatically on workers, soldiers, and progressive bourgeoisie. While this Menshevik government gave peasants the land, it viewed them with suspicion as a backward and potentially counterrevolutionary class. As Shanin says, this experience "should have changed the earlier theoretical constructions by the local Marxists, but, in this case, conceptual resilience proved stronger than revolutionary dreams." See Shanin, *Roots,*

2:227; also Suny, *Making.* The Italian Socialists were also a good illustration: massively successful among the agricultural proletariat of the Po Valley, the PSI proved uninterested in the differently based radicalism of the smallholding peasantry of the center and south of the country, which in the "red years" of 1919–20 was also extremely militant. See also Hussain and Tribe, *Marxism.*

24. The literature is vast. For a careful and sympathetic treatment, see Haupt, "Lenin."

25. Tseretelli, who was then minister of posts and telegraphs in the Provisional Government, was trying to silence criticism of Menshevik and SR participation in the governing coalition. The full record was as follows: " 'At the present moment there is no political party which would say: "Give the power into our hands, go away, we will take your place." There is no such party in Russia.' (Lenin from his seat: 'There is.')" See Carr, *Bolshevik Revolution,* 1:100.

26. Lenin, *Collected Works,* 24:419.

27. Aleksei Rykov, at the April Conference of the Bolsheviks, cited by Carr, *Bolshevik Revolution,* 1:95.

28. Löwy, *Politics,* p. 56.

29. Cited by Rabinowitch, *Bolsheviks,* p. 294.

30. In the Petrograd City Duma elections on 20 August 1917, the SRs had 37.4 percent of the popular vote, and in the Moscow City Duma elections of 25 June 1917, an imposing 58 percent. In the Constituent Assembly elections, the Mensheviks won only 3.1 percent in Petrograd, 2.8 percent in Moscow. See Radkey, *Election,* appendix. The comparison with the City Duma elections is added by Rosenberg, *Liberals,* p. 274.

31. For this and the above, see Carr, *Bolshevik Revolution,* 1:115–33.

CHAPTER 9

1. The first quotation comes from Davidson, *Antonio Gramsci,* p. 83. The others are assembled from Gramsci's articles "The Russian Maximalists" (28 July 1917) and "The Revolution against 'Capital' " (24 December 1917), in *Political Writings,* pp. 31–7.

2. As indeed the gendered language of the statements quoted from Gramsci plainly reveals. Given the massive recruitment of women into the wartime working class and their role in popular militancy, from the actions sparking the February Revolution in Russia to the earliest antiwar protests in Germany, the rent strikes on Clydeside, and the Turin Riots of 1917, the Left's neglect of women's questions becomes all the more striking.

3. True to their promises, the Bolshevik government entered peace negotiations with Germany at Brest-Litovsk in December 1917, accepting German terms in March. They originally treated negotiations as a propaganda exercise, hoping to galvanize German workers into revolution. The German government responded with intransigently tough demands, provoking the Austro-Hungarian strikes beginning on 14 January 1918.

4. A more radical chemistry of events—a railway strike spreading rebellion through the Habsburg Empire and preventing troop movements, plus mutinies, and possibly a turn by the imperial government to military dictatorship—might have escalated to a genuinely revolutionary crisis. See Schlesinger, *Central Euro-*

pean, pp. 135–9. In Sweden, conservative demands for military intervention against the Social Democrats in the Finnish Civil War also revived labor militancy, likewise in February–March 1918.

5. See Radziejowski, *Communist Party*.

6. For radicalization in the lesser states of Europe (Spain, Switzerland, Denmark, Sweden, Norway, Netherlands, Belgium, Luxemburg), see Schmitt (ed.), *Neutral Europe*; Meaker, *Revolutionary Left*; Nelson, "Labour Insurgency"; Andrae, "Swedish Labor"; Heerma van Voss, "Netherlands," pp. 44–52; Polasky, *Democratic Socialism*, pp. 160–90; Scuto, *Sous le signe*.

7. See Péteri, *Effects*, pp. 1–54; Hajdu, *Hungarian Soviet*; Tökes, *Béla Kun*; Kenez, "Coalition Politics"; Nagy, "Budapest"; Romsics, "Hungarian." Aleksandr Kerensky (1881–1970) was head of the Russian Provisional Government from April to its overthrow in October. Though originally aligned with the Socialist Revolutionaries, by 1917 he was identified with the Kadets.

8. Carr, *Bolshevik Revolution*, 3:200. Polish-Soviet relations worsened after an early clash on the Belorussian frontier in February 1919, as both states entered the vacuum left by the German military administration. Jozef Pilsudski launched an offensive (May 1920), which the Bolsheviks dramatically turned back. Davies, *White Eagle*, is overindulgent toward the Poles. For a more judicious summary, see Leslie (ed.), *History*, pp. 134–8.

9. See Hansen, "Between Reform."

10. Arthur Henderson, *The Aims of Labour* (London, 1917), pp. 20, 24, quoted by Hinton, *Labour*, p. 103.

11. Quoted in Abrams, "Failure," p. 46. For the long-term importance of these years, despite the disappointments of specific reforms, see Middlemas, *Politics*, pp. 120–51.

12. Hobsbawm, " 'New Unionism,' " p. 29.

13. A model of collaboration between employers and union leaders was the Stinnes-Legien pact in Germany on 15 November 1918. Named after its main negotiators, the heavy industrialist Hugo Stinnes and the veteran Free Union chair Karl Legien, it gave unions big concessions, including full legal recognition and unrestricted rights of recruitment, the eight-hour day, assured employment for returning soldiers, and full consultative arrangements in firms, including the elections of workers' committees. In return, union leaders opposed rank-and-file desires for nationalization and workers' control, producing great embitterment inside the labor movement. The pact's official name was the *Zentralarbeitsgemeinschaft* or Central Working Agreement.

14. Fox, *History*, p. 293; Middlemas, *Politics*, p. 143; Wrigley, *Lloyd George*.

15. See Cronin, "Coping"; Wrigley, "State"; Foster, "Working-Class."

16. See Liulevicius, *War Land*; Fischer, *Germany's Aims*, pp. 475–509; Borowsky, *Deutsche Ukrainepolitik*, pp. 166–262; Guratzsch, *Macht*, pp. 363–79.

17. See Reshetar, *Ukrainian Revolution*; Suny, *Baku Commune*; Upton, *Finnish Revolution*; Alapuro, *State*; Azergailis, *1917 Revolution*; Rauch, *Baltic States*; Suny, *Making*; Shanin, *Roots*, 2:261–79.

18. See above all Suny, "National Revolutions"; also Eley, "Remapping."

19. See Bell, *Peasants*, pp. 122–53; King, *History*, pp. 9–38; Hitchens, "Romanian Socialists"; Banac, *National Question*, pp. 328–39, and "Communist Party."

20. See above all Wheaton, *Radical Socialism;* McDermott, *Red Unions,* pp. 1–38.

21. For the British example, see Slatter, "Learning."

22. The far right Kapp Putsch (13 March 1920) was led by Wolfgang Kapp, a leading radical nationalist politician of the years 1912–18, and General Walther von Lüttwitz. The government retreated from Berlin to Stuttgart, but by 21 March the Putsch was defeated by a general strike. Mass actions were then hard to demobilize, and the returning government's attempts at military repression provoked civil war in large areas of industrial Germany. For the standard account, see Erger, *Kapp-Lüttwitz;* for events in the Ruhr, Lucas, *Märzrevolution 1920,* and Eliasberg, *Ruhrkrieg;* and for a compelling local analysis (Leipzig), Dobson, *Authority,* pp. 278–89.

23. Some indebtedness can be traced to syndicalism and similar pre-1914 movements. For example, one line ran from the "localism" of the Berlin metals and building trade unionism of the 1890s through the revival of direct accountability in the wartime shop stewards movement to the Räte that immediately followed. Berlin localism had counterposed the sovereignty of the branch general meeting to the victorious model of centralist unionism, in a rear-guard action finally defeated around 1907–8. See Müller, *Gewerkschaftliche Versammlungsdemokratie.*

24. The standard work on the German factory-based councils is von Oertzen, *Betriebsräte.* For an excellent, broadly contextualized account of the movement in Leipzig, see Dobson, *Authority,* pp. 223–77.

25. "Socialization" implies more than the English "nationalization." Where the latter signifies public ownership and central bureaucratic administration (as in British nationalized industry after 1945), the former foregrounds social ownership, with workers' control over production. In the British labor movement before 1914, nationalization was opposed precisely for its irrelevance for the worker at the point of production, simply substituting state bureacracy for private capitalists. Before 1914, the alternative was syndicalism stressing democracy in production, even to the exclusion of any centralized managerial framework. An absolute dichotomy of state ownership (nationalization) versus workers' control (in the localist syndicalist sense) was unnecessary, and the German socialization discussion of early 1919 characteristically combined both. For the classic British debate, see Morgan, "Socialism."

26. For Heiling and the *Freie Vereinigung der Bergarbeiter Deutschlands,* see Tampke, *Ruhr,* p. 101. For organizational and ideological context, see Bock, *Syndikalismus* and *Geschichte,* pp. 74–169; Thorpe, "Keeping."

27. For the broader context of labor militancy in Germany, see Weitz, *Creating,* pp. 83–141. For France in the same period: Magraw, "Paris 1917–20"; Amdur, *Syndicalist Legacy,* pp. 83–172.

28. Gramsci, "The Revolution against Capital" (24 December 1917), in *Political Writings,* p. 34.

29. Quoted from the anonymous autobiography of a council militant, "Erlebnisse und Schlußfolgerungen eines Revolutionärs," in *Proletarische Zeitgeist,* 10 (1931), p. 9, cited by Bock, *Geschichte,* p. 97.

30. Program of the Communist Workers' Party of Germany (KAPD), May 1920, cited ibid. The KAPD, founded April 1920, briefly focused the council-

communist militancy exploding across industrial Germany in 1919–21. Highly localized and politically amorphous, embracing direct action and armed defense, this neosyndicalist movement initially rivalled the KPD, before its different wings fragmented and the membership dispersed. See the works of Bock, and Hölz, *White Cross*.

31. Clark, *Antonio Gramsci*, pp. 112–5.

32. The German law is printed in an appendix to Moses, *Trade Unionism*, pp. 467–500. Moses gives a good summary of the discussions preceding the law, from a perspective sympathetic to the trade union leadership, pp. 291–320. The law created separate works councils for white-collar employees.

33. Ibid., p. 460. In an earlier conference (1–2 February 1919), Legien attacked decentralized systems of council sovereignty as privileging favorably placed workers, denying others the benefits of national bargaining and organization. He wished "to give expression to our trade union principles, that with the councils system only a few sections of workers under favorable conditions would be served, while the large mass of the working class would be disadvantaged." P. 437, note 46.

CHAPTER 10

1. When sailors learned of the Naval High Command's plans for a death-or-glory battle with the British on 27–28 October, they refused to put to sea. Once back in port, disciplinary actions provoked full-scale mutiny, which spread to the army and working class. The High Command had wanted to undermine the new constitutional government and disrupt armistice negotiations. As Horn aptly says: "It was the admirals' rebellion against the government that caused the mass disobedience of the sailors and stokers." See Horn, *Naval Mutinies*, p. 233.

2. The new climate was highly combustible. Naval mutinies were the necessary spark, rather than coming out of the blue. See Carsten, *War*, pp. 208–21.

3. For a careful and sympathetic explication of the pressures faced by the Ebert government, see Mathews, "Economic Origins"; also Bessel, *Germany*, pp. 194–219.

4. Kirby, *War*, p. 227.

5. However, this 12-person Executive Committee of the Workers' and Soldiers' Council of Berlin coopted 12 supposedly nonpartisan soldiers' delegates, for whom the principle of parity was waived. By controlling the Berlin garrison, the SPD had brought a clear majority of soldiers' delegates into its own camp, thereby ensuring a two-thirds majority in the Executive. See Winkler, *Revolution*, pp. 55–8. The USPD nominees to the new government were originally Haase, Georg Ledebour (the USPD's left-wing cochairman), and Liebknecht, but the latter two were opposed to participating on principle.

6. Carsten, *War*, p. 227. The best synthetic accounts of the German Revolution are Winkler, *Revolution*, pp. 19–150; Kluge, *Die deutsche Revolution*; Carsten, *Revolution*, pp. 32–49, 55–77, 127–223.

7. Miller, *Bürde*, p. 99.

8. See Winkler, *Revolution*, pp. 68–72; and Carsten, *Reichswehr*, pp. 10–37. For the soldiers' councils, Kluge, *Soldatenräte*; for demobilizing the troops, Bessel, *Germany*, pp. 69–90; and for the *Freikorps*, Schulze, *Freikorps*, and Waite, *Vanguard*. For the role of Gustav Noske, see Wette, *Gustav Noske*.

9. Winkler, *Revolution*, pp. 72–5.

10. The Agreement is printed in Moses, *Trade Unionism*, 2:454–6. See also Feldman, "German Business" and "Origins."

11. The KPD's founding Congress on 30 December 1918 was attended by 94 delegates from the Spartacus League, 29 from the International Communists of Germany (IKD), and four others. Since 11 November, the Spartacists had formed an organized caucus in the USPD; the IKD united radicals from Bremen, Hamburg, and Berlin on 23 November. "Order Rules in Berlin" was the title of Rosa Luxemburg's last article, published in *Rote Fahne*, 14 January 1919. See Luxemburg, *Gesammelte Werke*, 4:533–8. See Fowkes, *Communism*, pp. 10–23; Winkler, *Revolution*, pp. 114–33; Weber (ed.), *Gründungsparteitag*.

12. One study exploring the connections between exceptionally unstable socioeconomic and institutional circumstances and popular receptiviness to radical change, in a "world turned upside down," is Geyer, *Verkehrte Welt*. A similar argument is presented in exhausting and encyclopedic detail by Feldman, *Great Disorder*.

13. The pioneering accounts of the Räte as the basis for a "third way" were von Oertzen, *Betriebsräte*, and Kolb, *Arbeiterräte*. For critical overviews, see Rürup's two essays, "Problems" and "Demokratische Revolution." For a strong argument based on workers' democratic expectations, see Dobson, *Authority*, pp. 191–220.

14. For careful statements of this argument, see Geary, "Radicalism" and "Revolutionary Berlin." The classic studies of radicalization in the Ruhr are Lucas, *Märzrevolution 1920*; Eliasberg, *Ruhrkrieg*. The process can be tracked through the lens of the parties in Fowkes, *Communism*, pp. 24–53; and Morgan, *Socialist Left*, pp. 212–341.

15. The PSI's response to the postwar crisis is best followed through the literature on Gramsci: Cammett, *Antonio Gramsci*, pp. 65–155; Clark, *Antonio Gramsci*, pp. 46–209; Williams, *Proletarian Order*, pp. 95–301; also Davidson, *Theory*, pp. 75–101. For broader context, see the excellent regional studies by Corner, *Fascism*, pp. 76–136; Cardoza, *Agrarian Elites*, pp. 245–386; Snowden, "From Sharecropper;" Abse, "Rise"; Bell, "Working-Class Culture."

16. Clark, *Antonio Gramsci*, p. 34.

17. Corner, *Fascism*, p. 82.

18. Vivarelli, "Revolution," p. 246.

19. In the course of the debate, Ludovico D'Aragona, Secretary of the CGL, offered the CGL leadership's collective resignation if the PSI Directorate truly believed the moment for revolution had arrived. The PSI abjured and referred the decision back to the CGL National Council. Meanwhile, the Fascists were already seizing the initiative. By far the best discussion is Spriano, *Occupation*, pp. 86–93.

20. Egidio Gennari, a leading Maximalist in the PSI Directorate, made this argument in a speech of 20 April 1920, justifying the decision not to support the Piedmont general strike. Cited by Clark, *Antonio Gramsci*, p. 107.

21. Giacinto Menotti Serrati (1872–1926), Maximalist leader, in October 1919, cited by Lyttleton, "Revolution," p. 68. Given Marx's famous statement ("The philosphers have only interpreted the world; the point is to change it"), the irony in Serrati's words was cosmic.

22. Filippo Turati, quoted by Seton-Watson, *Italy*, p. 575.

23. Amadeo Bordiga (1889–1970) dominated the Communist group. There were actually *five* factions at Livorno: the others were the Intransigent Revolutionaries and the Communist-Unity Group. The leader of the former, Constantino Lazzari (1857–1927), PSI secretary 1912–1919, spoke brandishing all 40 of his membership tokens going back to 1882. Bordigans dominated the new party's five-person Central Executive, while Togliatti edited *Il Comunista* in Rome and Gramsci *l'Ordine nuovo* (now turned into a daily) in Turin. The best account of Livorno is in Cammett, *Antonio Gramsci,* pp. 141–55.

24. Spriano, *Occupation,* p. 135.

25. Another dimension of this political isolationism was the failure to develop a strategy for women. See especially Foot, "Socialist-Catholic."

26. See Foot, "Analysis."

27. For the specifically Italian revolutionary dynamic as a local chain reaction organized through the Chambers of Labor, see Lyttleton, "Revolution," p. 70. As secretary of the Turin Chamber, Angelo Tasca (1892–1960) argued against Gramsci that the analogue to the soviets in Russia was not the factory council but the geographically based camere del lavoro; he also gave greater priority to unions and cooperatives. See De Grand, *Stalin's Shadow,* pp. 21–33.

28. Vivarelli, "Revolution," pp. 242–5.

CHAPTER 11

1. Kirby, *War,* p. 190.

2. The founding of the Third International is taken up later in this chapter.

3. See Ritter (ed.), *Zweite Internationale;* Ritter, "Second International"; Wheeler, "Failure"; Morgan, *Socialist Left,* pp. 280–91.

4. See Carr, *Bolshevik Revolution,* 3:181–205.

5. In addition to the 58,000 who fell by the wayside during October–December, another 126,000 of the USPD's pre-Halle membership disclaimed affiliation with either side. Thus in the short term the split produced a net loss of 184,000 to the USPD rump and the united KPD combined. For details, see Winkler, *Revolution,* pp. 482–3; Morgan, *Socialist Left,* pp. 355–80.

6. The motion to accept the Twenty-One Conditions received 3,208 block votes, with 1,028 against and 397 abstentions. The new party kept 110,000 members, leaving 30,000 to the refounded SFIO. See Adereth, *French Communist Party,* pp. 22–28; Wohl, *French Communism,* pp. 158–207.

7. The Italian CP claimed 58,000 members, the Czechoslovak 170,000. See Cammett, *Antonio Gramsci,* pp. 141–55; Gruber (ed.), *International Communism,* pp. 231–66; Myant, *Socialism and Democracy,* pp. 5–14; Wheaton, *Radical Socialism,* pp. 75–101.

8. Winkler, *Revolution,* pp. 478–82; Morgan, *Socialist Left,* pp. 395–6; Steiner, "Internationale Arbeitsgemeinschaft"; Wheeler, *USPD.*

9. See Carr, *Bolshevik Revolution,* 3:404–9; Sukiennicki, "Abortive Attempt."

10. Central Committee of the Communist Party of Russia (Bolsheviks), 24 December 1918, "Against an International of Traitors," in Riddell (ed.), *German Revolution,* p. 442.

11. Full text, ibid., pp. 447–52.

12. The full proceedings of the Congress, including these various statements,

are now available in Riddell (ed.), *Founding*. The quoted phrases are taken from Trotsky's "Manifesto" (pp. 231, 238), except from the last, which comes from Lenin's "Theses" (p. 150).

13. Riddell (ed.), *Founding*, p. 139.

14. Details from Riddell's introduction, ibid., p. 12, where he also observes that two delegates were arrested on their way back—Platten in Finland and Steinhardt in Romania.

15. Lenin quoted by Mayer, *Wilson vs. Lenin*, p. 298. See also Boersner, *Bolsheviks*.

16. Vatislav Vorovsky, at 48 years old one of the senior participants in the Congress. See *Pravda*, 7 March 1919, quoted in the introduction to Riddell (ed.), *Founding*, p. 20.

17. Carr, *Bolshevik Revolution*, 3:132.

18. For the confusing histories of the KAPD and broader council-communist and syndicalist movements, see Bock, *Syndikalismus* and *Geschichte*, pp. 74–169; also Hölz, *White Cross*.

CHAPTER 12

1. Women also had the vote before 1914 in New Zealand (1893), Australia (1903), the prairie provinces of Manitoba, Saskatchewan, and Alberta in Canada, and 11 states to the west of the Mississippi in the United States. Among the 1918 successor states, Yugoslavia denied votes to women. Swiss women also lacked the franchise.

2. This anxiety about population was particularly salient in France. See Le Bras, *Marianne*; Teitelbaum and Winter, *Fear*; Huss, "Pro-Natalism"; Tomlinson, "Disappearance"; Offen, "Body Politics"; Thébaud, "Work"; and for the deeper context, Offen, "Depopulation."

3. For fascism: Nash, "Pronatalism"; Saraceno, "Redefining"; de Grazia, *How Fascism*, pp. 41–76; Bock, "Antinatalism"; Czarnowski, "Hereditary." For the Soviet Union: Goldman, *Women*, pp. 254–95. For France: Schneider, *Quality*; Carol, *Histoire*. For Britain: Searle, *Eugenics*; Soloway, *Demography*. For Weimar Germany: Grossmann, *Reforming Sex*. For Scandinavia: Broberg and Roll-Hansen (eds.), *Eugenics*; Blom, "Voluntary Motherhood." For Spanish anarchism: Cleminson, "Eugenics." For general overviews: Dikötter, "Race Culture"; Nye, "Rise"; Adams (ed.), *Wellborn Science*.

4. See especially Berezin, *Making*.

5. See Hong, "World War I."

6. See Heinen, "Kollontai."

7. See for example, Stoehr, "Housework"; Sachße, "Social Mothers."

8. Alexander, "Becoming," p. 247.

9. For the gendered contexts of consumption in the modern metropolis and their complex political implications, see Nava, "Modernity's Disavowal"; Rappaport, *Shopping*; Pumphrey, "Flapper"; Grossmann, "New Woman"; Roberts, *Civilization*; von Ankum (ed.), *Women*; Charney and Schwartz (eds.), *Cinema*; Matthews, "They Had"; Alexander, "Becoming."

10. John Sommerfield, *May Day* (London, 1936), p. 30, cited by Alexander, "Becoming," p. 246.

11. Lapidus, *Women*, p. 58.

12. See Goldman, "Women."

13. Lapidus, *Women,* p. 41. Kollontai headed the Commissariat for Social Welfare from October 1917 to March 1918.

14. Carr, *Socialism,* 1:44; Lapidus, *Women,* p. 89.

15. Lapidus, *Women,* pp. 66, 210. Zhenotdel was used for Soviet political campaigning in Muslim Central Asia, where women became prioritized as a "surrogate proletariat." See Massell, *Surrogate Proletariat.* The essential study of Zhenotdel and its context is Wood, *Baba;* also Goldman, *Women;* Wood, "Prostitution Unbound"; Naiman, *Sex.*

16. Lapidus, *Women,* p. 72.

17. See Carr, *Socialism,* 3:1014–24; Waters, "Shadow."

18. Figures from the printed record of the Fourth Congress of the Communist International, 4 December 1922, in the report of Hertha Sturm, cited by Bruley, *Leninism,* pp. 97–8. The Norwegian Labor Party (DNA), with 15 percent female membership, affiliated with the Third International *en bloc* in 1919 but then left it again in 1923.

19. Hellman, *Journeys,* p. 31.

20. See de Grazia, *How Fascism;* Caldwell, "Reproducers." For the broader context of Socialist neglect, see Foot, "Socialist-Catholic."

21. Bruley, *Leninism,* pp. 122–5, 118.

22. For the role of feminists in the CPGB's foundation, see ibid., p. 63. For Stella Browne, see Sheila Rowbotham, *New World.* For Sylvia Pankhurst, see Harrison, *Prudent Revolutionaries,* pp. 209–41.

23. See Bard, "Marianne" and "Proletarians."

24. This paragraph is based on Bard and Robert, "French Communist Party." For the stable masculinity of Communist political culture and its shifting representations of women between the 1920s and later 1930s (from strong and athletic women workers to conventional pronatalist and maternalist ideals of femininity), using visual evidence from the KPD, PCF, and PCI, see Weitz, "Heroic Man."

25. Quoted by Kontos, *Die Partei,* p. 134. Ruth Fischer (1895–1961) was part of the KPD's ultraleft leadership in 1924–25.

26. Details from Kontos, *Die Partei,* pp. 210–23.

27. Ibid., pp. 145–9.

28. For general accounts, see Grossmann, "German Communism"; Weitz, *Creating,* pp. 188–232.

29. Pedersen, "Gender," pp. 991–1000. See also Bland, "In the Name."

30. Daniel, *Arbeiterfrauen,* pp. 119, 77. For comparative treatment of "Welfare Supervision and Labor Discipline in Britain and France, 1916–1918," see Downs, *Manufacturing,* ch. 5, pp. 147–85. See also Roberts, *Civilization.*

31. Pedersen, "Gender," p. 1003.

32. Koven and Michel, "Womanly Duties," provides a valuable comparative survey of maternalist welfare politics but misses the decisive changes wrought by the First World War, which reconfigured the possible agency maternalism allowed to women, whether as social workers or mothers. For further debate, see Lewis, "Gender."

33. See Crew, "German Socialism," pp. 235–63.

34. Klenkes, *SPD-Linke,* 2:853.

35. In 1908, national legislation in Germany allowed women to join and form political organizations properly for the first time.

36. The strength of this generalization certainly needs detailed qualification. See von Saldern, "Modernization"; Blom, "Double Responsibility"; Christensen, "Socialist Feminists"; Frangeur, "Social Democrats." For the broader context of SPD welfare politics in the 1920s, see especially Eifert, *Frauenpolitik;* Hagemann, "Rationalizing"; Eifert, "Coming to Terms"; Rouette, "Mothers"; Crew, "Socialism" and *Germans.* For the Austrian case, see Gruber, *Red Vienna.*

37. Thane, "Women," p. 136. Graves calls this a "woman-centered socialism." See Graves, "Experiment" and *Labour Women.* See also Lebas, 'When Every-Street.'

38. The NUSEC was a reformation of the earlier NUWSS, the nonmilitant "Suffragist" umbrella founded in 1897, to which the "Suffragette" WSPU was the militant counterfoundation in 1903. See Smith, "British Feminism," pp. 47–65.

39. Pedersen, "Failure," p. 86.

40. Thus many equality feminists supported family allowances and contraception per se; likewise, they objected to the limiting of protective legislation to women workers in isolation rather than the extending of it to men and women workers in general. For these nuances, see Law, *Suffrage;* Smith, "British Feminism," p. 58.

41. Pedersen, "Failure," p. 105. For the most important general assessment of British feminism in this period, see Kent, *Making Peace* and "Politics."

42. A telling example was Marion Phillips (1887–1932), former suffragist, Labour MP, and the Labour Party's "Chief Woman Officer" in the 1920s, who controlled access of the women's sections to the agenda at the Annual Conference. Radical resolutions, as Pedersen says, "somehow never quite made it into the pre-arranged debate." See Pedersen, "Failure," p. 96.

43. For a survey of intewar feminism through an array of biographical portraits, see Harrison, *Prudent Revolutionaries.*

44. Francis, "Labour," p. 201. See also Law, *Suffrage.*

45. See Scott, *Only Paradoxes,* pp. 125–60; Boxer, "When Radical"; Gordon, *The Integral Feminist.*

46. Grossmann, "Gender," p. 14.

47. See Gruber, *Red Vienna,* pp. 156, 175.

48. Stella Browne, "The Sexual Variety and Variability among Women and their Bearing upon Social Reconstruction," in Rowbotham, *New World,* p. 92. See also Hall, "Impotent Ghosts."

49. See Grossmann, *Reforming Sex.*

50. Rowan, " 'Mothers,' " p. 82.

51. Sachse, *Siemens,* p. 256.

52. See especially Nolan, *Visions,* and " 'Housework' "; Reese et al. (eds.), *Rationale Beziehungen?* Grossmann, "Gender" and "New Woman"; Maier, "Between Taylorism"; Rabinbach, *Human Motor,* pp. 238–88.

53. Gramsci, "Americanism," pp. 297, 304.

54. Wollen, "Modern Times," p. 39.

55. Matthews, "They Had," p. 50

56. Ibid., pp. 43, 47. Matthews invokes a famous analysis of Siegfried Kra-

cauer from the 1920s, where the precision dancing of the Tiller Girls Dance Troupe was likened to the standardized procedures of Fordist mass production. See Kracauer, "Mass Ornament."

57. Helena Swanwick, *Manchester Guardian*, 24 August 1932, cited by Harrison, *Prudent Revolutionaries*, p. 320.

58. Orwell and Angus (eds.), *Collected Essays*, p. 207.

59. George Orwell, *The Road to Wigan Pier* (1937), quoted by Campbell, *Wigan Pier*, pp. 217, 227.

60. Marie Juchasz, quoted from the SPD's 1927 Kiel Congress by Winkler, *Schein*, pp. 353–5.

CHAPTER 13

1. See Schorske, *Fin de Siecle*; Eksteins, *Rites*, pp. 9–54.

2. Hobsbawm, *Age of Empire*, p. 233; also Hobsbawm, "Socialism."

3. See his two Berlin novels, *Mr. Norris Changes Trains* (London, 1935) and *Goodbye to Berlin* (London, 1939).

4. See Benjamin, "Paris," pp. 155–76.

5. "The Founding and Manifesto of Futurism," originally published in *Le Figaro*, 1909, in Kolocontroni et al. (eds.), *Modernism*, pp. 249–53. See also Williams, "Politics," p. 51; Adamson, "Modernism"; Adamson, *Avant-Garde;* Davies, "Futures Market"; Orban, "Women"; Forgacs, "Fascism"; Adamson, "The Impact."

6. Dada was a deliberately anarchical and "meaningless" movement, originating in a small group of artists and performers at the Cabaret Voltaire in Zurich in 1916. It migrated to Berlin in early 1918, where it drew a broader group, including John Heartfield and George Grosz, who moved into the orbit of the Communist Party.

7. Stites, *Revolutionary Dreams*, p. 38. See also Rosenberg (ed.), *Bolshevik Visions;* Clark, *Petersburg;* Gleason, Kenez, and Stites (eds.), *Bolshevik Culture*.

8. Quoted by Williams, *Russian Revolution*, p. 79.

9. Lunacharsky, statement of October 1920, quoted by McClelland, "Utopian," p. 123.

10. Fitzpatrick, *Commissariat*, pp. 124, 148, 130.

11. The *Vpered* (Forward) circle formed in 1908–9 among dissident Bolsheviks dissatisfied with Lenin's centralist leadership of the party. It centered on two party schools organized by Bogdanov in Capri (1909) and Bologna (1910–11) for worker students smuggled out of Russia. By 1913 the faction had fallen apart. See Sochor, *Revolution;* and above all Mally, *Culture*.

12. Gregorii Zinoviev, quoted by Fitzpatrick, *Commissariat*, p. 100.

13. Lenin's address to the First All-Russian Congress on Extra-Mural Education in early May 1919, cited in ibid., p. 106. The political heterogeneity of the delegates lent context to Lenin's attack on the "bourgeois intelligentsia": among 576 voting delegates there were only 156 Communists and another 70 sympathizers, the rest being SRs, Bundists, anarchists, and other non-Communists.

14. The quotations are all from Carr, *Socialism*, 1:33. Carr selects four areas to illustrate the cultural transition of NEP—policies toward the family, the Orthodox Church, literature, and the law (pp. 37–101). See further his chapter on "Class and Party" (pp. 102–50).

15. In no. 16 of his "Theses on the Philosophy of History," in Benjamin, *Illuminations,* p. 264.

16. Constructivism repudiated the "fine arts" tradition in painting, sculpture, and architecture in favour of the "practical arts" in metals, woods, ceramics, typography, and interior design. It was strongly oriented toward engineering and machines, with an emphasis on abstraction, utilitarianism, and the natural properties of materials. Tatlin's tower was meant to straddle the river Neva in Petrograd, designed as a huge spiral of iron and glass in which would be suspended a cylinder, a cube, and a sphere containing conference centers, offices, and a state-of-the-art communications center.

17. Carr, *Socialism,* 1:37.

18. Lukács, *Record,* p. 59. Details are taken from Zsuffa, *Béla Balázs,* p. 78; and Hajdu, *Hungarian,* pp. 73–8. According to Zsuffa, Balázs's illustrated fairy tales reached an audience of 120,000 children in Budapest every week—"in classrooms, parks, hospitals, and orphanages" (p. 416, note 43).

19. The Hungarian Soviet was composed of three main groupings: radicalized younger intellectuals who formed the key group in the CP in November 1918; trade-union leaders; and leftists influenced by Ervin Szabo, who formed the Left opposition in the prewar Social Democratic Party after 1903. See Tökes, *Béla Kun,* pp. 13–6.

20. Details from Löwy, *Georg Lukács,* pp. 72–90; also Midgely, "Communism"; Held, "Culture."

21. In general, see Müller, Ringer, and Simon (eds.), *Rise;* and Ringer, *Education.* For two excellent national studies, Jarausch, *Students;* Cohen, *Education.*

22. For an excellent illustration, see Jensen, *Marketing Modernism.*

23. They included the Commissars for Social Production in the Soviet government, 29-year-old Gyula Hevesi and 26-year-old Jozsef Kelen, who were both engineers, members of a grouping called the "revolutionary technocrats."

24. Willett, *New Sobriety,* p. 12.

25. George Bussmann, "Some Attitudes to Art and Politics in the Twenties," in Schneede, *George Grosz,* p. 160. Like Grosz, Vogeler was incarcerated in a mental institution for his inability to continue coping with the war. He was 42 when war began, at the peak of his renown.

26. Zsuffa, *Béla Balázs,* p. 58.

27. See Kerbs (ed.), *Gegen Kind,* p. 4.

28. Whyte, *Bruno Taut,* p. 20.

29. The cessation of construction until economic recovery in 1924 necessarily encouraged radical architects into literary or abstract activity: in Berlin, 18 buildings were started in the first quarter of 1919, only 9 in the last quarter, and a mere 5 in the first quarter of 1920. See Whyte, *Bruno Taut,* p. 169, and Willett, *New Sobriety,* p. 92. On finishing his utopian work, *Die Auflösung der Städte oder die Erde eine gute wohnung* (Hagen, 1920), Taut wrote to a friend: "With that, 'utopias' should come to an end, and I hope that I shall have some opportunities to work with my ideas in the realm of the practical." But while architect to the SPD city of Magdeburg in 1921–23, Taut saw only one of his projects built. See Whyte, *Bruno Taut,* p. 206.

30. The demand of the Revolutionary Central Committee of Dada for the organization of circuses for the "enlightenment of the proletariat" was a far more "realistic" idea in the circumstances.

31. The Malik-Verlag was founded in 1917 by the brothers John Heartfield and Wielande Herzfelde and became the premier publisher in the arts linked to the KPD during the Weimar Republic.

32. The PSI debates over culture began in 1912 at the instigation the Young Socialist Federation. See Gramsci's article, "For a Cultural Association," in the Piedmont edition of *Avanti!* on 18 December 1917, in Forgacs and Nowell-Smith (eds.), *Antonio Gramsci,* pp. 22–3.

33. Gramsci, "Philanthropy, Good Will and Organization," in ibid., 24 December 1917, p. 25.

34. Imprisoned from 1926, Gramsci elaborated his ideas in the famous *Prison Notebooks,* which became a legacy of enormous influence for the Left. They were initially planned by Gramsci in January 1927 immediately after his arrest, and the writing began in February 1929. After 1945 they were published in Italy, with a full edition in 1948–51. A new critical edition was issued in 1975. A first detailed translation appeared as *Selections from the Prison Notebooks,* edited by Quintin Hoare and Geoffrey Nowell-Smith (London, 1971), although a shorter selection appeared as *The Modern Prince and Other Writings* (New York, 1957). See also Forgacs (ed.), *Gramsci Reader,* Forgacs and Nowell-Smith (eds.), *Selections from Cultural Writings.*

35. Macintyre, *Little Moscows,* p. 173. "Little Moscows" was the sobriquet attaching to various small and usually single-industry communities with strong Communist or left Labour political cultures between the wars. Macintyre's three examples are the coal-mining towns of Mardy in South Wales and Lumphinnans in Fife and the textile company town of Vale of Leven in western Scotland.

36. Ibid., p. 172.

37. In 1924 Vienna had 1.8 million inhabitants in an Austrian population of 6.5 million; in the same year the Socialists had 266,415 members in the city, or one in five adults (nationally in 1924 membership was 566,124). In the municipal elections of 4 May 1919 (on a democratic franchise now extended to women and young adults), the SPÖ won 100 out of 165 seats on an absolute popular majority of 54 percent, rising in 1923 to two-thirds. The best general study is Gruber, *Red Vienna.*

38. Rabinbach, *Crisis,* p. 27.

39. For excellent discussion of this point, see von Saldern, "Sozialdemokratie" and "Workers' Movement."

40. See Gruber, "History," esp. pp. 52–4.

41. Eric J. Hobsbaum, introduction to Duczynska, *Workers,* p. 19.

42. Gruber, "History," pp. 50–1.

43. Valtin Hartig, director of the Leipzig Workers' Educational Institute, quoted by Langewiesche, "Working-Class Culture," p. 108.

44. Grossmann, " 'Satisfaction," p. 266. The best estimate for the overall membership of the extremely ramified sex reform movement seems to be around 150,000 in 1930–31.

45. See also Hopwood, "Producing."

46. For membership and capsule descriptions of the SPD's many cultural organizations, see Fricke, *Handbuch,* pp. 1022–42, and Ueberhorst, *Frisch,* p. 111. See the four-volume systematic study of SPD leisure organizations, Lösche (ed.), *Solidargemeinschaft.* For the sex reform movement: Grossmann, *Reforming Sex.* For the working-class freethinkers: Kaiser, *Arbeiterbewegung,* pp. 350–4. For the

speaking choirs: Clark, *Bruno Schönlank*. For general accounts: von Saldern, "Arbeiterkulturbewegung," pp. 29–70; Guttsman, *German*, pp. 167–218.

47. Langewiesche, "Working-Class Culture," p. 109.

48. For a detailed development of this argument, see Eley, "Cultural Socialism"; also Korff, "Brotherly Handshake"; Weitz, "Heroic Man" and "Communism."

49. For the general debate over the character of the SPD's labor movement culture in the 1920s, see Lösche and Walter, "Zur Organisationskultur"; von Saldern, "Arbeiterkulturbewegung"; Harsch, "Codes."

50. Details from the following: Langewiesche, "Working-Class Culture," p. 110; Jones, *British*, p. 7; Peterson, *Media*, p. 228. See also Crump, "Recreation," p. 266.

51. For radio, see Koon, *Believe*, p. 155; Peterson, *Media*, pp. 131, 136; Cronin, *Labour*, p. 90; LeMahieu, *Culture*, p. 12; and esp. Marßolek and von Saldern (eds.), *Zuhören*. For the new dance halls, see Crump, "Recreation," pp. 277–80; and for spectator sports see Jones, *Sport*, and Fishwick, *English Football*.

52. For a thoughtful discussion of the labor movement's response to cinema, see Langewiesche, "Massenmedium."

53. A 31-year-old Nottingham upholsterer responding to a 1939 Mass-Observation Survey of attitudes toward class, cited by Cronin, *Labour*, p. 73. The W.E.A. was the Workers' Educational Association.

54. Wickham, "Working-Class Movement," p. 335.

55. Ibid., pp. 337–8.

56. See Cronin, *Labour*, p. 86; Jones, *British*, p. 7; Miles and Smith, *Cinema*, p. 163.

57. The quotations (originating with the Marxist intellectuals Eden and Cedar Paul and a statement by the Llanelly Constituency Labour Party) are taken from Jones, *British*, pp. 53, 57.

58. See Bloch, *Erbschaft*. For the fascist politics of leisure, see esp. de Grazia, *Culture;* Passerini, *Fascism;* Mason, "Workers' Opposition," pp. 120–37.

59. See Williams, "Culture," esp. p. 3.

60. Wickham, "Working-Class Movement," p. 342.

CHAPTER 14

1. In Italy, the other country of more extreme working-class insurgency, the PSI stayed more sympathetic to the revolutionary mood of the wider movement, and this "maximalism" prevented the leaders from assuming the stabilizing role of the SPD or SPÖ. By neither acting on its revolutionary rhetoric nor forging the broader parliamentary coalitions needed to defend democracy, the PSI helped open the space during 1920–22 where Mussolini's Fascists could grow.

2. Lenin, *The State and Revolution* (1917), in *Selected Works*, 1:296. See Jessop, "Capitalism."

3. Lichtheim, *Short History*, p. 261.

4. See Lenin, *"Left-Wing Communism."* Lenin's pamphlet was handed out to all delegates at the Comintern's Second Congress in July. Its main target was the KAPD, which broke with the KPD in April 1920, threatening to shape council communist militancy into a distinct national movement. Briefly, the KAPD counted perhaps two hundred thousand supporters linked to the neosyndicalist

General Workers' Union of Germany formed in February 1920. The militancy involved was highly volatile, locally fragmented, and divided among competing neosyndicalist tendencies. By 1921, the potential rivalry with the KPD had dissipated. Lenin's fire was also aimed against the Dutch left Communists Hermann Gorter and Anton Pannekoek, associates of the extreme left in the prewar SPD, with a base in Bremen. See especially Gerber, *Anton Pannekoek*, pp. 132–62.

5. This official policy of United Front was hugely ambiguous. Taking cooperation with social democrats too seriously always rendered Communists liable to Bolshevik censure, and in his speech outlining the policy, Zinoviev stressed the instrumental quality: reformists could be supported "as a rope supports a hanging man," as Lenin disarmingly put it in *"Left-Wing Communism"—An Infantile Disorder*. At the same time, these tones were certainly reciprocated by social democrats in kind. Nonetheless, early Communists like Heinrich Brandler in Germany and Bohumir Smeral in Czechoslovakia, with long experience in prewar labor movements, sought to pursue the United Front in many creative ways. The same was true in myriad local settings. See Angress, *Stillborn Revolution*, pp. 223–53, esp. p. 227; Fowkes, *Communism*, pp. 74–90, 129–47; McDermott, *Red Unions*, pp. 63–95, 125–52; Meaker, *Revolutionary Left*, pp. 429–55; Wohl, *French Communism*, pp. 256–69, 328–31, 374–5; Calhoun, *United Front*; and Macintyre, *Little Moscows*.

6. For excellent examples of such local dynamics, permitting working-class Communists and left-wing socialists to work together even when their national parties were effectively proscribing cooperation, see Macintyre, *Little Moscows*.

PART III INTRODUCTION

1. My account of the Witenberg affair and the FPO is based on Arad, *Ghetto*, pp. 387–95, 234–62. There are briefer accounts in Dawidowicz, *War*, pp. 441–3; Hilberg, *Perpetrators*, pp. 180–1.

2. The Judenrat (Jewish council) was the form of ghetto self-administration imposed on the Jews by the Third Reich, growing in importance once the deportations and concentration of Jewish populations began in the autumn of 1939. See Trunk, *Judenrat*; Hilberg, *Perpetrators*, pp. 105–17.

3. Levy-Hass, "Interview," pp. 80–1. Levy-Hass was born in Sarajevo. In 1945 she returned to Yugoslavia and in 1948 emigrated to Israel, where she remained active as a Communist until 1968 and thereafter as a left-wing feminist.

4. Thompson and Thompson (eds.), *There Is*.

5. In August 1943 the Communist resistance in Vilna was reestablished through a City Underground Committee, to which Madeysker became the FPO representative. When the Vilna ghetto was liquidated in September 1943, she was living in the city and coordinated the FPO escapes to join the the partisans in the forests. She remained in the city Communist leadership until the eve of Liberation in July 1944, when she was captured by the Gestapo and died in hospital after a failed suicide attempt. See Arad, *Ghetto*, pp. 190, 409–10, 433, 456–7.

CHAPTER 15

1. See ch. 1 of Lukács, *Lenin*, pp. 9–13.

2. See Rabinbach, *Crisis*, esp. pp. 26–30.

3. See Lewis, *Fascism;* Jeffery, "Beyond."

4. For Hilferding, see Breitman, *German Socialism,* pp. 114–30; Smaldone, *Rudolf Hilferding.* For the SPD's strategizing more generally, see Heimann and Meyer (eds.), *Reformsozialismus;* Luthardt (ed.), *Sozialdemokratische Arbeiterbewegung.*

5. Naphtali et al., *Wirtschaftsdemokratie.* See Abraham, "Labor's Way," p. 8. See more generally Harsch, *German Social,* pp. 32–7; Winkler, *Schein,* pp. 606–13.

6. Esping-Anderson, *Social Class,* p. 36.

7. The WTB Plan was named after its three main promoters, Wladimir Woytinsky (head of the unions' statistics section, Fritz Tarnow, and Fritz Baade. See Schneider, *Brief History,* pp. 194–6; Moses, *Trade Unionism,* 2:385–96; James, *German Slump,* pp. 223–45, and "SPD"; Winkler, *Weg,* pp. 494–506. The standard monograph is Schneider, *Arbeitsbeschaffungsprogramm.*

8. See especially Harsch, *German Social,* pp. 203–46; Winkler, *Weg,* pp. 646–80, 693–7, 746–54, 802–9, 858–9, 867–75.

9. For Hendrik de Man (1885–1953): Dodge, *Beyond Marxism;* Dodge (ed.), *Documentary Study;* White, *Lost Comrades,* pp. 117–39.

10. See Horn, *European Socialists,* pp. 74–95.

11. Hall, "Rise," p. 41.

12. For an excellent account of the Greek case, see Mavrogordatos, *Stillborn Republic.*

13. This was true in Hungary under Istvan Bethlen, whose regime (1921–31) amnestied socialists under a pact of December 1921; unions were relegalized providing they abstained from organizing the countryside or civil servants and public employees like railway and postal workers. Similar corporative accommodations occurred in Spain under Primo de Rivera (1923–31), in Poland under Pilsudski after 1926, and in the Baltic states. For the Spanish case, see Ben-Ami, *Fascism,* pp. 282–318, 372–7; Winston, *Workers,* pp. 171–292.

14. Luebbert, *Liberalism,* p. 265. See also Eley, "What Produces."

15. Maier, *Recasting,* p. 580.

16. Ibid., pp. 580, 594.

17. Hall, "Rise," p. 43; Ramsden, *Age,* p. 265.

18. For the British corporatism, see Middlemas, *Politics;* Fox, *History,* pp. 280–372; Hall and Schwarz, "State"; Schwarz, "Corporate Economy"; Schwarz and Durham, "Safe."

19. Hall, "Rise," p. 8.

20. For this general argument, see Hall, "Rise"; Cronin and Weiler, "Working-Class Interests"; Cronin, "Coping"; Price, *Labour,* pp. 135–207; Wrigley, *Lloyd George;* Howell, *Lost Left,* pp. 229–80. See also Ryan, "Poplarism"; Gillespie, "Poplarism"; Branson, *Poplarism;* Marriott, *Culture,* pp. 69–183.

21. At the same time, the coercive resources of the British state remained extremely important. See Ewing and Gearty, *Struggle,* pp. 94–274.

22. Luebbert, *Liberalism,* p. 193.

23. The phrase "extra-systemic solution" is taken from the title of the penultimate section of the final chapter of Abraham, *Collapse.* See also Kershaw, *Weimar.*

24. Luebbert, *Liberalism,* p. 272.

CHAPTER 16

1. Stalin, *Leninism*, p. 156, cited by McLellan, *Marxism*, p. 122. Stalin's first reference to socialism in one country was in a newspaper article of 20 December 1924, reprinted as the introduction to a collection of his speeches and writings in January 1925.

2. Stalin, July 1924, quoted by Carr, *Socialism*, 3:12.

3. See Jacobson, *When*, esp. pp. 81–151.

4. Study of the Comintern has been transformed since the opening of the Soviet archives, starting in the late 1980s. See McDermott and Agnew, *Comintern*; Rees and Thorpe (eds.), *International Communism*; Saarelo and Rentola (eds.), *Communism*; Narinsky and Rojahn (eds.), *Center*; McDermott, "Rethinking." The old standard works include: McKenzie, *Comintern*; Gruber (ed.), *Soviet Russia*; Jackson, *Comintern*; Drachkovitch and Lazitch (eds.), *Comintern*.

5. During a period of radicalization in the summer and early fall of 1923, the KPD began preparing for armed insurrection. In October, this was called off, but in Hamburg the action went ahead anyway, with disastrous results. The "rightist" leader Brandler was made the scapegoat for this fiasco, although the uprising had been a "left" brainchild conceived against his advice with the help of Zinoviev through the Comintern. The best account is still Angress, *Stillborn Revolution*, especially pp. 426–74. More generally, see Weber, *Wandlung*; Fowkes, *Communism*, pp. 74–144; Weber (ed.), *Unabhängige Kommunisten*; Deutscher, "Record."

6. Examples included: Ernst Thälmann in the KPD (from 1925 till his arrest in 1933 and murder by the Nazis in 1944); Maurice Thorez in the PCF (1930–64); Harry Pollitt in the CPGB (1928–56); Klement Gottwald in the KSC (1929–53); and Palmiro Togliatti in the PCI (1928–64).

7. Carr, *Foundations*, 3/2:392; Morton and Macintyre, *T. A. Jackson*, p. 22. *Inprecorr* was the abbreviation for *International Press Correspondence*, which in its various language editions was the Comintern's official organ. Jackson's sarcasm targeted the creeping jargon and formulaic polemicizing of official Comintern language.

8. This account is based on the following: Davidson, *Theory*, pp. 206–13; Andreucci and Sylvers, "Italian Communists," p. 29; Ignazio Silone, in Crossman (ed.), *God*, pp. 106–12; Urban, *Moscow*, pp. 52–79.

9. Hobsbawm, *Revolutionaries*, p. 50; Davidson, *Theory*, p. 209.

10. Humbert-Droz joined the Zimmerwald-Kienthal movement as a young Christian Socialist and pacifist, advocated Swiss Socialist adherence to the Third International, and joined the latter's Secretariat at Lenin's invitation. From 1928 he opposed Stalin, returned to Switzerland (1931), and reemerged to direct the Swiss CP after the Seventh Comintern Congress (1935), until expelled on Stalin's instructions (1942). In 1946–59 he played a new role in the Swiss Socialist Party. Münzenberg was a German Zimmerwaldist and Spartacist, devoted to the Third International through the front activities of the IAH (formed 1921), which he directed with consummate administrative and diplomatic skill. Winning an exceptional degree of independence from the Moscow-based Comintern apparatus, he was especially adept at enlisting sympathetic non-Communist intellectuals. He became a byword for the "fellow traveling" success of such "front" activities.

11. See Rupnik, "Roots, pp. 304–7, 309, and *Histoire;* Wheaton, *Radical Socialism;* McDermott, *Red Unions.*

12. Rupnik, "Roots," p. 319, note 30.

13. For general reflections, see Anderson, "Communist Party History."

14. Spriano, *Stalin,* pp. 79, 82, 86.

15. Macintyre, *Little Moscows,* p. 44. For German "little Moscows," see Tenfelde, *Proletarische Provinz;* Althaus et al., *Da ist;* and for KPD local government: Herlemann, *Kommunalpolitik;* Wünderich, *Arbeiterbewegung.* For other examples: Boswell, *Rural Communism;* Downs, "Municipal Communism"; Alapuro, "Artisans." For a general argument about the community settings of Communist political culture: Mallmann, "Milieu"; Rosenhaft, "Communists."

16. Macintyre, *Proletarian Science,* pp. 239, 238. See also Rée, *Proletarian Philosophers.*

17. See Howkins, "Class"; Bodek, *Proletarian Performance,* pp. 80–158; Samuel, McColl, and Cosgrove, *Theatres,* pp. 33–73, 77–146, 149–63, 207–55; Hogenkamp, *Deadly Parallels,* pp. 29–135; Lewis, *Politics,* pp. 55–118.

18. See also Bruley, "Women."

19. For the neighborhood context of German Communist politics, with its confrontational command of the streets, militarized stylistics, and aggressive masculinity, see especially the work of Eve Rosenhaft: *Beating,* "Working-Class Life," and "Organizing"; also Wickham, "Social Fascism"; McElligott, "Mobilizing" and "Street Politics"; Weitz, *Creating,* pp. 132–79.

20. Grossmann, *Reforming Sex.*

21. Work on the British party provides a classic illustration: Samuel, "Lost World," "Staying Power," and "Class Politics"; Croft (ed.), *Weapon;* Fishman, *British Communist Party;* Morgan, *Harry Pollitt;* Saville, "May Day 1937"; Andrews, Fishman, and Morgan (eds.), *Opening;* Kingsford, *Hunger Marchers;* Srebnik, *London Jews.*

22. Works on the CPGB capturing both dimensions of Communist culture, the "national-particular" and the "Moscow-internationalist," include Samuel, "Lost World" and "Staying Power"; and Macintyre, *Proletarian Science* and *Little Moscows.* For the apotheosis of Stalinist internationalism, see Callaghan, *Palme Dutt.* For a French illustration: McMeekin, "From Moscow."

23. For this general argument, see Anderson, *Considerations.*

24. See New Left Review (eds.), *Western Marxism;* Howard and Klare (eds.), *Unknown Dimension;* Löwy, *Georg Lukács,* pp. 145–213; Arato and Breines, *Young Lukács,* pp. 75–209; Lukács, *Political Writings;* Goode, *Karl Korsch.*

25. See Jay, *Dialectical Imagination;* Dubiel, *Theory;* Roberts, *Walter Benjamin.*

CHAPTER 17

1. An emergency provision for the event of an attempted coup, article 48 of the Weimar Constitution (1919) allowed presidential government by direct decree if parliamentary process collapsed. From March 1930 to January 1933, it became the main tool of the right-wing clique around President Paul von Hindenburg, whose voice was Chancellor Heinrich Brüning (1930–32). Ironically, therefore, it

became a device for undermining Weimar democracy rather then ensuring its survival.

2. Figures taken from Eichengreen and Hatton, "Interwar Unemployment," pp. 6–7. See Horn, *European Socialists*, p. 6.

3. For the SPD during illegality and exile, see Edinger, *German Exile Politics;* Barclay, "Rethinking"; Horn, "Social Origins"; Winkler, *Weg,* pp. 867–949. For the KPD: Peukert, *KPD;* Merson, *Communist Resistance;* Weitz, *Creating,* pp. 280–310; Herlemann, "Communist Resistance."

4. See above all Horn, *European Socialists*, pp. 53–73. For the Austrian uprising: Rabinbach, *Crisis,* pp. 181–215; Lewis, *Fascism,* pp. 122–201; Duczynska, *Workers.* For the Asturias: Shubert, *Road* and "Revolution." For the reaction of a young British socialist to events in Vienna, see Williams, *Hugh Gaitskell.*

5. Horn, *European Socialists,* p. 127.

6. See Jackson, *Popular Front,* pp. 17–51

7. Adereth, *French Communist Party,* p. 49.

8. On 22 April 1934, in a key step in the Comintern's internal change, Dimitrov became director of the ECCI's Central European Section.

9. On 18–19 February 1933, the LSI Executive meeting in Zurich offered the Comintern an agreement, but the smaller Bureau (9 persons as against the 35 delegates in Zurich) decided not to renew the offer (Paris, 27 March). An LSI Left coalesced in protest against this bureaucratic maneuver. See Horn, *European Socialists,* pp. 40–45.

10. Between September 1931 and July 1932, three left-wing groupings were expelled or seceded from their national parties—the ILP in Britain, the Socialist Workers Party in Germany, and the Independent Socialist Party in the Netherlands. See Buschak, *Londoner Büro,* pp. 1–60. The process inside the LSI is best followed through Horn, *European Socialists,* pp. 17–52.

11. See Santore, "Comintern's"; Haslam, "Comintern."

12. Horn, *European Socialists,* p. 33.

13. At the Thirteenth Plenum of the ECCI on 28 November 1933, only 16 CPs were "more or less legal," 7 were "semi-legal," and 38 "totally illegal"; the review of the world movement recorded a catalogue of losses and defeats. Carr, *Twilight,* 106.

14. Hobsbawm, "Fifty Years," p. 240.

15. Carr, *Twilight,* p. 407.

16. See Heineman, "People's Front"; Rickaby, "Artists' International"; Morgan, *Against Fascism,* pp. 254–77; Stanton, "French Intellectual"; Clark et al. (eds.), *Culture;* Gloversmith (ed.), *Class;* Lucas (ed.), *1930s;* Heineman, *"Left Review";* Thompson, *"Left Review";* Barker et al. (eds.), *1936;* Hogenkamp, *Deadly Parallels,* pp. 136–75; Buchsbaum, *Cinema Engagé;* Sandy Holguín, "Taming." For debates among Marxist intellectual exiles over aesthetics and politics, see Lunn, *Marxism;* Bloch et al., *Aesthetics.*

17. Carr, *Twilight,* p. 10. See also Bauer, "Fascism"; Beetham (ed.), *Marxists.*

18. Hobsbawm, "Fifty Years," p. 245.

19. On the eve of the so-called Left Turn in 1928, which marked the high point of insurrectionary thinking among Communists in the new post-1917 era, the Comintern published a substantial handbook using case studies from the 1920s to guide CPs in how to organize uprisings. Its author, "A. Neuberg"; was a collective pseudonym. See Neuberg, *Armed Insurrection.*

20. Piero Gobetti (1901–26) died in exile in Paris; Carlo Rosselli (1899–1937), likewise in French exile, was assassinated by fascist agents. See Gobetti, *Liberal Revolution;* Rosselli, *Liberal Socialism;* Pugliese, *Carlo Rosselli.*

21. In the new legislature, the Left claimed 376 deputies, the Right 220. The Radicals dropped from 159 to 106 seats, while the SFIO rose from 97 to 147 and the PCF from only 10 to 72. For the context, see Jackson, *Popular Front,* pp. 1–13, 52–81; Colton, *Léon Blum,* pp. 92–197; Graham, *Choice,* pp. 7–76; Levy, "French Popular."

22. The best general studies are Jackson, *Popular Front,* and Gruber, *Léon Blum.*

23. The movement encompassed 1,830,938 strikers in 12,142 separate actions, as against 1,316,559 for the previous highest *annual* total, in 1920. See Jackson, *Popular Front,* pp. 85–112; Chapman, *State Capitalism,* pp. 75–100; Seidman, *Workers.*

24. Alexander Werth, *The Destiny of France* (London, 1937), p. 305, cited by Jackson, *Popular Front,* p. 86.

25. Jackson, *Popular Front,* pp. 264–8; Rossiter, "Blum Government."

26. The Right bitterly dubbed him the "Minister for Idleness." See Jackson, *"Le Temps."*

27. Levy, "French Popular," p. 76.

28. See Rossiter, "Blum Government"; Jackson, *Popular Front,* pp. 159–88.

29. Jackson, *Popular Front,* pp. 271–87; Graham, *Choice,* pp. 77–223.

30. Levy, "French Popular," p. 70.

31. Even during the Popular Front, the Radicals under Vice-Premier Edouard Daladier publicly criticized the Socialists. The Radical-dominated governments after June 1937 allowed employers to disavow Matignon and claw back the concessions. By late November 1938, police were forcing defeated strikers at Renault to march from the factory, giving the fascist salute, to cries of "Long Live the Police." See Jackson, *Popular Front,* p. 112.

32. See Jackson, *Popular Front,* pp. 190–212. For the response in Britain, where the Labour Party (then in opposition) resisted the pressure of its own supporters for aid to Spain, strongly backed by the CPGB and other independent Left groups, see Buchanan, *Spanish,* and the debate between Buchanan, "Britain's Popular Front," and Fyrth, "Aid Spain."

33. Between the Republican-Socialist Pact of San Sebastián (17 August 1930), which ensured a transition from the monarchy and swept the elections of June 1931, and the Left's debacle in the elections of November 1933, polarization occurred around the Constitution of 9 December 1931 and the Azana government's reform program. The original front comprised "the PSOE, the various left republican parties and a great pot-pourri of center and right-wing republicans including the Radical Party under Alejandro Lerroux," but by late 1931 the center-right had deserted the government. In March 1933, José María Gil Robles unified the Catholic Right in the *Confederación Espanola de Derechas Autónomas* (CEDA), and after November 1933 government was conducted by a coalition of Radicals and CEDA under Lerroux's premiership. The PSOE left became radicalized and broke with republicans in general for the 1933 elections. In the resulting defeat, PSOE support dropped from 116 deputies to 58, and the left republicans from 139 to 40. The ratio of seats to popular vote showed the usual inequities: Socialists needed 1,627,472 votes for their 58 seats, while the Radicals

won twice as many seats (104) with only half the vote (806,340). See Preston, "Creation."

34. See Preston, *Coming;* Preston (ed.), *Revolution;* Blinkhorn (ed.), *Spain;* Preston, "Creation"; Graham, "Spanish Popular."

35. See Preston, "Struggle"; Graham, *Socialism;* Heywood, *Marxism* and "Development"; Radcliff, *From Mobilization.*

36. See especially Graham, "Spanish Popular."

37. After Soviet aid, the International Brigades were the main expression of international support for the Republic. Recruited abroad via the national CPs and processed via the Comintern in Paris, the first arrivals were mainly exiled German and Italian antifascists, plus recruits from France, Britain, and Poland. By 8 November 1936, they were being deployed in Madrid. The Eleventh International Brigade, commanded by the Soviet general Emilio Kléber, in conjunction with the PCE's Fifth Regiment (by reputation the best disciplined unit of the Republican sector), was vital to the defense of Madrid. Soviet aid also began arriving at this time, paid for by shipment of the Republic's gold reserves to Moscow on 25 October. See Carr, *Comintern.*

38. See Kelsey, "Anarchism"; Seidman, *Workers.*

39. Fraser, "Popular Experience," p. 226. More generally on the revolutionary atmospherics, see Horn, "Language."

40. "The FAI wanted to make the libertarian revolution, to attain a society without God or Bosses, without laws or police forces, using human material that wasn't prepared for it. . . . The FAI was acting like a political group within the CNT, taking its own decisions and trying to impose them on the CNT, talking of liberty and acting like dictators." Josep Robuste, a CNT bookkeeper, quoted by Fraser, *Blood,* p. 546. See also Seidman, *Workers.*

41. *The Partit Socialista Unificat de Catalunya* (PSUC) was formed from the Socialists and Communists on the outbreak of the war, affiliating with the Comintern and becoming effectively the Catalan CP; the Esquerra was the Catalan left Republican party formed in 1931.

42. José Sandoval, organizer of Enrique Líster's Eleventh Division, quoted by Fraser, "Popular Experience," p. 231.

43. In a letter to Largo Caballero, 21 December 1936, quoted by ibid., p. 233.

44. Timoteo Ruiz, quoted by ibid.; also Graham, "Spain 1936," pp. 77–9.

45. See Haslam, *Soviet Union;* Hochman, *Soviet Union.*

46. Spain was also the first time Soviet advisors directed a foreign CP with access to state power, first through the PCE's Comintern representative, Vittorio Codovilla (also known as "Louis," an Italian Argentinian), between 1932 and the fall of 1937, and then via Soviet military and political advisors as the Republic fell dependent on Soviet aid. Some influence was constructive, especially that of Togliatti, Comintern representative from July 1937 to April 1939. The worst was the secret police created in October 1936, which persecuted the POUM and other enemies of the PCE after the 1937 May Days. The role of police methods in securing Communist political leadership and Soviet control was an ugly foretaste of Eastern European events after 1947. Carr, *Comintern,* pp. 27–36, 60, 85, 89–101.

47. Preston, *Spanish Civil War,* p. 104, 58–61.

48. See esp. Richards, *Time*.

49. Quoted in Preston, *Spanish Civil War*, p. 86.

50. The 37-year-old Tom Howell Jones, a miner and trade unionist from Aberdare, killed at the front on 25 August 1938, typified the self-conscious working-class militant who went to Spain: a keen gardener and mountain-climber, an avid reader of political texts, fiction, and poetry (learning German to read Goethe, Hegel, and Marx in the original), embedded in the working-class associational world (member of the Aberdare Left Book Club Circle, the YMCA, the Workers Educational Association, an Esperanto class, and National Council of Labour Colleges classes on economic theory), and member of the CPGB, he was not so much a working-class autodidact as a continuing student in the labor movement's culture of improvement. See Francis, *Miners*, p. 27, and " 'Say Nothing' "; also (for the north east England), Watson and Corcoran, *Inspiring Example*. For the International Brigades, with details of casualties and individual brigades and commanders, see Richardson, *Comintern Army*; Brome, *International Brigades*.

51. "Spain, 1937," in Robin Skelton (ed.), *Poetry of the Thirties*, pp. 133–6.

CHAPTER 18

1. See Haslam, *Soviet Union*.

2. Giulio Ceretti, quoted by Adereth, *French Communist*, p. 92. Ceretti was an Italian Communist exiled in France in 1927–39, where he became a PCF Central Committee member and close friend of Thorez, returning to Italy after the war.

3. Morgan, *Against Fascism*, p. 87.

4. Kettle, "Goodbye," p. 20. See King and Matthews (eds.), *About Turn*; Attfield and Williams (eds.), *1939*; Morgan, *Harry Pollitt* and *Against Fascism*, pp. 85–104; Johnstone, "CPGB."

5. If the Comintern was now silent about fascism, the LSI was no better. At its very last meeting (Brussels, 3 April 1940), the Executive issued a May Day manifesto that mentioned neither Hitler nor Stalin. See Spriano, *Stalin*, p. 133: "Meanwhile, the ill-famed Second International was truly outstanding in its reticence. It was motionless, silent, internally divided. . . . Social Democratic internationalism was completely exhausted." For the French Socialists, see Graham, *Choice*, pp. 224–53.

6. Fischer, *Opposing Man*, p. 358.

7. Getty, *Origins*, p. 177. For more detail: Getty and Manning (eds.), *Stalinist Terror*; Fitzpatrick, *Everyday Stalinism*; Suny, "Stalin."

8. Getty, Rittersporn, and Zemskov, "Victims," pp. 1020–5.

9. Kettle, "Goodbye," p. 20.

10. Ibid. See Callaghan, *Palme Dutt*.

11. *L'Humanité* (southern ed.), 12 December 1940, quoted by Kedward, "Behind," p. 107. See further Kedward, *Resistance* and *In Search*.

12. See Adereth, *French Communist*, pp. 91–116; Simmonds, "French Communist"; Pike, "Between." For the British CP in this period: Morgan, *Against Fascism*, pp. 105–253, 254–77; Croucher, *Engineers*, pp. 73–139. For the Italian: Davidson, *Theory*, pp. 223–70.

13. Spriano, *Stalin*, p. 167.

14. Churchill, *Second World*, p. 227. Churchill also proposed 75–25 for Russia in Bulgaria and 50–50 in Hungary. By that time Poland was assumed to be in the USSR's sphere.

15. For Eastern Europe during 1943–47, see Rothschild, *Return*, pp. 25–123; McCauley (ed.), *Communist Power*.

16. Spriano, *Stalin*, p. 179.

17. Adereth, *French Communist*, pp. 116–30; Sweets, *Politics*; Farmer, "Communist Resistance"; Taylor, "Collective Action."

18. Corni, "Italy"; Ellwood, *Italy*; Delzell, *Mussolini's Enemies*; Urban, *Moscow*, pp. 148–79; Sassoon, *Strategy*, pp. 8–28; Gundle, *Between Hollywood*, pp. 11–41; Wilson, "Saints"; de Grazia, *How Fascism*, pp. 272–88; Slaughter, *Women*; Absalom, *Strange Alliance*. See also Spriano, *Antonio Gramsci*.

19. France, Italy, and Czechoslovakia had the strongest European Communist movements emerging from the Resistance struggles of the Second World War. Czechoslovakia had Europe's strongest CP in the 1920s next to the German and one of the leading Social Democratic parties before 1914.

20. Bloomfield, *Passive Revolution*, pp. 29–105; also Mastny, *Czechs*.

21. See Iazhborovskaia, "Gomulka Alternative"; Coutouvidis and Reynolds, *Poland*; Polonsky and Drukier (eds.), *The Beginnings*, pp. 1–139; Kersten, *Establishment*; Toranska, *Them*.

22. See Banac, *With Stalin*, pp. 3–44; Clissold, *Djilas*, pp. 43–176; Volkov, "Soviet Leadership"; Djilas, *Wartime*; Shoup, *Communism*; Palmer and King, *Yugoslav Communism*; Bokovoy, "Peasants."

23. Fowkes, "Wartime National," p. 173.

24. See Hondros, *Occupation* and "Greek Resistance"; Clogg, "Pearls"; Iatrides, *Revolt*; Stavrakis, *Moscow*, pp. 1–126; Mazower, *Inside*.

25. See, for example, Gjelsvik, *Norwegian Resistance*; Grimnes, "Beginnings"; Kirchoff, "Denmark"; Moland, "Norway"; Haestrup, *Secret Alliance*.

26. See Valeva, "CPSU"; Oren, *Road*; Thompson, *Beyond*.

27. For general discussions, see Anderson, "Communist Party"; Sassoon, "Rise." See also Thompson, *Beyond*.

28. While federalist discussions became quickly supplanted in 1945 by the return of national politics, they reflected strong desires for pan-European cooperation after the war. Significantly, the Geneva conference convened Resistance movements from both Eastern and Western Europe, those dominated by CPs and those not, including Italy, France, Germany, the Netherlands, Czechoslovakia, Yugoslavia, Poland, Norway, and Denmark. For the broader context, see Lipgens, *History* and *Documents*. See also Bess, *Realism*, pp. 94–100; Thompson and Thompson, *There Is*.

29. The ideal of moral renewal quickly turned into a politics of retribution, marked as much by violence, vindictiveness, and opportunism as by clearheaded political ethics. See Deak et al. (eds.), *Politics*; Dunnage (ed.), *After*; Henke and Woller (eds.), *Politische Säuberung*; Kedward and Wood (eds.), *Liberation*; Novick, *Resistance*.

30. For general overviews of the Resistance, see: Moore (ed.), *Resistance*; Haestrup, *Europe Ablaze*; Semelin, *Unarmed*; Robertson (ed.), *War*; Judt (ed.), *Resistance*; also McLoughlin, "Proletarian Cadres." Historians increasingly focus on the complexities and ambivalence of the Resistance experience, deconstructing the meanings of collaboration and opposition, particularly in their relationship to

postwar political cultures. They emphasize both the importance of local settings and the social divisiveness resulting from the collapse of the pre-Occupation national states, with continuing fallout after the Liberation. See especially Lagrou, *Legacy;* Moore (ed.), *Resistance;* Mazower (ed.), *After;* Kedward and Wood (eds.), *Liberation.*

31. Anderson, "Communist Party," p. 153.

32. The most useful source for comparative CP membership in 1945–46 is Lazitch, *Les partis communistes;* also Tannahill, *Communist Parties,* pp. 249–64.

33. See Mazower, *Dark Continent,* pp. 185–214, ch. 6: "Blueprints for a Golden Age"; Smith and Stirk (eds.), *Making;* Lipgens, *History* and *Documents;* Shennan, *Rethinking;* Gundle, *Between Hollywood,* pp. 11–41. For a widely diffused contemporary text: Carr, *Conditions;* and Haslam, *Vices,* pp. 81–118.

34. For the rise of Christian Democracy, see Burgess, "Political Catholicism"; Irving, *Christian Democratic;* Fogarty, *Christian Democracy;* Hanley (ed.), *Christian Democracy;* van Kersbergen, *Social Capitalism;* Buchanan and Conway (eds.), *Political Catholicism;* Vinen, *Bourgeois Politics,* pp. 137–72.

35. Shennan, *Rethinking,* pp. 188–201, 224–86; Lagrou, "Belgium," pp. 53–8; Henau, "Shaping."

36. The following account is based on Hamrin, *Between Bolshevism;* Sassoon, *Strategy,* pp. 8–97; Urban, *Moscow,* pp. 179–224; Harper, *America;* Filippelli, *American Labor.*

37. Sassoon, introduction to Togliatti, *On Gramsci,* p. 12. See also, in the same volume, Togliatti's speech to PCI cadres in Naples, 11 April 1944, "The Communist Policy of National Unity," pp. 40, 61.

38. Adereth, *French Communist,* p. 135.

39. Sassoon, *Strategy,* p. 37.

40. Quoted by Ginsborg, *History,* p. 43.

41. Macciocchi, *Letters,* p. 130.

42. The new open recruitment departed from the deep traditions of the cadre party. The statutes adopted at the PCI's Fifth Congress in December 1945 welcomed "all honest laborers of either sex who have reached the age of 18 years, regardless of race, religious faith, or philosophical convictions." See Urban, *Moscow,* p. 213.

43. Ginsborg, *History,* p. 46. *L'Unità* was the PCI daily newspaper. Its annual festivals were the occasions not only of rallying the faithful but also for broader popular celebrations.

44. A not entirely unrealistic goal was fusion with the Socialists: the CGIL had unified the separate Communist and Socialist unions, and both UDI and ANPI were joint foundations. However, the PSIUP split in January 1947, when Giuseppe Saragat led half its deputies into the right-wing Social Democratic Party, which became an understudy of the Christian Democrats (DC). Pietro Nenni and Lelio Basso kept the PSIUP firmly in the PCI's shadow but also preserved its independence. A sharper dynamic occurred in France. The PCF proposed a draft unity charter in June 1945, which the Socialists rejected. Four times between October 1945 and November 1946, the PCF offered the SFIO a joint government, and each time the Socialists refused, thereby blocking a more decisive reformism. This isolated the PCF as the strongest Left party and gave the SFIO ever-diminishing credibility.

45. Ginsborg, *History,* p. 46.

46. Urban, *Moscow*, p. 180.

47. See Behan, " 'Going Further.' "

48. See Shenann, *Rethinking*, pp. 287–96, 106–286; Graham, *French Socialists* and *Choice*, pp. 267–365; Vinen, *Bourgeois Politics*.

49. For the shaping of the Labour Party's program during the war, see Brooke, *Labour's War;* and Addison, *Road*. For the record of the Attlee governments of 1945–51: Morgan, *Labour;* Hennessy, *Never Again;* Fyrth (ed.), *High Noon;* Fyrth (ed.), *Promised Land?* Tiratsoo (ed.), *Attlee Years;* Brett et al., "Planned Trade."

50. Elliott, *Labourism*, p. 58. See also Millward and Singelton (eds.), *Political Economy*.

51. Hinton, "Self-Help," p. 102. See also Hinton's analysis of the CPGB's role during the war, "Coventry Communism," and Hinton, *Shop Floor;* also Croucher, *Engineers*, pp. 197–362. For unrest in the Royal Air Force at the slowness of demobilization in 1945–46, see Duncan, *Mutiny*.

52. For the quality of discussion inside the Labour Party around "active citizenship," see Brooke, *Labour's War* and "Problems"; Francis, *Ideas* and "Economics"; Beach, "Forging."

53. Hinton, "Self-Help," p. 101.

54. Ibid., p. 120.

55. Shennan, *Rethinking*, p. 292.

56. For this much-neglected subject, see Niethammer et al., *Arbeiterinitiative 1945;* Naimark, *Russians*, pp. 251–71.

57. Shennan, *Rethinking*, p. 37.

CHAPTER 19

1. For Allied policy in postwar Germany, see Eisenberg, *Drawing;* Deighton, *Impossible Peace;* Turner (ed.), *Reconstruction;* Naimark, *Russians;* Sandford, *From Hitler;* Nettl, *Eastern Zone;* Weitz, *Creating*, pp. 311–56; Naimark, "Soviets."

2. Lane, *Europe*, p. 77.

3. Ibid., pp. 60, 59.

4. The 16 were: Britain, France, Belgium, the Netherlands, Luxemburg, Italy, Ireland, Portugal, Denmark, Norway, Sweden, Iceland, Switzerland, Austria, Greece, and Turkey, plus West Germany via its Allied military governors. The Plan was announced by U.S. Secretary of State George Marshall on 5 June 1947.

5. Truman, *Memoirs*, 2:121, quoted by Spriano, *Stalin*, p. 283. The political situation was also stamped by the disastrous winter of 1946–47. See the report of the editor of *Foreign Affairs*, Hamilton Fish Armstrong, on a visit to Europe (spring 1947): "the present currency for winning esteem is mainly material [so that] the advantage lies with us if we choose to exercise it . . . we can use our calories and our machines to reveal the weakness of the Communist apparatus of production and distribution." Quoted by Ellwood, *Rebuilding Europe*, p. 76.

6. For general treatments of the Cold War, see Cronin, *World;* Hunter (ed.), *Re-Thinking;* Reynolds (ed.), *Origins;* Kennedy-Pipe, *Stalin's Cold War*.

7. See Hogan, *Marshall Plan;* Ellwood, *Rebuilding Europe;* Milward, *Reconstruction* and *European Rescue;* Young, *Britain* and *France;* Becker and Knipping

(eds.), *Power;* Ellwood (ed.), *Marshall Plan;* Stirk and Willis (eds.), *Shaping;* Maier, "Politics."

8. In May 1950 the French foreign minister, Robert Schuman, proposed the European Coal and Steel Community, which pooled French and West German coal and steel production. It became the model for the Treaty of Rome, signed by France, West Germany, Italy, Belgium, the Netherlands, and Luxemburg in March 1957, which created the European Economic Community (EEC). The North Atlantic Treaty Organization (NATO) was the Western military alliance signed by 10 European countries, Canada, and the United States in April 1949.

9. Hogan, *Marshall Plan,* p. 428.

10. See Kofas, *Intervention.*

11. Alcide de Gasperi, the DC premier, told the US ambassador on 27 May 1947 that "[w]hat he needed for the survival of the new single party government, if he undertook it, was some new and substantial evidence of economic aid which could be supplied to the support of the lira and the financial position of the government." With that support, De Gasperi felt able to confront the Left. He had in mind direct aid to Italy, but the Marshall Plan did the trick. See Harper, *America,* p. 133.

12. Filippelli, *American Labor,* p. 212.

13. Ibid., p. 213. For an analogous argument about the foundations of Spanish modernization in a "culture of repression" after the Civil War, including the systematically instrumentalized purging of "Marxists" from Spanish society, see Richards, *Time.*

14. See Weiler, *Ernest Bevin.*

15. Weiler, *British Labour,* p. 9. For the role of Marshall Aid in protecting the Attlee government against the effects of the "shortage economy," see Tomlinson, "Marshall Aid"; and Chick, *Industrial Policy.* For the Attlee government, see Morgan, *Labour;* Hennessy, *Never Again;* Fyrth (ed.), *High Noon;* Fyrth (ed.), *Promised Land;* Tiratsoo (ed.), *Attlee Years;* Brett et al., "Planned Trade."

16. See also Saville, *Politics.*

17. Weiler, *British Labour,* p. 124.

18. See Wyman, *DPs;* Proudfoot, *European Refugees;* Schechtman, *Postwar Population.*

19. Here I follow the analytical framework in Jones, "Days," pp. 71–3. More generally, see Naimark and Gibianskii (eds.), *Establishment;* McCauley (ed.), *Communist Power;* Rothschild, *Return,* pp. 125–46.

20. Stalin approved the idea on Gottwald's visit to Moscow in July 1946, after which Rakosi in Hungary, Dimitrov in Bulgaria, and Gomulka in Poland all used the rhetoric, contrasting it with the Soviet model. For the Polish road, in Gomulka's words, "the dictatorship of the working class, and still more of a single party, would be neither useful nor necessary." See Spriano, *Stalin,* p. 276.

21. In the Czechoslovak elections (26 May 1946), Communists won 38 percent of the vote, joined by the Social Democrats (13 percent), and National Socialists (18 percent). In the Hungarian elections (4 November 1945), the Communists won only 17 percent, in coalition with the Social Democrats (17.4 percent), the Smallholders (57 percent), and the National Peasants (6.9 percent).

22. The intensity of purges varied. After the Bulgarian Fatherland Front took power in September 1944, the new people's courts tried 11,667 "collaborators"

and "war criminals" under the first six months of a decree of 6 October, officially sentencing 2,138 to death. This was the severest early Eastern European purge. For Poland, see Micgiel, "Bandits;" and for Hungary, Karsai, "People's Courts." For the equivalent process in Western Europe: Déak et al. (eds.), *Politics;* Laurens, " 'La Femme.' "

23. See Zhelitski, "Postwar Hungary."

24. Swain, *Hungary,* p. 46.

25. Charlton, *Eagle,* p. 68. Szasz (born 1910) joined the Hungarian Communist Party (KMP) in 1932 and emigrated to Argentina in 1939, where he edited an antifascist weekly and ran the Free Hungarian Movement in South America, returning to Hungary in 1946 on a government press appointment.

26. See Lukes, "Czech Road," pp. 250-1, 246-8; Parish, "Marshall Plan," pp. 274-87; Bloomfield, *Passive Revolution,* pp. 181-8.

27. Spriano, *Stalin,* pp. 292-306.

28. For the Czech events, see Lukes, "Czech Road," pp. 252-9; Myant, *Socialism,* pp. 131-242; Bloomfield, *Passive Revolution,* pp. 177-240; Kaplan, *Short March.*

29. Disciplining the working class in the interests of productivity was another dimension of this process barely addressed by historians. But see Kenney, *Rebuilding Poland* and "Working-Class Community."

30. See especially Gibianskii, "Soviet-Yugoslav Split."

31. This deterioration of language was marked by the Second Cominform Resolution against Titoism (27 November 1949), after a report by the Romanian General Secretary Gheorghiu-Dej called "The Yugoslav Communist Party in the Power of Murderers and Spies." See Banac, *With Stalin,* pp. 123-32.

32. Wood, *Communism,* p. 222.

33. See Hodos, *Show Trials;* Swain and Swain, *Eastern Europe,* pp. 65-72.

34. Rothschild, *Return,* p. 137. Admiral Miklós Horthy presided over the Hungarian counterrevolution of the summer of 1919 and governed until 1944.

35. This account is based on Pelikán (ed.), *Czechoslovak Political,* esp. pp. 69-114.

36. Westoby, *Communism,* p. 71.

37. Loebl, *Stalinism,* p. 46. Of the Slansky codefendants, Artur London was imprisoned by the Nazis in Mauthausen, Karel Svab in Sachsenhausen, and Josef Frank in Buchenwald. See London, *Confession.*

38. Loebl, *Stalinism,* p. 23. See also Goldstücker, "Kafka Returns," pp. 60-75.

39. Rupnik, "Roots," p. 312.

40. The OEEC (formed April 1948) outlasted the Marshall Plan itself, eventually transmuting in 1960 into the Organization for Economic Cooperation and Development (OECD), when the United States and Canada were added to the original Western European members, followed by Japan in 1964. The Council of Europe was created in May 1949 by 10 states (Belgium, the Netherlands, Luxemburg, France, Britain, Ireland, Italy, Denmark, Norway, Sweden), joined by Greece and Turkey (1949), Iceland (1950), West Germany (1951), Austria (1956), Cyprus (1961), Switzerland (1963) and Malta (1965). It comprised a committee of ministers and a public consultative body, with permanent offices in Strasbourg. Though conceived more ambitiously for the promotion of European unity, its effectiveness was limited.

41. For the influential British version, see Marshall, *Citizenship;* Titmuss, *Essays*. In general: Sassoon, *One Hundred*, pp. 137–66.

42. See Wilson, *Women* and *Only Halfway;* Moeller, *Protecting* and "Reconstructing"; Heineman, "Complete Families"; Schissler, "Social Democratic" and "Normalization"; Carter, *How German*.

43. Moeller, *Protecting*, p. 214.

44. Ibid., p. 208. The SPD spokeswoman was Elisabeth Selbert.

45. For the multivalency of welfare statism, see Harris, "Enterprise"; Tomlinson, "Welfare"; McIntosh, "The Family"; Baldwin, *Politics;* Esping-Anderson, *Three Worlds;* de Swaan, *In Care*.

46. Sweden's Communists achieved 10.3 percent (1944), Denmark's 12.5 percent (1945), and Norway's 11.9 percent (1945) in postwar elections, roughly doubling their previous best performances. With the Cold War, these CPs became remarginalized until their revival as Left Socialist parties after the 1970s.

47. Guy Mollet (1905–75), the schoolteacher son of a weaver, was secretary-general of the SFIO in 1946–69 and led the party to its demise. He served in five governments (1946–58), becoming prime minister at one of the several low points of postwar French politics (1956–57).

48. These parties formed the "north-central European social democratic core" forming the Left's heartland before 1914, which reemerged as a distinct bloc in subsequent periods. For a detailed survey of social democracy in the 1950s, see Sassoon, *One Hundred*, pp. 189–273.

49. Keynesianism took its name from the ideas of John Maynard Keynes (1883–1946), which were diffused during the war in British governing circles and in Western European governments in exile. They implied a range of macroeconomic policy innovations aimed at producing both regularized economic growth and social stability on the basis of full employment, some of which (like those in Sweden) originated independently of Keynes himself. The convenience of the generic term outweighs the loss of the complexity needed for full-scale treatment of postwar policy-making. For the latter, see Harris, "State"; Thompson, "Economic Intervention"; Booth and Pack, *Employment*.

50. For corporatism, see Jessop, *State Theory*, pp. 107–43; Maier, "Fictitious Bonds" and "Preconditions." For deployment of the concept in the British case: Middlemas, *Politics*, esp. pp. 371–85; Jessop, "Transformation."

51. Crosland, *Future*, p. 517. Anthony Crosland (1919–77) was a leading Labour politician and disciple of Hugh Gaitskell (1907–63), the party's leader during 1955–63. *The Future of Socialism* (1956) made him a key influence on social democratic thinking: against Marxist and other theories of class conflict, it proposed Keynsianism, a strong welfare state, and redistributive taxation. See Sassoon, *Hundred Years*, pp. 244–9; Harris, "Labour's Political," pp. 33–6.

52. See Sassoon, *Hundred Years*, pp. 249–54; Klotzbach, *Weg*, pp. 356–494.

53. For Swedish social democracy, see in general: Esping-Andersen, *Politics*, pp. 71–113; Pontusson, *Limits*, pp. 37–96; Korpi, *Working Class;* Misgeld et al. (eds.), *Creating;* Tilton, *Political Theory;* Tingsten, *Swedish;* Therborn, " 'Pillarization' "; Esping-Andersen and Korpi, "Social Policy."

54. Tilton, "Role," p. 411.

55. Therborn, "Unique," p. 4.

56. See also Elder et al., *Consensual Democracies;* Logue, *Socialism*.

57. Middlemas, *Politics*, p. 275.

58. Ackelsberg, "Women," p. 8. The AMA had 50,000 members in 255 locals by July 1936.

59. Ackelsberg, *Free Women*, p. 1. See also Mangini, *Memories*; Nash, *Defying*; Cabezali et al., "Myth."

60. The three subministers, Cécile Brunschvig (welfare), Irène Joliot-Curie (science) and Suzanne Lacore (education), were intended merely as public adornment and received no support. See Gruber, "French Women," p. 287.

61. Reynolds, "Women," p. 199.

62. Catherine Rhein, "Jeunes femmes au travail dans le Paris de l'entre-deux-guerres" (Doctorat de 3e cycle, University of Paris-VII, 1977), cited by Reynolds, "Women," p. 199.

63. See Weitz, "Heroic Man," p. 340; Bard and Robert, "French Communist," pp. 339–44.

64. Precursor organizations, the Groups for the Defense of Women and for Aid to the Volunteers for Liberty had been launched in the Nazi-occupied north (November 1943), formally affiliated with CLN (July 1944), before merging with the UDI (September 1944). An earlier "UDI" had been formed among PCI and PSI exiles in the 1930s in France.

65. Ginsborg, *History*, p. 85.

66. Hellman, *Journeys*, p. 35.

67. Ginsborg, *History*, p. 196.

68. Segal, " 'Most Important," p. 19.

69. Grossmann, *Reforming Sex*, p. 209. The quoted phrase was the title of the proceedings of the 1957 meeting of the European International Planned Parenthood Federation in Berlin, edited by Harmsen. Before *Pro Familia* was adopted, "Conscious Mothering" was considered as a title. Hans Harmsen had been the only major sex reformer to throw his lot in with the Nazis after 1933, but despite his involvement with Nazi population policy, he built an illustrious West German career after 1945; he was eventually deposed as honorary president of *Pro Familia*.

70. Keyworth, "Invisible Struggles," pp. 137, 135.

71. Bruzzone, "Women," p. 282. An estimated 623 women were executed or died in the field, while 7,403 were arrested or deported to Germany.

72. These examples, based on oral histories, are taken from Slaughter, *Women*, pp. 65, 55–6, 80. Weitz, "Heroic Man," pp. 344–8, found much greater flexibility in PCI gender politics during the Resistance than in German and French Communism during the antifascist period.

73. Keyworth, "Invisible Struggle," p. 139.

74. These figures are taken from slightly varying dates in the 1980s.

75. Einhorn, "Socialist Emancipation," p. 292. The statistics in this paragraph are taken partly from here and partly from Einhorn, *Cinderella*, pp. 262–74. See also Ansorg and Hürtgen, "Myth"; Langenhan and Roß, "Socialist Glass"; Lampland, "Biographies."

76. The 1950 Law provided protection for working mothers, including five months' compulsory paid leave surrounding childbirth and further provisions for the child's first year. The Equal Pay Convention was issued by the International Labor Organization in 1954 and ratified by Italy much earlier than elsewhere in Europe. Over the longer term, it allowed the CGIL's stress on "class unionism" (collective bargaining linked to social policies and weighted to improvements for

the lower-paid) to work for the benefit of working women. Gender differentials in Italian wages became especially low, with women's wages amounting to 70 percent of men's on average by 1969, rising to 85 percent by 1981. The figure for Britain in 1980 was 53 percent. See Beccalli, "Modern Women's," p. 91.

77. Hobson, "Feminist Strategies," p. 403. The Social Democratic Women's Union boosted its membership from 7,302 to 26,882 during 1930–40. The National Association of Housemothers, on the conservative end of this coalition, grew from 10,000 to 23,550.

78. Ibid., p. 412.

79. See Liddington, *Road,* pp. 130–94; Eglin, "Women and Peace"; Bruley, "Women."

80. For a complex discussion of the ideological context, see especially the writings of Riley, "Free Mothers" and *War.*

81. See this statement by a French expert, André Morali-Daninos, quoted by Copley, *Sexual Moralities,* p. 218: "If homosexuality received even in spirit a glimmer of approval, if it were even partially to be allowed to leave the bounds of pathology, then one would soon see the end of the heterosexual pair and the end of the family, which are the base of western society in which we live."

82. See especially here Sinfield, *Literature,* pp. 60–85; and Warner (ed.), *Fear.*

83. Pauline Long, "Speaking Out on Age," *Spare Rib,* 82 (May 1979), quoted by Braybon and Summerfield, *Out,* p. 280.

CHAPTER 20

1. Quoted by Childs, "Changing Face," p. 22.

2. See Suny, *Soviet Experiment,* pp. 387–403.

3. See Fulbrook, *Anatomy,* pp. 177–87; Diedrich, *17. Juni;* also Port, "When Workers."

4. Vidali, *Diary,* p. 35. Anastas Mikoyan (1895–1978), a longstanding member of the Soviet leadership under Stalin, delivered an earlier address on 16 February attacking the errors of a "certain personality."

5. Ibid., p. 97. Paolo Robotti, who survived arrest and torture in 1937, was Togliatti's brother-in-law.

6. For the full text of the speech, see "Special Report by Nikita S. Khrushchev, First Secretary of the Communist Party of the Soviet Union. Delivered at the Closed Session of the 20th Congress of the Communist Party of the Soviet Union. (24–25 February 1956)," in Ali (ed.), *Stalinist Legacy,* pp. 221–72.

7. Swain and Swain, *Eastern Europe,* pp. 92–6; Zinner (ed.), *National Communism.*

8. Felkay, *Hungary,* p. 53.

9. Swain and Swain, *Eastern Europe,* pp. 84–96; Lomax, *Hungary 1956;* Lomax (ed.), *Eye-Witness;* Kopacsi, *In the Name.*

10. "Through the Smoke of Budapest" was the title of the editorial written by Edward Thompson for the third and final issue of the *Reasoner,* the internal discussion journal produced illicitly by Thompson and John Saville during the crisis of 1956, against the ruling of the CPGB Executive Committee. In protest against events in Hungary, Saville, Thompson, and a large number of others resigned from the CP immediately rather than continuing the fight for internal reform. They relaunched the journal as the *New Reasoner* in summer 1957, con-

verging with *Universities and Left Review,* launched by a younger generation the previous spring, to form the *New Left Review* in January 1960. See Kenny, "Communism" and *First,* pp. 10–53; Archer et al. (eds.), *Out.*

11. The West German KPD was finally banned after a long legal battle in 1956, as it happened; the Portuguese CP had been illegal since the 1930s. See Major, *Death.*

12. Adereth, *French Communist,* pp. 161–3; Urban, *Moscow,* pp. 227–60; Sassoon, *Strategy,* pp. 98–139.

13. A minority report was issued by three members of the Commission— Malcom MacEwan (*Daily Worker* journalist and Central Committee (CC) member 1941–43), Christopher Hill (historian), and Peter Cadogan (teacher)—while two other critics, Kevin Halpin (industrial worker) and Joe Cheek (teacher), had been successfully detached by the leadership. All three dissenters resigned from the party. See McEwan, "Day"; Thompson, *Good Old,* pp. 91–133.

14. The quotation is adapted from Childs, "Changing Face," p. 25.

15. On returning from the 1957 world conference (attended by 12 ruling and 52 nonruling CPs), the Italian delegate declared: "It is not a question of a return to either the Comintern or the Cominform. Such forms of organization . . . no longer comply with present situations and needs." See Leonhard, *Eurocommunism,* p. 89. The Soviet leadership tried using the orthodox-loyalist PCF to convene another world conference in 1963, primarily to elicit a public condemnation of China, but the PCI blocked this maneuver. The next world meeting only convened in 1969.

16. The CWC drew on the militancy and political experience of working-class activists from the old Social Democratic Party and the CP, especially in the prewar Metalworkers' Union, together with younger workers in their twenties. As usual, skilled workers (engineers, metalworkers, toolmakers, electricians) were especially prominent, with a tolerated contingent of student and intellectual observers. They were all men. See Lomax, "Workers' Councils," p. 94.

17. Milch, "Eurocommunism," pp. 230–1. The first part of the *Hungaricus* pamphlets was translated as *Hungaricus: On a Few Lessons of the Hungarian National-Democratic Revolution* (Brussels, 1959); the second is available only in Hungarian. They are described in Lomax, *Hungary 1956,* pp. 182–92. See also Nagy, *On Communism.*

18. The main cases of colonial violence before Suez included the Madagascar Rebellion of 1947, the Indonesian war of independence (1945–49), the division of Vietnam (1945–54), the Malayan counterinsurgency, beginning in 1947, the Mau-Mau Insurgency in Kenya in 1952, and the Algerian War, beginning in 1954.

19. The contrast can be overdrawn. The extraordinarily vicious Algerian War (1954–62) spanned 1956, while colonial violence ravaged the Congo and southern Africa in the 1960s and 1970s, not to speak of the Indo-China War. But mainly these wars were waged by settler societies on the ground or by the dominant policy of the United States. Britain and France gave up their forward role.

20. Hall, " 'First,' " p. 23.

21. For a detailed picture of the apathy and decrepitude characterizing Labour Party branch life in the mid-1950s, see Black, "Still."

22. Hall, " 'First,' " pp. 16–17, 13. For a taste of the polarized rhetorical violence of the first half of the 1950s, which so brutally narrowed the space Hall

wished to create, see the overwrought but challenging treatment of French intellectual polemics in Judt, *Past Imperfect,* pp. 101–319.

PART IV INTRODUCTION

1. The Social Democratic Party (SDP) broke from the Labour Party in January 1981 with 29 MPs. For the 1983 general elections it formed a coalition with the Liberal Party under the common name of the Alliance. Demonized by the press and the Labour right, Militant dominated some local Labour organizations during the early 1980s, notably in Liverpool.

2. See Panitch and Leys, *End,* pp. 201–2, 206–7; Tatchell, *Battle.* Livingstone's GLC administration (1981–86) set a new standard of imaginative local government politics, attracting enthusiastic New Left support and equally passionate right-wing hostility. The GLC was abolished by Margaret Thatcher's Conservative national government (elected 1979) in 1986. *London Labour Briefing* was the left-wing organ of the Labour group in the GLC. See Mackintosh and Wainwright (eds.), *Taste;* Carzel, *Citizen Ken.*

3. Hall, *Hard Road,* p. 263.

4. Smith, *New Right,* p. 67. By that time the Labour Leader was Neil Kinnock, replacing Foot after Labour's ignominious election defeat in 1983. Kinnock led Labour to its third successive defeat in the elections of 1987.

CHAPTER 21

1. Fidel Castro (1927–) came to power through a guerilla war that toppled the regime of Fulgencio Batista in January 1959. After a flexible start, he moved strongly in a socialist direction, aligned internationally with the USSR. Che Guevara (1928–67), Castro's immediate comrade and minister in the revolutionary government, had left Cuba in March 1965 to organize revolutionary guerillas elsewhere. He was captured in Bolivia on 8 October 1967 and killed next day.

2. Cuba became a model of revolutionary insurgency for Latin America, attracting younger Leftists in Europe. Guevara became a primary icon of 1968 student movements.

3. Launched in January 1966, the War Crimes Tribunal was snubbed by Britain and France, convening in Stockholm in May 1967. It comprised 3 officers and 23 members from Britain, Cuba, France, Italy, Japan, Mexico, Pakistan, the Philippines, Sweden, Turkey, the United States, West Germany, and Yugoslavia. After a week's hearings, it found the United States government guilty of war crimes against Vietnam.

4. Hobsbawm, *Age of Extremes,* p. 446.

5. The following narrative is drawn from these general accounts: Caute, *Year;* Fraser et al., *1968;* Daniels, *Year;* Katsiaficas, *Imagination;* Ali and Watkins, *1968.*

6. See Eisler, "March 1968."

7. See Maravall, *Dictatorship.*

8. Piero Bernocchi, an engineering student leader, in Fraser et al., *1968,* p. 182. For the Italian context: Lumley, *States,* pp. 63–76; Portelli, *Battle,* pp. 183–98; Kurz, "Italienische Studentenbewegung"; Tarrow, *Democracy,* pp. 143–67.

9. See Marwick, *Sixties*, pp. 632–42; Fraser et al., *1968*, pp. 272–84; Halloran et al., *Demonstrations;* Students and Staff, of Hornsey College of Art, *Hornsey Affair.*

10. Ali and Watkins, *1968*, p. 64.

11. A sociology student at Nanterre, Cohn-Bendit's red hair and public flamboyance earned him international notoriety and the nickname "Dany the Red." The son of German-Jewish refugees, he grew up on both sides of the Rhine, electing German nationality to avoid military service. For his activism at Nanterre, the French authorities set about deporting him. He became vilified by the Right and the PCF as a foreign agitator, thereby prompting the Left's counterslogan "We are all German Jews."

12. Fraser et al., *1968*, p. 189.

13. Violence between student Left and radical Right was continuous in Paris in early 1968, with physical exchanges at the General Assembly of the National Union of Students on 21 April. Ultraright leaflets of 2 May called for a confrontation with the Left in Nanterre. Ibid., p. 203.

14. Caute, *Year*, p. 88.

15. See Gilcher-Holtey, *"Phantasie"* and "May 1968"; Schnapp and Vidal-Naquet, *French Student;* Bourges (ed.), *Student Revolt;* Fišera (ed.) *Writing;* Touraine, *May Movement;* Fraser et al., *1968*, pp. 203–30.

16. The leaflet was produced by the general student organization in Clermont-Ferrand (5 May), indicating how rapidly events spread to the rest of France. See Schnapp and Vidal-Naquet, *French Student,* p. 157. The *Compagnies Républicaines de Sécurité* (CRS) were the Ministry of the Interior riot police formed after 1945. Various police were used against students, including the armed *gardes-mobiles* of the army, but CRS became the generic term, embellished into "CRS-SS."

17. Fraser et al., *1968*, p. 204, also for the preceding quotation.

18. The main ultraleft sects were rival Trotskyist groups, *Jeunesse Communiste Révolutionnaire* (JCR) and *Fédération des étudiants révolutionaires* (FER), plus the Maoist *Union des Jeunesses Communistes, marxistes-léninistes* (UJC-ml). The Communist student organization was the *Union des étudiants communistes* (UEC). The 22 March Movement was the new nonsectarian coalition emerging from the events in Nanterre.

19. Fraser et al., *1968*, p. 212.

20. See Fraser et al., *1968*, p. 211. Cohn-Bendit had proposed occupying the Latin Quarter as a solution to the directionless frustration building in the crowd. As the barricades appeared, last-minute negotiations were proceeding between Geismar and the vice-chancellor.

21. Ibid., p. 213.

22. French trade unionism divided three ways: the Communist *Confédération Générale des Travailleurs* (CGT), with 1.5 million members, based in engineering, mining, railways, docks, automobiles, and aircraft; the Catholic pro-Socialist *Confédération Francaise Démocratique du Travail* (CFDT), whose 750,000 members were based more in electrotechnical sectors; and the anti-Communist, socialist-aligned *Force Ouvrière* (FO), with six hundred thousand members. The FO and CFDT responded more positively to the student movement, pulling CGT along for the strike of 13 May. For PCF response to student protests: Johnson, *French Communist.*

23. Fraser et al., *1968*, p. 216. Nantes events had the familiar pattern. When the prefect refused demands, the CGT delegate whispered to the student union leader, "Now tell them to go home." He refused, and fighting ensued. By participating, rank-and-file workers exceeded their union leaders' decisions, a process dramatically radicalized via the factory occupation next day. The entire *modus operandi* of Communist trade unionism was being left behind.

24. At Billancourt (35,000 workers), Sorbonne students found the occupied factory gates locked by the CGT union, with flyers warning workers against talking to students.

25. The full version of one of these—"I take my desires for reality because I believe in the reality of my desires"—was painted across the big ampitheater entrance at the Sorbonne.

26. See Caute, *Year*, pp. 225–31. On occupying the Odéon on 15 May, students declared: "The only theater is guerilla theater. Revolutionary art takes place in the street." Jean-Louis Barrault, the director of the *Théâtre de France*, endorsed the student occupation. After police reclaimed the theater on 14 June, he was dismissed.

27. For examples, see ibid., p. 220.

28. Schnapp and Vidal-Naquet, *French Student*, p. 41.

29. The French *chienlit* means literally "he who shits in the bed," or more loosely, "dog-shit." One of the more famous Atelier Populaire posters responded (beneath a cartoon silhouette), "He's shit-in-the-bed himself" (*La Chienlit c'est lui*).

30. Quotations from Fraser et al., *1968*, p. 226–7, and Caute, *Year*, pp. 247–8.

31. In the worst Flins incident on 10 June, police drove student supporters into the Seine, where Gilles Tautin, an 18-year-old lycée student and UJC-ml militant, was drowned. Factory and town were under massive police occupation, with systematic attacks on strikers and supporters, including by-now-familiar "rat hunts" of students. For descriptions, see the Open Letter by a participant, Jean Terrel, ex-president of the National Students Union, and the report from *Mouvement du 22 mars* (8 June 1968), in Schnapp and Vidal-Nacquet, *French Student*, pp. 387–8.

32. Caute, *Year*, p. 252.

33. Nelly Finkielsztejn, in Fraser et al., *1968*, p. 218.

34. See Lily Métreaux (lycée student), in Fraser et al., *1968*, p. 209.

35. See Brown, *Socialism*; Khilnani, *Arguing Revolution*, pp. 140, 182–3.

36. André Liber (lycée student, UJC-ml militant, and future high school teacher), in Fraser et al., *1968* p. 86.

37. Jupp, "Discontents," p. 73.

38. Caute, "Cohn-Bendit," p. xxx.

39. Touraine, *May Movement*, pp. 58–9. "Today socialization—the spread of society's values and norms—is no longer confined to specialized milieux, to home and school; it is part of everyday life. It is spread by radio and television, by posters and newspapers, by the audio-visual signals which constantly stimulate and direct."

40. Nairn, "Why," p. 147.

41. Daniel Cohn-Bendit, in Vuliamy, "Dany Le," p. xxxi.

42. Caute, "Cohn-Bendit," p. xxx. See also Shields, *Lefebvre*, pp. 81–108.

43. For postwar patterns of consumption, see Foot, "Mass Cultures" and "Family"; Forgacs, "Cultural Consumption"; Wildt, *Am Beginn* and "Plurality"; Obelkevich, "Consumption."

44. Ginsborg, *History,* p. 248. For the PCI response to consumerism and popular culture, see above all Gundle, *Between Hollywood.*

45. For debates about "Americanization" and the corruptions of commercialized popular culture, see Ellwood, "Comparative Anti-Americanism"; Wagnleitner, *Coca-Colonization;* Strinati, "Taste"; Kuisel, *Seducing;* Lüdtke et al. (eds.), *Amerikanisierung;* Sywottek, "Americanization"; Maase, "Establishing"; Poiger, *Jazz* and "Rebels." See also Stella, " 'Rebels Without.' "

46. The quotations are from Fraser et al., *1968,* pp. 76–7. Public commentary on teenagers was profoundly condescending, hardening in reaction to student revolt. See Laurie, *Teenage Revolution;* Wilson, "Trouble," pp. 23–4. An emblematic text was Abrams, *Teenage Consumer.* In 1960, after the Labour Party lost its third successive election (1959), Abrams coauthored *Must Labour Lose?* with Richard Rose (Harmondsworth, 1960), proposing an electoral strategy of classlessness, based on modernizing social change. He went on to plan Labour's campaign for the 1964 elections.

47. Fraser et al., *1968,* p. 78; also Waite, "Sex 'n' Drugs."

48. Portelli, "Luigi's Socks," p. 241.

49. Ibid., pp. 243–4. See also Marwick, *Sixties,* pp. 624–32.

50. Edward Short, education secretary in the Labour government in 1968, cited by Hoch and Schoenbach, *LSE,* p. 210.

51. Fiorella Farinelli, in Passerini, *Autobiography,* p. 29.

52. University attendence skyrocketed to 615,000 students in France by 1969, 488,000 in Italy, 376,000 in West Germany. For a full Western European tabulation, see Sassoon, *Hundred Years,* pp. 393–7.

53. The best account of the Underground is Green, *Days,* plus Fountain, *Underground;* also Stansill and Mairowitz (eds.), *Bamn.*

54. See Taylor, *Against;* Minnion and Bolsover (eds.), *CND Story;* Taylor and Young (eds.), *Campaigns;* Liddington, *Road,* pp. 172–99; Taylor and Pritchard (eds.), *Protest Makers;* Hinton, *Protests,* pp. 153–81; also Wittner, "Transnational Movement," "Nuclear Threat," and *Resisting;* Carter, *Peace Movements,* pp. 40–84.

55. Taylor, *Against,* p. 134. In 1959–60, a DAC team collaborated with the president of newly independent Ghana, Kwame Nkrumah, to protest French tests.

56. Dissenters left the CPGB in protest against the Soviet invasion of Hungary in 1956 and launched a journal called the *New Reasoner* in summer 1957, edited by the historians Edward Thompson and John Saville; meanwhile, younger socialist intellectuals at Oxford University had also started *Universities and Left Review* in the spring, edited by Stuart Hall, Gabriel Pearson, Raphael Samuel, and Charles Taylor. The two merged in January 1960 to form *New Left Review.* For a time, the latter sponsored local New Left Clubs, numbering around 40 by 1962. See Kenny, *First;* Chun, *British,* pp. 1–64; Archer et al. (eds.), *Out.*

57. Stuart Hall, in Fraser et al., *1968,* p. 30.

58. Fraser et al., *1968,* p. 35.

59. The phrase is David Widgery's, in Green, *Days,* p. 41. See also Fountain, *Underground,* p. 18. Widgery (1947–93) passed through all the cultural political histories mentioned here. Expelled from grammar school at 16 for sex writing in

an unofficial school magazine, he was already into jazz, blues, Beat poetry, Brecht, and Mayakovski, passing through the Young Communists and Trotskyist-dominated Labour Party Young Socialists before visiting the United States and Cuba in 1966, joining the civil rights movement in the South and Students for a Democratic Society in Chicago. Back in London, he joined International Socialism (the future Socialist Workers Party), hung out at LSE, and wrote regularly for Oz. He also went to medical school and became a socialist GP.

60. Miles, in Green, *Days,* p. 72. Miles dropped his given name, Barry, in 1961 as an 18-year-old Cheltenham art student, becoming a central figure of the Underground, where he organized the Poetry Festival and cofounded *International Times.* He came to London in 1964 and by January 1965 was running the paperback department of Better Books. He experimented with small magazines, from *Bomb* (1959) and *Tree* (1960), to Love Books (1964–65) and *Long Hair* (1965), as well as the abortive *East Village Other* (1965). Like his friend, collaborator, and fellow Beat John Hopkins, he entered this world partly via CND. He met his wife, Sue Miles, at a CND party. "To a lot of us the great thing about CND was that it was the force that actually got us out of our small towns." See Green, *Days,* p. 25.

61. Robin Blackburn, in Fraser et al., *1968,* p. 169. For additional context, see Cooper (ed.), *Dialectics;* Frith and Horne, *Art into Pop;* Paget, *True Stories?* pp. 59–76; Laing, "Banging In"; Crisell, "Filth"; Itzin, *Stages;* Hewison, *Too Much;* Hall and Whannel, *Popular Arts.* There is much rich detail buried in Marwick, *Sixties,* an otherwise opinionated and militantly underinformed book.

62. The following account is based on Skilling, *Czechoslovakia's Interrupted;* Williams, *Prague Spring;* Remington (ed.), *Winter;* Golan, *Reform Rule;* Kramer, "Czechoslovak Crisis"; Mylnár, *Night Frost;* Smrkovský, "How."

63. Josef Smrkovský (1911–74) joined the KSC in 1932, became a leader of the anti-Nazi resistance, and organized the Prague Uprising in 1945. He was imprisoned during the Purges (1951–55), eventually rejoining the Central Committee in the 1960s. President of the National Assembly from 8 April 1968, he strongly advocated reforms while defending the KSC's leading role, providing a vital link to wider publics between February and May. He was part of the four-person team negotiating with Soviet leaders between March and August. Zdenek Mlynár (1930–) headed a team of scholars formed to review the political system of socialism in the fall of 1966, who vitally influenced the Prague Spring, especially via their critiques of the cult of personality and proposals on federalism. A Central Committee member since 1964, Mlynár joined the KSC Secretariat in the April 1968 changes, becoming a radical reformer within a realist *modus operandi.*

64. The KSC Presidium and the Soviet leadership were in constant negotiation between February and July, through the Soviet Ambassador Stepan Chervonenko, directly with Brezhnev, and in a series of high-level conferences, culminating in a meeting on the Ukraine border at Cierná nad Tisou on 29 July.

65. *Literární listy* in particular, with its weekly critiques of the government by non-Communist intellectuals Antonín Liehm, Jaroslav Sedivý, and Vaclav Klaus under the collective pseudonym Dalimil, was anathema to Brezhnev and the Soviet leaders. Inside the government, Cestmir Císar (as secretary for mass media, science, education, and culture), and Jirí Pelikán (head of television) vitally helped democratization along.

66. Williams, *Prague Spring*, p. 78.

67. Ibid., p. 100. Kosygin continued: "we have only one border, the border with the West. . . . It is the border of the Second World War, it is a border from which we shall never retreat, I tell you that openly."

68. Smrkovský, "How," pp. 100–103.

69. The KSC Presidium's conservatives were Vasil Bilak, Drahonir Kolder, Jan Piller, Frantisek Barbirek, Oldrich Svestka, and Emil Rigo, plus the secretaries Alois Indra, Jozef Lenárt, Antonin Kapek, and Stefan Sádovský. The breadth of this grouping reemphasized the importance of pressures from below in stiffening the reformers' willingness to press ahead. In looking for a more compliant KSC leadership, Brezhnev had earlier offered an alliance to Smrkovský, who refused, defending Dubcek and reform. See Smrkovský, "How," p. 403.

70. Skilling, *Czechoslovakia's Interrupted*, pp. 217–21.

71. Ibid., p. 613.

72. At Cierna on 29 July, a request for Soviet intervention had been handed secretly to Brezhnev by Kapek. Once invasion began, the antireformers were supposed to seize the Presidium in the name of a "Revolutionary Workers' and Peasants' Government" modeled on the normalizing regime in Hungary after November 1956. When the crunch came, however, the conspiracy collapsed: Bilak and Indra took refuge in the Soviet Embassy, Kapek withdrew to his dacha, Piller left Prague for Kladno, and Kolder locked himself in his office with a bottle. Bilak's group had failed to establish any control in Prague or Bratislava.

73. Gustav Husák (1913–91) joined the KSC in 1929 and survived the War to play a key role in Slovakia during 1945–49. He was arrested as a Slovak nationalist in 1951 and reemerged in 1960 via the partial rehabilitation typical under Novotny. He built a Slovakian following and offered Dubcek support in December 1967. He published "the first clarion call for democratization in 1968" in *Kultúrny zivot,* the Slovak writers' weekly on 12 January. He joined the new Cernik government in April, as the third most popular figure in Slovakia after Dubcek and Svoboda. Initially hostile to the Soviet invasion, he then accepted power and presided willingly over normalization. He remained head of the KSC (1969–87) and president of Czechoslovakia (1975–89). See Williams, *Prague Spring,* pp. 48–9.

74. Among 5,469 party cells directly identified as proreform, one-third of the 220,000 members were expelled. See Williams, *Prague Spring,* pp. 226–36.

75. Ibid., p. 241.

76. Waterman, "Hopeful Traveller," p. 180. Born 1936, the son of London Jewish Communists (mother from an East End shopkeeper family, father an illegal Polish immigrant), Waterman worked for the Prague-based International Union of Students (1955–58), and then again for the World Federation of Trade Unions Education Department (also in Prague, 1966–69), before breaking with the CPGB in 1970.

77. Proreform representations by the PCI, whose general secretary, Luigi Longo, was in Moscow during the invasion, and the PCE were ignored. The Soviet chief ideologist, Mikhail Suslov, brushed the Spanish party aside: "as a tiny party, you count for nothing." Middlemas, *Power,* p. 250. Only a handful of CPs endorsed the Soviet invasion, those in Luxembourg, Cyprus, Portugal, and West Germany. The Dutch, British, Swedish, Norwegian, Swiss, Spanish, and Italian parties were strongest in opposition.

78. Triska, "Enrocommunism," pp. 73–5.

79. This was the case most famously developed by Sartre, *Communists*, originally published in *Le Temps Modernes*, 81 (July 1952), 84–5 (October–November 1952), 101 (April 1954), and 89 (April 1953). See also Rossanda, "Revolutionary Intellectuals."

80. Rossanda, "Power," p. 5.

81. In Poland, greater cultural pluralism was signaled by the journal *Pro prostu*, edited by Kolakowski in 1955–57; liberalization ended abruptly in March 1968 with repression in the universities, leading to Kolakowski's dismissal and exile. In Yugoslavia, the circle associated with the journal *Praxis* (founded 1963–64) were harassed after the crackdown on student protests in summer 1968. The "Belgrade Eight" were suspended from university posts, and the journal closed down in 1975. In Czechoslovakia, conditions supporting critical Marxism from 1963–64 came to an end in August 1968. For Castoriadis and Lefort, see van der Linden, "*Socialisme.*" More generally: Anderson, *Considerations, Arguments*, and *In the Tracks*; Khilnani, *Arguing Revolution*, pp. 49–117.

82. See especially Cockburn and Blackburn (eds.), *Student Power*.

83. Major examples were the West German Red Army Fraction and Revolutionary Cells (formed in 1968 and 1973, respectively) and the Italian Red Brigades and Front Line (1969 and 1976). Otherwise, terrorism achieved popular success only in the Basque region of Spain through the Euskadita Askatasuna or Basque Nation and Liberty (ETA); and in Northern Ireland, where repression of the Catholic Civil Rights movement in 1968–69 revived the Irish Republican Army (IRA).

84. See Dutschke, *Mein langer Marsch*.

85. See Williams (ed.), *May Day Manifesto*; Chun, *British*, pp. 86–7; Kenny, *First*, pp. 158–62. The *Manifesto* (which made no reference to women) was also left behind by the new women's movement developing in 1969–71. See Swindells and Jardine, *What's Left?*

CHAPTER 22

1. Rowbotham, "Beginnings," p. 36.

2. A French woman militant, writing in *Le Torchon brûle* (The Burning Rag), 2 (1971), the first French feminist newspaper, cited by Duchen, *Feminism*, p. 7. The revelatory dynamic of these experiences with sexism (based on the United States, Britain, France, and Italy) is well described by Marwick, *Sixties*, pp. 679–700.

3. For an edited version of Helke Sanders's speech, see Altbach et al. (eds.), *German Feminism*, pp. 307–10. I have slightly adapted the translation.

4. Reprinted in Miermeister and Staadt (eds.), *Provokationen*, p. 223. The name *Weiberrat* roughly translated as "Broads' Committee."

5. See Duchen, *Women's Rights* and *Feminism*; Jensen, "Representations"; Duchen (ed.), *French Connections*; Moi (ed.), *French Feminist*; Marks and de Courtivron (eds.), *New French*.

6. See Bono and Kent (eds.), *Italian Feminist*; Beccalli, "Modern Women's." The Italian case was complicated by the existence of the PCI-aligned *Unione Donne Italiane* (Union of Italian Women, UDI), a mass organization with some

two hundred thousand members in 1963 and in non-Scandinavian Western Europe by far the largest of the older "equality" organizations.

7. For general accounts of the origins of Women's Liberation, see Fraser et al., *1968*, pp. 340–7; Sassoon, *Hundred Years*, pp. 427–40; Jensen, "Representations," pp. 73–91; Maleck-Levy and Maleck, "Women's Movement," pp. 374–85 (with some inaccuracies).

8. Ali, *Street Fighting*, pp. 232–4; Rowbotham, "Beginnings," p. 35.

9. Coote and Campbell, *Sweet Freedom*, p. 7.

10. Christianson, "Making Choices." The Defence of Literature and the Arts Society was formed in 1968 by John Calder, a British publisher of avant-garde literature. Calder organized the writers' conference at the Edinburgh Festival (August 1962) and was a key bridge from the international avant-garde to the London Underground. The "files issue" developed in 1969–70, when evidence of political surveillance was uncovered during student sit-ins at Warwick and other universities, provoking a national chain of direct actions. See Thompson (ed.), *Warwick*.

11. Juliet Mitchell was on the Board of *New Left Review* and the author of *Women: The Longest Revolution*, originally published in *NLR*, 40 (November–December 1966), and *Women's Estate*, two early texts of the new British feminism. The former title was a play on a key work of the British New Left, "a small tribute to a heritage." See Williams, *Long Revolution*, and Mitchell's comment in Wandor (ed.), *Once*, p. 111.

12. See Belsize Lane Women's Group, "Nine Years," p. 566; Audrey Battersby, in Wandor (ed.), *Once*, pp. 115, 114.

13. Wandor (ed.), *Once*, p. 90; the earlier unattributed quotations are by Catherine Hall and Janet Hadley (pp. 174, 77). A few older women attended, including Raya Levin (born 1915 in Russia), a Communist lawyer active in CND, who came to Britain in 1936 after spells in Switzerland, Austria, Palestine, Heidelberg, and Paris. Typical biographies included some encounter with existing Left traditions, often through the arts, and radicalization via the student movement. Val Charlton (born 1942) came to graduate school in London from rural Yorkshire in 1965 and met a man from a CP family; she was arrested at one of the 1968 Vietnam demonstrations and joined the CP. Catherine Hall (born 1945) was a graduate student involved in the student movement in Birmingham, formng a women's group there in 1969. Working as a bank clerk and taking "A" levels at a college near the LSE, Janet Hadley (born 1950) was a student activist with connections to radical black politics. Sally Alexander (born 1943) had trained at the Royal Academy of Dramatic Art and was part of the left-wing arts network helping launch *Black Dwarf* in 1968; she went to Ruskin College in 1969 (as one of two women among a hundred male trade unionists) and helped organize the 1970 Conference. Charlton, Hall, and Alexander were all mothers.

14. The Second Conference in Skegness in September 1971 was blighted so badly by factionalism—Maoists seized control of the agenda—that the National Coordinating Committee dissolved. The Tenth National Women's Liberation Conference in Birmingham in 1978 proved the last, collapsing in conflicts over sexuality. Sectarianism also killed the Women and Socialism Conferences, which met during 1972–79.

15. Belsize Lane Women's Group, "Nine Years Together," p. 562.

16. Ibid., p. 565. The sociology of the original Women's Liberation activists

in Paris was similar: born in the 1940s, from all social classes, highly educated, and previously politically active in alternative Left groups, the student movement, and protests against the Algerian War. Three-quarters were from homes where the mother worked. On the other hand, they were slightly younger than the Belsize Laners, and very few had children. See Duchen, *Women's Rights,* p. 207.

17. Sheila Rowbotham, in Wandor (ed.), *Once,* p. 36.

18. Similar clusters of events formed "the identity-creating lore of the movement" elsewhere. In France these included "feminist attacks on the *Arc de Triomphe,* the *Petite Roquette* prison at the time of Alain Geismar's trial, and the spectacular offensive organized against *Elle* magazine's *Etats Généraux,* all in the fall of 1970." See Jensen, "Representations," p. 78.

19. The Ford women were awarded less than parity and continued to be classified as unskilled. Seventeen years later in winter 1984, they struck again for "equal pay for work of equal value" with male workers in the semiskilled grade, winning their demand on 25 April 1985.

20. O'Sullivan, "Passionate Beginnings," p. 55. Sue O'Sullivan (born in 1941 in the United States) came to Britain in 1961, danced, joined CND, met the president of the LSE Socialist Society, returned to New York during 1965–67, and moved in revolutionary Left circles on both sides of the Atlantic; in 1968 she had a baby, and she helped found the Tufnell Park group in 1969.

21. Ibid., p. 56, quoting the protesters' retrospective pamphlet, *Why Miss World?* See also Coote and Campbell, *Sweet Freedom,* p. 15.

22. The giant shoe was sculpted from papier-mâché by Val Charlton (see note 13). See Rowbotham, *Century,* p. 399.

23. Rowbotham, "Making Tracks," p. 80. Among the best local accounts are Segal, "Local Experience," on Islington; Rowbotham, "Women," on Islington-Hackney; and Belsize Lane Women's Group, "Nine Years."

24. Duchen, *Feminism,* p. 120.

25. Ibid., p. 9.

26. Rowbothan, *Century,* p. 408. See also Itzin, *Stages;* Wandor, *Carry On* and *Look Back.*

27. Lumley, *States,* p. 326.

28. Hazel Galbraith, describing the Peckham Rye group, one of the earliest London Women's Liberation groups. Quoted by Coote and Campbell, *Sweet Freedom,* p. 25.

29. The London Women's Liberation Workshop was a federation of small groups, which sent delegates to the all-city meetings.

30. Rowbotham, *Century,* p. 431.

31. Ibid., pp. 426, 429.

32. Coote and Campbell, *Sweet Freedom,* p. 250.

33. Ibid, p. 224.

34. Ibid.

35. The Brussels Tribunal was modeled on the Bertrand Russell Peace Foundation's War Crimes Tribunal to counter the 1975 United Nations Conference on the Decade for Women in Mexico City. It opposed Women's Liberation to the official party and government delegations composing the latter. In her keynote address, Simone de Beauvoir attacked the goals of integrating "Woman into a male society" and hailed the start of "a radical decolonization of women." Over two thousand women from 40 nations discussed "topics ranging from compul-

sory motherhood to compulsory heterosexuality, from clitoridectomies and child abuse to incest and rape." The Tribunal used the "speak-out" in dramatizing issues of sexual violence. See Anderson and Zinsser, *History,* 2:422.

36. Markovits and Gorski, *German Left,* p. 92. On the other hand, by demanding censorship and the implied strengthening of police powers, antipornography campaigning complicated alliances with the broader Left.

37. See especially Maria Rosa Dalla Costa's 1972 pamphlet *The Power of Women and the Subversion of the Community* (1972).

38. Kaplan, *Contemporary Western,* p. 156.

39. See in general Lovenduski and Outshoorn (eds.), *New Politics.*

40. The same tactic was repeated later in Spain in 1979, when 1,200 women published a statement "I too have had an abortion" in solidarity with nine women on trial in Bilbao. For the Bobigny case, see Marwick, *Sixties,* pp. 702–12.

41. Lumley, *States,* pp. 321–5; Caldwell, "Church" and "Abortion"; Tarrow, *Democracy,* pp. 326–30.

42. Boston Women's Health Book Collective, *Our Bodies, Ourselves* (New York, 1970).

43. Lumley, *States,* p. 323.

44. See the analyses in Science and Technology Subgroup, "In the Wake."

45. For the US women's movement, see Evans, *Personal Politics;* Echols, *Daring;* Rosen, *World.*

46. See Bennett and Nicholls, "We Are." Barreno, Horta, and da Costa, *New Portuguese Letters* (London, 1975; original Lisbon, 1973), was contemporary Portuguese feminism's founding document, itself unimaginable without the preceding five years' experience in the rest of Western Europe.

47. For the Netherlands, see de Vries, "Feminism."

48. See Morken and Selle, "Alternative Movement," p. 180.

49. See van der Ros, "State"; Karvonen and Selle, *Women;* Skjeie, "Uneven Advance."

50. See also Tarrow, *Democracy,* pp. 327–8, and Beccalli, "Modern Women's," p. 164, for a microcosm of such conflicts in Italy, involving a violent clash between male militants of *Lotta Continua* and the first national abortion demonstration in December 1975.

51. Hellman, *Journeys,* p. 216; also Beccalli, "Modern Women's," pp. 164–5.

52. Through Togliatti's and the PCI's alliance strategies, the UDI had acquired a prestigious presence on the Italian national stage, with a network of 1,253 local circles and 84 provincial offices, plus fiscal security and rent-controlled offices in Rome.

53. Hellman, *Journeys,* p. 198.

54. See Caldwell, "Courses"; Lumley, *States,* pp. 325–9; also Beccalli, "Modern Women's," pp. 177–82.

55. Wainwright, *Labour,* p. 179.

56. During 1976–78, the PCF was pushing strongly for alliance with Mitterrand's Socialist Party in the Union of the Left, with the next French elections in mind, but during 1978 the strategy fell apart. See Hellman, *Journeys,* p. 47; Jensen, "French Communist"; Jensen and Ross, *View,* pp. 63–70, 84–9, 199–205, 243–53.

57. Jenson, "Representations," p. 74; Coquillat, "Achievements"; Kaplan, *Contemporary Western*, pp. 171–3.

58. Threlfall, "Feminist Politics," p. 125 and "Social Policy"; Kaplan, *Contemporary Western*, pp. 200–210.

59. Dutch women increased their parliamentary presence from only 9.3 percent in 1975 to 27.3 percent in 1989, while in Austria percentages rose from 7.6 to 21.9 percent and in West Germany from 5.6 to 16 percent.

60. Kaplan, *Contemporary Western*, pp. 41–7, 58, 64, 75, 127, 160, 227, 256; Lovenduski, *Women;* Karvonen and Selle (eds.), *Women;* Skjeie, "Uneven Advance"; Haavio-Mannila (ed.), *Unfinished Democracy.*

61. Kaplan, *Contemporary Western*, pp. 88–9; Dominelli and Jonsdottir, "Feminist Political."

62. On 4 January 1969 militant Protestants and police auxiliaries violently attacked a civil rights march from Belfast to Derry organized by the student-based People's Democracy (PD). Modeling their strategy on the Selma–Montgomery civil rights march of 1965, PD hoped to precipitate British government intervention against the Protestant-dominated Northern Irish state. After further deterioration of the crisis, during which Protestants escalated attacks on Catholic areas of Belfast and Derry and the PD became supplanted by the IRA, British troops finally intervened in August 1969.

63. Mullan, "1968."

64. Rowbotham, "Mapping," p. 15. For analogous arumentation in the U.S. case, see Rosen, *World.*

65. Rowbotham, *Century*, p. 576.

CHAPTER 23

1. Here I've relied on Kitschelt, *Transformation*, pp. 42–3, based on the European Community Statistical Office *Yearbook of Labor Statistics: Retrospective Edition* (Geneva, 1990). See also Ambrosius and Hubbard, *Social*, p. 59. My discussion in this chapter is confined to capitalist Europe, although the argument in principle applies to the pre-1989 socialist countries too.

2. See Sassoon, *One Hundred*, p. 652.

3. See Coriat and Petit, "Deindustrialization"; Elger, "Flexibility"; Amin and Dietrich (eds.), *Towards;* Henry, "New Industrial."

4. See Jensen et al. (eds.), *Feminization;* Gubbels, "Female Labor"; Bakker, "Women's Employment"; Schmidt and Weitzel (eds.), *Sex Discrimination;* Hakim, "Explaining Trends" and "Myth." In 1982–86, 130,000 French women lost their full-time jobs, but 450,000 part-time positions were created. See Jensen, "Representations," p. 96.

5. The gross category of community, social, and personal services includes domestic services, public administration, social and health services, education, and entertainment. It excludes all financial and business services.

6. See Allen and Massey (eds.), *Economy;* Massey and Meegan, *Anatomy;* Hudson, *Wrecking* and "Rewriting History"; Cooke (ed.), *Localities;* Martin, "Deindustrialization"; Beynon et al., *Tale;* Foster and Woolfson, "Corporate Reconstruction"; Jessop, "Thatcherism."

7. For the nature of this restructuring, theorized as the post-Fordist transi-

tion, see Murray, "Fordism"; Lipietz, *Towards;* Harvey, *Condition;* Lash and Urry, *End* and *Economics;* Amin (ed.), *Post-Fordism;* Amin and Dietrich (eds.), *Towards;* Hirsch, "From"; Hirst and Zeitlin, "Flexible Specialization."

8. See Panitch, *Social Democracy;* Taylor, *Trade Union;* Hall, *Governing;* Krieger, *Reagan* and *British Politics;* Gamble, *Britain* and *Free Economy;* Gamble and Walkland, *British Party;* Fox, *History,* pp. 373–431; Currie, *Industrial Politics;* Crouch, *Politics.*

9. Head of the newly established Conservative Research Department after 1945, which redesigned the party's politics for the new Keynesian era, Butler was a dominant Conservative politician of the 1950s. His Labour Party counterpart was Hugh Gaitskell, leader from 1955 until his death in 1963. *The Economist* coined the term "Butskellism" in 1954. There were clear differences—though on the right of the Labour Party, Gaitskell epitomized the solid Keynesianism of the era, while Butler never accepted the forward role for planning this implied—but the sobriquet captured the contemporary political mood. For a portrait, see Cannadine, "R. A. Butler."

10. Morgan, *People's Peace,* pp. 298–305, 324–32, 375–81, 411–20; Taylor, *Trade Union,* pp. 134–44; Panitch, *Social Democracy,* pp. 63–165; Middlemas, *Politics,* pp. 430–63; Fox, *History,* pp. 387–414; Ludlam, "Norms," pp. 220–9; Regini, "Conditions."

11. In 1971, as part of an antiunion offensive, Edward Heath's conservative government passed the Industrial Relations Act, restricting the right to strike, only for punitive wage settlements in the public sector to provoke a chain of successful industrial actions by dockers, public service workers, postmen, electricians, shipbuilders, miners, and railwaymen. The government then reverted to an incomes policy, in the familiar cycle of failed negotiations and statutory restraint at the end of 1972, and 12 months later its policies were in shreds. After a further sequence of public sector strikes by gas workers, health workers, civil servants, and most famously the miners, who reduced the economy to a three-day week in the winter of 1973, Heath called an early election in February 1974 on the issue of "Who Runs Britain?" and lost.

12. Currie, *Industrial Politics,* p. 210.

13. Dating from 1973, the Alternative Economic Strategy became the Left's counterprogram, proposing a radicalized Keynesianism of planning, nationalization, public spending, strategic investment, and import regulation, linked to isolationist rejection of the Common Market (EEC) hostility to the IMF, and a partially acknowledged economic nationalism. The strongest intellectual statement can be found in Holland, *Socialist Challenge.*

14. The Labour movement was strongly opposed to the EEC, which the Heath government had joined in 1973. Although Labour was committed to renegotiating British membership, the Wilson-Callaghan leadership refused to observe this policy, and the Referendum massively endorsed the pro-EEC position, leading to the Left's marginalization in the government. Next year, the terms dictated by the IMF to the government, a deflationary package of public spending cuts, were a watershed in the abandonment of Keynesianism. After the crucial Cabinet decisions of December 1976, its advocates never recovered. For the British Left's debates over Europe, see Newman, *Socialism;* Nairn, *Left.*

15. Statement by Frank Cousins to the 1963 Trades Union Congress, in the same speech quoted earlier. See Currie, *Industrial Politics,* p. 210.

16. Quotations from speeches of union leaders at annual Labour Party Conferences: Clive Jenkins (Scientific, Technical, and Managerial Staffs, 1965); Danny McGarvey (Boilermakers, 1965); Frank Cousins (1966); and Danny McGarvey (1968). Ibid., p. 212.

17. Ibid., p. 211.

18. From the mid-1960s the "Broad Left" prevailed in British unions in varying coalitions mainly inspired by the CPGB. As Cold War conformities unfroze, the big unions moved left, including the TGWU, Engineers, Miners, Building Workers, Teachers, and the emergent bloc of white-collar unions and public employees. The Broad Left's organizing center was a Liaison Committee formed in 1967 to oppose first the incomes policy and then proposals for state regulation of strikes, including the 1971 Industrial Relations Act. Until the mid-1970s its leaders were Hugh Scanlon (Engineers president from 1967) and Jack Jones (TGWU general secretary, 1968–77). Its bête noire was the EETPU (Electricians and Plumbers) under the ruthlessly anti-Communist ex-Communists Les Cannon and Frank Chapple, which became notorious as a "rogue" union pursuing right-wing policies for militantly economistic aims.

19. Ludlam, "Norms," p. 237.

20. My figures are culled from the following sources. For unemployment: Fothergill and Vincent, State, pp. 50–1; Sassoon, One Hundred, p. 450; Therborn, Why Some, pp. 41, 49, 79. For union density and membership: Bain and Price, Profiles, p. 38; Berger and Broughton (eds.), Force, pp. 272, 107; Sassoon, One Hundred, p. 655; Wainwright, Labour, p. 242.

21. Wainwright, Labour, p. 227.

22. See ibid., pp. 206–51; Foster and Woolfson, "Corporate Reconstruction."

23. A majority of NALGO and NUPE, and from a quarter to a third of GMB, were women. The next largest unions organized tertiary workers in the private sector: Shop Workers (USDAW, 438,000 members), and Scientific, Technical, and Managerial Staffs (ASTMS, 432,000). They were followed by four industrial unions (Electricians and Plumbers, Building Workers, Miners, and Graphical Workers) and then four further unions in services: Health Employees, Teachers, Civil Servants, and Communications Workers. Figures (1981–82) are from Fothergill and Vincent, State, p. 53. The argument concerning dualism ("the existence of two *different* industrial relations systems in Britain") is made cogently by Lash and Urry, End, pp. 274–9.

24. Claims for the EETPU's greater democracy were specious. It was the most centralized British union, the least accountable to its rank and file, and the most egregiously indifferent to the sovereignty of the membership. For a succinct account of the union's history and structure, see Wainwright, Labour, pp. 213–9.

25. Ibid., p. 210.

26. "Eric Hammond [EETPU general secretary] treated the debate about the statutory minimum wage as a kind of trade-union virility test, implying that the advocates . . . were just covering up their own impotence." Ibid., p. 227.

27. For example, in 1964 the Labour Party returned to government committed to economic modernization, creating the new Department of Economic Affairs and announcing the National Plan in September 1965. Yet while the leading trade unionist of the day, Frank Cousins, TGWU general secretary, was appointed minister of technology, there was no involvement of the TUC in the machinery of planning, as against the "huge legion of Oxford and Cambridge econ-

omists and statisticians" on whom the Wilson government relied. By July 1966, the National Plan was abandoned and Cousins had resigned. See Morgan, *People's Peace,* p. 245.

28. Indeed, under actually existing circumstances (a workplace, a neighborhood, an event, an individual life), "social facts" and "sociopolitical understandings" were inextricably interlocked. The distinction between "social being" and "social consciousness" has typically invited a dichotomous choice (either one or the other is primary), but no such hard or hierarchical separation is intended here. For theoretical approaches to working-class formation and the associated debates, see Katznelson and Zolberg (eds.), *Working-Class Formation;* Somers, "Workers" and "Narrativity"; Berlanstein (ed.), *Rethinking;* Frader and Rose (ed.), *Gender;* Canning, "Gender" and "Feminist Theory"; Eley and Nield, "Farewell."

29. My discussion here follows the admirably succinct account in Anderson, Introduction.

30. See, for instance Therborn, "Two-Thirds"; Hutton, "Three Thirds."

31. See Jensen et al. (eds.), *Feminization;* del Boca, "Women"; Jensen, "Limits"; Ruggie, "Gender"; Erler, "German Paradox"; McDowell, "Women."

32. See Massey and Meegan, *Anatomy;* Hudson, *Wrecking* and "Rewriting History"; Cooke (ed.), *Localities.*

33. National divisions can be found earlier, like those of Polish and German workers in the pre-1914 Ruhr or in the massive coercion of foreign labor by Nazism in the Second World War. National integration can also occur, as in the loyalty to the British Labour Party not only of the Scottish and Welsh working class but also of the Irish in mainland Britain.

34. See Smith, "Politics"; Miles, *Migration;* Tabili, *"We Ask";* Paul, *Whitewashing Britain;* James and Harris (eds.), *Inside Babylon;* Solomos, *Race;* Rattansi and Westwood (eds.), *Racism;* Noiriel, *French Melting;* Wihtol de Wenden et al., "Post-1945 Migration"; Herbert, *History,* pp. 193–254; Bommes et al., "Structural Conditions."

35. For the examples cited, see Fink, "Forward March"; Rosenhaft, *Beating* and "Communists"; Bell, *Sesto San;* Balfour, *Dictatorship.* For additional British examples, see Macintyre, *Little Moscows;* Wyncoll, *Nottingham Labour;* Whiting, *View;* Savage, *Dynamics;* Marriott, *Culture.* For similar arguments, see Cronin, "Labor Insurgency"; Mallmann, "Milieu." For a case of working-class formation *without* the enabling context of municipal socialism and dissociated from labor movement institutions, see Waller, *Dukeries Transformed.*

36. Thompson, "Town," pp. 79–80.

37. Ibid.

38. Hobsbawm cites the example of the London County Council's massive rehousing project at semirural Becontree between the wars, when a population of some one hundred thousand provided the labor market for the newly established Ford plant at Dagenham. See Hobsbawm, "Labour," p. 48.

39. See Goodwin and Duncan, "Crisis."

40. Kitschelt, *Transformation,* pp. 40–66, presents the evidence for Western Europe. See also Sassoon, *One Hundred,* pp. 651–7.

41. Kitschelt, *Transformation,* p. 45.

42. The changing *size* of the working class alone can't explain the varying

strength of the Left. The fortunes of the Left depended on the complex interrelations between the movements of the economy and the social, cultural, and institutional histories of class formation on the one hand and the political strategies of left-wing parties on the other.

43. Hobsbawm, *Politics*, p. 64. The figures are adapted from pp. 23, 64, 203–5.

44. Crewe, "Disturbing Truth"; also Crewe, "Labour Party" and "Labor Force."

45. Sassoon, *One Hundred*, p. 654.

46. Touraine, *L'après socialisme*; Gorz, *Farewell*. For the cognate West German debate: Ebbighausen and Tiemann (eds.), *Ende*; and for the British: Hobsbawm et al., *Forward March*. For the general context: Gerry, "Small Enterprises"; Schneider, "In Search"; Merkel, "After."

47. The British debate began in the short-lived Labour discussion journal *New Socialist*, from 1981 until its independence was ended in the mid-1980s. It was then taken up by the CPGB in *Marxism Today* until its discontinuation in 1991. See Curran (ed.), *Future*; Hall and Jacques (eds.), *New Times*; Hobsbawm, *Politics*; Hall, *Hard Road*.

48. Hall and Jacques, introduction to *New Times*, p. 11.

49. Hobsbawm, *Age of Extremes*, p. 303.

CHAPTER 24

1. In conceptualizing the character of this post-Fordist transition, I've found the following most helpful: Lipietz, *Towards*; Lash and Urry, *End* and *Economics*; Harvey, *Condition*; Murray, "Fordism"; Amin, "Post-Fordism"; Elam, "Puzzling Out"; Hirst and Zeitlin, "Flexible Specialization"; Hirsch, "From the Fordist." For excellent guides to the new era opened in 1968–73, see Hobsbawm, *Age of Extremes*, pp. 403–32 ("The Crisis Decades"); and Mazower, *Dark Continent*, pp. 332–66 ("The Social Contract in Crisis").

2. For two versions of this argument: Lösche, "Is the SPD"; and Benton, "Decline."

3. See Amin and Dietrich (eds.), *Towards*; Gowan and Anderson (eds.), *Question*; Ross, "Confronting"; Marquand, "Reinventing."

4. The successor to Antonio de Oliveira Salazar, Portugal's ruler from 1932 to 1968, Caetano was toppled by fruitless colonial wars in Angola, Guinea-Bissau, and Mozambique. After the conservative general António Spínola's *Portugal and the Future* (April 1974) declared the wars unwinnable, younger officers proclaimed Portugal a democracy, legalized parties, and appointed a civilian government. The Greek colonels used the *enosis* (union) of Cyprus with the mainland to salvage their credibility but collapsed when Turkey invaded Cyprus in name of the Turkish minority. They invited the exiled conservative Kostantinos Karamanlis to introduce qualified democracy, whereupon he restored full political freedoms. In Spain, Franco's annointed successor, King Juan Carlos, abandoned limited liberalization and in July 1976 appointed the modernizing conservative Adolfo Suarez prime minister, who began a negotiated democratic transition.

5. Abse, "Italy," p. 108. The 953 names on P-2's list included 30 generals, 8 admirals, all the former and current heads of intelligence, sundry police chiefs,

the prefects of Brescia and Parma, leading businessmen, the editor of *Corriere della Sera,* and 43 parliamentary deputies. P-2's existence was exposed in 1981. See Bufacchi and Burgess, *Italy,* p. 23.

6. See Drake, *Revolutionary Mystique,* pp. 1–17.

7. For Berlinguer's three *Rinascita* articles, see Ginsborg, *History,* pp. 354–8; Sassoon, *One Hundred,* p. 574.

8. Amyot, *Italian Communist,* p. 203. Berlinguer explained the defensive purpose of this perspective in July 1970: "We cannot forget that there are forces which consciously aim at further worsening the present state of affairs, in order to use the economic difficulties and disorder as a pretext to attempt reactionary, adventurist, rightist political operations"; p. 200. See also Sassoon, *Strategy,* pp. 209–34; Amyott, *Italian Communist,* pp. 195–231; Hobsbawm and Napolitano, *Italian Road;* Hellman, *Italian Communism;* Middlemas, *Power,* pp. 147–87; Urban, *Moscow,* pp. 261–303; Lange, "Crisis."

9. The model was the 1958 constitutional crisis bringing de Gaulle to power in France. See Seton-Watson, "Terrorism," pp. 92–5.

10. Sassoon, *Hundred Years,* p. 577.

11. The term was coined on 26 June 1975 by the Croatian journalist Frane Barbieri in *Il Giornale nuovo,* an anti-Communist daily founded by prominent Italian journalists to combat the Left's growth. Berlinguer used it in a meeting with Georges Marchais in Paris on 3 January 1976. See Levi, "Eurocommunism," pp. 9, 31. For a typical statement of anti-Communist rejectionism, see Johnson, "Myth."

12. See Ranney and Sartori (eds.), *Eurocommunism;* Aspaturian et al. (eds.), *Eurocommunism;* Leonhard, *Eurocommunism;* Boggs and Plotke (eds.), *Politics;* Marzani, *Promise;* Tökes (ed.), *Eurocommunism;* Kindersley (ed.), *In Search.*

13. Sassoon, *Hundred Years,* p. 577.

14. Ginsborg, *History,* p. 379.

15. Italian terrorism—of both Right and Left—was the worst in Europe in the 1970s, exacerbated by the security forces' clear manipulations. There were 7,866 recorded acts of violence, including 362 killings (1969–80). In 1976–80, the Red Brigades were at their height, relying on the alienation of youth and many intellectuals and targeting progressives (magistrates, journalists, and active public figures, often PCI) rather than figures of the Right. See Sassoon, *Hundred Years,* p. 587; Ginsborg, *History,* pp. 379–87; Lumley, *States,* pp. 279–93; Silj, *Never Again;* Wagner-Pacifici, *Moro;* Drake, *Revolutionary Mystique* and "Why."

16. Sassoon, *Hundred Years,* p. 585.

17. Ginsborg, *History,* p. 379.

18. The *scale mobile* protected wages against inflation (then running at 20 percent) by flat-rate increases per percentage point.

19. Sassoon, *Hundred Years,* p. 590.

20. Ginsborg, *History,* p. 402.

21. Lieutenant-colonel Antonio Tejero Molina and two hundred Guardia Civil invaded Parliament as the new prime minister, Leopoldo Calvo-Sotelo, was being inducted on 23 February 1981. Backed by several generals and other Francoists, the coup lacked the support of King Juan Carlos, whose resolution helped rally the army behind Spain's democracy. Tejero surrendered next day. For Spain's democratic transition, see Preston, *Triumph;* Carr and Fusi, *Spain,*

pp. 206–58. For the PCE: Middlemas, *Power,* pp. 214–43; Mujal-León, *Communism;* Carrillo, *Dialogue.*

22. Camiller, "Spain," p. 246.

23. For the Stalinism of Carrillo's inner-party regime, see especially Semprun, *Communism.*

24. See Johnson, *Long March;* Ross and Jenson, "France"; Bell and Criddle, *French Socialist.*

25. See Middlemas, *Power,* pp. 111–46; Ross, *Workers,* pp. 215–335; Jensen and Ross, *View;* Adereth, *French Communist,* pp. 238–79, Brown, *Socialism;* Khilnani, *Arguing Revolution,* pp. 121–54, 179–86.

26. The European picture was more complicated. The PCP played a key role in the Portuguese revolution in 1975–76 and in the early 1980s stabilized its electorate at 15–18 percent. The Finnish CP joined coalition governments through its electoral front (1966–70, 1970–71, 1975–76, 1977–82), with 20–23 percent of the vote in seven elections (1945–66), and 16–19 percent in the next four (1970–79). In the small countries of Cyprus and Iceland, large CPs formed coalition governments, the Cypriot party recording 32.8 percent (1981) and the Icelandic party 17–23 percent in five elections (1971–83). The Finnish and Icelandic parties were among the earliest and strongest Eurocommunist CPs, dating from the mid-1960s and the Soviet invasion of Czechoslovakia. By contrast, the Portuguese and Cypriot parties were consistently Stalinist.

27. Ginsborg, *History,* pp. 387–401.

28. See Golden, *Labor Divided;* Salvati, "Muddling Through"; Regini, "Labour Unions."

29. Heywood, "Spanish Left," p. 67.

30. Daniels and Bull, "Voluntary Euthanasia," p. 4.

31. For the transnational ferment across Eurocommunist and left-socialist boundaries in the late 1970s, see Liebich (ed.), *Future;* Nicolic (ed.), *Socialism;* Curran (ed.), *Future; Il Manifesto* (ed.), *Power;* Medvedev, *Leninism.*

32. Sassoon, *Hundred Years,* pp. 307–19; Cioc, *Pax Atomica,* pp. 147–83.

33. See Markovits and Gorski, *German Left,* pp. 33–58; Cioc, *Pax Atomica,* pp. 116–50; Fichter, *SDS;* Schneider, *Demokratie;* Tent, *Free University,* pp. 277–444.

34. Fraser et al., *1968,* p. 87.

35. Ibid., p. 354.

36. Willy Brandt (1913–92) spent the Nazi years in Scandinavia and in the 1950s led the SPD in West Berlin. Mayor of West Berlin in 1957–66, he became vice-chancellor and foreign minister in the Grand Coalition (1966–69) and chancellor in the SPD-FDP coalition (1969–74). See Braunthal, *West German;* Paterson, "German Social Democratic," pp. 187–203.

37. Braunthal, *West German,* pp. 37–105; Markovits and Gorski, *German Left,* pp. 94–101.

38. See above all, Brand et al., *Aufbruch,* and Markovits and Gorski, *German Left.*

39. These protests—directed against the nuclear energy megaprojects at Wyhl in Baden-Württemberg (1973–75), Brokdorf on the Lower Elbe (1973–76), and Gorleben in Lower Saxony (1979–80)—vitally radicalized the Citizens' Initiatives. By 1977, the Union of Environmentalist Citizens' Initiatives (BBU, formed 1972) had 950 groups and over three hundred thousand members and the German As-

sociation for Environment and Nature Protection (1975) another one hundred thousand. The popular dynamism of these actions indicted the absence of democratic process—uncontrolled bureaucratic decision-making, interlocking of government and business, the parties' disregard for remarkably broad civic actions, and massive use of police. New coalitions formed, spreading from the local to the national. In Hanover, 100,000 people demonstrated against Gorleben (March 1979), and 150,000 rallied in Bonn (September). Some 5 million people were affiliated in 1,138 regional and 130 supraregional environmentalist groups by 1980. See Papadakis, *Green Movement*, pp. 64–70, 77–81; Markovits and Gorski, *German Left*, pp. 99–106; Hager, *Technological Democracy*.

40. Cooper, *Paradoxes*, p. 151.

41. After a meeting of West German, French, and British premiers with President Jimmy Carter in Guadeloupe (6 January 1979), NATO decided to deploy 108 Pershing II medium-range missiles in West Germany and 464 ground-launched cruise missiles in Britain and the Low Countries. A response to the Soviet deployment in Eastern Europe of SS-20s, this was meant to force the USSR into arms control. Instead it reescalated the Cold War in Europe, aided by the Soviet invasion of Afghanistan (December 1979) and the election of the crudely anti-Communist Ronald Reagan in the United States (November 1980). Much of the impetus behind NATO's decision came from Helmut Schmidt, the West German chancellor (1974–82). It galvanized a transnational peace movement, at its strongest in West Germany, the Netherlands, Italy, and Britain. Missiles were finally deployed in November 1983, whereupon the USSR left the arms talks, not returning until March 1985. See Herf, *War*, esp. pp. 45–66.

42. Cooper, *Paradoxes*, pp. 117–210; Markovits and Gorski, *German Left*, pp. 106–12; Papadakis, *Green Movement*, pp. 132–56; Herf, *War*, pp. 67–97.

43. Markovits and Gorski, *German Left*, pp. 80–7; Katsiaficas, *Subversion*, pp. 59–110; Papadakis, *Green Movement*, pp. 113–31; Lyons, *"Grassroots" Network*.

44. Kolinsky, *Parties*, pp. 194, 180.

45. Markovits and Gorski, *German Left*, p. 86. *Modell Deutschland* (Model Germany) became a familiar description in the 1970s for West Germany's success story of liberal democracy and economic growth.

46. Kolinsky, *Parties*, p. 170.

47. Markovits and Gorski, *German Left*, pp. 71–8; Braunthal, *Political Loyalty*.

48. Sassoon, *Hundred Years*, pp. 674–9; Markovits and Gorski, *German Left*, pp. 189–208; Kolinsky, *Parties*, pp. 292–338; Hülsberg, *German Greens*, pp. 77–139; Scharf, *German Greens*, pp. 64–124; Papadakis, *Green Movement*, pp. 157–86.

49. Markovits and Gorski, *German Left*, p. 189.

50. Ibid., pp. 107–12

51. Ibid., pp. 199, 203.

52. Preston, *Triumph;* Carr and Fusi, *Spain*, pp. 206–58.

53. See Sassoon, *Hundred Years*, pp. 617–27; Preston, "PCE"; Camiller, "Eclipse."

54. Gillespie, *Spanish Socialist*, pp. 299–419; also Share, *Dilemmas;* Camiller, "Spain," pp. 247–55.

55. Balfour, *Dictatorship*, p. 43.

56. Ibid., pp. 1–14; and esp. Richards, *Time*.

57. Balfour, *Dictatorship*, pp. 62–109.

58. Ibid., p. 69.

59. Ibid., p. 69.

60. Ibid., p. 83.

61. See Gillespie, *Spanish Socialist*, pp. 264–98.

62. For the social profile of the PSOE, including the sociology of its membership and electorate, see Gillespie, "Spanish Socialism," pp. 63–70; also Camiller, "Spain," p. 254.

63. By 1987, Spain had Europe's fastest growing economy but by far the highest unemployment. See Sassoon, *Hundred Years*, p. 627: "Gonzalez's success in 'modernizing' the Spanish economy was impressive, if by 'modernization' we mean economic restructuring, GNP growth, and a more flexible labor market. The context of the achievement, however, was massive unemployment, a large public sector deficit, growing corruption, and frequent devaluation of the peseta."

64. Camiller, "Spain," pp. 255–62.

CHAPTER 25

1. "[I] in the late 1970s it was estimated that the Soviet urban population spent about twenty billion roubles on private consumer, medical and legal services, plus about another seven billions in 'tips' to ensure service. This would at the time have been a sum comparable to the total of imports of the country." Hobsbawm, *Age of Extremes*, p. 385.

2. Ibid., p. 376.

3. For the character of Soviet-style political systems, see Holmes, *Politics;* Harding (ed.), *State*.

4. Swain and Swain, *Eastern Europe*, p. 159. For the period of détente between 1962–63 and the advent of the new Cold War in 1978–79, see Edmonds, *Soviet Foreign;* Gelman, *Brezhnev Politburo;* Dyson (ed.), *European Détente;* Banchoff, *German Problem*, pp. 61–96; Hanrieder, *Germany*, pp. 195–219; Newhouse, *Cold Dawn;* Haslam, *Soviet Union;* Prins (ed.), *Defended;* Holloway, *Soviet Union*.

5. For the following, see Kolankiewicz and Lewis, *Poland*, pp. 66–82; 101–8, 141–7, 159–62; Green, "Third Round"; Woodall (ed.), *Policy*.

6. Polish working-class militancy reflected a general European strike wave during 1968–74, matching the Italian and French unrest of 1968–69 and the British militancy of 1969–74. In scale and character, under analogous political circumstances of repression, it came closest to the Spanish militancy of 1966–76. Polish social transformation also resembled Spain's: population grew by 50 percent during 1950–80, with town-dwellers rising from 24 to 41 percent of the whole; agricultural work declined from 54 to 31 percent, while industry grew from 26 to 39, and services from 20 to 30 percent of general employment. During the 1960s, Poland entered the consumer economy: Television sets per thousand people increased from 10 to 230 during 1960–80, at a rate similar to that of Spain.

7. In the 1960s, 40 percent of the Polish CP's members were workers (930,000 in 1970), and another 450,000 workers were expelled during that decade, so the party's rank and file were inevitably drawn into the labor unrest,

often in prominent roles. Thus 7 of 38 members of the Szczecin strike committee in 1970 were past or present members, and the numbers in Gdansk were higher. See Green, "Third Round," p. 75.

8. For the Rise of Solidarity, see Lipski, *KOR;* MacDonald, "Polish Vortex"; Laba, *Roots;* Kubik, *Power;* Ost, *Solidarity.*

9. MacDonald, "Polish Vortex," p. 34. When police assaulted a Solidarity meeting in Bydgoszcz on 19 March, only intense efforts by Walesa and Jaruzelski averted a general strike. Neither national leadership were united enough to shape events, and both conceded the initiative to Brezhnev in a manner recalling the Czechoslovak crisis in 1968. Paralysis continued through the summer, until Kania was replaced by Jaruzelski in October. Security forces increasingly displaced the Party, which was deserted by half a million members during June-December 1981; p. 38.

10. Bogdan Borusewicz, Gdansk Solidarity adviser, quoted in ibid., p. 31.

11. "Solidarity's Program, 16 October 1981," in Stokes (ed.), *From Stalinism,* p. 212.

12. Since the late 1920s, democratic centralism had forbidden horizontal links among lower party organs in the Stalinized CPs, channelling all communications through the central committee, and the same rule banned links among national CPs not sanctioned by Moscow. This was designed to preempt alternative centers of opinion. See Kolankiewicz and Lewis, *Poland,* pp. 147, 150–1; Myant, *Poland,* pp. 140–75; Hahn, *Democracy;* Woodall (ed.), *Policy.*

13. See Michnik, "New Evolutionism"; and the critique by Walicki, "From Stalinism." In Michnik's argument, the system was incapable of reforming itself from within. Thus, society had to be organized independently beyond the party-state's control, forcing it into reactive concessions and an effective retreat. Cumulatively, society would pass beyond the system's control, and the latter would eventually collapse. See also Staniszkis, *Poland's Self-Limiting.*

14. On 2 May 1981, Kuron admitted: "This entire program (of self-limitation) has fallen to pieces, because a revolution has started in the party. . . . This revolution has reached the party and now it is proceeding inside the party. And I don't know yet what should be done in this situation." Interview with *Intercontinental Press,* 1 June 1981, quoted by MacDonald, "Polish Vortex," p. 37.

15. See Kolankiewicz and Lewis, *Poland,* pp. 148–52; Malcher, *Poland's Politicized;* Sanford, *Military Rule.*

16. See Bakuniak and Nowak, "Creation."

17. See Kennedy and Stukuls, "Narrative."

18. PCI Resolution on Poland, "The Struggle for Socialism—A New Start in a New Way," in Berlinguer, *After Poland,* p. 16.

19. See Suny, *Soviet Experiment,* pp. 449–506; White, *Gorbachev;* Lewin, *Gorbachev Phenomenon;* Bloomfield (ed.), *Soviet Revolution;* Dawisha, *Eastern Europe.*

20. Iurii Andropov (1914–84), the son of a railway worker, rose through the party in the wake of the Purges to become ambassador to Hungary after Stalin's death (1954–57). By 1961, he was elected to the Central Committee, becoming KGB head in 1967. Konstantin Chernenko (1911–85) was a Brezhnev loyalist and colorless bureaucrat, in the Central Committee since 1971 and the Politburo since 1978. Mikhail Gorbachev (born 1931) was raised on a collective farm and attended Moscow State University in law, joining the CPSU in 1952. He rose

through the party, joining the Central Committee in 1971. Andropov brought him to Moscow in 1978 as secretary for agriculture. He joined the Politburo in 1980.

21. A key architect of the Prague Spring, Zdenek Mlynár, was Gorbachev's close friend at Moscow University in 1952–55.

22. The Twenty-eighth Party Congress in 1990 entirely rebuilt the leadership: 28 of 35 Politburo and Secretariat members were new, and only two had party cards under Stalin, including Gorbachev himself. During 1986–89, all 14 republican first secretaries and two-thirds of secretaries at all other levels were replaced. Only 22 of the 115-strong Council of Ministers lasted during 1984–89; only 10 survived into the new Council of June 1989; none were in the Cabinet of December 1990. Two-thirds of industrial managers and farm directors were replaced. By 1991, the Politburo's average age was 55; almost half had higher degrees. Only 3 of 15 republican heads had held office before 1990.

23. Suny, *Soviet Experiment*, p. 452.

24. Ibid., p. 454.

25. The SDI, or "Star Wars," announced March 1983, envisaged a protective shield in space to intercept Soviet missiles, using the most advanced (and expensive) technologies. Touted as a defensive panacea, it would also have created immunity for a US first strike and thereby negated the tradition of deterrence, or "mutually assured destruction."

26. See White, *Gorbachev*, pp. 194–212; Haslam, *Soviet Union*.

27. White, *Gorbachev*, pp. 212–9; Dawisha, *Eastern Europe*; Gati, "Gorbachev." For the background of the new Cold War in the early 1980s, see Halliday, *Making* and *From Kabul*.

28. The attack on the rally, ordered by Ministry of Interior rather than Georgian officials, was allegedly a provocation by Kremlin conservatives seeking to destabilize Gorbachev's policies. The confused politics of the event were symptomatic of the flux that perestroika created.

29. Suny, *Soviet Experiment*, p. 456.

30. Ibid., pp. 461, 462, 467.

31. Ibid., p. 476. Boris N. Yeltsin (1931–) was briefly Gorbachev's ally in 1985–86, when he was recruited into the Central Committee (July 1985) and headed the Moscow party (December). In October 1987, he attacked the party leadership for dragging their feet and resigned from the Politburo, drawing unanimous condemnation and subsequent dismissal. He used the Party Conference of June 1988 and the Congress of People's Deputies as platforms for attacking Gorbachev. By the summer of 1990, he had established the Russian Republic as an alternative power base, from which he disputed Gorbachev's legitimacy.

32. Suny, *Soviet Experiment*, p. 457.

33. Yeltsin, quoted in ibid., p. 478.

34. Ibid., p. 483.

35. See, in general, Banac (ed.), *Eastern Europe*; Prins (ed.), *Spring*; Batt, *East Central*; Stokes, *Walls*; Wolchik, "Crisis."

36. They were also preceded by crisis in China, whose democratic inspiration and violent denouement were transferred to Europe via Television. Student protests interacted with divisions in the Chinese Communist Party (CCP) during the spring of 1989, leading to a protracted standoff and the forming of the Students Autonomous Federation, with signs of similar initiatives among workers. Troops

finally cleared Tiananmen Square on 3–4 June, amid many deaths. For Eastern Europe, these events were both inspiration and warning.

37. Speech to the United Nations, 7 December 1988. See Stokes, *Walls,* p. 99.

38. See Kolankiewicz and Lewis, *Poland,* pp. 82–96, 108–33, 165–73; Hahn, *Democracy;* Sanford, *Military Rule;* Stanizskis, *Dynamics;* Walicki, "Paradoxes."

39. Grósz had himself succeeded János Kádár in May 1988, encouraging a stronger reform course attuned to Soviet perestroika. However, Grósz combined support for radical economic reforms with protection of the CP's leading role, which precluded détente with the opposition. In contrast, Imre Pozsgay was close with some oppositionists and associated himself with the legacy of Imre Nagy. Grósz envisaged "power sharing" to coopt the pragmatic opposition, whereas Pozsgay pursued genuine liberalization. Pozsgay's reformers defeated Grósz's more "hardline" faction in June 1989, opening the way for Roundtable talks. See Bruszt and Stark, "Remaking"; Swain, *Hungary,* pp. 7–32.

40. Jarausch, *Rush,* pp. 15–32.

41. Maier, *Dissolution,* p. 155.

42. Jaurausch, *Rush,* pp. 33–72; Maier, *Dissolution,* pp. 108–67; Joppke, *East German,* pp. 133–82; Torpey, *Intellectuals,* pp. 118–83; Sandford, *Sword;* Philipsen, *We Were;* James and Stone (eds.), *When.*

43. Stokes, *Walls,* pp. 141–8; Todorova, "Improbable Maverick."

44. Judt, "Metamorphosis"; Stokes, *Walls,* pp. 148–57.

45. Ibid., 158–67.

46. Stokes, *Walls,* p. 237.

47. The breakdown of international federation in Yugoslavia began with greater Serb domination in the autonomous region of Kosovo, where Milosevic's repression of Albanian self-determination signified a broader pan-Serb project, in which Vojvodina was also annexed, Montenegro manipulated, and war eventually unleashed against Croatia and Bosnia-Hercegovina. This first destabilized the finely balanced machinery of the Yugoslav state and then drove the other nationalities into self-protection.

48. While the Romanian revolution resulted in the establishment of constitutional and juridical democracy, the new National Salvation Front was really the CP under another guise. Ceauşescu was deposed by a group of senior Communists, who preserved much of the party's institutional power.

49. In Poland, elections had already occurred, on the intermediate basis reserving two-thirds of Sejm seats for the Communist Party, in June 1989. The rest of Yugoslavia and Albania are excluded from this accounting, as warfare removed conditions of democratic consolidation. Nonetheless, formal democracy pertained, with elections in Croatia (April–May 1990), Macedonia (November–December), Bosnia-Hercegovina (November–December), Serbia (December), and Montenegro (December). Elections were held in Albania in March-April 1991.

50. See Konrad, *Anti-Politics.* Konrad was known for his book with Iván Szelényi, *The Intellectuals on the Road to Class Power,* composed in the early 1970s immediately before the crackdown against intellectuals. At that time, the Lukács school lost their university jobs: its elder members (Ferenc Fehér, Agnes Heller, György Márkus, Mária Márkus) went into exile, while their younger colleagues stayed (György Bence, János Kis, Mihály Vajdá). András Hegedüs, leading sociologist and prime minister in 1956, was expelled from the Party. In 1973, Miklós Haraszti received eight months in prison after writing about the experi-

ence of heavy industrial work, *A Worker in a Worker's State*. Szelényi went into exile.

51. Rupnik, *Other Europe,* p. 245.

52. Michnik, "New Evolutionism"; Havel, *Living*. See also Michnik, *Church, Prison,* and *Freedom*.

53. Signatories ranged from the ex-KSC high official Zdenek Mlynár and the critical Communist author Pavel Kohout through the Trotskyist Petr Uhl, to the Catholic writer Václav Benda and the philosopher-playwright Václav Havel. See Skilling, *Charter 77;* Semecka, *Restoration;* Deutscher et al. (eds.), *Voices;* Skilling, *Samizdat;* Tökés (ed.), *Opposition;* Johnston, "What Is"; Kaldor (ed.), *Europe*. See also Bahro, *Alternative*.

54. See Ryback, *Rock,* pp. 141–8; Kovac, "Slovene Spring," p. 116. In Slovenia, this cultural politics proceeded through the official Socialist Youth Alliance.

55. The phrase came from Václav Benda, a Catholic writer at the center of Charter 77. In 1979, Benda was imprisoned with Havel, Uhl, and three other activists. Havel was released in March 1983, Benda and Uhl in May. Stokes, *Walls,* p. 151.

56. See Maier, *Dissolution,* pp. 169–214; Jarausch, *Rush,* pp. 33–134; Joppke, *East German,* pp. 133–82; Torpey, *Intellectuals,* pp. 118–83; Rucht, "German Unification"; Osmond, "Yet Another."

57. The populist coalition formed the first democratically elected government. The renamed Communists, the Hungarian Socialist Party, who were excluded from both main camps, won 10.9 percent of the popular vote.

58. Mazowiecki had been prime minister in the first Solidarity government. In Bulgaria, the Union of Democratic Forces held together, forming a government after the next elections (October 1991), with 34.4 percent, but it too was more a coalition of disparate groups. In Romania, the National Salvation Front (NSF) swept the first elections with 66 percent, but by the next in 1992 it had split into Iliescu's governing Democratic NSF (28 percent) and ex–prime minister Roman's opposition NSF (10 percent). In July 1993, Iliescu's party renamed itself the Party of Social Democracy of Romania.

59. For the difficulties of late-Communist economic reform, see Kornai, "Hungarian Reform"; Szelenyi, "Eastern Europe"; Brus, " "Evolution."

60. See Baylis, "Transforming"; Jarausch, *Rush,* pp. 137–56; Maier, *Dissolution,* pp. 22–44, 290–303; Smith (ed.), *After;* Pohl, "Macroeconomic."

61. Stokes, *Walls,* p. 191. Klaus's Scenario for Economic Reform (September 1990) defeated the mixed economy advocated by Valtr Komárek, director of the pre-1989 Institute of Economic Forecasting and deputy prime minister in the post-1989 Civic Forum government. Klaus forced Komárek out after the June 1990 elections, split Civic Forum (early 1991), and won new elections with his neoliberal Civic Democratic Party (June 1992). As Komárek's deputy before 1989, Klaus had held extreme neoliberal economic views since the 1960s, influenced by Friedrich von Hayek and the Chicago economist Milton Friedman. Komárek became leader of the Social Democrats. See Gowan, "Neo-Liberal Economic"; Amsden et al., *Market Meets*.

62. Gowan, "Post-Communist Socialists," p. 156.

63. Invoking Karl Polanyi's classic analysis of the industrial revolution in Britain, various commentators have likened the post-Communist transition to a new "great transformation," where state intervention assembled the essential con-

ditions for laissez faire. See Glasman, "Great Deformation"; Bryant and Mokrzycki (eds.), *New Great;* Polanyi, *Great Transformation.*

64. Turnout was also low in post-1989 elections in Hungary (65 percent 1990) and exceptionally so in Poland (only 43 percent 1991 and 52 percent 1993), suggesting that many Communist supporters may have stayed at home.

65. See Gowan, "Post-Communist Socialists" and "Passages"; Waller et al. (eds.), *Social Democracy;* Waller (ed.), *Parties;* Ekiert and Kubik, *Rebellious.* For the political dynamics of democratization more generally: Ekiert, *The State;* Dawisha and Parrott (eds.), *Consolidation;* Nagle and Mahr, *Democracy;* Fowkes, *Post-Communist Era.*

66. See Dawson, *Eco-Nationalism.*

67. By the end of the 1990s, there were signs of greater openness on the SPD's part. See Olsen, "PDS" and "Seeing Red."

68. The indispensable starting point is provided by Gal and Kligman, *Politics,* and Gal and Kligman (eds.), *Reproducing Gender,* plus the earlier survey in Einhorn, *Cindarella,* and the detailed narative in Young, *Triumph;* also Funk and Mueller (eds.), *Gender Politics;* Berry (ed.), *Post-Communism.* See also Verdery, "From Parent-State," esp. pp. 81–2. Unfortunately, the relationship of the new post-Communist parties to a specifically "women's interest" is not dealt with in these sources.

69. This question has been best addressed by ethnographers. See Verdery, *What Was,* pp. 1–16, 19–38; Lampland, *Object;* Verdery, *National Ideology;* Burawoy and Lukács, *Radiant Past;* Burawoy and Verdery (eds.), *Uncertain Transitions.*

70. For the continuing renegotiation of the Eastern European social contract, see Cook et al. (eds.), *Left Parties;* Millar and Wolchik (eds.), *Social Legacy;* Adam, *Social Costs;* Gowan, "Neo-Liberal"; Glasman, "Great Deformation"; Bryant and Mokrzycki (eds.), *New Great;* Ekiert and Kubik, "Contentious Politics"; Ekiert, *State.* See also Swain, *Hungary,* pp. 185–224; Jarausch, "Care."

CHAPTER 26

1. The largest was the Communist League of West Germany (formed 1973) with a peak of 2,800 members; followed by the Communist League (1971) with 800–1,500; and the Communist Party of Germany, Marxist-Leninist (1968), with some 800. In 1971 the Communist Party of Germany (KPD) was founded to dispute the legacy of the earlier KPD, banned in 1956, competing with the officially refounded German CP (DKP); by 1977 it claimed eight hundred members. The Trotskyist International Marxist Group (formed 1969) claimed 400–600 members. See Markovits and Gorski, *German Left,* pp. 59–65.

2. Trotskyists defined themselves by splits in the Fourth International, launched by Trotsky's supporters in 1938. French groups included the International Communist Organization and the Revolutionary Communist League, dating from 1952, and Workers' Struggle, from 1939, each claiming five thousand members in the 1970s. The Fourth International's British section, the Revolutionary Communist Party, splintered in 1949: one offshoot eventually produced International Socialism; another the Socialist Labour League; and a third the secretive Revolutionary Socialist League, which worked inside the Labour Party under the name of its newspaper *Militant.* In the 1970s, they each drew several thousand

supporters. The smaller International Marxist group (750 members in 1978), dating from CPGB dissidence in 1956, exercised broader influence through the journals *Black Dwarf* (1968–70) and *New Left Review*. For details: Alexander, *International Trotskyism;* and Callaghan, *British Trotskyism.*

3. In Trotskyist theory, the *party* could be launched only if society was ripe for revolution; otherwise, revolutionaries organized inside larger movements with a newspaper as a front. Wishfully, the Socialist Labour League and International Socialism each declared Britain prerevolutionary, launching respectively the Workers' Revolutionary Party (1973) and the Socialist Workers' Party (1976), each reaching a membership of several thousand.

4. Alexander, *International Trotskyism*, p. 490.

5. See Ross and Jensen, "France," pp. 166–70; Lewis and Sferza, "French Socialists," pp. 101–7.

6. Seyd, *Rise*, pp. 37–75; Koelble, *Left Unraveled*, pp. 85–9; Thompson, *Good Old*, pp. 161–90; Andrews, "Young Turks."

7. Tarrow, *Democracy*, pp. 219–90; Lumley, *States*, p. 116.

8. For Italy: Lumley, *States*, pp. 279–93; Drake, *Revolutionary Mystique* and "Why." For Germany: Markovits and Gorski, *German Left*, pp. 65–78.

9. See Patterson, *Politics;* Clark, *Basque Insurgents;* Sullivan, *ETA;* Vague, *Anarchy.*

10. Katsiaficas, *Subversion*, pp. 87–8, 99–100, 128–31.

11. Ibid., pp. 39.

12. Lama, head of the CGIL, was attacked while seeking to end an occupation of Rome University in February 1977. When Metropolitan Indians, "armed with rubber tomahawks, streamers, and water balloons," threw Lama and his bodyguard out, police intervened, applauded by watching Communists, who denounced students as Fascists. The Indians' chanted: "In Chile tanks; in Italy, the Communists!" Ibid., pp. 42–50.

13. Ibid., pp. 115–27.

14. The scale of the violence also matched the uprisings of 1968—whether in the streetfighting of 12 December 1980 and 13 March 1981 ("Black Friday") in West Berlin or the Dutch *kraakers'* battles in the Coronation riots of April 1980, the pope's visit in May 1985, and police assaults in Nijmegen and Amsterdam in 1988.

15. Some northern socialist parties precipitously declined in membership: British Labour claimed 830,000 members in 1964 but only 277,000 in 1981; Dutch Labor dropped from 140,000 to 98,000 in 1965–76; Danish Social Democrats fell by half during 1960–80. Others, including the Austrian, Belgian, Swedish, and West German parties, enrolled higher membership but lost their subcultural supports. Some parties never possessed those subcultures to begin with: the socialist parties of France and Spain were plebiscitary machines, rallying voters merely for elections.

16. See Johnstone, *Politics;* Bess, *Realism*, pp. 124–54; Coates, *Most Dangerous;* Howarth, *France*. For END's founding "Appeal," see Thompson and Smith (eds.), *Protest*, pp. 163–5. For cooperation between peace movements in East and West: Baldwin et al. (eds.), *Documents;* Kavan and Tomin (eds.), *Voices;* Köszegi and Thompson, *New Hungarian;* Sandford, *Sword;* Kaldor (ed.), *Europe*. See also New Left Review (ed.), *Exterminism.*

17. Wainwright, *Labour*, p. 4; Rowbotham et al., *Beyond.*

18. Palmer, "Bread," pp. 134–5.

19. In 1981, this new urban Left added the GLC and Merseyside Metropolitan Council to strongholds in Wallsall, Stirling, Sheffield, and South Yorkshire. London boroughs of Camden, Greenwich, Hackney, Haringey, Islington, and Southwark followed in 1982, as did Liverpool in 1983 and Manchester in 1984, plus many smaller towns. The enemy was the older paternalism, which combined public spending with an authoritarian political style, further linked to the endemic corruption of many local Labour baronies.

20. Livingstone and Ali, *Who's Afraid,* jacket quotation. For the GLC, see Mackintosh and Wainwright (eds.), *Taste;* Carzel, *Citizen Ken.*

21. Cooper, "Engaged State," p. 197.

22. This was Labour's worst local performance since 1945 and traumatized local parties. In 1967, the party lost control of London, 10 county councils, and major cities, with a nationwide loss of 1,500 seats to the Conservatives. In 1968, Labour took only 17 percent of London seats, as against 63 percent to the Conservatives, with another net loss of 1,602 seats. In Sheffield, the Conservatives won control for only the second time in 41 years.

23. Wainwright, *Labour,* pp. 116–20.

24. Gyford, *Politics,* p. 43.

25. Maurice Stonefrost, GLC Director-General, *Sunday Times,* 16 September 1984, quoted by Gyford, *Politics,* p. 43. See also Seyd, *Rise,* pp. 137–58; Clarke, *Rise;* Lansley et al., *Councils;* Panitch and Leys, *End,* pp. 160–1.

26. After inheriting a peerage in 1961, Anthony Wedgwood Benn was required by constitutional rules to resign his parliamentary seat but fought instead for the right to renounce the title, winning in 1963. Minister for the post office (1964–66) and technology (1966–70) in the Wilson government, he remade himself after 1968 as the voice of "popular democracy," metamorphosing into "Tony Benn." He spoke for the left in the Wilson and Callaghan governments, as secretary of state for industry (1974–75) and energy (1975–79). After Labour's election defeat in 1979, he led the left attack on the government's record, driving for the party's constitutional reform and narrowly missing election as deputy leader in 1981. See Benn, *Parliament.*

27. Benn had a series of tense but important encounters in the early 1970s—a Yorkshire Labour Women's rally in June 1971, where he embraced feminism; the 1972 TUC Congress; an Institute of Workers' Control Conference in April 1973; and a National Community Action Conference in June 1973. See Panitch and Leys, *End,* p. 56. The quotations are from pp. 47, 49–51.

28. Speech to the Engineering Union's Foundry Section annual delegate meeting, May 1971. Ibid., p. 57. After the 1970 change of government, Benn addressed hundreds of meetings.

29. See Panitch and Leys, *End,* pp. 134–91; Seyd, *Rise,* pp. 76–136; Koelble, *Left Unraveled.*

30. Jenkins, Rodgers, and Williams were leading Gaitskellites; Owen was a younger pragmatist, unexpectedly appointed foreign secretary by Callaghan in 1977. Though the SDP was launched to great fanfare, as "breaking the mold" of British politics, it brought little new but belief in a third party per se, plus the commitment to electoral reform and proportional representation, essential if its popular votes were to be converted into parliamentary seats. For the 1983 elections it combined with the Liberals to form the Alliance.

31. On defeating Dennis Healey narrowly for the leadership (by a vote of the parliamentary party, under the old rules), Michael Foot immediately appointed Healey deputy leader and made a secret pact with leading trade unionists to oppose any challenge to the new Foot-Healey leadership, whatever the outcome of the upcoming Wembley Conference.

32. During the 1983 election, Healey and others campaigned freely against Labour's own Manifesto, even against Foot himself on the issue of nuclear arms. Labour won only 27.6 percent of the popular vote, barely ahead of the Alliance with 25.5 percent. See Panitch and Leys, *End,* pp. 192–213; Seyd, *Rise,* pp. 159–71; Hobsbawm, *Politics,* pp. 43–99; Hall, "Crisis," pp. 196–210.

33. Panitch and Leys, *End,* p. 172.

34. The Labour controlled GLC sought to reverse three decades of rising prices and deteriorating services in London transport. It lowered fares by 30 percent in 1981, with immediate impact on use and public support. Conservatives challenged this in the courts, leading to a doubling of fares and a new crisis of declining use. The GLC then produced a modified proposal for an integrated system on a 25 percent lower fare, which survived legal challenge in May 1983. Accordingly, the Conservative government removed control of London Transport from the GLC in July 1984. See Livingstone, *If Voting.*

35. Roseneil, *Disarming Patriarchy,* p. 165. Roseneil was a Greenham activist in 1983–84. By 31 December 1983, all nine gates into the base were camped. See Harford and Hopkins (eds.), *Greenham Common,* pp. iii–vi. After the last camp, at Blue Gate, was disbanded in February 1994, a handful of women still remained, 17 years after the Camp began. See Suzanna Chambers, "Last Greenham Women Demand Memorial Garden," *Independent on Sunday,* 19 July 1998. See also Thompson (ed.), *Over Our;* Liddington, *Road,* pp. 197–286; Kanter et al. (eds.), *Sweeping Statements,* pp. 10–26.

36. Segal, *Is the Future,* p. 167.

37. The best overall account is Richards, *Miners.* For local studies: Samuel et al. (eds.), *Enemy Within;* Gibbon and Steyne (eds.), *Thurcroft;* Welsh Campaign for Civil and Political Liberties and National Union of Miners South Wales Area (eds.), *Striking Back.* For the policing of the strike: Geary, *Policing;* Ewing and Gearty, *Freedom,* pp. 103–12.

38. Scargill, speech in Mansfield, 14 May 1984, Crick, *Scargill,* p. 152.

39. Beckett, *Enemy Within,* p. 207; Richards, *Miners,* p. 117.

40. See Fielding, *Labour,* pp. 50–53; and more generally, Taylor, *Trade Union.*

41. Mackey, "Women," p. 52. Kath Mackey grew up in Sheffield "amongst the steelworks" and worked with the unemployed. She was married to Paul Mackey, a trade unionist who led a successful 10-week occupation at the Firth Derihon steel works in 1983. See also Miller, *You Can't,* an account of the Abertillery Women's Support Group. Born in 1945, Jill Miller left South Wales in 1970, settling in Somerset and publishing her first novel, *Happy as a Dead Cat,* in 1983. Her local Women's Peace Group contacted miners picketing a cement works seven miles away. See also Massey and Wainwright, "Beyond"; Seddon (ed.), *The Cutting Edge;* Samuel et al. (eds.), *Enemy Within,* pp. 154–65.

42. Howells, "Stopping Out," p. 145. In July 1984, Government used new laws limiting picketing to sequester South Wales NUM funds, including those for food. To ensure the survival of the 20,000 mining families, support activity was intensified on a national and international scale.

43. Suddick, "Making," p. 26.

44. See James, "Working-Class Television."

45. Massey and Wainwright, "Beyond," pp. 154–7.

46. Sassoon, *One Hundred*, p. 724.

47. Ibid., pp. 713–29; Padgett, "German"; Meyer, "Transformation."

CHAPTER 27

1. See Kriesi, "New Social Movements"; Parkin, *Middle Class*.

2. See Touraine, *Post-Industrial* and *Self-Production*; Amin (ed.), *Post-Fordism*; Castells, *Rise*; Leadbetter, *Living*.

3. See Inglehart, *Silent Revolution* and *Culture Shift*; Beck, *Risk Society*; Beck al. (eds.), *Reflexive Modernization*; Franklin (ed.), *Politics*.

4. Jones, "Liverpool Socialist," pp. 92–101. In 2000, at age 87, Jones was still active as spokesman for the national old-age pensioners' movement.

5. Tarrow, *Democracy*, p. 227.

6. Brunt, "Politics," p. 151.

7. See especially Housee and Sharma, "Too Black"; also Sharma et al. (eds.), *Dis-Orienting Rhythms*; James and Harris (eds.), *Inside Baylon*.

8. Hall, "Ethnicity," p. 342; Hall, "Meaning," p. 120; Hall, "Old and New," p. 59.

9. Hugh Corbett, writing in the Campaign for Homosexual Equality's magazine *Lunch*, in 1972, quoted by Power, *No Bath*, p. 89.

10. Peter Tatchell, in Power, *No Bath*, p. 101. The *Gay Liberation Front Manifesto* is reprinted pp. 316–30.

11. Adam, *Rise*, p. 94.

12. Ibid., p. 90.

13. Tim Clark, in Power, *No Bath*, p. 240. This women's secession was paralleled in 1971–72 by similar lesbian breakaways in Paris, West Berlin, and Amsterdam.

14. The preceding account is based on the following: Power, *No Bath*; Cant and Hemmings (eds.), *Radical Records*; Healey and Mason (eds.), *Stonewall 25*; Rayside, *On the Fringe*; Adam, *Rise*.

15. Jeffrey Weeks, historian and gay activist, early member of GLF from 1970, interviewed 22 June 1992, in Rayside, *On the Fringe*, p. 31.

16. Ibid., pp. 19–101; Cooper, "Engaged State"; Thomson, "Unholy Alliances."

17. Details compiled from various sources, including: Kriesi et al., "Gay Subcultures"; *New York Times*, 13 September 2000; Adam, *Rise*; Hendrik et al. (eds.), *Third Pink*; International Lesbian and Gay Association, *ILGA Bulletin*.

18. See Watney, *Practices*, esp. pp. xi-xxii, 148–59, 231–43; Carter and Watney (eds.), *Taking Liberties*.

19. For Guérin, see Copley, *Sexual Moralities*, pp. 181–97.

20. See Jeffrey Weeks's comment in Power, *No Bath*, p. 285: "radicals were anti the family and that's reflected in the GLF *Manifesto*. . . . The commune movement was subconsciously an alternative way of living to the family. What I think has happened over the last two decades is that hostility to the family has gone and what people now talk about is alternative families."

21. See Storr, "New Sexual"; Mort, "Essentialism Revisited?" Warner (ed.), *Fear*.

22. For these antecedents, see McKay, *Senseless Acts,* pp. 11–44; Clarke, *Politics;* Rigby, *Communes;* Hind and Mosco, *Rebel Radio.*

23. During 1989–90, after long preparation, the traditional system of local taxation, the rates (a property tax assessed on households) was replaced by the flat-rate Community Charge, or "poll tax." This provoked major opposition, including organized nonpayment and the Trafalgar Square riot of 31 March 1990. See Burns and Simonns, *Poll Tax;* Bagguley, "Protest." The 1994 Criminal Justice Act was the latest in a chain of laws restricting civil liberties and strengthening police powers against ravers, travelers, squatters, and all kinds of direct action protests. See McKay, *Senseless Acts,* pp. 169–81; Redhead, *Unpopular Cultures.*

24. See Hemment, "Dangerous Dancing"; Collin, *Altered State;* Reynolds, *Generation Ecstasy;* Huq, "The Right."

25. Hemment, "Dangerous Dancing," pp. 209, 218, 226.

26. Protests began against the M3 at Twyford Down in 1991–92, continuing against the M11 Link Road in Wanstead, East London (1993–1995); the M65 in mid-Lancashire (1994–95); the M77 at Pollock, Glasgow (1994–95); the Newbury Bypass (1995–96); the Fairmile, Devon (1996); and the Birmingham Northern Relief Road (1998). Earth First! was founded in 1990 as a radical rival to Friends of the Earth. See Plows, "Earth First!"

27. The Dongas formed from early Twyford Down protesters (young "environmentalists, craftworkers and herbalists") during the year-long action and then dispersed into traveling along the so-called Freedom Trail in the West Country, "reclaiming our stolen countryside." According to Donga Alex, "our most direct ideological links are with the environmental movements of the late sixties, seventies and eighties; for example, CND, Greenpeace, and the Greenham Women's Movement. . . . Our tactics were also influenced by Earth First!; tree-sitting, climbing on machinery to stop it moving, etc." See McKay, *Senseless Acts,* pp. 138, 146, 137.

28. Jordan, "Art," p. 132; also Field, "Anti-Roads Movement." Reclaim the Streets was originally formed in 1991 and then relaunched in 1994.

29. See Wollen, "Situationist International"; Plant, *Most Radical.*

30. *Aufheben,* "Politics," pp. 100–102.

31. As the Paris 1968 slogan said: "Beneath the Cobblestones—the Beach." In the call to the West Berlin *Tunix* festival in January 1978, "Tunix Beach" was an alternative utopia "beneath the cobblestones of this country." See Jordan, "Art," p. 287; Markovits and Gorski, *German Left,* p. 86.

32. See Bey, *TAZ,* p. 106. TAZs were " 'pirate economics,' living high off the surplus of social overproduction—even the popularity of colorful military uniforms—and the concept of *music* as revolutionary social change—and finally their shared air of impermanence, of being ready to move on, shape-shift, relocate to other universities, mountain-tops, ghettos, factories, safe houses, abandoned farms—or even other planes of reality." Another example: the Haçienda club in Manchester was opened by Anthony Wilson, a Granada Television presenter and founder of Factory Records, who discovered the Situationists as a student in Cambridge. He took the name from Ivan Chtcheglov's 1953 tract *Formulary for a New Urbanism*: "The haçienda must be built." See Schlosser, "Saturday Night," p. 26.

33. This paragraph is based on McKay, *Senseless Acts,* pp. 73–90, including letters and interviews with the band's members. The Poison Girls were among the

original sponsors of the Peace March that led to Greenham Common. See Rimbaud, *Last* and *My Revolting;* also Savage, *England's Dreaming.*

34. See also Jordan, "New Space" and *Cyberpower;* Lee, *Labour Movement.*

35. The first description is quoted from *schNEWS,* 38 (1 September 1995), the second from *Aufheben.* See McKay, *Senseless Acts,* p. 175.

36. Luton car workers were subjects of a classic study of British sociology, which tested the effects of rising living standards in the 1950s and 1960s on working-class values. See Goldthorpe and Lockwood, *Affluent Worker.*

37. From a poem addressed "To the Leaser of Dis Place," left behind in the empty warehouse ("a monument to the disgrace that is wasted land") after an all-night squatted party. Malyon, "Tossed," p. 206.

38. The name played on the autonomist-cum-Situationist ideal of the TAZ, or Temporary Autonomous Zone.

39. The farm's purchase by the government for widening the M1 motorway highlighted the connections among environmentally irresponsible government policy, economic waste, and the absence of local productive investment, which galvanized the broadest social movements demanding democratic accountability.

40. Dunstable Chief Inspector Mick Brown initially negotiated with the Collective and appealed for public support in legalizing parties, before Conservative pressure overruled him. Equipment was seized and 36 arrested in January 1993. A crowd of some four thousand laid siege to Luton police station, turning on the music to dance. The people were released and the sound system returned. Further raids led to suspension of parties, until Paul Taylor was acquitted amid national controversy and public discrediting of the police.

41. Glenn Jenkins, Exodus spokesperson, quoted in Malyon, "Tossed," p. 200.

42. Ibid., p. 193.

43. Ibid., p. 206.

44. See Bowring, "LETS"; Fitzpatrick, "New Welfare"; Douthwaite, *Short Circuit;* Croall, *LETS Act;* Amin and Thomas, "Negotiated Economy."

45. Wainwright, *Arguments,* p. 286, note 3.

46. Technology Networks facilitated contacts between producers, consumers, and scientists: London Energy and Environment Network; London Transport Network; London Innovation Network; and three for North, South, and East London. Coin Street was an urban village of single dwelling houses, shops, and workshops near Waterloo Station, "a micro network of co-ops and community groups supported by Coin Street Community Trust." The GLC used planning powers to keep out property developers, while providing financial and expert support for community groups. See Wainwright, *Arguments,* pp. 164–8, 178–82. For the GLC, see Mackintosh and Wainwright (eds.), *Taste.*

47. Wainwright, *Arguments,* pp. 143–89.

48. See in general, Sassoon, *Hundred Years,* pp. 730–77.

49. Western European socialists governing in 1998—Blair in Britain, Jospin in France, Schröder in Germany—were ex-students in 1973, when Pinochet led the coup deposing Salvador Allende's Popular Unity government in Chile.

50. Peter Glotz, "What Is To Be Done?" *Socialist Affairs,* 1–2 (1988), pp. 25, cited in Sassoon, *Hundred Years,* p. 735.

51. Sassoon, *Hundred Years,* pp. 736, 746, and see pp. 706–13; Pontusson,

Limits, "Radicalization," and "Sweden"; Jenson and Mahon, "Representing Solidarity"; Mjoset et al., "Norway"; Christiansen, "Denmark."

52. The British Green Party formed in 1973 was a pressure group with non-existent electoral prospects given the absence of proportional representation, which elsewhere was vital in enabling new parties to take off.

53. Wainwright, *Argument,* p. 193.

54. See Rüdig, *Green Wave;* Richardson and Rootes (eds.), *Green Challenge;* Parkin, *Green Parties;* Parkin (ed.), *Green Light;* Feinstein, *Sixteen Weeks;* Philip, *Swedish Green.*

55. Wainwright, *Argument,* pp. 190–236; also Andersson, "Fundamental Values."

56. Grünen, *Think Globally,* p. 40.

57. After devolution failed in referenda in 1979 (comprehensively in Wales, more narrowly in Scotland), 10 years of industrial devastation under Thatcher fueled nationalist revivals, and by 1997 Conservatives failed to elect a single MP in either country. Scottish and Welsh Nationalists moved markedly to the Left during the 1980s. See Fevre and Thompson (eds.), *Nation;* Griffiths, *Thatcherism;* Andrews, *Wales Says;* Denver, *Scotland Decides;* Sillars, *Scotland.*

58. See Markovits and Silvia, "Green Trumps"; Markovits and Gorski, *German Left,* pp. 265–90.

59. In Austria, Switzerland, the Netherlands, Norway, Sweden, Finland, and Ireland, systems were more stable.

60. Bowd, "C'est la lutte," p. 73.

61. Jean-Pierre Chevénement's Citizens' Movement drew ex-Socialists, ex-Communists, feminists, and independent socialists. The PCF began its overdue renovation, replacing Georges Marchais as general secretary in 1993 with Robert Hue. Greens revived after dropping from 10.6 percent in the Euro-elections (1989) and 14.4 percent in regional elections (1992) to 7.6 percent in 1993. The maverick entrepreneur Bernard Tapie and the Radicals rallied "Ecologists, ex-Socialists, an ex-Communist Trade-union leader, feminists (such as Antoinette Fouque), and anti-racists." Ibid., p. 82.

62. The four thousand charged included 130 parliamentarians in networks of bankers, industrialists, administrators, and party officials linked to the Mafia and the Vatican. Corruption's reckless scale was Craxi's contribution to the history of Italian socialism. Trails led back to the "strategy of tension" and Licio Gelli's P-2 in the 1970s. See McCarthy, *Crisis,* pp. 61–102; also Bufacchi and Burgess, *Italy,* pp. 83–106. For Craxi's PSI, see Hine, "Social Democracy" and "Italian Socialist."

63. *Allianza Nationale* was the electoral front of the neo-Fascist MSI, formed by its leader Gianfranco Fini in the summer of 1993. The party reemerged fully as *Allianza* in January 1995.

64. Berlusconi made his fortune in Milan real estate, building a Television empire and purchasing the soccer team AC Milan by using his connections to Craxi in Milan and the Andreotti DC. See MacCarthy, *Crisis,* p. 82; Bufacchi and Burgess, *Italy,* pp. 191–217.

65. Born in 1936, Occhetto became secretary of the Young Communists (1963–66), PCI parliamentarian (1976), and Central Committee member (1979), succeeding Alessandro Natta as secretary (1988). Four days after the fall of the

Berlin Wall in November 1989, he announced the refounding of the PCI with a new name. This required 14 months of debate and two Congresses (March 1990, January 1991), which approved the change by 65 and 69 percent.

66. See Gundle, "Italian," pp. 21–3.

67. See the debate between Abse, "Leopard," and Salvati, "Travail."

68. Salvati, "Crisis," p. 80.

69. Occhetto resigned after the 1994 elections. Massimo D'Alema (born 1949) had headed the Young Communists and edited *L'Unità*. After the recent turmoil, he was "perceived as the candidate of the Communist tradition." He "defended the PDS apparatus, especially by leaving it alone. Where Occhetto called for daily transformation of the party, D'Alema said that the PDS must 'become what it is,' namely, a Social Democratic party with a strong organization. The second part of his strategy was that the PDS must form an alliance with the Center." See McCarthy, *Crisis*, pp. 186–7. In so doing, D'Alema followed in Togliatti's and Berlinguer's footsteps.

70. See Therborn, "Life."

71. See Ross, *Jacques Delors*, "Fin de Siècle," and "Confronting"; Marquand, "Reinventing Federalism"; Gowan and Anderson (eds.), *Question*; Grahl and Teague, "Cost"; Camiller, "Beyond 1992."

CONCLUSION

1. Carroll, " "Struggle"; Stanley, *"L'Unita"*; Lloyd, "Socialism," p. 23.

2. See Connolly, "Jiři Pelikan"; also Pelikan, "Struggle."

3. Partos, "Ladislav Lis."

4. Sassoon, "Nilde Iotti."

5. Christie, "Goliardo Fiaschi."

6. Baxell, "Bill Alexander." See his official history of the International Brigades from Britain and Ireland, Alexander, *British Volunteers*.

7. Bowyer, "Dora Cox."

8. Pimlott, "Joan Bourne."

9. Philpot, "Barbara Kahan."

10. MacCarthy, "Alix Meynell." See also Meynell, *Private Servant*.

11. Connolly, "Margarete Schütte-Lihotsky." See also Schütte-Lihotsky, *Memories*.

12. "If you look at the great causes in which people of my age have been involved, such as the war against Nazism, it is impossible to say that the price paid was higher than the results obtained. Would the world be better if we hadn't resisted? I don't believe that there is a single person involved in that battle that is willing today to say that it was not worthwhile." Hobsbawm, *On the Edge*, p. 161.

13. Hobsbawm, *On the Edge*, p. 159.

14. This expansion of politics into areas previously reserved for privacy or beyond the political sphere in its established definitions, particularly in sexuality and family life, proved double-edged. Right-wing drives to make "family values" and associated social issues into political priorities also worked in this new political space. The new interest in subjectivities, lifestyle, and personal growth could also depoliticize large areas of public debate, *removing* them from democratic advocacy rather than bringing them into the public sphere.

15. See Ross, *Jacques Delors,* "Fin de Siècle," and "Confronting"; Marquand, "Reinventing Federalism"; Gowan and Anderson (eds.), *Question;* Grahl and Teague, "Cost"; Camiller, "Beyond 1992."

16. For an example of carefully theorized and concretely specified strategizing, see especially Held, *Democracy;* and for broader debates, Held et al., *Global Transformations.* For a case of glibness, Giddens and Pierson, *Conversations,* pp. 151–93.

17. See especially Jameson, "Globalization," pp. 49–68.

18. For current usages of the "Third Way," see especially Giddens, *Third Way* and *Third Way and Its Critics;* Merkel, *Third Ways.* The basic arguments have been reiterated many times. For instance: "The Third Way Goes Global," *New Democrat,* 3 (May–June 1999), for an account of a 1998 Washington meeting of Bill Clinton (United States), Tony Blair (Britain), Gerhard Schröder (Germany), Massimo D'Alema (Italy), and Wim Kock (Netherlands). See also Zuege, "Chimera."

19. Until, of course, one remembers the earlier twentieth-century context of prevailing fascist dictatorship, which it was the Left's enduring achievement to have opposed and help sweep away.

Bibliography

Abraham, David. *The Collapse of the Weimar Republic: Political Economy and Crisis*, 2nd ed. New York: Holmes and Meier, 1986.
———. "Labor's Way: On the Successes and Limits of Socialist Politics in Interwar and Post–World War II Germany." *International Labor and Working-Class History* 28 (fall 1985): 1–24.
Abrams, Mark. *The Teenage Consumer*. London: London Press Exchange, 1959.
Abrams, Philip. "The Failure of Social Reform: 1918–1920." *Past and Present* 24 (April 1963): 43–64.
Absalom, Roger. *A Strange Alliance: Aspects of Escape and Survival in Italy 1943–45*. Florence, Italy: Olschki, 1991.
Abse, Tobias. "Italy: A New Agenda." In Perry Anderson and Patrick Camiller, eds., *Mapping the West European Left*. London: Verso, 1994.
———. "The Left's Advance in Italy." *New Left Review* 217 (May–June 1996): 123–30.
———. "The Rise of Fascism in an Industrial City: The Case of Livorno 1918–1922." In David Forgacs, ed., *Rethinking Italian Fascism: Capitalism, Populism and Culture*. London: Lawrence and Wishart, 1986.
———. "The Triumph of the Leopard." *New Left Review* 199 (May–June 1993): 3–28.
Accampo, Elinor A. *Industrialization, Family Life, and Class Relations in Saint-Chamond, 1815–1914*. Berkeley: University of California Press, 1989.
Ackelsberg, Martha A. *Free Women of Spain. Anarchism and the Struggle for the Emancipation of Women*. Bloomington: University of Indiana Press, 1991.
———. "Women and the Politics of the Spanish Popular Front: Political Mobilization or Social Revolution?" *International Labor and Working-Class History* 30 (fall 1986): 1–12.
Adam, Barry D. *The Rise of a Gay and Lesbian Movement*. 2nd ed. New York: Twayne, 1995.
Adam, Jan. *Social Costs of Transformation to a Market Economy in Post-Communist Countries: The Cases of Poland, the Czech Republic, and Hungary*. New York: St. Martin's Press, 1999.
Adams, Mark B., ed. *The Wellborn Science: Eugenics in Germany, France, Brazil, and Russia*. Oxford: Oxford University Press, 1990.
Adamson, Walter L. *Avant-Garde Florence: From Modernism to Fascism*. Cambridge: Harvard University Press, 1993.
———. "The Impact of World War I on Italian Political Culture," In Aviel Roshwald and Richard Stites, eds., *European Culture in the Great War: The Arts, Entertainment, and Propaganda, 1914–1918*. Cambridge, England: Cambridge University Press, 1999.
———. "Modernism and Fascism: The Politics of Culture in Italy, 1903–1922," *American Historical Review* 95 (1990): 359–90.

Adereth, Mazwell. *The French Communist Party: A Critical History (1920–84): From Comintern to "the Colours of France."* Manchester: Manchester University Press, 1984.

Addison, Paul. *The Road to 1945: British Politics and the Second World War.* London: Cape, 1977.

Adler, Friedrich., ed. *Victor Adler: Briefwechsel mit August Bebel und Karl Kautsky.* Vienna: Wiener Volksbuchhandlung, 1954.

Agulhon, Maurice. *The Republic of the Village: The People of the Var from the French Revolution to the Second Republic.* Cambridge, England: Cambridge University Press, 1982.

Alapuro, Risto. "Artisans and Revolution in a Finnish Country Town." In Michael Hanagan, Leslie Page Moch, and Wayne Te Brake, eds., *Challenging Authority: The Historical Study of Contentious Politics.* Minneapolis: University of Minnesota, 1998.

———. *State and Revolution in Finland.* Berkeley: University of California Press, 1988.

Alexander, Bill. *British Volunteers for Liberty, Spain 1936–1939.* London: Lawrence and Wishart, 1982.

Alexander, Martin, and Helen Graham, eds. *The French and Spanish Popular Fronts: Comparative Perspectives.* Cambridge, England: Cambridge University Press, 1989.

Alexander, Robert J. *International Trotskyism 1929–1985: A Documented Analysis of the Movement.* Durham, N.C.: Duke University Press, 1991.

Alexander, Sally. "Becoming a Woman in London in the 1920s and 1930s." In David Feldman and Gareth Stedman Jones, eds., *Metropolis—London. Histories and Representations since 1800.* London: Routledge, 1989.

———. "Women, Class and Sexual Differences in the 1830s and 1840s: Some Reflections on the Writing of a Feminist History." In Nicholas B. Dirks, Geoff Eley, and Sherry B. Ortner, eds., *Culture/Power/History: A Reader in Contemporary Social Theory.* Princeton: Princeton University Press, 1995.

Ali, Tariq. *Street Fighting Years: An Autobiography of the Sixties.* New York: Citadel Press, 1987.

———, ed. *The Stalinist Legacy. Its Impact on Twentieth-Century World Politics.* Harmondsworth: Penguin, 1984.

Ali, Tariq, and Susan Watkins. *1968: Marching in the Streets.* New York: Free Press, 1998.

Allen, J. and Doreen Massey, eds. *The Economy in Question: Restructuring Britain.* London: Sage, 1988.

Altbach, Edith Hoshino, Jeanette Clausen, Dagmar Schultz, and Naomi Stephen, eds. *German Feminism: Readings in Politics and Literature.* Albany: State University of New York Press, 1984.

Althaus, Hans-Joachim, et al. *Da ist nirgends nichts gewesen außer hier. Das "rote Mössingen" im Generalstreik gegen Hitler. Geschichte eines schwäbischen Arbeiterdorfes.* Berlin: Rotbuch Verlag, 1982.

Ambrosius, Gerold, and William H. Hubbard. *A Social and Economic History of Twentieth-Century Europe.* Cambridge: Harvard University Press, 1989.

Amdur, Kathryn E. *Syndicalist Legacy: Trade Unions and Politics in Two French Cities in the Era of World War I.* Urbana: University of Illinois Press, 1986.

Amin, Ash. "Post-Fordism: Models, Fantasies and Phantoms of Transition." In Ash Amin, ed., *Post-Fordism: A Reader*. Oxford: Blackwell, 1994.

———, ed. *Post-Fordism: A Reader*. Oxford: Blackwell, 1994.

Amin, Ash, and M. Dietrich, eds. *Towards a New Europe? Structural Change in the European Economy*. Aldershot, England: Elgar, 1991.

Aminzade, Ronald. *Ballots and Barricades: Class Formation and Republican Politics in France, 1830–1871*. Princeton: Princeton University Press, 1993.

Amsden, Alice, Jacek Kochanowicz, and Lance Taylor. *The Market Meets its Match: Restructuring the Economies of Eastern Europe*. Cambridge: Harvard University Press, 1994.

Amyot, Grant. *The Italian Communist Party: The Crisis of the Popular Front Strategy*. New York: St. Martin's Press, 1981.

Anderson, Bonnie S. and Judith P. Zinsser. *A History of Their Own: Women in Europe from Prehistory to the Present*. Vol. 2. 2nd edn. New York: Oxford University Press, 1988.

Anderson, Harriet. *Utopian Feminism: Women's Movements in Fin-de-siècle Vienna*. New Haven: Yale University Press, 1992.

Anderson, Perry. *Arguments within English Marxism*. London: Verso, 1980.

———. "Communist Party History." In Raphael Samuel, ed., *People's History and Socialist Theory*. London: Routledge, 1981.

———. *Considerations on Western Marxism*. London: Verso, 1976.

———. *In the Tracks of Historical Materialism*. London: Verso, 1983.

———. Introduction to Perry Anderson and Patrick Camiller, eds., *Mapping the West European Left*. London: Verso, 1994.

Anderson, Perry, and Patrick Camiller, eds. *Mapping the West European Left*. London: Verso, 1994.

Andersson, Jan Otto. "Fundamental Values for a Third Left." In *New Left Review* 216 (March–April 1996): 66–78.

Andrae, C. G. "The Swedish Labor Movement and the 1917–1918 Revolution." In S. Koblik, ed., *Sweden's Development from Poverty to Affluence, 1750–1970*. Minneapolis: University of Minnesota Press, 1975.

Andréas, Bert. *Le Manifeste Communiste de Marx et Engels. Histoire et Bibliographie 1848–1918*. Milan: Feltrinelli, 1963.

Andreucci, Franco. "The Diffusion of Marxism in Italy during the Late Nineteenth Century." In Raphael Samuel and Gareth Stedman Jones, eds. *Culture, Ideology and Politics, Essays for Eric Hobsbawm*. London: Routledge, 1983.

———. *Il marxismo collettivo. Socialismo, marxismo e circolzione delle idee dalla seconda alla terza internazionale*. Milan: Franco Angeli, 1986.

———. "Italy." In Marcel van der Linden and Jürgen Rojahn, eds., *The Formation of Labour Movements 1870–1914: An International Perspective*, Vol. 1. Leiden: Brill, 1990.

Andreucci, Franco, and Malcom Sylvers. "The Italian Communists Write Their History." *Science and Society*, 50, 1 (1976): 28–56.

Andrews, Geoff. "Young Turks and Old Guard: Intellectuals and the Communist Party Leadership in the 1970s." In Geoff Andrews, Nina Fishman, and Kevin Morgan, eds., *Opening the Books: Essays on the Social and Cultural History of the British Communist Party*. London: Lawrence and Wishart, 1995.

Andrews, Geoff, Nina Fishman, and Kevin Morgan, eds. *Opening the Books: Es-*

says on the Social and Cultural History of the British Communist Party. London: Lawrence and Wishart, 1995.

Andrews, Leighton. *Wales Says Yes: The Inside Story of the Yes for Wales Referendum Campaign*. Bridgend: Seren, 1999.

Angress, Werner T. *Stillborn Revolution: The Communist Bid for Power in Germany, 1921–1923*. Princeton: Princeton University Press, 1963.

von Ankum, Katherina, ed. *Women in the Metropolis: Gender and Modernity in Weimar Culture*. Berkeley: University of California Press, 1997.

Ansorg, Leonore, and Renate Hürtgen. "The Myth of Female Emancipation: Contradictions in Women's Lives." In Konrad H. Jarausch, ed., *Dictatorship as Experience: Towards a Socio-Cultural History of the GDR*. New York: Berghahn, 1999.

Arad, Yitzhak. *Ghetto in Flames: The Struggle and Destruction of the Jews in Vilna in the Holocaust*. Jerusalem: Yad Vashem, Martyrs' and Heroes; Remembrance Authority, 1980.

Arato, Andrew, and Paul Breines. *The Young Lukács and the Origins of Western Marxism*. New York: Seabury, 1979.

Arblaster, Anthony. *The Rise and Decline of Western Liberalism*. Oxford: Blackwell, 1984.

Archer, Robin et al., eds. *Out of Apathy: Voices of the New Left Thirty Years On*. London: Verso, 1989.

Ascari, Rosalia Colombo. "Feminism and Socialism in Anna Kuliscioff's Writings." In Robin Pickering-Iazzi, ed., *Mothers of Invention: Women, Italian Fascism, and Culture*. Minneapolis: University of Minnesota Press, 1995.

Aslund, Anders. *Private Enterprise in Eastern Europe: The Non-Agricultural Private Sector in Poland and the GDR*. London: Macmillan, 1985.

Aspaturian, Vernon V., Jiri Valenta, and David P. Burke, eds. *Eurocommunism between East and West*. Bloomington: University of Indiana Press, 1980.

Attfield, John, and Stephen Williams, eds. *1939: The Communist Party of Great Britain and the War*. London: Lawrence and Wishart, 1984.

Aufheben. "The Politics of Anti-Road Struggle and the Struggles of Anti-Road Politics: The Case of the No M11 Link Road Campaign." In George McKay, ed., *DiY Culture: Party and Protest in Nineties Britain*. London: Verso, 1998.

Azergailis, Andrew. *The 1917 Revolution in Latvia*. New York: Columbia University Press, 1974.

Bagguley, P. "Protest, Power and Poverty: A Case Study of the Anti-Poll Tax Movement." *Sociological Review* 43 (1995): 693–719.

Bahro, Rudolf. *The Alternative in Eastern Europe*. London: Verso, 1978.

Bailey, Stephen. "The Berlin Strike of 1918." *Central European History* 13 (1980): 158–74.

Bain, George Sayers, and Robert Price. *Profiles of Union Growth: A Comparative Statistical Portrait of Eight Countries*. Oxford: Oxford University Press, 1980.

Baker, Robert. "Socialism in the Nord 1880–1914." *International Review of Social History* 12 (1967): 357–89.

Bakker, Isabella. "Women's Employment in Comparative Perspective." In Jane Jensen, Elisabeth Hangen, and Ceallaigh Reddy, eds., *The Feminization of the Labor Force: Paradoxes and Promises*. London: Routledge, 1988.

Bakuniak, G., and K. Nowak. "The Creation of a Collective Identity in a Social

Movement: The Case of *Solidarnosc* in Poland." *Theory and Society* 16 (1987): 401–29.

Baldwin, Hugh, and END Hungary Working Group, eds. *Documents on the Peace Movement in Hungary.* London: Merlin, 1986.

Baldwin, Peter. *The Politics of Social Solidarity: Class Bases of the European Welfare State, 1875–1975.* Cambridge, England: Cambridge University Press, 1990.

Balfour, Sebastion. *Dictatorship, Workers, and the City: Labour in Greater Barcelona since 1939.* Oxford: Oxford University Press, 1989.

Balibar, Etienne. *On the Dictatorship of the Proletariat.* London: Verso, 1977.

Banac, Ivo, "The Communist Party of Yugoslavia during the Period of Legality (1919–1921)." In Ivo Banac, ed., *The Effects of World War I. The Class War after the Great War: The Rise of Communist Parties in East Central Europe, 1919–1921.* Brooklyn: Columbia University Press, 1983.

————. *The National Question in Yugoslavia: Origins, History, Politics.* Ithaca, N.Y.: Cornell University Press, 1984.

————. *With Stalin against Tito: Cominformist Splits in Yugoslav Communism.* Ithaca, N.Y.: Cornell University Press, 1988.

————, ed. *Eastern Europe in Revolution.* Ithaca, N.Y.: Cornell University Press, 1992.

Banchoff, Thomas. *The German Problem Transformed: Institutions, Politics, and Foreign Policy, 1945–1995.* Ann Arbor: University of Michigan Press, 1999.

Barclay, David E. "Rethinking Social Democracy, the State, and Europe: Rudolf Hilferding in Exile, 1933 to 1941," In David E. Barclay and Eric D. Weitz, eds., *Between Reform and Revolution: German Socialism and Communism from 1840 to 1990.* New York: Berghahn, 1998.

Bard, Christine, and Jean-Louis Robert, "The French Communist Party and Women: From 'Feminism' to Familialism." In Helmut Gruber and Pamela Graves, eds., *Women and Socialism/Socialism and Women: Europe between the Two World Wars.* New York: Berghahn, 1998.

Bard, Christine. "Marianne and the Mother Rabbits: Feminism and Natality under the Third Republic," In Maire Cross and Sheila Perry, eds., *Population and Social Policy in France.* London: Pinter, 1997.

————. "Proletarians of the Proletariat: Women's Citizenship in France," *International Labor and Working-Class History* 48 (fall 1995): 49–67.

Barker, Francis, et al., eds. *1936: The Sociology of Literature. Vol. 2. Practices of Literature and Politics.* Colchester: University of Essex Press, 1979.

Barnett, Anthony. *This Time: Our Constitutional Revolution.* London: Vintage, 1997.

Barnsley Women against Pit Closures. *Women against Pit Closures.* Barnsley, England, 1984.

Baron, Samuel H. *Plekhanov: The Father of Russian Marxism.* Stanford: Stanford University Press, 1963.

Barreno, Maria Isabel, Maria Teresa Horta, and Maria Velho da Costa. *New Portuguese Letters.* London: Readers International, 1994.

Barrow, Logie. "Determinism and Environmentalism in Socialist Thought." In Raphael Samuel and Gareth Stedman Jones, eds., *Culture, Ideology, and Politics.* Boston: Routledge, 1982.

————. "Socialism and Eternity: Plebeian Spiritualists 1853–1913." *History Workshop Journal* 9 (spring 1980): 37–69.

Barrow, Logie, and Ian Bullock. *Democratic Ideas in the British Labour Movement, 1880–1914.* Cambridge England: Cambridge University Press, 1996.

Batt, Judy. *East Central Europe from Reform to Revolution.* New York: Council on Foreign Relations Press, 1991.

Bauer, Otto. "Fascism." In Tom Bottomore and Patrick Goode, eds., *Austro-Marxism.* Oxford: Oxford University Press, 1978.

Baxell, Richard. "Bill Alexander: British Commander in the International Brigades Whose Concern for His Fellow Veterans Outlived the Spanish Civil War." *Guardian,* 14 July 2000.

Baylis, Thomas A. "Tranforming the East German Economy: Shock without Therapy." In Michael G. Huelshoff, Andrei S. Markovits, and Simon Reich, eds., *From Bundesrepublik to Deutschland: German Politics after Unification.* Ann Arbor: University of Michigan Press, 1993.

Beach, Abigail. "Forging a 'Nation of Participants': Political and Economic Planning in Labour's Britain," In Richard Weight and Abigail Beach, eds., *The Right to Belong: Citizenship and National Identity in Britain, 1930–1960.* London: Tauris, 1998.

Bebel, August. *Women and Socialism.* New York: Socialist Literature, 1917.

Beccalli, Bianca. "The Modern Women's Movement in Italy." In Monica Threlfall, ed., *Mapping the Women's Movement: Feminist Politics and Social Transformation in the North.* London: Verso, 1996.

————. "The Modern Women's Movement in Italy." *New Left Review* 204 (March–April 1994): 86–112.

Beck, Ulrich. *Risk Society: Towards a New Modernity.* London: Sage, 1992.

Beck, Ulrich, Scott Lash, and Anthony Giddens, eds. *Reflexive Modernization: Politics, Tradition, and Aesthetics in the Modern Social Order.* Cambridge, England: Polity Press, 1994.

Becker, Jean Jacques. *The Great War and the French People.* Leamingon Spa, England: Berg, 1986.

Becker, Josef, and Franz Knipping, eds. *Power in Europe? Great Britain, France, Italy and Germany in a Postwar World, 1945–1950.* Berlin: de Gruyter, 1986.

Beckett, Francis. *Enemy Within: The Rise and Fall of the British Communist Party.* London: Murray, 1995.

Beecher, Jonathan. *Charles Fourier: The Visionary and His World.* Berkeley: University of California Press, 1986.

————. *Victor Considérant and the Rise and Fall of French Romantic Socialism.* Berkeley: University of California Press, 2001.

Beetham, David, ed. *Marxists in Face of Fascism.* London: Manchester University Press, 1983.

Behagg, Clive. "Custom, Class and Change: The Trade Societies of Birmingham." *Social History* 4 (October 1979): 455–80.

Behan, Tom. " 'Going Further': The Aborted Italian Insurrection of July 1948." *Left History,* 3–4 (fall 1995–spring 1996): 168–203.

Bell, David S., and Byron Criddle. *The French Socialist Party: The Emergence of a Party of Government.* Oxford: Oxford University Press, 1988.

Bell, H. Donald. *Sesto San Giovanni: Workers, Culture, and Politics in an Italian Industrial Town 1880–1922*. New Brunswick, N.J.: Rutgers University Press, 1986.

———. "Working-Class Culture and Fascism in an Italian Industrial Town, 1918–22." *Social History* 9 (1984): 1–24.

Bell, John D. *Peasants in Power: Alexander Stamboliski and the Bulgarian Agrarian National Union, 1899–1923*. Princeton: Princeton University Press, 1977.

Belsize Lane Women's Group, "Nine Years Together," In Marsha Rowe, ed., *Spare Rib Reader*. Harmondsworth: Penguin, 1982.

Ben-Ami, Shlomo. *Fascism from Above: The Dictatorship of Primo de Rivera in Spain 1923–1930*. Oxford: Oxford University Press, 1983.

Benjamin, Walter. *Illuminations*. London: Fontana, 1973.

———. "Paris—The Capital of the Nineteenth Century." In *Charles Bandelaire: A Lyric Poet in the Era of High Capitalism*. London: Verso, 1973.

Benn, Tony. *Parliament, People and Power: Agenda for a Free Society*. London: Verso, 1982.

Bennett, Anita, and Jill Nicholls. ' "We Are All Criminals: Women's Liberation in Spain." In Marsha Rowe, ed., *Spare Rib Reader*. New York: Penguin, 1982.

Benton, Sarah. "The Decline of the Party." In Stuart Hall and Martin Jacques, eds., *New Times: The Changing Face of Politics in the 1990s*. London: Lawrence and Wishart, 1991.

Berenson, Edward. *Populist Religion and Left-Wing Politics in France, 1830–1852*. Princeton: Princeton University Press, 1984.

Berezin, Mabel. *Making the Fascist Self: The Political Culture of Interwar Italy*. Ithaca, N.Y.: Cornell University Press, 1997.

Berg, Maxine. *The Age of Manufactures, 1700–1820*. 2nd ed. London: Blackwell, 1994.

Berger, Stefan, and David Broughton, eds. *The Force of Labour: The Western European Labour Movement and the Working Class in the Twentieth Century*. Oxford: Berg, 1995.

Berlanstein, Leonard R., ed. *Rethinking Labor History: Essays on Discourse and Class Analysis*. Urbana: University of Illinois Press, 1993.

Berlinguer, Enrico. *After Poland: Towards a New Internationalism*. Nottingham: Spokesman Books, 1982.

Bernard, Philippe, and Henri Dubief. *The Decline of the Third Republic 1914–1938*. Cambridge, England: Cambridge University Press, 1985.

Bernstein, Samuel. *Auguste Blanqui and the Art of Insurrection*. London: Lawrence and Wishart, 1971.

Berry, Ellen E., ed. *Post-Communism and the Body Politic*. New York: New York University Press, 1995.

Bess, Michael. *Realism, Utopia, and the Mushroom Cloud. Four Activist Intellectuals and Their Strategies for Peace, 1945–1989: Louise Weiss (France), Leo Szilard (USA), E. P. Thompson (England), Danilo Dolci (Italy)*. Chicago: University of Chicago Press, 1993.

Bessel, Richard. *Germany after the First World War*. Oxford: Oxford University Press, 1993.

Bey, Hakim. *TAZ: The Temporary Autonomous Zone, Ontological Anarchy, Poetic Terrorism*. Brooklyn: Autonomedia, 1991.

Beynon, Huw, Ray Hudson, and David Sadler, *A Tale of Two Industries: The Contraction of Coal and Steel in the North East of England*. Milton Keynes, England: Open University Press, 1991.

Bezucha, Robert J. *The Lyon Uprising of 1834: Social and Political Conflict in the Early July Monarchy*. Cambridge: Harvard University Press, 1974.

Bezza, Bruno. "Social Characteristics, Attitudes, and Patterns of Strike Behavior of the Metalworkers in Italy during the First World War." In Leopold Haimson and Charles Tilly, eds., *Strikes, Wars, and Revolutions in an International Perspective: Strike Waves in the Late Nineteenth and Early Twentieth Centuries*. Cambridge: Cambridge University Press, 1989.

Biagini, Eugenio F. *Liberty, Retrenchment and Reform: Popular Liberalism in the Age of Gladstone, 1860–1880*. Cambridge, England: Cambridge University Press, 1992.

Biagini, Eugenio F., and Alastair J. Reid, eds. *Currents of Radicalism: Popular Radicalism, Organized Labour and Party Politics in Britain 1850–1914*. Cambridge, England: Cambridge University Press, 1991.

Bird, Tessa, and Tim Jordan. "Sounding Out the New Social Movements and the Left: Interview with Stuart Hall, Doreen Massey, and Michael Rustin." In Tim Jordan and Adam Lent, eds., *Storming the Millennium: The New Politics of Change*. London: Lawrence and Wishart, 1999.

Black, Lawrence. " 'Still at the Penny-Farthing Stage in a Jet-Propelled Era': Branch Life in 1950s Socialism." *Labour History Review* 65 (2000): 202–26.

Blackburn, Robin, ed. *After the Fall: The Failure of Communism and the Future of Socialism*. London: Verso, 1991.

Blackburn, Sheila C. "Ideology and Social Policy: The Origins of the Trade Boards Act." *Historical Journal* 34 (1992): 43–64.

———. ' "No Necessary Connection with Homework': Gender and Sweated Labour, 1840–1909." *Social History* 22 (1997): 269–85.

Blackmer, Donald L. M., and Sidney Tarrow, eds. *Communism in Italy and France*. Princeton: Princeton University Press, 1975.

Bland, Lucy. "In the Name of Protection: The Policing of Women in the First World War," In Julia Brophy and Carol Smart, eds., *Women-in-Law: Explorations in Law, Family, and Sexuality*. London: Routledge, 1985.

Blänsdorf, Agnes. *Die Zweite Internationale und der Krieg. Die Diskussion über die internationale Zusammenarbeit der sozialistischen Parteien 1914–1917*. Stuttgart: Klett-Cotta, 1979.

Blinkhorn, Martin, ed. *Spain in Conflict 1931–1939: Democracy and Its Enemies*. London: Sage, 1986.

Blobaum, Robert E. *Feliks Dzierzynski and the SDKPiL: A Study in the Origins of Polish Communism*. New York: Columbia University Press, 1984.

———. *Rewolucja: Russian Poland, 1904–1907*. Ithaca: Cornell University Press, 1995.

Bloch, Ernst. *Erbschaft dieser Zeit*. Frankfurt: Suhrkamp, 1962.

Bloch, Ernst, Georg Lukács, Bertolt Brecht, Walter Benjamin, and Theodor Adorno. *Aesthetics and Politics*. London: Verso, 1977.

Blom, Ida. "A Double Responsibility: Women, Men, and Socialism in Norway," In Helmut Gruber and Pamela Graves, eds., *Women and Socialism/Socialism and Women: Europe between the Two World Wars*. New York: Berghahn, 1998.

———. "The Struggle for Women's Suffrage in Norway, 1885–1913." *Scandinavian Journal of History* 5 (1980): 3–22.

———. "Voluntary Motherhood 1900–1930: Theories and Politics of a Norwegian Feminist in an International Perspective," In Gisela Bock and Pat Thane, eds., *Maternity and Gender Policies: Women and the Rise of the European Welfare States 1880s-1950s*. London: Routledge, 1991.

Bloomfield, Jon. *Passive Revolution: Politics and the Czechoslovak Working Class, 1945–1948*. London: Lawrence and Wishart, 1979.

———, ed. *The Soviet Revolution: Perestroika and the Remaking of Socialism*. London: Lawrence and Wishart, 1989.

del Boca, Daniela. "Women in a Changing Workplace: The Case of Italy." In Jane Jensen, Elisabeth Hangen, and Ceallaigh Reddy, eds., *The Feminization of the Labor Force: Paradoxes and Promises*. London: Routledge, 1988.

Boch, Rudolf. *Handwerker-Sozialisten gegen Fabrikgesellschaft. Lokale Fachvereine, Massengewerkschaft und industrielle Rationalisierung in Solingen 1870 bis 1914*. Göttingen: Vandenhoeck und Ruprecht, 1985.

———. "Lokale Fachvereine im Bergischen Land—eine vergessene Phase in der Geschichte der Gewerkschaftsbewegung," In Kurt Düwell and Wolfgang Köllmann, eds., *Rheinland-Westfalen im Industriezeitalter. Vol. 2. Von der Reichsgründung bis zum Weimarer Republik*. Wuppertal, Germany: Hammer, 1983.

Bock, Gisela. "Antinatalism, Maternity and Paternity in National Socialist Racism." In Gisela Bock and Pat Thane, eds., *Maternity and Gender Policies: Women and the Rise of the European Welfare States 1880s-1950s*. London: Routledge, 1991.

Bock, Manfred. *Geschichte des "linken Radikalismus" in Deutschland. Ein Versuch*. Frankfurt am Main: Suhrkamp, 1976.

———. *Syndikalismus und Linkskommunismus 1918–1923*. Meisenheim am Glan,: Hain, 1969.

Bodek, Richard. *Proletarian Performance in Weimar Berlin: Agitprop, Chorus, and Brecht*. Columbia, S.C.: Camden House, 1997.

Boersner, D. *The Bolsheviks and the National and Colonial Question, 1917–1928*. Westport, Conn.: Hyperion Press, 1981.

Boggs, Carl. *Social Movements and Political Power: Emerging Forms of Radicalism in the West*. Philadelphia: Temple University Press, 1986.

Boggs, Carl, and David Plotke, eds. *The Politics of Eurocommunism: Socialism in Transition*. Boston: South End Press, 1980.

Bokovoy, Melissa. "Peasants and Partisans: A Dubious Alliance." In Norman M. Naimark and Leonid Gibianskii, eds., *The Establishment of Communist Regimes in Eastern Europe, 1944–1949*. Boulder, Colo.: Westview Press, 1997.

Boll, Friedhelm. *Frieden ohne Revolution? Friedensstrategien der deutschen Sozialdemokratie vom Erfurter Programm 1891 zur Revolution 1918*. Bonn: Dietz, 1980.

———. "International Strike Waves: A Critical Assessment." In Wolfgang J. Mommsen and Hans-Gerhard Husung, eds., *The Development of Trade Unionism in Great Britain and Germany, 1880–1914*. London: Allen and Unwin, 1985.

———. *Massenbewegungen in Niedersachsen, 1906–1920: Eine sozialgeschichtliche Untersuchung zu den unterschiedlichen Entwicklungstypen Braunschweig und Hannover*. Bonn: Dietz, 1981.

Bommes, Michael et al. "Structural Conditions, Historical Contexts and Social Effects of Post-1945 Migration to Germany." In Michael Bommes, Stephen Castles, and Catherine Wihtol de Wenden, eds., *Migration and Social Change in Australia, France and Germany, IMIS-Beiträge,* Heft 13. Osnabrück, Germany: University of Osnabrück, 1999.

Bonnell, Victoria. *Roots of Rebellion: Workers, Politics, and Organizations in St. Petersburg and Moscow 1900–1914.* Berkeley: University of California Press, 1983.

Bono, Paolo, and Sandra Kent, eds. *Italian Feminist Thought: A Reader.* Oxford: Blackwell, 1991.

Booth, Alan, and Melvyn Pack. *Employment, Capital and Economic Policy: Great Britain 1918–1939.* Oxford: Blackwell, 1985.

Borón, Atilio. "Latin America: Between Hobbes and Friedman." *New Left Review* 130 (November–December 1981): 45–66.

Borowsky, Peter. *Deutsche Ukrainepolitik 1918.* Lübeck, Germany: Matthiesen, 1970.

Boston Women's Health Book Collective. *Our Bodies, Ourselves.* New York: Simon and Schuster, 1970.

Boswell, Laird. *Rural Communism in France, 1920–1939.* Ithaca, N.Y.: Cornell University Press, 1998.

Bottomore, Tom. "Social Democracy." In Tom Bottomore, Lawrence Harris, Victor Kiernan, and Ralph Miliband, eds., *A Dictionary of Marxist Thought.* Oxford: Blackwell, 1983.

Boulton, Marjorie. *Zamenhof, Creator of Esperanto.* London: Routledge, 1960.

Bourges, Hervé, ed. *The Student Revolt: The Activists Speak.* London: Cape, 1968.

Bowd, Gavin. " 'C'est la lutte initiale': Steps in the Realignment of the French Left." *New Left Review* 206 (July–August 1994): 71–85.

Bowring, Finn. "LETS: An Eco-Socialist Initiative." *New Left Review* 232 (November–December 1998): 91–111.

Bowyer, Fran. "Dora Cox: Communist Campaigner for the Workers and Women of Wales." *Guardian* 2 February 2000.

Boxer, Marilyn. "When Radical and Socialist Feminism Were Joined: The Extraordinary Failure of Madeleine Pelletier." In Jane Slaughter and Robert Kern, eds., *European Women of the Left: Socialism, Feminism, and the Problems Faced by Political Women, 1880 to the Present.* Westport, Conn.: Greenwood Press, 1981.

Brand, Karl-Werner, Detlef Büsser, and Dieter Rucht. *Aufbruch in eine andere Gesellschaft: Neue soziale Bewegungen in der Bundesrepublik.* Frankfurt: Campus, 1983.

Branson, Noreen. *Poplarism.* London: Lawrence and Wishart, 1979.

Braunthal, Gerard. *Political Loyalty and Public Service in West Germany: The 1972 Decree against Radicals and Its Consequences.* Amherst: University of Massachusetts Press, 1990.

———. *The West German Social Democrats, 1969–1982: Profile of a Party in Power.* Boulder, Colo.: Westview Press, 1983.

Braunthal, Julius. *History of the International.* Vol. 1. London: Gollancz, 1966.

Braybon, Gail, and Penny Summerfield. *Out of the Cage: Women's Experiences in Two World Wars.* London: Pandora, 1987.

Breitman, Richard. *German Socialism and Weimar Democracy*. Chapel Hill: University of North Carolina Press, 1981.

Brett, Teddy, Steve Gilliatt, and Andrew Pople. "Planned Trade, Labour Party Policy, and US Intervention: The Successes and Failures of Postwar Reconstruction." *History Workshop Journal* 13 (spring 1982): 130–42.

Briggs, Asa. "The Language of 'Class' in Early Nineteenth-Century England," In Asa Briggs and John Saville, eds., *Essays in Labour History*. London: Macmillan, 1967.

———. "The Language of 'Mass' and 'Masses' in Nineteenth-Century England." In David E. Martin and David Rubinstein, eds., *Ideology and the Labour Movement*. London: Croom Helm, 1979.

Broberg, Gunnar, and Nills Roll-Hansen, eds. *Eugenics and the Welfare State: Sterilization Policy in Denmark, Sweden, Norway, and Finland*. East Lansing: Michigan State University Press, 1996.

Brome, Vincent. *The International Brigades. Spain 1936–39*. London, 1965.

Brooke, Stephen. *Labour's War: The Labour Party and the Second World War*. Oxford: Oxford University Press, 1992.

———. "Problems of 'Socialist Planning': Evan Durbin and the Labour Government of 1945." *Historical Journal* 34 (1991): 687–702.

Brose, Eric Dorn. *Christian Labor and the Politics of Frustration in Imperial Germany*. Washington, D.C.: Catholic University Press, 1985.

Brown, Bernard E. *Socialism of a Different Kind: Reshaping the Left in France*. Westport, Conn.: Greenwood Press 1982.

Brüggemeier, Franz Josef. *Leben vor Ort: Ruhrbergleute und Ruhrbergbau 1889–1919*. Munich: Beck, 1984.

Brüggemeier, Franz Josef, and Lutz Niethammer. "Lodgers, Schnapps-Casinos and Working-Class Colonies in a Heavy-Industrial Region." In Georg Iggers, ed., *The Social History of Politics. Critical Perspectives in West German Historical Writing since 1945*. New York: St. Martin's Press, 1985.

Bruley, Sue. *Leninism, Stalinism, and the Women's Movement in Britain, 1920–1939*. New York: Garland, 1986.

———. "Women against War and Fascism: Communism, Feminism, and the People's Front." In Jim Fyrth, ed., *Britain, Fascism, and the Popular Front*. London: Lawrence and Wishart, 1985.

———. "Women and Communism: A Case Study of the Lancashire Weavers in the Depression." In Geoff Andrews, Nina Fishman, and Kevin Morgan, eds., *Opening the Books: Essays on the Social and Cultural History of the British Communist Party*. London: Lawrence and Wishart, 1995.

Brunt, Rosalind. "The Politics of Identity." In Stuart Hall and Martin Jacques, eds., *New Times: The Changing Face of Politics in the 1990s*. London: Lawrence and Wishart, 1989.

Brus, Wlodzimierz. "Evolution of the Communist Economic System: Scope and Limits." In Victor Nee and David Stark, eds., *Remaking the Economic Institutions of Socialism: China and Eastern Europe*. Stanford: Stanford University Press, 1989.

Bruszt, László, and David Stark. "Remaking the Political Field in Hungary: From the Politics of Confrontation to the Politics of Competition," In Ivo Banac, ed., *Eastern Europe in Revolution*. Ithaca, N.Y.: Cornell University Press, 1992.

Bruzzone, Anna Maria. "Women in the Italian Resistance." In Paul Thompson, ed., *Our Common History. The Transformation of Europe*. London: Routledge, 1982.

Bryant, Christopher G. A., and Edmund Mokrzycki, eds. *The New Great Transformation? Change and Continuity in East-Central Europe*. London: Routledge, 1994.

Buchanan, Tom. "Britain's Popular Front? Aid Spain and the British Labour Movement." *History Workshop Movement* 31 (spring 1991): 60–72.

———. *The Spanish Civil War and the British Labour Movement*. Cambridge, England: Cambridge University Press, 1991.

Buchanan, Tom, and Martin Conway, eds. *Political Catholicism in Europe, 1918–1965*. Oxford: Clarendon Press, 1996.

Buchsbaum, Jonathan. *Cinema Engagé: Film in the Popular Front*. Urbana: University of Illinois Press, 1988.

Bufacchi, Vittorio, and Simon Burgess. *Italy since 1989: Events and Interpretations*. 2nd ed. New York: St. Martin's Press, 2001.

Bull, Ann Cento. "The Lombard Silk Spinners in the Nineteenth Century: An Industrial Workforce in a Rural Setting." *Italianist* 7 (1987): 99–121.

Burawoy, Michael, and János Lukács. *The Radiant Past: Ideology and Reality in Hungary's Road to Capitalism*. Chicago: University of Chicago Press, 1992.

Burawoy, Michael, and Katherine Verdery, eds. *Uncertain Transitions: Ethnographies of Change in the Postsocialist World*. Lanham, Md.: Rowman and Littlefield, 1999.

Burgess, Keith. "The Political Economy of British Engineering Workers during the First World War." In Leopold Haimson and Charles Tilly, eds., *Strikes, Wars, and Revolutions in an International Perspective: Strike Waves in the Late Nineteenth and Early Twentieth Centuries*. Cambridge: Cambridge University Press, 1989.

Burgess, Michael. "Political Catholicism, European Unity and the Rise of Christian Democracy." In Michael L. Smith and Peter M. R. Stirk, eds., *Making the New Europe. European Unity and the Second World War*. London: Longman, 1990.

Burns, Danny and Mark Simmons. *Poll Tax Rebellion*. AK Press: Edinburgh, 1992.

Burton, Antoinette. *Burdens of History: British Feminists, Indian Women, and Imperial Culture, 1865–1915*. Chapel Hill: University of North Carolina Press, 1994.

———. "The Feminist Quest for Identity: British Imperial Suffragism and 'Global Sisterhood,' 1900–1915." *Journal of Women's History* 3 (1991): 46–81.

Buschak, Willy. *Das Londoner Büro*. Amsterdam: International Institute of Social History, 1985.

Bush, Julia. *Behind the Lines: East London Labour 1914–1919*. London: Merlin, 1984.

Cabezali, Elena, Matilde Cuevas, and Maria Teresa Chicote. "Myth as Suppression: Motherhood and the Historical Consciousness of the Women of Madrid, 1936–39." In Raphael Samuel and Paul Thompson, eds., *The Myths We Live By*. London: Routledge, 1990.

Cahm, Caroline. *Kropotkin and the Rise of Revolutionary Anarchism, 1872–86*. Cambridge, England: Cambridge University Press, 1989.

Caldwell, Lesley. "Abortion in Italy." *Feminist Review* 7 (1981): 49–63.

———. "Church, State, and Family: The Women's Movement in Italy." In Annette Kuhn and AnnMarie Wolpe, eds., *Feminism and Materialism: Women and Modes of Production*. London: Routledge, 1978.

———. "Courses for Women: The Example of the 150 Hours Movement in Italy." *Feminist Review* 27 (1983): 71–83.

———. "Reproducers of the Nation: Women and the Family in Fascist Policy." In David Forgacs, ed., *Rethinking Italian Fascism*. London: Lawrence and Wishart, 1986.

Calhoun, Daniel C. *The United Front: The TUC and the Russians, 1923–1928*. Cambridge, England: Cambridge University Press, 1976.

Callaghan, John. *British Trotskyism: Theory and Practice*. Oxford: Blackwell, 1984.

———. *Rajani Palme Dutt: A Study in British Stalinism*. London: Lawrence and Wishart, 1993.

Camiller, Patrick. "Beyond 1992: The Left and Europe." *New Left Review* 175 (May–June 1989): 5–17.

———. "The Eclipse of Spanish Communism." *New Left Review* 147 (September–October 1984): 122–8.

———. "Spain: The Survival of Socialism?" In Perry Anderson and Patrick Camiller, eds., *Mapping the West European Left*. London: Verso, 1994.

Cammett, John M. *Antonio Gramsci and the Origins of Italian Communism*. Stanford: Stanford University Press, 1967.

Campbell, Beatrix. *Wigan Pier Revisited: Poverty and Politics in the Eighties*. London: Virago, 1984.

Cannadine, David. "R. A. Butler." In *The Pleasures of the Past*. London: Penguin, 1989.

Canning, Kathleen. "Feminist Theory after the Linguistic Turn: Historicizing Discourse and Experience." *Signs* 19 (1994): 368–404.

———. "Gender and the Politics of Class Formation: Rethinking German Labor History." In Geoff Eley, ed., *Society, Culture, and the State in Germany, 1870–1930*. Ann Arbor: University of Michigan Press, 1996.

———. *Languages of Labor and Gender: Female Factory Work in Germany, 1850–1914*. Ithaca: Cornell University Press, 1996.

Cant, Bob, and Susan Hemmings, ed. *Radical Records: Thirty Years of Lesbian and Gay History*. London: Routledge, 1988.

Cardoza, Anthony L. *Agrarian Elites and Italian Fascism: The Province of Bologna, 1901–1926*. Princeton: Princeton University Press, 1982.

Carlisle, Robert B. *The Proffered Crown: St. Simonianism and the Doctrine of Hope*. Baltimore: Johns Hopkins University Press, 1987.

Carlson, Andrew R. *Anarchism in Germany*. Vol. 1. *The Early Movement*. Metuchen, N.J.: Scarecrow Press, 1972.

Carol, Anne. *Histoire de l'eugenisme en France: Les médecins et la procréation, XIXe–XXe siècle*. Paris, 1995.

Carr, Edward Hallet. *The Bolshevik Revolution 1917–1923*. Vol. 1. Harmondsworth: Penguin, 1966.

———. *The Bolshevik Revolution 1917–1923*, Vol. 3. Harmondsworth: Penguin, 1966.

———. *The Comintern and the Spanish Civil War*. New York: Pantheon, 1984.

———. *Conditions of Peace.* London: Macmillan, 1942.

———. *Foundations of a Planned Economy 1926–1929.* Vol. 3, part 2. London: Penguin, 1976.

———. *Socialism in One Country, 1924–1926.* Vol. 3. Harmondsworth: Penguin, 1972.

———. *The Twilight of the Comintern, 1930–1935.* New York: Pantheon, 1982.

Carr, Raymond. *Spain 1808–1975.* 2nd ed. Oxford: Oxford University Press, 1982.

Carr, Raymond, and Juan Pablo Fusi Aizpurua. *Spain: Dictatorship to Democracy.* 2nd ed. London: Allen and Unwin, 1981.

Carrillo, Santiago, with Régis Debray and Max Gallo. *Dialogue on Spain.* London: Lawrence and Wishart, 1977.

Carroll, Rory. "Struggle Over for Italy's Radical Daily." *Guardian,* 17 July 2000.

Carsten, Francis L. *The Reichswehr and Politics 1918–1933.* Oxford: Oxford University Press, 1966.

———. *Revolution in Central Europe 1918–1919.* Berkeley: University of California Press, 1972.

———. *War against War: British and German Radical Movements in the First World War.* Berkeley: University of California Press, 1982.

Carter, April. *Peace Movements.* London: Longman, 1992.

Carter, Erica, *How German Is She? Postwar West German Reconstruction and the Consuming Woman.* Ann Arbor: University of Michigan Press, 1997.

Carter, Erica, and Simon Watney, eds. *Taking Liberties: AIDS and Cultural Politics.* London, 1989.

Carzel, John. *Citizen Ken.* London: Hogarth Press, 1984.

Castells, Manuel. *The Rise of the Network Society: The Information Age.* Vol. 1. Oxford: Blackwell, 1996.

Castillo, Santiago. "Spain," In Marcel van der Linden and Jürgen Rojahn, eds., *The Formation of Labour Movements 1870–1914: An International Perspective,* Vol. 1. Leiden: Brill, 1990.

Caute, David. "Cohn-Bendit: the Greening of the Red." In *1968: I Love You!!! Oh, Say It with Cobblestones!!!* Supplement to *New Statesman* (December 1987): xxviii–xxx.

———. *The Left in Europe since 1789.* London: Weidenfeld and Nicolson, 1966.

———. *The Year of the Barricades: A Journey through 1968.* New York: Harper and Row, 1988.

Cecil, Lamar. *Wilhem II: Emperor and Exile, 1900–1941.* Chapel Hill: University of North Carolina Press, 1996.

Cerny, Philip G., and Martin A. Schain, eds. *Socialism, the State and Public Policy in France.* New York: Oxford University Press, 1985.

Chambers, Suzanna. "Last Greenham Women Demand Memorial Garden." *Independent on Sunday,* 19 July 1998.

Chapman, Herrick. *State Capitalism and Working-Class Radicalism in the French Aircraft Industry.* Berkeley: University of California Press, 1991.

Charlton, Michael. *The Eagle and the Small Birds. Crisis in the Soviet Empire: From Yalta to Solidarity.* Chicago: University of Chicago Press, 1984.

Charney, Leo, and Vanessa R. Schwartz, eds. *Cinema and the Invention of Modern Life.* Berkeley: University of California Press, 1995.

Chick, Martin. *Industrial Policy in Britain 1945–1951: Economic Planning, Na-*

tionalization, and the Labour Governments. Cambridge, England: Cambridge University Press, 1998.

Chickering, Roger. *Imperial Germany and the Great War, 1914–1918.* Cambridge, England: Cambridge University Press, 1998.

Childs, David. "The Changing Face of Western Communism," In Childs, ed., *The Changing Face of Western Communism.* London: Croom Helm, 1980.

Christensen, Hilda Romer. "Socialist Feminists and Feminist Socialists in Denmark 1920–1940." In Helmut Gruber and Pamela Graves, eds., *Women and Socialism/Socialism and Women: Europe between the Two World Wars.* New York: Berghahn, 1998.

Christiansen, Niels Finn. "Denmark: End of an Idyll?" In Perry Anderson and Patrick Camiller, eds., *Mapping the West European Left.* London: Verso, 1994.

Christianson, Aileen. "Making Choices—Scotland and the Women's Movement," In Amanda Sebestyen, ed., *'68,'78,'88: From Women's Liberation to Feminism.* Bridport, England: Prism Press, 1988.

Christie, Stuart. "Goliardo Fiaschi: Anarchist Loyal to His Cause against Fascist Italy and Franco's Spain." *Guardian,* 15 August 2000.

Chun, Lin. *The British New Left.* Edinburgh: Edinburgh University Press, 1993.

Churchill, Winston. *The Second World War.* Vol. 6: *Triumph and Tragedy.* London: Education Book, 1953.

Cioc, Mark. *Pax Atomica: The Nuclear Defense Debate in West Germany during the Adenauer Era.* New York: Columbia University Press, 1988.

Claeys, Gregory. *Citizens and Saints: Politics and Anti-Politics in Early British Socialism.* New York: Oxford University Press, 1989.

Clark, Anna. "Gender, Class, and the Nation: Franchise Reform in England, 1832–1928." In James Vernon, ed., *Re-Reading the Constitution: New Narratives in the Political History of England's Long Nineteenth Century.* Cambridge, England: Cambridge University Press, 1996.

———. *The Struggle for the Breeches: Gender and the Making of the British Working Class.* Berkeley: University of California Press, 1995.

Clark, Jon. *Bruno Schönlank und die Arbeitersprechchorbewegung der Weimarer Republik.* Cologne: Prometh, 1984.

Clark, Jon, Margot Heineman, David Margolies, and Carole Snee, eds. *Culture and Crisis in Britain in the Thirties.* London: Lawrence and Wishart, 1979.

Clark, Katerina. *Petersburg: Crucible of Cultural Revolution.* Cambridge: Harvard University Press, 1995.

Clark, Martin. *Antonio Gramsci and the Revolution That Failed.* London: Yale University Press, 1977.

Clark, R. *The Basque Insurgents: ETA, 1952–1980.* Madison: University of Wisconsin, 1980.

Clarke, Alan. *The Rise and Fall of the Socialist Republic: A History of the South Yorkshire County Council.* Sheffield: Nichols, 1986.

Clarke, Michael. *The Politics of Pop Festivals.* London: Junction Books, 1982.

Clarke, Peter F. *Lancashire and the New Liberalism.* Cambridge, England: Cambridge University Press, 1971.

———. *Liberals and Social Democrats.* Cambridge, England: Cambridge University Press, 1978.

Claudin, Fernando. *Eurocommunism and Socialism.* London: Verso, 1978.

Cleminson, Richard. "Eugenics by Name or Nature? The Spanish Anarchist Sex Reform of the 1930s." *History of European Ideas* 18 (1994): 729–40.

Clissold, Stephen. *Djilas: The Progress of a Revolutionary*. New York: Universe Books, 1983.

Clogg, Richard. " 'Pearls from Swine': The Foreign Office Papers, SOE and the Greek Resistance." In Phyllis Auty and Richard Clogg, eds., *British Policy towards Wartime Resistance in Yugoslavia and Greece*. London: Macmillan, 1975.

Close, David H. *The Origins of the Greek Civil War*. London: Longman, 1995.

Coates, Ken. *The Most Dangerous Decade*. Nottingham: Spokesman, 1984.

Cockburn, Alexander, and Robin Blackburn, eds. *Student Power: Problems, Diagnosis, Action*. Harmondsworth: Penguin, 1969.

Coddington, Ann, and Mark Perryman, eds. *The Moderniser's Dilemma: Radical Politics in the Age of Blair*. London: Lawrence and Wishart, 1998.

Coffin, Judith. *The Politics of Women's Work: The Paris Garment Trades, 1750–1915*. Princeton: Princeton University Press, 1996.

Cohen, Gary B. *Education and Middle-Class Society in Imperial Austria 1848–1918*. West Lafayette, Ind.: Purdue University Press, 1996.

Cole, G. D. H., and A. W. Filson, eds. *British Working-Class Movements: Select Documents 1789–1875*. London: Allen and Unwin, 1951.

Collette, Christine. "Socialism and Scandal: The Sexual Politics of the Early Labour Movement." *History Workshop Journal* 23 (spring 1987): 102–11.

Collier, Peter. "Dreams of a Revolutionary Culture: Gramsci, Trotsky and Breton." In Edward Timms and Peter Collier, eds., *Visions and Blueprints: Avant-Garde Culture and Radical Politics in Early Twentieth-Century Europe*. Manchester: Manchester University Press, 1988.

Collin, Matthew, with contributions by John Godfrey. *Altered State: The Story of Ecstasy Culture and Acid House*. London: Serpent's Tail, 1997.

Collins, Henry, and Chimen Abramsky. *Karl Marx and the British Labour Movement: Years of the First International*. London: Macmillan, 1965.

Colton, Joel. *Léon Blum: Humanist in Politics*. 2nd ed. Durham, N.C.: Duke University Press, 1987.

Communist Party, The. *Manifesto for New Times: A Strategy for the 1990s*. London: Lawrence and Wishart, 1990.

Connolly, Kate. "Jiři Pelikan: A Reform Communist of Czechoslovakia's Prague Spring, He Fought on from Italy and Became a Socialist MEP." *Guardian*, 30 June 1999.

———. "Margarete Schütte-Lihotsky: Socialist Beliefs were Central to the Life of Austria's First Female Architect, from Designing Mass-production Kitchens to Defying the Nazis." *Guardian*, 31 January 2000.

Conze, Werner. "From 'Pöbel' to 'Proletariat.' The Socio-Historical Preconditions of Socialism in Germany." In Georg Iggers, ed., *The Social History of Politics: Critical Perspectives in West German Historical Writing since 1945*. New York: St. Martin's Press, 1985.

Cook, Chris, and John Paxton. *European Political Facts 1848–1918*. London: Macmillan, 1978.

Cook, Linda J., Mitchell A. Orenstein, and Marilyn Rueschemeyer, eds. *Left Parties and Social Policy in Post-Communist Europe*. Boulder, Colo.: Westview Press, 1999.

Cooke, Philip, ed. *Localities*. London: Hutchinson, 1989.
———. "Radical Regions? Space, Time and Gender Relations in Emilia, Provence, and South Wales." In Gareth Rees, Janet Bujra, Paul Littlewood, Howard Newby, and Teresa L. Rees, eds., *Political Action and Social Identity: Class, Locality, and Ideology*. London: Macmillan, 1985.
Cooper, Alice Holmes. *Paradoxes of Peace: German Peace Movements since 1945*. Ann Arbor: University of Michigan Press, 1996.
Cooper, Davida. "An Engaged State: Sexuality, Governance, and the Potential for Change." In Joseph Bristow and Angelia R. Wilson, eds., *Activating Theory: Lesbian, Gay, Bisexual Politics*. London: Lawrence and Wishart, 1993.
Cooper, David, ed. *The Dialectics of Liberation*. Harmondsworth: Penguin, 1968.
Coote, Anna, and Beatrix Campbell. *Sweet Freedom: The Struggle for Women's Liberation*. Oxford: Blackwell, 1987.
Copley, Anthony. *Sexual Moralities in France 1780–1980: New Ideas on the Family, Divorce, and Homosexuality*. London: Routledge, 1989.
Coquillat, Michelle. "The Achievements of the French Ministry of Women's Rights, 1981–1986." In Mary Buckley and Malcom Anderson, eds., *Women, Equality and Europe*. London: Macmillan, 1988.
Coriat, B., and P. Petit. "Deindustrialization and Tertiarization: Towards a New Economic Regime?" In Ash Amin and M. Dietrich, eds., *Towards a New Europe? Structural Change in the European Economy*. Aldershot, England: Elgar, 1991.
Cornell, Richard. *Revolutionary Vanguard: The Early Years of the Communist Youth International 1914–1924*. Toronto: University of Toronto Press, 1982.
Corner, Paul. *Fascism in Ferrara 1915–1925*. Oxford: Oxford University Press, 1975.
Corni, Gustavo. "Italy." In Bob Moore, ed., *Resistance in Western Europe*. Oxford: Berg, 2000.
Cottam, Kazimiera Janina. *Boleslaw Limanowski (1835–1935)*. New York: Columbia University Press, 1978.
Coutouvidis, John, and Jaime Reynolds. *Poland 1939–1947*. Leicester: Leicester University Press, 1986.
Crew, David F. "German Socialism, the State, Family Policy, 1918–1933." *Continuity and Change* 1 (1986): 235–63.
———. *Germans on Welfare: From Weimar to Hitler*. New York: Oxford University Press, 1998.
———. *Town in the Ruhr: A Social History of Bochum 1870–1914*. New York: Columbia University Press, 1979.
Crewe, Ivor. "The Disturbing Truth behind Labour's Rout." *Guardian,* 13 June, 1983.
———. "Labor Force Changes, Working-Class Decline, and the Labour Vote: Social and Electoral Trends in Postwar Britain." In Frances Fox Piven, ed., *Labor Parties in Postindustrial Societies*. Cambridge, England: Polity Press, 1991.
———. "The Labour Party and the Electorate." In Dennis Kavanagh, ed., *The Politics of the Labour Party*. London: Allen and Unwin, 1982.
Crick, Martin. *The History of the Social-Democratic Federation*. Keele England: Keele University Press, 1994.
Crick, Michael. *Scargill and the Miners*. 2nd ed. Harmondsworth: Penguin, 1985.

Crisell, Andrew. "Filth, Sedition and Blasphemy: The Rise and Fall of Television Satire." In John Corner, ed., *Popular Television in Britain: Studies in Cultural History*. London: British Film Institute, 1991.

Croall, Jonathan. *LETS Act Locally*. London: Calouste Gulbenkian Foundation, 1997.

Croft, Andy, ed. *A Weapon in the Struggle: The Cultural History of the Communist Party in Britain*. London: Lawrence and Wishart, 1998.

Cronin, James E. "Coping with Labour, 1918–1926." In James E. Cronin and Jonathan Schneer, eds., *Social Conflict and Political Order in Modern Britain*. New Brunswick, N.J.: Rutgers University Press, 1982.

———. *Industrial Conflict in Modern Britain*. London: Croom Helm, 1979.

———. "Labor Insurgency and Class Formation: Comparative Perspectives on the Crisis of 1917–1920 in Europe." In James E. Cronin and Carmen Sirianni, eds., *Work, Community, and Power: The Experience of Labor in Europe and America, 1900–1925*. Philadelphia: Temple University Press, 1983.

———. *Labour and Society in Britain 1918–1979*. London: Croom Helm, 1984.

———. "Strikes and the Struggle for Union Organization: Britain and Europe." In Wolfgang J. Mommsen and Hans-Gerhard Husung, eds., *The Development of Trade Unionism in Great Britain and Germany, 1880–1914*. London: Allen and Unwin, 1985.

———. *The World the Cold War Made: Order, Chaos, and the Return of History*. New York: Routledge, 1996.

Cronin, James E., and Peter Weiler. "Working-Class Interests and the Politics of Social Democratic Reform in Britain, 1900–1950." *International Labor and Working-Class History* 40 (fall 1991): 47–66.

Crosland, Anthony. *The Future of Socialism*. London: Cape, 1956.

Crossman, Richard H., ed. *The God That Failed*. Freeport, N.Y.: Books for Libraries Press, 1972.

Crouch, Colin. *The Politics of Industrial Relations*. London: Fontana, 1979.

Croucher, Richard. *Engineers at War 1939–1945*. London: Merlin, 1982.

Crowder, George. *Classical Anarchism: The Political Thought of Godwin, Proudhon, Bakunin, and Kropotkin*. Oxford: Oxford University Press, 1991.

Crump, Jeremy. "Recreation in Coventry between the Wars." In Bill Lancaster and Tony Mason, eds., *Life and Labour in a Twentieth Century City: The Experience of Coventry*. Coventry, England: Cryfield Press, 1986.

Cummins, Ian. *Marx, Engels and National Movements*. New York: St. Martin's Press, 1980.

Curran, James, ed. *The Future of the Left*. London: Polity, 1984.

Currie, Robert. *Industrial Politics*. Oxford: Oxford University Press, 1979.

Czarnowski, Gabriele. "Hereditary and Racial Welfare (*Erb—un Rassenpflege*): The Politics of Sexuality and Reproduction in Nazi Germany." *Social Politics: International Studies in Gender, State, and Society* 4 (1997): 114–35.

Dalla Costa, Maria Rosa. *The Power of Women and the Subversion of the Community*. Bristol, England: Falling Wall Press, 1972.

Dallas, Gloden, and Douglas Gill. *The Unknown Army: Mutinies in the British Army in World War I*. London: Verso, 1985.

Dalotel, Alain, and Jean-Claude Freiermuth. "Socialism and Revolution." In Adrian Rifkin and Roger Thomas, eds., *Voices of the People: The Politics and*

Life of "La Sociale" at the End of the Second Empire. London: Routledge, 1988.

Daniel, Ute. *Arbeiterfrauen in der Kriegsgesellschaft. Beruf, Familie und Politik im Ersten Weltkrieg.* Göttingen: Vandenhoeck und Ruprecht, 1989.

Daniels, Philip, and Martin J. Bull. "Voluntary Euthanasia: From the Italian Communist Party to the Democratic Party of the Left." In Martin J. Bull and Paul Heywood, eds., *West European Communist Parties after the Revolutions of 1989.* London: Macmillan, 1994.

Daniels, Robert V. *Year of the Heroic Guerrilla: World Revolution and Counter-revolution in 1968.* Cambridge: Harvard University Press, 1989.

David-Fox, Katherine. "Czech Feminists and Nationalism in the Late Habsburg Monarchy: 'The First in Austria.' " *Journal of Women's History* 3 (1991): 26–45.

Davidson, Alastair. *Antonio Gramsci: Towards an Intellectual Biography.* London: Merlin, 1977.

————. *The Theory and Practice of Italian Communism.* Vol. 1. London: Merlin, 1982.

Davies, Andrew. *Leisure, Gender and Poverty: Working-Class Culture in Salford and Manchester: Manchester University Press, 1900–1939.* Buckingham, England: Open University Press, 1992.

Davies, Andrew, and Steven Fielding, eds. *Workers' Worlds: Cultures and Communities in Manchester and Salford, 1880–1939.* Manchester: Manchester University Press, 1992.

Davies, Judy. "The Futures Market: Marinetti and the Fascists of Milan." In Edward Timms and Peter Collier, eds., *Visions and Blueprints: Avant-Garde Culture and Radical Politics in Early Twentieth-Century Europe.* Manchester: Manchester University Press, 1988.

Davies, Norman. *White Eagle, Red Star: The Polish-Soviet War, 1919–1920.* London: Orbis, 1972.

Davis, Belinda J. *Home Fires Burning: Food, Politics, and Everyday Life in World War I Berlin.* Chapel Hill: University of North Carolina Press, 2000.

Davis, John A. "Socialism and the Working Classes in Italy before 1914." In Dick Geary, ed., *Labour and Socialist Movements in Europe before 1914.* Oxford: Berg, 1989.

Dawidowicz, Lucy S. *The War Against the Jews 1933–1945.* New York: Holt, Rinehart, and Winston, 1975.

Dawisha, Karen. *Eastern Europe, Gorbachev and Reform: The Great Challenge.* 2nd ed. Cambridge, England: Cambridge University Press, 1990.

Dawisha, Karen, and Bruce Parrott, eds. *The Consolidation of Democracy in East-Central Europe.* New York: Cambridge University Press, 1997.

Dawson, Jane I. *Eco-Nationalism: Anti-Nuclear Activism and National Identity in Russia, Lithuania, and Ukraine.* Durham, N.C.: Duke University Press, 1996.

Déak, István, Jan T. Gross, and Tony Judt, eds. *The Politics of Retribution in Europe: World War II and Its Aftermath.* Princeton: Princeton University Press, 2000.

De Grand, Alexander J. *In Stalin's Shadow: Angelo Tasca and the Crisis of the Left in Italy and France, 1910–1945.* Dekalb: Northern Illinois University Press, 1986.

Deighton, Anne. *The Impossible Peace: Britain, the Division of Germany, and the Origins of the Cold War*. Oxford: Oxford University Press, 1990.

Delzell, Charles. *Mussolini's Enemies: The Italian Anti-Fascist Resistance*. Princeton: Princeton University Press, 1961.

Denver, David. *Scotland Decides: The Devolution Issue and the 1997 Referendum*. London: Frank Cass, 2000.

Derfler, Leslie. *Alexandre Millerand: The Socialist Years*. The Hague: Mouton, 1977.

———. *Paul Lafargue and the Founding of French Marxism, 1842–1882*. Cambridge: Harvard University Press, 1991.

Deutscher, Isaac. "Record of a Discussion with Heinrich Brandler." *New Left Review* 105 (September–October 1977): 47–55.

Deutscher, Tamara, et al., for Committee to Defend Czechoslovak Socialists, eds. *Voices of Czechoslovak Socialists*. London: Merlin, 1977.

Diedrich, Torsten. *Die 17. Juni 1953 in der DDR. Bewaffnete Gewalt gegen das Volk*. Berlin: Ch.Links, 1991.

Dikötter, Frank. "Race Culture: Recent Perspectives on the History of Eugenics." *American Historical Review* 103 (1998): 467–78.

Djilas, Milovan. *Wartime: With Tito and the Partisans*. London: Secker and Warburg, 1977.

Dobson, Sean. *Authority and Upheaval in Leipzig, 1910–1920: The Story of a Relationship*. New York: Columbia University Press, 2001.

Dodge, Peter. *Beyond Marxism: The Faith and Works of Hendrik de Man*. The Hague: Mouton, 1966.

———, ed. *A Documentary Study of Hendrik de Man, Socialist Critic of Marxism*. Princeton: Princeton University Press, 1979.

Domansky, Elisabeth. "The Rationalization of the Class Struggle: Strikes and Strike Strategy of the German Metalworkers' Union, 1891–1922." In Leopold Haimson and Charles Tilly, eds., *Strikes, Wars, and Revolutions in an International Perspective: Strike Waves in the Late Nineteenth and Early Twentieth Centuries*. Cambridge: Cambridge University Press, 1989.

Dominelli, Lena, and Gudrun Jonsdottir. "Feminist Political Organization in Iceland: Some Reflections on the Experience of *Kvenna Frambothid*." *Feminist Review* 30 (1988): 36–60.

Dominick III, Raymond H. *Wilhelm Liebknecht and the Founding of the German Social Democratic Party*. Chapel Hill: University of North Carolina Press, 1982.

Douthwaite, Richard. *Short Circuit: Strengthening Local Economies in an Unstable World*. Dublin Ireland: Lilliput Press, 1996.

Downs, Laura Lee. *Manufacturing Inequality: Gender Division in the French and British Metalworking Industries, 1914–1939*. Ithaca, N.Y.: Cornell University Press, 1995.

———. "Municipal Communism and the Politics of Childhood: Ivry-sur-Seine 1925–1960," *Past and Present* 166 (2000): 205–41.

Drachkovitch, Milorad M., and Branko Lazitch, eds. *The Comintern: Historical Highlights: Essays, Recollections, Documents*. New York: Praeger 1966.

Drake, Richard. *The Revolutionary Mystique and Terrorism in Contemporary Italy*. Bloomington: University of Indiana Press, 1989.

———. "Why the Moro Trials Have Not Settled the Moro Murder Case: A

Problem in Political and Intellectual History." *Journal of Modern History* 73 (2001): 259–78.

Dubiel, Helmut. *Theory and Politics: Studies in the Development of Critical Theory.* Cambridge: MIT Press, 1985.

Duchen, Claire. *Feminism in France: From May '68 to Mitterrand.* London: Routledge, 1986.

———. *Women's Rights and Women's Lives in France 1944–1968.* London: Routledge, 1994.

———, ed. *French Connections: Voices from the Women's Movement in France.* Amherst, Mass.: University Press of New England, 1987.

Duczynska, Ilona. *Workers in Arms: The Austrian Schutzbund and the Civil War of 1934.* New York: Monthly Review Press, 1978.

Duncan, David. *Mutiny in the RAF: The Air Force Strikes of 1946.* London: Socialist History Society, 1999.

Dunnage, Jonathan, ed. *After the War: Violence, Justice, Continuity and Renewal in Italian Society.* Hull: Troubador, 1999.

Dutschke, Rudi. *Mein Langer Marsch: Reden, Schriften und Tagebücher aus 20 Jahren.* Edited by Gretchen Dutschke-Klotz, Helmut Gollwitzer, and Jürgen Miermeister. Hamburg, 1980.

Dyson, Kenneth, ed. *European Détente: Case Studies of the Politics of East-West Relations.* London: Pinter 1986.

Ebbighausen, Rolf, and Friedrich Tiemann, eds. *Das Ende der Arbeiterbewegung in Deutschland? Ein Diskussionsband zum sechzigsten Geburtstag von Theo Pirker.* Opladen: Westdeutscher Verlag, 1984.

Echols, Alice. *Daring to Be Bad: Radical Feminism in America, 1968–1975.* Minneapolis: University of Minnesota Press, 1988.

Edinger, Lewis J. *German Exile Politics: The Social Democratic Executive Committee in the Nazi Era.* Berkeley: University of California Press, 1956.

Edmonds, Robin. *Soviet Foreign Policy: The Brezhnev Years.* Oxford: Oxford University Press, 1983.

Eglin, Josephine. "Women and Peace: From the Suffragists to the Greenham Women." In Richard Taylor and Nigel Young, eds., *Campaigns for Peace: British Peace Movements in the Twentieth Century.* Manchester: Manchester University Press, 1987.

Ehrenberg, John. *Proudhon and His Age.* Atlantic Highlands N.J.: Humanities Press, 1996.

Eichengreen, Barry, and T. J. Hatton. "Interwar Unemployment in International Perspective: An Overview." In Barry Eichengreen and T. J. Hatton, eds., *Interwar Unemployment in International Perspective.* Dordrecht Netherlands: Kluwer, 1988.

Eifert, Christiane. "Coming to Terms with the State: Maternalist Politics and the Development of the Welfare State in Weimar Germany." *Central European History* 30 (1997): 25–47.

———. *Frauenpolitik und Wohlfahrtspflege: Zur Geschichte der sozialdemokratischen "Arbeiterwohlfahrt."* Frankfurt am Main: Campus, 1993.

Einhorn, Barbara. *Cinderella Goes to Market: Citizenship, Gender and Women's Movements in East Central Europe.* London: Verso, 1993.

———. "Socialist Emancipation: The Women's Movement in the German Democratic Republic." In Sonia Kruks, Rayna Rapp, and Marilyn B. Young, eds.,

Promissory Notes. Women in the Transition to Socialism. New York: Monthly Review Press, 1989.

Eisenberg, Caroline. *Drawing the Line: The American Decision to Divide Germany.* New York:, 1996.

Eisenstein, Elizabeth. *The First Professional Revolutionary: Filippo Michele Buonarroti.* Cambridge: Harvard University Press, 1958.

Eisler, Jerzy. "March 1968 in Poland." In Carole Fink, Philipp Gassert, and Detlef Junker, eds., *1968: The World Transformed.* Cambridge, England: Cambridge University Press, 1988.

Ekiert, Grzegorz. *The State against Society: Political Crises and Their Aftermath in East Central Europe.* Princeton: Princeton University Press, 1996.

Ekiert, Grzegorz, and Jan Kubik. "Contentious Politics in New Democracies: East Germany, Hungary, Poland, and Slovakia, 1989–1993." *World Politics* 50 (1998): 547–81.

———. *Rebellious Civil Society: Popular Protest and Democratic Consolidation in Poland, 1989–1993.* Ann Arbor: University of Michigan Press, 1999.

Eksteins, Modris. *Rites of Spring. The Great War and the Birth of the Modern Age.* Boston: Houghton Mifflin, 1989.

Elam, Mark. "Puzzling Out the Post-Fordist Debate: Technology, Markets and Institutions," In Ash Amin, ed., *Post-Fordism: A Reader.* Oxford: Blackwell, 1994.

Elder, Neil, Alastair H. Thomas, and David Arter. *The Consensual Democracies? The Government and Politics of the Scandinavian States.* Oxford: Blackwell, 1982.

Eley, Geoff. "Cultural Socialism, The Public Sphere, and the Mass Form: Popular Culture and the Democratic Project, 1900 to 1934." In David E. Barclay and Eric D. Weitz, eds., *Between Reform and Revolution: German Socialism and Communism from 1840 to 1990.* New York: Berghahn, 1998.

———. "Remapping the Nation: War, Revolutionary Upheaval, and State Formation in Eastern Europe, 1914–1923." In Peter J. Potichnyj and Howard Aster, eds., *Ukrainian-Jewish Relations in Historical Perspective.* Edmonton: Canadian Institute of Ukrainian Studies, 1988.

———. "What Produces Fascism: Pre-Industrial Traditions or a Crisis of the Capitalist State?" In Geoff Eley, *From Unification to Nazism: Reinterpreting the German Past.* London: Unwin Hyman, 1986.

Eley, Geoff, and Keith Nield. "Farewell to the Working Class?" *International Labor and Working-Class History* 57 (Spring 2000): 1–30.

Elger, Tony. "Flexibility and the Intensification of Labour in UK Manufacturing in the 1980s." In Anna Pollert, ed., *Farewell to Flexibility.* Oxford University Press, 1991.

Eliasberg, Georg. *Der Ruhrkrieg von 1920.* Bonn: Dietz, 1974.

Elliott, Gregory. *Althusser: The Detour of Theory.* London: Verso, 1987.

———. *Labourism and the English Genius. The Strange Death of Labour England?* London: Verso, 1993.

Ellwood, David W. "Comparative Anti-Americanism in Western Europe." In Heide Fehrenbach and Uta G. Poiger, eds., *Transactions, Transgressions, Transformations: American Culture in Western Europe and Japan.* New York: Berghahn, 2000.

———. *Italy 1943–1945.* Leicester: Leicester University Press, 1985.

————. *Rebuilding Europe. Western Europe, America, and Postwar Reconstruction*. London: Longman, 1992.

————, ed. *The Marshall Plan Forty Years After: Lessons for the International System Today*. Bologna, 1989.

Engels, Friedrich. *The Condition of the Working Class in 1844,* In Karl Marx and Friedrich Engels, *On Britain*. Moscow: Progress, 1962.

Epstein, James. "Some Organizational and Cultural Aspects of the Chartist Movement in Nottingham." In James Epstein and Dorothy Thompson, eds., *The Chartist Experience: Studies in Working-Class Radicalism and Culture, 1830–1860*. London: Macmillan, 1982.

Ergas, Yasmine. "1968–1979—Feminism and the Italian Party System: Women's Politics in a Decade of Turmoil." *Comparative Politics* 14 (1982): 253–80.

Erger, Johannes. *Der Kapp-Lüttwitz Putsch: Ein Beitrag zur deutschen Innenpolitik, 1919/20*. Düsseldorf: Draste, 1967.

Erler, Gisela. "The German Paradox: Non-Feminization of the Labor Force and Post-Industrial Social Policies." In Jane Jensen, Elisabeth Hangen, and Ceallaigh Reddy, eds., *The Feminization of the Labor Force: Paradoxes and Promises*. London: Routledge, 1988.

Esenwein, George. *Anarchist Ideology and the Working-Class Movement in Spain, 1868–1898*. Berkeley: University of California Press, 1989.

Esping-Andersen, Gosta. *Politics against Markets: The Social Democratic Road to Power*. Princeton: Princeton University Press, 1985.

————. *Social Class, Social Democracy and State Policy: Party Policy and Party Decomposition in Denmark and Sweden*. Copenhagen: New Social Science Monographs 1980.

————. *The Three Worlds of Welfare Capitalism*. Cambridge England: Polity Press, 1990.

Esping-Andersen, Gosta, and Walter Korpi. "Social Policy as Class Politics in Post-War Capitalism: Scandinavia, Austria, and Germany." In John H. Goldthorpe, ed., *Order and Conflict in Contemporary Capitalism: Studies in the Political Economy of Western European Nations*. Oxford: Oxford University Press, 1984.

Evans, David Owen. *Social Romanticism in France, 1830–1848*. Oxford: Oxford University Press, 1951.

Evans, Richard J. "Politics and the Family: Social Democracy and the Working-Class Family in Theory and Practice before 1914." In Evans, ed., *The German Family: Essays on the Social History of the Family in Nineteenth and Twentieth-Century Germany*. London: Croom Helm, 1981.

————. *Sozialdemokratie und Frauenemanzipation im deutschen Kaiserreich*. Berlin: Dietz, 1979.

Evans, Sara. *Personal Politics: The Roots of Women's Liberation in the Civil Rights Movement and the New Left*. New York: Pantheon, 1979.

Ewing, Keith D., and C. A. Gearty. *Freedom under Thatcher: Civil Liberties in Modern Britain*. Oxford: Oxford University Press, 1990.

————. *The Struggle for Civil Liberties: Political Freedom and the Rule of Law in Britain, 1914–1945*. Oxford: Oxford University Press, 2000.

Farmer, Sarah. "The Communist Resistance in the Haute-Vienne." *French Historical Studies* 14 (1989): 89–116.

Faure, Alain. "The Public Meeting Movement in Paris from 1866 to 1870." In

Adrian Rifkin and Roger Thomas, eds., *Voices of the People: The Politics and Life of "La Sociale" at the End of the Second Empire*. London: Routledge, 1988.

Feinstein, Mike. *Sixteen Weeks with European Greens: Interviews, Impressions, Platforms, and Personalities*. San Pedro Ca.: Miles, 1992.

Feldman, Gerald D. *Army, Industry and Labor in Germany, 1914–1918*. New ed. Providence R.I.: Berg, 1992.

———. "German Business between War and Inflation: On the Origins of the Stinnes-Legien Agreement." In Gerhard A. Ritter, ed., *Enstehung und Wandel der modernen Gesellschaft: Festschrift für Hans Rosenberg zum 65. Geburtstag*. Berlin: De Gruyter, 1970.

———. "Socio-Economic Structures in the Industrial Sector and Revolutionary Potentialities, 1917–22," In Charles L. Bertrand, ed., *Revolutionary Situations in Europe, 1917–22: Germany, Italy, Austria-Hungary*. Montreal: Centre interuniversitaire d'études européennes, 1977.

———. "The Origins of the Stinnes-Legien Agreement: A Documentation." *Internationale wissenschaftliche Korrespondenz zur Geschichte der deutschen Arbeiterbewegung* 19–20 (1973): 45–103.

———. *The Great Disorder: Politics, Economics, and Society in the German Inflation 1914–1924*. Oxford: Oxford University Press, 1993.

Felkay, Andrew. *Hungary and the USSR, 1956–1988. Kadar's Political Leadership*. Westport, Conn.: Greenwood Press, 1989.

Fevre, Ralph, and Andrew Thompson, eds. *Nation, Identity and Social Theory: Perspectives from Wales*. Cardiff: University of Wales Press, 1999.

Fichter, Tilman. *SDS und SPD: Parteilichkeit jenseits der Partei*. Opladen Germany: Westdeutscher Verlag, 1988.

Field, Patrick. "The Anti-Roads Movement: The Struggle of Memory Against Foregetting." In Tim Jordan and Adam Lent, eds., *Storming the Millennium: The New Politics of Change*. London: Lawrence and Wishart, 1999.

Fielding, Steven. *Class and Ethnicity: Irish Catholics in England, 1880–1939*. Buckingham: Open University Press, 1993.

———. *Labour: Decline and Renewal*. Manchester: Manchester University Press, 1995.

Figes, Orlando. *Peasant Russia, Civil War: The Volga Countryside in Revolution, 1917–1921*. Oxford: Oxford University Press, 1989.

Filippelli, Ronald L. *American Labor and Postwar Italy, 1943–1953: A Study of Cold War Politics*. Stanford: Stanford University Press, 1989.

Fink, Carole, Philipp Gassert, and Detlef Junker, eds. *1968: The World Transformed*. Cambridge, England: Cambridge University Press, 1988.

Fink, Leon. "The Forward March of Labour Started? Building a Politicized Class Culture in West Ham, 1898–1900." In John Rule and Robert Malcomson, eds., *Protest and Survival: The Historical Experience. Essays for E. P. Thompson*. London: Merlin, 1993.

Finn, Margot. *After Chartism: Class and Nation in English Radical Politics*. Cambridge, England: Cambridge University Press, 1993.

Fischer, Ernst. *An Opposing Man: The Autobiography of a Romantic Revolutionary*. New York: Liveright, 1974.

Fischer, Fritz. *Germany's Aims in the First World War*. London: Chatto and Windus, 1967.

Fišera, Vladimir, ed. *Writing on the Wall. France, May 1968: A Documentary Anthology*. London: Allison and Busby, 1978.

Fishman, Nina. *The British Communist Party and the Trade Unions 1933–1945*. Aldershot, England: Elgar, 1995.

Fishman, Robert M. *Working-Class Organization and the Return to Democracy in Spain*. Ithaca, N.Y.: Cornell University Press, 1990.

Fishwick, Nicholas. *English Football and Society, 1910–1950*. Manchester: Manchester University Press, 1989.

Fitzpatrick, Sheila. *The Commissariat of Enlightenment: Soviet Organization of Education and the Arts under Lunacharsky, October 1917–1921*. Cambridge, England: Cambridge University Press, 1970.

———. *Everyday Stalinism*. New York: Oxford University Press, 1999.

Fitzpatrick, Tony. "New Welfare Associations: An Alternative Model of Well-Being." In Tim Jordan and Adam Lent, eds., *Storming the Millennium: The New Politics of Change*. London: Lawrence and Wishart, 1999.

Fletcher, Ian Christopher. " 'Prosecutions . . . Are Always Risky Business': Labor, Liberals, and the 1912 'Don't Shoot' Prosecutions." *Albion* 28 (1996): 251–78.

———. " 'A Star Chamber of the Twentieth Century': Suffragettes, Liberals, and the 1908 'Rush the Commons' Case." *Journal of British Studies* 35 (1996): 504–31.

Fletcher, Roger. *Revisionism and Empire: Imperialism in Germany 1897–1914*. London: Unwin Hyman, 1984.

Fogarty, Michael Patrick. *Christian Democracy in Western Europe, 1820–1953*. London:Routledge, 1957.

Foot, John M. "Analysis of a Defeat: Revolution and Worker-Peasant Alliances in Italy, 1919–20." *Labour History Review* 64 (1999): 159–78.

———. "The Family and the 'Economic Miracle': Social Transformation, Work, Leisure, and Development at Bovisa and Comasina (Milan), 1950–1970." *Contemporary European History* 4 (1995): 315–38.

———. "Mass Cultures, Popular Cultures and the Working Class in Milan, 1950–1970." *Social History,* 24 (1999): 134–57.

———. "Socialist-Catholic Alliances and Gender. Work, War, and Family in Milan and Lombardy, 1914–21." *Social History* 21 (1996): 37–53.

Forgacs, David. "Cultural Consumption, 1940s to 1990s." In David Forgacs and Robert Lumley, eds., *Italian Cultural Studies: An Introduction*. Oxford: Oxford University Press, 1996.

———. "Fascism, Violence and Modernity." In Jane Howlett and Rod Mengham, eds., *Violence and the Artistic Imagination in Europe, 1910–1939*. Manchester: Manchester University Press, 1994.

———, ed., *A Gramsci Reader*. London: Lawrence and Wishart, 1999.

Forgacs, David and Geoffrey Nowell-Smith, eds., *Antonio Gramsci: Selections from Cultural Writings*. London: Lawrence and Wishart, 1985.

Forster, Peter G. *The Esperanto Movement*. The Hague: Mouton, 1982.

Foster, John. "Working-Class Mobilization on the Clyde 1917–1920." In Chris Wrigley, ed., *Challenges of Labour: Central and Western Europe 1917–1920*. London: Routledge, 1993.

Foster, John, and Charles Woolfson. "Corporate Reconstruction and Business Unionism: The Lessons of Caterpillar and Ford." *New Left Review* 174 (March–April 1989): 51–66.

Fothergill, Stephen, and Jill Vincent. *The State of the Nation*. London: Penguin, 1985.

Fountain, Nigel. *Underground: The London Alternative Press 1966–74*. London: Comedia, 1988.

Fowkes, Ben. *Communism in Germany under the Weimar Republic*. London: Macmillan, 1984.

———. *The Post-Communist Era: Change and Continuity in Eastern Europe*. New York: St. Martin's Press, 1999.

———. *The Rise and Fall of Communism in Eastern Europe*. London: Macmillan, 1993.

———. "The Wartime National Fronts in Eastern Europe: Ideal and Reality." In Michael L. Smith and Peter M. R. Stirk, eds., *Making the New Europe. European Unity and the Second World War*. London: Pinter, 1990.

Fox, Alan. *History and Heritage: The Social Origins of the British Industrial Relations System*. London: Unwin Hyman, 1985.

Frader, Laura L., and Sonya O. Rose, eds. *Gender and Class in Modern Europe*. Ithaca, N.Y.: Cornell University Press, 1996.

Francis, Hywel. *Miners against Fascism. Wales and the Spanish Civil War*. London: Lawrence and Wishart, 1984.

———. "The Origins of the South Wales Miners' Library." *History Workshop* 2 (autumn 1976): 183–205.

———. " 'Say Nothing and Leave in the Middle of the Night.' The Spanish Civil War Revisited," *History Workshop Journal* 32 (autumn 1991): 69–76.

Francis, Martin. "Economics and Ethics: The Nature of Labour's Socialism, 1945–51." *Twentieth-Century British History* 6 (1995): 220–43.

———. *Ideas and Policies under Labour, 1945–1951*. Manchester: Manchester University Press, 1997.

———. "Labour and Gender." In Duncan Tanner, Pat Thane, and Nick Tiratsoo, eds., *Labour's First Century*. Cambridge, England: Cambridge University Press, 2000.

Frangeur, Renée. "Social Democrats and the Woman Question in Sweden: A History of Contradiction." In Helmut Gruber and Pamela Graves, eds., *Women and Socialism/Socialism and Women: Europe between the Two World Wars*. New York: Berghahn, 1998.

Franklin, Jane, ed. *The Politics of Risk Society*. Cambridge England: Polity Press, 1997.

Fraser, Ronald. *Blood of Spain. The Experience of Civil War, 1936–1939*. London: Penguin, 1979.

———. "The Popular Experience of War and Revolution, 1936–39." In Paul Preston, ed., *Revolution and War in Spain 1931–1939*. London: Methuen, 1984.

Fraser, Ronald, et al. *1968: A Student Generation in Revolt*. New York: Pantheon, 1988.

Frevert, Ute. *Women in German History. From Bourgeois Emancipation to Sexual Liberation*. Oxford: Berg, 1989.

Fricke, Dieter. *Handbuch zur Geschichte der deutschen Arbeiterbewegung 1869 bis 1917*. 2 vols. East Berlin: Dietz, 1987.

Fridenson, Patrick. "The Impact of the War on French Workers." In Richard

Wall and Jay M. Winter, eds., *The Upheaval of War: Family, Work and Welfare in Europe, 1914–1918*. Cambridge, England: Cambridge University Press, 1988.

Frith, Simon, and Howard Horne. *Art into Pop*. London: Routledge, 1987.

Fulbrook, Mary. *Anatomy of a Dictatorship: Inside the GDR 1949–1989*. Oxford: Oxford University Press, 1995.

Funk, Nanette, and Magda Mueller, eds. *Gender Politics and Post-Communism: Reflections from Eastern Europe and the Former Soviet Union*. New York: Routledge, 1993.

Furlough, Ellen. *Consumer Cooperation in France: The Politics of Consumption 1834–1930*. Ithaca, N.Y.: London: Cornell University Press, 1991.

Furlough, Ellen, and Carl Strikwerda, eds. *Consumers against Capitalism? Consumer Cooperation in Europe and North America, 1840–1990*. Lanham, Md.: Roman and Littlefield, 1998.

Fyrths, Jim. "The Aid Spain Movement in Britain, 1936–39." *History Workshop Journal* 35 (spring 1993): 152–64.

———, ed. *Labour's High Noon: The Government and the Economy 1945–51*. London: Lawrence and Wishart, 1993.

———, ed. *Labour's Promised Land? Culture and Society in Labour Britain 1945–51*. London: Lawrence and Wishart, 1995.

Gal, Susan, and Gail Kligman. *The Politics of Gender after Socialism*. Princeton: Princeton University Press, 2000.

———, eds. *Reproducing Gender: Politics, Publics, and Everyday Life after Socialism*. Princeton: Princeton University Press, 2000.

Galenson, Walter. *The Danish System of Labor Relations*. Cambridge: Harvard University Press, 1952.

Gallagher, Tom, and Allan M. Williams, eds. *Southern European Socialism: Parties, Elections and the Challenge of Government*. Manchester: Manchester University Press, 1989.

Gallili, Ziva. *The Menshevik Leaders in the Russian Revolution: Social Realities and Political Strategies*. Princeton: Princeton University Press, 1989.

Gamble, Andrew. *Britain in Decline: Economic Policy, Political Strategy and the British State*. 4th ed. London: Macmillan, 1994.

———. *The Free Economy and the Strong State: The Politics of Thatcherism*. 2nd ed. London: Macmillan, 1994.

Gamble, Andrew, and S. A. Walkland. *The British Party System and Economic Policy 1945–1983: Studies in Adversary Politics*. Oxford: Oxford University Press, 1984.

Gankin, Olga, and H. H. Fisher, eds. *The Bolsheviks and the World War. The Origin of the Third International*. Stanford: Stanford University Press, 1940.

Garnett, Ronald G. *Cooperation and the Owenite Socialist Communities in Britain 1825–1845*. Manchester: Manchester University Press, 1972.

Gati, Charles. "Gorbachev and Eastern Europe," *Foreign Affairs* 65 (1987): 958–75.

Gay, Peter. *The Dilemma of Democratic Socialism: Eduard Bernstein's Challenge to Marx*. New York: Columbia University Press, 1952.

Geary, Dick. *Karl Kautsky*. Manchester: Manchester University Press, 1987.

————. "Karl Kautsky and 'Scientific Marxism.' " *Radical Science Journal* 11 (1981): 130–5.

————. "Radicalism and the Worker: Metalworkers and Revolution 1914–23." In Richard J. Evans, ed., *Society and Politics in Wilhelmine Germany.* London: Croom Helm, 1978.

————. "Revolutionary Berlin 1917–1920." In in Chris Wrigley, ed., *Challenges of Labour: Central and Western Europe 1917–1920.* London: Routledge, 1993.

Geary, Roger. *Policing Industrial Disputes 1893 to 1985.* London: Methuen, 1985.

Gelman, Harry. *The Brezhnev Politburo and the Decline of Détente.* Ithaca, N.Y.: Cornell University Press, 1984.

Gerber, John. *Anton Pannekoek and the Socialism of Workers' Self-Emancipation, 1873–1960.* Dordrecht Netherlands: International Institute of Social History, 1989.

Gerry, Chris. "Small Enterprises, the Recession and the 'Disappearing Working Class.' " In Gareth Rees, Janet Bujra, Paul Littlewood, Howard Newby, and Teresa L. Rees, eds., *Political Action and Social Identity.* London: Macmillan, 1985.

Getty, J. Arch. *The Origins of the Great Purges: The Soviet Communist Party Reconsidered, 1933–1938.* Cambridge, England: Cambridge University Press, 1985.

Getty, J. Arch, and Roberta T. Manning, eds. *Stalinist Terror: New Perspectives.* Cambridge, England: Cambridge University Press, 1993.

Getty, J. Arch, Gabor T. Rittersporn, and Viktor N. Zemskov. "Victims of the Soviet Penal System in the Pre-War Years: A First Approach on the Basis of Archival Evidence." *American Historical Review* 19, 4 (October 1993): 1020–5.

Geyer, Martin H. *Verkehrte Welt. Revolution, Inflation und Moderne: München 1914–1924.* Göttingen: Vandenhoeck und Ruprecht, 1998.

Gibbon, Peter, and David Steyne, eds. *Thurcroft. A Village and the Miners' Strike: An Oral History.* Nottingham: Spokesman, 1986.

Gibianskii, Leonid. "The Soviet-Yugoslav Split and the Cominform." In Norman M. Naimark and Leonid Gibianskii, eds., *The Establishment of Communist Regimes in Eastern Europe, 1944–1949.* Boulder, Colo.: Westview Press, 1997.

Giddens, Anthony. *The Third Way and Its Critics.* Cambridge England: Polity Press, 2000.

————. *The Third Way: The Renewal of Social Democracy.* Cambridge England: Polity Press, 1998.

Giddens, Anthony, and Christopher Pierson. *Conversations with Anthony Giddens: Making Sense of Modernity.* Stanford: Stanford University Press, 1998.

Gidlund, Gullan. "From Popular Movement to Political Party: Development of the Social Democratic Labor Party Organization." In Klaus Misgeld, Karl Molin, and Klas Amark, eds., *Creating Social Democracy: A Century of the Social Democratic Labor Party in Sweden.* University Park: Penn State University Press, 1992.

Gilcher-Holtey, Ingrid. *"Die Phantasie der Macht": Mai 1968 in Frankreich.* Frankfurt: Suhrkamp, 1995.

———. "May 1968 in France: The Rise and Fall of a New Social Movement." In Carole Fink, Philipp Gassert, and Detlef Junker, eds., *1968: The World Transformed.* Cambridge, England: Cambridge University Press, 1988.

———, ed. *1968: Vom Ereignis zum Gegnstand der Geschichtswissenschaft.* Göttingen: Vandenhoeck und Ruprecht, 1998.

Gildea, Robert. *Barricades and Borders: Europe 1800–1914.* Oxford: Oxford University Press, 1987.

Gillespie, James. "Poplarism and Proletarianism: Unemployment and Labour Politics in London, 1918–34," In David Feldman and Gareth Stedman Jones, eds., *Metropolis—London. Histories and Representations since 1800.* London: Routledge, 1989.

Gillespie, Richard. "Spanish Socialism in the 1980s." In Tom Gallagher and Allan M. Williams, eds., *Southern European Socialism: Parties, Elections and the Challenge of Government.* Manchester: Manchester University Press, 1989.

———. *The Spanish Socialist Party: A History of Factionalism.* Oxford: Oxford University Press, 1989.

Ginsborg, Paul. *A History of Contemporary Italy: Society and Politics 1943–1988.* London: Penguin, 1990.

Gjelsvik, Tore. *Norwegian Resistance 1940–1945.* Montreal: McGill-Queen's University Press, 1979.

Glasman, Maurice. "The Great Deformation: Polanyi, Poland, and the Terrors of Planned Spontaneity." *New Left Review* 205 (May–June 1994): 59–86.

Gleason, Abbott, Peter Kenez, and Richard Stites, eds. *Bolshevik Culture: Experiment and Order in the Russian Revolution.* Bloomington: University of Indiana Press, 1985.

Gleason, William. "The All-Russian Union of Zemstvos and World War I." In Terrence Emmons and Wayne S. Vucinich, eds., *The Zemstvo in Russia: An Experiment in Local Self-Government.* Cambridge, England: Cambridge University Press, 1982.

Gloversmith, Frank, ed. *Class, Culture and Social Change: A New View of the 1930s.* Brighton England: Harvester, 1980.

Gobetti, Piero. *On Liberal Revolution.* Edited by Nadia Urbinati. New Haven: Yale University Press, 2000.

Godfrey, John. *Capitalism at War: Industrial Policy and Bureaucracy in France, 1914–1918.* Leamington Spa, England: Berg, 1989.

Golan, Galia. *Reform Rule in Czechoslovakia: The Dubcek Era, 1968–1969.* New York: Cambridge University Press, 1973.

Goldberg, Harvey. *The Life of Jean Jaurès.* Madison: University of Wisconsin Press, 1964.

Golden, Miriam. *Labor Divided: Austerity and Working-Class Politics in Contemporary Italy.* Ithaca, N.Y. Cornell University Press, 1988.

Goldman, Wendy Z. "Women, the Family, and the New Revolutionary Order in the Soviet Union." In Sonia Kruks, Rayna Rapp, and Marilyn B. Young, eds., *Promissory Notes: Women in the Transition to Socialism.* New York: Monthly Review Press, 1989.

————. *Women, the State and Revolution: Soviet Family Policy and Social Life, 1917–1936.* Cambridge, England: Cambridge University Press, 1993.

Goldstücker, Eduard. "Kafka Returns to Prague." In G. R. Urban, ed., *Communist Reformation: Nationalism, Internationalism and Change in the World Communist Movement.* London: Temple Smith, 1979.

Goldthorpe, John H., and David Lockwood. *The Affluent Worker.* 3 vols. Cambridge, England: Cambridge University Press, 1968–69.

Goode, Patrick. *Karl Korsch: A Study in Western Marxism.* London: Macmillan, 1979.

Goodwin, Mark, and Simon Duncan. "The Crisis of Local Government: Uneven Development and the Thatcher Administration," In John Mohan, ed., *The Political Geography of Contemporary Britain.* London: Macmillan, 1989.

Gordon, Eleanor. *Women and the Labour Movement in Scotland, 1850–1914.* Oxford: Oxford University Press, 1991.

Gordon, Felicia. *The Integral Feminist: Madeleine Pelletier, 1874–1939.* Minneapolis: University of Minnesota Press, 1990.

Gorman, John. *Banner Bright.* London: Lane, 1973.

Gorz, André. *Farewell to the Working Class.* London: Pluto Press, 1982.

Gotthardt, Christian. *Industrialisierung, bürgerliche Politik und proletarische Autonomie. Voraussetzungen und Varianten sozialistischer Klassenorganisationen in Nordwestdeutschland 1863 bis 1875.* Bonn: Dietz, 1992.

Gowan, Peter. "Neo-Liberal Economic Theory and Practice for Eastern Europe." *New Left Review* 213 (September-October 1995): 3–60.

————. "Passages of the Russian and Eastern European Left." In Leo Panitch and Colin Leys, eds., *Socialist Register 1998.* London: Merlin, 1998.

————. "The Post-Communist Socialists in Eastern and Central Europe," In Donald Sassoon, ed., *Looking Left: Socialism in Europe after the Cold War.* New York: New Press, 1997.

Gowan, Peter, and Perry Anderson, eds., *The Question of Europe.* London: Verso, 1997.

Graham, Bruce D. *Choice and Democratic Order: The French Socialist Party, 1937–1950.* Cambridge, England: Cambridge University Press, 1994.

————. *The French Socialists and Tripartisme 1944–1947.* Toronto: University of Toronto Press, 1965.

Graham, Helen, and Paul Preston, eds. *The Popular Front in Europe.* New York: St. Martin's Press, 1987.

Graham, Helen. *Socialism and War: The Spanish Socialist Party in Power and Crisis, 1936–1939.* Cambridge, England: Cambridge University Press, 1991.

————. "Spain 1936: Resistance and Revolution: The Flaws in the Front." In Tim Kirk and Anthony McElligott, eds., *Opposing Fascism: Community, Authority and Resistance in Europe.* Cambridge, England: Cambridge University Press, 1999.

————. "The Spanish Popular Front and the Civil War." In Graham and Preston, eds., *Popular Front in Europe.* New York: St. Martin's Press, 1987.

Grahl, John, and Paul Teague. "The Cost of Neo-Liberal Europe." *New Left Review* 174 (March–April 1989): 33–50.

Gramsci, Antonio. "Americanism and Fordism." In *Selections from the Prison Notebooks,* edited by Quintin Hoare and Geoffrey Nowell Smith. London: Lawrence and Wishart, 1971.

————. *Selections from Political Writings 1910–1920*. London: Lawrence and Wishart, 1977.

————. *The Modern Prince, and Other Writings*. New York: International Publishers, 1957.

————. *Selections from the Prison Notebooks,* edited by Quintin Hoare and Geoffrey Nowell-Smith. London: Lawrence and Wishart, 1971.

Graves, Pamela. "An Experiment in Women-Centered Socialism: Labour Women in Britain," In Helmut Gruber and Pamela Graves, eds., *Women and Socialism, Socialism and Women: Europe between the Two World Wars.* New York: Berghahn, 1998.

————. *Labour Women: Women in British Working-Class Politics, 1918–1939.* New York: Cambridge University Press, 1993.

Gray, John. "After Social Democracy." In Geoff Mulgan, ed., *Life after Politics: New Thinking for the Twenty-First Century.* London: Fontana, 1997.

Grazia, Victoria de. *The Culture of Consent: Mass Organization of Leisure in Fascist Italy.* Cambridge, England: Cambridge University Press, 1981.

————. *How Fascism Ruled Women: Italy, 1922–1945.* Berkeley: University of California Press, 1992.

Green, Jonathan. *Days in the Life: Voices from the English Underground, 1961–1971.* London: Heineman Minerva, 1988.

Green, Peter. "The Third Round in Poland." *New Left Review* 101–2 (February–April 1977): 69–108.

Griffith, Gwilym O. *Mazzini: Prophet of Modern Europe.* New York: Fertig, 1970.

Griffiths, Dylan. *Thatcherism and Territorial Politics: A Welsh Case Study.* Aldershot, England: Elgar, 1996.

Grimnes, Ole Kristian. "The Beginnings of the Resistance Movement." In Henrik S. Nissen, ed., *Scandinavia during the Second World War.* Minneapolis: University of Minnesota Press, 1983.

Grossman, Atina. "Gender and Rationalization: Questions about the German/American Comparison." *Social Politics: International Studies in Gender, State, and Society* 4 (1997): 6–18.

————. "German Communism and New Women: Dilemmas and Contradictions." In Helmut Gruber and Pamela Graves, eds., *Women and Socialism/Socialism and Women: Europe between the Two World Wars.* New York: Berghahn, 1998.

————. "The New Woman and the Rationalization of Sexuality in Weimar Germany," In Ann Snitow, Christine Stansell, and Sharon Thompson, eds., *Powers of Desire: The Politics of Sexuality.* New York: Monthly Review Press, 1983.

————. *Reforming Sex: The German Movement for Birth Control and Abortion Reform, 1920–1950.* New York: Oxford University Press, 1995.

————. " 'Satisfaction Is Domestic Happiness': Mass Working-Class Sex Reform Organizations in the Weimar Republic." In Michael N. Dobkowski and Isidor Wallimann, eds., *Towards the Holocaust. The Social and Economic Collapse of the Weimar Republic.* Westport, Conn.: Greenwood Press, 1983.

Gruber, Helmut. "French Women in the Crossfire of Class, Sex, Maternity, and Citizenship." In Helmut Gruber and Pamela Graves, eds., *Women and Socialism/Socialism and Women: Europe between the Two World Wars.* New York: Berghahn, 1998.

————. "History of the Austrian Working Class: Unity of Scholarship and Practice." *International Labor and Working Class History* 24 (fall 1983): 43–60.

————. *Léon Blum, French Socialism, and the Popular Front: A Case if Internal Contradictions.* Ithaca, N.Y.: Cornell University Press, 1986.

————. *Red Vienna: Experiment in Working-Class Culture, 1919–1934.* New York: Oxford University Press, 1991.

————, ed. *International Communism in the Era of Lenin: A Documentary History.* Garden City, N.Y.: Doubleday, 1972.

————. *Soviet Russia Masters the Comintern.* New York: Anchor Press, 1974.

Grünen, Die. *Think Globally—Act Locally!* Statement for the European Elections of 17 June 1984. Bonn: Die Grünen, 1984.

Gubbels, Robert. "The Female Labor Force in Western Europe." In Lynn B. Iglitzin and Ruth Ross, eds., *Women in the World: A Comparative Study.* Santa Barbara, Calif.: Clio Books 1976.

Gullickson, Gay L. *Spinners and Weavers of Auffay: Rural Industry and the Sexual Division of Labor in a French Village, 1750–1850.* New York: Columbia University Press, 1986.

Gundle, Stephen. *Between Hollywood and Moscow: The Italian Communists and the Challenge of Mass Culture, 1943–1991.* Durham, N.C.: Duke University Press, 2000.

————. "The Italian Communist Party: Gorbachev and the End of 'Really Existing Socialism.' " In David S. Bell, ed., *Western European Communists and the Collapse of Communism.* Oxford: Berg, 1993.

Gupta, Partha Sarathi. *Imperialism and the British Labour Movement 1914–1964.* London: Macmillan, 1975.

Guratzsch, Dankwart. *Macht durch Organisation: Die Grundlegung des Hugenbergschen Presseimperiums.* Düsseldorf: Bertelsmann, 1974.

Guttsman, W. L. *The German Social Democratic Party 1875–1933. From Ghetto to Government.* London: Allen and Unwin, 1981.

Gyford, John. *The Politics of Local Socialism.* London: Unwin Hyman, 1985.

Haavio-Mannila, Elinia, ed. *Unfinished Democracy: Women in Nordic Politics.* Oxford: Pergamon Press, 1985.

Haestrup, Jorgen. *Secret Alliance: A Study of the Danish Resistance Movement 1940–1945.* 3 vols. Odense Denmark: Odense University Press, 1976–77.

————. *Europe Ablaze: An Analysis of the History of the European Resistance Movement.* Odense Denmark : Odense University Press, 1979.

Hagemann, Karen. "Rationalizing Family Work: Municipal Family Welfare and Urban Working Class Mothers in Germany," *Social Politics: International Studies in Gender, State, and Society* 4 (1997): 19–48.

Hager, Carol J. *Technological Democracy: Bureaucracy and Citizenry in the German Energy Debate.* Ann Arbor: University of Michigan Press, 1995.

Hahn, W. G. *Democracy in a Communist Party: Poland's Experience since 1980.* New York: Columbia University Press, 1987.

Haimson, Leopold. "The Problem of Social Stability in Urban Russia, 1905–1917." *Slavic Review* 23 (1964): 619–42 and 24 (1965): 1–22.

Hajdu, Tibor. *The Hungarian Soviet Republic.* Stanford, Calif.: Hoover Institution Press, 1970.

————. "Socialist Revolution in Central Europe, 1917–21." In Roy Porter and

Mikulas Teich, eds., *Revolution in History*. Cambridge, England: Cambridge University Press, 1986.

Hakim, Catherine. "Explaining Trends in Occupational Segregation: The Measurement, Causes, and Consequences of the Sexual Division of Labour." *European Sociological Review* 8 (1992): 127–52.

———. "The Myth of Rising Female Employment," *Work, Employment and Society* 7 (1993): 97–120.

Hall, Lesley A. "Impotent Ghosts from No Man's Land, Flapper's Boyfriends, or Cryptopatriarchs? Men, Sex and Social Change in 1920s Britain," *Social History* 21 (1996): 55–70.

Hall, Peter. *Governing the Economy: The Politics of State Intervention in Britain and France*. New York: Oxford University Press, 1986.

Hall, Stuart. "Blue Election, Election Blues." In Hall, *The Hard Road to Renewal: Thatcherism and the Crisis of the Left*. London: Verso, 1988.

———. "The Crisis of Labourism." In *The Hard Road to Renewal: Thatcherism and the Crisis of the Left*. London: Verso, 1988.

———. "Ethnicity: Identity and Difference." In Geoff Eley and Ronald Grigor Suny, eds., *Becoming National: A Reader*. New York: Oxford University Press, 1996.

———. "The 'First' New Left: Life and Times," In Robin Archer et al., eds., *Out of Apathy: Voices of the New Left Thirty Years On*. London: Verso, 1989.

———. *The Hard Road to Renewal: Thatcherism and the Crisis of the Left*. London: Verso, 1988.

———. "The Meaning of New Times." In Stuart Hall and Martin Jacques, eds., *New Times: The Changing Face of Politics in the 1990s*. London: Lawrence and Wishart, 1991.

———. "Old and New Identities, Old and New Ethnicities." In Anthony D. King, ed., *Culture, Globalization, and the World-System: Contemporary Conditions for the Representation of Identity*. Minnesota: University of Minnesota Press, 1997.

———. "The 'Political' and the 'Economic' in Marx's Theory of Classes," In Alan Hunt, ed., *Class and Class Structure*. London: Lawrence and Wishart, 1977.

———. "The Rise of the Representative/Interventionist State 1880s-1920s," In Gregor McLennan, David Held, and Stuart Hall, eds., *State and Society in Contemporary Britain. A Critical Introduction*. London: Polity, 1984.

———. "Then and Now: A Reevaluation of the New Left." In Robin Archer et al., eds., *Out of Apathy. Voices of the New Left Thirty Years On*. London: Verso, 1989.

Hall, Stuart, and Martin Jacques, eds. *New Times: The Changing Face of Politics in the 1990s*. London: Lawrence and Wishart, 1991.

Hall, Stuart, and Bill Schwarz. "State and Society, 1880–1930." In Mary Langan and Bill Schwarz, eds., *Crises in the British State 1880–1930*. London: Hutchinson, 1985.

Hall, Stuart, and Paddy Whannel. *The Popular Arts*. London: Pantheon, 1964.

Halliday, Fred. *From Kabul to Managua: Soviet-American Relations in the 1980s*. New York: Monthly Review Press, 1989.

———. *The Making of the Second Cold War*. 2nd ed. London: Verso, 1986.

Halloran, James D., Philip Elliott, and Graham Murdock. *Demonstrations and Communication: A Case Study*. Harmondsworth: Penguin, 1970.

Hamrin, Harald. *Between Bolshevism and Revisionism: The Italian Communist Party, 1944–1947*. Stockholm: Esselte studium, 1975.

Hanagan, Michael. *The Logic of Solidarity: Artisans and Industrial Workers in Three French Towns*. Urbana: University of Illinois Press, 1980.

Hanisch, Ernst. "Neuere Studien zur Marxismus-Rezeption in der deutschen und österreichischen Arbeiterbewegung." In Klaus Tenfelde, ed., *Arbeiter und Arbeitebewegung im Vergleich: Berichte zur internationalen historischen Forschung*. Munich: Oldenbourg, 1986.

Hanley, D. L., ed. *Christian Democracy in Europe*. London: St. Martin's Press, 1996.

Hanrieder, Wolfram F. *Germany, America, Europe: Forty Years of German Foreign Policy*. New Haven: Yale University Press, 1989.

Hansen, Erik. "Between Reform and Revolution: Social Democracy and Dutch Society, 1917–1921." In Hans A. Schmitt, ed., *Neutral Europe between War and Revolution 1917–1923*. Charlottesville: University of Virginia Press, 1988.

Haraszti, Miklós. *A Worker in a Worker's State*. New York: Universe Books, 1978.

Harding, Neil. *Leninism*. London: Macmillan, 1996.

———. *Lenin's Political Thought: Theory and Practice in the Democratic and Socialist Revolutions*. London: Macmillan, 1983.

———, ed. *The State in Socialist Society*. London: Macmillan, 1984.

Hardy, Dennis, and Lorna Davidson, eds. *Utopian Thought and Communal Experience*. Enfield, England: Middlesex Polytechnic, School of Geography and Planning, 1989.

Harford, Barbara, and Sarah Hopkins, eds. *Greenham Common: Women at the Wire*. London: Women's Press, 1984.

Harper, John Lamberton. *America and the Reconstruction of Italy, 1945–1948*. Cambridge, England: Cambridge University Press, 1986.

Harris, Jose. "Enterprise and Welfare States: A Comparative Perspective." *Transactions of the Royal Historical Society*, fifth series, 40 (1990): 175–96.

———. "Labour's Political and Social Thought," In Duncan Tanner, Pat Thane, and Nick Tiratsoo, eds., *Labour's First Century*. Cambridge, England: Cambridge University Press, 2000.

———. *William Beveridge: A Biography*. Oxford: Oxford University Press, 1977.

Harris, Laurence. "State and Economy in the Second World War." In Gregor McLennan, David Held, and Stuart Hall, eds., *State and Society in Contemporary Britain. A Critical Introduction*. London: Polity, 1984.

Harrison, Brian. *Prudent Revolutionaries: Portraits of British Feminists between the Wars*. Oxford: Oxford University Press, 1987.

Harrison, John F. C. *Robert Owen and the Owenites in Britain and America: The Quest for the New Moral World*. London: Routledge, 1969.

Harrison, Royden. "The War Emergency Workers' National Committee, 1914–1920." In Asa Briggs and John Saville, eds. *Essays in Labour History, 1886–1923*. London: Croom Helm, 1971.

Harsch, Donna. "Codes of Comradeship: Class, Leadership, and Tradition in Munich Social Democracy." *Central European History* 31 (1998): 385–412.

———. *German Social Democracy and the Rise of Nazism*. Chapel Hill: University of North Carolina Press, 1993.

Harvey, David. *The Condition of Postmodernity*. Oxford: Blackwell, 1989.

Hasegawa, Tsuyoshi. *The February Revolution: Petrograd 1917*. Seattle: University of Washington Press, 1981.

Haslam, Jonathan. "The Comintern and the Origins of the Popular Front." *Historical Journal* 22 (1979): 673–91.

———. *The Soviet Union and the Politics of Nuclear Weapons in Europe 1969–1987*. Basingstoke, England: Macmillan, 1989.

———. *The Soviet Union and the Struggle for Collective Security in Europe, 1933–1939*. London: Macmillan, 1984.

———. *The Vices of Integrity: E. H. Carr, 1892–1982*. London: Verso, 1999.

Hatry, Gilbert. "Shop Stewards at Renault." In Patrick Fridenson, ed., *The French Home Front*. Providence: Berg, 1992.

Haupt, Georges. *Aspects of International Socialism 1871–1914*. Cambridge, England: Cambridge University Press, 1986.

———. "Lenin, the Bolsheviks, and the Second International." In *Aspects of International Socialism 1871–1914*. Cambridge, England: Cambridge University Press, 1986.

———. "Marx and Marxism." In Hobsbawm, ed., *History of Marxism*. vol. 1. *Marxism in Marx's Day*. Bloomington: Indiana University Press, 1982.

———. "Model Party: The Role and Influence of German Social Democracy in South-East Europe." In *Aspects of International Socialism 1871–1914*. Cambridge, England: Cambridge University Press, 1986.

———. *Socialism and the Great War: The Collapse of the Second International*. Oxford: Oxford University Press, 1972.

Haupt, Georges, and Madeleine Rebérioux, eds., *La deuxiéme Internationale et l'Orient*. Paris: Mouton, 1967.

Hautmann, Hans, and Rudolf Kropf. *Die österreichische Arbeiterbewegung vom Vormärz bis 1945. Sozialökonomische Ursprünge ihrer Ideologie und Politik*. Vienna: Europaverlag, 1978.

Havel, Václav. *Living in Truth*. London: Faber, 1986.

Healey, Emma and Angela Mason, eds. *Stonewall 25: The Making of the Lesbian and Gay Community in Britain*. London: Virago Press, 1994.

Heimann, Horst, and Thomas Meyer, eds. *Reformsozialismus und Sozialdemokratie: Zur Theoriediskussion des Demokratischen Sozialismus in der Weimarer Republik*. Bonn: Dietz, 1982.

Heineman, Elizabeth. "Complete Families, Half Families, No Families at All: Female-Headed Households and the Reconstruction of the Family in the Early Federal Republic." *Central European History* 29 (1996): 29–60.

Heineman, Margot. "*Left Review, New Writing* and the Broad Alliance against Fascism," In Edward Timms and Peter Collier, eds., *Visions and Blueprints: Avant-Grade Culture and Radical Politics in Early Twentieth-Century Europe*. Manchester: Manchester University Press, 1988.

———. "The People's Front and the Intellectuals." In Jim Fyrth, ed., *Britain, Fascism and the Popular Front*. London: Lawrence and Wishart, 1985.

Heinen, Jacqueline. "Kollontai and the History of Women's Oppression." *New Left Review* 110 (July–August 1978): 43–63.

Held, David. *Democracy and Global Order*. Cambridge England: Polity Press, 1995.

Held, David, Anthony McGrew, David Goldblatt, and Jonathan Perraton, *Global Transformations: Politics, Economics and Culture.* Cambridge England: Polity Press, 1999.

Held, Joseph. "Culture in Hungary during World War I." In Aviel Roshwald and Richard Stites, eds., *European Culture in the Great War: The Arts, Entertainment, and Propaganda, 1914–1918.* Cambridge, England: Cambridge University Press, 1999.

Hellman, Judith Adler. *Journeys among Women: Feminism in Five Italian Cities.* New York: Oxford University Press, 1987.

Hellman, Stephen. *Italian Communism in Transition: The Rise and Fall of the Historic Compromise in Turin, 1975–1980.* New York: Oxford University Press, 1988.

Hemment, Drew. "Dangerous Dancing and Disco Riots: The Northern Warehouse Parties," In George McKay, ed., *DiY Culture: Party and Protest in Nineties Britain.* London: Verso, 1998.

Henau, Brigitte. "Shaping a New Belgium: The CEPAG—the Belgian Committee for the Study of Postwar Problems, 1941–44." In Michael L. Smith and Peter M. R. Stirk, eds., *Making the New Europe: European Unity and the Second World War.* London: Pinter, 1990.

Henderson, Arthur. *The Aims of Labour.* London: British W. Husbeck, 1917.

Henderson, William O. *The Life of Friedrich Engels.* 2 vols. London: Cass, 1976.

Hendrik, Aart, Rob Tielman, and Evert va der Veen, eds., *The Third Pink Book: A Global View of Lesbian and Gay Liberation and Oppression.* Buffalo: Prometheus Books, 1993.

Henke, Klaus-Dietmar, and Hans Woller, eds. *Politische Säuberung in Europa. Die Abrechnung mit Faschismus und Kollaboration nach dem Zweiten Weltkrieg.* Munich: Deutscher Taschenbuch Verlag, 1991.

Hennessey, Peter. *Never Again: Britain 1945–1951.* London: Cape, 1992.

Henry, N. "The New Industrial Spaces: Locational Logic of a New Production Era?" *International Journal of Urban and Regional Research* 16 (1992): 376–96.

Herbert, Ulrich. *A History of Foreign Labor in Germany, 1880–1980: Seasonal Workers/Forced Workers/Guest Workers.* Ann Arbor: University of Michigan Press, 1990.

Herf, Jeffrey. *War by Other Means: Soviet Power, West German Resistance, and the Battle of the Euromissiles.* New York: Free Press, 1991.

Herlemann, Beatrix. "Communist Resistance between Comintern Directives and Nazi Terror," In David E. Barclay and Eric D. Weitz, eds., *Between Reform and Revolution: German Socialism and Communism from 1840 to 1990.* New York: Berghahn, 1998.

———. *Kommunalpolitik der KPD im Ruhrgebiet 1924–1933.* Wuppertal, Germany: Hammer, 1977.

Hewison, Robert. *Too Much: Art and Society in the Sixties, 1960–75.* Oxford: Oxford University Press, 1987.

Heywood, Paul. "The Development of Marxist Theory in Spain and the *Frente Popular.*" In Martin Alexander and Helen Graham, eds., *The French and Spanish Popular Fronts: Comparative Perspectives.* Cambridge, England: Cambridge University Press, 1989.

———. "The Labour Movement in Spain before 1914," In Dick Geary, ed., *Labour and Socialist Movements in Europe before 1914*. Oxford: Berg, 1989.

———. *Marxism and the Failure of Organized Socialism in Spain, 1879–1936*. Cambridge, England: Cambridge University Press, 1990.

———. "The Spanish Left: Towards a 'Common Home'?" In Martin J. Bull and Paul Heywood, eds., *West European Communist Parties after the Revolutions of 1989*. London: Macmillan, 1994.

Hickey, Stephen H. *Workers in Imperial Germany: The Miners of the Ruhr*. Oxford: Oxford University Press, 1985.

Hilberg, Raul. *Perpetrators, Victims, Bystanders: The Jewish Catastrophe 1933–1945*. New York: Aaron Asher Books, 1992.

Hilden, Patricia Penn. *Women, Work, and Politics: Belgium, 1830–1914*. Oxford: Oxford University Press, 1993.

———. *Working Women and Socialist Politics in France, 1880–1914: A Regional Study*. Oxford: Oxford University Press, 1986.

Hill, Jeffrey. "Requiem for a Party? Writing the History of Social-Democracy," *Labour History Review* 61 (1996): 102–9.

Himka, John-Paul. *Socialism in Galicia: The Emergence of Polish Social Democracy and Ukrainian Radicalism 1860–1890*. Cambridge: Harvard University Press, 1983.

Hind, John, and Stephen Mosco. *Rebel Radio: The Full Story of British Pirate Radio*. London: Pluto Press, 1985.

Hine, David. "The Italian Socialist Party," In Tom Gallagher and Allan M. Williams, eds., *Southern European Socialism: Parties, Elections and the Challenge of Government*. Manchester: Manchester University Press, 1989.

———. "Social Democracy in Italy," In William E. Paterson and Alastair H. Thomas, eds., *Social Democratic Parties in Western Europe*. London: Croom Helm, 1977.

Hinton, James. "Coventry Communism: A Study of Factory Politics in the Second World War." *History Workshop Journal* 10 (autumn 1980): 90–118.

———. *The First Shop Stewards' Movement*. London: Allen and Unwin, 1973.

———. *Labour and Socialism: A History of the British Labour Movement 1867–1914*. Brighton England: Harvester, 1983.

———. *Protests and Visions: Peace Politics in Twentieth-Century Britain*. London: Hutchinson, 1989.

———. "Self-Help and Socialism. The Squatters' Movement of 1946." *History Workshop Journal* 25 (spring 1988): 111–20.

———. *Shop Floor Citizens: Engineering Democracy in 1940s Britain*. Aldershot, England: Elgar, 1994.

Hirsch, Helmut, ed. *Eduard Bernstein: Briefwechsel mit Friedrich Engels*. Assen, Netherlands: Van Gorcum, 1970.

Hirsch, Joachim. "From the Fordist to the Post-Fordist State." In Bob Jessop, H. Kastendiek, K, Nielsen, and O. Pedersen, eds., *The Politics of Flexibility*. Aldershot, England: Elgar, 1991.

Hirsch, Pam. *Barbara Leigh Smith Bodichon: Feminist, Artist and Rebel*. London: Chatto and Windus, 1998.

Hirst, Paul Q. and Jonathan Zeitlin, "Flexible Specialization versus Post-Fordism: Theory, Evidence, and Policy Implications." *Economy and Society* 20 (1991): 1–156.

Hitchens, Keith. "The Romanian Socialists and the Hungarian Soviet Republic." In Andrew C. Janos and William B. Slottman, eds., *Revolution in Perspective: Essays on the Hungarian Soviet Republic of 1919*. Berkeley University of California Press, 1971.

Hobsbawm, Eric, and Giorgio Napolitano. *The Italian Road to Socialism*. London: Journeyman Press, 1977.

Hobsbawm, Eric J. *The Age of Empire 1875–1914*. New York: Pantheon, 1987.

———. *The Age of Extremes: A History of the World, 1914–1991*. New York: Pantheon, 1994.

———. "Artisans and Labour Aristocrats." In *Workers: Worlds of Labour*. New York: Pantheon, 1987.

———. "Fifty Years of People's Fronts." In Jim Fyrth, ed., *Britain, Fascism and the Popular Front*. London: Lawrence and Wishart, 1985.

———. "The Fortunes of Marx's and Engels' Writings," In Hobsbawm, ed., *History of Marxism*. Vol. 1. *Marxism in Marx's Day*. Bloomington: Indiana University Press, 1982.

———. "Labour in the Great City." *Politics for a Rational Left: Political Writing 1977–1988*. London: Verso, 1989.

———. *Labouring Men: Studies in the History of Labour*. London: Weidenfeld and Nicholson, 1964.

———. "The Making of the Working Class 1870–1914." In *Workers: Worlds of Labor*. New York: Pantheon, 1984.

———. "Marx, Engels, and Politics." In Hobsbawm, ed., *The History of Marxism. Vol. 1. Marxism in Marx's Day*. Bloomington: Indiana University Press, 1982.

———. "Marx, Engels and Pre-Marxian Socialism." In Hobsbawm, ed., *The History of Marxism. Vol. 1. Marxism in Marx's Day*. Bloomington: Indiana University Press, 1982, pp. 1–28.

———. "Mass-Producing Traditions: Europe, 1870–1914." In Hobsbawm and Terence Ranger, eds., *The Invention of Tradition*. Cambridge, England: Cambridge University Press, 1983.

———. "The 'New Unionism' Reconsidered." In Wolfgang J. Mommsen and Hans-Gerhard Husung, eds., *The Development of Trade Unionism in Great Britain and Germany, 1880–1914*. London: Allen and Unwin, 1985.

———. "The 1970s: Syndicalism without Syndicalists?" In *Workers: Worlds of Labor*. New York: Pantheon, 1984.

———. *On the Edge of the New Century*. New York: New Press, 2000.

———. *Politics for a Rational Left: Political Writing 1977–1988*. London: Verso, 1989.

———. *Revolutionaries*. New York: Pantheon, 1973.

———. "Socialism and the Avant-Garde, 1880–1914." In *Uncommon People: Resistance, Rebellion, and Jazz*. New York: New Press, 1998.

———. *Workers: Worlds of Labor*. New York: Pantheon, 1984.

Hobsbawm Eric et al. *The Forward March of Labour Halted?* London: Verso, 1981.

Hobson, Barbara. "Feminist Strategies and Gendered Discourses in Welfare States: Married Women's Right to Work in the United States and Sweden." In Seth Koven and Sonya Michel, eds., *Mothers of a New World. Maternalist Politics and the Origins of Welfare States*. New York: Routledge, 1993.

Hoch, Paul, and Vic Schoenbach. *LSE: The Natives Are Restless: A Report on Student Power in Action.* London: Sheed and Ward, 1969.

Hochman, Jiri. *The Soviet Union and the Failure of Collective Security, 1934–1938.* Ithaca:, N.Y. Cornell University Press, 1984.

Hodos, George H. *Show Trials: Stalinist Purges in Eastern Europe, 1948–54.* New York: Praeger, 1987.

Hogan, Michael J. *The Marshall Plan: America, Britain, and the Reconstruction of Western Europe, 1947–1952.* Cambridge, England: Cambridge University Press, 1987.

Hogenkamp, Bert. *Deadly Parallels: Film and the Left in Britain 1929–39.* London: Lawrence and Wishart, 1986.

Hohorst, Gerd. Jürgen Kocka, and Gerhard A. Ritter, *Sozialgeschichtliches Arbeitsbuch. Materialien zur Statistik des Kaiserreichs 1870–1914.* Munich: Beck, 1975.

Holguín, Sandy. "Taming the Seventh Art: The Battle for Cultural Unity on the Cinematographic Front during Spain's Second Republic, 1931–1936." *Journal of Modern History* 71 (1999): 352–81.

Holland, Stuart. *The Socialist Challenge.* London: Quartet Books, 1975.

Holloway, David. *The Soviet Union and the Arms Race.* New Haven: Yale University Press, 1983.

Holmes, Leslie. *Politics in the Communist World.* Oxford: Oxford University Press, 1986.

Holton, Bob. *British Syndicalism 1900–1914: Myths and Realities.* London: Pluto Press, 1976.

Holton, Sandra Stanley. *Feminism and Democracy: Women's Suffrage and Reform Politics in Britain 1900–1918.* Cambridge, England: Cambridge University Press, 1986.

———. "The Suffragist and the 'Average Woman.' " *Women's History Review* 1, 1 (1992): 9–24.

———. *Suffrage Days.* London: Routledge, 1996.

Hölz, Max. *From White Cross to Red Flag: The Autobiography of Max Hoeltz: Waiter, Soldier, Revolutionary Leader.* London: Routledge, 1930.

Hondros, John L. "The Greek Resistance, 1941–1944: A Reevaluation," In John O. Iatrides, ed., *Greece in the 1940s: A Nation in Crisis.* Hanover: N. H. University Press of New England, 1981.

———. *Occupation and Resistance: The Greek Agony, 1941–1944.* New York: Pella, 1983.

Hong, Young-Sun. "World War I and the German Welfare State: Gender, Religion, and the Paradoxes of Modernity." In Geoff Eley, ed., *Society, Culture, and the State in Germany, 1870–1930.* Ann Arbor: University of Michigan Press, 1996.

Hopwood, Nick. "Producing a Socialist Popular Science in the Weimar Republic." *History Workshop Journal* 41 (spring 1996): 117–53.

Horn, Daniel. *The German Naval Mutinies of World War I.* New Brunswick, N.J.: Rutgers University Press, 1969.

Horn, Gerd-Rainer. *European Socialists Respond to Fascism: Ideology, Activism and Contingency in the 1930s.* New York: Oxford University Press, 1996.

———. "The Language of Symbols and the Barriers of Language: Foreigners' Perceptions of Social Revolution (Barcelona 1936–1937)." *History Workshop Journal* 29 (spring 1990): 43–64.

―――. "The Social Origins of Unity Sentiments in the German Socialist Underground, 1933 to 1936." In David E. Barclay and Eric D. Weitz, eds., *Between Reform and Revolution: German Socialism and Communism from 1840 to 1990*. New York: Berghahn, 1998.

Horne, John. *Labour at War: France and Britain, 1914–1918*. Oxford: Oxford University Press, 1991.

―――. *"L'Impot du Sang*: Republican Rhetoric and Industrial Welfare in France, 1914–1918." *Social History* 14 (1989): 201–23.

Housee, Shirin, and Sanjay Sharma, " 'Too Black Too Strong'? Anti-Racism and the Making of South Asian Political Identities in Britain," In Tim Jordan and Adam Lent, eds., *Storming the Millennium: The New Politics of Change*. London: Lawrence and Wishart, 1999.

Howard, Dick, and Karl E. Klare, eds. *The Unknown Dimension: European Marxism since Lenin*. New York: Basic Books, 1972.

Howarth, Jolyon. *Edouard Valliant. La création de l'unité socialiste en France*. Paris: Syros 1982.

―――. *France: The Politics of Peace*. London: Merlin, 1984.

―――. "French Workers and German Workers: The Impossibility of Internationalism, 1900–1914." *European History Quarterly* 15 (1985): 71–97.

Howell, Chris. *Regulating Labor: The State and Industrial Relations Reform in Postwar France*. Princeton: Princeton University Press, 1992.

Howell, David. *British Workers and the Independent Labour Party 1888–1906*. Manchester: Manchester University Press, 1983.

―――. *A Lost Left: Three Studies in Socialism and Nationalism*. Chicago: University of Chicago Press, 1986.

Howells, Kim. "Stopping Out: The Birth of a New Kind of Politics," In Huw Beynon, ed., *Digging Deeper: Issues in the Miners' Strike*. London: Verso, 1985.

Howkins, Alun. "Class against Class: The Political Culture of the Communist Party of Great Britain, 1930–1935," In Frank Gloversmith, ed., *Class, Culture and Social Change: A New View of the 1930s*. Brighton England: Harvester, 1980.

Hudson, Ray. "Rewriting History and Reshaping Geography: The Nationalized Industries and the Political Economy of Thatcherism," In John Mohan, ed., *The Political Geography of Contemporary Britain*. London: Macmillan, 1989.

―――. *Wrecking a Region*. London: Pion, 1989.

Hülsberg, Werner. *The German Greens: A Social and Political Profile*. London: Verso, 1988.

Hunecke, Volker. *Arbeiterschaft und industrielle Revolution in Mailand 1859–1892. Zue Entstehungsgeschichte der italienischen Industrie und Arbeiterbewegung*. Göttingen: Vandenhoeck und Ruprecht, 1978.

Hunt, Karen. *Equivocal Feminists: The Social Democratic Federation and the Woman Question*. Cambridge, England: Cambridge University Press, 1996.

Hunt, Richard N. *The Political Ideas of Marx and Engels*, Vol. 1. *Marxism and Totalitarian Democracy, 1818–1850*. London: Macmillan, 1975. Vol. 2. *Classical Marxism, 1850–1895*. Pittsburgh: University of Pittsburgh, Press, 1984.

Hunter, Allen, ed. *Re-Thinking the Cold War*. Philadelphia: Temple University Press, 1998.

Huq, Rupa. "The Right to Rave: Opposition to the Criminal Justice and Public Order Act 1994." In Tim Jordan and Adam Lent, eds., *Storming the Millennium: The New Politics of Change*. London: Lawrence and Wishart, 1999.

Hurd, Madeline. *Public Spheres, Public Mores, and Democracy: Hamburg and Stockholm, 1870–1914*. Ann Arbor: University of Michigan Press, 2000.

Huss, Marie-Monique. "Pro-Natalism in the Interwar Period in France," *Journal of Contemporary History* 25 (1990): 39–68.

Hussain, Athar, and Keith Tribe. *Marxism and the Agrarian Question, Vol. 1. German Social Democracy and the Peasantry 1890–1907*. London: Macmillan, 1981.

Hutton, John. "Camile Pissarro's *Turpitudes Sociales* and Late Nineteenth-Century French Anarchist Anti-Feminism," *History Workshop Journal* 24 (autumn 1987): 32–61.

Hutton, Patrick. *The Cult of Revolutionary Tradition: The Blanquists in French Politics, 1864–1893*. Berkeley: University of California Press, 1981.

Hutton, Will, interviewed by Mike Power. "Three Thirds Britain." In Stuart Wilks, ed., *Talking about Tomorrow: A New Radical Politics*. London: Pluto Press, 1993.

Hyman, Richard. "Mass Organization and Militancy in Britain: Contrasts and Continuities." In Wolfgang J. Mommsen and Hans-Gerhard Husung, eds., *The Development of Trade Unionism in Great Britain and Germany, 1880–1914*. London: Allen and Unwin, 1985.

———. *The Workers' Union*. Oxford: Oxford University Press, 1971.

Iatrides, John O. *Revolt in Athens: The Greek Communist "Second Round," 1944–1945*. Princeton: Princeton University Press, 1972.

Iazhborovskaia, Inessa. "The Gomulka Alternative: The Untravelled Road." In Norman M. Naimark and Leonid Gibianskii, eds., *The Establishment of Communist Regimes in Eastern Europe, 1944–1949*. Boulder, Colo.: Westview Press, 1997.

Il Manifesto, ed. *Power and Opposition in Post-Revolutionary Societies*. London: Ink Links, 1979.

Inglehart, Ronald. *Culture Shift in Advanced Industrial Society*. Princeton: Princeton University Press, 1990.

———. *The Silent Revolution: Changing Values and Political Styles among Western Publics*. Princeton: Princeton University Press, 1977.

Institut für Marxismus-Leninismus, ed. *Dokumente und Materialen zur Geschichte der deutschen Arbeiterbewegung*. Vol. 4. East Berlin: Akademie Verlag, 1967.

International Lesbian and Gay Association. *ILGA Bulletin*. Stockholm: Association, 1989–2000.

Internationaler Sozialisten-Kongress zu Amsterdam, 14. bis 20. August 1904. Berlin: Buchhandlung Vorwärts, 1904.

Irving, R. E. M. *The Christian Democratic Parties of Western Europe*. London: Allen and Unwin, 1975.

Isherwood, Christopher. *Goodbye to Berlin*. London: Hogarth, 1939.

———. *Mr. Norris Changes Trains*. London: Hogarth, 1935.

Itzin, Catherine. *Stages in the Revolution: Political Theatre in Britain since 1968*. London: Eyre Methuen, 1980.

Jackson, George D. *The Comintern and the Peasant in Eastern Europe, 1919–1930*. New York: Columbia University Press, 1966.

Jackson, Julian. *The Popular Front in France: Defending Democracy, 1934–1938*. Cambridge, England: Cambridge University Press, 1988.

———. *"Le temps des loisirs"*: Popular Tourism and Mass Leisure in the vision of the *Front Populaire*. In Martin Alexander and Helen Graham, eds., *The French and Spanish Popular Fronts: Comparative Perspectives*. Cambridge, England: Cambridge University Press, 1989.

Jacobson, Jon. *When the Soviet Union Entered World Politics*. Berkeley: University of California Press, 1994.

Jacques, Kergoat. "France." In Marcel van der Linden and Jürgen Rojahn, eds., *The Formation of Labour Movements 1870–1914: An International Perspective*. Vol. 1. Leiden: Brill, 1990.

Jallinoja, Riitta. "The Women's Liberation Movement in Finland: The Social and Political Mobilization of Women in Finland, 1880–1910." *Scandinavian Journal of History* 5 (1980): 37–49.

James, David E. "For a Working-Class Television: The Miners' Campaign Tape Project." In *Power Misses: Essays across (Un)Popular Culture*. London: Verso, 1996.

James, Harold. *The German Slump: Politics and Economics 1924–1936*. Oxford: Oxford University Press, 1986.

———. "The SPD and the Economic Depression, 1930–1933." In Roger Fletcher, ed., *Bernstein to Brandt: A Short History of German Social Democracy*. London: Arnold, 1987.

James, Harold, and Marla Stone, ed. *When the Wall Came Down: Reactions to German Unification*. New York: Routledge, 1992.

James, Winston, and Clive Harris, eds. *Inside Babylon: The Caribbean Diaspora in Britain*. London: Verso, 1993.

Jameson, Fredric. "Globalization and Strategy." *New Left Review* 4 (July–August 2000): 49–68.

Jarausch, Konrad H. "Care and Coercion: The GDR as Welfare Dictatorship." In Jarausch, ed., *Dictatorship as Experience: Towards a Socio-Cultural History of the GDR*. New York: Berghahn, 1999.

———. *The Rush to German Unity*. New York: Oxford University Press, 1994.

———. *Students, Society, and Politics in Imperial Germany*. Princeton: Princeton University Press, 1982.

Jay, Martin. *The Dialectical Imagination: A History of the Frankfurt School and the Institute of Social Research 1923–1950*. London: Heineman, 1973.

Jeffery, Charlie. "Beyond Red Vienna: New Perspectives on Social Democracy in the Austrian First Republic," *German History* 11 (1993): 81–92.

Jenkins, Mark. *Bevanism, Labour's High Tide: The Cold War and the Democratic Mass Movement*. Nottingham: Spokesman, 1979.

Jennings, J. R. *Georges Sorel: The Character and Development of his Thought*. London: Macmillan, 1985.

Jensen, Jane. "The Limits of 'and the' Discourse: French Women as Marginal Workers." In Jane Jensen, Elisabeth Hangen, and Ceallaigh Reddy, eds., *The Feminization of the Labor Force: Paradoxes and Promises*. London: Routledge, 1988.

———. "Representations of Difference: The Varieties of French Feminism." In

Monica Threlfall, ed., *Mapping the Women's Movement: Feminist Politics and Social Transformation in the North*. London: Verso, 1996.

———. "The French Communist Party and Feminism." In Ralph Miliband and John Saville, eds., *The Socialist Register 1980*. London: Merlin, 1980.

———. "The French Left: A Tale of Three Beginnings." In James F. Holifield and George Ross, eds., *Searching for a New France*. New York: Oxford University Press, 1991.

Jensen, Jane, Elisabeth Hangen, and Ceallaigh Reddy, eds. *The Feminization of the Labor Force: Paradoxes and Promises*. London: Routledge, 1988.

Jensen, Jane, and Rianne Mahon. "Representing Solidarity: Class, Gender and the Crisis in Social Democratic Sweden." *New Left Review* 201 (September–October 1993): 76–100.

Jensen, Jane, and George Ross. *The View from Inside: A French Communist Cell in Crisis*. Berkeley: University of California Press, 1984.

Jensen, Robert. *Marketing Modernism in Fin-de-Siècle Europe*. Princeton: Princeton University Press, 1994.

Jessop, Bob. "Capitalism and Democracy: The Best Possible Political Shell?" In Gary Littlejohn, Barry Smart, John Wakeford, and Nira Yuval-Davis, eds., *Power and the State*. London: Croom Helm, 1978.

———. *State Theory: Putting Capitalist States in Their Place*. University Park: Penn State University Press, 1990.

———. "Thatcherism and Flexibility: The White Heat of a Post-Fordist Revolution." In Bob Jessop, H. Kastendiek, K, Nielsen, and O. Pedersen, eds., *The Politics of Flexibility*. Aldershot, England: Elgar, 1991.

———. "The Transformation of the State in Post-War Britain." In Richard Scase, ed., *The State in Western Europe*. London: Croom Helm, 1980.

Johnson, Christopher H. *Utopian Communism in France: Cabet and the Icarians, 1839–1851*. Ithaca, N.Y.: Cornell University Press, 1974.

Johnson, Martin Phillip. *The Paradise of Association: Political Culture and Popular Organizations in the Paris Commune of 1871*. Ann Arbor: University of Michigan Press, 1996.

Johnson, Paul. "The Myth of Euro-Communism." In Ferdinand Mount, ed., *Communism: A TLS Companion*. Chicago: University of Chicago, 1993.

Johnson, Richard W. *The French Communist Party versus the Students*. New Haven: Yale University Press, 1972.

———. *The Long March of the French Left*. Manchester: Manchester University Press, 1981.

Johnston, Gordon. "What is the History of *Samizdat*? *Social History* 24 (1999): 115–33.

Johnstone, Diana. *The Politics of Euromissiles: Europe's Role in America's World*. London: Verso, 1984.

Johnstone, Monty. "The CPGB, the Comintern, and the War, 1939–1941: Filling in the Blank Spots." *Science and Society* 61 (1997): 27–45.

———. "Marx, Blanqui and Majority Rule." In Ralph Miliband and John Saville, eds., *The Socialist Register 1983*. London: Merlin, 1983.

———. "Marx, Engels and the Concept of the Party." In Ralph Miliband and John Saville, eds., *The Socialist Register 1967*. London: Merlin, 1967.

Joll, James. "Anarchism—A Living Tradition." In David E. Apter and James Joll, eds. *Anarchism Today*. London: Macmillan, 1971.

————. *The Anarchists*. London: Methuen, 1964.

————. *Europe since 1870: An International History*. Harmondsworth: Penguin, 1976.

————. *The Second International 1889–1914*. New York: Routledge, 1966.

Jones, Gareth Stedman. "Engels and the End of Classical German Philosophy." *New Left Review* 79 (May–June 1973): 17–36.

————. "Rethinking Chartism." In *Languages of Class: Studies in English Working-Class History 1832–1982*. Cambridge, England: Cambridge University Press, 1983.

————. *Outcast London: A Study in the Relationship between Classes in Victorian Society*. Harmondsworth: Penguin, 1976.

————. "Utopian Socialism Reconsidered." In Raphael Samuel, ed., *People's History and Socialist Theory*. London: Routledge, 1981.

Jones, Jack. "A Liverpool Socialist Education." *History Workshop Journal* 18 (autumn 1984): 92–101.

Jones, Mervyn. "Days of Tragedy and Farce." In Ralph Miliband and John Saville, eds., *The Socialist Register 1976*. London: Merlin, 1976.

Jones, Stephen G. *The British Labour Movement and Film 1918–1939*. London: Routledge, 1987.

————. *Sport, Politics and the Working Class: Organized Labour and Sport in Interwar Britain*. Manchester: Manchester University Press, 1989.

Joppke, Christian. *The East German Dissidents and the Revolution of 1989: Social Movement in a Leninist Regime*. New York: New York University Press, 1995.

Jordan, John. "The Art of Necessity: The Subversive Imagination of Anti-Road Protest and Reclaim the Streets." In George McKay, ed., *DiY Culture: Party and Protest in Nineties Britain*. London: Verso, 1998.

Jordan, Tim, and Adam Lent, eds. *Storming the Millennium: The New Politics of Change*. London: Verso, 1999.

Jordan, Tim. *Cyberpower: The Culture and Politics of Cyberspace and the Internet*. London: Routledge, 1999.

————. "New Space, New Politics: The Electronic Frontier Foundation and the Definition of Cyberpolitics." In Tim Jordan and Adam Lent, eds., *Storming the Millennium: The New Politics of Change*. London: Verso, 1999.

————. *Reinventing Revolution: Value and Difference in New Social Movements and the Left*. Aldershot, England: Elgar, 1994.

Judt, Tony. *Past Imperfect: French Intellectuals, 1944–1956*. Berkeley: University of California Press, 1992.

————. *Socialism in Provence 1871–1914: A Study in the Origins of the Modern French Left*. Cambridge, England: Cambridge University Press, 1979.

————, ed., *Resistance and Revolution in Mediterranean Europe, 1939–1948*. London, 1989.

Jupp, James. "The Discontents of Youth." In Bernard Crick and William A. Robson, eds., *Protest and Discontent*. Harmondsworth: Penguin, 1970.

Kaiser, Jochen-Christoph. *Arbeiterbewegung und organisierte Religionskritik. Proletarische Freidenkerverbände in Kaiserreich und Weimarer Republik*. Stuttgart: Klett-Cotta, 1981.

Kaldor, Mary, ed. *Europe from Below: An East-West Dialogue*. London: Verso, 1991.

Kanter, Hannah, Sarah Lefanu, Shaila Shah, and Carole Spedding, eds. *Sweeping Statements: Writings from the Women's Liberation Movement 1981–83*. London: Women's Press, 1984.

Kaplan, E. Ann, and Michael Sprinker, eds. *The Althusserian Legacy*. London: Verso, 1993.

Kaplan, Gisela. *Contemporary Western European Feminism*. New York: New York University Press, 1992.

Kaplan, Karel. *The Short March: The Communist Takeover in Czechoslovakia, 1945–1948*. New York: St. Martin's Press, 1987.

Kaplan, Temma. *Anarchists of Andalusia, 1868–1903*. Princeton: Princeton University Press, 1977.

———. *Red City, Blue Period: Social Movements in Picasso's Barcelona*. Berkeley: University of California Press, 1992.

Karrsholm, Preben. "The South African War and the response of the International Socialist Community to Imperialism between 1896 and 1908." In Fritz van Holthoon and Marcel van der Linden, eds., *Internationalism in the Labour Movement 1830–1940*. Vol. 1. Leiden: Brill, 1988.

Karsai, László. "The People's Courts and Revolutionary Justice in Hungary, 1945–56." In István Déak, Jan T. Gross, and Tony Judt, eds., *The Politics of Retribution in Europe: World War II and its Aftermath*. Princeton: Princeton University Press, 2000.

Karvonen, Lauri, and Per Selle, eds. *Women in Nordic Politics: Closing the Gap*. Brookfield, Vt.: Dartmouth, 1995.

Katsiaficas, George. *The Imagination of the New Left: A Global Analysis of 1968*. Boston: South End Press, 1987.

———. *The Subversion of Politics: European Autonomous Social Movements and the Decolonization of Everyday Life*. Atlantic Highlands N.J.: Humanities Press, 1997.

Katznelson, Ira, and Aristide R. Zolberg, eds. *Working-Class Formation: Nineteenth-Century Patterns in Western Europe and the United States*. Princeton: Princeton University Press, 1986.

Kautsky, Karl. *The Class Struggle (Erfurt Program)*. New York: Norton, 1971.

———. *Georgia*. London: International Bookshops, 1921.

Kavan, Jan, and Zdena Tomin, eds. *Voices from Prague: Documents on Czechoslovakia and the Peace Movement*. London: Merlin, 1983.

Kean, Hilda. "The Feminist and Socialist Response to Vivisection." *History Workshop Journal* 40 (autumn 1995): 16–38.

Keane, John. *Democracy and Civil Society*. London: Verso, 1988.

Kedward, H. Roderick. "Behind the Polemics: French Communists and Resistance 1939–41." In Stephen Hawes and Ralph White, eds., *Resistance in Europe 1939–1945*. Harmondsworth: Penguin, 1976.

———. *In Search of the Maquis: Rural Resistance in Southern France, 1942–1944*. Oxford: Oxford University Press, 1993.

———. *Resistance in Vichy France: A Study of Ideas and Motivation in the Southern Zone 1940–1942*. Oxford: Oxford University Press, 1978.

Kedward, H. Roderick, and Nancy Wood, eds. *The Liberation of France: Image and Event*. Oxford: Berg, 1995.

Kelly, Aileen. *Mikhail Bakunin: A Study in the Psychology and Politics of Utopianism*. Oxford: Oxford University Press, 1982.

Kelly, Michael. *Modern French Marxism*. Baltimore: Johns Hopkins University Press, 1982.

Kelsey, Graham. "Anarchism in Aragon during the Second Republic: The Emergence of a Mass Movement." In Martin Blinkhorn, ed., *Spain in Conflict 1931–1939: Democracy and its Enemies*. London: Sage, 1986.

Kenez, Peter. "Coalition Politics and the Hungarian Soviet Republic." In Andrew C. Janos and William B. Slottman, eds., *Revolution in Perspective: Essays on the Hungarian Soviet Republic Of 1919*. Berkeley: University of California Press, 1971.

Kennedy, Michael, and Daina Stukuls. "The Narrative of Civil Society in Communism's Collapse and Postcommunism's Alternatives: Emancipation, Polish Protest, and Baltic Nationalisms. *Constellations* 5 (1998): 541–71.

Kennedy-Pipe, Caroline. *Stalin's Cold War: Soviet Strategies in Europe, 1943–1956*. Manchester: Manchester University Press, 1995.

Kenney, Padraic. *Rebuilding Poland: Workers and Communists, 1945–1950*. Ithaca, N.Y.: Cornell University Press, 1997.

———. "Working-Class Community and Resistance in Pre-Stalinist Poland: The Poznanski Textile Strike, Lódz, September 1947." *Social History* 18 (1993): 31–52.

Kenny, Michael. "Communism and the New Left." In Geoff Andrews, Nina Fishman, and Kevin Morgan, eds., *Opening the Books: Essays on the Social and Cultural History of the British Communist Party*. London: Lawrence and Wishart, 1995.

———. *The First New Left: British Intellectuals after Stalin*. London: Lawrence and Wishart, 1995.

Kent, Susan Kingsley. *Making Peace: The Reconstruction of Gender in Interwar Britain*. Princeton: Princeton University Press, 1993.

———. "The Politics of Sexual Difference: World War I and the Demise of British Feminism." *Journal of British Studies* 27 (1988): 232–53.

———. *Sex and Suffrage in Britain, 1860–1914*. Princeton: Princeton University Press, 1987.

Kerbs, Diethart, ed. . . . *Gegen Kind und Kunst. Eine Dokumentation aus dem Jahr 1927, mit Kinderzeichnungen und Fotos der zerstörten Barkenhoff-Fresken von Heinrich Vogeler*. Wismar, Germany: Anabas-Verlag, 1974.

Kergoat, Jacques. "France." In Marcel van der Linden and Jürgen Rojahn, eds., *The Formation of Labour Movements 1870–1914: An International Perspective*. Vol. 1. Leiden: Brill, 1990.

van Kersbergen, K. *Social Capitalism: A Study of Christian Democracy and the Welfare State*. London: Lawrence and Wishart, 1995.

Kershaw, Ian, ed. *Weimar: Why Did German Democracy Fail?* London: Weidenfeld and Nicolson, 1990.

Kersten, Krystyna. *The Establishment of Communist Rule in Poland, 1943–1948*. Berkeley: University of California Press, 1991.

Kertzer, David I. *Comrades and Christians: Religion and Political Struggle in Communist Italy*. Cambridge, England: Cambridge University Press, 1980.

Kettle, Martin. "Goodbye to the Comintern." *London Review of Books,* 21 February 1991: 20.

Keyworth, Florence. "Invisible Struggles: The Politics of Ageing." In Rosalind

Brunt and Caroline Rowan, eds., *Feminism, Culture, and Politics*. London: Lawrence and Wishart, 1982.

Khilnani, Sunil. *Arguing Revolution: The Intellectual Left in Postwar France*. New Haven: Yale University Press, 1993.

Kindersley, Richard, ed. *In Search of Eurocommunism*. London: Macmillan, 1981.

King, Francis, and George Matthews, eds. *About Turn*. London: Lawrence and Wishart, 1990.

King, Robert R. *History of the Romanian Communist Party*. Stanford: Stanford University Press, 1980.

Kingsford, Peter. *The Hunger Marchers in Britain 1920–1939*. London: Lawrence and Wishart, 1982.

Kingston Mann, Esther. *Lenin and the Problem of Marxist Peasant Revolution*. Oxford: Oxford University Press, 1983.

Kirby, David. *War, Peace, and Revolution: International Socialism at the Cross-roads 1914–1918*. New York: St. Martin's Press, 1986.

———. " 'The Workers' Cause': Rank-and-File Attitudes in the Finnish Social Democratic Party 1905–1918." *Past and Present* 111 (1986): 130–64.

Kirchoff, Hans. "Denmark." In Bob Moore, ed., *Resistance in Western Europe*. Oxford: Berg, 2000.

Kitschelt, Herbert. *The Transformation of European Social Democracy*. Cambridge, England: Cambridge University Press, 1994.

Klenke, Dietmar. *Die SPD-Linke in der Weimarer Republik. Eine Untersuchung zu den regionalen organisatorischen Grundlagen und zur politischen Praxis und Theoriebildung des linken Flügels der SPD in den Jahren 1922–1932*. 2 vols. Münster: Lit, 1983.

Klotzbach, Kurt. *Der Weg zur Staatsparte: Programmatik, praktische Politik und Organisation der deutschen Sozialdemokratie 1945 bis 1965*. Berlin: Dietz, 1982.

Kluge, Ulrich. *Die deutsche Revolution 1918/19: Staat, Politik und Gesellschaft zwischen Weltkrieg und Kapp-Putsch*. Frankfurt: Suhrkamp, 1985.

———. *Soldatenräte und Revolution: Studien zur Militärpolitik in Deutschland 1918/19*. Göttingen: Vandenhoeck und Ruprecht, 1975.

Kocka, Jürgen. *Klassengesellschaft im Krieg: deutsche Sozialgeschichte 1914–1918*. Göttingen: Vandenhoeck und Ruprecht; 1973.

Koelble, Thomas A. *The Left Unraveled: Social Democracy and the New Left Challenge*. Durham, N.C.: Duke University Press, 1991.

Koenker, Diane P. *Moscow Workers and the 1917 Revolution*. Princeton: Princeton University Press, 1981.

Koenker, Diane P., and William G. Rosenberg. *Strikes and Revolution in Russia, 1917*. Princeton: Princeton University Press, 1989.

Kofas, Jon V. *Intervention and Underdevelopment: Greece During the Cold War*. University Park: Penn State University Press, 1989.

Kolankiewicz, George, and Paul G. Lewis. *Poland: Politics, Economics and Society*. London: Pinter, 1988.

Kolb, Eberhard. *Die Arbeiterräte in der deutschen Innenpolitik*. Düsseldorf: Droste, 1962.

Kolinsky, Eva. *Parties, Opposition, and Society in West Germany*. New York: St. Martin's Press, 1984.

————. *Women in West Germany*. Oxford: Berg, 1989.

Kolmerton, Carol A. *Women in Utopia: The Ideology of Gender in the American Owenite Communities*. Bloomington: University of Indiana Press, 1990.

Kolocotroni, Vassiliki, Jane Goldman, and Olga Taxidou, eds. *Modernism: An Anthology of Sources and Documents*. Chicago: Chicago University Press, 1998.

Kongress-Protokolle der Zweiten Internationale. Vol 1. *Paris 1889 — Amsterdam 1904*. Glashütten im Taunus Germany: Auvermann, 1975.

Konrad, György. *Anti-Politics*. New York, 1984.

Konrad, György, and Iván Szelényi. *The Intellectuals on the Road to Class Power*. New York: Harcourt Brace Jovanovich, 1979.

Kontos, Silvia. *Die Partei kämpft wie ein Mann. Frauenpolitik der KPD in der Weimarer Republik*. Frankfurt: Campus, 1979.

Koon, Tracy H. *Believe, Obey, Fight: Political Socialization of Youth in Fascist Italy, 1922–1943*. Chapel Hill: University of North Carolina Press, 1985.

Kopacsi, Sandor. *In the Name of the Working Class: The Inside Story of the Hungarian Revolution*. New York: St. Martin's Press, 1986.

Kořalka, Jiři. "The Czech Workers' Movement in the Habsburg Empire." In Marcel van der Linden and Jürgen Rojahn, eds., *The Formation of Labour Movements 1870–1914: An International Perspective*. Vol. 1. Leiden: Brill, 1990.

Korff, Gottfried. "From Brotherly Handshake to Clinched Fist: On Political Metaphors for the Worker's Hand." *International Labor and Working-Class History* 42 (fall 1992): 70–81.

Kornai, János. "The Hungarian Reform Process: Visions, Hopes, and Reality." In Victor Nee and David Stark, eds., *Renaking the Economic Institutions of Socialism: China and Eastern Europe*. Stanford: Stanford University Press, 1989.

Korpi, Walter. *The Working Class Class in Welfare Capitalism*. London: Routledge, 1978.

Kossmann, E. H. *The Low Countries 1780–1940*. Oxford: Oxford University Press, 1978.

Köszegi, Ferenc, and Edward P. Thompson. *The New Hungarian Peace Movement*. London: Merlin, 1983.

Kovac, Miha. "The Slovene Spring" (interview). *New Left Review* 171 (September–October 1988): 115–28.

Koven, Seth, and Sonya Michel. "Womanly Duties: Maternalist Politics and the Origins of Welfare States in France, Germany, Great Britain, and the United States, 1880–1920." *American Historical Review* 95 (1990): 1076–1108.

Kracauer, Siegfried. "The Mass Ornament." *New German Critique* 5 (1975): 67–76.

Kramer, Mark. "The Czechoslovak Crisis and the Brezhnev Doctrine." In Carole Fink, Philipp Gassert, and Detlef Junker, eds., *1968: The World Transformed*. Cambridge, England: Cambridge University Press, 1988.

Krieger, Joel. *British Politics in the Global Age: Can Social Democracy Survive?* New York: Oxford University Press, 1999.

————. *Reagan, Thatcher, and the Politics of Decline*. New York: Oxford University Press, 1986.

Kriesi, Hanspeter. "New Social Movements and the New Class in the Netherlands," *American Journal of Sociology* 94, 5 (March 1989): 1078–1116.

Kriesi, Hanspeter, Ruud Koopmans, Ian Willem Dyvendak, and Marco G. Giugni. *New Social Movements in Western Europe: A Comparative Analysis.* Minneapolis: University of Minnesota Press, 1995.

Kruse, Wolfgang. *Krieg und nationale Integration: Eine Neuinterpretation des sozialdemokratischen Burgfriedensschlusses 1914/15.* Essen Germany: Klartext, 1993.

Kubik, Jan. *The Power of Symbols against the Symbol of Power: The Rise of Solidarity and the Fall of State Socialism in Poland.* University Park: Penn State University Press, 1994.

Kuczynski, Jürgen. *Der Ausbruch des Ersten Weltkrieges und die deutsche Sozialdemokratie. Chronik und Analyse.* East Berlin: Akadamie Verlag, 1957.

———. *Die Geschichte der Lage der Arbeiter unter dem Kapitalismus.* Vol. 4: *Darstellung der Lage der Arbeiter in Deutschland von 1900 bis 1917/18.* East Berlin: Akadamie Verlag, 1967.

Kuisel, Richard. *Seducing the French: The Dilemma of Americanization.* Berkeley: University of California Press, 1993.

Kulczycki, John J. *The Foreign Worker and the German Labor Movement: Xenophobia and Solidarity in the Coal Fields of the Ruhr, 1871–1914.* Oxford: Berg, 1994.

———. *The Polish Coal Miners' Union and the German Labor Movement in the Ruhr, 1902–1934: National and Social Solidarity.* Oxford: Berg, 1997.

Kurz, Jan. "Die Italienische Studentenbewegung 1966–1968." In Ingrid Gilcher-Holtey, ed., *1968: Vom Ereignis zum Gegnstand der Geschichtswissenschaft.* Göttingen: Vandenhoeck und Ruprecht, 1998.

Laba, Roman. *The Roots of Solidarity.* Princeton: Princeton University Press, 1991.

Lagrange, Hugues. "Strikes and the War." In Leopold Haimson and Charles Tilly, eds., *Strikes, Wars, and Revolutions in an International Perspective: Strike Waves in the Late Nineteenth and Early Twentieth Centuries.* Cambridge, England: Cambridge University Press, 1989.

Lagrou, Pieter. "Belgium," In Bob Moore, ed., *Resistance in Western Europe.* Oxford: Berg, 2000.

———. *The Legacy of Nazi Occupation: Patriotic Memory and National recovery in Western Europe, 1945–1965.* Cambridge, England: Cambridge University Press, 2000.

Laing, Stuart. "Banging In Some Reality: The Original 'Z Cars.' " In John Corner, ed., *Popular Television in Britain: Studies in Cultural History.* London: British Film Institute, 1991.

Lambertz, Jan. "Sexual Harassment in the Nineteenth-Century English Cotton Industry." *History Workshop Journal* 19 (spring 1985): 29–61.

Lampland, Martha. "Biographies of Liberation: Testimonials to Labor in Socialist Hungary." In Sonia Kruks, Rayna Rapp, and Marilyn B. Young, eds., *Promissory Notes: Women in the Transition to Socialism.* New York: Monthly Review Press, 1989.

———. *The Object of Labor: Commodification in Socialist Hungary.* Chicago: University of Chicago Press, 1995.

Lancaster, Bill. "The Rise of Labour." *Labour History Review* 57 (1992): 97–100.

Lanchester, Elsa. *Elsa Lanchester Herself*. London: Michael Joseph, 1983.

Lane, David. *The Rise and Fall of State Socialism*. Oxford: Blackwell, 1996.

Lane, Peter. *Europe since 1945: An Introduction*. Totowa, N.J.: Barnes and Noble, 1985.

Lange, Peter. "Crisis and Consent, Change and Compromise: Dilemmas of Italian Communism in the 1970s," In Peter Lange and Sidney Tarrow, eds., *Italy in Transition: Conflict and Consensus*. London: Cassell, 1980.

Lange, Peter, and Maurizio Vannicelli, eds. *The Communist Parties of Italy, France, and Spain: Postwar Change and Continuity. A Casebook*. London: Allen and Unwin, 1981.

Langenhan, Dagmar, and Sabine Ro, "The Socialist Glass Ceiling: Limits to Female Careers." In Konrad H. Jarausch, ed., *Dictatorship as Experience: Towards a Socio-Cultural History of the GDR*. New York: Berghahn, 1999.

Langewiesche, Dieter. "Das neue Massenmedium Film und die deutsche Arbeiterbewegung in der Weimarer Republik," In Jürgen Kocka, Hans-Jürgen Puhle, and Klaus Tenfelde, eds., *Von der Arbeiterbewegung zum modernen Sozialstaat: Festschrift für Gerhard A. Ritter zum 65. Geburtstag*. Munich: Oldenbourg, 1994.

———. "Working-Class Culture and Working-Class Politics in the Weimar Republic." In Roger Fletcher, ed., *Bernstein to Brandt: A Short History of German Social Democracy*. London: Arnold, 1987.

Langewiesche, Dieter, and Klaus Schönhoven. "Arbeiterbibliotheken und Arbeiterlektüre im wilelminischen Deutschland," *Archiv für Sozialgeschichte*, 16 (1976): 135–204.

Lansley, S., S. Goss, and C. Wolmar, *Councils in Conflict: The Rise and Fall of the Municipal Left*. London: Macmillan, 1989.

Lapidus, Gail Warshafsky. *Women in Soviet Society: Equality, Development, and Social Change*. Berkeley: University of California Press, 1978.

Lash, Scott, and John Urry, *Economics of Signs and Space: After Organized Capitalism*. London: Sage, 1993.

———. *The End of Organized Capitalism*. Madison: University of Wisconsin Press, 1987.

Laubier, Claire, ed. *The Condition of Women in France 1945 to the Present*. London: Routledge, 1990.

Laurens, Corran. " 'La Femme au Turban': Les Femmes tondues." In H. Roderick Kedward and Nancy Wood, eds., *The Liberation of France: Image and Event*. Oxford: Berg, 1995.

Laurie, Peter. *The Teenage Revolution*. Barcelona: Fontanella, 1969.

Law, Cheryl. *Suffrage and Power: The Women's Movement, 1918–1928*. London: Routledge, 1999.

Lawrence, Jon. *Speaking for the People: Party, Language and Popular Politics in England, 1867–1914*. Cambridge, England: Cambridge University Press, 1998.

Laybourn, Keith. "The Failure of Socialist Unity in Britain c.1893–1914." *Transactions of the Royal Historical Society*, sixth series, 4 (1994): 153–75.

———. "The Rise of the Labour Party and the Decline of Liberalism: The State of the Debate." *History* 80 (1995): 207–26.

————, ed. *A Centennial History of the Independent Labour Party: A Collection of Essays*. Halifax England: Sutton, 1992.

Lazitch, Branko. *Les partis communistes d'Europe 1919–1955*. Paris: Iles d'or, 1956.

Leadbetter, Charles. *Living on Thin Air: The New Economy*. London: Viking, 1999.

Lebas, Elizabeth. " 'When Every Street Became a Cinema': The Film Work of Bermondsey Borough Council, 1923–1953." *History Workshop Journal* 39 (spring 1995): 42–66.

Le Bras, Hervé. *Marianne et les lapins: L'obsession démographique*. Paris: Hachette, 1991.

Lee, Eric. *The Labour Movement and the Internet: The New Internationalism*. London: Pluto Press, 1997.

Lehning, Arthur. *From Buonarroti to Bakunin: Studies in International Socialism*. Leiden: Brill, 1970.

Leighten, Patricia. *Re-Ordering the Universe: Picasso and Anarchism, 1897–1914*. Princeton: Princeton University Press, 1989.

LeMahieu, D. L. *A Culture for Democracy. Mass Communication and the Cultivated Mind in Britain between the Wars*. Oxford: Oxford University Press, 1988.

Lenin, Vladimir I. *Collected Works*. Vol. 24. London: Lawrence and Wishart, 1964.

————. *Imperialism, the Highest Stage of Capitalism*. New York: International publishers, 1939.

————. *The State and Revolution* (1917). In Lenin, *Selected Works*. Vol. 1. Moscow: Progress, 1963.

————. *Selected Works*. Vol. 1. Moscow: Progress, 1963.

————. *"Left-Wing Communism"—An Infantile Disorder* (April–May 1920). In Lenin, *Collected Works*. Vol. 31. Moscow: Progress, 1970.

Leonhard, Wolfgang. *Child of the Revolution*. Chicago: University of Chicago Press, 1958.

————. *Eurocommunism: Challenge for East and West*. New York: Holt, Rinehart, and Winston, 1978.

Leslie, R. F., ed. *The History of Poland since 1863*. Cambridge, England: Cambridge University Press, 1980.

Levi, Arrigo. "Eurocommunism: Myth or Reality?" In Paolo Filo della Torre, Edward Mortimer, and Jonathan Story, eds., *Eurocommunism: Myth or Reality?* Harmondsworth: Penguin, 1979.

Levine, David. *Family Formation in the Age of Nascent Capitalism*. New York: Academic Press, 1977.

Levy, Carl. "Education and Self-Education: Staffing the Early ILP." In Carl Levy, ed., *Socialism and the Intelligentsia 1880–1914*. London: Routledge, 1987.

————. "Italian Anarchism 1870–1926," In David Goodway, ed., *Anarchism: History, Theory and Practice*. London: Routledge, 1989.

Levy, David A. L. "The French Popular Front, 1936–37." In Helen Graham and Paul Preston, eds., *The Popular Front in Europe*. New York: St. Martin's Press, 1987.

Lévy-Hass, Hanna. "Interview between Hanna Lévy-Hass and Eike Geisel." In Lévy-Hass, *Inside Belsen*. Totowa, 1982.

Lewin, Moshe. *The Gorbachev Phenomenon.* New York: Pantheon, 1988.

Lewis, Helena. *The Politics of Surrealism.* New York: Paragon, 1988.

Lewis, Jane. "Gender, the Family and Women's Agency in the Building of 'Welfare States': The British Case." *Social History* 19 (1994): 37–55.

Lewis, Jill. *Fascism and the Working Class in Austria 1918–1934.* Providence: Berg, 1991.

Lewis, Steven C., and Serenella Sferza, "French Socialists between State and Society: From Party-Building to Power," In George Ross, Stanley Hoffmann, and Sylvia Malzacher, eds., *The Mitterand Experiment: Continuity and Change in Modern France.* New York: Oxford University Press, 1987.

Lichtheim, George. *Marxism: An Historical and Critical Study.* London: Routledge, 1961.

———. *The Origins of Socialism.* New York: Praeger, 1969.

———. *A Short History of Socialism.* London: Fontana, 1975.

Liddington, Jill. *The Life and Times of a Respectable Rebel: Selina Cooper (1864–1946).* London: Virago, 1984.

———. *The Road to Greenham Common: Feminism and Anti-Militarism in Britain since 1820.* Syracuse, N.Y. Syracuse University Press, 1991.

Lidtke, Vernon. *The Alternative Culture: Socialist Labor in Imperial Germany.* New York: Oxford University Press, 1985.

———. *The Outlawed Party: Social Democracy in Germany, 1878–1890.* Princeton: Princeton University Press, 1966.

Liebich, André, ed. *The Future of Socialism in Europe?* Montreal: Centre interuniversitaire d'études europeénnes, 1979.

Liepitz, Alain. "Governing the Economy in the Face of International Challenge: From National Developmentalism to National Crisis." In James F. Holifield and George Ross, eds., *Searching for a New France.* New York: Oxford University Press, 1991.

Lindenberger, Thomas. *Straßenpolitik: Zur Sozialgeschichte der öffentlichen Ordnung in Berlin 1900 bis 1914.* Bonn: Dietz, 1995.

van der Linden, Marcel. "Second Thoughts on Revolutionary Syndicalism." *Labour History Review* 63 (1998): 182–96.

———. "*Socialisme ou Barbarie*: A French Revolutionary Group (1949–65)." *Left History* 5 (1997): 7–37.

van der Linden, Marcel, and Jürgen Rojahn, eds. *The Formation of Labour Movements 1870–1914: An International Perspective,* Vol. 1. Leiden: Brill, 1990.

Lipgens, Walter. *Documents on the History of European Integration.* Vol. I: Continental Plans on European Union, 1939–1945. New York: de Gruyter, 1985.

———. *A History of European Integration.* Vol. I: 1945–1947. Oxford: Oxford University Press, 1982.

Lipietz, Alain. *Towards a New Economic Order: Post-Fordism, Ecology and Democracy.* Oxford: Oxford University Press 1992.

Lipski, Jan Jozef. *KOR: A History of the Workers' Defense Committee in Poland, 1976–1981.* Berkeley: University of California Press, 1985.

Liu, Tessie P. *The Weaver's Knot: The Contradictions of Class Struggle and Family Solidarity in Western France, 1750–1914.* Ithaca, N.Y.: Cornell University Press, 1994.

———. "What Price a Weaver's Dignity? Gender Inequality and the Survival of Home-Based Production in Industrial France." In Laura L. Frader and Sonya O. Rose, eds., *Gender and Class in Modern Europe*. Ithaca, N.Y.: Cornell University Press, 1996.

Liulevicius, Vejas Gabriel. *War Land on the Eastern Front: Culture, National Identity and German Occupation in World War I*. Cambridge, England: Cambridge University Press, 2000.

Livingstone, Ken. *If Voting Changed Anything, They'd Abolish It*. London: Collins, 1987.

Livingstone, Ken, in conversation with Tariq Ali. *Who's Afraid of Margaret Thatcher? In Praise of Socialism*. London: Verso, 1984.

Lloyd, John. "Socialism Loses Another Old Star." *New Statesman*, 7 August 2000.

Loebl, Eugen. *Stalinism in Prague: The Loebl Story*. New York: Grove Press, 1969.

Logue, John. *Socialism and Abundance: Radical Socialism in the Danish Welfare State*. Minneapolis: University of Minnesota Press, 1982.

Lomax, Bill. *Hungary 1956*. New York: St. Martin's Press, 1976.

———. "The Workers' Councils of Greater Budapest." In Ralph Miliband and John Saville, eds., *Socialist Register 1976*. London: Merlin, 1976.

———, ed. *Eye-Witness in Hungary: The Soviet Invasion of 1956*. Nottingham: Spokesman, 1980.

London, Artur. *The Confession*. New York: Morrow, 1970.

Lorreck, Jochen. *Wie man früher Sozialdemokrat wurde. Das Kommunikationsverhalten in der deutschen Arbeiterbewegung und die Konzeption der sozialistischen Parteipublizistik durch August Bebel*. Bonn: Dietz, 1977.

Lösche, Peter. "Is the SPD Still a Labor Party? From 'Community of Solidarity' to 'Loosely Coupled Anarchy.' " In David E. Barclay and Eric D. Weitz, eds., *Between Reform and Revolution: German Socialism and Communism from 1840 to 1990*. New York: Berghahn, 1998.

———, ed. *Solidargemeinschaft und Milieu: Sozialistische Kultur-und Freizeitorganisationen in der Weimarer Republik*. Vol. 1. Franz Walter. *Sozialistische Akademiker-und Intellektuellenorganisationen in der Weimarer Republik*. Bonn: Dietz, 1990. Vol. 2. Franz Walter, Viola Denecke, and Cornelia Regin. *Sozialistische Gesundheits-und Lebensreformverbände*. Bonn: Dietz, 1991. Vol. 3. Dietmar Klenke, Peter Lilje, and Franz Walter. *Arbeitersänger und Volksbühnen in der Weimarer Republik*. Bonn: Dietz, 1992. Vol. 4. Siegfried Heimann and Franz Walter. *Religiöse Sozialisten und Freidenker in der Weimarer Republik*. Bonn: Dietz, 1993.

Lösche, Peter, and Franz Walter. "Zur Organisationskultur der sozialdemokratischen Arbeiterbewegung in der Weimarer Republik." *Geschichte und Gesellschaft* 15 (1989): 511–36.

Loubère, Leo O. *Louis Blanc: His Life and His Contributions to the Rise of French Jacobin Socialism*. Evanston, Ill.: Northwestern University Press, 1961.

Lovenduski, Joni. *Women and European Politics: Contemporary Feminism and Public Policy*. Brighton England: Harvester, 1986.

Lovenduski, Joni, and Joyce Outshoorn, eds. *The New Politics of Abortion*. London: Sage, 1986.

Löw, Raimund. *Der Zerfall der "Kleinen Internationale." Nationalitätenkonflikte in der Arbeiterbewegung des alten Österreich (1889–1914)*. Vienna: Junius, 1984.

Löwy, Michael. *Georg Lukács—From Romanticism to Bolshevism*. London: Verso, 1979.

———. *The Politics of Combined and Uneven Development: The Theory of Permanent Revolution*. London: Verso, 1981.

Lucas, Erhard. *Märzrevolution März/April 1920*. 3 vols. Frankfurt am Main: Verlag Roter Stern, 1970–78.

———. *Zwei Formen von Radikalismus in der deutschen Arbeiterbewegung*. Frankfurt am Main: Verlag Roter Stern, 1976.

Lucas, John, ed. *The 1930s: A Challenge to Orthodoxy*. Brighton England: Harvester, 1978.

Ludlam, Steve. "Norms and Blocks: Trade Unions and the Labour Party since 1964." In Brian Brivati and Richard Hefferman, eds., *The Labour Party: A Centenary History*. London: Macmillan, 2000.

Lüdtke, Alf. *Eigen-Sinn: Fabrikalltag, Arbeitererfahrungen und Politik vom Kaiserreich bis in den Faschismus*. Hamburg: Ergebnisse, 1993.

———. "Organisational Order or *Eigensinn*? Workers' Privacy and Workers' Politics in Imperial Germany." In Sean Wilentz, ed., *Rites of Power: Symbolism, Ritual, and Politics Since the Middle Ages*. Philadelphia: University of Pennsylvania Press, 1985.

Lüdtke, Alf, Inge Marßolek, and Adelheid von Saldern, eds. *Amerikanisierung: Traum und Alptraum in Deutschland des 20. Jahrhunderts*. Stuttgart: Steiner, 1996.

Luebbert, Gregory M. *Liberalism, Fascism, or Social Democracy: Social Classes and the Political Origins of Regimes in Interwar Europe*. Oxford: Oxford University Press, 1991.

Lukács, Georg. *Lenin: A Study in the Unity of His Thought*. London: New Left Books, 1970.

———. *Political Writings, 1919–1929: The Question of Parliamentarianism and Other Essays*. Edited Rodney Livingstone. London: New Left Books, 1972.

———. *Record of a Life: An Autobiographical Sketch*. Edited by Istvan Eorsi. London: Verso, 1983.

Lukes, Igor. "The Czech Road to Communism." In Norman M. Naimark and Leonid Gibianskii, eds., *The Establishment of Communist Regimes in Eastern Europe, 1944–1949*. Boulder, Colo: Westview, 1997.

Lumley, Robert. *States of Emergency: Cultures of Revolt in Italy from 1968 to 1978*. London: Verso, 1990.

Lunn, Eugene. *Marxism and Modernism: An Historical Study of Lukács, Brecht, Benjamin, and Adorno*. Berkeley: University of California Press, 1982.

Luthardt, Wolfgang, ed. *Sozialdemokratische Arbeiterbwegung und Weimarer Republik: Materialien zur gesellschaftlichen Entwicklung 1927–1933*. 2 vols. Frankfurt am Main: Suhrkamp, 1978.

Luxemburg, Rosa. *Gesammelte Werke*. Vol. 4. Berlin: Dietz, 1974.

Lyons, Matthew Nemiroff. *The "Grassroots network": Radical Nonviolence in the Federal Republic of Germany, 1972–1985*. Ithaca, N.Y.: Center for International Studies, Cornell University, 1988.

Lyttleton, Adrian. "Revolution and Counter-Revolution in Italy, 1918–1922." In

Charles L. Bertrand, ed., *Revolutionary Situations in Europe, 1917–1922: Germany, Italy, Austria-Hungary*. Montréal: Centre interuniversitaire d'études europeénnes, 1977.

Maase, Kaspar. "Establishing Cultural Democracy: Youth, 'Americanization,' and the Irresistible Rise of Popular Culture." In Hanna Schissler, ed., *The Miracle Years: A Cultural History of West Germany, 1949–1968*. Princeton: Princeton University Press, 2001.

MacCarthy, Fiona. "Dame Alix Meynell: A Towering Pioneer for Women in the Civil Service and an Unconventional Figure in British society." *Guardian*, 2 September 1999.

Macciocchi, Maria Antonietta. *Letters from Inside the Italian Communist Party to Louis Althusser*. London: New Left Books, 1973.

MacDonald, Oliver. "The Polish Vortex: Solidarity and Socialism." *New Left Review* 139 (May–June 1983): 5–48.

Machin, Howard, ed. *National Communism in Western Europe*. London: Methuen, 1983.

Macintyre, Stuart. "Joseph Dietzgen and British Working-Class Education." *Bulletin of the Society for the Study of Labour History* 31 (autumn 1974): 50–4.

———. *Little Moscows: Communism and Working-Class Militancy in Inter-War Britain*. London: Croom Helm, 1980.

———. *A Proletarian Science: Marxism in Britain, 1900–1933*. Cambridge, England: Cambridge University Press, 1980.

Mack Smith, Denis. *Mussolini*. New York: Knopf, 1983.

Mackey, Kath. "Women against Pit Closures: From Local Groups to National Organization." In Vicky Seddon, ed., *The Cutting Edge: Women and the Pit Strike*. London: Lawrence and Wishart, 1986.

Mackintosh, Maureen, and Hilary Wainwright, eds. *A Taste of Power: The Politics of Local Economics*. London: Verso, 1987.

MacMillan, James F. *Housewife or Harlot: The Place of Women in French Society, 1870–1940*. New York: St. Martin's Press, 1981.

Magnusson, Lars. *The Contest for Control: Metal Industries in Sheffield, Solingen, Remscheid and Eskilstuna during Industrialization*. Oxford: Berg, 1994.

Magraw, Roger. *France 1815–1914: The Bourgeois Century*. London: Fontana, 1983.

———. "Paris 1917–20: Labour Protest and Popular Politics." In Chris Wrigley, ed., *Challenges of Labour: Central and Western Europe 1917–1920*. London: Routledge, 1993.

———. "Socialism, Syndicalism and French Labour before 1914." In Dick Geary, ed., *Labour and Socialist Movements in Europe before 1914*. Oxford: Berg, 1989.

Maier, Charles S. "Between Taylorism and Technocracy." In *In Search of Stability: Explorations in Historical Political Economy*. Cambridge, England: Cambridge University Press, 1987.

———. *Dissolution: The Crisis of Communism and the End of East Germany*. Princeton: Princeton University Press, 1997.

———. " 'Fictitious Bonds . . . of Wealth and Law': On the Theory and Practice of Interest Representtation." In Suzanne Berger, ed., *Organizing Interests in*

Western Europe: Pluralism, Corporatism, and the Transformation of Politics. Cambridge, England: Cambridge University Press, 1981.

———. "Preconditions for Corporatism." In John H. Goldthorpe, ed., *Order and Conflict in Contemporary Capitalism: Studies in the Political Economy of Western European Nations.* Oxford: Oxford University Press, 1984.

———. *Recasting Bourgeois Europe: Stabilization in France, Germany, and Italy in the Decade after World War I.* Princeton: Princeton University Press, 1975.

———. "The Politics of Productivity: Foundations of American International Economic Policy after World War II." In *In Search of Stability: Explorations in Historical Political Economy.* Cambridge, England: Cambridge University Press, 1987.

Maitland, Sarah, ed. *Very Heaven: Women's Voices from the 1960s.* London: Virago, 1988.

Major, Patrick. *The Death of the KPD: Communism and Anti-Communism in West Germany, 1945–1956.* Oxford: Oxford University Press, 1997.

Malcher, G. C. *Poland's Politicized Army: Communists in Uniform.* New York: Praeger, 1984.

Maleck-Levy, Eva, and Bernhard Maleck. "The Women's Movement in East and West Germany." In Carole Fink, Philipp Gassert, and Detlef Junker, eds., *1968: The World Transformed.* Cambridge, England: Cambridge University Press, 1988.

Maleckova, Jitka. "The Emancipation of Women for the Benefit of the Nation: The Czech Women's Movement." In Bianka Pietrow-Ennker and Sylvia Paletschek, eds., *Women's Movements in Europe in the Nineteenth Century: A Comparative Perspective.* (Forthcoming).

Mallmann, Klaus-Michael. "Milieu, Radikalismus und lokale Gesellschaft: Zur Sozialgeschichte des Kommunismus in der Weimarer Republik." *Geschichte und Gesellschaft* 21 (1995): 5–31.

Mally, Lynn. *Culture of the Future: The Proletkult Movement in Revolutionary Russia.* Berkeley: University of California Press, 1990.

Malyon, Tim. "Tossed in the Fire and They Never Got Burned: The Exodus Collective." In George McKay, ed., *DiY Culture: Party and Protest in Nineties Britain.* London: Verso, 1998.

Mandel, David. *The Petrograd Workers and the Fall of the Old Regime: From the February Revolution to the July Days, 1917.* New York: St. Martin's Press, 1983.

———. *The Petrograd Workers and the Soviet Seizure of Power: from the July Days 1917 to July 1918.* New York: St. Martin's Press, 1984.

Mandel, Ernest. *From Stalinism to Eurocommunism: The Bitter Fruits of "Socialism in One Country."* London: Verso, 1978.

Mangini, Shirley. *Memories of Resistance: Women's Voices from the Spanish Civil War.* New Haven: Yale University Press, 1995.

Manuel, Frank E. *The New World of Henri Saint-Simon.* Notre Dame, Ind.: Notre Dame University Press, 1963.

Maravall, José. *Dictatorship and Political Dissent: Workers and Students in Franco's Spain.* New York: St. Martin's Press, 1978.

Markoff, John. "Really Existing Democracy: Learning from Latin America in the 1990s." *New Left Review* 223 (May–June 1997): 48–68.

————. *Waves of Democracy: Social Movements and Political Change*. Thousand Oaks, Calif.: Pine Forge & Press 1996.

Markovits, Andrei S., and Philip S. Gorski. *The German Left: Red, Green, and Beyond*. Cambridge, England: Cambridge University Press, 1993.

Markovits, Andrei S., and Steven Silvia. "Green Trumps Red? Political Identity and Left-Wing Politics in United Germany." In Christopher S. Allen, ed., *Transformation of the German Political Party System: Institutional Crisis or Democratic Renewal?* New York: Berghahn, 1999.

Marks, Elaine, and Isabelle de Courtivron, eds. *New French Feminisms: An Anthology*. Amherst: University of Massachusetts Press, 1980.

Marquand, David. "Reinventing Federalism: Europe and the Left." *New Left Review* 203 (January–February 1994): 17–26.

Marriott, John. *The Culture of Labourism: The East End between the Wars*. Edinburgh: Edinburgh University Press, 1991.

Marshall, T. H. *Citizenship and Social Class, and Other Essays*. Cambridge, England: Cambridge University Press, 1950.

Marßolek, Inge, and Adelheid von Saldern, eds. *Zuhören und Gehörtwerden I: Radio im Nationalsozialismus. Zwischen Lenkung und Ablenkung*. Tübingen: Edition Diskord, 1998.

Martin, Ron. "Deindustrialization and State Intervention: Keynesianism, Thatcherism and the Regions." In John Mohan, ed., *The Political Geography of Contemporary Britain*. London: Macmillan, 1989.

Marwick, Arthur. *The Sixties: Cultural Revolution in Britain, France, Italy, and the United States, c.1958–c.1974*. Oxford: Oxford University Press, 1998.

————. *Women at War 1914–1918*. London: Croom Helm, 1977.

Marx, Karl. *Capital. A Critique of Political Economy*. Vol. 1. Harmondsworth: Penguin, 1976.

————. *Early Writings*. Edited by Lucio Colletti. Harmondsworth: Penguin, 1975.

————. *The First International and After: Political Writings*. Vol. 3. Edited by David Fernbach. Harmondsworth: Penguin, 1974.

————. *The Revolutions of 1848: Political Writings*. Vol. 1. Edited by David Fernbach. Harmondsworth: Penguin, 1973.

————. *Surveys from Exile: Political Writings*. Vol. 2, Edited by David Fernbach. Harmondsworth: Penguin, 1973.

————. *Selected Correspondence*. Moscow: Progress, 1965.

Marzani, Carl. *The Promise of Eurocommunism*. Westport, Conn.: Greenwood, 1980.

Mason, Tim. "The Workers' Opposition in Nazi Germany." *History Workshop Journal* 11 (1981): 120–37.

Massell, Gregory. *The Surrogate Proletariat: Moslem Women and Revolutionary Strategies in Soviet Central Asia, 1919–1929*. Princeton: Princeton University Press, 1974.

Massey, Doreen, and Hilary Wainwright. "Beyond the Coalfields: The Work of the Miners' Support Groups." In Huw Beynon, ed., *Digging Deeper: Issues in the Miners' Strike*. London: Verso, 1985.

Massey, Doren, and Richard Meegan. *The Anatomy of Job Loss: The How, Why and Where of Employment Decline*. London: Routledge, 1982.

Mastny, Vojtech. *The Czechs under Nazi Rule: The Failure of National Resistance, 1939–1942.* New York: Columbia University Press, 1971.

Mathews, William Carl. "The Economic Origins of the Noskepolitk." *Central European History* 27 (1994): 65–85.

Matthews, Jill Julius. "They Had Such a Lot of Fun: The Women's League of Health and Beauty between the Wars." *History Workshop Journal* 30 (autumn 1990): 22–54.

Mattl, Siegfried. "Austria." In Marcel van der Linden and Jürgen Rojahn, eds., *The Formation of Labour Movements 1870–1914: An International Perspective.* Vol. 1. Leiden: Brill, 1990.

Mavrogordatos, George Th. *Stillborn Republic: Social Coalitions and Party Strategies in Greece, 1922–1936.* Berkeley: University of California Press, 1983.

Mayer, Arno J. *Wilson vs. Lenin: Political Origins of the New Diplomacy, 1917–1918.* New York: World, 1964.

Mayhall, Laura E. Nym. "Reclaiming the Political: Women and the Social History of Suffrage in Great Britain, France, and the United States." *Journal of Women's History* 12 (2000): 172–81.

Mazower, Mark. *Dark Continent: Europe's Twentieth Century.* Harmondsworth: Penguin, 1999.

———. *Inside Hitler's Greece: The Experience of Occupation, 1941–1944.* London: Yale University Press, 1993.

———, ed., *After the War Was Over: Reconstructing the Family, Nation, and the State in Greece, 1943–1960.* Princeton: Princeton University Press, 2000.

McCarthy, Patrick. *The Crisis of the Italian State: From the Origins of the Cold War to the Fall of Berlusconi and Beyond.* New York: St. Martin's Press, 1997.

McCauley, Martin, ed. *Communist Power in Europe 1944–1949.* London: Macmillan, 1977.

McClelland, James C. "The Utopian and the Heroic: Divergent Paths to the Communist Educational Ideas." In Abbott Gleason, Peter Kenez, and Richard Stites, eds., *Bolshevik Culture: Experiment and Order in the Russian Revolution.* Bloomington: University of Indiana Press, 1985.

McDermid, Jane, and Anna Hillyar. *Midwives of the Revolution: Female Bolsheviks and Women Workers in 1917.* London: UCL Press, 1999.

McDermott, Kevin, and Jeremy Agnew. *The Comintern: A History of International Communism from Lenin to Stalin.* Basingstoke: Macmillan, 1996.

McDermott, Kevin. *The Czech Red Unions, 1918–1929. A Study of their Relations with the Communist Party and the Moscow Internationals.* New York: Routledge, 1988.

———. "Rethinking the Comintern: Soviet Historiography, 1987–1991." *Labour History Review* 57 (1992): 37–58.

McDowell, Linda. "Women in Thatcher's Britain," In John Mohan, ed., *The Political Geography of Contemporary Britain.* London: Macmillan, 1989.

McElligott, Anthony. "Mobilizing the Unemployed: The KPD and the Unemployed Workers' Movement in Hamburg-Altona during the Weimar Republic." In Richard J. Evans and Dick Geary, eds., *The German Unemployed: Experiences and Consequences of Mass Unemployment from the Weimar Republic to the Third Reich.* New York: St. Martin's, Press 1987.

———. "Street Politics in Hamburg, 1932–1933." *History Workshop Journal,* 16 (1983): 83–90.

McEwan, Malcom. "The Day the Party Had to Stop." In Ralph Miliband and John Saville, eds., *Socialist Register 1976*. London: Merlin, 1976.

McIntosh, Mary. "The Family, Regulation, and the Public Sphere." In Gregor McLennan, David Held, and Stuart Hall, eds., *State and Society in Contemporary Britain: A Critical Introduction*. Oxford: Blackwell, 1984.

McKay, George. *Senseless Acts of Beauty: Cultures of Resistance since the Sixties*. London: Verso, 1996.

McKenzie, Kermit E. *Comintern and World Revolution 1928–1943: The Shaping of a Doctrine*. New York: Columbia University Press, 1964.

McKibbin, Ross. *The Evolution of the Labour Party 1910–1924*. Oxford: Oxford University Press, 1974.

McLellan, David. *Marxism after Marx*. London: Macmillan, 1979.

McLeod, Hugh. *Piety and Poverty: Working-Class Religion in Berlin, London, and New York 1870–1914*. New York: Holmes and Meier, 1996.

———. *Religion and the People of Western Europe, 1789–1970*. Oxford: Oxford University Press, 1981.

———, ed. *European Religion in the Age of Great Cities, 1830–1930*. London, 1995.

McLoughlin, Barry. "Proletarian Cadres en Route: Austrian NKVD Agents in Britain 1941–43." *Labour History Review* 62 (1997): 296–317.

McMeekin, Sean. "From Moscow to Vichy: Three Working-Class Militants and the French Communist Party, 1920–1940," *Contemporary European History* 9 (2000): 1–38.

McPhee, Peter. *The Politics of Rural Life: Political Mobilization in the French Countryside, 1846–1852*. Oxford: Oxford University Press, 1992.

Meaker, Gerald H. *The Revolutionary Left in Spain, 1914–1923*. Stanford: Stanford University Press, 1974.

Medvedev, Roy. *Leninism and Western Socialism*. London: Verso, 1981.

Melling, Joseph. *Rent Strikes: Peoples' Struggle for Housing in West Scotland 1890–1916*. Edinburgh: Polygon Books 1983.

———. "Welfare Capitalism and the Origins of Welfare States: British Industry, Workplace Welfare and Social Reform, c.1870–1914." *Social History* 17 (1992): 453–78.

Merkel, Wolfgang. "After the Golden Age: Is Social Democracy Doomed to Decline?" In Christiane Lemke and Gary Marks, ed., *The Crisis of Socialism in Europe*. Durham, N.C.: Duke University Press, 1992.

———. *The Third Ways of European Social Democracy at the End of the Twentieth Century*. Heidelberg; University of Heidelberg, 1999.

Merriman, John M. *The Margins of City Life: Explorations on the French Urban Frontier, 1815–1851*. New York: Oxford University Press, 1991.

———. *The Red City: Limoges and the French Nineteenth Century*. New York: Oxford University Press, 1985.

Merson, Allan. *Communist Resistance in Nazi Germany*. London: Lawrence and Wishart, 1985.

Meyer, Thomas. "The Transformation of German Social Democracy." In Donald Sassoon, ed., *Looking Left: Socialism in Europe after the Cold War*. New York: New Press, 1997.

Meynell, Alix. *Private Servant, Public Woman: An Autobiography*. London: Gollancz, 1988.

Micgiel, John. " 'Bandits and Reactionaries': The Suppression of the Opposition in Poland, 1944–1946." In Norman M. Naimark and Leonid Gibianskii, eds., *The Establishment of Communist Regimes in Eastern Europe, 1944–1949*. Boulder, Colo.: Westview, 1997.

Michnik, Adam. *The Church and the Left*. Chicago: University of Chicago Press, 1993.

————. *Letters from Freedom*. Berkeley: University of California Press, 1998.

————. *Letters from Prison and Other Essays*. Berkeley: University of California Press, 1985.

————. "A New Evolutionism," *Survey* 22 (1976): 267–77.

Middlemas, Keith. *Politics in Industrial Society: The Experience of the British System since 1911*. London: Deutsch, 1979.

————. *Power and the Party: Changing Faces of Communism in Western Europe*. London, 1980.

Midgely, David. "Communism and the Avant-Garde: The Case of Georg Lukács." In Edward Timms and Peter Collier, eds., *Visions and Blueprints: Avant-Garde Culture and Radical Politics in Early Twentieth-Century Europe*. Manchester: Manchester University Press, 1988.

Mielke, Siegfried, ed. *Internationales Gewerkschafts-Handbuch*. Opladen Germany: Westdeutscher Verlag, 1983.

Miermeister, Jürgen, and Jochen Staadt, eds. *Provokationen: Die Studenten und Jugendrevolte in ihren Flugblättern 1965–1971*. Darmstadt and Neuwied: Luchterhand, 1980.

Milch, Paul R. "Eurocommunism and Hungary," In Vernon V. Aspaturian, Jiri Valenta, and David P. Burke, eds., *Eurocommunism Between East and West*. Bloomington: University of Indiana Press, 1980.

Miles, Peter, and Malcolm Smith, *Cinema, Literature and Society. Elite and Mass Culture in Interwar Britain*. London: Croom Helm 1987.

Miles, Robert. *Migration and European Integration: The Dynamics of Inclusion and Exclusion*. London: Routledge, 1995.

Miliband, David, ed. *Reinventing the Left*. Cambridge England: Polity, 1994.

Millar, James R., and Sharon Wolchik, eds. *The Social Legacy of Communism*. Cambridge: Cambridge, England University Press, 1994.

Miller, James Edward. *From Elite to Mass Politics: Italian Socialism in the Giolittian Era, 1900–1914*. Kent, Ohio: Kent State University Press, 1990.

Miller, Jill. *You Can't Kill the Spirit: Women in a Welsh Mining Valley*. London: Women's Press, 1986.

Miller, Martin A. *Kropotkin*. Chicago: University of Chicago Press, 1976.

Miller, Suzanne. *Die Bürde der Macht. Die deutsche Sozialdemokratie 1918–1920*. Düsseldorf: Droste, 1978.

————. *Burgfrieden und Klassenkampf. Die deutsche Sozialdemokratie im Ersten Weltkrieg*. Düsseldorf: Droste, 1974.

Millward, Robert, and John Singleton, eds. *The Political Economy of Nationalisation in Britain 1920–1950*. Cambridge, England: Cambridge University Press, 1995.

Milner, Susan. *The Dilemmas of Internationalism: French Syndicalism and the International Labor Movement*. Oxford: Berg, 1990.

Milward, Alan S. *The European Rescue of the Nation-State*. Berkeley: University of California Press, 1992.

————. *The Reconstruction of Western Europe 1945–51.* London; Methuen 1984.

Minnion, John, and Philip Bolsover, eds. *The CND Story.* London: Allison and Busby, 1983.

Misgeld, Klaus, Karl Molin, and Klaus Åmark, eds. *Creating Social Democracy. A Century of the Social Democratic Labor Party in Sweden.* University Park: Penn State University Press, 1992.

Mitchell, Juliet. *Women: The Longest Revolution.* New York: Pantheon, 1984.

————. *Women's Estate.* Harmondsworth: Penguin, 1973.

Mjoset, Lars, Adne Cappelen, Jan Fagerberg, and Bent Sofus Tranoy, "Norway: Changing the Model," In Perry Anderson and Patrick Camiller, eds., *Mapping the West European Left.* London: Verso, 1994.

Mlynar, Zdenek. *Night Frost in Prague.* New York: Karz, 1980.

Moeller, Robert G. *Protecting Motherhood: Women and the Family in the Politics of Postwar West Germany.* Berkeley: University of California Press, 1993.

————. "Reconstructing the Family in Reconstruction Germany: Women and Social Policy in the Federal Republic, 1949–1955." In Moeller, ed., *West Germany under Construction: Politics, Society, and Culture in the Adenauer Era.* Ann Arbor: University of Michigan Press, 1997.

Moi, Toril, ed. *French Feminist Thought: A Reader.* Oxford: Blackwell, 1987.

Moland, Arnfinn. "Norway." In Bob Moore, ed., *Resistance in Western Europe.* Oxford: Berg, 2000.

Mommsen, Hans. "Otto Bauer, Karl Renner und die sozialdemokratische Nationalitätenpolitik in Österreich 1905–1914." In Mommsen, *Arbeiterbewegung und Nationale Frage: Ausgewählte Aufsätze.* Göttingen: Vandenhoeck und Ruprecht, 1979.

————. *Die Sozialdemokratie und die Nationalitätenfrage im habsburgischen Vielvölkerstaat.* Vienna: Europa-Verlag, 1963.

Moore, Bob, ed. *Resistance in Western Europe.* Oxford: Berg, 2000.

Morgan, David. *The Socialist Left and the German Revolution: A History of the German Independent Social Democratic Party, 1917–1922.* Ithaca, N.Y.: Cornell University Press, 1975.

Morgan, Kenneth O. *Labour in Power 1945–1951.* Oxford: Oxford University Press, 1984.

————. *The People's Peace: British History 1945–1989.* Oxford: Oxford University Press, 1990.

————. "Socialism and Syndicalism: The Welsh Miners' Debate, 1912." *Bulletin of the Society for the Study of Labour History* 30 (spring 1975): 22–37.

Morgan, Kevin. *Against Fascism and War: Ruptures and Continuities in British Communist Politics, 1935–41.* Manchester: Manchester University Press, 1989.

————. *Harry Pollitt.* Manchester: Manchester University Press, 1994.

Morken, Kristin, and Per Selle. "An Alternative Movement in a 'State-Friendly' Society: The Women's Shelter Movement." In Lauri Karvonen and Per Selle, eds., *Women in Nordic Politics: Closing the Gap.* Brookfield, Vt.: Dartmouth, 1995.

Morland, David. *Demanding the Impossible: Human Nature and Politics in Nineteenth-Century Social Anarchism.* London: Cassell, 1997.

Mort, Frank. "Essentialism Revisited? Identity Politics and Late Twentieth-Century Discourses of Homosexuality." In Jeffrey Weeks, ed., *The Lesser Evil and the Greater Good: The Theory and Politics of Social Diversity*. London: Lawrence and Wishart, 1994.

Morton, Vivien, and Stuart Macintyre. *T. A. Jackson. A Centenary Appreciation*. London: Lawrence and Wishart, 1979.

Moses, Claire Goldberg. *French Feminism in the Nineteenth Century*. Albany: State University of New York Press, 1984.

———. "Saint-Simonian Men/Saint-Simonian Women: The Transformation of Feminist Thought in 1830s France." *Journal of Modern History* 54 (1982): 240–67.

Moses, John A. *Trade Unionism in Germany from Bismarck to Hitler 1869–1933. Vol. 2. 1919–1933*. Totowa, N.J.: Barnes and Noble, 1982.

Moss, Bernard H. *The Origins of the French Labor Movement 1830–1914: The Socialism of Skilled Workers*. Berkeley: University of California Press, 1976.

Mujal-León, Eusebio. *Communism and Political Change in Spain*. Bloomington: Indiana University Press, 1983.

Mulgan, Geoff, ed. *Life after Politics: New Thinking for the Twenty-First Century*. London: Fontana, 1997.

———. *Politics in an Antipolitical Age*. Cambridge England: Polity, 1994.

Mullan, Mary Kay. "1968: Burntollet Bridge," In Amanda Sebestyen, ed., *'68,'78,'88: From Women's Liberation to Feminism*. Bridport, England: Prism Press, 1988.

Müller, Detlef K., Fritz Ringer, and Brian Simon, eds. *The Rise of the Modern Educational System*. Cambridge, England: Cambridge University Press, 1987.

Müller, Dirk H. *Gewerkschaftliche Versammlungsdemokratie und Arbeiterdelegierte von 1918. Ein Beitrag zur Geschichte des Lokalismus, des Syndikalismus und der entstehenden Rätebewegung*. Berlin: Colloquium Verlag, 1985.

———. "Syndicalism and Localism in the German Trade Union Movement." In Wolfgang J. Mommsen and Hans-Gerhard Husung, eds., *The Development of Trade Unionism in Great Britain and Germany, 1880–1914*. London: Allen and Unwin, 1985.

Murray, Robin. "Fordism and Post-Fordism." In Stuart Hall and Martin Jacques, eds., *New Times: The Changing Face of Politics in the 1990s*. London: Lawrence and Wishart, 1991.

Myant, Martin. *Poland: A Crisis for Socialism*. London: Lawrence and Wishart, 1982.

———. *Socialism and Democracy in Czechoslovakia, 1945–1948*. Cambridge, England: Cambridge University Press, 1981.

Nagle, John D, and Alison Mahr. *Democracy and Democratization: Post-Communist Europe in Comparative Perspective*. London: Routledge, 1999.

Nagy, Imre. *On Communism in Defense of the New Course*. New York: Praeger, 1957.

Nagy, Zsuzsa L. "Budapest and the Revolutions of 1918 and 1919." In Chris Wrigley, ed., *Challenges of Labour: Central and Western Europe 1917–1920*. London: Routledge, 1993.

Naiman, Eric. *Sex in Public: The Incarnation of Early Soviet Ideology*. Princeton: Princeton University Press, 1997.

Naimark, Norman M. *The History of the "Proletariat": The Emergence of*

Marxism in the Kingdom of Poland. New York: Columbia University Press, 1979.

———. *The Russians in Germany: A History of the Soviet Zone of Occupation, 1945–1949.* Cambridge: Harvard University Press, 1995.

———. "The Soviets, the German Left, and the Problem of 'Sectarianism' in the Eastern Zone, 1945 to 1949." In David E. Barclay and Eric D. Weitz, eds., *Between Reform and Revolution: German Socialism and Communism from 1840 to 1990.* New York: Berghahn, 1998.

Naimark, Norman M., and Leonid Gibianskii, eds. *The Establishment of Communist Regimes in Eastern Europe, 1944–1949.* Boulder, Colo.: Westview, 1997.

Nairn, Tom. *The Left against Europe?* Harmondsworth: Penguin, 1973.

———. "Why It Happened." In Angelo Quattrocchi and Tom Nairn, *The Beginning of the End: France, May 1968.* London: Panther 1968; new ed. London: Verso, 1988.

Najdus, Walentyna. "The Relation of the Polish Social Democrats in Galicia to the Habsburg Empire and the Austrian Social Democratic Workers' Party." In Keith Hitchens, ed., *Studies in East European History.* Vol. 1. Leiden: Brill, 1977.

Naphtali, Fritz et al. *Wirtschaftsdemokratie: Ihr Wesen, Weg und Ziel.* Berlin: Diet–1928.

Narinsky, Mikhail, and Jürgen Rojahn, eds. *Centre and Periphery: The History of the Comintern in the Light of New Documents.* Amsterdam: International Institute of Social History 1996.

Nash, Mary.*Defying Male Civilization: Women in the Spanish Civil War.* Denver Colo:, Arden Press, 1995.

———. "Pronatalism and Motherhood in Franco's Spain." In Gisela Bock and Pat Thane, eds., *Maternity and Gender Policies: Women and the Rise of the European Welfare States 1880s–1950s.* London: Routledge, 1991.

Nation, R. Craig. *War on War: Lenin, the Zimmerwald Left, and the Origins of Communist Internationalism.* Durham, N.C.: Duke University Press, 1989.

Nava, Mica. "Modernity's Disavowal: Women, the City and the Department Store." In Mica Nava and Alan O'Shea, eds., *Modern Times: Reflections on a Century of English Modernity.* London: Routledge, 1996.

Nelkin, Dorothy, and Michael Pollak. *The Atom Besieged: Antinuclear Movements in France and Germany.* Cambridge,: Harvard University Press, 1981.

Nelson, Styen Sparre. "Labour Insurgency in Norway: The Crisis of 1917–1920," *Social Science History* 5 (1981): 393–416.

Nettl, J. P. *The Eastern Zone and Soviet Policy in Germany, 1945–50.* London: Routledge, 1951.

———. *Rosa Luxemburg,* 2 vols. Oxford: Oxford University Press, 1966.

Neuberg, A. *Armed Insurrection.* Translated by Quintin Hoare. London: New Left Books, 1970.

Newhouse, John. *Cold Dawn: The Story of SALT.* Washington, D.C.: Pergamon-Brassey's, 1989.

New Left Review, ed. *Exterminism and Cold War.* London: Verso, 1982.

———. *Western Marxism: A Critical Reader.* London: Verso, 1977.

Newman, Michael. *Socialism and European Unity: The Dilemma of the Left in Britain and France.* London: Junction Books, 1983.

Newton, Douglas J. *British Labour, European Socialism and the Struggle for Peace 1889–1914.* Oxford: Oxford University Press, 1985.

Nicolic, Milo, ed. *Socialism on the Threshold of the Twenty-First Century.* London: Verso, 1985.

Nield, Keith. "Edward Carpenter: The Uses of Utopia." *Prose Studies* 13 (May 1990): 18–32.

Niethammer, Lutz et al. *Arbeiterinitiative 1945: Antifaschistische Ausschüsse und Reorganisation der Arbeiterbewegung in Deutschland.* Wuppertal, Germany: Hammer, 1976.

Noiriel, Gérard. *The French Melting Pot: Immigration, Citizenship, and National Identity.* Minneapolis: University of Minnesota Press, 1996.

Nolan, Mary. " 'Housework Made Easy': The Taylorized Housewife in Weimar Germany's Rationalized Economy." *Feminist Studies* 16 (1990): 549–77.

———. *Social Democracy and Society: Working-Class Radicalism in Düsseldorf, 1890–1920.* Cambridge, England: Cambridge University Press, 1981.

———. *Visions of Modernity: American Business and the Modernization of Germany.* New York: Oxford University Press, 1994.

———. "Workers and Revolution in Germany, 1918–1919: The Urban Dimension." In James E. Cronin and Carmen Sirianni, eds., *Work, Community, and Power: The Experience of Labor in Europe and America, 1900–1925.* Philadelphia: Temple University Press, 1983.

Nolte, Claire E. "Every Czech a *Sokol!* Feminism and Nationalism in the Czech *Sokol* Movement." *Austrian History Yearbook* 24 (1993): 79–100.

Novick, Peter. *The Resistance versus Vichy: The Purge of Collaborators in Liberated France.* London: Chatto and Windus, 1968.

Nye, Robert. "The Rise and Fall of the Eugenics Empire: Recent Perspectives on the Impact of Bio-Medical Thought in Modern Society." *Historical Journal* 36 (1993): 687–700.

Obelkevich, James. "Consumption." In James Obelkevich and Peter Catterall, eds., *Understanding Post-War British Society.* London: Routledge, 1994.

von Oertzen, Peter. *Betriebsräte in der Novemberrevolution: Eine politikwissenschaftliche Untersuchung über Ideengehalt und Struktur der betrieblichen und wirtschaftlichen Arbeiterräte in der deutschen Revolution 1918/19.* Düsseldorf: Droste, 1963.

Offen, Karen. "Body Politics: Women, Work, and the Politics of Motherhood in France, 1920–1950." In Gisela Bock and Pat Thane, eds., *Maternity and Gender Policies: Women and the Rise of the European Welfare States 1880s–1950s.* London: Routledge, 1991.

———. "Depopulation, Nationalism, and Feminism in Fin-de-Siècle France." *American Historical Review* 89 (1984): 648–76.

Offermann, Toni. *Arbeiterbewegung und liberales Bürgertum in Deutschland 1850–1863* Bonn: Dietz, 1979.

———. "The Lassallean Labor Movement in Germany: Organization, Social Structure, and Associational Life in the 1860s." In David E. Barclay and Eric D. Weitz, eds., *Between Reform and Revolution: German Socialism and Communism from 1840 to 1990.* New York: Berghahn, 1998.

Oliver, Hermia. *The International Anarchist Movement in Late Victorian London.* London: Croom Helm, 1983.

Olsen, Jonathan. "The PDS after Gysi: A Report from the PDS Congress in Cottbus." *German Politics and Society* 19 (2001): 61–79.

———. "Seeing Red: The SPD-PDS Coalition Government in Mecklenburg-West Pomerania." *German Studies Review* 23 (2000): 557–80.

Orban, Clara. "Women, Futurism, and Fascism." In Robin Pickering-Iazzi, ed., *Mothers of Invention: Women, Italian Fascism, and Culture*. Minneapolis: University of Minnesota Press, 1995.

Oren, Nissan. *Bulgarian Communism: The Road to Power 1934–1944*. New York: Columbia University Press, 1971.

Orwell, George. *The Road to Wigan Pier*. London: Gollancz, 1937.

Orwell, Sonya, and I. Angus, eds. *The Collected Essays, Journalism and Letters of George Orwell*. Vol. 1. Harmondworth: Penguin, 1970.

Osmond, Jonathan. "Yet Another Failed German Revolution? The German Democratic Republic 1989–90." In Moira Donald and Tim Rees, eds., *Reinterpreting Revolution in Twentieth-Century Europe*. New York: St. Martin's Press, 2001.

Ost, David. *Solidarity and the Politics of Anti-Politics*. Philadelphia: Temple University Press, 1990.

O'Sullivan, Sue. "Passionate Beginnings: Ideological Politics 1969–72." In Feminist Review, eds., *Sexuality: A Reader*. London: Virago, 1987.

Padgett, Stephen. "The German Social Democrats: A Redefinition of Social Democracy or Bad Godesberg Mark II." *West European Politics* 16 (1993): 20–38.

Paget, Derek. *True Stories? Documentary Drama on Radio, Screen and Stage*. Manchester: Manchester University Press, 1990.

Pakulski, J. "Social Movements and Class: The Decline of the Marxist Paradigm." In L. Maheu, ed., *Social Movements and Social Classes*. London: Routledge, 1995.

Palmer, Bryan D. "Bread and Roses: Sheila Rowbotham, an Introduction, an Appreciation, and an Interview." *Left History* 2 (spring 1994): 119–38.

Palmer, Stephen E., and Robert R. King. *Yugoslav Communism and the Macedonian Question*. Hamden, Conn.: Archon Books, 1971.

Panitch, Leo. *Social Democracy and Industrial Militancy: The Labour Party, Trade Unions and Incomes Policy, 1945–74*. Cambridge, England: Cambridge University Press, 1976.

Panitch, Leo, and Colin Leys. *The End of Parliamentary Socialism: From New Left to New Labour*. London: Verso, 1997.

Papadakis, Elim. *The Green Movement in West Germany*. London: Croom Helm, 1984.

Parkin, Frank. *Middle Class Radicalism*. Manchester: Manchester University Press, 1968.

Parkin, Sara, ed. *Green Light on Europe*. London: Heretic Books, 1991.

———. *Green Parties: An International Guide*. London: Heretic Books, 1989.

Parrish, Scott. "The Marshall Plan, Soviet-American Relations, and the Division of Europe." In Norman M. Naimark and Leonid Gibianskii, eds., *The Establishment of Communist Regimes in Eastern Europe, 1944–1949*. Boulder, Colo.: Westview, 1997.

Partos, Gabriel. "Ladislav Lis: Charter 77 Reformer Who Survived Persecution after Prague Spring to Witness Czech Democracy." *Guardian*, 25 March 2000.

Passerini, Luisa. *Autobiography of a Generation: Italy, 1968.* Hanover, N.H.: University Press of New England, 1996.

———. *Fascism in Popular Memory: The Cultural Experience of the Turin Working Class.* Cambridge, England: Cambridge University Press, 1987.

Paterson, William E. "The German Social Democratic Party." In Paterson and Alastair H. Thomas, eds., *Social Democratic Parties in Western Europe.* London: Croom Helm, 1977.

Patterson, Henry. *The Politics of Illusion: A Political History of the IRA.* London: Hutchinson Radius, 1997.

Paul, Kathleen. *Whitewashing Britain: Race and Citizenship in the Postwar Era.* Ithaca, N.Y.: Cornell University Press, 1997.

Pedersen, Susan. "The Failure of Feminism in the Making of the British Welfare State." *Radical History Review* 43 (1989): 86–110.

———. "Gender, Welfare, and Citizenship in Britain during the Great War." *American Historical Review* 95 (1990): 983–1006.

Pelikán, Jirí. "The Struggle for Socialism in Czechoslovakia." Interview. *New Left Review* 71 (January–February 1972): 3–35.

———, ed. *The Czechoslovak Political Trials 1950–1954. The Suppressed Report of the Dubcek Government's Commission of Inquiry, 1968.* Stanford: Stanford University Press, 1971.

Pelling, Henry. *The Origins of the Labour Party.* Oxford: Oxford University Press, 1965.

Pennybacker, Susan D. *A Vision for London 1889–1914: Labour, Everyday Life and the LCC Experiment.* London: Routledge, 1995.

Pepper, Hugo. "Die frühe österreichische Sozialdemokratie und die Anfänge der Arbeiterkultur." In Wolfgang Maderthaner, ed., *Sozialdemokratie und Habsburgerstaat.* Vienna: Löcker Verlag, 1988.

Pérez-Díaz, Víctor M. *The Return of Civil Society: The Emergence of Democratic Spain.* Cambridge: Harvard University Press, 1993.

Pernicone, Nunzio. *Italian Anarchism 1864–1892.* Princeton: Princeton University Press, 1993.

Perryman, Mark, ed. *The Blair Agenda.* London: Lawrence and Wishart, 1996.

Péteri, György. *Effects of World War I: War Communism in Hungary.* Vol. 16 of *War and Society in East Central Europe.* New York: Columbia University Press, 1984.

Peterson, Bo. *Media, Minds and Men: A History of Media in Sweden.* Uppsala: Alniquist and Wileseli International 1988.

Peukert, Detlev. *Die KPD im Widerstand: Verfolgung und Untergrundarbeit an Rhein und Ruhr 1933 bis 1945.* Wuppertal, Germany: Hammer, 1980.

Philip, John Gaiter. *The Swedish Green Party: Responses to Parliamentary Challenge 1988–1990.* Stockholm: Norstedt, 1991.

Philipsen, Dirk. *We Were the People: Voices from East Germany's Revolutionary Autumn of 1989.* Durham, N.C.: Duke University Press, 1993.

Philpot, Terry. "Barbara Kahan: Childcare Pioneer Whose 'Pindown' Scandal Report Prompted Residential Care Reform." *Guardian,* 8 August 2000.

Piccone, Paul. *Italian Marxism.* Berkeley: University of California Press, 1983.

Pierson, Stanley. *Marxism and the Origins of British Socialism: The Struggle for a New Consciousness.* Ithaca: Cornell University Press, 1973.

Pike, David Wingeate. "Between the Junes: The French Communists from the Collapse of France to the Invasion of Russia." *Journal of Contemporary History* 28 (1993): 465–85.

Pimlott, Ben. "Joan Bourne: Labour Stalwart Who Made Policy and Suffered Prejudice." *Guardian,* 9 June 2000.

Pinder, John. *The European Community and Eastern Europe.* New York: Council on Foreign Relations Press, 1991.

Pipa, Arshi. "The Political Culture of Hoxha's Albania." In Tariq Ali, ed., *The Stalinist Legacy: Its Impact on Twentieth Century World Politics.* Harmondsworth: Penguin, 1984.

Plant, Sadie. *The Most Radical Gesture: The Situationist International in a Postmodern Age.* London: Routledge, 1992.

Plows, Alex. "Earth First! Defending Mother Earth, Direct-Style." In George McKay, ed., *DiY Culture: Party and Protest in Nineties Britain.* London: Verso, 1998.

Pohl, Rüdiger. "The Macroeconomis of Transformation: The Case of Eastern Germany." *German Politics and Society* 18 (2000): 48–93.

Poiger, Uta G. *Jazz, Rock, and Rebels: Cold War Politics and American Culture in a Divided Germany.* Berkeley: University of California Press, 2000.

———. "Rebels with a Cause? American Popular Culture, the 1956 Youth Riots, and New Conceptions of Masculinity in East and West Germany," In Reiner Pommerin, ed., *The American Impact on Postwar Germany.* Providence: Berghahn, 1995.

Polanyi, Karl. *The Great Transformation* New York: Farrar and Rinehart 1944.

Polasky, Janet. *The Democratic Socialism of Emil Vandervelde: Between Reform and Revolution.* Oxford: Berg, 1995.

Pollard, Sidney. *A History of Labour in Sheffield.* Liverpool: Liverpool University Press, 1959.

Polonsky, Antony, and Boleslaw Drukier, eds. *The Beginnings of Communist Rule in Poland, December 1943 – June 1945.* London: Routledge, 1980.

Pontusson, Jonas. *The Limits of Social Democracy: Investment Politics in Sweden.* Ithaca, N.Y.: Cornell University Press, 1992.

———. "Radicalization and Retreat in Swedish Social Democracy." *New Left Review* 165 (September–October 1987): 5–33.

———. "Sweden: After the Golden Age." In Perry Anderson and Patrick Camiller, eds., *Mapping the West European Left.* London: Verso, 1994.

Port, Andrew. "When Workers Rumbled: The Wismut Upheaval of August 1951 in East Germany," *Social History* 22 (1997): 145–73.

della Porta, Donatella. *Social Movements, Political Violence, and the State: A Comparative Analysis of Italy and Germany.* Cambridge, England: Cambridge University Press, 1995.

Portelli, Alessandro. *The Battle of Valle Giulia: Oral History and the Art of Dialogue.* Madison: University of Wisconsin Press, 1997.

———. "Luigi's Socks and Rita's Makeup: Youth Culture, the Politics of Private Life, and the Culture of the Working Classes." In *The Battle of Valle Giulia: Oral History and the Art of Dialogue.* Madison: University of Wisconsin Press, 1997.

Power, Lisa. *No Bath but Plenty of Bubbles: An Oral History of the Gay Liberation Front, 1970–73.* London: Cassell, 1995.

Preston, Paul. *The Coming of the Spanish Civil War: Reform, Reaction and Revolution in the Second Republic 1931–1936*. London: Macmillan, 1978.

———. "The Creation of the Popular Front in Spain." In Graham and Preston, eds., *Popular Front in Europe*. New York: St. Martin's Press, 1987.

———. "The PCE in the Struggle for Democracy in Spain," In Howard Machin, ed., *National Communism in Western Europe*. London: Methuen, 1983.

———. *The Spanish Civil War 1936–39*. Chicago: HarperCollins, 1986.

———. "The Struggle against Fascism in Spain: *Leviatán* and the Contradictions of the Socialist Left," In Martin Blinkhorn, ed., *Spain in Conflict 1931–1939: Democracy and its Enemies*. London: Sage, 1986.

———. *The Triumph of Democracy in Spain*. London: Methuen, 1986.

Preston, Paul, ed. *Revolution and War in Spain, 1931–1939*. London: Methuen, 1984.

Price, Richard. *An Imperial War and the British Working Class: Working-Class Attitudes and Reactions to the Boer War 1899–1902*. London: Routledge, 1972.

———. *Labour in British Society: An Interpretative History*. London: Routledge, 1986.

Prins, Gwyn, ed. *Defended to Death: A Study of the Nuclear Arms Race by the Cambridge University Disarmament Seminar*. Harmondsworth: Penguin, 1983.

———. *Spring in Winter: The 1989 Revolutions*. Manchester: Manchester University Press, 1990.

Procacci, Giovanna. "Popular Protest and Labour Conflict in italy, 1915–18." *Social History* 14 (1989): 31–58.

Prothero, Iorwerth J. *Artisans and Politics in Early Nineteenth-Century London: John Gast and his Times*. Folkestone, England: 1979.

Proudfoot, Malcom J. *European Refugees, 1939–1952: A Study in Forced Population Movement*. Evanston, Ill.: Northwestern University Press, 1956.

Pugh, Martin. "The Rise of European Feminism," In Pugh, ed., *A Companion to European History 1871–1945*. Oxford: Blackwell, 1997.

Pugliese, Stanislao. *Carlo Rosselli: Socialist Heretic and Antifascist Exile*. Cambridge: Harvard University Press, 1999.

Pumphrey, Martin. "The Flapper, the Housewife, and the Making of Modernity," *Cultural Studies* 1 (1987): 179–94.

Quataert, Jean H. "The Shaping of Women's Work in Manufacturing: Guilds, Households, and the State in Central Europe, 1648–1870." *American Historical Review* 90 (1985): 1122–48.

Quist, Gunnar. "Policy towards Women and the Women's Struggle in Sweden." *Scandinavian Journal of History* 5 (1980): 51–74.

Rabinbach, Anson. *The Crisis of Austrian Socialism: From Red Vienna to Civil War 1927–1934*. Chicago: Chicago University Press, 1983.

———. *The Human Motor: Energy, Fatigue, and the Origins of Modernity*. Berkeley: University of California Press, 1992.

Rabinowitch, Alexander. *The Bolsheviks Come to Power: The Revolution in 1917 in Petrograd*. New York: Norton, 1976.

Radcliff, Pamela Beth. "The Emerging Challenge of Mass Politics." In José Alvarez Junco and Adrian Shubert, eds., *Spanish History since 1808*. London: Arnold, 2000.

——. *From Mobilization to Civil War: The Politics of Polarization in the Spanish City of Gijón, 1900–1937.* Cambridge, England: Cambridge University Press, 1997.

Radkey, Oliver H. *The Election to the Russian Constituent Assembly of 1917.* Cambridge, England: Cambridge University Press, 1950.

Radziejowski, Janusz. *The Communist Party of the Western Ukraine 1919–1929.* Edmonton: Canadian Institute of Ukrainian Studies, 1983.

Ramsden, John. *The Age of Balfour and Baldwin.* London: Longman, 1978.

Ranney, Austin, and Giovanni Sartori, eds. *Eurocommunism: The Italian Case.* Washington, D.C.: American Enterprise Institute 1978.

Rappaport, Erika Diane. *Shopping for Pleasure: Women in the Making of London's West End.* Princeton: Princeton University Press, 2000.

Rattansi, Ali, and Sallie Westwood, eds. *Racism, Modernity, Identity on the Western Front.* Cambridge, England: Cambridge University Press, 1994.

von Rauch, Georg. *The Baltic States. The Years of Independence: Estonia, Latvia, Lithuania 1917–1940.* London: Hurst, 1974.

Ravindranathan, T. R. *Bakunin and the Italians.* Kingston, Ontario: McGill-Queen's University Press, 1988.

Rayside, David. *On the Fringe: Gays and Lesbians in Politics.* Ithaca, N.Y.: Cornell University Press, 1998.

Redhead, S. *Unpopular Cultures.* Manchester: Manchester University Press, 1995.

Redzic, Enver. "Die österreichische Sozialdemokratie und die Frage Bosniens und der Herzegowina," In Keith Hitchens, ed., *Studies in East European History.* Vol. 1. Leiden: Brill, 1977.

Rée, Jonathan. *Proletarian Philosophers: Problems in Socialist Culture in Britain, 1900–1940.* Oxford: Oxford University Press, 1984.

Rees, Tim, and Andrew Thorpe, eds. *International Communism and the Communist International 1919–1943.* Manchester: Manchester University Press, 1998.

Reese, Dagmar, Eve Rosenhaft, Carola Sachse, and Tilla Siegel, eds. *Rationale Beziehungen? Geschlechterverhältnisse im Rationalisierungsprozeß.* Frankfurt am Main: Suhrkamp, 1993.

Regini, Marino. "The Conditions for Political Exchange: How Concertation Emerged and Collapsed in Italy and Great Britain." In John Goldthorpe, ed., *Order and Conflict in Contemporary Capitalism: Studies in the Political Economy of Western European Nations.* Oxford: Oxford University Press, 1984.

——. "Labour Unions, Industrial Action, and Politics." In Peter Lange and Sidney Tarrow, eds., *Italy in Transition: Conflict and Consensus.* London: Cassell, 1980.

Reid, Alastair. "Dilution, Trade Unionism and the State in Britain during the First World War." In Steven Tolliday and Jonathan Zeitlin, eds., *Shop Floor Bargaining and the State.* Cambridge, England: Cambridge University Press, 1985.

Reid, Donald. *The Miners of Decazeville: A Genealogy of Deindustrialization.* Cambridge: Harvard University Press, 1985.

Remington, Robin Alison, ed. *Winter in Prague: Documents on Czechoslovak Communism in Crisis.* Cambridge: Harvard University Press, 1969.

Reshetar, J. S. *The Ukrainian Revolution, 1917–1920: A Study in Nationalism.* Princeton: Princeton University Press, 1952.

Reynolds, David, ed. *The Origins of the Cold War in Europe: International Perspectives.* New Haven: Yale University Press, 1994.

Reynolds, Siân. "Women, Men and the 1936 Strikes in France." In Martin S. Alexander and Helen Graham, eds., *The French and Spanish Popular Fronts. Comparative Perspectives.* Cambridge, England: Cambridge University Press, 1989.

Reynolds, Simon. *Generation Ecstasy: Into the World of Techno and Rave Culture.* New York: Routledge, 1999.

Riasonovsky, Nicholas V. *The Teaching of Charles Fourier.* Berkeley: University of California Press, 1969.

Richards, Andrew J. *Miners on Strike: Class Solidarity and Division in Britain.* Oxford: Berg, 1996.

Richards, Michael. *A Time of Silence: Civil War and the Culture of Repression in Franco's Spain, 1936–1945.* Cambridge, England: Cambridge University Press, 1998.

Richardson, Dick, and Chris Rootes, eds. *The Green Challenge: The Development of Green Parties in Europe.* London: Routledge, 1995.

Richardson, R. Dan. *Comintern Army: The International Brigades and the Spanish Civil War.* Lexington: University Press of Kentucky, 1982.

Rickaby, Tony. "The Artists' International." *History Workshop Journal* 6 (autumn 1978): 154–68.

Riddell, John, ed. *The Communist International in Lenin's Time. Lenin's Struggle for a Revolutionary International. Documents 1907–1916. The Preparatory Years.* New York: Monad Press, 1984.

———. *Founding the Communist International: Proceedings and Documents of the First Congress, March 1919.* New York: Monad Press, 1987.

———. *The German Revolution and the Debate on Soviet Power. Documents 1918–1919: Preparing the Founding Congress.* New York: Monad Press, 1986.

Rigby, Andrew. *Communes in Britain.* London: Routledge, 1974.

Rigby, T. H. *Communist Party Membership in the USSR, 1917–1967.* Princeton: Princeton University Press, 1968.

Riley, Denise. "The Free Mothers: Pronatalism and Working Mothers in Industry at the End of the Last War in Britain." *History Workshop Journal* 11 (spring 1981): 59–118.

———. *War in the Nursery. Theories of the Child and the Mother.* London: Virago, 1983.

Rimbaud, Penny. *The Last of the Hippies: An Hysterical Romance.* Columbus, Ohio: Anok and Peace Press, 1982.

———. *Shibboleth: My Revolting Life.* Edinburgh: AK Press, 1999.

Ringer, Fritz. *Education and Society in Modern Europe.* Bloomington: Indiana University Press, 1979.

Ritter, Gerhard A. "The Second International 1918–1920: Attempts to Recreate the Socialist International and to Influence the Peace Treaties." *Europa: Revue d'études interdisciplinaires* 2 (1978): 11–33.

———, ed. *Die Zweite Internationale 1918/19: Protokolle, Memoranden, Berichte und Korrespondenzen.* 2 vols. Berlin: Dietz, 1980.

Ritter, Gerhard A., and Klaus Tenfelde. "Der Durchbruch der Freien Gewerk-schaften Deutschlands zur Massenbewegung im letzten Viertel des 19. Jahr-hunderts." In Heinz O. Vetter, ed., *Vom Sozialistengesetz zur Mitbestimmung.* Düsseldorf: Bund-Verlag, 1975.

———. *Arbeiter im Deutschen Kaiserreich 1871 bis 1914.* Bonn: Dietz, 1992.

Rizzi, Franco. "Socialist Propaganda in the Italian Countryside." In Jim Obelkov-ich, Lyndal Roper, and Raphael Samuel, eds. *Disciplines of Faith: Studies in Religion, Politics and Patriarchy.* London: Routledge, 1987.

Robert, Jean-Louis. "Mobilizing Labour and Socialist Militants in Paris during the Great War," In John Horne, ed., *State, Society and Mobilization during the First World War.* Cambridge, England: Cambridge University Press, 1997.

Roberts, Julian. *Walter Benjamin.* Atlantic Highlands N.J.: Humanities, 1983.

Roberts, Mary Louise. *Civilization without Sexes: Reconstructing Gender in Post-war France 1917–1927.* Chicago: Chicago University Press, 1994.

Robertson, K. G., ed. *War, Resistance and Intelligence: Essays in Honour of M. R. D. Foot.* Barnsely, Pen and Sword Books England: 1999.

Rojahn, Jürgen. "Poland." In Marcel van der Linden and Jürgen Rojahn, eds., *The Formation of Labour Movements 1870–1914: An International Perspec-tive.* Vol. 1. Leiden: Brill, 1990.

Romera Maura, Joaquín. "Terrorism in Barcelona and Its Impact on Spanish Pol-itics 1904–1909." *Past and Present* 41 (1968): 130–83.

Romsics, Ignác. "The Hungarian Peasantry and the Revolutions of 1918–19." In Chris Wrigley, ed., *Challenges of Labour: Central and Western Europe 1917–1920.* London: Routledge, 1993.

van der Ros, J. "The State and Women: A Troubled Relationship in Norway." In Barbara Nelson and Najma Chowdury, eds., *Women and Politics Worldwide.* New Haven: Yale University Press, 1994.

Rose, R. B. *Gracchus Babeuf: The First Revolutionary Communist.* Stanford: Stanford University Press, 1978.

Rose, Sonya O. " 'Gender at Work': Sex, Class and Industrial Capitalism," *His-tory Workshop Journal* 21 (spring 1986): 113–31.

———. *Limited Livelihoods: Gender and Class in Nineteenth-Century England.* Berkeley: University of California Press, 1992.

Rosen, Ruth. *The World Split Open: How the Modern Women's Movement Changed America.* New York: Penguin, 2000.

Rosenberg, William G. *Liberals in the Russian Revolution. The Constitutional Democratic Party, 1917–1921.* Princeton: Princeton University Press, 1974.

———. "The Zemstvo in 1917 and Its Fate under Bolshevik Rule." In Terrence Emmons and Wayne S. Vucinich, eds., *The Zemstvo in Russia: An Experi-ment in Local Self-Government.* Cambridge, England: Cambridge University Press, 1982.

———, ed. *Bolshevik Visions: First Phase of the Cultural Revolution in Soviet Russia.* Ann Arbor: University of Michigan Press, 1984.

Rosenberg, William G., and Diane P. Koenker. "The Limits of Formal Protest: Worker Activism and Social Polarization in Petrograd and Moscow, March to October 1917." *American Historical Review* 92, 2 (April 1987): 296–326.

Roseneil, Sasha. *Disarming Patriarchy: Feminism and Political Action at Green-ham.* Buckingham, England: Open University Press, 1995.

Rosenhaft, Eve. *Beating the Fascists? The German Communists and Political Violence, 1920–1933.* Cambridge, England: Cambridge University Press, 1983.

———. "Communists and Communities: Britain and Germany between the Wars." *Historical Journal* 26 (1983): 221–36.

———. "Organizing the 'Lumpenproletariat': Cliques and Communists in Berlin during the Weimar Republic." In Richard J. Evans, ed., *The German Working Class 1888–1933: The Politics of Everyday Life.* London: Croom Helm, 1982.

———. "Working-Class Life and Working-Class Politics: Communists, Nazis and the State in the Battle for the Streets, Berlin 1928–1932." In Richard Bessel and Edgar J. Feuchtwanger, eds., *Social Change and Political Development in Weimar Germany.* London: Croom Helm, 1981.

Ross, Ellen. *Love and Toil: Motherhood in Outcast London, 1870–1918.* New York: Oxford University Press, 1993.

Ross, George. "Confronting the New Europe." *New Left Review* 191 (January–February 1992): 49–68.

———. "Fin de Siècle Globalization, Democratization, and the Moore Theses: A European Case Study." In Theda Skocpol, ed., *Democracy, Revolution, and History.* Ithaca, N.Y.: Cornell University Press, 1998.

———. *Jacques Delors and European Integration.* New York: Oxford University Press, 1995.

———. *Workers and Unionists in France: From Popular Front to Eurocommunism.* Berkeley: University of California Press, 1982.

Ross, George, Stanley Hoffmann, and Sylvia Malzacher, eds. *The Mitterand Experiment: Continuity and Change in Modern France.* New York: Oxford University Press, 1987.

Ross, George, and Jane Jensen. "France: Triumph and Tragedy." In Perry Anderson and Patrick Camiller, eds., *Mapping the West European Left.* London: Verso, 1994.

Rossanda, Rossana. "Power and Opposition in Post-Revolutionary Societies." In Il Manifesto, ed., *Power and Opposition in Post-Revolutionary Societies.* London: Ink Links, 1979.

———. "Revolutionary Intellectuals and the Soviet Union." In Ralph Miliband and John Saville, eds., *The Socialist Register 1974.* London: Merlin, 1974.

Rosselli, Carlo. *Liberal Socialism.* Edited by Nadia Urbinati. Princeton: Princeton University Press, 1994.

Rossiter, Adrian. "The Blum Government, the *Conseil National Economique* and Economic Policy." In Martin Alexander and Helen Graham, eds., *The French and Spanish Popular Fronts: Comparative Perspectives.* Cambridge, England: Cambridge University Press, 1989.

Roth, Roland, and Dieter Rucht, eds. *Neue soziale Bewegungen in der Bundesrepublik Deutschland.* Frankfurt: Campus, 1987.

Rothschild, Joseph. *Return to Diversity: A Political History of East Central Europe since World War II.* New York: Oxford University Press, 1989.

Rouette, Susanne. "Mothers and Citizens: Gender and Social Policy in Germany after the First World War." *Central European History* 30 (1997): 48–6.

Rowan, Caroline. " 'Mothers, Vote Labour!' The State, the Labour Movement, and Working-Class Mothers, 1900–1918." In Rosalind Brunt and Caroline

Rowan, eds., *Feminism, Culture and Politics*. London: Lawrence and Wishart, 1982.

Rowbotham, Sheila. "The Beginnings of Women's Liberation in Britain." In *Dreams and Dilemmas: Collected Writings*. London: Virago, 1983.

———. *A Century of Women: The History of Women in Britain and the United States*. London: Penguin, 1997.

———. *Friends of Alice Wheeldon*. London: Pluto Press, 1986.

———. "In Search of Carpenter," *History Workshop Journal* 3 (spring 1977): 121–33.

———. "Making Tracks: Women's Liberation 1972–82." In *Dreams and Dilemmas: Collected Writings*. London: Virago, 1983.

———. "Mapping the Women's Movement," In Monica Threlfall, ed., *Mapping the Women's Movement: Feminist Politics and Social Transformation in the North*. London: Verso, 1996.

———. *A New World for Women: Stella Browne—Socialist Feminist*. London: Pluto Press, 1977.

———. "Our Party Is the People: Edward Carpenter and Radicalism in Sheffield." In *Threads through Time*. London: Penguin, 1999.

———. "Storefront Day Care Centers, the Radical Berlin Experiment." In *Dreams and Dilemmas: Collected Writings*. London: Virago, 1983.

———. "Strategies against Sweated Work in Britain, 1820–1920." In *Threads through Time: Writings on History and Autobiography*. London: Penguin, 1999.

———. "Travellers in a Strange Country: Responses of Working-Class Students to the University Extension Movement, 1873–1910," In *Threads through Time*. London: Penguin, 1999.

———. "Women . . . How Far Have We Come?" In *Dreams and Dilemmas: Collected Writings*. London: Virago, 1983.

Rowbotham, Sheila, Lynne Segal, and Hilary Wainwright. *Beyond the Fragments: Feminism and the Making of Socialism*. London: Merlin, 1979.

Rowbotham, Sheila, and Jeffrey Weeks. *Socialism and the New Life: The Personal and Sexual Politics of Edward Carpenter and Havelock Ellis*. London: Pluto Press, 1977.

Royle, Edward. *Robert Owen and the Commencement of the Millennium: A Study of the Harmony Community*. Manchester: Manchester University Press, 1998.

Rucht, Dieter. "German Unification, Democratization, and the Role of Social Movements: A Missed Opportunity." *Mobilization* 1 (1996): 36–62.

Rüdig, Wolfgang. *The Green Wave: A Comparative Analysis of Ecological Parties*. Cambridge, England: Cambridge University Press, 1991.

Ruggie, Mary. "Gender, Work and Social Progress: Some Consequences of Interest Aggregation in Sweden." In Jane Jensen, Elisabeth Hangen, and Ceallaigh Reddy, eds., *The Feminization of the Labor Force: Paradoxes and Promises*. London: Routledge, 1988.

———. *The State and Working Women: A Comparative Study of Britain and Sweden*. Princeton: Princeton University Press, 1984.

Rupnik, Jacques. "The Czech Socialists and the Nation (1848–1918)." In Eric Cahm and Vladimir Fišera, eds., *Socialism and Nationalism in Contemporary Europe (1848–1945)*. Vol. 2. Nottingham: Spokesman, 1979.

————. *Histoire du Parti communiste tchecoslovaque*. Paris: Fondation nationale des sciences politiques, 1981.

————. *The Other Europe: The Rise and Fall of Communism in East-Central Europe*. London: Weidenfeld and Nicolson, 1988.

————. "The Roots of Czech Stalinism." In Raphael Samuel and Gareth Stedman Jones, eds., *Culture, Ideology and Politics: Essays for Eric Hobsbawm*. London: Routledge, 1983.

Rupp, Leila J. *Worlds of Women: The Making of an International Women's Movement*. Princeton: Princeton University Press, 1997.

Rürup, Reinhard. "Demokratische Revolution und 'dritter Weg': Die deutsche Revolution von 1918/19 in den neueren wissenschaftlichen Diskussion," *Geschichte und Gesellschaft* 9 (1983): 278–301.

————. "Problems of the German Revolution 1918–19." *Journal of Contemporary History* 3 (1968): 109–35.

Ryan, P. A. " 'Poplarism' 1894–1930." In Pat Thane, ed., *The Origins of British Social Policy*. London: Croom Helm, 1978.

Ryback, Timothy W. *Rock around the Bloc: A History of Rock Music in Eastern Europe and the Soviet Union*. New York: Oxford University Press, 1990.

Saarelo, Tauno, and Kimmo Rentola, eds. *Communism: National and International*. Helsinki: Suomen Historiallinen Seura, 1998.

Sabel, Charles, and Jonathan Zeitlin. "Historical Alternatives to Mass Production: Politics, Markets, and Technology in Nineteenth-Century Industrialization." *Past and Present* 108 (August 1985): 133–76.

Sachse, Carola. *Siemens, der Nationalsozialismus und die moderne Familie. Eine Untersuchung zur sozialen Rationalisierung in Deutschland in 20. Jahrhundert*. Hamburg: Rausch und Rîohring Verlag, 1990.

Sachße, Christoph. "Social Mothers: The Bourgeois Women's Movement and German Welfare State Formation, 1890–1929." In Seth Koven and Sonya Michel, ed., *Mothers of a New World: Maternalist Politics and the Origins of Welfare States*. New York: Routledge, 1993.

von Saldern, Adelheid. "Arbeiterkulturbewegung in Deutschland in der Zwischenkriegszeit." In Friedhelm Boll, ed., *Arbeiterkulturen zwischen Alltag und Politik. Beiträge zum europäischen Vergleich in der Zwischenkriegszeit*. Vienna: Europaverlag, 1986.

————. *Auf dem Wege Zum Arbeiter-Reformismus. Parteialltag in sozialdemokratischer Provinz Göttingen: Vandenhoeck and Ruprecht, 1870–1920*. Frankfurt: Materialis, 1984.

————. *Häuserleben: Zur Geschichte städtischen Arbeiterwohnens vom Kaiserreich bis heute*. Bonn: Dietz, 1995.

————. "Modernization as Challenge: Perceptions and Reactions of German Social Democratic Women." In Helmut Gruber and Pamela Graves, eds., *Women and Socialism/Socialism and Women: Europe between the Two World Wars*. New York: Berghahn, 1998.

————. "Sozialdemokratie und kommunale Wohnungsbaupolitik in den 20er Jahren—am Beispiel von Hamburg and Wien." In *Archiv für Sozialgeschichte*, 25 (1985): 183–237.

————. "The Workers' Movement and Cultural Patterns on Urban Housing Estates and in Rural Settlements in Germany and Austria during the 1920s." *Social History* 15 (1990): 233–55.

Salvadori, Massimo. *Karl Kautsky and the Socialist Revolution*. London: Verso, 1979.

Salvati, Michele. "The Crisis of Government in Italy." *New Left Review* 213 (September–October 1995): 76–95.

———. "Muddling Through: Economics and Politics in Italy 1969–1979." In Peter Lange and Sidney Tarrow, eds., *Italy in Transition: Conflict and Consensus*. London: Cassell, 1980.

———. "The Travail of Italian Communism." *New Left Review* 202 (November–December 1993): 117–24.

Samuel, Raphael. "Class Politics: The Lost World of British Communism." Part 3. *New Left Review* 165 (September–October 1986): 52–91.

———. "The Lost World of British Communism." *New Left Review* 154 (November–December 1985): 3–53.

———. "Staying Power: The Lost World of British Communism." Part 2. *New Left Review* 156 (March–April 1987): 63–113.

———. "The Workshop of the World: Steam Power and Hand Technology in Mid-Victorian Britain." *History Workshop Journal* 3 (1977): 6–72.

Samuel, Raphael, Barbara Bloomfield, and Guy Boanas, eds. *The Enemy Within: Pit Villages and the Miners' Strike of 1984–85*. London: Routledge, 1986.

Samuel, Raphael, Ewan McColl, and Stuart Cosgrove. *Theatres of the Left 1880–1935: Workers' Theatre Movements in Britain and America*. London: Routledge, 1985.

Sandford, Gregory W. *From Hitler to Ulbricht: The Communist Reconstruction of East Germany*. Princeton: Princeton University Press, 1974.

Sandford, John. *The Sword and the Ploughshare: Autonomous Peace Initiatives in East Germany*. Nottingham: Spokesman, 1983.

Sanford, G. *Military Rule in Poland; The Rebuilding of Communist Power, 1981–1983*. New York: St. Martin's Press, 1986.

Santore, J. "The Comintern's United Front Initiative of May 1934: French of Soviet Inspiration?" *Canadian Journal of History* 16 (1981): 405–21.

Saraceno, Chiara. "Redefining Maternity and Paternity: Gender, Pronatalism and Social Policies in Fascist Italy." In Gisela Bock and Pat Thane, eds., *Maternity and Gender Policies: Women and the Rise of the European Welfare States 1880s–1950s*. London: Routledge, 1991.

———. "Shifts in Public and Private Boundaries: Women as Mothers and Service Workers in Italian Daycare." *Feminist Studies* 10 (1984): 7–29.

Sarti, Roland. *Mazzini: A Life for the Religion of Politics*. Westport, Conn. Greenwood, 1997.

Sartre, Jean-Paul. *The Communists and Peace. With an Answer to Claude Lefort*. London: Hamilton, 1969.

Sassoon, Donald. "Nilde Iotti: Italy's Leading Postwar Woman Politician and a Founding Mother of the Republic." *Guardian*, 9 December 1999.

———. "The Rise and Fall of West European Communism 1939–48." *Contemporary European History* 1 (1992): 139–69.

———. *One Hundred Years of Socialism: The West European Left in the Twentieth Century*. London: Tauris, 1996.

———. *The Strategy of the Italian Communist Party: From the Resistance to the Historic Compromise*. London: St. Martin's, Press, 1981.

Savage, Jon. *England's Dreaming: Sex Pistols and Punk Rock*. London: Faber, 1991.

Savage, Mike. *The Dynamics of Working-Class Politics: The Labour Movement in Preston, 1880–1940*. Cambridge, England: Cambridge University Press, 1987.

Savage, Mike, and Andrew Miles. *The Remaking of the British Working Class 1840–1940*. London: Routledge, 1994.

Saville, John. "May Day 1937," In Asa Briggs and John Saville, eds., *Essays in Labour History 1918–1939*. London: Croom Helm, 1977.

———. *The Politics of Continuity: British Foreign Policy and the Labour Government 1945–46*. London: Verso, 1993.

Scharf, Thomas. *The German Greens: Challenging the Consensus*. Providence: Berg, 1994.

Schechtman, Joseph B. *Postwar Population Transfers in Europe, 1945–1955*. Philadelphia: Temple University Press, 1962.

Schissler, Hanna. " 'Normalization' as Project; Some Thoughts on Gender Relations in West Germany during the 1950s," In Schissler, ed., *The Miracle Years: A Cultural History of West Germany, 1949–1968*. Princeton: Princeton University Press, 2001.

———. "Social Democratic Gender Policies, the Working-Class Milieu, and the Culture of Domesticity in West Germany in the 1950s and 1960s." In David E. Barclay and Eric D. Weitz, eds., *Between Reform and Revolution: German Socialism and Communism from 1840 to 1990*. New York: Berghahn, 1998.

Schlesinger, Rudolf. *Central European Democracy and Its Background*. London, 1953.

Schlosser, Eric. "Saturday Night at the Hacienda." *Atlantic Monthly* 282, 4 (October 1998): 22–34.

Schmidt, Günther, and Renate Weitzel, eds. *Sex Discrimination and Equal Opportunity. The Labour Market and Employment Policy*. Aldershot, England: Elgar, 1984.

Schmitt, Hans A., ed. *Neutral Europe between War and Revolution 1917–1923*. Charlottesville: University of Virgina Press, 1988.

Schnapp, Alain, and Pierre Vidal-Naquet. *The French Student Uprising, November 1967–June 1968: An Analytical Record*. Boston: Beacon Press 1971.

Schneede, Uwe M. *George Grosz: His Life and Work*. New York: Macmillan, 1979.

Schneer, Jonathan. "The War, the State and the Workplace: British Dockers during 1914–1918." In James E. Cronin and Jonathan Schneer, eds., *Social Conflict and the Political Order in Modern Britain*. New Brunswick, N.J.: Rutgers University Press, 1982.

Schneider, Michael. *Das Arbeitsbeschaffungsprogramm des ADGB. Zur gewerkschaftlichen Politik in der Endphase der Weimarer Republik*. Bonn: Dietz, 1975.

———. *A Brief History of the German Trade Unions*. Bonn: Dietz, 1991.

———. *Die Christlichen Gewerkschaften 1894–1933*. Bonn: Dietz, 1982.

———. *Demokratie in Gefahr? Der Konflikt um die Notstandsgesetze: Sozialdemokratie, Gewerkschaften und intellektueller Protest (1958–1968)*. Bonn: Dietz, 1986.

———. "In Search of a 'New' Historical Subject: The End of Working-Class Culture, the Labor Movement, and the Proletariat." *International Labor and Working-Class History* 32 (fall 1987): 46–58.

————. "Religion and Labor Organization: The Christian Trade Unions in the Wilhelmine Empire," *European Studies Review* 12 (1982): 345–69.

Schneider, William H. *Quality and Quantity: The Quest for Biological Regeneration in Twentieth-Century France.* Cambridge, England: Cambridge University Press, 1990.

Scholliers, Peter. "The Social-Democratic World of Consumption: The Path-Breaking Case of the Ghent Cooperative *Vooruit* Prior to 1914," *International Labor and Working-Class History* 55 (spring 199): 71–91.

Schönhoven, Klaus. *Expansion und Konzentration. Studien zur Entwicklung der Freien Gewerkschaften im Wilhelminischen Deutschland 1890 bis 1914.* Stuttgart: Klett-Cotta, 1980.

————. "Localism—Craft Union—Industrial Union: Organizational Patterns in German Trade Unions." In Wolfgang J. Mommsen and Hans-Gerhard Husung, eds., *The Development of Trade Unionism in Great Britain and Germany, 1880–1914.* London: Allen and Unwin, 1985.

Schorske, Carl E. *Fin de Siecle Vienna: Politics and Culture.* New York: Vintage Books, 1980.

————. *German Social Democracy 1905–1917: The Development of the Great Schism.* New York: Wiley, 1955.

Schöttler, Peter. *Die Entstehung der "Bourses du Travail." Sozialpolitik und französischer Syndikalismus am Ende des 19. Jahrhunderts.* Frankfurt on Main: Campus, 1982.

————. "Syndikalismus in der europäischen Arbeiterbewegung. Neuere Forschungen in Frankreich, England und Deutschland," In Klaus Tenfelde, ed., *Arbeiter und Arbeitebewegung im Vergleich: Berichte zur internationalen historischen Forschung.* Munich: Oldenbourg, 1986.

Schröder, Hans-Christoph. *Gustav Noske und die Kolonialpolitik des Deutschen Kaiserreiches.* Berlin: Dietz, 1979.

————. *Sozialistische Imperialimusdeutung: Studien zu ihrer Geschichte.* Göttingen: Vandenhoeck und Ruprecht, 1973.

————. *Sozialismus und Imperialismus. Die Auseinandersetzungen der deutschen Sozialdemokratie mit dem Imperialismusproblem und der "Weltpolitik" vor 1914.* Hanover, Germany: Verlag für Literatur und Zeitgeschehen, 1968.

Schulze, Hagen. *Freikorps und Republik 1918–1920.* Boppard, Germany: Bundesarchiv, 1969.

Schütte-Lihotsky, Margarete. *Memories from the Resistance: The Aggressive Life of an Architect between 1938 and 1945.* London: Weidenfeld and Nicolson, 1985.

Schwarz, Bill. "The Corporate Economy, 1890–1929." In Mary Langan and Bill Schwarz, eds., *Crises in the British State 1880–1930.* London: Hutchinson, 1985.

Schwarz, Bill, and Martin Durham. " 'A Safe and Sane Labourism': Socialism and the State, 1910–24." In Mary Langan and Bill Schwarz, eds., *Crises in the British State 1880–1930.* London: Hutchinson, 1985.

Schwarzkopf, Jutta. *Women in the Chartist Movement.* London: Macmillan 1991.

Science and Technology Subgroup, The. (Maureen McNeil, Wendy Fyfe, Deborah Lynn Steinberg, Sarah Franklin, Tessa Randles.) "In the Wake of the Alton Bill: Science, Technology and Reproductive Politics." In Sarah Franklin, Celia

Lury, and Jackie Stacey, eds., *Off-Centre: Feminism and Cultural Studies.* London: Hutchinson, 1991.

Scott, Joan Wallach. *The Glassworkers of Carmaux: French Craftsmen and Political Action in a Nineteenth-Century City.* Cambridge: Harvard University Press, 1974.

———. "Men and Women in the Parisian Garment Trades: Discussions of Family and Work in the 1830s and 1840s." In Pat Thane, Geoffrey Crossick, and Roderick Floud, eds., *The Power of the Past: Essays for Eric Hobsbawm.* Cambridge, England: Cambridge University Press, 1984.

———. *Only Paradoxes to Offer: French Feminists and the Rights of Man.* Cambridge, England: Cambridge University Press, 1996.

———. "Social History and the History of Socialism: French Socialist Municipalities in the 1890s." *Mouvement Social,* 111 (1980): 145–53.

Scuto, Denis. *Sous le signe de la grande grève de mars 1921: Les années sans pareilles du mouvement ouvrier luxembourgeois 1918–1923.* Esch-sur-Alzette: Edit press, 1990.

Searle, Geoffrey R. *Eugenics and Politics in Britain.* Leiden: Brill, 1976.

Seddon, Vicky, ed. *The Cutting Edge: Women and the Pit Strike.* London: Routledge, 1986.

Segal, Lynne. *Is the Future Female? Troubled Thoughts on Contemporary Feminism.* New York: Peter Bedrick Books, 1987.

———. "A Local Experience." In Sheila Rowbotham, Lynne Segal, and Hilary Wainwright. *Beyond the Fragments: Feminism and the Making of Socialism.* London: Merlin, 1979.

———. " 'The Most Important Thing of All'—Rethinking the Family: An Overview." In Segal, ed., *What Is To Be Done about the Family?* Harmondsworth: Penguin, 1983.

Seidman, Michael. *Workers against Work: Labor in Paris and Barcelona during the Popular Fronts.* Berkeley: University of California Press, 1991.

Semelin, Jacques. *Unarmed against Hitler: Civilian Resistance in Europe, 1939–1943.* New York: Praeger, 1993.

Semprun, Jorge. *Communism in Spain in the Franco Era: The Autobiography of Federico Sanchez.* Brighton England: Harvester, 1980.

Service, Robert. *The Bolshevik Party in Revolution 1917–1923.* London: Macmillan, 1979.

Seton-Watson, Christopher. *Italy from Liberalism to Fascism 1870–1925.* London: Methuen, 1967.

———. "Terrorism in Italy." In Juliet Lodge, ed., *The Threat of Terrorism.* Brighton England: Harvester, 1988.

Sewell, Jr., William J. *Work and Revolution in France: The Language of Labor from the Old Regime to 1848.* Cambridge, England: Cambridge University Press, 1980.

Seyd, Patrick. *The Rise and Fall of the Labour Left.* London: Macmillan, 1987.

Shunin, Teodor. *The Roots of Otherness: Russia's Turn of the Century.* Vol. 2. *Russia 1905–07. Revolution as a Moment of Truth.* New Haven: Yale University Press, 1986.

———, ed. *Late Marx and the Russian Road: Marx and "the Peripheries of Capitalism."* London: Routledge, 1983.

Share, Donald. *Dilemmas of Social Democracy. The Spanish Socialist Workers Party in the 1980s.* Westport, Conn.: Greenwood Press, 1989.

Sharma, Sanjay, John Hutnyk, and Ashwani Sharma, eds. *Dis-Orienting Rhythms: The Politics of the New Asian Dance Music.* London: Zed Books, 1996.

Shennan, Andrew. *Rethinking France: Plans for Renewal 1940–1946.* Oxford: Oxford University Press, 1989.

Shields, Rob. *Lefebvre, Love and Struggle: Spatial Dialectics.* London: Routledge, 1999.

Shoup, Paul. *Communism and the Yugoslav National Question.* New York: Columbia University Press, 1968.

Shubert, Adrian. "Revolution in Self-Defence: The Radicalization of the Asturian Coal Miners, 1921–34." *Social History* 7 (1982): 265–82.

———. *The Road to Revolution in Spain.* Urbana: University of Illinois Press, 1987.

Siegelbaum, Lewis. *The Politics of Industrial Mobilization: A Study of the War Industries Committees in Russia, 1914–1917.* New York: St. Martin's, Press, 1983.

Siegenthaler, Jürg. "Producers' Cooperatives in Switzerland." *International Labor and Working-Class History* 11 (May 1977): 19–25.

Silj, Alessandro. *Never Again without a Rifle: The Origins of Italian Terrorism.* New York: Karz, 1979.

Sillars, Jim. *Scotland: The Case for Optimism.* Edinburgh: Polygon, 1986.

Simecka, Milan. *The Restoration of Order: The Normalization of Czechoslovakia 1969–1976.* London: Verso, 1984.

Simmonds, J. C. Don. "The French Communist Party and the Beginnings of Resistance." *European Studies Review* 11 (1981): 517–42.

Simonson, Birger. "Sweden." In Marcel van der Linden and Jürgen Rojahn, eds., *The Formation of Labour Movements 1870–1914: An International Perspective.* Vol. 1. Leiden: Brill, 1990.

Sinfield, Alan. *Literature, Politics, and Culture in Postwar Britain.* Berkeley: University of California Press, 1989.

Skilling, H. Gordon. *Charter 77 and Human Rights in Czechoslovakia.* London: Macmillan, 1981.

———. *Czechoslovakia's Interrupted Revolution.* Princeton: Princeton University Press, 1976.

———. *Samizdat and Independent Society in Central and Eastern Europe.* London: Macmillan, 1989.

———. *T. G. Masaryk: Against the Current, 1882–1914.* University Park: Penn State University Press, 1994.

Skjeie, Hege. "The Uneven Advance of Norwegian Women." *New Left Review* 187 (May–June 1991): 79–102.

Skelton, Robin, ed. *Poetry of the Thirties.* Harmondsworth: Penguin, 1964.

Slatter, John. "Learning from Russia: The History of Soviets in Britain." *Labour History Review* 61 (1996): 5–29.

Slaughter, Jane. *Women and the Italian Resistance 1943–1945.* Denver: Arden Press, 1997.

Smaldone, William. *Rudolf Hilferding: The Tragedy of a German Social Democrat.* DeKalb: University of Northern Illinois Press, 1998.

Smith, Angel. "Anarchism, the General Strike, and the Barcelona Labour Movement 1899–1914." *European History Quarterly* 27 (1997): 5–40.

Smith, Anna Marie. *New Right Discourse on Race and Sexuality: Britain, 1968–1990.* Cambridge, England: Cambridge University Press, 1994.

Smith, Bonnie G. *Changing Lives: Women in European History since 1700.* Lexington, Mass.: Heath, 1989.

Smith, Dennis. *Conflict and Compromise: Class Formation in English Society 1830–1914.* London: Routledge, 1982.

Smith, Harold L. "British Feminism in the 1920s," In Smith, ed., *British Feminism in the Twentieth Century.* Aldershot, England: Elgar, 1990.

Smith, Joan. "Labour Traditions in Glasgow and Liverpool." *History Workshop Journal* 17 (spring 1984): 32–54.

Smith, Michael L. and Peter M. R. Stirk, eds., *Making the New Europe: European Unity and the Second World.* London: Pinter Publishers, 1990.

Smith, Patricia J., ed. *After the Wall: Eastern Germany since 1989.* Boulder, Colo.: Westview, 1998.

Smith, Steve A. *Red Petrograd: Revolution in the Factories 1917–1918.* Cambridge, England: Cambridge University Press, 1983.

Smith, Susan J. "The Politics of 'Race' and a New Segregationism." In John Mohan, ed., *The Political Geography of Contemporary Britain.* London: Macmillan, 1989.

Smrkovsk, Josef. "How They Crushed the Prague Spring." In Tariq Ali, ed., *The Stalinist Legacy: Its Impact on Twentieth-Century World Politics.* Harmondsworth: Penguin, 1984.

Snowden, Frank M. "From Sharecropper to Proletarian: The Background to Fascism in Rural Tuscany, 1880–1920." In John A. Davis, ed., *Gramsci and Italy's Passive Revolution.* London: Croom Helm, 1979.

Soboul, Albert. *The Sans-Culottes: The Popular Movement and Revolutionary Government 1793–1794.* Princeton: Princeton University Press, 1980.

Sochor, Zenovia A. *Revolution and Culture: The Bogdanov-Lenin Controversy.* Ithaca, N.Y.: Cornell University Press, 1988.

Šolle, Zeněk. "Die tschechische Sozialdemokratie zwischen Nationalismus und Internationalismus." *Archiv fur Sozialgeschichte* 9 (1969): 181–266.

Solomos, John. *Race and Racism in Britain.* 2nd ed. New York: St. Martin's Press, 1993.

Soloway, Richard A. *Demography and Degeneration: Eugenics and the Declining Birthrate in Twentieth-Century Britain.* 2nd ed. Chapel Hill: University of North Carolina Press, 1995.

Somers, Margaret R. "Narrativity, Narrative Identity, and Social Action: Rethinking English Working-Class Formation." *Social Science History* 26 (1992): 591–630.

———. "Workers of the World, Compare!" *Contemporary Sociology* 18 (1989): 325–30.

Sommestad, Lena. "Gendering Work, Interpreting Gender: The Masculinization of Dairy Work in Sweden, 1850–1950." *History Workshop Journal* 37 (spring 1994): 57–75.

Sonn, Richard D. *Anarchism and Cultural Politics in Fin de Siècle France.* Lincoln: University of Nebraska Press, 1989.

Sowerwine, Charles. *Sisters or Citizens? Women and Socialism in France since 1876.* Cambridge, England: Cambridge University Press, 1982.

Spencer, Michael Clifford. *Charles Fourier.* Boston: Twayne, 1991.

Spitzer, Alan B. *The Revolutionary Theories of Louis Auguste Blanqui.* New York: Columbian University Press, 1957.

Spriano, Paolo. *Antonio Gramsci and the Party: The Prison Years.* London: Lawrence and Wishart, 1979.

———. *The Occupation of the Factories: Italy 1920.* London: Pluto Press, 1975.

———. *Stalin and the European Communists.* London: Verso, 1985.

Srebnik, Henry. *London Jews and British Communism.* London: Lawrence and Wishart, 1995.

Stafford, David. *From Anarchism to Reformism: A Study of the Political Activities of Paul Brousse 1870–90.* Toronto: Unviersity of Toronto Press, 1971.

Stalin, Joseph. *Leninism.* London: Allen and Unwin, 1940.

Stanizskis, Jadwiga. *The Dynamics of Breakthrough in Eastern Europe: The Case of Poland.* Berkeley: University of California Press, 1991.

———. *Poland's Self-Limiting Revolution.* Princeton: Princeton University Press, 1986.

Stanley, Alessandra. "*L'Unita,* Leftist Italian Paper, Halts Publication." *New York Times,* 29 July 2000.

Stansill, Peter, and Savid Zane Mairowitz, eds. *Bamn: Outlaw Manifestos and Ephimera 1965–70.* Harmondsworth: Penguin, 1971.

Stanton, Martin. "French Intellectual Groups and the Popular Front: Traditional and Innovative Uses of the Media." In Martin Alexander and Helen Graham, eds., *The French and Spanish Popular Fronts: Comparative Perspectives.* Cambridge, England: Cambridge University Press, 1989.

Stavrakis, Peter J. *Moscow and Greek Communism, 1944–1949.* Ithaca, N.Y.: Cornell University Press, 1989.

Steedman, Carolyn. *Childhood, Culture and Class in Britain: Margaret McMillan, 1860–1931.* New Brunswick, N.J.: Rutgers University Press, 1990.

Steenson, Gary. *Karl Kautsky 1854–1938: Marxism in the Classical Years.* Pittsburgh: University of Pittsburgh Press, 1978.

Steinberg, Hans-Josef. "Workers' Libraries in Germany before 1914." *History Workshop Journal* 1 (spring 1976): 166–84.

Steiner, Herbert. "Die Internationale Arbeitsgemeinschaft Sozialistischer Parteien (2½ Internationale)." In Enzo Collotti, ed., *L'Internationale Operaia e Socialista tra le due guerre.* Milan: Feltriuelli, 1985.

Stella, Simonetta Piccone. " 'Rebels Without a Cause': Male Youth in Italy around 1960." *History Workshop Journal* 38 (Fall 1994): 157–78.

Stirk, Peter M. R., and David Willis, eds. *Shaping Postwar Europe: European Unity and Disunity 1945–1957.* London: Pinter, 1991.

Stites, Richard. *Revolutionary Dreams: Utopian Vision and Experimental Life in the Russian Revolution.* Oxford: Oxford University Press, 1989.

Stoehr, Irene "Housework and Motherhood: Debates and Policies in the Women's Movement in Imperial Germany and the Weimar Republic." In Gisela Bock and Pat Thane, eds., *Maternity and Gender Policies: Women and the Rise of the European Welfare States 1880s–1950s.* London: Routledge, 1991.

Stokes, Gale. *The Walls Came Tumbling Down: The Collapse of Communism in Eastern Europe*. New York: Oxford University Press, 1993.

———, ed. *From Stalinism to Pluralism: A Documentary History of Eastern Europe since 1945*. 2nd ed. New York: Oxford University Press, 1996.

Stone, Norman. *Europe Transformed: 1878–1919*, 2nd ed. Oxford: Blackwell, 1999.

Storr, Merl. "New Sexual Minorities, Opposition and Power: Bisexual Politics in the UK." In Tim Jordan and Adam Lent, eds., *Storming the Millennium: The New Politics of Change*. London: Lawrence and Wishart, 1999.

Strikwerda, Carl. *A House Divided: Catholics, Socialists, and Flemish Nationalists in Nineteenth-Century Belgium*. Lanham, Md:Roman and Littlefield, 1997.

Strinati, Dominic. "The Taste of America: Americanization and Popular Culture in Britain." In Dominic Strinati and Stephen Wagg, eds., *Come On Down? Popular Media Culture in Post-War Britain*. London: Routledge, 1992.

Stuart, Robert. *Marxism at Work: Ideology, Class and French Socialism during the Third Republic*. Cambridge, England: Cambridge University Press, 1992.

Students and Staff of Hornsey College of Art. *The Hornsey Affair*. Harmondsworth: Penguin, 1969.

Sturmthal, Adolf. *Left of Center: European Labor since World War II*. Urbana: University of Illinois Press, 1983.

Suddick, Anna. "Making the Links: Women against Pit Closures." In Raphael Samuel and Hilary Wainwright, eds., *A Nuclear Future?* London: Merlin, 1986.

Sukiennicki, Wiktor. "An Abortive Attempt at International Unity of the Workers' Movement: The Berlin Conference of the Three Internationals, 1922)." In Alxander Rabinowitch, Janet Rabinowitch, and K. D. Kristof Ladis, eds., *Revolution and Politics in Russia: Essays in Memory of B. I. Nicolaevsky*. Bloomington: University of Indiana Press, 1972.

Sullivan, J. *ETA and Basque Nationalism: The Fight for Euskadi 1890–1986*. London, 1988.

Suny, Ronald Grigor. *The Baku Commune 1917–1918: Class and Nationality in the Russian Revolution*. Princeton: Princeton University Press, 1973.

———. *The Making of the Georgian Nation*. 2nd ed. Bloomington: University of Indiana Press, 1994.

——— "National Revolutions and Civil War in Russia." In *The Revenge of the Past: Nationalism, Revolution, and the Collapse of the Soviet Union*. Stanford: Stanford University Press, 1993.

———. *The Soviet Experiment: Russia, the USSR, and the Successor States*. New York: Oxford University Press, 1998.

———. "Stalin and His Stalinism: Power and Authority in the Soviet Union, 1930–1953," In Ian Kershaw and Moshe Lewin, eds., *Stalinism and Nazism: Dictatorships in Comparison*. Cambridge, England: Cambridge University Press, 1997.

———. "Toward a Social History of the October Revolution," *American Historical Review* 88, 1 (February 1983): 31–52.

Swaan, Abram de. *In Care of the State: Health Care, Education and Welfare in Europe in the Modern Era*. Cambridge, England: Polity, 1988.

Swain, Geoffrey, and Nigel Swain. *Eastern Europe since 1945*. New York: St. Martin's Press, 1993.

Swain, Nigel. *Hungary. The Rise and Fall of Feasible Socialism*. London: Verso, 1992.

Sweets, John F. *The Politics of Resistance in France (1940–1944): A History of the Mouvements Unis de la Résistance*. Dekalb: University of Northern Illinois Press, 1976.

Swindells, Julia, and Lisa Jardine. *What's Left? Women in Culture and the Labour Movement*. London: Routledge, 1990.

Sywottek, Arnold. "The Americanization of Everyday Life? Early Trends in Consumer and Leisure Time Behavior," In Michael Ermarth, ed., *America and the Shaping of German Society 1945–1955*. Providence: Berghahn, 1993.

Szelenyi, Ivan. "Eastern Europe in an Epoch of Transition: Toward a Socialist Mixed Economy?" In Victor Nee and David Stark, eds., *Renaking the Economic Institutions of Socialism: China and Eastern Europe*. Stanford: Stanford University Press, 1989.

Tabili, Laura. *"We Ask for British Justice": Workers and Racial Difference in Late Imperial Britain*. Ithaca, N.Y.: Cornell University Press, 1994.

Tampke, Jürgen. *The Ruhr and Revolution: The Revolutionary Movement in the Rheinish-Westphalian Industrial Region, 1912–1919*. London: Croom Helm, 1979.

Tannahill, R. Neal. *The Communist Parties of Western Europe*. Wesport, Conn.: Greenwood, 1978.

Tanner, Duncan. *Political Change and the Labour Party 1900–1918*. Cambridge, England: Cambridge University Press, 1990.

Tarrow, Sidney. *Center and Periphery: Grassroots Politicians in Italy and France*. New Haven: Yale University Press, 1977.

———. *Democracy and Disorder: Protest and Politics in Italy 1965–1975*. Oxford: Oxford University Press, 1989.

———. *Power in Movement: Social Movements, Collective Action and Politics*. Cambridge, England: Cambridge University Press, 1994.

Tatchell, Peter. *The Battle for Bermondsey*. London: Heretic Books, 1983.

Taylor, Anne. *Visions of Harmony: A Study in Nineteenth-Century Millenarianism*. Oxford: Oxford University Press, 1987.

Taylor, Barbara. *Eve and the New Jerusalem: Socialism and Feminism in the Nineteenth Century*. New York: Pantheon, 1983.

———. "Socialist Feminism: Utopian or Scientific?" In Raphael Samuel, ed., *People's History and Socialist Theory*. London: Routledge, 1981.

Taylor, Lynn. "Collective Action in Northern France, 1940–1944," *French History* 11 (1997): 190–214.

Taylor, Richard. *Against the Bomb: The British Peace Movement 1958–1965*. Oxford: Oxford University Press, 1988.

Taylor, Richard, and Colin Pritchard, eds. *The Protest Makers: The British Nuclear Disarmament Movement of 1958–1965, Twenty Years On*. Oxford: Oxford University Press, 1980.

Taylor, Richard, and Nigel Young, eds. *Campaigns for Peace: British Peace Movements in the Twentieth Century*. Manchester: Manchester University Press, 1987.

Taylor, Robert. *The Trade Union Question in British Politics: Government and Unions since 1945*. Oxford: Oxford University Press, 1993.

Teitelbaum, Michael, and Jay M. Winter. *The Fear of Population Decline*. New York: Academic Press, 1985.

Tenfelde, Klaus. *Proletarische Provinz. Radikalisierung und Widerstand in Penzberg/Oberbayern 1900–1945*. Munich: Oldenbourg, 1982.

Tent, James F. *The Free University of Berlin: A Political History*. Bloomington: University of Indiana Press, 1988.

Thane, Pat. "The Women of the British Labour Party and Feminism, 1906–1945." In Harold L. Smith, ed., *British Feminism in the Twentieth Century*. Aldershot, England: Elgar, 1990.

Thébaud, Françoise. "Work, Gender, and Identity in Peace and War: France 1890–1930," In Billie Melman, ed., *Borderlines: Genders and Identities in War and Peace, 1870–1930*. New York: Routledge, 1998.

Therborn, Göran. "The Life and Times of Socialism." *New Left Review* 194 (January–February 1992): 17–32.

———. " 'Pillarization' and 'Popular Movements.' Two Variants of Welfare State Capitalism: The Netherlands and Sweden." In Francis G. Castles, ed., *The Comparative History of Public Policy*. Oxford: Oxford University Press, 1989.

———. "The Rule of Capital and the Rise of Democracy." *New Left Review* 103 (May–June 1977): 3–41.

———. "The Two-Thirds, One-Third Society." In Stuart Hall and Martin Jacques, eds., *New Times: The Changing Face of Politics in the 1990s*. London: Lawrence and Wishart, 1991.

———. "A Unique Chapter in the History of Democracy: The Social Democrats in Sweden," In Klaus Misgeld, Karl Molin, and Klaus Åmark, eds., *Creating Social Democracy. A Century of the Social Democratic Labor Party in Sweden*. University Park: Penn State University Press, 1992.

———. *Why Some Peoples Are More Employed Than Others: The Strange Paradox of Growth and Unemployment*. London: Verso, 1986.

Thom, Deborah. *Nice Girls and Rude Girls: Women Workers in World War I*. London: Routledge, 1998.

Thompson, Dorothy. *The Chartists: Popular Politics in the Industrial Revolution*. New York: Pantheon, 1984.

Thompson, Edward P. "Homage to Tom Maguire." In Asa Briggs and John Saville, eds., *Essays in Labour History*. London: Macmillan, 1967.

———. *Beyond the Frontier. The Politics of a Failed Mission: Bulgaria 1944*. Stanford: Stanford University Press, 1997.

———. "Homage to Tom Maguire." In Asa Briggs and John Saville, eds., *Essays in Labour History*. London: Macmillan, 1967.

———. "*Left Review.*" In *Making History: Writings on History and Culture*. New York: New Press, 1994.

———. *The Making of the English Working Class*. London: Gollancz, 1963.

———. *William Morris: Romantic to Revolutionary*. 2nd ed. London: Merlin, 1977.

———, ed. *Warwick University Ltd., Industry, Management, and the Universities*. Harmondsworth: Penguin, 1970.

Thompson, Edward P., and T. J. Thompson. *There Is a Spirit in Europe: A Memoir of Frank Thompson*. London: Gollancz, 1947.

Thompson, F. L. M. "Town and City." In F. M. L. Thompson, ed., *The Cambridge Social History of Britain 1750–1950.* Vol. 1. *Regions and Communities.* Cambridge, England: Cambridge University Press, 1990.

Thompson, Grahame. "Economic Intervention in the Postwar Economy." In Gregor McLennan, David Held, and Stuart Hall, eds., *State and Society in Contemporary Britain. A Critical Introduction.* Oxford: Blackwell, 1984.

Thompson, Willie. *The Good Old Cause: British Communism 1920–1991.* London: Pluto Press, 1992.

Thomson, Rachel. "Unholy Alliances: The Recent Politics of Sex Education." In Joseph Bristow and Angelia R. Wilson, eds., *Activating Theory: Lesbian, Gay, Bisexual Politics.* London: Lawrence and Wishart, 1993.

Thorpe, Wayne. "Keeping the Faith: The German Syndicalists in the First World War." *Central European History* 33 (2000):195–216.

———. *"The Workers Themselves:" Revolutionary Syndicalism and International Labour, 1913–1923.* Dordrecht Netherlands: Kluwer, 1989.

Threlfall, Monica. "Feminist Politics and Social Change in Spain." In Monica Threlfall, ed., *Mapping the Women's Movement: Feminist Politics and Social Transformation in the North.* London: Verso, 1996.

———. "Social Policy towards Women in Spain, Greece and Portugal," In Tom Gallagher and Allan M. Williams, eds., *Southern European Socialism: Parties, Elections and the Challenge of Government.* Manchester: Manchester University Press, 1989.

Tichelman, Frijtof. "Socialist 'Internationalism' and the Colonial World: Practical Colonial Policies of Social Democracy in Western Europe before 1940 with Particular Reference to the Dutch SDAP." In Fritz van Holthoon and Marcel van der Linden, eds., *Internationalism in the Labour Movement 1830–1940.* Vol. 1. Leiden: Brill, 1988.

Tickner, Lisa. *The Spectacle of Women: Imagery of the Suffrage Campaign 1907–14.* Chicago: University of Chicago Press, 1988.

Tierskey, Ronald. *Ordinary Stalinism: Democratic Centralism and the Question of Communist Political Development.* Boston: Unwin Hyman, 1985.

Tilly, Charles. "Britain Creates the Social Movement." In James Cronin and Jonathan Schneer, eds., *Social Conflict and the Political Order in Modern Britain.* New Brunswick, N.J.: Rutgers University Press, 1982.

———. "Contentious Repertoires in Britain, 1754–1834." *Social Science History* 17 (1993): 253–80.

———. "Demographic Origins of the European Proletariat." In David Levine, ed., *Proletarianization and Family History.* Orlando, Fla.: Humanities, 1984.

———. "Social Movements and National Politics." In Charles Bright and Susan Harding, eds., *Statemaking and Social Movements: Essays in History and Theory.* Ann Arbor: University of Michigan Press, 1984.

Tilly, Louise A. *Politics and Class in Milan 1881–1901.* New York: Oxford University Press, 1992.

Tilton, Tim. *The Political Theory of Swedish Social Democracy: Through Welfare State to Socialism.* Oxford: Oxford University Press, 1990.

———. "The Role of Ideology in Social Democratic Politics." In Klaus Misgeld, Karl Molin, and Klaus Åmark, eds., *Creating Social Democracy. A Century of the Social Democratic Labor Party in Sweden.* University Park: Penn State University Press, 1992.

Tingsten, Herbert. *The Swedish Social Democrats*. Totowa, N.J.: Barnes and Noble, 1973.

Tiratsoo, Nick, ed. *The Attlee Years*. London: Pinter, 1991.

Titmuss, Richard. *Essays on the Welfare State*. London: Routledge, 1963.

Tobin, Elizabeth. "War and the Working Class: The Case of Düsseldorf, 1914–1918." *Central European History* 13 (1985): 257–98.

Todorova, Maria. "Improbable Maverick or Typical Conformist? Seven Thoughts on the New Bulgaria." In Ivo Banac, ed., *Eastern Europe in Revolution*. Ithaca, N.Y.: Cornell University Press, 1992.

Togliatti, Palmiro. *On Gramsci and Other Writings*. London: Lawrence and Wishart, 1979.

Tökes, Rudolf L. *Béla Kun and the Hungarian Soviet Republic: The Origins and Role of the Communist Party of Hungary in the Revolutions of 1918–1919*. New York: Praeger, 1967.

———, ed. *Eurocommunism and Détente*. New York: New York University Press, 1978.

———. *Opposition in Eastern Europe*. London: Macmillan, 1979.

Tomac, Elza. "Die sozialdemokratische Partei in Kroatien und die Krise des Dualismus Österreich-Ungarns vom Jahre 1903 bis zum I. Weltkrieg." In Keith Hitchens, ed., *Studies in East European History*, Vol. 1. Leiden: Brill, 1977.

Tomassini, Luigi. "Industrial Mobilization and the Labour Market in Italy during the First World War." *Social History* 16 (1991): 59–87.

Tomlinson, Jim. "Marshall Aid and the 'Shortage Economy' in Britain in the 1940s." *Contemporary European History* 9 (2000): 137–55.

———. "Welfare and the Economy: The Economic Impact of the Welfare State, 1945–1951." *Twentieth-Century British History*, 6 (1995): 194–219.

Tomlinson, Richard. "The Disappearance of France, 1896–1940: French Politics and the Birth Rate." *Historical Journal* 28 (1985): 405–16.

Toranska, Teresa. *Them: Stalin's Polish Puppets*. New York: Pantheon, 1987.

Torpey, John C. *Intellectuals, Socialism, and Dissent: The East German Opposition and its Legacy*. Minneapolis: University of Minnesota Press, 1995.

della Torre, Paolo Filo, Edward Mortimer, and Jonathan Story, eds. *Eurocommunism: Myth or Reality?* Harmondsworth: Penguin, 1979.

Touraine, Alain, Zsuzsa Hegedus, François Dubet, and Michel Wieviorka. *Anti-Nuclear Protest: The Opposition to Nuclear Energy in France*. Cambridge, England: Cambridge University Press, 1983.

Touraine, Alain. *L'après socialisme*. Paris: Grasset, 1983.

———. *The May Movement: Revolt and Reform*. New York: Random House, 1971.

———. *Post-Industrial Society: Tomorrow's Social History: Classes, Conflicts, and Culture in Programmed Society*. New York: Random House, 1971.

———. *The Self-Production of Society*. Chicago: University of Chicago Press, 1977.

Trotsky, Leon. *The Permanent Revolution and Results and Prospects*. New York: Merit Publishers, 1969.

Truman, Harry S. *Memoirs*. Vol. 2. *Years of Trial and Hope, 1946–1953*. London: Hodder and Stoughton, 1956.

Trunk, Isaiah. *Judenrat: The Jewish Councils in Eastern Europe under Nazi Occupation*. New York: Macmillan, 1972.

Tudor, Henry, and J. M. Tudor, eds. *Marxism and Social Democracy. The Revisionist Debate 1896–1898*. Cambridge, England: Cambridge University Press, 1988.

von Tunzelman, Nicholas. *Steam Power and Industrialization to 1860*. Oxford: Oxford University Press, 1978.

Turner, H. A. *Trade Union Growth, Structure, and Policy*. London: Allen and Unwin, 1962.

Turner, Ian D., ed. *Reconstruction in Post-War Germany: British Occupation Policy and the Western Zones 1945–1955*. Oxford: Berg, 1989.

Ueberhorst, Horst. *Frisch, Frei, Stark und Treu. Die Arbeitersportbewegung in Deutschland 1893–1933*. Düsseldorf: Droste, 1973.

Ullrich, Volker. *Die Hamburger Arbeiterbewegung vom Vorabend des Ersten Weltkrieges bis zur Revolution 1918/19*. Hamburg, 1976.

Umansky, Lauri. *Motherhood Reconceived: Feminism and the Legacies of the Sixties*. New York; New York University Press, 1996.

Upton, Anthony F. *The Finnish Revolution 1917–1918*. Minneapolis: University of Minnesota Press, 1980.

Urban, Joan Barth. *Moscow and the Italian Communist Party: From Togliatti to Berlinguer*. Ithaca, N.Y.: Cornell University Press, 1986.

Vague, Tom. *Anarchy in the UK: The Angry Brigade*. Edinburgh: AK Press, 1997.

Valeva, Yelena. "The CPSU, the Comintern, and the Bulgarians." In Norman M. Naimark and Leonid Gibianskii, eds., *The Establishment of Communist Regimes in Eastern Europe, 1944–1949*. Boulder, Colo.: Westview, 1997.

Vandervort, Bruce. *Victor Griffuelhes and French Syndicalism 1895–1922*. Baton Rouge, La.: Louisianna Stare University Press, 1996.

Vecernik, Jiri. *Markets and People: The Czech Reform Experience in a Comparative Perspective*. Aldershot, England: Elgar, 1996.

Vecernik, Jiri, and Petr Matejn, eds. *Ten Years of Rebuilding Capitalism: Czech Society after 1989*. Prague: Academia, 1999.

Verdery, Katherine. "From Parent-State to Family Patriarchs: Gender and Nation in Contemporary Eastern Europe." In *What Was Socialism and What Comes Next?* Princeton: Princeton University Press, 1996.

———. *National Ideology under Socialism: Identity and Cultural Politics in Ceauşescu's Romania*. Berkeley: University of California Press, 1991.

———. *What Was Socialism and What Comes Next?* Princeton: Princeton University Press, 1996.

Verhey, Jeffrey. *The Spirit of 1914: Militarism, Myth and Mobilization in Germany*. Cambridge, England: Cambridge University Press, 2000.

Vernon, Richard. *Commitment and Change: Georges Sorel and the Idea of Revolution*. Toronto: University of Toronto Press, 1978.

Vidali, Vittorio. *Diary of the Twentieth Congress of the Communist Party of the Soviet Union*. Westport, Conn.: Greenwood Press, 1974.

Vincent, John R. *The Formation of the British Liberal Party, 1857–68*. Harmondsworth: Penguin, 1972.

Vincent, K. Steven.*Between Marxism and Anarchism: Benoît Malon and French Reformist Socialism*. Berkeley: University of California Press, 1992.

———. *Pierre-Joseph Proudhon and the Rise of French Republican Socialism*. New York: Oxford University Press, 1984.

Vinen, Richard. *Bourgeois Politics in France, 1945–1951.* Cambridge, England: Cambridge University Press, 1995.

Vivarelli, Roberto. "Revolution and Reaction in Italy, 1918–1922." *Journal of Italian History* 1 (1978), 235–63.

Volkov, Vladimir. "The Soviet Leadership and Southeast Europe." In Norman M. Naimark and Leonid Gibianskii, eds., *The Establishment of Communist Regimes in Eastern Europe, 1944–1949.* Boulder, Colo.: Westview, 1997.

Voss, Lex Heerma van. "The Netherlands." In Stefan Berger and David Broughton, eds., *The Force of Labour: The Western European Labour Movement and the Working Class in the Twentieth Century.* Oxford: Berg, 1995.

Vries, Petra de. "Feminism in the Netherlands." *Women's Studies International Quarterly* 4 (1981): 389–407.

Vuliamy, Ed. "Dany Le Vert." In *1968: I Love You!!! Oh, Say It With Cobblestones!!!,* Supplement to *New Statesman* (December 1987): xxi.

Wagner-Pacifici, Robin Erica. *The Moro Morality Play: Terrorism as Social Drama.* Chicago: University of Chicago Press, 1986.

Wagnleitner, Reinhold. *Coca-Colonization and Cold War: The Cultural Mission of the United States in Austria after the Second World War.* Chapel Hill: University of North Carolina Press, 1994.

Wainwright, Hilary. *Arguments for a New Left: Answering the Free Market Right.* Oxford: Blackwell, 1994.

———. *Labour: A Tale of Two Parties.* London: Hogarth Press, 1987.

Waite, Mike. "Sex 'n' Drugs 'n' Rock 'n' Roll (and Communism) in the 1960s." In Geoff Andrews, Nina Fishman, and Kevin Morgan, eds., *Opening the Books: Essays on the Social and Cultural History of the British Communist Party.* London: Lawrence and Wishart, 1995.

Waite, Robert G. L. *Vanguard of Nazism: The Free Corps Movement in Postwar Germany 1918–1923.* Cambridge Harvard: University Press, 1952.

Walicki, Andrzej. "From Stalinism to Post-Communist Pluralism: The Case of Poland." *New Left Review* 185 (January-February 1991): 92–121.

———. "The Paradoxes of Jaruzelski's Poland." *Archives Européens de Sociologie* 26 (1985): 125–51.

Walkowitz, Judith. "Science, Feminism and Romance: The Men's and Women's Club 1885–1889." *History Workshop Journal* 21 (spring 1986): 37–59.

Waller, Michael, ed. *Parties, Trade Unions and Society in East Central Europe.* Ilford, England: 1994.

Waller, Michael, Bruno Coppieters, and Kris Deschouwer, eds. *Social Democracy in a Post-Communist Europe.* Ilford, England: 1994.

Waller, Robert J. *The Dukeries Transformed: The Social and Political Development of a Twentieth-Century Coalfield.* Oxford: Oxford University Press, 1983.

Wandor, Michelene. *Carry On, Understudies: Theatre and Sexual Politics.* London: Routledge, 1986.

———. *Look Back in Gender: Sexuality and the Family in Post-War British Drama.* London: Routledge, 1987.

———, ed. *Once a Feminist: Stories of a Generation.* London: Virago, 1990.

Ward, J. T. *Chartism.* London: Batsford, 1973.

Warner, Michael, ed. *Fear of a Queer Planet: Queer Politics and Social Theory.* Minneapolis: University of Minnesota Press, 1993.

Waterman, Peter. "Hopeful Traveller: The Itinerary of an Internationalist." *History Workshop Journal* 35 (spring 1993): 165–83.

Waters, Chris. *British Socialists and the Politics of Popular Culture, 1884–1914.* Stanford: Stanford University Press, 1990.

Waters, Elizabeth. "In the Shadow of the Comintern: The Communist Women's Movement, 1920–43." In Sonia Kruks, Rayna Rapp, and Marilyn B. Young, eds., *Promissory Notes: Women in the Transition to Socialism.* New York: Monthly Review Press, 1989.

Watney, Simon. *Practices of Freedom: Selected Writings on HIV/AIDS.* Durham, N.C.: Duke University Press, 1994.

Watson, Don, and John Corcoran. *An Inspiring Example: The North East of England and the Spanish Civil War 1936–1939.* Newcastle, England: McGuffin, 1996.

WCCPL and NUM South Wales Area, eds. *Striking Back.* Cardiff: Welsh Campaign for Civil and Political Liberties, 1985.

Weber, Hermann. *Die Wandlung des deutschen Kommunismus. Die Stalinisierung der KPD in der Weimarer Republik.* 2 vols. Frankfurt: Campus, 1969.

———, ed. *Der Gründungsparteitag der KPD: Protokoll und Materialien.* Frankfurt: Campus, 1969.

———. *Unabhängige Kommunisten. Der Briefwechsel zwischen Heinrich Brandler und Isaac Deutscher 1949 bis 1967.* Berlin: Dietz, 1981.

Weeks, Jeffrey. "Havelock Ellis and the Politics of Sex Reform." In Sheila Rowbotham and Jeffrey Weeks, *Socialism and the New Life: The Personal and Sexual Politics of Edward Carpenter and Havelock Ellis.* London: Pluto Press, 1977.

Wehler, Hans-Ulrich. *Sozialdemokratie und Nationalstaat. Nationalitätenfragen in Deutschland 1840–1914.* Göttingen: Vandenhoeck und Ruprecht, 1971.

Weil, Kari. "Feminocentric Utopia and Male Desire: The New Paris of the Saint-Simonians." In Libby Falls Jones and Sarah Webster Goodwin, eds., *Feminism, Utopia, and Narrative.* Knoxville: University of Tennessee Press, 1990.

Weiler, Peter. *British Labour and the Cold War.* Stanford: Stanford University Press, 1988.

———. *Ernest Bevin.* Manchester: Manchester University Press, 1993.

Weitz, Eric D. "Communism and the Public Spheres of Weimar Germany." In David E. Barclay and Eric D. Weitz, eds., *Between Reform and Revolution: German Socialism and Communism from 1840 to 1990.* New York: Berghahn, 1998.

———. *Creating German Communism, 1890–1990: From Popular Protests to Socialist State.* Princeton: Princeton University Press, 1997.

———. "The Heroic Man and the Ever-Changing Woman: Gender and Politics in European Communism, 1917–1950." In Laura L. Frader and Sonya O. Rose, eds., *Gender and Class in Modern Europe.* Ithaca, N.Y.: Cornell University Press, 1996.

Weller, Ken. *"Don't be a Soldier!" The Radical Anti-War Movement in North London 1914–1918.* London: Journeyman Press, 1985.

Wenger, Beth S. "Radical Politics in a Reactionary Age: The Unmaking of Rosika Schwimmer, 1914–1930." *Journal of Women's History* 2, 2 (fall 1990): 66–99.

Westoby, Adam. *Communism since World War II*. New York: St. Martin's Press, 1981.

Wette, Wolfram. *Gustav Noske. Eine politische Biographie*. Düsseldorf: Droste, 1987.

Wheaton, Bernard. *Radical Socialism in Czechoslovakia: Bohumír Šmeral, the Czech Road to Socialism and the Origins of the Czechoslovak Communist Party, 1917–1921*. New York: Columbia University Press, 1986.

Wheeler, Robert F. "The Failure of 'Truth and Clarity' at Berne: Kurt Eisner, the Opposition and the Reconstruction of the International." *International Review of Social History* 18 (1973): 173–201.

———. *USPD und Internationale. Sozialistischer Internationalismus in der Zeit der Revolution*. Frankfurt am Main: Ullstein, 1975.

White, Alan. " '. . . We Never Knew What Price We Were Going To Have Till We Got to the Warehouse': Nineteenth-Century Sheffield and the Industrial District Debate," *Social History* 22 (1997): 306–17.

White, Dan S. *Lost Comrades: Socialists of the Front Generation 1918–1945*. Cambridge, England: Cambridge University Press, 1992.

White, Joe. "1910–1914 Reconsidered," In James E. Cronin and Jonathan Schneer, eds., *Social Conflict and the Political Order in Modern Britain*. New Brunswick, N.J.: Rutgers University Press, 1982.

White, Stephen. *Gorbachev and After*. Cambridge, England: Cambridge University Press, 1992.

Whiting, R. C. *The View from Cowley: The Impact of Industrialization upon Oxford 1918–1939*. Oxford: Oxford University Press, 1983.

Whyte, Iain Boyd. *Bruno Taut and the Architecture of Activism*. Cambridge, England: Cambridge University Press, 1982.

Wickham, James. "Social Fascism and the Division of the Working-Class Movement: Workers and Parties in the Frankfurt Area 1928–30." *Capital and Class* 7 (1979): 1–34.

———. "Working-Class Movement and Working-Class Life: Frankfurt am Main during the Weimar Republic," *Social History* 8 (October 1983): 325–43.

Wildt, Michael. *Am Beginn der "Kosumgesellschaft": Mangelerfahrung, Lebenshaltung, Wohlstandshoffnung in Westdeutschland in den fünfziger Jahren*. Hamburg: Ergebnisse, 1994.

———. "Plurality of Taste: Food and Consumption in West Germany during the 1950s." *History Workshop Journal* 39 (spring 1995): 23–41.

Wilks, Stuart, ed. *Talking about Tomorrow: A New Radical Politics*. London: Pluto Press, 1993.

Willett, John. *The New Sobriety: Art and Politics in the Weimar Period, 1917–1933*. London: Thames and Hudson, 1978.

Williams, Beryl. *The Russian Revolution 1917–1921*. Oxford: Oxford University Press, 1987.

Williams, Gwyn A. *Artisans and Sans-Culottes: Popular Movements in France and Britain during the French Revolution*. London: Arnold, 1968.

———. "Eighteenth Brumaire: Karl Marx and Defeat." In Betty Matthews, ed., *Marx: A Hundred Years On*. London: Lawrence and Wishart, 1983.

———. *Proletarian Order: Antonio Gramsci, Factory Councils and the Origins of Communism in Italy 1911–1921*. London: Pluto Press, 1975.

Williams, Kieran. *The Prague Spring and Its Aftermath: Czechoslovak Politics 1968–1970.* Cambridge, England: Cambridge University Press, 1997.

Williams, Philip M. *Hugh Gaitskell.* Oxford: Oxford University Press, 1982.

Williams, Raymond. *Culture and Society.* Harmondsworth: Penguin, 1961.

———. "Culture is Ordinary." In *Resources of Hope: Culture, Democracy, Socialism.* London: Verso, 1989.

———. *Keywords.* Rev. ed. New York: Oxford University Press, 1985.

———. *The Long Revolution.* Harmondsworth: Penguin, 1961.

———. *May Day Manifesto.* Harmondworth: Penguin, 1968.

———. "The Politics of the Avant-Garde." In *The Politics of Modernism: Against the New Conformists.* London: Verso, 1989.

Wilson, Bryan. "The Trouble with Teenagers." In *The Youth Culture and the Universities.* London: Faber, 1970.

Wilson, Elizabeth. *Only Halfway to Paradise: Women in Postwar Britain 1945–1968.* London: Methuen, 1980.

———. *Women and the Welfare State.* London: Methuen, 1977.

Wilson, Perry R. "Saints and Heroines: Rewriting the History of Italian Women in the Resistance." In Tim Kirk and Anthony McElligott, eds., *Opposing Fascism: Community, Authority and Resistance in Europe.* Cambridge, England: Cambridge University Press, 1999.

Winkler, Heinrich August. *Der Schein der Normalität. Arbeiter und Arbeiterbewegung in der Weimarer Republik 1924 bis 1930.* Bonn: Dietz, 1985.

———. *Der Weg in die Katastrophe: Arbeiter und Arbeiterbewegung in der Weimarer Republik 1930 bis 1933.* Bonn: Dietz, 1987.

———. *Von der Revolution zur Stabilisierung. Arbeiter und Arbeiterbewegung in der Weimarer Republik 1918–1924.* Bonn: Dietz, 1984.

Winston, Colin M. *Workers and the Right in Spain, 1900–1936.* Princeton: Princeton University Press, 1985.

Winter, Jay M. *Socialism and the Challenge of War: Ideas and Politics in Britain 1912–18.* London: Routledge, 1974.

———. "The Webbs and the Non-White World: A Case of Socialist Racialism." *Journal of Contemporrary History* 9 (1974): 181–92.

Wintle, Michael J. *Pillars of Piety: Religion in the Netherlands in the Nineteenth Century, 1813–1901.* Hull, England: Hull University Press 1987.

Wittner, Lawrence S. "The Nuclear Threat Ignored: How and Why the Campaign against the Bomb Disintegrated in the Late 1960s." In Carole Fink, Philipp Gassert, and Detlef Junker, eds., *1968: The World Transformed.* Cambridge, England: Cambridge University Press, 1988.

———. *Resisting the Bomb: A History of the World Nuclear Disarmament Movement, 1954–1970.* Stanford: Stanford University Press, 1998.

———. "The Transnational Movement Movement against Nuclear Weapons, 1945–1986: A Preliminary Survey." In Charles Chatfield and Peter van Dungen, eds., *Peace Movements and Political Cultures.* Knoxville: University of Tennessee Press, 1988.

Wohl, Robert. *French Communism in the Making 1914–1924.* Stanford: Stanford University Press, 1966.

Wolchik, Sharon L. "The Crisis of Socialism in Central and Eastern Europe and Socialism's Future." In Christiane Lemke and Gary Marks, eds., *The Crisis of Socialism in Europe.* Durham, N.C.: Duke University Press, 1992.

Wollen, Peter. "Modern Times: Cinema/Americanism/the Robot." In *Raiding the Icebox: Reflections on Twentieth-Century Culture*. Bloomington: University of Indiana Press, 1993.

———. "The Situationist International: On the Passage of a Few People through a Rather Brief Period of Time." In *Raiding the Icebox: Reflections on Twentieth-Century Culture*. Bloomington: University of Indiana Press, 1993.

Wood, Elizabeth A. *The Baba and the Comrade: Gender and Politics in Revolutionary Russia*. Bloomington: University of Indiana Press, 1997.

———. "Prostitution Unbound: Representations of Political and Sexual Anxieties in Post-Revolutionary Russia." In Jane Costlow, Stephanie Sandler, and Judith Vowles, eds., *Sexuality and the Body in Russian Culture*. Stanford: Stanford University Press, 1993.

Wood, Neal. *Communism and British Intellectuals*. London: Gollancz, 1959.

Woodall, Jean, ed. *Policy and Politics in Contemporary Poland: Reform, Failure and Crisis*. London: Pinter, 1982.

Woodcock, George. *Anarchism: A History of Libertarian Ideas and Movements*. Cleveland: Meridian Books, 1962.

Woollacott, Angela. *On Her Their Lives Depend: Munitions Workers in the Great War*. Berkeley: University of California Press, 1994.

Wrigley, Chris. *Lloyd George and the Challenge of Labour: The Post-War Coalition 1918–1922*. Hemel Hempstead, England: Wheatsheaf, 1990.

———. "The State and the Challenge of Labour in Britain 1917–1920." In Chris Wrigley, ed., *Challenges of Labour: Central and Western Europe 1917–1920*. London: Routledge, 1993.

Wünderich, Volker. *Arbeiterbewegung und Selbstverwaltung*. Wuppertal, Germany: Hammer, 1980.

Wyman, Mark. *DPs: Europe's Displaced Persons, 1945–1951*. Ithaca, N.Y.: Cornell University Press, 1998.

Wyncoll, Peter. *The Nottingham Labour Movement 1880–1939*. London: Lawrence and Wishart, 1985.

Yeo, Eileen. "Culture and Constraint in Working-Class Movements, 1830–1855." In Eileen Yeo and Stephen Yeo, eds., *Popular Culture and Class Conflict 1590–1914: Explorations in the History of Labour and Leisure*. Brighton England: Harvester, 1981.

———. "Some Practices and Problems of Chartist Democracy." In James Epstein and Dorothy Thompson, eds., *The Chartist Experience: Studies in Working-Class Radicalism and Culture, 1830–1860*. London: Macmillan, 1982.

Yeo, Stephen. "A New Life: The Religion of Socialism in Britain, 1883–1896." *History Workshop Journal* 4 (autumn 1977): 5–56.

Young, Brigitte. *Triumph of the Fatherland: German Unification and the Marginalization of Women*. Ann Arbor: University of Michigan Press, 1999.

Young, John W. *Britain, France and the Unity of Europe 1945–51*. Leicester: Leicester University Press, 1984.

———. *France, the Cold War and the Western Alliance, 1944–49*. Leicester: Leicester University Press, 1990.

Zappi, Elda Gentili. *If Eight Hours Seem Too Few: Mobilization of Women Workers in the Italian Rice Fields*. Albany: State University of New York Press, 1991.

Zarnowska, Anna. "Religion and Politics: Polish Workers c.1900." *Social History* 16 (1991): 299–316.

Zhelitski, Bela. "Postwar Hungary, 1944–1946." In Norman M. Naimark and Leonid Gibianskii, eds., *The Establishment of Communist Regimes in Eastern Europe, 1944–1949.* Boulder, Colo.: Westview, 1997.

Zinner, Paul, ed. *National Communism and Popular Revolt in Eastern Europe.* New York: Columbia University Press, 1986.

Zsuffa, Joseph. *Béla Balázs: The Man and the Artist.* Berkeley: University of California Press, 1987.

Zuege, Alan. "The Chimera of the Third Way." In Leo Panitch and Colin Leys, eds., *Socialist Register 2000: Necessary and Unnecessary Utopias.* New York: Monthly Review Press, 1999.

Index

abortion, 375–76
Acheson, Dean, 300
Adenauer, Konrad, 417
Adler, Friedrich, 178, 179, 279
Adler, Victor, 42, 89, 92
Adorno, Theodor, 259
Agnelli, Giovanni, 415
Aguilera, Gonzalo de, 276
Aksel'rod, Pavel, 129
Albertini, Ave, 323
Aldermaston March, 356
Alexander, Bill, 494
Alexander, Sally, 369
Algeria, 335
Americanization, 353
anarchism, 26, 64, 87, 95–97, 98
Andreotti, Giulio, 412, 487
Andropov, Iurii, 437
Antal, Frigyes, 208
"April Theses" (Lenin), 141
artisans. *See* skilled workers
arts, 201–19
Asia, 299, 301
association, 29
Atlee, Clement, 303
Austria
    broadening discontent, 138
    economic reforms, 236
    multinational movement, 92, 93
    Red Vienna, 212–13, 222, 237
    and Serbia, 124–25
    and social democracy, 226
    women in, 106, 198
authoritarianism, 242
autonomists, 459–60
Azana, Manuel, 271–72

Baader, Andreas, 420
Babeuf, Gracchus, 25
Badajoz (Spain), 276
Badoglio, Pietro, 284, 285
Bakunin, Michael, 26, 35, 39, 95, 96
Balázs, Bela, 207, 208, 209
Balcerowicz, Leszek, 450, 451
Baldesi Project, 163
Barcelona (Spain), 273, 274, 423–24
Barnes, George, 193
Barth, Emil, 166

Basnett, David, 393
Basso, Lelio, 285
Battersby, Audrey, 368
Bauer, Otto, 213, 266, 410
Bebel, August, 42, 45, 87, 90, 99, 100,
    115, 258
Belgium, 68, 101, 239–40, 241
Bell, Tom, 252
Bellamy, Edward, 46, 115
Benes, Edward, 285
Benjamin, Walter, 206
Benn, Tony, 462, 463, 468
Bergson, Henri, 211
Beria, Lavrenty, 329
Berlin (Ger.), 202, 300, 330
Berlinguer, Enrico, 409–12, 415, 489, 494
Berlusconi, Silvio, 487
Bermondsey (London), 337–38
Bernstein, Eduard, 42, 90, 91
Bertrand Russell Peace Foundation, 341
Bevin, Ernest, 303, 316, 319–20
Bibó, István, 306
Bickerstaffe, Rodney, 393
Bierut, Boleslaw, 331
blacks, 473
Blanc, Louis, 29
Blanqui, Auguste, 25, 36, 87
Blanquism, 26, 31, 37, 39
Blatchford, Robert, 14
Blok, Alexander, 203
Blum, Léon, 268, 269–70, 271, 321
Bogdanov, Aleksander, 204
Bolshevism, 123, 152
    and culture, 204–7
    and revolution, 145–50, 223–25
    and women, 188
    and Zimmerwald movement, 129, 130
Bondfield, Margaret, 195
Bonomi, Ivanoe, 285
Bordiga, Amadeo, 171, 254
Bordoni, Gaetano, 354
Börner, Holger, 422
Bourne, Joan, 495–96
Bowlby, John, 326
Boyer, Miguel, 426
Brandler, Heinrich, 250
Brandt, Willy, 418, 419
Branting, Hjalmar, 154

Brezhnev, Leonid, 358, 359, 437, 439
Britain. *See* Great Britain
British Social Democratic Federation
    (SDF), 13–15
Brousse, Paul, 86
Browne, Stella, 190
Buchez, Philippe, 28
Bulgaria, 445, 451
Buonarroti, Filipo, 25
Buozzi, Bruno, 134
Burns, John, 14
Burrows, Herbert, 14
Bush, George, 444
Butler, R.A., 387

Cabet, Étienne, 28–29, 31, 36
Caetano, Marcelo, 409
Callaghan, James, 337, 388, 392
Capital (Marx), 35, 36, 37, 38, 42, 43, 45
capitalism
    Bernstein on, 90
    and class consciousness, 50
    and democracy, 301–4
    and early industry, 18–20, 49–50, 60
    Keynesian, 316, 317, 318, 319
    and Marx, 37
    and social democracy, 316–17
capitalist stabilities, 235–48
Carnot, Sadi, 96
Carpenter, Edward, 99, 115
Carrillo, Santiago, 409, 411, 415, 423
Castro, Fidel, 341
Ceausescu, Nicolae, 446
Cerník, Oldrich, 357, 359, 360
Chamberlain, Neville, 280
Chartism, 19, 22, 28, 32, 34, 53, 54
Chernenko, Konstantin, 437
Chernobyl (Soviet Union), 438
Chiaromonte, Geraldo, 379
Chile, 409
Christianson, Aileen, 369
Churchill, Winston, 158, 283, 299, 308
Císar, Cestmír, 357
Clarion (British newspaper), 14
class, 39, 50, 52, 80, 88
    as analytic category, 394
    consciousness, 50, 77, 81, 93
    and identity, 464
    loosening of affiliations, 399–402
    political dimension, 395
    voting, 401
    See also working class
Class Struggle, The (Kautsky), 89
Clementis, Vladimir, 309
Cocchi, Romano, 279
Cohn-Bendit, Daniel, 343, 345, 346, 348–
    49, 351, 352

Cold War, 288, 298, 301–4, 307, 311,
    313, 315, 327, 329, 429
collectivism, 312, 481
colonialism. *See* imperialism
Cominform, 300, 307–8
Comintern, 182, 183, 252, 256–57, 263–
    64, 266–67, 275, 281, 282, 284, 308
    See also Second Comintern Congress
Communism, 9, 180, 250
    Cold War, 288, 298, 301–4, 307, 311,
        313, 315, 327, 329, 429
    containment, 300
    crisis of, 333–35, 500
    in Czechoslovakia, 254, 285, 493–94
    demonizing of, 301
    in Eastern Europe, 306–11, 499
    end of, 429–56, 483
    Eurocommunism, 408–17
    in France, 350, 413–14, 416
    future of reform, 454–55
    in Great Britain, 252, 256, 494–95
    in Italy, 291–95, 415, 491
    and Left, 360–63
    left-wing, 152–64
    "Little Moscows," 256
    national, 255–57, 283–87
    and Nazi-Soviet Pact, 279–83
    in Poland, 433–34
    and Popular Front, 263–67
    post-Second World War, 290–98
    revolutions of 1989, 443–46
    in Second World War, 278–89
    shaping tradition, 253–55
    and social democracy, 225–29, 499
    in Soviet Union, 249–53, 430
    split with socialism, 121, 124
    and women, 188–92
Communist International, 176–84, 249,
    250
Communist Manifesto (Marx), 36, 43
Communist parties, 176–84, 407, 452–53
conflict, and democracy, 4
constitutional states, 220–29, 239–41, 447
consumerism, 187–88, 353–54
cooperation, 27, 29
Cooper, Selina, 104
Cornforth, Maurice, 281
corporatism, 241–45, 247, 316–17, 319,
    387–90, 396
council communism, 162
counterculture, 459–60
Cousins, Frank, 389
Cox, Dora, 495
Cox, Idris, 495
craftsmen, 19, 52–54
Craxi, Bettino, 487
Croce, Benedetto, 211

Crosland, Anthony, 317
Cuba, 341
culture, 201–19
Cunhal, Alvaro, 409
Cyprus, 335
Czechoslovakia
    Communism in, 254, 285, 307, 310,
        493–94
    economy, 450, 451
    feminism in, 106
    multinational movement, 92, 93
    Prague Spring, 342, 357–60, 363, 493,
        499
    revolution of 1989, 445–46
    in Second World War, 278
    socialists in new nationalist
        framework, 159–60
    Soviet invasion, 358–63, 408, 431, 435

D'Alema, Massimo, 489
Darwin, Charles, 45
David, Eduard, 126, 166
Davison, Emily Wilding, 103
De Gaulle, Charles, 284, 344–46, 348–
    50, 363, 486
deindustrialization, 386–87, 399
Delmar, Rosalind, 368
de Man, Hendrik, 239, 240
democracy
    broadening boundaries of, 220–29
    and capitalism, 301–4
    definitions of, 3–4, 22
    early fronts, 85–108
    in Eastern Europe, 304–7
    economics of, 21, 238
    in Europe, 3–12, 447
    in Italy, 409–10
    Marx on, 40
    in Poland, 431–37
    radical, 18–19, 111, 295–98
    remaking, 405–28
    and social history, 20
    socialist parties as torchbearers, 109
    strong drives for, 116
    transnational dimension, 4–5
    visions of, 18–20
    and women, 22–24
    See also social democracy
Denmark, 67, 68, 377, 460
Derossi, Laura, 354
dictatorship, 305
Dimitrov, Georgii, 263, 264–65, 281,
    284, 310
Dini, Lamberto, 488
Dittmann, Wilhelm, 166
Dohnanyi, Klaus von, 422
Dongas Tribe, 477

Dubcek, Alexander, 342, 357–60, 445,
    446
Duclos, Jacques, 282
Dutschke, Rudi, 343, 364, 418
Dutt, Rajani Palme, 282
dyarchy, 155, 156

Eastern Europe
    Communist bloodletting in, 309–10
    economy, 449–54
    industrial unrest, 330
    politics, 305, 439, 492–93
    post-Communist revolutions, 443–49,
        499
    prospects of democracy, 304–7
    Soviet-style centralism, 429
    Stalinization of people's democracies,
        307–11
    women in, 324
    See also specific countries
Ebert, Friedrich, 165, 166, 167
economics, 21, 38, 236–38, 283, 449–54
Edmunds, John, 393
Egypt, 332
Eisenhower, Dwight D., 332
Engels, Friedrich, 27, 33–38, 40–42, 45,
    62
England. See Great Britain
Ensslin, Gudrun, 420
entertainment, 187, 215–17
Erfurt Program, 89, 99
Eurocommunism, 408–17
"Eurocommunism" and the State
    (Carrillo), 411
Europe
    broadening of discontent, 135–38
    democracy in, 3–12, 447
    early democratic fronts, 85–108
    feminism in, 196–97
    First International, 31, 35, 36, 38, 39,
        62
    geography of socialism, 64–65
    industrialization and working class, 47–
        61
    Left in, 220–29, 467–68
    parliamentary government in, 66–69
    revolutionary circumstances in, 120–
        21, 153–60
    rural areas, 94, 385
    Second International, 86–93
    trade unionism in, 70–74
    See also Eastern Europe; Western
        Europe; specific countries
evolution, 45
Exodus Collective, 479–81
extraparliamentary movements, 500

family, 30, 54–56, 102, 186–87, 194, 218, 312–13
fascism, 242, 245, 246, 261, 266, 280, 288, 495, 499
Female Eunuch (Greer), 368
feminism
  in Czechoslovakia, 106
  early attempts, 30
  in Great Britain, 103–5, 106, 195–97, 368–75
  and labor, 322
  post-1960, 24, 313, 326, 366–83
  of pre-1914 labor movements, 100
  radical, 472
  social, 187
  and socialism, 99, 112–13
  Women's Liberation Movement, 367–81, 461
  between world wars, 195–98
  See also women; women's suffrage
Fernbach, David, 354
Ferri, Enrico, 45
Fiaschi, Goliardo, 494
films. *See* movies
First International, 31, 35, 36, 38, 39, 62, 95
First World War, 118, 121, 123–38, 186, 192, 209, 499
Fischer, Ruth, 251
Fiszbach, Tadeusz, 434
Fogarasi, Béla, 208
Foot, Michael, 337, 463
Ford, Henry, 199
"Forums," 448–49
Fourier, François-Charles, 27–28, 29, 30
France
  Communism in, 350, 413–14, 416
  labor in, 53, 69, 268–69, 270
  Left in, 32
  moves toward unity, 263, 284
  politics in, 486–87
  Popular Front, 268–70
  postwar, 290–91
  in Second World War, 284
  socialism in, 29, 64
  social reforms in, 87–88, 89
  student protests (1968), 343–53
  Trotskyism, 458
  Vichy regime, 282
  women in, 190, 321, 379
Franco, Francisco, 422, 423
Frank, Ludwig, 126
Frankfurt School, 259, 362
Franko, Ivan, 95
French Revolution, 5, 17, 18, 25
From Trotsky to Tito (Klugman), 309

Gaitskell, Hugh, 387
Galicia (Habsburg Empire), 95
Gallacher, William, 280
Gallifet, Gaston, 87
Geismar, Alain, 345, 346
generation gap, 354–55, 458
Gens, Jacob, 231–32
George, Henry, 46
George V (King of England), 157
German Communist Party (KPD), 190–92, 250–52, 257, 261–262
German Social Democratic Party (SPD), 59, 67, 83, 262
  conflicts in, 116
  and culture, 213–15, 216, 217
  and economy, 238–39, 317
  and First International, 39
  and First World War, 125, 126, 128, 129–30, 132, 135
  formation, 79–80
  in Göttingen, 82
  as main governing party, 418–19
  and Marxism, 42, 44–45, 68
  peasant-based strategy, 93, 94
  plurality of outlooks, 43
  as protector of working-class family, 194
  in Remscheid and Hamborn, 57
  revisionism, 417
  and Second International, 86, 88, 91
  and Social Democratic Republic, 165–69
  as strongest socialist party, 89–90
  and women, 99, 100, 102, 200, 313
Germany
  arts and intellectuals in, 208–11, 213–16
  broadening discontent in, 136, 137, 138
  East German Uprising, 330
  economy, 237, 238–39, 450
  First World War, 125–38, 158
  labor in, 70–71, 73–74, 76–78, 119, 161–64, 167
  Nazi-Soviet Pact, 279–83
  postwar, 297
  revolutionary turbulence, 165–69, 172–75
  rural areas, 93–95
  and social democracy, 225–26
  socialist subculture, 79–80
  suffrage in, 67
  unification, 5, 38, 67
  women in, 99, 190–92, 193
  working class in, 56–57, 59
  See also German Social Democratic Party; Nazism; West Germany

Gerö, Ernö, 332
Gierek, Edward, 431, 432
Gladstone, William Ewart, 31
glasnost, 438
globalization, 501, 502
Glotz, Peter, 467–68, 482
Goegg, Marie, 107
Goldet, Hélène, 345
Gomulka, Vladislav, 309, 310, 331, 332, 431
Gonzalez, Felipe, 423, 425–27
Gorbachev, Mikhail, 437–43, 444, 451, 454, 455, 483, 484, 500
Gormley, Joe, 390
Gorz, André, 403
Göttingen (Ger.), 82
Gottwald, Klement, 254, 307, 309
Gramsci, Antonio, 162, 171, 254, 255, 266, 267, 323, 491
  cultural and educational initiatives, 211, 214, 215, 217
  on Lenin, 152
  and Marxism, 258–59
  on sexuality, 199
  on women's issues, 189
Grand Alliance, 283–84, 288
Gray, Mary, 15
Gray, Willie, 15
Great Britain
  artisans in, 19
  Chartism, 19, 22, 28, 32, 34, 53, 54
  and Cold War, 303
  Communism in, 252, 256, 494–95
  deindustrialization, 386–87
  "Do-It-Yourself" politics, 476–81
  egalitarianism, 312
  homosexuality in, 474
  industrialization in, 19, 51
  labor in, 53, 97, 101–2, 133–34, 157–58, 387–94, 465–66
  Labour Party, 244, 295–96, 337–38, 461–64, 474
  Lanchester case, 13–15
  Left in, 462–67
  liberalism in, 67
  nationalization in, 295–96
  New Left, 355–56
  preconditions for capitalist industrialization, 49
  socialism in, 13–15, 99, 319–20
  student protests (1968), 342
  trade unionism in, 71, 72, 101–2
  Trotskyism, 458
  women in, 101–7, 189–90, 192, 194–97, 323, 368–75
  working class in, 59

Great Scourge and How to End It, The (Pankhurst), 105
Greece, 286, 291, 302, 310, 409
Green parties, 421–22, 453, 468, 484–86, 500
Greer, Germaine, 368
Grimm, Robert, 128
Groener, Wilhelm, 167
Grosz, George, 209, 211
Grósz, Karoly, 444
Guesde, Jules, 86, 87, 88, 89, 127
Guevara, Ernesto Che, 341
Gullo, Fausto, 292
Gurney, Jason, 276
Gysi, Gregor, 452

Haase, Hugo, 125, 166
Haase, Klara, 100
Hall, Stuart, 335, 362, 491
Hamborn (Ger.), 56–57
Hammesfahr, Gottlieb, 78
Hansson, Per Albin, 318, 325
Hardie, Keir, 14, 323
Harding, Thomas, 479
Havel, Václav, 445–46, 448
Heartfield, John, 209
Hewitt, Patricia, 338
Hilferding, Rudolf, 91, 237, 238
Hitler, Adolf, 275, 278, 279, 280
Hölz, Max, 119–20
homosexuality, 327, 337–38, 472, 473–76
Honecker, Erich, 444, 445
Horkheimer, Max, 259
Horovitz, Michael, 356
Hoxha, Enver, 309
Hué, Otto, 76–77
Hungary
  Communism in, 306
  Communist purges in, 309, 310
  difference from Russia, 307
  exodus to West Germany, 444
  intellectuals and arts, 207–8
  1956 uprising, 331–32
  Soviet invasion of, 333, 334, 335, 362
  Soviet Republic, 155
  women in, 107–8
Husák, Gustav, 360, 446

Icarian movement, 28, 36
identity, 464, 472–76
Illyes, Gyula, 306
imperialism, 91, 112, 299, 301, 335
independent mass party of labor, 39
individualism, 21
industrialization
  British deindustrialization, 386–87
  early, 19

industrialization (*continued*)
  and making of working class, 47–61
  militant, 117
  and skilled workers, 52–54
  Soviet, 430
  unevenness of, 48, 51
  and women, 54–56
Industrial Syndicalist Education League, 97
Ingrao, Pietro, 411
insurrection, 25–26
intelligentsia, 207–10
International Brigades, 276
International Working Men's Association. *See* First International
Iotti, Nilde, 494
Ireland, 381
Isherwood, Christopher, 202
Israel, 332
Italian Socialist Party (PSI), 88–89, 98, 116, 170–74
Italy
  anarchists in, 64
  arts in, 211
  broadening discontent, 136, 137
  Communism in, 291–95, 415, 491
  democracy in, 409–10
  labor in, 72, 134, 163, 302–3
  politics, 458–59, 487–89
  revolutionary turbulence, 169–75
  in Second World War, 284–85
  socialism in, 45, 65
  social reforms in, 88–89
  student protests (1968), 342
  unification, 5, 38
  women in, 321–22, 378, 379

Jackson, Tommy, 252
Jaruzelski, Wojciech, 433, 434, 444
Jaurès, Jean, 21, 86, 87–88, 89, 90, 126, 263
Jeffreys, Sheila, 373
Jenkins, Glenn, 480
Jenkins, Roy, 463
Jews, 304, 310–11
Jogiches, Leo, 114
John Paul II (Pope), 432
Jones, Jack, 388, 389, 471
Jospin, Lionel, 487
Juan Carlos (King of Spain), 422, 423
Julián, Narciso, 273
July Days, 146

Kádár, Janos, 332, 334
Kahan, Barbara, 496
Kamenev, Lev, 146, 205, 249, 280
Kania, Stanislaw, 432, 434

Kapp Putsch, 119, 120, 169, 227
Karolyi, Michael, 155
Kassak, Lajos, 207
Katayama, Sen, 86
Kautsky, Karl, 42, 45, 78, 88–91, 93–95, 99, 110, 114, 179, 235, 239
Kennan, George F., 294
Kerensky, Alexander, 125
Keynesianism, 316, 317–18, 319, 389, 396–97, 453, 481, 501
Keyworth, Florence, 323
Khrushchev, Nikita, 329, 330–31, 333, 362, 439, 441, 455
Kienthal international conference, 128, 129, 130
Kiesinger, Kurt Georg, 418
Kinnock, Neil, 458, 463
Kissinger, Henry, 410
Klaus, Václav, 450, 451, 493
Klugman, Jack, 309
Kobitsch-Meyer, Herbert, 120
Koedt, Anne, 370
Kohl, Helmut, 448
Kohout, Pavel, 358
Kollontai, Aleksandra, 187, 188, 189
Konrad, György, 447
Kornilov rising, 141, 142
Korsch, Karl, 258–59
Kossuth, Lajos, 111
Kostov, Trajco, 309, 310
Kovner, Abba, 231, 232
KPD. *See* German Communist Party
Krasnov, Petr, 150
Kravchuk, Leonid, 442
Krenz, Egon, 445
Kriegel, Frantisek, 357, 359, 360
Kropotkin, Peter, 95
Kuliscioff, Anna, 114
Kun, Bela, 155
Kuron, Jacek, 434

labor
  bifurcation with industry, 45
  in Europe, 38
  expansion of, 74–79
  in France, 53, 69, 268–69, 270
  in Germany, 119, 161–64
  in Great Britain, 53, 97, 101, 157–58, 387–94, 465–66
  in Italy, 72, 134, 163, 302–3
  Marx on, 37
  and national economies, 243
  nineteenth-century, 31
  in Poland, 431–37
  politics of, 384–404
  pre-1914 values, 44
  radicalization of, 131–35

rise of, 62–84
and skilled workers, 52–53
in Spain, 424
in Western Europe, 312
and women, 22–23, 100–102, 322,
324–25
workers' councils, 160–64
See also trade unions; working class
Labor and Socialist International (LSI),
264, 279
Labour Party (G.B.), 244, 295–96, 337–
38, 461–64, 474
Lafontaine, Oskar, 467
Lama, Luciano, 412, 415
Lanchester case (Great Britain), 13–15
Lansbury, George, 15
Largo Caballero, Francisco, 272–74, 275
Laval, Pierre, 268
Lawrence, Susan, 195
Left
and Communism, 360–63
contemporary, 471
in culture, 201–19
definition of, 17
in Eastern Europe, 305
in Europe, 220–29, 467–68
future of, 364, 464–67
in Great Britain, 462–67
and liberalism, 30
"loony Left" syndrome, 338
and Marxism, 33–45
of parliament and people, 467–69
post-Second World War, 406
radicalizing, 116
regrouping during First World War,
127–31
remaking, 483–89
and Russian Revolution, 123
and social democracy, 110–11
and socialism, 6–9, 407
in Spain, 423, 425
and women, 185–200, 378–81
Legien, Karl, 134
Lenin, Vladimir, 91, 142, 236, 249, 253
"April Theses," 141
criteria for affiliation with Comintern,
182
Gramsci on, 152
and power of workers, 146–49
and Proletkult, 205
on Soviet benefits for women, 188
and Third International, 176–77, 179
and Vienna Union, 178
What Is to Be Done?, 143, 146, 148
Leroux, Pierre, 28
Levi, Paul, 250
Lévy-Hass, Hanna, 232–33

liberal constitutionalism, 5, 39, 80
liberalism, 30–31, 67
Liebknecht, Wilhelm, 42, 88, 154, 166,
168, 258
Linz Program, 213, 262
Lis, Ladislav, 493–94
Litvinov, Maxim, 278
Livingstone, Ken, 338, 461
localism, 173
local workers' associations, 25, 36, 67
Loebl, Eugen, 310
Longuet, Jean, 179
Loos, Alfred, 497
Löwenthal, Richard, 422
LSI. See Labor and Socialist International
Lukács, Georg, 207, 208, 258–59, 362
Lunacharsky, Anatoly, 204–5, 206
Luxemburg, Rosa, 90, 91, 98, 114, 154,
168
Lyon Theses, 254

MacDonald, Ramsay, 244
MacGregor, Ian, 466
Máchová, Karla, 106
Macleod, Iain, 388
Madeysker, Sonia, 233
Madrid (Spain), 272–73, 274
Makarios, Archbishop, 335
Malatesta, Errico, 95
Malenkov, Georgii, 329
Mann, Tom, 97
Mansfield, Michael, 480
Mansfeld-Halle region (Ger.), 119
manufacturing, 385, 399
Manuilski, Dimitri, 263, 278, 284
March Action, 120
Marchais, Georges, 413–14
Marcuse, Herbert, 259
Marinetti, Filippo Tommaso, 203
marketization, 449–54
Marosán, György, 306, 332
Marshall, George C., 294
Marshall Plan, 300, 302–4, 307, 315
Marx, Eleanor, 30, 42
Marx, Karl, 25, 27, 33–45, 49, 62, 94
Marxism, 27, 41–46, 93, 94, 255–56,
258–60, 362–63, 384
Maslow, Arkadi, 251
mass production, 51
Mass Strike, Party and Trade Unions
(Luxemburg), 98
Masur, Kurt, 444
materialism, 38, 40
maternalism. See motherhood
Matignon Agreement, 269
Maximalism, 171–72
May, Ernst, 497

Mazowiecki, Tadeusz, 449
Mazzini, Giuseppe, 111
McGahey, Mick, 466
McMillan, Margaret, 102
Meciar, Vladimir, 449
Mediterranean area, 64
Mellish, Bob, 337
Mendès-France, Pierre, 348–49
Menshevism, 129, 142–45
Merrheim, Albert, 127
Meyer, Ernst, 250, 251, 252
Meynell, Alix, 496–97
Meynell, Francis, 497
Miaja, José, 273
Michnik, Adam, 434, 447–48
Mihailovic, Dragoljub-Draza, 286
Mikardo, Ian, 295
Millerand, Alexandre, 69, 87, 89
Millerand Affair, 87–88, 90
mineworkers, 76–77, 80–82, 119, 391,
    465–66, 467
Mitchell, Juliet, 368
Mitterrand, Francois, 348, 413–14, 458,
    487
modernism, 202
Mollet, Guy, 335
Molotov, Viacheslav Mikhailovich, 279
Monnet, Jean, 291
Moore, Bill, 281
Moro, Aldo, 412, 459
Morris, William, 115
motherhood, 186, 187, 188, 194, 195,
    197, 313, 325, 326
movies, 207, 215, 216–17
Mullan, Mary Kay, 381
Münzenberg, Willi, 253
Mussolini, Benito, 280, 284, 293
mutualism, 29, 53

Nagy, Imre, 330, 331, 332, 334, 444
Naphtali, Fritz, 237, 238
national fronts, 284
nationalism, 123, 127–28
nationalization, 295–96
nation-states, 220–29, 408
Nazism, 231–32, 262, 278, 284, 288,
    289, 304–5, 492
Nazi-Soviet Pact, 279–83
Negrín, Juan, 274
Netherlands, 128, 154, 156
New Harmony (Ind.), 28, 29
Nicholas II (Tsar of Russia), 139
Nineteen fifty-six, 329–36
Nineteen sixty-eight, 341–65
Norway, 67, 380, 483
Novotny, Antonin, 342, 357

Occhetto, Achille, 487–88
Ochab, Edward, 331
O'Connor, Paul, 479
oil crisis (1973–74), 406
Origins of the Family, Property and the
    State (Engels), 100
Orwell, George, 200
Owen, David, 463
Owen, Robert, 27–28, 29, 30, 36

Pankhurst, Christabel, 103, 104, 105
Pankhurst, Emmeline, 103
Pankhurst, Sylvia, 104, 323
Pannekoek, Anton, 114
Paris Commune, 26, 29, 35, 36, 40, 43,
    69, 85, 87, 95, 268
parliamentary government, 66–69, 88,
    241–45
Paul, Cedar, 190
Paul, Maurice Eden, 190
peace movements, 419–20, 461, 464–65,
    466–67
Pelikan, Jiri, 493
Pelletier, Madeleine, 197
Pelloux, Luigi, 88
People's Front, 265
perestroika, 438, 440
Petöfi Circle, 331–32
Pinochet, Augusto, 482
Plättner, Karl, 120
Poland
    Communism in, 331, 499
    economy, 450, 451
    labor in, 431–37, 447
    post-Communist, 444
political class movement, 39
political parties, 24–27, 117
    Communist, 176–84, 407, 452–53
    independent mass party of labor, 39
    invention of modern, 113
    organizationally united but
        ideologically diverse, 85
    See also socialist parties; specific
        parties and countries
politics
    and class, 395
    counterculture, 459–60
    Eastern European, 305, 439, 492–93
    of identity, 472–76
    new (1970–90), 405–28
    of refusal, 460–62
    and socialism, 79–82
    working-class, 56–60, 384–404
    See also political parties; specific
        countries
Pollitt, Harry, 280, 329

polycentrism, 333
Pompidou, Georges, 345, 346–47, 350
popular culture. *See* entertainment
Popular Front, 263–77, 279, 284
Populism, 94
post-materialist values, 470–71
postwar boom, 406
Poszgay, Imre, 451
Prague Spring, 342, 357–60, 363, 455, 493, 499
Prieto, Indalecio, 272
primitive accumulation, 49
private property, 21
Prodi, Romano, 488
productivism, 162
progressivism, 392–94
Proletkult, 204–5, 206
protelarianization, 48, 49
Proudhon, Pierre-Joseph, 29, 31, 36, 39, 95
PSI. *See* Italian Socialist Party
public sector unions, 392–94

race, 473
radical democracy, 18–19, 111, 295–98
radicalism, 116, 117, 131–35, 181, 341, 355, 363, 457, 472, 499
radical planism, 240, 241
radio, 215, 216
Rajk, László, 309, 310, 331, 332
Rákosi, Mátyás, 306, 309, 330, 331, 332
Rakovsky, Christian, 91, 129
Rakowski, Mieczyslaw, 451
Raspe, Jan-Carl, 420
Rathbone, Eleanor, 195, 196, 197
Ravera, Camilla, 189
Reagan, Ronald, 439
Red Vienna (Aus.), 212–13, 222, 237
reform
  economic, 236
  social, 87–88, 89
  versus revolution, 295
  Western European, 311–13
Remscheid (Ger.), 56–57, 59
Resistance movements, 287–88, 289, 296, 297
revolution
  circumstances for in Europe, 120–21, 153–60
  post-Communist of 1989, 443–49
  rethinking meanings of, 236–39
  versus reform, 295
Right, 17, 116, 186
Rimbaud, Penny, 478, 479
Rivera, Primo de, 272
Rocard, Michel, 413, 458, 487

Rodgers, William, 463
Röger, Sigrid, 367
Rokossovski, Marshall Konstantin, 331
Roman, Petre, 446
Romania, 446
Roudy, Yvette, 379
Rousseau, Jean-Jacques, 111
Rowbotham, Sheila, 368, 461
Royden, Maude, 195
Ruhr (Ger.) coal miners, 76–77
rural areas, 93–95, 111, 385
Russia
  cultural revolution, 203–7, 210
  dual power, 139–42
  extremism and opportunities for Left, 152
  Populism, 94
  See also Russian Revolution; Soviet Union
Russian Revolution, 118, 121, 123, 139–52, 236, 249
  and arts, 203–4
  Bolshevism, 145–50
  from dual power to dictatorship of proletariat, 150–51
  Menshevism, 142–45
  radicalizing effects, 97
  See also Bolshevism

Saint-Simon, Claude Henri de, 27, 28, 29
Salengro, Roger, 270
Sander, Helke, 367
Sauvageot, Jacques, 345
Sawyer, Tom, 393
Scandinavia, 64, 106, 245, 246, 247, 317–19
Scargill, Arthur, 465
Scheidemann, Philipp, 165, 176
Schleyer, Hanns Martin, 420, 459
Schmidt, Helmut, 418
Schütte-Lihotsky, Margarete, 497–98
Schwimmer, Rosika, 107–8
SDF. *See* British Social Democratic Federation
Second Comintern Congress, 155, 177, 189
Second International, 86–93, 96, 97, 114, 124–27, 177, 178, 182, 384
Second World War, 278–98, 320, 323, 324, 495, 498
Segal, Lynne, 461
Séguy, Georges, 346, 348
Sembat, Marcel, 127
Serbia, 124–25
Serrati, Giacinto, 135, 179
service industries, 386–87

sexuality, 198–99, 214, 322, 327
Simon, Bohumil, 357, 359
skilled workers, 19, 52–54
Slansky, Rudolf, 309, 311
Slavík, Václav, 357
Sling, Otto, 309
Smeral, Bohumir, 254
Smrkovsky, Josef, 357, 358, 359
Soares, Mário, 415
social citizenship, 312, 313
social class. *See* class
social democracy
  and anarchism, 95
  and capitalism, 316–17
  and Communism, 225–29, 499
  constitutionalizing of, 226, 239–41
  and gendering of citizenship, 192–95
  and Left, 85, 110–11
  making of, 21–22
  postwar, 314–19
  progress before 1914, 66
  of Russian Empire, 92
  Scandinavian, 317–19
  and working class, 93, 403
socialism
  and capitalism, 238
  contemporary, 483, 490, 501
  in context, 503
  and culture, 210–19
  culture of, 113–15
  deepening crisis of, 115–18
  divisions of international, 177–79
  early, 21, 85–108
  and First World War, 123, 125, 127–28
  in France, 29, 64
  geography of, 64–65
  in Great Britain, 13–15, 99, 319–20
  in Italy, 45, 65
  and Left, 6–9, 407
  limits of, 110–13
  models of goals, 89
  moderate, 121
  national politics and everyday life, 79–82
  for neo-liberal times, 481–83
  and parliamentary government, 66–69
  remaking, 405–28
  and skilled workers, 52–54
  in Soviet Union, 249–60
  in Spain, 422–28
  split with Communism, 121, 124
  strengths, 109–10
  utopian, 27–30, 114–15
  and women, 100, 103, 112–13
  See also socialist parties
Socialism (Engels), 27

socialist constitutionalism, 27, 31, 62
socialist parties
  as agents of class formation, 400
  and decentralization, 110
  early, 85, 86
  first nationally organized, 63
  foundations of, 65
  in governing role, 467
  and mass strike tactic, 91–92
  obstacles to, 115
  and parliamentary government, 67
  as torchbearers of democracy, 5–6, 109
Solidarity (trade union), 433–37
Sorbonne University, 344, 345, 347, 349, 352
Sorel, Georges, 98, 211
Sossi, Mario, 409
Soviet Union
  from Bolshevization to Third Period, 250–54
  Churchill on, 299
  Cold War, 288, 298, 301–4, 307, 311, 313, 315, 327, 329
  Communism in, 249–53, 430
  de-Stalinization, 330–32, 361
  and Eastern Europe, 306–11
  economy, 438, 441
  Gorbachev, 437–43, 500
  invasion of Czechoslovakia, 358–63, 408, 431, 435
  invasion of Hungary, 333, 334, 335, 362
  Nazi invasion of, 282–83
  in Second World War, 284
  socialism in, 249–60
  Stalinism, 255, 281, 282, 298, 307–11, 329
  women in, 188
Spacek, Josef, 357, 359
Spain
  anarchists in, 26, 64, 65
  and Eurocommunism, 411, 413, 415
  labor in, 424
  Left in, 423, 425
  Popular Front, 271–76
  socialism in, 422–28
  women in, 320
Spanish Civil War, 271–76
SPD. *See* German Social Democratic Party
stabilization patterns, 244–48
Stalin, Joseph, 275, 279, 283, 284, 300, 307, 308, 329–31, 333
Stalinism, 255, 281, 282, 298, 307–11, 329, 429–31, 492
Steinhardt, Karl, 180
Strachey, Pippa, 196

student movements, 342–53, 355, 364
Stuttgart resolution, 92
Suarez, Adolfo, 422, 423
Suddick, Ann, 466
Suez Crisis, 332, 335, 336
suffrage. *See* voting; women's suffrage
Sukhanov, Nikolai, 150
Svoboda, Ludvík, 359
Sweden, 67, 98, 317–19, 325
Switzerland, 128, 377
syndicalism, 97–98
Szabó, Ervin, 208
Szasz, Bela, 307

Tasca, Angelo, 252
Tatchell, Peter, 337–38, 474
Taut, Bruno, 210
Taylor, Barbara, 30
Taylor, Frederick, 199
Taylor, Paul, 480
terrorism, 420, 459
Testa, Teresa, 323
textile industry, 101
Thälmann, Ernst, 251
Thatcher, Margaret, 386, 390–91, 392, 466
theater, 207, 208
Theunis, Georges, 240
Third International. *See* Communist International
Thomas, Albert, 176
Thorez, Maurice, 264, 266, 282, 292, 333
Tito, 286, 308–10
Togliatti, Palmiro, 252, 254, 267, 280, 281, 284, 291–93, 321, 333–34, 489, 494
Tökés, László, 446
Tolstoy, Leo, 46
Touraine, Alaine, 403
trade unions, 69–76, 117
  and class, 401–2
  and corporatism, 316, 387–90, 396
  in Germany, 167
  in Great Britain, 390–94
  in Italy, 163
  public sector, 392–94
  and syndicalism, 98
  and women, 100–101
Troelstra, Pieter, 128, 154
Trotsky, Leon, 147, 149, 182, 236, 249, 255
Trotskyism, 458
Truman, Harry, 300
Truman Doctrine, 300, 307
tsarism, 91, 142, 143
Turati, Filippo, 88–89, 90, 114, 170

Twentieth Congress (Communist Party of the Soviet Union), 330–31
Two-and-a-Half International. *See* Vienna Union

unions. *See* trade unions
United Kingdom. *See* Great Britain
urban radicalism, 472
USSR. *See* Soviet Union
utopian socialism, 27–30, 114–15

Vaculík, Ludvík, 358
Vaillant, Edouard, 87, 88, 89, 92
vanguardism, 26, 37
Vidali, Vittorio, 330
Vienna Union, 178–79, 183
Vietnam War, 341
Viková-Kunetická, Bozena, 106
Vilna (Lith.), 231–32
Viviani, Luciana, 323
Vogeler, Heinrich, 209, 210, 211
voting, 85, 315, 401
  See also women's suffrage

Wainwright, Hilary, 461
Waldeck-Rousseau, René, 87
Walesa, Lech, 432, 433, 436
Weber, Henri, 346
Weiss, Peter, 452
welfare state, 312–13, 318–19
Western Europe, 499
  consumerism in, 353
  patterns of reform, 311–13
  student movements, 342, 363
  women in, 312, 324
  working class in, 385
  See also specific countries
West Germany, 417–22
  "German Autumn," 420
  Green movement, 421–22
  immigration into, 444
  peace movement, 419–20
What Is to Be Done? (Lenin), 143, 146, 148
Wheeldon, Alice, 107
white-collar workers, 398
Widgery, David, 356
Wilde, Oscar, 14
Wilkinson, Ellen, 195
Williams, Shirley, 463
Witenberg, Itzhak, 231–32, 233
Woman under Socialism (Bebel), 99, 115
women
  in Austria, 198
  and democracy, 4, 22–24
  emancipation of, 99–107, 198–200
  and First World War, 186, 192–93

women (*continued*)
in France, 190, 321, 379
gendered traditions, 55–56
in Germany, 99, 190–92, 193
in Great Britain, 13–15, 54, 101–2,
189–90, 192, 194–95, 323, 368–75
in Hungary, 107–8
and industrialization, 54–56
in Italy, 321–22, 378, 379
and labor, 22–23, 100–102, 324–25
and Left, 185–200, 378–81
between Popular Front and Cold War,
320–26
post-Second World War, 322, 324, 326–
28
in Second World War, 320, 323, 324
and social democracy, 192–95
and socialism, 100, 103
in Spain, 320
in Sweden, 325
and utopian socialism, 29–30
in Western Europe, 312, 324
See also feminism; women's suffrage
Women's Liberation Movement. *See*
feminism
Women's Peace Camp (Greenham
Common, Great Britain), 464–65
women's suffrage, 116
in Austria, 106
and Chartism, 22
early opposition, 22, 23
in France, 321

in Great Britain, 103–5, 107, 323
in Western Europe, 312
workers' councils, 160–64
working class
decline of, 385–87, 397–99, 402–4
"historic," 400
and industrialization, 47–61
Marxist definition, 49
miners, 76–77, 80–82, 119, 391, 465–
66, 467
in Poland, 431–37
politics of formation, 56–60
politics of labor, 384–404
socialist definition, 394
in Spain, 424
See also labor
World War I. *See* First World War
World War II. *See* Second World War

Xoxe, Koçi, 309

Yagüe, Juan de, 276
Yeltsin, Boris, 442, 443, 455
Yugoslavia, 286, 291, 308, 342

Zetkin, Clara, 30, 189
Zhdanov, Andrei Alexandrovich, 300
Zhivkov, Todor, 445
Zimmerwald movement, 128–30, 136,
148, 176, 177, 178, 266
Zinoviev, Grigory, 146, 177, 182, 249,
280